UNITED STATES

SUBMARINE
OPERATIONS

IN

WORLD WAR II

LOCKWOOD

UNITED STATES

SUBMARINE OPERATIONS

IN

WORLD WAR II

By Theodore Roscoe

Written for
THE BUREAU OF NAVAL PERSONNEL
from material prepared by
REAR ADMIRAL R. G. VOGE, USN
CAPTAIN W. J. HOLMES, USN (RETD.)
COMMANDER W. H. HAZZARD, USN
LIEUT. COMDR. D. S. GRAHAM, USN
LIEUT. H. J. KUEHN, USNR
★
DESIGNED AND ILLUSTRATED BY
LIEUT. COMDR. FRED FREEMAN, USNR
PHOTOGRAPHS BY THE U. S. NAVY

Published by
Naval Institute Press
Annapolis, Maryland

Library of Congress Catalog Card Number 50-5198

ISBN 0-87021-731-3

PRINTED IN THE UNITED STATES OF AMERICA ON ACID-FREE PAPER ∞

20   19   18   17   16   15

FOREWORD

☆☆☆☆☆

Future students and historians of our naval war in the Pacific will inevitably conclude that the Japanese commander of the carrier task force which wrought so much damage at Pearl Harbor on 7 December 1941 missed a golden opportunity in restricting his attack to one day's operations, and in the very limited choice of his objectives. The capital ships he sank or severely damaged could not have operated effectively in the far western Pacific for many, many months, whereas our submarines began unsupported operations in Japanese home waters immediately after the commencement of the war. How effective were those submarine operations against his Fleet and against his vitally important shipping is dramatically told in the following pages.

That the Japanese Naval High Command failed to evaluate at their true worth the potentialities of our submarines is incredible. Up to the shattering blow at Pearl Harbor the Japanese had accurate and up-to-the-minute intelligence of the situation at Pearl Harbor. They knew of our dependence on the dockyard, on the fuel supplies and on the Submarine Base, all of which were objectives of the first importance. They knew that they had taken out practically all our Air on 7 December. They knew that all our fuel storage was above ground and very vulnerable. Also known to them was our great dependence on the dockyard facilities, the destruction of which would have thrown us back on the West Coast for many months and possibly years. Finally, they were aware of our submarine establishment and they must have known that only that branch of the Service could operate effectively *at once* in the critical waters between Japan and the Netherlands East Indies.

Fortunately for the United States, our great Submarine Base in Hawaii with its supplies and facilities and our submarines were undamaged. When I assumed command of the Pacific Fleet on 31 December 1941 our submarines were already operating against the enemy, the only units of the Fleet that could come to grips with the Japanese for months to come.

It was to the Submarine Force that I looked to carry the load until our great industrial activity could produce the weapons we so sorely needed to carry the war to the enemy. It is to the everlasting honor and glory of our submarine personnel that they never failed us in our days of great peril. The world will now learn from the following pages how well they did their work in spite of real hardships and heavy losses.

C. W. Nimitz

FLEET ADMIRAL, U. S. NAVY

DEDICATION

. . . . . to the

valiant submariners

of the United States Navy

who lost their lives

in World War Two . . . . .

Acknowledgment is gratefully made for permission to reprint the following selections: Part I, page 1, verse by Robert Haven Schauffler from "Divers," Dodd, Mead and Company; Part II, page 47, verse by Ridgley Torrence from "Hesperides," copyright 1925 by The Macmillan Company; Addenda, page 498, verse by Leslie Nelson Jennings from "Lost Harbor," Third Book of Modern Verse, Houghton-Mifflin Company.

CONTENTS

PART I

SUBMARINES TO WAR
(DECEMBER 1941)

PART II

THE FIGHTING DEFENSE
(1942)

PART III

ALL-OUT ATTRITION
(1943)

PART IV

PACIFIC SWEEP
(1944)

PART V

JAPANESE SUNSET
(1945)

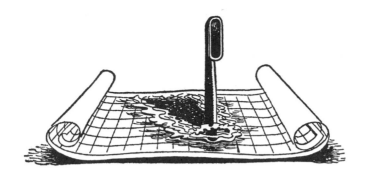

C H A R T S   A N D   P I C T U R E S

ILLUSTRATIONS   *Facing Page*

PHOTOGRAPHS

The photographs in this book were collected from various sources. Most of them are official Navy photographs by official Navy photographers. Many were taken by the famous Steichen Photographic Unit under the direction of Captain Edward Steichen, USNR. Some were taken through periscopes or on deck by amateur photographers of the Submarine Service. A few are from the private collections of submariners who took them with their own cameras—pictures released to their owners after the war. Space does not permit a complete listing of credits. One way or another, the photographs are all Navy pictures.

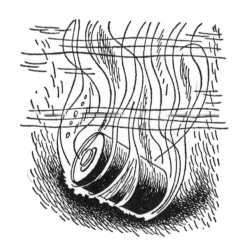

P R E F A C E

U. S. SUBMARINE OPERATIONS IN WORLD WAR II tells the story of the United States Submarine Service and its accomplishments in the greatest undersea war in world history.

This volume is not the official operational history. Strictly speaking, it is not a history, nor is it to be studied as such. Herein, in narrative form, the reader will find the inspiring saga of submarining. For the student, the technical side is featured. And many aspects of submarine warfare which would ordinarily be excluded from a purely historical text are detailed and discussed. Produced by the Training Division, Bureau of Naval Personnel, the volume's primary mission is to serve as an informative, instructive, and inspirational text for those in Naval Service who are interested, directly or indirectly, in submarines. The United States Naval Academy, NROTC Units, members of the Navy's various training schools, officers and men on active duty in submarines and many components of the Naval Reserve will employ (and enjoy) this book. The veteran submariner and the submariner of the future will cherish the achievements of the Submarine Service recounted in this volume.

Beginning with the opening gun at Pearl Harbor, the book details the submarine counter-attack in the Philippines, the launching of the attrition war on enemy shipping, the pioneering invasion of Empire waters, the battle for the Malay Barrier. The fighting retreat to Australia, the Battle of Midway, the bitter Aleutian struggle, the tidal turn in the Solomons, the Central Pacific offensive—these follow in chronological sequence. The battles fought by Submarines, Atlantic, the Homeric tale of the "sugar boats" from Panama, the memorable endeavors and accomplishments of the tenders are included. The big year of 1944 featuring the drive through the Mandates, the thundering torpedo attack on the Imperial Japanese Navy, the invasion of the Japan Sea, the sinking of Japan's economy with the liquidation of her merchant fleet—the story moves to its final climax, with a ring of submarines embracing Japan, a prostrate enemy whose war effort lay at sea-bottom.

Interwoven through the narrative are the dramatic special missions which demonstrated the submarine's versatility as blockade-runner, scout, transport, supply ship and rescue vessel capable of operating at will in enemy-controlled waters. Submarine reconnaissance, submarine support of fleet operations, submarine lifeguarding are subjects fully covered. Valuable for students of submarining are the sections devoted to tactics, detailing the various approach and attack techniques favored by commanding officers in action and illustrative of the methods of torpedo warfare. The "end-around," the "down-the-throat shot"—these and other tactics come to the reader straight from the patrol reports of experts who successfully employed them. For student reference, discussions of submarine tactics have been sub-titled throughout this volume and are noted under "Tactics" in the Index.

Many brilliant successes highlight this dramatic history, but losses and failures are included, as must be done in the authentic recording of any war effort. Commodore Luce (founder of the Naval War College) recommended the study of naval history "with the cold eye of professional criticism," so that one might learn "where the principles of science have been illustrated, or where a disregard for the accepted rules of the art of war has led to defeat and disaster." The officers of the United States Submarine Service subscribe to this forthright doctrine. Thus, recounted in this text are the trials and tribulations experienced with an undependable weapon. Attacks on friendly vessels and attacks made on submarines by friendly forces are included. From these mistakes lessons were learned, which may serve to guide submariners of the future.

But, although informative and instructive, this volume is not to be read as a textbook. It is to be read as a story—the epic story of the U. S. submarine war against the Axis—an heroic drama composed of, by, and for the submariners of the United States Navy. The volume is based on the official operational history compiled under ComSubPac direction by Captain R. G. Voge, Captain W. J. Holmes, Commander W. H. Hazzard, and (for SubLant) Lieutenant Commander D. S. Graham. Additional material was drawn from work prepared by Lieutenant H. J. Kuehn, from patrol reports, from current historical data, from conversation with submarine officers. Pertinent statistics and ship-sinking assessments are based on records compiled by the Submarine Operations Research Group, the United States Strategic Bombing Survey, and the Joint Army-Navy Assessment Committee. The volume was prepared in its final form by Theodore Roscoe of the Training Publications Section, Training Division.

This book was designed and illustrated by Lieutenant Commander Fred Freeman, USNR. The photographs were selected by Freeman from thousands sighted in the photograph libraries at Anacostia, New London Submarine Base, the Bureau of Naval Personnel and from private collections. The drawings were reconstructed from patrol and action reports.

The Steichen Photographic Unit, whose battle action shots were used in the film "Fighting Lady," took many of the photographs herein. The unit was under the direction of Captain Edward Steichen, USNR.

Technical reading and assistance by Vice Admiral C. A. Lockwood, Admiral R. S. Edwards, Commander W. B. Sieglaff, Commander J. S. McCain, Commander S. D. Cutter, Commander E. T. Shepard, Commander D. G. Irvine, and Lieutenant Commander C. E. Bell improved the manuscript. The manuscript was most capably edited by Miss Theresa Gettings of the Training Publications Section under direction of Dr. Kenneth Gayer. Publication of the work was fostered, sponsored, and supervised by Captain J. M. Will, Director of Training, Bureau of Naval Personnel.

N A V A L

W A R

C O L L E G E

1 9 4 2

O R

"Old Fuds, Young Studs and Lieutenant Commanders"

Battleships are title B,
That's Lesson One in strategy.
They are the backbone of the Fleet,
Their fighting power can't be beat.
They dominate the raging Main,
While swinging round the anchor chain,
And bravely guard your home and mine,
While anchored out there all in line.
They fill the Japs with fear and hate,
From well inside the Golden Gate.

Now Lesson Two in strategy—
Our subs and planes are title C.
Just send them out on any mission,
And win your battles by attrition.
Where'er you send the subs or planes,
You're bound to chalk up lots of gains—
And losses, too, but what the hell,
Who cares about their personnel?
For planes are chauffered by young studs,
Lieutenant Commanders run the subs.

RICHARD G. VOGE
Lieutenant Commander, USN

REAR ADMIRAL RICHARD G. VOGE, USN
Captain of USS Sealion and USS Sailfish, and SubPac Operations Officer, Who Planned Many of the Operations Reported in This Volume

☆☆

U. S. SUBMARINE OPERATIONS IN WORLD WAR II is "Dick" Voge's book. He compiled much of the background material, edited the technicalities of submarining in the final draft of the manuscript, advised in the matter of art-work, and selected many of the photographs which illustrate the text. Moreover, as Vice Admiral Lockwood's Operations Officer, he devised the strategy and planned many of the operational moves which carried Submarines Pacific to the forefront in the great offensives of the war. He was Captain of Sealion when the Japanese bombers first struck Manila. He then made several fighting patrols as Captain of Sailfish. As a submarine commander and as a member of ComSub-Pac's staff, "Dick" Voge won the respect and affection of all who knew him.

Before the book went to press, Rear Admiral Voge died at his home in Port Chester, N.Y.—a casualty of the war's afflicting strain and the many stresses he had endured. The introduction to this volume is the last article he wrote. The volume remains as a memorial to his service in the United States Navy and his fine record as a submariner.

INTRODUCTION

In a democracy such as ours National Defense policies are set by the general public. The Secretary of Defense, the Secretaries of the Army, the Navy, and the Air Force, the Joint Chiefs of Staff may make their recommendations, but it is the public, acting through its representatives, that makes the final decisions. The people elect their representatives to Congress, and Congress appropriates the money for military expenditures. In so doing, the elected representatives follow the will of their constituents. This may not be strictly true in time of war when military expenditures are hidden in a cloak of secrecy, but in time of peace the budget is a matter of public domain, and an unpopular or little-understood weapon is apt to be paid scant heed by the lawmakers. As a consequence, with the world in its present stage of political unrest, and with the various world powers girding for, or to avoid, another conflict, it is incumbent upon the layman, as well as the militarist, to have a clear understanding of the capabilities and limitations of each weapon in the National Defense arsenal.

If public opinion is to decide the issue, that opinion must be based on fact rather than fiction. Neither publicity nor propaganda must be permitted to sway the Nation into placing undue emphasis on any one weapon at the expense of others of relative importance. Hitler made that fatal mistake and thereby lost a war and a world empire. Yet even a superficial study of the history of World War I would have pointed out to him the road to success. Germany, on February 1, 1917, declared unrestricted submarine warfare. By April of that year British ship losses had reached such proportions that Admiral Jellicoe, First Sea Lord of the Admiralty, declared,

"They will win unless we stop these losses and stop them soon." The record was available that all might read, but Hitler chose to follow his intuition rather than the lessons of history. Naval protagonists were given but little voice in matters of high policy. The democracies of the world may well pray that their future enemies will have such a bigoted viewpoint. It is common knowledge how perilously close the German submarines came to winning the Battle of the Atlantic in World War II. Yet Germany started that war with but 76 submarines in commission. Think what the ultimate outcome would have been had Hitler had 500 submarines available at the outset, a force that would not have been out of proportion to the size of his army and his air force.

The mistakes that a dictator makes through bigotry can be duplicated in a democracy through ignorance or misunderstanding on the part of the populace. The public cannot properly evaluate a weapon about which it knows nothing, and no authoritative and comprehensive account of the work of U.S. submarines in World War II has heretofore been published. The Submarine Service has too long been content to let the record speak for itself. A record buried deep in the classified files of the Department of the Navy speaks only in a whisper, and then only to the archivist or researcher. It is the purpose of this volume to bring that record to public view.

The book had its beginning in July 1945. At that time the Submarine Service found itself, like Alexander, with no more worlds to conquer, or, more accurately, no more Japanese ships to sink. The last big submarine offensive—the penetration of the Sea of Japan—had been successfully completed in June. Japanese shipping had been driven from the seas. Submarines were going to every extreme to stir up a little excitement and at the same time harass the enemy. One submarine put a landing party ashore to blow up a Japanese railroad bridge and followed that exploit by bombarding several coastal towns with rocket and machine-gun fire. Another submarine, patrolling off the coast of southern China, sighted two Japanese destroyers at anchor in a harbor, and brazenly patrolled on the surface in broad daylight in full view of the enemy, trying to entice him to come out and fight. The bulk of the submarines were engaged in lifeguard missions for the B-29 raids on Japan. In short, submarine operations were in the doldrums.

It was then that Vice Admiral C. A. Lockwood, Jr., Commander Submarine Force, Pacific Fleet, on board his flagship, USS HOLLAND, at Guam, sent for his Operations Officer. From his two and one-half years of association with the Admiral the Operations Officer had learned to expect almost any type of order, but this time it was something radically different: "You've been handling operations long enough to know the score. Pack up your duffle, thumb a ride to Pearl Harbor and then sit down and write the submarine history."

Admiral Lockwood, one of God's true noblemen, was not one to surround himself with "yes" men. If any member of his staff disagreed with his decisions he expected that staff officer to tell him so, and why. The reaction in this case was immediate: "Admiral, I have never written a book. I don't know how to write a book. I don't want to write a book." As is usual in such cases, three stars prevailed over four stripes, and a few days later I was on board a plane en route to Pearl Harbor.

It was my original intention to limit the scope of the work to the operations of the Submarine Force, Pacific Fleet. However, it soon became evident that such a limitation was not feasible. There were three U.S. Submarine Forces in existence during World War II, and although each force constituted a separate entity, their operations were so coordinated and interrelated that it was impossible to treat independently any one force and still present a complete picture. A call for assistance was sent out to the other force commanders, and Commander W. H. Hazzard and Lieutenant Commander Donald S. Graham were assigned to record the deeds of Submarines, Southwest Pacific and Submarines, Atlantic Fleet, respectively.

In December 1945, Captain W. J. Holmes, USN (Ret.), was assigned to SubPac to assist with the enterprise. A few months later, upon my detachment, he took charge of the entire project. Captain Holmes was preeminently qualified for the task assigned. Until his retirement for physical disability in 1935 he had been a submarine officer of outstanding ability. In 1941 he was recalled to active duty with Naval Intelligence at Pearl Harbor and his duties there gave him an intimate knowledge of the daily doings of all the submarines throughout the war. In addition, during the years of his retirement, and while serving as a professor of engineering at the University of Hawaii, he attained considerable renown as a writer of submarine fiction under the pen name of Alec Hudson. Since mid-1943 Vice Admiral Lockwood had tried, without avail, to have Holmes assigned to him to write the submarine history while that history was in the making. Fleet Admiral Nimitz, knowing the value of Holmes' services to the Intelligence organization, refused to release him until some months after the cessation of hostilities.

Under Holmes' direction the compilation was completed and sent on to Washington in the fall of 1946—some ten pounds, more or less, of typewritten manuscript. Almost simultaneous with its arrival in Washington the office of Coordinator of Submarine Warfare was created in the Navy Department. Prior to that time there had been no central agency in Washington charged with submarine affairs, and the new office of Coordinator had neither the personnel nor the funds available to undertake the publication of the history. In addition, the manner in which the manuscript had been prepared precluded its issue to the public in its original form. The original outline called for covering the subject matter from the point of view of the strategy or tactics involved. This resulted in a lack of continuity and considerable repetition.

The manuscript thereupon proceeded to gather dust on the shelves of the Navy Department while its advocates searched for a sponsor, or, in theatrical parlance, an "angel" who would finance the show. The "angel" was eventually found in the person of Rear Admiral T. L. Sprague, Chief of Naval Personnel. Admiral Sprague detailed the project to Captain J. M. Will, veteran submariner and just the officer to blow the dust off such a manuscript.

Captain Will, in his capacity as Director of Training, was, among many other things, in charge of the preparation of textbooks and training manuals for naval personnel. He wished to develop a textbook to point up the operational lessons of World War II to future submariners, and the submarine history appeared to be the answer to the problem. He assigned Mr. Theodore Roscoe, then under contract to the Bureau of Naval Personnel, to the project of rewriting the text, with the dual objective of having it serve as an account to the layman in addition to its prime purpose as a textbook for submarine personnel. Mr. Roscoe, a writer of established reputation and unquestioned ability, little knew what he was letting himself in for when he accepted the assignment. The deeper he delved into the subject the deeper he became engrossed, and the project which was originally scheduled to take but a few months extended over eighteen. It must be emphatically pointed out that while the combine of Holmes, Hazzard, Graham, and Voge compiled the record upon which this history is based, the text as herein presented is entirely the work of Theodore Roscoe.

The text had to include enough technical data to satisfy the needs of the future submariner, but not too much to bore the layman. It was my pleasure and privilege to assist the writer in the final stages of editing this volume—my job was to check his writings for errors of fact, or phraseology, both nautical and subnautical. The job was a sinecure. The few errors that I did detect could readily be traced to source material. On the other hand, during the course of his work the writer had become such an ardent admirer of the submariners' work in the war that my hardest task was in getting him to tone down some of his panegyrics. Then, too, there was the weather to contend with. Those unfamiliar with the climate of our national capital will find it difficult to understand the occupational hazards of creative writing in midsummer Washington. The sun, with no thought of protocol, beats down on mighty and commoner alike, but the seats of the mighty are all located in air-conditioned offices. Not so were Roscoe's and Voge's, and the sultry air resembled nothing so much as a hot towel in a barber shop. That, in a small measure, accounts for some of the delay in getting this volume to press.

It is human nature to learn more from our mistakes than from our successes, and for that reason, although a few toes may be stepped on, this book presents a candid picture of submarine operations as they were and not always as we might have wished them to be. Thus the full story of the submarine torpedo has been included. It contains a lesson too valuable to be buried in the archives. It should be required reading for every officer in the Navy.

RICHARD G. VOGE.
Rear Admiral, USN

PART I

SUBMARINES TO WAR
(DECEMBER 1941)

Stumbling we grope and stifle here below
In the gross garb of this too cumbering flesh,
And draw such hard-won breaths as may be drawn,
Until, perchance with pearls, we rise and go
To doff our diver's mail and taste the fresh,
The generous winds of the eternal dawn.

R. H. SCHAUFFLER

CHAPTER 1

HOLOCAUST AT PEARL HARBOR

Two-ocean War

The Japanese strike in the Pacific immediately involved the United States in a two-ocean war.

To many Americans it seemed as if the Japanese had run amuck. This was an insular view. Those who took a global view of the situation realized the Pacific strike was shrewdly calculated.

In December 1941, England was holding on by little more than the skin of a bulldog's teeth. The Axis partners held Western Europe prisoner in Hitler's Fortress Europa. Rommel's army was on its way to Cairo. London was a city of bleeding ruins, the Royal Navy was striving desperately to retain control of the Atlantic, and Nazi shipyards were launching U-boats by the squadron.

In Russia, German invasion forces hurled thunderbolts at the gates of Moscow. Allied experts, who had predicted the collapse of the Soviet Army by the end of September, now gave the Russians until Christmas. The expected Nazi conquest of the USSR would remove a potential enemy from Japan's back door and release thousands of Japanese troops from Manchuria for use against Chinese and American forces.

The major portion of the U.S. Navy's strength was gathered in the Atlantic—eight battleships, including the new NORTH CAROLINA, four aircraft carriers, 13 cruisers, some 90 destroyers and 60 submarines. In the Pacific, the U.S. Navy could muster about 100 surface warships, and expect support from some 50 British and Netherlands naval vessels. Against these the Imperial Navy could pit about 170 warships. There were 51 American submarines in the Pacific and a few British and Dutch submersibles. The Japanese considered these inconsequential. In December 1941, they themselves had 63 ocean-going submarines in commission, and their shipyards were spawning schools of "baby" submersibles for use in coastal defense.

Analysis of all these factors shows that the Japanese, far from running amuck, timed their strike for a most opportune hour. Add in the logistics factor—Japan's relatively short communication lines, and the oceanic stretch from America to the Philippines—and the Tokyo war plan seems anything but miscalculated.

The American industrial potential was a matter to be considered. But it had to produce for a war on two fronts which were separated by oceans from the production center. And against this factor stood German and Japanese labor, already operating in high gear on a totalitarian basis. Such raw material disparity as existed, the Japanese intended to balance by seizure of the immense oil and rubber resources of the East Indies, and capture of the world's supply of quinine, vital to troops operating in the tropics. With everything to gain, Tojo and Yamamoto struck.

Four days after the Pearl Harbor raid, Germany and Italy, in accordance with their Axis pact, declared war on the United States. The squeeze-play was on.

Washington strategists, however, had long foreseen the possibility of a two-ocean war with the Axis nations, and had determined on a concentration of effort to defeat Nazi Germany while the Japanese offensive was contained by a holding action in the Pacific. This strategic plan recognized Germany as the most formidable Axis power and the Atlantic threat as the one more immediately menacing the security of the United States. Defeat of Japan was considered inevitable once the Nazis were beaten, whereas a victory over the Japanese forces in the Pacific did not assure defeat of Germany, were the Nazis able to crush Britain and Russia in the meantime. Hence, the American war plan—to sustain Great Britain and Soviet Russia until an all-out offensive against Hitler's Fortress Europa could be mounted and launched. This meant winning the Battle of the Atlantic while American naval forces in the Pacific went on the defensive.

Defensive strategy did not preclude the possibility of aggressive tactics. In holding the line, the United States Pacific Fleet was supposed to engage the Japanese vigorously, blocking the enemy advance wherever possible. It was realized that shipping would be the weakest link in the chain drive of a Japanese seaborne offensive. On December 1, 1941, Japanese merchant shipping was estimated as approximating 6,000,000 tons of ocean-going, steel ships (vessels over 500 tons). During the 1930's, the Japanese had worked with Trojan energy to build up this large and modern merchant fleet, for no nation on the globe was more dependent upon ocean shipping than Dai Nippon. Neither in foodstuffs for civilian consumption nor in raw materials for industry were the home islands self-sufficient. Rice, tea, beef, dozens of other staples had to be imported for Mr. Moto's table. Scrap iron, aluminum, coal of coking quality had to be shipped in for Brother Mitsui's blast furnaces. Dependent upon imports during peacetime, Japan was doubly so when dedicated to a war of conquest. Nearly all of the basic raw materials for the munitions industry alone had to be brought in by water, and the Imperial Navy, merchant marine, and air force operated literally on seas of imported oil.

War added to the shipping burden in another respect, demanding vessels for the transport of troops, supplies and munitions to overseas bases and fronts. The Japanese merchant fleet was divided into separate Army, Navy and civilian pools. Allocated some 4,000,000 tons at the word "Go!", the military obtained the bulk of available merchantmen, and civilian shipping was expected to carry on with about 1,900,000 tons. This imposed a serious strain on Japanese commerce at the start. But the war-planners in Tokyo hoped to relieve this strain with ships acquired by conquest. And it was presumed that vessels which went out with military cargoes could come home with cargoes for civilian use.

Aware of the Japanese War Machine's dependence on shipping, the U.S. Navy's strategists had planned to block the enemy's sea lanes with strong units of the Pacific Fleet. United States submarines were expected to play a stalwart part in the Pacific defense —by aggressively reducing Japan's marine tonnage, harrying and delaying convoys, and slowing the enemy's military transport service to a walk. But the stunning strike at Pearl Harbor, which resulted in the complete immobilization of the battleship force, and the overwhelming Japanese onslaught on the Philippines and Malaya deranged American-Pacific strategy. The stupendous break-through, immediately menacing Hawaii, India and Australia, had not been anticipated. It could not be allowed to dislocate America's two-ocean war plan. But the Pacific defense plan had to be at once readjusted.

Nobody could pretend that the Japanese smash at Pearl Harbor did not present the U.S. Navy with an appalling situation. The surface fleet, which had been counted on to defend the Central Pacific, was "out of it" and would remain so for a long time. In the Philippines, Admiral Hart's small surface force could not hope to cope with the mighty armadas storming down from Japan. Months would pass before adequate air, land and naval reinforcements could reach the Central and Southwest Pacific fronts. But one naval arm remained unimpaired by the Pearl Harbor smash—an arm capable of striking at the Japanese naval and merchant fleets with some chance of success and survival. That arm was the United States Navy's Submarine Service.

On the eve of the war's outbreak, the U.S. Navy's submarine strength was 111 in commission and 73 building. Of the 51 submarines on duty (or available for duty) in the Pacific, 29 were attached to the Asiatic Fleet based at Manila, and 22 operated with the Pacific Fleet based at Pearl Harbor.

To United States submarines, then—those 51 submersibles on duty or available for duty in the Pacific —fell the major portion of the improvised defense. To them fell the task of intercepting the Japanese naval forces plunging down on the Philippines— of slashing at Tojo's communication line—of running interference for the Allied naval forces fighting to hold the Malay Barrier—of dealing with that 4,000,000 some-odd tons of merchant shipping allocated to the enemy's War Machine and the approximate 2,000,000 tons devoted to the maintenance of Japan's home economy.

At best, this was a large order for 51 submersibles! And it was soon apparent that circumstances were far from "best." But the submariners took the circumstances as they took the order—standing up. They knew they were in for a war big enough for two oceans, right there in the Pacific, when they received

4

SUBMARINE BASE PEARL! Alongside finger-pier Narwhal escapes December 7th destruction. Aboard her, a gun crew waits its chance at the low-flying enemy invader. With a near-by destroyer, and the submarine Tautog in a neighboring berth, Narwhal shared credit for the kill of a Japanese torpedo plane.

BATTLESHIP ROW! *December 7, 1941. This Jap photo was captioned: "... in picture clearly appear outlines of* two of our Sea Eagles who are carrying out a daring low-level attack, reminiscent of the performance of the gods."

JAPANESE MIDGET! *This 2-man sub, raised by Navy tug* Ortolan, *is similar to one that sneaked into Pearl.*

MIDGET CONNING TOWER. *The Jap 2-man sub, a claustrophobia nightmare, operated as a human torpedo.*

USS TAUTOG—*Navy's top-scoring submarine. In action from start, she single-handedly downed a Jap plane at Pearl. While under Comdr. J. H. Willingham, she sank* 2 Jap subs, 3 merchantmen. Under Comdr. W. B. Sieglaff: 2 Jap destroyers, 11 merchantmen. Under Comdr. T. S. Baskett: 2 naval craft, 6 merchantmen. Total: 26 ships.

the fighting directive which was issued by the Chief of Naval Operations the afternoon of December 7:

EXECUTE UNRESTRICTED AIR AND SUBMARINE WARFARE AGAINST JAPAN

Underwater Attack (December 7th)

Contrary to popular opinion, the first angry shot at Pearl Harbor was fired at, and not by, the attacking intruder.

At 0342 on the morning of December 7, 1941, the USS CONDOR, a minesweeper, nearly collided with a small submarine traveling at periscope depth not far from the Pearl Harbor entrance buoys. When sighted, the periscope was skulking through the dark water about 100 feet dead ahead of CONDOR, the feathery arrow of its wake aimed directly at the harbor entrance. Shadow in the night, the periscope was gone. This was in a defensive sea area—a zone where American submarines were restricted to surface operation—and a moment later the startled minesweeper's blinker was flashing a message to the destroyer (DD) WARD.

SIGHTED SUBMERGED SUBMARINE ON WESTERLY COURSE . . . SPEED NINE KNOTS

A DD of the Inshore Patrol engaged in guard duty off the harbor entrance, WARD immediately began a search for the unidentified submarine. After combing a wide area in an hour or so of futile hunt, WARD asked the minesweeper for more detail. CONDOR answered with information that convinced WARD's captain that he had been searching in the wrong direction. But a hasty probe of the waters indicated failed to locate the trespasser. This invited the conclusion that the minesweeper's lookout had been mistaken concerning the unidentified sub.

Meanwhile, CONDOR proceeded to the harbor entrance where the channel was protected by an antitorpedo net. The gate vessel, charged with the opening and closing of the net, opened for the incoming minesweeper at 0458. Day was a faint tint in the east when CONDOR entered the harbor. The channel was placid, and the early sky gave promise of a halcyon Sunday morning.

Some thirty minutes later, the USS ANTARES with a 500-ton steel barge in tow was standing in. At 0630, ANTARES' lookout sighted what appeared to be a small submarine about 1,500 yards off her starboard quarter. Her bridge blinkered this information to WARD, and at 0640 WARD sighted the submarine which seemed to be trailing ANTARES into Pearl Harbor.

WARD's captain sounded General Quarters and sent the destroyer steaming for the submarine at top speed. Beating the DD to the gun, a Navy PBY, returning from long-range patrol, circled the area and dropped two smoke pots to mark the submarine's location. In murky dawn-light the silhouetted conning tower was seen as unfamiliar.

At 0645, range approximately 100 yards, WARD opened point-blank fire. Her first shot missed, but her second punctured the submarine's conning tower (and in all probability its occupant) just below the waterline.

Immediately the injured boat heeled over and sank. Charging forward, the destroyer thrashed the swirling water with depth bombs. Four "ashcans" blasted geysers from the area where the submarine had plunged, and then a surge of oil swam to the surface and spread a somber stain across the tide.

At 0653, WARD sent the following radio message to the Commandant, Fourteenth Naval District:

WE HAVE ATTACKED FIRED UPON AND DROPPED DEPTH CHARGES UPON SUBMARINE OPERATING IN DEFENSIVE SEA AREA

Received by the Bishop's Point radio station, this message was at once relayed to the Officer in Charge, Net and Boom Defenses, Inshore Patrol; the Communications Officer, Fourteenth Naval District; and the ComFourteen Duty Officer. At 0712 the ComFourteen Chief of Staff was notified, and the Duty Officer of the Commander-in-Chief, Pacific Fleet, at 0715. Subsequently, Admiral Bloch, Commandant of the Fourteenth Naval District, received word of WARD's message. The relief ready duty destroyer MONAGHAN was dispatched to join forces with WARD. But no alert was sounded. There had been previous reports of submarine contacts off Hawaii—reports which had proved unfounded—and the impression persisted that WARD had been mistaken.

Apparently previous cries of "Wolf!" had deadened the impact of any submarine alarm. Other modulating factors influenced the situation. Although strained to the breaking point, Tokyo-Washington relations—thanks to the suave diplomacy of Nomura and Kurusu—did not appear on the verge of a violent fracture. Taking their orders from Washington, the military and naval guardians of Pearl Harbor had been somewhat misled by dispatches received on November 7th. At that date Admiral Husband E. Kimmel, Commander-in-Chief of the United States Fleet with Headquarters at Pearl Harbor, had been advised, "Japan is expected to make an aggressive move within the next few days." But reference was made to "an amphibious expedition against either the Philippines, Thai or Kra Peninsula, or possibly Borneo." At the same time, Lieutenant General

Walter C. Short of the Hawaiian Department received official warning that a hostile Japanese move was "possible at any moment." However, he was ordered to take defense measures in a manner that would not "alarm the civilian population or disclose the intent." Thereupon General Short alerted his department against sabotage and placed Hawaii under a condition of "limited preparedness."

It is not within the province of this volume to criticize American defense measures, or lack of them, which permitted a large Japanese carrier force to attain striking distance of the Hawaiian Islands and launch a devastating surprise attack. Errors in judgment were not confined to any one department or branch of the Armed Services—radar detection of the approaching planes at 0702 was ignored, and the anti-torpedo net which had been opened for the mine-sweeper CONDOR remained open for nearly an hour after the attack began. Of concern to students of submarining, however, is the build-up to the surprise assault and the part played therein by strategically employed submarines.

Admiral Yamamoto, Commander-in-Chief of the Combined Japanese Fleet, had formulated the Pearl Harbor attack plan the preceding January. As early as July, Japanese submarines were reported in Hawaiian waters, apparently keeping the approaches to Pearl Harbor under surveillance.

Yamamoto completed his planning by mid-September. Submarine contacts were sporadically reported by American destroyers in the Hawaiian area during the ensuing autumn weeks.

Details of the surprise raid and date of its execution were promulgated to all Japanese fleet and task force commanders on November 5th. As previously mentioned, there was increasing evidence of Japanese submarine activity off Hawaii in November.

On November 22 Yamamoto's striking force assembled in the Kuriles, and on the 26th it set out on a circuitous North Pacific course for the target islands. On December 6 the Japanese commanders received the fateful code-phrase:

CLIMB   MOUNT   NITAKA

Early morning, December 7, the carriers were in range, some 200 miles north of Oahu. And a squadron of Japanese submarines (Sixth Fleet Submarine Force) was in position off the entrance to Pearl Harbor. With this squadron were five midget or "baby" submarines. It was one of these babies which WARD had sunk at dawn, thus drawing first blood and giving the assailant the dubious honor of enduring the first casualty in the Pacific War.

Meanwhile, a midget submarine slipped undetected into the open harbor entrance, and eased into the inner harbor early that Sunday morning. This pocket-size submarine's casual junket around Pearl Harbor is a feat every submariner will recognize as remarkable. Its presence unsuspected, the underwater foot-pad was hugging the bottom off Ford Island when the air attack began. While the harbor was being bombed, this submarine launched both of its torpedoes. The first passed between the seaplane tender CURTISS and the cruiser RALEIGH, and exploded on the Ford Island shore. The other burrowed into the mud not far from the old timber-covered target ship UTAH. The Japanese announced a battleship of the OKLAHOMA class torpedoed by a midget submarine, but records cancel the report as hearsay. Promptly sunk by CURTISS for its pains, the midget in question constituted the enemy's second submarine loss. It is possible this submarine was the one originally sighted by CONDOR.

One small submersible, soon to be a needle under a haystack of shattered American warships, might seem of little account. But this sinking of an enemy submarine in the heart of Pearl Harbor emphatically underlines that most important faculty of the undersea boat—its ability to penetrate naval defenses, conduct an unobserved approach and deliver a surprise attack. While the attack in this instance failed, the approach was nonetheless successful. In this respect it gave observers a hint of the undersea warfare to come.

Another Japanese midget submarine lost its bearings and crawled up on a reef near Bellows Field southeast of Kaneohe Bay. There, the day following the raid, it was captured intact. Also captured intact was the Japanese commanding officer, Sub Lieutenant Sakamaki, who swam ashore and surrendered, preferring Hawaii to *hara-kiri*. A product of the Japanese Naval Academy, class of 1940, Sakamaki dolefully informed his interrogators that he had failed in his mission. His mission, of course, had not been to become America's first Japanese P.O.W.

Leery of the freak submersible, Army officials wanted to blow it off the reef with gunfire. Timely intervention of Captain F. A. Daubin, commander of the Submarine Base at Pearl Harbor, and his executive officer, Commander M. M. Stephens, rescued the miniature submarine for scientific examination. Quick work by Lieutenant Commander D. T. Eddy, engineer and repair officer at the Pearl Harbor Submarine Base, salvaged the craft.

The captured midget submarine bore the designation "I-18," obviously relating it to a Japanese I-class ocean-going submarine which must have served as its "mother." Found on a chart recovered from the midget were notations, "IZ16," "I-20," "—22," "I-18," "I-24," spotted in the entrance channel between Hammer Point and Hospital Point. However dubious its origin and unique its design, every baby must have a mother, and the implications were clear. At least five Japanese "mother" submarines had been lurking in the waters off Pearl Harbor.

The mother submarine carried her dwarf offspring on the main deck abaft the conning tower where it was fastened to the pressure hull by heavy clamps. Tied to its mother's apron strings by a 200-mile cruising radius, the baby had to be "piggy-backed" close to its objective before launching.

The Japanese midget submarine captured at Bellows Field was approximately 79 feet long, with a 6-foot beam, electrically powered, and capable of a maximum speed of 24 knots and a cruising speed of 4 to 6 knots. Thin hull-plating limited the boat to shallow submergence. A forward compartment carried torpedo tubes and compressed air tanks. Electric motors and propeller drive shaft were compartmented in the stern. At either side of the conning tower were the battery compartments. The periscope, projecting five feet above the conning tower, could not be raised or lowered.

The little craft was equipped with a gyro compass, a magnetic compass, radio (made in the U.S.A.) and underwater sound gear. It was armed with two 18-inch torpedoes, and a demolition charge capable of converting the midget itself into a giant torpedo.

(The two-man submarine was designed primarily for hit-and-run tactics, and its hazardous operational features seem to have been counter-balanced by the possibilities for its mass production. With considerable foresight the Japanese, in 1941, were building scores of midgets for defense of the homeland's beachheads.)

While the midgets at Pearl Harbor were generally regarded as minor novelties, the mothering I-boats in the waters off Oahu constituted a major menace to the assailed Pacific Fleet. The I-boats were submarines of the long-range reconnaissance type. The typical I-16 class had a surface displacement of 2,180 tons, and was 348 feet in length, with a 30-foot beam. With a total horsepower of 9,000, the boats attained a surface speed of around 22 knots. Eight 21-inch tubes gave them a firepower equal to that of all but the newest American submarines.

For a number of days these big submarines had been off Oahu in company with their midget brood. Reconnoitering, their periscopes spied on the approaches to Pearl Harbor, marking the movements of the American fleet. But midget-tending and scouting for Yamamoto's carrier force were only part of this squadron's mission. Its chief mission, revealed in a captured copy of the Japanese plan of operation, was concisely stated as follows:

"Will observe and attack American fleet in Hawaii area. Will make a surprise attack on the channel leading into Pearl Harbor and attempt to close it. If the enemy moves out to fight he will be pursued and attacked."

The menace of this deadly backfield deployed to trap any warship attempting to escape the harbor is obvious. Had the U.S. Pacific Fleet sortied under fire on the morning of December 7, many of its warships might have been sunk in waters too deep for recovery.

From the above and foregoing detail, an interesting highlight emerges.

The war in the Pacific began as a contest between surface forces and submarines.

In this preliminary foray the eluded and deluded surface forces remained at a disadvantage. That they were American and the submarines were Japanese was a factor awaiting speedy revision. But a change of denominators did not alter the values in the submarine vs. surface-force equation.

Submarines, Pacific Fleet

The Pearl Harbor Submarine Base was home for the 22 submarines which, under the command of Rear Admiral Thomas Withers, operated with the Pacific Fleet. The base (commanded by Captain F. A. Daubin) contained machine shops, a torpedo plant, supply stores, major repair installations, an escape training tank and other training devices, berthing facilities for submarines and tenders, and housing facilities for 2,400 men and 98 officers. Here the submarines could put in for fuel and provisions, a refit or a complete overhaul. Here crews were groomed for patrol and brushed up on the latest techniques of submarining. Like the force itself, the base reflected the efficient hand of Admiral Withers, who had pushed a rigorous program for material improvement as well as stringent drills and trials to test equipment and men. The Pacific Fleet submariners were proud of their Pearl Harbor base. Perhaps it was fortunate that, on the morning of December 7, not many of the submarines were home.

On that fateful Sunday of December 1941, the submarines of the Pacific Fleet were widely dispersed. Of the 22 which comprised the force, 16 were modern fleet-type submarines, and six were S-boats of older vintage. These last, being shorter of wind and leg than the moderns, were at that date on the American Pacific coast, several undergoing repair, and others employed in training exercises at San Diego. The fleet-type submarines (the layman may recognize them as being named after fish) were, in the main, on duty in the Central Pacific.

At the hour when the Japanese struck, the submarines ARGONAUT and TROUT were already conducting defensive patrols near Midway Island. TAMBOR and TRITON were patrolling off Wake. THRESHER was en route to Pearl Harbor after a 43-day training patrol in the Midway vicinity. POLLACK, POMPANO and PLUNGER were en route from San Francisco to Pearl Harbor. TUNA and NAUTILUS were being overhauled at Mare Island Navy Yard. Not far from Pearl Harbor, GUDGEON was conducting aircraft-submarine training exercises at Lahaina, Maui.

Five submarines, all in various stages of overhaul, were at the Pearl Harbor Submarine Base when the murderous attack came thunderbolting out of the blue. These were the first submarines in the Pacific to hear the fury of guns and bombs and see the raging fires of Armageddon ignited by an enemy determined to plunge the United States into the Second World War.

The Air Strike

At 0750 the first wave of Japanese planes struck Kaneohe Naval Air Station on the eastern side of Oahu. Incendiary bullets slashed the seaplanes ranged along the ramp or moored in the bay. Through clouds banked over the Koolau Range the bombers stormed on westward to attack Pearl Harbor. Hickam Field, the Naval Air Station at Ford Island, and the Marine Corps station at Ewa were marked as primary targets for this Oriental version of the German *blitz*. Aircraft were demolished where they stood on the ground. Hangars and barracks were strafed. Following this thunderbolt assault on the airfields, Japanese dive bombers and torpedo planes swept in to pound the fleet at anchor in the harbor. Armed with torpedoes which had been provided with wooden fins for shallow running, the planes roared in from two directions to strike Battleship Row.

Seven battleships (BB's) were moored in Battleship Row and BB PENNSYLVANIA was sitting helpless in drydock. These eight composed the battleship force of the United States Pacific Fleet. Nine cruisers, 28 destroyers, tenders, minesweepers, supply ships, auxiliaries—a total of 86 naval vessels—crowded the harbor. The accompanying map shows the disposition of the major naval units which suffered the punishing onslaught.

The five submarines at Pearl Harbor Submarine Base were the CACHALOT, CUTTLEFISH, DOLPHIN, NARWHAL and TAUTOG—with the submarine tender PELIAS located as shown in the inset. Situated on the south side of the harbor, the Submarine Base was a box seat flanking the bombing-run of the planes which came hurricaning over Hickam Field on their way to Ford Island. Skimming the tip of Kuahua, the Japanese torpedo planes launched their torpedoes into the exposed beam of Battleship Row.

Like many of the fleet units caught at Pearl, the five submarines of Task Force Seven were in harbor for rest and reconditioning after strenuous exercises and patrols. Officers and men had been granted liberty, and repair crews had come aboard. One of the submarines was at the Navy Yard undergoing a major overhaul. Tied up at their finger-piers with hatches open and gear dismantled, the other four were equally disarmed. Few naval vessels are as vulnerable to air attack as surfaced submarines, and a submarine tethered to a pier by charging cables and water lines is as helpless as a moored canal barge. Fish in a barrel made difficult targets compared to these fish "out of water." Yet the submariners caught at their Pearl Harbor base were to give a good account of themselves.

Typical of their precarious situation was TAUTOG's. On October 21, she and her sister submarine, THRESHER, had left Pearl Harbor to conduct the first full-time, simulated war patrol made by Pacific submarines. Both submarines carried full torpedo loads. The patrol, conducted in waters off Midway, gave captains and crews a sharp taste of realism. Wartime conditions were observed—the submarines remained submerged by day and surfaced at night. Men and material were put through gruelling tests. Proceeding home to Pearl three days ahead of THRESHER, TAUTOG entered the harbor in need of overhaul and supplies, her crew worn to the bone by the exhausting trials. Now, Sunday morning of the 7th, few of her complement were aboard. Of her submarine sailors on hand, several were readying for church, others were thinking about breakfast, and undoubtedly someone was listening to "Music for Your Morning Mood." It was almost time for the routine sounding of Colors at 0800.

When a familiar drone of planes invaded the peaceful sky, it sounded like a flight returning to Hickam—perhaps a squadron of Flying Forts expected from the mainland.

Husky explosions growled in echo across the south. Men looked up surprised. "Say, this is right on the beam! Just what this Navy needs! Sunday morning practice! Realistic stuff!"

So thought a number of submarine officers at first

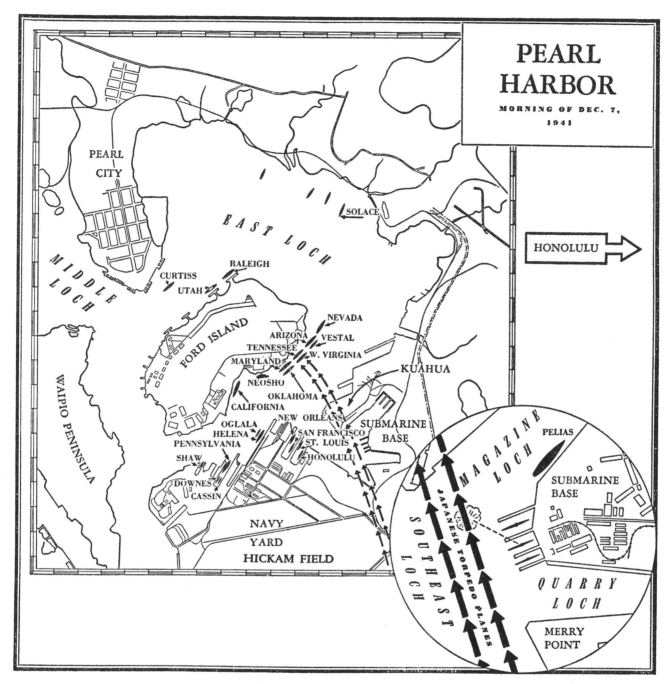

PEARL HARBOR

MORNING OF DEC. 7, 1941

glimpse of the oncoming bombers. To several, like Lieutenant W. B. (Barney) Sieglaff, duty officer aboard TAUTOG, this touch made a fitting climax for weeks of extensive drill. But someone was overdoing it. These planes looked too much like business. Somewhere a man shouted, "Japs! This is it!" Then a low-flying torpedo plane roared by, and stunned submariners stared in shock at the red fireball.

Alarm bell! General Quarters! "Man all battle stations!" Snapping commands through pandemonium, Sieglaff mustered a gun crew as TAUTOG's sailors boiled out on deck. Weapons had to be broken out

of lockers; ammunition passed up from below. Nearby anti-aircraft opened up with shattering volleys as the submariners manned TAUTOG's 3-incher. Aboard the submarine NARWHAL, a gun crew opened fire as a Jap torpedo plane came hurtling over Merry Point. TAUTOG's gunners blazed at the plane. A destroyer berthed near the Submarine Base opened fire. The plane burst into flames and crashed in the channel 50 yards from the Submarine Base. The two submarines shared credit with the DD for this first kill.

Now tumultuous explosions rumbled from the direction of Ford Island. In a matter of moments,

9

each of the outboard battleships moored in the Row was hit. Mountains of smoke, lit by gouts of dark fire, surged into the sky. Blast after blast shook the harbor. From the Navy Yard to Pearl City, anti-aircraft were barking like frantic dogs at the invader. Klaxons, bells, whistles, sirens, a bedlam of human and mechanical outcry loudened and swelled as Pearl Harbor entered its morning of travail. Another flight of torpedo planes came racing in. On Tautog's deck a machine gun chattered.

A Browning .50-cal. machine gun was strictly improvisation in the face of this tornado. But it proved the best thing at hand. Tautog's deck gun was frozen, unable to elevate after days of submergence during that long trial patrol. While gunner's mates worked desperately over the malfunctioning 3-incher, Torpedoman Pasqual Mignon manned the machine gun and opened up on the Jap planes.

A low-flying "V" of torpedo planes was storming up the track for Battleship Row. Two destroyers which had been covering the zone immediately beyond the Submarine Base simultaneously ceased fire. In that few seconds' interval, Torpedoman's Mate Mignon got in his shot. Observers of the action (among them, Rear Admiral Thomas Withers, Commander Submarine Force, Pacific) saw the fiery whip of bullets lash out from Tautog's deck and lick across the Jap plane's fuselage. A binding flash—then, streaming a plume of smoke, the plane nose-dived into the channel.

This was the first Japanese warrior destroyed, single-handed, by a U.S. submarine in World War II.

Ordeal by Fire

Despite the heavy screen of anti-aircraft fire thrown up by the warships in the harbor, Battleship Row was hard hit. Stabbed by four torpedoes, Oklahoma rolled over. West Virginia, battered and aflame, wedged neighboring Tennessee in a fiery grip against the concrete quay. Torpedoed, California settled in a lake of blazing oil. Maryland was blasted. Nevada was struck. On the north side of Ford Island, old Utah, mistaken for an aircraft carrier, capsized and sank under a bombing. A freak mischance sent a bomb down one of Arizona's stacks, and the battleship's forward boilers and magazine exploded. In this one horrendous blast, 1,100 officers and men, including Rear Admiral Isaac C. Kidd and Captain Franklin Van Valkenburgh, were slain.

At Ten Ten Dock, the cruiser Helena and minelayer Oglala were wounded by a torpedo blast. Oglala capsized. Curtiss and Raleigh were disabled. The destroyer Shaw was almost torn to pieces. Destroyers Cassin and Downes were scorched in drydock as though in a furnace. California, already injured, was speared by a 15-inch armor-piercing shell which had been adapted for use as a bomb. Although damaged, Nevada managed to escape her moorings and start for the harbor entrance. As she reached the channel she suffered five more bomb hits. To keep her from sinking in the narrows, her commander deliberately ran her aground.

A few Army fighter planes rising to meet the attackers were quickly eliminated. So were several unarmed Flying Fortresses which blundered into the melee. Naval planes from the aircraft carrier Enterprise, which was at that time 200 miles off Oahu, ran into Jap dive bombers and indiscriminate anti-aircraft fire, and 11 were shot down. Some 18 enemy planes also perished in that morning's inferno, and the submariners could look back with pride on their contribution to the attacker's casualty list.

Throughout the Pearl Harbor blasting, the officers and men at the Submarine Base were in the thick of the fight. Those who were not manning guns aboard the submarines were rushing ammunition, serving in the Navy Yard with fire details, or laboring with hospital crews and rescue parties. Some 1,500 blankets and 2,000 mattresses were distributed to sailors of the shattered surface fleet. Clothing was doled out, and food was prepared for exhausted crews. Loaded with gear borrowed from the escape training tank, the submarine rescue vessel Widgeon and the Submarine Base diving ship rushed to assist in the rescue of the men trapped in the capsized Oklahoma.

The attack subsided around 10:00 A.M., and the last Japanese plane was reported over the harbor about noon. Littered with burning hulls and calcined wreckage, its piers and quays strewn with scrap iron, Pearl Harbor was a weltering Aceldama. Of the capital ships, only Pennsylvania, in drydock, had come through without serious damage. Nineteen warships had been sunk, gutted, or savagely mangled. Shore installations on Ford Island were reduced to shambles. Over 3,000 Navy and Marine Corps officers and men had been killed.

To the submariners who witnessed the debacle, this reduction of the U.S. Navy's great Central Pacific base came as a staggering initiation to modern warfare. On that black day there were few, if any, who did not realize that History hung in the balance. Setting out to make history—their own undersea brand of it—the submariners were to be weighed in this balance. And they would not be found wanting.

Pearl Harbor Aftermath

At the Pearl Harbor Submarine Base the crews reassembled, and technicians worked at top speed to ready the boats for departure. Engines and motors were groomed, batteries were serviced, loading operations went forward on the double. By evening of the 7th, several of the submarines were fueled and ready to go.

But a number of days would pass before one of these submarines would venture out on war patrol. Expected follow-up raids on Pearl Harbor did not materialize, and the submariners welcomed the opportunity to complete the overhauling of their boats. It was a fortunate feature of the Pearl Harbor onslaught that the Submarine Base escaped a bomb hit. The torpedo shop on the ground floor of the submarine administration building and munition dumps on neighboring Kuahua were overlooked by the enemy planes which thundered over Southeast Loch.

Although prepared with meticulous care and masterfully executed by the pilots, the Japanese attack-pattern neglected this vital detail. Bombs and torpedoes were specifically marked for expenditure on the battleships in the Row and the carriers thought to be moored off Ford Island. Submarines and submarine repair facilities were presumed to be minor targets. It was a presumption the Japanese High Command would eventually regret.

Under the driving leadership of Rear Admiral Thomas Withers, submarines of the Pacific Fleet operating out of Pearl Harbor would presently launch an undersea offensive that would more than return the bread so ruthlessly cast upon the waters by the Japanese militarists. And the war was but a few days old when the Pearl Harbor submariners arranged for the Imperial Navy a meaningful epitaph.

The midget submarine sunk by CURTISS was raised from the mud and found to be wrecked beyond useful examination. At the Submarine Base a new pier was under construction. Fill-in material was needed, and the midget submarine's hulk made fitting residue for the excavation. A military funeral ceremony preceded the burial. Then the battered little boat—a coffin for its two-man crew—was cemented into the foundations of the Submarine Base pier.

CHAPTER 2

CENTRAL PACIFIC FRONT

Japanese Myopia

In their all-out, surprise smash at Pearl Harbor, the Japanese evidently hoped to copy their successful Port Arthur performance which opened the Russo-Japanese War of 1904. Intention was to deal the U.S. Pacific Fleet a blow that would paralyze American sea power for months to come. Gaining the initiative, the forces of Dai Nippon would gather the Southwest Pacific into the embrace of the "Greater East Asia Co-Prosperity Sphere" and fortify this territory before the U.S. Navy could strike back.

The master minds in Tokyo assumed that American naval forces (divided between Atlantic and Pacific as the Czarist Russian fleets had been) would then concentrate for a strike at the Japanese homeland. Yamamoto intended to meet this attack with minefields, dive bombers and a superior concentration of naval power. Lured into Empire waters, this United States fleet, far from its home base, would be destroyed. Thus victory would be assured the Japanese. Interesting plan—but it seems the Japanese War Lords overlooked the venerable adage about counting chickens before they were hatched.

In their over-all war plan the Imperial strategists also overlooked the U.S. submarine fleet, even as the five submarines at Pearl Harbor were blandly ignored. For several generations Japan's Shinto-inspired militarists had been plotting Pacific conquest. Before the turn of the century Viscount Tani had counselled, *"Japan must with patience wait for the time of confusion to gain its ends."* During World War I, Premier Shigenobu Okuma had said in the face of the Allies, *"In the middle of the Twentieth Century Japan will meet Europe on the plains of Asia and wrest from her the mastery of the world."* Abrupt substitution of the Pacific Ocean for the plains of Asia may account for some of the Japanese nearsightedness concerning the American submarine potential. But even in the 1930's, when fleet-type

submarines were replacing the older S-boats, Japanese Foreign Minister Baron Kijuro Shidehara declared, *"The number of submarines possessed by the United States is of no concern to the Japanese inasmuch as Japan can never be attacked by American submarines."*

The baron's view appears to have been shared by the Imperial Navy's leaders, who failed to see that an island is a body of land completely surrounded by a submarine's favorite element. Notoriously myopic, the Japanese. Yet their underestimation of the submarine is a strategic error difficult to comprehend. In World War I Japan's naval observers had seen the U-boat blockade bring England to the verge of defeat. Again in 1940 the undersea fleet of Nazi Admiral Doenitz all but sank the United Kingdom. The similarity of Japan's insular position to that of the British Isles is apparent on any map. Certainly the U.S. Navy was aware of the analogy.

However, the Japanese may have judged American undersea power by the U.S. submarine fleet which existed in 1939 when World War II exploded in Europe. On September 8, 1939, when President Roosevelt declared a limited national emergency, there were only 55 U.S. submarines in active commission. But the Nazi conquests in Europe and the spread of U-boat warfare in the Atlantic set a pace for American submarine building. The old R-boats—coastal submarines built during World War I—were soon to be relegated to the status of training ships. Refits were rushed to place decommissioned boats back in operating condition. Work was accelerated on submarines then building in the yards, and an energetic construction program was implemented by emergency appropriations voted by Congress.

With the development of a two-ocean Navy, a two-ocean undersea fleet was organized, the submarine force being divided between the Atlantic and the Pacific. Axis agents might have observed that, despite the growing U-boat menace in the Atlantic, a formidable number of American submarines were heading for waters under the sundown. Perhaps the secretive nature of the service, indoctrinated in the arts of concealment, frustrated such observation.

In gratuitously ignoring this undersea fleet, the Samurai leaders of Dai Nippon displayed an antediluvian kind of thinking that was going to cost them the sea lanes of the Pacific. Had the raiders at Pearl Harbor erased the Submarine Base, and the bombers that struck the Philippines concentrated on the boats and tenders in Manila Bay, the "Greater East Asia Co-Prosperity Sphere" could unquestionably have prospered longer than it did. And an Allied come-back in the Pacific would have been far more costly for the delay.

But the milk was spilled in the War Plans Section of the Imperial High Command before even the first shot was fired. American submarines were considered secondary targets, and the Imperial Navy was confident it could win control of the sea and escort Japan's convoys without difficulty to the farthest Pacific horizon.

United States fleet-type submarines and S-boats set out to correct these miscalculations on the afternoon of December 7 when the Chief of Naval Operations sent the undersea forces into action with the order to execute unrestricted submarine warfare against Japan.

Fleet-type Submarines and S-boats

To Mr. Average American on Main Street, an aircraft is no longer a novelty. During World Wars I and II, he became acquainted with armored vehicles and tanks. If he lived on the seaboard or patronized the movies, he doubtless saw naval vessels on occasion and had some knowledge of the workings of battleships, cruisers and destroyers. But to the citizen on Main Street, submarines (and submariners) operated in a realm of mystery as remote as the deep blue sea. After the strike at Pearl Harbor the mystery deepened, for the "Silent Service" wasn't talking. To understand submarine operations, however, the layman should have at least a bowing acquaintance with the submersibles which featured in this history. For the uninitiated reader, a brief review—

At the time of the Pacific War's outbreak the U.S. Navy's submarines were of two general classes—the long-range, fleet-type submarines (bearing the name of fish), and the older shorter-range S-boats which were numerically designated.

While not of one homogenous type, the modern fleet submarines had one common feature. Representing the results of 20 years of experiment to determine the best design for a Pacific-going submarine, all were capable of long periods of sustained cruising. Able to remain at sea for approximately 75 days, they could cover some 10,000 or more miles at normal cruising speeds without refueling.

Largest of the Navy's submarines, ARGONAUT (V-4) was 385 feet in length, with a displacement of 2,710 tons surfaced and 4,000 tons submerged. Armament consisted of four 21-inch torpedo tubes, plus two 6-inch guns mounted fore and aft of the conning tower. She was designed primarily for minelaying. Her capacious quarters provided for a complement of 89.

NARWHAL and NAUTILUS (V-5 and V-6) shared honors for size with ARGONAUT. They were 371 feet in length, with surface displacement of 2,730 tons. Each had six torpedo tubes—four in the bow and two in the stern—and two 6-inch deck guns.

These three large submarines (designated as V-boats) were built in the decade which followed World War I. Their construction was preceded by that of BARRACUDA, BASS and BONITA (V-1, V-2 and V-3)—somewhat smaller submarines, which carried complements of 75 men, and were armed with six torpedo tubes, one 3-inch gun, and two machine guns.

Acting upon experience gained from these big V-boats, naval designers concluded that size and heavy deck guns were more of a burden than a benefit to the combat submarine. During World War I the British had built M-1, a large submersible mounting a 12-inch gun in a watertight deck housing. Before she could be effectively tested, she was sunk in a collision. Completed in 1929, the French submarine SURCOUF, carrying two 8-inch guns mounted in a turret, plus an anti-aircraft battery and a small seaplane, had proved the world's largest Jonah. Such ultra-large submarines sacrificed maneuverability for size, were comparatively difficult to handle and required too much time for submerging. Greater bulk made them easier to detect. And heavy guns for surface action competed with the submarine's No. 1

function—the delivery of an undersea attack. Priority was therefore given by American submarine designers to diving speed, cruising range and torpedo power. DOLPHIN (V-7), CACHALOT (V-8) and CUTTLEFISH (V-9) built in 1932, 1933 and 1934, were the last of the V-boats.

The PIKE and PERCH classes, constructed between 1935 and 1936, had a displacement of some 1,320 tons. In length 300 feet, beam 25 feet, they were capable of a surface speed of 20 knots, submerged speed of 10 knots, and had a 12,000-mile cruising radius. PIKE-class submarines were equipped with an all-electric drive. Whereas the Diesels had formerly been connected directly to the propellers, those installed in the PIKE class drove generators whose power was converted into electricity which in turn drove motors connected to the propeller drive shaft.

Eight torpedo tubes, a 3-inch deck gun and a machine gun gave greater firepower to SALMON and SARGO-class submarines built in 1938 and 1939. Displacement of these boats was 1,450 tons. This class was succeeded in 1940 by the TAMBORS which were 308 feet in length, with 27-foot beam, and a displacement of 1,475 tons. TAMBOR was driven by four Diesels, totaling 6,400 H.P., at a surface speed of 21 knots. A 3-inch deck gun and two machine guns armed her against attack. Ten torpedo tubes carried this class to the fore in striking power.

Newest of the fleet-type submarines, the GATO class, built in 1941, was to remain standard for eventual wartime construction. Including GREENLING and GROUPER, this class embodied the best features of the previously built long-range submarines—all-welded construction, all-electric drive, oceanic cruising range, ten torpedo tubes. Minor refinements would be made after war experience, but there were no basic changes in the design of these boats which had a displacement of 1,500 tons; length, 307 feet; beam, 27 feet; horsepower, 6,400; and surface speed, 20 knots. This was the submarine produced by American builders throughout World War II.

The older S-class submarines, constructed primarily for defense purposes in the decade following World War I, were not designed to cruise the vast expanses of ocean which had to be covered by Pacific patrols. The early S-boats, modeled after the S-1, were capable of only limited cruising and comparatively brief submergence. Stowage space, at a premium on any submarine, was restricted to absolute necessities, and quarters were cramped beyond comfort. Even in the later S-boats, lack of air-conditioning made the atmosphere mephitic and the heat overpowering during prolonged submergence in tropic waters. In this regard, the S-boat more than lived up to the

nickname "pig boat." But for all its deficiencies, the S-boat was to demonstrate hardy sea-keeping qualities that made "pig boat" a shining *nom de guerre*.

Last of the S-boats, the S-42 type was 225 feet in length with a 21-foot beam and a surface displacement of 906 tons. Two Diesel engines produced 1,200 H.P. to drive the boats at a maximum speed of 14½ knots. Electric motors of 1,500 H.P. gave them a maximum submerged speed of 11 knots. Structurally, S-48 was similar to the larger V-boats—divided into six watertight compartments with double hull construction amidships and single hull construction at bow and stern. Her armament consisted of five 21-inch torpedo tubes (four at the bow and one at the stern) and a 4-inch deck gun. Her complement numbered 44 men.

Longer legged, longer winded, with firepower heavier than the S-boats, the modern fleet-type submarine was, of course, better equipped for combat and in all respects a superior "weapon." Its "habitability"—that is, "living space" and "breathing space" —was the last word in submarine achievement. Its sea-keeping—and, one might say, undersea-keeping— qualities were second to none. The maximum diving depth of this fleet-type submarine was, and still is, labeled "secret." But it could go down under the sea to a depth well below 200 feet (greater depths will be reported in this history), and it could remain submerged as long as any rival at that time operating.

Like all submarines of the period, American fleet-types and S-types were engine-driven on the surface and driven by motors when submerged. The layman will note that the Diesel engine's dependence on fuel and the motor's dependence on battery "juice" limit the surface and undersea cruising ranges of all submarines. Engines must have air as well as fuel. As the batteries which ran the motors were charged by generators run by the engines, the submarine had to surface after a number of hours' submergence in order to charge the batteries. (Thus, to conserve their batteries, submarines ran on the surface as much as possible. The submerged runs were made when stalking the enemy, avoiding detection, or evading counter-attack.)

Ton for ton, the modern submarine is without question the most compact and complicated man-of-war ever conceived by man's inventive mind. Reference to the plan drawing on page 15 will give the reader an idea of the World War II (fleet-type GATO class) submarine's interior.

As shown in the drawing, the submarine contains as many compartments and cubicles as a fighting ship two or three times its size. Tucked into a space approximately twice as large as the average six-room

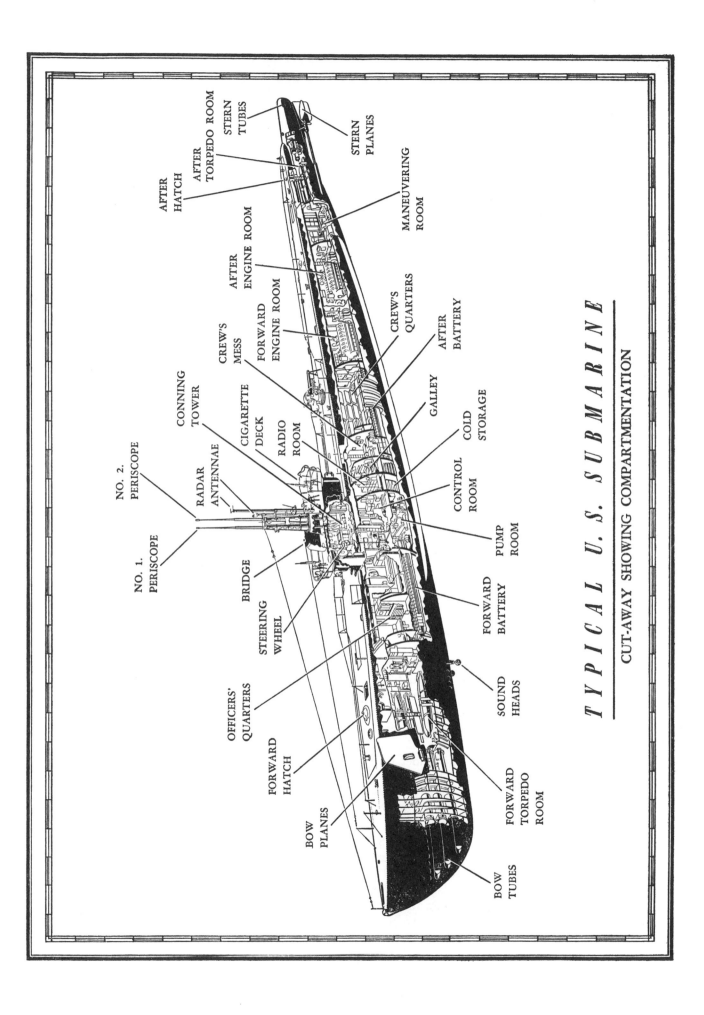

NO. 1.
PERISCOPE

NO. 2.
PERISCOPE

CONNING
TOWER

RADAR
ANTENNAE

CIGARETTE
DECK

RADIO
ROOM

CREW'S
MESS

FORWARD
ENGINE ROOM

AFTER
ENGINE ROOM

AFTER
HATCH

AFTER
TORPEDO ROOM

STERN
TUBES

STERN
PLANES

MANEUVERING
ROOM

CREW'S
QUARTERS

AFTER
BATTERY

GALLEY

COLD
STORAGE

CONTROL
ROOM

PUMP
ROOM

FORWARD
BATTERY

SOUND
HEADS

FORWARD
TORPEDO
ROOM

BOW
TUBES

BOW
PLANES

FORWARD
HATCH

OFFICERS'
QUARTERS

STEERING
WHEEL

BRIDGE

TYPICAL U. S. SUBMARINE

CUT-AWAY SHOWING COMPARTMENTATION

house, there are living accommodations for a crew of 80 or 90 men, a control room, Diesel engines and electric motors, fuel and water tanks, and 252 battery cells, each cell weighing in excess of one ton. There are air compressors and high-pressure air banks for blowing tanks and charging torpedo air flasks. There are torpedo rooms fore and aft, 10 torpedo tubes, stowage space for 24 torpedoes. Crammed into the remaining nooks and crannies are refrigerated and dry stores, stills for manufacturing fresh water, air-conditioning and air-purifying equipment, ice machines, shower baths, main ballast tanks to give "positive buoyancy" when cruising on the surface and "neutral buoyancy" when running submerged, variable ballast tanks for adjusting trim, electrical equipment for operating bow and stern planes, and wells for the periscopes. Lazaret, chain locker, ammunition magazines, galley. Navigational instruments, fire control instruments, radio and radar and sonar gear. Some of this paraphernalia is indicated in the illustration. Only a complicated blueprint could show the multiplicity of valves, gages, meters and operating levers which are the sensitive organs of this undersea vessel; the maze of oil, air and water lines that are its veins and capillaries; the electric cables that are its nervous system. All this within a watertight hull capable of withstanding tremendous pressures deep under the sea! One may believe the submariner who asserts that his is the most complex war engine of all.

Command Organization

With a picture of a submarine in mind, the layman will be interested in the force organization and in a brief detail on the Command.

At the outbreak of the war, submarines of the U.S. Navy were divided among the three existing fleets—Atlantic, Pacific and Asiatic. Each submarine group had its own administrative command: Submarines, Atlantic Fleet, with headquarters at New London, Connecticut; Submarines, Scouting Force, Pacific Fleet, with headquarters at the Submarine Base, Pearl Harbor; Submarines, Asiatic Fleet, with headquarters on board the submarine tender CANOPUS in Manila Bay.

Shortly after the Pearl Harbor attack, it was determined that the submarines of the Pacific Fleet would operate directly under CinCPac rather than under Commander Scouting Force. Commander Submarines, Scouting Force, Pacific Fleet, then became Commander Submarines, Pacific Fleet (ComSubPac). Less than a year later the title was again changed to Commander Submarine Force, Pacific Fleet. Commander Submarines, Asiatic Fleet, eventually became Commander Submarines, Southwest Pacific (ComSubSoWesPac). When all naval forces operating in the Southwest Pacific were designated as the Seventh Fleet he received the alternate title of Commander Submarines, Seventh Fleet.

Each of the three submarine force administrative commands functioned as a separate entity under its own fleet commander, and there were no official ties that bound them together. All of the cooperation, coordination, and standardization of doctrine among the three forces was effected by mutual consent of the force commanders rather than by high command edict. Commander Submarines, Atlantic (ComSubLant) controlled all submarines operating in the Atlantic and in European waters. He also had operational control over Panama-based submarines patrolling the Pacific approaches of the Panama Canal.

The boundary line between the areas patrolled by Submarines, Pacific Fleet, and Submarines, Asiatic Fleet, at the start of the war was subject to revision as the conflict widened. The boundary finally stabilized at a line drawn along the parallel of 20° north from the coast of China to a point a few miles east of the easternmost point of the Philippine Archipelago, thence directly south to the equator, and then eastward along the equator. While this was the established line, temporary exchanges of areas were made from time to time to meet the needs of any particular operation or tactical situation. Normally, those waters to the north and east of the line were patrolled by Pacific Fleet submarines, those to the south and west by SubSoWesPac.

New-construction submarines, after being fitted out and trained by ComSubLant, reported for duty and became units of SubPac upon passing through the Panama Canal. In accordance with a plan developed some months after the war's outbreak, ComSubPac operated under a directive from the Chief of Naval Operations to keep SubSoWesPac up to a fixed numerical strength. Whenever a submarine was lost in the Southwest Pacific or became due for an overhaul in the States, ComSubPac would furnish a submarine from his command to serve as a replacement.

To decentralize the administrative organization and relieve the force commander of unnecessary details, submarines are organized into divisions and squadrons. The normal division consists of six submarines, and two divisions form a squadron. Each squadron is either assigned its own tender or is assigned to a submarine base. In either case the functions of the tender and the base are the same—to supply office space and quarters for the squadron and division commanders and their staffs, to billet repair personnel and relief crews, to undertake all submarine repairs, short of complete overhauls. Everything from the replacement of a damaged propeller to the adjustment of a cranky sextant, the supplying of all necessary food, fuel, clothing, spare parts, munitions, medical stores—the care of all the material needs of the submarines and physical needs of the submariners—these are the tasks accomplished by submarine tender or submarine base.

In peacetime the squadron and division commanders exercise a considerable degree of operational control over their boats. During the war they served in a wholly administrative capacity. The force commanders controlled all combat operations, and in so doing, they dealt directly with the submarine captains—there were no intervening command echelons. A submarine returning from patrol in enemy waters was assigned to a squadron commander for refit. (Not necessarily his own squadron commander, as the refit workload had to be equalized.) The submarine was also assigned to one of the division commanders of that squadron for training. A relief crew from the squadron would take over the submarine while the regular crew was ashore. After a period of rest and recreation, the regulars would return on board. One day would then be spent in testing machinery and equipment, and in making a trim dive. Four days would be devoted to refresher training at sea under the division commander. Two days would be spent loading stores, food, fuel, and torpedoes, and in getting ready for sea. Finally on the "readiness-for-sea day," the submarine would pass to the direct command of the force commander, who would issue the operation order to the submarine's captain and send the submarine on her way.

Unless unusual repair work or special training was required, the period of refit and training covered three weeks. With the patrol then lasting anywhere from 45 to 60 days, the normal patrol cycle was 75 days. Standard procedure was to send the submarine from the Pacific to a navy yard on the West Coast for complete overhaul after five patrols had been made. During these overhaul periods, the crews were granted leave in the States.

Internal Submarine Organization

The submarine's crew is an organization of specialists. Brain rather than brawn is the selection criterion. There are many "sergeants" but few "privates"—non-rated men constitute less than 20% of the entire complement. Each officer and man must be a specialist in his own job, but he must know his shipmate's job as well. Before an officer or man can be designated as "qualified in submarines" he must pass a rigid written and oral examination on all machinery, piping and equipment throughout the boat. The electrician's mate must know how to fire the torpedo tubes, the torpedoman's mate how to charge batteries. There are no spare parts in a submarine's crew—each member is a cog in the wheel, and each cog must do its job to perfection if the organization is to function smoothly, efficiently, and above all, safely.

From a numerical standpoint, motor machinist's mates, electrician's mates and torpedoman's mates predominate in the crew. These three groups approximate half of the enlisted personnel. Next come radiomen and operators of the submarine's electronic gear. Three quartermasters or signalmen, two ship's cooks, two steward's mates, one pharmacist's mate, one gunner's mate, one yeoman and a number of firemen and seamen complete the complement. The senior chief petty officer on board, usually a chief torpedoman's mate, is designated the "Chief of the Boat."

The senior officer on board is, of course, the submarine's captain. ("Old Man" to the crew, he was, at the outbreak of World War II, a lieutenant commander whose age was probably 34 or 35). He is followed in seniority by the executive officer who also serves as navigator. Aside from these two—captain and exec—seniority does not enter the picture. The submarine captain assigns officers to the various ship's duties in accordance with their experience and capabilities. There are the chief engineer, torpedo and gunnery officer, communications officer and commissary officer. (When radar equipment was installed during World War II there was sometimes a radar officer.) The officers may be, and frequently are, assigned more than one of the above-listed duties.

In the pre-war days the complement of a fleet-type submarine consisted of five officers and 54 enlisted men. As newly developed fire control, radar, radio and sound equipment was added to the submarines, and as war experience dictated the need for more personnel, the complement grew. At war's end it approximated eight officers and 75 enlisted men.

For purposes of watch-standing, the submarine crew is divided into three sections. All hands, the captain excepted, stand watches "one in three" with four hours on duty and eight hours off. The work of the captain, in the words of the well-known sideshow pitch, "is goin' on all the time." He must be constantly on the alert and always on call. Each section is organized to man all necessary stations for diving, surfacing, and surfaced or submerged cruising. With the exception of routine cleaning and minor repair jobs, little work is done on a submarine at sea, and sections off watch occupy their time with eating, reading, acey deucey, and sleeping.

Torpedo or gun attacks are, of course, all-hands evolutions. When contact with the enemy is made, the general alarm is sounded and everyone mans his battle station. The captain takes over the periscope and conducts the approach and attack. Breathing over his shoulder is the exec who, as assistant approach officer, is the "official kibitzer." It is his job to check the captain's observations and estimates, and to assist with the adroit mental gymnastics required for a submarine approach. In pre-war days the assistant approach officer was called the "yes man." The term fell into disrepute because of its unintended connotation with obsequious kowtowing. There is no time for "yessing" in a submarine when the life of all on board may depend on "flooding negative." The only answer permitted in submersible operations is the right answer.

On board the submarine going into action, other officers serve as diving officer, torpedo data computer operator, and plotting officer. One officer is usually assigned to each torpedo room to supervise the readying of the tubes, or to take charge of torpedo reloads. The battle station duties of the crew keep the enlisted men busy. Some serve as members of the approach and fire control party, others as telephone talkers, timekeepers, or recorders. Torpedoman's mates, of course, man their torpedo rooms, and all men not otherwise specifically assigned proceed to these rooms to assist with reloads. When attack and inevitable counter-attack are concluded, the word is passed, "Secure from battle stations—first [or second, or third] section on watch." Normal routine is resumed.

The stranger on board a submarine on war patrol might have difficulty distinguishing between captain and seaman. Both eat the same food and wear similar garb—shorts and leather sandals being standard costume for patrols in the tropics. And both might be found engrossed in a fast game of chess on the control room deck. Submarines and submarining do not provide space for the protocol of rank. Each member of the crew, from cook to captain, stands on his own two feet as an individual.

Warfare Unrestricted

The unrestricted warfare directive issued by the Chief of Naval Operations on December 7 was as startling as the Japanese attack on Pearl Harbor. To many in the submarine forces it was as unexpected. It meant "total war" on the sea—a war in which a fishing boat or freighter was to be considered a target as legitimate as an enemy battleship.

Although the Axis Powers had for many months been conducting total war in the Atlantic and the Mediterranean, indiscriminate war on merchant shipping had never been advocated by American naval authorities. Veteran submariners recalled America's abhorrence for the unrestricted German campaigns of 1917-1918 when the U-boat was denounced as the "stiletto of the seas." The Nazi sinkings of the ATHENIA, the ZAMZAM, the ROBIN MOOR and the SESSA had revived American protests against submarine attacks on passenger and cargo ships.

Neither by training nor indoctrination was the U.S. Submarine Force readied for unrestricted warfare. The Service was prepared for battle action. In connection with lend-lease operations, submarines in the Atlantic were already conducting what amounted to war patrols. In the Pacific, "Readiness for War Trials" had been strenuous and not without hazard. Officers and men prided themselves in their efficiency and were confident that American scientific and technological genius had given them weapons superior to any on or under the sea.

But the submariners had trained to fight a war of their own conception—a campaign against enemy combat ships—occasional surface engagements—tactical scouting—a few minelaying missions to harass enemy harbors. The war contemplated was an orthodox one in which the naval combatants observed "ethical" tactics based on rules which had been devised for sea conflict by such idealists as Hugo Grotius.

Among the official publications allowed to each submarine was a small volume entitled: "INSTRUCTIONS FOR THE NAVY OF THE UNITED STATES GOVERNING MARITIME AND AERIAL WARFARE." When war appeared imminent, this volume was studied assiduously. Submarine captains were taught to respect its word. The Service was subject to many legal limitations and treaty restrictions, and submarines guilty of violating these could be *hunted down and captured or sunk as pirates.*

Such paragraphs as the following were impressed on the memory of every submarine commanding officer:

"In their action with regard to merchant ships, submarines must conform to the rules of International Law to which surface vessels are subject.

"In particular, except in the case of persistent refusal to stop on being duly summoned, or of active resistance to visit or search, a warship, whether surface vessel or submarine, may not sink or render incapable of navigation a merchant vessel without having first placed passengers, crew and ship's papers in a place of safety."

On the opening day of World War II, the Nazi U-boat which sank the ATHENIA torpedoed these legal niceties. And the Mikado's military leaders, for all their reverence for the Code Bushido, had long shown little respect for rules of "civilized" warfare.

In any event, realistic thinking demanded recognition of the fact that a nation's economic forces and its fighting forces bear the inseparable relationship of Siamese twins. Any reduction of a nation's economic resources weakens its war potential. Sever the commercial arteries of a maritime nation and its industrial heart must fail, while the war effort expires with it. Therefore, it was not reprisal so much as military imperative that caused Washington to reverse its opinion on the already abrogated naval laws.

Webster defines a merchant vessel as "a ship employed in commerce." There were to be no merchant ships in the Pacific for the duration of the war—cargo carriers were merchantmen by genesis only. The U.S. Navy was to consider all Japanese shipping as engaged in prosecution of the war effort—either carrying men, munitions, and equipment to areas under attack or occupation, or freighting home the plundered raw materials from conquered territory.

Armed or not, these merchantmen were in effect combatant ships. "Transports," "freighters," "tankers" were hollow titles for auxiliaries of war, and it was the realistic duty of the submarine forces to reduce these ships to hulls as hollow as their titles. The polite little law book went overboard. Converted by a directive into commerce raiders, American submarines in the Pacific went to war to sink everything that floated under a Japanese flag.

Action at Midway and Wake

Timed with the attack on Pearl Harbor, surprise blows were landed by the enemy on America's outpost islands—Midway—Wake—Guam. At Midway and Wake, American submarines had their opening encounter with Japanese surface forces.

Flying the Rising Sun flag, a powerful Japanese naval force bore down on Midway in the afternoon of December 7th. A coral group composed of two atolls (Sand and Eastern islands) too small to accommodate a battle fleet, Midway was nonetheless important as a stepping stone strategically located on an invasion route from (or to) Japan via the Bonin Islands. Despite the island's salient position, Midway's fixed defenses were of insufficient caliber to meet any determined Japanese assault.

The defenders had been alerted by the first radio alarm from Hawaii which came that morning at 0630, Midway time. Throughout the day Marines stood

tensely at their battle stations. When night extinguished the brief twilight, the defenders were still waiting in suspense.

The little harbor was blacked out, but a bright tropic moon whitewashed the beach and revealed shore installations in stark silhouette. For the Japanese naval gunners Midway was a beautiful target.

The first projectiles fell in the lagoon at 2130, shattering the silence with the sudden violence of rocks dropped on a mirror. Lookouts in the communication tower spotted the flash of turret guns far to the southwest and beyond range of Midway's shore batteries.

Another salvo flashed. This time the shells struck the beach not far from the artillery installations.

A third salvo struck the Midway hangar, starting a furious conflagration.

The Marines now saw the answer to the ease with which the distant warships got on target. A Japanese destroyer and what appeared to be a light cruiser (CL) were closing in at top speed, and spotting for the warships on the horizon.

As the DD and the CL raced in they opened up on the American shore batteries. The Marines returned a blistering fire. A searchlight on Sand Island illuminated the destroyer for a moment, spotlighting the red sun flying from her main truck. The light was promptly blown out by a salvo from the Jap cruiser.

Salvos from the distant warships smashed the Marine command post and exploded near the burning hangar while the racing destroyer and light cruiser traded fire with the shore batteries. The Marines lashed the enemy warships with heavy machine-gun fire, and the shore guns hit both targets. But the set-up favored the heavier naval guns. And Midway's defenders were steeled for an all-out bombardment, when the destroyer and the cruiser veered away and retired as suddenly as they had charged. As abruptly, the ships on the horizon ceased fire and executed a high-speed withdrawal.

The sudden retirement of this Japanese force from Midway Island has been remarked as one of the major mysteries of the war. Apparently the Japanese were not bent on seizing Midway. Had they continued their initial attack they could have won the island at comparatively minor cost. When they returned six months later, Midway's defenses were tremendously strengthened, and the Imperial Navy suffered the worst defeat it had up to that time ever encountered. Many strategists have put a big question mark behind the withdrawal of the first Japanese striking force from Midway's waters. While Midway was not on Yamamoto's agenda for early conquest, it seems possible that U.S. submarine action

19

may have interfered with the December 7th bombardment.

As remarked in the previous chapter, the submarines TROUT and ARGONAUT were conducting defensive patrols in the Midway area on that momentous date. Both submarines were on the surface that Sunday evening. Both sighted ominous flashes on the horizon. The red breath of the guns! The enemy was shelling Midway from the west.

TROUT (Lieutenant Commander F. W. Fenno) had received news of the Pearl Harbor bombing that morning. Then had come a radio dispatch ordering her to locate ARGONAUT. All day she had tried to contact the big submarine which was patrolling south of her. But ARGONAUT, in accordance with training routine, had submerged for the day, and TROUT could only wait for sundown when the big V-boat would come to the surface.

Now, sighting the gun flares against the evening sky, Fenno drove his submarine at top speed to the north of Midway, hoping to intercept the enemy in that direction. Meantime, ARGONAUT, cruising off Sand Island, had picked up word of the Pearl Harbor raid when she surfaced just after sunset. Not long after that she sighted the Japanese force shelling Midway. This was it! ARGONAUT's captain, Lieutenant Commander S. G. Barchet, ordered the submarine under, and began an approach on the enemy vessels.

TROUT, north of Midway, was unable to close with the warships. But ARGONAUT's submerged approach brought her within attack range. Before diving, however, she had been sighted in the brilliant moonlight, and one enemy warship rushed to search the area, while the other Jap ships raced away at 30-knot speed. With a cruiser or large destroyer probing for the submarine with echo-ranging gear, Barchet gave the order to rig for depth charges, and ARGONAUT, in the parlance of the submariners, "went deep." The first days of the war were trial-and-error ones for American submarine captains and crews, who had not yet fired a torpedo in anger and were unacquainted with the devices of the enemy. So ARGONAUT's brush with the foe at Midway resulted in no material damage to either side. But the Midway bombardment was broken off while the hunt for the submarine began. Here at the outset of the war was an example of the submersible's ability to divert surface forces and disrupt an enemy attack.

Unfortunately, submarine action at Wake Island, while more aggressive than that at Midway, was unable to fend the enemy's blow.

Flanked by the Japanese Mandates—the Marshalls and the Caroline Islands—Wake was decidedly vulnerable. And the island's defenses, despite belated reinforcement, were weaker than Midway's. Originally designated a bird sanctuary by the U.S. Government, and later employed as a Pacific way-station by Pan-American Airways, Wake was not armed until early in 1941. To any determined Japanese assault, the defenders could offer only back-to-the-wall resistance. The war-makers in Tokyo had determined to seize Wake Island.

About 0700, December 8 (Wake time), the Wake garrison received word of the Pearl Harbor attack. Mid-morning, Wake was struck by enemy bombers from Kwajalein.

Two days of aerial pounding preceded the arrival of a Jap task force consisting of three light cruisers, six destroyers, two transports and two scouting submarines. Before this overpowering force the island was to fall after 16 days of sacrificial resistance by its handful of Marines.

U.S. submarines TAMBOR and TRITON were on practice war patrols off Wake when the Japanese struck. TRITON played a fighting part in the desperate defense.

TAMBOR (Lieutenant Commander J. W. Murphy) was some 40 miles northeast of Wake when word of the Pearl Harbor strike came in by radio. On the night of December 8-9, TAMBOR's bridge watch could see fires bursting out on Wake Island, and during the ensuing onslaught the watch had periscope views of air raids and a glimpse of the attacking warships. TAMBOR was unable to close the range and attack the Jap naval force.

Patrolling south of Wake, TRITON found herself in position to intercept the enemy naval force. Just before midnight on December 10, TRITON was on the surface finishing a battery charge. Suddenly two bright flashes lit the horizon, and the officer of the deck made out a Jap man-of-war silhouetted against the illumined sky. A large destroyer or light cruiser, it appeared to be heading toward the submarine. TRITON had been ordered not to attack unless attacked, so her skipper, Lieutenant Commander W. A. Lent, gave the command to go deep, and the submarine submerged to start evasive tactics.

The crew rigged for depth charges, and there was a harrowing wait while the sound operator at the listening gear reported a rush of high-speed screws, indicating the enemy was on the hunt. Nerves tightened as the warship's propellers could be heard closing in, fading off, returning. As the hunter closed in once more, TRITON's commanding officer may have recalled Farragut's classic theory that the best defense is a well-directed fire. At any rate, Lent decided to attack the hunter. At 0317, after more than three hours of lethal hide-and-seek, he maneuvered

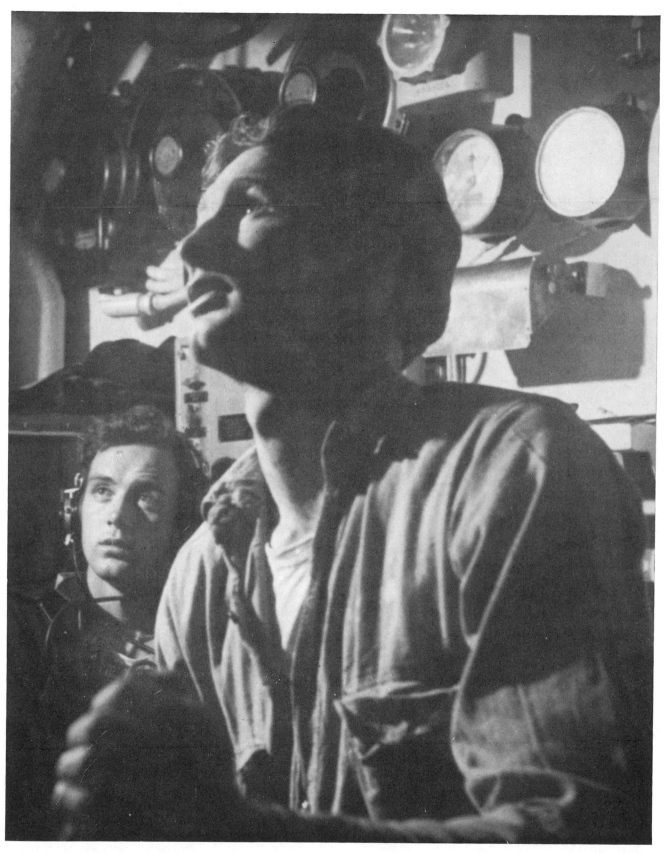

MORE THAN DRAMA and tense excitement is expressed by these men in the maneuvering room of a submarine. Steady hand on the controls—knowing eye on the gauges—instinct for every necessary move—these "musts" for submarining come from training, discipline and high morale under expert leadership.

FLEET TYPE AND S-BOAT—The two subs, tied up at a repair base, show striking contrast of the old and new.

Vintage of the 20's, the S-boat (foreground) looks small beside the modern. But the little "pig-boats" fought big.

GUDGEON—before her bridge was given a slender silhouette.

GUDGEON—After 1943 conversion. Note added machine guns.

S-44—Photograph shows typical "sugarboat" conning tower and gun mounts.

DECK GUNS. In foreground, submariners man a 50 cal. AA-type machinegun mounted on a stanchion. Above on "cigarette deck" looms a 20mm.

FLEET-TYPES tied up alongside tender Proteus. Submarines built during war were modeled after the Gato-class. Roomy enough below decks, but a tight line-up for the crew topside.

TRITON into position, and fired four after-tubes at the stubborn enemy.

Fifty-eight seconds after the first torpedo was fired, a blunt explosion was heard. The muffled blast sent vibrations through the submarine, and there seemed little doubt that the enemy was hit. The chase was over. TRITON was credited with damaging one Japanese warship. This was the first torpedo attack made by a Pacific Fleet submarine in World War II.

Thus U.S. submarines began unrestricted warfare in the Pacific by exchanging blows with the Imperial Japanese Navy. But the war was soon to expand at four-engine speed into an epic conflict of attrition.

Pearl Harbor Postscript

Guam, practically defenseless and within easy striking distance of Saipan, was captured by the Japanese early in the morning of December 10th. Bluejackets and Marines died fighting a hopeless battle to hold Agaña, and the Rising Sun flag climbed over the island at dawn.

"So sorry," said a Japanese naval captain to Ensign Leona Jackson of the U.S. Navy Nurse Corps. "Sorry to tell you all your fleet sunk. All your ships on bottom. No more."

Braggadocio. The Japanese High Command knew better. Yamamoto and his staff had obtained a fairly accurate estimate of the damage done to the United States Pacific Fleet, and Jap announcements of its total destruction were so much propaganda.

Yet the Imperial Navy's leaders did miscalculate. They failed in their estimation of the speed with which the United States Navy could make a comeback.

Immediately after the strike at Pearl Harbor, Yamamoto's carrier force made a high-speed withdrawal to the northwest. About three hours later, Japanese Imperial Headquarters, with a sense for the anti-climactical, issued a rescript from Tokyo declaring war on the United States and Great Britain. The following day Washington and London formally acknowledged the existing state of war with Japan. The embattled U.S. Navy, with no time for diplomatic formalities, was already in action.

At the Pearl Harbor Submarine Base preparations were rushed for a counter-attack on the enemy. Submarine supplies were distributed to various depots around the harbor—a dispersal dictated by the possibility of another air assault and, perhaps, a bombing of the base. Follow-up raids were expected, and the harbor defenses were hair-triggered. THRESHER, approaching Hawaii, ran into some of these keyed-up defenses.

THRESHER was about 60 miles off Barber's Point, the southwest corner of Oahu, when she received the alarm which was broadcast on the morning of the Japanese strike.

PEARL HARBOR ATTACKED . . . THIS IS NO DRILL

The submarine was at that time under escort of the destroyer LITCHFIELD. Lieutenant Commander W. L. Anderson, THRESHER's captain, intending to submerge until nightfall, released the destroyer to join a surface task force scouting for the Jap attackers. The DD raced off. Then, just as THRESHER was going under, she picked up a radio dispatch cautioning her not to release her escort. The submarine promptly sent a radio message to the destroyer, arranging for a rendezvous at the diving point. Two hours later, at the rendezvous position, Anderson ran up the periscope. A destroyer—an old "four piper"—was on the spot. But this DD was not the LITCHFIELD, as THRESHER discovered when her conning tower broke water.

Gunfire blazed from the destroyer, and machine-gun bullets drove THRESHER under. Anderson took her deep, and did not attempt to approach the Pearl Harbor entrance until the morning of December 8th.

In accordance with orders received some hours before, the submarine surfaced at 0600, off the harbor entrance. Again she was attacked by friendly forces—this time by bombing planes. Driven under by this slashing attack, THRESHER remained submerged until the destroyer THORNTON came steaming out to escort her home. It was not until mid-afternoon that the assailed submarine finally entered the base and tied up under the wing of the tender PELIAS.

Fortunately, GUDGEON, entering Pearl Harbor the following day, was unmolested. One by one the other submarines arrived—POLLACK, POMPANO and PLUNGER from San Francisco, and later that month, TAMBOR, recalled from Wake, and TROUT and ARGONAUT from Midway, and finally TRITON. One by one they slid in from the sea, and their crews stared in shock at the harbor's devastation, and boats and crews were readied to go out again and fight the war.

First to leave were GUDGEON and PLUNGER, heading out on December 11th. With but 24 hours' lay-over, GUDGEON, captained by Lieutenant Commander E. W. Grenfell, set a course for Japan to conduct a pioneer patrol in Empire waters off the Bungo Suido —the strait between Shikoku and Kyushu. She was provisioned for a 51-day patrol (some three-fourths of which would be spent in the long haul, going and coming). Like Columbus, Grenfell and the submarine skippers who followed him to make those first patrols in Japan's home waters were setting out for the Unknown. They were not faced with "going over the edge," perhaps. But ahead of them lay the mystery of the enemy's home defenses—a dark mystery of minefields, anti-submarine patrols, air screens. Defenses to be tested and penetrated. Dangerous ventures to try the steel of American submarines and submariners.

PLUNGER (Lieutenant Commander D. C. White) headed for the Kii Suido—the passage between Shikoku and Honshu. When only a few miles out of Pearl Harbor, she was forced to return to base for repairs to a leaky after-battery hatch. Three days later she made a fresh start. Heading once more for Japan, PLUNGER carried the first radar set into battle —the SD aircraft warning installation.

On December 13, POLLACK (Lieutenant Commander S. P. Moseley) left Pearl Harbor to strike out for the Tokyo Bay area—waters lying at the very mouth of the Japanese dragon. The submariners could count on those waters being closely guarded. Would the dragon jaws snap on the invading submersible? Would she run into tongues of flame, or be caught by teeth of steel? POLLACK would soon find out.

On the 18th, POMPANO, captained by Lieutenant Commander L. S. Parks, went pioneering in another direction. Her voyage of discovery was to take her southwest to the Marshall Islands where she was to investigate the Japanese defenses in that area—defenses no less mysterious and baleful than those which guarded the Empire waters off the home coasts of Japan.

To the Marshalls in POMPANO's wake went DOLPHIN (Lieutenant Commander G. B. Rainer), departing Pearl Harbor on Christmas Eve.

TAUTOG (Lieutenant Commander J. H. Willingham) presently followed DOLPHIN, bent on another perilous exploratory mission.

So the Pacific Fleet submarines were under way. The New Year would see these pioneers from Pearl Harbor torpedoing the Japanese High Command's high hope that the Imperial Navy could handily cope with American undersea power.

But the enemy had yet to ride the crest of triumph before descending into the trough of defeat. Before the U.S. submarine forces could counter-attack effectively, the invader's tidal-wave offensive swamped the Philippines. Caught in the storm that broke around Manila were the submarines of the United States Asiatic Fleet.

CHAPTER 3

PHILIPPINES INVASION

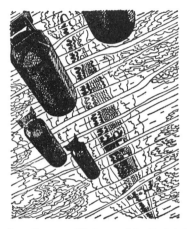

Situation SoWesPac

With Pearl Harbor shattered, Midway dented, Guam captured and Wake's fall a certainty, the Japanese were satisfied that America's mid-Pacific outposts were canceled for the opening phase of the war, if not permanently. The Yamamoto-Tojo war plan now called for an amphibious offensive against the Philippine Islands, Indonesia, and the Netherlands East Indies.

For months the U.S. authorities had anticipated a Japanese strike in this area. Bogged down in China and hard-pressed for petroleums, the Japanese War Machine was slated for a sooner-or-later drive at the oil-rich Netherlands East Indies. Such a drive would mean head-on collision with British and American forces based at Singapore and Manila on the flanks of Java and Sumatra. And the U.S. embargo on Japanese war materials, along with the reopening of the Burma Road, timed the drive at sooner rather than later.

Extension of Philippine fortifications had long been prohibited by treaty with Japan—diplomatic commitments which the U.S. Government had observed while the militarists of the Mikado secretly fortified the Mandates and engaged in unrestricted naval building. Attempting last-minute defense measures, the War Department in 1941 began a program of reinforcement. General Douglas MacArthur was appointed Commander of U.S. Army Forces in the Far East. Fortifications were rushed at Corregidor, guarding the entrance to Manila Bay, and at Mariveles Bay, sheltered by Bataan Peninsula, while the U.S. Navy labored to strengthen its facilities at Cavite. That these impromptu reinforcements might prove too little and too late was a probability generally recognized. Yet their inadequacy was to prove nearly as shocking as the unpreparedness at Pearl Harbor.

Headquartered in the Marsman Building in Manila, Admiral Thomas C. Hart had taken all possible emergency steps to prepare his naval forces for the expected blow. His fleet consisted of the cruisers HOUSTON, MARBLEHEAD and BOISE, 13 over-age destroyers, a flotilla of small gunboats and auxiliary vessels, a squadron of 30 slow, cumbersome PBY's, six PT-boats and the previously mentioned 29 submarines with their tenders HOLLAND, OTUS and CANOPUS and the submarine rescue vessel PIGEON.

Admiral Hart was fully aware that his fleet would face appalling odds were it isolated in combat with the naval forces of Japan. The Japanese had ten battleships for action against the three American cruisers. Three Japanese heavy or light cruisers were available for battle against each over-age Asiatic Fleet destroyer. For good measure the Imperial Navy of Nippon boasted nine aircraft carriers, 113 destroyers, 63 submarines and hundreds of aircraft waiting to strike from near-by bases. It was obvious that when war eventuated, the Asiatic Fleet could do little more than fight a delaying action in an attempt to hold the Philippines until the Pacific Fleet arrived from Pearl Harbor.

Meantime Admiral Hart counted on support from Dutch and British allies—in particular the British with their base at Singapore backed up by Britain's most powerful battleship, HMS PRINCE OF WALES, and the battle cruiser HMS REPULSE. It was realized, however, that a three-pronged Japanese attack, stabbing at Malaya, the Philippines and the East Indies simultaneously, could pin the British and Royal Netherlands naval squadrons in their own waters. In any case, the Americans would have to bear the brunt of battle. And for shock troops to slow the drive he suspected was imminent, Admiral Hart was relying on his fleet's strongest element—the submarine forces.

Himself a veteran submariner, Admiral Hart was superlatively qualified to devise the strategy and direct the submarine defenses for the Philippines. Although he had never commanded an individual submarine or served in one as a detailed ship's officer, he had as wide an acquaintance with submarines as any officer in the Navy.

This experience began in 1915 when Hart, then a lieutenant commander, was serving as the executive officer of the battleship MINNESOTA. The ship was due to be placed in reserve commission, and Lieutenant Commander Hart requested a livelier billet. He had qualified as a torpedo expert, and it was undoubtedly this distinction that won him an assignment to the Hawaiian Islands to command the small submarine squadron of K-boats at that time based in Honolulu Harbor.

As commodore, a courtesy title given to squadron commanders, he raised his flag over the antiquated submarine tender ALERT—a vessel whose brightwork soon began to gleam and whose operations quickened to keep pace with her name. However, Commodore Hart was something more than a spit-and-polish officer. World War I was engulfing Europe, and the U-boats of Von Tirpitz were sinking British merchantmen at a rate that presaged defeat for the Allies. Then—as in 1939—a program of American naval expansion was hastily launched. Undersea warfare was revising naval strategy, and priority thinking was concentrated on submarines.

Among the World War I Allies this thinking centered on the problem of combating the undersea boat rather than developing submarine forces to carry the war to the enemy. Nevertheless, American submarines were readied for active duty. One of Commodore Hart's first moves was to take his K-boats around to Pearl Harbor where he installed a torpedo shop and laid the groundwork for a new submarine base.

When the United States entered the conflict, the Navy Department selected Hart to lead America's first submarine squadron to Europe. His flag transferred to the tender BUSHNELL at Philadelphia, the commodore ordered submarines K-1, K-2, K-5 and K-6 prepared for the Atlantic run.

On the date set for departure, the submarine commanders informed the commodore that two additional weeks would be needed to ready the boats. At the expiration of this period the boats were not yet ready, and the commanders requested a few more days.

"I'll give you one more week," Commodore Hart declared. "If you're not ready by that time, you're going to sea if I have to take you out on a towline."

On October 7, 1917, the K-boat squadron went to sea. And one of the K-boats started on a towline. But the commodore's flagship did not haul this cripple for long. When the four boats reached the Azores three weeks later they cruised in under their own power—a sample of the leadership provided by Thomas C. Hart.

In 1918 he was made Director of Submarines in Washington—the first naval officer to occupy that post. During his incumbency, many improvements in engine and torpedo design were projected. In 1921 he led ten S-boats from Portsmouth, N.H., to Manila, the longest submarine cruise accomplished by Americans up to that date.

Eight years later, as admiral, he was commander of the Submarine Force, Battle Fleet, with his flag in the tender HOLLAND. He next served as commander of the Control Force, directing Atlantic and Pacific Fleet submarines and the operation of their bases at New London, Coco Solo and Pearl Harbor. It was an officer thoroughly conversant with undersea boats and undersea warfare who, wearing the stars of full admiral, became Commander-in-Chief of the Asiatic Fleet.

"I was convinced in June of 1941," Admiral Hart said some months later, "that Japan intended to go to war."

With invasion seen as inevitable, submarines and submariners were put through intensive trials and long days of target practice. Emergency supplies were stowed aboard the tenders. In company with Admiral Hart, officers and men of SubsAsiatic took a candid view of the sullen clouds on the horizon. Observers had seen the Japanese legions smashing their way into China, and veterans on Asiatic station could tell anybody about the savagery and power of the land, air and sea forces of Nippon. The glass was falling. Throughout the autumn, the atmosphere in the Far East was electric—sultry as the lull before the tempest.

In November, en route to Manila from Pearl Harbor, the tender HOLLAND, escorted by submarines SALMON, SWORDFISH, STURGEON and SKIPJACK had an encounter with a Japanese vessel which might at that date have sparked the war. With her clipper bow, HOLLAND's unique silhouette made her an outstanding target. In view of this and the deteriorating Far East situation, her submarine escort carried warheads.

Orders were for HOLLAND to proceed with a submarine off either bow and a submarine trailing off either flank. In event of possible trouble, the submarines were to dive and the tender was to continue on course. If an attack developed, she was to execute a fast reverse and run back to her submerged escort for protection.

Some 300 miles off Guam, SWORDFISH sighted a large ship on the horizon, steaming on a parallel course. HOLLAND proceeded according to plan. Then the unidentified ship made a sudden turn toward the tender, and HOLLAND immediately reversed, heading back for the submarine line—the emergency signal.

SWORDFISH, STURGEON, SKIPJACK and SALMON had promptly "pulled the plug." Now all hands went to battle stations, the submarine commanders believing the tender under attack.

The ship failed to attack, doubtless identifying HOLLAND and suspecting a submarine escort in the tender's vicinity. But SALMON's skipper, Lieutenant Commander Eugene B. McKinney, had given orders to load, and the submariners were ready for instant action when the big ship, instead of attacking, veered away. Whether a torpedo would have detonated the Pacific War at that moment remains a matter for conjecture, but the incident illustrates the fact that the submarine force was on the alert. Reinforcements for the Asiatic Fleet, HOLLAND and her escort reached Manila on November 18th.

On November 27 Admiral Hart received from the Chief of Naval Operations the following message:

THIS DISPATCH IS TO BE CONSIDERED A WAR WARNING. NEGOTIATIONS WITH JAPAN LOOKING TOWARD STABILIZATION OF CONDITIONS IN THE PACIFIC HAVE CEASED AND AN AGGRESSIVE MOVE BY JAPAN IS EXPECTED WITHIN THE NEXT FEW DAYS. THE NUMBER AND EQUIPMENT OF JAPANESE TROOPS AND THE ORGANIZATION OF NAVAL TASK FORCES INDICATE AN AMPHIBIOUS EXPEDITION EITHER AGAINST THE PHILIPPINES, THAI OR KRA PENINSULA, OR POSSIBLY BORNEO. EXECUTE AN APPROPRIATE DEFENSIVE DEPLOYMENT

Admiral Hart readied his sea forces. Security was tightened at the Cavite Naval Base and at Manila Headquarters where discussions were held with British and Royal Netherlands naval representatives devising moves for joint action. To cover the Celebes area and the western approaches to the Philippines, Admiral Hart ordered the PBY's of Patwing Ten to fly extensive patrols.

On December 2, the scouting planes brought in word that a large Japanese convoy was assembling in Camranh Bay on the southeast coast of French Indo-China. The following day this convoy was counted as 50 Japanese ships, including cruisers and destroyers. The train and its escort were gone on December 4, disappearing ominously in foul weather that prevented aerial reconnaissance.

With Manila Headquarters waiting tensely for further news of this Japanese armada, Admiral Sir Tom Phillips arrived at Cavite on December 5, to convey to Admiral Hart the alarming information that only four British destroyers were available as a screen for HMS PRINCE OF WALES and HMS REPULSE. The British admiral requested four American destroyers. But Admiral Hart was faced with the problem of diplomatic punctilio—the United States was not an active belligerent in alliance with Great Britain. Furthermore, a loan of four destroyers would seriously weaken the vulnerable American force.

While the admirals' staffs were conferring over the matter, reconnaissance planes discovered the Japanese armada in the Gulf of Siam, heading for the Malay Peninsula. Admiral Phillips was forced to leave at once by plane for Singapore.

As the British flag officer departed, Admiral Hart assured him that four American destroyers would be in Singapore as fast as their engines could move them there from the Dutch port of Batavia.

Two days later (December 8) the Japanese landed on beachheads 400 miles north of Singapore, and the invasion of Malaya was begun.

Simultaneously (about 0300, December 8) news of the Pearl Harbor raid reached Manila. The storm had broken.

Submarines Asiatic

The Asiatic Fleet Submarine Force comprised the following roster:

SUBMARINE DIVISION 21 (COMMANDER S. S. MURRAY)

SALMON, Lieutenant Commander Eugene B. McKinney
SEAL, Lieutenant Commander Kenneth C. Hurd
SKIPJACK, Lieutenant Commander Charles L. Freeman
SARGO, Lieutenant Commander Tyrrell D. Jacobs
SAURY, Lieutenant Commander John L. Burnside
SPEARFISH, Lieutenant Roland F. Pryce

SUBMARINE DIVISION 22 (COMMANDER J. A. CONNOLLY)

SNAPPER, Lieutenant Commander Hamilton L. Stone
STINGRAY, Lieutenant Commander Raymond S. Lamb
STURGEON, Lieutenant Commander William L. Wright
SCULPIN, Lieutenant Commander Lucius H. Chappell
SAILFISH, Lieutenant Commander Morton C. Mumma
SWORDFISH, Lieutenant Commander Chester C. Smith

SUBMARINE DIVISION 201 (COMMANDER R. B. VANZANT)

S-36, Lieutenant John R. McKnight, Jr.
S-37, Lieutenant James C. Dempsey
S-38, Lieutenant Wreford G. Chapple
S-39, Lieutenant James W. Coe
S-40, Lieutenant Nicholas Lucker, Jr.
S-41, Lieutenant Commander George M. Holley

SUBMARINE DIVISION 202 (COMMANDER W. M. PERCIFIELD)

SEADRAGON, Lieutenant Commander William E. Ferrall
SEALION, Lieutenant Commander Richard G. Voge
SEARAVEN, Lieutenant Commander Theodore G. Aylward
SEAWOLF, Lieutenant Commander Frederick B. Warder

SUBMARINE DIVISION 203 (COMMANDER E. H. BRYANT)

PERCH, Lieutenant Commander David A. Hurt
PICKEREL, Lieutenant Commander Barton E. Bacon
PORPOISE, Lieutenant Commander Joseph A. Callaghan
PIKE, Lieutenant Commander William A. New
SHARK, Lieutenant Commander Louis Shane, Jr.
TARPON, Lieutenant Commander Lewis Wallace
PERMIT, Lieutenant Commander Adrian M. Hurst

TENDERS

HOLLAND, Captain Joseph W. Gregory
CANOPUS, Commander Earl L. Sackett
OTUS, Commander Joel Newsom
PIGEON (rescue vessel), Lieutenant Commander Richard E. Hawes

To all intents and purposes, this force had been operating under "Condition Zed" for many days. On practice patrols the submarines had traveled with darkened ship. Night lookouts had been posted, and the boats kept in battle trim with war shots ready.

The force was charged with the defense of the Philippines by patrolling northern Philippine waters and specified areas off Japanese bases. The strategic plan was to send 21 of the boats (or as many of that number as were available) into immediate action, while a reserve of eight submarines would be held in readiness for use as a striking force or to augment patrols.

On that Monday morning of December 8, some of these submarines were out on patrol, and a few were on their way to designated stations. And a considerable concentration had gathered in Manila Bay for loading or repair.

Two of the long, black, fleet submarines were at Cavite undergoing a complete yard overhaul.

SEAWOLF lay at anchor off Cavite, waiting her turn in the harbor for scheduled repairs.

SCULPIN, SALMON, SAILFISH and PERMIT were among others in the Manila vicinity taking on supplies and readying for action.

The captains knew it was coming. For several days the tenders had been working on the double, dispensing torpedoes and ammunition. But Manila Bay was as peaceful as the somnolent dark before dawn when CANOPUS suddenly fractured the calm with a flashing message from her searchlight.

FROM COMMANDER ASIATIC FLEET . . . TO ASIATIC FLEET . . . URGENT . . . BREAK . . . JAPAN HAS COMMENCED HOSTILITIES . . . GOVERN YOURSELVES ACCORDINGLY

The submariners of the United States Asiatic Fleet governed themselves accordingly. Orders relayed from the headquarters of Captain Wilkes set in motion the previously planned defensive moves, and loading and repair work was stepped up to racing speed aboard the submarines in Manila Bay.

S-36 and S-39 were in the vicinity of their assigned patrol stations when they received word that the war was on. Both boats immediately began the well-rehearsed maneuvers of war patrolling. S-36 was covering the approaches to Bolinao Harbor on the west coast of Luzon in the Lingayen Gulf area. Off the southern end of Luzon, S-39 had been standing by at Sorsogon Bay. Now she moved out to play sentry in San Bernardino Strait—the passage between Luzon and the island of Samar.

S-38 was dispatched to patrol the Verde Island Passage between Luzon and Mindoro. At Port Gulero, S-37 sidled out to team up with S-38.

To harass the enemy's communication lines, PIKE headed northwestward to patrol the eastern entrance to Hainan Strait. To the same area went SWORDFISH, her destination the approaches to Sama Bay on the south coast of Hainan Island.

Southwest to the Indo-China coast raced PICKEREL to conduct a patrol off Camranh Bay. Further south, SARGO headed to take up a beat off the coast of Cochin China at the mouth of the Gulf of Siam. SPEARFISH steamed out to patrol the waters off the Indo-China coast between the areas covered by PICKEREL and SARGO.

To waters lying between the Pescadores and the Formosan port of Takao went STURGEON. Off the north coast of Luzon, the approaches to Lingayen Gulf were to be patrolled by SEAWOLF and SAURY. SCULPIN raced through San Bernardino Strait to begin a patrol off the east coast of Luzon.

In Manila Bay a conference of submarine captains was held aboard the tender CANOPUS. Here several of the boats were assigned special duty, and the unrestricted warfare directive was relayed.

YOU WILL SINK OR DESTROY ENEMY SHIPPING WHEREVER ENCOUNTERED

Among the first submarines to leave Manila Bay were SCULPIN and SEAWOLF, ordered to escort a convoy made up of the aircraft tender LANGLEY, the tanker PECOS, and the destroyer tender BLACK HAWK,

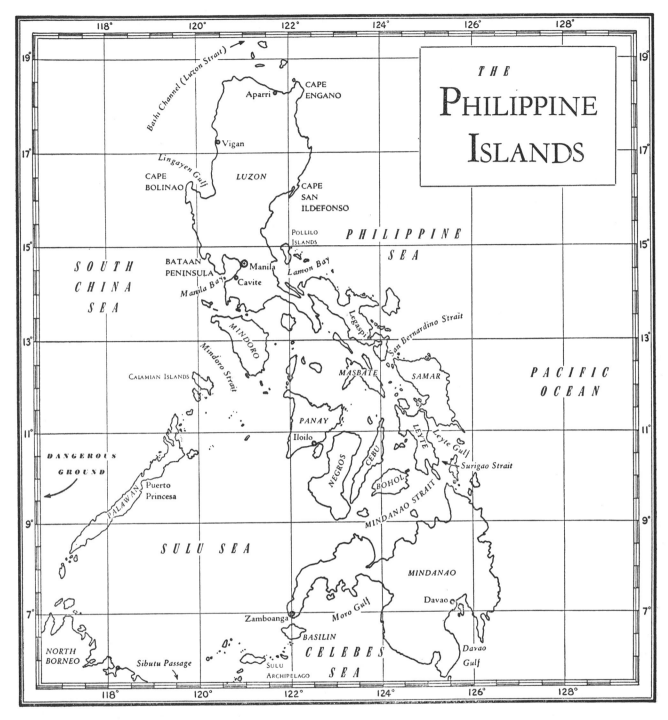

THE

PHILIPPINE

ISLANDS

heading south. Skippered by Lieutenant Commanders F. B. Warder and Lucius Chappell, the WOLF and SCULPIN stood out with darkened convoy that night, slipped through the Manila Bay minefields, then headed seaward at the best speed the surface ships could maintain. S-boats and fleet submarines followed throughout the night and ensuing day, in purposeful procession departing Manila Bay.

On December 9 the situation's gravity demanded that the eight "reserve" submarines be sent out on patrol. These were dispatched to add the final links to the chain of submarine patrols around Luzon. S-40 went out to Verde Island Passage. S-41 was assigned the approaches to Looc Bay, Tablas Island. SHARK was stationed in Santa Cruz Harbor, Marinduque Island. TARPON was positioned in Masbate Harbor to guard that sector of San Bernardino Strait. PERMIT and PERCH were assigned areas off the west coast of Luzon. SAILFISH and STINGRAY were started for the Lingayen Gulf area.

Beyond this defense ring of patrol areas which embraced Luzon, still other submarines were rushed to cover the enemy's possible roads of advance. SEARAVEN went north to patrol off Formosa Strait. SKIPJACK headed eastward toward the Pelews where the enemy base at Palau lay off the flank of Mindanao. SNAPPER was sent out to relieve PIKE in the Hainan Gulf area.

Meantime, the Japanese assault on the Philippines had begun. Jap aircraft were bombing and strafing the outlying Philippine bases. Coordinated sea-air attacks slashed at Mindanao Island, the enemy bombers concentrating on the Navy's PBY base at Davao. Against a horde of fighters, bombers and dive bombers, the Navy's 30 seaplanes rose like a covey of eagles winging up to fight clouds of predatory hawks and condors. Overwhelmingly outnumbered, the Navy pilots fought against immolating odds. Perhaps the hopelessness of their situation is best described in a message which is said to have been radioed back to his base by the pilot of a PBY a number of days later:

HAVE SIGHTED ENEMY PLANES . . . PLEASE NOTIFY NEXT OF KIN

While the Japs struck the Philippine fringe, the expected attack on Manila, Corregidor and Cavite was delayed. The reason, somewhat obscure, seems in part attributable to bad weather over Formosa which grounded the Japanese air forces in the north for a number of hours. But rather than disrupting the Japanese schedule, this postponement served to disarm the U.S. Army Air Force on Luzon. Around noon of December 8, Army planes which had been out on early war patrol came in to refuel. On Clark and Iba Fields they were parked wing to wing when the bombers from Formosa finally arrived. Dive bombers and strafers blasted landing strips, hangars and planes out of existence. A follow-up raid smashed Nichols Field south of Manila. By midnight of December 8 the Philippine Islands were practically without air cover.

This was grim news for the Asiatic Fleet. It was particularly dismaying to the submarine forces which had been hopefully relying on land-based aircraft to keep enemy bombers out of tropic skies which looked down on some of the clearest coastal waters in the world. Now the submariners knew they must advance into the narrow Philippine straits and the glassy shallows of Lingayen Gulf with little more protection against aircraft than that afforded by risky emergency dives or suicidal surface fighting with Browning machine guns.

Grim news—but it was of small import compared

with the appalling word which came to them from Pearl Harbor.

THE PACIFIC FLEET HAS BEEN IMMOBILIZED

On December 10, the Japanese onslaught struck Manila.

The Strike at Manila

Flying at about 20,000 feet, two waves of Japanese bombers, accompanied by fighter escorts, appeared over the Philippine capital early in the afternoon of December 10th.

The attack lacked the shock of surprise that had stunned Pearl Harbor. The war was in its third day, and air-raid sirens and ack-ack greeted the invader. The Japanese air armada came sailing down the sky as though each echelon were in a groove. The attack was characterized by the leisurely manner in which the two bomb groups circled the city in perfect V-formation, unperturbed by anti-aircraft fire and undeterred by the few planes which rose to meet them. Against the blue of broad daylight they might have been performing for an air show. They were casual about it. They took their time. The few American fighter planes were scattered and shot down. One Japanese "V" proceeded to Nichols Field to add a neutralizing bombing to previous devastation. The other proceeded to bomb the shipping in Manila Harbor. The two "V's" then converged over Cavite to blast the Navy Yard.

Strategically dispersed, the Asiatic Fleet cruisers were not in the Manila area. HOUSTON had been dispatched to Iloilo. BOISE was at Cebu. MARBLEHEAD had gone to Tarakan, Borneo, with four destroyers. For defense, the Navy Yard depended on recently installed anti-aircraft batteries.

The Japanese bombers had the afternoon at their disposal. Cavite, under their bomb-sights, was as helpless as a blueprint with targets embossed for easy pinpointing. Docks, oil tanks, repair shops, radio stations squatted in the brilliant sunshine, waiting. Cavite's anti-aircraft batteries—nine 3-inch guns— barked in a desperation of futility. With a maximum range of 15,000 feet, they might as well have sent up a barrage of popcorn against the high-flying Japanese planes.

In the sky above the naval base the bombing planes moved back and forth at a sauntering pace. Sticks of bombs, seemingly slow, drifted down with murderous accuracy. Oil tanks began to explode, sending up mountainous eruptions of smoke. Machine shops, docks and storehouses burst and crumbled. Within half an hour Cavite was a molten furnace. A third formation of Japanese bombers came down

DIRECT HIT! Two bombs strike Sealion almost simultaneously. First U.S. submarine casualty of the war, she went down in the shambles of Cavite—was later raised from the shallows off Machina Wharf and sunk in Manila Bay to prevent capture. USS Seadragon (shown at right) narrowly escaped the blast.

ATTACK TEAM in action in the conning tower. Skipper at periscope eyes target, directs approach.

APPROACH PARTY in control room. A submarine attack is a problem in math. Instruments aid, but luck remains "X" factor.

DIVING OFFICER AND MEN at control room diving station. Men are at trim manifold, operating trim pump controls.

MANNING the air manifolds controlling high and low pressure air. Operator eyes the pressure gauges.

THE "CHRISTMAS TREE INDICATOR." Red and green lights show when hull openings are open or closed. (Man at ballast tank vents.)

TORPEDO ROOM. Torpedoman (center) is manning tube blow-and-vent manifold, standing by to fire, while "talker" at right gets orders from conning tower. Above and below, sub-crew acts as unified team from the north to join in the carnival of destruction.

From a window at Headquarters in the Marsman Building overlooking Manila Bay, Admiral Hart had a dramatic view of the bombing. He noted the unhurried, methodical progress of the attack. The Japanese airmen were precise about it.

"If they were not completely satisfied with their aim," he told reporters, "they held their bombs and kept making runs until they were satisfied."

Three or four enemy dive bombers were shot down. But crowded Manila Harbor and defenseless Cavite remained at the mercy of the attackers. Tons of bombs crashed into the harbor, and Cavite Navy Yard was reduced to a fire-swept limbo.

Here again—as at Pearl Harbor—the Japanese bombers concentrated on obvious targets and overlooked the American submarines. A number of submarines were loading and fueling at Manila when the raiders arrived. Several lay alongside a tender, hatches open, crews topside, taking aboard ammunition and supplies. Decks were burdened with boxes of food and crates of gear. As the attack began, the submarines left their mooring places at buoys and alongside tenders, and evacuated the danger area at four-engine speed, submerging as soon as they cleared the harbor's breakwater.

Lieutenant Commander C. A. Ferriter, captain of the small minesweeper WHIPPOORWILL, steered his vessel through a traffic jam of angry submarines.

"Every once in a while a submarine would show his conning tower so we would not run over them," he wrote later, understandably uncertain of his pronouns. "They became quite a nuisance. It seemed we annoyed some sub or other every time we turned."

All but one of the Asiatic Fleet submarines escaped into Manila Bay's deeper waters. The submarine unable to escape was one of the two undergoing overhaul at Cavite. There, tied up at Machina Wharf, was SEADRAGON. Alongside lay SEALION. Outboard of SEALION was the minesweeper BITTERN. Not far distant in the harbor were the submarine rescue vessel PIGEON and the minesweeper QUAIL.

PIGEON (Lieutenant R. E. Hawes) was standing by with a crippled rudder in need of repair. Since receiving word of the Pearl Harbor raid, she had maintained a steaming watch and was on the alert for air attack. QUAIL and BITTERN were also in for repairs. Yard workmen were rushing the finishing touches on the submarine overhauls scheduled for completion on December 12th. Squeezed in against the wharf by the vessels lying outboard, the two submarines were in a tight spot when the Jap bombers struck.

About half an hour after noon, the air-raid alarm sounded. Over Manila Bay, in two groups of 27 each, came 54 Japanese twin-engine bombers. Out in the harbor QUAIL and PIGEON opened fire at the high-flying planes, but the range was too great for their guns. After a few futile bursts, the gunners ceased fire, and the vessels began evasive maneuvers, PIGEON's crew working her tiller with a winch. At the wharf the two submarines were boxed in. The first stick of bombs landed some 150 yards astern of SEALION. The day burst asunder with a cataclysmic roar, and Cavite Navy Yard was doomed.

Loss of Sealion

When the air-raid alarm split the quiet with its banshee wail, SEALION's captain, Lieutenant Commander R. G. Voge, her executive officer, Lieutenant Albert Raborn, and a number of her men were on the submarine's bridge. All hands went below except Voge, Raborn and three gunners, who remained topside to man the machine gun.

The planes droned overhead, and the bombs came laddering down. The blasting shook Machina Wharf. Noting that anti-aircraft fire was unable to touch the high-altitude bombers, Voge ordered the submarine's bridge cleared. Officers and gunners went below—a most fortunate move for those concerned. A few minutes later, the planes made another bombing run, and two bombs struck SEALION almost simultaneously.

One struck the after end of the conning-tower fairwater. The explosion wrecked the main induction, the battery ventilation and the after conning-tower bulkhead, and completely demolished the machine-gun mount which had just been vacated. Bomb fragments ripped through SEALION's pressure hull, wounding three men in the control room. Another fragment of this bomb penetrated the conning tower of SEADRAGON near by, instantly killing Ensign Samuel H. Hunter of SEADRAGON's crew—the first submarine casualty of the war.

An instant later, the second bomb smashed through SEALION's main ballast tank and pressure hull, and exploded in the maneuvering space in the after end of the engine room. Four men who had been working in that compartment were killed—Chief Electrician's Mates S. C. Foster and M. D. O'Connell; Third Class Electrician's Mate V. L. Paul; and Motor Machinist's Mate E. E. Ogilvie.

The after engine-room flooded immediately, and SEALION settled by the stern. In the after torpedo-room and forward engine-room, water surged in through holes ripped in the bulkheads. As the submarine settled, the living crew escaped through the hatches which were still above water. With a list to starboard, SEALION sank by the stern and finally came to rest on the bottom with about half of her main deck submerged.

Several days after the bombing, divers cut a hole aft of the conning tower, and entered the flooded submarine. The bomb which burst in SEALION's after engine-room could not have hit a more vital spot. All motor controls, reduction gears and main motors were wrecked, totally immobilizing the submarine. Had overhaul facilities been available, however, she might have been repaired. But the bombing which wrecked SEALION also obliterated the Cavite Navy Yard. With nearest overhaul facilities at Pearl Harbor, 5,000 miles away, SEALION's case was hopeless. Her radio, gyro and sonar instruments were removed. Then, to prevent her from falling into enemy hands, ComSubsAsiatic ordered her destroyed. Three depth charges were rigged in her compartments, and on Christmas Day, 1941, the charges were exploded. So went down SEALION, the first U.S. submarine lost in World War II.

Escape of Seadragon

Although scarred by the blasting which wrecked SEALION and the crimson tempest which swept Machina Wharf, SEADRAGON managed to get away. Flying fragments of steel and iron slashed her conning tower, ripped away part of her bridge and punctured her tanks. Around her the Cavite yard was blowing to pieces. BITTERN was afire. Bombs were falling dangerously close to a barge loaded with torpedoes. Not far from the wharf, a torpedo shop was struck. Air flasks exploded, and warheads detonated, adding their fury to the storm of destruction. Defying this inferno, the rescue vessel PIGEON moved in and passed a towing line to the threatened submarine. Men from SEALION clambered on SEADRAGON's deck. Slowly she was jockeyed away from the wharf, towed from her berth to a position where she could back out into the channel.

During this tight maneuver, a big oil tank exploded, throwing a wave of fire at SEADRAGON and PIGEON. A gust of heat scorched the paint on the submarine's superstructure and blistered the hull of the rescue vessel. Had PIGEON delayed in her race to the submarine's rescue, both vessels might have perished in the holocaust.

Once she reached the channel, SEADRAGON was able to continue under her own power. Leaking and lamed, she retained her sea legs, and her skillful crew worked her out into the Bay. That night she was once more taken under PIGEON's valiant wing, and Lieutenant Hawes and his technicians contrived a repair job described by observers as miraculous.

SEADRAGON was in need of more than a miracle she needed a careful overhaul. Undoubtedly in peacetime she could not have passed her "physical." But this was war. Her leaks plugged, her pressure hull patched, the SEADRAGON was available when the time came to remove part of Admiral Hart's staff from Manila; after which she went out on war patrol to become a legend off the Indo-China coast and a thorn in the side of such propagandists as Tokyo Rose.

Brave little PIGEON was the first ship of the U.S. Navy to be awarded the Presidential Unit Citation. In Manila Bay to the last, on May 6, 1942, she was sunk off Corregidor.

Philippine Twilight

In spite of time and opportunity, the Japanese air strike at Manila on December 10 was strangely ineffective. Damage in Manila Harbor was relatively minor—one merchantman sunk in a nest of some 40 ships, and one minesweeper put out of action. At Cavite the devastation was absolute. The yard was in black ruins, and the charred shops and wrecked piers could only be abandoned. Over 1,000 people were killed in the Cavite bombing, and 400 died later in the hospital. Yet the Cavite ammunition depot was missed by the airmen. They failed to hit the submarine tenders. And with the exception of SEALION and SEADRAGON, the submarines in the Bay remained unscathed.

Succeeding daylight raids were to make Manila Harbor untenable for the submersibles, but the enemy relinquished an initial chance to deal the submarine forces a deadly blow. This substantiates the assumption that the naval strategists in Tokyo considered American submarines to be of secondary account, and the Japanese airmen were instructed to expend their bombs on surface vessels and shore installations.

Had the bombers concentrated on the undersea boats, or even on the submarine tenders, the Pacific War might have been lengthened by many months. The sinking of HOLLAND alone would have deprived the Asiatic submarines of their mainstay for supply and maintenance. The big tender was loaded to the gunwales with stores, repair gear and torpedoes, and she had been on the point of transferring some of her equipment to CANOPUS when the war's outbreak deferred the operation. A bomb through her decks or a hit on the other torpedo-heavy tenders, would have left the submarines intolerably handicapped. But HOLLAND and OTUS remained on duty to support the submarine forces through the hardest phase of the war. And CANOPUS remained with her submariners to go down in history as the indomitable "Old

Lady," supporting not only the hard-driven boats but the embattled defenders who fought to the last at Bataan.

Nevertheless, the strike at Manila Bay was sufficiently effective in its immediate consequences. The Asiatic Fleet submarines were deprived of major repair facilities at Cavite. Installations at Olongapo were inadequate for refit or overhaul, and the boats were left wholly dependent on the tenders.

Furthermore, the bombing of December 10 resulted in a decision to move HOLLAND and OTUS south to the Malay Barrier. The following morning Admiral Hart called a conference of merchant captains and agents, and offered a destroyer escort for the cargo ships if they would leave the exposed harbor at once. Along with a flotilla of naval vessels, the two tenders joined this convoy as it left Manila Bay. Only CANOPUS and little PIGEON were retained at Manila to service the submarines returning from war patrols.

By the morning of December 11, the submariners of the Asiatic Fleet realized they were going to war against unimaginable odds. While the Japanese bombers had been bearing down on Manila Bay, another Japanese air armada was winging over the Gulf of Siam. Shortly before noon of the 10th, this second air armada sighted HMS REPULSE and HMS PRINCE OF WALES off the Malay coast. The news reached the Philippines while the raid was on at Manila. PRINCE OF WALES and REPULSE had been sunk!

The Japanese invasion was roaring down from the north like a typhoon. And *the Allies were without a single capital ship in the Far East!*

Without air cover, without battleship support, its Cavite base burned behind it, the Asiatic Fleet was left to fight off the Philippines invasion "like a man with bare fists fighting a killer with a tommy-gun." The description was Admiral Hart's.

Assigned to the front line were the Manila-based submarines.

Submarines into Battle

The Manila submarines went out in the dark like cats, walking softly to go far.

Submarine commanding officers had been advised to use extraordinary caution and feel the enemy out on their first patrol, for it was realized this would be the most perilous encounter of all. The enemy was an unknown adversary—a foe whose power was recognized, but whose methods and equipment had been developed in secrecy and whose fighting techniques had yet to be discerned. Japanese electronic devices were a mystery. What was their destroyer strength?

Had they acquired secret weapons from Germany? Answer to these and similar questions could only be obtained by exploratory probing—a process that demanded steel nerve and the utmost care on the part of the explorer. The Asiatic Fleet submariners were not disposed to underestimate the enemy.

Original plan was to limit the first patrols to about three weeks to enable the collection of first-hand information on enemy tactics at an early date. By analysis of such data the enemy's measure could be taken and the submarine forces could devise counter-strategy accordingly.

This policy could not be carried out, however, and the submarines had to enter the conflict "b'guess and b'God," individually learning of the enemy from close-contact experience and fragments of information dispatched from other boats. Weeks would pass before a definite assessment of Japanese matériel and tactics could be made. Meanwhile, the enemy's naval strength and attack patterns in the Philippines had to be discovered by periscope. Allied air reconnaissance was practically nil from the start of the war.

Hampered by the loss of the Cavite yard, the submariners looked to CANOPUS at Manila for repairs. But adequate servicing at Manila became impossible. Japanese bombing raids harried the harbor daily and kept the submarines constantly on the move in Manila Bay, rigged for dives. Only minor repair work could be accomplished at night. It was evident from the first that the Philippines capital could not long hold out. The submariners who cruised from Manila in these opening days of the war took with them uncertainty and apprehension—uncertainty as to how, where or when they could again be supplied and serviced—apprehension of an enemy of unknown capabilities.

But these were men schooled to face uncertainties and apprehensions. Pick of a service wherein many are called, but few are chosen, they had been indoctrinated in emergency and inoculated against defeatism. Engineering officers and motor macs, who were hair-line perfectionists, now took the view that repairs could be made with anything at hand. Torpedoman's mates were confident that somewhere they could find replacements. Cooks trained to serve the finest fare in the Navy craftily hoarded against possible famine and rolled up their sleeves to invent new dishes from yesterday's hash. Best acquainted with all facets of the situation, the captains tautened ship for what they knew was in prospect. From bridge to galley all hands were aware that they faced an unprecedented ordeal. Over the ship radio came the dispatches from HQ, the somber news bulletins and broadcasts from Don Bell at Manila.

The enemy was bombing Hong Kong and Singapore. Jap amphibious troops were landing near Vigan. Immense invasion forces were approaching the Philippines. Japanese infantry was ashore at Legaspi. Another fire raid was striking Manila.

"Where is the United States Fleet?" jeered Tokyo Rose, introduced by a jiujitsu rendition of *It's Three o'clock in the Morning*. "I'll tell you where it is, boys. It's lying at the bottom of Pearl Harbor."

The Asiatic Fleet submariners knew better. They knew that S-boats and fleet submarines of their own force were entering Davao Gulf, probing through San Bernardino Strait, patrolling off Indo-China, advancing to meet the foe in northern Philippine waters.

Foraying in this fortnight before Christmas were boats that would carve famous names across the oceanic reaches of the Pacific, and captains and crews who would be remembered for waging some of the greatest sea-fights in history.

Among the pioneer captains who drove first blows at the enemy in the Southwest Pacific were Lieutenant Commander Frederick B. (Fearless Freddie) Warder; Lieutenant Commander Chester (Chet) Smith; Lieutenant Commander Eugene McKinney (SALMON became known as the "submersible PT-boat"); Lieutenant Commander Kenneth C. Hurd; Lieutenant Commander Richard G. Voge, who survived the blasting of SEALION; Lieutenant Commander William Leslie (Bull) Wright; Lieutenant Commander Tyrrell D. Jacobs; Lieutenant James W. (Red) Coe; Lieutenant Commander William E. (Pete) Ferrall; Lieutenant Commander David A. Hurt; Lieutenant Commander Barton E. Bacon; Lieutenant Wreford G. (Moon) Chapple.

While these skippers conducted eminently daring and successful patrols, there was scarcely a captain of the SubsAsiatic Force who did not merit acclaim for the manner in which he took his submarine out to do undersea battle with the overwhelming forces of the Unknown. With those of Grenfell, Lent, Mosely, White, Willingham and other Pearl Harbor pioneers, the cruises of the pioneer SubsAsiatic skippers set patterns in courage and resourcefulness to be followed throughout the war and remain as an inspiration to the Service.

One of the veteran Manila boats had already featured in a memorable chapter of submarine history. When she headed out for her first war patrol, her officers and men may have been thinking of that other time she was rigged for a dive—May 23, 1939.

She was making a test dive off Portsmouth, N.H. Everything checked before the order came to take her down. The klaxon sounded. Kingstons and vents were opened and the bow planes set. Engines were stopped, valves closed, battery engine inductions presumably closed. The board showed green to the diving officer. "Pressure in the boat, sir." The submarine started down.

Then instead of leveling off, she kept on going. Water in the engine room. Down by the stern. Mechanical failure in the operating gear of the main-engine air induction valve. Seven men escaped the flooded engine room and after battery compartment —the bulkhead door had to close on 27—and the submarine hit bottom at 240 feet.

Thirty-three submariners including the commanding officer and a naval architect were imprisoned at sea bottom. Few men had ever survived such a disaster, but miraculously these were saved. The sunken boat was located by the submarine SCULPIN, and a salvage rescue ship raced to the scene. Divers attached a McCann diving bell to the forward escape-hatch. Four times the bell was raised to the surface, bringing up the men who had been trapped. On the last trip the cable fouled. When at length it was freed by the divers, the remaining survivors were recovered. So ended the tragic dive of the USS SQUALUS.

She was raised by Navy salvage engineers three months later and hauled into Portsmouth Navy Yard. Eleven months went into the submarine's reconditioning. Then completely overhauled and refitted, she was recommissioned for active service as the USS SAILFISH.

But submariners remembered. A shadow lingered over this boat—a shadow undispelled by the wonder of her resurrection. Among the men she was known as the SQUAILFISH.

To dispel the ghosts of uneasiness, she was given to a master tough and exacting and a chosen crew with no time for dark imaginings under the sea. SAILFISH joined the SubsAsiatic Force with Lieutenant Commander Morton C. Mumma as her captain and Lieutenant Hiram Cassedy as her exec.

While the Japs were bombing Manila, she set out to put an end to any lingering superstitions. During a short 9-day trial patrol she made contact with an enemy convoy and burrowed in to fire two torpedoes at the troopships.

The torpedoes missed. SAILFISH had no time to dive before a Japanese destroyer charged up through the dusk to trample her with ash-cans. In the periscope the DD loomed as large as an onrushing bogie when SAILFISH fired two more torpedoes. There was a geyser and a roar, and the officer at the periscope reported a hit as the submarine went deep.

The hit could not be confirmed, and subsequent reports do not credit SAILFISH with either damaging or sinking this enemy. Possibly the torpedoes were prematures. But her performance satisfied her complement—she had stood the test of battle and come through. The captain, who had exorcised the shades, transferred to the PT-boats. Under Lieutenant Commander Richard Voge, who was given her command, and later under Lieutenant Commander R. E. M. Ward, SAILFISH was to win the name of one of the great fighting submarines of the war.

SEAWOLF, another of the great, encountered her first enemy off the northeastern coast of Luzon, not far from Aparri. On the morning of December 14, about 0900, she sighted a Japanese destroyer, portside to, bearing three one zero relative.

"Down periscope! Battle stations!"

Down she went, her men racing through the boat to their stations as the bell bonged the alarm. The approach party crowded about the plotting table in the control room. In the torpedo room, the chief radioman listened to the destroyer's searching "pings."

Warder described the enemy over the intercom. A big DD—AKASAKI class—multiple torpedo tubes amidships—depth charge racks—estimated course, zero seven zero—estimated speed, fifteen knots—range 3,000 yards. She was patrolling outside a cove.

Walking the periscope, Warder watched this target closely. She seemed a fat prize. He weighed her value against the fact that she must be guarding even fatter, more valuable prizes in the cove. Should SEAWOLF try for the bird in the hand or attempt to snare two in the bush? Sea conditions were unfavorable for immediate attack—high seas in which the torpedoes might broach. Warder decided to wait and try for what he scented in the cove.

Battle stations secured, SEAWOLF drew off to wait. Mountainous seas walloped the coast throughout the night, but the following dawn the waves flattened considerably, and SEAWOLF crept into the cove with torpedoes ready.

Warder had been right. Almost immediately SEAWOLF's periscope was focused on what looked like a Japanese seaplane tender, about 12,000 tons. Guns fore and aft. Two stick mast cranes.

"Make ready the bow tubes! Open outer doors! Stand by!"

A moment later Warder gave the order, and two torpedoes sped at the silhouetted tender. Then the skipper, watching through the periscope, shouted in wrathful disappointment.

"They've missed! Make ready the after tubes. Open outer doors in after room. Right full rudder!"

Full speed ahead, SEAWOLF turned. Warder reduced speed to one-third as the submarine once more got on target and periscope observation showed the tender trying to get under way.

"Fire—!"

This time the submariners heard thudding blasts, and at the periscope Warder saw the Japanese tender rock behind explosions of white water. The torpedoes may have hit. But Warder was not certain. With a destroyer in the vicinity it was time to go deep and quit the neighborhood. Positive proof of a sinking could not be established, and Warder did not even claim damage.

SARGO, under Lieutenant Commander Tyrrell D. Jacobs made her first attack (day-submerged) on December 14th. Her target was a corpulent cargo carrier sighted at lat. 08-05 N., long. 109-06 E. She fired one torpedo at this AK and missed.

Ten days later she sighted a convoy. Jacobs maneuvered the submarine into this herd of Nipponese ships, and fired five torpedoes at three AK's. Each torpedo missed its mark. Seventy-two hours later, SARGO's shots missed two more Japanese freighters and a tanker. Baneful luck seemed to follow the submarine. On this, her first patrol, she made a total of eight day-submerged attacks—fired thirteen torpedoes with zero results and zero in the hearts of her crew. However, there was fire in the heart of SARGO's commander, and Jacobs was credited with 100% aggressiveness. His patrol report was soon to feature in one of the war's more startling disclosures.

Meantime, another aggressive anti-*maru* campaign was begun by Chester Smith and crew of SWORDFISH. They began it on December 9 at lat. 14-30 N., long. 119-00 E., burrowing into a big, destroyer-screened convoy that came down across the seascape, ugly and pugnacious. Smith directed a night-surface approach, firing one torpedo at a fat supply ship (AK). Destroyers charged SWORDFISH to ram her, and "Sound" heard a loud explosion as Smith gave the order to take her down. The DD's lost her, and Smith brought her up to periscope depth to fire another shot at the big AK. He reported a sinking, but the vessel's destruction could not be confirmed.

On the night of the 11th, SWORDFISH again made a surface attack on this convoy. Aimed at another AK, two torpedoes missed.

On the 14th (area: South China Sea) SWORDFISH made three successive attacks on the same convoy or one similar. Sound reported a swelling chorus of low-speed screws, and a periscope sweep revealed a dark parade of ships in parallel columns behind a formidable destroyer screen. The opening attack was night-surface. Smith fired two torpedoes at a large freighter. He reported the ship as sunk, but again confirmation was lacking.

33

Evading a furious counter-attack, SWORDFISH bored in after daylight, making a submerged approach. Smith picked two targets carefully, firing two torpedoes at the first and one at the second. Sound reported explosions, and the periscope saw a stampede of Japanese ships rushing away from two wallowing, smoke-wrapped freighters. With Japanese destroyers bearing down full speed on the hunt, there was no time for further observation. SWORDFISH went deep and commenced evasive action. Apparently these ships were only damaged.

December 15 (16 in her locality) was another day. This time she got her big one. She trapped her target off the coast of Hainan Island, made a submerged approach, and Smith fired three torpedoes. An undoubted hit roared in the sound gear, followed by the clash, crackle and static of breaking-up noises. Shrouded in smoke and fire, the large freighter was seen going down by the stern. This vessel was identified as the 8,663-ton ATSUTUSAN MARU. And SWORDFISH (Chester Smith and crew) won credit for the first confirmed sinking of a Japanese ship by a U.S. submarine.

These maiden war patrols of SAILFISH, SEAWOLF, SARGO and SWORDFISH were more or less typical of those accomplished by the other SubsAsiatic boats which joined battle with the Japanese forces plunging down on the Philippines.

A number of these first patrols were, like that of SAILFISH, brief in duration. Others lasted anywhere from 40 to 55 days. Some of the submarines "got in where they were," and others scouted into areas which afforded few targets. One consistent adversity plagued all the submarines that entered combat during this desperate period. Like a dark thread in a pattern, it is woven through the record of the hard-pressed SubsAsiatic Force. Discernible in the patrol reports of SAILFISH, SEAWOLF, SARGO and SWORDFISH, it is apparent in the summarized experiences of the following submarines:

S-38 (Lieutenant W. G. Chapple) sighted a transport on December 12th. Directing a night-surface attack, Chapple fired one torpedo at the target. It sounded like a hit, but the damage could not be confirmed and the torpedo may have prematured.

S-39 (Lieutenant Coe) sighted a 5,000-ton AK on December 13th. Coe sent his S-boat boring in, and fired four torpedoes at the unsuspecting merchantman. He reported a solid hit. Damage or sinking could not be subsequently verified.

PICKEREL (Lieutenant Commander Bacon) sighted a Jap patrol craft on December 19th. Bacon fired a total of five torpedoes at this vicious little vessel— for a total of five zeroes.

SPEARFISH (Lieutenant Pryce) encountered a Japanese submarine on December 20th. Pryce directed a submerged approach, and fired four torpedoes. All torpedoes missed.

STURGEON (Lieutenant Commander Wright) delivered a surface attack on a large cargo carrier on the night of December 21st. Four torpedoes were fired at the bulky target. No hits.

SEARAVEN (Lieutenant Commander Aylward) struck at a good-sized freighter on the night of December 22nd. In this, a surface attack, Aylward fired two torpedoes. Both missed. Three days later (Christmas), during a day-submerged attack on another AK, one torpedo was fired. The torpedo missed.

SNAPPER (Lieutenant Commander Stone) engaged in a submerged attack on a cargo ship the same day. Two torpedoes were fired. Both failed to score.

PERMIT (Lieutenant Commander Hurst) on December 23 delivered a submerged attack on a Japanese destroyer. Two torpedoes were fired at the DD. The destroyer was not hit.

SKIPJACK (Lieutenant Commander Freeman) sighted a heavy cruiser on the night of December 25th. This was one for the stocking, and Freeman directed a surface attack. A spread of three torpedoes rushed at the Japanese cruiser. Not one found the mark.

PERCH's Christmas luck was equally foul. It began with the sighting of an enemy convoy and a night-surface attack on a 4,000-ton freighter. Four torpedoes missed this target. Stubbornly, the submarine's captain, Lieutenant Commander David Hurt, hung on. The following day (submerged attack) two torpedoes missed. Two more torpedoes were fired in an attack on December 27th. Hurt reported one enemy ship sunk, but the sinking could not be verified.

TARPON (Lieutenant Commander Wallace) sighted a Japanese light cruiser on New Year's Eve. Wallace directed a night-surface attack. The enemy warship was not hit by what seems to have been the last undersea shot fired in the defense of the Philippines that year.

The dark thread woven through the record delineates the didoes of a defective torpedo.

Action in Lingayen Gulf

It would have taken more than 28 submarines to stem the titanic Japanese offensive which stormed down on Luzon. Swimming into this tidal wave of enemy transports and warships under a scudding screen of aircraft, the Manila submarines were as a squadron of cavalrymen deployed in the face of a charging army. They were to fight delaying actions.

But, much less than delay the invader, the SubsAsiatic Force was scarcely able to interrupt his landing operations.

In Lingayen Gulf, where the Japanese made their main landing, the submarines were balked at every turn. The experience proved the more bitter in that the landing at this point had been long expected. In anticipation of the enemy's move, S-36 (Lieutenant J. R. McKnight) had been dispatched to guard the area early in December. On the night of December 11, the boat was ordered to patrol inside the Gulf. The order was not acknowledged. Continued silence from S-36 led to the belief that she was either in trouble or had been lost. Presuming the S-boat to be in difficulty, ComSubsAsiatic, on December 16, ordered her to return to Manila Bay. When she arrived back at base, the trouble was disclosed as a faulty radio. She could receive, but was unable to transmit.

Meantime, STINGRAY (Lieutenant Commander R. S. Lamb) was shifted up to Lingayen to keep the Gulf under surveillance. She arrived in time to find the Gulf aswarm with Japanese, their transports crowding the inner bay, their troops going ashore. Her report, radioed on December 21, was the first indication that the invader had reached Lingayen Gulf. It was also an indication of the absence of Allied air reconnaissance. Had aircraft been on hand to observe the enemy's advance on the Gulf, a strong group of submarines could have been mustered to intercept the invasion forces.

As it was, four more submarines were rushed to Lingayen's waters in answer to STINGRAY's report. These were S-38 (Lieutenant W. G. Chapple), S-40 (Lieutenant Nicholas Lucker, Jr.), SAURY (Lieutenant Commander J. L. Burnside), and SALMON (Lieutenant E. B. McKinney). Here, for the first time in the war, submarines had an opportunity to disrupt a full-scale enemy landing. The counterstrike failed for a number of reasons.

First, the move was belated—the thieves were in the barn and had a halter on the horse by the time the owners arrived to lock the door. Then, the invading force was legion, and could gang up on the scattered defenders in such fashion that the contest would be all but suicidal. Finally, shallow Lingayen Gulf did not lend itself to submarine defense. Submariners know it as a dangerous cruising ground with a tricky bottom and an entrance laced with a snarl of reefs. The Japanese exploited the obvious marine advantage with an invasion fleet composed of small vessels which could barge around in four or five fathoms of water. The transports were herded into the Gulf by diverse routes, each herd under heavy escort. After convoying one group of transports to its destination, the escort vessels would steam out to the gulf mouth to pick up another. In the background were heavy units of Vice Admiral Kondo's Second Fleet which was supporting the Philippines invasion. The massive transport and landing operation, carefully planned and well rehearsed, plus the other hostile elements involved, went far to frustrate the submarine effort at Lingayen. Inject into the equation an undependable torpedo, and the plight of the submarines is evident.

But two of the five at Lingayen traded hard blows with the enemy, and only one of the five managed to penetrate the Gulf. One of the hard blows was struck by SALMON late in the evening of December 22, when, patrolling the approaches to the Gulf, she engaged in a scrimmage with the enemy in the backfield.

The scrimmage began when SALMON's lookouts spotted a ship off in the gloom. In the thickening twilight the vessel was not at once recognized as a Japanese destroyer, and by the time SALMON made identification, the warship was up ahead and turning toward the submarine. Simultaneously a companion destroyer hove into view.

There followed a nerve-wracking game of tag, SALMON remaining stubbornly on the surface while the two destroyers maneuvered off the port bow, giving the submarine a long-distance inspection. Then, keeping a wide berth, the twin DD's circled astern and came nosing up like a pair of stiff-legged dogs, curious but wary.

McKinney kept SALMON on course while the destroyers advanced slowly, boxing her in. For perhaps half an hour this game went on, the DD's and the submarine withholding fire while the dusk darkened and the atmosphere was like a drawn breath. Certainly the Japs by this time had recognized the American conning tower.

"I confess I felt a lot like diving," McKinney said later. "But I was curious, too. We stayed on the surface and the DD's came on. I guess the Jap skippers were just as inexperienced and puzzled as I was."

Sooner or later this prickly armistice was bound to burst—the surface was not big enough for a submarine and two enemy destroyers. And SALMON's bridge personnel, including her exec, Lieutenant I. H. Hartman, and Ensign Walter Sharer, were feeling the strain when McKinney decided to end the byplay.

The criss-crossing warships had come too close for comfort, and the range was too good for further delay. One of the destroyers was crossing SALMON's stern. McKinney gave the order to fire two torpedoes.

The DD saw them coming, and veered aside. The torpedoes missed. The "party" was over now, and SALMON braced herself for a first-class brawl. Down on her track the destroyers came charging, one behind the other, to ram and blast the submarine out of the picture.

McKinney clung to the bridge. If he took SALMON down (a suggestion made by several of his officers) she would be in for a depth-charge lambasting. With two "fish" remaining in the stern tubes, he could get in a solid shot at the rampaging "cans."

The leading destroyer was charging head-on, growing bigger and bigger in the dusk, like the Twentieth Century Limited coming down a straightway. Plumes of spray made flying wings under her bow, and her smoke streamed back flat. McKinney gave the order "Fire—!" The torpedo sped on its way, trailing a luminous streak.

In the last of the gloaming the destroyer saw the deadly wake, and started a swing to starboard. McKinney and his bridge personnel saw a geyser spout high where the torpedo must have struck the DD directly under her bridge.

The second torpedo was on its way, heading straight for the No. 2 destroyer which had swung to port. McKinney "pulled the plug" at this moment, and Sound reported echoes of demolition as SALMON went deep.

Three days later, having avoided a hunting party of patrol boats, corvettes and destroyers, SALMON was on the track of an enemy transport. McKinney directed a night-surface attack, and fired four torpedoes at the silhouetted AP. The torpedoes failed to register a hit.

The waters off Lingayen Gulf were boiling when SALMON finally quit the area. But crew and captain were satisfied they had done a good week's work. All were convinced they had left one Japanese DD on the bottom and damaged another.

SALMON's encounter with the two destroyers remains unique in several respects. Ordinarily, only the officer at the periscope witnesses such a drama. In this case SALMON's bridge personnel had a topside view of the action. Again, in firing at the oncoming lead destroyer, McKinney launched one of the first "down-the-throat" shots on record—a torpedo aimed squarely at the nose of a vessel and calculated to strike her if she veers either way.

Yet, the sinking of a Japanese destroyer during the Lingayen invasion could not subsequently be corroborated. Evidence indicates that many sinkings reported in the pioneer period were illusory—straining eyesight is frequently perverse, and a torpedo, exploding prematurely, can shower a target with a water blast that looks like the real thing. According to Japanese records, examined after the war, the Imperial Navy did not lose any destroyers on that date in Lingayen Gulf.

While SALMON was not credited with a sinking, her captain and crew were credited for a display of what it takes to run a fighting submersible—guts. A submarine is no stronger than the viscera of her personnel, and SALMON's personnel had their share of what it took. Their torpedoes may have missed or misbehaved at Lingayen, but McKinney and crew went on from there with high confidence, and the next six vessels attacked by SALMON were cruisers.

Meanwhile, SAURY had a brush with the enemy in the Lingayen area when she sighted a Jap destroyer on the evening of December 22nd. Her captain, Lieutenant Commander Burnside, directed a night-surface attack and launched one torpedo at this DD. The torpedo failed to strike, and SAURY went under to evade a depth charging.

Three of the other submarines at Lingayen had indifferent luck. But S-38 got in where they were, and her battle inside the Gulf remains one of the outstanding submarine forays of the war.

S-38 vs. All the Odds

On the evening of December 21, S-38 received radio orders to proceed into Lingayen Gulf. Early the following morning, she entered that baleful body of water, crossing the seaward end of the reef that extends north from Cape Bolinao. By taking his submarine across the reef in this fashion, S-38's skipper, Lieutenant Wreford (Moon) Chapple, probably outflanked the destroyer patrol that was barring the entrance of the other submarines.

In the dark before dawn the S-boat submerged. By 0615 it was light enough for a periscope survey of the situation, and the scope was quickly focused on a clutter of Japanese transports. The transports were guarded by circling destroyers and several large motor launches laden with depth charges. Chapple immediately began approach maneuvers, and, undetected by the escort vessels, S-38 gained firing position.

Chapple fired four torpedoes at four selected targets. Aimed at a 5,000-ton transport, the first torpedo missed. The second torpedo missed. The third torpedo missed. The fourth torpedo missed. S-38 was experiencing the plague which ruined the bravest efforts of the war-going submarine forces. Unbeknown to Chapple and crew, the Mark 10 torpedo carried by the S-boats was running four feet deeper than set. And each of the four torpedoes just fired had passed impotently under its intended target.

Chapple presumed he had misjudged the draft of the Jap vessels, estimated as 12 feet. His next torpedo was set for a depth of nine feet. The S-boat, of course, had only four tubes, and Chapple had ordered her deep under for a reload after the firing of her opening salvo.

All chance for a surprise attack went glimmering with the four misses. Sighting the torpedo wakes, enemy lookouts raised the alarm. As the S-boat's crew rushed reload operations, a Jap destroyer raced over on the hunt and dropped three fairly close depth charges. The other escorts began a search for the intruding submarine, the DD's probing with supersonic. For three-quarters of an hour, the S-boat dodged and veered this way and that, evading her furious pursuers. She managed to elude them in this game of tag, and at 0758 Chapple had her once more at periscope depth, stalking an anchored transport—a "sitting duck."

Moving in on this unsuspecting target, Chapple fired two torpedoes at close range. Thirty seconds later there was a boat-rocking explosion, and three minutes after that, Jap destroyers were blasting the tide around the S-boat, attempting to gouge her out of the water.

Rigged for depth charges, the submarine went deep—that is, as deep as a submersible could go in those turbulent shallows. For the next hour and a half, S-38 burrowed in one direction and then another, striving to escape the "pinging" destroyers which were determined to track her down. While thus maneuvering to evade, she sideswiped a submerged ledge and threatened to broach. Chapple ordered the auxiliary tanks flooded, and the submarine groped her way along the bottom, bumping as she coasted.

Presently she ran into a mud bank. Chapple stopped all machinery except the motor generator on the lighting circuits. Men took off their shoes and conversed in whispers. The S-boat "played possum," listening. Sometimes the depth charges sounded distant and sometimes they sounded close aboard as the destroyers continued a frantic hunt. The DD's were persistent, and S-38 could do nothing but sit it out.

Moon Chapple started a cribbage game in the control room, but no player could honestly say he was interested. Varnished cards stick to perspiring fingers, and the aces were soon gummy and hard to shuffle.

In other quarters of the submarine the men began to think about the S-boat's lack of air conditioning. Nobody talked much or moved about—at their stations the men remained silent, conserving oxygen. Time dragged. One hour. Two hours. Small boats

passed overhead at regular intervals. Some large vessel fouled the clearing lines and bent the submarine's forward stub mast. Was her number up? Another tense wait in perspiration and inertia.

Moisture condensed on the bulkheads and began to drip as the air thickened, becoming mephitic. It was as though the submarine herself were sweating in the stifling heat. Soda lime was sprinkled to absorb the carbon dioxide. The gesture was something, but it failed to sweeten the sour air.

Sound reported high-speed screws coming back again. Chapple ordered the sound man to stow his phones. What couldn't be cured had to be endured, and it was easier to endure it without hearing it. In a process that seemed as slow as erosion, the afternoon wore away.

The "pinging" continued for most of the day, but died out after sundown. The deck was greased with sweat, the heat becoming unendurable and the air unbreathable when Chapple finally decided it was dark enough to surface. Exhausted men blew her ballast as her skipper backed her out of the mud. The port propeller was damaged, but S-38 got clear, and at 2100 was proceeding submerged toward the west side of the Gulf. There were 11 inches of mercury pressure in the boat when Chapple finally ordered her to the surface. After 12 hours of submergence, all hands were wilting, and it was high time for fresh air and a battery charge.

At 2300 the boat was on the surface, going ahead on one engine and charging batteries with the other.

Her conning tower had not been long in the fresh air when S-38 was sighted by a patrolling destroyer, and once more she had to go under. The boat had been aired somewhat, but her weary crewmen could have used more relief, and now they were in for another ordeal.

So, S-38 received another "going over," laconic enough in her patrol report, but extensively punishing in reality. Again she managed to evade. Finally she reached a position a mile off the beach where she was anchored in 18 fathoms of water. At dawn Chapple ordered a stationary dive to the bottom, and the submarine remained there throughout that day, giving the crew a chance to rest. At sunset the S-boat surfaced and remained at anchor, charging batteries. She was forced under once by a patrol boat, and it was not until 0500 on December 24 that the battery charge was completed and the air tanks were filled.

With night fading in the east, Chapple started S-38 on a tour of the Gulf. Cautious periscope exposures were made now and then, and a distant destroyer was finally sighted. Then six transports trudged into view, heading south. Chapple was maneuvering to close the range when a thunderclap explosion—probably an aircraft bomb—blasted the water not far from the submarine. Both control room depth gages were put temporarily out of commission. Chapple took her down to 90 feet and headed north, evading by silent running.

From noon until sunset, patrol boats hounded her. At intervals depth-charge barrages would boom down as she crawled from one Gulf-bottom foxhole to another. Skillful submarining got her out from under this storm, and early evening found her running for the west side of the Gulf. At 2230 on that Christmas Eve she ran aground a second time. The jolt gave her a shaking up, but the crew brought her clear, and Chapple ordered her to the surface off Hundred Islands.

No sooner had the water drained from the superstructure with the boat riding high, than there was an explosion in the after battery! Chapple had given the order to ventilate the hull outboard and the battery into the engine room.

Apparently someone started the blowers too soon, before the air had time to circulate and freshen the gaseous atmosphere in the battery room. A spark from the thrown blower-switch may have caused the blast. Chapple rushed below. Thick smoke was surging from the compartment, and fire flickered in its gloomed interior.

Two men had been painfully burned by the explosion, and Chief Machinist's Mate Harbin had suffered a broken spine. The captain and a young electrician's mate carried out the badly wounded petty officer.

Two or three of the battery cells were found to be cracked, and the electricians worked at top speed to cut the damaged cells out of the circuit. Daylight of December 25 was graying the east before the mangled battery room was cleaned up. There was one relieving note—a radio dispatch ordering the S-boat to leave the Gulf. Then it was discovered that the engine-room hatch, which had been opened, could not be tightly closed because of deteriorated gaskets. While the men struggled to dog down the hatch, the lookouts sighted a destroyer squadron bearing down. Just in time the hatch was secured.

S-38 got deep enough to evade, but thanks to her damaged and noisy propeller, she was presently picked up by a patrol boat that drove her to the bottom. Then for a third time, she ran aground! Chapple and crew worked every maneuver to get her clear. She refused to budge. The pumping system proved unavailing. The submarine was jammed on a mud bank with her bow angled up 50 feet higher than her stern. But the crewmen kept the pumps going, and finally she worked free. Only to slide down the mud bank to a depth of 350 feet— one hundred and fifty feet deeper than her tested depth. The ballast tank compressed enough to cause the battery decks to buckle up, but they expanded as she surfaced. Then, in coming to periscope depth, the submarine broached.

Every Japanese lookout in the harbor must have seen this spectacle, and the S-38 crew expected the Japs to attack with the enthusiasm of harpooners who have sighted a spouting whale. In desperation, Chapple held the submarine on the surface. She was on the reef north of Bolinao, and nothing was in sight. Then two destroyers appeared about 12 miles distant on the other side of the reef. Chapple sent her down under once more, hoping to evade detection. While the submarine was creeping forward she struck an underwater obstruction.

The jolt smashed the outer glass of several gages, splintered the paint on bulkheads, shook the boat from stem to stern. But to offset this last blow, there was one Christmas gift. Chapple sent S-38 to the surface, determined to run for it, and the two destroyers turned out to be one auxiliary vessel which failed to sight the sub.

Hours later, S-38 worked her way out of Lingayen, and headed for Manila. Only Spartan courage, surpassing skill and a relenting smile from Lady Luck brought her through. Depth bombs, groundings, underwater collision, a broaching, mechanical maladjustments and an internal explosion had been defeated by all hands and a boat remarkable for stamina.

Her foray in Lingayen was not futile. Official records credit S-38 with sinking the second Japanese ship on the American undersea score—Hayo Maru, freighter, 5,445 tons—the transport torpedoed at its anchorage inside the Gulf.

Guarding the approaches to Vigan, north of Lingayen Gulf, the submarine Seal (Lieutenant Commander Hurd) torpedoed and sank the third and last Japanese ship destroyed by American submarine fire in December 1941. This vessel, sunk on the 23rd, was Hayataka Maru, a small 856 ton freighter.

The transport downed by S-38 was the only ship sunk by the Asiatic Fleet submarines dispatched to intercept the Japanese invasion forces at Lingayen. One transport out of an armada which numbered more than 80 ships, including cruisers, does not stand as impressive on the record. To the submariners Lingayen Gulf was a crucible of frustration. What stands as impressive is the performance of the crews who manned such boats as S-38, and the fact that, outnumbered scores to one, and handicapped by a defective weapon, the submarines that met the enemy in the Philippines survived at all.

Strategic Withdrawal

December 25th Manila was declared an open city. With the Japanese Army in northern Luzon, the Imperial Navy controlling the archipelago, Japanese planes raking the interior and Japanese bombers pounding Manila Bay, the Philippine capital was militarily indefensible. General MacArthur had already begun his withdrawal toward the Bataan Peninsula where he hoped his troops could maintain a stand until the arrival of reinforcements. Rear Admiral Francis W. Rockwell had gone to Corregidor to establish a naval headquarters. And to prevent a wholesale slaughter of the Manila populace, the remaining American military and naval forces were ordered to evacuate. Admiral Hart made preparations to fly to Java on Christmas morning.

Loss of Manila was a severe blow to the submarine command, given but 24 hours' notice. Not only did it disorganize the operational plan, but it compelled the abandonment of practically all S-boat spares and many Mark 14 torpedoes—an extremely serious deprivation to a force already worried about replacements. Ingenuity alone kept some of the S-boats going thereafter, and the torpedo shortage continued to hamper the submarine effort for the next year and a half.

Before leaving Manila, the SubsAsiatic Command Staff was divided into two groups. This would prevent a fatal bomb or torpedo hit from wiping out the entire higher echelon at one stroke.

Captain John Wilkes, due for transfer, had been retained in command of the SubsAsiatic Force by Admiral Hart. It was decided that the S-boats and some of the fleet submarines should use the facilities of the Dutch Submarine Base at Soerabaja in the Netherlands East Indies. Captain Wilkes was assigned to this base with the operational part of the divided Submarine Command Staff.

Meantime, the tender HOLLAND had been ordered to leave the Malay Barrier and proceed to Darwin, Australia, where a service base was planned. As head of the administrative part of the divided staff, Captain James Fife, Jr., was to establish headquarters in Darwin.

Admiral Hart's plane flight to Java was canceled by Japanese airmen who discovered the mooring place of the four old Catalinas awaiting the Admiral's party, and smashed them into scrap. Admiral Hart perforce left Manila by submarine, traveling on SHARK (Lieutenant Commander Shane.)

The day after Christmas, SEAWOLF prowled into Mariveles Bay. That midnight she picked up Captain James Fife and his staff and set out for Australia.

On December 29 and 30, the SubsAsiatic boats at sea were ordered to go south to the Malay Barrier when their patrols were completed. On December 31, the last submarine left Manila Bay. She was SWORDFISH, heading for Soerabaja with Captain John Wilkes and his operational staff.

Senior naval officer in a unified command organized under General MacArthur, Rear Admiral Rockwell at Corregidor commanded the remnant units of the Asiatic Fleet in the Manila area. Among those few remaining units were the submarine rescue vessel PIGEON and the submarine tender CANOPUS.

MacArthur's forces on Bataan would hold out for a number of blood-stained weeks, but the Philippine Islands and the waters of the archipelago were lost. General Homma marched into Manila the day after New Year's, and the Imperial Japanese Navy forged an iron ring around the islands.

It remained for American submarines to lead the counter-offensive that smashed that ring.

CHAPTER 4

UNDERSEA LANES TO VICTORY

Axis Design for World Conquest

"Heute gehört uns Deutschland, Morgen die ganze Welt—!" So sang the Nazi legions going to war under Hitler. Once it had been the Drang Nach Östen—a push from Berlin to Bagdad. Now it was an ambition to conquer Europe, the Middle East and North Africa and gain control of the Atlantic Ocean.

Beginning with open violation of the Versailles Treaty (and continuing behind the legalistic camouflage of a bilateral agreement with Great Britain) the German War Lords had been building up a navy since 1934. It seems to have been Hitler's original intention to create a small fleet capable of countering the naval power of Soviet Russia or France. This fleet expanded with the Führer's bloating ambitions.

U-boat construction was rushed after all quantitative restrictions on naval building were removed by the Treaty of 1936. Calculated to seem small to the eye of superficial observation, the U-boat arm was capable of swift development into a formidable undersea force which could challenge any power on the Atlantic. Behind the submarine pens of Heligoland, lay the industrial and scientific resources of a nation devoted to war and long an advocate of the undersea offensive. Schooled in World War I submarining, the German Navy possessed an invaluable technical and tactical reserve fund of experience. Whereas peacetime building had been limited to a monthly output of two or three U-boats, wartime construction could (and did) step up the output to 25 submarines a month.

With sham gestures similar to those which duped many Western diplomats into believing he planned an attack on the USSR, Hitler paid pious homage to International Law and expressly agreed to adhere to the provisions of Article 22 of the London Naval Treaty of 1930 which outlawed unrestricted submarine warfare. To the U-boats at sea on September 3, 1939—the day Great Britain and France declared war on Germany after the Nazi invasion of Poland—the German Naval Staff dispatched orders to the effect that merchant ships were to be attacked only in accordance with the rules of International Law. Nine hours later a U-boat sank the British passenger liner ATHENIA off the north coast of Ireland. Whether the ATHENIA sinking was deliberately manufactured or not, London's reaction was as anyone would have foreseen. The British armed their merchantmen, and this gave Germany an excuse to announce unrestricted submarine warfare on merchant shipping and to start a blockade of the British Isles.

German submarine tactics were highly aggressive, favoring day-submerged attacks made at periscope depth. The U-boats scored heavily against Allied shipping, and the Royal Navy suffered immediate and severe losses. One of the earliest U-boat successes was dated September 17, 1939, when the aircraft carrier HMS COURAGEOUS, operating with British anti-submarine forces in the western approaches of the Atlantic, was torpedoed and sunk. This signal success incited the U-boat Command to open a bold drive against shipping in British harbors.

On October 14th, U-47, under Kapitan-Leutnant Gunther Prien, entered Scapa Flow and destroyed the British battleship ROYAL OAK. Torpedo failures prevented Prien from wreaking further havoc upon the anchored British Fleet, but this one expertly delivered blow was a cold-water shock to the Lords of the Admiralty.

In the Firth of Forth the cruiser BELFAST was torpedoed, and at Lock Eue the NELSON was hit. Both warships were eventually repaired.

These initial U-boat blows were spectacular and staggering. But the Nazi submarines were unable to reap such a harvest as their forerunners garnered in the opening months of World War I. This, despite the fact that the 1939 U-boat was far superior to the 1914 model and Hitler's submarine fleet much larger than the Kaiser's original.

British warship losses (from all causes) during the first six months of World War II totaled approximately 63,000 tons—about half the total of the first six months of World War I. Prompt institution of the convoy system and the rapid organization of all available anti-submarine forces into an Anti-Submarine Warfare Command served to hold down Allied merchant-shipping losses in the fall of 1939 and the ensuing winter and spring. Improvement of the hydrophone, the "Asdic," and development of other electronic devices had stiffened the British defense. This apparent countering of the U-boat effort seemed to substantiate a statement made by Churchill eight months before the war's outbreak. Churchill observed that *the undoubted obsolescence of the submarine as a decisive war weapon should give further confidence to the English-speaking democracies."*

But the Allied shipping toll soon increased to a figure that controverted this hopeful view. And when France fell in June 1940, Germany became an Atlantic power.

The Nazi naval chiefs lost no time in capitalizing on the strategical advantages afforded them by possession of the French coast. U-boat pens were built at Lorient, St. Nazaire and other coastal ports, and squadrons of German submarines were soon operating from these bases.

Then, timing the play with the German breakthrough, Mussolini threw Fascist Italy into the war on June 10, 1940. This move completely neutralized the French Navy, which was soon withdrawn from the war by Admiral Darlan. The British were compelled to weaken their Atlantic lifelines by rushing sea forces to the Mediterranean, the Adriatic and the Aegean. British surface forces were able to handle the second-class Italian Navy, which represented a "fleet in being" rather than a powerful adversary. But the transparent waters of Mare Nostrum afforded poor cover for submarines, and of the first four large British submarines which went out on patrol from Malta after Italy entered the war, three were lost.

In the Atlantic the U-boats launched an all-out campaign to sever England's shipping arteries while Goering's Luftwaffe smashed at England's heart. Lend-lease had gone into effect in September 1940 with the American loan of 50 over-age destroyers to Great Britain and President Roosevelt's announcement that the United States would serve as the "Arsenal of Democracy." To stop the flow of munitions, guns and foodstuffs from that arsenal to Britain was the U-boat's mission. The phlebotomy began in earnest.

During the first ten months of the war the average number of U-boats on patrol in the Atlantic had been six. Average number of ships sunk by them monthly had been 26, totaling an approximate 106,000 tons. By the summer of 1941 the average number of U-boats in the Atlantic was 36. And in April alone of that year nearly 600,000 tons of British-controlled shipping had gone to the bottom —more than twice the replacement capacity of British and American shipyards combined.

Much of this U-boat success can be attributed to the tactic of "wolf-packing" introduced by the German Submarine Force at that time. Devised to counter Britain's wide-ranging air patrols, the wolf-pack system featured a group control which permitted wide dispersion of the submarines for search over a broad area, and provided a means for their concentration for attack. In this method of operation there were numerous advantages. For one, the group could be commanded by an ace U-boat captain whose abilities had heretofore been confined to the operation of an individual submarine. This meant that a Gunther Prien or a Joachim Schepke controlled a dozen U-boats instead of one. For another, the limited vision of the individual submarine was extended by the periscopes of many. Coupled with this advantage, the eyes of the long-range reconnaissance plane could guide the pack to distant prey. Once a convoy was located, the pack-leader would direct the U-boats to a point of interception where they could assemble and deliver a mass attack. Mass attack scattered the convoy's defenses, forcing the escort to disperse, pell-mell. The submarines could then dodge in and strike through holes in the screen.

In company with the wolf-pack tactic, the U-boats employed the night-surface approach. They might track a convoy for days, keeping well beyond the horizon, then close in for an after-dark kill. Trimmed down to decks awash, they would use their high surface speed to charge in, attack, escape. Diving was resorted to only in dire emergency.

41

The Allied answer to the mounting U-boat toll was the establishment of American bases in Iceland and Greenland. United States naval vessels were already convoying British shipping to the edge of the 300-mile safety belt established in the western Atlantic at the start of the war. When Secretary of the Navy Knox declared, *"We cannot allow our goods to be sunk in the Atlantic. We must make good our promise to Britain,"* these patrols were extended. American naval vessels were not permitted to attack enemy ships, but were to report the presence of any raiders sighted.

On September 4, 1941, a German U-boat commander fired two torpedoes at the veteran destroyer GREER, which had been tracking his submarine. GREER countered with a depth charge barrage. The U-boat escaped from the old four-piper, having fired the first German shot at the U.S. Navy in World War II.

One week later President Roosevelt ordered Navy patrollers to shoot on sight any U-boat or other raider attacking merchant ships of any flag inside American defense areas.

"From now on, if German or Italian vessels of war enter waters the protection of which is necessary for American defense, they do so at their own peril."

Isolationists and other critics protested, unwilling to believe that the waters off Greenland and Iceland lay in the United States defense periphery. Skeptics were equally unready to recognize the West African "bulge" as a possible base for a future Nazi thrust into the Western Hemisphere. But early in 1940, German Grand Admiral Erich Raeder had endorsed a proposal to seize Iceland and occupy the Canary Islands for use as bases from which an attack on the U.S. Navy could be launched. A Nazi naval staff paper written at this time declared that with England's defeat the United States and the remnants of the British Empire would remain Germany's "natural enemies," and recommended a huge naval building program to implement strategy devised to crush the "enemy's" sea power. Hitler tentatively approved the building program, at the same time refusing to sanction a proposal made by Admiral Raeder in February 1940, recommending the dispatch of two U-boats to attack shipping off Nova Scotia and lay mines off Halifax. According to the records, Der Führer put the cancel on this operation "in view of the psychological effect on the United States." It seems obvious that Hitler hoped to disarm American opinion before the strike at American sea power was made.

During the planning of Operation Seeloewe (the invasion of England) the Nazi High Command discussions turned to a possible invasion of Ireland. German naval chiefs demurred, fearing a Nazi Dunkirk. Raeder opposed Operation Seeloewe in its entirety, insisting that the U-boat and naval-air blockade could starve the British Isles into surrender.

Postponing the invasion of England after the Luftwaffe failure, Hitler and his advisers (in late November, 1940) next contemplated seizure of the Azores. Intent was to employ the Azores as a base for a long-range Messerschmidt bomber capable of striking the Atlantic seaboard of the United States.

Hitler vacillated. He favored a strike at America from the Azores, but in the spring of 1941 his intuition advised him to attack Soviet Russia first.

Against vociferous opposition from his naval advisers, Hitler cranked up the German War Machine in the summer of 1941 and sent it roaring on its way to Moscow. Russian wheat, Russian ores and Russian oil were the objectives. Once supplied by an inexhaustible reservoir of raw materials from the greatest land mass on the globe, the *herrenvolk* could conquer Great Britain and dispose of American sea power in their own good time.

For the latter project, Hitler did not count on German force alone. Conversations had gone forward with Tokyo. The Japanese strike at Pearl Harbor apparently came as a surprise to the Nazi chiefs, but they could only have been more pleased than surprised. The blasting of the United States Pacific Fleet and the crushing of the Americans in the Philippines gave the Nazis reason to hope their U-boats could win control of the Atlantic.

On New Year's Day, 1942, representatives of 26 Allied countries convened in Washington. There, in the White House, they signed the document which founded the United Nations. But there were grave expressions among the signers. This two-ocean war against the Axis was going to be a long war. A horde of U-boats was cutting the Anglo-American lifeline in the Atlantic. In the Pacific a small fleet of American submarines was the mainstay of the Allied naval defense.

Could the U-boats be defeated? Could the American submarines hold the Pacific defense line until reinforcements arrived? On these two questions hinged the outcome of the two-ocean war.

Pacific Defense Line

Following the Pearl Harbor debacle, President Roosevelt appointed Admiral Ernest J. King Commander-in-Chief of the U.S. Fleet with Headquarters in Washington, D.C. Vice Admiral Royal E. Ingersoll replaced Admiral King as Commander-in-Chief of the Atlantic Fleet and Admiral Hart remained in command of the Asiatic Fleet. And Admiral Chester W. Nimitz, making a secret flight from Washington to Pearl Harbor in civvies, on the last day of December 1941 became Commander-in-Chief of the Pacific Fleet.

Submariners noted that both Admiral King and Admiral Nimitz were, like Admiral Hart, veterans of the undersea service. Thus, of the four top-ranking admirals of the Navy, three were prominent submarine officers.

Admiral King had been in the Submarine Service during the 20's. In 1922, after a tour of duty at the Submarine Base, New London, he was made commander of SubDiv 2. Later he commanded SubDiv 3. From 1923 to 1926 he occupied various posts at New London. He received the DSM citation for exceptional service in the S-51 salvage operation, of which he had charge. In 1927 he received the Distinguished Service Medal for similar action in raising the S-4.

Admiral Nimitz, a fully qualified submariner, entered that service in the experimental days of 1909 —as Lieutenant Nimitz reporting for duty with the First Submarine Flotilla. In April 1909 he was placed in command of the First Flotilla and served as commander of PLUNGER (A-1)—the second submersible of that name, and one of the few U.S. submarines not named after a fish. In 1910 Nimitz went to Boston to fit out the submarine SNAPPER (C-5), built by the Fore River Shipbuilding Company. He served as the first commanding officer of SNAPPER, and the following year commanded NARWHAL (D-1). In September 1911, he was assigned additional duty commanding SubDiv 3, Atlantic Torpedo Fleet. Later that year he was transferred to Quincy, Massachusetts, to fit out SKIPJACK (E-1). He assumed her command early in 1912. May 1912, he became Commander Atlantic Submarine Flotilla.

In 1916 he was transferred to the USS CHICAGO for duty in connection with submarines. During World War I, he served on the staff of the Commander of the Submarine Force, Atlantic, later becoming Chief of Staff. In May 1918, he was assigned additional temporary duty in connection with submarines operating in European waters. He was also a member of the Board of Standardization of Submarines, and Senior Member of the Board on Submarine Design. In 1920 he officially established the Submarine Base at Pearl Harbor, T.H., and served as its first commanding officer.

No naval officer in submarines was better qualified to wear the dolphins than Fleet Admiral Chester W. Nimitz. It was a submariner who took hold at Pearl Harbor on that black New Year's Eve of 1941.

Before he left Washington for Pearl Harbor Admiral Nimitz realized he was facing an unparalleled defense problem. Given a depleted force to work with, he had to do much with little and make that little last.

Important surface units of the Pacific Fleet had been at sea on the morning of December 7, and thus escaped the Pearl Harbor bombing. Composed of three heavy cruisers, nine destroyers and the aircraft carrier ENTERPRISE, Task Force Eight, under Vice Admiral William F. Halsey, had been en route to Hawaii from Wake. Task Force Three—one heavy cruiser and a minelaying squadron, under Vice Admiral Wilson Brown—was at Johnston Island. Task Force Twelve—three heavy cruisers, five destroyers and the aircraft carrier LEXINGTON, under Rear Admiral Newton—was some 400 miles off Midway. SARATOGA, the third Pacific Fleet aircraft carrier, had been in drydock at San Diego.

From these elements and undamaged units of the fleet at Pearl Harbor, a Central Pacific battle force could be assembled to meet the onrushing Japanese. But even as the Navy reeled back before the Japanese offensive in the Far East, it suffered another stunning blow. Racing to the relief of Wake Island, a small task force had gone steaming at top speed across the Pacific. One of the vessels in this force was SARATOGA, fresh out of drydock and primed for battle. When reconnaissance indicated the rescue attempt would prove futile, the task force turned back. It was heading for safer waters when the SARA was torpedoed by a Japanese submarine. Damage was serious enough to keep the badly needed aircraft carrier out of action for many weeks.

Months would pass before the Pacific Fleet could be strongly reinforced. Naval units could not be withdrawn from the vital Battle of the Atlantic. Replacements from American shipyards, like the salvage operations at Pearl, would take time. With its surface arm broken and its air arm badly wounded, the Pacific Fleet could only retreat before the Japanese juggernaut.

Retreat how far? The juggernaut was bearing down on the Netherlands East Indies. Its spearheads were aimed at New Guinea. Keeping pace with the Philippine drive, Japanese forces advanced from the Marshalls to the near-by Gilbert Islands, evidently heading for the Solomons, the New Hebrides and New Caledonia on the flank of Australia. Conferring in Washington late in December 1941, American and Allied leaders had decided that the Philippines and the East Indies could not be held, but the supply lines from the United States to Australia must at all cost be maintained. The Japanese must not be permitted to break through the Central Pacific or the island chains flanking Australia. Nor could they be allowed to gain a foothold in the Aleutians. A line drawn from Dutch Harbor to Midway, to Samoa, to New Caledonia, to Australia marked the frontier to be held by American and Allied forces. The sea defense, of course, was up to the United States Pacific Fleet.

But this defense could not remain static. It is an old American truism that touchdowns are made (and games are won) by the side which carries the ball. The Navy could not stand stationary and inert like a seagoing Maginot Line, waiting for the enemy onslaught. The inflexible wall is too likely to give under pressure built up at one point, as the Maginot Line had demonstrated.

"When driven back," said Ferdinand Foch in World War I, "attack!"

As the calendar turned from 1941 to 1942, the bulk of the defensive attack in the Pacific was shouldered by the one fleet-arm which had not been incapacitated by the enemy smash—the one arm capable of driving hard punches at the onrushing foe: The Submarine Force.

Submarine Strategy

This is an axiom of warfare: Where concealment is equally available to both sides, it favors the inferior force.

Certainly the American submarines in the Pacific at war's beginning were by far the inferior force. The Japanese offensive came striding down from the north like a giant in seven-league boots. Never before had the world witnessed such an exhibition of amphibious might. The colossus scooped up Hong Kong on Christmas Day. His club smashed Singapore as though that stronghold were made of pottery. Cast by the Rising Sun, his shadow stretched across the whole Southwest Pacific as his boots trampled the Philippine Sea and waded on down to Borneo, Sumatra, Java.

The Japanese offensive, seaborne, was supplied by shipping and sustained by shipping. Fleets, therefore naval and merchant—were the boots in which the amphibious giant walked. In the van of this sea-air-land drive (an operation Churchill termed "triphibious") were the warships and aircraft carriers of the Imperial Navy. At its center were scores of shallow-draught transports, small gunboats, power boats and droves of light, fast craft which could invade a bay like a swarm of beetles. Behind these shock-troop laden armadas came the heavy transports, the supply and munition ships, the destroyer-screened AP's, AO's, and AK's. And in the offensive's wake came the loot-hungry hordes of merchantmen, oil tankers, ore ships, cattle boats, junks, sampans and coastal steamers, herded along by the guarding DD's.

The Philippines invasion supplied naval strategists with a notable demonstration of concealment favoring the force inferior. True, it was not equally available to both sides, surface craft being the least concealable of targets. Vulnerability in this respect can be offset by firepower, protective armor, speed, sheer weight of numbers. Still, the inferior force, given the advantage of concealment, can get in. Where Allied surface forces fell precipitously back and Allied air forces were swept away, American submarines went in.

Submariners will note that concealment may permit a penetration of enemy lines, but it does not preclude the possibility of discovery thereafter. Getting in is one thing—getting out is another. Especially after one's entry has been revealed by a torpedo's wake. The submarine, however, was the only warcraft in existence which could penetrate and escape, undetected by human eyesight. Consider the many submarine-detection devices, and this concealment advantage seems a slim one. Yet it gave American submarines a narrow margin which enabled them to operate in enemy-infested seas and carry out their primary mission—the destruction of Japanese shipping.

Only by shipping could the Japanese front be maintained and the conquered areas exploited. Only by destruction of that shipping—as the war leaders in Washington realized—could the Japanese offensive be halted, the front line cut off, Japan herself isolated and disarmed with her industry dead-stalled.

During the Nineteenth Century, naval strategists had concluded that the *guerre de course*—commerce raiding—could never decide the issue between maritime powers. The "war of the chase" was resorted to (they contended) by the inferior belligerent attempting to deprive the enemy of sea lanes he had already won. Commerce raiding merely postponed inevitable defeat, for command of the sea was gained and held not by raiders, but by men-of-war. Only *guerre d'escadres*—battle of naval squadrons—would result in a decision. In proof of this, the strategists pointed to the American Civil War in which Confederate raiders all but drove northern shipping off the sea, but the Federal Navy's blockade clinched the issue. Mahan himself inclined to this line of reasoning. Allied strategists were consequently dismayed by the devastating U-boat raids of World War I.

By 1918 it was apparent that there was an ocean of difference between the lone-wolf ALABAMA, a fugitive the moment she was sighted by an enemy naval

THE HUNTERS! All looks peaceful in this camera masterpiece. But in this scene all may not meet the eye. Still waters run deep in war-time. Surface haze may screen an enemy convoy—or lurking destroyer. The tide may conceal a mine. The submarine's bridge watch scans the horizon for targets—and foes.

CONSTRUCTION. *Women drillers at Electric Boat Co., Groton. Lady at left seems able to chat above chatter of drill!*

LAUNCHING! *A new submarine goes down the ways at Portsmouth, N.H. Date: December 7, 1942.*

PROVISIONS. *Work party carrying stores aboard submarine at Pearl. Good grub is featured in the underwater Navy.*

LOADING "AMMO." *Shells go aboard a submarine for stowage in magazine below. Many subs on special mission carried munitions to Corregidor, later to Filipino guerillas.*

"CAST OFF ALL LINES!" *Submarine under way for patrol. Leaving home base, a raider would be gone for many days, usually returned with a display of Jap flags.*

squadron, and the lone-wolf submarine, capable of attacking a squadron and sinking its largest battleship. The undersea commerce raider was a threat to man-of-war and merchantman alike, and ships in either category could be driven from the sea by the side which launched a sufficient submarine offensive.

Such had been the contention of French Admiral Aube, speaking to deaf conservatism back in the 1880's. Such was the contention of submarine designers and submarine men in the 1920's and 1930's, who discerned the fallacy in the argument against the commerce raider (had the Union been dependent on commercial shipping, she might have lost to the Confederacy), and remembered Churchill's comment that the U-Boat campaign of World War I was, in his opinion, *"the gravest peril that we faced in all the ups and downs of that war."*

Conservatives, however, had continued to favor surface navies with their high-speed cruisers and destroyers and mastodonic capital ships. By such proponents the lessons of World War I were largely forgotten or misread—after all, had not the U-boat been beaten by mine barrages and the convoy system? Had not Britannia's Navy ultimately ruled the waves? Invention of magnetic and acoustic mines, electronic detectors and other anti-submarine devices, the development of evasive routing and aerial protection for convoys seemed the final answer to submarining. In particular, the airplane was seen as ending the war career of the submersible. If the dive bomber could sink a battleship, what couldn't it do to a submarine which, even when submerged to periscope depth, remained a visible target to the airman? To evade the plane, the submarine would have to cruise far below the surface. And eventually it must surface for a battery charge and expose its conning tower to the deadly air bomb.

These opinions had their reflection in the United States. They were mirrored in the naval building program rushed by the Government in 1940 and 1941. On December 1, 1941, the Navy was building 15 battleships, 11 aircraft carriers, 54 cruisers, 191 destroyers and 73 submarines. Separated into categories, the figures read: 271 surface craft and 73 submarines. But in weight of steel, armament, equipment and cost, the surface building heavily overbalanced the submarine. In capital ships alone the difference was enormous, for in the yards were the giants South Dakota, Indiana, Massachusetts, Alabama, Iowa, New Jersey, Missouri, Wisconsin, Kentucky, and the unnamed No's. 65, 67, 68, 69, 70, 71. Add the great North Carolina and Washington, completed the previous July, and the BB's loom as mammoth whales above the minnow submarine boats.

In this building equation the expenditure for naval aircraft must be included, for President Roosevelt had promised the nation the world's biggest air force, and millions had been appropriated for naval aviation. Couple the naval aircraft to the surface-craft building program, and the construction of 73 submarines is seen as a minuscule project.

Seen against this background, the situation of the U.S. Submarine Force as it entered a two-ocean war is plainly evident. There were too few submarines. The future of submarining was uncertain. The submarine itself was a sort of "second cousin" at the naval board where the BB sat austerely at table's head, with the large carrier and cruiser (CVB and CB) at either hand and the new naval aircraft as guest of honor. The SS was admired, respected, but considered something of a radical.

So the American SS's immersed in the Battle of the Pacific were inclined to insert an "O" as a middle initial. Especially in the Philippine area where, after the loss of Sealion, there were only twenty-eight (28) of these. Twenty-eight (28) Manila submarines. The number is repeated for emphasis, and it was due to grow smaller before reinforcements arrived. The Manila submarines were supported by a small Dutch submarine squadron—a Dutch submarine (Captain A. J. Bussemaker, RNN) broke up a convoy entering the Gulf of Thailand in the first night of the war, drawing first blood for the Allies in Asiatic waters. And an unidentified Netherlands submarine sank the first Japanese warship to go down from torpedo fire in World War II (the destroyer Sagiri, sunk off Kuching, Borneo, on December 26, 1941). But the little Netherlands force soon melted away, and Subs-Asiatic bore the brunt thereafter.

The Imperial Navy did not lose a single major unit during the Philippines invasion. But as the Japanese moved down on the Malay Barrier they began to lose merchant ships here and there. And with the advent of the New Year, ships started going down off the coasts of Japan. American submarines were beginning the war of attrition.

Preview of Victory

The submarine forces in the Pacific "got in there" and fought. The Manila boats diverted the enemy's naval vanguard, harried the flanks of the Japanese Second Fleet, and impeded the drive on the Netherlands East Indies. Pearl Harbor submarines joined battle in the Central Pacific, patrolled the line extending from Australia to the Aleutians, drove over to the East China Sea and cut the shipping lanes to Japan.

With mid-Pacific bases lost—with Asiatic bases lost

—with air cover lost—the Pacific Fleet immobilized—supplies cut off—spare parts lost—Manila torpedoes captured—reinforcements and replacements leagues away—with all these disadvantages, the submariners entered the conflict and kept on going.

They kept on going, despite the fact that the enemy had the initiative. The fact that the S-boats were old and the enemy destroyers new—that operational plans, like repairs, had to be improvised—that Japanese anti-submarine tactics were a mystery to be solved by trial and error—that Japanese bombs were known to contain an explosive charge greater than any at that time developed by the Allies. The submariners kept on going despite an unreliable weapon. Loss of forward bases, fleet support, repair facilities, stores—these never imperilled the submarines as did torpedo failure. *And for almost two years American submarines went into action handicapped by a defective torpedo!*

In spite of this and all other handicaps, the submariners led the United States offensive. Through reeling winter seas and the burnished waters of the tropics, through berserk typhoons, arctic storms of white wickedness and foaming venom, steaming equatorial calms, blazing days, impenetrable nights, through ocean deeps black with silence, through waters blasted by depth charge and air bomb, the U.S. submarines carried the fight to the enemy. From the glacial coasts of Greenland to the boiling shoals of the South Seas they fought the two-ocean war. They aided in the defense of Midway and battled the foe in the Aleutians. They helped to parry the enemy's thrust at Guadalcanal. They blockaded the ports of the Jap home Empire. Cut the sea lanes to the China Coast and the Mandates, to Malaya, the Netherlands East Indies and New Guinea. Laid mines. Reconnoitered for air strikes. Rescued refugees. Served as lifeguards. Struck the Imperial Navy some of the hardest blows it ever received. Swept the merchant fleets of the Rising Sun from the Central and Southwest Pacific. Penetrated the Sea of Japan. And finally halted (presumably for lack of wheels) at the beachheads of Kyushu, Shikoku, Hokkaido and Honshu.

Above all, the U.S. submarines accomplished the No. 1 mission of submarining. They sank ships!

In the Addenda the reader will find the score sheet of those sinkings—indelible testimony to the ruthless efficiency and superb valor of the U.S. Submarine Force. Composed of no more than 1.6% of the Navy's personnel, this incomparable service arm accounted for 73% of Japanese ship losses from all causes during the first two years of the Pacific War. The final score, verified by post-war inquest, credits U.S. submarines with sinking 54.7% of the Japanese merchantmen and 29% of the Japanese naval vessels sunk in World War II.

The figures sum up the record. The following chapters detail the manner of its making.

46

PART II

THE FIGHTING DEFENSE
(1942)

Though I Be Wounded, I Am Not Slain!
I'll Lie Me Down To Bleed Awhile,
And Then I'll Rise And Fight Again!

EARLY ENGLISH BALLAD

CHAPTER 5

PIONEERS PACIFIC

Operations, January 1942

"The true speed of war," said Mahan, "is not headlong precipitancy, but the unremitting energy which wastes no time."

Track men will recognize the truth of this aphorism, as will boxers and those skilled with the foils. Boiled down, it may be taken to mean that the rush is not so effective as the steady drive. The rush is spectacular—may sweep an opponent off his feet—but it is a tactic which frequently ends in exhaustion, leaving the rusher little in reserve for a follow-through. Service veterans, watching the Japanese offensive smash forward in the New Year of 1942, may have thought of the time Firpo knocked Jack Dempsey out of the ring. The champion was badly hurt, but the Wild Bull of the Pampas put everything in his Sunday punch and had little left over for Monday. In the end the implacable fighter with the unremitting energy beat the slugger.

However, exceptions plague all generalities, and the laws of probability sometimes give before the improbable. A blind swing *might* fell a champion, or cripple him beyond ultimate recovery. And a wild rush might, through virtue of surprise, drive an opponent so far down the field that the cost of recapturing the lost ground would frustrate its eventual retrieval. Hence many American observers faced the New Year with pessimism, foreboding, or excruciating anxiety. Seemingly unstoppable, the Japanese offensive plunged forward. When would this headlong charge be slowed? Where could it be halted? Had the U.S. Navy been irreparably crippled? If Japan seized the Philippines, Indonesia, the Netherlands East Indies and the islands on down to the Solomons, how could the United Nations hope to retrieve so vast a territory?

Many failed to realize that the territory marked for immediate conquest by Japan represented an empire vast in extent, but small in land area. This expansive territory was not unlike the sort of real estate which looks impressive on paper but is largely aquatic. Sea empires are conquered only when the surrounding seas are conquered, and so long as the United States had naval forces in action, the Pacific, far or near, did not "belong" to the Japanese.

Witness the fact that units of the U.S. Navy were on duty in Philippine waters on New Year's Day, 1942. Other units were in action off the coasts of China and Indo-China. Others were at Wake and Midway. And still others were cruising in waters off Japan's home islands, within sight of the lighthouses of Shikoku and Honshu. While the Japanese were subjugating conquered islands they were unable to subjugate the surrounding ocean, much less its deeps. In these unconquered regions the war was carried by the 50 U.S. submarines of the Pacific Fleet based at Pearl Harbor and the Asiatic Fleet which had based at Manila.

So the Philippines were not abandoned by the Navy to lie within reach of the Japanese grab like a pot of gold at the end of Operation Rainbow Five. Wake and the islands of the Western Pacific were not deserted. ComSubPac's original supporting plan to Rainbow Five (the Pacific Fleet war plan) had provided for submarining patrol areas around the Empire, in the Marianas and Marshalls, and off Truk,

Ponape and Kusaie. This plan included a series of intermediate stages leading up to unrestricted submarine warfare—an eventuality not discounted by the Submarine Command. However, with the immediate declaration of unrestricted submarine warfare (which came at the beginning of hostilities rather than as a climax) the submarine operating areas were changed to cover important shipping lanes, in conformance with the directive to blast the enemy's merchant fleets out of the sea. Areas on the skirts of Japan were little altered, but areas in the Yellow Sea, the East China Sea and the Mandates were completely revised. Those in the Mandates were altered to cover both naval bases and shipping centers. Defensive patrol areas around Wake and Midway were to be maintained.

At the war's outbreak, Asiatic Fleet submarines were operating off the China Coast and covering the shipping lanes below Formosa and on down to the Malay Barrier. In November 1941, the northern boundary for the SubsAsiatic Force had been established at 30° N. Shortly before the Pearl Harbor attack, the Pacific Fleet Force was given a small strip extending to 28°-30° N., and in January 1942, the boundary was lowered to 26° N. to give the Pacific Fleet submarines easier access to the shipping lanes of the East China Sea.

Meanwhile it became necessary to patrol the Aleutian archipelago. Coverage of North Pacific areas was incumbent on the force based at Pearl Harbor, and with the activation of Rainbow Five, two S-boats were dispatched from Hawaii to Dutch Harbor in the Aleutians. Arriving late in January, these S-boats reported to the Commander, Pacific Northern Naval Front, and prepared for war patrol.

With patrol areas extending from the Aleutians southward to the Solomons, New Guinea, and the Dutch East Indies, and from Midway westward to the coast of China and Indo-China, the American submariners in the Pacific had a whale of a job on their hands. One square mile of land (640 acres) is a sizable piece of real estate. A square mile of ocean is even larger, for the nautical mile is longer than the statute mile. A million square miles adds up to a lot of acreage by land or sea. With these figures in mind, one can appreciate the task detailed to the Pacific and Asiatic Fleet submarines—the task of driving Japanese shipping from some 8,000,000 square miles (over 5,000,000,000 acres) of ocean. Evenly divided among the 50 starting submarines, this oceanic sphere would have yielded 100,000,000 acres apiece!

Of course, the Pacific vastness was not apportioned in such fashion. In general, the patrolling Pacific Fleet (Pearl Harbor) submarines restricted their operations to the areas assigned, covering waters where enemy ship traffic was anticipated, and focal points where shipping lanes converged. The Asiatic Fleet (Manila) submarines were detailed to strategic sectors of a fluid front that constantly shifted with the advance of the Japanese offensive. Where opportunity presented they might penetrate this front to harry the sea lanes behind the lines or raid the harbors captured by Jap invasion forces.

With but 50 submarines to do the job (and experience soon revealed that not more than one-third of these could be maintained on patrol station simultaneously—the other two-thirds being either en route to or from the area, or undergoing refit or overhaul) the submarine effort had to be spread exceedingly thin. At the start of 1942 there were not enough submarines available for effective patrol of the areas delineated, and throughout the greater part of the year the problem of area coverage remained an equation in which pressures had to be balanced against probable results.

As the Japanese offensive stormed forward through the first weeks of 1942, the pressures were easier to discern than the results of counter-action. Japanese strategy was determinable as a three-prong drive to pin Malaya and Sumatra in the west; the Philippines, Borneo, Celebes and Java in the center; and New Guinea and Rabaul in the Bismarck Archipelago to the east. Once these objectives were impaled on the fork, the Orient would be practically secured. Protected by bases on New Guinea, New Britain, and New Ireland, the East Indies would be made impregnable against attack from that direction. Malaya would serve as either a wall or a door on the British-India border. Wake, the Marshalls, and the Gilberts would serve to guard the expanded empire's northeast flank.

Spearing through the Philippines, the central prong of the Japanese offensive had Luzon and Mindanao pinned by the first of January, and the spearhead in this sector had advanced to Jolo in the Sulu Archipelago. Heaviest fighting in the Pacific fell to United States forces in this central arena where the seas were defended by Admiral Hart's Asiatic Fleet.

Admiral Hart arrived at Soerabaja on New Year's Day, 1942, and immediately set up provisional headquarters for the Asiatic Fleet. Provisional because the Navy and War Departments, foreseeing the impossibility of holding the Malay Barrier, had selected Port Darwin, Australia, for development as a major base, and fleet auxiliaries were already being sent there. But as Port Darwin was too distant for effective operations in the Java Sea area, the operational command was located at Soerabaja where Dutch basing facilities could be used to good advantage for the time being.

In supreme command of Allied forces in this theater, British General Sir Archibald P. Wavell appointed Admiral Hart to the operational command of the American-British-Dutch-Australian (ABDA) Fleet. Under Admiral Hart was Vice Admiral Conrad Helfrich, Dutch Commander-in-Chief, a hard-fisted sea dog who knew the waters of the East Indies from long experience. Helfrich stubbornly opposed the concept of a fighting retreat, but with the odds overwhelmingly against the Allied forces, he could only agree to strategic withdrawals. It was not easy to put in gear the machinery of a unified command which spoke two different languages and included four differing systems of fleet tactics. Exchange of signalmen among the flagships aided somewhat, but a smooth-functioning, integrated command was not readily achieved under stress of emergency. For the first month or so the various elements of the ABDA fleet continued to operate more or less independently, with the U.S. Asiatic Fleet in the eastern arenas of the theater, and the British and Dutch in the Malaya and Sumatra sectors.

The ABDA fleet was composed of Admiral Hart's three American cruisers and 13 destroyers; three Dutch light cruisers, DE RUYTER, JAVA, and TROMP, and six destroyers; the British heavy cruiser EXETER; and the Australian light cruisers, PERTH and HOBART, with seven destroyers. Its undersea force consisted of some submarines—28 American, three British, nine Dutch.

January found MacArthur's forces digging in for the defense of Bataan. Admiral Rockwell had shifted his headquarters to Corregidor. In Malaya the British were fighting desperately to stem the enemy advance on Singapore. The Japanese drive was crashing into Borneo, concentrating on the oil port of Tarakan. Admiral Hart disposed his hopelessly outnumbered naval forces with the care of a chess master maneuvering pawns against a powerhouse of bishops, knights and castles. On January 8, 1942, SubsAsiatic was designated as Task Force Three of the Asiatic Fleet, and assigned the mission of stopping the enemy north of the Malay Barrier.

Meantime, the enemy's home waters were being invaded. This counter-invasion was begun by Pacific Fleet submarines.

Pioneer Tactics (Day-periscope Attack)

The first three submarines to go out on war patrol from Pearl Harbor—GUDGEON, PLUNGER and POLLACK —were pioneers in a number of respects. They were the first Pacific Fleet submarines to make the long and hazardous 3,400-mile voyage from Oahu to Japan. As such, they were the first American submarines to invade Empire waters. And they were first in other militant ways and means.

PLUNGER, patrolling the Kii Suido Area with the first radar set carried into action, was first to test the air defenses of the Japanese homeland. POLLACK, in the Tokyo Bay Area, sank the No. 1 Japanese merchantman on the Pacific Fleet Submarine Force list. GUDGEON, returning from the Bungo Suido area, scored a first that was original in the annals of the U.S. Navy—by sinking the first enemy warship in history to go down from the fire of a United States submarine.

Firsts are noteworthy for something more than mere originality. They point the way. They prove a possibility (or an impossibility, as the case may be). They may establish a precedent, furnish a foundation for something previously confined to the realm of theory, or set a mark for others to shoot at. The Pearl Harbor submariners pioneering in Empire waters blazed a trail for their companions in the Service. They showed what they and their submarines were made of. They demonstrated what could be done by those determined to do it.

Blazing the trail from Pearl Harbor to Japan's doorstep, PLUNGER had an adventurous maiden patrol. While she tested Japan's air defenses with her novel radar equipment, she underwent the first depth-charging sustained by a Pacific Fleet submarine. On January 4, evading an enemy destroyer, PLUNGER was subjected to this rigorous "going over." Twenty-four depth charges sought her life, and one exploded close aboard with a violence that split an alcohol tank in her after torpedo-room.

Absorbing this punishment, PLUNGER's pioneers learned a number of things about the enemy's anti-submarine tactics. It was evident that Japanese underwater listening gear was efficient. In fact, experience was to prove that at the start of the war it was the equal of contemporary American equipment. While Japanese echo-ranging apparatus was only fair (with a maximum range of around 3,000 meters, and effective at a speed of 12 knots) Japanese hydrophones could obtain a bearing at about 5,000 meters at a speed of approximately 5 knots. Such warcraft as assailed PLUNGER repeated, demonstrated a facility for locating submerged submarines by means of sonar. The Japanese were to lag behind in wartime development of electronics, but at the war's beginning their sonic devices were good. Good enough, at any rate, to worry PLUNGER.

Twenty-four depth charges are a lot of T.N.T. in

any language, and those which thundered around PLUNGER amounted to something like 2½ tons of explosive. The depth charge was the favorite anti-submarine weapon of the Japanese, and the Imperial Navy was later known to feature a king-size model weighing close to 1,000 pounds. The charges dropped on PLUNGER, however, were probably the standard Type 2, Model 2—350-pounders which had an explosive charge of about 230 pounds. Japanese fleet destroyers carried 30 depth charges. The DD hunting for PLUNGER must have nearly unloaded the rack, but she was unable to knock out the submarine.

For the submariners the experience was a gruelling one, but PLUNGER's captain, Lieutenant Commander David C. White, brought her through. Submarine, skipper, and all hands showed the Force that Pearl Harbor boats and those who manned them could take it.

Two weeks later PLUNGER's submariners demonstrated that they could deal it out as well. Sighting a Japanese freighter, White sent his crew to battle stations and directed a day-periscope attack. Early battle reports were as brief as these Pacific pioneers were stoic, and the official account of PLUNGER's action is as bare of drama as a recital in arithmetic. Latitude and longitude. So many tons. Such and such a bearing. Estimated range. Fired two.

Between the lines, however, a reader can visualize half-naked men racing through the submarine's interior as the alarm sends them to battle stations. The approach party in a huddle over the plotting table in the control room. Hands working the wheel that opens the outer doors to the bow tubes. Torpedomen tense at their stations. The sound man crouched at his gear. Engineers at their posts in the forward and aft engine rooms. Electricians at the controls. The glistening metal shaft of the periscope gliding up and down in its well in answer to sharp orders from the captain. Up periscope! Down periscope! Up periscope! The commanding officer pressing his forehead to the sponge-rubber eyepiece for another look at the nearing target. Rotating the pillar with his arms draped over the training handles. Steady! Stand by to fire one! Now—! Action, suspense, lightning decision, and reflex action high geared into a teamwork that made of submarine and submariners a unified precision machine.

Apparently White's direction of the approach was conventional as to method, ending in a demonstration of the normal daytime periscope attack. The day-periscope attack—as distinguished from the deep submerged attack in which fire control depended solely on sound apparatus, and the night-surface, or night-periscope attack—remained the fundamental method of torpedo attack throughout the early part of the war. Contrary to pre-war expectations, sound attacks conducted from deep submergence soon proved to be of minor importance. There had been little training for the night-periscope attack, which was always limited by visibility conditions. And the night-surface attack, conducted from the submarine's bridge, did not come into its own until 1943 when fire control was considerably advanced by radar.

Before the war, the day-periscope attack had been featured as the chief battle tactic to be mastered by combat submarines. As such, it had engaged much of the training effort, although overestimation of aircraft as a submarine menace had caused strong emphasis to be placed on daytime attacks conducted by sound at deep submergence. The fire control instruments were developed as adapted to the periscope attack. Interior communication systems were arranged and conning towers laid out to accommodate operations in which the fire control party worked in synchronic organization around the central figure of the commanding officer at the periscope.

This proved fortunate, for the problems presented by the periscope attack were fundamental to the torpedo fire control problem. With good instruments for the conduct of the periscope attack, only minor adaptations remained necessary to meet new developments. As designed and devised by U.S. submariners and technicians, American torpedo fire control instruments and methods were second to none. A brief historical review furnishes a glimpse of the science and invention which lay behind the equipment and tactics of such a submarine as USS PLUNGER.

The early American forefather of all submarine weapons (1775) was a time-bomb which the submersible operator attempted to attach to the hull of the enemy ship. A similar Russian device appeared during the Crimean War, the underwater bomb being attached by means of a pair of gutta-percha gloves which protruded like hands from the submarine's hull. During the Civil War, contact bombs (called torpedoes) were towed beneath the target vessel's hull by the submarine. Later the Confederates employed the "spar torpedo"—a bomb which was fixed to a long pole or spar on the submarine's nose and was literally punched at the target (with fatal results to both target and submersible).

The original mobile or automotive torpedo was designed and constructed at Fiume, Austria, in 1864 by the Englishman, Robert Whitehead, who based his invention on the work of Austrian experimenters. The Austrian torpedo, propelled by steam and clockwork, was steered toward the target by means of a guide-rope manipulated from shore. Whitehead's big contributions were a hydrostatic valve and pendulum balance connected to a horizontal rudder for depth-control, and a compressed-air engine for propulsion.

Directional accuracy remained an unsolved problem until the middle 1880's when an American naval officer, Lieutenant Howell, suggested that a gyroscope be used to control the torpedo's vertical rudder. Gyroscopic steering apparatus was installed in torpedoes during the next decade, and by the turn of the century the torpedo was established as one of the deadliest of naval weapons.

The fire control problem was another matter. Early submarines of the HOLLAND type had to be maneuvered into position so that their bow tubes aimed directly at the target and the torpedo was fired point-blank—in effect, the submarine served as a gun which was trained on target for the firing of a projectile. Improvement of the gyroscopic steering apparatus permitted the setting of gyro angles which determined the torpedo's course. According to the gyro angle which was set, the torpedo could be made to run dead ahead, or veer off on a tangent. But target bearing, range, speed and accommodating gyro angles were variables which had to be computed by the captain at the periscope and his party. Perhaps the submarine's best fire control device was the human cerebrum which worked as a lightning calculator.

At the end of World War I, mechanical fire control devices were a-borning. However, about the only instrument then in use aboard American submarines was the "Is-Was" or Submarine Attack Course Finder. Surface vessels in submarine zones had adopted the zigzag as an evasive tactic, and when it came to torpedo fire a ship's position was liable to be "was" a lot more frequently than "is."

At this date the general method of attack was for the submarine to get within 500 yards of the target and fire a straight bow shot on about a 90° track. Gyro angles could not be set on torpedoes after they were loaded into the tubes, and all hands breathed a sigh of satisfaction if the torpedoes ran "straight and hot."

By 1925 American submarines were fitted with "outside gyro-setting devices" by means of which the gyro angle could be set on the torpedo after the "fish" was loaded into the tube. However, the periscope angle (formed by the periscope's line-of-sight to the target, and the track of the torpedo) could only be computed by means of a series of tables. It was therefore necessary to decide what gyro angle was to be used, then compute the required periscope angle, set the gyro angle, set the periscope to the computed angle and fire when the target passed the crosswire of the periscope scale.

In practice the gyro angles commonly used were either zero or 90°, with the zero angle generally preferred. To hit with an angled shot it was necessary to know the range, and submarines were particularly weak in range determination. Targets of this period were zigzagging, some of them screened, and speeds were low and prescribed within narrow limits for each practice. A sound shot was required at a target on a straight course, and sound gear was used during an approach, enabling the operator to obtain a turn-count of the target ship's propellers. Firing ranges were usually about 1,000 yards, and penalties were imposed for firing inside 500 yards.

Targets had been speeded up considerably by 1930 and were better screened. Air observation had been introduced into the defense. The "banjo" angle solver (forerunner of the Mark VIII angle solver) was in use, and angled shots other than zero and 90° were frequently made. Stern tubes had been installed in submarines, adding tremendous firepower to the undersea boats which had been formerly limited to bow-tube shots.

Increased emphasis on "sound shots" developed with the conviction that submarines would have to fire by sound from deep submergence when air screens were present. The executive officer was now required to fire a certain number of practices—a notable advance in the training program. Fire control instruments were improved, but far from perfected. Many homemade instruments, some of them exceedingly ingenious, were employed to solve such problems as range vs. periscope angle, distance to the track, and so on. A few submarines had stadimeter range-finders built into the periscope. The firing of a spread (torpedoes launched at the target, fan-wise, on the assumption that one out of two or more set at varying angles would find the mark) was recommended. Even when it was discovered that the torpedo warhead then in use would counter-mine at 200 yards, submarines were required to fire each torpedo to hit. To do so and still space the torpedoes 200 yards apart demanded the rapid solution of a complicated problem based on the assumption that a target, after receiving one torpedo hit, would continue on its former course and speed until it had collected the succeeding three torpedoes, properly spaced at 200 yards apart. Happily, the torpedo data computer was in the offing.

By 1940, targets were traveling at high speed and screened on the surface and in the air. Sonar had entered the picture as both an anti-submarine device and a device employed in torpedo fire control. Submarines were ordered to run deep between periscope exposures to escape air observation. Firing by sound from deep submergence was encouraged. While it reduced the chances of a hit by about one-half, an attack made without any periscope exposure also greatly reduced the possibility of air detection.

The torpedo data computer (T.D.C.) now made its appearance. This device continuously computed the hitting gyro angle, and either transmitted it to the torpedo room or automatically set the angle on the torpedo. Installation of the T.D.C. revolutionized submarine tactics, as the robot computer ended the necessity of maneuvering a submarine into position on a predetermined course in order to launch torpedoes on a selected track with a selected gyro angle. With the torpedo data computer in use, last-minute submarine maneuvers were practically eliminated once a favorable firing position had been obtained. The torpedo was angled to suit the condition of fire.

Although new fire control devices were to be developed, the standard doctrine for making a submerged daylight periscope attack, as practiced by the Pacific pioneers, was to undergo little change throughout the remainder of the war. When a submarine established contact with enemy smoke or masts on the horizon, the first problem was to determine the target's direction by a few observations in the change in true bearing. When this was done, the submarine came to the "normal approach course," closing the target's track on a course at right angles to the true bearing.

During the approach the submarine endeavored to draw within 1,000 yards of the target's track, at a range equal to about 7½ minutes of the target's run and within two minutes since the last zigzag. From such a position (and barring unforeseen eventualities), the submarine's attack was assured. The approach phase was now ended, and the submarine commenced maneuvers to gain the best possible firing position.

The ideal firing position would place the submarine on a course for the optimum track angle (a little more than 90°) with small or zero gyro angles and a firing range of about 1,000 yards. This ideal, however, was not an imperative. As the war progressed and sufficient data became available for statistical analysis of torpedo shots, several surprising facts were disclosed. Post-war findings are ahead of the story at this point, but those concerning torpedo fire control provide some interesting story, as well as gyro, angles.

Throughout the war the percentage of hits was more or less constant for track angles between 60° and 120° and ranges between 1,000 and 3,000 yards. Within this region the scored hits averaged 36%.

The percentage of hits was independent of the gyro angle for values of the gyro angle between zero and 40°.

While the above was contrary to pre-war prediction, the reasons are not obscure. The effect of gyro can easily be explained. As the accuracy of angled shots depends upon the accuracy of range estimations, and as submarine range estimates were known to be weak, it was considered best to use as small a gyro angle as possible. But experience proved that a submarine could, with absolute safety, take a "single ping" range with sonar equipment just before firing. It was practically impossible for an enemy vessel to locate the source of this one "ping," while it gave the attacking submarine the enemy's range with great accuracy. Any errors that remained, inherent in angle shots, were no more than those incidental errors introduced by feverish efforts to reduce the gyro angle by last-minute changes in the submarine's position by altering the course.

The tendency for percentage hits to hold up with increased range proves more difficult to explain. Introduction of radar after some months of warfare offers partial explanation, as radar meant accurate range-finding, particularly at night, and the data employed in post-war analysis cover both the radar and pre-radar period. Theoretically, an increase in range should mean a decrease in hits, but actually a falling off in percentage hits at close range is revealed by the statistics. It can only be assumed that control errors mount rapidly with the heightening of emergency as range is reduced, and that the incidental errors are caused by the rapid rate of change of bearing incident to close ranges.

The statistics on which the foregoing conclusions are based admit to errors of observation, particularly in regard to the number of torpedo hits scored. Nevertheless, if the conclusions are approximately correct, they indicate that many harsh criticisms given early patrol reports resulted from erroneous tactical assumptions. Doctrine is one thing, and doing it is something else. Perhaps the officer in direct contact with the enemy is better able to arrive at correct tactical conclusions than is the analyst provided with more data but less opportunity to observe.

In any event, on January 18, 1942, PLUNGER was operating in the realm of actuality, not theory. And Lieutenant Commander White, at the periscope, was observing the course, speed, range and size of a Jap cargo ship (AK). His estimate of her size, recorded as 7,200 tons, was on the heavy side—a common error in the guesswork of those days. But his other figures were right "on the beam." Appropriate data were fed into the T.D.C. Gyro angles were set automatically. PLUNGER was maneuvered into the best possible firing position. And two torpedoes were fired for two hits.

Down at sea went EIZAN MARU, 4,700 tons. "X" marked the spot at lat. 33-30 N., long. 135 E. Score one for PLUNGER.

Of more significance than this successful day-periscope attack (SWORDFISH had already scored the first) was PLUNGER's pioneer work with radar. Making no contacts on her SD aircraft warning installation, PLUNGER substantiated supposition that the Japanese had not set up extensive air patrols over the Empire. Despite PLUNGER's report in this regard, submarines were for some time thereafter constrained to remain submerged during daylight in areas where air coverage was likely. The plane vs. submarine question had not yet been answered by experience, and it was a matter wherein experience might prove a fatal teacher.

PLUNGER's pioneers learned and lived. They came out of the Kii Suido area gaunt and game, and returned to Pearl Harbor after 52 days with the assurance of explorers who have accomplished a voyage of discovery. Successful patrol!

Pioneer Tactics (Night-periscope and Night-surface Attack)

Another adventurous pioneer patrol was POLLACK's, skippered by Lieutenant Commander Stanley P. Moseley. POLLACK was cruising off the south coast of Honshu on New Year's Eve.

Lookout sighted a small Japanese destroyer bustling across the dark seascape, and Moseley sent his men to battle stations. Attempting a surface approach, he found visibility conditions demanded a submerged attack, and he gave the order to take her down. As POLLACK slid under the waves, she began the first night-periscope attack made by a SubPac submarine.

POLLACK's pioneers encountered a difficulty which troubled many submarines early in the war. The periscope then in use was inadequate for night operations. Only on clear, bright moonlight nights was the instrument wholly effective.

Here was another submarine device due to undergo wartime rectification and improvement. Associated with submarine tactical developments, the periscope's story is interesting.

Obviously the success of the combat submarine depends largely on its ability to see without being detected. In 1854 the inventor, Marie Davy, designed a sight tube for the submersible. Consisting of two small mirrors fixed at either end of a vertical tube at 45° angles (so that a horizontal beam of light, striking the upper mirror, would be reflected down to the lower mirror which reflected it to the observer's eye) this primitive instrument embodied the essential features of the modern periscope.

The first periscope used in the U.S. Navy made its appearance in 1864. Necessity was certainly the mother of this device which was invented under fire aboard the Federal monitor OSAGE, ambushed by Confederates in the Red River. The gunners in the monitor turret were unable to see the enemy snipers on the river bank. And it looked as if OSAGE was going to be shot to junk when her chief engineer, Thomas Doughty, constructed a tube with reflecting mirrors which he thrust up from the engine-room hatch. His observations of the enemy's position, relayed to the gun turret, saved the day for the Federal warship—the first example of the periscope's use in fire control.

In 1872 prisms were introduced—a great improvement, as the prism transmitted more light than a mirror. High-powered lenses were the next major advance, extending the sight range, and magnifying and clarifying the image. Simon Lake invented a collapsible periscope for the submarine he designed in 1893, and he was the first to use a rotating periscope which gave the submarine operator a view of the entire horizon. Despite these developments, John Holland did not install a periscope in the first naval submarine he designed in 1900. But only seven years later two periscopes were installed on several submarines—one periscope for surveying the entire horizon, and the other for conning the target.

World War I compelled many improvements in the submarine periscope—devices for rapidly raising and lowering the tube—better lenses—double-tube construction to resist water pressures. The periscope tube was also considerably lengthened. Yet throughout the First World War poor vision hampered the submersible. Even when awash the submarine was nearsighted, and when submerged its field of vision was restricted by lack of sufficient periscope elevation. At night the periscope went blind, or nearly so, and the submarine had to grope its way through darkness, or surface and operate with lookouts on the bridge.

The periscope in use at the outbreak of World War II was a scientific marvel in comparison with the World War I model. Automatically raised and lowered in its well, the modern scope could be elevated to a height which afforded vision to a submerged submarine operating at a "keel depth" of over 50 feet. The best in optical science had gone into the lens system, employing devices which absorbed excess light and greatly clarified the image. On some of the large submarines three periscopes had been installed.

Because the day-periscope attack was featured in peacetime training, pre-war periscope development was chiefly directed toward producing an instrument for daytime operation. In several respects, day-periscope requirements differ widely from those of night. Different lens systems are necessary. The night periscope needs a large head for maximum light transmission, whereas the day periscope must employ a small head which lessens the chance of detection by enemy observers. American submarines entered the war with a periscope designed primarily for daytime use—a periscope with a lens system for extended range of vision, and a small head to frustrate enemy detection. Both of these features reduced the high light transmission expressly needed by the night periscope.

Pioneering into combat, the submariners were soon aware of the periscope's nocturnal shortcomings, and took steps to correct them. Original efforts to improve the periscope's light transmission were concerned with "light treating" the optical system with anti-reflection film. This considerably increased the percentage of light transmitted. But it was not until the summer of 1942 that such light-treated periscopes were obtainable, and for a long time after that they remained at a premium. A true night periscope with a large head and a shorter optical system did not become available until late in 1944. Attention was also given the matter of night camouflage for the scope, experiments producing a gray paint which made the tube and head difficult to detect in moonlight. These improvements were a considerable aid to night operations. And they developed from such experiences as POLLACK had when she made one of the war's first night-periscope attacks.

Pre-war doctrine gave preference to the night attack conducted on the surface where the submarine could take advantage of high surface speed. If light conditions proved unfavorable for a surface attack—as was often the case when bright moonlight threatened to expose the submarine—it was considered good tactics to track until the target's base course and speed had been determined. The submarine would then run up ahead to submerge on the enemy's track. This tactic usually assured a sufficiently reduced target range for an effective night-periscope attack.

Directing POLLACK's attack on the DD off the Honshu coast, Lieutenant Commander Moseley followed the preconceived rules. He began with a surface approach conducted from the bridge, then ordered the submarine under for the periscope attack. By periscope he found it impossible to distinguish enough of the target's features to make an accurate estimation of course or range. As the destroyer blurred off in the night, Moseley fired two torpedoes, hoping for a hit. Both missed, and the opportunity was gone. Figuratively as well as literally, the experience gave Moseley a dim view of night-periscope attacks. He resolved to avoid the tactic thereafter unless conditions were extremely favorable.

January 3, POLLACK was on the track of a Japanese freighter. Moseley directed a day-submerged approach. Stalking a merchantman in broad daylight off the coast of Japan was perilous business, and conditions were unfavorable in the bargain. Moseley fired one torpedo, and the freighter escaped. A miss.

Traffic in the waters off Tokyo Bay kept POLLACK stubbornly on the job despite this initiation in disappointments. Dogged persistence seemed rewarded on the night of January 5 when another Japanese ship hove in view. Moseley, directing a surface attack, fired six torpedoes at this merchantman. Three explosions looked like hits, and POLLACK's submariners cheered a sinking. But the sinking of this vessel on the night in question could not be confirmed.

POLLACK's luck was in on the seventh of the month, however. That was the day she got her official first. Lat. 34-27 N., long. 138-59 E., Moseley fired two torpedoes at a 2,225-ton freighter after a skillfully executed day-submerged approach. One torpedo struck home with a fatal blast, and the AK went under. She was DAI I UNKAI MARU, a pioneer in her own right as the first victim of the Pacific Fleet Submarine Force.

On the night of January 9, POLLACK did some more pioneering. This consisted of a night-surface attack which Moseley culminated successfully by sinking another Jap freighter. So POLLACK scored another No. 1. Records show that the first three attacks made by American submarines in the Pacific were night-surface attacks conducted from the bridge. Two of these were made by SWORDFISH (on December 9 and 11, 1941) and one was made by S-38 on December 12th. While both SubsAsiatic boats reported a sinking, the sinkings could not be verified by post-war investigation. The first vessel to be positively identified as sunk in a night-surface attack by a U.S. submarine was the one torpedoed by POLLACK on January 9, 1942.

As was the case with the majority of submarines of this period, POLLACK was not equipped with radar. Her night-surface attack furnishes a thumbnail sketch of the tactic as practiced by the pre-radar pioneers. It was a tactic which required the utmost in competence and daring in any circumstance, and double skill was demanded of the pioneer operating in enemy waters.

American submarines had not been adequately

prepared for night warfare—nor had such preparation been possible. Due to the hazards inherent in night exercises, and the difficulties involved in simulating a submarine attack, pre-war training in night-surface tactics had been superficial. It was not until the late 1930's that night practices were held, and they remained elementary and inconclusive.

Rehearsals are never as drastically instructive as the real thing. In simulated combat, artificialities must be imposed for reasons of safety—for example, in night exercises the submarines carried dimmed running lights to avert a possible collision. Moreover, the submariners were limited to using torpedoes which carried dummy warheads. Obviously an enemy's reactions can hardly be approximated by the maneuvers of a practice target ship. And determining the results of counterfeit torpedo fire at night is something like estimating the marksmanship of a sniper firing blank cartridges at an imaginary bull's-eye.

An attempt was made to equip practice torpedoes with headlights so that observers might mark their course in the dark. The lighted torpedo was not entirely reliable, and a certain amount of guesswork could not be eliminated from the marksmanship equation. In 1940 and 1941 night practice was still in the experimental stage of development. Although German submarines were at that time employing the night-surface attack with some success, night practice was not a requirement in the training of U.S. submarines. Only 23 out of a possible 69 submarines fired it.

Lack of night experience saddled the American submariners entering the war with a heavy cargo of unsolved combat problems. One problem had to do with the submarine's silhouette—under varying conditions of dark and moonlight how far was it visible at night? Before the war, submarine silhouettes were the fat and lazy peacetime kind. With the beginning of hostilities a lot of this corpulence was peeled off and jettisoned by the ship's force. On the first navy yard availability, the submarine underwent a reducing process. Bridge structures were cut down, deck gear was dispensed with wherever possible, and outlines were smoothed and flattened. Miss SS America emerged with a slimmed silhouette calculated to deceive the watchful mariner's eye. But there were still some noticeable bulges to her whaleboned figure.

Then there remained the matter of her paint. Night camouflage was an unsolved problem, and months were to pass before discovery of the fact that a coat of sable black was easier to spot at night than were various modified shades. Pre-war studies of submarine visibility had been concerned with submerged submarines. More night practice might have directed attention to the need for better protective coloration.

Perhaps the most serious deficiency, and one to be coped with immediately, was the lack of a proper instrument for taking target bearings from the bridge at night.

The torpedo directors designed for surface ships were not adaptable for submarine use. In 1941 the Bureau of Ships designed for submarines a dummy pelorus, and this was in the process of manufacture and distribution when the Pacific War broke out.

Serviceable for daylight action, this dummy pelorus was practically useless for nocturnal warfare. Few submarine skippers would risk fracturing a surface blackout with a flashlight, yet the dummy pelorus could not be read by braille, and its reading necessitated a light on the bridge. The urgent need, therefore, was for an unlighted instrument capable of transmitting bearings from the bridge to the fire control party in the conning tower. This need was met by the "Mare Island" type target bearing transmitter (T.B.T.).

A somewhat makeshift affair, this T.B.T. was designed and produced by submarine personnel working in cooperation with Mare Island Navy Yard technicians. It served a dual purpose in permitting the operator to take target bearings in a blackout and in transmitting those bearings to the fire control party below. Despite impromptu construction, the Mare Island T.B.T. filled the bill, and it did yeoman service on U.S. submarines throughout the early part of the war. At the war's outbreak, however, no more than a few of these instruments had been installed. Most of the S-boats were equipped with the "night blind" dummy pelorus. Only a small minority of the fleet submarines had the Mare Island T.B.T., or a "reasonable facsimile" thereof—some local adaptation of the device.

At any rate, at the start of the Pacific War, torpedo fire control was in a formative stage of development and so were the tactics of night warfare. For night firing on the surface, experienced submarine officers recommended that the periscope angle computed for a straight bow shot be set as a gyro angle on the torpedoes, and the order to fire be given as the point of aim passed the jackstaff.

These or similar methods were employed by Moseley on that night of January 9 when POLLACK made contact with a merchantman off Inubo Saki, Honshu. Target was picked up at 0050. In spite of the fact that DAI I UNKAI MARU had been torpedoed in this vicinity two nights before, the Jap steamer was burning dimmed running lights. Evidently this freighter's captain did not believe lightning could strike twice in the same place. Moseley undertook to prove the old rule by an exception.

Translating the Roman adage, *"Carpe diem"* (seize the day) into advice to seize the night, Moseley sent POLLACK closing in swiftly at surface speed. In this maneuver POLLACK was testing a number of doubtful factors such as submarine visibility and merchant ship vulnerability at night.

At 0130, after a 40-minute surface approach, Moseley fired two torpedoes from the bow tubes—and missed! Whether the failure lay in faulty torpedoes or faulty fire control, the records fail to indicate. If faults there were, Moseley managed to correct them. Swinging POLLACK around, he brought her stern tubes to bear. Two more torpedoes rushed at the target, and one hit the target squarely. TEIAN MARU, 5,387 tons, went down by the stern.

Later that same night Moseley ordered a submerged attack on a DD which came foaming out on the prowl. Again he was presented with a difficult night-periscope problem. He fired one torpedo at the destroyer —missed—and then removed POLLACK from the neighborhood.

That concluded the drama in his submarine's first patrol. But she had experienced enough. Having sunk two ships totalling some 11,000 tons, with the possible addition of a 4,000-tonner, POLLACK returned to home base, after 39 days, with all torpedoes expended. Successful patrol!

Gudgeon vs. I-173

First of the Pacific Fleet submarines to leave Pearl Harbor for a foray into Japan's home waters, GUDGEON patrolled the Bungo Suido area in comparative peace and quiet. This was not the fault of her skipper, Lieutenant Commander Elton W. Grenfell. Doughty as they make 'em, Grenfell (known to the force as "Jumping Joe") was looking for action. And he kept GUDGEON on her toes, so to speak, and ready for the gong. But, predictions to the contrary, ship traffic was almost conspicuous by its absence from the western entrance to the sea of Japan. For GUDGEON the gong rang only twice in the Bungo Suido area, and both rounds were to prove disappointment. On January 4, contact was made with a cargo ship. Grenfell directed a day-submerged attack on this AK, and fired two torpedoes for two misses. On the 10th of January another freighter was sighted. Directing a night-surface attack, Grenfell maneuvered GUDGEON into position and fired three shots at this likely target. Two torpedoes appeared to hit. A sinking was cheerfully reported but it could not be confirmed by the investigation made later. Things were like that with submarines and ships that passed in the night.

As were her companion pioneers in those early days, GUDGEON was hampered by lack of radar, by night-periscope difficulties, by inadequate fire control apparatus, and by torpedo trouble. Her operations were also inhibited by headquarters instructions which read: *"When within radius of enemy patrol planes (about 500 miles) it will generally be advisable to remain submerged during daylight, proceeding on the surface during dark."* Accompanying these instructions was a list of Japanese bases from which enemy planes could be expected to operate, and a routing through these areas to and from the submarine's patrol station.

GUDGEON's instructions were in keeping with that pre-war doctrine which overestimated the aircraft as a submarine foe. In anticipation of heavy losses, submarine skippers were ordered to proceed with "extreme caution." Headquarters believed that the only hope of inflicting serious damage on the enemy lay in the use of such tactics as firing by sound from deep submergence, and avoiding surface exposure as much as possible. GUDGEON's submariners were indoctrinated accordingly. But peacetime doctrine and authoritative tactical concept were soon to undergo speedy revisions, and GUDGEON's practical experiences played a part in the changes made.

Commander Submarines, Pacific Fleet, was to comment on GUDGEON's patrol report:

It is noted that the GUDGEON spent a total of 51 days from base to base, of which only 12 were submerged on station. Eight days prior to the arrival on station, and seven days after departure from station or a total of 15 days, GUDGEON submerged during daylight. This represents a terrific overhead in time, a great part of which should have been spent on station. It is realized GUDGEON did not have radar for plane detection, but it is considered that with efficient lookouts more surface cruising could have been done prior to and after departure from station. The GUDGEON reports only two aircraft having been sighted, and these in the operating area.

Here is an indication of the rapidity with which tactical concepts can shed peacetime theory for wartime practice. Within a period of 51 days, ComSubPac was able to criticize adversely a patrol carried out in conformance with original operational instructions.

However, the sharpest of lookouts and the best of electronic devices cannot produce ships in areas where they are absent. After days of unproductive search GUDGEON was forced to head homeward with an empty bag and a large supply of unused torpedoes. So she said good-bye to Japan, as the travelogues put it, and regretfully set a course for Pearl Harbor.

Then, on January 25, when GUDGEON was about 600 miles off Midway, events took another turn. The turn began when GUDGEON's radio intercepted a message from the Naval Air Station to CinCPac, reporting three Japanese submarines heading westward from the Midway area. One of the Jap subs had shelled Midway Island in passing. GUDGEON's crew snapped into a fast alert. With the Japs coming westward and GUDGEON on an easterly course, a meeting in mid-ocean was possible.

On January 26—time: 2320—GUDGEON received a message from ComSubPac. When last located, one of the three enemy submarines was on a track which had her heading for GUDGEON's immediate vicinity.

Grenfell and his officers eagerly studied the chart. True enough, if the enemy sub continued on her present course, she would all but collide with GUDGEON the following morning. Here was the opportunity begged for by every submarine skipper—a chance to bag an enemy warship! Grenfell decided to maintain a submerged patrol and attempt to nail the Jap submarine from ambush. Thank God for those remaining torpedoes! Take her down!

To anyone uninitiated in undersea warfare, this submarine attack on another submarine might seem as novel in the news as the classic "man bites dog." Actually, it was more a case of tiger biting tiger, for the submarine had long been recognized as the enemy submersible's natural foe. During World War I, British submarines took a sharp bite out of the Kaiser's U-boat fleet, and again in 1939 and 1940 Allied submarines had battled U-boats in their common element, patrolling offshore to engage them as they stole out of their pens on the French coast.

Submarine warfare against submarines is warfare in a medium of fast action—sudden contacts, snap decisions, lightning attacks. It calls for flexible organization and iron nerves. The duelists are more or less evenly matched and each is acquainted with the methods and capacities of submarining. The submersible is the only naval craft which can pursue an enemy submarine beneath the sea, and a deadly underwater contest can develop after contact.

It seems probable that more than a few U-boats listed as "Spurlos Versenkt" and Allied submarines reported as "lost without trace" were destroyed in deep-sea combat with opposing submarines. Results of such combat are most difficult to ascertain. But when the submarine attacked is on the surface, and the attacker is the one submerged, the target may be watched by periscope and the outcome discerned. Such was the case with GUDGEON and the Japanese submarine which came junketing over the horizon on the morning of January 27th.

At 0859 GUDGEON's sound man detected the enemy's screw. Periscope contact followed immediately. At the scope, GUDGEON's exec, Lieutenant H. B. Lyon, could hardly believe the luck. As though without a care in the world, the big I-boat was excursioning along in the morning sunshine, cutting the surface at a speed of around 15 knots, her prow pointed for Japan.

Men raced to battle stations as Captain Grenfell took over the periscope to direct GUDGEON's approach. Praying that the enemy's sonar man might be slightly deaf, he set GUDGEON on the enemy's track. Course, speed and other factors were rushed through the T.D.C. Down periscope! Up periscope! Grenfell, too, could hardly credit his vision as he watched the Japanese submarine grow on the periscope scale—saw the Jap officers standing on the bridge—brown faces in a cluster—men around the conning tower, sunning.

Time: 0908. Fire one! Fire two! Fire three! Streaking the surface with a frothy ribbon, the first torpedo ran straight for the mark as GUDGEON's periscope went down. Sound heard the roar of a violent explosion, and a tremor went through the American submarine. A moment later there was another detonation. Then silence in the listening gear—only the sound of GUDGEON's motors running.

Grenfell kept her under, thinking of those other Jap subs in the area. And two could play at this game. But when he raised the periscope after a cautious interval for a look-see, it was no-see. Nothing more than an empty expanse of Pacific where the Jap submarine had been.

But it was not until GUDGEON reached Pearl Harbor that the crew of Grenfell's boat shook hands all around—the first U.S. submariners in history to score the first confirmed sinking of an enemy warship. Grenfell had reported only damage, but ComSubPac had the word. The trio of Japanese submarines reported off Midway had been traced there from the American Pacific coast. Evidently, triumphant after an invasion of American waters, they had been returning to home base. Radio had traced two of the trio all the way home, but the third I-boat had evaporated somewhere around lat. 28-24, N., long. 178-35 E.—where GUDGEON fired those three torpedoes. Subsequently identified by post-war investigation, GUDGEON's victim proved to be I-173, a Japanese cruiser submarine, 1,785 tons.

In company with Lieutenant Commanders David White and Stanley Moseley, Elton Grenfell received the Navy Cross for his successful patrol in Empire waters.

The Navy Department announcement read:

ALL BUT THE SUBMARINE CREDITED TO LIEU-TENANT COMMANDER GRENFELL WERE AT-TACKED IN JAPANESE WATERS, AND IN ALL BUT THAT INSTANCE THE ATTACKS WERE DRIVEN HOME IN THE FACE OF INTENSIVE ENEMY AIR AND SURFACE PATROLS. ONLY ONE OF OUR SUB-MARINES WAS DAMAGED—THAT DAMAGE WAS SLIGHT—WHILE THERE WAS NO INJURY TO PER-SONNEL.

Other Pearl Harbor submarines were to follow the trail blazed by PLUNGER, POLLACK and GUDGEON. TUNA reached the Bungo Suido area in February. DRUM got in there fighting a few weeks later. By the late spring of 1942, Japanese merchant skippers were aware of a serious discrepancy between the propaganda broadcasts of Radio Tokyo (American Navy all at sea bottom) and the ship losses in Empire waters.

Those losses would have been much higher had Japanese shipping been normal in the area. Its scarcity, discovered by the pioneers, was to send American submarines to better hunting-grounds. An early surprise of the Pacific War was this scantiness of Japanese ship traffic in the waters off Hokkaido and Honshu—apparently the Nipponese merchant fleets were with the invasion forces far from home. But they had to return to their home ports eventually, and when they did return they found American submarines waiting for them. The pioneers had showed the way and demonstrated how it could be done.

A Fleet Headquarters release packed into the following paragraph the story of those pioneer submariners who blazed that perilous Pearl Harbor-Japan trail.

THEY CAME BACK TO THEIR BASE—GRINNING, TRIUMPHANT, TACITURN. MOST OF THEM HADN'T SEEN THE LIGHT OF DAY FOR WEEKS. THEY HAD CARRIED THE WAR RIGHT TO THE ENEMY'S FRONT DOORSTEP, TORPEDOED HIS SHIPS, SOMETIMES ALMOST IN VIEW OF LOOK-OUTS AT HIS PRINCIPAL HOME PORTS, AND SUSTAINED THE WORST DEPTH CHARGE AT-TACKS HE COULD LAUNCH.
THEY WERE THE SUBMARINES OF THE PACIFIC FLEET.

TORPEDO! The arrowing wake promises a direct hit. Frantic crewmen of Jap submarine I-173 see their doom written in froth. USS Gudgeon (Commander Grenfell) was victor in this sub vs. sub battle west of Midway. Downed in January 1942, I-173 was the first warship ever sunk by a United States submarine.

BRIDGE OF JAP SUBMARINE. *Compared with streamlined super-structure of American sub, this seems junky. Note odd basketwork.*

BRIDGE OF JAP DESTROYER, *Maikaze class. Note rigging, bamboo splinter shields.*

CONTROL ROOM *of Jap submarine. Although inferior to U. S. fleet-type, I-boats struck hard blows early in war.*

ENGINE ROOM *of Jap submarine. I-boat Diesels were modern, crews well-trained. But strategy was under par.*

SUBMARINE CAMERA-SHOT! *This early periscope photo, taken by USS Pollack, profiles an unsuspecting freighter. Periscope photography is tricky, hazardous. Good shots were snapped at ranges under a mile, best at 500 yards. For photo reconnaissance, U. S. submarines preferred the hard-to-get German Primarflex camera.*

CHAPTER 6

PIONEERS SOWESPAC

Soerabaja

Captain John Wilkes, a Carolinian with an angular jaw, was another submarine officer who could revise a theory in the interests of practicality. For instance, he managed to improve on Mahan's aphorism about the true speed of war by combining "headlong precipitancy" with "unremitting energy" and wasting no time whatever in transferring SubsAsiatic headquarters from Manila, P.I., to Soerabaja, N.E.I.

Faced by such a situation as confronted ComSubsAsiatic on New Year's Day, 1942, a Hamlet might have lost the name of action in pale casts of thought. Captain Wilkes had no time for introspection.

HOLLAND and OTUS had gone. CANOPUS was at Corregidor. Cavite was wiped out, and Manila had been declared an open city. And the 28 submarines of the Asiatic Fleet had been ordered to the Malay Barrier. Cutting red tape with the knife of initiative, Captain Wilkes boarded SWORDFISH with his operational staff and headed for Soerabaja.

Captain Wilkes, in tourist parlance, traveled light. Squadron files had been left aboard HOLLAND, and all needless paper work dispensed with. In fact, the staff carried just three essential items: the pay accounts for the force—one typewriter (treated like a mascot)—and one radio receiver from CANOPUS. Which might lead one to remark that the true speed of war does not depend on nine carbon copies of everything. At any rate, what the staff lacked in paper work, it made up for in acumen—the sort of acumen exhibited by Captain John Wilkes, ComSubsAsiatic.

His trip to Soerabaja in SWORDFISH was not his first sea voyage in a submarine. He had come up the Navy ladder through the conning tower. As Lieutenant John Wilkes, he had stepped from the Naval Academy into the Mexican "trouble," serving aboard the cruiser MARYLAND on patrol duty off the coast of lower California. Ordered to the Submarine

School, New London, in the summer of 1919, he was assigned to R-3 in November of that year, and two years later he had his first command in K-7.

Later, after a tour of duty as Assistant Inspector of Machinery at the Electric Boat Company in Groton, Connecticut, he commanded S-47 and then was made skipper of BARRACUDA. In 1935 he became navigator aboard the USS INDIANAPOLIS, but his heart was in a submarine's control room. In 1939, after serving as Aide to Commandant, Navy Yard, Mare Island, he was ordered to command SubDiv Fourteen, USS PICKEREL (flag), based at San Diego as part of Submarine Squadron Six, Pacific Fleet.

September 1939, he departed for Asiatic station, via Pearl, with his division. Arriving in Manila, he presently assumed command of Submarine Squadron Five operating in Philippine waters. This squadron consisted of six PERCH-class submarines and six S-boats.

The following year the squadron was strengthened by the arrival of SHARK and four submarines of the SEADRAGON class. Then in November 1941, Submarine Squadron Two and the tender HOLLAND arrived in Manila under Captain W. E. Doyle.

December 1, 1941 (six days before the Pearl Harbor attack) the submarines operating out of Manila were combined into Submarines, Asiatic Fleet, under command of Captain Doyle. Wilkes was relieved for return to the United States. The Japanese onslaught interrupted his departure. With the enemy roaring down on the Philippines, Admiral Hart retained Wilkes in command, and Wilkes relieved Captain Doyle as ComSubsAsiatic. Now, as the year edged into 1942 and the offensive came on like an avalanche, he was a submarine force commander with a payroll, one typewriter and one radio receiver, all at sea in one submarine.

SWORDFISH made a fine taxi—no better skipper in the service than Chester Smith—and the Java base was reached on January 7th. There, disembarking amidst an excited chatter of Dutch, *bêche-de-mer* and Javanese, Captain Wilkes' staff must have experienced several misgivings. From the first it was apparent that the Malay Barrier might be a language barrier. Submarines cannot be dispatched and repaired by sign language. Repairs, in particular, demand technical terminology. The stout Dutch colonial with his *reis taffle* and his Bols, as hospitable as he was rotund, could speak only broken English. The average American submarine officer could speak no Dutch at all. Dutch naval technicians were good, but their methods were indigenous to the Royal Netherlands Navy, and Dutch submarine parts, like Dutch adjectives, were not designed for American use.

Under ordinary circumstances Soerabaja would have been an excellent submarine base. The harbor embraced a sheltered overhaul basin, ample docking space, some of which was roofed over, a floating drydock, and fine machine shops with modern equipment. But in January 1942 the circumstances were far from ordinary. Dutch submarines, in from war patrol, were booked for repairs. Overhaul facilities were taxed to the breaking point by the inrush of Allied naval vessels. A few S-boats and one or two fleet submarines were jammed in for sketchy refits, but the arrival in January of one American submarine after another soon swamped the capacities of the Dutch naval base.

By the time Captain Wilkes reached Soerabaja the submarines were crowded in like so many SS SARDINES. Spare parts could not be had. Docking space was at a premium. Dutch technicians and native mechanics were baffled by American machinery, and submarine repairs were far behind schedule. As though to cork the bottleneck, the Navy Yard did not work on weekends (*Ja, Mynheer,* the situation is serious, but here everything must go by custom).

Admiral Hart had already established Fleet Headquarters in a house on the outskirts of Soerabaja,

and there Captain Wilkes installed his staff, his payroll and his typewriter. The radio receiver was set up in a garage behind the house. Captain Wilkes rolled up his sleeves and went to work. ComSubsAsiatic was in business.

And business was booming. Booming with the thunder of Japanese naval salvos and air bombs crashing down around the Philippines, Borneo and the Celebes—the thud and smash of shell fire from the handful of American warships fighting their hearts out to stem the enemy drive. Relentlessly the Japanese advanced. Any hour now the vanguard might strike at Sumatra and Java. Lights burned late behind the black-out curtains of ComSubsAsiatic's Headquarters, and officers and men worked day and night on the submarines crowding the base.

Fleet submarines came back from the front, some needing little more than fuel and supplies, some with lamed engines and burnt-out gear, their hulls dimpled by the blasts of depth bombs. Tired S-boats limped in, foul from lack of air conditioning, a few with jammed bow planes, out-of-kilter periscopes, malfunctioning motors, leaking bulkheads. All needed careful inspection. And the captains and crews who crawled up out of the innards of these subs and stood blinking and staring in the sunshine (not all of them grinning and triumphant)—these captains and crews needed rest.

But at Soerabaja, with the Japs booming down, there was little rest for the weary. Java was too close to the front line. Bearded, unwashed, as famished and slow-footed as refugees, the American submariners were hustled into the mountains behind the town and taken to Malang where there was a rest camp operated by the Dutch Submarine Force. Thrown open to the Americans, this camp offered splendid facilities for recuperation—if the submariner had the time.

The captains and crews of the SubsAsiatic Force did not have the time. Officers and men had to remain aboard the submarines to oversee repairs and handle work details. Lacking spare parts, engineers had to manufacture them out of this and that and thin air. Electricians contrived jobs that rivalled the inventive works of Edison and Marconi. Torpedomen, motor macs, all hands up to the cook pitched in to scour the boat and get her out into action. At best the crews obtained no more than three days at the Malang rest camp.

At SubsAsiatic Headquarters the typewriter went like a machine gun and the radio in the garage was hot. Staff heard that the Japs had landed on the coast of Sarawak in northwest Borneo and captured Tarakan on January 11, gaining possession of some of the richest oil wells in the world. Strong units of the Imperial Navy were operating in the Celebes Sea, and fresh invasion forces were gathering for a drive at Kendari on the southeast peninsula of Celebes, ominously close to Bali and eastern Java. Soerabaja was growing warm.

ComSubsAsiatic had his problems. The administrative staff had gone to Darwin under Captain Fife, and while both operational staff and administrative staff had been organized to function if necessary as independent operational-administrative units, this separation of staffs threw some wrenches in the machinery. Loss of personal contact among operational staff, overhaul staff and submarine commanding officers created slow-ups in administration. No one knew when the radio equipment might peter out, and things can be on tenterhooks when communications depend on a couple of irreplaceable vacuum tubes.

Fortunately, close liaison could be maintained with Admiral Hart, although CinCAF spent a good part of his time at Batavia where Dutch Admiral Helfrich was headquartered. Less fortunately, the degree of operational control to be exercised by ComSubsAsiatic was not clearly defined and the extent of Captain Wilkes' command was more or less ambiguous. While Captain Wilkes was technically in command of the submarine forces, CinCAF (in command of the ABDA fleet) issued directives that were so specific as to permit little interpretation or flexibility in the execution of the tasks assigned. Thus, submarines were ordered to specific positions in defense of points where enemy landings were expected. Perhaps convinced they could have been used to better advantage if aggressively employed to cut enemy supply lines, ComSubsAsiatic was, nevertheless, without authority to alter their disposition.

Inexperience in the strategic and tactical aspects of submarine warfare was partly responsible for the ineffectiveness of the Asiatic submarines in this period. Again, the pre-war concept of the submarine as a fleet adjunct served to restrict operations. Finally, the Allied Fleet Commander was faced with a desperate crisis which impelled him to muster all available forces for a showdown battle with the enemy. With Allied naval forces driven back everywhere, and Dutch Admiral Helfrich pounding the table and demanding a stand, Admiral Hart groped for every warship available and issued the directive ordering the submarines to defend the Malay Barrier.

With Supreme Allied Commander General Wavell setting up Soerabaja headquarters in the house occupied by Admiral Hart and Captain Wilkes, the ABDA command became a fairly compact body. But its forces, only skeletal to begin with, were rapidly shrinking. Battered by the Japanese sea-air drive, the surface squadrons of ABDAFLOAT retreated and dwindled. Only the submarines escaped this piecemeal destruction. But every beachhead lost brought the enemy closer to Java. The few PBY's and Allied planes which constituted ABDAIR were far short of the number needed to provide coverage for Soerabaja.

On February 3 the first enemy aircraft roared over, and bombs crashed into the harbor. The attack on Soerabaja had begun.

Australia and Down Under

Darwin, Australia (population 600), was not the best submarine base in the Pacific. Selected because it seemed a sheltered harbor, it was within coverage of Allied fighter strips on the northern coast of Australia, and at the war's beginning it was the focal point for water-borne supply ships routed through Torres Strait. But Captain James Fife had hardly entered the port with his administrative staff aboard SEAWOLF before he recognized the deficiencies.

As a base for submarine tenders (HOLLAND was already there) the harbor was vulnerable. For one thing it was deep with a four-fathom tide—which meant submarines or tenders sunk by enemy bombing would be beyond salvage. For another thing, it alternately broiled or squalled in some of the worst weather in the book. Rail connections with Brisbane and Perth were nonexistent. Air protection was inadequate, and the port would be within range of enemy bombers if the Japanese push reached Timor. And the waters off Darwin were mineable—another feature calculated to make the base unsatisfactory. Boarding HOLLAND with his staff, Captain Fife was not too favorably impressed with Port Darwin.

The submariners found Darwin a ghost town—Main Street deserted, stores boarded up, stray dogs slinking along the curbstones. Red dust smoked up under the blazing sun and the local thermometer bubbled at 110 degrees. A few British, Dutch, Indian and American soldiers drifted around in the heat, and a sailor asked a G.I. Joe where the Australians were. He was told that most of the townspeople had headed for the interior. Word that the Japs had bombed Rabaul in New Britain and Tulagi and Kieta in the Solomons had sent the populace packing. A glass of beer? Hell, you couldn't even buy a kangaroo. Darwin was expecting invasion.

A ghost town expecting invasion was hardly the place to revitalize exhausted submarine crews, and the harbor was scarcely suitable for the overhaul of submarines. But Captain Fife and his staff pitched in. The Salvation Army turned up with a hut on the town's outskirts, and there was plenty of desert available for a baseball diamond. HOLLAND was ready to take on the submarines. The plan called for two-thirds of the SubsAsiatic Force to base at Soerabaja, the remaining third at Darwin, the submarines to rotate between these bases. Darwin wasn't Utopia, but there was a war going on.

Having delivered the SubsAsiatic administrative staff, SEAWOLF loaded anti-aircraft and machine-gun ammunition—cargo for Corregidor. Taking on this freight, she was one of the pioneers to prove the submarine's versatility as fighting ship, passenger carrier, scout, merchant raider, rescue vessel, ferry, freighter and whatever else was demanded of her on or under the sea.

While the WOLF was loading at Darwin, USS TARPON hobbled in, looking as though she had been on a cruise in Hades. Her skipper, Lieutenant Commander Wallace, reported that he had been forced by a low battery to surface in a typhoon. TARPON had nearly foundered when a monster wave climbed over the open conning-tower hatch, flooding the control room and short-circuiting the radio and the motors. Unable to dive after that, the submarine rode out the storm on the surface, rolling like a log in weather that must have made Old Neptune seasick. TARPON was in bad shape, and the repair forces at Port Darwin had a job to do.

Not long after TARPON's arrival, SCULPIN (Lieutenant Commander Lucius H. Chappell) came rolling in. Chappell delivered an interesting battle report.

SCULPIN had been patrolling Lamon Bay. Proceeding from there to Darwin, she had been running submerged during daytime and making what distance she could on the surface at night. On the night of January 10, somewhere around lat. 10-05 N., long. 123-55 E., she had encountered a couple of Japs.

SCULPIN surfaced that evening at 1840. At 2304 the officer of the deck called Chappell to the bridge and reported sighting a darkened ship, bearing 195°T, at a range of 2,000 yards.

Chappell peered through the darkness. "I can't see a damned thing! Are you sure there's something off there?"

The officer of the deck was sure. This was in the days before much was known about the protection of night vision. Blue lights were still in use aboard darkened ships, and red glasses were unheard of. Night vision devices for submarine lookouts and bridge personnel had yet to be introduced. Chappell was unable to discern the target, and SCULPIN's approach depended almost entirely on the 20-20 vision of the O.O.D.

Target range was a matter of estimation. With the simple pelorus it was difficult to take accurate bearings. But a ship was out there, and about one minute after this first vessel was sighted, the O.O.D. picked up a second, bearing 165°T.

SCULPIN eased around to course 290°, closing the range on the first target. The target's speed was estimated at 12 knots, and the course at 290°. It was impossible to get much out of the torpedo data computer. Periscope angle was estimated by rule of thumb, and a 30° right gyro angle was set on two torpedoes. The range closed to 1,000 yards.

Chappell gave the order to fire as the target's bow passed the jackstaff. Two torpedoes were launched from the bow tubes in a longitudinal spread (one directly behind the other) with a four-second firing interval. Silence grew oppressive as the seconds ticked off and there were no torpedo detonations.

Chappell ordered 45° right gyro angle on a second pair of forward torpedoes, and fired again. These torpedoes were hardly out of the tubes when the explosion came—55 seconds after the initial salvo, and just three minutes after the target was sighted.

Chappell now maneuvered SCULPIN to attack the second ship with stern tubes. At 2307 the vessel which had been hit opened fire with a pompom or a battery of small guns. Chappell cleared the submarine's bridge and gave the order to take her down. Breaking-up noises roared into the sound gear as SCULPIN's diving officer "pulled the plug."

Tracking the second ship by sound proved difficult, and SCULPIN was unable to obtain an attack position. A few depth charges were dropped helter-skelter to drive her off, but the counter-attack was not pressed home. With the targets fading away, the submarine remained submerged and continued on her course for Port Darwin.

Scoring two hits out of four torpedoes fired, Chappell did not report a sinking, although a sunken *maru* seemed likely. Post-war records disclose the names of three Japanese ships lost in submarine attacks on January 10, 1942. Although the positions of the attack and the reported sinkings do not agree, it is possible that SCULPIN sank the 3,817-ton merchantman AKITA MARU.

PICKEREL and STINGRAY were the other SubsAsiatic scorers on the date in question. PICKEREL (Lieutenant Commander Bacon) got hers in lat. 6-12 N., long. 125-55 E., up north of the Solomons. Making a night-submerged attack, Bacon identified his target as a 5,000-ton merchantman, and fired two torpedoes for two resounding hits on this vessel. The target broke up with a fireworks roar, and the submarines were elated over PICKEREL's first bag. Victim was later identified as a 3,000-ton ex-gunboat, KANKO MARU.

STINGRAY (Lieutenant Commander R. J. Moore) sank the transport HARBIN MARU, 5,100 tons, in lat. 17-40 N., long. 109-20 E. This was one of the first good-sized troopships to go down in the Pacific War, and January 10 must have seemed an ominous date on the Japanese calendar. If the little men with the charts and colored pins were on the job in Tokyo, they must have noted that American submarines were in action all the way from Empire waters to the seas off Australia and down under.

North of the Malay Barrier

When Japanese invasion forces appeared off Tarakan on January 10, three submarines—S-37, S-41 and SPEARFISH—were ordered to intercept the enemy landing. The three submarines headed for the point at top speed, but arrived too late to inflict damage.

With the Japanese holding Tarakan and swarming ashore at Kendari, Admiral Hart deduced that the enemy would now advance through either Makassar or Molukka straits. On January 11, Japanese forces landed at Menado and Kema, Northeast Celebes, and according to report they were assembling an invasion fleet at Kema. Again ComSubsAsiatic was directed to dispatch three submarines to intercept the invaders.

A striking force of destroyers, with the cruiser MARBLEHEAD in support, was to deliver a night torpedo attack on the enemy's shipping concentration at Kema. This surface force was withdrawn when the submarines PIKE and PERMIT, scouting ahead, reported no large enemy concentration at the northeast Celebes port.

As it turned out, the surface force was withdrawn too soon. Scouting off Kema a few days later, SWORDFISH discovered the harbor alive with Japanese shipping which had arrived at a later date than had been expected. As was the case at Tarakan, there had been no Allied air reconnaissance. Japanese troops were firmly established on the beachheads, and it was too late for the submarines to impede the landings.

This deployment of submarines to defend points open to invasion was the sort of strategy the force commander might have altered had he possessed full operational control. However, the dispatching of submarines to Kema resulted in the penetration of that enemy harbor—another feat of submarine pioneering which showed the force what could be done.

Prowling off Kema on January 24, SWORDFISH observed two freighters anchored in the roadstead north of the port. Lieutenant Commander Chester Smith quickly sized up the situation.

An anti-sub surface patrol had been previously spotted, and a flying boat had been seen patrolling offshore. To the submarine these spelled danger in capital letters. But the chart showed the water deep enough for a submerged approach, and Smith calculated that mines were unlikely as they would interfere with Japanese invasion shipping.

To get at one of the freighters, the submarine would have to go through the lower part of narrow Lembeh Strait—a squeeze the enemy could easily have defended with channel barriers. But no boom defenses were in evidence, and the target was waiting.

"All right, boys," Smith told his men. "We're going in."

Three years in submarines on the China Station had provided Chester Smith with a fund of skill and know-how that had already won him recognition as one of the ablest skippers in the Service. From successful personal performance he had acquired that confidence which lent assurance to those under him. "Smitty," they would tell you, "knows what he's doing."

This confidence of skipper in self, and crew in skipper, was matched by "Smitty's" confidence in all hands, and the confidence of all hands in SWORDFISH. Perhaps submarining demands a purer amalgam of these confidences—leader in self and crew; crew in leader; and all in boat—than any other service in the Navy. More than in any other, its practitioners *are* all in the same boat. The submarine is by nature a lone wolf. Usually it operates in an isolation unknown to surface vessels and aircraft. Bereft of companionship beneath the sea, the submersible is entirely "on its own." Its war patrols may be utterly solitary, and its cruises as lonely as Magellan's voyage to the Ladrones. Entering combat alone, it must fight its own battles without aid or succor from supporting forces. Thus of every submariner from cook to exec is required the utmost in personal responsibility, while the captain must shoulder the heaviest weight of individual responsibility in the Service.

The exactions demanded by such requirements are plainly manifest—submariners and submarine welded into a unit—brain-power, machine-power and firepower incorporated by the brand of leadership exhibited by pioneering Chester Smith. Given such leadership (and good equipment) submarines are not dominated by the factor of luck. This uncomfortable indeterminable (referred to by submariners as the "Jesus Factor"—in polite company, the "Jay Factor") is present, of course, in every operation. Napoleon put much confidence in generals he considered lucky. But it might be remarked that Napoleon ended up on Elba, and the Jay Factor may be manipulated and frequently controlled by those who make few errors in judgment and can confidently act on their own decisions with appropriate know-how and skill.

So SWORDFISH went forward at Kema, proceeding northward and making periscope observations every 20 or 30 minutes, and running at 90-foot depth between exposures. Smith was not depending on any Jay Factor to save him from detection by enemy patrols.

Entering the channel, the submarine hugged the Lembeh shore. The day was bright with tropic noon, the water brassy in hot sunlight. Ashore, the Celebes landscape seemed to dream as though it had remained undisturbed since the time of the Portuguese and Dutch explorers. Doubtless old Von Tromp had waddled into this port with his square-nosed Dutch galleon on the search for spices, and Seventeenth Century pirates had raided the jungly coves on the hunt for gold and teak. Now, concealed by the forested beachheads, other invaders were on the shore. Their ships lay down-channel in view of SWORD-FISH's periscope. Smith directed a wary approach.

Accurate determination of the channel's current (a factor to be estimated in torpedo fire on an anchored target) was impossible. For this reason Smith decided to fire two torpedoes at each target. Anchored in the roadstead, the ships were "sitting ducks," and four shots ought to get them.

"Stand by to fire . . . Steady, now! . . . Steady!" Then, with the clock at 1238: "Fire one! Fire two!"

Streaking the channel's surface with wakes of froth, the torpedoes rushed at the No. 1 target. Smith swung SWORDFISH toward the second ship. About two minutes after the first salvo, he heard the rumbling explosion. Two torpedoes raced toward the second target—straight bow shots at a range of 3,600 yards. A moment later came another detonation.

Smith took SWORDFISH down to 180 feet and headed her out of the channel for open water. A spatter of explosions crackled in the sound gear—some not far distant, and a few overhead. They may have come from gunfire or light aircraft bombs. Small-boat propellers were heard, and angry depth charges blew holes in the tide well astern. These anti-submarine measures were futile in the face of a *fait accompli*. For SWORDFISH was already safe on her way, leaving behind her the remains of MYOKEN MARU—4,000 tons of Japanese invasion shipping—on the bottom.

Two days later, SWORDFISH attacked an enemy destroyer (day-submerged approach), firing two torpedoes with zero results. The following day she attacked and missed a shot at a freighter. Valentine's Day she tackled still another freighter, and Smith fired two torpedoes for a hit. And on February 19,

Smith reported the sinking of an oil tanker. While the sinkings of these last two vessels could not be corroborated, the *maru* torpedoed at Kema went down without any doubt. For this daring foray, SWORDFISH was credited with a successful patrol. Lieutenant Commander Chester Smith was awarded the Navy Cross, *"for especially meritorious conduct as commander of a submarine operating in the Southwest Pacific."*

Another pioneering SubsAsiatic skipper who struck hard uppercuts at the oncoming enemy was Lieutenant Commander William L. Wright, captain of STURGEON. Affectionately known throughout the Service as "Bull"—a sobriquet which paid tribute to his talents as a raconteur—Wright could make history as well as recount it. Under Wright's command, STURGEON won early laurels as a fighting submarine. Like Chester Smith, he was able to inspire confidence and indoctrinate his men in that sense of individual responsibility so requisite for successful submarining.

Typical of Wright and his captaincy was the episode which resulted in the naming of STURGEON's mess boy as "Me Too." The mess attendant was new to submarining, and the skipper wanted to impress upon him the unique responsibility which every man aboard STURGEON had to bear.

"It's all for one and one for all, aboard a submarine," the captain told the boy, who had reported topside for his first go at night lookout duty. "Night vision is damned important. You've got to look sharp out there. Remember, when you're up here on this watch, you're responsible for a six million-dollar submarine. All this fine equipment—the lives of all those men down below—everything depends on you. So you've got to keep your eye peeled. We can run into the enemy mighty sudden on a night like this, and whether we sink or swim is up to the watch!"

The mess boy nodded solemnly, peering ahead.

"Don't forget," the captain warned, looking back from the conning tower hatch. "You're responsible for six million bucks worth of sub—everything in it—the lives of all of us down below."

"Yes, sir, Captain," the boy assured. "An' then there's me, too."

So there were Me Too and all of them on wartime duty aboard STURGEON as she knifed her way through the Asian seas to seek out and fight the enemy.

After the Japanese seizures of Tarakan and Kema, American and Dutch submarines were stationed in the Straits of Makassar. Dutch air patrols had reported a large enemy convoy moving southward down the strait, apparently heading for the oil port of Balikpapan. Here, again, three U.S. submarines—

PORPOISE, PICKEREL and STURGEON—were dispatched to intercept the invasion forces. Stationed in the strait between North Watcher and Mangkalihat, PORPOISE and PICKEREL scouted the forward line, while STURGEON played the backfield in reserve.

On January 22 the forward submarines reported the Japanese convoy steaming south in full array. An umbrella of planes, screening the convoy train, had made daylight attack most hazardous. Now dusk was dimming the seascape when STURGEON received the word from PORPOISE and PICKEREL. Almost simultaneously her sound gear picked up the murmur of ship's screws. Excited, the sound man reported the vessel was probably a carrier or a cruiser.

The STURGEON, as the old song had it, needed no urgin'. Wright rushed the men to battle stations, and the submarine squared away for a surface attack.

Five nights before, Wright had directed a surface gun attack on an oil tanker. The quarry escaped. Tonight, with multiple ship screws droning in Sound's ear, and what looked like a 10,000-tonner coming down through the gloom, Wright determined to nail the target.

Big as a barn door may seem an exaggeration for a vessel coming over the night horizon. But to those sweating it out on a submarine's bridge, a blurred silhouette—cruiser, or carrier?—may have the menacing loom of an oncoming mastodon. STURGEON's crew waited in tightening tension. Target bearing, speed, range went into the T.D.C. Gyro angles were set on the torpedoes. Submarine and everything were at stake, including Me Too, when Wright gave the order to fire.

Four torpedoes raced from the tubes. Two hits roared in the sound gear. Wright "pulled the plug." Because of darkness and the advisability of leaving the vicinity, results of the torpedo fire could not be observed. But all hands aboard STURGEON were confident that they had sent a big Jap vessel to the bottom.

Although post-war inquest failed to identify a Japanese carrier or cruiser sunk at lat. 01 N., long. 199 E., and Wright reported STURGEON's target as "unknown," it is possible that the enemy lost a large ship in Makassar Strait. If not sunk, a ship was undoubtedly hit and damaged, and STURGEON was entitled to that classic characterization dispatched by Wright in his memorable radio report:

STURGEON NO LONGER VIRGIN

Other reports from STURGEON enlivened the reading matter at SubsAsiatic Headquarters. She was one of the first vessels to conduct a sound attack from deep submergence. This attack and a similar one made by SEAL furnish good examples of the tactic as practiced by the pioneers.

Pioneer Tactics (The Sound Attack)

By pre-war definition, a sound attack was one delivered from deep submergence, the approach officer depending solely on "sound information." On submerged approach, the JK and QB listening devices were manned in the torpedo room or conning tower, and the JP listening device was manned in the torpedo room. It was up to Sound to maintain a continuous and accurate flow of data to the approach officer. One listener kept continuously trained on the nearest escort if the target was screened, while the JP was frequently used for all-around sweeps. These assignments were occasionally varied, and the JP followed the target while one of the conning tower listeners was used for search. Changes in target bearing, speed and range were relayed by Sound to the fire control party, and the attack was made with the submarine maneuvering far below the surface.

The following excerpts from the Report of Gunnery Exercises, 1940-1941, disclose pre-war concepts concerning the proper conduct of a sound attack:

> *A submarine attacking a target protected by supersonic screen has a 50-50 chance of penetrating screen without detection. It has a 1 in 4 chance of escaping detection and making successful sound attack on target.*
> *If detected while penetrating sound screen it has 1 chance in 7 of evading depth charge attack and completing successful attack on target.*
> *If detected by sound screen it has a 1 in 7 chance of successfully attacking target but receiving depth charge damage in return.*
> *On 1 out of 8 attempted attacks submarines will receive fatal damage and if detected by sound screen there is 1 chance in 4 of submarine's receiving fatal damage by depth charge attacks.*
> *Results indicate that submarines making sound attacks on an unscreened target in an area where good sound conditions exist, regardless of whether target is periodically making small or large changes of course, can expect about one-half of attacks to be successful. . . .*
> *It is bad practice and is contrary to submarine doctrine to conduct an attack at periscope depth when aircraft are known to be in the vicinity. . . .*

Here again is evidence that anti-submarine measures were overestimated before the war, and danger of detection by aircraft was particularly exaggerated. At the same time, peacetime target practice had invited confidence in the submarine's ability to hit with "sound shots." Combat experience soon proved these pre-war concepts faulty. Concerning them, a submarine captain was to write, *"They should forever stand as monuments to the dangers inherent in reaching sweeping conclusions, as regards tactics, from target practices conducted under artificial conditions."*

The quoted criticism was substantiated by statistical analyses made by the Submarine Operations Research Group (SORG) during and after the war. This body, organized in Washington and later installed with an IBM machine at Pearl Harbor, analyzed 4,873 submarine attacks, and listed only 31 of these as conducted by sound. Moreover, many of the 31 attacks listed do not meet the precise definition of a "sound attack." Data on numerous pioneer approaches is incomplete, and probably a higher percentage of legitimate sound attacks was made in the early war period than SORG's figure indicates. But the number is surprisingly small, considering pre-war emphasis on the tactic.

In the 31 sound attacks listed by SORG, seven credited sinkings are included. But positive identification of the vessels sunk could not be made. Japanese records are garbled, and there may have been more sinkings than met SORG's eye. On the other hand, there may have been fewer. The sound attack made from deep submergence did not lend itself to observation of the target, and the accuracy of torpedo fire could be judged only by "breaking-up noises" and the fade-out of ship's screws in the listening gear. So evidence of a sinking after a sound attack was apt to be wholly circumstantial.

Results of the sound attack made by STURGEON on January 26, 1942, were never conclusively determined. On this date (four days after her graduation from maidenhood) she was in the vicinity of Balikpapan. Early in the morning she sighted a transport screened by four minesweepers. Wright sent the men to battle stations, and STURGEON closed on the normal approach course to a range of 800 yards.

Then, to avoid detection, Wright sent STURGEON to 100 feet. Three minutes later, firing by sound, the submariners launched four bow shots at the troopship. There was one timed hit—an explosive roar and crackle in the sound gear. And STURGEON's crew was convinced she had done it again.

Japanese records failed to show a transport lost at the time and place in question. Again, STURGEON may have only damaged the enemy—or the torpedo may have prematured. In a similar attack made by SEAL a month later, the outcome was equally uncertain.

On February 24, SEAL (Lieutenant Commander K. C. Hurd) was patrolling submerged north of Lombok. At 0800 Sound heard pinging, and shortly thereafter smoke was sighted.

SEAL came to a normal approach course, and about an hour later a convoy of four cargo vessels escorted by three destroyers was sighted. Hurd gave the order to go deep, and then speeded up in an effort to close the track. Ten minutes later he ordered SEAL to periscope depth. The range was now 5,800 yards, angle on the bow 50° port, and speed 13 knots. Hurd selected the biggest ship as SEAL's target, and went to 110 feet to attack by sound.

In order to attain firing range, Hurd had to keep the submarine boring in, as frequent rising to periscope depth would mean loss of time and distance. SEAL was after an important target which was protected by a supersonic screen—the sea was smooth and dangerous—the freighter's port escort was defensively in the way. As Sound had been tracking the target when SEAL was at periscope depth, an attack from deep submergence seemed feasible as well as imperative.

Dismayingly enough, Sound lost the target on the high-speed run in. Therefore, at 0940, when T.D.C. generated gyro angles were approaching zero, SEAL slowed to pick up the target once more. Contact was successfully made, but the bearing, compared with the generated bearing, indicated that the target had zigged to the left.

Four minutes later, with T.D.C. matching continuous bearings from Sound, Hurd fired four torpedoes. Some of the crew reported hearing two explosions, but Hurd was not satisfied that hits had been scored—not until an hour later, when he ordered SEAL to periscope depth and no sign of the target could be seen. But if victim there was, she was erased from Japanese records as well as the surface of the sea. Because the vessel's loss could not be verified, SEAL was not officially credited with a sinking. But her sound attack is noteworthy as one conducted exactly in accordance with the accepted pre-war doctrine.

As combat experience was gained, and the danger of being detected by air screens or supersonic screens was more realistically evaluated, the "doctrine of sound approach" became extinct. By the late summer of 1942, a submarine commander who conducted his patrol in conformance with the doctrine expounded at the war's beginning would undoubtedly have been relieved of command. Tested by the pioneer submariners, sound attacks conducted from deep submergence did not meet the requisites of battle, and in final summary the total amount of damage inflicted by such attacks on the enemy proved negligible.

TENDER SERVICE. Two fleet-type submarines alongside USS Proteus *(AS19). Home and mother to subs and submariners, the tenders provided the un-* *dersea forces with food, ammunition, medical supplies, spare parts—everything* and *the kitchen stove. Repairs by tender-men kept the submarines going.*

TENDER HOLLAND *with S-boats alongside. Holland's clipper bow gave her a notable silhouette. But the Japs failed to pick her off. Escaping Manila, she serviced subs throughout war.* "Ma" *Holland was no Mother Hubbard.*

"THE OLD LADY." *Sometimes called* "Mama San." *Portrait of tender* Canopus *and her brood in the Asiatics, 1940. At Bataan she proved one of the war's greatest fighting ships—a sub tender with the heart of a battlewagon.*

TENDER ORION. *Photographed at Saipan in Sept. 1944, she has 7 fleet-type subs alongside. Submarine tender-men had no soft berths. Operating at advanced bases, they did not serve by standing and waiting.*

TENDER BUSHNELL. *Named after Yankee submarine inventor of the Revolution, she is shown with 3 Marine Turtle descendents.*

Such hard-hitting combat skippers as Smith and Wright favored other tactics. Conducting STURGEON's forays in early 1942, Wright came to favor the night-submerged approach and night-periscope attack.

Pioneer Tactics (Night-periscope Attack)

As the war advanced into 1942, a number of night-periscope attacks were attempted in the Philippine and Dutch East India areas. No sinkings could be confirmed by post-war inquest. But there was reasonable evidence of several, and although the attacking submarines were not officially credited, three or four of the Jap vessels involved undoubtedly failed to reach their destinations.

STURGEON made some of these night attacks. And Wright, arriving at conclusions which differed from those reached by POLLACK's Captain Moseley, became enthusiastic over the tactic. He wrote:

"I don't know whether or not everyone fully appreciated the possibilities and advantages of periscope approaches in moonlight. I believe that, in most cases, it is the ideal condition, if a few principles are followed:

"1. *Get a good estimate of the target course before submerging. This can usually be done with pretty narrow limits, and it is not likely that target will be zigzagging.*

"2. *Use periscope freely and feed bearings to TDC constantly. This is important because range (mostly estimates at best) is likely to be out.*

"3. *Close to a good firing range. You can generally choose your position far better than in a daylight approach.*

"4. *Fire straight shots. Then a range error makes no difference.*

"A great many of my pre-war ideas as to night visibility have been knocked into a cocked hat by experience. For instance, the idea that the sector toward the moon is always the sector of best visibility. This is very often not at all so. Generally speaking, the sector of best visibility is that sector where there is the greatest contrast between color of sky and water, that is, where the horizon is most definitely defined. More often than not, the sectors bordering the path of the moon are the sectors of poorest visibility.

"Also, I am convinced that, except on a very dark night, a surface attack on almost any target will be detected before a decent firing range can be reached. On an escorted target, it will almost certainly be detected."

Wright's remarks constituted a blueprint of the accepted method of conducting a night-periscope attack. Perhaps STURGEON's periscopes were better than those of POLLACK and, in the latitude in which she operated, light conditions may have been better than those prevailing in the Tokyo Bay area. As to the chance of being detected in a night-surface attack, Wright's estimate was probably at that time justified. As previously noted, night camouflage was as yet undeveloped, and submarine visibility was a moot question.

The first identified ship to be sunk in a night-submerged attack was torpedoed by SEADRAGON on February 2, 1942. Therein lies not only a study in tactics, but a saga concerning camouflage.

The matter of protective coloration may have had considerable influence on SEADRAGON's skipper, Lieutenant Commander W. E. Ferrall, when it came to a choice of tactics. On her first three war patrols, dated between early January and late July 1942, SEADRAGON made 19 attacks. Of these only two were night surface. The remainder, with the exception of the submerged attack on the night of February 2, were day submerged. Apparently SEADRAGON was all for keeping under the surface, day or night. In this regard, Ferrall was dutifully following the accepted doctrine. But circumstances seem to have impelled him to pay it scrupulous respect. For tactics can hinge on such matters as camouflage, and when it came to paint, SEADRAGON had a problem uniquely her own.

The problem had its beginnings on that morning when she was lying alongside ill-fated SEALION in the harbor at Cavite. The blasts which wrecked the LION scorched the DRAGON's hull and blistered the paint on her superstructure. She had entered Cavite in need of a paint job, and when she left Manila Bay, such paint as she had left was cracked and flaking off around her patched-up wounds, and blotches of red lead primer were showing through.

She was spotted like a leopard when she reached her station off the coast of Luzon. Some members of her crew considered her conspicuous. A leopard cannot change its spots, and it may be remarked that the feat is equally difficult for a dragon dodging about in hostile seas. Ferrall might well have ordered his diving officer, "Take her down, and keep her down!"

On January 10, 17, 23 and 25, SEADRAGON delivered a series of attacks on the invasion shipping which swarmed down on Luzon. Her adventures resembled those of the other SubsAsiatic boats battling the Japanese tidal wave. She harassed the convoys. She eluded depth bombs and patrols. She stalked and evaded. She prowled along the surface, and belly-crawled in the bottom mud, and generally behaved like any normal submersible in action.

In her January attacks she fired 15 torpedoes for one hit—a single out of that batch! On this hit she reported the sinking of FUKUYO MARU. Even so she was robbed, for investigation failed to reveal the downing of a Japanese freighter by that name. SEADRAGON's fire controlmen may have been nervous in their peculiarly freckled submarine. But other submariners were not hitting with the Mark 14 torpedo. Nerves or no, the fault probably did not lie with Ferrall's fire control party.

Luck relented, however, on the morn of February 2nd. A bright tropic moon was gilding the water, and the submarine, on the hunt off the western Luzon coast, sighted five ships coming over the sharp horizon.

Contact was made at 0416. Japanese transports—five of them in column!—carrying troops and equipment to reinforce General Homma. Ferrall decided to bore in for a periscope attack. SEADRAGON went to periscope depth, and the approach was begun.

Ferrall put the submarine on the convoy's track and chose his target—the fourth ship in the column. The approach lasted a little over an hour. At 0522 SEADRAGON was in firing position and two torpedoes were launched. The torpedo run was 500 yards.

Two hits were observed—geysers spouting high —bursts of water and fire. Eight minutes later Ferrall sent one torpedo racing at the fifth ship in column. Making a run of 1,200 yards, the torpedo missed.

At 0653 the transport which had been torpedoed was still afloat, and Ferrall attempted to deliver a *coup de grâce*, firing one torpedo at a range of 800 yards, depth-setting eight feet. This torpedo also missed.

Daylight on the water, it was time for SEADRAGON to leave the vicinity. And her continued presence in the Jap transport's neighborhood was unnecessary. A periscope view showed the transport settling by the stern. Lifeboats were overside, brown figures scrabbling down from the listing decks. As SEADRAGON left the scene, TAMAGAWA MARU was going under— a 6,441-ton APK with military cargo that never reached the Philippines.

Radar and improved submarine camouflage would popularize the night-surface approach, but the night approach and attack made at periscope depth were by no means to be discounted.

Submarine Camouflage (Dragon in Pirate Costume)

The subject of submarine camouflage was of more than passing interest to the pioneers. Many a wardroom discussion waxed hot on the topic of war paint.

Some advocated this color and some advocated that as the proper protective coat for a combat submarine.

An unrelieved black had been considered the best color for defeating aircraft observation of a submerged submarine. With pre-war doctrine emphasizing aircraft evasion, U.S. submarines entered World War II wearing the darkest coats available. Hence the nickname, "Black-bottom Boats," for these black-painted submersibles.

A black coat was good for concealment in deep water, but it was as obvious as India ink when the submarine was on the surface in tropic daylight or silhouetted against a yellow Asian moon. A number of the pioneer captains in the Pacific preferred battleship gray or some other less Stygian shade. The painting of the periscope provided a secondary topic to be hotly argued over a cup of "jamoke." Many of the skippers took the matter in their own hands, and periscopes were painted according to individual convictions.

The coming of radar loudened the demand for improved camouflage—a paint job which would afford submarines more protection and permit them to forego submerged approaches in favor of radar-guided approaches on the surface. But it was not until July 1943 that Lieutenant Dayton R. E. Brown, with the cooperation of Commander Elton W. Grenfell, who was at that time SubPac tactical officer, began experimenting with night and surface camouflage for submarines.

Necessity mothering invention (with experience as father) the work went forward. Result of this experimenting was to have a decided effect on night tactics. Out of the workshop came a smoke-gray paint which blended so admirably with Pacific backgrounds that submarines were often able to operate boldly on the surface with the enemy in full view. Many attacks, which would formerly have required submergence to escape detection, could be made on the surface—a tremendous advantage which permitted the submarine to maneuver at high surface (Diesel engine) speed and make the most of surface radar.

These boons, however, were not enjoyed by the Pacific Fleet and SubsAsiatic pioneers. Patrolling the waters off Japan and cruising in the glassy seas of the Southwest Pacific, the submariners of 1942 went into action with the uneasy conviction that their boats were about as inconspicuous as light-ships and carnival floats. Should a submarine be painted the color of Charon's Ferry in a latitude where the sun blazed like a spotlight? Wouldn't a stove-black conning tower be silhouetted in star-shine? How about coffee color for muddy tides? Blue, like the Britishers used in the Mediterranean? Or slate gray?

While captains argued, their crews joining in as art critics, all were in agreement on one point. No combat submarine should be Baker red.

And therein lay a tale—one of the early submarine stories emanating from the Southwest Pacific. A yarn, perhaps—all wool and a yard wide—but there were sailors who said it was true, or mostly true.

The tale seems to have come from the crew of SEADRAGON, whose members to a man were convinced that carmine was not an appropriate color for a submarine. Gloomy for interior lighting, shades of red were absolutely depressing on a submarine's exterior. SEADRAGON's complement knew that for a fact. In the boisterous shallows off Luzon, in the saline tides below the Philippines, SEADRAGON's worn paint had been peeling off like sunburn. Every wave seemed to remove more of her black integument, and where the paint flaked off, her red-lead undercoat was exposed. The DRAGON had been spotty when she left Manila with part of Admiral Hart's staff. Entering Soerabaja, she resembled a shedding lizard.

The story goes that she had no time for paint in Soerabaja. Not with the Japs rushing down on Java like bulls descending on a china shop. Out she went at top speed to join the other SubsAsiatic boats that were fighting to defend the Philippines.

Running supplies and ammunition to Corregidor. Passenger service to Australia. Ferrall and his boys had little sleep and less rest—no time to get into port for a good brushing up. Hardly time to paint the periscope. They had to get back up there in the waters west of the Philippines and below Indo-China, where the Japanese ship traffic was thick.

SEADRAGON had been at sea 84 days by the end of her second patrol, and somewhere in this period a strange report began to circulate on the air. It was circulated by Radio Tokyo, and the circulator was a lady known as Tokyo Rose. Gist of her broadcasts was that the United States was sponsoring piracy. The U.S. Navy was not only violating the "civilized rules of warfare" by attacking troopships and transports carrying helpless soldiers and honest munition cargoes to the Japanese front line, the U.S. Navy was outraging humanity by sinking Japanese freighters lawfully employed in carrying plunder from conquered territory in the Philippines, Malaya and Indo-China. The Americans had sent a fleet of red submarines to raid in the South China Sea. These raiders—Red Pirates, the lady in Tokyo called them —would be properly exterminated for their nefarious forays. Honorable destroyers and airmen of the Imperial Navy were waiting for them. America would regret this piracy. Death to the red submarines!

American radio monitors heard this short-wave tirade, and undoubtedly were surprised by its content. Few reports on submarine activity had come from Fleet Headquarters, and here was Japanese propaganda admitting that American submarines were in the Far East doing damage. But what were these red submersibles! Was crimson a new color camouflage? Had Rose of Tokyo mistaken a report from Japanese lookouts? Perhaps the Soviet Navy was involved, and these were Russian submarines.

The radio monitors were mystified—could only conclude that Tokyo Rose was "seeing red."

Aboard USS SEADRAGON (the story has it) there was no such mystification. Everyone knew the answer —Lieutenant Commander Ferrall; Engineer Officer Lieutenant Charles C. Manning; Motor Machinist's Mate, First Class, Earl Oeschner; Pharmacist's Mate Wheeler B. Lipes—to take a cross-section of SEADRAGON's personnel. According to the story, they suspected the answer when they first heard Rose's broadcast.

"We used to keep the radio going all the time," MotorMac Oeschner told a war correspondent later "Working the radio didn't tell the Japs anything they didn't know. They'd figured it out that we were in there."

It seemed the enemy observers did not have to do a great deal of figuring. When Tokyo Rose launched her diatribe about American pirates in red submarines, SEADRAGON's crew perceived the cause. A storm in the South China Sea had scoured away the last of the submarine's black paint. If the DRAGON at Soerabaja had been a shedding lizard, off French Indo-China she was a boiled lobster.

"Nobody had to use sound gear on us," swore one of the crew. "They could see us no matter where we went."

Thus are legends born and reputations made. Her hull a garish crimson, SEADRAGON continued to patrol the Indo-China coast, delivering her attacks from understandable submergence.

And that's the story—a carmine submarine with a conning tower that stood out like a sore thumb. She escaped the promised punishment. Colors flying, she got back to base. But hers was an embarrassing experience, as any lady would know had she been forced to run down Main Street without her camouflage.

The costume is not recommended for the publicity-shy submersible. Thanks to her unabashed personnel, SEADRAGON survived the exposure and sank three merchantmen on her third patrol. But she was never a pirate fleet. She was just one fleet submarine. If the story is true, she was the only red submarine in the history of naval warfare.

CHAPTER 7

BATTLE FOR THE MALAY BARRIER

Submarine vs. Destroyer

The first enemy destroyer to be sunk by a U.S. submarine was torpedoed on February 8, 1942, by S-37. For an S-boat this was a doubly notable performance.

For she was, as her designation indicates, one of that veteranly vintage launched in the decade following World War I. This was not to say such boats were superannuated, senescent and fit only for shore duty in a marine museum. Nor were they constantly opening their seams in a high sea, or smothering their crews in a Turkish bath of sweat. Yet, uncomfortably deficient as they were in air conditioning, they occasionally harbored an atmosphere which would have been recognized by Jean Valjean. Their rivets were apt to weep a little if a depth charge came too close, or the oceanic pressure was too great. Lacking the latest in fire control apparatus and gear, they were not the equal of fleet submarines. And in selecting a destroyer for a target, S-37's skipper, Lieutenant James Charles Dempsey, took his risks.

Destroyers, it goes without saying, were the "born enemy" of submarines. Shallow craft, light and agile, hard to hit with a torpedo and swift on the counter-attack, they had come into their own in World War I as submarine hunters and killers. The first two years of World War II did not deprive them of their formidable reputation. One of their primary duties was screening larger vessels from submarine attacks. And in breaking the U-boat's Atlantic blockade in the winter of 1941-1942, they were proving as successful as their forerunners of 1918.

The old "four-piper" which bested the Kaiser's undersea fleet was slow and spavined compared to the World War II model engaged in battling Hitler's. Equipped with search radar, electronic fire control gear and high-powered guns, the modern DD was as far ahead of its predecessor as a fleet-type submarine was ahead of an S-boat. While reference is made to British and American destroyers, the point concerns all warships in this category—the Japanese were not behind in the development of the DD. Japanese destroyers were fast and tough. They threw their depth charges with modern throwing and launching apparatus. All were equipped with improved listening gear. A Japanese destroyer, bearing down on the attack with a bone in her teeth and her sonar pinging as she bore, was as dangerous a foe as a submersible would wish to meet. (But in the Pacific war the hunted turned hunter.)

Characterized as deadly dangerous, the destroyer was also considered a secondary target over which transports, troopships, oil tankers and other surface vessels were given high priority. The duty of the submarine was to get in under the destroyer screen and attack the convoy. This was in keeping with strategy designed to cut the enemy's supply lines and deprive his offensive and home fronts of necessary sustenance.

The destroyer, therefore, hard hitting and hard to hit, was considered a savage whose downing was hardly worth the risk of attack. Destroyers were to be attacked only when encountered alone, or when convoy targets could not be reached and the submarine could get no farther than the escort screen.

The DD, however, could be downed. One had been

72

sunk by a Dutch submarine the day after Christmas, and now on the 8th of February an S-boat was squaring away for an American performance. It looked tough, but the captain's name was Dempsey.

S-37 had been patrolling off Makassar City. After the Japanese landings in the Celebes, six submarines had been stationed in Makassar Strait and three had been stationed off Ambon, south of Molucca Passage. STURGEON had disputed the enemy's advance to Balikpapan, but the Japanese sea-air drive had relentlessly smashed forward. Thinking the next invasion step would be the island of Timor, CinCAF directed ComSubsAsiatic to dispose his submarines accordingly. Whereupon the undersea force in the Strait of Makassar had been withdrawn with the exception of S-37 left behind on guard.

Again, deprived of sufficient air reconnaissance, the Allied command was unable to apprehend the enemy's intentions. Instead of stabbing directly across the Banda Sea at Timor, the Japanese drive swung westward around the lower end of Celebes. Veering northwestward in the Flores Sea, a strong-arm invasion fleet headed for Makassar City. S-37 was all by herself in the path of this armada.

Off Makassar City Dempsey's submarine had been keeping a periscope watch on the harbor. On the February evening in question, her exec, Lieutenant W. H. Hazzard, was at the periscope. Twilight was graying into dusk when the scope spied a pigstick on the horizon—a minuscule splinter about the size of an exclamation point on the skyline. It might have been the tip of a lugger's mast, the foremast of a cruiser, or the main topmast of the immortal Flying Dutchman. It developed into the mast of a Jap destroyer that came roaring forward in the gloaming at bat-out-of-hell speed.

The DD was heading for Makassar City at a pace too fast to be overhauled. Hazzard decided it was a high-speed scout—a deduction in which Captain Dempsey concurred. The destroyer was hardly abeam before four more came nosing over the horizon in a slow-moving column barely visible in the last of the evening light. Then, as the submariners watched in fascination, a dark caravan of larger ships formed in the far-off gloom. These silhouettes were too blurred and distant for periscope identification. But there could be no doubt that S-37 was standing in the road in front of an invasion convoy.

Someone may think of a Model-T Ford packed in a maze of switchtracks in a night-gloomed terminal yard with a host of trains coming in from five directions. So it may have sounded—like scores of clashing wheels and crackling switches—in the S-boat's saturated listening gear. And so it may have looked to the S-boat's periscope watchers, with signal lights beginning to twinkle here and there in the darkness and black shades looming left and right. Somewhere over the horizon a pale searchlight fanned across the sky. That was probably a cruiser. The S-boat (as would the Model-T in the analogous situation) began to move. With traffic closing in, it was time to get off the Main Line.

The clock had been at 1947 when the submarine sighted the destroyer column. Now that the night was thickening, Dempsey ordered the S-boat to the surface, and started on the trail at top speed. He was unable to run around the destroyer column for an attack on the larger ships beyond, and resenting this interference, he decided to attack the destroyers.

This decision was not too easy. While range, gyro angles and other mathematical computations were deftly handled by the fire control party, probable risks, choice of tactics, and other abstract factors had to be computed in the head of Lieutenant James Charles Dempsey. A spread of black clouds shot through with dark lightning hovered in the east. Would the flashings reveal the submarine? In these tropic waters, torpedoes left a phosphorescent wake. Could the S-boat get away with it?

The opportunity vs. risk equation was solved by determination to seize the former. Attack on an escort when a convoy could not be reached was in accordance with doctrine. Night-surface attack gave the submarine advantage of high speed. And Dempsey probably preferred the risk of gunfire to that incurred by a creeping submerged approach which might mean sonar detection followed by enemy counterattack.

So S-37 ran in for a night-surface attack. Dempsey fired one torpedo at each of the destroyers in column. Fire control depended largely on the night vision of Lieutenant Hazzard, who was operating the dummy pelorus on the bridge. The ingenious lieutenant had fitted the brass rim of this device with an embossment of brads for finger-reading in the dark. Crude though it was, it "put the finger" on one of the DD's. The third destroyer in the column was hit.

The blast buckled the vessel in the middle, heaving the amidships section a good 20 feet above the bow and stern. Evidently the torpedo exploded in the fire room, as a cloud of soot burst from the destroyer's stack in a gust of orange light. Wrapped in a shroud of flame and smoke, the destroyer started down.

S-37 went under at safe distance and burrowed deep to evade. The DD's hunted, but could not find her. They next heard of her three nights later when she attacked another destroyer in the Strait of Makassar.

She missed that one. But an S-boat could hardly be expected to sink every destroyer in the Pacific, although it would seem that S-37 tried. She ended her 18-day third patrol with a record of five straight attacks on destroyers. The one that went down off Makassar City was the Imperial Navy's NATSUSHIO.

Dempsey's attack in that instance was exactly patterned to conform with pre-war concepts of the method to be employed. As the war progressed, destroyers were awarded a higher priority on the target list, and almost any submarine commander in the latter part of the war would have picked a single DD for target and let her have the whole salvo.

Statistics: In 1941 American submarines fired 1.85 torpedoes per attack on targets identified as destroyers. In 1942 they fired 2.45 torpedoes per destroyer attack. And in 1944 they fired 3.29 at destroyer targets.

The figures dramatize the trend of official opinion on the value of the DD as a target, and the trend of the submariner's opinion of the destroyer as a foe. No doubt the available supply of torpedoes had some influence on this trend, but experience proved that the enemy DD with her pinging sound gear and booming depth charges was not the ferocious opponent anticipated.

U.S. submarines sank only four destroyers in 1942. During the year they made 82 attacks on targets identified as destroyers. Identification was apt to be faulty, for the Japanese employed torpedo boats which were smaller than destroyers but of similar silhouette, and as the war went on they built a great number of craft classified as *kaibokan*, or coast defense vessels, which closely resembled American destroyer escorts. There was also a small combat transport which was easily mistaken for a DD.

At war's end, SORG would count 349 American submarine attacks on Japanese destroyers. Due to the aforementioned difficulties of identification, reported sinkings were considerably higher than the number verifiable. Even so, the figure officially confirmed was a remarkable one, considering the destroyer's pre-war reputation as a submarine killer—its armament, firepower and speed—and the American submarine's slow start, lack of radar, and unreliable torpedo. Altogether 39 Japanese destroyers were confirmed as sunk by U.S. submarines in the Pacific War.

Going to the bottom, the 1,900-ton NATSUSHIO was leader of a long parade.

Submarine Aground

One of the major hazards which imperilled the pioneer submarine in the Philippines-Netherlands East Indies area was grounding. Off Luzon, Mindanao, Borneo and Java, the coastal waters are shallow. Among the archipelagoes lies a treachery of bars and reefs, dangerous to the surface vessel and a menace to the submersible which must often grope its way below the surface without the aid of lookouts aloft or a leadline.

Dutch charts were good, but at the war's beginning not all of the American submarine skippers were provided with them. To many, the seas which lapped the Malay Barrier, the straits and passages and channels between Java and the Philippines were as mysterious as the waterways the early explorers followed to Zipangu. Off the Bali coast or beneath the tides south of Celebes, there were bottoms as unknown as the other side of the moon. Attacked by aircraft or enemy's DD's, a submarine had no opportunity for soundings. A growl of gravel under keel—a jammed rudder—a sudden, butting shock—these might be the undersea navigator's first indication he was caught on a bar or clutched by a rocky snare.

Four U.S. submarines were lost from groundings during World War II. Only expert handling reduced the losses to this remarkably low figure. Many submarines ran aground. But these were able to get off. Some were damaged severely, a number lost their keel-mounted sonar heads, and some escaped with scarcely an abrasion, despite the fact that nearly every get-off demanded the utmost in skilled submarining.

In 1942 two S-boats (S-36 and S-39) were lost by stranding in the Southwest Pacific and one (S-27) was lost in the Aleutians. As has been noted, the S-boats lacked radar and a bridge pelorus that could be read in the dark. Neither fathometer nor pitometer log was aboard to indicate depth, speed and distance. Fortunately all hands survived these S-boat disasters, and also the grounding of DARTER, the fourth submarine so lost (in 1944). That personnel losses were not suffered in these incidents bespeaks the skill and resourcefulness of those who manned the afflicted submarines.

Loss of S-36

The first submarine lost from grounding during the war was S-36. On her second patrol, having completed a successful attack on a small transport moored in Calapan Harbor, Mindoro, in the Philippines, she was proceeding to Soerabaja, Java. Just before dawn on the morning of January 20, she ran hard aground on Taka Bakang Reef in Makassar Strait.

Currents in this area are strong and hard to predict. S-36 had traveled at least 100 miles since last she had been able to fix her position. When the blow came, she was standing south at standard speed in the tropic night. Taka Bakang, awash at low water, could not be seen. A sudden violent jolt—a grinding snarl—propellers churning futile froth—S-36 was stranded.

Her forward battery, flooded, appeared to be generating chlorine gas. All efforts to move the boat proved unavailing. And the alarming situation impelled the submarine's commander, Lieutenant J. R. McKnight, Jr., to send out a plain language message that S-36 was aground and sinking.

SARGO, at that time nearing Soerabaja, received the message and tried to relay it. After five hours of unsuccessful trying, she turned back to help the stranded S-boat.

When ComSubsAsiatic at Soerabaja finally received the message, SARGO was recalled and a PBY was sent to survey the stranded submarine's situation. By the time the plane arrived, McKnight was confident that with assistance he could salvage his submarine. The plane raced to Makassar City to request aid from the Dutch authorities. A Dutch launch was dispatched the following morning.

The launch took off two officers and 28 men, the remainder of the submarine's crew staying aboard in the hope S-36 could be hauled clear. But conditions steadily worsened. When the Dutch ship, SS SIBEROTE, arrived that afternoon, McKnight decided to abandon. S-36 was rigged for flooding, and the submariners transferred to the SIBEROTE which took them to Makassar City.

All hands reached Soerabaja on February 25th.

Escape of USS Tarpon

The loss of S-27 in the Aleutians, S-39 in the Louisade Archipelago, and DARTER on Bombay Shoal will be related in subsequent chapters. Relative to the subject at this point is the grounding of TARPON—a misadventure in which loss of the submarine was averted.

TARPON's escape furnishes a good example of the intestinal fortitude which kept the submariners going in the early months of the war.

She was the boat that had staggered into Darwin after swallowing a lot of sea water in a typhoon. There a repair crew got her back on steady legs, and later in January TARPON returned to war patrol.

On the night of February 22 she was ordered to a new patrol area north of the Malay Barrier. When these orders were received she was south of the Barrier, and her skipper, Lieutenant Commander Lewis Wallace, selected Boling Strait for the transit. Although adjacent Alor Strait was easier to navigate, PIKE was expected in that waterway the same night, and Boling was the nearer passage.

Whereas three-quarters of the southern approach to Boling Strait is wide and steep-shored, the navigable channel narrows to about a mile's width in the northern end of the strait. A course due north leads to the narrows, and when this euripus is entered, a course of about 035 parallels its axis.

TARPON had to depend on a low-lying tangent of land, Point Tusk, for a turning point. A higher ridge of the land was mistaken for the point, and as she waited for its silhouette to come abeam, TARPON grounded at 12 knots on the reefs bordering the western shore of the channel.

Boling Strait was no place for a submarine to be aground. The Japanese offensive was probing for the Malay Barrier, and any hour a fusillade from the dark might announce the arrival of the enemy. TARPON's crew lightened ship by blowing her remaining reserve fuel and fresh water and lowering both anchors. Three torpedoes were jettisoned forward after their exploders had been removed. Still the submarine could not be budged.

With daylight making and the tide ebbing out from under, the remaining torpedoes were retained aboard. During the morning both forward normal fuel tanks were blown. Lube oil was shifted aft. Two hundred rounds of 3-inch ammunition were tossed overside. On the reef TARPON mulishly remained, exposed in a glare of tropic day, obstinate, impervious to persuasion.

The port anchor chain was slipped, and the starboard anchor hauled aft about three-quarters the length of the ship in an attempt to kedge. Strive as they would, TARPON's crew could not get her clear. With the submarine apparently fastened to the reef, plans were made to blow her to Kingdom Come to prevent her from falling into enemy hands. A warhead was suspended by oil-soaked line above several small blocks of T.N.T. In event of imminent capture, the oil-soaked line could be set afire to burn through and drop the warhead on the explosive blocks. To insure a detonation, the crew planned to rig an air hose to the warhead's exploder device so that a jet of air might spin the propeller and rapidly arm the warhead.

Meanwhile, a native boat had been sighted and the boatmen prevailed upon to take an officer ashore. After a visit to the island of Adunara, the boat returned bearing the island's sole white occupant, Mynheer H. Van Den Hulst, a missionary. The arrival of a "sky pilot" may have seemed fitting at this juncture. Emphatically so when the missionary informed the stranded submariners that Jap planes had been over the Strait during the past four days and enemy ships were to eastward. However, by way of better news he assured TARPON's sailors there would be a high tide from 1600 to 1800.

These tidings, good and bad, prompted the submariners to stick by their guns. Three engines were backed, and the crew heaved in on the anchor windlass, and TARPON was finally moved. Aided by Providence and the flooding tide, the crew got her off at 1600—a pioneer exploit which showed the Force that submariners capable of surviving hell and high water could also live through hell and low. And the patience and perseverance which move mountains may also move submarines from a reef.

Tjilatjap

With the Japanese ashore in Borneo, Celebes and the Moluccas, their forces swarming into Balikpapan and Ambon, the hot breath of invasion began to scorch Java.

Defense of the Netherlands East Indies with a skeleton force had been a forlorn hope at best. On February 4, the Japanese struck Admiral Hart's ABDA Fleet a blow that all but broke the back of the skeleton.

The bombing of Soerabaja had begun the day before, and the enemy's air fleets were raiding the island of Timor where a base would put them within bomber range of northern Australia. Obviously the enemy was preparing to drive at Java or Timor, perhaps both simultaneously. To fend the thrust at Java, Admiral Hart gathered the heaviest surface force he could muster and dispatched it, under command of Dutch Rear Admiral Karel Doorman, to attack the invasion forces assembling at Balikpapan.

Decks cleared for a showdown, the ABDA squadron stood out from Madoera Strait. The force consisted of the Dutch cruiser DE RUYTER (Doorman's flagship) plus the USS HOUSTON, USS MARBLEHEAD, RNN VON TROMP and several destroyers.

Provided air protection, this striking force might have had a fair chance to deal with the enemy. But air cover was not available. The Japanese, on the other hand, were all over the sky, and a flight of Japanese planes on their way to bomb Soerabaja spotted the ABDA squadron in Madoera Strait. Realizing his ships had been seen, the Dutch admiral hoped he could elude detection under cover of night, and his force made the run for Makassar after sundown. The following morning, off the Kangean Islands north of Bali, the force was rediscovered by enemy planes, and four or five bomber formations roared down on the attack.

For more than two hours the warships dodged, veered and zigzagged, throwing up a thunder storm of anti-aircraft fire. Several enemy planes were shot down, but it took more than one swallow to make a summer, and the Japanese airmen were out for a Roman holiday.

The bombers concentrated on the cruisers. Zigzagging at top speed, HOUSTON evaded all but the last bomb aimed at her. This bomb, hurtling down from a straggler, struck the leg of her mainmast and exploded in a ricochet near the after turret. The blast ignited the ready powder in the gun turret, and the turret blew up, instantly killing 48 men.

MARBLEHEAD received even worse punishment. Landing on her fantail, a bomb penetrated the main deck, smashed her steering gear and punctured several fuel tanks. Spurts of flaming oil fired the ship. Another bomb blasted the officers' quarters and sick bay. A third ruptured her hull below the waterline. Fires raged fore and aft, and her jammed rudder sent the cruiser in a helpless circle to port. She took a sharp list to starboard, began to settle by the head and only heroic work by the damage control party managed to keep her afloat. Bailed by pumps and bucket brigades, and steered by her engines, she limped off down through Lombok Strait, and, escorted by wounded HOUSTON, headed for Tjilatjap on the southern coast of Java.

Lying at the head of a long, narrow, river entrance, Tjilatjap (pronounced "Chilachap") had already been selected as a reserve base to be used in the event that Soerabaja became untenable. It was thought, perhaps wishfully, that submarines and other units might employ the port as a temporary base for a few weeks, at least, without detection by the enemy. Accordingly on February 4, tenders HOLLAND and OTUS were dispatched to Tjilatjap from Darwin, Australia, as CinCAF perceived that Darwin was unsatisfactory as a submarine base. The north Australian port had come under the shadow of the Japanese air advance, and the moving of HOLLAND and OTUS to Tjilatjap proved providential. Delayed by foul weather, the tenders arrived in the Javanese port on February 10th. Nine days later, enemy aircraft struck Darwin. High-level bombers blasted the shore installations to rubbish. Nearly every ship in the harbor was sunk, losses including the destroyer USS PEARY. Strafed and set afire, the town was practically wiped out. As a base for submarine overhaul Darwin, Australia, was eliminated.

Tjilatjap was by no means secure. The submarine tenders found a grim harbor—MARBLEHEAD battle-scarred and fire-blackened in the floating drydock; HOUSTON's crew burying her dead; submarines coming in from patrol, haggard and hungry for supplies; every hour bringing word that the enemy was drawing nearer. ComSubsAsiatic was preparing to leave

Soerabaja. Daily air raids were leveling the Dutch naval base, and work on submarines was becoming impossible. The catastrophic situation was made apparent by the fact that the cruiser HOUSTON, even with her after turret destroyed, was the strongest warship remaining to the ABDA Fleet. After makeshift repairs at Tjilatjap she was rushed to Darwin, to escort troops to Timor where it was hoped Allied forces could try to stand. MARBLEHEAD, her wounds patched, was sent to Trincomalee, Ceylon, under escort of the submarine tender OTUS. An unusual assignment for a submarine tender, but the crippled cruiser could not proceed alone, and no other escort could be spared.

Whittled down to the bone, Admiral Hart's skeletal fleet was disposed to defend Java. Operations at Soerabaja were coming to a standstill, as Japanese bombings grew in frequency and violence. Submarines were ordered to clear the restricted overhaul basin and submerge in the outer harbor during air raids. One Dutch submarine, tardy in complying with the order, was bombed and sunk inside the basin. Daylight refits could no longer be accomplished, and the SubsAsiatic boats were ordered to Tjilatjap.

OTUS gone, only HOLLAND remained to serve the SubsAsiatic Force—a single tender for all the submarines in the Southwest Pacific Area. The one small drydock at Tjilatjap was given over to destroyers, and shore repair facilities consisted of a railroad shop whose capacities were decidedly limited. The tender force rolled up its sleeves, and somehow the boats were refitted as they came in from patrol. Among those which made port at Tjilatjap were SAILFISH, SALMON, SEAL, SNAPPER and STINGRAY.

In the mountains behind Tjilatjap a hotel was available for a rest camp, and there the submariners had a few moments to catch their breath. But the rumbling of the bombs at Soerabaja echoed over the mountains in radio reports that were consistently discouraging.

On February 14 came the word that Admiral Thomas C. Hart had been relieved of command of the ABDA Fleet—the command going to Dutch Admiral Helfrich. For the American admiral it had been a heartbreaking battle. He had sent his forces out to fight a delaying action, knowing that retreat and defeat were inevitable—that victory would be won by other forces later. There is no harder individual role than the one of loser so that others may win, and Admiral Hart, veteran submariner, accepted it with that sense of duty appreciated by every man in submarines.

On February 18 Japanese invasion forces landed on the island of Bali. The following night an ABDA surface force fought a savage battle in Badoeng Strait with the enemy's invasion convoy. In the melee the Dutch destroyer PIET HIEN was sunk, the cruiser TROMP seriously damaged, and the cruiser JAVA wounded. Two Japanese destroyers were badly battered—small consolation. The blows struck the little Allied fleet were all but paralyzing at a moment when every ship was needed.

It was now realized that Soerabaja must be abandoned and Tjilatjap could not long be held. The channel entering Tjilatjap was a snare. Entry at night was navigationally unsafe, and one sunken ship could block the entrance and trap the vessels in the harbor. These dangers, plus a total lack of air protection, resulted in the dispatch of HOLLAND (February 20) to Exmouth Gulf.

On February 26 the last effort at refitting submarines at Soerabaja was concluded when S-37 precipitately departed for patrol. Admiral Wilkes and the remaining members of the staff set out over the mountains by automobile. There was still some hope of holding on at Tjilatjap. Help was on the way.

To Java were coming two Allied aircraft tenders—USS LANGLEY and HMS SEAWITCH. Between them they carried 59 fighter planes with munitions, pilots and ground personnel. But LANGLEY was destined never to arrive. About 100 miles off Tjilatjap, she was sighted by a Japanese scouting plane. Summoned to the target, nine enemy bombers roared over, and with a single salvo of nine bombs scored five direct hits on LANGLEY. Parked aircraft were blown to pieces and volcanic fires set raging. Somehow the vessel remained afloat. But she was too badly damaged to make port. The command was given to abandon. LANGLEY was sunk by shellfire from the destroyer WHIPPLE—a tragic ending for the old "Covered Wagon," the U.S. Navy's first aircraft carrier.

Two days later HMS SEAWITCH arrived at Tjilatjap unharmed. But the reinforcements she brought were too little and too late. The Japanese drive designed to roll over the Malay Barrier was beginning. The harbor of Tjilatjap was too hot for the submarines.

Among the submariners there was a famous rhyme about Tjilatjap, suggesting that they would endure a lot of discomfort in preference to spending a night there. But the Battle of the Java Sea was in the making, and the nights of the SubsAsiatic Force in Tjilatjap were numbered.

Pioneer Special Missions

The French term for it in World War I was *"mission extraordinaire."* An air pilot was detailed the job of dropping a secret agent behind enemy lines— a soldier disguised as a peasant was sent out to carry a message across Belgium—a navy crew was dispatched to do a little gun-running or blow up a harbor obstruction.

The submariner's designation for it in World War II was "Special Mission." This applied to a variety of non-routine tasks assigned submarines—tasks which deviated from the primary mission of sinking enemy ships. Scores of these missions (see Addenda) were carried out during the war—there was a demand for the execution of many more—and in the variety of tasks detailed and hazards faced and overcome, the submarine missions were certainly "special." Perhaps the more appropriate adjective would be "extraordinary."

At best the apportionment of submarine patrol objectives had to be a compromise measured by long-range considerations concerning effective damage to the enemy. Frequently the consideration of direct and immediate damage had to be by-passed in favor of rescuing endangered American or Allied personnel or rushing relief to some beleaguered outpost. The support of Philippine guerrillas, transportation of intelligence operators, establishment of lifeguard patrols, reconnaissance of prospective invasion beaches—these were vitally important activities which linked in with major military and naval projects and resulted in the saving of many lives. Because they seldom afforded an opportunity to sink enemy ships, special missions were as a rule disliked by the submariners. But, although difficult to measure by percentages and cold sums, their value in promoting the ultimate defeat of the enemy will be seen as immense.

Never a holiday excursion, the special mission usually demanded a perilous penetration of enemy territory—a venture frequently far more hazardous than the normal war patrol. Whereas a ship attack was generally a matter of "hit and git," the landing of a shore party on an enemy-held beach, or the rescue of personnel from a port under fire called for the last belt-notch of courage and no end of resourcefulness.

Submarine special missions may be divided into the following general types: reconnaissance, supply, evacuation or rescue, transportation of coast watchers and intelligence agents, lifeguarding, mining. Miscellaneous tasks included weather reporting, minefield detection, anti-picket boat sweeps, shore bombardment, support of commando raids, and serving as marker beacons for surface ships. Any submarine in accomplishing a special mission might perform more than one of these enumerated tasks.

As the war continued and the submarine's versatility became recognized, the undersea force was called upon to undertake all manner of special missions. At war's end, submarines were ready to play the part of aircraft-warning radar pickets—a role formerly detailed to destroyers. Less vulnerable when it came to aircraft observation, submarines were readied for this new task after tests with the submarine FINBACK had proved highly successful. Plans were made to furnish 24 submarines with the necessary radar equipment and employ them as pickets in the invasion of Japan. This novel employment of submarines, and, in fact, many of the extraordinary special missions to which they were assigned, must have surprised the pre-war conservatives who thought of the submersible as a warcraft whose operations were limited to torpedo attacks. But those who knew them best had been otherwise confident about their capacities. By the end of the war, submariners had gone far to convince the world that (to paraphrase Kipling) "there isn't a thing under heaven or sea the beggar can't learn to do."

The first missions, executed by the SubsAsiatic pioneers, involved the carrying of supplies to the defenders of Corregidor, and the evacuation of personnel. Relief and personnel rescue missions continued as the Japanese offensive crashed over the Malay Barrier and eddied around the island stepping-stones to Australia. Transportation of intelligence agents to and from enemy-held territory was the next undertaking. Strewn with islands which were populated in the main by friendly or passively disinterested natives, the Southwest Pacific offered unusual opportunity for intelligence operations. One of the more important services accomplished was the relaying of information on enemy ship movements as observed by coast watchers. Many agents of the Allied Intelligence Bureau and Netherlands Field Intelligence Service were transported to and from their dangerous posts by American submarines. Other early special missions included a search for refugees and a shore bombardment.

Few special missions were more dramatic than those accomplished in the war's opening weeks. Every mission demanded iron nerve from all hands, and all the imagination and initiative the commanding officer could muster. Again, these "firsts" were ventures into the Unknown, and the perils inherent in all were magnified by lack of experience and precedent.

The first submarine to perform a special mission in the Southwest Pacific was SEAWOLF. As previously related, she loaded anti-aircraft ammunition at Darwin, Australia, and departed on January 16 for Corregidor. If her skipper, Lieutenant Commander Warder, was uneasy sitting on top of 37 tons of

.50-caliber ammunition, he did not wear the fact on his sleeve. But he must have entertained a few anxious doubts. Crammed "to the gills" with such cargo, SEA-WOLF, under a depth-charging, might blow up like a giant grenade. The crew was indisposed to worry. As one of them stoically expressed it, "If they hit us, they'll just blow us a little higher, that's all."

Although the WOLF on her northward journey sighted a flock of enemy ships, the depth-charging failed to eventuate. Traveling submerged by day and on the surface at night, she pursued a cautious and steady course. One night she spied a Japanese task force—three or four cruisers, a squadron of destroyers, seven transports. Here was the sort of situation which made special missions unattractive to submariners—a whole gallery of targets, and not a chance to shoot. The mission was primary, and SEAWOLF perforce continued on her way. But when the Jap ships were under the horizon, Warder brought his submarine to the surface and radioed a detailed description of the enemy force to the Submarine Command.

Not long after that, the WOLF had to dive to evade a destroyer which loomed up out of nowhere, late for the task force rendezvous. The DD failed to detect the submarine, and SEAWOLF went on her way. The Japanese had fastened a blockade on the Philippines, but Warder took the WOLF through without detection, and a PT-boat escorted her in through the minefields to Corregidor.

On leaving, SEAWOLF took out with her 25 Army and Navy aviators, a load of submarine spare parts and 16 torpedoes for delivery to Soerabaja. Once more the Japanese blockade had to be run, and again the WOLF slipped through. When she tied up at Holland Pier in Soerabaja, she had her first real breather since December 8th. Aside from the brief stop at Darwin, SEAWOLF had been steadily on the go for two months.

Trout Goes to Rainbow's End

The second U.S. submarine to pioneer a special mission was TROUT (Lieutenant Commander F. W. Fenno). Of the Pacific Fleet Force, she enters this SubsAsiatic chapter by way of orders dispatching her to Corregidor with 3,500 rounds of desperately needed anti-aircraft ammunition. Return trip, she was to carry what was undoubtedly the most valuable ballast ever loaded into a submarine. Certainly TROUT's was a mission extraordinary.

Having glimpsed the Jap strike at Midway, she was home at the Pearl Harbor Submarine Base, where technicians were reducing her superstructure's silhouette, when she received the orders which rushed her to the Philippines. To provide stowage space in the torpedo rooms for the ammunition cargo, the heavy torpedo skids had to be shifted topside and carried in the superstructure. This was done at the base by Lieutenant Commander Tom Eddy's repair gang. The "ammo" was then stowed at special-delivery speed, and TROUT was standing out to sea on the morning of January 12th.

First stop, Midway, where she replenished her fuel supply ("topped off," in seagoing vernacular). Then she headed on a great circle course north of Wake and Marcus, following a route calculated to take her through Balintang Channel above Luzon. Running south through enemy-patrolled waters west of Luzon, she was off Corregidor on February 3rd. Japanese bombers were hammering the Rock, so TROUT remained submerged until nightfall when a patrol boat came out to guide her in through the minefields.

Jap planes were winging across the sky and fiery tracers were soaring up from PT-boats in Manila Bay as the submarine groped her way into the lagoon and tied up at South Dock. Immediately the submariners pitched in to unload the precious ammunition—a tedious job, as the shells had to be passed one by one through the hatches, hand to hand. A party of Philippine Scouts joined the stevedoring, and some war-worn Army trucks lumbered out on the dock to pick up the dangerous cargo.

Grapefruit, cigarettes, canned food and news were also passed out to Corregidor's hungry defenders. Ammunition ashore, the crew's next job was returning the skids to the torpedo rooms. There were six of these to be moved, each weighing over 900 pounds, and no cranes on the dock to lend a hand. Elbow grease and callus got the skids down a narrow torpedo-room loading hatch, and then there were six 3,000-pound torpedoes to be lugged aboard and stowed below. All this under the compulsion of making haste slowly, while the gunfire over on Bataan fluttered like summer lightning and any moment a shower of bombs might fall from the night sky. By 0300 every man aboard TROUT was ready to "hit the sack."

Such jobs as the foregoing were soon to be commonplace undertakings for submariners on special mission assignments. But TROUT's mission did assume a peculiar distinction. En route to Corregidor, Fenno felt that his submarine could use more ballast.

"Our weight conditions had been figured out on paper," he remarked afterwards. "We were supposed to have had a leeway of about five thousand pounds. This, as we approached Corregidor, seemed hardly enough. Consequently, with our arrival report, we requested twenty-five tons of ballast, preferably sand bags so that we could move them around as necessary to effect a trim."

Reporting in person to Admiral Rockwell at Corregidor Naval Headquarters, TROUT's captain learned that sandbags were not to be had on the embattled Rock. How about cement bags? Admiral Rockwell shook his head. Every last stick and stone on Corregidor was shoring up the fortifications. Neither cement nor sandbags could be spared. But wait—

In the bank vaults at Manila there had been a large gold store. This bullion, along with a fortune in silver, currency and securities, had been spirited to Corregidor for safekeeping. If TROUT could use bars of gold for ballast—

TROUT could, and did! Two tons of gold bars. And 18 tons of silver pesos, plus stacks of negotiable securities and bags of vital State Department documents and U.S. Mail. Throughout the night of February 4, in a dark scene lit by the gunfire on Bataan, gleaming yellow bars and clinking sacks of silver were stowed in the submarine's holds. Freighted with this treasure, TROUT submerged off Corregidor at dawn, and the following evening she went out through the minefields and stood seaward like a submersible National Bank.

Her orders called for a brief war patrol in the East China Sea area, and Fenno headed her northward on the hunt for enemy shipping. Twice enemy vessels were sighted, and each time TROUT rose to the occasion. Gold or no gold, Fenno was ready for a fight. Five days out of Corregidor, with a Japanese freighter in view, he directed a submerged attack and pitched three torpedoes at the target. Two explosions sent the AK under. Post-war inquest identified the vessel as CHUWA MARU, 2,718 tons.

That night TROUT received orders to head back for Pearl. Homeward bound, off the Bonin Islands she sighted a small Jap patrol craft. Three torpedoes were fired, one struck the mark, and the 200-ton PC was blown from the Pacific's surface.

The remainder of the voyage was uneventful. Reaching Pearl Harbor, TROUT's fabulous ballast was unloaded for transshipment to the States. On a mission which lasted 57 days, she had been to Rainbow's End, picked up the jackpot, made a home-run through enemy infested waters and sunk two Jap vessels along the way.

As some sailor remarked, there may have been gold bricks aboard TROUT on that special mission, but there was no gold-bricking.

Other Pioneer Missions

While TROUT had been loading gold at Corregidor, SEADRAGON arrived at the Rock. Up from Soerabaja on passenger and freight service, she took aboard 19 members of a Naval Radio Intelligence Unit, an Army major, two naval officers, 23 torpedoes, 3,000 pounds of radio equipment and two tons of submarine spares. All of which she delivered to Soerabaja on schedule.

Between February 5 and February 22, SARGO (Lieutenant Commander Tyrrell D. Jacobs) carried one million rounds of .30-caliber ammunition from Soerabaja to the hard-pressed Philippine forces at Paraug, Polloc Harbor, Mindanao. On return runs she brought out 24 American soldiers and conveyed them to Soerabaja.

For Commander Jacobs these special missions must have been trying in the extreme. For SARGO was the submarine that had ended her first patrol with a zero score after making eight attacks in which 13 torpedoes were fired for a straight string of 13 misses. With that sort of jinx aboard, another skipper might have hesitated at attempting to breach the enemy's Philippine blockade. But SARGO delivered the goods and scored a successful patrol. Ironically enough, it was when she reached friendly water at the conclusion of these missions that Dame Fortune turned against her and almost "did her in."

Late February she left the Philippine-Netherlands Indies area for Fremantle, West Australia. On March 4, about a half-day's run from Fremantle, the clock at 1338, she sighted a two-engine land plane some five miles distant. Jacobs gave the order, "Take her down!" and SARGO immediately submerged—a maneuver that proved most fortunate.

The plane was hunting a Japanese submarine which had been reported by the destroyer WHIPPLE. Although the Submarine Command had informed the Air Wing Headquarters, the RAAF pilot had not been briefed on SARGO's arrival in the area. Having sighted SARGO at an estimated range of nine miles, he made a bee-line for the submarine.

SARGO submerged sluggishly. She had been bucking a heavy sea, all main ballast tanks blown dry, and safety and negative tanks dry.

To quote Jacob's patrol report:

At about 1341 heard one bomb explode on port quarter, no damage to ship. Stern planesman allowed down angle to get away from him. Stopped motors, blew bow buoyancy and forward group, checked descent at 170 feet. Vented tanks at fraction of a second too late and broached. Believe ship was at 50 feet when a second bomb exploded over the conning tower. This was a terrific explosion, glass rained down, power and lighting lost, depth gauges were put out of order, various other casualties.

The blast came within an ace of sinking the submarine. The after end of the conning tower was badly sprung, and at depths short of 80 feet the lower part of the conning-tower door failed to seat. Gallons of water poured into the control room. Both periscope exit windows and prisms were broken. Three-fourths of the light globes were shattered, and three toilet bowls were broken. Other internal injuries were suffered by SARGO. Only expert submarining on the part of her captain and all hands prevented black tragedy.

They brought her to the surface that night and reached port the next day. All hands probably agreed they would rather undertake special missions than undergo bombing by friendly aircraft.

While SARGO had been on her missions to Mindanao, SWORDFISH ran the blockade to Corregidor. At the Rock on February 19, she took aboard a distinguished list of passengers—Emanuel Quezon, President of the Philippines, and party of nine. Destination, San Jose, Panay, was reached on February 22nd.

SWORDFISH then returned to Corregidor to evacuate the United States High Commissioner, Mr. Francis B. Sayre, and party of eleven, plus five Navy men. The passengers were to be taken to Fremantle.

"You're going out with an ace submarine skipper," Admiral Rockwell said to Commissioner Sayre in parting. "He'll get you through."

The skipper was Chester Smith. He got them through.

Another special mission drama was enacted at this time by S-39—Lieutenant James W. (Red) Coe and Company. Like the other pioneers in the Philippines-Netherlands Indies theater, S-39 had been having her ups and downs in the battle against the Japanese offensive. In the first week of the war she had attacked a big AK without verifiable result. On her second patrol in January she had fired a shot at and missed an enemy submarine.

February she was wandering through the war-swept seas with all hell loose around her. No one knew when a submarine could get back to base, or if the base would be on hand when one got there. Soerabaja was disintegrating. Admiral Hart was gone. Singapore fell on February 15th. ABDACOM, General Wavell, departed for India on February 24th. Only Bataan and Corregidor were holding out as the Japanese pincers closed on Java.

Then it was that ComSubsAsiatic assigned S-39 to her mission. A mission to rescue Rear Admiral Spooner, RN, and a large party of British refugees from Singapore who had landed on minuscule Chebia Island in the South China Sea.

Among the refugees, apparently, were a number of Australian aviators. Somehow they had rigged a transmitter and sent out a plaintive S.O.S. Japanese scouts were in the neighborhood, and if rescue were effected it would have to be soon. S-39 was ordered to locate the marooned Britishers and bring them off to safety.

Locating a fly-speck island in a zone teeming with enemy patrols demanded a high order of submarining. Locating a party of refugees in an island hideout demanded something more. Coe and company answered the demand by reaching the island on February 27 in plenty of time for the rendezvous.

Periscope view showed a palm-jungled shoreline, a strip of white beach, no sign of Japs. No sign of refugees either, but Coe assumed they were hiding in the bush.

After nightfall he maneuvered the old S-boat close in and flashed a message through the tropic dark. No answer. He kept the signal going while all hands waited with crossed fingers, hoping the light would not be spotted by lurking enemies. The light remained unanswered.

At daybreak Coe withdrew. The sun blazed up, and S-39 waited offshore, submerged. At nightfall she moved in for a repeat performance—furtive signals—no answer—another flash of code—finally a radio call. Chebia Island remained as silent as an oil painting.

"Tomorrow night," Coe told his crew, "we go ashore."

There was no lack of volunteers. Special missions had their drawbacks, but an opportunity to get out in the air and stretch one's legs on a tropic beach was not one of them.

The men crowded forward. Automatics were buckled on. Coe briefed them on what might happen —Japs—anything. They launched a boat, Coe with them, and paddled in.

Beginning at one end of the island, they started working through the brush to the other end. Tiger-striped in moonlight, the island lay as though asleep —make a wrong step and it would rouse with a roar.

Its nocturnal slumbers continued undisturbed. The submariners could find no human occupant. All they found was a trample of footprints on a sandy beach—footprints driven to the water's edge where undoubtedly a Japanese small boat had been grounded.

"We were sorry for those people," Coe commented later. "The Japanese prisons were tough."

Five days later S-39 repaid the futile mission to Chebia by penetrating a destroyer screen and torpedoing the 6,500-ton Japanese oil tanker ERIMU. As the tanker sank under a cloud of flame, the destroyers rushed over to attack the S-boat. Coe got her out from under a furious depth-bomb barrage, and the mission ended as a successful patrol.

PERMIT, under Lieutenant Wreford (Moon) Chapple, was the next submarine to visit Corregidor on special mission. The submarine was to be placed in the service of General MacArthur.

Chapple was the skipper who brought S-38 through a murderous depth-charging in Lingayen Harbor. After that experience, Hades would have been a pleasant port of call, and the veteran Chapple was prepared for anything the Japs could throw when he set out to take PERMIT through the blockade to the Rock. The enemy had tightened the anti-submarine screen to stop the undersea traffic to Corregidor, but PERMIT was there at the end of February. She delivered to the defenders most of her service allowance of ammunition. In return she received three torpedoes, ten naval officers and 41 enlisted men.

PERMIT was not employed by General MacArthur. Entering passenger service, she left Corregidor for Fremantle. She reached that Australian port on April 7th.

Meanwhile Chapple's old boat—the indestructible S-38—was also on special mission under command of Lieutenant Henry G. Munson. Patched and perhaps a little shaky after her Lingayen Gulf foray, S-38 had gone to Java to fight in the battle for the Malay Barrier.

The Japanese advance down Makassar Strait was one prong of a coordinated attack on the Netherlands East Indies. On February 18, submarines were stationed in Lombok Strait to oppose the invasion of Bali. Later in February, ComSubsAsiatic stationed five submarines in the Java Sea to cover the approaches to Soerabaja. One of these was staunch S-38. Then on February 26 she was assigned her special mission. She was to patrol a line from Bawean Island to Soerabaja and to investigate a reported landing on Bawean Island. Her primary mission was to bombard the radio station on that island.

This was the first submarine bombardment mission of the war. S-38 was fortuitously close to her objective at the time she received her orders, and four hours later Bawean was in sight.

Munson set the course for a point off the town of Sangapura on the southern coast where the radio station was located. As the submarine approached the anchorage in the misty twilight of early morning, a slow, steady signal light was observed signaling to seaward from the center of the town. The code was unfamiliar. Reasoning that the signals were intended for Japanese submarines or surface craft somewhere seaward, Munson gave the order to dive.

Submerged, S-38 loitered off shore, awaiting a clearer view of the situation. At 0600 periscope scrutiny revealed the harbor occupied by two auxiliary schooners and a number of small sailing craft, the schooners standing to the westward inside the reefs.

Munson gave the order, "Battle stations!"

S-38 surfaced. Gunners hit the deck on the double. They opened up with a slow, controlled fire at an average gun range of 5,100 yards. A radio station could not be discovered, so the gun crew, using a white house on the pier as point of aim, systematically swept the shoreline, up, down, right and left, in 100 yards and 2 mil steps respectively.

Fire was returned from a small gun on the beach. After two shots it was summarily extinguished by a shell from the submarine. The deck gun had fired 42 rounds when a destroyer was sighted bearing in. Munson ordered a fast dive. The enemy ship materialized as a sailboat, and S-38 again battle-surfaced.

Thirty rounds were fired at an average range of 4,300 yards. European houses were picked as main targets, and ten rounds were fired at the native settlement where it was thought troops might be quartered. Several large conflagrations were started, and one shell apparently hit a small ammunition dump. The bombardment thereupon ceased as all ammunition had been expended.

Military damage to enemy installations—if any—was probably negligible. But S-38 had demonstrated the submarine's capacity for shore bombardment. And the demonstration was made in the face of enemy forces on the very eve of the Battle of the Java Sea. As that battle opened, S-38 distinguished herself by accomplishing an extraordinary rescue.

Blockade running—evacuation of personnel—transport of supplies—search for marooned refugees—shore bombardment—in hazards encountered and difficulties overcome, the special mission episodes related are typical of the many which followed. Altogether, American submarines accomplished 289 special missions during World War II. Those successfully undertaken by the pioneers set the pace.

Entering the Java Sea Battle, S-38 set the pace for a new type of special mission—life-saving.

The Battle of the Java Sea

S-38's crew were unaware that they were about to set a pace. Life-saving duty as a submarine assignment was in the future. Having carried out orders concerning Bawean Island, S-38 resumed war patrol.

Nor were her submariners aware that a great sea battle was in the making. The world outside the pressure hull is remote to those in a submersible. Particularly so when the "pressure" outside the hull dictates precautionary radio silence and submergence during daylight. Information then comes in brief radio fragments at night, and the day's war picture can only be surmised.

On the night of February 28, nearing the end of her patrol, S-38 was on the surface, homeward bound. The Diesels were drumming a good sound, and the old S-boat was going like a horse to its stable. Then—

A call from the lookout. Captain on the bridge with focussed glasses. A dark blur on the water off the starboard bow—a low, flat, unidentifiable silhouette that might be drifting wreckage, a mat of seaweed or a huddle of sampans.

Wreckage, Munson decided. But he couldn't take chances. Ordering out the gun crew, he held the submarine at top speed, veering over for a look-see.

As the submarine neared the blurred mass, a voice cried out of the darkness, "My God, they're not finished with us yet!"

Astounded at hearing English, Munson answered the cry with a hail. "Who are you?"

A weird chorus of muffled voices rose in the dark. Someone shouted, "We're men of His Majesty's Ship ELECTRA!"

S-38 hove to. The sea seemed alive with struggling men. Men clinging to life rafts, floating timbers, clutched together in a sprawl of debris. It was necessary to launch a boat to get them aboard. They were sighted around 0400, and dawn was tinting the sky when the last man was picked up.

Plucked as from a common grave, they crowded the submarine—fifty-four of them. They were oil smeared, lacerated, sick, half-drowned, burnt from fire and sea salt and thirst. Tottering anatomies, they had to be carried down the hatch. Seventeen were badly wounded. One of them was dying. They were the men of HMS ELECTRA, sunk by Japanese destroyers in the Battle of the Java Sea.

The men of the S-38 took them in, fed them, tended their wounds, and carried them to safety—the first of many open-sea rescues to be accomplished by submarines. By way of an encore, S-37 (Lieutenant J. C. Dempsey) in the same area rescued two American sailors, survivors of the cruiser DE RUYTER, and supplied a boatload of the Dutch cruiser's men with five days' provisions.

This human flotsam was the residue of a violent naval engagement which cost the ABDA Allies their last foothold on the Malay Barrier. Loss of Java and Sumatra had been foreordained by the fall of Singapore and the Japanese occupation (February 18) of Bali. American submarines stationed in Lombok Strait to oppose the Bali landing were unable to stem the enemy's all-out drive. The Japanese

already controlled the beachheads when SEAL, SEAWOLF and SAILFISH got there.

The five U.S. submarines stationed in the Java Sea were also unable to slow the Japanese advance. Several British and Dutch submarines on Java Sea patrol were similarly ineffective. Shallow waters in the area greatly hampered submarine operations. In pushing through the East India archipelagoes, the Japanese made good use of this hindering factor by moving their convoys close inshore.

On February 25 strong reinforcements reached the Japanese on Bali. In command of the ABDA Forces, Admiral Helfrich determined to make a final stand. Commanding the ABDA Fleet, Admiral Doorman patrolled the Java Sea, prepared to engage the invader.

On the afternoon of February 27, Doorman retired to Soerabaja to refuel his destroyers. While there, he learned that a Japanese invasion fleet was off Bawean. Immediately he headed his flagship out of Soerabaja, signalling to his naval force,

AM PROCEEDING TO INTERCEPT ENEMY UNIT . . . FOLLOW ME

Doorman's force consisted of the Dutch light cruisers DE RUYTER and JAVA, the British heavy cruiser EXETER, the Australian light cruiser PERTH, and USS HOUSTON up from Timor. Supporting destroyers were the Dutch KORTENAER and WITTE DE WITH; the British ENCOUNTER, JUPITER and ELECTRA; and the American four-stackers EDWARDS, ALDEN, FORD and PAUL JONES. Steaming from Soerabaja, the five cruisers and nine destroyers constituted the strongest surface force the Allies could at that hour muster in the Southwest Pacific.

It was zero hour. The Japanese armada north of Java proved to be a convoy of transports escorted by several cruisers and destroyers, plus a covering force of three heavy cruisers and a number of destroyers, plus a support force of two heavy cruisers and four destroyers.

Outnumbered, the ABDA Force was at another disadvantage. Bilingual, it lacked a common language necessary for rapid communication. Without common flag signals (and some of the ships lacked the code books needed for translation), communications were slowed to a stutter. Fast tactical moves were accordingly impossible. The results proved tragic.

Enemy was sighted some 30 miles southeast of Bawean. Time: about 1600. The Japanese opened fire at 30,000 yards as Doorman drove forward to close the range. During the gun duel that followed, DE RUYTER suffered a damaging hit, and JAVA was also struck. A short time later HOUSTON was pierced by an

8-inch dud which smashed through to her engine room.

A confused maneuver followed, in which EXETER was disabled by a shell that blasted her boiler room. KORTENAER was struck and sunk by a destroyer torpedo. ELECTRA, rushing to EXETER's aid, ran into three Japanese destroyers. Multiple shell hits blasted ELECTRA, sending her to the bottom.

About 1930 the battle slacked off, and Doorman maneuvered his battered force toward Soerabaja. Their torpedoes expended and fuel tanks almost empty, the four American destroyers left the column and went on ahead.

As Doorman's force moved on to the west, HMS JUPITER was torpedoed and sunk, apparently by a Japanese submarine. Japanese destroyers were encountered in the night, and fire from the ABDA cruisers put two out of action. According to Japanese assertions, this was the only damage suffered by their fleet during the battle.

At 2315 Japanese warships, closing in, reopened fire on the ABDA column. Under a blaze of star shells the Allied cruisers were exposed. While the column turned away, JAVA was struck (apparently by a torpedo) and flames burst from her stern. While JAVA was sinking, DE RUYTER was hit by a torpedo. Explosion and fire made a volcano of Doorman's flagship, and she sank a few moments later.

Of the ABDA force only USS HOUSTON and the Australian cruiser PERTH remained. Doorman got off a message to these cruisers just before DE RUYTER went down. "Do not stand by for survivors. Proceed to Batavia." Running along the coast of Java, they managed to reach Sundra Strait. There they raced headlong into a Japanese invasion force—five cruisers, eleven destroyers, armed transports. Struck by a

hurricane of shells, PERTH went to the bottom. HOUSTON fought it out for over an hour. In spite of her useless after turret, she sank two transports and scored hits on the Japanese warships. But she was one against a fleet. Lamed by torpedoes, her topside shot to shambles, afire, listing, her ammunition running out, she finally went down. Over half of her crew went down with her. The remainder were picked up and spent the rest of the war in Japanese prison camps.

So ended the Battle of the Java Sea, and with it the Malay Barrier was lost. The battle was hardly over before Japanese troops occupied beachheads west of Soerabaja. The following morning (March 1) the ABDA Fleet was dissolved. Admiral Glassford ordered the remaining American ships to proceed to Australia.

That same day, the submarine SEAL (Lieutenant Commander Hurd) attacked and possibly damaged a Japanese light cruiser in Lombok Strait. In the waters off Bali, SEAWOLF attacked a destroyer, a transport and two other ships, probably hitting them for damage. In the waters off Java, S-38 reported a torpedo hit on a YUBARI-class cruiser, but this, too, could not be confirmed.

Confirmable, however, is the fact that while the Japanese conquered the Netherlands East Indies, they had yet to conquer the surrounding seas. The ABDA surface fleet was gone. But the submarines remained.

They remained to slash the Japanese communication lines. To penetrate the enemy-held harbors. To litter the beaches with water-logged supplies and wrecked ships. To strew the sea bottom with the hulks of sunken merchantmen and the bones of Imperial naval vessels.

JUNGLE WARFARE! Crew of S-39, led by Skipper "Red" Coe, searches for Singapore refugees on tropic island. Had the enemy intercepted the call for help? *Were Jap marksmen waiting in ambush? (Story is told on page 81.) This was but one of many dangerous special missions performed by submariners.*

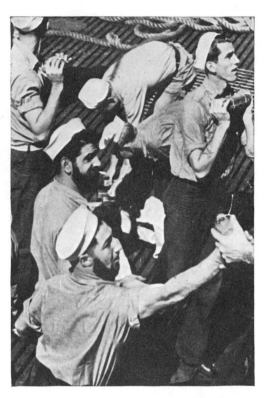

FORTUNE ABOARD! All that glitters isn't gold on deck of USS Trout—but a lot of it is! She won a jackpot on this special mission!

PIRATES? No, men of Trout unloading gold from the Philippines! Are they goldbricking!

RECONNAISSANCE PHOTOGRAPH taken by the USS Pollock off the North East Coast of Honshu Island, Japan, shows shore installations and a beached Japanese freighter.

This picture, taken March 17, 1943 is typical of the intelligence missions which were constantly undertaken by U. S. submarines. Such information was assessed by ONI.

CHAPTER 8

SUBMARINES ATLANTIC

The Atlantic Front

When the prospect of a two-ocean war loomed as a thunderhead on America's horizon, naval strategists began to think in terms of a dual fleet. Actually the Navy's forces were divided three ways when, on February 1, 1941, three fleets were organized: United States Atlantic Fleet, United States Pacific Fleet, United States Asiatic Fleet. With this new organization, Submarines, Patrol Force, came to be designated Submarines, Atlantic Fleet.

Rear Admiral Richard S. Edwards, formerly in command of Submarines, Patrol Force, became Commander Submarines, Atlantic Fleet (ComSubLant). Admiral Edwards was a square-jawed officer who had captained his first submarine, C-3, in the winter of 1912-1913. In 1913 he commanded the first submarine division to be based in the Panama Canal Zone. During World War I, he saw active duty aboard USS Kentucky, USS Kansas and USS Arkansas. Later in his career he did a tour of duty in the Pacific and attended the Naval War College at Newport, R.I. In June 1935, he assumed command of Submarine Squadron Six with additional duty as Commander SubDiv Twelve. In 1937 he was commander of the Submarine Base at New London. And in December 1940, after six months as captain of the USS Colorado, he became Commander Submarines, Patrol Force.

As ComSubLant in February 1941, Admiral Edwards faced the task of readying his Atlantic submarine force for the impending war. It was a task as broad and latitudinal as the Atlantic. At this date the iron-fisted Nazi *Wehrmacht* was hammering Europe to a crimson welter. England was on one knee, bloody but unbowed, fighting desperately for survival. In North Africa, German and Italian tanks were smashing their way toward Suez. U-boats roamed the Atlantic from Norway to Dakar and from Greenland to Tierra del Fuego. German shells had swept the West Indies port of Curacao and torpedoes were sinking ships off Brazil, in the Caribbean and off the Florida Keys. The American Merchant Marine left our piers with Lend-Lease goods and many of its freighters did not come back. In cities on the Atlantic seaboard, people discussed blackout curtains, and heard lectures on how to extinguish thermite bombs with sand. Americans were fast becoming aware that the Atlantic, once leagues wide, was only a few hours from the European front—a fact they had dimly perceived in 1918, but had neglected to remember afterward.

May 1918—that was when the first German cruiser-type submarine, U-151, crossed the Atlantic to strike at American coastal shipping. Under Herr Kapitan von Nostitz, this daring raider sank dozens of vessels, small and large, in United States waters.

The sinking of the heavy cruiser USS San Diego off Fire Island, and the hulling of a battleship in waters off Delaware were attributed to mines laid by Von Nostitz' U-boat. Four others followed U-151 to play havoc off the eastern seaboard that last summer of the First World War. Would Nazi submarines achieve a repeat performance? Could modern U-boats launch planes to bomb coastal cities? In Boston, New York City, Jacksonville, anxious citizenry looked to the Navy for defense. And the Navy, facing conflict on two oceans, was now called upon to defend the world's longest coastline—a line that extended from Newfoundland to Panama, and from Panama to Alaska. With the forces available, it would have to make its defensive measures stretch a long, 7,000-mile way.

This problem was particularly pressing on ComSubLant. With the exception of the two new coastal submarines, MACKEREL and MARLIN, the submarine organization in the Atlantic consisted entirely of the older B-, O-, R-, and S-class boats. Some of these old-timers were veterans of World War I, rugged enough in their day, and still serviceable for training purposes, but hardly up to trading blows with the stream-lined sea and air forces of Nazi Germany. The newer S-boats were ocean-goers but limited by the deficiencies common to their class. Instructed to groom these submarines for combat duty, Admiral Edwards was presented with a tremendous job. To it he brought a salty sense of humor and a capacity for work that, coupled with experience, spelled success.

New-construction submarines, commissioned on the East Coast, became temporarily part of Submarines, Atlantic Fleet, for training purposes only. MACKEREL and MARLIN, experimental-type submarines launched in 1941, were assigned to the Submarine School Squadron. In April 1941, Admiral King, Commander-in-Chief of the Atlantic Fleet, proposed that one division of six fleet-type submarines be retained in the Atlantic to serve as components of a "striking force." Chief of Naval Operations disapproved the proposal, as the modern, long-legged submarines were needed for duty in the Pacific.

It was originally planned to divide Submarines, Atlantic Fleet, into three groups—Submarine Force One, Submarine Force Two, Submarine Force Three.

This plan did not assign a task to Submarine Force One. Nor did it define this force, other than to state: "Submarine Force One will be composed of submarines, submarine tenders and submarine bases not assigned to Submarine Force Two. Not less than five submarines must remain based on the Submarine Base, Coco Solo." Presumably Submarine Force One was to be used strategically in the defense of home waters and the Panama Canal, and to furnish services to the Submarine School, Sound School and various anti-submarine groups.

Submarine Force Two was to be composed of submarines destined for overseas duty. Intentions were to base this force at Gibraltar. As a task force it would raid enemy shipping in the Mediterranean. It would operate under the British Commander-in-Chief, Mediterranean, while remaining a part of the U.S. Atlantic Fleet for administration purposes.

Submarine Force Three would be detached from the U.S. Atlantic Fleet and be assigned to the U.S. Naval Force, North Europe. Basing in British home waters, it would raid enemy shipping in an area to be designated by the British Vice Admiral, Submarines.

These plans were later modified and to some extent redesigned, but the over-all tasks assigned the submarines in the Atlantic remained much as described.

On March 17, 1941, CNO directed CinCLant to form a task force within the Atlantic Fleet. This force was to be entitled the Submarine Patrol Group, and it was to be made up of Submarine Squadron Twenty and Submarine Divisions Eleven, Forty-three and Forty-one. As such it would be part of the Support Force, and operate from two bases—one at Gibraltar, the other in England.

After a careful review of the units available for this group, Admiral Edwards proposed to exclude the R-boats, deficient in size, spare parts and sea-keeping qualities. He proposed a reorganization which would provide for the Patrol Group two squadrons—one composed of 17 S-class submarines which would operate from the base in England, and the other composed of three B-class and seven S-class submarines which would operate from the base at Gibraltar. The GRIFFIN was selected as tender for the former group, and the BEAVER would serve the group at Gibraltar. Admiral Edwards' proposal was accepted, and the submarines were readied and trained for their Patrol Group assignment.

Plans for the submarine bases in Europe went forward. Gare Lock in the Clyde area was chosen for a base in England. The location was relatively secure against enemy action, and ample overhaul and repair facilities could be maintained in this shipbuilding littoral. Quarters for the submariners were located, and storerooms and magazines planned for supply.

Gibraltar, on the other hand, seemed too exposed to enemy action to warrant establishment of extensive overhaul facilities. With France crumbling at its back, and Franco Spain standing by like a gunman, Gibraltar might be felled at any moment. Accordingly, plans for a submarine base called for tender maintenance only and the construction of huts to augment the housing, storage and repair facilities on hand.

High priority was given the construction of these overseas bases. To serve as coordinator in all matters relating to the project, Commander J. P. Compton was assigned to the Office of the Chief of Naval Operations as ComSubLant's representative. Lieutenant L. D. Follmer was assigned to ComSubLant's staff as planning officer. Equipment was assembled at Quonset Point, R.I., and at State Pier, New London. Consumable supplies and maintenance materials were gathered at the Naval Supply Depot at Norfolk and the Naval Depot at Bayonne.

While the Gibraltar and Gare Lock projects were on the planning table, attention was focused on Bermuda. War plans called for the establishment of a submarine group to enter intensive training for defense operations in the Bermuda area. Therefore CinCLant, late in May 1941, urged the acquirement of Ordnance Island, St. George's Harbor, Bermuda, for development as an advance submarine base.

In June, Ordnance Island was leased from the Corporation of St. George's and construction of a temporary base to accommodate six submarines was begun. R-boat and S-boat repair facilities were installed, and a detachment of boats from Submarine Squadron Seven was sent to Bermuda.

Meantime, Submarines Atlantic was getting a taste of realistic action. The United States, making good as the Arsenal of Democracy, was sending ton after ton of food and munitions to embattled Britain. In the spring of 1941 the U-boats began their "wolf-pack" tactics which threatened to sever the trans-Atlantic supply lines. In June 1941, United States submarines commenced anti-submarine patrols in search for German and Italian undersea raiders in the Atlantic and Caribbean. These patrols were not established as a regular and continuous operation, but they were ordered from time to time as intelligence reports indicated that belligerent submarines were operating within the extended American "safety belt."

In 1940 the Caribbean Naval District had been established under command of Rear Admiral Raymond A. Spruance, with headquarters at San Juan, Puerto Rico. Covered by this district were the new West Indies anchorages leased to the U.S. in return for the 50 destroyers sent to Britain. In June 1941, submarines from the Submarine Base at St. Thomas, Virgin Islands, operating under Commander Caribbean Sea Frontier, began patrols in the Virgin Passage. German or Italian submarines were reported seen in this area where ship traffic was heavy.

On September 11, after the American merchantman STEEL SEAFARER was sunk by German aircraft in the Red Sea, President Roosevelt issued his "shoot-on-sight" order. Thereafter, Navy patrol craft were directed to open fire on any submarine or commerce raider attacking merchantmen of any flag inside American defense areas. Before the issuance of this decree, United States vessels on patrol had been instructed to trail naval vessels of belligerent powers and report their movements in plain language. Now

the submarine forces were ordered to destroy any German or Italian combatant naval vessel that was encountered.

This was tantamount to war. And the open break almost came when wolf-packing U-boats attacked a convoy bound for Iceland in mid-October. Acting as escort, the new destroyer USS KEARNEY was damaged by a German torpedo. Eleven men were killed by the blast which wrecked the KEARNEY's forward engine room.

Then the naval tanker SALINAS and the destroyer REUBEN JAMES were torpedoed in the Atlantic. Although hit three times, the tanker managed to reach port. REUBEN JAMES, struck amidships while escorting a convoy, went to the bottom, taking 100 lives with her. After this—the first sinking of a U.S. naval vessel in the Second World War—open hostilities were expected hourly.

The waters were hot in the North Atlantic where U-boats were boldly making surface attacks on shipping off Newfoundland. Accordingly, late in the autumn of 1941 five submarines of Squadron Five, plus MACKEREL, were ordered to Argentia, N.F., where plans to establish an anti-submarine patrol were in prospect. GRIFFIN went along to act as tender, and Admiral Edwards accompanied the group in VIXEN. No patrols were made, however, and shortly after the Pearl Harbor raid this force returned to New London.

Its pre-war activities had the Atlantic Submarine Force on the alert and in fighting trim for the full-dress conflict that came on the heels of the Japanese attack. When Germany and Italy, in conformance with the Tripartite Pact, declared war on the United States on December 11, 1941, Submarines, Atlantic Fleet, was ready.

Perhaps in the readying of these submarines and submariners, the Atlantic Submarine Command made its major contribution to the war effort. A testing ground for the submarine patrolling under authentic wartime conditions, the Atlantic also served as a training school for officers and crews going into battle. In the Atlantic most of the Pacific Fleet submarines first tried their sea legs. A great many submariners who went to Hawaii, Australia, the Philippines and beyond were schooled in the waters off Maine, Rhode Island, Connecticut, Florida, Puerto Rico, Panama. As the war developed, and Atlantic targets were found fewer and farther between, the S-boats and fleet-type submarines were dispatched from the "Western Ocean" to fight in the Pacific.

The Atlantic was a hard and exacting Alma Mater, and its undersea graduates soon proved the value of their education. Thanks to Admiral Edwards and his staff, the submarines and submariners had solid ground under their sea legs.

Atlantic Operations (Anti-Submarine Training and Fleet Sonar School)

Although history may to some extent repeat itself, its wars are cut to unique patterns based on the varying capabilities of the opposing leaders and on the weapons newly developed and available. No war follows the design of the previous one. Each has its individual features.

One peculiar feature of World War II concerned undersea warfare. Whereas U.S. submarines, riding an up-curve on the graph, were devoted to the sinking of surface vessels in the Pacific, U.S. surface forces in the Atlantic concentrated on an all-out war to sink submarines. In either case, the Navy bore down on the priority target. In the Pacific that target was composed of the Japanese merchant fleet and the Imperial Japanese Navy. In the Atlantic it was the Nazi U-boat. Submarine war in the Pacific—anti-submarine war in the Atlantic—it seems safe to assume that failure to win one or the other could have resulted in the loss of both. And in the Battle of the Atlantic, the United States anti-submarine forces were aided by Submarines, Atlantic Fleet.

Working "arm in arm" with the destroyer-man, the submariner revealed to his surface comrade the tricks of the undersea trade. With the step-up in anti-submarine activity in the months just before and immediately after America's entry into World War II, the submarine forces were called upon to furnish regular services to anti-submarine forces at a number of training centers established on the East Coast and in the Caribbean. Such service (with the Fleet Sonar School, for example) had been furnished anti-submarine units during peacetime. War enormously expanded the demand. Not only were submarines used in these training projects, but they were employed in the research and development of instruments to be employed in detecting and destroying undersea craft.

In addition to the services extended anti-submarine air forces, submarines at New London were made available for other activities. Commander Destroyers, Atlantic Fleet, used them for refresher training given DD's and DE's which were sent to this area from East Coast bases. In November 1941, the Underwater Sound Laboratory at Fort Trumbull, New London, launched a series of experiments with various sonic devices. Several submarines entered into the conduct of these experiments.

Submarines were detailed to Casco Bay in Maine, to St. Thomas, Guantanamo, Trinidad and Coco Solo for anti-submarine training work. The operations at these bases began in the fall of 1941. Normally one submarine was assigned to each base for the activity, and convoy escorts and other anti-submarine vessels were given refresher training.

Submarine activity at the Naval Station, Key West, Florida, began with the moving of the East Coast Sound Operator and Material School from New London to Key West. Dictated by bad operating conditions in Long Island Sound, this move was made in December 1940. At that date three submarines of Experimental Division One were ordered to Key West to furnish services. In Key West the Fleet Sonar School was established.

On June 1, 1941, SubDiv Twelve, under Commander W. A. Gorry, replaced the submarines of Experimental Division One. SubDiv Twelve—later designated SubDiv Seventy-three—remained at Key West throughout the war. Commander Gorry was to remain in command of submarines at Key West until April 1943 when he was relieved by Commander W. W. Weeden. On February 27, 1942, all submarines of this division were assigned to the Fleet Sound School Squadron.

As activity at the Sound School progressed, the regular employment of modern fleet submarines in exercises involving listening gear and echo-ranging apparatus became imperative. A modern submarine was also required for occasional experimental operations conducted at Fort Lauderdale, Florida. As a consequence, late in 1943 CinCLant directed that each new submarine sailing from the East Coast to the Pacific should be made available to the Fleet Sound School for a short period of time.

Submarine School

The Submarine School at New London was, of course, the mainspring of the submarine training activity. Established in December 1915, it had developed rapidly into one of the finest technical schools in the world. Its graduates numbered practically all submariners of the U.S. Navy, and included the submariners of several foreign navies.

Situated at the Submarine Base on the Thames River—a site donated the Navy by the State of Connecticut in 1867—the school expanded to embrace Diesel and sound laboratories, torpedo shops, periscope shops, attack teachers, compression chamber and escape tank, and other educational facilities which kept pace with the advance of submarining. Engineering, electronics, radio, navigation, gunnery, torpedo overhaul and repair, the strategy and tactics of undersea warfare—these were major courses in the curriculum.

Expansion of the Submarine School to accommodate the wartime demand for submarine personnel was a task ably accomplished by the Submarine Command. Difficulties to be overcome included lack of classroom space, lack of textbooks, lack of time, and lack of new equipment—in particular "school boats." When the R-boats which had been serving as training submarines at New London were sent to Key West for service with the Fleet Sound School, they were replaced by antiquated O-type submarines, in mothballs since World War I and recommissioned in 1941 and 1942. ComSubLant made persistent appeals for a division of modern submarines to be used in instruction at New London. But the Pacific War demanded every fleet-type submarine available. It was not until December 1942 that CACHALOT and CUTTLEFISH were sent to New London, the first of a number of modern submarines to be used for training purposes.

War in the "Western Ocean"

When the United States entered World War II, Atlantic Fleet submarines were assigned to Task Force Five and ComSubLant was designated Task Force Commander. After Admiral Ingersoll relieved Admiral King as CinCLant, this task force was numbered Twenty-five. It was to hold that designation throughout the war.

Shortly after the war's outbreak, the administrative offices of ComSubLant were moved to the State Pier, New London, which had been leased by the U.S. Navy. On January 3, 1942, Rear Admiral Edwards became Deputy Chief of Staff to Admiral King, and ComSubLant was taken over as additional duty by Captain E. F. Cutts.

A few weeks later Captain Cutts was relieved by Rear Admiral Freeland A. Daubin, who was to serve as ComSubLant until late November 1944, when he was relieved by Rear Admiral Charles W. Styer. On Admiral Daubin's shoulders rested the responsibility of directing the Atlantic submarine forces during the stress and strain of wartime expansion—organizing the personnel procurement program, and developing new training projects to keep pace with the war's demand.

The submarine sailor (officer or man) is a specialist. Rank or rate, he must meet the highest qualifications in the Naval Service—more than answer the basic requisite, *mens sana in corpore sano*. Sound mind in sound body is not the whole requirement, for blended with these attributes must be a cooperative, democratic spirit, an ability to get along with one's fellow man in weeks of confined association. Joe Blowhard, John Gripe, Jr., and Pat the Egotist are anathema down below. So is Captain Jynx, the sadistic sun-downer. Officer or man, the submariner must be a "right guy." At the same time—true of Bushnell and the men who manned the *Davids*—the submariner is an individualist, a man who can (as he frequently must) think for himself. No "his-not-to-reason-why" mentality will do for the submersible operator whose intelligence must be energized by imagination and initiative. The procurement and training of this superior brand of personnel, for both Atlantic and Pacific submarine duty, were ComSubLant's primary task. It was to be accomplished by the training force under Daubin's, and later under Admiral Styer's direction.

In the period between wars, Daubin, a veteran submariner, had served with the surface fleet. Returning to submarines in January 1941 as Commander Submarine Squadron Four at Pearl Harbor, he was selected for promotion to rear admiral on November 27, 1941. At Pearl when the Japanese attacked, he was an officer with first-hand knowledge of submarines and warfare when he took hold in March 1942 as ComSubLant.

Atlantic pioneers were already out on war patrol. Operating from Bermuda under Commander Bermuda Task Group, the Squadron Seven submarines started a hunt for Nazi U-boats which were preying on American coastwise traffic. Patrol areas could not be covered continuously. Venerable and vulnerable, the R-boats were exceedingly limited in cruising range, and the old-type S-boats good only for intermittent patrols. The submarines were dispatched to areas where U-boats were reported, but intermittent patrols averaged only 12 days' duration.

In January and February 1942, Nazi U-boats were prowling in United States coastal waters from Maine to Miami. That the situation was serious is attested by the ease with which they landed a party of saboteurs on Long Island, and littered the sands of Cape May, the Carolina beaches and the strands of lower Florida with forlorn mats of wreckage. Apprehension and blackout darkened the ports of the eastern seaboard. Hitler was here.

In February, a submarine patrol line extending from Bermuda toward Nantucket Light was established. Submarines were stationed on this patrol line where good hunting was indicated by several reports. R-5 (Lieutenant D. W. Morton) made the only contact in this area. On the evening of February 10 a German submarine was sighted on the surface. Lieutenant Morton drove in on the attack. Four torpedoes were fired at the U-boat. All missed, and the invader escaped in the darkness while R-5 was making a torpedo reload. (But note the name: D. W. Morton.)

Because of the urgent demand for submarines to be used in training, and the few submarines available for combat duty, it was impossible to maintain the long Bermuda-Nantucket patrol line. However, patrols continued to the north and east of Bermuda until the summer of 1942.

R-1 (Lieutenant James D. Grant) encountered a U-boat in these waters late in April. The meeting took place about 300 miles northeast of Bermuda. There were no war correspondents and news photographers on hand to publicize the incident, and the patrol report leaves much to the imagination. The R-boat made contact with a U-boat. The R-boat skipper's nickname was "Gunboat." He decided to attack. One torpedo (Mark 10) was fired. Explosion and founting water. Breaking-up noises. Disappearance of a Nazi submarine from the vicinity of Bermuda. Grant did not claim a sinking, and the destruction of the U-boat was never confirmed.

The old R-boats were in there fighting. Two other enemy contacts were made north of Bermuda in April and May 1942. One of them was made by R-5, but she was unable to develop an attack. R-7 featured in the second skirmish. Commanded by Lieutenant W. T. Nelson, she fired four torpedoes at a U-boat but missed. Contact was lost while R-7 reloaded.

In waters closer to home, experimental MACKEREL had a brush with the *unterseebooten*. On the night of April 14, MACKEREL, minding her business, was proceeding on the surface from New London to Hampton Roads. While following this southbound course, she may have come upon the ghostly trail of the ALLIGATOR, first Federal submarine of the Civil War. It was ALLIGATOR's fate to be cut adrift by her towing vessel during a storm, after her crew abandoned ship because she threatened to founder. Never to be seen again, she submerged in the Atlantic gale. And MACKEREL might have joined her in her deep Valhalla, but for quick work on the part of bridge personnel and crew.

The clock was at 2310, no sign of trouble from the stars, when the lookout spied two ribbons of froth racing across the dark water at the submarine.

"Torpedo!"

The cry sent the bridge into instant action. Helmsman spun the wheel, and, as MACKEREL swerved to avoid, the crew rushed to battle stations. Luminous tracks in the night, the torpedo wakes whispered by, deadly as streaks of poison. Simultaneously the Axis submarine was sighted. MACKEREL's skipper, Lieutenant Commander J. F. Davidson, returned the fire with two torpedoes from the stern tubes. The enemy evaded, fleeing in the darkness. MACKEREL gave chase, but was unable to regain contact.

At 0503 the following morning, MACKEREL sighted another submarine. It might have been a U-boat, a friendly submarine, or, spectral in the morning mist, the long-gone ALLIGATOR. Accordingly, MACKEREL challenged. The challenge was not answered. Davidson could only assume the silhouette in the vapor was a U-boat.

Remaining on the surface, MACKEREL squared away to duel. "Fire One!" One torpedo sped at the misty target. The shot failed to hit, and the target evaporated in the surface haze.

Under the Spanish Main

When James Monroe presented Congress with the famous doctrine that bears his name, the Panama Canal (dream of the Spanish explorers) was still in the idea stage. But it was enough of an idea to invite cogitations concerning naval defense of the Caribbean approach.

As the canal idea neared realization, the German Government, in company with the British and Italian, decided to try the Monroe Doctrine's sincerity. First Grover Cleveland, then President "Teddy" Roosevelt assured the Europeans the Doctrine was sincere. The Kaiser, unconvinced, dabbled on a Venezuela beachhead—and thrust his toe into hot water. He withdrew it hastily as a naval squadron under Dewey assembled in the vicinity of Cuba.

One of the two most strategic short-cuts on the globe, the Panama Canal was vigilantly guarded during World War I. Construction of a submarine base was begun at Coco Solo Point in the Canal Zone in 1916, and the base went into operation in 1917 when a squadron of C-boats was sent there to guard the Canal.

In the First World War the Germans did not come close. But at the start of World War II, Nazi penetration had reached the Mosquito Coast. U-boats were poking up their periscopes all over the Caribbean, prowling through the Windwards and Leewards, and stalking the approaches to Cristobal. While the watch on the Canal was hair-triggered, strategy called for a forward submarine base in the eastern Caribbean. Need for this base became urgent after President Roosevelt's Declaration of National Emergency.

At that date, the Submarine Base, Coco Solo, was the only submarine base in the Caribbean area with war-scale supply and repair facilities. Therefore the Secretary of the Navy appointed a board to investigate and make recommendations for selection of a site at St. Thomas in the Virgin Islands. The board was headed by Captain Sherwood Picking, Commander Submarine Squadron Three and C.O. of the Submarine Base at Coco Solo. After exploring all possibilities the board recommended Little Krum Bay, West Gregorie Channel, St. Thomas, as site for the proposed submarine base. Construction plans were begun in the summer of 1939, and the Submarine Base, St. Thomas, was officially established on March 1, 1941, under Lieutenant Commander H. C. Fish.

Three R-boats of Division Thirty-two (Lieutenant Commander R. A. Knapp) arrived at the St. Thomas base that May. In the autumn a group of S-boats from Squadron Seven, Coco Solo, arrived. Thereafter, R-boats and S-boats rotated between the St. Thomas and Coco Solo bases. By December 1941, Submarines Atlantic was prepared to support the Monroe Doctrine.

Shortly after the German and Italian declaration of war, patrols were made around the Virgins by submarines from the St. Thomas base. Conducting one of these patrols, S-17 made two submarine contacts in the Anegada Passage.

First contact was made on March 4, 1942—a day that was going like any other on the calendar—the S-boat running submerged—nothing to report—another Caribbean cruise. Then Sound went tense at the listening gear. A vessel in the vicinity! Up periscope! Nothing in view. Down periscope! Up scope! Nothing in sight. So that murmur in the sound gear must be coming from the propellers of an Axis submarine. "Battle stations!"

Unable to make a sight contact, S-17's skipper, Lieutenant Commander T. B. Klakring, attempted to ram. A blind rush proved unsuccessful, and the quarry escaped.

The following day at morning twilight, S-17 on the surface picked up a U-boat. The Nazis were beyond torpedo range, and apparently the two submarines sighted each other simultaneously, for the U-boat promptly dove. S-17 followed her under. Ensued a game of blind-man's buff, the U-boat "pinging" frequently as the S-boat attempted to close in. The German could not be located. But a moment or two before contact was lost, something sounded like a torpedo passing close aboard S-17. In such incidents a miss may be as good as a mile, but when he thinks about it afterwards the submariner takes his coffee black.

Submarines from St. Thomas were also dispatched to keep an eye on the French cruiser JEANNE D'ARC moored at Gaudeloupe and the French aircraft carrier BEARN moored at Martinique. Loyal to the dubious Vichy Government, the French authorities in the West Indies were suspected of Nazi leanings, and it was necessary to keep the Vichy warships under surveillance. Ordered to report any movement of these ships, S-12, S-14 and S-16 picketed the waters off Martinique and Guadeloupe. The observation patrols were discontinued when the United States and Vichy France came to a diplomatic understanding, the gentlemen of Vichy promising to immobilize the warships in question.

Farther south in the Caribbean, submarines were sent from Coco Solo to patrol the waters off St. Andrews, Old Providence and other islands north of Panama. Although there were persistent reports of U-boat activity in this area, no invading submarines were sighted. If Nazis remained in the neighborhood that summer, they failed to interrupt operation of the Canal, and the patrols were discontinued in September 1942 when Intelligence reported that the Germans were no longer in the area.

Meantime, Captain T. J. Doyle, who had relieved Captain Picking in July 1941 as ComSubRon Three and C.O. of the Coco Solo base, was presented with a dual problem. A canal has two ends, and the Japanese on December 7 had made it a two-ocean war.

Word of the Pearl Harbor raid had hardly been confirmed before Captain Doyle, acting under the authority of Commander Panama Sea Frontier, ordered submarines to patrol off the Pacific entrance to the Canal. Extending about 800 miles from Balboa, C.Z., a patrol line was established to guard the canal approaches. This line, which covered a sector normally devoid of traffic, was set up on the assumption that a Jap surprise attack would sidestep a busy sea lane in favor of a more secretive route. Patrols were to average 30-day duration, with the submarines remaining 22 days on station.

Starting in December 1941, these patrols from Balboa continued throughout the first year of the war. No enemy vessels were sighted. It was in this area, however, that the United States Submarine Force suffered its first operational fatality of the war.

Loss of S-26

Victim was S-26, lost on January 24, 1942, in the Gulf of Panama. She had previously made one war patrol when, in company with S-21, S-29, S-44 and escort vessel PC-460, she was proceeding from Balboa to her patrol station. About 14 miles west of San Jose Light—time: 2210—the escort vessel flashed a visual message to the surfaced submarines, stating that she was leaving the formation and they were to proceed on duty as assigned. S-21 was the only submarine that received this message.

Shortly thereafter PC-460 collided in the dark with S-26, ramming her on the starboard side of the torpedo room. The S-boat sank within a few seconds.

On the bridge were Lieutenant Commander E. C. Hawk; his executive officer, Lieutenant R. E. M. Ward; and two enlisted men. Only the two officers and J. B. Hurst, Seaman First Class, survived the disaster.

Salvage operations were started immediately under Captain Doyle, but the submarine had sunk in 300 feet of water, and rescue attempts were unsuccessful. S-26's was a tragic loss. And although she did not go down from enemy action her men gave their lives in the relentless battle to stop the Japanese offensive.

To Crack the Axis

In the spring of 1942 the Navy began construction of a submarine operating base at Balboa. Previously, submarines based at Coco Solo were forced to transit the canal to make Panama-Pacific patrols. The establishment of a Balboa operating base would give the submarine forces a stronger home port on the Pacific side, and provide a training center for Pacific-bound submarines.

The Balboa operating base was not completed until late 1943, at which time it added a high card to the hand of the Pacific submarine forces. Meanwhile, the Panama-Pacific sector remaining quiescent, patrols in defense of the Canal were discontinued late in 1942. By that time submariners from Balboa were consistently following the advice of the early navigators. One must travel west—to find the Far East.

In the Spanish Main, as in the Panama-Pacific area, patrolling submarines reported a diminishing number of contacts. And in the western Atlantic, as in the Caribbean, the U-boats were "hunter-killer" game. As a result, late in 1942 anti-submarine patrols by ComSubLant submarines in the Caribbean and Atlantic were discontinued. By that time air and surface anti-submarine forces were well organized and taking a heavy toll of the undersea raiders who ventured over from Europe.

A menace when America entered World War II, the *unterseebooten* eventually retreated before the American anti-U-boat drive. The Nazis failed to produce a Von Nistitz—were unable to repeat their U-boat performance of World War I. Even before the end of 1942, U.S. submarines had quit coast defense operations to inaugurate an aggressive campaign. In the Atlantic and Pacific the policy was, "Go get 'em!"

Footnote to Atlantic Operations

The Atlantic Ocean was the training school of the American Submarine Service. Baptized by fire and water in this cradle of the deep, such undersea aces as D. W. Morton and T. B. Klakring went westerward with crack crews to carve great names across the far Pacific. From the Atlantic came the first inkling of the torpedo's faulty exploder device. Early in the war the British had rejected the magnetic exploder, pointing out its flaws to an American observer, Lieutenant D. G. Irvine, who reported the matter from England. Another observer, veteran Commander James Fife, Jr., had learned much in the Atlantic and Mediterranean where (August 1940-March 1941) he made war patrols in British submarines. Returning to the States, Fife promoted a training campaign that put the American submariners "on their toes." Thanks to his reports on combat techniques, habitability, durability and other aspects of submarining, the Pearl Harbor and Manila submarines were ready for action in December 1941. An astute teacher from a realistic school, Fife was to serve in the Southwest Pacific as one of the war's finest force commanders.

And so the deep-sea tide turned west against Japan, where, to paraphrase Admiral King, "men in little boats could not handle an opponent as tough as the submarine."

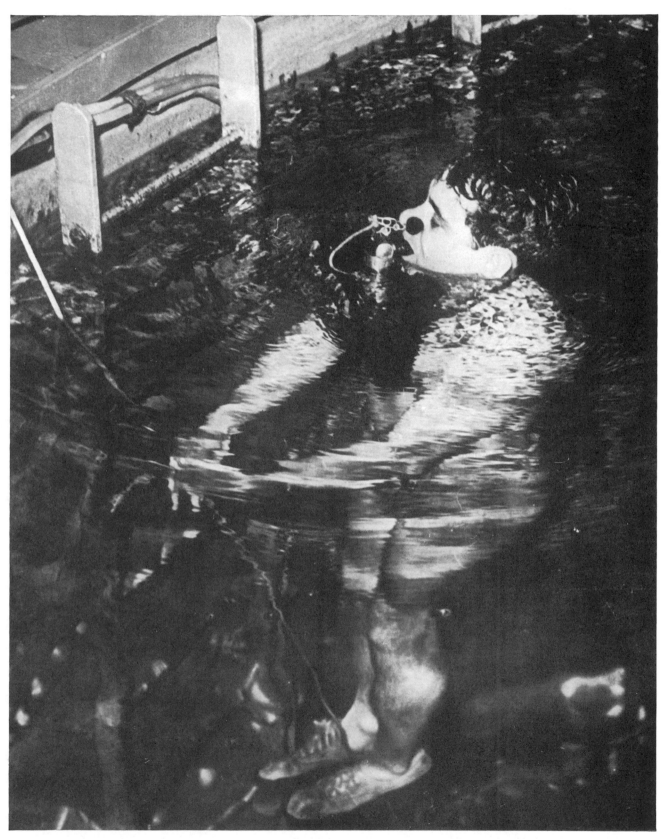

UNDERWATER TRAINING. Wearing a Momsen lung, this student comes to the surface in the Escape Training Tank at New London, Connecticut. Es-tablished in 1915, the New London Submarine School is the Alma Mater of most of the Navy's dolphin-wearers. Graduates step from there into deepsea duty.

HERE'S HOW. *A communications officer shows the ropes to a radioman striker. Shipboard training is thorough for the Navy's sub-sea sailors.*

TRAINEES *boarding an O-boat during the war. Practice and drill soon turned such picked men as these into competent, hardy submariners.*

TRAINING. *Student officers and men on O-boat training cruise out of New London.*

ESCAPE TRAINING TANK *at New London towers against sky. Trainees learn to surface from depth of 100 feet.*

MODERN ATTACK TEACHER, *New London. Student officer trains periscope on model ships moving realistically across sea scene. Maneuvers are rehearsed; checked for accuracy by comparison with actual target track.*

T H U N D E R   D O W N   U N D E R

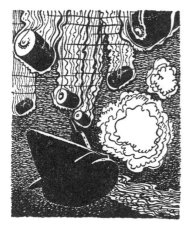

Skirmish in the Mandates (Pioneer Reconnaissance)

The war was only a few days old when the first submarine reconnaissance missions were ordered. On December 18, 1941, POMPANO (Lieutenant Commander L. S. "Lew" Parks) left Pearl Harbor to patrol off the Marshall Islands. *"Primary mission: To sink Jap ships, and secondary to find out what the Nips have at their various bases."* Four days later her orders were changed, and reconnaissance was made her primary mission.

Pre-war planning and training had included the matter of submarine reconnaissance. In a pamphlet, "Current Submarine Doctrine," issued in January 1942 after its pre-war preparation, Commander Submarines, Pacific Fleet, made the statement:

Submarines are capable of performing three types of reconnaissance missions:
(a) Visual reconnaissance through periscope,
(b) Photographic reconnaissance through periscope,
(c) Reconnaissance by landing party.

All three types were to be conducted by submarines during the war. A fourth type—known as minefield reconnaissance—was developed in the later stages of the war.

The early reconnaissance missions, conducted by Pearl Harbor submarines, were, like the early combat missions, simple operations in comparison to those that came later. Simple, and beset with all manner of complexities for their very simplicity. The tools were crude and the task was difficult. The operations were exploratory. Techniques were new and untried. The operator, delving into mystery, had no idea of what he might find. In short, he reconnoitered into the Unknown where the Unexpected may lie.

In particular the islands which had been under Japanese mandate were question marks. Heavily fortified, concealing supply bases and airfields, the Mandates—the Marianas, Marshalls and Carolines—had been cloaked in secrecy for two decades. It was the submarine's business to poke holes in the cloak and spy out military installations, harbor defenses and beachheads for possible landings.

Normally, the main source of such information would be aerial reconnaissance. Aerial photography for intelligence purposes was ordinarily far superior to periscope photography. And in the opening months of the Pacific war, submarines were not fitted for this scientific camera-work. However, the presence of aircraft performing photographic reconnaissance over enemy islands has one drawback—it alerts the enemy against a possible strike. The submarine, on the other hand, may reconnoiter without being detected.

And there was one type of information impossible for planes to obtain—aircraft were unable to check the accuracy and orientation of charts. Aircraft compasses were not sufficiently accurate for this detail, and it was accordingly assigned to submarines. This type of information became vitally important when amphibious landings were contemplated. In the Gilberts, for example, available hydrographic charts, generally correct concerning the contour of the various islands, were found to be as much as 11° out of orientation—

a flaw revealed by submarine reconnaissance. Correction was made by rotating the compass rose on the charts to the degree necessary to bring the charts into alignment with true north. A trifle, indeed—meaning all the difference between landing or shipwreck.

POMPANO, ordered out on the first submarine-reconnaissance mission, was slated to visit Wake, Ujelang, Ponape, Rongelap and an insignificant atoll named Bikini. Before departing on the mission, her skipper, Lew Parks, visited the Emergency and Repair Shop at the Pearl Harbor Submarine Base, in search of an adapter to hold a camera.

"I want a rig for periscope photography," Parks explained. He added that he didn't have time to go to Rochester, N.Y., and discuss the matter with Eastman-Kodak.

It was suggested that the fitting of an adapter necessitated the discovery of the periscope's focal point—an exacting business that would consume long hours. Parks did not have the hours, but he did have a knowledge of photography. Taking the matter in his own hands, he himself made tests to find the periscope's focal point, and succeeded in installing a small camera on the scope. POMPANO thereby became a pioneer in submarine periscope photography as well as the first frontiersman on reconnaissance.

Facing an extremely hazardous venture, she was almost eliminated when but two days out. The eliminators in this case were not Japanese, but American—dive bombers from the aircraft carrier ENTERPRISE. Trouble began at 0700 on December 20 when a PBY patrol bomber spotted the submarine and rushed over to lay an egg on POMPANO. Fortunately the egg hatched some distance away, but the worst was yet to come. Racing off to the blue horizon, the PBY informed the aircraft carrier of POMPANO's position. Three enterprising flyers from ENTERPRISE arrived overhead at 1400, and three bombs were dropped—one—two—three—on the submarine. The second bomb was close enough to loosen rivets in her mid-section and loosen the mid-sections of her disconcerted crew. They escaped by the proverbial hair, but for the remainder of the cruise POMPANO trailed fuel oil from a leaky tank.

Nevertheless, she visited the islands on her itinerary, and Parks recorded what there was to see. One of the things to be seen was the Jap flag flying over the Pan-Am Airways Administration Building at Wake. A few Japanese ships were sighted. POMPANO launched four shots at a minelaying destroyer—two torpedoes were prematures and two missed the target —and her crew experienced the metallic taste of a depth-bombing.

It was dangerous work, prowling into island waters that might be mined or otherwise set with traps. Running up the scope for a look-see. Peering into coves and harbors where anti-submarine patrols might be lying in ambush. In spite of Jap patrols and leaking oil, POMPANO accomplished the reconnaissance mission.

Shortly after POMPANO left Pearl, DOLPHIN (Lieutenant Commander G. B. Rainer) departed on similar scouting detail. TAUTOG (Lieutenant Commander J. H. "Joe" Willingham, Jr.) soon followed DOLPHIN.

DOLPHIN and TAUTOG concentrated on the mysterious Marshalls. DOLPHIN was past due for an overhaul when she put out on this patrol, and her mechanical condition was somewhat shaky. Nothing shaky about her personnel, however. Rainer and crew trained the periscope on the beaches of Arno, Maloelap, Wotje, Kwajalein and Jaluit, at ranges as close as 500 yards. TAUTOG's submariners made periscope observation of Bikar, Bikini, Rongelap, Kwajalein, Ujae, Utirik and Taongi.

Much of the work was boresome. The captains slid their submarines into uncharted shallows, dodged over knife-edged coral reefs and prowled around dark headlands. They sighted enemy warships and went under to avoid detection. One day Willingham fired a shot at a nosey patrol boat, and another day he took TAUTOG to the entrance of a lagoon and fired two at a ship going in. Destroyers rushed out with their depth charges, and TAUTOG suffered a ferocious "going over." The submariners survived the punishment, and TAUTOG got back to Pearl Harbor little the worse for wear.

DOLPHIN got back. Bearded, famished and as full of adventure stories as a pirate novel, each submariner climbed out into the sunshine and headed for the Royal Hawaiian. The captains turned in their reconnaissance reports. Admiral Withers directed three more submarines to investigate the Japanese Mandates.

On February 1, 1942, Rear Admiral Halsey's carrier task force made the Navy's first retaliatory strike on enemy territory, attacking the Marshall Islands. Shore installations, air strips and shipping at Wotje and Taroa in the Maloelap Atoll and air and naval bases in the Kwajaleins were shelled and bombed. Simultaneously a force under Rear Admiral Frank J. Fletcher raided Jaluit and Mille in the Marshalls and Makin Island in the Gilberts. After blasting the enemy at Kwajalein, Halsey's force steamed over to bomb and shell the Japs on Wake. Late in February the same force pounded the enemy on Marcus.

While these punitive raids failed to interrupt the Japanese offensive in the Southwest Pacific, they did serve early notice on the enemy that the U.S. Navy remained to be dealt with. They also heartened the home front in that darkest period of the war.

Retreat to Australia

For the United States forces in the Southwest Pacific, the month of March 1942 came in like a lion and went out like a lion. Japanese troops swarmed into the Malay States and walked across the Netherlands East Indies where a small Dutch army of some 75,000 colonials was able to offer little more than token resistance. An iron clamp tightened around the American forces in the Philippines. With the exception of Bataan and Corregidor, the Japanese were now in virtual control of a vast segment of the Orient extending from the conquered shores of China to Timor below the Banda Sea and from the Kurile Islands in the far north to Wake, the Marshalls, the Gilberts, and Rabaul in the Bismarck Archipelago. In a little over three months, the enemy had completed the first phase of the strategic war plan devised by Imperial General Headquarters.

The second phase of this plan called for stabilization of the conquered territory and construction of strong defenses for the island outposts of its Pacific perimeter. A third phase was in a process of incubation on the planning table. This phase concerned the expansion of the Japanese front—conquest of the Solomon Islands and New Guinea, a thrust into the New Hebrides and possible invasion of Australia. A drive at India might be simultaneously launched. Meantime, the Philippines remained as a mopping-up operation—an annoyance, but of no great concern to Tojo, Yamamoto and the Mitsui Brothers. The Pacific was their oyster, and they had all but pried it open. Captured Sumatra, alone, was as large as California—bigger than Japan proper. Java, the size of New York State, and Dutch Borneo, in area greater than Old Germany, contained enough rubber, oil, tin and other minerals to supply the Mikado's war machine for years to come. Singapore could be turned into a Japanese Gibraltar, and Manila would make a splendid colonial capital. Anticipating Axis victory in Europe, a stalemate in the Pacific and eventual Allied peace-feelers, Tokyo was jubilant. Already the riches of the Co-Prosperity Sphere had begun to flow toward Japan. The Sons of Heaven were coming into their own. *Banzai!*

There was no elated cheering in the Allied camp. Rather there was stern determination to hold on until reinforcements arrived. At all cost, an enemy drive at Australia must be beaten back. He must not be allowed to consolidate his gains, and he must be deprived of the raw materials he was gathering for shipment to Japan. But there was no Allied air force on

hand to raid his lines. The ABDA Fleet was gone. To block the enemy's advance, to stop his ships in their business of loot-carrying there were only the submarines. In the Southwest Pacific there were all too few of these—a half-dozen or so remaining to the British and Dutch, and the small SubsAsiatic Force now based in Australia.

Leaving Tjilatjap on February 20, HOLLAND had headed for Exmouth Gulf in company with the old destroyer tender BLACK HAWK, escorted by STINGRAY and STURGEON. But Exmouth Gulf, western Australia, was unsuitable for a submarine base. The port was swept by bitter windstorms, and heavy swells rolled in from the sea, making anchorages difficult and unhandy. HOLLAND was therefore ordered to take aboard a load of passengers (refugees from Java) and move south to Fremantle.

Arriving in Fremantle on March 3, she was met by Admiral Glassford, Captain W. E. Doyle, who had come down from Darwin, and Captain E. H. Bryant and Commander R. B. VanZant who had flown in from Java. Fremantle, near the southwest corner of the continent, had the look of a hospitable base.

Loaded with food and submarine spares, two supply ships from the States were already in the harbor. To "Ma" HOLLAND these were a most welcome sight. At the war's start she had been carrying a full supply of food, munitions and spares—enough to last her normal complement of 12 submarines a good six months. However, in Darwin and Tjilatjap she had serviced any submarine that came alongside. She had doled out her stores sparingly, and many submarines had been forced to leave on patrol with short provisions. Boats that would normally take aboard 1,600 pounds of meat received as little as 600 pounds at Darwin and Tjilatjap. Nevertheless "Ma" HOLLAND's supplies had run low, and she reached Fremantle in a condition approximating Mother Hubbard's.

Now her cupboards were once more filled, and Captain Pendleton and his tender force could dispense to the submarines adequate rations as well as service. Work went forward to establish in Fremantle the first American submarine base in Australia. Two wheat-loading sheds, 50 feet high, 800 feet long, were leased for shop space. Twelve miles up the Swan River from the Port of Fremantle, the city of Perth opened its doors and its heart to the submariners. Machine shops, a rail head and recreational facilities were at last available in a secure location. Over Manila, Soerabaja, Darwin and Tjilatjap there had hovered the constant threat of air attack. Submarines had hugged bottom during daylight, daring to expose themselves on the surface only at night. At Fremantle repair work could go on a 24-hour shift, Sundays included. All hands heaved a sigh of relief and shook hands with the realistic Aussies.

A few days after HOLLAND's arrival, Captain Wilkes and the remainder of his Operational Staff reached Fremantle. They had come down from Java aboard SPEARFISH, STURGEON, SARGO and SEADRAGON. And Fremantle began to look like Old Home Week to the submariners when OTUS put in, after her long excursion to Ceylon with MARBLEHEAD.

Shortly after OTUS made port, HOLLAND again weighed anchor. Leaving Fremantle, she steamed for Albany, West Australia, 300 miles farther south. As she was the only fully equipped submarine tender in the Southwest Pacific, the force commanders were taking no chances with her security. Although Albany contained no facilities for servicing submarines, it possessed a sheltered harbor and good rail and highway connections with Perth. Also, excellent living and recreational facilities were there to service the submariners. The port won the sobriquet of "Little Siberia," but the boats and men it harbored went out on war patrol in better condition than at any time since the war's outbreak.

At Perth, Captain Wilkes reestablished Submarine Headquarters. After Soerabaja, the city's telephones, radio station, office space and other accommodations seemed an embarrassment of riches. Driven from pillar to post, the force had at last found sanctuary. Here, in reasonable security, the tenders could devote all their time and effort to caring for the submarines —the submarines still fighting north of the Barrier, delaying the enemy's advance, and winning time. Time for planes and surface ships, troops and supplies to reach the Southwest Pacific front. Time for Nimitz, Spruance, Halsey and MacArthur to mount a counter-offensive.

Time. The submarines had to win it. There could be no further retreat. Australia was the end of that line.

But some of the SubsAsiatic boats were a long time reaching Australia, and some were destined never to make port. March was a dark month on the submarine calendar—a month in which the force lost two fleet-type submarines.

Loss of Shark

After transporting Admiral Hart and his staff from Manila to Soerabaja on her first patrol, SHARK (Lieutenant Commander Lewis Shane, Jr.) had entered the thick of the fighting early in January. In a skirmish on January 6 she was barely missed by a torpedo from a Jap submarine. A few days later she was ordered to Ambon Island, where enemy invasion was expected. On January 27 she was directed to take station with the submarines patrolling in Molucca Passage. Then she was ordered to cover the passage east of Lifometola, and twenty-four hours later her patrol area was extended to include Banka Passage.

On February 2 she reported to Soerabaja that she had been depth-charged off Tifore Island, and had missed on a torpedo attack. Five days later she reported an empty cargo ship heading northeast. Thereafter no messages were received from SHARK.

She was told on February 8 to proceed to Makassar Strait via the north coast of Celebes. A later message from Soerabaja asked her for information. SHARK made no reply. On March 7, 1942, she was reported as presumed lost.

Post-war examination of Japanese records reveals three anti-submarine attacks which may have been made on SHARK. The Japanese depth-charged a submarine east of Menado, northern Celebes, on February 11th. They attacked an unidentified submarine off Kendari on February 17, and another off Kendari on February 21st. A Japanese press release claimed the ramming of a U.S. submarine by an enemy sub-chaser in Manipa Strait that month, but this report could not be confirmed.

If SHARK was lost through enemy action, the depth-charging at Menado on February 11 seems to be the attack responsible. On the 8th she had been ordered to that vicinity. But the exact date of her loss and the specific cause remain beyond mortal determination. She went out. She was in the fight. She did not come back. If destroyed by depth charges, she was the first U.S. submarine to be sunk by enemy surface craft in the Pacific.

Loss of Perch

Tragic, although many of her crew survived, was the loss of PERCH. On her first patrol, conducted west of the Philippines, she attacked and possibly sank a 5,000-ton Jap freighter. In February she was ordered into the Java Sea. There Lieutenant Commander David A. Hurt and crew waded into the engagement that developed into the savage Java Sea Battle.

They scouted in Makassar Strait. Performed reconnaissance in the area. And on February 25 they were directed to go through Sallier Strait and patrol along the 100-fathom curve northeast of the Kangean Islands as part of the force at that time fighting to defend Java.

While making a surface attack on an enemy force that night, PERCH was struck in the conning-tower fairwater by a shell. The explosion ruptured the antenna trunk, the standard compass flooded, and

96

minor damage was sustained. After the antenna trunk was repaired a message was sent to ComSubsAsiatic telling him that radio reception was possible, but transmission was uncertain. Three nights later, in the vortex of the Java Sea Battle, PERCH got a message directing all submarines to disregard assigned areas and attack the invading convoy at the landing point.

On the night of March 1, she was on the surface, steaming on a westerly course approximately twelve miles northwest of Soerabaja, when she sighted two Jap destroyers. Hurt ordered a dive. The destroyers passed well clear astern, but after going on for four or five miles suddenly turned and came back toward the submarine. It was a bright moonlight night with good periscope vision, and one of the destroyers was seen maneuvering itself into a position suitable for a stern-tube attack. But when the range was down to 600 yards, the destroyer suddenly changed course, presenting a zero angle on the bow and coming in at high speed. Hurt ordered 180 feet, thinking he had 200 feet of water under him.

PERCH had reached 100 feet, when the destroyer came over and dropped a string of depth charges. The submarine hit bottom at 147 feet with the motors still turning over. No damage resulted from this depth-charging or from the accidental bottoming. But the destroyer returned.

On the DD's second run, four depth charges were dropped. PERCH was punished by this barrage. Maximum damage and shock was in the motor room and engine room. All motor-field relays tripped and were reset. Power was lost on one shaft. Ninety percent of the engine-room gages were broken. The hull ventilation supply-stop valve was frozen closed. The high-pressure air bank in the after battery started a bad leak. Number Five main-ballast vents were frozen closed. The engine air-induction inboard-stops were jammed closed. Both batteries showed a full ground. In the after battery the hull was compressed for about 6 feet by 1 foot, to a depth of 2½ inches. The crew's toilet bowl was broken to fragments.

The third string of charges came while PERCH was nestled in the mud with motors stopped. Maximum damage and shock hit amidships. In the control room the hull exhaust-duct section flooded, soaking the fire-control panel. The battery exhaust valve apparently opened and reseated. Several depth gages were broken. The conning tower was compressed to a depth of 2 inches over an area about 3 feet by 1 foot. Number Two periscope was frozen. Number One periscope would raise, but required four men to turn it. The engine-room hatch, conning-tower hatch and conning-tower door gaskets were crimped so that they leaked steadily. The air-conditioning water-supply flange cracked at the weld and leaked copiously.

Shortly thereafter the crew freed PERCH from the mud, and Hurt commenced evasion tactics. In about two hours PERCH managed to shake the destroyers. It was discovered later that loss of air and oil had convinced the enemy that the submarine had been demolished, and the Japs had discontinued the attack accordingly. However, their depth charges had been set shallow and detonated above. Reason: Japanese depth charges were designed for a limited number of settings and would not detonate if they bottomed before making their set depth. Therefore, when dropped on a submarine on the bottom, the charges had to be set shallow. For her part, PERCH could only lie on the bottom and take it. Stuck in the mud, she was unable to attempt evasion. Most submariners concede that it is psychologically harder to take a severe depth-charging when lying helplessly on the bottom than it is when maneuvering to evade. In this, PERCH's crew concurred.

At 0300 PERCH surfaced. All the antenna insulators were found broken. A bushel of depth-charge fragments was picked up on deck. Both periscope windows were broken and both periscopes were flooded. The blinker light was flattened as though by a giant fist. Number One main engine ran away on starting. Number Four main-engine camshaft was broken. Number Two main engine was put on battery charge. Number Three main engine was put on propulsion. Lieutenant Commander Hurt headed PERCH for the position of the Japanese landing. The submarine had been down, but she was far from "out" as she drove back in to the attack.

About an hour later, with dawn two hours away, a pair of enemy destroyers hove in sight. PERCH made for the bottom. Hurt figured she had a better chance on the bottom. To run submerged in the condition PERCH was in, the noisy trim pumps had to be operated, but on the bottom all machinery could be stopped, and the submarine could lie quietly. Unfortunately, she had been sighted, and the Jap destroyers were on top of her with a vengeance.

The first string of charges dealt her no additional damage. She was on the bottom in 200 feet of water. But efforts to move her from this precarious location proved unsuccessful. And the second attack was murderous. One underwater blast after another shook the submarine. The air-conditioning circulating-water-supply flange leaked quarts as the flange studs elongated under successive shocks. The same casualty caused bad leaks on the suction and discharge lines of the high-pressure air-compressor circulating water system. Number One main-ballast vent was damaged —or the tank was cracked—for it proved impossible to blow the tank. Air could be heard passing up alongside the hull when blowing, but the tanks would not hold air.

There were leaks in the engine circulating water line and in various high-pressure air lines. Toilet bowls in the maneuvering room and after battery were shattered. The antenna trunk leaked. PERCH was badly injured, hemorrhaging internally when a third string of five charges was laid directly overhead from stern to bow. The bow planes, on a 20° rise, were rigged in by force of the explosions, a violence that burned up the bow-plane rigging panel. The JK soundhead went out of commission. Torpedoes No. 1 and No. 2 made hot runs in the tube.

Another depth-charge barrage came down. As explosion followed explosion, the support studs on the bow-plane tilting motor elongated and the shim dropped out. Bow planes had to be operated by hand from then on. The officers' toilet bowl was shattered and thrust out into the passageway. PERCH shook as though in the grip of an earthquake.

The final run of three charges proved the most severe of all. This came at about 0830 on the morning of March 2nd. At one blast, the depth gage suddenly changed from 200 to 228 feet. For an area of some 6 feet by 2½ feet the hull in one of the officers' staterooms was dished in at least 1½ inches. A cell cracked in the after battery (19 cells had previously cracked in the forward battery). All the electric alarm system and telephone circuits went dead, their cables being cut when instruments were flung off the bulkheads. On the engine-room deck the supporting stanchions between the overhead and the deck were broken at the hull weld. Air banks No. 1 and No. 2 were emptied by leaks. After this savage attack the Jap destroyers steamed away, confident of a kill.

But there was life in the old boat yet. And PERCH's submariners were not dead. In their broken iron tube they were in Purgatory, but like Grifhelm, the legendary Briton, each man determined to escape this limbo. Now the Japs were gone, the specter of slow suffocation appeared. Its grisly countenance was determinedly ignored. The men went about their jobs. David Hurt spoke a quiet word here and another there. "We've got to conserve air, so we won't try to get off the bottom until tonight."

During the day, damage to one of the main motors was isolated, returning power to both shafts. Bilges were kept pumped down to avoid the grounding of electrical machinery. Forward and after trim and No. 2 auxiliary were pumped dry. Efficiently the men went about their jobs, sweating it out as best they might.

At 2100, PERCH surfaced after about an hour's struggle. The main vents would not hold air, and emergency vents had to be closed. The barometer in the boat was broken and no one knew what the pressure was. There was a 240-volt ground on both batteries. By going ahead and astern at maximum power on both shafts, the submarine was finally broken from the mud. Somehow she reached the upper night and breathable air.

After successively trying all engines, the reprieved submariners finally got one on the line, and PERCH was under way, making 5 knots. One auxiliary engine was capable of charging batteries. Fifty percent of the holding-down studs on Number Three main engine had snapped, and this engine vibrated so badly that the head covers raised one inch. There were numerous short circuits caused by spray from salt water leaks under pressure. Strips a quarter of an inch square in cross-section had been cut from the gaskets of the conning tower and escape-trunk doors by the force of explosions which squeezed the gasket between door and knife-edge. Many gaskets were badly crimped. Port reduction-gear casing was cracked, and lost lube oil constantly. The steering gear was badly damaged. On left rudder, the rudder could be moved only with difficulty, then upon reaching the amidships position it would suddenly snap over against the stops on the starboard side. Main ballast tank No. 2 was leaking grievously. On deck, the crew was unable to elevate the gun, and the sights were discovered shattered. Hull leaks proved so bad on the surface that both trim and drain pumps were required at full capacity to keep bilges from flooding.

Hurt decided they would have to make a trim dive before sunrise. About 0400, before daybreak of March 3, he ordered a running dive. In spite of every effort to make the ship light, and catch a trim by flooding in, she was found logily heavy on the dive. Before the descent could be checked, the injured submarine went down to 60 feet. Conning-tower and engine-room hatches failed to seat and leaked dangerously. The diving officer started blowing as soon as they were under. By the time they regained the surface, water in the engine-room bilges was up to the generators. After surfacing it was possible to expose only the forward half of the deck. Her stern under water, PERCH chugged ahead like a wounded whale.

The crew discovered that the conning-tower hatch was badly twisted, and there was an opening three-eighths of an inch wide that could not be closed.

Handicapped by darkened ship, they tried to adjust the dogs on the hatch. While they were busy on the hatch the officer of the deck reported three Japanese destroyers in sight. Purgatory was not yet over.

The nearest Jap opened fire with one gun. The first shell fell 300 yards short. The next was on in deflection and still short. But daylight was coming and the enemy would soon find the range. For PERCH the situation was hopeless. None of her tubes could be fired. Her deck gun was out of commission. It was obvious that she could not dive.

No use standing by to be massacred. Captain Hurt decided to abandon ship, and ordered the submarine scuttled. All the men got into the water safely. From a distance they watched PERCH start for the bottom, the sea pouring into her open conning-tower hatch. A moment later she was gone.

Then the weary submariners watched the Japs close in. All were picked up by the enemy destroyermen, who may have regarded the submariners with some of that respectful awe which those who know the sea bestow on its survivors.

They were not respectfully regarded by the landside Japanese, however. Taken to the questioning camp at Ofuna, Japan, the men of PERCH were ruthlessly grilled, then hustled off to the Ashio mines. There, nine of their number were to perish as prisoners of war. Fifty-three, including Lieutenant Commander Hurt, survived imprisonment.

The Ides of March

Loss of SHARK and PERCH in the wake of S-36 came as painful blows to the submarine forces. The submariners struck back hard.

On the day PERCH was lost, SAILFISH was getting in some hard hits at lat. 08-16 S., long. 116-50 E., in Lombok Strait. Having located a Japanese destroyer, Lieutenant Commander Richard Voge made a daylight-submerged attack on the DD, firing twice for zero hits. He followed up this attack with a night-submerged strike at a larger ship identified as an aircraft carrier. Voge fired four torpedoes at this target. Explosions rumbled into the sound gear. SAILFISH took the necessary evasion measures, and her skipper, with characteristic diffidence, reported two hits.

Post-war inquest bettered this modest report. Comparing losses with latitudes and longitudes, researchers found that on the night of March 2, 1942, the Japanese aircraft ferry KAMOGAWA MARU, 6,440 tons, had been sunk at the spot in question.

S-39 ("Red" Coe and crew) sighted a tanker (AO) on March 4th. Scene of action was lat. 04-19 S., long. 108-25 E., where the waters were still littered with the flotsam of the Java Sea Battle. The Japanese tanker joined the jetsam. Coe directed a day submerged attack, and fired four torpedoes for three hits on the volatile target. Belching fire, the AO—later identified as the 6,500-ton ERIMO—went under.

SALMON (Eugene McKinney) was doing her best to torpedo the Japanese Navy in a near-by area. McKinney's second patrol report is distinguished by a string of five straight night-submerged attacks on Jap light cruisers (CL's). McKinney fired twice at each cruiser, and eight torpedoes missed. But on March 3, date of SALMON's fifth cruiser attack, the two shots seemed to hit. SALMON reported the CL as sunk, and while official Japanese reports fail to agree, it is possible the cruiser was seriously damaged.

The Asiatic submariners continued plugging. Theirs was a discouraging prospect—Jap invasion forces entering New Guinea and the Bismarcks—cannon to the right of them, cannon to the left of them, and God knew what behind. The Java Sea Battle had been a gruelling experience. But it had been experience, and it had taught a lesson in submarine strategy. The lesson: That a small number of submarines were relatively impotent in the face of well-organized convoys in the vicinity of landing points, particularly when the submarines were operating in shallow coastal waters.

This lesson took effect on March 6 when Vice Admiral H. Fairfax Leary, Commander U.S. Naval Forces, Southwest Pacific, advised the Commander-in-Chief that the Asiatic Fleet submarines could best be employed along enemy supply lines linking Japan to the Netherlands Indies and Malaya. Oil supply routes from Borneo and Sumatra, and material routes from Saigon and Singapore were vital arteries that could be severed by submarines. Roving patrols at focal points in the South China Sea, the Celebes, and waters east of the Philippines were recommended—patrols that steered clear of enemy anti-submarine concentrations in narrow straits and off main bases.

In general these recommendations were followed, and submarines in the Philippines-Netherlands East Indies theater were employed as advised. The change in strategy was to prove most expedient.

In the deeper but no less dangerous waters of the Central Pacific the submarines from Pearl Harbor were fighting hard battles in the March seas. TUNA (Lieutenant Commander J. L. DeTar) had carried the undersea war to Japan, arriving at the Bungo Suido Area in February. POLLACK (Lieutenant Commander Moseley) was revisiting the waters off Honshu. In the vicinity was Lieutenant Commander Grenfell with GUDGEON. Elsewhere in the Pacific, among others, were GAR, GRAMPUS, GRAYBACK and NARWHAL.

99

GRAMPUS, making her first war patrol under Lieutenant Commander E. S. Hutchinson, led the month's score sheet. After missing three shots at an AK on February 27, Hutchinson and crew turned the tables to their account on the first of March, making a night-submerged attack on a fat oil tanker. Three shots. Two hits. Down at sea went KAIJO MARU NO 2, 8,636 tons, lost to the Japanese off Borneo.

TUNA got hers on March 4th—a 4,000-ton cargo carrier whose name went to the bottom with her. NARWHAL (Lieutenant Commander C. W. Wilkins) scored a sinking on the same date, hitting twice with four torpedoes shot at a waddling AK. The cargo ship, which went under at lat. 28-37 N., long. 129-10 E., was identified as TAKI MARU, 1,244 tons.

On March 11, POLLACK torpedoed FUKUSHU MARU, another small cargo vessel, to keep things going off the coast of Nippon.

GAR, on March 13, while making her maiden patrol under Lieutenant Commander D. (Don) McGregor, caught up with CHICHIBU MARU, cargo, 1,520 tons. McGregor fired four torpedoes for three hits, and the Japanese lost another link in their supply line off the China coast.

GRAYBACK, north of the Bonin Islands, sank a Japanese freighter on the 17th. On contact, Lieutenant Commander W. A. Saunders directed a day-submerged approach to put a torpedo into ISHIKARI MARU, 3,921 tons.

For the Pearl Harbor submarines, GUDGEON ended the month's box score by sinking an unknown *maru* on the 26th (4,000 tons), and repeating the performance on another *Maru*, 4,000-ton passenger-cargo carrier, on the 27th.

So in March 1942 the pioneers from Pearl accounted for eight Japanese ships. It is the effort which is impressive, not the tonnage total which scarcely equals that of lost HOUSTON. The score may not seem to justify the exhausting patrols, the many attacks which ended in failure, the overhead in risk to submarines and submariners. But the accomplishments of these pioneers were not to be measured by the ton. Their achievements were comparable to those of the pre-Columbus navigators who proved the earth was round—the forgotten explorers who located the Antilles long before 1492. In March 1942, the Pacific and Asiatic Fleet submarines blazed similar trails. If they did not sink many ships in that month, they sank a number of myths (such as vulnerability to aircraft detection) and added to the store of information.

From the dangerous corners of the Malay Barrier the Asiatic Fleet submariners extricated themselves. They dodged enemy destroyers and booming ashcans.

They fought their way through the enemy's lines, striking where and when they could. They navigated through seas of adversity, and despite consistent torpedo failures they harried the enemy.

One of the last March sinkings was scored by STURGEON. On the 30th she made contact with a small AK in Makassar Strait. Wright fired two and scored a hit. Down at sea went CHOKO MARU's 800 tons.

Then, as a March finale, there was SEAWOLF at Christmas Island.

Seawolf at Christmas Island

She had moved into those waters south of Java after patrol in the vicinity of Bali. And there she was to be the last submarine to oppose an enemy landing at an invasion point in the Java area. Her opposition at Christmas Island was the sort that will live in history as an undersea warfare classic.

Already her captain, Freddie Warder, was becoming known in submarine circles as an "artist of submarining." A native of Grafton, West Virginia, he had been in submarines since 1928, and in the war since the first bomb dropped on Manila Bay. With deft artistry he had been operating SEAWOLF around the Philippines and Java fronts from that date. His Christmas Island operation was by way of an artistic masterpiece.

Shortly before SEAWOLF's visit to Christmas she picked up a radio message from SALMON giving the position and approximate bearing and speed of a large enemy convoy moving in SEAWOLF's general direction. Skipper McKinney, author of this message, was unaware of SEAWOLF's presence beyond the horizon and never knew until weeks later that his news dispatch had been of interest to Lieutenant Commander Warder. SALMON had been concentrating on another Jap cruiser which was somewhere overhead at the time Sound heard the advancing convoy. McKinney's message, sent out later, was more inspirational than operational. Someone might pick it up and find it useful.

In relaying this chance information, McKinney employed a tactic practiced by the German wolf-packs in the Atlantic. It was soon to be adopted by U.S. submarines. For the WOLF, listening in on the "party line," got the word. And Warder put it to good use.

SEAWOLF intercepted the invasion force, and there was a battle royal in which torpedo explosions and the watery smash of depth bombs echoed to Tokyo. While official records based on post-war inquest fail to credit SEAWOLF with a sinking at this time, there seems no doubt that enemy ships were damaged.

ABANDON SHIP! USS Perch *in extremis. Mortally injured by depth charges, her hull maimed and leaking, her engines crippled, periscopes blinded, torpedo tubes paralyzed and deck gun frozen, she is trapped by approaching enemy. Her captain orders the crew overside and gives the word to scuttle.* Perch *is lost.*

DOGGING the conning tower hatch. It has to be closed fast when the sub starts a dive.

SMILING GENERAL HOMMA (Jap photo) landing on Luzon, December, 1941. Should have been captioned: "Came, saw, did not conquer!"

EARLY RECONNAISSANCE PHOTOS of Rat Islands, Kiska Island (Leif Cove) taken by submarine. Note how pictures are joined to make panorama. Note also the barren Aleutian terrain. A storm-thrashed, bleak frontier.

USS SEAWOLF—as she looked in 1942. One of the war's great fighting submarines, she made her first patrols under one of the war's great under-sea skippers—"Fearless Freddie" Warder. Few subs had more adventures than the "Wolf", bagged more game. Under hardhitting Comdr. R. L. Gross she sank 12 Jap vessels. But tragedy stalked her.

Some torpedoes may have missed and others, erratic as they were, prematured. But a number were heard to run straight and hot, and in the volley of blasts several ships were probably holed and put out of action.

Protests to the contrary by Radio Tokyo certainly pointed to American submarine successes in the Malay Barrier area. One had only to put reverse English on the propaganda.

"Our fleet has again shown its superiority over the Allied submarines!" (Tokyo Rose speaking.) *"In a recent landing on the island of Bali our forces ran into a nest of them. Not one enemy submarine was able to accomplish a successful attack. It will not be long before we have eliminated the last Allied submarine from Pacific waters."*

Listening in on this bedtime story, SEAWOLF's crew was unimpressed. They had lived through some tremendous depth-chargings. Their submarine was whole. Far from eliminated, they were on their way to Christmas Island, a British flyspeck off the southwest coast of Java, to do some eliminating. The island, valuable for its phosphate mines, was a logical enemy objective. Orders directed SEAWOLF to patrol the area and then proceed to Australia.

Running submerged by day and on the surface at night, SEAWOLF arrived off the island in due time. Due time was early morning on the last day of March. Warder moved up cautiously, wary of possible Allied batteries. To shore gunners fighting for their lives, all submarines tend to look alike. But periscope inspection could detect no life on the island. Warder studied the chart. The island's only dock facilities were in an inlet called Flying Fish Cove. Obviously the enemy had not yet arrived.

He discussed the matter with his officers. "We could go in there tonight and blow up that dock. But there might be some natives on the island. They might be killed on the waterfront."

Reported in a book about the SEAWOLF by her Chief Radioman, Joseph Melvin Eckberg, Warder's comment, as quoted, tells a whole volume about "Fearless Freddie" Warder. A humane man who, in the teeth of hell and high water, could find time to think about the natives on a picayune island, time to see them as fellow humans experiencing life on a common star, and, as such, deserving of consideration. But Warder walked on a star unknown to the officers of conquest coming down from Tokyo. Already their forces, on a rampage of exploitation, were pillaging Java. And on the night of March 31, their invasion ships were sighted on the way to Christmas Island.

The contact report came by radio, and Warder immediately started defensive patrolling. Assuming the enemy would head into Flying Fish Cove, SEAWOLF patrolled the inlet throughout the night, and submerged the following dawn. At 0730 the enemy hove in sight—four cruisers in column, lined up as though contemplating a shore bombardment.

Light cruisers—two turrets forward, one aft—typical Jap bow—raked stern—pagoda-style fire control tower—plane catapults—the column grew in the periscope scale. Upping and downing the scope, Warder maneuvered the WOLF forward to intercept, and sent the crew to battle stations. He chose a target and described her over the intercom.

"Cruiser NATORI class. Angle on the bow, five starboard. Range 3,000. Seems to be making medium speed."

A moment later, "This ship is patrolling. Planes are still on deck. Range 2,300. Left full rudder. Ahead two-thirds. Come to course three four zero."

Then, "I can see a command pennant. There's an admiral aboard this baby. Down periscope! Forward room, make ready the bow tubes!"

The tubes were made ready. Sound, feeding information to the skipper, reported the target bearing as three five two. She was getting close. "Open the outer doors! Up periscope! Here she comes! Down periscope! Stand by to fire. Fire one!" A whispery cough as the torpedo sprinted on its way. "Fire two!"

Third and fourth shots were fired for good measure. At the periscope Warder saw one hit—a spout of water—jets of steam—Jap officers and men racing about in pandemonium. The cruiser kept on coming.

It was time to go deep. Warder dived down the conning-tower ladder to the control room; the conning tower was sealed off; the WOLF, rigged for depth charges, began evasion tactics.

Explosions slammed somewhere to starboard. Then *slam! slam! slam!* Timed at 15-second intervals they came closer. The submarine vibrated and heaved. SLAM! Locker doors flew open, and flakes of paint and cork scattered across the control room. The men clutched at hand-holds, swaying, grimacing. The explosions faded off to starboard. Then *slam! slam!* they began somewhere to port.

SEAWOLF was not eliminated by that first barrage off Christmas Island. Nor was she eliminated by the follow-up depth-chargings which continued throughout that day. Warder maneuvered the submarine to a position some 15 miles offshore, and waited for nightfall. A brilliant moon held the WOLF at bay until about 0200. After moondown, Warder started in toward Flying Fish Cove.

At 0400, when the submarine was about 11 miles offshore, a cruiser was sighted. SEAWOLF took a dive.

The warship was moving slowly—no hurry. At daybreak she was off the port beam. Warder ran up the periscope for a look.

"I'll be damned!" he gripped the training handles, "this cruiser is like the one we hit yesterday! They've got a doggone command pennant flying. Did we shift that admiral around, or are they trying to trick us?"

But it seemed unlikely that the Japs were aware of the significance of April First. Warder peered again. The morning light was trying to fool him? The cruiser with the command pennant was plainly there. He began a submerged approach.

On yesterday's target he had expended four torpedoes. With the supply running low, he could afford only three on this CL. The firing began at 0513. A few seconds later there was a jarring explosion. The WOLF went under to listen. Breaking-up noises rattled, clashed, crackled and popped in the sound gear. There was a final crunching roar—then silence. Warder upped the periscope. Where the cruiser had been he could see no cruiser. A broom might have swept her away. There was not a visible particle of debris.

The time was 0517. At 0522 Sound heard high-speed screws. Two DD's came into the scene, and SEAWOLF departed therefrom. She departed in the direction of Flying Fish Cove.

As the morning advanced, the little inlet became busy with Jap ships. Loitering offshore, SEAWOLF watched them. Business was leisurely until about noon when some angry-looking destroyers came out on patrol. Sound could hear them "pinging." They were followed by a cruiser which launched a patrol plane. At the periscope Warder made out a herd of transports getting up steam in the cove. It looked as if the convoy was preparing to come out and the Imperial Navy was setting up a big anti-submarine screen.

As Warder watched these preparations, the cruiser which had launched the plane nosed over in SEA-WOLF's direction, zigzagging. Warder eyed her in fascination. Had he seen that pennant somewhere before? Well, the bunting might be imaginary, or the Japs might be April fooling, but this was certainly another CL and she was lining up as a perfect target.

Warder rushed the crew to battle stations, bore in for the attack, and fired two. An explosion was heard as the submarine dove for cover, but there was no time for periscope observation of the damage. And there wasn't much cover.

Goaded to fury by the persistent submarine activity off Christmas Island, the enemy determined to put an end to it. Smashing the water with depth bombs, the destroyers raced up and down trying to locate the submersible.

SEAWOLF went under and stayed under, sweating it out. Time dragged. The air conditioning had to be turned off, and the humidity thickened to an almost visible fog. Men and machines began to drip. A reek of perspiration, warm oil, and battery gases coagulated in muggy heat. The refrigerator had to be switched off and the drinking water became as warm as weak tea. The toilet tanks could not be emptied as betraying air bubbles would have traveled to the surface. Gasping for air, the men sprawled in their bunks or moved slowly through tiring little tasks. Chief Pharmacist's Mate Frank Loaiza passed out saline tablets. Some of the men became nauseated.

In this sewer-like atmosphere minds went sluggish and voices were reduced to a squeaky whisper. Warder moved here and there with a forced, "How you doing?" no better off than any of them. They had to take it. The Jap hunters were up there, and they were down here, all in the same boat, enduring.

They endured. One hour. Two. Three. But finally the lights went dim, and they had to surface to charge the batteries. If they didn't get up there before the batteries died, they, themselves, would go out with the lights. Warder gave the order, and they climbed.

But they did not reach fresh air. Not yet. The periscope found a destroyer on the surface, waiting for them in the dusk, listening.

"Take her down," Warder ordered. And they started the descent.

Then the depth gage jumped—the deck slid in the wrong direction—they were broaching!

Warder shouted, "Flood negative!" and there was a tumult of escaping air as water flooded into the negative tank. SEAWOLF's conning tower broke the surface, showering spray.

"All ahead, emergency! Bow planes, stern planes, hard dive!"

Motors shocked to action, and the WOLF went down, plunging. The dive had to be checked by blowing negative and, "All back, emergency!" A swirl of froth and bubbles eddied to the surface, and the enemy was overhead directly.

The first depth charge sounded like World's End. Thrown from their footing, the men collided with bulkheads and caromed off greasy wheels and slippery gear. Glass splintered and there was a sound of groaning metal. But the submarine held together, and that introductory blast was the worst.

The WOLF found deeper water. Again the men waited at their stations, wilting in the suffocating murk. They learned they had broached because an order had been misinterpreted and too much water had been blown from the bow buoyancy tank. That wouldn't happen again.

It was after midnight when three blares on the diving alarm announced Warder's order to surface. Without misadventure she climbed—cool night air poured in—all clear. Warder headed for Australia. The Battle of Christmas Island was over.

The following night, SEAWOLF received a radio message from the High Command:

A WONDERFUL CRUISE . . . CONGRATULATIONS

Captain Warder posted a copy on the bulletin board, amending the message with a note.

"To all hands: I want to take this opportunity to express my deepest thanks for your ability and your conduct, and above all, your devotion to duty. It is my firm hope that I will be with you all when we put out to sea on the next patrol. Respectfully, F. B. Warder."

Some time later, the Navy Department issued a communique which stated:

DURING THE JAPANESE LANDING OPERATIONS ON CHRISTMAS ISLAND . . . THE SEAWOLF PLAYED HAVOC AMONG THE ENEMY CRUISERS. DURING THE EARLY MORNING OF MARCH 31, A JAPANESE LIGHT CRUISER WAS HIT BY ONE AND POSSIBLY TWO TORPEDOES. ALTHOUGH POSITIVE CONFIRMATION IS LACKING, IT IS PROBABLE THAT THIS SHIP SANK. DURING THE NIGHT OF MARCH 31-APRIL 1, A LIGHT CRUISER WAS SUNK BY THE SEAWOLF. ON THE AFTERNOON OF THE NEXT DAY, APRIL 1, THE SUBMARINE DAMAGED A THIRD LIGHT CRUISER. . . .

ALL ATTACKS WERE FOLLOWED UP TO SHORT RANGE IN THE FACE OF ACTIVE ENEMY OPPOSITION AND AFTER EACH ATTACK HIS SUBMARINE WAS THE TARGET OF HEAVY, PROLONGED DEPTH CHARGE COUNTER ATTACKS BY THE ENEMY. LIEUTENANT COMMANDER WARDER BROUGHT HIS CRAFT THROUGH UNSCATHED.

Japanese records do not admit loss of a light cruiser at Christmas Island, and a sinking is not down on the official record, although a cruiser may be down under the waters off Christmas. Certainly something happened there on April First. The Admiral's pennant may have been a trick, but SEAWOLF and Freddie Warder were not fooling.

Retreat from the Philippines (Good-bye to a Great Old Lady)

The Ides of March boded ill for the defenders of Bataan and Corregidor. Ordered to delay the conquest of the Philippines, American and Filipino troops—60,000 against Tojo's legions—turned the defense into an Asian Verdun. So long as the Bataan flank was held, Corregidor could block the entrance to Manila Bay, and the Jap offensive would be stalled in the center until the Americans and Filipinos were dispossessed. Accordingly, the Japanese launched a spring drive that reached its fiery summit at the beginning of April. Battered by massed artillery, under constant bombardment from the air, Wainwright's army stood backed to the wall. History has few chapters as tragic and courageous as that written by the men who held out to the last in the Philippines. And while land forces bore the brunt of the bloody battle, Navy and Marine Corps personnel—3,500 fighters—did their last-inch share.

Perhaps they did more than that, considering their number and the tasks accomplished. The Naval Defense Battalion on Bataan, Lieutenant Bulkeley's PT-boaters and the sailors at Corregidor put up a fight that will long remain a synonym for human valiance and endurance. And in the vortex of this battle, unpublicized at the time, were the submariners who ran the blockade—the special missioners who carried food, medicine, munitions to the besieged troops and took out the evacuees—the men who made a battleship of a tender. The Army could not have achieved its four-month Bataan stand without the Navy at Corregidor, and Corregidor could not have been held without the support of the submariners.

Early in March, General MacArthur, Rear Admiral Rockwell and their staffs said good-bye to those they had to leave behind, and made their dash to the southern Philippines and away. On the 31st of that month, SEADRAGON received orders to go to Cebu and ferry rations from there to starving Corregidor. Ferrall and his boys were at Cebu on April 3. Thirty-four tons of food waited delivery to Corregidor's last standers. Twelve torpedoes and 250 rounds of 3-inch ammunition had to be unloaded from the DRAGON to make room for this shipment.

The Jap vise was closing on Corregidor when SEADRAGON got there on the 6th. Working at aching speed, the submariners had only time to unload seven tons of cargo before Commandant Sixteenth Naval District ordered her away from the dock. She stood by off Corregidor for 48 hours, after which time Ferrall was informed that further unloading was not feasible. With a passenger list which included 30 communication officers, 18 enlisted men and an Army colonel, she headed south for Fremantle.

SNAPPER (Lieutenant Commander H. L. Stone) arrived off Corregidor on April 9. She had come up from Cebu with 46 tons of food. Stone and his crew were able to deliver about 20 tons of food to the rescue vessel PIGEON. The submarine then went up to the Rock to take aboard seven naval officers and 20 enlisted men. With these evacuees she was ordered to shove off for Fremantle.

Loaded with 40 tons of food, SWORDFISH set out on April 1 for Corregidor. This cargo was never to reach its intended destination. Bataan was surrendered at long last on April 9. Chester Smith and crew were ordered to conduct a short patrol and return to Fremantle with the undelivered cargo.

In the meantime, SEARAVEN had left Fremantle on April 2 with 1,500 rounds of 3-inch anti-aircraft ammunition for Corregidor. On April 10, after the surrender of Bataan, she, too, was directed to conduct a short patrol and return to Australia.

On April 11, she was ordered to attempt the rescue of 33 Australian Army personnel on Timor just north of Koepang. This proved to be a ticklish operation that might have failed but for the cold-steel nerve of skipper Hiram Cassedy and crew.

Lieutenant Commander Hiram Cassedy had started the war as executive officer aboard SAILFISH when that submarine made her first patrol. After various patrols around the Philippines, he had been put in command of his own submarine.

SEARAVEN arrived off Timor in good time, and Cassedy maneuvered her into a cove at the entrance of a large lagoon. Shallow water prevented the submarine's entry into the lagoon, but there was nothing to prevent the submariners from going ashore—except the Japs. The Japs had been puttering around Timor for a number of weeks. Cassedy had no way of knowing their whereabouts—and little means of ascertaining the whereabouts of the Australians marooned in the vicinity. He had been briefed on recognition signals and warned of a possible trap. The only way to rescue the Aussies, if any, was to risk the trap.

Two successive night attempts to communicate with the unseen Australians failed. Finally Ensign George C. Cook volunteered to take a small boat in to the beach. Rough surf forced the boat to stand off, and young Cook dived in and swam through the breakers.

A campfire had been seen in the bush, and Cook, believing the Australians were at hand, walked boldly forward. In the laconic wording of SEARAVEN's report:

He noted about 12 men standing around. When within about twenty-five yards of the campfire he turned his flashlight upon himself and shouted, at which all hands near the fire scattered. He searched the surrounding area for about an hour and then reported he was unable to make contact.

Cook's one-hour search of the jungle in which a dozen men had disappeared (or were they phantoms?) is one of those individualistic dramas that men write home about—or do when they aren't submariners in a silent service. Struggling and splashing through the swampy jungle-fringe, the ensign flashed his light on vines that looped down like giant pythons and grotesque mats of foliage in which anything might have crouched in ambush. Strange birds flew up screaming in the night. Floundering in mud, he stumbled over something—probably a crocodile.

Cook returned empty-handed from this nightmare limberlost, wondering if his imagination had played him tricks. Later that night SEARAVEN made radio contact with Headquarters and learned that the Australians were camped on the other side of the lagoon. Their plight was desperate, and Japs were in the neighborhood. Cook's scalp must have prickled a little. Of what origin were those shades he had seen around the campfire?

The following night, Cassedy surfaced the submarine, and the indomitable Ensign Cook once more went in with the small boat. Again heavy surf held the boat offshore. So Cook swam in to the beach. And this time he found the Australians.

Suffering from malaria, tropical fever, ulcers and battle wounds, the Australians came out of the bush as figures from a grave. A haggard lieutenant reported that Jap scouts were close by in the jungle. Quick getaway was imperative, but getting the wounded men out to the submarine proved a Herculean task. The small boat capsized in the surf. Lifelines parted, and several of the emaciated men were nearly drowned. But heroic work by Cook and his shore party contrived the rescue. Two trips were made. Cook swam through the surf with one badly wounded Australian on his back, and another submariner—whose name also was Cook—went through the surf with a wounded man. Before the Japs got to the scene, 33 Australians were saved.

For the Aussies and Searaveners the adventure was not yet over. On the run back home to Fremantle a serious fire broke out in the maneuvering room. Smoke choked the after quarters of the submarine. Power went out, and SEARAVEN was immobilized for a number of hours while Cassedy and crew fought to bring the blaze under control. But when SEARAVEN was eventually towed into port, the rescued Australians were convalescing, and the submariners had written another saga for the Silent Service.

In the Philippines the chapter had been closing with still another.

SPEARFISH (Lieutenant Commander J. C. Dempsey) was the last submarine to visit crumbling Corregidor.

On May 3 she evacuated 12 Army and Navy officers, 11 Army nurses, a Navy nurse and a civilian woman. Up to that date, ladies were uncommon submarine passengers, but these, who had remained in bomb-hammered Corregidor, were uncommon ladies.

And then there was *the* Old Lady—herself, a submariner—who remained in the Philippines to the very last. Her story—part and parcel of any chronicle on submarining—deserves a chapter to itself.

She was the submarine tender CANOPUS—a product of 1919, originally built for the merchant service. The Navy acquired her from the Grace Line in 1921, and converted her into a tender of "pig boats." Supplied with forges, machine shops, oil tanks and other vitals necessary for her trade, she had been mothering her submarine broods for some 20 years when the war broke around her at Manila.

The night before General Homma marched in, she moved down to Mariveles Bay to tend the Asiatic Fleet submarines which had been driven from Manila and Cavite. On December 29 Jap aviators spied her and hit her with an armor-piercing bomb that wrecked her propeller shaft, started fires that threatened to explode the magazines, and killed a number of men in the engine room. Her skipper, Commander E. L. Sackett, and her crew put out the fires and kept her afloat. This was a job on an old vessel like CANOPUS, but her people were artisans, technicians and mechanics whose specialty was damage control and repair.

On January 1, 1942, when the Asiatic submarines were ordered to Java, CANOPUS found herself left behind. Lamed as she was, she would have made a floating bull's-eye for enemy planes, and a dash for Soerabaja was out of the question. Her crew hoped she might be able to limp down there later, but an air attack in early January settled the matter. Striking the tender's old-fashioned smokestack, a fragmentation bomb clawed her upper decks to ruin and left her listing and battered with 15 casualties.

"The tough old girl was not ready for her grave yet," Captain Sackett recounted in a biographic article. *"But if she were to continue in a career of usefulness, it seemed best to make the Japs think the last salvo of bombs had done the trick. . . . The next morning, when 'Photo Joe' in his scouting plane came over, his pictures showed what looked like an abandoned hulk . . . from which wisps of smoke floated up for two or three days. What he did not know was that the smoke came from oily rags in strategically placed smudge pots, and that every night the 'abandoned hulk' hummed with activity, forging new weapons for the beleaguered forces of Bataan."*

Unable to sail, she was nevertheless able to operate. Sackett and crew kept her going in high gear. About 100 of the tender-men took up lodgings in a capacious storage tunnel which the Army had dug in a cliff flanking the bay. Bunks, a dressing station and a radio were installed in the tunnel. And old CANOPUS, listing in the shallows, was turned into a general machine shop, smithy and manufactory, working on a 24-hour shift to aid and succor the defenders of Bataan and Corregidor.

One of her first jobs was to turn her own 40-foot motor launches into armored craft for the harrying of Jap beachheads. The shipfitters on CANOPUS cut up boiler plate to make gun shields and body armor for the three launches which comprised a tiny task force that won fame as "Uncle Sam's Mickey Mouse Battle Fleet."

To CANOPUS, then, came guns in need of repair, radios in want of gadgets, Marine gear requiring some gizmo, watches that failed to keep time. Word hurried around that the tender was staffed with blacksmiths, tinkers and plumbers capable of anything. What was more, her refrigerators were working and she was chock full of ice cream and ham sandwiches. Want some dungarees? They got 'em on that submarine tender. You broke a finger? They'll fix it for you aboard CANOPUS.

"Nearly every evening, Army officers and nurses who were able to snatch a few hours leave from their duties, gathered on board the CANOPUS," wrote Captain Sackett. *"To enjoy a real shower bath, cold drinking water, well-cooked meals served on white linen with civilized tableware, and greatest luxury of all, real butter, seemed almost too much for them to believe. When these favored ones returned to their primitive surroundings and described these 'feasts' topped off with ice cream and chocolate sauce, they were often put in the same 'dog house' as the optimists who claimed to have seen a fleet of transports steaming in."*

So, sitting in the bay like a stranded river-steamer, all Hades exploding around her and the next bomb liable to blast her into the Hereafter, CANOPUS became a king-pin in the last ditch Philippine defense. Her engineers, who had repaired the Diesels of fleet submarines, now worked on the firing mechanisms of Army pistols. Her undersea technicians built a spare part for an Army plane. Her cooks served hot victuals to Leathernecks and cold drinks to Filipino Scouts. To her radiomen came runners with messages for dispatch. Wounded and dying troopers were cared for by her pharmacist's mates. Her storekeepers distributed skivvies to anyone in need. One of her artisans built for an Army dentist an upper plate.

One hundred and thirty of her sailors joined the Naval Defense Battalion to fight ashore.

"Occasionally, our submarines, which were prowling the sea lanes looking for Jap ships to sink, would pay us a visit while en route from patrol stations back to their new southern bases. Other submarines also made special visits when required, bringing in vital medical supplies or ammunition of any kind which happened to be urgently needed. Nearly all of these submarines took out passengers when they left—high political personages, Army and Navy officers, and specially trained enlisted men who were badly needed to carry on the war elsewhere. Greatest comfort of all to those left behind were the letters these submarines carried to their loved ones at home."

The men on the tender could receive no mail, but they could write to their families in the States and tell the world they were holding the fort. Through burning February and blasted March, CANOPUS stuck it out at her bomb-thrashed anchorage. Hospital, machine shop, P.X., communications center, supply store, U.S.O.—she was all things to all forces fighting on Bataan and the Rock. They called her the "Old Lady," and like her famous namesake in fiction, she "showed her medals." Her submarine technicians labored like giants with the craft of jewelers, and her forges were turning out mechanical gems when the Japs guns were right on top of Mariveles.

On April 8 the end came.

"All hope of holding Bataan was gone, leaving us with the grim duty of destroying everything that might be of value to the Nipponese. . . . Around the shores of Mariveles Bay, Navy men blew up the Dewey floating drydock, which had served the Asiatic Fleet for so many years, and scuttled the ships which had no part to play in defending Corregidor. The CANOPUS seemed reluctant to go, but her crew could still take pride in the fact that the Japs had been unable to knock her out—she was still able to back out under her own power to deep water. There she was laid to her final rest by the hands of the sailors she had served so faithfully."

She was gone, but the human part of her—her people—remained. They joined the naval forces for the last-stand fight at Corregidor. The tender's versa-

tile launches were turned over to Mine Force sailors to serve as miniature minesweepers. Machinists, engineers, every hand of the CANOPUS crew who was physically able, supported the Marines manning Corregidor's beach defenses. There was no such thing as sinking the spirit of the "Old Lady."

During the remainder of April and the first days of May, the Japs sledge-hammered the Rock with countless tons of air bombs and monster shells.

"Flesh and blood could not endure the merciless pounding indefinitely, nor could the concrete and steel of the forts stand forever. One by one, pill boxes and gun emplacements were knocked out, leaving little to resist when the yellow horde should finally pour from boats in the final assault. . . . Two nights before that landing, a submarine slipped through the screen of Jap destroyers clustered around the entrance to Manila Bay, and the last group of passengers raced out the new channel to meet their rescue ship. . . . As their little boat bobbed its way through the darkness, they found it almost impossible to convince themselves that the long months of trial were actually nearing an end. Suppose something had happened to keep that submarine from reaching the appointed spot? Could she get through the cordon of enemy destroyers searching only a few miles outside? What a wonderful relief was the sight of that low black hull looming through the darkness, waiting exactly at her station!"

That submarine, as previously mentioned, was SPEARFISH—there on the spot to pick up this group of Navy and Army nurses and officers who were the last of Corregidor's defenders to be reprieved. Here again was proof of the submersible's ability to operate unsupported in waters under enemy control. With Japanese warships on every hand, SPEARFISH got in and got out, accomplishing one of the war's most perilous rescue missions.

Among those on Corregidor when the Japs arrived were men of the submarine tender CANOPUS—the "Old Lady" who was named after a star of the first magnitude, and who more than lived up to her name.

Corregidor fell on May 6, and the Philippine Islands were lost to the Japanese.

MacArthur said he would be back. But the submariners never left the Philippines.

CHAPTER 10

STAND TIDE

Weather Report

Spring 1942. Stormy weather for the Allies—a winter of defeats, reluctant to loosen its grip on the battle fronts of the United Nations. In the Pacific the Japanese offensive rolled on, its spearheads thrusting toward Australia, stabbing into New Guinea and the Bismarck Archipelago. To observers in Washington and London there seemed no break, no slowing of the titanic forces unleashed by Tokyo. Studying the war maps, Americans on the home front (and many in the field) were unable to perceive any change, or hint of change, in the war's weather.

But there were hints of change that spring. Nothing that showed up in banner headlines. No abrupt stoppage of storm and flood. But a faint jolting somewhere out there in the Pacific—or, rather, under it. Muffled seismic disturbances—a series of them—perceptible to those with the proper measuring instruments. Crepitations which could be registered on charts and graphs—charts on the wall of Imperial Naval Headquarters in Tokyo, for example; graphs in Submarine Headquarters at Pearl, and on the desk of ComSubs-Asiatic.

It may be that the submarine force commanders were the first to be aware of the break—the undersea phenomena that invited hopeful prophecy. On the surface April and May were bad months for the Allies. Under the surface there was a U.S. submarine rally.

Perhaps it had its source in the fact that by the end of March 1942 the pattern of undersea warfare in the Pacific had begun to clarify. Nearly all of the Central Pacific areas had been covered except those north of Tokyo and in the Sea of Japan. It was certain that the Yellow Sea and the East China Sea were going to prove productive in the war against merchant shipping. Areas south of Honshu were recognized as potentially good hunting grounds for combat and merchant ships. In the Southwest Pacific the enemy's supply lines had been discerned and marked for submarine attention. That was the strategic summary.

On the tactical side, battle tactics had been tested and altered where found wanting. Surface running wherever possible was now advised, and trust was placed in the SD radar aircraft-warning device. Jap methods had been evaluated and Jap stratagems countered. The enemy destroyer no longer enjoyed its former reputation as the submarine's Nemesis.

Concerning matériel, the lasting power of fleet submarines had been tested and found up to the mark, and the sea-keeping qualities of the S-boats had bettered expectation. Pressure hulls had withstood depths and depth-charge barrages formerly considered fatal.

Most important, the submariners, themselves, had met the fitness test of action, and come through. They'd been able to take it and survive. A program designed to give each crew two weeks' rest and recuperation between patrols was showing excellent results. Morale was on the rebound from initial shock and discouragement. A tendency at war's outbreak to underestimate the enemy can result in consternation at early losses, and consequent overestimation of the opponent's prowess. Now the enemy's character

107

was more realistically appraised. The submarine forces had taken his full measure and found him neither from Lilliput nor Brobdingnag. He was ruthless, clever, skillful, well-trained, courageous. A tigerish foe. But prone to errors of judgment, to weaknesses and miscalculations, and as vulnerable to a bullet as any man.

In short, the submarine forces were acquiring experience and self-confidence. These had their reflection in the patrol reports of April and May.

STURGEON, on the prowl in Makassar Strait, picked up some targets on April 3rd. "Bull" Wright directed a night-submerged attack on a Japanese destroyer. Three torpedoes were fired at the DD. One sounded like a square hit, and Wright reported a sinking which was never officially verified. Later, he fired four torpedoes at what looked like a freighter. On the record STURGEON is credited with the "probable" sinking of a small frigate. Later, on this April patrol, she made an unsuccessful attempt to locate some 53 RAF and RAAF personnel on an island at the entrance to Tjilatjap, Java.

Far to the north, off the southern coast of Kyushu, GRAYLING went into action. On her second patrol from Pearl, under Lieutenant Commander E. Olsen, she scored her first sinking on April 13th. Four torpedoes registered one hit on a big freighter to climax a day-submerged attack. Down in Empire waters went RYUJIN MARU, 6,000 tons, with the usual breaking-up noises.

SPEARFISH (Lieutenant Commander Dempsey of S-boat experience) struck in Philippine waters on April 17th. Dempsey put two out of four torpedoes into an AP for the credited sinking of an "unknown *maru*." Eight days later, in another day-submerged attack, SPEARFISH stabbed a torpedo into a freighter identified as TOBA MARU, 6,995 tons—"probably sunk."

So far, the April submarine score is not spectacular. But at this time the submarines in the Pacific were unable to concentrate on ship-hunting, and many were engaged in activities which did not show on the surface. In mid-March the Navy had launched raids on enemy fleet units at Lae and Salamaua on the north coast of New Guinea, and submarines had performed reconnaissance missions which paved the way for these strikes. They also reconnoitered for a strike which was planned against Rabaul. This strike was thwarted when Japanese patrol planes sighted Vice Admiral Wilson Brown's task force within 350 miles of the objective. The aircraft carrier LEXINGTON was held at bay by enemy Zeros, and the Rabaul raid was frustrated. Submarines, however, continued to furnish Naval Intelligence with information that surface scouts and aircraft were unable to obtain.

Enough data had been gleaned by the pioneers in Empire waters to implement the planning of the first American air strike at the Japanese homeland. As early as January 25, submarine patrols had been shifted in preparation for this retaliatory strike. Weather conditions, of vital import in such an undertaking, demand study. Into Japanese waters went THRESHER, under Lieutenant Commander W. L. Anderson, to play aerographer and forecaster.

While engaged in this pursuit, THRESHER took up another that terminated on April 10 with the sinking of SADO MARU, 3,000-ton Japanese freighter. Her back broken by a torpedo, this AK went down off Yokohama Harbor a few miles south of Tokyo—objective of the coming air strike. Having completed her weather observations, THRESHER moved out to a safety zone and relayed her reports. They were of interest to an aircraft carrier named HORNET.

THRESHER's weather reports timed a storm over Tokyo for April. On the 18th, HORNET, supported by ENTERPRISE, was 700 miles off Japan. Led by Lieutenant Colonel "Jimmie" Doolittle, sixteen Army B-25's took off from HORNET's flight deck, and the thunderbolt hit Dai Nippon in the heart. Jap submarines had pried into Hawaiian waters, scouting for an air strike. On similar mission, Pearl Harbor submarines scouted off Tokyo Bay. Two could play at this game of submarine reconnaissance.

And now, deep in the Pacific, there was another contest between submarines. The winner was TAUTOG—the submarine which had brought down a torpedo plane at Pearl and had since been on reconnaissance mission in the Marshalls.

Sub vs. Subs

TAUTOG had returned to Pearl to complete the overhaul interrupted by the Japanese raid, and now she was ordered to the Southwest Pacific to add her weight to the Allied defenses in that quarter.

While reconnoitering in the Marshalls, TAUTOG had sighted a pair of Japanese submarines loafing on the surface. Lieutenant Commander "Joe" Willingham maneuvered in for an attack, but the Jap submarines spotted the American, dived for cover, and escaped.

She was to have better hunting on this, her second patrol. On April 26 she was cruising on the surface in the vicinity of lat. 18-11 N., long. 166-54 W. Suddenly the officer of the deck saw a flash on the water—a flying fish?—his imagination?—or a periscope? The glimmer persisted. Neither flying fish nor imagination, the object proved to be a Jap submarine about one point on TAUTOG's bow.

Willingham put the rudder over, cleared the bridge, sounded the diving alarm, sent the crew to battle stations and ordered the stern tubes ready, all in the same rush of breath. When TAUTOG swung around on target, he fired one torpedo and saw the white tail of froth head straight for the enemy submersible. A moment later, water piled up in a foamy explosion. The Jap periscope disappeared.

Wary of other Jap subs which might be in the immediate neighborhood, Willingham held TAUTOG at safe distance. When it became apparent she had the sea to herself, TAUTOG moseyed back up to the surface. A few minutes after that a U.S. plane was sighted. TAUTOG signaled the aircraft to search the area. The plane spied a mess of oil and debris drifting where the target had been, and the sinking was thus verified. Official records credit TAUTOG with the destruction of the 965-ton Japanese submarine RO-30.

Twenty days more of TAUTOG's second patrol passed more or less uneventfully. On May 16, off a coral island no bigger on the chart than a grain of salt, the lookout sighted a large freighter. TAUTOG waded in, and Willingham fired two. One torpedo hit. The freighter, however, refused to sink. With flames surging from her bow, she headed full speed for the island and thrust her blazing prow on a reef.

TAUTOG moved on, and presently ran into a tropical squall. After this the tumbled sea was hazed by a humid mist. Jap shipping was glimpsed in this vapor, but the ships were gone like smoke before TAUTOG could get in an attack. But Willingham could bide his time. And he was biding it when the lookout sighted a Japanese submarine—another!—off the bow.

This submersible's silhouette was about the size of an S-boat's, which suggested caution. Willingham maneuvered in with appropriate care. After a two-hour approach, he drove TAUTOG forward on the attack and fired two torpedoes. The target went under as the first one missed. No. 2 sounded like a hit. However, a sinking in this instance could not be verified.

Two hours later, contact was made on still another submarine! Directing a day-submerged approach, Willingham launched three torpedoes at this undersea boat. Two rousing explosions roiled the water. Evidence was more than circumstantial this time. The Imperial Navy was minus one more submarine, and the records credit TAUTOG with sinking I-28, 2,212 tons.

The records also credit her with sinking SHOKA MARU, 4,467-ton cargo carrier, in the same island area on May 25th. Ending her second patrol with this gesture, she reached her base with a figurative if not a literal broom at her masthead. Two enemy subs and a freighter were sharp shooting for any pioneer.

More Sharpshooting

While TAUTOG was blasting the enemy's submarine force in the Marshalls, TRITON, in the East China Sea, was blowing up units of his merchant marine. Steaming out under Lieutenant Commander C. C. Kirkpatrick, this submarine put on a water carnival that must have dampened the spirits of a good many Japanese merchant seamen.

Kirkpatrick was a salty destroyer-man who knew the surface as well as what lay under it. He had been hand-picked for TRITON's command, and he had a topnotch crew to work with. The result was a series of sinkings that topped the submarine score to that date.

TRITON's score sheet (see table below) provides an interesting statistical review. Behind the statistics, or, rather, beneath them, ones sees a coterie of submariners who went out looking for a fight and found one.

Month	Day	Year	Latitude	Longitude	Type of Attack	Target	Name	Sunk or Damaged	Tons	Shots	Hits
4	23	42	2822N	15318E	Night surface	Trawler	....	.....	....	2	0
4	23	42	2822N	15318E	Gun	Trawler	Unknown	Sunk	1100	x	x
5	01	42	2806N	12347E	Day submerged	AK	....	.....	5300	4	0
5	01	42	2806N	12347E	Day submerged	APK	Calcutta Maru	Sunk	5300	2	1
5	06	42	2842N	12350E	Night surface	AK	Taei Maru	Sunk	2209	2	1
5	06	42	2842N	12350E	Night surface	AK	....	.....	7000	2	0
5	06	42	2819N	12328E	Night submerged	APK	Taigen Maru	Sunk	5660	3	1
5	15	42	2822N	13302E	Gun	Sampan	....	Sunk	100	x	x
5	15	42	2822N	13302E	Gun	Sampan	....	Sunk	100	x	x
5	17	42	2925N	13409E	Day submerged	SS	I-164	Sunk	1635	1	1
5	21	42	2909N	13657E	Day submerged	SS	....	.....	....	4	0

(Note: The table is an excerpt from the records of the Submarine Operations Research Group—SORG. It is presented in official form to show the layman reader the exactitude with which the Submarine Service compiled combat statistics. Based on submarine patrol reports and data from other available sources, SORG's wartime records do not in all cases agree with the post-war compilations of the Joint Army-Navy Assessment Committee.)

A trawler, a freighter, two passenger-cargomen and a submarine, with two sampans thrown in for good measure! Kirkpatrick and his crew bade fair to chase the season's shipping from the East China Sea, and TRITON's was another pioneer exploit that boosted morale in the Service—specifically, in the American Submarine Service. Hirohito's submariners were not at all heartened by the loss of I-164 in the waters south of Kyushu.

The memorable April-May patrols of TAUTOG and TRITON were not the only indications of a change in the undersea weather. Another indication had its source in the submarine DRUM. And it was a fairly noisy indication.

DRUM was skippered by Lieutenant Commander Robert H. (Bob) Rice, who took command of this sleek new submarine in Portsmouth Navy Yard and drove her out to Pearl at a speed which guaranteed she would not be late for the war. She got there in time.

She was out on her first war patrol in the latter part of April. May found her in the neighborhood of lat. 34-26 N., long. 138-14 E.—not too far from Osaka and on a sea lane that led to Yokohama. In fact, if the periscope were pushed up far enough in those waters, one might obtain a free, postcard view of the sacred mountain Fujiyama. On whose flank (if the lens were strong enough) an observer might have glimpsed the high priests of Shinto praying for the health of the god-Emperor, victory in the war, and for the spirits of Japanese mariners lost at sea. Some of these mariners were lost in the neighborhood of lat. 34-26 N., long. 138-14 E.

The record discloses a fact which the gods of Fujiyama were unable to reveal. Nemesis in that particular locality and season was DRUM. If the Imperial Navy failed to confide this phenomenon to the gods, it was probably because Lieutenant Commander Rice refused to confide his identity to the Imperial Navy. He might captain a DRUM, but he was indisposed to beat his own. DRUM's May 1942 patrol did not appear in headlines. But let the record compiled by SORG speak for DRUM.*

Six attacks—four sinkings, including a 9,000-ton seaplane tender downed in a night-surface action—two ships sunk, each by a single torpedo blast—this was submarining of a high order. DRUM's patrol left an echo in Empire waters.

(Five months later, when DRUM revisited the waters off Honshu, Rice elevated the periscope and obtained a fine view of the Sacred Mountain. Rice and company paid their respects to the scenery by removing three more marus from the vista.)

While DRUM's torpedoes were booming off Honshu, TROUT (Lieutenant Commander Fenno) was firing away in an adjacent patrol area. She had fought her way through a run of dreary luck in April—nine attacks with persistent torpedo misses, and no confirmed sinkings for her pains. But on May 2 and May 4 the "fish" ran straight and hot. UZAN MARU, 5,000-ton merchantman, followed by KONGOSAN MARU, converted gunboat, traveled to the bottom.

GREENLING (Lieutenant Commander H. C. Bruton) got hers on the 4th of May in Caroline waters. She, too, had experienced the capricious workings of luck. These workings began on the evening of April 30 when GREENLING, on patrol off Eniwetok, encountered a 7,000-ton armed merchantman. Her ensuing tangle with the Japanese and the Jay Factor resulted in an action which featured one of the early gun attacks of the war.

Pioneer Tactics (The Gun Attack)

In the opening months of the war most submarines, when operating within 500 miles of enemy bases, submerged during daylight. Under these aquatic circumstances, there was no opportunity for employment of the deck gun. But there was a tantalizing plentitude of targets.

*Month	Day	Year	Longitude	Latitude	Type of Attack	Target	Name	Sunk or Damaged	Tons	Shots	Hits
5	02	42	3426N	13814E	Night surface	AV	Mizuho	Sunk	9000	2	1
5	02	42	34N	137E	Night submerged	DD	....	Missed	....	4	0
5	09	42	34N	137E	Day submerged	AK	Unknown	Sunk	4000	4	1
5	13	42	34N	139E	Day submerged	AK	Shonan Maru	Sunk	5264	1	1
5	25	42	34N	139E	Day submerged	AK	Kitakata Maru	Sunk	2380	1	1
5	28	42	34N	139E	Twilight submerged	AK	....	Missed	....	5	0

Submarines pioneering in Empire waters encountered whole schools of sampans, fishing boats, trawlers, skiffs and small vessels of nondescript character. A ring of these craft encompassed Japan. Ranged some 600 miles off the coastline, they swarmed in the submarine operating areas and sailed in front of the periscopes with the nonchalance of clay pigeons in a shooting gallery. The resemblance was not lost on the American sailor whose favorite pastime was ten shots for two bits on the boardwalk. Yet this Japanese Penny Arcade had to be passed up by the submarine gunners. The targets seemed worth neither a torpedo nor the risk of battle-surfacing for gunfire.

However, the submariners suspected that many of these innocuous-looking craft were on duty as naval lookouts and some were serving as anti-submarine pickets. At the time of the Doolittle raid on Tokyo the suspicions were confirmed. The carrier task force met a clutter of sampans several hundred miles from the objective. Two sampans were sunk and prisoners were taken. These specimens confirmed the supposition that the sampans were conducting organized picket-boat watches to guard the approaches to the Empire. Many spent long periods at sea, fishing while they watched. Some sampans carried a naval signal party.

By April 1942, the submarine forces determined to take a hand in the situation. Although the patrol craft were too picayune for torpedo attack, they were worth a few machine-gun bursts or a 3-inch shell. Periscope inspection showed the average sampan picket was either feebly armed or feigning innocence by drifting around without arms. In the last week of April, three or four of the snooping craft were sunk by gunfire from patrolling submarines.

Tactics of these early gun attacks were fairly simple. They consisted chiefly of approaching the target submerged, then quickly surfacing, and sweeping the target with gunfire. It was soon discovered that small wooden vessels of a few hundred tons burden were not easily sent to the bottom by a fusillade. They could be riddled with .30- and .50-caliber machine-gun bullets, and holed several times by 3- or 5-inch shells and remain afloat like a box of Swiss cheese. Quickest method of destruction was to set them afire, but burning a boatload of fish or wet seaweed was not easy.

At the start of the war there was some question as to the value of submarine deck guns. And as the war progressed, attacks on sampans and small patrol craft seemed to accomplish little. Amphibious Japan spawned sampans the way a stocked aquarium spawns guppies. Sink one, and another took its place.

It is possible the attacks made throughout the war forced the Japs to arm their patrol craft, thereby depleting arsenal stocks. Yet the outer ring of pickets which vigilantly patrolled off Japan contained few innocently unarmed "fishermen," to begin with. War against these nuisances was costly in time and effort. They were like mosquitoes—necessary to destroy because a few might be malarial. But eventually it became imperative to clear certain areas with a campaign of extermination, and submarine deck guns did the job.

Gun attacks were something of a tonic for men who had been committed to long weeks of confinement below decks. A glimpse of the enemy was vitalizing, and "Battle surface!" sounded as a welcome break in the routine. In the minds of many submariners the gun also served, perhaps, as a subconscious anchor to windward. If the going were tough, or depth charges came too close, they could surface and fight it out with the artillery. The weapon's value was psychological as well as military, and on several occasions during the war, the deck gun, used in desperation, was credited with saving the submarine.

On a number of occasions the gun attack was resorted to in exasperation after failure to score with torpedoes. Case in point is that of GREENLING, entering action on the evening of April 30, 1942.

Sighting the large freighter, as previously described, Bruton ordered a submerged approach, and maneuvered nicely into attack position. Sunset. The target at appropriate range. Everything clicking, Bruton fired four torpedoes. A tense wait for the explosions was rewarded by elongating silence. The ship sailed majestically on. So, apparently, did the futile torpedoes.

Dusk on the water and the target fading over the hill, Bruton ordered GREENLING to the surface in top-speed pursuit.

The night hung out her moon, and the submarine had no difficulty overhauling the ship. Passing the target 6,000 yards abeam, Bruton tracked her as making 17 knots. As the moon was rising high, he closed to 2,500 yards on a 110° track, and sent GREENLING under for another submerged attack.

The target was clearly visible in the periscope. GREENLING bored in until pinging established the range as 1,350 yards. Bruton ordered two shots. The first torpedo whispered on its way. The second torpedo whispered on its way. And so did the unperturbed freighter.

It was now apparent that something was somewhere askew. Lieutenant Commander Bruton's comments on the subject are not available for publication, but it is logical to assume they were red, white and blue in accordance with naval customs, traditions and usage. Having spoken, he waited until the target range increased to 7,000 yards, and then brought GREENLING up for air.

On the surface the submarine was sighted by the cargo ship. Opening fire with a stern gun, the Japs uncorked two rounds, both of which fell short. The moon edged into a nest of cloud, and visibility was decreasing, if Bruton's temper was not. Ordering the gun crew out on deck, he drove GREENLING forward to do some shooting on a 180° track. When the range closed to 5,000 yards the visibility suddenly cleared. The Jap lookouts spotted the submarine, and the freighter promptly zigzagged. Bruton set his jaw, driving in to 4,500 yards—4,000 yards—3,500 yards. At every yard the submariners expected a shell, and when the expected didn't happen, Bruton concluded the merchantman's stern gun must have suffered a casualty.

GREENLING's gun crew pointed and trained. Range closed to 3,250.

"Fire!"

Six shots blazed in the night. At the sixth, the Jap freighter opened up in return. Shells splashed the moonlit water off GREENLING's bow. The duel continued slam-bang as the submariners fired four more rounds from the 3-incher.

One shot hit the freighter without notable effect, and one Jap shell struck the submarine a glancing blow. Ricocheting off the submarine's side, the projectile whistled over the heads of the gunners on a trajectory too close for comfort. Unwilling to risk a direct hit on his submarine, Bruton decided to knock off the action. The merchantman ceased fire when the submarine's gun crew secured, so Bruton held GREENLING on the surface.

Ensued a five-hour game of tag that ended in the darkness before the dawn of May 1st. With the moon obscured by clouds, Bruton determined to try once more with torpedoes. Holding the bridge, he steered GREENLING in to attack position. Clock at 0547, he fired one torpedo. Its wake high-tailed across the water and went on going—ahead of the ship! Bruton fired again. This torpedo rushed straight at the target for a bull's-eye hit. Then, at 500 yards, the torpedo prematured.

Saved by this exploding squib, the Jap ship executed a fast reverse. A moment later GREENLING's aircraft warning installation picked up an approaching plane. Bruton was probably ready to attack the enemy with sling-shots, but with things going the way they were, a dive seemed only circumspect.

"Take her down!"

Reviewing Bruton's patrol report, a submarine tactician wrote: *"It is entirely possible that all these torpedo misses were caused by control errors, but the torpedoes fired were set at a depth five feet greater than estimated draft in accordance with current directives. A short time later it was learned that depth control of torpedoes was erratic, with torpedoes often running ten feet deeper than set."*

On May 4 GREENLING put one over on the statistics. On this date Bruton fired a single, and sank KINJOSAN MARU, 3,262-ton AK, with one shot.

If nothing else, the gun attack of April 30 proved the aggressiveness of Bruton and crew—aggressiveness which eventually paid off.

Pioneer Tactics ("Down-the-throat" Shot)

SKIPJACK went into battle in May under Lieutenant Commander J. W. (Red) Coe. Already acknowledged as one of the outstanding submarine skippers, Coe was to distinguish this patrol with another outstanding performance.

The ability to analyze a difficult situation and improvise emergency measures to offset the difficulties is an invaluable asset to the submariner. Frequently an introvert, the analyst may lack the extrovert's punch which translates thought into action. Coe could act and think, too (or think and act, too)—a faculty nicely demonstrated during SKIPJACK's May 1942 patrol.

In pre-war practice it was usually conceded that if a submarine making a torpedo approach were caught at close range dead ahead of the target, the appropriate tactic was to go deep and pray. The prayer might be answered by a reprimand and advice on the right method of making an approach. In any event, doctrine deplored a maneuver which placed the submarine directly ahead of an enemy ship at close range.

War experience, however, was to prove that such a situation was by no means fatal for the sub. On the contrary, if the submarine gained a position in which she could exploit small gyro angles at a firing range of 1,500 yards or less, the chances of hitting were nearly as good as the chances presented by more conventional attacks which provided broader track angles.

Boiled down, the problem was basically one of marksmanship. Was it easier to hit a wide target with a long-range shot, or a narrow target at short range? Reverse the English, and the aspect of safety becomes involved. Firing at distance, the submarine itself is hard to hit. Conversely, at close range it is an easier target for the enemy advancing head-on.

A torpedo shot fired at close range under the circumstances described was labeled a "down-the-throat" shot. While this shot was seldom, if ever, deliberately chosen in preference to the more conventional, many commanding officers learned to use it with telling effect. If able to maneuver the submarine into a dead-ahead position, they would head straight for the target. Then, if the target zigged to right or left, a normal attack position was set up under conditions most favorable to torpedo fire. If the target did not zig, and the range closed to 1,500 yards or less, a down-the-throat shot had an excellent chance of punching the ship on the prow.

SORG records show 167 attacks with track angles less than 20°. In these attacks, 452 torpedoes were fired for 104 credited hits. This percentage of hits compares favorably with the average for the total number of torpedo attacks, in which 14,343 torpedoes were fired for 4,790 credited hits. By war's end, the down-the-throat technique had become as established in submarining as the tonsillectomy in surgery.

The first successful down-the-throat shot on official record was fired by Lieutenant Commander Coe, early in SKIPJACK's third patrol. Date: May 6, 1942. Locale: off Indo-China, near Camranh Bay.

POMPANO (Lieutenant Commander Parks) and SALMON (Lieutenant Commander McKinney) had entered previous engagements in which such shots were fired; by Parks at a minelaying DD in the Marshalls, and by McKinney off Lingayen. But SKIPJACK's torpedoes were the first to score.

Target was sighted at 0300, about seven miles distant with a 90° angle on the bow. A luminous moon was astern of the submarine, and Coe did not want to risk a night-surface approach. Putting all four engines on propulsion, he made a high-speed run to get ahead of the target—a position he hoped to gain by daybreak. Traveling at a good 16.5 knots, SKIPJACK handily outdistanced the Jap freighter, and Coe eased over ahead by 10° increments of course.

At 0436, the submarine was 18,000 yards ahead, and 20° on the target's port bow. Target's speed was estimated at 11 knots. Coe planned to fire straight bow shots, using the Mark VI angle-solver which he at that time preferred to the T.D.C. But in the resulting maneuvers he discovered he had overrun the position for straight bow shots.

Overestimation of the target's size may have caused the error in Coe's calculations. Silhouettes in moonlight are often deceptive, and the vessel he had sized up as a 6,000-tonner proved to be a small cargoman of some 2,500 tons. The submariners, deluded by a trick of perspective, bored in for the attack with a speed that took SKIPJACK to a point only 300 yards from the track.

Here was a situation that demanded instantaneous adjustment. The Jap freighter might be armed, and the submarine, almost dead ahead, was in that tactical position deplored by pre-war doctrine. According to current theory, Coe should have gone deep and prayed. He did neither.

While the target swelled in size on the periscope scale, Coe's mind raced through some fast analysis. She's coming at 11 knots. The torpedoes must have time to arm. Sufficient range for arming means a new set-up. Take it or leave it? We'll take it.

In order to fire with a range that permitted arming, he had to accept a 20° track with a 50° gyro angle. Abandoning the Mark VI angle-solver for the Torpedo Data Computer, Coe became a convert to the T.D.C. from there on out. The robot came through with the set-up in jig time, and three torpedoes were fired accordingly. One struck home with a geysering smash. And under by the head went a ship later identified as KANAN MARU—the first of many to succumb to the lethal down-the-throat shot.

Torpedoes for Taiyo Maru

Throughout May 1942, Japanese ships continued to go down. SKIPJACK sank another—BUJUN MARU, 4,804-ton AK—on May 8th. Nine days later she torpedoed TAZAN MARU, a 5,478-ton passenger and cargo carrier. Altogether Coe directed eight day-submerged attacks on shipping off the Indo-China coast, and undoubtedly SKIPJACK's score would have been higher, given a square-shooting torpedo.

Having consistently sabotaged the efforts of the pioneer submariners, this Mark 14 torpedo nearly undid the work of Lieutenant Commander "Pilley" Lent and the men who served under him in GRENADIER.

Lent took her out on her second patrol to hunt in the East China Sea southwest of Kyushu. At 1852, late in the afternoon of May 8, she encountered a convoy of six freighters and a large passenger ship which Lent correctly identified as the 14,457-ton TAIYO MARU. GRENADIER had been patrolling submerged. As soon as he established the fact that the convoy was southbound, Lent came to the normal approach course. No escorts were sighted, although their presence in the vicinity was assumed. The assumption proved correct, as events were to disclose.

The possibility of air cover induced Lent to keep periscope exposures to a minimum despite the failing light. Also to run deep between exposures. This was precisely the sort of attack dictated by peacetime training, and it was conducted as though TAIYO MARU were playing target for GRENADIER in a war game.

Ignoring the other ships present, Lent concentrated

on the big passenger liner. At 1931 he fired the first of four torpedoes in a salvo from the bow tubes, 105° starboard track, range 1,500 yards. The first and last torpedoes were set for a depth of 24 feet, and the second and third for 28 feet. Time of explosion indicated that the first and fourth torpedoes hit, and the other two missed, although the spread indicated that they should have hit.

Trailed down the home stretch by Sound, the torpedoes had apparently run straight and hot. Lent concluded that something had gone wrong with the magnetic exploders. These finicky devices could be "duds" for a variety of reasons, and Lent determined to make a note of it for the attention of ComSubPac.

Perhaps he made these notes while GRENADIER had her "going over." Two minutes after firing, she was burrowing deep and changing course when a stick of bombs exploded overhead. A few minutes later, fast screws were heard, and the ash-cans started coming down. Thirty-six depth charges roared in the deeps around her. Lent brought her undamaged through the barrage, although several blasts were close.

Nerves may have received another jarring after Lieutenant Commander Lent, mistrusting the Mark 14's exploder, reported his suspicions to Submarine Headquarters. Coming on the heels of other reports protesting the behavior of the Mark 14, Lent's comments sparked prompt reaction. Evidence of torpedo malfunction was summed up for review. Unfortunately the conclusions drawn by the analysts were as wide of the mark as the torpedoes. Rejecting evidence which indicated a bug in the machinery, ComSubPac ordered the depth-settings maintained as before (five feet greater than maximum depth of the target).

The big passenger liner was the only ship sunk by GRENADIER on that patrol. In fact, the liner was to be the only vessel officially credited to her record. A few months later, GRENADIER herself was sunk.

But in sinking the 14,457-ton TAIYO MARU, Lent's submarine dealt a crippling blow to the masters of the Co-Prosperity Sphere. The liner had been en route to the East Indies with a group of Jap scientists, economists and industrial experts bent on expediting exploitation of the conquered territory. Most of these experts went down with the torpedoed liner. Their liquidation undoubtedly slowed up the Jap looting effort.

"Sugar Boats"* to Brisbane

Following the enemy seizure of the Netherlands East Indies, the war moved front and center into the Solomons-Bismarck area.

Long before the cherry blossoms were out it was apparent that Tojo and Yamamoto were contemplating further expansion of the so-called Co-Prosperity Sphere. Such expansion was, in fact, a military imperative. For if conquerors are to capitalize on gains already made, they must protect the conquered areas until the raw materials therein can be exploited. Exploitation is difficult under fire (witness the difficulties experienced by the experts aboard TAIYO MARU). Therefore, outer bases must be established to defend the captured areas. In turn, outposts must be set up to secure the defense bases. This imperative is particularly pressing on the conqueror of insular territories wherein one island lies within striking distance of another. To protect Java, for example, it was necessary to seize and establish strongholds on all neighboring islands. And to maintain these strongholds it was necessary to occupy and set up bases on the islands that neighbored the neighboring islands. Thus the Celebes group could be secured from attack only by seizure of bases in New Guinea. The New Guinea bases could be held only by securing the Bismarck Archipelago. And Rabaul in the Bismarck Archipelago could be secured only by seizure of bases in the Solomon Islands.

The Jap militarists, therefore, were in the position of the liar who must devise one falsehood after another to support an original untruth. The analogous business of conquest—the strategic need for continued expansion—has embarrassed conquerors throughout history. For it must go on *ad infinitum* which leads to a military *reductio ad absurdum*. In Japan's case the *"absurdum"* was conquest of eastern New Guinea and the Solomons to control the approaches to Australia.

Nevertheless, the military necessity remained. So long as the American-Australian lifeline operated, Australia would be a standing threat to Japan's hold on the East Indies. And in the early spring of 1942, a Japanese drive on Australia seemed far from absurd. The Anzac Army was fighting in North Africa. Australian naval units had all but melted away in the crucible of the Java Sea. A skeleton air force and only a smattering of anti-aircraft guns were on guard in the east coast cities, and in the Perth and Fremantle area there were more kangaroos than troops.

The continent was looking invasion squarely in the teeth, and it was evident that Australia's defense was up to the U.S. Navy. It was equally apparent that the only U.S. naval units immediately

---

* "Sugar" is the code name for the letter "S" in "S-boats."

114

available for that defense were those which could be mustered by the submarine forces.

Plans were accordingly pushed to meet the emergency. The submarines in the Southwest Pacific were divided into two task forces—one to be based at Fremantle, the other to operate from Brisbane on Australia's east coast. That at Fremantle was composed of the SubsAsiatic Force under Captain Wilkes. The Brisbane Force was to be composed of S-boats—several to be detached from Wilkes' command, and a division which was being rushed into the breach from Panama. This force would be commanded by Captain Ralph W. Christie.

At the war's start, Christie was commander of Submarine Squadron Five, with 17 S-class submarines under his command. A veteran submariner who had assumed his first command in C-1 during the First World War, Christie knew undersea boats as the average citizen knows the inside of his sedan. He was also an acknowledged torpedo expert—from Torpedo School aboard USS MONTANA in 1916 to Officer in Charge, Torpedo Section, Bureau of Ordnance, 1936 to 1938. In Panama, February 1942, Christie received orders to proceed with SubDiv 53 "toward Australia."

The race run by these Panama boats—12,000 miles from Balboa to Brisbane—was another operational classic due to live in submarine history. Hazardous enough in peacetime, the voyage across the war-rocked Pacific tested the metal of every boat and man that made it. And there were no weaklings in either category in Panama S-class Submarine Division 53, under Lieutenant Commander E. E. Yeomans. All of them made it.

Led by Captain Christie aboard the new submarine tender GRIFFIN, the S-boats set out for Australia in early March. They were S-42 (Lieutenant O. G. Kirk); S-43 (Lieutenant E. R. Hannon); S-44 (Lieutenant J. R. Moore); S-45 (Lieutenant I. C. Eddy); S-46 (Lieutenant R. C. Lynch); and S-47 (Lieutenant J. W. Davis).

The old World War I "sugar boat" had not been designed for a 12,000-mile run—or a 6,000-mile run, for that matter. Now, called upon to hike from Panama to Australia, with but one fueling stop en route—Bora Bora in the Society Islands—the S-boaters must have experienced some private qualms. Time for worry, however, was one of the things the SubDiv 53 submariners did not have. Among other items lacking were air-conditioning systems for the submarines, and the well-known comforts of home. As for the operating condition of the S-boats, "bugs" were anticipated. In this regard, the crews were by no means disappointed.

S-43 and S-47 had run down to Panama from Argentia, Newfoundland—a strain to begin with. Overhauls had been rushed at the Philadelphia Navy Yard where the boats were reconditioned for war duty, and at Balboa there had been time for only sketchy repairs. But no one expected an overhaul to modernize elderly submarines constructed with single hulls and riveted fuel tanks which tended to leak and leave oil slicks. Modern submarines could not be made of old-timers whose bow and stern planes were noisy—boats with only two motors to get them out from under sharp-eared DD's. Could they make the long haul to Australia?

They could try.

One day the Society Islands turned up, and the Pacific racers had a three-day breather. Submarines did not make port in Bora Bora every Thursday, and the islanders regarded the S-boaters in much the same manner as the aborigines regarded mariners in the time of Melville.

Then, with the submarines running ahead of GRIFFIN in two groups, the little convoy headed for Brisbane. Making an average 8.7-knot speed, they trooped into Morton Bay, Brisbane, on the 15th of April. The epic voyage was over—42 days at sea without a major breakdown.

Awaiting the Panama boats at Brisbane was battle-scarred S-38. At intervals in the next three weeks, other S-boats from Fremantle came migrating across the Great Australian Bight to join the Brisbane Task Force. Under the command of Captain Christie, the S-boats of the former Asiatic Fleet and the Panama "sugar boats" were welded together into Task Force Forty-two.

At the time the Panama boats reached Brisbane the Japs were moving strong forces into the Bismarcks and the Solomons, and the Australian-American lifeline was seriously jeopardized. Task Force Forty-two was promptly ordered into action. Six days after arrival in Australia, the first Panama S-boat left Brisbane on war patrol. She was S-47, skippered by Lieutenant J. W. Davis. The rest of the force was in action by mid-May.

The "sugar boaters" went out from Brisbane, and they met more enemies than one. They battled weather, humidity, fatigue, mechanical difficulties and a large assortment of attendant mental hazards. On early patrols anywhere north of 15° south, the submarines were forced to run submerged all day, surfacing only at night. Temperatures averaged 95° F., and humidity averaged over 85% in S-boats running submerged. Throughout the day the submariners were in a soak of sweat, and often enough at night when engine trouble or failing electrical gear kept them working overtime. A three-week patrol in equatorial water was enough to wilt the most stalwart crew.

Both engines out of commission, S-43 (Lieutenant Commander Hannon) drifted helplessly for three days in enemy-infested seas off the lower tip of New Ireland. Other boats experienced battery trouble and oil leaks. But, with all these adversities to battle, the Brisbane submariners still found time to battle the Japs.

Patrolling off New Ireland on May 11, S-42 (Lieutenant O. G. Kirk) got off a brace of four torpedoes for three hits on a Japanese minelayer. She was the Imperial Navy's 4,400-ton OKINOSHIMA, and she obliged S-42 by sinking on the spot. First blood for the task force from Brisbane.

The Brisbane S-boaters would presently draw more. Armed with the reasonably reliable Mark 10 torpedo, they dealt a telling punch in Australia's defense. And in keeping the old S-boats in there fighting, they made what has been called a remarkable demonstration of the "mastery of mind over matter." They also put on a remarkable demonstration of "guts."

Battles Above and Below

Ju Island, located between New Guinea and Halmahera, is not prominent on the map. But it was as unforgettable as Manhattan to five U.S. Army aviators whose plane made a crash landing in its jungles early in May. The flyers got off a call for help, and waited. There might be Japs, cannibals, head-hunters and other bogies in that neighborhood. But presently a periscope peered up at the beach, and there was PORPOISE on hand to rescue the Crusoes. Picking up the aviators, she took them to Darwin—all part of the submariners' work.

Meantime, another submarine was going into action—one whose name was to be engraved in gleaming chirography across the broad Pacific. The name: SILVERSIDES. The engravers: Creed Burlingame and crew.

Burlingame had come up through the conning tower of an S-boat—the old S-30—and he knew the ups and downs of submarining. The war was not three months old when, at Mare Island, he assumed command of SILVERSIDES, newest of the Pacific Fleet's new-construction submarines.

Sleek, streamlined and modern to the last fitting, she was a magnificent engine of war. And her launching boded ill for the Japanese, although her trial run had not been entirely successful. During a quick dive her stern planes had jammed. As she went down and kept on going, Burlingame "blew everything," but the water wasn't there to save her, and she slammed her nose into the bottom. Torpedomen caromed off the bulkheads. Crockery crashed in the galley. Burlingame and crew managed to back the submarine out of the silt, and she returned to dock with nothing much worse than a muddy nose. But a sailor with nautical superstitions might have wished her a more auspicious beginning.

On their way out to Hawaii they almost lost their radioman striker, Sam Remington. New man in submarines (he had joined the Navy but a year before), Remington was standing lookout on the bridge when the order came, "Take her down!" Remington heard the yell as his companion lookouts raced for the hatch. But he had tied the leather thongs of his binoculars to the "A" frame, and now, hasty-fingered, he was unable to untie the knot.

A frantic yank failed to break the leather thongs. Unwilling to leave the binoculars, Remington fought the knot and finally loosened it. Then, in confusion, he raced to the after ladder instead of leaping down to the bridge forward. Diving across the "cigarette deck," he plunged through the wheelhouse for the conning-tower hatch.

He found the hatch sealed. SILVERSIDES was going down.

"Halloo!" Remington shouted in the bridge telephone. "I'm up here! Man topside!"

No answer on the phone. Green seas were slapping under the deck boards and a burst of spray scudded into the fairwater. The lad stared appalled as the deck came awash. Lonely ocean and sky. He'd better climb to the lookout tower and jump. And it looked like a long swim to nowhere when the submarine suddenly lurched upward and the deck rose clear. The button on the conning-tower phone had been taped down that night, and Remington's yell in the mouthpiece had been heard.

No one aboard SILVERSIDES was going to loiter on her bridge after that, but it was her subsequent misfortune to lose one of the few deck gunners killed in action during a "battle surface." Late in April she was assigned to her first patrol in an area off the coast of Japan. Burlingame told all hands they were shoving off for the real thing, and they headed out of Pearl Harbor into tumbling seas.

Rough voyage to Midway gave the crew authentic sea legs, and then, about 540 miles north of Marcus and 600 from Japan, SILVERSIDES waded into the tag end of a typhoon. On May 10, about 0800, with high seas combing the superstructure, a hail was raised by the lookout.

"Two masts! Four points on the starboard bow! Crossing!"

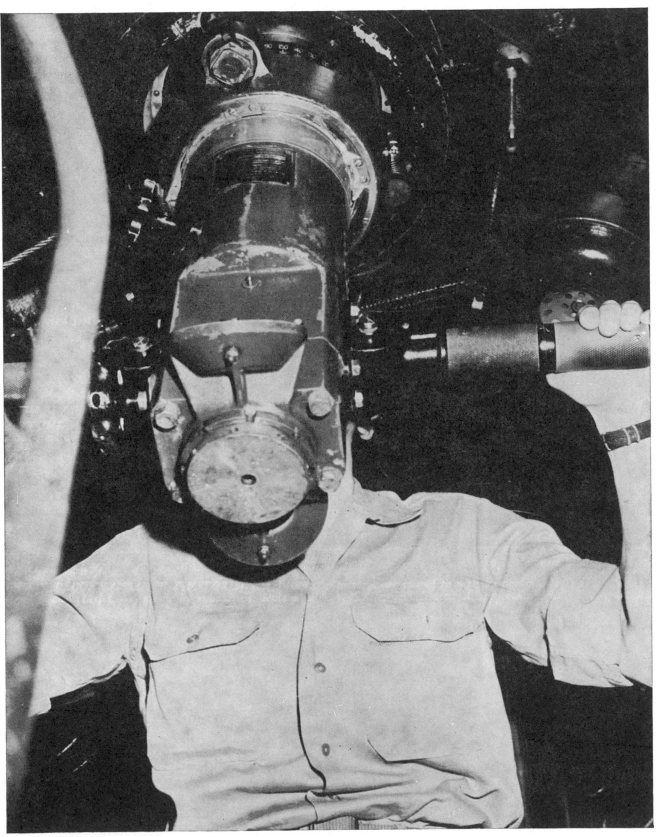

MAN FROM MARS? No, from Neptune. A sub-mariner's view of the skipper in conning tower performing familiar feat of "walking the periscope around." The order, "Up periscope!" or "Down periscope!" elevates or lowers the scope in its well. The periscope is revolved by moving the training handles.

SUBMARINE GUN CREW in action! Manning a 4-incher, these deep-seamen are duelling on the surface. Hot-shell man removes shell case as third loader passes up shell. Greenling's gunners staged similar scene, night in April '42.

SOUVENIR. Silversides *man recovers life-ring from torpedoed* Tairin Maru.

ANOTHER SOUVENIR. Silversides *was a champion ship-sinker. Here two of crew pick up a Jap invasion barge.*

CREW OF S-42 *on deck of sub which sank Jap mine-layer Okinoshima off New Ireland. Leaky and cranky, S-42 was one of old "sugar boats" that helped stem Jap drive toward Australia. She drew first blood for the Brisbane Force.*

Burlingame was topside on the double. Binocular inspection revealed the target as a Japanese trawler, maybe 300 tons.

"Patrol boat! We'll sink her with gunfire!"

Burlingame ordered battle stations for gun attack and the gun crew hit the deck. The target—a big, sea-going sampan with sail and auxiliary engines—was soon in range. The submariners opened fire with machine guns and the 3-incher. The trawler replied with rifle and machine-gun fire.

SILVERSIDES' gunners had to fight to keep their feet on the pitching deck, and the first shots went wild. The sight-setter, struck by a wall of swooping water, went acrobating to the forward engine-room hatch. The shell-passers struggled, fell, hung on. Burlingame drove to closer range, and the gun crew found the target with a succession of hits. Fire burst from the trawler, but she refused to sink. Machine-gun bullets whipped across the submarine's deck. Second loader, Mike Harbin, TM3, fell with a bullet in his temple.

Retaliating, the submarine gunners pumped shells into the Jap trawler. Riddled, spouting flames, the sampan remained afloat like so much burning cork. As the target was wrecked beyond repair, Burlingame broke off the engagement. Further expenditure of ammunition would have been futile. The action had lasted over an hour, the gun crew was close to exhaustion, and the loss of a man had made the battle painfully costly.

Submariners, usually fatalists, expect to meet death when their number comes up. But they seldom conceive of death as an individual matter. All in the same boat, they think of themselves as "all going out together," and Harbin's solitary loss was a shock to the crew. The torpedoman's body was commended to the deep at sunset. Harbin's mates in the after torpedo room served as pallbearers. Burlingame read the service. Afterwards he addressed the crew at general quarters. "The first fish we fire will have Harbin's name on it."

The torpedo with Harbin's name on it was fired at a Japanese submarine on the afternoon of May 13th. The enemy's conning tower was sighted across an expanse of rough water, and Burlingame directed a surface approach. The torpedo raced on its way and an explosion was heard. The enemy's periscope disappeared. SILVERSIDES cheered a sinking.

While the sinking of this submarine was never confirmed, there was no doubt about the destruction of a 4,000-ton Japanese merchantman in the same area on May 17th. In itself unremarkable, this torpedoing was attended by the sort of incident that spices the conversation of undersea mariners.

On the day in question SILVERSIDES was cruising submerged in a locale that seemed to have been taken over by half the sampans of Nippon. Normally, a ship-hunting submarine would avoid such a raffish fishing fleet. Some of the small boats were undoubtedly naval patrols. Others were just fishing. But the area promised bigger game, and Burlingame remained on the lookout, raising his periscope cautiously in white-capped water that made its "feather" less detectable.

Each time he upped the periscope there seemed to be another sampan in view. Then he spied a medium-sized cargo vessel advancing into the scene. Alerting the crew, he headed SILVERSIDES for the target, which was several miles away.

A couple of patrol vessels were easily dodged, and SILVERSIDES was making a businesslike approach when Burlingame was suddenly aware of a peculiar noise in the conning tower. Something rustling against the superstructure? Weeds slapping the hull?

"Up periscope!" Burlingame barked at his executive officer. "What the devil is that?"

SILVERSIDES' exec, Lieutenant Commander Roy M. Davenport, didn't know.

Then walking the periscope, the skipper halted abruptly. Pointing aft, the periscope was focused on a great, flapping, winglike appendage which was trailing from the submarine's stern. Weaving and dripping—a weird marine creature with a blur of red in its heart, and a tail of bobbling tentacles—it might have been some species of octopus or fantastic ray.

Burlingame glared in a dismay which turned to outrage.

"Down periscope! Take her down!" he roared. "We've tangled into a fishnet! We're dragging a blank-blank Japanese flag!"

Marked by flags held aloft on tall bamboo poles, the native Japanese fishnet was usually visible from a distance. This one, snaring SILVERSIDES, had escaped attention as the submariners concentrated on the target. But the submarine's collision with the net did not escape the attention of the Jap fishermen. Burlingame caught a periscope glimpse of a sampan heading over to warn a patrol boat. With the latter less than a quarter of a mile away, he sent SILVERSIDES deep, hoping to dislodge the trailing net.

Little time was lost, as this submerged run was in the direction of the target. And during this approach another freighter was contacted on the same course as the first. Patrol boats were in the van of these merchantmen, and it was a locale where anything untoward might happen. Undeterred, Burlingame sent SILVERSIDES boring in, fishnet and all.

He hit the first AK with two torpedoes out of three.

The explosions roared in the sound gear and merged in a blast that shook the submarine. Periscope view showed the ship burst open at the stern, a tower of flame and smoke erupting from her mid-section.

"Munitions ship!" Burlingame cheered to his crew. "Let's get her sister!"

Two shots appeared to hit this second vessel—an 8,000 tonner—and another violent blast was heard. This second sinking was never verified, but damage, at least, seems a certainty. The submarine was not afforded the leisure for a periscope check. Patrol boats were closing in, and it was time to quit the vicinity.

When SILVERSIDES surfaced that night, her superstructure was subjected to examination. Strands of fishnet were found snagged in the topside gear—some cordage and a glass ball and a splintered bamboo pole topped by a tassel. The Rising Sun was gone. But, as Lieutenant Commander Davenport remarked, SILVERSIDES was probably the only American submarine to make an approach while flying the Japanese flag.

American submarines were beginning to fly facsimiles of that flag, however. Miniatures painted in neat array on the conning towers. As May advanced on the calendar, the list of torpedoings lengthened. Before the month was out, six more Japanese vessels went down.

POMPANO (Lieutenant Commander Parks) sank one on the 25th and another on the 30th. Her first was TOKYO MARU, a 902-ton tanker. The second was ATSUTA MARU, an 8,000-ton transport. Two down in the Nansei Shoto area.

SALMON (Lieutenant Commander McKinney) on May 25 sent ASAHI to the China Sea bottom. There a big 11,441-ton repair ship could make no more repairs for the Emperor's navy. Three days later in the same area, SALMON torpedoed and sank GANGES MARU, a 4,382-ton transport.

On that same day, SEAL (Lieutenant Commander Hurd) sent TATSUFUKU MARU, a 1,946-ton cargoman, to the bottom of the sea off Palawan.

And therein lies a tale—another undersea story to add flavor to a submariner's coffee. Pioneer sinkings were often difficult to verify. Prematuring torpedoes, dim periscope vision, scrambled Japanese records and official reluctance on the part of Tokyo to admit shipping losses made accurate sinking assessments a job for SORG. But the sinking in question was easy to confirm. This particular *maru* was double sunk!

Two Subs, Two Hits, No Errors

On the night of May 28, SEAL was en route to a patrol station off the coast of French Indo-China. She had just transited Balabac Strait when, at 2127, the lookout sighted the target.

Bright moonlight abetted a night-periscope attack. Hurd sounded the diving alarm, and SEAL went under to commence a submerged approach. Thirty minutes later she gained good attack position, and Hurd fired two torpedoes. Seconds ticked away. Two misses!

A quick report from Sound—the torpedoes had missed astern. Hurd calculated the target was traveling three knots faster than he had originally estimated, and he fired two more torpedoes, adding three knots into the fire control equation. This time there was a thudding explosion. Periscope view showed the ship hit just forward of the bridge, settling by the bow, her progress slowed.

Hurd lowered the periscope, and resumed the submerged approach to close the target. Either the tide or the target, or both, wandered in an erratic course that proved puzzling to the submariners, and Hurd was forced to surface to regain position. With a new bead on the target, he sent SEAL once more to periscope depth and bored in to deliver the *coup de grâce*.

At 6,000 yards Hurd trained the periscope on the damaged target. The freighter's bow was almost under water. Like a dying cow, head down, she was dragging herself backward at a speed of about 6 knots. Hurd sent his submarine deep and put on speed to get in.

Some nine minutes later, as SEAL was drawing close, a sharp explosion was heard in the direction of the target. This was followed by a series of lesser detonations. The ship's screw was heard to start up and then abruptly stop.

After a wait of several minutes, Hurd decided to go up to periscope depth for a look-see. As SEAL was climbing surfaceward, a tremendous undersea thunderclap shook the submarine. The men in SEAL's control room could almost taste the powder. Trailing explosions gradually petered out. Hurd put up an inquisitive periscope. The target had gone down. Moonlight and water—the sea was bare.

But it has previously been remarked that pioneer periscope vision was on occasion astigmatic, and in any event this was a matter for sonar. The sea's surface was bare, but the sea has a dimension beneath its surface. Unbeknownst to SEAL, she was not alone in this undersea dimension.

While Hurd's submarine had been closing in on the wounded freighter, the submarine SWORDFISH (Chester Smith) had glimpsed the quarry. She was on that side of the freighter directly opposite to SEAL, and her periscope had sighted the target just after

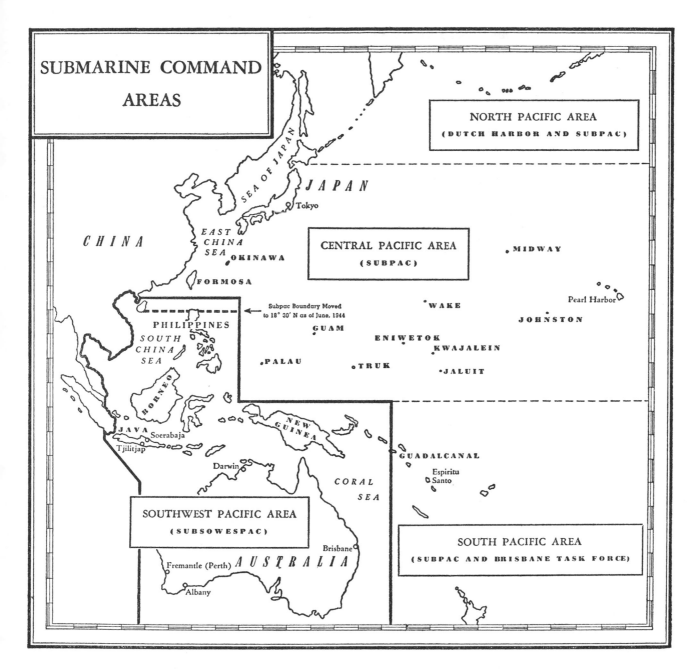

SUBMARINE COMMAND AREAS

NORTH PACIFIC AREA
(DUTCH HARBOR AND SUBPAC)

SEA OF JAPAN

JAPAN

Tokyo

CHINA

EAST CHINA SEA

OKINAWA

FORMOSA

CENTRAL PACIFIC AREA
(SUBPAC)

MIDWAY

Pearl Harbor

WAKE

JOHNSTON

Subpac Boundary Moved
to 18° 30' N as of June, 1944

PHILIPPINES

SOUTH CHINA SEA

GUAM

ENIWETOK

KWAJALEIN

PALAU

TRUK

JALUIT

BORNEO

JAVA Soerabaja

Tjilitjap

NEW GUINEA

Darwin

CORAL SEA

GUADALCANAL

Espiritu Santo

SOUTHWEST PACIFIC AREA
(SUBSOWESPAC)

Brisbane

Fremantle (Perth) AUSTRALIA

Albany

SOUTH PACIFIC AREA
(SUBPAC AND BRISBANE TASK FORCE)

SEAL had put a fatal hole in the vessel's head. Driving SWORDFISH in, Smith had fired three torpedoes at the silhouetted ship. Three torpedoes that were headed straight for, and might have demolished, SEAL—if TATSUFUKU MARU had not been there to stop them.

Submarine Command Areas

The foregoing anecdote should not suggest that submarine operating areas in the Pacific had become so constricted in the spring of 1942 that patrols were overlapping and there were two U.S. submarines for every unwary enemy freighter. Obviously the situation was quite the reverse.

In the Southwest Pacific the war was spreading like a forest fire. Submarines were not only called upon to defend an expanding front, but were faced with the problem of covering the conquered territory behind that front—an oceanic "hinterland" that broadened by many acres as the enemy advanced. Strictly speaking, there is no "front line" for the Submarine Force. It plays the entire field. And this field had expanded to such an extent by the spring of 1942 that adequate area coverage was out of the question.

To begin with, there were far too few submarines. Loss of SEALION, S-36, S-26, SHARK and PERCH was felt in every theater. Replacements had arrived—SILVER-SIDES and other new-construction submarines had

119

reached Pearl, and the Panama S-boats were at Brisbane. Staunch as were these and later reinforcements, months would pass before the pressure was relieved and there were sufficient submarines to patrol the vast network of sea lanes open to enemy ship traffic.

The chart on page 119 shows the Submarine Command Areas—Central Pacific, South Pacific and Southwest Pacific—as established for coverage by the Pacific Fleet (SubPac) Force based at Pearl Harbor, Task Force Forty-two (Brisbane), and Southwest Pacific (SoWesPac) Force based at Fremantle.

As indicated on the chart, the Pacific Fleet Force patrolled the Mandates, the sea lanes to and around Japan in the waters off Formosa, the Nansei Shoto and the Bonins, the East China and Yellow Sea, and the coastal waters of Japan's home islands. The area covered by the Pacific Fleet Force would soon include the North Pacific where Aleutian and northern Kurile patrols were assigned to submarines from Pearl Harbor.

The task force at Brisbane—a port destined to serve as a submarine operating base until March 1945—was devoted primarily to assignments on the Solomons-Bismarck front. The S-boats from the Philippines and Panama had their work cut out for them in this theater, for the waters they patrolled were shadowed by Japanese aircraft that roamed as far south as Tulagi and Guadalcanal in the Solomons, hovered over the Bismarck Archipelago, the Louisiade Archipelago and the Faisi-Shortland sector, and ranged the northeast coast of New Guinea.

To the submarines based at Fremantle fell the task of patrolling the long road back to the Philippines—the intricate waterways of the Malay Barrier, the Arafura Sea, the Flores Sea, the Banda Sea, the Java and Celebes Seas, the Sulu Sea, the South China Sea as far north as Hainan and as deep as the Gulf of Siam. Had all the U.S. submarines in the Pacific been concentrated in this one area that spring, there would scarcely have been enough of them to patrol the maze of traffic routes linking the ports of the Southwest Pacific. That there were not enough submarines for this prodigious region is evidenced by the fact that, as the Japanese offensive swept into the Solomons, submarines from Fremantle were rushed as reinforcements to Brisbane. And by the end of 1942 only eight or nine submarines were operating out of Fremantle. These few for the whole Southwest Pacific Area!

No, the Pacific was not teeming with U.S. submarines in May 1942. And while many leagues of ocean demanded patrol, submarines were also called upon to perform a multiplicity of special missions which diverted them from ship-hunting. In addition, they were hampered by the torpedo shortage (which remained critical for another year). Yet Japanese ships were going to the bottom, and the economists in Tokyo were already beginning to worry about rice, oil, nickel, tin and other imports required by the voracious War Machine.

So May warmed toward June. And as the springtide deepened, a drastic change in the war weather was in the making. All indications pointed to a violent upheaval—a climacteric storm moving with cyclonic velocity toward a vital mid-Pacific area. The area: Midway.

CHAPTER 11

THE BATTLE OF MIDWAY

Coral Sea Overture

For some time in the spring of 1942 a contentious debate had engaged Japan's grand strategists in Imperial General Headquarters. Question: to outflank Australia by a drive through eastern New Guinea, the Solomons and the New Hebrides, or to buttress Japan's Wake-Gilberts defense line by seizure of Midway in the Central Pacific and the western Aleutians in the far north?

There was much to be said on both sides. The South Pacific adventure appealed to those who favored the securing of the Philippines-Netherlands East Indies territory. With a spearhead already in Rabaul, aggressive forces should be able to sweep the weakened Allies from the South Pacific and cut the American-Australian supply line with relative ease.

Popular Admiral Yamamoto sponsored the Midway-Aleutians drive. For one thing, the securing of Japan's mid-Pacific defense line would reduce the threat of such air raids as Doolittle's on Tokyo, and strengthen the screen which American submarines, Japan bound, had been shooting full of holes. For another, the logistic problem in the South Pacific was becoming overly complicated. An Australian offensive meant a lengthened transport service. A lengthened transport service meant more *marus*. Conservative General Staff officers insisted that shipping facilities ought to be augmented before the logistics problem was extended in the direction of Australia.

Meanwhile, time and tide refused to wait for Japan's grand strategists. Following the raids on Lae and Salamaua, a strong American naval force was assembling in the New Hebrides where bases had been established at Efate and Espiritu Santo. On hand was the task force built around the aircraft carrier LEXINGTON, commanded by Rear Admiral Aubrey W. Fitch, plus Rear Admiral Frank J. Fletcher's task force—the aircraft carrier YORKTOWN, supported by two cruisers, and destroyers.

The attempted raid on Rabaul in the Bismarcks and the blistering attacks on the Japanese bases in New Guinea forced the Jap hand in the South Pacific. Early in April, Japanese shock troops landed on beachheads in the upper Solomons, and established a seaplane base on Tulagi Island in the eastern end of the group. Simultaneously a drive was mounted with Port Moresby in southeast New Guinea as its objective. Invasion forces were assembled at Rabaul on New Britain and at Buin on Bougainville Island. At Truk in the Carolines a naval striking force was readied. Escorted by three cruisers, two DD's and the small aircraft carrier SHOHO, the invasion convoy was to rendezvous in the Solomon Sea. The naval striking force—aircraft carriers SHOKAKU and ZUIKAKU, two cruisers, seven destroyers and a tanker—was to steam around the eastern end of the Solomons and attack the Allied surface forces in the Coral Sea.

The resulting Battle of the Coral Sea blocked the Japanese drive. Informed of the enemy's intentions, the Allied High Command ordered the forces under Fitch and Fletcher into action. On May 4, YORKTOWN headed for the Solomons, her planes taking off for three lightning strikes at Tulagi. This surprise raid accounted for a Jap destroyer and a minelayer.

After the Tulagi strike, the YORKTOWN force joined the LEXINGTON force, and on the morning of May 7, planes from the American carriers found the Japanese carrier SHOHO off Misima Island. Zero fighters rose to intercept, but the American dive bombers got in deadly hits. In a short time SHOHO was burning like a haystack. Coming in low under thunderheads of smoke, American torpedo planes finished the job. SHOHO went down with some 200 of her crew.

The Japanese invasion force fled north. The SHOKAKU-ZUIKAKU striking force, however, had already skirted the eastern Solomons and was in the Coral Sea. The large Japanese carriers were blanketed by concealing cloud-cover, and their scouts were able to surprise the Americans off Misima. Seventy Jap planes streaked in to attack the U.S. destroyer SIMS and the tanker NEOSHO. Hit three times, SIMS broke in two and sank. Only 13 of her crew were saved. Struck by seven bombs and a burning plane, NEOSHO, drifting inferno, was eventually sunk by an American destroyer. One hundred and seventy-six of her complement were lost.

Throughout that day and the night of May 7-8 the opposing carrier forces maneuvered for position at long range. Air battle exploded on the morning of the 8th when both forces simultaneously located each other with scouting planes, and the carriers launched their aircraft in a criss-cross attack.

From LEXINGTON and YORKTOWN 82 planes took off, and about 70 zoomed from the decks of ZUIKAKU and SHOKAKU. Far at sea the air squadrons passed each other at a distance beyond contact range. The clock was nearing 1100 when the Jap and American aircraft screamed down on their targets.

YORKTOWN's planes struck at the aircraft carrier SHOKAKU. LEXINGTON's slashed down through a break in the clouds to strike at ZUIKAKU. Two 1,000-pound bombs struck SHOKAKU squarely, wrecking her flight deck and starting gasoline fires. Zigzagging desperately, the wounded carrier managed to evade the American torpedo planes that raced in for the kill. Attacking ZUIKAKU, the planes from LEXINGTON encountered heavy opposition, and seven were lost. Less than half were able to locate the cloud-screened target. The bombers failed to get in a deadly hit, and this carrier also evaded the torpedo planes. Apparently she suffered only minor damage.

Sheltered by an overcast sky, the Japanese carriers had the advantage of their American rivals over the horizon. Exposed beneath blue skies, the YORKTOWN and LEXINGTON were the easier targets. Hard-fighting interceptor groups, effective anti-aircraft fire and expert ship-handling saved YORKTOWN's life after an air bomb exploded in her aviation storeroom.

LEXINGTON was less fortunate. The larger of the two aircraft carriers, she became the primary target of the attacking planes. Misinterpreted orders held the lion's share of escorting cruisers with YORKTOWN. Battle maneuvers separated the carrier groups, and LEXINGTON faced the major attack with an inferior defense force.

Jap torpedo planes raced in, and two torpedoes struck LEXINGTON's port side. A moment later she was staggered by a 1,000-pound bomb which demolished her port forward battery. A smaller bomb exploded inside her funnel. Fire spurted from her superstructure. Damage control parties downed the flames, and LEXINGTON kept on going. But the bomb hits had sprung her gasoline pipes, and shortly after 1300, escaping fumes caused a fatal explosion. Fires raced through the gaseous flat-top, and as the flames ate their way toward the magazines, an order was given to abandon ship.

A molten furnace, LEXINGTON was sunk that night by an American destroyer. In her flaming and exploding hull over 200 men had lost their lives. This number was equalled by the Japanese fatalities aboard SHOKAKU.

Comparing the loss of the 33,000-ton LEXINGTON with the 12,000-ton SHOHO, the destruction of two American destroyers with the one Japanese lost at Tulagi, and the loss of 66 U.S. planes with the 60 Japanese planes reported lost, the Japanese claimed a decisive victory. But the Battle of the Coral Sea— the first naval engagement in history in which the opposing surface forces never sighted each other— was a strategic victory for the Allies. The Japanese invasion of Port Moresby by sea was frustrated. Japan learned that the U.S. Navy, far from *hors de combat*, was able to muster strong surface forces in the Pacific only six months after Pearl Harbor. The Japanese lost much more than a small carrier and one destroyer in the Battle of the Coral Sea. They lost face.

To salvage that face—restore to it the lineaments of implacable conqueror—Imperial Headquarters turned to Admiral Yamamoto. At Admiral Yamamoto's disposal were more than 100 warships, including 11 battleships and four aircraft carriers. The U.S. Navy had lost LEXINGTON. The carrier YORKTOWN (as seen through Japanese spectacles) was severely crippled. Aircraft carriers HORNET and ENTERPRISE had raced to the South Pacific where they had arrived too late to join the Coral Sea Battle. When last accounted for (by Japanese Intelligence) SARATOGA was on the American West Coast undergoing repairs. Thus (according to Japanese deduction) there were no U.S. aircraft carriers in the Central Pacific. Now was the time to seize Midway.

Submarine Support of Fleet Operations

Prior to May 1942, U.S. submarines (with the exception of those on special mission) had operated as free agents on combat patrols in which the primary mission was the sinking of enemy shipping, merchant and naval. Acting under broad directives from CinC-Pac or ComSoWesPac, and assigned patrol areas at the discretion of force commanders, they went out free-lancing to spear their quarry.

This sort of offensive patrolling was to continue throughout the war. But as the conflict went on, a gradually increasing percentage of submarine effort was diverted to the support of fleet operations. In each major carrier strike, and in the amphibious operations that were developed, submarines had their part to play. Concentration along the enemy's trade routes and supply lines fell into the category of normal patrolling. On such patrols the submarine generally operated as a "lone wolf," or, when the tactic was adopted, as the member of a pack. But in scouting, running interference and guarding the backfield, submarines team-working with the Fleet made a cardinal contribution to the Navy's battle record.

With the Battle of Midway on the horizon, the SubPac Force was called upon *en masse* to support fleet operations. This was to be the first time that Pearl Harbor submarines interrupted their raiding patrols to operate as a task force with the Pacific Fleet. In the Java Sea Battle, groups of Asiatic Fleet submarines had entered action in conjunction with the ABDA Fleet. But in that battle the submarines were chiefly employed as scouts—the force was widely dispersed and many of the boats remained on patrol. At Midway the Pearl Harbor Force converged to operate as a fleet arm—the first instance in the Pacific war wherein submarines were so employed.

After the engagement in the Coral Sea, a two-prong Japanese thrust at the Aleutians and Midway was seen as in the cards. By the middle of May 1942 the pattern of the attack became clear. The thrust at Dutch Harbor would be by way of a diversion, and the enemy's main attack and invasion effort would be aimed at Midway.

CinCPac mustered his defense forces for deployment. Naval units in the Aleutians were alerted and reinforced, and all available surface and air forces in the Central Pacific were assembled in Hawaiian waters. HORNET and ENTERPRISE were recalled from the South Pacific. YORKTOWN made a top-speed run to Pearl Harbor for emergency repairs. By the last week in May, three aircraft carriers, eight cruisers

and 14 destroyers composed the surface fleet which was readied for Midway's defense.

In the meantime, on May 14 orders had been dispatched to 25 Pacific Fleet submarines, assigning them to stations in the Midway area. In essence, the submarine captains were told that a full-scale invasion of Midway was expected, and the enemy would probably consist of an invasion convoy backed up by aircraft carriers, cruisers and destroyers. The submarines were to scout and report the location of the Japanese ships, and to intercept and attack.

At this date SubPac was in the strongest and by far the most advantageous position which that organization had achieved since the war's outbreak. Twelve new subs from construction yards back in the States had been added to the original Pearl Harbor Force. Four submarines had been ordered to the Southwest Pacific to replace the number lost by that Command, but not one Pacific Fleet submarine had been lost since the beginning of the war. When zero hour was set for Midway, ComSubPac had 29 submarines under his operational control.

Early in May, Admiral Withers had been ordered to the States to command the Navy Yard, Portsmouth, N.H., where he was to supervise the submarine building program. To Admiral Withers all submariners were indebted for the fine recuperation program which included the leasing of Honolulu's Royal Hawaiian Hotel for a rest camp de luxe. The first of such camps, it inaugurated a broad project which was to prove worth its weight in wildcats when it came to physical reconditioning and morale-maintenance in the undersea service. All hands wished Admiral Withers a heartfelt Godspeed. He was relieved by Rear Admiral Robert H. English, who had been serving as Commander Submarine Squadron Four and Commander Submarine Base, Pearl Harbor.

As ComSubPac, Admiral English stepped into the task of directing the Pacific Fleet submarines in the Midway engagement. English needed no introduction to submarine warfare. He had been immersed in submarining since 1914, the year he reported for duty in the old D-3, one of the gasoline-driven breed which antedated the Diesel. He was commander of D-3 when the United States entered World War I, after which he placed O-4 in commission and commanded her throughout that war.

Director of submarines in the Office of CNO—commander of T-boats in SubDiv Fifteen—commander of SubDiv Eight, which included ten O-class submarines—English climbed the undersea ladder. There followed several tours of duty ashore, command of SubDiv Eight (six S-boats) at Pearl Harbor, the post of Chief of Staff to the Commander Submarine Force, U.S. Fleet, and a desk job as Director of Fleet Maintenance. July 1941 he assumed command of the cruiser HELENA; March 1942 he was commanding the Submarine Base at Pearl; May 1942, he was ComSubPac, deploying the Pacific Fleet submarines for the Midway showdown.

Of the 29 submarines which comprised SubPac, only four were to remain out of the Midway battle. THRESHER and ARGONAUT were undergoing overhaul. TRITON, returning from patrol in the East China Sea, was too low on fuel and torpedoes to participate in the battle. SILVERSIDES was ordered to maintain her patrolling of the Kii Suido entrance to Japan's Inland Sea.

Among the 25 submarines available for the Midway engagement, six had never made a war patrol. And four of these novices were newcomers from the West Coast whose crews had not had time for battle training at Pearl Harbor. Eight of the 25 were just in from patrol and needed repair. Six others were out on patrol when the Midway crisis developed, and they would have to stretch their legs to reach the battle area in time to attempt the interception of retiring units of the enemy fleet. The remaining five had just departed on routine patrol or were on the point of departure when ComSubPac ordered them to Midway. These were able to reach their assigned stations and begin defensive patrols with time at their disposal.

Previously designated as Task Force 7, the Pacific Fleet submarines were divided by ComSubPac into three task groups. These task groups did not include those submarines which were on patrol in areas far from Midway.

Task Group 7.1 formed the Midway patrol group. It was composed of the following submarines:

CACHALOT	(Lieutenant Commander G. A. Lewis)
FLYINGFISH	(Lieutenant Commander G. R. Donaho)
TAMBOR	(Lieutenant Commander J. W. Murphy)
TROUT	(Lieutenant Commander F. W. Fenno)
GRAYLING	(Lieutenant Commander E. Olson)
NAUTILUS	(Lieutenant Commander W. A. Brockman)
GROUPER	(Lieutenant Commander C. E. Duke)
DOLPHIN	(Lieutenant Commander R. L. Rutter)
GATO	(Lieutenant Commander W. G. Myers)
CUTTLEFISH	(Lieutenant Commander M. P. Hottel)
GUDGEON	(Lieutenant Commander H. B. Lyon)
GRENADIER	(Lieutenant Commander W. A. Lent)

West of Midway these submarines of Task Group 7.1 were to converge and patrol on stations that were located like the points of an opening fan. A fan that was intended to screen the face of Midway from the oncoming Japanese hurricane.

The second task group—Task Group 7.2—was composed of three submarines. These were:

NARWHAL	(Lieutenant Commander C. W. Wilkins)
PLUNGER	(Lieutenant Commander D. C. White)
TRIGGER	(Lieutenant Commander J. H. Lewis)

These three submarines were to cover an area to the east and a little north of Midway, on a scouting line about halfway between Midway Island and Oahu. There was a possibility that Yamamoto might launch a diversionary strike at Oahu, and the Task Group 7.2 trio were to serve as roving shortstops in this east-of-Midway area where they could run in an arc to intercept any Oahu attackers and warn the task group in the backfield.

This third group—Task Force 7.3—covered a position some 300 miles north of Oahu. The group was composed of four submarines.

TARPON	(Lieutenant Commander L. Wallace)
PIKE	(Lieutenant Commander W. A. New)
FINBACK	(Lieutenant Commander J. L. Hull)
GROWLER	(Lieutenant Commander H. W. Gilmore)

Accordingly, on the morning of June 4, the three task groups and their submarine units were in position as shown in the accompanying diagram. (See page 125.)

With the exception of CACHALOT, FLYINGFISH and CUTTLEFISH, the Task Group 7.1 submarines were ordered to patrol a line perpendicular to the median of their assigned sectors. The three submarines named were to conduct station patrol. They were ordered to conduct periscope patrol during daylight and remain ready to surface and pursue the enemy when contact report was received. Note that CUTTLEFISH was on station some 700 miles west of Midway.

Task Group 7.2 and Task Group 7.3 were directed to conduct submerged patrol on station and move in line or pursue the enemy when ordered. All three groups were instructed to disregard station boundaries when in contact with the enemy.

Meanwhile, there were six other Pacific Fleet submarines at sea. These were the ones returning from long-distance patrols. They included:

GREENLING	(Lieutenant Commander H. C. Bruton)
DRUM	(Lieutenant Commander R. H. Rice)
POLLACK	(Lieutenant Commander S. P. Moseley)
TUNA	(Lieutenant Commander J. L. De Tar)
POMPANO	(Lieutenant Commander L. S. Parks)
PORPOISE	(Lieutenant Commander J. R. McKnight)

Of the above, DRUM, POLLACK, TUNA and POMPANO were coming east from Japanese waters. GREENLING was en route from a patrol in the Carolines and Marshalls. PORPOISE, due a State-side overhaul, was heading for Pearl from Fremantle. These submarines were to be supplied with all available information

NAUTILUS SINKS SORYU! The periscope looks on as a killing torpedo strikes the damaged carrier. Sole SubPac success at Midway, the Soryu sinking presaged the shape of things to come. A faulty torpedo lowered the score until 1944—then boom! More than one U.S. periscope saw a Jap carrier torpedoed.

JAP CRUISER MOGAMI. *In such a hurry to get away from* Tambor's *periscope, she rammed sister cruiser* Mikuma. *Damaged ships were later caught, pounded by U. S. bombers.* Mikuma *was sunk—thanks to submarine scare.*

NAUTILUS IN DRYDOCK. *At Philadelphia Navy Yard. Picture gives good view of big V-boat's underwater body, torpedo tubes and deck tubes. One of Navy's 3 largest subs, she was modernized in autumn of 1941—in time for Midway. She and Narwhal carried 6-inch guns. After Midway,* Nautilus *proceeded to Empire waters, sank DD Yamakaze.*

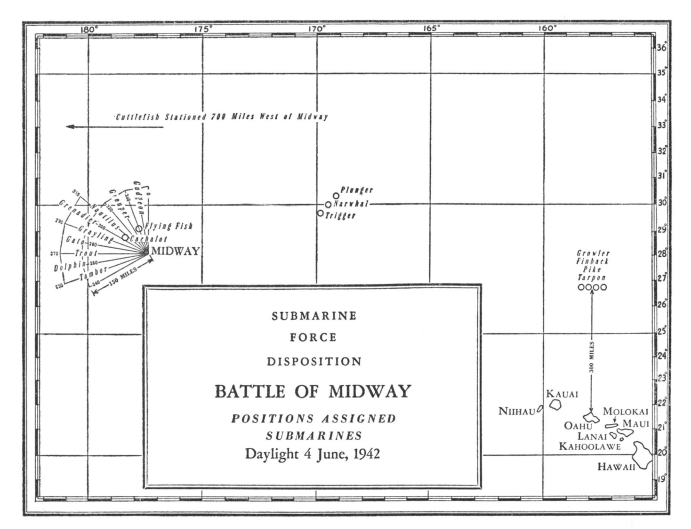

SUBMARINE

FORCE

DISPOSITION

BATTLE OF MIDWAY

*POSITIONS ASSIGNED
SUBMARINES*
Daylight 4 June, 1942

on the location of Japanese fleet units and they were ordered to attempt the interception of such units as retreated.

On June 1, Task Group 7.1 was advised that American surface forces, including aircraft carriers, might operate west of Midway. The submarines would be notified by CinCPac if positional changes were demanded.

By the morning of June 3, all task group submarines were on station. That night the word was flashed to the three task groups and to the six submarines heading for Midway—*"Enemy planes attack Dutch Harbor."*

So the Aleutian thrust was underway. The Midway "haymaker" could not be far off.

Its direction previously detected, the haymaker was a "telegraphed" punch. During the morning of June 3, a lone PBY patrol plane had spotted the main Japanese attack force 700 miles west of Midway. Flying Fortresses took off from Midway's airstrip to bomb the Jap armada that afternoon, but the bombers succeeded in doing little damage. Unaware of

what was waiting for him, Yamamoto kept on coming. His presence in the Midway theater was revealed to the waiting submarines shortly after they heard the word about Dutch Harbor.

Captain to cook, the submariners tightened their belts.

"Here it comes!"

The Battle

One of the war's decisive battles, Midway developed as an air show. Planes did most of the attacking, aircraft carriers were the major targets, and there were no blows traded between surface craft. But submarines on both sides dealt deadly torpedoes, and throughout the combat their influence was as a strong undercurrent on the battle's tide.

In over-all tactical command at Pearl Harbor Headquarters, Admiral Nimitz had dispatched the ENTERPRISE-HORNET force to the Midway area on May 28. This force was commanded by Admiral Raymond A. Spruance. It was followed by YORKTOWN and her escorts. The two carrier forces rendezvoused on June 2, and, under command of Admiral Fletcher, steamed to a position north of Midway.

On Midway Island a handful of Army B-26 bombers and B-17's had been mustered. On station were 27 Marine Corps dive bombers and 27 fighters (under command of Lieutenant Colonel Ira L. Kimes), six Navy torpedo planes, and some old Catalinas.

The land-based air and the carrier forces enumerated, plus the submarines of Task Group 7.1 and Task Group 7.2, comprised the bulk of Midway's defense. Rushing from San Diego was the aircraft carrier SARATOGA, but she did not arrive in time for the battle.

Converging on Midway in three groups, the Japanese armada advanced as a champion heavyweight on a fighter of the middleweight class. Approaching Midway from the northwest was the Striking Force which would spearhead the attack. This force was composed of destroyers, cruisers and two battleships supporting the four aircraft carriers, AKAGI, KAGA, HIRYU and SORYU—all veterans of the Pearl Harbor assault. A Main Body composed of seven battleships, cruisers and destroyers, led by Yamamoto himself, aboard the battleship YAMATO, was to approach from the west and stand off Midway until the island had been softened up by the Striking Force. After the island had been softened up by the Striking Force and presumably been reduced by the Main Body, the Occupation Force was to move in. This force, coming up from the Marianas, contained transports carrying 3,500 invasion troops, freighters loaded with supplies, tankers with fuel. It was accompanied by two battleships, several cruisers and a number of destroyers. Japanese submarines scouted ahead of the armada with orders to take a line west of Pearl Harbor and intercept any American forces sent to Midway's defense.

The defense forces got there ahead of the Jap submarines. Even so, Midway's defenders did not enjoy any supreme advantage. Fast action had pulled the teeth of surprise from the Japanese offensive, but the enemy's 11 battleships, four aircraft carriers and accompanying cruiser squadrons, destroyer squadrons and invasion ships remained to be dealt with. In the Midway area there was not a single U.S. battleship. YORKTOWN's repairs had been superficial, and her men still showed the strain of the Coral Sea engagement. Of the submariners at Midway, those who were not novices had been on the go from hell to breakfast. And now, on the morning of June 4 it didn't look as if they were going to get any breakfast.

At sunrise that morning the submarine task groups were in their assigned positions: Task Group 7.3 some 300 miles north of Oahu; Task Group 7.2 between Oahu and Midway; Task Group 7.1 spread out as a fan screening the island's western approaches.

In this fan-shaped sector, CACHALOT and FLYINGFISH were about 60 miles northwest of Midway. Some 150 miles farther out, in a sweep that covered the area from north to southwest, were GUDGEON, GROUPER, NAUTILUS, GRAYLING, TROUT and TAMBOR. Fifty miles beyond this screen, GRENADIER, GATO and DOLPHIN were making wide sweeps. And 450 miles farther west, a solitary sentry, patrolled CUTTLEFISH.

Breakfast? Not with stomach muscles as tight as whalebone corsets, throats dry and teeth gritty from the tension of waiting. During the night, four torpedo-rigged Catalinas from Midway had found the enemy Occupation Force and stopped a tanker. First blood. But it was a drop in the bucket to Yamamoto, directing the armada's steady advance. Inexorably the Japs came on, moving under a concealing weather front. Two hundred miles northeast of Midway, the American aircraft carriers were under blue sky—another disadvantage. Under water, the submariners in their pressure hulls could only guess the situation, but guesses did not make for hearty appetites. When does the show begin? Let's go!

For the submariners the show began at 0700. At that hour USS CUTTLEFISH sent out a radio report that she had contacted an enemy tanker bearing 260°, six hundred miles from Midway. ComSubPac ordered her to trail. But the approach of daylight and enemy combatant ships forced CUTTLEFISH to dive. Running submerged, she was unable to regain contact. Two hours later all submarines were given the position, course and speed of the Occupation Force, as reported by scout planes, and were ordered to close the enemy.

Meantime, the island's PBY search patrol, which had been flying the cloudy fringe of the weather-front some 150 miles northwest of Midway, sighted the Japanese Striking Force. Jap bombers were in the air. This news was flashed to Midway. Every plane on the island took off with orders to intercept the enemy planes. Fifteen Flying Forts, already aloft, were directed to bomb the Japanese carriers.

Simultaneously, all submarines in the Midway defensive patrol, with the exception of CUTTLEFISH, CACHALOT and FLYINGFISH, were ordered to attack the Jap carriers. The aforenamed submarines were to maintain their stations.

TAMBOR, TROUT, GRAYLING, NAUTILUS, GROUPER, DOLPHIN, GATO, GUDGEON and GRENADIER pointed their bows toward the enemy, and headed for him at best speed. The planes, of course, were first in action, and they collided full-gun with the Jap air squadrons buzzing toward Midway.

Numbering nearly 100 dive bombers and torpedo planes, escorted by about 50 Zero fighters, the Jap raiders swept in. They were met by the Americans about 30 miles offshore. Marine pilots dived into the enemy bomb groups, and shot down several bombers before the Zeros could interfere. Then while the Zeros tackled the Marines, the bombers broke through to punish Midway. Avoiding airstrips which they expected to use later, they bombed a power plant, near-by buildings and oil tanks. The Marine pilots fought with unparalleled valor, but their planes were no match for the faster Zeros. Before the Japs retired, 15 Marine planes were lost and seven were forced down, damaged.

Far at sea the American B-26's and Navy torpedo planes were diving on the Japanese carriers. Swarms of Zeros rose to defend the Jap flat-tops. All but three of these American planes were swept away. Then the 27 Marine dive bombers and 15 Flying Fortresses arrived on the scene. Zigzagging, throwing skyward umbrellas of anti-aircraft fire, the Jap carriers raced through evasion maneuvers while the Zeros battled the attackers. Eight Marine bombers were shot down. The remainder, riddled, barely made it back to Midway. The Flying Forts emptied their bomb-racks, but not a Japanese carrier was hit.

So far, Yamamoto's armada had come through practically unscathed, while Midway had received a blasting and its land-based air force had been severely pummeled. But the best-laid plans of mice and Yamamotos gang aft a-gley.

About the time the land-based American planes were beaten back, Jap air scouts sighted the ENTERPRISE-HORNET-YORKTOWN threat on the horizon. This news reached the Japanese Striking Force around 0900. The Jap carrier group promptly veered northeastward to meet the American. Jap bombers which had been loading for a Midway strike were ordered to change their bomb-loads for torpedoes. Ensued a delay which was to benefit the Americans.

ENTERPRISE, HORNET and YORKTOWN had been steaming forward to attack ever since the first contact report. YORKTOWN's planes were to be held in reserve while those from HORNET and ENTERPRISE were to take off as soon as they were within attack range. When the Jap Striking Force made its sudden change of course, squadrons from ENTERPRISE and HORNET were in the air. Bee-lining for the enemy's former position, they found nothing but sea water. In the resulting confusion and search, the HORNET fighter planes ran out of gas and were forced down at sea. HORNET bombers, low on fuel, had to land at Midway. Bombers from ENTERPRISE flew off westward. But a squadron of fighters, launched at this juncture by YORKTOWN, climbed to an altitude that gave view of the vagrant Japanese carriers. Steering the scattered HORNET and ENTERPRISE planes to the target, YORKTOWN's fighters timed the attack at that providential moment when the Japs were reloading their bombers.

At 0920, HORNET Torpedo Squadron 8, which had become separated from the searching groups, raced in to make the first run over the Japanese Striking Force. Met by a whirlwind of Zeros and a cyclone of anti-aircraft fire, the torpedo planes were unable to score. The entire squadron of 15 planes was destroyed. Sole survivor was Ensign George H. Gay, who struggled free from his sinking plane and managed to cling to a rubber life-raft. Thus clinging between life and death, he was to witness the dramatic climax of the battle.

He saw the torpedo squadron from ENTERPRISE roar in at 1000. Saw the planes from YORKTOWN storm into view a moment later. Jap planes and American spun through a pyrotechnic maelstrom of aerial fire. The aircraft carrier KAGA was hit—a tremendous explosion that shattered her island. Three more bombs struck the carrier. Then, a floating oven of flame and smoke, she stopped dead in the water.

Ten YORKTOWN planes came swirling down, afire. Ten ENTERPRISE torpedo bombers came spinning down. But now smoke was surging up from two other Jap carriers—AKAGI and SORYU. Explosions hurled planes from their flight decks and showered the sky with rocketing fragments of men and metal. Hit twice, AKAGI lay helpless in the sea, a fiery derelict. SORYU, struck by three air bombs, spouted gaseous flame clouds and wallowed in the water like a wounded leviathan.

Some 200 miles away, YORKTOWN came under attack a little after noon, when 18 Jap dive bombers and a like number of Zeros found her over the horizon. Radar detected the enemy planes, and 12 American fighters soared to intercept. In the resulting aerial battle, over half of the enemy bombers were bulleted down. Blasting the sky with anti-aircraft fire, YORKTOWN's gunners put up a shrapnel screen that tore the remnant Jap squadron to pieces. Either felled by American fighters or blown apart by anti-aircraft fire, all of the Japanese bombers were shot down.

But YORKTOWN was struck by three bombs. Two exploded on her flight deck, and one burst in a funnel, blowing out her fires. Damage control parties made valiant repairs, but these were hardly completed when a flight of Jap torpedo planes swept in.

In the ensuing aerial melee, every torpedo plane was shot into the sea. However, two torpedoes stabbed YORKTOWN in the side. Holed to port amidships, with her engines paralyzed and her funnels vomiting smoke, she threatened to capsize. As her planes veered away to land on the decks of HORNET and ENTERPRISE, Captain Elliott Buckmaster gave the order to abandon.

Mid-afternoon, YORKTOWN abandoned. And, 200 miles to the west, KAGA, AKAGI and SORYU in wrack and ruin. There Ensign Gay, still clutching his life-raft, saw the climax. He saw the burning carriers—saw the fourth carrier, HIRYU, retreat with her escorts to the northeast—saw the remaining Japanese ships drift off like so much litter on the tide. The mid-afternoon sun scorched a seascape strewn with wreckage, mats of oil, black flotsam. The carrier, SORYU, came drifting near, flame-scorched and smoking like a great iron stove. Men were swarming like ants on her forecastle and a clutter of small boats were hugged up under her bow, apparently working with a towing hawser. She seemed to be moving under her own power, crawling at the pace of a water-buffalo through sludge. Two miles ahead, a pair of cruisers waited to assist.

Then, in this vista of desolation, Ensign Gay saw something else.

Nautilus vs. Soryu

Of the Task Group 7.1 submarines participating in the daytime action of June 4, only three made contact with the enemy.

The first was CUTTLEFISH, contacting a tanker of the Jap Occupation Force. As related, this contact was lost.

The second was GROUPER. As she was diving early in the morning of that day she was sighted and strafed by a Japanese plane. She remained at deep submergence until late in the day, and so was out of the action.

The third submarine to contact the enemy was NAUTILUS. Making her first patrol under Lieutenant Commander William H. Brockman, she was to deal the one decisive blow struck the enemy at Midway by the U.S. Submarine Force.

One of the Navy's three largest submarines, the big V-boat had gone to Mare Island in the autumn of 1941 for an overhaul that amounted to virtual reconstruction. Her old engines were removed and a complete new plant was installed. Her superstructure was streamlined, her air-conditioning apparatus was improved and she was otherwise modernized. Reconditioned, re-engined and rejuvenated, she reached Pearl Harbor in April 1942—big, fast, and ready to

go. All she needed was the same sort of a skipper.

She got that sort in Brockman. Wide-shouldered, muscular, a man whose head had a bowing acquaintance with the tops of doors, this stalwart officer was as husky as NAUTILUS herself. He had been a submarine relief skipper during the war's first weeks, impatient in San Francisco. Then, driving NAUTILUS out to Hawaii, he had his boat, and a crew to match. That combination—good boat, good skipper, good crew—inevitably adds up to unbeatable submarining.

The winning figures began to show on the morning of June 4, at 0755. Patrolling northward of Midway as a unit of Task Group 7.1, NAUTILUS had submerged at 0420. About an hour and a quarter later, with her mast above water, she intercepted a wireless report that planes were bearing 320° T, 150 miles off Midway. This plotted close to NAUTILUS' estimated position. Brockman alerted the crew and maintained a vigilant periscope watch. About an hour later a flight of B-17's were seen against the dawn dead ahead. Then at 0710 NAUTILUS had a glimpse of aircraft bombing some target beyond range of the periscope horizon. Brockman changed course to head the submarine full speed toward the action.

At 0755 the periscope picked up ships' masts on the horizon. Simultaneously, a plane skimmed into view and opened fire on the periscope. Bombs tossed up fountains close aboard as Brockman roared the order to go down. Down went NAUTILUS to 100 feet. After a five-minute run submerged, Brockman sent her up again. Raising the periscope, he peered into a picture calculated to do the same to his hair.

Four large Japanese warships swam into the foreground as the periscope revolved. The largest Brockman identified as a battleship of the ISE class (she may have been a HARUNA-class BB or a TONE-class heavy cruiser). The other three Brockman identified as cruisers.

While Brockman was busy with his inventory of this heavyweight quartet, NAUTILUS was spied by a Jap plane. Having determined to attack the battleship, Brockman was beginning the approach when the air bombs came pelting down. At the same time one of the cruisers charged straight for the submarine, and at least two other warships were echo-ranging in an attempt to locate NAUTILUS.

Brockman ordered her to a depth of 90 feet, and the submariners set their teeth as the charges started to explode. At 0810, five depth bombs were dropped. Six more blasted the water a few minutes later, and then a pattern of nine boomed and crashed. Few of the explosions were close. The close ones, however, buffeted the submarine. NAUTILUS was equipped with "deck tubes" from which torpedoes could be fired.

These tubes were loaded at the time, and the depth-bomb barrage carried away a retaining pin in one of the tubes, starting the loaded torpedo on a "hot run" in the tube. The noise of the running torpedo must have made a beautiful sound target for Japanese listeners, and the exhaust gases released were trailing the submarine like a marker buoy. Nevertheless, 14 minutes after the first ash-can was dropped, NAUTILUS was again at periscope depth and Brockman was continuing his observations.

"The picture presented on raising the periscope," he wrote afterwards in his report, *"was one never experienced in peacetime practice. Ships were on all sides, moving across the field at high speed and circling away to avoid the submarine's position. A cruiser had passed over us and was now astern. Flag hoists were going up, blinker lights were flashing and the battleship on our port bow was firing her whole starboard broadside at the periscope."*

Certainly peacetime practice had never trained the submariners to face broadsides from an infuriated BB. Nor had it produced a set of rules on what a submarine captain was to do when he found his boat in the middle of an enemy fleet like a champagne bottle in a log-jam.

Actually, Brockman had run up his periscope in the midst of the Japanese Striking Force. And at that hour of the morning, the force had not yet been splintered to pieces by American planes. Vice Admiral Nagumo was proudly flying his flag from AKAGI. KAGA, SORYU and HIRYU paraded in company with the flagship. Battleships HARUNA and KIRISHIMA; heavy cruisers CHIKUMA and TONE; the light cruiser NAGARA and about eleven destroyers—these were the other Jap warships in the picture. Brockman selected a battleship for his target.

Range 4,500. Angle on the bow 80° starboard. Speed 25 knots. T.D.C. and fire control party worked at lightning speed. Brockman gave the order.

"Fire one! Fire two!"

The battleship side-stepped, veering leftward and heading directly away. A salvo from her main battery had almost straddled the submarine. Only one torpedo had raced at the BB—the other had stuck in the tube—and with the range extended to 6,000 yards and a 180° track angle, Brockman ceased fire. The BB's screening vessels had spotted the torpedo wake and were charging in for a kill. Brockman gave the order to go deep. As she slid down to lower levels another ash-can storm broke around her.

But at 0846 she was again at periscope depth with her scope out of water. Brockman was for giving the Japanese not an inch in this matter. Bombed by

air and surface ships, fired at by a BB, NAUTILUS could not be kept down.

Making periscope observation at 0846, Brockman discovered that the battleship and her companions had departed, leaving a destroyer to hunt the submarine. The hunter was evaded, and at 0900 Brockman sighted a Jap aircraft carrier—distance 16,000 yards. Flocks of anti-aircraft shell bursts hovered over the flat-top, indicating she was under bomber attack. Brockman headed NAUTILUS for the carrier.

Before NAUTILUS could close, her periscope was sighted by the rear-guard huntsman. The destroyer (or light cruiser) charged for the submarine at bone-in-teeth velocity. Promptly Brockman maneuvered to meet this attack. He waited until the enemy was 2,500 yards away, and then fired one torpedo. The attacking vessel dodged the "fish" and came on. Again NAUTILUS ducked. As she slid down deep, six depth charges exploded close astern.

Brockman held her deep under until the echo-ranging faded out. He managed to combine evasion tactics with approach maneuvers that took the submarine nearer the carrier. 0955. Sound reported all quiet on the NAUTILUS front. But anything was possible on the surface. Brockman ordered the submarine to climb, waited for the periscope to break water, and then walked it around to see the possibilities.

At 1029 ships' masts reappeared on the horizon. The submarine's vertical antenna picked up a message from an American plane reporting damage to a Jap carrier. Great trees of smoke were now towering up on the horizon, spreading gray limbs across the sky. Brockman headed NAUTILUS for the nearest smoke at best speed.

As the submarine ploughed forward, three planes were sighted. Running submerged reduced the speed, and the batteries caused some worry—at 1145 the target was still some eight miles distant. But Brockman was able to identify the smoke-pot as a burning Japanese carrier, apparently disabled but traveling slowly under her own power.

Three-quarters of an hour later the range had not been appreciably reduced, and Brockman decided to increase the speed to two-thirds, whether the batteries could afford it or not. By 1253 NAUTILUS was near enough for close-up identification of the carrier. Carrier was recognized as one of the SORYU class, and her disablement was evident. Smoke rolled up from her decks, and she was blundering along at a speed of two or three knots. However, she was on even keel, no flames were visible and her hull appeared undamaged. Work crews on her forecastle were apparently making preparations to pass a towing hawser. About two miles ahead, a pair of Jap cruis-

129

ers waited. As NAUTILUS watched, the carrier came to a dead stop. Obviously the hawser was ready for the hitch-up and tow.

During the long approach, the submariners had anxiously studied the silhouette book. As U.S. carriers were known to be in the area, Brockman had to be certain. But now there could be no doubt about the target's identity. Such doubts as there were concerned the other targets—the cruisers.

Lieutenant Thomas Hogan, diving officer aboard NAUTILUS, confided these misgivings later. Hogan remarked, in substance:

"We'd been taking a pretty bad beating that morning. The men weren't used to it. Somebody suggested to Captain Brockman that it might be better to go deep until things looked better topside. 'Hell no!' Brockman said. 'We're going to get a couple of these things.'"

Problem: Attack the cruisers standing by for the tow, and then come back to strike at the stalled carrier; or attack the carrier immediately, and then go after the cruisers.

Not an easy matter to decide. For a strike at the carrier meant that the cruisers, alerted, would come rushing over hell-bent, and NAUTILUS' batteries were getting dangerously low. On the other hand, much battery capacity would be expended in an approach on the cruisers. Swift and powerful, they might evade, and NAUTILUS would be left with a cruiser battle on her hands and no chance to get at the carrier. It was Hobson's choice, either way. Brockman decided to take the bird in hand.

Prowling forward at periscope depth, NAUTILUS advanced steadily on the carrier. The plan was to attack from the carrier's starboard side, her island side.

At 1359, range 2,700 yards, track angle 125° starboard, three torpedoes went speeding on their way. The ribboning wakes were seen to head straight for the target. Three thunderous explosions rocked the aircraft carrier. The men in the submarine took turns looking through the scope. Red flames spouted the length of the carrier, scattering the small boats under her bow. Ant-like figures raced across her decks. They were abandoning!

All this was observed before the cruisers, reversing course, came storming into the foreground. At 1410 NAUTILUS was again submerged beneath a depth-charge barrage. Brockman took her down to 300 feet, while the charges volleyed and thundered overhead.

About 1800—silence. Brockman ordered the boat to periscope depth for a look around. The cruisers had quit the scene. Only the carrier remained, a drifting smelter-furnace under a mountain of dense black smoke.

Then Brockman—perhaps because he was hungry—gave the scope to the O.O.D. and stepped into the wardroom with his exec for a bite to eat. They were just sitting down when the submarine was shaken by a shocking blast. Who was bombing them now? Racing into the control room, Brockman found the sound man staring in astonishment and the O.O.D. glaring into the scope.

"There's not a thing up there!" the O.O.D. cried. "No ships! Nothing!"

Brockman was reaching for the scope-handles when another underwater blast sent NAUTILUS rolling. Juggling the scope, the skipper could see no sight of attacking cruisers—or burning carrier. But a dark litter of flotsam and acres of oil carpeted the sea. Underwater, the detonations continued. They came from SORYU's 17,500 tons, exploding as they went to the bottom.

At 1941 NAUTILUS surfaced to revive her exhausted batteries and men. In the twilight she had the seascape to herself. After a day-long battle which included air bombs, "hot-running" torpedoes, broadsides from a battleship, and 42 depth charges, she was entitled to a breather.

Not until some days afterward did her submariners know that their reported sinking of the carrier had been confirmed. It was confirmed by the survivors of SORYU and by eye-witness Ensign Gay.

End of the Battle

Not long after the SORYU sinking, the bombed-out hulk that was KAGA went down. AKAGI, a burning derelict, was sunk by her own destroyer escort that same evening.

In the meantime, the fourth Jap Striking Force carrier, HIRYU, had come to grief. Escaping northwestward in the afternoon, she had been sighted by scouting planes from YORKTOWN. Soon afterward, dive bombers from HORNET and ENTERPRISE were on location. The carrier and her escorts—two battleships, three cruisers and four destroyers—raised a roof of fire, but the American bombers broke through. Less than a dozen Zeros rose in HIRYU's defense. One ENTERPRISE bomber was shot down, but its mates succeeded in making six hits on the carrier. The planes from HORNET attacked the flat-top's escorts. The surface ships received a blasting, and near hits scarred the battleship HARUNA. That ended HIRYU's retirement. At nightfall she was burning like a wooden barn, abandoned.

Aboard the battleship YAMATO, Admiral Yamamoto did not enjoy his supper of *suki yaki*. Advised that his four carriers were lost, he immediately canceled his invasion plans and ordered his residual armada to retreat westward. To cover this retirement, he ordered four heavy cruisers from the Occupation Force to move in and shell the Midway Island airstrips—a measure calculated to protect the retreating fleet from attack by American land-based planes. This move was foiled by the U.S. Submarine Force.

Fearing that the Jap Occupation Force might attempt a landing despite the Striking Force disaster, Pearl Harbor Headquarters rearranged the Midway defense. Early in the morning of June 5, ComSubPac ordered the Task Group 7.1 submarines back to their original sector to patrol a tight arc in the ten-mile circle from Midway. Task Group 7.2 was ordered to proceed west at best speed until further orders. The submarines raced to their assigned positions. And the Japanese bombardment group, steaming for Midway, ran headlong into the submarine screen.

At 0215, morning of June 5, TAMBOR (Lieutenant Commander Murphy) about 89 miles off Midway sighted four large ships bearing 279° T, course 050°. Warned that U.S. forces might be operating in this area, Murphy paced the warship formation, holding TAMBOR on a parallel course while he tried to identify the ships.

Night vision being what it was, friend-or-foe identification was not readily made. However, at 0300 TAMBOR sent out a contact report.

The cruisers she had sighted were the CA's SUZUYA, KUMANO, MIKUMA and MOGAMI—a formidable quartet. TAMBOR contacted them on several different courses as they swung toward the north and then veered west. At 0412, visibility had increased and the silhouettes were identifiable as Japanese. Like a team of horses drawing a chariot, the cruisers came racing, swerving this way and that.

With dawn in the making, TAMBOR was forced to dive. Then, running submerged, she was unable to close for an attack. The next time Murphy elevated the periscope he found only two of the cruisers in sight. One cruiser had a damaged bow. And they were heading away from the dawn-light.

The cruisers were, in fact, retreating. At about the time TAMBOR had sighted them, they had detected TAMBOR. With the submarine on their starboard bow, all four cruisers had executed an emergency turn to the left. On the turn, MOGAMI rammed MIKUMA on the port quarter, full tilt. The collision shattered MOGAMI's bow. Damage was reported by radio, and at 0300 the cruisers had been ordered by Yamamoto to abandon the Midway bombardment operation and retire.

Thereupon SUZUYA and KUMANO had withdrawn at top speed. MOGAMI and MIKUMA, their speeds reduced to 17 knots, were left in the rear. Crippled and leaking oil, MOGAMI was a drag on her companion—a drag that was to prove fatal.

Because the cruisers had made several fast turns after contact, TAMBOR had given no course in her original contact report. As no course was given, ComSubPac was unable to determine whether the ships were hostile or friendly. By the time their enemy character was established, opportunity for submarine attack was gone. Nevertheless, the MOGAMI-MIKUMA collision was tantamount to damage by a torpedo. Marine and Army bombers from Midway came across the wounded cruiser's oil slick the following day. Caught by the planes, MOGAMI was pounded by bombs, and MIKUMA was mortally hit. According to Rear Admiral Soji, on MOGAMI's bridge at the time, a Marine pilot crashed his plane into the neighboring cruiser's after turret. A crucible of flames, MIKUMA was to sink that afternoon.

MOGAMI came within an ace of suffering a like fate. TAMBOR's contact report had reached Admiral Spruance, who brought HORNET and ENTERPRISE into the chase. Dive bombers from these carriers located the two Jap cruisers and gave MIKUMA her death blow. MOGAMI absorbed a terrific beating. With one turret smashed, her after mast blown down, her funnel half gone and her decks a fiery shambles, she managed to crawl away after the planes were gone. Somehow she reached Truk.

Only one blow was struck at Midway by the enemy on June 5, and that by a Japanese submarine. To cooperate in the Midway offensive, three I-boats had been deployed on a scouting line to the north of Yamamoto's Main Body. Possibly it was one of these scouts which moved in on June 5 and fired a few futile shots at the island.

On June 6 the Japanese Submarine Force succeeded in striking a final blow. Herculean work by salvage crews had prevented disabled YORKTOWN from capsizing, and the carrier had been headed for Pearl Harbor under escort with the destroyer HAMMANN alongside. Early afternoon, June 6, the Japanese submarine I-168 made swift attack, firing four torpedoes. Two struck YORKTOWN and two hit HAMMANN. The destroyer's depth charges exploded as she sank, killing many of her crew and fatally blasting the damaged carrier. The other U.S. destroyers rushed the submarine, unleashed a tempest of T.N.T., and reported a kill. But there was no saving the carrier. At 0500 the following morning YORKTOWN rolled over and went down.

Pyrrhic victory.

Yamamoto had long since had enough, and his forces were in full retreat. Four first-line carriers sunk, a heavy cruiser on the bottom, another pounded to scrap, and 4,500 sailors and airmen killed had reduced his Midway drive to an appalling fiasco.

Assessment

Against the Japanese ship losses, the United States was forced to balance the loss of YORKTOWN and HAMMANN. One hundred and fifty U.S. planes were lost (the Japanese lost 258) and 307 Americans lost their lives in action. For Americans the battle had been costly, but the price paid by Japan, in contrast, was stunning. Plus the men and material thrown away in the Midway maelstrom, the Japanese lost the initiative in the Central Pacific. They would never be able to regain it.

Hindsight views of the battle suggest Yamamoto was overly impetuous. Perhaps deluded by faulty Intelligence, he underestimated the U.S. Navy's recuperative powers, its ability to fight without the battleships immobilized at Pearl Harbor. Japanese reconnaissance was insufficient, failing to detect the American carrier forces in the area until the Jap Striking Force itself was exposed. It might be said that in neglecting to seize Midway in December 1941 (when TROUT and ARGONAUT alone stood as naval forces in the way) the Japanese made their basic strategic error.

On the other hand, it might be held that American reconnaissance was insufficient. The American forces, anticipating Yamamoto's intentions, should have waylaid a greater portion of the Japanese armada and inflicted heavier damage. Yamamoto's Main Body escaped virtually unscathed, and the damage wrought upon MOGAMI and MIKUMA came by way of a lucky break. Such breaks, however, work both ways throughout a battle—certainly the U.S. submariners were entitled to a little help from Fate.

Critics of submarine strategy have suggested that the showing made by the 25 U.S. submarines in the battle was somewhat disappointing. Of course, not all 25 were in the battle area. Task Group 7.2 and Task Group 7.3, stationed east of Midway and off Oahu, respectively, were unable to join the battle, as were the six steaming in from distant patrol areas. However, of the 12 in intercepting position west of Midway, only NAUTILUS (and, indirectly, TAMBOR) managed to score.

For several days after the battle's June 4 climax, the submarines near Midway and those coming in from patrol were given a number of contact reports concerning damaged Jap vessels in retreat. In the main these reports, which came from aircraft, were erroneous or misleading. MOGAMI was the only crippled vessel retreating, and although others among the retiring fleet may have been struck, their scars did not amount to serious damage. On the basis of the reports that were made, the pursuing submarines were unable to overtake and come in contact.

On June 7 GRAYLING, making a dive, was bombed by a group of B-17's which reported her as an enemy cruiser. Fortunately she gained depth and no damage. CUTTLEFISH, bombed the following day by a Japanese plane, likewise escaped without damage.

On June 9 TROUT fished two Japs from the sea—forlorn survivors of defunct MIKUMA. These were apparently the first Japanese Navy men to be taken prisoner by a U.S. submarine.

By June 10 the enemy was far beyond range of submarine contact. The Pacific Fleet submarines received orders from ComSubPac to continue patrols as assigned, and resume the war of attrition interrupted by the Midway battle. The home-coming boats headed for Pearl and the outgoing patrollers proceeded on their way.

The only defensive battle of the Pacific War in which submarines were extensively employed, Midway served to point out lessons which were heeded in later engagements. Lack of search radar for night tracking was seen as a primary reason for submarine frustration at Midway. And the SJ radar—the first directional radar used by the undersea force—was installed on most of the submarines within a few months.

Too, it was obvious that if submarines were to use their capabilities to the fullest when participating in fleet actions, some method would have to be devised for designating specific areas in which they could attack freely without fear of sinking friendly ships. Necessity for positive silhouette identification—a time-consuming endeavor in which the opportune moment for attack might be lost (witness TAMBOR's predicament)—could then be largely obviated.

Finally, their deployment in close-in defensive positions in a battle which would be fought out in daylight, left submarines few attack opportunities and seriously curtailed their mobility. These factors were noted and taken into account when submarines were thereafter employed to support fleet operations.

For the submariners the Midway Battle was a new experience—more pioneering. Their influence on the battle—remarked as that of an undercurrent—certainly helped to turn the tide. Unquestionably the Japanese task groups were forced to move with caution after the first submarine alert. The TAMBOR contact frustrated a shore bombardment and set in motion a chain of events which brought disaster on two warships. NAUTILUS dislocated the maneuvers of a striking force, threw a battleship out of line, created day-long pandemonium, and finished off an escaping carrier. More than an undercurrent—a tide rip!

And with Midway the entire Pacific war-tide was to turn. Japan's offensive had reached its height, and failed to break the American sea wall. Midway, the bastion of Hawaii, would stand. The manifest importance of this naval base is underlined by the fact that, immediately after the battle, FLYINGFISH put in at Midway and received the first submarine refit accomplished there. Six months later, Midway was refitting two submarines at a time, and by the end of the war 12 submarines could simultaneously undergo refitting at Midway. The Midway submarine base went far to solve the SubPac logistic problem by providing a fueling station 1,100 miles from Pearl on the main line to Japan. Supplied at Midway, Japan-bound submarines were able to spend more time on patrol in Empire waters than their pioneer fore-runners, who had to make the long haul, non-stop, from Pearl Harbor.

Aside from its strategic implications, the Midway victory had an impact psychological. Flushed with triumph at the start, the drivers of Japan's war machine were left to explain a monumental wreck, and the people of the god-Emperor were given their first taste of disillusion. For the first time since 1592 a Japanese war fleet had been smashingly defeated. In the shambles of Yamamoto's armada the Imperial Navy not only lost face—it lost heart. It would continue to fight with iron fists and pagan fury. Attempting to recover position and prestige, it would lash out and strike destructive blows. But never again would it wear the features and display the gusto of implacable, invincible conqueror.

For the heart of the U.S. Navy the Midway victory was plasma. With renewed élan the submarines resumed their patrols. NAUTILUS, for example, put in to Midway to refuel, then she hiked off in the direction of Tokyo to carry the fight into Japan's home waters. On June 25 Brockman had his periscope trained on a Japanese destroyer. Then down at sea—lat. 34-34 N., long. 140-26 E.—went the Imperial Navy's 1,580-ton DD, YAMAKAZE. A fitting sequel for the torpedoing which finished off SORYU.

Interrogated by American officers (United States Strategic Bombing Survey) after the war, Captain Hisashi Ohara, surviving executive officer of SORYU, was asked what effect the loss of the carriers at Midway had upon the Imperial Navy's future plans.

"Loss of the carriers meant loss of control of the air," he admitted. *"We did not think we could capture Midway after we lost control of the air so we returned to Japan. The loss of the carriers and the planes also slowed up the occupation of the Solomons."*

The sinking of the aircraft carrier SORYU was a sizable contribution to the events which resulted in ultimate defeat for Japan.

CHAPTER 12

THE ALEUTIAN MAELSTROM

"IF JAPAN SEIZES ALASKA SHE CAN TAKE NEW
YORK . . . THEY WON'T ATTACK PANAMA."

GENERAL WILLIAM E. MITCHELL

Pioneers Alaska

When Russia offered to sell Alaska to the United States in 1867 Congress dilly-dallied. Ever since Monroe's Administration or thereabouts, the Russians had been trying to sell, but the territory was considered "too far north" to be of any consequence. And in 1867 the ask-price—$7,200,000—was considered exorbitant. Eventually negotiated by Secretary of State Seward, the purchase was ridiculed as extravagant folly and Alaska was called "Seward's Ice Box."

Few foresaw the future value of this immense country purchased at a figure which was probably below the royalties of James Oliver Curwood and Robert W. Service. As late as 1920 the public mind was picturing Alaska as a yowling wilderness of snow populated by Esquimaux, a few Sourdoughs and Dangerous Dan McGrew. Nome was the end of the world, and the Aleutian Islands seemed as remote as the Pleiades.

The U.S. Navy was somewhat better informed. Its early sailing ships had visited Alaska's icy waters, and at a later date U.S. patrols had chased seal-poachers from the Bering Sea. But by 1920 the Aleutian Chain, a U.S. possession for over sixty years, was still unrecognized as a strategic bastion of the North American Continent. Militarily Alaska and her outer islands remained neglected until noticed by airminded General William (Billy) Mitchell.

Held insubordinate for his outspoken intelligence, this prophet was to prove so right that his detractors would live to see his grave decorated with a tardy medal. Yet even farsighted General Mitchell, remarking Alaska's importance as an air base, never guessed the submarining that would one day go on in Alaska's waters—the undersea warfare that would be fought in Alaska's defense. Meantime, little was done by the Government to develop Alaska's military potential. With the exception of a few radio and radio direction finder stations set up for weather observation and navigational information, the Navy, as late as the middle 1930's had not established any posts in the Aleutians.

The Japanese conquest of Manchuria, however, and the increasingly warlike attitude of Tokyo brought home the importance of Alaska and the Aleutian Islands. Late in 1937, in conjunction with a plan for bases at Sitka and Kodiak, Unalaska Island was investigated by the Navy.

The sole naval activity on Unalaska at that date was a radio and weather station located at Dutch Harbor. Although 100 square miles of land had been pegged for a naval reservation, the site had not been exploited. Similarly undeveloped was a coaling station on the Anaknak side.

Fleet maneuvers were scheduled for northern Pacific waters early in 1938. This gave several units an opportunity to reconnoiter the Unalaska coast to determine the best harbor sites for a naval base. As part of the fleet problem, the necessary reconnaissance was carried out by Submarine Squadron Six, acting with a unit of the Air Scouting Force. HOLLAND tended these exploring submarines.

April 1939, Submarine Squadron Six completed its mission. The submariners recommended Akutan Harbor and Anderson Bay as best suited for the basing of submarines. Dutch Harbor and Iliuliuk Bay were named as second choices. Other harbors in the area were reported as too hazardous for consistent navigation—icy and treacherous when flailed by the vicious Williwaws which stormed across the northern islands. The submarine patrols also disclosed the need for accurate charts of the area. Existing charts were deficient, and the waters would have to be carefully surveyed before any large naval force could safely operate in the Aleutian Chain.

Acting on this information, the Chief of Naval Operations proceeded to establish operational bases at Kodiak and Dutch Harbor. But work on the proposed submarine bases was not begun until after the war's outbreak.

Repair facilities installed at Kodiak were to equal those of a submarine tender, and the shops and living quarters erected at this base were designed to accommodate one squadron of S-boats. Dutch Harbor was also set up to provide normal base facilities for a squadron of six S-class submarines. As the war went forward, action eventually centered around Attu and Kiska, and Kodiak's importance as a submarine base diminished. Dutch Harbor became the chief submarine base in the Aleutians.

However, at the beginning of World War II, Dutch Harbor bore a close resemblance to those frosty gold-rush towns featured in wolf-and-dog-team movies. Arriving at this bleak port on January 27, 1942, the submarines S-18 (Lieutenant W. J. Millican) and S-23 (Lieutenant J. R. Pierce) were to be the first to conduct pioneer war patrols in the area.

It was a rugged area for pioneering—a wilderness of gray, blizzard-swept seas studded by islands as inhospitable as rocks. The days were brief and the nights bitter black, deafened by wind-howl and the thunder of surf. Across the archipelago unpredictable storms raged in sudden tantrum. Worse were the fogs which curdled over the reefs like the blinding vapors of ammonia.

In the boreal water the submarines shivered. A business of constant dunking was necessary to de-ice the scope and scour the frozen snow-bergs from bridge and decks. In the tropical Pacific the S-boaters had prayed for air-conditioning. Now, in this arctic limbo, their prayers were for steam heat.

Aboard S-23, beginning her first Aleutian patrol

on February 7, Lieutenant Pierce and crew slept in their clothing to keep warm. Compartments in the boat were as cold and dank as duck-blinds in a marsh. At the same time there was enough "body-warmth" in the submarine's hull to cause a heavy condensation of atmospheric moisture when the vessel submerged under icy waves. Cold sweat dripped in a constant rain from the bulkheads, wetting everything in the submarine's interior.

And if conditions below decks were as evil as influenza, those encountered on the bridge were as wicked as pneumonia. On their maiden pioneer patrols, S-18 and S-23 made no verifiable contact with the enemy. The submariners standing bridge watch saw little more than ice-glaze and reeling water. Much of the time they could see no farther than the bow of the boat. When the islands were not imbedded in wintry fog they were whipped by the polar Williwaws which scourged the area. Even when the weather cleared, which was seldom, the hours of daylight were short and the horizon was engloomed. Snow-capped breakers showered the conning tower with brine that stung like shot salt, and the wind stabbed into a man's lungs like an icicle. In anything like a gale the bridge was almost untenable.

Entry in S-23's log, dated February 13, 1942:

Shipped heavy sea over bridge. All hands on bridge bruised and battered. Officer of Deck suffered broken nose. Solid stream of water down hatch for 65 seconds. Put high pressure pump on control room bilges; dry after two hours. . . . Barometer 29.60; thirty-knot wind from northwest. . . .

Submarine navigation in this area demanded skill with a capital S. Off Unalaska, Kiska and Attu the water lies in strata of varying density—a phenomenon which made every dive a problem in unpredictables. Radio reception was eccentric and sonar sometimes behaved queerly. On her first patrol S-23 encountered a continuous series of barometric lows, at one- to three-day intervals, accompanied by foul weather, moving rapidly from west to east. Typical Aleutian weather. Shooting the sun was a feat comparable to shooting a sea lion in a blizzard—when the sun did appear it loomed in the oceanic mist as dim and opaque as a cataract-blinded eye. Celestial navigation at night was practically impossible.

Other operational problems were introduced by the S-boats themselves—engine breakdown, battery trouble, malfunctioning gear. S-23 had seen two decades of undersea service, and age was in her frame. But S-23, and the other old-timers that pioneered after her from Dutch Harbor on war patrol, kept on plugging.

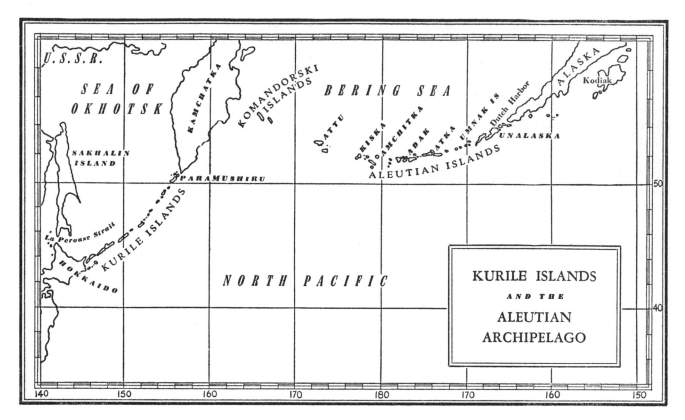

On her first patrol—an 11-day exploration that took her down through Unalaga Pass—S-23 had only one glimpse of what might have been the enemy. Somewhere between Kodiak and Dutch Harbor a submarine silhouette was sighted. A Jap I-boat? It may have been a walrus. It was gone before the submariners could be certain. Thereafter they beheld no sign of an enemy ship.

S-23's patrol was far from fruitless, however. In company with S-18 (Lieutenant Millican), her companion Aleutian explorer, she brought back valuable information. Information concerning winds and tide-rips—navigational difficulties—the need for arctic clothing for all hands, parkas and ski masks for the protection of bridge personnel. Not the least of this information concerned the condition of the S-boats— the fact that they and the submariners in them could meet the worst and take it.

Meantime, construction work was in high gear at the Dutch Harbor base. Despite the fact that Japanese naval scouts, first detected in the area shortly after the Pearl Harbor raid, seemed to have withdrawn, the Navy prepared to counter an Aleutian-Alaska thrust. By mid-April 1942 the base at Dutch and the one at Kodiak were ready for full-time operations. S-boat refits could be handled at Dutch Harbor, and when overhaul was demanded, the submarines could be sent south to the Destroyer Base, San Diego. At 'Dago an overhauled submarine would

serve for a month or so with the Sound School. This policy was designed to permit the S-boats of the Aleutian Force to rotate between the North Pacific and California. It remained in effect throughout the period that the S-boats campaigned in the Aleutian-Kurile area.

On the 3rd of April, S-34 (Lieutenant T. L. Wogan) and S-35 (Lieutenant J. E. Stevens) arrived at Dutch Harbor to strengthen the undersea defense. These S-boats were soon followed by two more. A list of the S-boats patrolling in the Aleutians by the end of May includes:

S-23	*(Lieutenant Commander J. R. Pierce)*
S-18	*(Lieutenant Commander W. J. Millican)*
S-34	*(Lieutenant R. A. Keating, Jr.)*
S-35	*(Lieutenant Commander J. E. Stevens)*
S-27	*(Lieutenant H. L. Jukes)*
S-28	*(Lieutenant Commander J. D. Crowley)*

The pioneer war patrols of these S-boats were meager in result when it came to targets, but mountainous in effort. In addition to scouting in the North Pacific, they opened a campaign to whittle down the enemy's food supply by depriving his fishing fleet of runs in those waters. They sank few fishermen, and during their early patrols made no contact with enemy men-of-war. But their mere presence in the area forced the Japanese to delay its penetration. And fighting fog, sleet, high seas, blizzards and some of the wildest storms in the book, they won the opening battle against the Aleutian weather—a victory that made an important contribution to the ultimate defeat of the Japs in that strategic theater. The stage was set in June when the Jap drive, timed with the Midway offensive, began.

War on the Northern Front

To fend off the expected Alaska thrust, Admiral Nimitz dispatched a sizable surface-air force to the endangered area. Welded into a single task force, its units included five cruisers, 11 destroyers, a large flotilla of smaller warcraft, and 169 planes. Then there were the aforementioned six submarines. Rear Admiral Robert A. Theobald was placed in command of all United States and Canadian forces in the area.

On June 1 the coastal defenses from Nome to Seattle were alerted, and aircraft joined the submarines in sweeping searches for the enemy's vanguard. Japanese scout submarines were detected making periscope reconnaissance off Cold Bay, Kodiak and Kiska. Jap seaplanes scouted off Dutch Harbor and Seattle. The enemy was coming!

For this diversionary drive Admiral Yamamoto had mustered a powerful striking force composed of the aircraft carrier RYUJO, the aircraft carrier HAYATAKA (sometimes called the JUNYO), two heavy cruisers, three destroyers and auxiliaries. The diversion was to be more than a feint, and this striking force moved in advance of two small but sturdy occupation flotillas—one to seize Kiska, the other to seize Adak and Attu. Entrenched in these outer islands, the invaders were to set up bases which would presumably control the Aleutian Chain and serve as springboards for drives at Dutch Harbor, Kodiak and the Alaskan mainland.

American scouting planes sighted the Jap striking force on June 2nd. Most of the defending planes in the area were Army aircraft, and foul weather pinned these to the ground the next day while the enemy advanced to within 150 miles of Unalaska. The Jap carriers launched two bomber squadrons. Fog turned back most of the pilots, but a few got as far as Dutch Harbor and bombed the naval installations there. At nearby Fort Mears they pelted the barracks, radio stations and warehouses. The raid cost the Japanese two planes—one shot down, another badly damaged.

During clearer weather on the following day, the enemy struck again at Dutch Harbor, setting oil tanks afire and demolishing an old station ship. Two fighters and two bombers were shot down when the raiders side-tracked to bomb an air base at Fort Glenn. Meanwhile, American and Canadian planes were attacking the enemy carriers. But the carriers managed to evade, and at nightfall the Jap striking force withdrew toward Attu and Kiska.

This was the evening of Yamamoto's bad day at Midway. Despairing of the entire offensive, the retreating Jap admiral was ready to call off the Aleutian drive. However, at the advice of his staff he decided to save some of the Imperial Navy's countenance, and orders for an Aleutian retirement were canceled. The Adak invasion was deleted from the plan, but on June 6 and 7, Attu and Kiska were seized by the Japanese occupation forces.

Thereupon Kiska and Attu became two of the hottest spots on the globe. Subjected to continual blastings by American aircraft, these islands were from the first a migraine headache to the Imperial High Command. Supply and maintenance of the exposed bases cost the Japanese dearly in time, material and effort. Of course, much effort, material and time were expended by the Americans in holding the Aleutian invader at bay. Toward his frustration the submarine forces contributed heavily.

When the S-boats first entered the Aleutian area, ComSubPac stated that if the North Pacific should become an active war theater, the S-boat force could be bolstered by fleet boats from Pearl Harbor. Dutch Harbor was approximately the same distance from Pearl as from Seattle, and fleet submarines could readily go to Alaskan waters from their Hawaiian base. With the enemy occupying Attu and Kiska, the time had arrived for the fleet boats to step in.

Loss of S-27

Loss of S-27 to the S-boat force intensified the urgent need of reinforcements. This occurred on the night of June 19, 1942.

Freak weather conditions and navigational hazards, from which approaching summer had brought little respite, were responsible. S-27 had been on reconnaissance mission to Constantine Harbor on Amchitka Island. This bleak isle was only 60 miles from Jap-held Kiska. Enemy plane observation was a constant threat during the arctic day which the midnight sun had lengthened to 18 hours. This meant 18 hours of submergence for the patrolling submarine, and only six hours of darkness for surface running and battery charge.

S-27's skipper, Lieutenant Commander Herbert L. Jukes, had planned to circle the island upon completion of the reconnaissance mission, then travel onward for a look at things around Kiska. Accordingly, the submarine started around the island that afternoon. At dusk Jukes ordered the S-boat to the surface for a battery charge. The twilight was dim, and S-27 lay to in a concealing surface haze while the "cans" were being charged. Unfortunately the haze which screened the submarine from possible air observation, also screened the landfall from the submarine.

Unnoticed, a furtive current gripped the S-boat and bore her shoreward. Darkness closed in, blotting out the visibility. Without radar or fathometer to warn her crew, the submarine was swept some five miles from her DR position. She was going ahead on one engine when, at 2200, she grounded 400 yards off Amchitka Island.

She was fast almost immediately, aground on a reef of solid rock. Throughout the brief night the submariners tried every device to move her. S-27 could not be budged.

By the next afternoon, high seas were breaking over the exposed submarine, her propellers were hiked in the air and she had assumed a 12° list. The motor room was flooded. The after battery, holed, threatened to generate chlorine gas. Jukes prepared to abandon.

With one three-man rubber lifeboat and no end of determination, the submarine captain and his entire crew relayed across 400 yards of boiling surf, and safely reached shore. Wet and shivering, they searched the barren tundra cross-island to Constantine Harbor. There they found a village which had been bombed out by the Japs and deserted by its inhabitants. The submariners took over.

Before abandoning S-27, the communication officer had been able to send off six messages reporting the situation. One of these was received, and six days later a searching PBY located the marooned submariners. They were flown by aircraft to Dutch Harbor, where they surprised the medical examiners by reporting, one and all, in good physical condition.

Torpedoes for Invading DD's

The loss of S-27 created a gap in the Aleutian defenses. Fortunately, reinforcements from Pearl Harbor were already on the way. Into Dutch Harbor on June 28 steamed GROWLER, fresh from Midway. On July 3, TRITON and FINBACK arrived. TRIGGER, GRUNION and GATO came in on the 5th, 9th and 12th, respectively. TUNA arrived a week later, and HALIBUT in mid-August. Thus, by late summer eight modern fleet boats were in Aleutian waters. They were:

GROWLER	(Lieutenant Commander H. W. Gilmore)
TRITON	(Lieutenant Commander C. C. Kirkpatrick)
FINBACK	(Lieutenant Commander J. L. Hull)
TRIGGER	(Lieutenant Commander J. H. Lewis)
GRUNION	(Lieutenant Commander M. L. Abele)
GATO	(Lieutenant Commander W. G. Myers)
TUNA	(Lieutenant Commander A. H. Holtz)
HALIBUT	(Lieutenant Commander P. H. Ross)

Four S-boats also added their weight to the Aleutian defense that summer. S-31 (Lieutenant Commander T. E. Williamson), S-32 (Lieutenant Commander M. G. Schmidt) and S-33 (Lieutenant Commander W. P. Schoeni) came around from the Atlantic Command to join the Dutch Harbor Force in July. In August, S-30 arrived under Lieutenant Commander F. W. Laing. These S-boat newcomers, plus the eight fleet submarines and the five remaining S-boat pioneers combined to give Admiral Theobald a powerful undersea force for Aleutian operations.

This force began to exert heavy pressure on the Japanese even before it was fully assembled. Hindered by antiquated gear, two-engine speed, and poor habitability, the S-boats scored no sinkings that summer. However, they conducted daring patrols, kept the enemy under periscope observation, chased Japanese fishermen away from the Aleutian runs and put a strain on the enemy's supply lines.

The fleet boats began to score almost as soon as they arrived. The first to down an enemy ship was TRITON. Conducting her fourth war patrol, she was run by a crew of bearded veterans, and commanded by that same Kirkpatrick who had littered the springtide off Japan with five torpedoed ships. Ordered to patrol off the south coast of Aggatu, she was on station as of July 3, hunting the invader.

Blinding fog blotted out the seascape throughout that day and night. But early next morning the fog dissolved long enough to reveal a Japanese destroyer's silhouette fading off in the mist. Kirkpatrick set TRITON on the trail of this target, and for ten hours the submarine pursued the DD through gusting vapor—Doom in pursuit of a phantom.

Late in the afternoon, Doom overtook the quarry. Kirkpatrick fired two torpedoes. One struck the destroyer amidships, the blast leaving the warship with a portside list. Through the periscope TRITON's submariners watched the stricken vessel put her port beam under and begin the long roll. As the destroyer gradually capsized, some 100 Japanese sailors and officers in white uniform walked down her starboard side and jumped into the surging water. Then down at sea went the Imperial Navy's DD NENOHI—1,600 tons, bottom up. The date was July 4th. TRITON celebrated appropriately.

On the day following TRITON's knockout performance, GROWLER pitched into the Aleutian Battle. This was the submarine's first patrol, and a first patrol for her captain, Lieutenant Commander Howard W. Gilmore. GROWLER and Gilmore—both names were to become immortalized in submarine history.

Ordered to patrol the waters off Kiska, GROWLER

was on station early in the morning of July 5th. The dawn was clear and cold, and the watch had a sharp periscope view of Kiska's barren peaks some five miles distant. As the periscope watch maintained a sweeping scrutiny, three Japanese destroyers were detected outside of Kiska Harbor. Gilmore ordered slow speed and silent running, and GROWLER began a direct but cautious approach.

Closer scrutiny revealed the DD's as 1,700-tonners of the AMAGIRI or FUBUKI class. Attaining attack position, Gilmore fired one torpedo at each of the first two destroyers. Two more torpedoes were fired at the third destroyer. The first torpedo missed the mark, but the second was seen to strike the target under the foremast. Flame spouted in a bright explosion, and then Gilmore gave the order to go deep. From its tube nest between the stacks, the destroyer had launched two torpedoes at the submarine.

GROWLER went down to 100 feet. Passing with the swish of speeding skiis on snow, the enemy torpedoes shot by on either side of the submarine and close enough to be heard without the aid of sound gear. A moment later depth charges were coming down. A Jap seaplane joined the enemy hunter-killer group determined to blow GROWLER to the bottom. Gilmore maneuvered the submarine through skillful evasion tactics, and surfaced when the storm was over. A great funnel of smoke was seen billowing up from the destroyer anchorage. The smoke was a funeral shroud for the Imperial Navy's 1,850-ton DD ARARE. Her companion destroyers were towed back to Japan.

GROWLER's advent in the area was a lesson to the enemy. A Japanese officer afterwards remarked, *"This was a daring and skillful attack by the American submarine and was admirably executed."*

On that same July 5, FINBACK (Lieutenant Commander J. L. Hull) attacked an ASHIO-type destroyer southeast of Aggatu. Hull fired three torpedoes at this DD and reported one hit for damage. Ten days later, FINBACK was racing like an ambulance for Dutch Harbor. Appendicitis case. The man was transferred to a hospital, and FINBACK continued her patrol. On August 8 she was dispatched from Dutch on special mission to taxi a survey party to Atka Island, a desolate rock in the Andreanof Group.

En route to Atka, FINBACK was spotted by a Japanese plane and forced to dive. One bomb exploded close enough to scale flakes of paint from the overhead and rupture a water line to the refrigerating plant. Spurting water grounded a number of electrical circuits, but the damage failed to ground FINBACK. After a seven-hour delay, she continued on her way, and on the night of August 10 the survey party of naval officers and Marines was put ashore at its

destination. The surveyors were spirited back aboard at 2210 the following night, and FINBACK made a fast run home to Dutch Harbor. Mission successfully completed.

Accounting for two Jap destroyers, and dealing damage to several more, the U.S. submarines played a leading part in stalling the Jap drive. Yamamoto was compelled to reinforce his Kiska-Attu supply line by rushing additional naval units to the area. To protect cargo vessels and troop transports, the aircraft carriers ZUIKAKU and ZUIHO were dispatched with a pair of battleships to the North Pacific front. This, at a time when the Imperial Navy was hard-pressed in the Central and South Pacific.

Either hot water or cold—the Pacific was becoming unpleasant for the Japanese.

Loss of Grunion

A price was to be paid for Alaska's security. There were casualties among the American and Canadian air, surface and ground forces. Native Aleuts died in bombings and scrimmages. And in Aleutian waters the SubPac Force suffered its first submarine casualty.

Reporting for duty in the Pacific War, GRUNION, novice from a new-construction yard, arrived in Pearl Harbor on June 20, 1942. She was given ten days of pre-patrol training, then, on the 30th, she left for the Aleutian front. She was captained by Lieutenant Commander Mannert L. Abele.

On July 10 GRUNION received orders to patrol the waters north of Kiska. Five days later she radioed Dutch Harbor that she had been attacked by an enemy DD. Abele had fired three torpedoes at the destroyer, and all had missed.

On that same day (July 15) Dutch Harbor received another battle report from GRUNION. The message was somewhat garbled, and exact details of the action were never learned. Post-war investigation revealed that GRUNION had pitched into an anti-submarine patrol. Two 300-ton patrol boats (Sub-chaser No. 25 and Sub-chaser No. 27) were sent to the bottom, and a third was badly damaged.

On July 19, GRUNION, S-32, TRITON and TUNA were assigned areas in the approaches to Kiska. Japanese forces had occupied the island only six weeks before, and there was a strong concentration of enemy vessels in the neighborhood. American aircraft were scheduled to bomb the island on the afternoon of July 22, and the submarines were to ambush enemy warships leaving the assailed harbor.

The bombardment was unexpectedly canceled, but the submarines were on the spot as ordered. On July 28 GRUNION was detailed to guard the exits from Kiska Harbor. She reported an attack on unidentified enemy ships off Sirius Point that day. Two torpedoes had missed the targets, and she had evaded a depth-charge barrage.

Her last transmission to Dutch Harbor was received on July 30th. She reported a tight anti-submarine screen off Kiska and but ten torpedoes remaining aboard. In reply, Headquarters ordered her to return to Dutch Harbor. GRUNION never returned.

Her fate remains a mystery. She was not contacted or sighted after July 30, and all efforts to locate her proved unavailing. With negative results, planes searched the waters off Kiska, and Headquarters sent out calls. On August 16 GRUNION was reported lost.

Examined after the war, Japanese naval records failed to reveal an anti-submarine attack in the Aleutians during the time in question. Apparently there were no minefields in the area. Either GRUNION was the victim of an unrecorded attack, or her loss was "operational." She went out. She was in the fight. She did not come back. Her requiem remains in the mourning of the northern winds and the "solemn surge of strange and lonely seas."

Cutting the Japan-Aleutian Supply Line

By late summer the Japanese occupiers of Kiska and Attu were beginning to experience some pangs of malnutrition. Little food could be scavenged on these wind-blighted islands. The natives, themselves, had survived mainly on a thin, raw diet of fish. And now the fishing grounds were under fire, practically all of the provisions for the occupying forces had to be imported from Japan. U.S. submarines were making importations increasingly difficult. Transports had to run into the harbors at dusk, unload under cover of night, and leave before dawn. Late in August, United States forces occupied Adak, and the Japanese supply situation became critical.

While harrying the Kiska-Attu transport service, submarines engaged in special missions in conjunction with the U.S. Army's occupation of Adak. TUNA (Lieutenant Commander A. H. Holtz) carried an Army colonel and a party of enlisted men from Dutch Harbor to Adak, putting these troops ashore at Kuluk Bay on the night of August 25th. Two days later TRITON carried another party of Army personnel, plus 8,700 pounds of equipment, to the same beachhead. The Army's advance to Adak threatened the invader's base at Kiska, and air raids on incoming ship traffic reduced his supplies to driblets.

In the autumn the submarine forces applied more pressure. This in spite of the fact that GROWLER, TRIGGER, FINBACK and other fleet boats were moved south to patrol stations off Formosa and other Central Pacific areas. The remaining Aleutian patrollers

kept the Jap ships on the run. On October 26, S-31 (Lieutenant Commander R. F. Sellars) sank the 2,800-ton cargoman, KEIZAN MARU. This sinking, in the neighborhood of Paramushiru some 500 miles west of Attu, came as a storm warning to the fishermen down through Japan's Kurile Islands.

Throughout the following late autumn and winter months, submarines from Dutch Harbor were to keep the Kurile Island fishermen on tenterhooks. Striding down through the Aleutians and across the North Pacific to the Kuriles, the submarines were hacking at the enemy's supply line where it was rooted in his home waters. For the S-boats engaged in this operation it was rough going. Lieutenant Commander Vincent A. Sisler, who made one of the later Aleutian-Paramushiru patrols in command of S-28, gave a vivid description of the rigorous submarining involved in these northern waters.

Hull-sweating he described as one of the worst plagues endured by the S-boaters.

> There were two ways to combat this. One way was to operate the air-conditioning unit, to evaporate the water and lower the boat temperature, which reduced sweating but forced everyone to wear more clothes. The other way was to rig canvas shields with funnel arrangements to keep the water from dripping on the bunks. But eventually, regardless of the precautions taken, the mattresses, blankets, sheets and everything became soggy, wet and damp. The habitability of S-boats in northern waters was terrible.

With winter's onset, the submariner dressed for bridge duty in heavy woolen underwear, a woolen hunting shirt, two pairs of woolen submarine trousers, three pairs of heavy wool socks, aviator's fleece-lined boots, plus flexible rubber boots. He climbed into a pair of trousers lined with sponge rubber and put on more sweaters and a parka. Regular-issue rain gear might be added if the weather were particularly inclement. Two pairs of wool mittens were worn and sometimes covered with rubber surgical gloves. A diving suit could hardly have been more cumbersome than this garb. Sisler reported:

> It was necessary to lash lookouts, the officer of the deck and the quartermaster to the bridge to keep them from being bashed around by the waves that rolled over the boat. Amazing that all hands didn't have severe colds and pneumonia, but health in general was excellent. The big problem turned out to be teeth. They decayed quickly for lack of calcium. Calcium pills soon became standard issue as did sun lamps. Without them, men soon developed a green, washed-out appearance.

Submarining without regular arctic clothing, calcium pills and sun lamps, the S-boaters who

THE ALEUTIAN FRONT. Ice on the conning tower—but such "sugar boats" as S-32 (seen entering Dutch Harbor) made these arctic waters hot for the enemy invader. S-boat patrols were daredevil in this maelstrom area. Surfacing in high seas to charge batteries, S-32 three times rolled 65°. Sailors, these men!

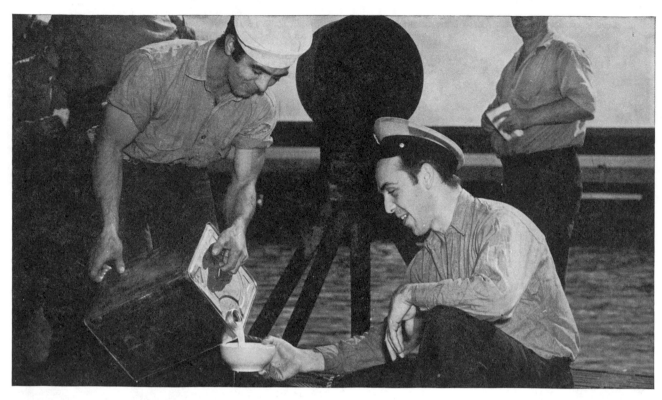

FUEL FOR THE INNER MAN. S-boaters share a can of milk after a cruise. There were no cows aboard American warships—especially subs—but lacteal nourishment wasn't lacking. Modern subs were equipped to make ice cream.

TRITON at Dutch Harbor. Aleutian patrols were rough on elderly S-boats. Subs from Pearl joined the northern force to stem the invasion. Triton celebrated July 4, 1942 by sinking destroyer Nenohi.

FUBUKI CLASS destroyer. Similar to that sunk by Growler off Kiska Island, dawn of July 5, 1942.

S-44 SURFACING. She did not reach the Aleutians until 1943. In 1942 she was busy elsewhere (see next chapter). A small sub with a big punch.

opened the Aleutian campaign will be remembered as rugged pioneers.

Fire and Ice

In the Aleutian Battle there were always two enemies—the Japanese and the weather. Relentless as was the human foe, he was never so dangerous as the inhuman. Wind and tide joined in winter-long conspiracy against the submarines. And in their war with these elemental forces, the S-boaters put up a fight that was almost superhuman. This conflict reached its summit in the battle waged and won by S-35 during the week preceding Christmas 1942.

The struggle began on the afternoon of December 21 when the Aleutian storm-gods unleashed such an offensive as only the North Pacific and Bering Sea could mount against a lonely submarine. It was the sort of weather when whalers stayed in port and landlubbers lay down below. Gigantic seas rolled through the archipelago where the surf burst like gunfire and the wind-whipped waves released a scud as ferocious as shrapnel. The sky was frozen, the horizon obscured as though by a sandstorm, and a spatter of spume, striking a man's naked cheek, burned like liquid fire.

Patrolling in the vicinity of Amchitka Island, S-35 forged her way along the surface through hills of cannonading water and valleys of scalding spray. In this tempest of heaving sea and flying brine the submarine climbed and staggered and drove forward, fighting to keep on course. Late afternoon, the storm worsened. At one-third speed, heavy seas were engulfing the bow and ploughing over the bridge. Water gushed down into the control room, and sometime around 1800 a geysering sea buried the bridge, and the control room was drenched by a cataract.

Topside, the submarine's captain, Lieutenant H. S. Monroe, ordered his men to close the conning-tower hatch. He had hardly given this order when a mountainous sea (time: 1805) charged the conning tower and burst across the bridge in exploding fury. Hurled from his footing, Monroe was flung into the hatch. Agonized by a sprained arm and leg, he made his way to his quarters, leaving the command to his second officer, Lieutenant O. H. Payne.

Monroe had just crawled into his bunk when, at 1830, he was roused by the cry, "Fire in the control room!" Lurching into the control room, the injured captain saw an alarming display of electric arcs and blue flames sputtering out of the main power cables from the forward battery.

Apparently salt water had soaked into the cables, causing a short and igniting the insulation. There was an acetylene-like flare—acrid smoke—the crackle of sparks and hiss of burning rubber. At the same time water was rising in the control-room bilges. Although he was scarcely able to stand, Monroe immediately took charge of the fight to save his ship from this dual peril.

Chief Electrician's Mate E. J. Bergero and others of the crew attacked the flames with fire extinguishers. But no sooner had this fire in the after starboard corner of the control room been extinguished than a similar fire broke out in the forward starboard corner. When this second fire was extinguished, arcing and flames were reported in the forward battery room.

Extinguishers smothered the battery-room fire, but could do nothing about the choking smoke and fumes of charred cork and burnt rubber. Blinded and coughing, the fire-fighters retreated aft. The forward battery-breaker and forward power-switch on the main board were pulled to remove the electrical load forward. The forward battery room and torpedo room were abandoned and sealed. Then again, "Fire in the control room!" clamored through the submarine. Two extinguishers were emptied on this new outbreak, but the electrical fire sizzled unabated, and in a pall of asphyxiating smoke the crew was driven back.

The engines were secured and the control room abandoned and sealed. Crowded into the S-boat's after quarters, the ship's company groped through a haze that thickened as smoke contamination and moisture produced large grounds on most of the electrical circuits in the boat. One short circuit after another disabled the electrical equipment. Gyro compass, radio transmitter, electric steering system, engine-order-annunciators and the bow and stern planes were put out of commission. A hole was burned in the top of No. 2 main ballast tank and the lines from No. 1 and No. 5 air banks were burned through. Storming seas above-decks and a choking hell of smoke, chemical fumes and eerie pyrotechnics below—S-35's crew was all but ready to abandon hope.

All but—!

And this introduces a point (call it an exclamation point) which was inserted more than once in the patrol reports of American submarines operating in World War II.

Submarine warfare is a science, and many of its material and operational problems can be solved by engineers, physicists, strategists and mathematicians. But in submarining, as in all forms of warfare, there is one most important factor that baffles the scales and calipers of the scientist, and even mystifies the psychologist given to dealing with abstractions. That factor is the human factor. In particular, one element of the human factor. The British call it morale. The French know it as *élan*. Americans have described it as "fighting heart"—that manifestation of grit or optimism or stubbornness that never says die.

Whatever its composition, this will to win (or, basically, will to live) has throughout history upset the certainties of mathematics, the laws of probability, the limitations of handicaps, the opposition of long odds. Every war furnishes a dozen examples. Paul Jones in a riddled and disabled hulk tells the world he has just begun to fight, and, defying the very laws of flotation, defeats SERAPIS. The Schlieffen Plan, devised by Europe's greatest military scientists, collapses like hollow nonsense under the weight of a single phrase, "They shall not pass!" Time and again "fighting heart" has overcome obstacles thought insurmountable, and won the day after all but hope was lost.

Submarine operations in World War II taught many lessons. One lesson learned was that successful submarining depended largely on an attitude that never said die. There were many instances wherein skill and seamanship alone would not have been enough, but with "fighting heart" coupled in, the submariners won through. Reversing the plaintive, "Where there's life there's hope," they proved a better adage—where there's hope there's life. No ship is lost until commanding officer and crew give up hope. This truism was courageously demonstrated by S-35.

At 1855 a party using smoke-lungs attempted to enter the control room. Not enough oxygen, but a wall of fumes that stifled the men and drove them out. To hell with the fumes. The escape lungs were charged with oxygen, and the men made another try. This time they were able to stay in the compartment long enough to flood the magazines and partially blow No. 3 main ballast tank to increase the submarine's freeboard. They were also able to close the auxiliary induction and completely seal the forward battery.

With her electrical controls burned out, her steering gear disabled, her radio transmitter dead, her interior a Black Hole of Calcutta, and a raving storm driving her through midnight, S-35 was in a bad way—few submarines were ever in a worse. Captain Monroe, Lieutenant Payne and the fighters under them refused to despair of it. They held the icy bridge. They fought the below-deck inferno. They met the test of fire and ice, and in the bleak light of morning the crew and their submarine were still there.

Meantime, the boat had been flogged off course. It was necessary to get propulsion on her screws to keep her clear of the deadly beaches of Amchitka. The crew tried to make an air start on the engines, taking a suction through the induction outlets aft. The engines were too cold to start. So the smoke-filled control room was reentered, and gasping electricians and motor macs made a desperate attempt at starting the motors. These were finally started, and S-35 crawled slowly eastward through the raging storm.

At 0700 a new fire flared up in the control room. As the fire extinguishers had been emptied the night before, the crew could only retreat from the smoke-fogged compartment. Soon the after quarters of the submarine were choked by the stifling smudge. All hands had to clear below deck and go up to the bridge into breathable air.

Lights out—the men groping about with hand lanterns—struggling into bulky arctic clothing—going topside to cling to the bridge and face the polar storm—here was an extremity beyond human endurance. From the frying pan into icy fire, the submariners endured it. Topside they were flayed by a cat-o'-nine-tails wind, and drenched by sheets of frigid water. For an hour and a half they suffered this punishment, hoping that the closure of the conning-tower hatch would smother the fire below.

Then electricians and motor macs entered the control room and the Diesels were started. The cables to the forward battery continued to flash and arc as the battery discharged. But the smoke was to some extent cleared by the running engines, and the crew was able to work below for several hours.

At 1100 all hands were once more forced topside by the suffocating smoke. Again the control room was sealed off. By 1330 it was possible to reopen the control room and go ahead on one engine, taking a suction through the induction outlets aft. Smoke from melted rubber, charred cork and fused metal continued to fog the submarine's interior, and the air became stifling every time the conning-tower hatch was closed—which was each time a heavy sea broke over the bridge. But somehow the engine was kept running, and S-35 kept going through the slow hours of December 22nd. After which, she continued to push ahead through the even slower ones of December 23rd.

At long last, on the day before Christmas, she staggered into Kuluk Bay, Adak Island. There she found the USS GILLIS, and the exhausted submariners were given first aid while emergency repairs were made on the S-boat. S-35 then proceeded to Dutch Harbor, arriving at home base on December 29th.

Concerning the 50-hour ordeal endured by S-35, Lieutenant Monroe had this to say:

I had opportunity to observe the reactions on numerous occasions of submarine personnel under various conditions of strain, both physical and mental, which attended the counter-measures employed by the enemy following an attack. None of the conditions prevailing during or after encounters with the enemy could compare with the hardships met during this patrol with a smoke-filled boat in a severe three-day storm.

In spite of the seeming hopelessness of our condition, there was, throughout the entire return trip, an outward calm and an efficient, tireless performance of duties by all hands.

Lieutenant O. H. Payne, second officer who took charge while the captain was incapacitated by a sprained arm and leg, Chief Electrician's Mate Bergero, who suffered severely from smoke, and many others who remained at their posts and performed their duties "without regard for personal danger or hardships" were mentioned in the captain's report. It is obvious that the personnel of S-35 had morale, *élan*, "fighting heart," to a man.

It was such submariners as these who cut the Japanese transport lines to Attu and Kiska and, before the end of 1942, reduced the invader's supplies to the famishing point.

The term *heroics* has been defined as the accomplishment of the impossible. Certainly that applies to the S-boaters who outfought the Japanese and the weather in the Aleutians.

CHAPTER 13

COUNTER-OFFENSIVE

Lockwood

Captain John Wilkes, who had held the SubsAsiatic Force together in the long retreat from Manila to Australia, was relieved in May 1942 by Captain Charles A. Lockwood, Jr. When Wilkes departed on a tour of various duties that eventually took him to England, he was confident that he left the submarines at Fremantle in competent hands. Competence and submarining were two words long associated with the name Lockwood.

Presently to become a rear admiral, and later to be the youngest vice admiral in the Navy, Lockwood had already composed his naval career of chapters that read like episodes of an adventure story.

He was born in Virginia, but Lockwood was from Missouri. From there he went to the Naval Academy in 1908, and from the Naval Academy he went into submarines. From September 1914 to August 1918 he was here and there under the sea in command of A-2 and B-1. During World War I he went out to the Philippines. At Cavite, where they still talked of Dewey, he commanded the first Asiatic Submarine Division and USS MONADNOCK. Later on he served as assistant naval attache in the U.S. Embassy, Tokyo —experience he would remember.

In 1918 and 1919 he commanded G-1 and N-5, and then he was on the bridge of the ex-German minelayer UC-97. After that, to the conning tower of R-25, and in April 1920 to the command of S-14, from Bridgeport, U.S.A., back to Manila. Then up the Yangtze River as skipper of the ex-Spanish gunboat QUIROS, after which he commanded the old ELCANO of the Yangtze Patrol.

From China to Portsmouth Navy Yard and the post of repair superintendent—from there to the command of V-3—then rolling down to Rio, where he spent two years (1929 to 1931) with the Naval Mission to Brazil—Lockwood continued up the ladder. Seamanship instructor at the Naval Academy; ComSubDiv 13 at San Diego; Submarine Desk of

Fleet Maintenance in the Office of CNO; Chief of Staff to Rear Admiral W. L. Friedell, Commander Submarines, Scouting Force—the year was 1941. In January of that year he went to London as Naval Attache, and he arrived in the British capital in time to see a close-up of the Nazi blitz.

Now, late in May 1942, after relieving Captain Wilkes in Fremantle, Australia, he received the stars of rear admiral and the toughest assignment he had ever faced. As ComSubSoWesPac and Commander Task Force Fifty-one, he was to take over the war-torn submarines of the Asiatic Force now based at Fremantle and Albany. Take over and start an undersea blitz, American version, against the Japanese.

The Southwest Pacific picture was far from encouraging. The defeat handed Yamamoto at Midway on June 4 electrified the weary SoWesPac submariners. In the Central Pacific the Japanese drive had come a cropper. But in the South Pacific the enemy's offensive continued to advance like a slow, dark stain, spreading around New Guinea, enveloping the Bismarck Archipelago, creeping through the Solomons. Although the Midway victory had stopped the Jap thrust at Hawaii, the Australian situation remained critical. Down from Java, down from the Philippines, down from Japan came ship after ship, piling up

144

men and guns in the islands flanking Australia. It would take something more than armchair submarining to blitz these invasion fleets out of the Southwest Pacific. Lockwood, no armchair submariner, walked into the job, swinging.

He began by installing in Fremantle such drivers as Commander John M. Will—a matériel and maintenance officer, tough and exacting, who could find a pump in the bottom of an Australian gold mine on Thursday and have it inside a submarine before the week-end. The captains were praying for search radar, better fire control equipment, periscope cameras, good ammunition. Lockwood and staff launched an all-out, let's go, bottleneck-breaking campaign to answer these prayers.

Headquarters in the Commercial Mutual Life Insurance Building in Perth hit a stride that should have warned Yamamoto (had he been properly advised) to take out some new policies. In every large organization—and the U.S. Navy was swiftly becoming one of the world's largest—there is a necessary amount of paper work and the sort of detail known as tape. There comes a point in administration where carbon copies may clog operations, and detail, becoming red tape, threatens to tangle in the machinery and cause slow-downs. One of Admiral Lockwood's specialties was the cutting of red tape and the elimination of excess paper work.

That the situation needed the Lockwood treatment is evidenced by the following letter which was written before the Admiral's methods were in effect:

Concerning Paper Work

#3s184/L8   S36-1   June 11, 1942
From: The Commanding Officer
To: Supply Officer, Navy Yard, Mare Island
Via: Commander Submarines, Southwest Pacific
Subject: Toilet Paper
Reference: (a) (4608) USS HOLLAND (S184) USS SKIPJACK Req. 7042 of July 30, 1941
           (b) SO NYMI Canceled invoice No. 272836
Enclosure: (A) Sample of canceled invoice.
           (B) Sample of material required.

1. This vessel submitted a requisition for 150 rolls of toilet paper on July 30, 1941, to USS HOLLAND. The material was ordered by HOLLAND to the supply officer, Navy Yard, Mare Island, for delivery to USS SKIPJACK.

2. The supply officer Mare Island on November 26, 1941, canceled Mare Island Invoice No. 272836 with the stamped notation "Canceled. Cannot Identify." This canceled invoice was received by SKIPJACK June 10, 1942.

3. During the eleven and a half months elapsing from the time of ordering the toilet paper to the present date, USS SKIPJACK personnel, despite their best efforts to await delivery of the subject material, have been unable to wait on several occasions, and the situation is now acute,

particularly during depth-charge attacks by the "back stabbers."

4. Enclosure (B) is a sample of the desired material provided for the information of the supply officer, Navy Yard, Mare Island. The commanding officer of USS SKIPJACK cannot help but wonder what is being used at Mare Island as a substitute for this unidentifiable material once well known to this command.

5. Boat's personnel during this period has become accustomed to the use of ersatz in proportion to the vast amount of incoming paper work generally nonessential, and in so doing feels that the wish of the Bureau of Ships for the reduction of paper work is being complied with, thus killing two birds with one stone.

6. It is believed by this command that the stamped notation "Cannot Identify" was possibly an error, and that this is simply a case of shortage of strategic war material, USS SKIPJACK probably being low on the priority list.

7. In order to co-operate in the war effort at small local sacrifice USS SKIPJACK desires no further action be taken until the end of the current war, which has created a situation so aptly described as "war is hell."

(Signed) J. W. COE

Torpedo Test at Albany

One of Admiral Lockwood's first moves was to investigate the Mark 14 torpedo. Ever since SARGO's experience in December 1941, when Lieutenant Commander T. D. Jacobs had fired 13 shots for a string of zero hits, evidence of torpedo malfunction had continued to pile up. During the desperate six months of retreat from the Philippines and the Netherlands East Indies, there had been no time for experimental tests and investigation at Soerabaja, Darwin and other Southwest Pacific bases. That the Mark 14 torpedo was prematuring, failing to explode, and otherwise sabotaging the best efforts of the submariners was apparent in anguished patrol reports and bitter appeals from veteran captains.

Late in the spring, reports from SALMON (McKinney) and SKIPJACK (Coe) joined those written earlier in the war to support SARGO's claim that the Mark 14, along with its other defects, was running deep. Convinced that all this circumstantial evidence meant guilt, Admiral Lockwood promptly arranged to bring the torpedo to trial.

The trial, begun on June 20, 1942, at Albany, Australia, was designed to end all conjecture concerning the torpedo's faulty depth-setting device. A large fishnet was anchored offshore in the quiet waters of Frenchman's Bay. SKIPJACK and Coe were chosen as submarine and skipper to make the test, and Captain James Fife officiated.

A Mark 14 torpedo that had been aboard SKIPJACK was fitted with an exercise head which was filled with calcium chloride solution to simulate in weight a Mark 16 warhead. The torpedo was set for 10-foot depth, and SKIPJACK fired on the surface at the net which was 850 yards distant. The torpedo cut a hole in the net at a depth of 25 feet!

The following day two more torpedoes were fired from SKIPJACK. The first one, set for 10-foot depth, cut the net at 18 feet, having reached that depth at a range of about 700 yards after making its initial deep dive. The second torpedo, set for zero feet, cut the net at a depth of 11 feet. When recovered and examined, this torpedo displayed evidence of having struck the bottom at 60 feet on its initial deep dive.

Admiral Lockwood lost no time in reporting these findings to the Bureau of Ordnance. On the heels of this report, the Bureau of Ordnance received one from Admiral English. The SubPac force commander reported that a Mark 14 exercise torpedo, inadvertently fired at a zero-feet depth-setting, had hit its destroyer target approximately eight feet below the waterline. Information regarding depth performance of all submarine torpedoes, and in particular the Mark 14, was urgently requested. Depth performance for torpedoes set between zero and 10 feet was specifically in question. ComSubPac inquired:

HAVE NET TESTS INDICATED THAT TORPEDOES RUN GREATER THAN FOUR FEET BELOW SET DEPTH

Dispatched on June 24, ComSubPac's message reached BuOrd some 48 hours after the one from Lockwood's Headquarters. Substantiating the report from ComSubSoWesPac, the message from Pearl should have gone far to settle the issue. However, on June 30 the Bureau of Ordnance informed Admiral Lockwood that no reliable conclusions could be reached from the Albany tests because improper torpedo trim conditions had been introduced.

Admiral Lockwood might have shelved the matter at this juncture. But Australia was too near the firing line. Into Fremantle were coming captains like Coe and Warder—war-wearied veterans who had risked their submarines and the lives of all on board, on the caprices of an unreliable torpedo. On July 11 Lockwood informed the Bureau of Ordnance that the tests would be repeated with an exercise-head lengthened to match as nearly as possible the trim and buoyancy characteristics of a Mark 16 warhead. The admiral urged the Bureau to make conclusive tests with its own equipment and inform him of the results by dispatch.

At Albany on July 18 a second depth test was conducted. This time SAURY (Lieutenant Commander L. S. Mewhinney) did the firing. Four Mark 14 torpedoes were fired. The torpedoes were set for 10 feet and fired at a net which was 850 to 900 yards from the firing point.

The first shot was wasted because the net had carried away during the night. But the remaining three torpedoes all penetrated the net at 21 feet. Here was proof positive, and in a July 20 dispatch the Bureau of Ordnance was informed accordingly. Admiral Lockwood also requested the Bureau to conduct tests using equivalent Mark 16 heads to determine depth performance with zero setting.

Meantime the torpedo problem had come to the attention of Admiral King, Commander-in-Chief, United States Fleet. On July 21 the Commander-in-Chief dispatched a letter to the Chief of the Bureau of Ordnance requesting action. Specifically BuOrd was told to immediately re-check the tactical data for the Mark 14 torpedo fitted with the Mark 15 or Mark 16 warhead. Cominch noted that BuOrd, in conducting additional tests of Mark 14's depth performance, had fired the torpedoes from a torpedo-barge and not from a submarine. Cominch also stated that submarine patrol reports continued to indicate lack of confidence in the Mark 14 and its depth performance, and it was apparent that there were valid reasons for this lack of confidence. In conclusion, Cominch stressed the need for accurate assessment and correct tactical data concerning the torpedo.

On July 29 Admiral English informed his force that torpedoes ran 11 feet deeper than set, and issued orders to set all torpedoes to run about five feet but no more than 10 feet deeper than the target's estimated draft, then to subtract 11 feet to obtain the correct depth-setting.

And on August 1, 1942—almost eight months after the war's outbreak—the Bureau of Ordnance announced that tests conducted at Newport corroborated reports concerning the faulty depth performance of the Mark 14. Fired from the tubes of a submarine near periscope depth, the torpedoes, fitted with Mark 16 warheads, had run 10 feet deeper than set!

Official confirmation! What this meant to the submariners, who had seen their marksmanship consistently betrayed by a defective weapon, may be imagined. Some of the pioneer captains, discouraged by repeated torpedo misses, had come to doubt their own ability. Several had left the Submarine Service. Hundreds of hours had been expended in fruitless approaches, and many thousands of dollars worth of ammunition had gone down the drains. To Jacobs—Bruton — Lent — Bacon — Parks — Coe — McKinney — Wright — Smith — Warder — Aylward — Rice —Voge—all of the skippers who fought the battle in the first months of the war, the Mark 14's exposure came as a boon and a relief—one that restored the self-confidence of captains and crews.

Deep-running, however, was not the Mark 14's sole malfunction. The torpedo harbored other defects. Tracked down by consistent inquiry, and finally cornered by the submarine TINOSA (in July 1943—almost a year after the Albany trials), these will be detailed in the chapter devoted to torpedoes. A lot of war would be fought with this erratic "tin fish" in the meantime. But the flaw revealed by the fishnets at Albany was corrected to a degree that greatly benefited fire control. Indicative of Admiral Lockwood's character, nine weeks after he took command at Fremantle the Mark 14's depth-setting deficiency was exposed.

Inspired by this brand of leadership, the SoWesPac Force went into battle with renewed morale. There were no more pestiferous shortages of the sort that had bothered SKIPJACK. Shortages there were in spare parts, munitions, time. But that was war. There was no dearth at all of determination to stop the enemy—to cut his Southwest Pacific supply lines—to counter the offensive which the turning tide of conflict was channeling into the Bismarcks and the Solomons.

Raiders to Asia

Cartoonists drew Japan as an octopus—a monster kraken with tentacles reaching in all directions. Thick coils were looped around the Philippines and Netherlands East Indies. Others were cupped on Malaya, Siam, the China Coast. Long arms writhed down through the Marianas and Carolines, Marshalls and Gilberts to fasten on the islands flanking Australia. In the north a thin appendage adhered to the tip of the Aleutians. And one thick tentacle had been amputated as it stretched for Midway.

This picture of Nippon as a giant cephalopod is apt in more than one respect. Japan, in the summer of 1942, was feeding on many shores far distant from its body. Chopped through at Midway, in the Central Pacific, one arm had been reduced to a bloody stump. But the kraken cannot be slain by the amputation of a single limb. It draws nourishment by means of many tentacles, and grows new ones even as one is cut away.

The monster can be slain by a mortal body-thrust, but the body, lying in a sheltered lair, can be protected by withdrawing the arms which will muscle up as they are shortened. However, the creature can be paralyzed and brought to death's door by anemia. Let shipping represent blood in the outstretched arm, and each ship represent a corpuscle, and the caricature assumes significance for submariners. Anemia can be induced by a war of attrition in which every merchantman sunk means one less corpuscle in the kraken's blood system, and every naval vessel to go down weakens an arm muscle. Paralyze the arms, destroy enough corpuscles, and the body with the heart in Tokyo will be unable to fend the final thrust.

Hence submarine strategy was designed to keep Japanese shipping under continuous attack—operations based on that No. 1 mission to sink everything afloat under the Rising Sun. All Japanese sea lanes were to be covered wherever they extended—south, north, east, west, near or far from Nippon. Submarines would go on special missions—would scout, lay mines, reconnoiter, operate with the fleet as at Midway. But the war of attrition went on around the clock. And throughout the remainder of the conflict (summer of 1942 to August 1945) hardly a day went by without the sinking of some Japanese vessel somewhere in the Pacific.

By the summer of 1942, U.S. submarines were conducting attrition campaigns in six regional patrol areas. These may be roughly described as the Empire Patrol, the South China Sea Patrol, the Netherlands East Indies-Philippines Patrol, the New Guinea-Bismarck-Solomons Patrol, the Mandates Patrol, and the Aleutian Patrol. As previously noted, Central Pacific submarines conducted the patrols in Empire waters and the Mandates, and operated with the Dutch Harbor Force in the Aleutians. Task Force Forty-two (Brisbane) patrolled the New Guinea-Bismarck-Solomons triangle. Patrolling the Netherlands East Indies, Philippines and South China Sea were the submarines from Fremantle, Australia.

Thus, while the Pearl Harbor Force had converged for the defense of Midway, Submarines SoWesPac were giving the enemy no respite in Asian waters. Far behind the enemy's Southwest Pacific Lines, SWORDFISH (Chester Smith) roamed the Gulf of Siam. A long haul from Fremantle. Dangerous every mile. But not so dangerous for SWORDFISH as it proved for BURMA MARU, a 4,584-ton freighter torpedoed and sunk by Smith and company off the coast of Thailand on June 12th.

SEAWOLF (Freddie Warder) was at this time off the southwest coast of Luzon where, on June 15, she sank NAMPO MARU, converted gunboat, 1,206 tons.

STINGRAY (Lieutenant Commander R. J. Moore) roamed the waters due east of the Philippines. So did SAIKYO MARU, converted gunboat, 1,292 tons. Meeting occurred at 12-41 N., 136-22 E. Torpedoed June 28, another converted gunboat was subtracted from the Imperial Navy.

Off Lingayen Gulf in the South China Sea was STURGEON under command of "Bull" Wright. Down the track came MONTEVIDEO MARU, a big 7,267-ton transport in the service of Homma and Hirohito.

147

STURGEON sent this liner to the bottom on the first day of July—a loss that added a sizable figure to the enemy's casualty list.

SEADRAGON (Ferrall and crew) shot to pieces a Jap convoy off the Indo-China coast, July 12, 13 and 16th. Down at sea went HIYAMA MARU, SHINYO MARU and HAKODATE MARU—one, two, three—a total of 15,636 tons.

And in the meantime, Pearl Harbor submarines had left Midway to resume their attrition missions. On the last day of June, PLUNGER fired a tricky shot that should have convinced the enemy that nowhere were his defenses wholly secure. The tactic employed by PLUNGER merits description.

Submarine Tactics—The "Up-the-kilt" Shot

Comparable to the down-the-throat shot, which took the target head-on, was the shot which, fired on a 180° track, caught the target from the opposite direction. The shot aimed at a ship's oncoming prow, and the shot aimed at a ship's retiring stern had one advantage in common—in either case, target speed was canceled out of the fire control problem, and the target's course could usually be estimated accurately from the position in which the torpedo attack was delivered.

The shots had a common disadvantage. Were the attack discovered in time, maneuvers to evade were comparatively simple. However, this disadvantage was offset by the fact that a tardy evasive maneuver was worse than none at all, for in zigging or zagging, the target ship presented a broader mark to the torpedo.

An attack from ahead was more likely to be discovered than one from astern. It was also subject to more immediate and efficient counter-measures. On the other hand, in a head-on attack the target's advance decreased the torpedo run, or, as the mathematicians put it, the target's speed and the torpedo's speed were additive. The reverse was true when the attack was from astern and the target was running away from the torpedo.

Target maneuvers to avoid were usually successful when the torpedo had to make a long run. To hit, the down-the-throat shot and the shot at a ship's stern had to be fired at relatively close range. In either case the target was narrow, and submarine captains generally preferred the more conventional approaches "on the beam"—attacks which gave the submarine a broader target and normal firing-range.

So the shot at a vessel's stern, like its down-the-throat opposite, was seldom deliberately courted by the submariners. In most cases it was a resort tried when opportunities for a conventional approach had been missed. In the pre-radar days of the war, the attack from directly astern was sometimes favored for a night approach. A number of these early attacks were reported as successful, but in the majority of instances it was impossible to verify the sinking. The Mark 14 was undependable. The exploders in use were apt to premature in the turbulence of the target vessel's wake. And it is usually difficult to identify a stern silhouette—as any sailor knows.

However, on June 30, 1942, UNKAI MARU No. 5 went down from a torpedo hit under her taffrail. The shot was fired by PLUNGER, and seems to be the first identifiable sinking of its kind in the Pacific War.

Captained by Lieutenant Commander D. C. (Dave) White, PLUNGER was patrolling in the East China Sea. About midway between Nagasaki and Shanghai, UNKAI MARU No. 5 came steaming along under the Asian moon. PLUNGER sighted the freighter at 0200 and White decided to try a surface approach. He fired the four bow tubes at a range decreasing from 2,500 to 1,500 yards. The four torpedoes were fired on conventional track angles between 90° and 110° port. All missed the target. Moonlight threatened to silhouette the submarine, and White feared detection if he closed the range from a position on the target's beam. But he ordered the forward tubes reloaded, and sent PLUNGER in pursuit of the Jap freighter which was travelling at an estimated 12-knot speed.

Heavily loaded, PLUNGER could make no better than 14.5 knots, a speed which gave her little latitude for maneuver against the 12-knot ship. The submarine was able to overhaul, however, and close in on the freighter's stern. At a range of 400 yards, White fired one torpedo on a 170° track. The torpedo struck home, the freighter blew up, and five minutes later the *maru's* 3,282 tons were under the surface.

White tried the tactic again when PLUNGER picked up a four-ship convoy in the same area two nights later. Handicapped by her 14.5-knot speed, PLUNGER was unable to gain a conventional attack position on the convoy. While the submarine attempted to close in, one of the four ships retired to the northward. This ship, it seemed, was the convoy's escort.

The other three vessels continued on a southeast course, apparently heading for the Central or South Pacific. Determining to interrupt the voyage, White sent PLUNGER in pursuit of the trailing cargo vessel, and fired two torpedoes on a 180° and 170° track.

One shot hit. The freighter, playing a frightened searchlight, circled left with a jammed rudder. White fired a torpedo from the stern tubes. It struck the freighter amidships; there was a geysering explosion and the ship went down.

The remaining freighters ran on their southeast

course, and PLUNGER gave chase at best speed. Once more she gained position for a stern attack. At a range of 500 yards, White fired two shots at one of the ships and a single at the other, on tracks of approximately 170°. The three torpedoes missed.

At this juncture a lookout sighted a ship on PLUNGER's port quarter—apparently the escort summoned by an alarm from the vessel which had first been attacked. White continued the attack on the freighters, driving in to fire a torpedo on a 180° track at 600-yard range. The torpedo made an erratic run, and White sent PLUNGER hard left to investigate the ship reported on her port quarter.

The escort was lost to sight, and PLUNGER returned to the freighter chase. After a few minutes of best-speed running, the submarine gained position for another stern attack, and White fired still another torpedo on a 170° track. There was an explosion which shook the submarine, but the torpedo may have prematured.

Attacking the remaining vessel, White swung PLUNGER on a hard left turn, and fired the last two torpedoes. One of these appeared to hit, but there was no way in which the damage could be assessed. Confident of at least one sinking in that night's melee, White took his submarine out of there. Post-war records confirmed his patrol report. The ship that went down on July 2 was UNYO MARU No. 3, 2,997 tons.

PLUNGER's performance would seem to indicate that the attack from astern was decidedly effective. Certainly it was efficacious, when driven home by White and crew. Throughout the war there were probably no more than 50 of these attacks essayed—torpedoes fired at close range on track angles between 170° and 180°. Only five or six proved successful, and the method is accordingly recognized as an expedient employed in a forced tactical situation.

Yet the possibility of such an attack was enough to keep the Japanese merchant marine looking back over an uneasy shoulder. A sailor never could tell. The attack from astern was an omnipresent threat. The name for the tactic—apparently British in origin —is self-explanatory. UNKAI MARU No. 5 and UNYO MARU No. 3 were victims of the "up-the-kilt" shot.

Lull Before Storm

While Fremantle submarines were sinking ships from the Gulf of Siam to the Philippine Sea, and PLUNGER was sinking them below Nagasaki, the Aleutian Battle was in full swing and there was a lull in the Central and South Pacific—"lull" meaning there were no major naval engagements in those areas in late June and July 1942. But Pearl Harbor submarines were in there free-lancing, and THRESHER, NARWHAL and SILVERSIDES scored sinkings in this period.

THRESHER scored hers in the Marshalls. Her skipper was W. J. Millican, veteran of Aleutian warfare in pioneering S-18. Date: July 9. Target: SHINSHO MARU, motor torpedo boat tender, 4,836 tons. Millican fired a brace, and the tender went down. "X" marked the spot about midway between Kwajalein and Wotje.

NARWHAL (Lieutenant Commander C. W. Wilkins) was concurrently heading for the Kuriles. July 24, lat. 45-05 N., long. 147-27 E., she sank a 1,500-ton cargo vessel whose name went unrecorded to the bottom.

SILVERSIDES (Creed Burlingame) torpedoed an unidentified transport off the Bungo Suido for an estimated 4,000 tons on July 28. Eleven days later (August 8) she torpedoed and sank NIKKEI MARU, 5,811-ton passenger-cargoman in the Bungo Suido area.

So the war of attrition went on beneath the lull— the lull that presaged a South Pacific storm. Midway had been secured. And before the end of July the Japanese Aleutian thrust had been parried. But in July the enemy landed on Guadalcanal. Jap labor battalions were constructing an airfield at Lunga Plain on the island's north coast. Jap shipping was concentrating in the Bismarcks and gathering in New Guinea. The storm in the Solomons was coming.

The glass was falling, but this time with a difference. Heretofore, Japan's rampaging forces had raised the storm. Now the storm was to be raised by the forces of the United States. Jap bases in the Solomons would seriously threaten Allied bases in Australia, and the Allies decided to strike before the enemy's foothold was established. This time the Americans would take the offensive.

Planning was supervised by Vice Admiral R. L. Ghormley, Commander South Pacific Forces, with headquarters in Auckland, New Zealand. In the first U.S. amphibious operation of World War II, Marines were to land and occupy Guadalcanal, Tulagi, Florida and Gavutu in the Solomons. The Marine landing force of 19,500 men would be commanded by Major General A. A. Vandergrift. Twenty-three troop transports escorted by five U.S. and three Australian cruisers and 15 destroyers would be under Vice Admiral Frank J. Fletcher and Rear Admiral R. K. Turner. Aircraft carriers ENTERPRISE, SARATOGA and WASP, supported by the new battleship NORTH CAROLINA and by cruisers and destroyers would comprise a carrier air force under Rear Admiral Leigh Noyes. Land-based air support would be given by planes based at New Caledonia, Samoa, and in the New Hebrides, Tonga and Fiji Islands under command of Rear Admiral John S. McCain. Army planes based in New Guinea and Australia under General MacArthur's command would add their weight to the attack.

Strictly speaking, the Solomons campaign may be referred to as a defensive, or counter-offensive. It was designed to relieve Japanese pressure in Burma, and to stymie the enemy in the South Pacific rather than hurl back a solidified front. It was also designed as a shot in the arm for the United Nations public, engloomed by European reverses. A tough campaign was seen in prospect, for the Marines would be facing seasoned veterans who were thus far undefeated. Infuriated by the Midway fiasco, Yamamoto would order the Imperial Navy to fight to the last gun. Accordingly, U.S. surface and air forces girded for a gruelling contest. And U.S. submarines were readied for rough assignments in what promised to be one of the bloodiest battles of the war.

The Boats from Brisbane

The Brisbane S-boats of Captain Christie's Task Force Forty-two had been covering the Bismarck-New Guinea area since early May. Assigned to regularly defined patrol areas, which were shifted as the situation warranted, they were to enter the undersea war of attrition and do their best to harry enemy shipping. Strategy also called for the covering of the enemy's bases—Rabaul, New Britain; Kavieng, New Ireland; Buin, Bougainville; Lae and Salamaua in Northeast New Guinea. Available intelligence information was given the captains, and they were expected to act upon it to the best of their ability.

By this time every submariner knew that these old "sugar boats" were not up to long patrols and difficult missions—so they stayed out on patrol anywhere from 10 to 45 days. Which could seem like so many years to those aboard a weary, old boiler whose seams trailed oil slick and whose engines might die of asthma at any crisis. And they performed missions which would have been a credit to submarines with four engines, radar and modern air conditioning.

For example, S-42 (Lieutenant O. G. Kirk)—the submarine that distinguished her first patrol by sinking the minelayer OKINOSHIMA. On her second patrol, begun early in July, she landed and embarked a special agent at Adler Bay, near Rabaul, practically on the doormat of enemy headquarters in New Britain.

Old S-43 (Lieutenant E. R. Hannon) planted an RAAF officer on the hostile shore of New Ireland to contact Allied agents operating on that Jap-held island. The date: July 19-20—one night after S-42's extraordinary mission.

S-43 went on from there to put a special agent ashore at Feni Island in the Bismarcks. Here she encountered trouble—was unable to recover this RAAF officer. They could gray a captain's hair, these missions wherein the submariners put an agent on a beach in enemy territory and then waited offshore for his return. If the agent were captured, anything could happen. A long wait, futile signals, no answer save dead silence—such a situation frayed the nerves.

The Brisbane S-boats did more than perform special missions. On June 21, old S-44 (Lieutenant Commander J. R. Moore) torpedoed KEIJO MARU, 2,626-ton converted gunboat, just south of Guadalcanal Island. The vessel blew up with a blast that convinced the submariners they had exploded a munitions ship. Chunks of metal and burning timbers splattered down around the submarine. She dove out from under the falling scrap iron, and came to periscope depth some time later at a comfortable distance. Raising the No. 1 periscope, Moore was surprised to discover that he could not see a thing. The No. 2 scope was put up, and it gave him a clear view in all directions. Moore ordered his submarine to the surface, and went topside to inspect the No. 1 periscope. The scope was blindfolded by a Japanese seaman's coat which was wrapped around its head.

On July 8, the old S-37 (Lieutenant J. R. Reynolds) sank TENZAN MARU, 2,776-ton passenger-cargo carrier, in the waters of the Bismarck Archipelago.

S-38 (Lieutenant Commander H. G. Munson) followed through on August 8 by sinking MEIYO MARU, 5,628-ton transport, in the same torrid area.

Four sinkings were almost more than could have been expected of S-boats whose cruising capacities were strained by a run from Brisbane to Rabaul. And these submarines accomplished more than the score would indicate. At a time when it was S-boats or nothing, they stepped in to hold the front against the first-class forces of the enemy. Patrolling the hottest water south of Midway, they harried the enemy's communications lines, badgered his convoys, reported on his movements. And finally, at an hour when the Japanese were mustering every resource for the Solomons battle, one of the Brisbane boats shot an 8,800-ton hole in the Imperial Navy. This shot, alone, made the sweat-and-be-damned efforts of all the sugar-boaters worth while.

It was fired by Moore and crew of the valiant S-44.

S-44 vs. Kako

U.S. Marines hit the beachheads of Guadalcanal on the morning of August 7, 1942. Jap Headquarters at Rabaul was taken by surprise. By nightfall 11,000 Marines were ashore on a three-mile front, and 20 hours later they were working on the unfinished Jap airstrip, renamed Henderson Field after the major who died leading a Marine bomber squadron at Midway. Simultaneous landings were made on Tulagi, Gavutu and Florida Islands. Jap torpedo bombers struck at the Florida occupation forces, blasted a transport and torpedoed the destroyer JARVIS. The planes were driven off with sharp losses, and the amphibious unloadings went on. So began the battle for the Solomons.

In the Bismarck Archipelago four Japanese heavy cruisers of the KAKO class, one light cruiser and two or three destroyers were available for counter-action. This force (designated Cruiser Division Six) was ordered into Savo Sound to strike at the Guadalcanal occupation fleet which was lying just east of Lunga Point. The division was underway on August 8, heading for Savo Island which is situated like an outpost in the western entrance of the Sound.

Japanese submarines were already in these waters between Guadalcanal and Florida Island. Warned of their presence, Admiral Noyes had obtained from Admiral Ghormley permission to move the carrier force and its escorts from the Sound. This left the surface forces of Admiral Fletcher and Admiral Turner to hold the waterway soon to become famous as "The Slot."

The advancing Japs were sighted off Bougainville, and again off Savo Island by Army aircraft. Unfortunately the fliers failed to recognize all of the cruisers, mistaking several for DD's. The Japanese made a deceptive reverse toward Rabaul which served to screen their intentions, and then came back at top speed. As a result, the Allied forces in the

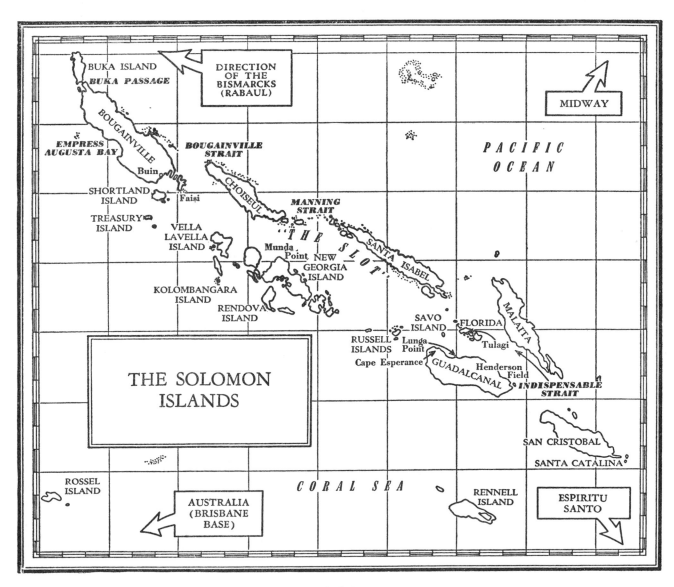

151

Sound were caught off guard, and the consequences were disastrous.

The cruisers CANBERRA, CHICAGO and AUSTRALIA, screened by destroyers PATTERSON and BAGLEY, were patrolling a line between Savo Island and Guadalcanal. Cruisers SAN JUAN and HOBART, with two DD's, patrolled a north-south line between Florida and Guadalcanal. Cruisers ASTORIA, QUINCY and VINCENNES with DD's WILSON and HELM patrolled between Florida and Savo. Two destroyers, BLUE and RALPH TALBOT, were stationed northwest of Savo.

About 0130 on August 9 the enemy column came straight down the track on a line between the TALBOT and BLUE. Although the enemy ships passed within 500 yards of BLUE, the destroyer failed to detect them. The Japanese cruisers continued without interruption down the west side of Savo Island, swung eastward into the Sound, and ran into the destroyers PATTERSON and BAGLEY.

Time 0143. PATTERSON cried the alarm over TBS, and opened fire on the leading cruiser. Return fire smote the destroyer as the cruisers steamed by. BAGLEY was unable to load in time for a shot. Jap seaplanes, launched from the cruisers, illuminated the scene with parachute flares, and the fireworks' glare revealed the Australian CANBERRA and heavy cruiser CHICAGO within range.

Some four hours previous to this, British Rear Admiral V. A. C. Crutchley, commanding the Allied escort groups, had gone with the cruiser AUSTRALIA to hold conference with Admiral Turner who was with the transports east of Lunga Point. Hence CANBERRA and CHICAGO were left to face the Japanese cruiser force, two against five.

Concentrated fire wrecked CANBERRA before her gunners could reach their mounts. Disabled and burning, the Australian cruiser wallowed helplessly until the following morning when her derelict hulk was sunk by U.S. destroyers. CHICAGO was hit by a torpedo. Veering, she raced westward, turned about in confusion and opened fire on PATTERSON. The destroyer returned the fire until her nationality was recognized.

The Japs swept counter-clockwise around Savo, and plunged into head-on contact with the cruisers QUINCY, ASTORIA and VINCENNES. Main batteries blazing, they shelled the trio out of action in a half-dozen minutes. Return fire swept the Japanese flagship CHOKAI, killing 30 men—the only major damage suffered by the Japs in this foray. Steaming on out of the Sound, they brushed into the TALBOT once more and battered the destroyer aside. Then away they rushed into the western night.

The United States-Australian forces had suffered a terrible setback. Three U.S. cruisers, QUINCY, VINCENNES and ASTORIA, and the Australian CANBERRA went to the bottom. About 1,500 American officers and men were killed in action. From the Allied surface forces the Japanese escaped practically unharmed. The U.S. Navy was staggered by this defeat in the Battle of Savo Island, which has been attributed to the weakness of early radar, insufficient reconnaissance, insufficient night training and lack of experience in amphibious operations. It might stand as the worst setback experienced by the American Navy in action, were it not for the pay-off. Japanese Cruiser Division Six was not permitted to escape scot free.

On the morning of August 10 a lone submarine was patrolling the waters off Kavieng Harbor at the northwestern end of New Ireland. She was an old submarine—an 850-tonner—product of the World War I building program, begun before the Armistice and completed in 1925. Her hull leaked oil. Her engines were tired. Only the ingenuity of an expert tender repair force, and the skill and seamanship of well-trained submariners had kept her going. She was S-44, making her third patrol from Brisbane commanded by Lieutenant Commander J. R. (Dinty) Moore.

One might expect to find a Dinty Moore in the vicinity of a New Ireland. But Japanese logic, apparently, did not admit to such a premise. On the day after its Savo triumph, Japanese Cruiser Division Six was doubtless still congratulating itself, polishing the brightwork and swabbing down for a victory parade into Kavieng Harbor. Here they were safe home, and not a plane had pursued them. The damage to the flagship was nothing. "Banzai!"

So at 0750, on August 10, 1942, the periscope of S-44 sighted two heavy cruisers coming out of the sun at a distance of some 9,000 yards. Two more heavy cruisers hove into view, the ships in column in two sections, line of bearing 45° relative, and angle on the bow 5° starboard. This put S-44 about 800 yards from the enemy track. Moore put the submarine on a course 70° divergent in order to open the distance to the track a trifle and give her a little more sea room for the approach.

After due deliberation, Moore decided to attack the rear ship in the rear section. The approach party got to work, the fire controlmen manned their instruments, the torpedomen stood by their tubes. Five minutes of maneuvering brought S-44 around to the firing course for an 80° track.

The leading cruisers steamed by. The third cruiser passed. At 0808 the last heavy cruiser was only 700 yards away.

"We were close enough to see the Japs on the bridge using their glasses," Moore recalled afterwards. And that was proximity from an old S-boat's point of view. The enemy cruiser looked bigger than the Pentagon Building and the submarine seemed smaller than a barrel.

Moore fired four torpedoes, zero gyro angle, 80° track. Thirty-five seconds after firing, the first torpedo hit. The explosion thunderclapped in the sound gear as the S-boat went down to 130 feet.

The trailing torpedoes slammed into the warship's hull. "Evidently all her boilers blew up," Moore related. "You could hear hideous noises that sounded like steam hissing through water. These noises were more terrifying to the crew than the actual depth charges that followed. It sounded as if giant chains were being dragged across our hull, as if our own water and air lines were bursting."

These were the breaking-up noises of the Imperial Navy's heavy cruiser KAKO—8,800 tons of machinery and steel tearing themselves to pieces as they went to the bottom. So was sunk the second Japanese cruiser to be downed by any agency in the war, and the first major naval vessel to be sunk by the single-handed action of a U.S. submarine. When torpedoed by NAUTILUS, the carrier SORYU was already disabled. At Christmas Island SEAWOLF had hit something, but post-war research was never able to identify the target. There was no doubt at all about what happened to KAKO.

The Savo Island setback was a shock that threatened to throw the Guadalcanal amphibious machine out of gear. Marines and Seabees on the beaches east of Lunga Point were isolated for several days, as Admiral Turner had to withdraw his transport flotilla from the danger zone. The ground forces were left short-rationed, with insufficient ammunition on beachheads relatively unprotected. Had the Japs struck again in the week following their Savo raid, they might have wiped out the Guadalcanal vanguard.

But Cruiser Division Six at Kavieng was unable to estimate the damage it had wrought at Savo. Japanese Headquarters at Rabaul was disposed to caution. The cruiser division was the only one immediately available in those waters, and undoubtedly the loss of KAKO and the knowledge that U.S. submarines were patrolling in the Bismarck-Solomons area caused the Japanese to be doubly cautious.

Thus it may well be that the blow struck by S-44 not only accounted for a heavy cruiser, but delayed a second Japanese attack at an hour when the fate of Guadalcanal hung in the balance. It may well be that other submarines from Brisbane caused the

enemy's hand to hesitate at that moment when success was within its grasp. Impossible to assess the precise "threat in being" value of the unseen submarine.

It remains obvious that the old sugar boat was worth its salt.

Loss of S-39

Casualties could be expected among old-timers fighting in World War II with World War I equipment. Case in point: S-39. She had come a long, hard way since her pioneer entry into the war under the red-headed leadership of Lieutenant Coe. Although she had but one sinking to her official credit, her torpedoes had damaged at least a dozen enemy ships. Her special mission to Chebia Island was a well-remembered exploit. And in May, under Lieutenant F. E. Brown, she went out of Fremantle on her fourth patrol to reconnoiter Deboyne Island in the Louisiades.

Later she traveled to Brisbane where her fifth patrol was delayed by a major breakdown. Early in August she was ready to start again, and she headed off for the Bougainville area. Then her executive officer developed pneumonia. Brown radioed for instructions and was ordered into Townsville, Australia, where the sick officer was put ashore. On August 10 she made a second start for her patrol area.

At 0000 hours on the night of August 13-14 she was east of Rossel Island in the Louisiade Archipelago. With the clock at midnight, her course was altered to take her clear of the island and well beyond it to the westward. But time and tide were not working in behalf of S-39. For two days the wind and sea had been coming from the southeast quadrant. Consequently the submarine was farther west than her navigator estimated. At 0220 there was a sullen growl under her keel. A butting shock, and she was hard aground on a reef south of Rossel Island.

The submarine listed to port, and following seas swooped over her stern. Backing the screws failed to budge her. Fuel and ballast tanks were blown dry. Everything that could go overside was jettisoned. But the lightened ship only swung broadside to the seas which drove her farther up on the rocks.

Brown ordered all fuel and ballast tanks flooded to hold her steady, and at high tide on the morning of August 14 the screws were backed until the low-voltage limit showed on the batteries. S-39 crawled backward about fifty feet, but once more listed heavily to port under pounding surf. Ballast tanks were ruptured by the jagged rocks as the seas beat against the submarine.

153

Throughout the day the submariners waited while breakers as high as haystacks smashed over and around the conning tower. Afternoon brought word that HMAS KATOOMBA would arrive and lend aid the following morning. Brown and crew set their teeth and hung on.

By the morning of the 15th the old S-boat had a 60° port list, and was threatening to roll over. Shortly after dawn the torpedoes were inactivated and fired, and Brown, still unwilling to abandon, gave his men permission to swim to a near-by reef if anyone wanted to make the attempt.

Lieutenant C. N. G. Hendrix volunteered to swim to the reef with a line and then haul the two mooring lines to the reef as a riding line for the rest of the crew. Hendrix made it to the reef like an Olympic champion, but had trouble with the heavy mooring lines. So into the surf plunged Chief Commissary Steward W. L. Schoenrock.

Between them, the two managed to secure the lines to a torpedo which had lodged on the reef.

Thirty-two of the crew went safely across on the lines, and the remaining 12 stayed on board with the captain until KATOOMBA arrived that noon. By 1000 the following day all hands were aboard the Australian ship. As S-39 was breaking to pieces under battering waves, no ammunition was spent in destroying her. The S-boat's complement arrived in Townsville on August 19th. "There," says one laconic report, "they were assigned further duty on other submarines."

The Truk Blockade

Before the Solomons offensive could be effectively launched and the drive on Guadalcanal set in motion, there was one most important Japanese base that had to be blockaded. This was the powerful naval base at Truk, centered in the eastern Caroline Islands.

When the Carolines, Marshalls and Marianas were relieved of German rule and mandated to Japan after World War I, the switch was of small benefit to civilization. The "Little Prussians of the East" immediately violated their diplomatic promises not to fortify these island groups, and set out to turn Truk into a west-central Pacific Gibraltar. How the Japanese could build this oceanic fortress behind a veil of secrecy remains one of those mysteries of the armament world, but the fact is that Truk was still an enigma to the Allied naval leaders at the start of World War II. It was soon suspected, however, as harboring one of the major bases of the Imperial Navy's fleet.

A glance at the Pacific map will show Truk's dominating location. Lying about midway on an arc between the Marianas and the Bismarcks, Truk was on the main line running from Japan to Rabaul—a strategic assembly point for shipping which came down via the Bonins, Saipan and Guam. At Truk the heavy-laden supply ships and troop transports could pick up escorts for the run to Rabaul or Bougainville, approximately 900 miles southward. Japanese warships or carrier forces based at Truk could be speedily rushed to the Solomons front, and the distance was not too great for long-range aircraft. At the outbreak of the war, Truk's defenses were believed to be invulnerable. But the waters off Truk were not immune to submarine penetration.

Pioneering submarines from Pearl Harbor had reconnoitered this Caroline stronghold, and now the SubPac Force was to conduct the blockade which was vital to the Solomons campaign. In July, while the Brisbane boats of Task Force Forty-two were attacking the enemy in the Bismarck-Solomons area, five fleet submarines from Pearl Harbor were sent to patrol off Truk.

These blockaders were GREENLING (Lieutenant Commander H. C. Bruton); DRUM (Lieutenant Commander R. H. Rice); GUDGEON (Lieutenant Commander W. S. Stovall, Jr.); GRENADIER (Lieutenant Commander B. L. Carr); and GRAYLING (Lieutenant Commander E. Olsen).

GUDGEON, under Lieutenant Commander Stovall, was first to score. In waters southwest of Truk on August 3, she sank NANIWA MARU, a 4,858-ton passenger-cargo vessel which had perhaps been scheduled to visit Rabaul. GUDGEON pitched into two other large AK's and probably sent them to the yards for repairs.

On August 5, two days before the Guadalcanal landing, GREENLING, patrolling northwest of Truk, sank the 12,752-ton BRASIL MARU. A survivor, fished from the sea which had swallowed this big transport, identified the ship and told the interested submariners it had carried over 400 troops and much valuable cargo.

The next day GREENLING sank another passenger-cargoman—4,500-ton PALAO MARU. Bruton and company sank a large fisherman on this same patrol, and went on to take periscope photographs of Truk.

DRUM, GRENADIER and GRAYLING all sighted, attacked and probably damaged large ships. Their reports, in addition to those from GREENLING and GUDGEON, strengthened the suspicion that Truk was a Japanese imitation of Pearl Harbor. The base was considered a tough nut to crack, for the waters around it were strongly defensible. But the island's approaches were open to submarine warfare and promised big game. The blockade was tightened.

154

A program was devised to permit submarines traveling to or from Australia to spend part of their time in the Truk area, en route. TAMBOR (Lieutenant Commander S. H. Ambruster) was heading for the Carolines in early August. On August 7, while weaving her way through the Marshalls, she paused to sink a small, converted net tender. August 21, southeast of Truk, she sighted, shot at and sank SHINSEI MARU No. 6, a 4,928-ton passenger-cargoman.

Periscopes maintained a vigilant watch on the road coming down from Guam, and patrollers lay in ambush along the south-bound sea lanes to Rabaul. As September came up on the calendar the submarine blockade of Japan's Central Pacific Gibraltar was in full swing. The guns which thudded on Guadalcanal were echoed by torpedoes off Truk.

Attrition without Intermission

The Allied counter-offensive in the South Pacific is described by some authorities as the U.S. Navy's first major offensive in the Pacific War. Others term it a limited operation, as its scope was restricted by the Anglo-American decision to strike the enemy at the other end of the Axis with a heavyweight invasion of North Africa.

But U.S. submarines had been on the offensive in the Pacific since the first bomb thundered in Pearl Harbor. Without air support, without fleet support, they had been striking at the enemy from Hawaii to Hokkaido, torpedoing his ships from Brisbane to Bataan, fighting the attrition war 'round the clock in accordance with the unrestricted warfare directive.

From the opening gun, they had pushed the attack. Invading Empire waters in January 1942, submarines from Pearl Harbor were menacing the enemy's homeland before the war was four weeks old. Off Hainan and the northern Philippines, the boats from Manila were making an up-the-kilt drive on the rear of the Co-Prosperity Sphere even as the Japanese vanguards stormed the Malay Barrier. Naval battles were won and lost—the Allied lines fell backward—the shock troops of the foe reached the marge of the Coral Sea. But at no time were his communication lines wholly secure. At no time were his transports and supply ships freed of the torpedo threat established at war's beginning by the United States submarine offensive.

Dedicated to a war of attrition to deprive the enemy of sustenance, the submarine offensive with its first shot had put a drain on the Japanese merchant marine. In *The War Against Japanese Transportation*, published in 1947 by the United States Strategic Bombing Survey, the authors have this to say:

Even during the retreats through the Philippines, Malaya and the Indies, significant damage was done by Allied air power and the submarines soon began to harass Japanese shipping lanes from Tokyo to Singapore, albeit in weak force and scattered fashion. Nevertheless, despite all of Japan's shipbuilding efforts and despite the weakness of available Allied offensive forces early in the war, the balance of shipping available to Japan began to decline as early as April 1942.

That this decline continued at an accelerating rate through the spring and summer of 1942 must be apparent to the reader of the preceding chapters of the present volume. The part played by U.S. submarines in inducing that decline is graphically portrayed in the accompanying chart (prepared by the United States Strategic Bombing Survey).

The reader will note that the chart indicates merchant sinkings only, and does not include Japanese naval losses in the period delineated. Several of the sinkings in Indonesian and Netherlands Indies waters were the work of Dutch and British submersibles. And, due to the difficulties of identification and verification of tonnages, not all of the sinkings are marked in this and similar charts which follow in this volume. The submarine patrols are nicely indicated, however, and one sees from the map the extent and approximate locale of the sinkings accomplished in the attrition war up to the end of August 1942.

Yet symbols on a chart—each one representing a merchantman—tell little of the story. Nor do tonnages complete the picture. One must visualize each sinking as a cargo or shipload going under—tons of rice, oil, bauxite, clothing, iron ore, cobalt, beef, coal. Boxes of tea, rifles, shoes, hand grenades, radio gear, revolvers, beer, anti-aircraft shells. Barrels of aviation gasoline, fish, cereal, lubricants, paint, chemicals. Cases of medicine and cartridges. Crates of machinery. Tanks, howitzers, tractors, field pieces, anti-aircraft guns. Each sinking sends to ocean bottom another mass of raw materials or manufactured goods—or strews the sea with a soggy Sargasso of wreckage and drifting men.

By the end of August 1942, when United States forces, turning from the defensive, were girding for the Solomons campaign, United States submarines had sunk a total of 82 Japanese merchant ships.

The enemy's transportation facilities were showing signs of strain, and the drivers of Japan's War Machine were beginning to worry about the supply lines to such distant outposts as Guadalcanal.

CHAPTER 14

GUADALCANAL CAMPAIGN

Diversionary Raid—Nautilus and Argonaut to Makin

NAUTILUS and ARGONAUT, under Group Commander J. M. Haines, stood out of Pearl Harbor on August 8 and headed for the Gilbert Islands. The Marines had landed on Guadalcanal the day before, and the previous evening they had landed on the decks of ARGONAUT and NAUTILUS.

Boarding ARGONAUT, seven officers and 114 men crowded into the submarine's interior. Six officers and 84 men were packed into NAUTILUS. These Marines were the pick of the Corps—Companies A and B of the famous 2nd Raider Battalion, trained and led by hard-hitting Colonel Evans F. Carlson—and they quickly had the submarine situation well under control. "Gung ho!"

Their objective in the Gilberts was Makin Island. Mission: a commando raid. This raid on Makin was primarily planned to create a diversion—scramble the enemy's plans and make him re-deploy strong forces which were known to be concentrating for an attack on Guadalcanal. The raiders were to strike Makin a savage blow, do as much damage as possible, and gather information on the island.

The run to Makin was accomplished without misadventure. ARGONAUT, under Lieutenant Commander J. R. Pierce of Aleutian experience, was making her second patrol after complete overhaul and modernization at Mare Island. Captain of NAUTILUS was Lieutenant Commander Brockman, and her ace crew had topped their big exploit at Midway with a rampage patrol in Empire waters. So the Marines as well as the submarines were in good hands.

Early in the morning of August 16, Makin was sighted. Periscope reconnaissance commenced at daylight. Rendezvous was accomplished at dusk, and plans for the attack were passed to ARGONAUT. The submarines waited offshore while the twilight thickened into darkness. The Marines shouldered into their gear and huddled, tense, as their officers briefed them on the final details. Shortly after midnight NAUTILUS put her rubber boats overside and the first group of raiders disembarked.

By 0421 all Marines were clear of the submarine, and the bridge personnel watched the last boat paddle off in the graying mist. For about an hour the submariners waited, while the gloaming seemed to listen with drawn breath. Then at 0513 word came by voice radio. The Marines were on the beach.

Thirty minutes later a pessimistic and cryptic message was received from Colonel Carlson. *"Everything lousy!"* Four minutes after that the news brightened with, *"Situation expected to be well in hand shortly."* Following this message, there was a blur of static and voice-radio reception deteriorated. Evidently the walkie-talkies had run into trouble. But a few snatches of English got through, and it became apparent that the raiders wanted fire support to neutralize the Ukiangang Point Lake Area where Jap reserves were thought to be.

NAUTILUS promptly opened up with her deck gun, and was on target with the third salvo. She had been firing for a short time when word came through that a merchant ship was sitting in the harbor 8,000 yards from the government pier. Fire was checked at the 24th round, and NAUTILUS maneuvered to fire on this new target.

S-44 VS. KAKO. Patrolling off New Ireland, the veteran S-boat ambushes enemy cruiser division at entrance to Kavieng Harbor. Four torpedoes (range 700 yards) send IJN Kako to the bottom—an 8,800-ton warship sunk by an 850-ton sub! This sinking of first Japanese heavy cruiser avenged defeat at Savo Island.

DESTINATION DAVY JONES LOCKER! *This periscope photo, dated spring of 1942, remains unidentified. But picture is clear.*

GOING DOWN! *Ship shown above, torpedoed, is on her way. Camera addicts in U. S. subs had many chances to take such shots.*

MAIL CALL! *After a long, hard-fighting sub cruise, nothing was better than a good word from home.*

SUNDOWN AT SEA. *Camera bears witness to the sinking of IJN destroyer* Yamakaze, *torpedoed by USS* Nautilus *off Tokyo Bay, June 25, 1942. Trained by pre-war doctrine to avoid enemy DD's, American submarines soon learned that the Jap destroyer's bark was worse than its bite. By V-J Day, U. S. submarines had eliminated 39 of the breed.*

Lieutenant Commander Thomas Hogan, the submarine's diving officer, recalled the shooting afterwards:

"Our area for the purposes of the raid was outside the lagoon. Ships were inside behind a wooded island in a harbor that we couldn't even see. We had suspected they were in there—a suspicion verified by the raiders.

"We sent a couple of men ashore to spot bursts for us, but there was plenty of hell going on, and they got out of communication. It's pretty hard to shoot blind when you can't be sure of your adjustment, but eventually we worked it out with a sort of zone fire. We picked out a tree in the distance, first as a registration point and then as an aiming point. After we got the range on it, we came up a little and traversed right and left from it."

This served to compensate for the disadvantages of blind firing. Spotters or no, the gunners did pretty well. The initial range of 14,000 yards was laddered up and down as the deflection was changed. After 65 rounds the gun crew was ordered to cease fire as the expenditure of ammunition had begun to appear unwarranted. But later word from the Marines assured the submariners that their gunnery had rung the bell. Their shells had disabled a 3,500-ton transport and smashed up a small patrol yacht.

Hogan said later, "We didn't need anybody to tell us about it. When the ships were hit we could see the smoke and flame shooting up over the trees."

Both NAUTILUS and ARGONAUT endeavored to remain on the surface throughout the morning. Several times they were forced under by enemy planes. Marines were strafed coming out from the shore in rubber boats, and one boatload was killed to a man. With Jap aircraft in the sky, the submarines went down for the afternoon and remained submerged until nightfall.

The submarines surfaced early in the evening, and four boats laden with weary raiders were recovered by 2130. More were due to arrive, and the submariners spent the remainder of the night in a futile search for these.

The 53 Marines who had made it told stories of desperate fighting ashore and the struggle to launch their boats after dark in wild surf. Many boats had capsized. Guns and gear had been lost. Aboard NAUTILUS and ARGONAUT, the Marine doctors and pharmacist's mates had their work cut out for them. One young Marine had eight wounds in his chest. A sergeant walked aboard with a bullet buried deep in his back. "I got a scratch somewhere," he told the surgeon, "and I can't bend forward." The submariners were not going to leave such men behind at

Makin, and at daybreak they were still on the surface, searching.

Then several boats were spotted on the beach, the Marines waiting to run the gantlet through the breakers. NAUTILUS closed to within half a mile of the reef, and by 0800 two more boatloads of Carlson's Raiders were aboard. One of the rubber boats was manned by volunteers and sent back to shore with extra weapons, paddles and a line-throwing gun. The volunteers carried a message advising Colonel Carlson that NAUTILUS, if forced by aircraft to submerge, would be back at 1930 and remain offshore indefinitely thereafter. A man from the boat swam in through the surf to deliver this message, and then swam back out to NAUTILUS. But the rubber boat and its complement of volunteers never returned. NAUTILUS was forced to submerge that morning, and apparently the aircraft which drove her under spotted and strafed the boat in the shallows. Carlson reported afterwards that he was certain the landing party was strafed by aircraft machine-gun fire.

Meanwhile, two more boats were recovered by ARGONAUT. She, too, was forced under by enemy planes. As the submarines surfaced later in the morning, they were again driven down by a plane which dropped two random bombs from high altitude. After this attack, the two submarines remained submerged.

At evening they surfaced once more, and Colonel Carlson was contacted ashore. A new rendezvous point was set for two hours later. The submarines maneuvered in, and the remaining five boatloads of Marines battled out through the surf. When the last man was aboard, both submarines set a course for Pearl Harbor. NAUTILUS was home on the 25th. ARGONAUT arrived the following day. It had been a tough assignment, but all hands had played their part, and the mission was highly successful.

Just how successful, the submariners were not to know until long afterward. The Makin Raid is predominantly a Marine story—a brilliant exploit in the career of the 2nd Raider Battalion and its famous leader, Colonel Carlson. The Marines wiped out the enemy garrison practically to a man. They destroyed a radio station, two planes, military installations and stores including some 900 barrels of gasoline. Thirty Marines were slain in the action, but the raid accomplished its primary objective by disrupting enemy plans to reinforce Guadalcanal and diverting Jap guns and aircraft to the Gilberts.

The crews of ARGONAUT and NAUTILUS could take pride in their part of this high exploit. They carried the Marines to Makin, and they brought them back. They shot up shipping in the harbor. From this pioneer operation they gained invaluable experience which would later aid the planning of full-fledged island invasions. By future submariners, NAUTILUS and ARGONAUT will be remembered as the valiant V-boats which participated in the greatest commando raid carried out in the Pacific during World War II.

The Truk Blockade

Down from Pearl Harbor to join the Truk blockaders in September came THRESHER. She was captained by Lieutenant Commander W. J. Millican, veteran from the Aleutians. Tropical Truk was a far cry from icy Attu. But in the torrid zone of the Carolines, THRESHER's crew underwent an experience as blood-chilling as a brush with an iceberg.

The experience began in the dark of 0300 one morning when THRESHER was moving quietly along on the surface. Stars gleamed overhead, but a wispy surface haze obscured the horizon. Lieutenant L. V. Julihn, executive officer, was on the bridge. Nothing was visible in any quarter when suddenly the sonar operator spoke a sharp alarm.

"Fast screws on the starboard bow!"

Sleeping at the time in the conning tower, the submarine commander was shocked awake. On the bridge Lieutenant Julihn ordered left full rudder, all ahead emergency, hoping to swing THRESHER clear of the reported sound bearing. Then, sweeping the horizon with his glasses, Julihn tried to find the reported ship. Starlight and mist revealed nothing. The exec was beginning to wonder if the "ping jockey" hadn't contacted a school of fish, when a gray silhouette loomed abruptly in the haze and came rushing at the submarine's starboard beam.

Millican, by that time on deck, ordered all back emergency. Materializing into a large patrol vessel, the oncoming craft bore down on the submarine as though bent on ramming.

"I ordered the collision alarm sounded," Julihn recalled afterward. "And I accidentally kicked the general alarm. With both alarms going off, the men below were as scared as they'd ever been in their lives."

The powerful patrol boat came charging down the track. Then suddenly the craft made a hard right turn and ran parallel to the submarine, no more than a grenade-throw away. With the two vessels running beam to beam, THRESHER's bridge personnel could see the Jap sailors gesturing, chatting together.

"Our quartermaster had come topside with a Tommy-gun. He requested permission to fire it. I wouldn't grant it because I had a feeling that if we started shooting, those Japs would wake up and shoot right back at us."

The patrol boat veered off, and the submariners cleared the bridge at acrobatic speed as Millican gave the order to go down. As THRESHER was nosing under there was a crash that sounded like a four-inch shell bursting forward of the conning tower. Down in the forward torpedo room several men were thrown off their feet by the concussion. The patrol boat had circled and raced back, dropping a string of ash-cans. The submariners were unimpressed by these Johnny-come-lately explosions.

"They didn't bother us at all," Lieutenant Julihn noted, "after what had just happened."

It may be supposed that the blasts which failed to jolt THRESHER had their repercussions in IJN Headquarters at Truk. Another submarine warning—more patrol boats called for—traffic re-routed—anti-submarine screens enlarged. While THRESHER and a number of the submarines which followed her into the Carolines failed to sink ships in the Truk area, their menace value could not be measured in tons. Forced to augment his anti-sub patrols and double his watch, the enemy paid the price in delays, side-tracking and anxiety.

Throughout the autumn of 1942 while the Guadalcanal battle was touch-and-go, the Truk blockade went on. TROUT (Lieutenant Commander L. P. Ramage) downed a small net tender in the area on September 21st. SKIPJACK (Lieutenant Commander Coe) caught the 6,781-ton freighter SHUNKO MARU about midway between Truk and Palau on October 14, and the enemy was minus another cargoman. On November 10, GRAYLING (Lieutenant Commander J. E. Lee) sank an unidentified 4,000-tonner off Truk.

Submarines would continue to patrol the Truk approaches until that stronghold was neutralized late in the war. When the Japs were thrown back to the upper Solomons in October 1943, the task of detecting enemy fleet units coming down from the Caroline base was a major mission assigned submarines. Long distances involved and the possibilities for evasive routing militated against such "offensive reconnaissance" patrols conducted in open sea by relatively few submarines. As will be seen, the high-speed warships eluded the submarine vedettes at that time. However, the 1942 blockaders put a crimp in the enemy's Truk-to-Solomons transport service. Anything which interfered with the Japanese service of supply was immensely valuable to the Allies during the Guadalcanal crisis. In this respect, the results obtained by forcing the enemy to institute defensive measures at Truk were well worth the effort required to produce them.

The strong Jap arm reaching down from the Caroline base to the Solomons-Bismarck front was not entirely paralyzed. But the tourniquet applied on Truk by the submarine forces was numbing, and the flow of war materials to the Solomons was appreciably reduced.

Undersea War in the Solomons

After the Battle of Savo Island, the opposing forces had recoiled, then come back to battery, crashing.

Determined to retake lost ground, Japanese Headquarters dispatched 1,000 crack troops to Guadalcanal. A massive fleet was assembled for a follow-up strike—four transports, four destroyers, a cruiser and an accompanying carrier force built around the large ZUIKAKU and SHOKAKU and the smaller RYUJO. Japanese submarines screened the advance of this armada which was 200 miles north of Guadalcanal by the morning of August 23rd.

Admiral Ghormley had countered by rushing his ENTERPRISE-NORTH CAROLINA-SARATOGA forces to the Eastern Solomons. WASP was in the backfield, and HORNET with her escorts was steaming hell-for-leather down from Pearl Harbor.

The Marines on Guadalcanal obliterated the crack Japanese 1,000, and the battle passed to the carrier forces which fought it out August 23-25. In this engagement, SARATOGA's airmen smashed and sank the carrier RYUJO. Bombers from Guadalcanal disabled the light cruiser JINTSO. A Jap destroyer and a large transport were sunk by planes from Espiritu Santo and Henderson Field. ENTERPRISE was damaged by bomb-hits, but only three of the 80 planes that attacked her survived. Altogether, nearly half of the Jap carrier planes engaged in this three-day battle were demolished. Badly beaten, the Japanese withdrew.

Japanese submarines, however, were somewhat more successful in their Solomons operations at this time. Planes from ENTERPRISE sighted a number of them, and bombed them without scoring hits. Their presence in the area was a threat to American convoys and slowed the reinforcement of the Marines holding Henderson Field.

Submarines from Brisbane similarly hampered Japanese efforts to reinforce their Guadalcanal vanguard. Fighting the war of attrition, they damaged enemy merchantmen on the fringe of the Solomons area, patrolled the Rabaul road to Guadalcanal and countered "threat" with menace. Due to a number of hindering factors, results on the American side of the Solomons undersea war were disappointing. Although there was a heavy flow of enemy traffic in the area, most of it traveled at high speed and at night. Until mid-autumn the submarines operating from Brisbane were without surface radar, and only a few

arrived with radar during the remainder of the year. Consequently the high-speed, night-going traffic was most difficult to locate and hard to hit.

The running of small destroyer groups and speedy landing craft down the "Slot" to Guadalcanal was more by way of a resort than a stratagem devised by the Japanese. For the Imperial Navy was unwilling to risk large fleet units in the Guadalcanal area. Nevertheless, the resort proved moderately successful. Jap forces came dashing down the "Slot" with such consistent regularity that the Marines dubbed the operation the "Tokyo Express." Land-based American aircraft wrecked the "Express" time and again. But as often it got through under cover of night, and the reinforcements delivered enabled the Imperial troops on the island to make a stubborn stand.

Endeavoring to reinforce the American position at this time, the U.S. Navy lost the destroyer BLUE and two destroyer transports. These were sunk during encounters with enemy warships in Savo Sound. A third destroyer transport was sunk by Japanese aircraft. But it was chiefly the Japanese submarine force which held American shipping at bay in this phase of the Guadalcanal campaign. In this period the I-boats scored their greatest strike of the war.

Scouting east of San Cristobal at the end of August, SARATOGA was attacked by submarines and struck by a torpedo which inflicted minor damage. In waters south of SARATOGA's position, HORNET was barely missed by a submarine torpedo a few days later. Then, on September 14, a large convoy carrying Marines and gasoline set out from Espiritu Santo to reinforce the hard-pressed Guadalcanal garrison. HORNET, WASP and NORTH CAROLINA provided air cover for the convoy.

On the afternoon of the 15th the carrier forces ran into a school of submarines. WASP, NORTH CAROLINA and the destroyer O'BRIEN were all hit by torpedoes within a bracket of ten minutes. A single torpedo blasted an enormous hole in the battleship's hull, the explosion killing five of NORTH CAROLINA's men. O'BRIEN, badly disabled, sank after she limped back to port. Three torpedoes struck WASP in her magazine and gasoline-storage holds. Nearly 200 men lost their lives in the explosions and fires which resulted. When the ready ammunition began to detonate, tearing out the vessel's vitals, Captain Forrest P. Sherman gave the order to abandon. That night a U.S. destroyer sank the gutted aircraft carrier. Her assailant was the Japanese submarine I-19.

WASP was the second U.S. aircraft carrier to meet destruction at the hands of the Japanese submariners. Credit has been given the Japanese torpedo which at that time contained an explosive charge almost

159

twice as great as that of the American torpedo. The Japanese torpedo also developed greater speed than the American, left less wake, and was generally the superior weapon.

But in the many months of war that followed the WASP torpedoing, the Japanese Submarine Force failed to approach its early successes. On October 26, during the Battle of Santa Cruz Islands, a Jap submarine torpedoed the destroyer PORTER. Disabled, the vessel had to be abandoned and sunk. And on November 13, in the wake of the furious naval battle off Guadalcanal, a spread of Japanese submarine torpedoes struck the damaged American cruiser JUNEAU. The blasting broke the cruiser in two, and she went down immediately—a disaster which took nearly 700 American lives. During the remainder of the war, Japanese submarines were able to sink but two major U.S. naval vessels—the escort carrier LISCOME BAY (November 1943) and the heavy cruiser INDIANAPOLIS (July 1945). Improved anti-submarine defenses, search radar, inferior Japanese submarine strategy— many factors contributed to this phenomenal decline.

One contributing factor was the anti-submarine campaign begun by GUDGEON, TAUTOG and TRITON and continued in the Solomons-Bismarck theater by SEADRAGON (Lieutenant Commander Ferrall) and GRAYBACK (Lieutenant Commander E. C. Stephan). Patrolling from Brisbane late in 1942, SEADRAGON sank the Japanese submarine I-4 off New Ireland. GRAYBACK sank I-18 south of New Georgia a fortnight later. These I-boat sinkings, presently to be discussed in detail, point up an interesting statistic.

By the war's end the U.S. Submarine Force had accounted for 26 Japanese submarines—one-fifth of the number lost by the Japanese from all causes during the war. In the blazing light of WASP's destruction and the hot glare from PORTER and JUNEAU, the figure may be seen as vitally significant.

Retirement of the Sugar Boats

The old S-boats at Brisbane could not keep the pace. The stranding of S-39 off Rossel Island was a straw in the wind. She was the third submarine so lost, and the previous two were S-boats. These strandings, attributable to antiquated equipment, low engine-power and lack of sonic depth-finding gear, hastened a decision to withdraw the S-boats from front-line duty as soon as possible.

One by one the more battle-worn were sent to the States as fleet-type submarines arrived in Brisbane to replace them. Among the first of these replacements were GRAMPUS, GRAYBACK and GROWLER. Entering the Guadalcanal campaign, they found the South Seas boiling. Throughout the autumn of 1942

replacements continued to come in as the struggle in the Solomons grew hotter. STURGEON, SAILFISH, SAURY, SNAPPER, SEADRAGON, SCULPIN, GROUPER, PLUNGER, GUDGEON, SWORDFISH, TUNA, FLYINGFISH, SARGO, GATO, AMBERJACK and ALBACORE patrolled out of Brisbane that fall. Altogether some 24 fleet-type submarines, about half of them "temporary loans" from Pearl Harbor, comprised the new Brisbane Force.

The retiring S-boats went home to serve as training vessels at submarine and anti-submarine warfare schools. A few were dispatched to the Aleutians. By the end of October 1942 nearly all of the old "sugar boats" had been withdrawn. Three or four remained to complete late autumn patrols. Then they, too, departed from the South Pacific.

S-31 and S-47 served at Brisbane later in the war— reminders of the veteran force which had been rushed to the defense of eastern Australia. The old "sugar boats" had held the line. From Manila to Fremantle, from Panama to the Bismarcks they had pioneered through the war's worst months. In the South Pacific and in the North Pacific they had met the enemy and taken the hardest blows he could give. They had raided and reconnoitered and run blockades, stuck it out and fought it out. They had downed Japanese ships. In sinking the cruiser KAKO and delaying the enemy's advance on Guadalcanal, the S-boats climaxed one of the great chapters in submarine history.

No force could be more deserving of the Navy's commendation, "Well done!"

Guadalcanal Undercurrent

The Battle of Cape Esperance was fought on October 11-12. In this hammer-and-tongs naval engagement, the Japanese crippled the cruiser BOISE and landed three shells on SALT LAKE CITY. An erroneous maneuver by the destroyers FARENHOLT, DUNCAN and LAFFEY brought them under a withering fire from American cruisers, and resulted in the disablement of FARENHOLT and the ultimate sinking of DUNCAN.

The battle cost the Japanese the cruiser FURUTAKA, several destroyers, and heavy damage to cruisers KINUGASA and AOBA. Despite this destructive blow, the Japs hit back fiercely, sending a striking force into Savo Sound on October 13 to bombard Henderson Field. Every plane but one on the field was demolished by the barrage, and the enemy followed through on the 15th by landing strong reinforcements to attack the American defenders.

The Guadalcanal situation was extremely serious at this juncture when Admiral William F. Halsey, replacing Admiral Ghormley, became Commander

South Pacific. Both sides were racing to shore up their Guadalcanal positions, and again the Japanese were amassing invasion forces at Rabaul and Truk. These focal points were becoming increasingly important as the pressure heightened in the Solomons. The Truk blockade and submarine patrols in the Bismarck area were of paramount consequence.

To protect the convoy trains to Guadalcanal, the Japanese were compelled to dispatch larger and heavier naval forces to the Solomons front. In turn, Task Force Forty-two at Brisbane was called upon to disrupt the influx of enemy traffic. Brisbane submarines were also called upon to support Admiral Halsey's fleet operations, and perform numerous special missions. But the routine war of attrition was to continue without let-up in the Solomons-Bismarck-New Guinea theater.

Operating far from Savo Sound, submarines STURGEON, SCULPIN and GUDGEON scored sinkings in the Bismarck area which had an undercurrent influence on the tide of battle at Guadalcanal.

STURGEON, veteran Asiatic raider, was making her first cruise (fifth patrol) under Lieutenant Commander H. A. Pieczentkowski. October 1, off New Britain, she was on the track of a large vessel which proved to be the 8,000-ton aircraft ferry KATSURAGI MARU. The submarine bored in, and so did the torpedoes fired by Pieczentkowski. Under a smudge of smoke, the aircraft ferry went down. On some flying field somewhere a group of Jap pilots were grounded for lack of planes.

October 7, SCULPIN was out on her fifth patrol under Lieutenant Commander Lucius H. Chappell. She had been in many battles and had her share of "goings over." Her share, too, of torpedo trouble and difficulties with Lady Luck. But this was her lucky day—the day she scored her first official sinking. Target, NAMINOUE MARU, was a 4,731-ton transport. SCULPIN's torpedoes ran straight and hot, and the transport went down, hot and straight, in the heart of the Bismarcks.

Seven days later SCULPIN sank a small freighter in the same area—SUMIYOSHI MARU, approximately 2,000 tons. Another cargo down under the Bismarck Archipelago.

GUDGEON, captained by Lieutenant Commander W. S. Stovall, Jr., followed SCULPIN into the Bismarck area. There, on October 21, she sank CHOKO MARU, 6,783-ton passenger-cargo carrier.

Meantime, submarines from Brisbane were performing special missions which were fitted into the Solomons campaign strategy like the pieces of a jigsaw puzzle. Supporting fleet operations, they scouted, reconnoitered and escorted convoys. They carried coast watchers to secret stations, and reported on enemy ship movements.

In the thick of the struggle for Guadalcanal was AMBERJACK, one of the new-construction submarines sent to Brisbane. At the height of the Guadalcanal crisis she was given a perilous assignment.

Gasoline to Tulagi

Under Lieutenant Commander J. A. Bole, Jr., who commissioned her in the States, AMBERJACK left Brisbane on September 3 to patrol traffic lanes angling from Rabaul and Buka to the Shortland Basin.

AMBERJACK's submariners won their combat insignia on this first patrol. On September 19 she attacked and sank SHIROGANE MARU, 3,130-ton passenger-cargo carrier. And on October 7 she sank SENKAI MARU, passenger-cargo carrier, 2,095 tons.

She was just setting a course for Pearl Harbor when she received orders to head for Espiritu Santo, the American base in the New Hebrides. The situation had reached the climax stage at Guadalcanal where General Vandegrift and his Marines were holding on by little more than their shoestrings. A gasoline famine was threatening to ground the planes on Henderson Field. Practically the only aviation gasoline on the island was that remaining in the tanks of the planes which had reached the defenders. Tankers attempting a run into Savo Sound were almost certain to be sunk by enemy submarines or aircraft, and Halsey was indisposed to risk strong surface escorts in the danger zone.

Such was the emergency which sent AMBERJACK on a tangent to Espiritu Santo. Three days after receiving the order, the submarine was weaving her way through the minefields into the naval base where she moored alongside LACKAWANNA. Lieutenant Commander Bole was notified that he was now assigned to ComAirSoPac. AMBERJACK was to take on 9,000 gallons of high-octane gasoline, plus 15 Army fighter personnel and two hundred 100-pound bombs, to be run, Special Delivery, to Guadalcanal.

If anyone was worried about a load of highly volatile gasoline, and touchy air-bombs, it was not AMBERJACK's submariners. The Marines at Guadal were hard-pressed, and all hands aboard AMBERJACK worked on the double to get in the gas.

Two full tanks were steamed out, and fuel connections closed by welding. The joints were found to leak, and these had to be plugged and welded to hold a 40-pound pressure. While this work was going on, the bombs were carried aboard and stowed in the forward torpedo room. Finally the gasoline was pumped in, the Army personnel came aboard and on October 22 AMBERJACK set out for Guadalcanal.

She had almost reached her destination when she received orders to deliver the bombs and gasoline to Tulagi, off Florida Island. The reason for this switch became apparent the following morning.

With time to spare, AMBERJACK was off Lunga Point on this morning of October 25th. She had submerged at daybreak and was standing over toward the point, when the periscope watch sighted the fleet tug SEMINOLE across the misty water.

In that perilous area the lightning might strike anywhere at any moment. Bole decided to reverse course to avoid complications which could arise if the submarine were sighted near the tug. He was to regret this decision. Thirty minutes later three Japanese destroyers came down the "Slot" in broad daylight and were seen, hull down, shelling the Marine positions on Guadalcanal. They crossed Lunga Point twice, laid a smoke screen, and retired at 30-knot speed. AMBERJACK was unable to get within torpedo range of this hit-and-run trio.

Obviously the Japs were launching a drive to recover Henderson Field, and AMBERJACK's orders had been changed to prevent her cargo from falling into enemy possession. Regretfully Bole and crew saw their chance to enter the battle fade over the horizon. At sunset of that day AMBERJACK steamed into Tulagi Harbor to unload cargo and passengers. Shortly after midnight she set out for Brisbane, her mission completed.

Once more the undersea boat had demonstrated its versatility. Warship and raider, it had also proved its capabilities as freighter and blockade-breaker, passenger ferry and munitions ship, troop transport, gun-runner and galleon. AMBERJACK's was a singular role. Carrying a bulk cargo of gasoline, she was the only U.S. submarine in World War II to operate as an oil tanker.

Subs to New Guinea and Palau

On October 26 the Japanese were badly mauled in the sea battle off Santa Cruz Islands. Simultaneously Marine and Army forces regained lost ground on Guadalcanal where the Imperial troops met defeat in a carnage that ended all Japanese hopes of winning the island without a major land-sea-air offensive.

The Japanese Army had suffered a staggering setback, but Japanese naval forces, despite severe damage to two carriers and a cruiser in the Santa Cruz engagement, remained formidable. And the Santa Cruz victory cost the U.S. Navy a high price—ENTERPRISE damaged by dive bombers—the destroyer PORTER torpedoed—loss of the aircraft carrier HORNET, destroyed by bomb hits and suicide planes. Carrier

strength reduced to ENTERPRISE, Halsey's fleet recoiled. The mauled Japanese force recoiled. Both sides rushed reserves into the Guadalcanal breach and gathered naval reinforcements for a showdown fight.

After the Java Sea Battle the Japs had seized a large portion of New Guinea. During the spring and summer of 1942 they had pushed the Allies out on the southeast peninsula, and by September they were threatening the Australian-American base at Port Moresby.

To counter this threat, General MacArthur, in supreme command of the Australia-New Guinea Area, planned an autumn drive across the Owen Stanley Mountains to capture the enemy's advance bases at Buna and Gona. This move was coordinated with Admiral Halsey's drive in the Solomons. Timed as it was, the New Guinea push was calculated to relieve the pressure in the Solomons while Halsey's campaign concurrently diverted enemy strength from New Guinea. Thus the two operations were meshed into gear, the military and naval commands agreeing to mutual support.

Submarines from Brisbane were assigned the task of stopping enemy naval vessels which were operating off the New Guinea coast near Buna. A number of Japanese destroyers had been sighted offshore at night, and it was believed they were running in reinforcements. Accordingly, the submarines were employed to patrol close-in positions off Buna, Casamata and Vitiaz—Dampier Straits. The directive under which they worked prescribed that the defense of the New Guinea coast was the primary mission and that destruction of enemy shipping was secondary.

Among the submarines participating in the New Guinea operation was ALBACORE, one of the new fleet-types which had arrived in Pearl Harbor in the summer of 1942. From the SubPac command she had been transferred to the Brisbane Force, and in November she was dispatched to the New Guinea front. Patrolling off New Guinea, ALBACORE was to combine the "defense" and "destruction" clauses of the directive by destroying one of the major enemy warships campaigning in those waters.

Into the South Seas the Japanese had rushed all available naval units, including as many light cruisers as the Imperial Navy could spare for duty in that theater. The Imperial Navy's CL's were a motley lot, ranging all the way from AGANO and OYODA, comparable in strength to heavy cruisers, to the training cruiser KASHII, hardly a match for a modern destroyer. Motley though the CL's were, the Japanese placed much faith in these craft, and all of them were pressed into active service, regardless of

162

age or size. They escorted convoys, occasionally transported troops and sometimes lugged freight. As units of the task forces that carried the Japanese offensive into the Southwest Pacific, they were much in evidence the first year of the war.

Among the oldest and busiest of the IJN cruiser divisions was CruDiv Eighteen, consisting of TATSUTA and TENRYU. Dating back to 1916, these 3,300-tonners were nonetheless capable of firing guns and dropping modern depth charges, and they performed ably as the major Japanese naval units in the New Guinea campaign. Belying reports that they had been bombed, disabled, blown up and sunk, they continued to ply their trade along the New Guinea coast throughout the autumn of 1942. And they were going strong in early December while MacArthur's forces were driving through the Owen Stanley Mountains.

Enter ALBACORE. Under Lieutenant Commander R. C. Lake, she had won her combat insignia on the Truk blockade by damaging three ships to make her first patrol a success. Now on her second patrol, she was looking for more action. She found it off the northeast coast of New Guinea.

The date: December 18. Lookout sighted a sizable AP, and Lake directed a day-submerged attack. He fired three shots at this target, and one torpedo hit for probable damage.

After nightfall, ALBACORE attacked a destroyer which came steaming out of the dark. Lake fired a single and the torpedo missed. Then he put the submarine on the track of a larger target which proved to be one of the busybodies of Japanese Cruiser Division Eighteen. Although immediate identification of this rakish silhouette was impossible, ALBACORE's crew realized they were after something big. Tense at the periscope, Lake sent ALBACORE boring in. Two torpedoes were fired. Two hits roared in the sound gear. Down went the light cruiser TENRYU —a link removed from the Jap chain holding New Guinea.

And with this, the first ship officially credited to her record, ALBACORE began an extraordinary career. That it began with the sinking of a CL was presageful. Two months later (February 20, 1943) she sank the Japanese destroyer OSHIO, farther up the New Guinea coast. Having destroyed two warships in South Seas waters, she went on to become a Nemesis to the Imperial Navy. Although she sank but ten ships before her final chapter was written, ALBACORE sent more enemy naval vessels to the bottom than any other U.S. submarine in the war.

While ALBACORE and her mates from out of Brisbane were operating off New Guinea, raiding in the Bismarcks and fighting in the Solomons, two Fremantle submarines were sent to investigate another quarter. This long-distance reconnaissance operation was related to the Solomons campaign much as was the Truk blockade. Its concern was the enemy naval base at Palau.

During the first months of the war, the Palau area had been patrolled by Asiatic Fleet submarines with disappointing results. Later, the area was shifted into the orbit of the submarines operating from Pearl Harbor. Although patrolled by SubPac boats and some of the Fremantle submarines en route to Hawaii, the waters off Palau provided few targets for the hunters.

This apparent lack of game mystified submariners and strategists alike. Before the war's outbreak there had been many indications of the Japs' intent to use this mandated island group as a major base for naval vessels and merchant ships. And information received during the Japanese offensive in the Southwest Pacific confirmed these pre-war indications. Where, then, was the expected ship traffic? Enemy vessels seemed to be coming from and heading for Palau, yet submarines patrolling the area were unable to contact them.

A clue to the mystery was uncovered in October 1942, during the Guadalcanal campaign, when a secret chart was captured from the enemy. The chart provided the answer to the Palau enigma. The SoWesPac and Pearl Harbor submarines had been watching the Malakal Passage entrance to the Palau Group. Lying in the southeast barrier, this was the only entrance known to the Allies. The captured chart revealed that Malakal Passage was too shallow for ships of deep draft, and it was not the only passage into Palau. Another entrance, Toagel Mlungui Passage, about 17 miles north of Malakal, in the mid-section of the western coral barrier, was the passage employed by the Japanese.

Submarines SEAWOLF and SEAL were ordered to Palau to investigate this "secret door."

Philippine Sideline—Seawolf at Davao Gulf

On this, her seventh patrol under Lieutenant Commander F. B. Warder, SEAWOLF had already been doing some high-class investigating. Her luck had been indifferent during her two previous patrols —HACHIGEN MARU, a small passenger-cargo carrier and SHOWA MARU, a tramp steamer, torpedoed and sunk in August in Makassar Strait.

Departing from Fremantle on October 7 to patrol in Philippine waters, Warder promised the WOLF's crew a lively cruise.

"We'll get some big ones this time, boys. You'll see."

November 1 the boys were seeing the jungly shore-line of Mindanao and the broad, blue entrance of Davao Gulf. The following morning Warder set a course into the Gulf. Early in the afternoon Lieutenant James Mercer at the periscope sighted a two-masted freighter climbing over the horizon about six miles from Cape San Augustin Light.

Warder directed a submerged approach, and fired a brace of torpedoes. A prodigious explosion blew the ship's lifeboats into the air, and left her sinking in a fiery shroud. Mercer clipped a camera to the periscope eyepiece to take a picture as Warder held the submarine in the vicinity, hoping a destroyer might come to the rescue and provide another target.

At nightfall he ordered SEAWOLF to the surface, and the crew made an attempt to rescue two Jap survivors. One swimmer floundered off in the darkness, courting suicide. The other refused to catch a lifeline, and the submariners had no time to argue. The incident was typical of many occasions during the war wherein Japanese seamen chose drowning for the Emperor in preference to rescue. Warder's reaction was typical of Warder. He ordered a life jacket and a bottle of whiskey tossed to the Jap, who caught them and held them up with a nod. The current swept the man on out to sea, and SEA-WOLF proceeded into the moonlit Gulf, heading for Davao Harbor. Post-war records would reveal that she had torpedoed and sunk GIFU MARU, 2,933 tons, at the mouth of the Gulf on November 2nd.

November 3rd. A hint of dawn was in the sky and the harbor was 12 miles farther on when Warder gave the order to submerge. At periscope depth the WOLF stalked cautiously forward. Several hostile aircraft drifted across the sky like roaming bumble-bees. Minefields, if any, were another hazard to be avoided, and the WOLF's first task was to find a swept channel. Keeping out beyond the 300-fathom curve, she scouted the approaches to Davao. Then, finding no evidence of mines, she pushed on toward the harbor.

Davao Gulf is deep right up to its shores. Walking the periscope, the skipper scanned the scenery.

"I can see a church steeple and some houses," he reported. "Several masts—there's a lot of shipping in there."

But the prize was a big ship at anchor in Talomo Bay.

"Man look at that! Motor ship with a cruiser's stern—heavy guns aft—a brand-new job—beautiful camouflage!"

The submariners took turns in looking at the beautifully camouflaged ship, which resembled nothing so much as a vessel painted for a water carnival. Tied up at, or anchored alongside a busy wharf, she seemed to be loading hemp.

Warder wanted to try a zero angle shot. Tide and current drift were estimated, and the usual figures were fed to the T.D.C.

"Sound, I want you to track the fish as we fire them. Bow tubes ready? Open the outer doors. Up periscope! Come left more—left just a hair. Are you ready—?"

Time: 1050. Warder had the position he wanted. He started firing the torpedoes with careful deliberation—one—two—three. Establishing the range by ping-ranges with supersonic and keeping the target under periscope observation as he watched torpedo performance.

Range varied from an initial 1,100 yards down to 880 yards. Set for 18-foot draft, the first torpedo ran deep and exploded on the beach. Warder set the second torpedo for eight feet. The wake ran straight for the target and the torpedo hit squarely, exploding at point of aim.

Water spouted high in the air, and the blast rolled the ship over on her starboard beam. Then she righted herself and steadied in the muddy roil with little visible change of draft.

Warder fired a third torpedo. He saw it run up to the target. Sound heard it running beyond the time it should have exploded. This torpedo proved to be a dud, and so did the fourth torpedo. The Japs were now manning bow and stern guns, and wild shots were splashing in the submarine's general direction. Warder noted that the Jap shells made bigger splashes and more noise than equivalent American projectiles. The Jap gunners, however, were too excited for equivalent accuracy.

SEAWOLF withdrew, reloaded, bored in a second time. The Japs fired steadily at her periscope as she approached, their forward gun dropping shells about 900 yards to starboard of the submarine, and their after gun dropping shells about the same distance to port. Paced by explosions off either beam, the WOLF ran the gantlet down the middle groove. Warder made this approach from the port side.

He fired one torpedo. It struck the after part of the camouflaged ship—bawhoom! When the smoke cleared away, Warder could see the vessel's after gun had been blown from its mounting. A dazed crew stood around the forward gun, which had ceased firing. Five boats were frantically busy carrying sailors from anchored ship to dock. Spectators lined the wharf, gesticulating and shouting.

Warder glared through the periscope. "That damned craft must be full of watertight compartments—she doesn't seem to be sinking. We'll throw

LOGISTICS. *Submarine Diesels are thirsty. Motor-macs fuel up a fleet-type sub before she sets out on war patrol. Empire-bound raiders from Pearl usually* *refueled ("topped off") at Midway, where refits were accomplished as of June 1942. Above picture would have made the oil-thirsting Imperial Navy envious.*

RETURN OF CARLSON'S RAIDERS. *Marines on deck of* Argonaut, *back from Makin and happy to see Pearl.*

The Macs had rough time of it; so did the Japs. Argonaut *and* Nautilus *carried the raiders to hot Makin Island.*

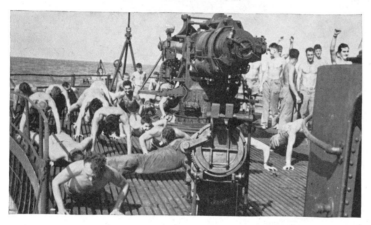

MARINES ABOARD NAUTILUS *limber up on way to Makin.* Nautilus *aided raiders with fire support at Ukiangang Point.*

SUNK BY ALBACORE *off New Guinea—light cruiser* Tenryu. Albacore *was bane of IJN.*

SEEN BY SEAWOLF *at Davao Gulf—*Sagami Maru *in Talomo Bay. Periscope snapshot shows jungly shoreline; camouflaged ship loading hemp. Then she got a load of—*

FISH FROM FREDDIE WARDER! *Down goes* Sagami *as out goes* Seawolf, *chased by Zeros. Photo bears out text (p. 165) "maru loading hemp can come to end of rope."*

one more at her and see what happens. We've got to work fast!"

He swung SEAWOLF completely around to aim her stern tubes at the target. This time he fired a Mark 9 torpedo which had been loaded in one of the tubes aft. Trailing its ribbon of froth, the torpedo ran straight and hot to strike the ship's forward quarter. Flame roared up out of her forward hold, and the vessel began to settle by the bow.

"She's going under," Warder cried. "Let's go under with her." He gave the order to secure battle stations, and then, "Here come some Zeros to pepper us! Down periscope! We're due out of here!"

Three planes came storming down from the blue. One zoomed the periscope as SEAWOLF started down to 120 feet. The crew could hear the staccato rataplan of machine-gun fire. Then, as SEAWOLF headed for the mouth of the Gulf, five depth charges thundered in the channel behind her. Sound reported the screws of anti-sub boats, but neither patrol craft nor depth charges were close.

Racing under a flat sea of sun-polished brass, the WOLF had almost completed the 50-mile run to open water when Warder put up the periscope and spied a seagoing freighter. Immediately he commenced approach maneuvers. Evidently the WOLF's presence was detected, for the *maru* began to zigzag wildly as the submarine closed in. Swinging her around for a stern-tube attack, Warder fired three Mark 9's at the weaving cargoman. Properly timed explosions were heard, but observation was impossible as SEAWOLF had to go deep to avoid a circular torpedo-run. Thus evading one of her own torpedoes, she made a hasty exit from Davao Gulf.

But she was not yet finished with Davao. Five days later, patrolling the Gulf's mouth, she found another target. At the periscope Warder described this vessel.

"Two goal posts—stack amidships—looks like a coal-burner! Estimated speed nine knots. Course, three five zero. Looks like her decks are loaded with invasion barges—crew in white uniform—she's probably a Jap naval reserve ship. We'll plunk her!"

They plunked her with two Mark 14's that registered two smashing hits. Down at sea with her load of invasion barges went KEIKO MARU, converted gunboat, 2,929 tons.

The patrol was almost over—SEAWOLF was due for a run to Pearl Harbor—when new orders arrived. En route to Hawaii she was to visit the mysterious waters off Palau. Orders called for an investigation of Toagel Mlungui Passage—the secret passage being used by the Japs. The course was charted, and SEAWOLF headed eastward.

On the bottom behind her lay three enemy ships and possibly a fourth, although the one attacked on the afternoon of November 3 remained a "doubtful." The large vessel sunk in Talomo Bay was SAGAMI MARU, passenger-cargo carrier, 7,189 tons. Proof that even in the snuggest of harbors, loading hemp, a Japanese ship might come to the end of her rope.

Palau Mystery Solved

SEAWOLF's three-day run to Palau was uneventful. Then, at nightfall on November 11, she raised one of the outer Pelews, and things began to happen. As the submarine moved in cautiously, the watch sighted a fast patrol boat.

Then something faster came over the horizon – a Jap destroyer. Warder rushed the crew to battle stations. A tropical squall wiped out visibility, and the DD was gone before SEAWOLF could get on her track.

Warder was deploring the weather when two more destroyers were sighted, charging along through the rain. He sent SEAWOLF charging after the destroyers at a pace that shook the submarine. Five minutes later, making a sweep with the periscope, he uttered an exclamation—one with a pyrotechnic point.

"There's an aircraft carrier up here! She's as big as a new barn, and those DD's have sucked us out of position! We've got to pour on the coal!"

Ordering SEAWOLF to the surface, he set her on the carrier's tail. The silhouette faded in the darkness. Suspecting that the carrier and her escorts were heading for a rendezvous—perhaps units of a task force assembling for a run to the Solomons—Warder hung on. At four-engine speed, the submarine raced in pursuit of the flat-top. She was still at the carrier's heels on the morning of November 12 when the main motor generator cables went bad. Forced by this electrical casualty to give up the chase, SEAWOLF radioed the carrier's course and apparent destination to the Allied command, and slowed to make repairs. A few hours later she set a course for Pearl Harbor.

Meantime, SEAL (Lieutenant Commander Hurd) had been dispatched from Fremantle to Palau to probe the waters off Toagel Mlungui Passage. Patrolling the area on November 15, SEAL sighted a large freighter and a tanker. On the horizon, both ships were too far distant for an attack.

Assured they were on a bustling sea lane, Hurd and company kept an alert vigil throughout the night. Their watch was amply rewarded. Out from Palau the next day paraded a convoy of nine cargo ships escorted by two destroyers.

As the vessels trooped into view, Hurd ordered his submarine to periscope depth and started a submerged approach. Everything clicking in the T.D.C., he maneuvered into attack position and fired two torpedoes at the chosen target—a sizable transport. Explosions thundered as the torpedoes struck home. To the bottom went BOSTON MARU, 5,477 tons.

SEAL herself was nearly sunk in the resulting melee. While maneuvering to evade, she was rammed by one of the ships in the milling convoy. With the overhead roar of an express train speeding across a trestle, the ship skimmed the submarine's conning tower. Both periscopes were damaged and put out of commission. It was a close shave for Hurd and crew. And with depth charges adding insult to injury, it took a fine blend of skill, grit and Jay Factor to save SEAL's skin.

But the Palau investigation had been completed. That the Japanese were entering the lagoon by the western passage was a fact established by submarine observation. Thereafter the Toagel Mlungui route would become a hunting ground for U.S. submarines and a burying ground for Japanese ships.

Guadalcanal Secured

In a series of rapid-fire naval actions fought in Savo Sound, November 12-15, the Japanese were defeated in the sea battle of Guadalcanal by the forces of Admiral Halsey. The battle cost the enemy his two battleships, HIEI and KIROSHIMA, and several destroyers. Of a ten-ship convoy sent to reinforce the Imperial troops on Guadalcanal, only four transports reached the beaches of Tassafaronga west of Lunga Point. These were soon bombed to a shambles by planes from Henderson Field.

American casualties were heavy. The cruiser ATLANTA was gutted by fire. SOUTH DAKOTA was badly damaged. Destroyers BARTON, CUSHING, LAFFEY, MONSSEN, PORTER, WALKE and BENHAM were lost, and three other DD's were crippled.

Two weeks later, the Japanese made another attempt to run reinforcements to Tassafaronga. Informed on the move, Admiral Halsey rushed from Espiritu Santo the cruisers MINNEAPOLIS, NEW ORLEANS, PENSACOLA, HONOLULU and NORTHAMPTON, with four destroyers, to meet the enemy. Two more destroyers were picked up en route, and on November 30 this force, under Rear Admiral C. H. Wright, was steaming off Lunga Point.

Down the "Slot" came eight Japanese destroyers. Mid-morning, they ran headlong into the American force, and delivered a devastating torpedo attack. One Jap DD was smothered by gunfire and sunk. But the Americans fared badly. MINNEAPOLIS had her bow blasted off by torpedoes. NEW ORLEANS suffered similar damage. PENSACOLA was also disabled by a torpedo. And the heavy cruiser NORTHAMPTON,

after a confused maneuver, was struck by two torpedoes and sunk. Of the five U.S. cruisers only HONOLULU escaped unscathed. In an action that lasted only 16 minutes, over 400 Americans lost their lives.

Although a severe setback for the American cruiser force, the Tassafaronga engagement served to prevent Jap reserves and supplies from reaching the Imperial Army on Guadalcanal. The Japanese destroyer force retired. With the exception of a few small blockade-running groups, it was the last to come down the "Slot."

In December, U.S. Army forces on the island unleashed a sledge hammer drive. The Jap troops were flung westward, and by Christmas the Guadalcanal Campaign was at the mopping-up stage. While the Imperial soldiery made suicidal "banzai" charges as they waited in vain for the "Tokyo Express," U.S. naval forces swept into Savo Sound and U.S. submarines closed in on the upper Solomons to cut off the escape routes.

On December 10, the submarine WAHOO, captained by Lieutenant Commander M. G. Kennedy, who brought her out from Mare Island, began a distinguished career by sinking KAMOI MARU, 5,355 tons, off the southern tip of Bougainville.

Ten days later, the indefatigable SEADRAGON, making her fifth patrol under Lieutenant Commander Ferrall, sighted a Japanese submarine in St. George's channel heading for Rabaul. Ferrall fired four Mark 10's at the shadowy silhouette. In an explosion of fire and water the Imperial Navy's I-4 went down for the last time.

GRAYBACK, too, on her fifth patrol, was thrusting her periscope into the Solomons panorama on the hunt for the retreating enemy. For GRAYBACK this was proving to be a lively and colorful patrol. Her experiences bore a curious parallel to SEADRAGON's—and SEADRAGON's adventures were not the sort easily duplicated.

Here is another case wherein fact surpasses fiction to prove that anything could—and did—happen in submarines.

Submarine Operations (for Appendicitis)

In common with the practitioners of most highly technical and exclusive professions, the Navy's submariners developed a succinct vernacular peculiarly and distinctively their own. There was "can" for battery. "Boiler" for "pig boat." "Ladder chancre" for bruises caused by barking the shins. "Spread," meaning torpedoes fired in series at various angles. "Pulling the plug" for submerging. "Ping jockey" for the operator of sonic "pinging gear." "Brass pounder" for radioman. A variety of names for other technicians of the crew. And the pharmacist's mate was frequently dubbed "Quack."

In the case of Wheeler B. Lipes, PhM1, member of the crew of SEADRAGON, the title was respectfully altered to "Doctor."

Entering the Navy before the war, Lipes had trained as a corpsman in San Diego. Transferred to a service hospital in Philadelphia, he qualified as a lab technician and acquired a special rating as cardiographer. When he reported for duty in submarines he had seen appendectomies performed. But he never, as he admitted afterward, expected to pinch-hit for surgeon and remove a human appendix.

SEADRAGON was patrolling far behind enemy lines in the Southwest Pacific when the crisis arose. The date, September 11, 1942, was one Lipes—and Darrell Dean Rector, Seaman 1—would not soon forget. Someone rushed to Lipes and told him that young Rector had fallen unconscious to the deck. Submariners had passed out before—from heat, fatigue, too thin a diet. But the pharmacist's mate recognized the high temperature and symptomatic pains.

"Appendicitis," he reported to Lieutenant Commander Ferrall. "It may be peritonitis. He'll have to be operated on at once."

SEADRAGON's captain put the question bluntly. "Can you do it?"

"Yes, sir," Lipes stated. "It's his only chance."

Ferrall ordered the submarine submerged in quiet water. Lipes, empowered to select an operating staff, chose Lieutenant Norvell Ward to act as his chief assistant. Communications Officer Lieutenant Franz Hoskins served as anesthetist. Engineer Officer Lieutenant Charles C. Manning, played the part of chief nurse.

Surgical instruments had to be improvised. Lipes fashioned a handle for the scalpel. Bent spoons served as muscular retractors. A tea strainer became an ether mask. The instruments were sterilized in a solution of torpedo alcohol mixed with water and boiled. A searchlight was rigged over the wardroom table.

Rector was carried in and stretched out on the table. Before proceeding with the operation, Lipes roused the patient.

"I've never performed an appendectomy on anybody," he told Rector. "I can do it, but it's a chance. If you don't want me to go ahead—"

The patient whispered, "Let's go."

Pharmacist's Mate Lipes went ahead. As best they could, the men at the controls held the submarine level, and the motors droned a murmurous monotone. Like a veteran Lipes made the incision, found

and removed the appendix, sewed up the incision with catgut. An antiseptic powder made of ground-up sulfa tablets was applied. Bandages were fastened in place. The sponge count came out even. Darrell Rector lived to tell about his operation.

The Press got hold of the story, and the SEADRAGON appendectomy was featured in headlines. Lipes' expert surgery was lauded by the medical profession and cited as an example of Navy training and salty submarine grit, and by the time of the Jap retirement from Guadalcanal the story was a household as well as submarine force legend. Few suspected that this remarkable episode would be repeated in other submarine patrol reports. That their own boat would stage such a drama probably never occurred to GRAYBACK's busy crew—least of all to Harry B. Roby, PhM1.

Groans from Torpedoman's Mate W. R. Jones were the first indication, and Pharmacist's Mate Roby's thermometer registered a second. By morning, December 13, Jones was decidedly on the binnacle list. Roby diagnosed acute appendicitis, and reported the emergency to the submarine's captain, Lieutenant Commander E. C. Stephan.

"Jones's appendix is already ruptured or due to burst soon."

"Can you operate?"

Roby answered in the affirmative of Wheeler B. Lipes.

So the scene from SEADRAGON was shifted to GRAYBACK. The improvised surgery in the wardroom—the spotlight over the operating table—the sailors with scrubbed hands standing by with bandages, haemostats, sponges, sulfa. Spiva L. Buck, MoMM1 acted as assistant surgeon, and Lieutenant J. A. Davis administered the ether.

Roby's commands crackled through an atmosphere of frozen tension. "Retractors!"—"Sponge!"—"Scalpel!"—"Give him more ether!" The operation lasted an hour and thirty-two minutes. Both patient and doctor recovered nicely.

As a singular footnote to the GRAYBACK case, a third undersea appendectomy was reported before year's end by the submarine SILVERSIDES (Lieutenant Commander Burlingame). The patient was George Platter, F1. The surgeon, Thomas Moore, PhM1. SILVERSIDES, making a run from Australia, was far out on the high seas on December 22, 1942, when Platter suffered the symptomatic pains. And Pharmacist's Mate Moore, assisted by Lieutenant Commander R. M. Davenport, Radioman First Class Albert H. Stegall and others of the crew, performed the necessary operation. Six days later the patient was on his feet, standing watch.

The foregoing might lead one to believe that submarine operations in World War II developed into a series of appendectomies. But with the arrival of penicillin, the necessity for emergency appendectomies was largely alleviated.

Statistic: Before the war was over, 11 cases of acute appendicitis were diagnosed and treated by pharmacist's mates aboard U.S. submarines. Pioneering the emergency appendectomy, Wheeler B. Lipes, Harry Roby, and Thomas Moore established a tradition that will inspire every pharmacist's mate and corpsman. Not a single death resulted from appendicitis originating on a submarine in war patrol in World War II. Proof of superlative Navy training and the submariner's intestinal fortitude.

But an appendicitis case did not constitute the only parallel in the patrols of SEADRAGON and GRAYBACK. On special mission to serve as a beacon ship for a task force bombardment of Munda Bar, off New Georgia, GRAYBACK was nearing her destination on Christmas Day. Off the southern tip of New Georgia, her lookouts sighted four Jap landing barges moving along in column. Stephan gave the order to battle surface. Her deck guns manned, GRAYBACK circled the miniature convoy, riddling the barges with machine-gun bullets. The Jap answered with revolver fire while one of the barges attempted to ram. All four barges were sunk. Seven days after this gunbattle, GRAYBACK's lookout sighted the prowling shadow of a submarine. Stephan fired a brace of torpedoes, and the Imperial Navy's I-18 went down off the coast of New Georgia—not many miles from the spot where SEADRAGON sank I-4.

After serving as beacon vessel for the Task Force Sixty-seven bombardment of Munda, GRAYBACK steamed south to Rendova Island on orders to rescue six Army airmen who had crashed near Banyetta Point. Enemy planes made it a hazardous adventure, but the rescue was successfully accomplished on January 5, 1943.

One rescue mission—one task force operation—one enemy submarine downed—one four-barge convoy shot up—one appendix removed—all this in one successful patrol accomplished by one submarine. But, with the exception of the appendectomy, GRAYBACK's patrol was not untypical of submarine operations in the Solomons.

Guadalcanal Conclusion

Their exit from the Solomons under fire, the Japs strove desperately throughout January and February 1943 to evacuate their forces from Guadalcanal. Japanese planes slashed at advancing American convoys, and at the end of January, Jap dive bombers succeeded in sinking the heavy cruiser CHICAGO. Two days later they sank the destroyer DeHAVEN. But Japanese naval units were withdrawing from the Guadalcanal area, and resistance on the island collapsed by the end of February. As the Jap guns went silent in the jungle, the major threat to Australia evaporated.

A summary of the Guadalcanal campaign must highlight two features. In the five-month struggle for control of Guadalcanal (August-December 1942) United States surface forces suffered drastic casualties. These included the loss of two aircraft carriers, four heavy cruisers, two light cruisers and 14 destroyers—22 warships in all. The Imperial Navy's losses were somewhat lighter: two battleships, one aircraft carrier, two heavy cruisers, two light cruisers and 12 destroyers—a total of 19 warships.

But under the surface, Japanese losses in this critical five-month period were far heavier than the American. Between August 7 (the day the Americans landed on Guadalcanal) and January 1, 1943, the enemy lost eight submarines in the South Pacific area. Not a single United States submarine was lost through enemy action in this theater, or elsewhere in the Pacific, during this period. GRUNION, lost in the Aleutians, was last heard from on July 30, and probably went down shortly thereafter. Sole loss in the South Pacific, S-39 was abandoned without a personnel casualty, after stranding. Silhouetted against the violence of the Guadalcanal conflict and the extensive submarine participation, these statistics speak volumes for the skill of the U.S. Submarine Force and the capabilities of the submersible.

But the Guadalcanal campaign was essentially an amphibious struggle—one that resolved into a race to reinforce the air and ground forces on the island. Cargo ships, transports, tankers and auxiliaries were of supreme importance in the contest. And in this race to supply and maintain an effective Guadalcanal garrison, the Japanese were unable to keep pace. In the merchant ship and auxiliary vessel category, Japanese losses far outweighed the American.

"I look upon the Guadalcanal and Tulagi operations as the turning point from offense to defense," said Japanese Fleet Admiral Osami Nagano in postwar recollection. *"The cause of our setback there was our inability to increase our forces at the same speed that you Americans did."*

In torpedoing such vessels as the aircraft ferry KATSURAGI MARU, the transport BOSTON MARU and the freighter KAMOI MARU, the submariners in the Solomons-Bismarck Area contributed generously to the Japanese setback. The sinkings of KAKO, TENRYU, I-18 and I-4 were further contributions.

168

CHAPTER 15

THE EMPIRE BLOCKADE

(WITH SIDE GLANCES AT RADAR, MINES AND ATLANTIC OPERATIONS)

Tourniquet on Tokyo

During the summer and autumn of 1942 the Pearl Harbor submarines clamped and tightened a blockade on the home islands of Japan. This blockade amounted to a submarine offensive—the one offensive which the Navy was able to launch in the Central Pacific in 1942.

Deserving as it was of applause, the Doolittle raid was but a single blow, a spectacular strike calculated to hearten the American home front even as it disheartened the civilian Japanese. The continuous submarine blockade delivered upon the enemy's home front a series of blows that landed with increasing frequency and impact as the war went on. And while the spectacle of these sinkings was not described by the "Silent Service" for the edification of the American home front, it was not missed by the Emperor's subjects who witnessed the destruction at their maritime doorstep and saw their beaches littered with the iron bones of broken vessels and the sea-bleached bones of brother Japs. The Empire blockade, therefore, was a dual-purpose operation which placed a drain on Japan's shipping resources and a strain on Papa San's mystical belief in the Empire's invulnerability.

Long before the Japanese strike, it had been evident to American naval leaders that a submarine blockade of Japan should counter that nation's plunge into World War II. The monstrous Japanese offensive had delayed blockade operations, and in the spring of 1942 Pearl Harbor submarines had been deployed on a wide front, engaged in reconnaissance and other special missions which took precedence over the patrols planned for Empire waters. Large expanses of ocean were added to the Central Pacific operating area as the enemy drive rolled forward. When the SubsAsiatic Force fell back to Australia a portion of the northern part of its operating area was shifted into the SubPac orbit. In April 1942, when the Japanese offensive was at its height, the Central Pacific operating area was expanded to include Formosa and Palau. In May, ComSubPac recommended, and CinCPac approved, a plan whereby submarines en route to or from the Southwest Pacific could be ordered to reconnoiter in the Marshalls, Carolines or Gilberts. This fitted into the program devised for the supplying of submarines for the Southwest Pacific Force through Pearl Harbor. In accordance with directives from CinCPac and Cominch, ComSubPac maintained submarine strength in the Southwest Pacific at the level necessary to meet the demand in that area, and SoWesPac submarines slated for major repairs were returned to SubPac for overhaul on the West Coast.

The Battle of Midway interrupted Empire patrols in early June. And immediately following the Midway engagement, a number of Pacific Fleet submarines were sent to reinforce the Aleutian front. Then the South Pacific crisis developed, and Pearl Harbor submarines were drawn into that area as "loans" to the Brisbane Force. These emergency moves reduced the number of submarines available

169

for patrols off Japan and temporarily weakened the grip of the blockade.

In the summer of 1942, however, the blockade took hold. A priority patrol plan gave areas off Honshu, Shikoku and Kyushu precedence over others covered by the SubPac Force. Top priority went to the Honshu area which embraced the approaches to Tokyo and Yokohama.

As submarines were not immediately available for continuous patrol of these areas, the recommendation was made to CinCPac that the number of submarines patrolling the Mandates be reduced and their weight shifted to the Empire blockade. But the pressure had to lessen in the Aleutians and the Solomons before the SubPac Force could go "all out" in applying the vise to Japan.

GUDGEON, POLLACK and PLUNGER had pioneered the way. TRITON, TROUT, GRENADIER, POMPANO, DRUM and others had gone out in the spring. SILVERSIDES had held on during Midway. Now in July the waters northeast of Tokyo were invaded for the first time when NARWHAL, making her third patrol under Lieutenant Commander C. W. Wilkins, stalked shipping off the southern coast of Hokkaido. On July 24 she sank a small and anonymous freighter. August 1 she sank MEIWA MARU, 2,921 tons. Seven days later she accounted for BIFUKU MARU, 2,559 tons. Total cost to the enemy: approximately 7,500 tons.

In August, GUARDFISH (Lieutenant Commander T. B. Klakring) made her first patrol in the hitherto unexplored waters off northeast Honshu. When the patrol was over, five Japanese ships were on the bottom, and GUARDFISH was topping the list of the season's high-scoring submarines. The GUARDFISH story presently.

While the GUARDFISH invasion was going on, SILVERSIDES (Lieutenant Commander Burlingame) was patrolling off the Kii Suido. She sank a 4,000-ton transport, name unknown, on July 28, and followed through on August 8 by sinking NIKKEI MARU, 5,811-ton passenger-cargo carrier.

A few days later, HADDOCK (Lieutenant Commander A. H. Taylor) was slicing through the East China Sea below Japan, the northern approaches to Formosa Strait. This was HADDOCK's maiden patrol, and she was the first submarine to go on war patrol equipped with SJ (search) radar. However, she was able to contact but seven ships in the area assigned. But of these seven she sank two. The actions are memorable as the first submarine radar attacks.

Submarine Tactics—The Radar Attack

The air search radar (SD) installed on a number of submarines at the beginning of the war, had little or no effect on the offensive tactics of submarining. As suggested by its name, this "aircraft warning installation" was used only to supplement lookout detection of enemy aircraft. Even there it often served in a supernumerary capacity, for its radar "pips," revealing the presence of aircraft and their distance from the submarine, failed to indicate the direction from which the planes were flying. Stormy seas interfered with the operation of this instrument. Traversing the hills and valleys of a roughened ocean, the rolling submarine could not depend on the SD, and the lookout in oilskins or the watch at the periscope remained the submarine's best eyes.

However, technicians of the Western Electric Company had long been working to develop a radar device which could locate surface vessels and indicate directional bearings as well as range. Result was the SJ radar which was ready for installation in submarines by the summer of 1942. With this product of electronic wizardry it was possible to "put the finger" on a target far beyond the range of visibility. Not only were accurate ranges and reasonably accurate bearings obtainable, but an experienced operator could often determine the approximate size of the target and identify it (by speed estimates and with the aid of sonar information) as a freighter, passenger liner, destroyer, cruiser or aircraft carrier.

The SJ's operation was independent of visibility conditions. Raised into daylight or pitchy dark above the surface, the parabolic antenna would continue to register "sweeps" so long as it was revolved by the operators.

Low-power vision had limited the submarine's combat capacities since the day of Bushnell's TURTLE. Myopic at best, the periscope was less efficient than the human eye at night, and could be totally blindfolded by fog. Here was an electronic lookout that could not only "see in the dark" but could indicate the invisible vessel's bearing, range and category. As sonar was the submarine's superhuman ear, search radar was to serve as its all-seeing eye. The changes wrought in the tactics of submarine warfare by this device were revolutionary.

Obviously many ships which would otherwise have "passed in the night" undetected, were now exposed to the submarine equipped with search radar. Moreover, having picked up the target, the SJ could guide the submarine's approach. Heretofore the periscope stadimeter, of limited accuracy, had been the only ranging instrument available for use during the tracking phase of the approach. It had, of course, been useless at night. In the attack phase, "ping" ranges on supersonic equipment had been employed, but the sonar instrument's short range, and the fact that it might disclose the submarine's presence and position, put stringent restrictions on this usage. Radar replaced the inaccurate, night-blind stadimeter and eliminated the necessity for continuous "pinging." For the first time the submarine had an efficient and accurate ranging device, available for tracking as well as detecting.

Neither surface haze nor sundown afforded concealment from the penetrating SJ. And as it increased the number of target contacts and implemented the ways and means of approach and attack, it influenced

tactics profoundly. Night no longer provided cover for enemy shipping, but it still served to cloak the hunting submersible. Therefore, targets contacted during daylight could be trailed until after nightfall when the submarine, tracking by radar, could launch an attack under the relative security of darkness. Thus the SJ's installation resulted in a marked increase of night attacks. Concurrently the night-surface approach came into its own as the favored night tactic.

This tactical trend did not develop until after

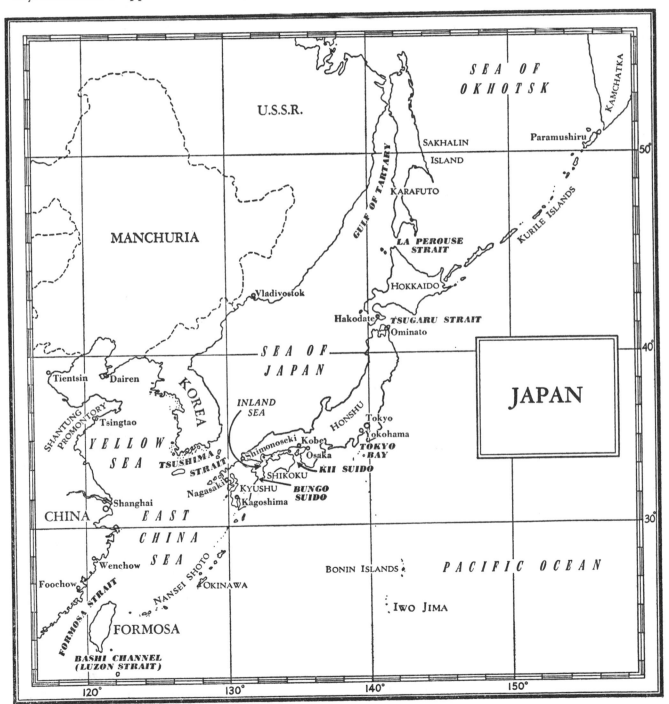

1942, for only a few submarines were equipped with search radar that year. However, the percentage of night attacks made in 1942—30% of the year's attack total—provides a basis for comparison. In 1944, with the SJ then installed, the number of night attacks had increased to 57%. Facility acquired from experience in radar operation was one contributing factor. But the advantages to be gained from a night attack, with a high-speed surface approach guided by radar's "electronic eye," inclined many submarine captains to employ the tactic. Before the war's end, opportunities for day-periscope attack were being deliberately passed up by commanding officers who preferred to defer their attack until they were protected by darkness.

These figures and facts were all in the future when HADDOCK left Pearl Harbor on August 12, 1942, with the Force's first SJ aboard. The instrument embodied mystery as well as novelty. The idiosyncrasies of radar along with its capabilities had yet to be understood.

Lieutenant Commander Taylor and crew also had to learn of the capabilities and idiosyncrasies of the Japanese in the East China Sea area north of Formosa. Pioneering in two activities—warfare and search radar—HADDOCK's maiden patrollers were disposed to be conservative in regard to tactics. When, en route to the area, the submarine sighted a loaded freighter on August 22, Taylor conducted a daylight periscope attack in accordance with established rules. One torpedo hit the target. But the damaged vessel corrected a list and kept on going.

Taylor ordered HADDOCK to the surface, and gave chase. The race ran into a dark and moonless night, and the SJ was called upon to demonstrate its capabilities.

The instrument and its operators performed like veterans. Radar picked up the target at 13,600 yards, and gave continuous ranges and bearings for the T.D.C. from there on in. Information is lacking on the range at which the target became visible, but HADDOCK overhauled her swiftly, and Taylor opened fire at 1,300 yards on a 180° track.

Apparently the submarine was sighted. Blowing a frantic whistle, the freighter started a turn to starboard which would have put HADDOCK in line for a shot from the stern gun. Taylor ordered submergence. Two timed hits were heard as HADDOCK slid down under. Taylor reported a sinking. Although Japanese records failed to provide a name for the abolished vessel, it was eventually credited to HADDOCK as a nameless transport.

On August 26 while still patrolling in Formosa Strait, HADDOCK picked up a radar contact at 12,000 yards. There was a full moon and a cloudless sky which made an undetected surface approach impossible. The enemy's course and speed were plotted by radar. Taylor sent HADDOCK to full speed to gain position ahead for an early morning attack. At daybreak Taylor submerged the submarine on the target's track. It was 0820 in the morning before the target was sighted for the first time. (All previous tracking had been by radar.) Taylor fired four torpedoes from the stern tubes. All missed. The submarine was swung hard under full rudder, and the bow tubes were brought to bear. Two more torpedoes were fired. One of these hit, and the freighter was seen to sink. She was TEISHUN MARU, 2,251 tons.

HADDOCK's first patrol may be remarked as a historic episode in submarining and an important turning point in the Pacific War. Search radar expanded the horizon of submarine warfare by many leagues, and its successful introduction dated the beginning of the end for thousands of tons of Japanese shipping, which, in pre-radar days, might have reached its intended destination.

Links in the Chain

While NARWHAL, GUARDFISH and HADDOCK were on patrol in their respective areas, POMPANO (Lieutenant Commander W. M. Thomas) was patrolling the sea lanes off Bungo Suido. Her luck that summer was consistently indifferent, but on August 12 she sank an anonymous freighter in those waters.

At the summer's close, GROWLER, making her second patrol under Lieutenant Commander H. W. Gilmore, hit a fast stride in the waters off northwest Formosa. Returned to SubPac from the Aleutian front, GROWLER added sharp teeth to the Empire blockade. In the Formosan area she sank the powerful ex-gunboat SENYO MARU (August 25); the freighter EIFUKU MARU (August 31); the supply ship KASHINO (September 4); the freighter TAIKA MARU (September 7). Adding a large sampan for good measure, she concluded one of the summer's best patrols by sending to the bottom over 15,000 tons of enemy shipping.

But it was the GUARDFISH patrol that set the seasonal pace for the Empire blockade. Returning to home base in mid-September, Klakring and crew turned in one of the most dramatic patrol reports to date. Only DRUM and TRITON the previous spring had sunk more tonnage in Empire waters. But in accounting for five ships, a trawler and a sampan, and hitting two freighters for heavy damage, GUARDFISH was not far behind these tonnage leaders. In battle action (twelve attacks) she was not behind at all. And her patrol, herewith related in some detail, contained another of those episodes that keeps the "Silent Service" talking over its coffee.

Guardfish Goes to the Races

On March 4, 1942, Lieutenant Thomas Burton Klakring, captain of S-17, attempted to ram a U-boat raider in the Virgin Islands. Six months later (August 6, 1942) Lieutenant Commander Thomas Burton Klakring took his new submarine GUARDFISH out of Pearl Harbor, T.H., to conduct a raid of his own off the home islands of Japan.

The northeast coast of Honshu had not previously been visited by a patrolling submarine. GUARDFISH's visit was to come as a surprise—one the natives were going to remember. GUARDFISH's submariners were going to remember it, too. They were going to remember that patrolling without benefit of search radar they made 77 enemy-ship contacts in half as many days. And they made some other contacts never to be forgotten.

After running out a storm en route to the area, GUARDFISH made her first contact on August 19. At 0625 an 8,000-ton naval auxiliary was sighted, and shortly thereafter an escorting destroyer poked its nose out beyond the target. Fifteen minutes after first sighting the target, Klakring fired three torpedoes from 1,300 yards. Three explosions were heard, but the ship in question merely put on steam and turned away. The torpedoes may have missed and then detonated, or one warhead might have gone off magnetically and set off the others.

The destroyer promptly headed for GUARDFISH. Klakring held the submarine at periscope depth, hoping for a shot. At 2,000 yards the DD wheeled, dropped two depth charges, and steamed off to join her cohort. GUARDFISH went down to 180 feet for a reload. That evening she quietly entered her area.

On August 22 the lookout sighted three vessels which were either too far away for attack, or too small for valuable torpedoes. That evening Klakring ordered the gunners on deck, and GUARDFISH set a small trawler ablaze in her first gun action. The following evening she repeated the performance on a large sampan.

After sighting three freighters, which she was unable to close on the 24th, GUARDFISH struck a merchantman coming out of Kinkasan Harbor. At 1657 three torpedoes netted two hits on the unwary vessel. The third torpedo exploded against the bluff of the island. The ship's bow was blown almost completely off, and she nose-dived with her screws still turning. That was the last of SEIKAI MARU, 3,109 tons.

This sinking put an end to ship operations in the vicinity of Kinkasan Harbor for the rest of the day.

A ship GUARDFISH had sighted coming out of Kinkasan just before the attack decided discretion was the better part of valor, and retreated into the harbor. GUARDFISH evaded a patrol boat and stood northward.

The next morning Klakring directed a submerged attack on another freighter. Of two torpedoes fired, one proved a dud and the other porpoised and failed to explode. A third torpedo appeared to premature, for the target, apparently undamaged, was seen to head for the beach. About to surface in pursuit, GUARDFISH made four plane contacts on her SD. Not long after that, one of GUARDFISH's torpedoes drifted into view, floating vertically, without its warhead. This depressing sight was followed by a sound of fast screws which, together with the previous plane contacts, left no doubt in Klakring's mind that GUARDFISH was "it" in a fast game of hunt-the-submarine. He ordered her down to 120 feet, at which depth she eluded the hunting party.

Followed a week of heavy seas and thick fog in which GUARDFISH made no contacts. Then, on September 2, while patrolling on the surface, she sighted a freighter eight miles distant. Directing a submerged attack, Klakring fired three torpedoes for two smacking hits on the target. The ship took a 50° starboard list, but did not appear to be sinking. So another torpedo was fired. No torpedo wake was seen in the rough seas, and no explosion was heard, but the freighter's crew began to abandon ship, and ten minutes later the vessel broke squarely in half and sank. She was TEIKYU MARU, 2,332 tons.

Around midday, September 4, GUARDFISH sighted three freighters heading northwest about half a mile offshore. At 1246, with GUARDFISH unable to close to less than 5,000 yards submerged, Klakring wound up and let one torpedo loose at this range. The forward room reported hearing an explosion, and one of the AK's turned beachward, belching smoke. She was probably damaged, and soon disappeared in the offshore haze.

Klakring assumed the freighter trio might be the advance section of a convoy. At 1634 his hopes were confirmed by the appearance of two large ore ships. He sent GUARDFISH boring in. At 1744 he fired one torpedo at the leading ship, range 500 yards. The torpedo hit 27 seconds later with a terrific explosion. Two shots at the second target resulted in another thunderous blast. Both vessels sank spectacularly while the submarine's crew took turns viewing the scene through the periscope. The obliterated ore ships were CHITA MARU, 2,276 tons, and TENYU MARU, 3,738 tons.

During the attack on the ore carriers, Klakring had

spied two more AK's heading out of Kuji Wan. These, in turn, spied the submarine's handiwork, and thereupon reversed course. One anchored off the town of Minato, while the other remained on the move in the bay. Clearing the rocks to seaward of the bay, GUARDFISH stalked in to a point 6,500 yards from the anchored ship, and fired a long shot. Seven minutes and 27 seconds later an explosion, probably in the vessel's boiler room, flung a spout of smoke and steam several hundred feet in the air. A bull's-eye at over three miles! This was one of the longest torpedo shots of the war. Klakring and company watched the ship sink stern first until she rested on bottom with 100 feet of her bow slanting up out of water.

At this juncture another ship was sighted, steaming into view from the southeast. Klakring sent GUARDFISH racing to meet this newcomer. The submarine closed at high speed, submerged, and Klakring fired two torpedoes from 1,000 yards range. One hit—another GUARDFISH-shaking explosion—and the target began to settle by the bow. To hurry the settlement, Klakring fired another torpedo. It missed, but a moment later the target, KEIMEI MARU, 5,254 tons, went nose-diving to the bottom.

As darkness fell, the patrol boats came out in force. Concerning the end of this epic day, Klakring wrote, *"Propellers could be heard starting and stopping at frequent intervals until 2042 hours, when, it being all quiet and pitch black, Guardfish surfaced and cleared out on three engines. 2112: Two patrols sighted. 2220: A third patrol vessel sighted. Steered semi-circular avoiding course and left them all astern."*

Brazen submarine! But boldness justified by the confirmed sinking in one day of three enemy ships, and the positive sinking of another (which, however, was probably raised and repaired by the enemy, and so is not listed in the record). Yet the performance might have been expected of a submarine captain who had tried to ram a Nazi U-boat.

For the next two days, GUARDFISH was plagued by patrol vessels that hunted her in swarms. She made 19 patrol-vessel contacts in this time, and avoided all. Then, on September 9, with two torpedoes forward and one aft, she sighted a northbound freighter in the mid-morning seascape. At 1103 she fired her two bow tubes. No explosions. The torpedoes probably ran deep, for the range was only 500 yards, and Klakring felt that they couldn't have missed. The "fish" may not have reached set depth after the initial dive. It proved impossible to maneuver submerged for a stern-tube shot, and when target opened fire with a deck gun, Klakring sent GUARDFISH down

to 150 feet. As she climbed to periscope depth some time later, a heavy explosion was felt—probably a bomb from an unseen aircraft. Klakring called off the approach, and took her down to let the situation cool off. That evening he headed her for Midway. As she left the area she was forced down and held down for nine hours by three more patrol boats. She won the endurance test, and arrived at Midway on September 15.

It was an excited complement of submariners who climbed out into the sunshine. They knew they'd sunk a lot of Jap tonnage and made a lot of attacks and survived their share of "goings over." But the topic for general discussion—the episode for remembrance—concerned the day GUARDFISH, investigating the coast of Japan, drew so near to land that captain and crew were able to watch a horse race.

Ponies and cheering fans, flags and dust—they could almost see the expressions of the losers. Lest the horse story be taken for a fish story, they snapped periscope photographs of Japs, jockeys and nags. If there were any skeptics at Midway, the snapshots settled the issue.

The pictures were eventually published, and Lieutenant Commander Klakring was made an honorary member of the New York State Racing Commission, and there was a Commander Klakring Day at Pimlico near his home town, Annapolis. But, due to wartime censorship, the details of GUARDFISH's patrol were not revealed to American racing fans—and therein lay the bigger story. In jockeying GUARDFISH into twelve attack positions that ended in the sinkings enumerated, Klakring and crew won for their submarine her first Presidential Unit Citation. They would win for her a second! GUARDFISH was one of the two United States submarines so honored during the war.

The Blockade Tightens

Blockade strategy called for a chain of submarine patrols which would embrace the Japanese home Empire from the Kuriles in the north down to the Nansei Shoto, and reach across the East China and Yellow Sea to the China coast. Although the shortage of available submarines continued throughout the autumn of 1942 as the war was concentrated in the Solomons, new links were forged in the Empire chain and the blockade was on for the duration.

Both GUARDFISH and HADDOCK returned to Japanese waters. Among other blockaders on station off Japan that fall were NAUTILUS, GROUPER, KINGFISH, GREENLING, DRUM, FINBACK and TRIGGER.

Not all of these patrols were to prove as action-packed as the one instituted by GUARDFISH. Most of them were made up of long, grinding hours of work-a-day detail—days of monotonous routine—nights of tedious cruising in a blackout under the stars. The long and usually uneventful haul from Pearl Harbor or Midway to patrol area might end in days of fruitless, eye-straining watch and nerve-straining vigilance as the submarine "made the rounds" like a policeman on a quiet suburban beat. Then a glimpse of smoke would come as a relief to tedium, interrupting a card game or a doze. Or radar or sonar contact might be followed by a rush to battle stations. But frequently such contacts were lost before the target could be closed. Distant ships would fade in the surface haze, or—worse—manage to escape by an unexpected turn after the submariners had covered miles in an exacting approach.

And in some areas targets were as hard to locate as needles in a haystack. In no submarine operation does Dame Fortune play a larger part than in the matter of locating enemy shipping. Sometimes it goes one way, and sometimes it travels another. Like pheasants in the hunting season, ships may disappear from a promising area, taking cover after the first shot. Luck is where one finds it, and in this regard some submarines were luckier than others.

Yet, considering the happenstance involved, the submarines blockading the Empire found surprisingly good hunting in the autumnal season. Not all could make 77 contacts in a single patrol—for the simple reason that there were not that many ships in every area to contact. But the record indicates that every submarine made the most of its contact opportunities.

NAUTILUS (Lieutenant Commander Brockman) was on station off northeast Honshu in mid-September. Three Japanese freighters went down to her hard-hitting torpedoes: TAMON MARU No. 6, 5,000 tons (September 28)—TOSEI MARU, 2,432 tons (October 1)—KENUN MARU, 4,643 tons (October 24). This tonnage was disappointing to the submariners who had struck the forces' hardest blow at Midway and operated with Carlson's Raiders in the Makin attack. But Lady Luck was indisposed and kicking up high seas which made patrolling at periscope depth impossible and torpedo fire out of the question. Although 63 ship contacts were made, only a few approaches could be developed, and breakdowns in operating gear hampered these.

Beset with difficulties external and internal, NAUTILUS had an all-out fight on her hands throughout the patrol. But in addition to the three ships downed, she battle-surfaced to sink three sampans. The aggressive work of Brockman and crew in behalf of the blockade was not to go unrecognized.

GROUPER (Lieutenant Commander R. R. McGregor) was simultaneously patrolling in the East China Sea. In the waters off Shanghai she sank a freighter and a good-sized transport: TONE MARU, 4,070 tons (September 21) and LISBON MARU, 7,053 (October 1).

KINGFISH, making her first war patrol under Lieutenant Commander V. L. Lowrance, downed a freighter and an ex-gunboat in the waters off southern Kyushu. These were: YOMEI MARU, 2,860 tons (October 1) and SEIKYO MARU, 2,608 tons (October 23).

GREENLING (Lieutenant Commander H. C. Bruton) raised an October storm in the waters off Honshu north of Inubo Saki. Bruton and crew were on location the morning of the 3rd. After a futile attempt to overhaul a small freighter, they sighted a 5,000-tonner against the dawn, and proceeded to get on target. At 0700 Bruton fired three torpedoes. One exploded in the vessel's engine room, and six minutes later the ship was under the rolling sea. The Japanese owners recorded the loss of KINKAI MARU.

The following day GREENLING evaded a patrol yacht and went on to pursue another freighter. After an approach that lasted for an hour and fifteen minutes, Bruton fired three shots at this target. Two torpedoes hit the mark, the vessel's screws came to a dead stop, and down by the stern went the 4,147-ton SETSUYA MARU.

For the next six days the submarine was buffeted by furious seas tumbling under dense fog. Bruton and crew had to devote their time to riding out the waves and repairing minor storm damage. But at dawn's early light on the 14th they were on the track of another AK. After a nineteen-minute approach they reached attack position, and two out of three torpedoes hit the target. Down went TAKUSEI MARU, 3,500 tons.

Four days later (October 18) after a lively interval of playing tag with sampans, patrol craft, a small destroyer and other submarine hunters, contact was made with another large cargo carrier. At 0255 GREENLING's periscope was trained on the target—a big freighter steaming southward. Bruton directed a surface approach. In the dark of 0325 he fired three torpedoes at the vessel's silhouette. A blast flared in the gloom, the ship stopped with a screech from her whistle, and sat down on her haunches.

As flame spouted from the vessel's stern, GREENLING skirted the burning ship, and Bruton fired two more torpedoes for a *coup de grâce*. The expected death-blow boomeranged as both torpedoes made circular runs, missing the target and rounding on the submarine to pass close aboard. The burning ship began to crawl ahead, and Bruton had to maneuver astern to deliver the finishing shot. One torpedo served. Hakonesan Maru, 6,673 tons, broke in two and went down.

On October 20, after the submarine weathered a light depth-charge attack from a patrol vessel, Bruton decided to beat along the Tokyo-Aleutian traffic lanes for a few days. Two days later a destroyer was contacted. Then an aircraft carrier or auxiliary carrier hove in sight. Bruton was on the track immediately. Heavy seas hampered the mid-morning approach. As the target swung by, Bruton fired five bow shots at a range of 2,800 yards, angle on the bow 130° starboard. Then he ordered deep submergence to evade the inevitable counter-attack, and as Greenling went down the slope two torpedo hits were heard. Three minutes later the depth-charge barrage began. It lasted for an hour—no submarine bones broken—after which Greenling climbed to periscope depth. Target and escorting destroyer were nowhere in view. Greenling was therefore credited with damaging a 22,000-ton auxiliary carrier.

She departed the area that night and arrived home at Pearl Harbor on November 1. She had run into a lot of action for a submarine patrolling without benefit of SJ radar, and her performance—which is to say the performance of her captain and crew—would be remembered.

While Greenling was harrying the enemy's sea lanes off northern Honshu, Drum (Lieutenant Commander R. H. Rice) had been beating around the approaches to Tokyo Bay. This was the patrol in which Rice and company enjoyed scenic views of Mount Fujiyama.

For Drum the targets were fewer than those donated to Greenling, but Rice and his submariners did their share to tighten the blockade. Holed by Drum's torpedoes, three merchantmen sloughed under to sleep in the deep: Hague Maru, passenger-cargo carrier, 5,641 tons (October 8)—Hachimanzan Maru, freighter, 2,461 tons (October 9)—Ryunan Maru, freighter, 5,106 tons (October 20).

Linked up with Drum's patrol was the one conducted by Trigger in the Bungo Suido area. Skippered by Commander R. S. Benson, Trigger went out looking for trouble—and found all she could handle of a sort she wasn't courting.

Indications began after sundown on October 5 when Benson and his boys tracked down a medium-sized freighter. Benson directed a night-surface attack and fired five torpedoes. Only two out of the five hit the target and the ship escaped in the night, probably damaged.

October 17 was Trigger's busy day. The morning was still in night when the watch spotted a large merchantman's silhouette off in the gloom. Benson rushed the crew to battle stations, directing another surface approach. Four shots were fired. Two explosions blasted the dark. Down went the 5,869-ton cargo ship, Holland Maru.

Shortly after the sinking, Trigger was hot on the track of another AK. A day submerged approach brought the submarine to attack position. Benson fired three. The target kept on going. No hits.

The ship may have sighted the torpedo wakes, or the early morning sinking may have been seen, for a Japanese destroyer came steaming at top speed out of the Bungo that evening. At any rate, the lookout spied the DD in the twilight at a range of about three miles—angle on the bow, cold zero—bearing down like an express train.

The destroyer announced it had seen the submarine by opening fire. Benson gave the order, "Take her down!" As Trigger plunged downgrade, the DD passed close astern and dropped depth charges. Ensued a deadly game of tag, the destroyer circling to locate the submarine and the submarine maneuvering to get in a shot at the destroyer. Some depth charges were close and others were wide of the mark as the surface craft and the submersible sparred in this play of catch-as-catch-can.

Finally Benson upped the periscope and saw his opponent start a run. He swung Trigger head-on toward the destroyer. With zero angle on the bow, zero relative bearing, he waited deliberately until the range decreased to 2,500 yards. At this moment the game of tag assumed the aspect of a shotgun duel at five paces. In perfect position for a down-the-throat shot, the submarine was practically looking into the destroyer's tonsils. And the destroyer, so to speak, was looking the submarine squarely in the eye. But Trigger had the advantage of the first shot. Benson snapped the command "Fire one! Fire two! Fire three!"

With a spread of three torpedoes rushing at him, there was exactly nothing the destroyer commander could do to evade. Change of speed was futile, and change of course would only present a broader target. There was, of course, the last resort of prayer. Perhaps the Japanese commander in this instance prayed.

Sixty seconds after firing, the submariners saw a terrific explosion throw up a hill of water in line with target. When the smoke and spray cleared, the destroyer was still there, although she had turned away. Benson concluded that one torpedo had prematured, and the other two had exploded on entering the swirl. He also concluded it was his turn to pray. For a missing down-the-throat shot leaves

176

a destroyer in the best possible position for a depth-charge attack. TRIGGER was now in line for a blasting from the opponent's "shotgun."

The blast did not come. Apparently the Jap destroyer-men were confused by the premature, or suspected some sort of trick. Having turned away, the DD kept on going. TRIGGER kept on going, too. And so did her torpedo difficulties.

Three nights later, attacking a 10,000-ton oil tanker, she scored two hits out of four shots but was unable to sink the tanker. In attacking another large tanker on October 24, four torpedoes were fired and only one hit the target. This tanker also escaped.

In commenting on TRIGGER's down-the-throat attack, a submarine officer wrote later: *"Never would the Japanese suspect the truth so apparent from many patrol reports of that date. American submarines were sent to sea with grossly defective torpedoes."*

Obviously the submariners pioneering the Empire blockade were surmounting obstacles. FINBACK (Lieutenant Commander J. L. Hull) surmounted hers in an October patrol in the Formosa area. Her torpedoes performed erratically, and she reported 13 "misses" out of 20 shots. Yet the seven that hit put a large hole in the enemy's shipping. In this, her second patrol, she led the blockade's tonnage score by sinking the 7,000-ton transport TEISON MARU (October 14) and the freighters YAMAFUJI MARU, 5,359 tons, and AFRICA MARU, 9,475 tons (October 20). Loss to Japan: 21,840 tons.

The day following FINBACK's double-sinking, GUARDFISH, patrolling in the East China Sea, west of the Nansei Shoto, scored a double. Klakring and crew had once more struck a "hot" shipping run. Again they turned in a dramatic patrol report.

Leaving Midway on September 30, after a two-week breather, GUARDFISH moved out of Midway's lagoon and headed west for her newly assigned hunting ground. Three days later she was back in Midway for repairs to her SD radar, her pitometer log and her T.D.C. Evening of October 3 she was under way again.

As during her maiden patrol, she ran into rambunctious weather that lasted until she reached her area. In addition, the fractious radar gear continued to give trouble. However, she reached the Nansei Shoto archipelago in good time, and drove on into the East China Sea.

Early in the morning of October 19, lookout sighted a large freighter steaming along under plane cover. At 1025, after a five-hour approach, Klakring decided he had obtained the best position possible under the circumstances, and fired four bow shots at 1,600 yards, 95° starboard track.

No explosions were heard although Klakring was certain at least two torpedoes passed directly beneath the target. Rechecking the set-up, he fired the remaining two bow tubes at 2,000 yards. The last torpedo exploded at the freighter's stern with a bright orange flash. While her scope was trained on the target, GUARDFISH sustained the first explosion of a bomb-attack delivered by the escorting plane. As three more depth bombs exploded, Klakring sent the submarine down to 200 feet. Fifteen minutes later she climbed to periscope depth, and the target was seen on a new track, heading for Kume Shima. Believing the freighter severely damaged and probably heading over to beach herself, Klakring took GUARDFISH to deep submergence and reloaded bow tubes while maneuvering for a new attack position. At 1148 the target was seen about eight miles distant, smoking heavily. GUARDFISH surfaced and commenced chase.

At 1310, two planes were sighted at six miles, heading toward the submarine. Klakring took her down. She was passing 125 feet when a heavy explosion shook her hull. Depth control was lost momentarily and GUARDFISH rose at a steep angle to something less than 90 feet, before she could be levelled off. A second explosion shook GUARDFISH. This one, fortunately, drove her down instead of up, and she descended to 250 feet. At this depth, Klakring decided to spend the remainder of the afternoon, "inspecting for damage, pulling ourselves together, and clearing the locality." That evening GUARDFISH surfaced to conclude what was far from a perfect day. Klakring recorded the imperfections as:

(a) Faulty torpedo performance which prevented destruction of a valuable target.
(b) The damaged target had to be let go due to the severe bombing attack.
(c) The radar failed so completely that GUARDFISH would have been destroyed by the attacking planes except for the vigilance of the topside watch.

But a better day was coming up. It began on the morning of October 21 when GUARDFISH sighted the smoke of a seven-ship convoy. Submerging at 1045—range to the van of the convoy at 3,500 yards—Klakring fired four torpedoes at the leading four ships, which were bunched together like a covey of quail. Two explosions stopped one freighter, which sank in a few minutes. She took her name down with her, and an estimated 4,000 tons.

The other vessels dispersed and opened fire on GUARDFISH. With her periscope fully exposed, GUARDFISH headed for the center of the milling convoy, and gained firing position on one of the freighters. The target wheeled around and forced the submarine to wheel to avoid a collision. However, the maneuver gave Klakring a stern-tube set-up, and he was able to fire three torpedoes at 1,000 yards, on an 80° track. A hit blew the freighter's after gun crew 40 feet in the air, demolished the vessel's stern, and put her under in two minutes. She was NICHIHO MARU, 6,363 tons.

The remaining vessels now presented their sterns to the submarine and delivered a fusillade that sent GUARDFISH deep for a reload. With torpedoes in the tubes, GUARDFISH surfaced to chase, and discovered a patrol vessel picking up survivors. The patrol craft opened fire at 6,000 yards, and GUARDFISH made a strategic withdrawal. Twenty-five minutes later two bombers came in and forced the submarine down, dropping a dozen depth charges in her wake. With aircraft overhead, the chase had to be abandoned.

The following day a smoke contact petered out and evening brought a northeast gale and high seas, which lasted for the next ten days. No shipping was sighted and it was doubtful if a torpedo attack could have been made in the gale's heavy seas. When the storm finally abated, all hands were worn as ragged as the weather. On November 9 another approach ended in disappointment when the range could not be closed for an attack.

On the 10th of November GUARDFISH cleared her area, spent four days patrolling east of the Nansei Shoto, and headed for the barn. On November 21 she was surprise-attacked by a roving airman. Her stern planes failed, and two close misses gave Klakring and crew a bad moment. They stopped for fuel at Midway on the night of November 23, and arrived at Pearl on the 28th.

GUARDFISH was to receive high honors for this, her second patrol. For her display of *"extreme aggressiveness and tenacity in the face of heavy anti-submarine activity and extremely adverse weather"* she was recognized as *"one of the Submarine Force's most valuable units."* In token of that recognition she was awarded the Presidential Unit Citation—the first of the two she was to receive.

For similarly outstanding performance on their first three patrols, NAUTILUS (Lieutenant Commander Brockman) and GREENLING (Lieutenant Commander Bruton) also received the citation. Thirty-five Presidential Unit Citations (see Addenda) were awarded to submarines before the end of the war. But only two submarines—GUARDFISH and TANG—won it twice. Only one other vessel in the entire U.S. Navy was thus honored.

Haddock in the Yellow Sea

On October 11, 1942, Lieutenant Commander A. H. Taylor took HADDOCK out of Midway on her second patrol. The area assigned to him was the Yellow Sea.

Embraced by Korea and the China mainland, and laced by main-line shipping routes to Nanking, Kiaochow and Taku, this body of water was geographically as dangerous to an American submarine as the Caribbean would have been to a Japanese I-boat. HADDOCK, with her SJ radar as a chip on her shoulder, was due for some action.

October 27, on location, she contacted two patrol boats and sighted a steamer's smoke, but was unable to close for an attack. The shooting began on the morning of the 31st when she contacted a large freighter. Taylor and crew maneuvered the submarine into a good attack position. At 0924 Taylor fired three stern shots at the target. The freighter made a radical zig to the left, and the torpedoes missed—one—two—three. Before the bow tubes could be brought to bear, the ship swung hard right and stood off. HADDOCK was unable to overtake her.

Near midnight of that same day, two large freighters with a DD escort were sighted. For two hours HADDOCK played hide-and-seek with the moon and the convoy. The convoy won. At 0200, convinced that a night-surface attack would not be feasible, and that a submerged attack would not be possible with HADDOCK's batteries running low, Taylor gave up the chase.

But early in the morning of November 3 the luck changed. At 0210 HADDOCK made SJ contact on a "large tanker" at 9,050 yards. Crossing the track at full speed to silhouette the target against the moon, HADDOCK closed to 1,700 yards. Taylor fired three shots. One hit amidships and was followed by a tremendous explosion. The target broke in two, and sank in four minutes. She was later identified as TEKKAI MARU, 1,925-ton cargoman.

Three days later Taylor directed a submerged attack on a 5,000-ton freighter. A trio of torpedoes, loosed from 1,250 yards, missed the mark. Apparently they ran too deep. Again, on the 8th, three stern shots missed a 6,500-ton freighter. In turn, HADDOCK was missed by two bombs from a patrol plane.

November 11 brought more encouraging results. While making a radar sweep at 40 feet, just before surfacing at evening, HADDOCK contacted a ship at 1,800 yards. Letting it pass, Taylor surfaced the submarine into a clear starlit night, waited for moonset and struck. At 2115 he fired four torpedoes on an 80° track, range 1,900 yards. One hit blew the vessel's stern off, and she settled rapidly, sending S.O.S. signals to HADDOCK by flashing light. In 15 minutes the ship was under the sea. She was VENICE MARU, 6,571-ton passenger-cargo carrier.

On the 13th HADDOCK had another radar contact. Taylor closed to fire three bow tubes at a LIMA MARU freighter from 1,450 yards. One hit—a thudding explosion—the vessel began to settle. As the submarine watched, the SJ picked up another target at 4,200 yards. HADDOCK swung to attack what appeared to be a tanker, and Taylor fired three torpedoes from 1,400 yards. Again one hit with a muffled explosion. This vessel slowed to three knots, and began to zigzag like a running steer. While Taylor considered the advisability of closing to finish off the tanker with the remaining two (stern) torpedoes, the lookout observed gun-flashes dead astern. As no radar pip came in from this direction, Taylor assumed an escort was firing and decided to clear the area at high speed. No Japanese record shows a ship sunk in this attack, but Japanese records were far from complete, and it seems probable that HADDOCK sank more ships in the Yellow Sea than the two officially credited.

On November 16 a submerged periscope attack at 1650 netted HADDOCK two hits on a large, empty tanker. No above-water damage was apparent as the target circled at 2 knots for over an hour after the attack, while HADDOCK stood helplessly by, out of torpedoes, observing. At sundown, the tanker slowly stood off to the northeast—no fire or list, but settled about three feet by the stern. That night HADDOCK cleared the area and headed for Pearl. She arrived at home base on December 4, out of ammunition.

So the Empire blockade tightened during October and November 1942. And in the meantime a new type of link was added to the chain being forged around Dai Nippon. While not so effective as the submarine patrol, it was to take its toll of enemy shipping and serve as another shackle on Japan's commerce. That "link" was the submarine minefield.

Submarine Mine Plants

As early as July 1941 plans had been made to lay submarine minefields in the event of war with Japan. When the Pearl Harbor attack crippled the U.S. Pacific Fleet an unanticipated workload gave the Submarine Force little opportunity for minelaying. Not until the autumn of 1942 did the force commanders feel that submarines could be spared for mine plants. In the category of special missions, such an operation monopolized the submarine's time and effort by limiting the number of torpedoes the undersea minelayer might carry, and thus restricting the submarine's combat potential. And in the early months of the war, torpedo attacks on enemy shipping were awarded the priority.

Paradoxically, the torpedo shortage that developed as the war expanded implemented the long-awaited opportunity for minelaying. As there were not enough torpedoes to fully load all submarines going out on patrol, space became available for mines. Available time for mine planting was not so readily provided. However, during October and November 1942, while the vortex of the Pacific War swirled in the Solomons, six submarines were dispatched on mine-planting missions. The results of these missions furnished basic data for operational analysis, and opened the field for effective expansion and development of submarine minelaying operations.

The first submarines sent out to mine the enemy's waters were THRESHER, TAMBOR, GAR, TAUTOG, WHALE and GRENADIER. All plants except WHALE's were to be made in the Southwest Pacific. WHALE's destination was the Kii Suido—the eastern entrance to the Inland Sea—deep in the inner ring of the Japanese homeland sea frontier.

THRESHER (Lieutenant Commander W. J. Millican) steamed west to the coast of Asia to lay her mines in the Gulf of Siam. October 16 she was on location. There, in the northernmost waters of the Gulf at the doorstep of Bangkok, this submarine made the first mineplant of the Pacific War.

Three days later, GAR (Lieutenant Commander Donald McGregor) laid mines in waters adjacent to the THRESHER field.

On October 29, GRENADIER (Lieutenant Commander B. L. Carr) sowed the waters in the heart of the Gulf of Tonkin with mines.

TAMBOR (Lieutenant Commander S. H. Ambruster) repeated the performance on November 2, laying her mines in the eastern waters of the Tonkin Gulf.

And on the same day, TAUTOG (Lieutenant Commander Willingham) planted a field in the waters off Cape Padaran, French Indo-China.

These strategic plants covered important Japanese shipping lanes which had previously been patrolled by submarines of the SoWesPac Force. When, to meet the Solomons emergency, many of the Fremantle boats were transferred to Task Force Forty-two at Brisbane, the coastal waters of Malaya, Siam and Indo-China had to be neglected. Mines, however, could bridge the hiatus until the submarine patrols were resumed. A minefield could scarcely pinch-hit for a wide-ranging submarine, but it did constitute a standing menace that forced the enemy to search, sweep or detour. Armed with the element of surprise, it could exact a sizable shipping toll.

In respect to surprise, the submarine mine plant has a decided edge on the field sewn by surface or aircraft. On the other hand, observation of the minefield's "activities" remains difficult. After planting

179

mines in some remote area deep in enemy waters, a submarine could not loiter at leisure in the neighborhood to watch results. Eye-witness, on-the-spot reports of minefield sinkings are few and far between. In the case of the pioneer plants enumerated, observations were sketchy.

THRESHER reported two prematures. GAR reported four. GRENADIER and TAMBOR reported singles. Three prematures were reported by TAUTOG. WHALE was the only pioneer who did not report a premature. The mines she laid had contact exploders.

Completing the war's first mine plant in Empire waters, WHALE turned in an interesting and informative report. Under Lieutenant Commander John B. Azer, the mine-loaded submarine had headed out for Japan on her maiden patrol. Most of the long haul from Pearl Harbor to Japan was made on the surface—a run which would have violated the rules in effect in the opening days of the war. WHALE cruised on top by day as well as night, evading Jap search planes by fast dives and making bold observations at periscope depth. Her men enjoyed the sun along with the stars, and she reached her destination with time to spare.

Pre-war shipping curves had indicated the Kii Suido passage as a main line for Japanese maritime traffic. WHALE's periscope watch confirmed the pre-war indications. Merchantmen and naval vessels were seen hugging the shoreline, running parallel to the coast about one mile off the beach. Evidently the pioneer raids earlier in 1942 had alarmed the local authorities.

Azer determined to alarm them further. Orders called for the mine plant in waters near the Kii Suido entrance but farther offshore. But at the suggestion of Executive Officer Lieutenant Fritz Harlfinger, WHALE's skipper decided to act on the initiative permissible in such circumstances.

"If we move in closer and plant the mines across their track just off the beach in that cove near the lighthouse, we'll scare them into a conniption," Harlfinger pointed out. "They'll never expect a sub to get in that close, and afterwards they'll have to sweep every foot of the coastline."

Azer liked the idea. Throughout that day of October 25, he held the submarine offshore, making periscope observations. The Japanese shipping path was carefully plotted and alternate routes were noted. Three minefield locations were chosen—one on the main line and two to cover possible detours.

At moonrise WHALE moved in warily. Azer himself was on the lookout for mines, aware of the irony involved in a mine-planting submarine creeping through a minefield to lay mines. One Japanese mine was detected. The Imperial Navy had laid its specimens well offshore, however, and there was little danger of mines close in where the Jap ships were traveling.

Under a full moon the first field of Mark 10-1's was planted. The second was laid closer to the shore, and the third was sewn across the traffic lane that paralleled the beach. With ships in the immediate vicinity, she had to do some expert maneuvering to extricate herself from the area. Thanks to Japanese navigation lights, she was able to grope her way out across the channel.

Just before sunrise the following morning, the lookout sighted a Jap convoy. Azer rushed the crew to battle stations and sent WHALE boring in on the attack. Torpedo fire was answered by a bedlam of explosions, but it was too dark for positive identification of the targets, and no sinkings could be ultimately confirmed.

Two of the ships were damaged, however. In the morning light these were seen limping off, surrounded by swarms of sampans which had scuttled out from shore to rescue survivors. WHALE's periscope watch was fascinated. The damaged vessels were caught between Scylla and Charybdis—either they veered in and grounded on a rocky shore, or they ran into the Mark 10-1 minefields.

Before WHALE could observe the outcome of the situation, she was driven under by a destroyer that came tearing out of the harbor on the hunt. While the submariners were under, making a reload, two heavy explosions rumbled from the direction of the minefields. Presently there were two more explosions. Busy with evasive maneuvers, Azer and company were unable to determine the upshots of these detonations. But all were convinced the mines had finished off a freighter or two, if not the pugnacious DD. After the war the Japanese admitted the sinking of a cargo ship by a mine in this area.

WHALE remained for several days in these dangerous waters, taking periscope pictures of headlands and beaches, gun emplacements and naval installations, anything of value for the Navy's future reference. In the teeth of Jap flying boats, sampans and harbor patrols, camera shots were made of the shoreline between Ashizuri Zaki and Murato Zaki, WHALE poking up her periscope at some points only 500 yards offshore.

In leaving for home she encountered a CHIDORI patrol boat just outside the 100-fathom curve, and the craft gave her a strenuous "going over." The first spread of depth charges flooded the inductions, opened valves and sent WHALE plunging toward seabottom with a 20° up-angle. As the blasts went off

GUARDFISH GETS A "GOING OVER." Under-water explosion forms huge bubble and sends out percussion waves. Blast close aboard could crush pres-sure hull. Here the sub sustains a near miss. On same patrol Guardfish *watched a Honshu horse-race, sank 4 ships in day, scored one of war's longest torpedo shots.*

A T T R I T I O N !

around the submarine, her light bulbs were pulverized, glass and paint chips flew into the faces of the men, and the boat pitched like a wild seesaw.

Harlfinger reported afterward, *"We barely held our own with the leaks. All available spare men were sent to the forward part of the boat in a desperate effort to regain an even keel. Charge after charge was dropped. We were pursued by the patrol boat for seventeen hours. The Nips were a little mad, I suppose, because we'd invaded their home territory."*

Finally the submarine shook her hunter and headed seaward. Azer and crew spent a night on the surface, repairing damage. Then they hit for home, photographs secure and minefields planted for the harvest season.

Aided by the experiences of the first six mine plants, a second group of submarine minelayers headed for Japan in December 1942, in compliance with a request from CinCPac. The submarines in this second group were SUNFISH (Lieutenant Commander R. W. Peterson), DRUM (Lieutenant Commander B. F. McMahon) and TRIGGER (Lieutenant Commander R. S. Benson).

SUNFISH planted mines in Empire waters at the entrance to Iseno Imi, completing the operation on December 17. DRUM, on the 17th, laid mines in the Bungo Suido passage between Shikoku and Kyushu. TRIGGER placed a mine pattern off Inubo Saki some 60 miles east of Tokyo on December 20.

TRIGGER's experience was unique in that she was able to witness some of the results of her handiwork. She arrived on station off Inubo Saki on December 16. Her orders were to conduct a reconnaissance mission a few days to determine the traffic route and then to lay two minefields along that route.

TRIGGER performed the preliminary reconnaissance. Four contacts were made, indicating that traffic was rounding Inubo Saki along the 20-fathom curve. No attacks were made as Benson did not want to alert the Japs before the minefields were laid. On the night of the 20th TRIGGER submerged in bright moonlight, and began her nocturnal planting. The first field had been sown, and the second one started when a ship was sighted approaching from the southward, heading almost straight for TRIGGER.

The mine plant was discontinued and TRIGGER hauled clear. As the ship approached it was seen to be a large freighter accompanied by a small escort vessel farther inshore. The ship passed astern in perfect position for a torpedo attack. But Benson allowed it to pass as he had been given to understand that TRIGGER's primary mission was to plant a minefield before risking detection.

About five minutes after the freighter passed astern, the submarine heard a violent explosion. A moment later the freighter, turned 90° from her course, was seen lying in the sea, helpless, with a broken back. She sank rapidly, folding up like a jackknife, with her bow and stern in the air. Score one for the mines.

Eighteen minutes later, TRIGGER heard another explosion, but was unable to discern the cause. The minefield might have caught something else, perhaps the escort. In the meantime, Benson had ordered the submarine seaward, to get her out of 15 fathoms into deeper water as fast as possible. About an hour and a half later she surfaced. Those on deck could see a sullen cloud of smoke bulging over the minefield.

Three days later, TRIGGER was patrolling outside her minefield in order to intercept any ships that might be detoured around it. In the middle of the afternoon, smoke was sighted to the northwest. TRIGGER commenced an approach on a southwesterly course which would pass her well to the southward of her mines. The smoke broke up into four separate columns, advancing toward Inubo Saki.

At this instant [Benson wrote in his patrol report] the leading ship which had reached the exact bearing of our mine plants, commenced smoking at least five times as great as before and the three other ships scattered to the northward. The smoke of our mine plants lasted only a few minutes while the other three columns of smoke disappeared to the northward. Consider that a freighter of at least 5,000 tons was damaged, if not sunk, by this mine.

Such long-distance observation could not be conclusive. But about two hours later, after nightfall, a searchlight opened up on Inubo Saki and began to sweep the water off the point. TRIGGER's submariners could reasonably deduce that something had happened in the minefield neighborhood—perhaps coast patrols were looking for survivors.

The submariners noted another aftermath resulting from their mine plant. Coastwise shipping hugged the shoreline with greater tenacity than before. Lights strung out along the beach were apparently employed as marker beacons for this nervous inshore traffic. Evidently Japanese mariners in the locality had been warned to remain within easy swimming distance of the homeland.

While observing these phenomena, Benson and company took the opportunity to attack several convoys. On December 22 they sank TEIFUKU MARU, freighter, 5,198 tons. And before quitting the Empire area they downed the Imperial Navy destroyer OKIKAZE, 1,300 tons. These torpedo sinkings caused TRIGGER's sharpshooters to regret that they had passed up three good targets before making their mine plant. In consideration of this lost opportunity, and the fact that the minefield drove ship traffic inshore where the shallow water made submarining overly hazardous, TRIGGER's experience created some doubt as to whether such a mine plant was worth the effort.

An analysis of the minelaying operations of SUN-FISH, DRUM and TRIGGER invited three general conclusions. First: Priority should be given the mining of harbor approaches, and sea-lane plants should be relegated to a later phase of the war. Second: A study of areas should be inaugurated to determine the best possible location for minefields, wherein economic planting might reap the best possible harvest. Third: Mining operations should be conducted with the aim of destroying the maximum number of ships before the fields were rendered impotent by enemy sweeping.

In consequence of these pioneer efforts, CinCPac established an analytical section on mine warfare with Dr. (later Lieutenant Commander) W. C. Michels as senior technician. Dr. Michels was to act as consultant with ComSubPac to determine best locations for future submarine minefields.

Strategists came to the conclusion that minefields laid close inshore in shallow water would force enemy ship traffic into deeper water where submarine attacks were more feasible. Future mine plants would be made accordingly.

Improvements were made on the Mark 12 magnetic mine, and its defects were eventually corrected. The Mark 10 had also prematured and countermined, and in addition its defectives had included "floaters." The type was finally abandoned in favor of the Mark 12.

Although the pioneer submarine mine plants seemed relatively unprofitable, it was realized that a conclusive assessment could not be made until the war's end. The minefield is a "long term" investment. The field may lie fallow for weeks, and in some instances the harvest may not come for several seasons.

On February 25, 1945, the U.S. submarine BECUNA sighted a small tanker in flames and stranded in the shallows southwest of Cape Padaran, off Indo-China. The tanker's position was estimated as within a mile of the minefield planted by TAUTOG on November 2, 1942.

Kingfish Sweeps with SJ

One of the submarines on blockade in December was KINGFISH. Patrolling off Shikoku in October, she had sunk a freighter and an ex-gunboat. Sallying forth in late November, she was twice as formidable.

As on her previous (first) patrol, she was skippered by Lieutenant Commander V. L. Lowrance. She carried the same crew of submariners. But there was a difference in her silhouette. Aft of the periscope a stainless steel tube had been reared—a device that could be raised or lowered in a watertight housing. Top of the tube was a large, metal parabola—the "reflector," or parabolic antenna of the SJ. Electronic technicians, working night and day at Pearl Harbor, were installing this gear on submarine after submarine. Within four momentous months, search radar had become indispensable.

Indispensable, but not to the elimination of sonar, periscope observation or even the 20-20 vision of the bridge lookout. Radar was not infallible—could go off whack or otherwise break down like any sensitive instrument. Moreover, it had its "blind spots," and there were numerous situations wherein the submarine had to go deep and rely on sonic information, or surface and observe by lookout. Sound and sight would continue to play important roles in the tactical gambit, in supporting teamwork with radar. The attacks made by KINGFISH on her pioneering radar patrol are illustrative.

Her area was a rectangular strip of ocean extending from Okinawa in the Nansei Shoto to the China coast directly north of Formosa Strait. Early in the morning of December 7, while running submerged about 200 miles west of Iwo Jima, KINGFISH picked up a lone freighter by periscope contact. The closest she could come to her target on a submerged approach was 6,000 yards. At 0815 Lowrance ordered her to the surface and made a top-speed run to gain attack position ahead, on the target's track. At 1510 KINGFISH submerged for the attack, and an hour later Lowrance fired three torpedoes. He saw the track of two torpedoes pass close to the stern of the target, but there were no explosions. This was not to be the only disappointment in that respect. KINGFISH was harassed by erratic exploder performance throughout the patrol.

Again waiting for the target to get over the horizon, Lowrance surfaced the submarine at 1727 and commenced chase. Here the radar began to pay dividends. The light was failing, but with some coaching from the bridge, radar picked up the target at 11,000 yards. From 9,000 yards on in, radar stayed right on the target. At 1936 Lowrance fired one torpedo on a 180° track at 1,200-yard range, from the surface. The torpedo prematured at 30 seconds. KINGFISH submerged as Japs were seen to be manning the vessel's deck gun. Ten minutes later, the submarine was on the surface again, giving chase.

The third approach was accomplished almost

entirely by radar. The target was picked up at 7,900 yards. The range opened to 9,300 and then started closing. Radar had no difficulty obtaining accurate ranges during attack maneuvers. At 2103 two torpedoes were fired at 1,400 yards on 110° starboard track, depth-setting six feet. Both hit. The ship, enveloped in flames, got off one salvo from the forward deck gun at the surfaced submarine. Lowrance then took her down, and allowed all hands a periscope view of the burning and sinking vessel. This was HINO MARU No. 3—a 4,391-ton cargo vessel.

December 28, off the coast of Formosa, Lowrance and crew sank the 5,328-ton freighter CHOYO MARU. Night-surface approach was conducted with the aid of the SJ. Lowrance fired six shots at the target. The radar worked better than the torpedoes, for only one of the six scored a hit.

The submariners wound up their patrol ten days later by sinking two sub-chasers (200-tonners) with gunfire. This gun battle, of course, was fought on the surface. Thus the periscope and 20-20 vision joined with radar in contacting and tracking down a number of enemy vessels. And sonar came into play in tracking torpedoes and "timing" prematures. In few cases would radar take over the entire operation—contact, tracking, fire control, everything down to the last shot. But it would happen—and the enemy would never know what hit him.

Blockade Statistic

Ardent nationalists tend to believe their own propaganda, but post-war inquiry reveals the fact that in Imperial Japanese Headquarters, as of December 1942, there were one or two skeptics unable to see the war through Tokyo Rose's colored glasses. The Japanese have a knack for juggling, but no matter how one rearranges the digits in a given column, they add up to the same total. Total in this case (the number of ships sunk by U.S. submarines in Empire waters in the last half of 1942) must have convinced the realistic Jap that all was not quiet on the Western Pacific front.

"Submarines initially did great damage to our shipping, and later, combined with air attack, made our shipping very scarce." Admiral (former Ambassador to the United States) Nomura speaking. *"Our supply lines were cut and we could not support these supply lines. . . . Our experts knew that it was necessary to have 3,000,000 tons of shipping just for civilian living in Japan."*

Admiral Nomura's statement clearly indicates that Japan's shipping losses in Empire waters (inclusive of the Formosa and Kurile areas) between July 1 and the end of 1942 had considerably reduced the Japanese civilian's standard of living. Three ships sunk in July. Nine in August. Eight in September. Nineteen in October. Three in November. Not so many bottoms for a maritime nation, perhaps—not beyond Japan's capacity for replacement—but hundreds of tons of irreplaceable coal, oil, fish, iron ore, rice.

Then KINGFISH contributed her three in December. And while KINGFISH was contributing, HALIBUT (Lieutenant Commander P. H. Ross) arrived in those December seas and added three more to the total. Making her third patrol under Ross—her previous one had been in the Aleutians—she took up the beat off the northeast coast of Honshu. On December 12 she tracked down and sank GYOKUZAN MARU's 1,970 tons. Four days later she made a double killing— SHINGO MARU, 4,740 tons, and GENZAN MARU, 5,708 tons. Including TRIGGER's sinking of TEIFUKU MARU on the 22nd, the month's total was six.

Sum total: 48 Japanese merchantmen sunk by Sub-Pac submarines on Empire patrol, July-December, 1942. Perhaps as many ships damaged and sent hobbling into harbor for costly repair. Estimated tonnage sunk: 203,000 tons.

Thousands of tons of cargo irretrievably destroyed, and hundreds of Japanese seamen irretrievably "lost at sea."

United States submarine losses in area: None.

In the light of this war effort accomplished by some 16 submarines (approximately 1,000 officers and men) a layman might logically wonder why the U.S. Navy was not ordered lock, stock and barrel to the shores of Japan. Why its entire submarine fleet and all its surface and air forces were not concentrated *en masse* to blockade and reduce the enemy's home islands. Forget the Japs stymied in Attu and Kiska—let them die on the Aleutian vine. Ignore the Solomons entirely. By-pass the Netherlands Indies and the Philippines. Assemble a great armada of submarines, warships and aircraft around Japan, and close in. If a handful of submarines shuttling back and forth from Pearl Harbor could penetrate the enemy's inner defense ring as if it were so much tissue, loiter off Tokyo Bay, photograph a Honshu horse race and chase shipping right up to the headlands—if a few boys in pressure hulls could play such havoc, why not assail Nippon with a mighty naval force and crush her in one massive embrace?

There were arm-chair and even editorial-chair strategists who made such proposals, forgetting that the submarine's singular ability to operate unseen behind enemy lines was a feature not enjoyed by surface and air craft. The undersea blockader could get in where battleships, like angels, might fear to tread.

Also there was that similarity of Japan's to an octopus—a many-armed kraken which could recoil and gather muscle in so doing—a beast which must first be weakened by attrition before cornering for a mortal thrust. And the Japanese arm extending into the Solomons was too dangerous a threat to Allied communications to ignore.

Finally, the Navy did not yet have the forces available for a mass attack on the enemy's homeland in the Pacific. Yamamoto's battle fleets remained to be dealt with. Japan's air arm was formidable. The citadel's outposts would have to fall before its bastions could be stormed—an offensive that would demand an army. And before this all-out offensive could be launched in the Pacific, there was "unfinished business" elsewhere on the Navy's agenda. The United States was engaged in a global conflict—the Navy was fighting a two-ocean war.

In the autumn of 1942 Nazi U-boats were making a fight of it in the Battle of the Atlantic. Behind the U-boat front lay Hitler's Festung Europa with its monstrous West Wall reared as a battlement against the Allied world. England was only holding on. France was prostrate under the rule of Vichy. Russia, locked in a death-grip with the German invader, was holding on in the bloody welter of Stalingrad, but the outcome was far from decided. Fascist Italy still held a club over the Mediterranean, and Nazi legions stood in North Africa.

As decided by the Allied leaders at the war's beginning, the defeat of Nazi Germany and Fascist Italy was the immediate objective. To this end, American forces were assembled in England in the autumn of 1942, others were concentrated at Hampton Roads, Virginia, and the invasion of North Africa was mounted.

Submarines of the Atlantic Command were slated to light the way in "Operation Torch."

North African Invasion—Operation Torch

Submarine Squadron Fifty was formed on September 3, 1942, at New London, Connecticut, with Captain N. S. Ives in command. It consisted of the tender BEAVER, under Commander M. N. Little, and the following submarines:

BARB	(Lieutenant Commander J. R. Waterman)
BLACKFISH	(Lieutenant Commander J. F. Davidson)
SHAD	(Lieutenant Commander E. J. MacGregor, III)
HERRING	(Lieutenant Commander R. W. Johnson)
GUNNEL	(Lieutenant Commander J. S. McCain, Jr.)
GURNARD	(Lieutenant Commander C. H. Andrews)

In late October the tender departed in convoy for U.S. Base Two, Roseneath, Scotland. With the exception of GURNARD, all submarines in the squadron proceeded for the coast of northwest Africa as part of the "Torch" movement.

One of the war's famous feats of submarining was performed on October 23 when the British submarine SERAPH landed Major General Mark W. Clark and staff on the Barbary Coast near Cherchel (about 75 miles from Algiers) to conduct secret negotiations with French General Maste. These negotiations paved the way for the invasion and brought General Giraud in as an ally.

The success of the amphibious Anglo-American landings in Morocco depended in a large degree on the weather. Arriving on station four days preceding D-day, the five submarines participating in "Operation Torch" conducted reconnaissance patrols off the northwest African coast and furnished the Allied fleet with weather information. SHAD patrolled off Mehediya, BARB off Safi, GUNNEL off Fedala, and HERRING off Casablanca, French Morocco. BLACK-FISH patrolled the coast of Senegal, off Dakar. In addition, the submarines were to act as beacons to mark the exact location of the landings which were made on November 8th. They also served as a potential intercepting force against possible enemy breakout. A British naval officer and a British radio-man were placed on each submarine to assure that communications with the British forces engaged would function without any hitch.

Unfortunately, neither the sea nor the communications set-up operated as smoothly as the submarines would have liked. Ground swells, high surf and strong tides create a problem in unpredictables along the Moroccan-Atlantic coast in the autumnal season. The swells, soaring as high as 20 feet, often prevail in fair weather and pound the beaches with crashing combers. Moving toward Spain from the Azores, a low atmospheric pressure foments a booming surf off Safi, Casablanca and Fedala, and 36 hours after a similar atmospheric depression between Bermuda and Newfoundland, the Moroccan coast may be swept by a high-sea gale.

Therefore meteorological conditions demanded careful study and vigilant watch as the Allied invasion forces advanced. The amphibious landing had to be timed with utmost care. Sudden wind or weather change could kick up a freakish surf capable of swamping the landing craft and completely extinguishing "Operation Torch." The vital need for accurate weather information from the submarines is manifest.

On November 6, heavy seas off the Moroccan coast caused Admiral Hewett, in command of the Western Naval Task Force, to consider an alternate plan for shifting the landings to the Mediterranean. Thanks to information from the submarines, and other meteorological data, the task force aerologist, Lieutenant Commander R. C. Steere, was able to predict that the high seas would moderate and the Moroccan landings would encounter better weather. On November 7 the submarines reported calm sea and a moderate ground swell. The task force advanced as planned.

The position of the submarines standing as twinkling beacons between the Moroccan shoreline and the oncoming Allied invasion fleet was not exactly comfortable. This was the first major amphibious operation of the war and every gun involved was hair-triggered. Morocco was a mystery, French reaction another unpredictable. Token resistance by the Vichy command at Casablanca was expected. But if the resistance were more than token, the French fleet lying in the harbor—battleship JEAN BART, light cruisers GLOIRE and PRIMAGUET, three flotilla leaders, six destroyers and twelve submarines—could put up a savage battle. Particularly dangerous were the twelve French submarines which might sortie and invite American and British gunners to shoot at every periscope in sight. In addition, a U-boat or two might have crept into the area. The situation had volcanic possibilities, and the U.S. submariners, maneuvering between the French coastal batteries and the guns of Task Force Thirty-four, were in something of a spot.

There were some tense individuals aboard BARB as darkness blacked out the evening of November 7th. Hallowe'en had been a week ago, but some of its atmosphere lingered in this gloom off the beaches of Safi. Tomorrow was D-Day and anything might happen tonight.

Waterman's submarine had a special mission to perform. BARB carried a group of four Army scouts under command of Army Lieutenant W. G. Duckworth. Duckworth and scouts were to disembark in a rubber boat, and paddle in to the Safi Breakwater Buoy with a radio and blinker. There they were to coach in the two assault destroyers BERNADOU and COLE, assigned to seize the harbor off Safi early the next morning.

Waterman took BARB shoreward on the surface, and at 2200 the scouts disembarked. Unfortunately the distance to the breakwater, estimated as three and one-half miles, was miscalculated, or the Army scouts miscalculated the current-and-paddle equation. At any rate, the rubber-boaters failed to reach the breakwater until six hours later, just as the firing began. Machine-gunners blazing away from shore peppered the rubber boat as the group dived overside. Luckily the beach was not far, and Duckworth and his scouts survived the incident with nothing

much worse than a hair-raising scare and a ducking.

As the naval bombardment opened up and the landings began, the submarines withdrew to relatively secure positions. However, in the Casablanca area where all hell was breaking loose and the approaches were congested with landing craft, transports and maneuvering warships, no water was overly secure for submarining.

Here communications and recognition became a life-and-death matter, and in this respect GUNNEL's submariners had a hair-raising experience. Surfacing off Fedala, McCain's submarine stood by to watch the shooting at Casablanca. Suddenly they were under the guns of a passing cruiser—so obviously under the cruiser's guns that McCain, with no chance to exchange signals, had to bellow his submarine's identity through a megaphone.

"And if those boys shoot," he shouted down the conning tower, "we'll give them a torpedo!"

Happily the megaphone carried the word to the cruiser's bridge and GUNNEL was recognized. A close call! It seemed the British Admiralty had changed the recognition signals during the night, and the beacon submarines were not advised of the switch!

D-Day provided some other close calls for the beacon submarines. Flying in from the sea, an Army bomber let fly at GUNNEL, and later she was strafed by an American fighter plane. McCain took her down and kept her down for the rest of the day.

SHAD, BARB and HERRING also had their troubles. Mainly these were located in the engines which powered the Squadron Five submarines. Frequent breakdowns developed as the submarines, after the D-Day bombardment, moved to positions on a line between Cape Sim and Madeira. For the next three days they patrolled this line on the lookout for Vichy French forces which might come north from Dakar. BLACKFISH, off Dakar, conducted a patrol in that strategic area during this time.

On November 8, HERRING (Lieutenant Commander Johnson) sank a 5,750-ton French merchantman off Casablanca. On the following day, BLACKFISH (Lieutenant Commander Davidson) probably damaged another Frenchman off Point Alamadies.

Spelling doom for Rommel's Afrika Korps, General Patton's troopers had a firm foothold on the beachheads of Morocco when the Squadron Fifty submarines were ordered to Roseneath, Scotland. Off the coast of Spain—a dangerous area—GUNNEL's engines expired, leaving her with low batteries and nothing but a Winton "dinky" engine for surface propulsion. While she was crawling along the surface at 5 knots, a British escort vessel picked her up and escorted her into Falmouth.

The other Squadron Fifty submarines proceeded to Base Two, Roseneath. Released by Commander Task Force Thirty-four, Submarine Squadron Commander Captain Ives, who was in the AUGUSTA during the "Torch" strike, reported to Commander U.S. Naval Forces in Europe (Admiral H. R. Stark) for duty. All units of SubRon Fifty were assigned to duty under British Admiral Sir Max Horton, Flag Officer (Submarines), Admiralty. This assignment of the submarines to the British permitted the Royal Navy to shift a number of units from the Atlantic to the Mediterranean at a time when warships were urgently needed for the African Campaign.

The Squadron Fifty submarines were ordered to patrol areas in the Bay of Biscay. GURNARD (Lieutenant Commander Andrews) made the first patrol early in December. Located close to the Spanish coast, the Biscay areas covered shipping lanes to Bilbao, Vigo, Gijon and El Ferrol—backdoor Spanish ports which Franco was holding wide open to the Nazis. Patrolling in the waters designated, the U.S. submarines were in position to intercept this Axis ship traffic. British air patrols covered the sea lanes farther out and acted as "spotters" for the submarines. The submarine patrol directive stated the primary mission was to "attack and destroy enemy blockade runners after making positive identification."

By year's end the Biscay Bay operation was a going concern. That Franco was working hand-in-glove with Hitler became plainly apparent to the submariners who saw the evidence through their periscopes.

According to Submarine Squadron Commander Captain Ives: *"As many as six hundred contacts, of which two hundred were vessels of over one thousand tons, were made by a single submarine during one patrol. There was obvious violation of neutrality by Spain in permitting German air patrols and A/S vessels to operate in her territorial waters. This use of the Spanish flag was common, as might be expected. Positive identification was difficult for the commanding officers, as both identification data and intelligence of neutral movements were lacking or late."*

Throughout the winter of 1942-1943, SubRon Fifty continued to operate in the Biscay area. During the nine patrols conducted at that time in those waters, SHAD (Lieutenant Commander MacGregor) sank a 700-ton ore barge, probably sank a small towing vessel and damaged a 1,200-ton destroyer escort. BLACKFISH sank a 1,000-ton anti-submarine vessel, after Davidson and crew received a ferocious "going over" from two disguised German trawlers. And HERRING (Lieutenant Johnson) encountered and probably sank a 517-ton U-boat.

Thus in the Atlantic as well as the Pacific the U.S. Submarine Force was carrying the torch.

End of 1942

The autumn calendar has shed its leaves and the first long year of war draws to a close.

Off the coasts of Imperial Japan, blockading submarines plough through the wintry seas. Other submarines of the Central Pacific Force are patrolling off lower China and Formosa, roaming in the Carolines, Gilberts and Marshalls, and keeping a watch on Palau.

Far to the north in the Arctic cauldron of the Aleutians, dogged S-boats from Dutch Harbor beat the storm-thrashed approaches to Attu and Kiska, and range as far as the northern Kuriles.

In the South Seas, below the equator, the submarine war pitches up, crescendo, as the enemy, driven from the central Solomons, turns at Bougainville to claw at his pursuers, and rushes reinforcements from the Bismarcks, from Truk, from Palau. Here the Task Force Forty-two submarines from Brisbane are in the battle's epicenter and on its circumference, lashing at the enemy's retreating "Tokyo Express," harrying his convoys to Bougainville, patrolling off his bases in the Bismarck Archipelago.

Off New Guinea the six submarines supporting MacArthur's offensive hack at the enemy's naval forces and convoys in that area.

SoWesPac submarines from Fremantle and Albany are in action as far west as the South China Sea, hunting merchantmen off Siam, transports off the Philippines, tankers off Borneo and Java.

In mid-December three submarines were performing a new type of special mission. Strung out in a trans-oceanic line, TRITON (Lieutenant Commander Kirkpatrick), FINBACK (Lieutenant Commander Hull) and PIKE (Lieutenant Commander New) were stationed along the route between Midway and Wake Island. There they marked the way for a Liberator strike at Wake. Mission of the submarines was to aid the aerial navigators by "homing" them on the target with radio information if so requested by the planes. Maintaining a lookout, they were to rescue the crews of any planes forced down at sea. No rescues were called for. (But submariners will rescue many an aviator before war's end.)

The submariners watch the departure of 1942 without regret. It has been a bitter year—a year of smarting disappointments, frustrating shortages, desperate makeshifts—of one-sided battles against long odds—of galling retreats in which the Manila veterans, falling back from the Philippines and Netherlands East Indies to Australia, perhaps suffered most.

But the school of hard knocks issues a *cum laude* diploma—its graduate submariners have learned much, and profited thereby. Confidence has been gained in the fighting and staying qualities of the submarine. New tactics have been developed to exploit those qualities. The enemy's measure has been taken, and the submariners have "learned their own strength."

Pioneering, they have invaded the home waters of the invader—established a combat "frontier" along Japan's coastline. They have explored the enemy's island outposts and discovered the keys to his secret island bases. They have successfully conducted scores of special missions, engaged in difficult fleet operations, and successfully carried on the undersea war through the long and gruelling Aleutian and Guadalcanal campaigns. In these manifold operations they have proved their versatility as commerce raiders, vedettes, scouts, blockade-runners and sea fighters capable of tackling the enemy's toughest warships.

Material improvements are coming in. Most important of the innovations, the two radars have been tested under battle conditions and found satisfactory. More than satisfactory, the SJ, now a "must," is changing tactical concepts in revolutionary fashion.

With or without benefit of radar, the day-periscope, night-periscope, and night-surface attacks are now established routines, the basic maneuvers becoming as standardized as the opening moves of chess.

Established also as routines are the submarine training programs, the programs for rotating submarines between various bases for overhaul or replacement, and the program for personnel recuperation providing rest and recreation for submarine crews between patrols.

Thus, in this year of trial, all has not been error—even the deplorable shortcomings of the defective Mark 14 have been partially rectified. And while it still seems as long a way to Tokyo as to Tipperary, submarines are getting there. The submarine repair base at Midway is a step in the right direction. A fueling station set up at Johnson Island in late November is another right step, in the direction of the Southwest Pacific.

The war panorama is not discouraging. The enemy has been decisively defeated at Midway, dead-stopped in the Aleutians, hurled back in the Solomons. The Alaska-Midway-Australia defense line has solidified. The Empire blockade is under way and the submarine war of attrition is shifting into high gear.

Looking back on 13 months of pitch-battle warfare, the submariners can take pride in their accomplishments. They have sunk scores of enemy merchant ships and damaged dozens more. Trading blows with the Imperial Navy, they have sunk a heavy cruiser, a light cruiser, six submarines, four destroyers and numerous auxiliaries, plus a damaged aircraft carrier.

Three fleet-type submarines—SEALION, SHARK and PERCH—and two S-boats have been lost in the Southwest Pacific. GRUNION and S-27 have been lost in the Aleutians, and S-26 off Panama. In the Philippines, the tender CANOPUS is a memory.

But not a single U.S. submarine has been lost in Central Pacific waters. Meantime, new-construction submarines from the States have been arriving in Pearl Harbor with almost week-in week-out regularity —a total of 37 since the war's December 1941 outbreak. In addition, three new tenders—GRIFFIN, FULTON and SPERRY—have arrived to ease the burden borne by the veterans PELIAS, HOLLAND and OTUS.

As the year ends, ComSubPac has 51 fleet-type submarines and eight S-boats under his operational control. Eight fleet-type submarines are operating out of Fremantle. The Brisbane task force, composed of "loans," remains a variable figure due to the constant shifting of its units and interplay of commands, but it contains the remainder of the 80 U.S. submarines now fighting in the Pacific.

Never able to compete with American construction yards, Japanese shipyards are slave-laboring to fill the gaps blown in the Emperor's merchant and naval fleets. In comparison with the eight U.S. submarines lost in the Pacific (from all causes), Japanese submarine losses since the war's beginning (exclusive of the midgets lost at Pearl Harbor) add up to 22. Almost three times the American figure!

Japanese submarine replacements—a total of 20— are two short of the number lost.

In major combat craft losses (exclusive of submarines) the U.S. Navy and Imperial Navy losses are an even 37. But United States replacements in this category are far ahead of the Japanese—138 to 20.

However, it is the enemy's merchant-ship losses that cause him greatest concern as he summarizes the war's first year. For he concedes the American superiority in naval building, but trusts the far-flung reaches of his conquered outer Empire to hold against assault—so long as its fortified island bases and outlying strongholds remain supplied. Crux of the logistics problem is the lasting power of his merchant marine. And between January 1 and December 31, 1942, United States submarines alone have sunk a total of 147 Japanese vessels (including such naval auxiliaries as aircraft ferries, ex-gunboats and patrol craft) of over 500 tons.

187

These figures loom as a shadow over Japan—a shadow in the shape of things to come.

As the Old Year moves out, making way for 1943, United States Submarine Forces in the Pacific are ready for an all-out offensive. The days of testing are over. The days of exploratory reconnaissance and pioneering are ended. The submariners are now in waters they know.

Given the tools—in particular, a reliable torpedo—they will do the job!

NEW SUBMARINES COMMISSIONED IN 1942

NAME	FIRST COMMANDING OFFICER
BUILT AT ELECTRIC BOAT COMPANY	
GREENLING	*Lt. Comdr. H. C. Bruton*
GROUPER	*Lt. Comdr. C. E. Duke*
GROWLER	*Lt. Comdr. H. W. Gilmore*
GRUNION	*Lt. Comdr. M. L. Abele*
GUARDFISH	*Lt. Comdr. T. B. Klakring*
ALBACORE	*Lt. Comdr. R. C. Lake*
AMBERJACK	*Lt. Comdr. J. A. Bole, Jr.*
BARB	*Lt. Comdr. J. R. Waterman*
BLACKFISH	*Lt. Comdr. J. F. Davidson*
BUILT AT PORTSMOUTH NAVY YARD	
DRUM	*Lt. Comdr. R. H. Rice*
FLYINGFISH	*Lt. Comdr. G. R. Donaho*
FINBACK	*Lt. Comdr. J. L. Hull*
HADDOCK	*Lt. Comdr. A. H. Taylor*
HALIBUT	*Lt. Comdr. P. H. Ross*
HERRING	*Lt. Comdr. R. W. Johnson*
KINGFISH	*Lt. Comdr. V. L. Lowrance*
SHAD	*Lt. Comdr. E. J. MacGregor*
BUILT AT MARE ISLAND NAVY YARD	
SILVERSIDES	*Lt. Comdr. C. C. Burlingame*
TRIGGER	*Lt. Comdr. J. H. Lewis*

NAME	FIRST COMMANDING OFFICER
WAHOO	*Lt. Comdr. M. G. Kennedy*
WHALE	*Lt. Comdr. J. B. Azer*
BUILT AT ELECTRIC BOAT COMPANY	
GUNNEL	*Lt. Comdr. J. S. McCain, Jr.*
GURNARD	*Lt. Comdr. C. H. Andrews*
HADDO	*Lt. Comdr. W. A. Lent*
HAKE	*Lt. Comdr. J. C. Broach*
HARDER	*Lt. Comdr. S. D. Dealey*
HOE	*Lt. Comdr. E. C. Folger, Jr.*
BUILT AT MANITOWOC SHIPBUILDING CO.	
PETO	*Lt. Comdr. W. T. Nelson*
RUNNER	*Comdr. F. W. Fenno, Jr.*
SAWFISH	*Lt. Comdr. E. T. Sands*
BUILT AT PORTSMOUTH NAVY YARD	
SCAMP	*Lt. Comdr. W. G. Ebert*
SCORPION	*Lt. Comdr. W. N. Wylie*
SNOOK	*Lt. Comdr. C. O. Triebel*
BUILT AT MARE ISLAND NAVY YARD	
SUNFISH	*Lt. Comdr. R. W. Peterson*
TUNNY	*Lt. Comdr. E. W. Grenfell*

PART III

ALL-OUT ATTRITION

(1943)

Swift flame—then shipwrecks only
Beach in the ruined light;
Above them reach up lonely
The headlands of the night.
RIDGELY TORRENCE

CHAPTER 16

BATTLE BENEATH THE SOUTH SEAS

Wrestler vs. Judo Expert

One of the livelier debates which entertained sports editors in the placid pre-war era concerned the relative merits of wrestling and jiujitsu. Pit a headlock champion against a Japanese judo expert, and who would conquer? Exponents of the Western sport predicted certain defeat for the Oriental. Others averred the wrestler would be swiftly mastered.

In January 1943 a cartoonist might have pictured the Pacific struggle as such a match. Japan, the judo expert, agile, guileful, highly skilled in the twists, dodges and jabs of jiujitsu, locked in mortal combat with tall Uncle Sam, sinewy athlete in Navy tights.

The match was staged in the South Seas arena of the Pacific War Theater. On the sidelines a bizarre and bewildered audience of Melanesian fuzzy-wuzzies—Solomons aborigines, New Guinea natives, Trobriand Islanders.

This illustration would be apt in several respects. Not only would it depict something of the character of the fighting—the tactics and strategy involved—but the portrayal of the Jap as a squat, bandy-legged figure in a breech-clout, and Uncle Sam, bared to the waist in the togs of a Navy grappler, aptly illustrates the weight, size and make-up of the opposing forces that battled it out in the opening weeks of 1943 in the Bougainville-Bismarck-New Guinea area.

Wrestling is essentially an offensive endeavor. Judo is defined as a "Japanese science of mental and physical development, including the art of self-defense (jiujitsu) in which one's opponent is compelled to use his strength to his own disadvantage." Thrown back from Guadalcanal to Bougainville, the Jap wheeled on the defensive, and with what might be called jiujitsu tactics—break, twist and savage counter-thrust—strove to block the U.S. Navy's advance. American strategy was to keep up offensive pressure and wear the enemy down. Sew a pair of gold dolphins on Uncle Sam's tights, and the analogous figure is complete. The Navy wrestler who bore the brunt at this time was a submariner.

On January 1, 1943, Japan had an estimated 500,000 gross tons of merchant shipping over and above the minimum requirement necessary to maintain the Empire's war economy. Despite losses sustained in the previous year, the enemy was able to prosecute the war with little dimunition in front-line supply. On the home front, Papa and Mama Moto were standing in line for ration tickets. But the merchant fleet was still well organized. No vital shortages faced the industrial machine as yet (although Japanese Imperial Headquarters was worried about oil). And as yet there was nothing to prevent the allocation of tonnages necessary for the fortification of the Mandate bases and the supply of strategic areas. In brief, the Japanese were still able to handle the logistics problem.

They handled it by moving their cargoes in relatively small convoys—four or five ships to a convoy with from one to four DD or DE escorts. As at the war's beginning, these convoys traveled close inshore wherever possible, and ran from port to port down through the island archipelagoes, whenever practicable making long runs at night.

In the Southwest Pacific much of the shipping

which supplied Bougainville in the upper Solomons and the enemy's bases in the Bismarcks and New Guinea came east from Manila. In the Philippines it was normally routed north of Mindoro, through the Visayan Sea, out through San Bernardino Strait, or south *via* passes east of Cebu and out through Surigao. Shipping farther south frequently took the shallow water east of Palawan, crossed the Celebes Sea to transit the passes south of Sangi Island, and from there proceeded to the Bismarcks, New Guinea or the Solomons. At Palau and Truk important convoys might pick up heavy surface escorts for protection going southward.

In the New Guinea-Bismarck-Solomons area convoy units were often dispersed to travel under strong air cover or powerful individual escort. Cargoes were frequently transshipped from major bases in barges and small coastal craft which moved beetle-like along the shoreline, usually at night. To the Japanese the safe arrival of their southbound convoy trains and the ultimate disposal of oil, munitions and other war supplies to garrisons on the front were of paramount importance. The importance of this traffic was equally clear, in reverse English, to the Allied forces in the Southwest Pacific. It was up to the Allies to break up this transportation system. Land-based aircraft, striking from Guadalcanal and Allied bases in eastern New Guinea, handled some of the job. But essentially it was a naval operation, squarely up to the United States Navy.

New Year's Day, 1943, the United States Navy was Herculean compared to the broken force which faced the Axis enemy on the New Year of the war's beginning. Four new battleships, a new aircraft carrier, 11 escort carriers, 9 light cruisers, 84 destroyers and the aforementioned 37 submarines had added massive muscles to the shoulders of the USN. In addition, four of the battleships damaged at Pearl Harbor were repaired and back in service, and the fleet air arm had been built up to a force of some 5,000 planes.

However, the Battle of the Atlantic engaged a large number of the newly launched warships. Pacific operations would therefore remain limited throughout the first half of 1943. A spring drive to expel the Japs from the Aleutians was on the agenda. Meantime, plans called for the consolidation of the Guadalcanal foothold in the Solomons, a campaign to cut the enemy's South Sea supply lines, and continuance of the attrition war against his merchant fleet.

Thus, with the winning of Guadalcanal, the immediate Pacific war effort was centered in the South Seas. The major job was Navy's. But the surface Navy would not engage in a major offensive until late June when an amphibious drive to take Rendova Island was scheduled for launching. The war of attrition, featuring the campaign to cut down the enemy's South Sea supply, was prosecuted largely by U.S. submarines.

Hence the figure of Uncle Sam in the Southwest Pacific Theater as a wrestler in Navy tights—from chin-whiskers to champion's belt, a submariner. From January to June 1943, during one of those "lulls" referred to by Admiral Nimitz, the submarines kept on going. And they continued to go in the summer, autumn and remaining months of the year.

For the young men wearing the dolphins there was no cessation of patrols, no respite in the undersea war. Week in, week out, the submariners fought the Battle of the South Seas against the Jap. At stake were Japan's forward bases—the chief prize, Rabaul, a gateway to the Philippines. Defending Rabaul, the enemy employed every stratagem at his command.

To counter the Jap's jiujitsu, Uncle Sam, Submariner, developed some shrewd stratagems of his own. One of these, a maneuver which came to be known as the "end-around," was the tactical innovation of 1943. The Jap hit back, striking painful blows.

It was a tough fight with no holds barred.

Nautilus Celebrates New Year's

At that midnight moment when 1942 passed into history, Guadalcanal land operations were nearing a conclusion, and Allied surface and air forces were still hard on the heels of the retreating enemy. Submarines were laying for the convoys retiring from Guadalcanal. At Bougainville the Japanese Command was assembling all available reinforcements to make a stand. In Tokyo the glib news-casters were doubtless resorting to the double talk of propaganda—that device so patently employed to obscure an issue or sugar-coat a bitter pill of truth. "Our forces have just completed a victorious, strategic withdrawal. Defeating the enemy on every hand, we have triumphantly retired to a previously prepared position."

At this hour the submarine GRAYBACK was on her way to Munda Bar off New Georgia where she was to play beacon-ship for the task force due to bombard Munda airfield. Other Brisbane-based submarines were engaged in performing those special missions which were a prominent feature of the submarine effort in this area. Coast watchers to be transported—spies to be carried to enemy beaches—airmen to be rescued from hostile jungles—refugees to be evacuated. Such missions had become commonplace to the submariners. Excursions to be accomplished between shots in the constant night-and-day war of attrition.

Typical was the one performed by NAUTILUS in the opening hours of the year. Ordered to Bougainville to rescue 29 refugees, the now-famous submarine captained by Lieutenant Commander Brockman crept into the very heart of the enemy's upper-Solomons territory on New Year's Eve to evacuate these imperiled civilians.

"My first greeting to these people when they came aboard," Brockman related, "was Happy New Year!"

To the fourteen nuns, three married women, three children and nine men who comprised the refugee party, NAUTILUS' arrival came as a deliverance from the jaws of a concentration camp.

"On the way to Australia we taught some of the passengers how to play the old Navy games of cribbage and acey-deucey. After that, their one fear seemed to be they might be unable to buy cribbage boards when they reached Australia."

The baby of the party, aged three, was one of the youngest individuals ever to cruise the ocean at a depth of 150 feet—an adventure unmatched by anything in fiction, including the fantastical "Swiss Family Robinson."

The voyage to Australia was accomplished without mishap. The submariners who had transported Carlson's Raiders were not to be dismayed by a curly-haired toddler.

Loss of Argonaut

NAUTILUS made her run through deadly dangerous waters. Driven from Guadalcanal, the enemy bent every effort to rush fresh forces into the upper Solomons while covering the withdrawal of his battered Guadalcanal garrison. Japanese planes roamed the skies from New Guinea to Bougainville on the lookout for periscope "feathers" or tell-tale oil slicks. Convoys traveled under heavy escort, powerfully armed DD's and alert DE's ready to launch their depth charges at the first alarm. It was a perilous area for Jap convoys—equally perilous for U.S. submarines.

Deep within this area bored ARGONAUT, hunting the enemy in the vicinity of Rabaul at the time her sister ship and former team-mate, NAUTILUS, was completing the dangerous run from Bougainville. ARGONAUT was making her third war patrol—her second under Lieutenant Commander J. R. Pierce, veteran of the Aleutian campaign.

On August 10, ARGONAUT made contact with a Japanese convoy, lat. 05-15 S., long. 153-50 E. The convoy—five vessels escorted by three destroyers—was sighted some time later by a U.S. Army plane which was returning with empty bomb racks to its base. This aerial observer saw one of the destroyers hit by a torpedo—flash!—and immediately the two other DD's raced across the water, releasing depth charges.

As the furious barrage blasted the surface, a submarine's bow broke water and remained thrust above the waves at a steep up-angle. The plane could only watch helplessly as the destroyers circled, pumping shells into their obviously disabled foe. After several smashing hits, the submarine was gone from view. With this grim story the plane returned to base.

In the week that followed, all efforts to contact ARGONAUT by radio proved fruitless. To the Submarine Command it was evident that she had gone down with all hands in this pitched battle. Japanese records corroborated the evidence, reporting a submarine sunk between Lae and Rabaul on January 10, 1943, by a depth-charge attack followed by artillery fire on the damaged target.

ARGONAUT's loss was a hard blow to the Submarine Force, and indicative of the desperate fighting to come. In the ensuing season it was to suffer the severest casualties it had yet endured in the war.

Searaven Develops a New Tactic

In the second week of January 1943, SEARAVEN was patrolling off Palau, keeping a watch on the approaches to Toagel Mlungui Passage—that recently disclosed "secret door" for Japanese shipping in the Pelews.

Both the submarine and her skipper, Commander Hiram Cassedy, were veterans from Manila—old hands at this deep-sea game of hide-and-seek. SEARAVEN, making her sixth war patrol (her fourth under Cassedy), had been through her share—perhaps more than her share—of action. Her crew could remember their second patrol under Lieutenant Commander T. C. Aylward, when the submarine crawled into Fremantle after 43 days at sea on short rations, and made port with little more than a spoonful of coffee in the larder. Throughout 1942 the submarine had experienced the usual torpedo troubles, hazardous missions and "goings over." On the hunt for targets it had been her luck to prowl a number of those areas so tersely described by submariners as "unproductive." Cassedy had attacked when opportunity presented, fired long shots and short shots, and scored many hits. But the RAVEN had yet to score a confirmed sinking (at least one that would show on the post-war record). Such were the shortcomings of the Mark 14 torpedo and the hit-or-miss workings of chance.

Now, on station off Toagel Mlungui—after the successful accomplishment of a mission ended on December 30, when she landed seven agents and a British officer on Ceram Island—SEARAVEN's luck was to change. The change came on the morning of January 13th.

About 0900, when the submarine was patrolling submerged, a periscope sweep picked up several columns of smoke to the southeast, distance about 10 miles. Cassedy attempted to close, but was unable to get much nearer than 7,000 yards. He decided to trail submerged and ascertain the convoy's base course and speed. The chase was on.

By noon Cassedy had figured out that the convoy was on base course 300° and making a speed of 9 to 10 knots. It was out of the question for SEARAVEN to surface and chase during daylight with the convoy in sight. Cassedy therefore held the submarine submerged until dusk. He now calculated the convoy would be 54 miles ahead, and given good luck he could overtake it by morning.

On the surface, SEARAVEN got underway at three-engine speed with the fourth engine charging batteries. Mile after mile the submarine ran steadily through the night. By 0200 the next morning Cassedy reckoned he was again within ten miles of the convoy. He changed course six degrees to the right of the convoy's estimated base course, intending to pass to starboard. Two hours later he figured SEARAVEN was abeam, and came back to the base course of 300°. All this was done on dead reckoning. SEARAVEN was not equipped with search radar, and nothing had been sighted since the previous afternoon.

And at dawn nothing was in sight. However, Cassedy estimated that the convoy was bearing 161°, distance about 15 miles. He brought SEARAVEN to a normal approach course based on that assumption. An hour later the convoy was still nowhere in sight. Cassedy slowed to 12 knots and changed course to run for the 8-knot position circle of the Palau-Surigao route. If contact had not been made by the time SEARAVEN reached that point, Cassedy decided he would make a try at the 10-knot position circle. Then, at 0740 smoke was sighted bearing 160°, distance 15 miles.

SEARAVEN built up speed to 16 knots and ran for position ahead. At 0907, with the convoy 15 miles away, Cassedy took her down to commence a submerged approach. Two hours later SEARAVEN was in attack position with her torpedo tubes trained on a large cargo ship (AK).

This all-night, surface pursuit, culminating in an attack made from a position ahead of the convoy, was not an original tactic. Early in 1942 a number of submarine captains had employed this stratagem of running ahead of a target at night to dive on the target's projected route and launch a morning attack.

The maneuver invalidated a tenet of peacetime training which held that a submerged approach which failed to close the target's track was an opportunity irretrievably lost. The tenet holds good for high-speed targets—task forces which move through submarine danger zones at top speed and may not be overtaken. Pre-war training had concentrated on attacks against such targets. But the slow-speed Japanese convoy presented the submarines with a different tactical set-up. To the captains it was soon apparent that when contact was made on a train of slow merchantmen, it was possible to make a surface run to a position ahead—a point on the track where the target might be "ambushed" and the submarine enjoyed positional advantage.

At the start of the war, submarines on patrol had remained submerged during the day. At night, operating without radar, they were pretty much "in the dark." Contacts were made at close range and opportunities for maneuver were limited. Surface running was particularly hazardous in the Philippines, the East Indies, and in the Solomons-Bismarck area where Japanese aircraft were an omnipresent threat. But the open sea gave the submariners an opportunity to try surface runs around slow-moving targets. The maneuver was in the experimental stage at the time Cassedy put SEARAVEN through its paces.

Attempted at night without radar the tactic was comparable to a fast game of blind-man's buff. It demanded astute guesswork as well as expert mathematical calculating. Cassedy was able to meet both requisites.

At 1132 he opened fire at the freighter—the largest vessel in the convoy. Three shots were fired at the AK, and one at an anti-submarine vessel in line with the target. Timed explosions boomed in SEARAVEN's sound gear as she went deep. There followed the electronic pandemonium caused by the crumpling of steel plates and machinery deep under the sea.

Forty minutes later SEARAVEN returned to periscope depth. Nothing in sight but an anti-submarine vessel which appeared to be picking up survivors. The victim, later identified, was SHIRAHA MARU, 5,693-ton cargo carrier. In sinking this vessel Cassedy provided the submarine forces with a peerless demonstration of that new tactic, soon to be perfected with the benefit of radar—the "end around."

Silversides Has an Iron Lining

Standing watch on the sixth day after the removal of his vermiform appendix, George Platter, Fireman 3, had recovered from his appendectomy with greater celerity than some of those who presided over the operation. Briefly noted in a previous chapter, the SILVERSIDES appendicitis case occurred on a patrol that was memorable for a number of emergencies. The patrol is worthy of elaboration as it portrays some of the hazards indigenous to submarining and exemplifies the grit and acumen with which such adversities were overcome.

To conduct her fourth war patrol, SILVERSIDES had put out from Brisbane on December 17, 1942. She was cruising off the coast of Bougainville on the 22nd when the appendicitis crisis arose. By anyone acquainted with the cutting of an abdominal incision and the slow, tedious process of shearing loose an appendix which has adhered to the intestine in six places, the Platter operation will be appreciated.

Altogether the appendectomy, performed on the night before Christmas Eve, took about five hours. The submarine, running submerged, all but used up the batteries which had been only partially charged at the time of diving. At 0400, advised the operation was over, Commander Burlingame brought SILVERSIDES to the surface. Battery charge was imperative, and it had to be accomplished before daybreak.

The submarine's conning tower was hardly out of water when it was spotted by a Japanese destroyer. The DD flashed a signal which Burlingame did not bother to acknowledge, and SILVERSIDES had a fracas on her hands. Burlingame wanted to run for it on the surface. But the destroyer came loping up astern at overhauling speed.

Burlingame fired two at this gray menace, praying for luck as the torpedoes left the stern tubes. The prayer was filed somewhere, perhaps in a far-distant Bureau. The first torpedo seemed to pass directly in front of the destroyer's bow, but it failed to explode. The second exploded right in line with the DD's bow-wave—a premature.

"Take her down!"

Alarm blaring, SILVERSIDES burrowed under. She was down to about 150 feet and going deeper when the enemy passed overhead. Depth charges thrashed the surrounding sea. The DD circled about for a time, then drew off to a distance of six or seven miles. Having won this round of hide-and-seek, Burlingame gave the order to secure from battle stations, and all hands except the duty watch turned in. "Hitting the sack" was a relief. With the exception of Fireman Platter, dreaming in his bunk, the entire ship's company had not slept for 40 hours.

The night had been somewhat nerve-wracking for Pharmacist's Mate Thomas Moore, Chief Radioman A. H. Stegall, Lieutenant Roy Davenport and others who had participated in the Platter operation. But its events were no more than a prologue to the episodes of a serial. The crew had hardly relaxed on the horizontal when thunder shook the submarine by the scruff and all hands were thrown off balance by a 30° angle on the boat. Weary men piled out of their bunks to grope about in confusion. The deck was covered with powdered glass, and some of the crew were bleeding from cuts. Someone said the submarine had been bombed by a plane. Then the bell was clanging the summons to battle stations. In the conning tower the radioman got the story. SILVERSIDES had surfaced after a long wait, only to find the DD still there. A Jap plane winged out to join the hunting destroyer, and the airmen spied the submarine's periscope. Three bombs had come down. The blasting had snapped the periscope and broken the pins in the bow planes. When the diving officer ordered, "Flood negative! Take her down!" the bow planes had locked on hard dive. SILVERSIDES went down like a bobsled on an Olympic slide and kept on going. The bombing, incidentally, had tumbled George Platter out of his bunk.

"The only amusing thing about any of it," a man said in reminiscence, "was one of the junior officers who ran to the forward torpedo room and asked Chief Torpedoman Andy Smiley to do something about those bow planes. Smiley said he was doing all he could—he was praying."

They finally managed to level her off at a depth just this side of destruction. The Jap destroyer "fooled around" for a time, dropping a depth charge here and there while SILVERSIDES played possum. On Christmas Eve SILVERSIDES reached the surface where the air was breathable and the engines could charge the batteries. There was barely enough juice in the cells to make the grade. Some of the human batteries aboard were also a little low at this time.

But there was George Platter standing watch six days later—testimony to the hardihood of "black gang" members and an inspiration to firemen of the future. And he was there at his battle station on January 18, three weeks after that, when SILVERSIDES, patrolling off Truk, picked up a likely target and stalked into action.

The target, a big tanker, was loaded to the Plimsoll mark, zigzagging in bright moonlight with a patrol boat pacing alongside. Burlingame drove SILVERSIDES forward at best surface speed to head her off. Then, ordering the submarine to periscope depth, he directed a submerged approach which brought the tanker within firing range. The bow tubes were ready. Everything clicked in the T.D.C. Burlingame snapped the order, and the firing officer, Lieutenant Tom Keegan, pressed the key.

Through the periscope Burlingame saw a blast at the tanker's bow—a geysering burst of white spray in the moonlight. Torpedo No. 2 hit amidships. A tower of black smoke reared up from the tanker's deck and loomed against the night sky. Crimson vines of flame climbed the smoky battlement, and then the fires of Vesuvius burst from the tanker's holds.

As the patrol boat raced out, savage as an angered watchdog, SILVERSIDES went deep. Sound heard the tanker crackling and breaking up beneath the sea like a crushed bushel basket. At war's end she was identified as TOEI MARU, 10,023 tons.

SILVERSIDES remained submerged throughout the following day. In the forenoon a Zero float plane drifted over and dropped a bomb, apparently on the off-chance of hitting something. After surfacing that evening the submariners understood the Zero's maneuver. An oil tank had been damaged and the tell-tale leakage left a slick on the ocean's surface. The enemy had spied this oil slick and sent the Zero out to investigate.

The leak was immediately reported to Chief Motor Machinist's Mate Theodore Duncan. Duncan contrived repairs, but this damage control was no sooner accomplished than another emergency developed. After closure, the valve to the damaged oil tank started a leak. The dribble soaked into the terminal connection of the Number One main generator. The resulting "short" sent a spark crackling from the positive to the negative terminal. The overload tripped out the generator, but not before the bakelite block took fire.

A shout of alarm brought three men plunging into the engine room with fire extinguishers. Roy Riser, MotorMac 1, was spraying the burning block when the hose of his extinguisher broke and a spurt of carbon dioxide gas struck him in the face. Momentarily asphyxiated, Riser crumpled to the deck.

The fire was finally smothered, but the bakelite block was a ruin, and the flames had damaged the main battery cables near the terminal. Arthur Clark, Electrician's Mate 1, and Howard Calver, EM2, got to work on this repair job. Before the task was completed, a bakelite switch in the maneuvering room was found burning. Calvin Lloyd, Electrician's Mate 2, on watch in the compartment, put in a hurry call for First Class Electrician's Mate Gutzmer. After cutting down the power load, Gutzmer called Ensign Donald Finch, the electrical officer, and Lieutenant John Biena, the engineer.

Finch, who had been promoted from chief electrician's mate to ensign after SILVERSIDES' previous patrol, snapped an order to stop the engines. A set of cables was run from the main supply panel to another switch. The submarine got once more under

way, but she could operate only three engines until new cables were installed. As they feverishly worked to fashion a set of cables from portable wire, Gutzmer and Clark were probably wondering what would have happened if the electrical fire had occurred while they were under attack.

But later that night everything was going smoothly as SILVERSIDES continued her nocturnal cruising. Burlingame and company relaxed. Not that submariners on war patrol in waters off an enemy base the size of Truk could devote much time to acey-deucey, but—consternation! Here was another joker in the cards for SILVERSIDES.

This time it was the main induction valve slamming shut and choking off the air supply to the engines. Deprived of oxygen, the big Fairbanks-Morse Diesels coughed and slowed. An alert watch stopped the panting engines.

The immediate problem was to ascertain the cause for the induction valve's malfunctioning. Breakfast-food manufacturers would be interested. SILVERSIDES' main induction-line valve was located at the after end of the galley. There also was the trouble located. The trouble was a box of cereal which had tumbled from a stack and lodged in the valve's hydraulic operating mechanism.

It seemed that anything could happen aboard a submarine. Some time later Lieutenant Davenport on the bridge saw a chunk of metal lying on SILVERSIDES' foredeck. A man was sent forward to pick up the metal shard. Davenport thought it a fragment from a depth charge. It turned out to be a fragment of a Mark 14 torpedo—a six-pound wedge of jagged steel, flung some three-quarters of a mile to SILVERSIDES' foredeck the previous evening when she torpedoed the big tanker.

The crew was still discussing this "made in America" meteorite when SILVERSIDES, moving southward in early morning, ran into a column of three enemy destroyers. Burlingame ordered periscope depth. The DD's disappeared over the horizon. SILVERSIDES surfaced and proceeded on a sea of undulating glass. Sunrise flamed in the east, and then tendrils of smoke appeared in the distance. Tips of merchantman masts came into view. A convoy!

Daylight attack was too risky—in this flat water a one-eyed lookout could spot a periscope feather. Sending SILVERSIDES on a tangent, Burlingame let the masts go over the horizon, then cautiously paralleled the convoy's course, following the smoke.

Some seven miles apart, submarine and convoy cruised through the heat of an equatorial morning. By midday SILVERSIDES was leading, and she maintained the lead through the afternoon. At sundown

196

Burlingame took her under to periscope depth, and closed on the target's track. At moonrise SILVERSIDES was lying beneath the sea, her scope trained on the advancing file of merchantmen.

Here is another example of the end-around tactic as performed by the submarine without radar. And SILVERSIDES put on a flawless performance. In yellow moonlight the ships came on like a procession of elephants, trunk-to-tail. SILVERSIDES had only to wait for the parade. The set-up would have been too easy had not a patrol boat suddenly picked up the submarine's screws and dashed inquisitively forward. The pachydermline of freighters broke up as each vessel wheeled on an oblique zig.

A periscope could not have found a prettier picture. Star-spangled sky. Placid sea. And down a path of moonlight a series of targets overlapping.

Burlingame opened fire, shooting to hit all ships in the convoy. Six in succession, the torpedoes could not miss. Lowering the periscope, the skipper sent SILVERSIDES deep. Five timed explosions shook the submarine. There was no sixth.

For the next half-hour the submariners listened to the racket of sinking vessels. Only "probables" could be reported because ComSubPac was reluctant to credit sinkings without eye-witness verification, and Burlingame wisely refused the hazard of thrusting a periscope into the gun sights of the convoy's maddened escort. But Burlingame and company were certain they had sunk two Japanese ships. And postwar records disclosed the number as three. Sunk by SILVERSIDES on the night of January 20, 1943 were SOMEDONO MARU, passenger cargo-carrier, 5,154 tons; SURABAYA MARU, freighter, 4,391 tons; MEIU MARU, freighter, 8,230 tons.

"We heard them going down all right," one of the crew related afterwards. "And then we heard something else. Chief Torpedoman Smiley came bursting into the control room, and Smiley wasn't smiling. He reported to Lieutenant Davenport that an armed torpedo was stuck in one of the forward tubes!"

Dangling Torpedo!

Lieutenant Robert Worthington, the diving officer, had already noted the forepart of the submarine was abnormally heavy. Water entering the torpedo tubes at time of firing had flooded the forward torpedo-room bilges. To balance this weight, Worthington sent some men aft, and formed a bucket brigade to tote the water from the forward bilges to the engine-room and after torpedo-room bilges. This redistribution of bilge water was to give the submarine an even trim.

While the bucket brigade was laboring, Davenport went forward to inspect the torpedo tubes. The outer door of the tube in question was jammed open. This, plus the fact that Smiley could push in the tripping spindle, indicated that a torpedo was halfway out of the tube and jutting from the bow like a gigantic stick of dynamite. Here was the explanation for the lack of a sixth explosion. And a distressing explanation it was. For the live torpedo was still capable of detonating. If the sixth explosion occurred now, it was the last they would hear aboard SILVERSIDES.

Davenport reported the situation to Worthington. "I've tried to pass it off—we can't alarm the crew. Told them maybe the door was jammed by barnacles or something. But it looks as if we've got a fish dangling out there."

And as Worthington succinctly put it, there was not a blank-blank thing they could just now do about it. In the distance, depth charges had started to slam. Let one of those slams come near enough, and that torpedo might take it into its warhead to go off. SILVERSIDES would blow apart like a hollow egg. They could only sit tight and wait until the patrol boats were gone.

Some three hours later the patrol boats obliged. During the interim, bucket brigade had moved hundreds of gallons of bilge water, mixed with a considerable quantity of sweat. Some of this perspiration came from the brows of the informed torpedomen and officers.

A night and another day went by before Burlingame could surface the submarine long enough for removal of the refractory torpedo. When SILVERSIDES had to herself a flat, clear sea, Burlingame led the officers and torpedomen topside for a look. All could see the Mark 14 jutting from the bow tube.

First Class Torpedoman Walter Czerwinski was lowered overside to disarm the torpedo. He found the torpedo lodged in a position that made it impossible to detach the arming gear. The only way to clear the torpedo from the tube was by refiring it.

A dangerous resort, but the last one. The torpedo might explode in the tube or immediately ahead of the submarine after leaving the tube. However, it had to be removed. Volunteers for the ticklish station in the forward torpedo room were Chief Torpedoman Smiley, First Class Torpedoman Duckworth, Third Class Torpedoman Paul Dennis and Ensign G. C. Clark.

The forward torpedo room was made watertight and the four volunteers stood ready. Burlingame's voice came over the intercom, "All back emergency!" As the submarine moved in a top-speed reverse, Burlingame gave the order to fire. Duckworth pressed

197

the key. The torpedo shot from the tube and its wake traced its journey to the horizon.

That night a serious oil leak was discovered, and the hull was found to be trailing air bubbles. Burlingame decided to call it a day.

"With a dangling torpedo," he wrote, *"a fuel and air leak, fire in the main generator and Cream of Wheat in the main induction, it was decided to leave the area two days ahead of schedule."*

This summary of mishaps and malfunctions might well have included the appendectomy of George Platter. Burlingame did not forget that hardy convalescent whom he later recommended for the Navy and Marine Corps Medal. For his part in the drama, Moore was promoted to chief pharmacist's mate.

Burlingame himself was decorated with the Silver Star for this successful patrol. The decoration was also pinned on Lieutenants Keegan and Worthington, Chief Radioman Stegall, Chief Torpedoman's Mate Anderson and Chief Motor Machinist's Mate Duncan. Lieutenants Biena and Nichols and Ensign Finch were awarded the Navy and Marine Corps Medal at the same ceremony.

So ended one of the work-a-day submarine patrols of the war. For, aside from the appendectomy and the dangling torpedo, the adventures of SILVERSIDES were not uncommon. Rather, they were typical of those experienced by the majority of submarines fighting the Battle of the Pacific. An iron crew in a steel ship, the SILVERSIDERS were typical of hundreds of submariners who went out from Pearl, Dutch Harbor, Brisbane, Fremantle, to meet the enemy above and below.

The end-around, ably demonstrated by Burlingame, was soon to be a major tactic of submarine warfare.

Sound Attack—The "Single Ping" Range

While the end-around was in the developmental stage, another tactic was becoming popular. This concerned a unique method of fire control.

As previously pointed out, sound gear was not shelved by the advent of radar. Radar or no, the sonic and supersonic submarine devices remained a vital part of the fire control organization.

On practically all submerged attacks (and throughout the war the majority of submarine attacks were in this category), Sound was the first to make contact with the target when the submarine was patrolling submerged. This was often the case when the target was escorted by craft which were making sonar search—"pinging" for submarines.

The sound men did more than to keep tabs on the target while the periscope was down. Having detected the target's maneuvers, they reported on changes of the escort's disposition. Listening to the throbbing of a ship's screws, the trained operator could count the turns, make an independent check of the vessel's speed, and advise of any changes in speed. Thus the approach officer was able to follow the maneuvers of target and escorts without making an undue number of periscope exposures.

And if sound gear aided and abetted an approach, it was essential during retirement. When under attack by escorts, a submerged submarine had no recourse but to go deep. Once below periscope depth, sound was the sole means by which the enemy's moves could be ascertained.

Sea water lies in strata of varying density, a phenomenon which has to do with temperature. Currents may be involved, but as a rule surface water is warmer than the water 50 feet down. A thermometer lowered into the Tuscarora Deep would register temperature changes at various depths below sea level. Varying with the gradient is the water's density.

Evading at deep submergence, then, the submarine seeks the protection of a "density layer." Such a layer, determinable by the temperature gradient, serves to deflect or "bend" a probing sonic wave. If the wave is deflected, it may not find the submarine. Or the "echo" may ricochet at a tangent that deceives the enemy sender in regard to the submarine's range and location. The sound men in the submarine concentrate on listening to the enemy's "pings." The commanding officer, following what might be called "sound advice," maneuvers to put the submarine's attackers astern. Gradually the submersible withdraws from the danger area.

Sound can also play a leading role when the submarine does the attacking. Angled shots using the larger gyro angles demand a particularly accurate computation of the firing range. For such computation, the periscope stadimeter was undependable. Radar, of course, was not operative when the submarine was submerged. Here Sound stepped in as a range-finder. By bouncing a supersonic echo off the target, the sound man could obtain the range with the nicest degree of accuracy.

The device had undergone pre-war experimentation. Opinion had differed concerning its practicability. Some believed it a resort that jeopardized the submarine. Others thought there was little chance of the enemy's locating a submersible which sent out one darting "ping." So the "single ping range" was a moot question at the war's beginning. However, several of the pioneer skippers tried it, among them Lieutenant Commander Warder taking SEAWOLF into action in Davao Gulf.

A few weeks later TAUTOG in the Southwest Pacific

neatly demonstrated the technique. Closing in on the attack, she bounced a "ping" off the target to obtain a check on the firing range. After which she bounced two torpedo explosions off the target's hull.

This successful performance, following SEAWOLF's, established the "single ping" as a handy aid for fire control.

Tautog Gets Two (and Throws One Back In)

"Christmas comes but once a year," wrote Lieutenant Commander W. B. (Barney) Sieglaff on the midnight of December 25, 1942. The comment reflected mild misanthropy—a suspicion concerning the authenticity of Santa Claus. True, bells had been jingling for the past 24 hours, lights had twinkled on the Christmas Tree, and there had been Donner and Blitzen. But these manifestations were more reminiscent of Fourth of July than Yuletide. TAUTOG had just been on the receiving end of another depth-charge barrage. Her commander thought gloomily of the home folks in the States. It had been a tough day.

TAUTOG may be remembered as one of the five submarines which began the war at Pearl Harbor—the submarine which single-handedly shot down a Japanese plane. Sieglaff was the duty officer on her bridge that fateful morning. Fate and the Fremantle Command had reestablished the relationship, and TAUTOG was once more under Sieglaff's able direction, cruising the Southwest Pacific on the hunt for some of that enemy traffic which filtered through the Netherlands Indies.

Her present mission to patrol off the northwest coast of Timor, reconnoiter Waingapu and Soemba Island and proceed to the vicinity of Ambon, TAUTOG was on the prowl in Ombai Strait. Christmas Eve she spotted a freighter apparently heading east for the port of Dili. Sieglaff surfaced the submarine in dusk to give chase. The strait was narrowing, and there was risk of observation from shore. But fearing his quarry would disappear against a background of dark mountains, the commander held TAUTOG in dogged pursuit.

The submarine had been equipped with search radar before leaving Fremantle. Now that it was needed, the gear was not functioning, and the chase had to be conducted by eyesight. Shortly after midnight a Japanese plane droned across the sky, and TAUTOG ducked under to evade detection. Three-quarters of an hour later she was again running on the surface. At 0140 the target's silhouette came into view off the port beam. Sieglaff ordered periscope depth, and the approach was started.

For several minutes after submergence, TAUTOG was unable to pick up the quarry again. Coastal mountains loomed like condensations of midnight, and against this Stygian shore the freighter and its escort were blacked out. Then, straining at the scope, Sieglaff saw a white glimmer in the darkness ahead—the unwary ship was signaling to her companion. Whatever the message, it spelled *finis* for the sender.

Driving full speed ahead, Sieglaff put the submarine on a course to cross the target's projected track, intending a stern-tube attack. Sound bearings started at a range of 3,000 yards. As the range closed, the sound operator dealt information to the fire control party. During the last few minutes of the approach the target was clearly seen in a bath of moonlight—a single-stack freighter with stick masts fore and aft, and a plumb bow. A moment before the firing key was pressed, the sound man "pinged" the target. The range obtained—1,900 yards—checked with the T.D.C. Sieglaff gave the order to fire. Three torpedoes trailed their luminous wakes.

Two hit. The third missed and exploded at the end of its run. Squatting in a wallow of turgid smoke, BANSHU MARU No. 2, freighter, 1,000 tons, would soon be at the bottom. Employing the "single ping range," Sieglaff had scored a bull's-eye.

Sound now had an opportunity to exercise listening faculties as TAUTOG submerged to escape the inevitable counter-attack. In a passage as narrow as Ombai, a submarine's position is a matter of simple mathematics to an alerted enemy. Theoretically TAUTOG was in a Panama Canal, her movements limited to a restricted channel. Obviously a submarine would not run toward an angered patrol boat. But as TAUTOG retired westward, Sieglaff and company could be uncomfortably certain the patrol was running toward them. A spatter of explosions, followed by the sound of the enemy's "pinging," left as little room for doubt as there was for maneuver.

At 0315, Christmas morning, TAUTOG was outrunning the pursuit. Ten hours later she was still down underneath, and Sound was listening to two vessels astern. At long last these echo-rangers were gone, and the submarine surfaced in twilight.

Dusk blurred the shoreline and a moon was coming over the mountain. Ombai Strait was a channel of blue gauze. Sieglaff decided to swing northward into Alors Strait, an intersecting passage. TAUTOG could then circuit Alors Island and reenter Ombai Strait east of Dili. Although the port was in the Portuguese half of Timor Island there was little doubt it was harboring Japanese ships. Sieglaff determined to investigate the port.

Then, heading for Alors Strait in the night, TAUTOG sighted a vessel coming west. The moon was under a cloud and the silhouette was hazed, but the

199

ship appeared to be a dumpy little freighter as high in the stern as in the bow. While the submariners studied this vessel, a craft which resembled a PC-boat bustled out in front of the target, turned, and passed behind the freighter's stern. Both the freighter and the smaller craft then veered abruptly in the submarine's direction.

Time: 2311. TAUTOG went under. Sound reported "pinging." TAUTOG was spotted. At 2315 eight depth charges, the blasts strung together in a volley of rapid-fire explosions that indicated the enemy was using Y-guns. It was now apparent that the high-rumped "freighter" was an anti-submarine vessel, stoutly armed and equipped with echo-ranging gear. The Japanese had underestimated the submarine's range. As their "pinging" continued, TAUTOG went deep to take refuge below a 5° temperature gradient.

At 2335, Sound heard the enemy pass astern. Sieg-laff moved his submarine—slowly—slowly—in a direction calculated to keep the enemy astern. It was not until 0127 the following morning that TAUTOG could safely surface for a breather. The night had clouded over. Showers dimmed the shoreline. The enemy was gone.

Thus it had come to TAUTOG's captain that his submarine had spent all of Christmas Day dodging charges and destruction. Yet submarining had its lighter moments, even in areas where freighters turned into anti-submarine vessels and the next encounter might be the last. Eleven days after Christmas, while en route to Ambon, TAUTOG sighted a sail on the port bow and promptly headed for the craft. In these East Indies waters were all manner of vagrant luggers and junks—shipping as colorful as Joseph's coat. But Joseph's coat might have a pistol in its pocket. Here as in Empire waters the Japanese employed some of these ragtag vessels as lookouts and patrol craft. The shabbiest might conceal a radio transmitter, or hide an enemy agent among its crew. Accordingly U.S. submarines were ordered to overhaul and sink the more suspicious-looking.

Seen through the azure mists of early morning, the specimen overtaken by TAUTOG looked as evil and verminous as something in a Grade B pirate movie. Sieglaff drove the submarine forward with all machine guns manned. By hand signal he ordered the native craft to lower sail and steer alongside.

About a dozen Mohammedan sailors squinted up at TAUTOG's bridge. And to cap the climax they broke out and hoisted a Japanese flag. The flag came as something of a surprise to the submariners who might have shot first and asked afterwards had their skipper been a less perceiving man.

"We had the flag lowered and delivered to TAUTOG along with the boat's papers," Sieglaff related. "She was named the BINGTANG BARAT, and registered as six or eighteen tons. What could you do with such a vessel? We ordered all hands aboard, intending to sink the BINGTANG and deposit the natives on the nearest land. Then we discovered four women aboard, and some babies and an infant only a month or so old."

A small *banca* was the vessel's only lifeboat. A live rooster was tied by its feet to the bowsprit. Chickens and a goat roamed the forecastle. Perhaps it was the month-old infant, or possibly the rooster that decided the issue. Jap flag or no, TAUTOG would not make war against this miniature Noah's Ark.

"Apparently the BINGTANG was a seagoing home for a tribal family. None of the batch could speak English. Her Dutch papers were dated 1930, with Japanese clearances of various ports during the past year. After a look in the hold, we felt sorry for the goat. We ordered the Mohammedans back aboard, but kept the papers on the chance they might be of some value to our Intelligence."

An old patriarch wearing a red fez stood on the forecastle head with a babe in his arms. As TAUTOG drew away, he tucked the babe under one arm and gave the submarine captain a smart Dutch salute.

"Tabay, tuan."

The submarine left BINGTANG BARAT astern and continued on to Ambon.

Off Ambon four days later, Sound heard something more than the squawking of chickens and the wailing of nursery babes. At 0938 TAUTOG sighted a NATORI-class cruiser, angle on the bow about 80° port, range about 3,000 yards.

Directing a daylight approach, Sieglaff sent TAUTOG boring in with nine feet of periscope exposed. Long swells climbed over the periscope, swamping the view. At 0941 Sieglaff opened fire. About two minutes later a booming explosion was heard. Sound reported the cruiser's screws had dead-stopped.

However, the target was seen to swing left and move off at reduced speed. Sieglaff fired two more torpedoes at 0948, "spread 25 seconds apart." Two minutes and five seconds after the last torpedo was fired, Sound heard a muffled blast preceded by a "definite detonation wave."

At 0951 the cruiser opened up on TAUTOG with all seven 5.5 guns, delivering four full salvos in rapid succession. Again screws could be heard. But when advised the cruiser had four, Sound reported only half the number previously heard were in operation. Sound also heard three or four loud explosions, either depth charges or torpedoes detonating.

At 0952 the cruiser hauled away at about 10 knots,

still firing at the submarine. A series of explosions sounded like shell detonations or aircraft bombs. The cruiser carried a plane on a catapult, and the plane may have taken to the air. The sea was too rambunctious for close periscope observation without risk of broaching—a risk to be declined in the face of hot gunfire. So Sieglaff held her under for the next hour while Sound listened to intermittent thunder. When the shooting was finally silenced, TAUTOG's periscope went up.

As the cruiser could not be located, the submarine went to 80 feet for a torpedo check and reload. Thanks to Sound, the submariners had remained informed on the cruiser's movements and material condition, and were able to report this warship as "definitely damaged."

A few days after the brush with the cruiser, TAUTOG's radiomen and electricians managed to revive the baulky SJ radar. With the SJ in operation, TAUTOG had little difficulty in tracking down a freighter sighted in Saleier Strait on the night of January 22nd. During a submerged attack, the target remained clearly visible in the periscope. Sieglaff fired a three-torpedo spread at 1,200 yards range. Two explosions flamed vividly in the moonlight and the ship went down with a rush. Four Malay seamen picked up from a life raft identified the vessel as HASSHU MARU, a former Dutch passenger-cargoman, 1,873 tons. She had been bound for Ambon, loaded with drums of aviation gasoline.

The following morning brought clear sunshine and glass-smooth sea. About five miles east of Saleier Strait, two ships sauntered over the blue horizon. The smaller ship was soon identified as an escort, and the larger proved to be another NATORI-class cruiser. A plane hovered over the cruiser.

Only the briefest of periscope exposures could be made in the translucent water, and an attack demanded a swift approach. The set-up would have been ideal for a shot from the stern, but there were no torpedoes in TAUTOG's stern tubes. To obtain a firing course and bring the bow tubes to bear, Sieglaff sent the submarine down to 70 feet for a full-speed turn of 115°.

About 0900 the escort passed ahead of TAUTOG, near enough for the submariners to hear the propellers through the hull. A moment later Sieglaff thrust up the scope for a quick look and a firing bearing. The cruiser had already crossed TAUTOG's bow and was beyond the desired firing point. Large gyro angles were now necessary, and the shooting had to be fast.

At 0908 Sieglaff fired the first shot of a four-torpedo spread. As the torpedoes trailed their wakes the cruiser opened fire with her after-guns. Simultaneously the

plane spotted the submarine. Sieglaff gave the order to go deep.

Two aircraft bombs and nine depth charges chased TAUTOG on down. At deep submergence the submarine headed south. The escort could be heard "pinging," and Sound reported this echo-ranging for the next two hours.

At 1140 the "pings" were far away. Seven depth charges exploded in the distance. At 1235 five explosions rumbled faintly. Three hours later the periscope showed a clean horizon, and at 1850 TAUTOG surfaced and headed for Fremantle, all torpedoes expended.

Five hours later the submarine ran headlong into a Jap convoy off Tiger Islands. One of the silhouettes shaped up into an aircraft carrier. Another materialized as a destroyer, heading at top speed for TAUTOG. The submarine dived. At a considerable depth the destroyer's "pinging" could be plainly heard. TAUTOG went deeper. Then, for the first time on this patrol, the submariners encountered water in which there was no temperature gradient.

Sound listened to the destroyer's "pinging," and it was evident these Japs knew their business. "The destroyer probably had an accurate range when we dove," Sieglaff reported, "but she certainly ranged us on her supersonic gear." Down came four depth charges—slam—slam—slam—slam. The barrage jostled the submarine, snapped fixtures from the bulkheads, pulverized light bulbs and wrecked the after antennae cable. Four more near explosions caused minor damage.

The hunters continued to "ping" for the next hour and a half, while TAUTOG, the hunted, worked her way toward open sea. Then, at 2330, Sound reported the enemy's "pinging" had ceased. Evidently the DD had turned back to rejoin the convoy. Two hours after that, TAUTOG surfaced in the night and had the sea to herself as she headed for home.

The foregoing TAUTOG episodes illustrate the submarine's dependence on sound gear. Radar was indeed the seventh wonder of the submarine world. But that world is three-dimensional. In its third and basic dimension—depth—the submarine at deep submergence would be deaf as well as blind were it not for Sound. Certainly Shakespeare's line applies to the alert sound man listening at the phones.

"A friend is an ear."

Loss of Admiral English

Returning from patrols late in January, the submariners who had been at sea during the first weeks of the year found changes in each of the Force Commands.

Routine advices had conveyed word of the change

at Brisbane where, on December 23, 1942, Captain James Fife, Jr., had relieved Captain Ralph Christie as Commander Task Force Forty-two. But the word from Pearl Harbor came to returning submariners as a shock. On January 19 Admiral English had been killed in a plane crash near San Francisco.

The SubPac commander had been flying to the States to attend a series of important conferences. The plane, a Pan-Am Clipper on loan to the Navy, encountered dense fog over the California coast. Unable to land at 'Frisco, the Clipper apparently headed for Crystal Lake to attempt a landing. Ceiling zero, visibility extinguished, the plane crashed blindly in the mountains behind the city. The thickly forested mountainside hampered the search parties. More than a week passed by before the tragic wreckage was found.

Lost with Admiral English were Commander J. J. Crane, force engineer; Lieutenant Commander John O. R. Call, force gunnery and torpedo officer; Commander W. G. (Billy) Myers, prospective relief for Commander Crane; and Captain Robert H. Smith, commander of Submarine Squadron Two. The disaster came as a gratuitous blow to the entire Submarine Force.

Rear Admiral Charles A. Lockwood succeeded Admiral English as ComSubPac, and left Fremantle for Pearl Harbor that same month. Captain Ralph Christie was promoted to rear admiral and ordered back to Australia to replace Admiral Lockwood at Fremantle.

Trout Develops a New Technique

On January 11, 1943, TROUT under the captaincy of Lieutenant Commander Lawson P. Ramage, entered an enemy harbor and torpedoed a vessel at anchor. The exploit featured a novel attack technique.

The target, a big tanker, was discovered moored off Miri, northwest Borneo. TROUT had been patrolling the area with indifferent luck, and Ramage and company jumped at this chance. They did not, however, immediately jump the target.

The vessel was sighted in broad daylight. Ramage sent the submarine sidling forward cautiously. He closed the range to 4,000 yards, then paused to study the tanker's anchorage. She was too far inside the ten-fathom curve to permit a closer submerged approach. TROUT might try some sharpshooting, but there was a strong and variable tidal current and an offshore swell. Ramage decided that a long-range attack had less chance than a short-range attack made at night after a run in on the surface.

"So we'll wait out here where she can't spot us,"

he concluded. "After dark we can go up and pick her off. Secure!"

About 1930, he surfaced the submarine and sent the crew to battle stations. The battery was low, so he put two engines on charge and two on the screw. An hour later, he secured the charge and shifted to the battery for propulsion. Silent running was in order, and the submarine's motors whispered.

Surprisingly, the target was picked up on the starboard quarter when expected on the port bow. As Ramage prepared to fire, the SJ, which had been unable to pick up the target, suddenly found her and revealed the range as 4,000 yards. Ramage maneuvered for a 90° starboard track. When the range was closed to 1,700 yards, he fired three straight bow shots. Two torpedoes hit. One prematured or counter-mined at 1,000 yards. Ramage then swung TROUT around and fired one stern-tube shot at a range of 1,400 yards. This torpedo failed to explode. But as TROUT retired, there were voluminous explosions astern and the tanker vomited spurts of dazzling flame.

The tanker's destruction was highly probable. But TROUT was unable to linger in the firelight for further observation, and a confirmed sinking was not officially credited. Japanese records fail to mention a large tanker sunk at Miri.

However, TROUT received credit for sinking an anonymous 3,000-ton freighter in the area on January 21st. If the tanker at Miri escaped total destruction, the deliverance was due to no flaw in the method of attack. Red-headed Lawson P. Ramage was recognized as a skipper possessed of those two qualities which make for success in submarine warfare. The qualities? Sagacity and audacity.

GREENLING, GROWLER, GATO, GUARDFISH and SWORDFISH were other submarines to up the periscope in the South Seas Battle that heightened during January 1943.

Action around the Bismarcks

As the last trains of the "Tokyo Express" were pulling out of Guadalcanal, the submarine effort concentrated on the Bismarck Archipelago where the enemy's bases were literally boiling with activity. Hub of this strategic area was the Island of New Britain with its anchorage at Rabaul. Little more than a name on the map before the war, this port had grown overnight from a harbor visited by trading schooners to a terminal for Japanese shipping and a base for the Imperial Navy. Out of Rabaul steamed the "Tokyo Express" with war freight for the Solomons front. Out of Rabaul ran fast convoy trains for New Guinea. Bristling with guns and naval installations, the port accommodated some of Yamamoto's strongest naval units. Long before Guadalcanal was secured, U.S. submarines were slashing at the sea lanes to this major Japanese base.

GREENLING (Lieutenant Commander Bruton) was patrolling the area early in January. On the 16th she got her ship—KINPOSAN MARU, 3,261 tons.

On that same day GROWLER (Lieutenant Commander Gilmore) caught, torpedoed and sank the passenger-cargoman CHIFUKU MARU—5,857 tons erased from the Rabaul area. On June 19 GROWLER again bared her teeth, and down at sea went MIYADONO MARU, another passenger-cargo carrier of similar size and tonnage.

SWORDFISH (Lieutenant Commander J. H. Lewis) removed another vessel from the Rabaul vicinity on the 19th—MYOHO MARU, 4,122 tons.

GATO (Lieutenant Commander R. J. Foley) sank the 4,575-ton transport, KENKON MARU, on the 21st; the freighter NICHIUN MARU, 2,723 tons, on the 29th; and the small tramp steamer SURUGA MARU a fortnight later. Adventurous GATO! She was not the luckiest of submarines, although later in the war she was to find an unexploded depth charge sitting prettily on her foredeck. Her patrols were not among the most "lucrative." Yet she hunted the north entrance of Bougainville Strait with a pertinacity that led Admiral Halsey to nickname her "The Goalkeeper." And her rescue missions in the Bougainville area were classics. The Japs might have redoubled their efforts to depth-charge GATO had they known her for what she was—the prototype for the fleet submarines under mass production in the United States since the start of the war.

On the night of January 28, GUARDFISH (Lieutenant Commander Klakring) made a valiant attempt to enter Rabaul's harbor. She had already (January 12) sunk a combative patrol boat classified as an "old destroyer" of some 750 tons. On the 22nd she had downed an anonymous 4,000-ton freighter. And on the 23rd she had sunk the Imperial Navy's destroyer HAKAZE, 1,300 tons. Then there was Rabaul itself in plain view one evening—a nest of targets seething and fuming in the sullen light of sundown.

Klakring determined to enter that distant bay of smokes. It would be on a par with raiding the courtyard of an enemy castle. But hazardous exploits were a submarine's business, and Klakring considered the target possibilities worth the risk.

Early in the morning of January 27, GUARDFISH made a high-speed approach from the Bismarck Sea side of St. George's Channel. This run was frustrated by a chance encounter with a pair of rambling small boats. On the following evening Klakring made

another try. This time he succeeded in gaining the lee of Watom Island without detection. Sunrise was coming. GUARDFISH's commander sent her to periscope depth and headed her for the objective.

During the morning, she evaded one echo-ranging patrol. Periscope exposures were limited to a few quick sweeps, hastily made in the face of bustling aircraft. One approach on a freighter was broken off because the target appeared too small to warrant the submarine's exposure in the position she had gained. A "pinging" destroyer was successfully passed.

The sea was a lake of glass. GUARDFISH prowled in at silent running speeds. Three or four echo-ranging patrols played sentry off the harbor entrance. At this point, periscope exposures every 15 minutes were necessary in order to check the submarine's position in relation to the beach, for currents off Rabaul are strong and erratic. Upping the scope under the eyes of the patrols was a test for steel nerves.

As GUARDFISH crept into Blanche Bay, two groups of ships in the lower reaches of Simpson Harbor could be seen. Bunched together, they made an overlapping target some 1,750 feet in length. Klakring decided to fire long-range, slow-speed shots at the multiple target, and began maneuvering for position. The six bow tubes were ready. In 60 seconds the submarine would reach the target's 8,000-yard circle.

With everything primed and cocked, Klakring ran up the periscope for a final bearing to fix his position before steadying on the firing course. Instantly the periscope was zoomed by a Japanese plane. Shore batteries opened up with the roar of a munitions plant exploding on a Sunday. Two patrol vessels rushed straight at GUARDFISH. The torpedo room reported the submarine had been struck over the wardroom. Shells were smashing the glassy mirror of the sea, and Rabaul was hotter than the core of the sun. Klakring headed GUARDFISH for cooler waters.

Lesson in Logistics

As suggested by SILVERSIDES' patrol off Truk, TAUTOG's foray around Timor, and TROUT's invasion of Miri, Borneo, the Japanese were losing ships on the lanes to the South Seas arena. All roads were leading to the Bismarck-Solomons-New Guinea front. And while the battle centered around Rabaul and Bougainville, submarines from Fremantle, Brisbane and Pearl Harbor continued to range the periphery and waylay enemy traffic behind the front lines.

The Japanese General Staff had long been worried about the transport problem resulting from the advance to the Solomons. It may be recalled that Yamamoto sponsored the Solomons drive against the advice

203

of the conservatives who foresaw the logistic difficulties involved. Yamamoto, of course, would never have to crouch hungry in a foxhole, waiting for a bowl of rice that wouldn't come. Nor would the Japanese admiral stand lookout on the bow of a rusty freighter crawling through a submarine zone. Militarists, like mathematicians, sometimes lack imagination. Yet the starving trooper and the sweating lookout are figures as intrinsic to the logistics equation as the numerals that add up into miles or tonnage. Raiding the shipping routes to Rabaul and Bougainville, American submarines were bent on animating these logistic figures.

There was WHALE, making her second patrol under Lieutenant Commander Azer. Cruising off Kwajalein, she sighted an old freighter outward bound for Truk. Promptly she smashed the AK's bottom out with four torpedoes. Down at sea January 13 went IWA-SHIRO MARU, 3,550 tons, the crew pulling away in lifeboats to report another hole in the Emperor's merchant marine.

Some time later, WHALE sighted a Jap patrol boat which was making squares around an apparently defined latitude and longitude. After watching this antic for awhile, Azer decided the craft was waiting for another vessel. From the patrol boat's location, he deduced that the other vessel was heading down from Saipan. Actually it was more a hunch than a deduction, but some submariners acquire a seventh sense for such things. Azer was such a submariner. He directed WHALE up the hypothetical track, and on January 17 a large passenger-cargo ship loomed on the horizon and advanced toward WHALE's periscope.

A transport! And it was a big one. Rushing the crew to battle stations, Azer sent the submarine boring in on the approach. As the liner grew on the periscope lens he could see the decks crowded with brown troops, helmeted gunners lounging at the gunmounts, officers in white on the bridge. He could almost see the course worked out in the chart room. There could be no doubt about it, these reinforcements were on their way to Bougainville.

"This sinking which would save the lives of our own Marines was a pleasure," Azer wrote in his patrol report.

Closing the range, he maneuvered WHALE into attack position. The patrol report vividly describes the action:

Fired three torpedoes. Three hits. One hit aft of his stack, the second blew wreckage up through forward hold; and the third hit aft. Target started turning toward us. Swung hard right and set up for a stern tube shot.

Fired single stern shot at range of 600 yards. Hit aft. This was a good hit, stopping the target cold. The target

was sinking by the stern, taking considerable port list and smoke billowed from after part of the ship. Took pictures, firmly convinced this was the graveyard of another Japanese ship. Many of the crew had an opportunity to view the sinking ship through the periscope.

Having worked up to windward to observe target better, was astonished to find the fire under control and the list corrected. Water was being pumped over the side through portable hoses. Fired another torpedo from the stern tubes, but this missed. Target was dead in the water, shooting wildly with deck guns.

Crew and passengers abandoned ship, although gun crews remained at posts. Target settled about ten feet over-all and then maintained its depth. Closed and fired sixth torpedo from bow tubes. This hit aft of superstructure deck.

Target still floating. Fired seventh torpedo from bow tubes. This hit with terrific concussion, but did not change trim or draft of ship appreciably.

Fired eighth torpedo from stern tubes. This was heard to hit, but very little concussion was felt.

Getting dark. Target sinking slowly on an even keel, but still looks salvageable. There was no sign of life on board, although it was believed gun crews had not yet abandoned ship. Wishing to dispose of it before arrival of planes or rescue ships, fired ninth torpedo. This hit right under stack and the explosion rippled away both sides of vessel about ten feet below the main deck.

Target now settled more rapidly, the main deck being few feet from wash condition at last observation. This vessel had absorbed seven and possibly eight torpedo hits. The cargo must have been of such nature as to prevent her from sinking more rapidly. Target was identified as the HEIYOU MARU, 9,815 tons.

On retiring we found ourselves in the midst of eight boats full of survivors, approximately fifty men to each boat. These men were dressed in both white and blue uniforms. One boat was passed close aboard, and survivors made ready to hit the periscope with their oars.

On January 27, WHALE gave the enemy another logistics lesson. The locale in this instance was 14-15 N., 153-43 E. The transport sunk was SHOAN MARU, 5,624 tons.

When WHALE ended her second patrol, Japanese shipping in the Truk area was minus 18,989 tons. Following the 27,708-ton subtraction made earlier in January by SILVERSIDES, the WHALE reduction—the second largest made by a U.S. submarine that month—must certainly have come to Yamamoto's attention.

Many a mickle makes a muckle. Even the 749-ton steamer USHIO MARU, sunk by GRAYLING on the 26th far to the west of the South Seas front, put another minus quantity in the Japanese supply problem. Still another was inserted on January 26 when FLY-INGFISH and SNAPPER teamed up to sink the passenger

"TAKE HER DOWN!" Commander H. W. Gilmore, wounded on Growler's bridge, makes heroic sacrifice by ordering an immediate dive. The submarine, bad- *ly damaged by collision with Jap gunboat, was saved. In giving up his life for his ship, Commander Gilmore followed the highest traditions of naval service.*

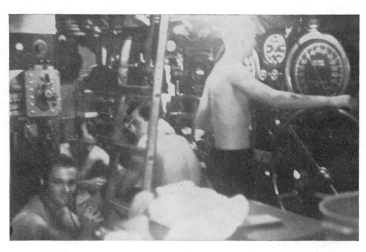

WAHOO'S CONTROL ROOM—and all under control. Taken during "Destroyer-gunnin' Wahoo-runnin'" battle. Morale high.

COMDR. HOWARD W. GILMORE. Posthumously awarded Congressional Medal of Honor.

TROUT'S HANDIWORK—a burning Jap trawler. The craft was set ablaze by gunfire from the attacking sub. Note sub's wake.

GROWLER ALONGSIDE TENDER, after ramming. Note submarine's crumpled bow, bent sideways like a broken nose. Comdr. A. F. Schade and plucky crew saved sub.

GROWLER GETS NEW BOW in Brisbane. Heroic work by Schade and crew got battered submarine home. Miracle job by repair forces put Growler once more in action.

cargoman Tokai Maru at lat. 13-27 N., long. 144-37 E. The dual attack cost the enemy's transport system a gross 8,358 tons.

Altogether the 26th of January 1943 was an ominous day for those who had to solve Japan's South Seas logistics problem. It was on this date that a Japanese convoy met Dudley W. Morton and USS Wahoo.

Wahoo vs. Convoy

Lieutenant Commander Dudley W. Morton was a submariner born. Which is to say his family were Kentuckians, he was born in Virginia, appointed to the Naval Academy from the state of Florida (Class of 1930) and walked into the conning tower from there. He commanded his first submarine, the R-5, in the Atlantic, and was transferred to the Pacific after two fast-action patrols.

Nothing particularly uncommon about this A. & P. routine. Nothing unusual about his serving as executive officer of Wahoo when she made her first two patrols under Lieutenant Commander M. G. Kennedy. But Morton, endeared to his Annapolis classmates as "Mushmouth" (abbreviated "Mush") because of a knack for yarn-spinning, was an uncommonly talented submarine officer. Combining capability with dynamic aggressiveness, Morton feared nothing on or under the sea. Torpedoings were guaranteed when he assumed command of Wahoo early in 1943 and took her out of Brisbane on her third war patrol.

Morton's orders were to patrol off Palau. Wahoo was en route to the Pelews when she received orders to investigate Wewak Harbor on the northeast coast of New Guinea. Wewak lies between two small islands. One is named Kairiru. The other—odd coincidence—Mushu.

"Mush" was confident he could locate any island named Mushu. But Wewak could be found on no available American chart. This made an approach exceptionally hazardous for a submarine, especially as the harbor was suspected of being strongly fortified. While Wahoo's officers puzzled over the problem of exploring an uncharted port, someone remembered that D. C. Keeter, MotorMac 1, had a grade-school atlas in his sea bag. From this pocket edition Morton contrived a navigational chart by tracing the map on a slide and projecting the same, by means of a camera and signal light, upon a large-scale chart. There might be hidden reefs and shifting bars in the harbor mouth; if so, they could be located by sonar search. Wewak, at any rate, was charted.

Early morning, January 24, Wahoo was off the dark coast of New Guinea. And there, as specified by the atlas, was the "off the map" harbor. Were Japanese ships in port? Wahoo's periscope found the answer in a pair of Chidori torpedo boats and a couple of snub-nosed harbor tugs.

"This was encouraging," Morton noted, "because patrol boats were likely to mean shipping."

He avoided these craft assiduously, moving Wahoo on a creep into the inner harbor. Wewak's bay proved disappointing. Although the periscope found a conspicuous lack of targets, Morton was convinced there were ships in the vicinity, and he sent the submarine over to Kairiru Island to wait.

About noon a tripod mast appeared on the far side of Kairiru, and Morton began a furtive approach. A meandering patrol boat intervened. Wahoo's captain then decided to take the target unawares by circumnavigating the island. The move was blocked by a reef which barred the passage—one of those barriers unrecorded in the pocket-edition atlas.

Deprived of a prize target, Morton determined to go five miles farther down harbor—there might be something to shoot at near Mushu Island. There was. It looked like a DD. Although the submarine was deep within the harbor when the periscope found this warship, Morton kept Wahoo going. Her excursion down the harbor covered about seven miles, a long run for a submarine in enemy water guarded by sharp-eared patrol vessels and men-of-war. Slowly the submarine bore down on the quarry. Cautiously Morton raised the periscope for another look. This time he was able to identify the target as a Fubuki-class destroyer. A curl of white froth at the warship's bow told Morton she was under way.

Obviously the DD was on the hunt, and Morton could only believe she was hunting a submerged submarine named Wahoo. Hastily lowering the periscope, he swung Wahoo into attack position and fired four torpedoes at a range of 3,000 yards. The four torpedoes missed! But the DD's lookouts did not miss the four torpedo wakes. The destroyer, having veered to avoid, now rushed straight for the submarine, a bone as big as a gorilla's shin in her teeth. With but two torpedoes remaining in the bow tubes, Morton had to do some lightning calculating.

Reporting this climax, he observed: "In order not to lose the initiative we continued to be aggressive. So we decided to shoot the remaining torpedoes down the enemy's throat as he came in to depth charge us."

Wahoo retained the initiative. Morton opened fire at a range of 1,200 yards. This torpedo missed. The range had dwindled to 800 yards when he fired the remaining torpedo. Wahoo dug under as the blast of a hit rolled its thunder down the channel.

On the way out of Wewak, Morton raised the periscope for a parting look. The destroyer no longer had a bone in her teeth. Her bow was completely blown off and she had come to a stunned halt. Sailors clung to her turret tops and swarmed monkey-fashion up her rigging.

Morton paused to let a periscope camera admire this view, then it was time to say farewell to Wewak. Japanese naval records do not list a DD sunk on that date in Wewak Harbor—evidently the enemy was able to beach and salvage the torpedoed vessel. Maimed as she was, she must have remained out of action for a long period. Rapid repair work was unlikely in that remote backwater of New Guinea.

Two days after the Wewak raid, WAHOO was about 450 miles off the New Guinea coast. The day, January 26, brought a morning benign with sunshine and a sea as calm as peace. At 0800 the lookout reported smoke on the horizon. Morton began tracking. He held the submarine on the surface, and drove ahead of the smoke to dive for a periscope attack. The smoke branched into two plumes—a two-ship convoy. A freighter and a transport, the two vessels were steaming in column. Morton rigged the set-up for a double salvo from the stern tubes. When WAHOO gained attack position, he fired two torpedoes at the leading ship and two at the ship astern. Two explosions stopped the first ship dead. The fourth torpedo struck the second ship in the quarter.

Swinging WAHOO to bring her bow tubes to bear, Morton raised the scope to check on the targets. The second ship wheeled and headed for the submarine to ram. At this juncture a third ship was sighted. Morton had to do some fast sharpshooting with the rammer heading for WAHOO. He did it. He fired three torpedoes at the newcomer, stopped her with a hit, then turned and fired two down-the-throat shots at WAHOO's nearing assailant. Explosions rumbled in a spreading wave of sound as WAHOO went deep.

Eight minutes later Morton ordered her back to periscope depth. A swift look showed the first ship had gone under. The second was crawling away. The third ship was at a standstill in the water like a model stuck in a sea of papier-mâché. "This ship was quickly dispatched and hundreds of Japs, evidently soldiers, were jumping over the sides like ants off a hot plate," Morton described the sinking. WAHOO stood by long enough to certify the transport as a goner. Then Morton ordered the submarine to the surface and set off in pursuit of the wounded freighter.

WAHOO was overtaking the fugitive when a fourth ship appeared on the horizon. A tanker. This was almost an embarrassment of riches. But before an attack could be made on either of these vessels a battery charge was necessary.

The tanker was then selected as the immediate target. The approach consumed most of the remaining day as Morton maneuvered to get ahead of the two vessels which were drawing together. With but seven torpedoes left, Morton made certain no shots should be wasted. At sundown WAHOO was in attack position, and he fired three shots at the tanker. The torpedoes hit, but the tanker kept on going.

Taking WAHOO to the surface, Morton closed the range. The tanker zigzagged frantically. A study of the zigzag plan ended in its frustration. An hour and a half after the first salvo, WAHOO had another bead on the target and Morton fired another torpedo. The shot struck home and the tanker folded at the middle like a closing jackknife.

This left WAHOO with but two torpedoes, and the crippled freighter seemed aware of the fact. Like a cornered badger, the AK turned to fight. Jets of flame spurted from her deck guns, and shells began to smash the water around the submarine. One shell ricochetted over the conning tower. Morton ordered WAHOO under, brought her back to the surface when the freighter ceased fire, and headed her toward the enemy.

As the submarine closed the range, a ghostly spoke of light rayed up on the horizon and fanned back and forth across the night sky. A searchlight! The crippled freighter had summoned an escort, and WAHOO would have to finish this target in a hurry, or the opportunity might evaporate. The freighter was already headed for the searchlight.

Morton sent WAHOO racing in to cut her off. Range 3,000 yards, he fired the last two torpedoes. Both hit the mark.

Later that night, Morton dispatched this crackling message:

IN TEN HOUR RUNNING GUN AND TORPEDO BATTLE DESTROYED ENTIRE CONVOY OF TWO FREIGHTERS ONE TRANSPORT ONE TANKER . . . ALL TORPEDOES EXPENDED . . . RETURNING HOME

The tanker's sinking could not be subsequently confirmed. But the stringent post-war inquest conducted by the Joint Army-Navy Assessment Committee in Japan credited WAHOO with a 4,000-ton cargo carrier (name unknown); the transport BUYO MARU, 5,447 tons; and the freighter FUKUEI MARU No. 2, 1,901 tons.

Thus three enemy ships fell to WAHOO in one scrimmage and a fourth limped away to the repair yards. If the tanker reached Wewak, she probably found the repair crews overburdened by a paralyzed

DD. Apparently the convoy off Wewak had been expecting an escort to usher it into port, and it was the torpedoing of this destroyer that permitted WAHOO to surprise an unguarded quartet of merchantmen.

There was a third act to this WAHOO drama. The morning after the convoy battle, WAHOO sighted another convoy! Six ships! Without a single torpedo left, and no more than 40 rounds of 4-inch ammunition aboard, Morton headed the submarine toward the train of freighters, hoping to pick off a straggler by gunfire. He was maneuvering into position for a gun attack when a Japanese destroyer steamed over the horizon. The convoy's lookouts had sighted WAHOO, the ships were stampeding, and the DD opened fire at the submarine without ado. As shells ripped up the sea directly ahead, Morton gave the order to go deep and rig for depth-charging.

The DD came over and dumped her bombs. For an hour she continued the search while the submariners lay low, holding their breath. Finally the enemy departed, and Morton dispatched his famous curtain-line:

ANOTHER RUNNING GUN FIGHT . . . DESTROYER GUNNING . . . WAHOO RUNNING

So WAHOO ran home to Hawaii with a broom at her masthead. Discussing this 22-day patrol which took his submarine from Brisbane to Pearl Harbor, Morton said the nerves in his necknape spent a week untangling themselves. A fortnight later WAHOO was off again, on a warpath that was to go like that of a tornado through the Japanese merchant fleet. Few skippers equalled Morton's initiative, and none had a larger reserve of nerve.

The judo expert in the Southwest Pacific had met a master grappler. Applied to "Mush" Morton, this was no figure of speech. He had been a champion wrestler at the Naval Academy.

Commander Howard W. Gilmore

GROWLER's fourth patrol was nearing its conclusion. She had departed Brisbane on New Year's Day to harry the enemy's traffic lanes between Rabaul and the Western Solomons. No sooner had she reached this area than her periscope was up to its neck in torpedo attacks.

As previously recounted, she downed a transport on January 16 and another on the 19th. Then she headed westward toward New Hanover to waylay traffic from Truk and Palau.

On January 30 she attacked and damaged a freighter. During this action she was driven deep by a tempest of gunfire and depth charges. The following day she struck at a heavily armed gunboat, only to have her life endangered by a defective torpedo.

The area seethed with enemy shipping and pugnacious patrol craft. At this date the Japanese were making a last desperate effort to evacuate the remnants of their Guadalcanal garrison. To the storm center the Imperial Navy was rushing every gun, bomb and depth charge it could muster. As GROWLER continued to contact enemy vessels on every hand, it was apparent to her captain, Commander Howard W. Gilmore, that the anti-submarine measures were boiling the water off the Bismarcks. The skipper who had invaded an Aleutian harbor to sink a Japanese destroyer was undismayed at this display of enemy force. Patrols meant convoys. Convoys were GROWLER's business. Gilmore drove her into the center of the seething area.

On the night of February 4, south of Steffen Strait, he put GROWLER on the trail of a convoy which was heading for Gazelle Channel, probably en route to Rabaul. Two merchantmen under escort of two patrol craft. Estimating their speed and course, Gilmore sent his submarine on a fast run southward— a run calculated to give GROWLER an ahead position on the convoy's projected track. True to Gilmore's estimates, the convoy came steaming down the track about 0300 the next morning. Gilmore had accomplished a perfect end-around.

Two ships were sighted. Poor visibility necessitated a surface attack, and Gilmore directed a wary approach. Radar went into action to guide the submarine and coach fire control. GROWLER was closing the target, and the torpedoes were ready to go when the lead ship suddenly opened fire at 5,000 yards.

Gilmore ordered a quick dive, and the submarine went under. Almost as soon as she coasted beneath the waves, Sound reported high-speed screws closing in on either bow. The submarine was rigged for depth-charging, and the submariners braced themselves for a blasting. They got it for about an hour.

Sometime between 0402 and 0413 a concussion ruptured a manhole gasket in the forward main ballast tank. Water sprawled into the forward torpedo-room at the rate of 1,000 gallons an hour. Emergency repairs stemmed this flood, but the damage control party would be a Dutch boy with finger in a crumbling dyke until the submarine could surface for an adequate repair job.

At 0539 the patrol boats seemed to have withdrawn, and Gilmore sent GROWLER to periscope depth. A sweep of the scope disclosed the presence of a vessel about five miles distant. The convoy's smoke was visible against the sky beyond. The torpedo-room bilges were being held at a reasonable level by the drain pump, and the damage control party had managed to cover the leaking manhole with sheet rubber and deck plates held in place by shores and jacks. The violent hemorrhaging had stopped, but the leakage remained dangerous.

With a patrol boat lurking in the vicinity, Gilmore held the submarine under and headed her westward to evade. At nightfall he brought her to the surface. The ruptured manhole was opened and a new gasket installed. Midnight found GROWLER once more roaming on the hunt.

At 0110 on the morning of February 7 a ship was sighted on the starboard bow, on an opposite course, range 2,000 yards. Gilmore turned the submarine away, ordered all tubes readied, and then swung about to close for an attack. As GROWLER reduced the range to 2,000 yards on a 130° starboard track, she was sighted. The enemy, a 2,500-ton gunboat, reversed course and rushed. Radar immediately detected the gunboat's course-change, but poor visibility screened the enemy's attack maneuver and it was not at once discerned by the bridge personnel.

On GROWLER's bridge were Commander Gilmore, the officer of the deck, the assistant O.O.D., the quartermaster and three lookouts. At 0134 radar indicated that the range was too short to allow the torpedoes to arm. From the bridge came the order, "Left full rudder!" A moment later the collision alarm sounded. Then GROWLER crashed into the Jap gunboat head on at 17 knots. The impact was stunning. Every man in the submarine was thrown off his feet. GROWLER heeled over, and as she righted like a rolled log, the gunboat opened fire at point blank range.

A whip of .50-caliber machine-gun bullets lashed across the submarine's bridge. Ensign W. W. William, assistant officer of the deck, was killed. W. F. Kelley, Fireman 3, standing lookout, died at his post. Commander Gilmore, badly wounded, clung to the bridge frame.

Gunfire blazed in the night; dark spray showered the bridge; steel whined and moaned, skimming the conning tower. Above the pandemoniac slam-bang of the guns and the deeper roaring of the sea, the commander's voice came clear.

"Clear the bridge!"

Officer of the deck and quartermaster descended, followed by two bleeding lookouts who were pulled through the hatch.

Then came the order, *Take her down!*

At the aperture the men hesitated. Seconds ticked by—the commander did not appear. A hurricane of machine-gun fire was sweeping GROWLER's superstructure. They closed the hatch and took her down.

A bullet punctured the conning tower as the submarine went under, and a stream of water shot into the hatch, forced through the bullet-hole at fire-hose pressure. All gyro, inter-communication, lighting and heater circuits were put out of commission by the spurting flood.

Lieutenant Commander A. F. Schade, who had been Gilmore's second, now assumed command. The collision with the gunboat had thrown him from the conning-tower hatch to the deck of the control room. Painfully bruised, dazed, he forced himself to meet the emergency presented by a lost captain and a seriously damaged submarine. With water in the control room and the pump room half flooded, GROWLER was levelled off, and Schade held her submerged while temporary repairs were contrived. Some 30 minutes after the smashing dive, Schade gave the order to "battle surface." It was a crippled submarine that went up to fight it out with the enemy. Eighteen feet of her bow was bent at right angles to port. The outer doors of two torpedo tubes could not be closed. About 35 feet of the bow, including the bow buoyancy tank, had been crumpled like so much cardboard.

Fortunately the enemy was nowhere in sight. In the night the rammed gunboat had gone—presumably to the bottom. Gone, too, were those who had been on GROWLER's bridge—the dead, and Commander Gilmore.

Schade put the battered submarine on a home course at dawn. Endorsing GROWLER's fourth patrol report, Commodore Fife commended: *"The performance of the officers and crew in effecting repairs and bringing the ship safely back to base is one of the outstanding submarine feats of the war to date. . . .* GROWLER *will be repaired and will fight again."*

Admiral Halsey wrote: *"The force commander is proud to extend his congratulations and commendation to this valiant ship and her courageous crew."*

To Commander Howard W. Gilmore went the first Congressional Medal of Honor to be awarded a submariner. *"For distinguished gallantry and valor, above and beyond the call of duty,"* the posthumous citation read. *". . . In the terrific fire of the sinking gunboat's heavy machine guns, Commander Gilmore, refusing safety for himself, remained on deck while his men preceded him below. . . ."*

Gilmore and GROWLER. In the memory of the U.S. Submarine Force the names are welded, inseparable. Mention either, and submariners think of gunfire and chaos in a roaring sea—a submarine's life threatened—and a voice speaking out of the night.

"Take her down!"

CHAPTER 17

JAPANESE ANTI-SUBMARINE WAR

Japanese A/S Effort

Guadalcanal was declared secured on February 7, 1943, and Japan had suffered her second catastrophic defeat since the war's beginning.

The little man in the breech-clout did not take the setback sitting down. Wheeling to defend his Upper Solomons front, he struck back hard. His blows fell hardest on that inexorable antagonist pursuing him from corner to corner of the South Seas arena—the United States Submarine Force.

It was evident in January that the Japanese were intensifying their anti-submarine war and employing every possible means to protect their shipping in the Bismarck-Solomons area. The opposition encountered by GUARDFISH, TAUTOG, GATO, ARGONAUT, GROWLER and other submarines in the Southwest Pacific bore testimony to the tightening defense. The enemy was straining his every muscle now, resorting to every dodge in the book. He, too, had learned from experience a lesson in the potentialities of undersea warfare.

Given greater industrial and technological support and the initiative in science, the Japanese might have won the anti-submarine battle at this juncture and delayed Allied victory for many months. Had U.S. submarines been forced to contend with an approximation of Allied anti-submarine measures, the enemy's grip on the Pacific would have been well-nigh unbreakable. Certainly the United States would have paid a much higher price in submarine losses.

As the war raged into its second year it was possible to assess the Japanese anti-submarine effort and draw a fairly conclusive picture of the enemy's ways and means in this aspect of warfare. The U.S. Submarine Force was now aware that it was up against nothing particularly novel or original. The Japanese possessed no "secret weapon." They employed no original tactic or unique device to combat the submersible. Japanese anti-submarine measures were copies, for the most part, of those developed by the Allies. But they were not what might be called "reasonable facsimiles." Due to a number of factors, the Japanese were unable to equal the Allied effort and maintain its pace.

Scientific and technological inferiority handicapped the enemy. In the development of electronic apparatus he lagged behind. Some of his equipment was good, but his technique in employing it was often faulty. He was late on the scene with such basic counter-measures as a convoy system and adequate air cover. Playing on his home field, he might have exploited a natural advantage, but with the exception of the area east of northern Honshu, where several submarine invaders were destroyed, Japan's coastal waters were indifferently defended. Merchant shipping was consistently torpedoed off Japan, and, as will be related, Japanese warships were attacked by submarines at the very entrance of Tokyo Bay.

Altogether, the Japanese Anti-Submarine War (naval abbreviation: ASW) was a jerry-built enterprise conducted at times in a most helter-skelter fashion. The Little Prussian of the East had perhaps grown too fast and was somewhat too big for his sea boots. Taking giant strides across the Southwest Pacific, he had failed to prepare a substantial footing—at least in the matter of anti-submarine warfare. In part responsible for this failure was a facet of the Japanese character. An overdose of nationalism, Shinto fanaticism, something in the Japanese make-up tended to breed a superiority complex which led to over-optimism. As will be seen, this exaggerated self-assurance had a direct bearing on his mediocre anti-submarine effort.

Japanese anti-submarine (A/S) devices and measures might have proved effective against submarines operating on a World War I scale. To facilitate discussion, they are herewith considered topically, although many were interrelated and all come under the general A/S heading.

For enlightenment on Allied submarine activities the Japanese A/S commands relied on Naval Intelligence—espionage to spy on submarine movements and operational facilities, and examination of captured documents and material, plus interrogation of prisoners to uncover inside information. Japanese offensive devices for anti-submarine warfare included contrivances for detecting submarines (radar, supersonic gear and so on) and such standard weapons for attack as depth charges and bombs. Defensive mining was relied upon to protect important harbors and shipping lanes. Other anti-submarine stratagems and measures for the protection of fleet units and convoys formed a part of the A/S panorama that had clarified by January 1943. The Japanese would contrive a few innovations and revisions. But by the end of 1943 the picture was much as it would remain for the duration of the war.

During 1942 but three U.S. submarines were lost in battle with the Pacific enemy. Fifteen went down in action in 1943. From the offensive measures encountered and the heavy casualties sustained in the Southwest Pacific Area in the first quarter of 1943, it may be assumed the Japanese A/S effort reached its peak of efficiency in this period. An examination of that effort provides background for the broadening picture of U.S. submarine operations.

Japanese Naval Intelligence

Post-war evidence indicates that Japanese intelligence sources failed to contribute anything of notable value to their anti-submarine effort. The ubiquitous Japanese spy system proved to be largely mythical. At Cavite the Japanese were able to raise SEALION, but they could not have learned much from her as her radio, sound and fire control gear had been removed before she was scuttled. Later in the war several U.S. submarines were lost in shallow water under circumstances that prevented the disposal of classified material and documents. The Japanese were unable to salvage any vital information from these submarines.

Suspected at the outset, the mediocrity of Japanese Intelligence became evident as the war progressed. It was openly, if accidentally, displayed in the spring of 1944 when Japanese Headquarters published a report by the so-called Battle Lessons Investigation Committee. This report concerned the submarine situation as it existed from June 1943 through March 1944. The document was captured, translated and studied by the Allies. Japanese estimates of the current strategic disposition of U.S. submarines were found to be fairly accurate. These estimates were undoubtedly based on information obtained from Japanese Radio Intelligence. But so long as the Japanese remained on the defensive this information on opposing strategy was of little value. An analysis of U.S. submarine tactics was lengthy, but hardly revelatory. The report contained some flagrant errors. Several anti-submarine attacks were described, and in each case the number of submarines involved was greatly overestimated.

The following excerpt is typical. It had reference to an incident which began on the morning of November 9, 1943, at lat. 214 N., long. 118-26 E. At this time and place AKATSUKI MARU was proceeding independently at 13 to 15 knots when she was attacked by what was estimated as three submarines. According to the Japanese document:

At 0539 three torpedo wakes were sighted 500 meters away on a bearing of 35° to port. Immediately turned to port to try to evade, when three more torpedo wakes were seen 500 meters away on a bearing of 50° to port, and the wakes of still another two torpedoes were seen 500 meters off the starboard beam bearing 100°. The first torpedo passed ahead. One of the second group of torpedoes passed under the vessel, and one, though it struck the vessel near the bridge, failed to explode. Although one of the third group of torpedoes also struck the vessel amidships it also was a dud. Another two additional torpedoes which failed to explode struck the stern. Damage was slight.

In reality, this attack was made by SEAWOLF on her eleventh patrol. She fired four torpedoes from the bow tubes, range 1,600 yards, 80° port track, depth setting 10 feet. Torpedoes were seen running hot and normal, on the right track. Her commanding officer, Lieutenant Commander R. L. Gross, rightly concluded the torpedoes must have been deep runners or duds.

An egregious shortcoming of Japanese Intelligence was its failure to obtain valid evidence upon which an accurate evaluation of anti-submarine attacks could be based. Contrary to American thoroughness which demanded evidence of the most reliable sort. Japanese credulity, rooted perhaps in egotism, accepted the flimsiest clue as an indication of success. As a result, the Japanese credited themselves with sinking about ten times the number of submarines actually sunk. Obviously they saw no need to modify the methods they thought were obtaining such happy results. And the U.S. Submarine Force did not talk down the enemy's exaggerated claims. As bombast was preferable to bombs, the "Silent Service" was more than willing to let the enemy enjoy this form of self-deception.

While silence paid generous dividends in the above respect, there was one feature of enemy Intelligence which could make it unbearable. This concerned the extraction of information from captive submariners under torture. Undoubtedly the Japanese obtained a few morsels of technical information by this means. Such fragments were worthless for the most part. Information given by submarine crews was generally sprinkled with all kinds of misleading or inaccurate details. Experience in questioning Japanese prisoners of war disclosed the fact that a captive could safely supply much technical data, sufficient in volume and so accurate in minor detail that the interrogator was enabled to make a long and impressive report. Boiled down, such a report would tell the enemy next to nothing. A broad gap exists between the knowledge of a design engineer and that of the usual interrogator, and the prisoner of war who is a technician may easily beguile the inquisitor who is not.

There were a few submarine secrets worth guarding to the bitter end. Maximum diving depth was one. Knowledge of future plans and operations was another. Technical features of material still in the development stage was perhaps a third. It was also important to keep the Japanese in ignorance respecting the ineffectiveness of their anti-submarine effort. Throughout the war these secrets remained unforfeited.

At war's end it was apparent that the Japanese had expended much effort in attempting to extort submarine information. And an excess of blood, sweat and tears had been endured in withholding information that would have availed the enemy little. Submarine Headquarters came to the conclusion it would have been better to brief submarine personnel to be more voluble—avoid beatings and torture by volunteering enough accurate information to satisfy the interrogator and impress his superiors. Altogether, the enemy's Inquisition was as futile as it was brutal.

In summary, Japanese Naval Intelligence was a dud when it came to supporting the anti-submarine effort.

Submarine Detection Devices

The Japanese had no shipborne radar during the early part of the war. A shore-based Japanese radar was captured on Guadalcanal. Apparently it had been used since January 1942 as an aircraft warning device. At the beginning of 1943 they installed a 10-CM radar on the battleship HYUGA. But even when possessed of a moderately satisfactory shipborne radar, the Japanese were slow to equip escort vessels with the device. Not until September 1944 did the lowly Japanese escort put to sea with radar.

Airborne radar was installed in Japanese medium bombers in the autumn of 1943. In December of that year the 901st Air Fleet was organized solely for the purpose of escorting convoys. But this radar-equipped group was composed of obsolescent aircraft, and it was the fall of 1944 before a large number of radar-equipped planes were pitched into the A/S war.

Japanese radar was inferior to Allied radar in every field. Japanese airborne radar was reputedly able to pick up a submarine at 12 miles, and toward the end of the war radar-equipped planes were making numerous night contacts on submarines. Japanese doctrine, however, called for only night or low-visibility radar use—visual search was persistently considered more reliable. And on many occasions the Japanese secured their radar, even at night, fearing radar-search would lead to the user's detection.

The Japanese themselves were early in the field with radar detector. It seems they had shipboard detectors in 1942. The date these detectors first appeared on escort vessels remains unknown, but evidence indicates that most of their escort vessels were so equipped by the end of 1944. Japanese radar detectors on surface ships had directional characteristics. Some of the detectors found on Japanese submarines at the end of the war were also directional.

Japanese radar search receivers were not installed in aircraft until late in 1944. Priority was given to carrier task force planes, and few were installed in anti-submarine aircraft. After V-J Day it was learned with certainty that Japanese aircraft never reached the stage of "homing" on U.S. submarine radar.

The enemy's radio direction finder net was well developed. At any time from the first day of the war until its last, an Allied submarine commander who made a radio transmission could count on the enemy to fix his position. This did not, of course, apply to very low or very high frequencies with transmission ranges commonly limited to visual distance. A good cut by well-located stations might fix the transmitting station as being within an area 100 miles square. A more accurate fix was usually unobtainable.

This fix could be broadcast to all ships at sea in a few hours' time. Frequency of the transmission would identify its source as a submarine transmitter, and it was impractical to change submarine frequencies often enough to obfuscate such identification. Accordingly, radio direction finders provided a means of keeping tabs on the number of submarines attached to each operating base, as well as the number on patrol and their general distribution throughout the Pacific.

As a tactical aid, the direction finder was decidedly limited. Submarine transmission within air-search range of a Japanese air base would receive special attention during the day's search. But the inaccuracy of the usual fix and the steaming distances involved ordinarily prevented the concentration of surface anti-submarine forces on the transmitting submarine. A secret monthly chart of all submarine contacts was issued in Tokyo and distributed to many operating commands. Several of these charts were captured during the war. The chart did little more than disseminate general information on the submarine war, and its security classification must have seriously interfered with that usage.

The Japanese were particularly proud of a device they called the *jikitanchiki*. This was a magnetic airborne submarine-detector somewhat similar to one developed by the Allies. The apparatus was capable of detecting a submersible at a distance of some 500 feet directly beneath the plane. Expert Japanese pilots flew magnetic search planes 30 to 40 feet above the surface. The average pilot maintained an altitude of 150 to 200 feet. By the end of the war, about a third of the shore-based anti-submarine planes were equipped with *jikitanchiki*, another third carried radar, a few had both, and the remainder carried neither.

Japanese optical equipment was good, and much effort was devoted to the training of lookouts. After the middle of 1943, however, U.S. submarine camouflage was greatly improved. This, and the submarine's reduced silhouette, went far to frustrate visual detection. The A/S vessel which depended solely on the man with binoculars seldom surprised the modern submersible.

The A/S vessel equipped with sonar apparatus proved a formidable foe from the first. As discussed in an earlier chapter, Japanese underwater listening gear was excellent. Japanese supersonic devices were also efficient. "Echo-ranging" destroyers and patrol craft presented a standing threat to the attacking or retiring submersible and were thoroughly respected by the submariners who sought to evade the probing "ping."

Offensive A/S Weapons

The Japanese produced nothing new in anti-submarine weapons. As was to be expected, their destroyers and larger escort vessels greatly outclassed submarines in gun-power. In a few instances submarines, damaged by depth charges from smaller escort vessels, surfaced and outfought their tormentors, gun for gun. But in all cases wherein a submarine was forced to fight it out on the surface with a destroyer, the battle ended quickly and disastrously for the submarine.

The Japanese were singularly tardy in the arming of their merchant marine. At the outset of the war their merchant vessels were not armed, and many remained unarmed for months thereafter. Japanese arsenals seem to have been entirely unprepared for this exigency. Priority went to merchantmen allotted to the Navy. Many ships in the Army pool went to sea with field guns on deck for protection. And some of the ships in the civilian fleet were reduced to the hopeless resort of dummy wooden guns.

These deficiencies were gradually rectified as the war went on. But the guns given the Japanese merchant fleet were too little and too late. In the previously mentioned Battle Lessons Investigation Committee report of April 1944, the Japanese stated:

> U.S. submarines have observed the guns with which our ships are equipped. Although our large vessels have one gun at both bow and stern, our small vessels have only one small caliber gun at the bow, with which the submarine's guns are fully capable of dealing. Therefore they seem to think that it is easy to make a close range gun attack especially from abaft the beam. Furthermore it is said that they are learning that the anti-submarine defensive power of our ships is less than at first imagined. The occasions at which gun engagements are carried out are steadily increasing.

But the gun-power of armed merchant ships, escort vessels and patrol craft was usually formidable enough to dictate caution on the part of the attacking submarine. Always at disadvantage in a gun duel, the thin-skinned submersible cannot survive many direct hits. Nevertheless, before the war ended, 939 gun attacks were made by U.S. submarines on enemy craft of all sizes and classes, and 722 vessels were reported sunk in these actions. As a number of these vessels were heavily armed, it would seem that Japanese firepower was not backed up by marksmanship of equivalent caliber.

The enemy's depth charge was perhaps his most

formidable A/S weapon. The 350-pounder carrying a 230-pound explosive charge was standard—and always dangerous. Yet it was not the deadly weapon that had been anticipated. While insufficient depth-settings, over-optimism, and lack of tenacity contributed to the lackluster results obtained, the chief reason for the weapon's feeble showing probably lay in its unwieldy characteristics. (Try to drop a can of beans on a fish at the bottom of a pond. Similar "X" factors enter the depth-charge equation.)

Early in the war depth charges were placed on practically every kind of Japanese ship that could lug them. The smallest and frailest of patrol craft might carry a few. Slow vessels carried depth charges equipped with parachute devices to decelerate the sinking and thereby give the vessel time to get well clear of the explosion. Many merchant ships were equipped with Y-guns and other depth-charge throwing apparatus. Japanese fleet destroyers carried 30 depth charges. Japanese frigates or *kaibokan* could carry as many as 300.

One of the busy Japanese PC-boats (the PC-13 class) was equipped with two depth-charge throwers and a stern tube rack. These 167-foot vessels could carry 36 charges. Their gun armament consisted of one 8-cm. dual-purpose and one dual-mount 13-mm. machine gun.

Japanese aircraft carried standard bombs, modified for use as anti-submarine weapons. Small planes carried 150-pound bombs, and larger ones carried 625-pound bombs. The bombs were equipped with delayed-action time fuses which could be set to explode the charge at a predetermined depth. Fuse settings were good for 80-foot, 150-foot or 250-foot depths. The 625-pound bomb was considered lethal at 60 feet. The smaller bomb had to make a direct hit.

During 1943 Japanese inventors were working on a circular-run torpedo to be used by aircraft against submarines. This torpedo was to be dropped about 200 yards in advance of the submersible. It was designed to travel in a reducing spiral, making four complete circles. While circling, it sank to a depth of 200 meters. It employed a contact exploder. (Records intimate mediocre performance.)

During the forepart of the war, the Japanese occasionally employed an explosive sweep. This mine-like contraption was towed astern, usually by slow patrol craft or merchantmen. It was fitted with a contact fuse. There is no record of any U.S. submarine coming into contact with this contrivance.

Japanese Mine Warfare

The most important Japanese mine was the Type-93—a moored contact mine. These mines were laid in great numbers with the purpose of closing off large sea-areas from submarine approaches. Behind such mine barriers Japanese merchant traffic could presumably proceed in safety.

One great minefield which blanketed the East China Sea extended from Formosa to Kyushu. The shallow water of the East China Sea was ideal for mine warfare. Another large minefield blocked Formosa Strait. To prevent submarines from entering the Sea of Japan, the straits of Tsushima, La Perouse and Tsugaru were mined. Other minefields guarded the coasts of Honshu, and many of the navigable channels in the Netherlands East Indies, in the Sulu Archipelago and in the Philippines were sown with mines intended to frustrate submarine navigation.

The Type-93 mine could be anchored in water of 550 fathoms. But these mines were usually planted in waters less than 100 fathoms, for in deeper water the cables sagged or were drawn askew by undersea currents. Such "mine dip" reduced the field's efficiency to the vanishing point and lengthy mine cables lasted only a short time. In an anti-submarine field the mines watched at various depths and might be placed as deep as 40 fathoms. Often they were planted in rows at staggered depths. The Type-93's were fired by means of "chemical horns"—tubes of acid which were activated by contact. Meeting the requirements of International Law, they were also equipped with a device designed to disarm them when the mooring cables were broken.

The Japanese possessed another type of anti-submarine mine. This was the Type-92—a moored, controlled mine which was used for mining harbor entrances and channels. This mine contained an 1,100-pound explosive charge and was fitted with a hydrophone detector. The mines were laid and controlled in clusters of six. They were fired from a control station when their hydrophones and magnetic loops gave warning that a submarine had entered the mine group. An ingenious weapon, but so far as is known it failed to score against a U.S. submarine.

Fields of moored contact mines laid in the open sea were another matter. Evidence indicates that three American submarines were lost to such minefields during the war, and they may have accounted for other submarines which vanished while on patrol. The large, open-sea minefield was laid in the expectancy that one submarine out of ten would be sunk while traversing it. Obviously the results obtained fell short of expectations. One reason: the field's efficiency was much reduced by time as the cables broke away and the mines became drifters, or sank from leaks or accumulated fouling.

An impartial weapon, the mine can be dangerous

to friend and foe alike—another drawback to the extensive use of minefields. More than one *maru* fell victim to a Japanese mine, and, as is common with widespread mining operations, the Japanese were faced with the necessity of constantly informing their merchant marine on the location of the fields. Widely disseminated information always jeopardizes security. Notices to mariners frequently fell into Allied hands, along with navigators' notes, old charts and other documents that betrayed minefield locations. These data were promptly relayed to the submarine commanders. In consequence, the most important Japanese minefields were as scrupulously avoided by U.S. submarines as they were by Japanese ship traffic.

By this it may be deduced that the Japanese mine as a defensive or tactical A/S weapon was ineffectual. Its teeth were drawn by the operational difficulties and inhibitions inherent to its usage. Strategic minefields succeeded in forcing U.S. submarines to avoid defined areas, and they remained a mental hazard for submariners operating in mineable water. Yet even in this regard the mine was far from invincible. In most instances the submarine could navigate with safety where merchant or naval vessels navigated, and that was exactly where the submersible wanted to be. And, as will be recounted in a later chapter, the Japanese mine was decisively vanquished by the U.S. Submarine Force in the last six months of the war.

Japanese Anti-submarine Tactics

Major combatant ships, military convoys, expeditionary forces and other important seagoing detachments were given a fair amount of anti-submarine protection from the first. But the enemy did not anticipate an aggressive submarine offensive in his home waters. Blockade Tokyo Bay? Impossible!

During the first year of the war, many Japanese vessels proceeded from Japan independently, without escort of any kind. Near the terminal points of the voyage such ships would be met by local anti-submarine patrols, but for the open-sea portion of the journey, they relied upon strategic routing and zigzagging.

Japanese zigzag plans were commonplace. A number of these plans were captured during the war. The Allies employed them in submarine training to give it a semblance of realism. Developed during World War I as an anti-submarine tactic, zigzagging proved an incompetent defense against the modern submarine, and Japanese zigzag tactics were notably ineffective. Increasing the time and distance steamed in submarine waters, zigzagging decreased the net speed of advance—a situation which favored the stalking submersible. The zigzag problem inspired an axiom popular in submarines circles. "For every ship saved by a fortuitous zig, another is lost by an unfortunate zag."

Japanese Patrol Craft

In the vicinity of important bases, in the approaches to busy ports and in similarly strategic locations Japanese anti-submarine patrol vessels were to be found. They might escort shipping clear of the port, but the majority maintained a day-in-day-out station patrol. Most of these patrol vessels were small, slow-speed craft. They ranged in size from sampans just large enough to carry a depth charge which could be rolled over the side, to ships of 400 or 500 tons' burden. On the small boats, listening gear was rare. A few were equipped with a crude microphone which could be lowered over the side. But the SHONAN MARU class, active around Truk and Palau, carried hydrophones, two-way radios, a depth-charge thrower, two depth-charge dropping platforms, one 3-inch gun and a machine gun. These craft were capable of 14 knots, and they were not to be "sneezed at" by any visiting submarine.

Small or large, the vessels on station patrol compelled the submarine to remain submerged and exert caution to prevent detection. Ordinarily they were not worth a torpedo attack, and a surface gun attack invited an immediate concentration of A/S vessels and aircraft from the nearby base. And the depth charges they carried were potentially just as dangerous to the submerged submarine as those carried by Japanese fleet destroyers. Had these patrol craft been faster and equipped with better sonar gear they would have proved a menace most difficult to overcome.

In some of the Malay Barrier passes, notably in Lombok Straits where the current forced submarines to make the northward passage on the surface, patrol craft were used in conjunction with shore batteries. Around the home Empire, at a radius of six hundred miles, stretched a ragged and broken line of surface pickets. As described in an earlier chapter these boats combined fishing and picketing. They were organized as regular patrols, and occupied regular stations. The picket usually carried a naval rating whose job was to watch and report any enemy activity in the vicinity of the picket line. The reporting of submarine activity was only incidental to their major job of locating and reporting surface task forces approaching the Empire. When air raids were striking at Japan, these pickets became an important element in the air-raid warning system.

In common with the Japanese patrol boat, pickets

were not worth a torpedo. Submarines frequently engaged them in gun battle. Dealt an odd assortment of weapons, they were pestiferous, hard to sink, and —as is always the case with an armed foe—dangerous. Their extermination was in order when the time was ripe for the Third Fleet's advance on Japan.

Japanese Escorting of Fleet Units

It was the responsibility of the Japanese Combined Fleet to furnish the anti-submarine screen for fleet units. Combat vessels and fleet oilers were usually escorted by fleet destroyers, although the Commander-in-Chief of the Combined Fleet might call upon an "area fleet" commander—such as Commander Fourth Fleet in Carolines and Marshalls—for occasional assistance. Normally the area fleet commander was responsible only for escorting within his area.

Apparently the Japanese did not follow any general doctrine for the guidance of these fleet-unit anti-submarine screens. The screens were tailored to fit the occasion, and were instructed in accordance with the views of the officer in tactical command. The instructions, therefore, were as varied as individual views. However, the Imperial Navy's major fleet units were usually well screened. Ordinarily the heavyweight warship or auxiliary had a fleet destroyer delegated to each bow, and if possible one was placed ahead. Japanese fleet destroyers also escorted important convoys.

The Jap DD was a redoubtable A/S vessel. Not the implacable killer pre-war doctrine led the submariners to expect (by the end of January 1943, five DD's had succumbed to U.S. submarine torpedoes), but an antagonist never to be taken lightly—as the ARGONAUT sinking brought home. A day would come when ARGONAUT's destruction would be repaid with a vengeance, but the attention then given the Japanese destroyer force emphasized its importance as a naval arm. Ultimately it was paralyzed to the point of complete atrophy, but before that upshot the Jap DD, acting as fleet-unit screen or convoy escort, did its share of damage.

The Japanese Convoy System

For the masters of a maritime nation launching a seagoing war, Japan's military leaders were strangely remiss in the matter of protection for their merchant marine. Their negligence in this regard seems as stupid as it was costly. They had only to refer to Britain's experience in World War I—to recall Jellicoe's frantic appeal, "We must stop these losses and stop them soon!" Unbelievably they discounted the lesson taught England at that time. More incredible

still, they ignored the current Battle of the Atlantic. That undersea warfare could seriously threaten Japan's own communication lines and economy apparently never occurred to the master minds in Tokyo. If it did occur, the thought was hastily discarded as too unpleasant for continued contemplation. Evidently the possibility of defeat seemed so remote in December 1941 that Nippon's domineering militarists felt they could dispense with elementary measures for the protection of Japanese shipping.

Not only did Japanese merchant vessels go to sea unarmed in the early months of the war, but no efficient convoy system was devised for their security. Some escortage was provided in the slapdash manner described. Troop transports and important military cargoes traveled under guard. But for the first two years of the war most of the Japanese merchantmen went unescorted.

Construction of special convoy vessels was started late in 1942. By that time the submarine attack had already blown a critical hole in the Japanese merchant marine. Merchant vessels and escorts now traveled in small groups, but regular convoying was not begun until 1943, and then it was confined to the Singapore run. Another year went by before the dire necessity for systematic convoying finally impelled the Japanese to establish a network of convoy routes. (See chart, page 340.) In the meantime the merchant marine had suffered irreparable damage; the war was rushing westward. Consequently, many convoy routes were abandoned shortly after being set up.

Japanese convoy methods were also belatedly devised. It was not until early 1944 that Number One Coast Convoy Unit issued an operation plan delineating ten or more standard formations designed to suit the number of ships in the convoy. In general, this Johnny-come-lately plan called for the formation of the convoy in a block to be surrounded by a ring of escorts. If enough escorts were available, a screen was to be placed in advance about 10,000 meters.

By this late date the shortage of escorts had become acute. But from the first, there had been an absurd insufficiency. The fault lay with Japan's leaders who had foolishly belittled the submarine. At the outset their shortsightedness forced transports to delay in port while commandants rummaged for escort vessels. Makeshift remedies could not cure the malady. Escort commanders did the best they could with the little at hand, and deployed their escort vessels according to whim, hunch and the craft available. Results were grab-bag. Large convoys might be efficiently screened by alert and aggressive escorts. Again a convoy would be trailed by a single escort vessel which could do little more than harass a submarine after an attack had been made. Sometimes one flank of a convoy would be left unguarded. Or, as in the WAHOO episode, a convoy might come waddling over the horizon without any guard at all. Throughout the Pacific War the behavior of the Japanese escort was completely unpredictable.

Surface Escort for Convoys

It was finally apparent to the Japanese High Command that area fleet commanders and commandants of naval stations acting on their own discretion were unable to supply adequate convoy protection. To rectify the situation, a Grand Escort Fleet was organized in 1943. Under command of a senior admiral, this fleet was independent of the Combined Fleet. The Commander-in-Chief of the Grand Escort Fleet was empowered to issue instructions on matters of convoy and was given authority in this respect over commandants of all naval stations. His principal forces, as eventually constituted, were the First Escort Squadron, the Second Escort Squardon and the 901st Air Squadron.

The First Escort Squadron developed into the First Escort Fleet with a vice admiral in charge. It was responsible for convoy escorts between the Empire and the Philippines, the East Indies and Palau. The Second Escort Squadron was responsible for escorting to the Marianas and Carolines. (After Saipan fell in 1944 its problems were over.) At Singapore, Soerabaja, Ambon, Manila and other Southwest Pacific bases, the area fleet commander retained responsibility for escort duty. Commander Sasebo Naval Station was made responsible for escorting to the Nansei Shotos.

In spite of its somewhat grandiloquent title, the Grand Escort Fleet could muster no more than 25 or 30 vessels for regular convoy escort duty until the spring of 1944. With the establishment, then, of convoy routes to Saipan, Manila, Saigon, North Borneo and Formosa, the escort fleet was expanded. Even so, its some 150 vessels were inadequate.

Originally the senior commanding officer of the escort acted as both escort and convoy commander. By late 1943, a convoy commander with the rank of captain was assigned to each major convoy. When the Allies finally closed in on the Philippines and Japan, 15 Imperial Navy captains and four rear admirals were acting as escorting group commanders in charge of both convoy and escort.

At that date the First Escort Fleet totaled but 60 vessels—four destroyers, 45 frigates, two sub-chasers, four minesweepers and some assorted gunboats. Backbone of the belated surface escort force was the *kaibokan* (known to the U.S. Navy as a frigate or

a coast defense vessel). There were several types of these vessels, the most numerous being a 220-footer. About half were steam-propelled and the remainder Diesel-powered.

The *kaibokan* carried two 4.7 guns, one forward and one aft, two light machine guns, and eleven 25-mm. guns. Fifty-two feet of the stern were occupied by the depth-charge installation which consisted of 12 depth-charge throwers, ranged in batteries of six on a side, and one stern rack from which the charges could be dropped singly. With the exception of the ready-service charges, all depth charges were stowed below and brought up by a hoist of the dumb-waiter variety. Loaded to the gills with 300 depth charges, these frigates were floating munition dumps. Their speed was somewhere between 16 and 20 knots, and their sonar gear topnotch. Despite deficient radar and a lack of modern A/S weapons, the *kaibokan* was an opponent no submarine would trifle with.

But the surface escort fleet, like the convoy system, was improvised and makeshift—a last-minute effort to rescue a foundering merchant service. When the Grand Escort Fleet was finally assembled, scores of freighters, tankers, passenger ships and transports were resting their torpedoed bottoms on the ocean's floor. The convoy escorts arrived too late. Deep-sea divers and salvage vessels were in order.

Air Escort for Convoys

It was not until December 1943 that the Japanese got around to organizing the 901st Air Fleet at Tateyama. As has been noted, this group was devoted to convoy service and its planes were among the first equipped with radar. The planes were old-timers; many of the pilots were second string. Results were third rate. From the beginning of the war to its end, communications between anti-submarine planes and anti-submarine surface vessels proved so difficult that there was little cooperation between the two. The Japanese Army Air Forces did some escort work at such remote bases as New Guinea, but there were never any joint escort operations between the Imperial Army and the Imperial Navy. Along with the communication difficulties, the pilots' unfamiliarity with the problems of overwater flying prevented coordinated effort.

Ordinarily when a Japanese plane made contact with a submarine, it attacked immediately. Anti-submarine planes did not carry guns as a rule, so there was no strafing. The airmen dropped one or two bombs. After the attack was made, the contact was reported and the estimated position was marked. If opportunity presented, the plane might visually guide a surface vessel to the contact.

Japanese pilots were indifferently trained in the tactics of anti-submarine warfare. After attacking a submarine, the pilot might remain on the scene until his plane was relieved or its fuel exhausted. But, having sighted oil or rubbish in the water, he was likely to depart elatedly, certain of of a kill. In the early part of the war many contacts were broken off after a few hours. Doctrine in the latter part of the war was for the plane to continue following the submarine for two or three days.

Usually, planes equipped with magnetic detector devices did not fly on area search, because the range of this equipment was limited to about 150 yards. When the magnetic detectors picked up a submarine, a red light showed on the pilot's instrument panel, and an aluminum powder-marker was automatically dropped. The indicated position of the submarine was then approached by the pilot who flew in four times from four different directions, dropping powder-markers each time his *jikitanchiki* picked up the submersible. In the center of the marker pattern the submarine was supposed to be situated. On a number of occasions the target turned out to be a sunken hulk—*jikitanchiki's* mistake. However, the Japanese claimed several U.S. submarines were sunk in the manner described.

To give a 10-knot convoy complete coverage, six planes equipped with magnetic detectors would have had to cover continuously the area ahead of a convoy. And an additional radar-equipped plane would have had to guard the convoy at night. Seven planes were rarely available for this duty, but major convoys sometimes were given two or three planes for air cover. Frequently the waters ahead of a convoy were searched by aircraft before the ships advanced.

Late in the war the Japanese planned to search a 30-mile-wide channel through the East China and the Yellow Sea. For a daily sweep of this extent some 80 planes were necessary. The planes were never forthcoming. When the carrier strikes on Formosa were unleashed in the fall of 1944, the losses of A/S planes outnumbered their replacements. Finally, U.S. Army Air Force planes, flying out of the Philippines, all but abolished the Japanese A/S aircraft. By V-J Day the bird was practically extinct.

A like fate awaited the Japanese land-based plane's seagoing counterpart. The Japanese started the war with five escort carriers. These at first were used exclusively as plane ferries. After Saipan fell, the four escort carriers which at that time remained were added to the convoy escorts. These carriers did not survive overly long. Three were sunk by submarines during 1944. There remains no evidence to indicate that carrier planes were any more efficient as convoy

protectors than shore-based planes would have been. Apparently the Japanese made no attempt to organize "hunter-killer" groups around an escort carrier.

The Japanese Counter-attack

At the beginning of 1943 the U.S. Submarine Force knew just about what it could expect in the way of Japanese A/S measures. The Japanese Grand Escort Fleet, organized convoying and aircraft equipped with radar and *jikitanchiki* were still in the future. However, the basic ingredients of the Japanese anti-submarine effort were in the pot. And there was no indication that the cooks would or could contrive a more lethal broth for Allied consumption.

Japanese ineptitude in this field of undersea warfare was, of course, recognized by the submarine Navy and exploited. The war was not many weeks old before the Americans realized "those guys up there" were setting their depth charges too shallow, breaking off their A/S attacks too soon and indulging in heady optimism concerning the results. Japanese airmen were not the only wishful thinkers. Imperial Navy men aboard destroyers, gunboats, sub-chasers and escort vessels frequently secured and sailed away in a glow of triumph entirely unjustified by the facts. A cheerful battle report always made good reading at Headquarters and enabled Tokyo Rose to broadcast an auspicious list of U.S. submarine obituaries. Many an embattled submarine owed its deliverance to Japanese presumption. And more than one submarine skipper could have quoted Mark Twain's, "The reports of my death are greatly exaggerated."

However—

Although the Japanese anti-submarine effort was haphazard and at times almost lackadaisical, it managed to exact a punishing toll. Inferior though they were in many respects, the component A/S forces constituted a menace that meant trouble whenever encountered. The heavily armed destroyer, the ugly CHIDORI "pinger," the lethal mine and zooming plane could be as deadly as lightning which strikes at random but kills when it hits.

In February, March and April 1943, Japanese A/S forces struck with tempestuous violence and ferocity.

Loss of Amberjack

AMBERJACK—the submarine that had substituted for an oil tanker—went back into the Solomons from Brisbane on her third war patrol. She could have used a longer stay in port, but the Japanese were not taking a holiday, and neither were the submarines of Task Force Forty-two. So the crew had hardly got around to "Waltzing Matilda" before the skipper had his orders and AMBERJACK was off again.

Her refit and rest period abbreviated to 12 days, the submarine was not quite up to the mark when she started out on January 24th. During a deep dive she started several minor leaks; had to put back into Brisbane for repairs. She was at sea again on the 26th, and five days later she was patrolling the western approaches to Buka Passage.

Southeast of Treasury Island she contacted a Japanese submarine. The contact faded, but Lieutenant Commander Bole knew AMBERJACK had moved into lively waters. On the afternoon of February 3, the submarine battle-surfaced to attack a large schooner. AMBERJACK's deck guns barked, and the two-master went down, a shambles of sailcloth and kindling.

Later that day the submarine received orders to move south along the Buka-Shortland traffic lane and concentrate on the area east of Vella Lavella Island. As she swung down this South Seas trail on the night of February 4, her lookout sighted a 5,000-ton freighter, and Bole immediately began the chase. The night-surface attack exploded into a slam-bang gun battle as the freighter materialized into a heavily armed munitions ship. Bole fired five torpedoes at this target, while the munitions vessel replied with shot and shell. Machine-gun bullets zipped around AMBERJACK's conning tower, and an officer on the submarine's bridge was struck in the hand. Going topside, Chief Pharmacist's Mate Arthur C. Beeman was killed by a vicious fusillade. The munitions ship was hit, and Bole reported her as sunk. Japanese records do not disclose the loss of a ship at the point indicated, but the vessel was unquestionably struck and a munitions cargo is particularly vulnerable.

On February 13 AMBERJACK was notified that her patrol was to include the entire Rabaul-Buka-Shortland Sea area. The next night she reported that she had plucked a half-drowned Japanese aviator from the sea during the afternoon and been attacked and forced down by two destroyers that evening. This was the last message received from AMBERJACK.

Further attempts to establish radio communication with the submarine proved unavailing. On March 22 she was 12 days overdue at Brisbane and so was reported lost.

Eventually it was learned that the Japanese torpedo boat HAYODORI, in company with Sub-chaser No. 18, attacked a U.S. submarine on February 16 in the area assigned to AMBERJACK. The submarine had previously been bombed by a Japanese patrol plane. Oil and wreckage swirled to the surface, and the Jap A/S vessels reported a sinking.

While evidence points to AMBERJACK as the victim of the anti-submarine attack described, the submarine under fire could have been GRAMPUS, lost in mid-February in that area. Whatever the date, it is certain that AMBERJACK's captain and crew went down fighting. The enlisted men's recreation center at the Submarine Base, Pearl Harbor, is named for Chief Pharmacist's Mate Arthur Beeman who was killed on the night of February 4 during the gun battle with the munitions ship.

Loss of Grampus

To conduct her sixth war patrol, GRAMPUS departed for the Solomons area on February 9th. On the 10th she was ordered to return to Brisbane. She started out again on February 11th. After leaving her exercise target the following day, she was never heard from again.

Under the captaincy of Lieutenant Commander J. R. Craig, GRAMPUS had accomplished several important special missions during the Guadalcanal campaign. She landed coast watchers on Vella Lavella and Choiseul Islands, struck at the enemy's convoys and probably damaged a good-sized transport and a destroyer. On February 14 she was directed to patrol in the Buka-Shortland-Rabaul area, the southern part of which was simultaneously patrolled by TRITON. A week later GRAMPUS was ordered to hunt in the waters east of Buka and Bougainville. On March 2 she was told to proceed toward Vella Lavella and enter Vella Gulf on the afternoon of March 5th. Her mission was to sink enemy shipping which might try to run westward through Blackett Strait in an attempt to escape United States surface forces scheduled to bombard Vella Lavella on March 6th. GRAYBACK was to team up with GRAMPUS in this operation, and each was informed of the other's assignment.

Both submarines were warned on the evening of March 5 that two enemy destroyers had been spotted heading from Faisi, off southeastern Bougainville, toward Wilson Strait, the passage between Vella Lavella and Canongga. As it eventuated, these DD's steamed through Blackett Strait into Kula Gulf where they were trapped and sunk by Allied surface forces.

GRAYBACK was apparently unable to contact this pair of destroyers. But on the night the warning was radioed, she sighted a silhouette in that part of Vella Gulf assigned to GRAMPUS. Assuming it was her sister submarine, GRAYBACK gave the silhouette a wide berth. She was unable to exchange recognition signals. Whether the vessel she sighted that night was Craig's submarine remains a mystery.

On March 7, Brisbane Headquarters, disturbed by the fact that no word had as yet come in from GRAMPUS, ordered the submarine to report her position. No answer. Again on the 8th Brisbane requested word from GRAMPUS. The submarine made no reply. She was officially reported lost on March 22nd.

The Japanese reported one of their convoys attacked by a submarine in the Rabaul area on the afternoon of February 18th. In this action a freighter was damaged by torpedo fire, and the escorts delivered a fierce counter-attack. The assaulted submarine may have been GRAMPUS.

According to Japanese records two of their seaplanes sighted and attacked a U.S. submarine in the same area the following afternoon. Afterward a large spread of oil was sighted on the surface. The seaplanes were confident of a kill. It seems possible, however, that GRAMPUS was caught and sunk by the two destroyers which passed through Blackett Strait on the night of March 5th. An ominous oil slick was sighted in Blackett Strait the following day. Submariners believe that GRAMPUS went down fighting in a night-surface action with these men-of-war en route to their own destruction in Kula Gulf.

Loss of Triton

The loss of ARGONAUT in January and AMBERJACK in February, followed by that of GRAMPUS, came as a direful indication of Japanese A/S reinforcements in the Bismarck-Solomons area. In the wake of this triple disaster TRITON was lost with all hands.

Captained by Lieutenant Commander G. K. MacKenzie, Jr., TRITON left Brisbane on February 16 to hunt enemy traffic running between Rabaul and the Shortland Basin. On March 6 she reported a battle royal with a Japanese convoy of five ships escorted by a destroyer. In this battle TRITON sank KIRIHA MARU, freighter, 3,057 tons, and damaged another cargo vessel. One of her torpedoes made a circular run which forced her to go deep. Two days later she rose to the occasion and attacked another escorted convoy. A destroyer rushed TRITON, and she was forced under before she could observe the results of eight torpedoes fired at the stampeding ships.

The last message received from TRITON reached Brisbane on March 11th. *"Two groups of smokes, 5 or more ships each, plus escorts. . . . Am chasing."*

She was ordered to stay south of the equator, and informed that TRIGGER was operating in an adjacent area. Two days later she was sent a message informing her that three Japanese destroyers had been sighted in her area, evidently on a submarine hunt. Subsequent radio dispatches failed to elicit any response.

The submarine was told to clear her area on March 25 and return to Brisbane. When TRITON made no reply to this order, and did not reach Australia on the date expected, the Brisbane Task Force realized it had lost another hard-fighting submarine.

Information made available after the war's end leaves little doubt as to the time and place of TRITON's last battle. Just north of the Admiralty Islands she went down fighting on March 15, in combat with the three destroyers which had been reported in her area. Veteran of the war's beginning, TRITON had sunk 11 Japanese vessels since the day she first contacted the enemy off Wake Island. Among her victims were the Japanese destroyer NENOHI and the submarine I-164. Altogether she had cost Japan 31,788 tons of shipping. But the DD's she attacked were apparently on the alert. Three against one, they unloosed upon TRITON an avalanche of depth bombs. Their battle reports described the barrage as strewing the ocean's surface with "a great quantity of oil, pieces of wood, cork and manufactured goods bearing the legend, 'Made in U.S.A.'"

"Made in U.S.A." Fitting epitaph for a valiant submarine.

Loss of Grenadier

In April 1943, GRENADIER, under Lieutenant Commander J. A. Fitzgerald, was patrolling in Malacca Strait. Although this waterway, lying between the Malay Peninsula and Sumatra, was deep in enemy territory, targets had proved disappointingly scarce to this veteran submarine on her sixth war patrol. But by every indication there was Japanese shipping in the vicinity of Penang. Dangerous hunting ground, but Fitzgerald determined to investigate the approaches to that Malay seaport. Early in the morning of the 21st, a few miles off Penang, GRENADIER sighted and set out on the trail of a two-ship convoy. At 0800 she had about 15 minutes to go to obtain a strategic position on the convoy's track, when the lookouts reported, "Plane on the port quarter." Fitzgerald gave the order to dive.

A few seconds after GRENADIER submerged, the executive officer remarked, "We ought to be safe enough now. We're between 120 and 130 feet." His statement was punctuated by a blast that sounded as if a munitions vessel had blown up immediately overhead. A bomb had exploded near the bulkhead between the maneuvering room and after torpedo room. In the conning tower the lights blacked out and power was lost. GRENADIER heeled over about 15°, and coasted helplessly—down—down—coming to rest on the sea floor under some 270 feet of water.

Communication with the after compartments went out of kilter. Then the alarming word came through, "Fire in the maneuvering room!" Smoke surged from the compartment, men groped about blindly, coughing, and as the fire got out of hand, Fitzgerald ordered the compartment sealed.

Some 30 minutes later the compartment was opened and entered by a damage control party using "lungs" and respirators. Flames were eating into the hull-insulation cork, cables, stores and cleaning rags. The main motor cables had been gashed when the submarine heeled over, and arcing and sparks from the resulting short circuit had started the blaze.

Two fire fighters were overcome by the suffocating smoke. Crew members went about their duties, tight-lipped, or sat staring dazedly at the overhead. Fitzgerald spoke quietly over the inter-com, "Steady men. Everything is under control."

But when the fire was finally smothered, the maneuvering room was a wreck. The induction valve had been knocked off its seat, and a two-inch stream of water was pouring in. The hard patch above the main motor-controller had ruptured, admitting a spray that soaked the maze of electrical apparatus. Short circuits and grounds started a pyrotechnic sputter, and no sooner was one blaze extinguished than another cropped out.

Meantime, a bucket brigade hustled between the maneuvering room and the forward torpedo room, trying to keep the water level below the main motors. In the fouling air, men slumped from heat prostration and physical exhaustion. Eventually a jury rig was installed between the main battery and a drain pump, so that the pump could be put on the motor room bilge. The bucket line was secured, and the submariners turned to other emergency repair tasks.

GRENADIER had suffered serious internal injuries. In the forward end of the after torpedo room the hull on the starboard side had been dished in from four to six inches. The after tubes had been forced to port, bending the main shafts. All the hull frames in the maneuvering room and the after torpedo room were bent inward. The door between the maneuvering room and the after torpedo room was sprung and would not close properly. The strongback in the after torpedo room loading hatch was bent. Water sprayed in through the damaged hatch. Later the crew discovered that about two-fifths of the gasket in this hatch was chopped up. The hatch had been wrenched into an elliptical shape, and a man could put his hand between the knife-edge and the hatch cover.

All hydraulic lines to the tubes, vents and steering mechanisms in the after torpedo room were broken. Many of the gages in the after room were knocked acockbill. In the maneuvering room the control gage was twisted askew. Deck plates and supporting frames were warped. The engine room had also suffered damage, and hydraulic lines to the main vents were discovered broken.

The radio transmitter in the conning tower had been jarred from its foundation and the insulators in the antenna trunk were fractured. The SJ radar appeared to be unharmed, but it could not be tested. Minor damage extended all the way to the forward battery room where dishes and phonograph records had been shattered.

GRENADIER's company worked throughout the day, laboring to regain propulsion. Electricians did everything they could to shield vulnerable equipment from the salt bath showering from the maneuvering room overhead, but intermittent electrical fires and persistent leaks frustrated their best efforts. The radio, however, was put back in commission, and the motors were at last revived. At 2130 the submarine struggled to the surface. Somehow Lieutenant H. B. Sherry, the diving officer, managed to keep her on an even keel.

Fitzgerald had hoped that on the surface they could stem the leakage and restore the electrical equipment. The submarine was cleared of smoke, and the engineers and electricians got to work on the damaged power plant. By means of jury rigs they finally managed to turn over one shaft at slow speed. But the shaft was badly bent and it was impossible to get the contact levers into the second stage of resistance. Approximately 2,750 amperes were required to turn the shaft, whereas the normal was 450. After a heartbreaking attempt, the engineering officer, Lieutenant Alfred J. Toulon, and the electricians reported to Fitzgerald on the bridge that their efforts were stymied. Everything possible had been done to establish propulsion, and it was literally no go.

With her deck gun out of commission, GRENADIER could neither fight nor run away—a desperate situation for a submarine far behind the enemy's lines in the hottest kind of water. Morning was coming, and it would certainly bring with it a horde of Japanese sub-hunters. In this extremity Fitzgerald was not for sitting on his hands. He soon had the crew working on a sail which might take GRENADIER in closer to the beach where the crew could be disembarked and the submarine blown up. But the sail proved useless in the breathless doldrum of a tropic sunrise. As daylight burned through the eastern mists Fitzgerald decided it was high time to scuttle the helpless submarine and strike out for shore.

A radio message was dispatched, describing the submarine's condition and the captain's intent to abandon. All confidential papers were destroyed. Radio, radar, T.D.C. and sound gear were demolished. While these acts of abandonment were in progress a merchant ship and an escort vessel hove in sight. A few minutes later a Japanese plane came droning over the horizon.

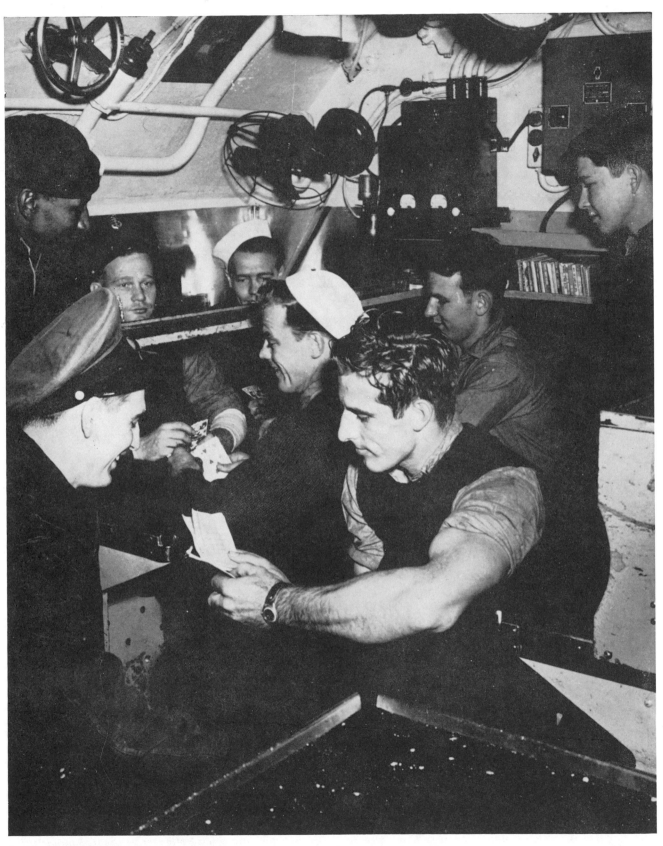

RELAXATION DOWN BELOW. Men off watch in the USS Tarpon *enjoy a breather. All is not work in the pressure hull, where there is elbow room for a game of acey deucy, a letter from home, some casual banter, or a bit of shut-eye. But "Battle Stations!" could turn the above scene into a blur of motion.*

KAIBOKAN FRIGATES. The quartet shown in this post-war photo typifies the breed. Though raffish in aspect and relatively slow, they were not to be ignored by subs. They usually carried two 4.7-inch guns and 300 depth-charges.

TORPEDOED BY GUDGEON, Meigen Maru sinks off Mangkhalihat. Same sub and Skipper Post sank biggest liner in Jap service.

TORPEDOED BY KINGFISH, transport Takachiho Maru, loaded with troops, goes down.

VICTIM OF WAHOO. Unidentified maru plays target for "Mush" Morton and company in January 1943. Wahoo raid in Yellow Sea served notice on Tokyo that cargoes from Manchuria could no longer be counted on. Attrition war began to pinch Empire's economy in spring of 1943. In autumn, subs hacked vital Singapore-Japan oil line.

The plane made a beeline for the stricken submarine. But GRENADIER was not entirely paralyzed. Withholding fire until the position angle was about 65°, Fitzgerald ordered the gunners to open up with two 20-mm. and two .30-cal. machine guns. The attacking plane was hit. It pulled up sharply and the pilot changed course to the left to try a run up GRENADIER's port side. Again the embattled submariners blazed away as the plane roared in. The pilot dropped a bomb that exploded in the water about 200 yards from GRENADIER. The miss cost the airman his life—he died that night as a result of bullet wounds and a crash landing when he returned to base.

The enemy surface vessels were not to be thus driven off. Closing in relentlessly, the Japanese saw GRENADIER's crew lined up with life jackets on her forecastle. Fitzgerald moved among the men, stalwart and reassuring. "Take it easy, boys. We'll come through." Those who were sick or unable to swim were assigned to rubber lifeboats. The chief of the boat W. C. Withrow, was below, manning the vents. Fitzgerald gave the order to abandon. The crew went overside. The chief opened the vents. GRENADIER began to sink by the stern. Fitzgerald waited for Withrow to come up from below, then he and the chief went over.

The Japs circled GRENADIER taking pictures. Lieutenant Kevin D. Harty clung to a mattress and read aloud to the crew from a popular magazine. All hands, and presumably the periodical, were picked up by the enemy.

GRENADIER's submariners were more fortunate than some. Despite long imprisonment and barbarous treatment at the hands of frustrated inquisitors, all but four survived and were recovered from Japanese prison camps at the end of the war.

Battle without Quarter (Gudgeon Gets a Liner)

GRENADIER's story serves to illustrate the point that the random bullet which hits can be as fatal as the sharpshooter's. And the Japanese A/S effort, although inconsistent and disorganized, constituted a standing menace which never permitted any relaxation of vigilance. From the war's first day until its last the submarine on war patrol could not let down its guard.

The loss of three submarines in St. George's Channel in the spring of 1943 marked those waters south of Rabaul as poison. Submariners returning from the area with stories of close-shave encounters and prolonged depth chargings confirmed previous indications that the enemy had launched a furious antisubmarine campaign in the Rabaul area. As a result

of mounting casualties, the commander of the Brisbane Force (which was now designated as Task Force Seventy-two) ordered his submarines to steer clear of confined waters. Daytime surface runs near the equator were tabooed, and restrictions on the use of the SD radar were imposed as it had been learned that shore and shipboard detectors could pick up and presumably take bearings on the SD at ranges up to 150 miles. Use of the SD aircraft-warning device had for some time occasioned controversy. While the restrictions applied principally to submarines on offensive reconnaissance, and were limited to clear days when aircraft could be spotted by vigilant lookouts, they were generally considered a wise precautionary measure in the Solomons-Bismarck area.

Precautionary measures did not mean a lessening of the pressure on Rabaul and Bougainville. As the casualty reports came in, the battle continued unabated, the Brisbane Force redoubling its efforts to wreck the enemy's South Seas transport system.

Long before ARGONAUT, AMBERJACK and the others were officially announced as lost, their "going west" was common knowledge to the force. A gap in the nightly dispatch which had previously mentioned the submarine's whereabouts. Grapevine. A crew came in from patrol, saw a vacant mooring place where a familiar boat was expected. "Hasn't GRAMPUS come in yet?" Blank looks from the hands aboard a tender. The word got around.

The submariners tightened their belts and set out with renewed determination to paint the conning towers with Japanese flags. To hell with the A/S war! The patrols went on. The battles went on. And throughout the worst of it in the Southwest Pacific, submariners continued to excursion through the enemy's lines on special missions that were Odysseys of daring and adventure.

There was GUDGEON (Lieutenant Commander Stovall) coming back from a voyage to Negros where, on January 14, she landed a ton of underground equipment, six Filipinos and a Major Villamor. There was GREENLING (Lieutenant Commander Bruton) returning from a reconnaissance mission in the Admiralties and a perilous junket to the east coast of New Britain where she landed a party of intelligence agents on February 2nd. On February 10, GROUPER (Lieutenant Commander R. R. McGregor) rescued an aviator from Rengi Island. Simultaneously, GUDGEON was at Timor, evacuating 28 refugees from that island's hostile south coast. Farther west went THRESHER (Lieutenant Commander Millican) to reconnoiter Christmas Island These missions were typical of the many accomplished by submarines from Brisbane and Fremantle while the Southwest Pacific Battle was at tempest pitch.

The force that could take it could also deal it out. On February 20 ALBACORE (Lieutenant Commander R. C. Lake) hit a bull's-eye in the Admiralties and downed the Imperial Navy's destroyer OSHIO. On April 9 TAUTOG (Lieutenant Commander Sieglaff) overtook the destroyer ISONAMI off Boston Island, Celebes, and three torpedoes sent this Japanese warship sloughing to the bottom. The 5,214-ton freighter PENANG MARU followed as a chaser.

In the Bismarck-Solomons cauldron the thunder of American torpedoes was not drowned by the boom of Japanese depth bombs as the anti-submarine storm raged on through February, March and April. On February 19 GATO (Lieutenant Commander Foley) in cooperation with land-based Navy aircraft sank the 6,550-ton freighter HIBARI MARU off Bougainville. Downed north of the Bismarcks in mid-April by DRUM (Lieutenant Commander B. F. McMahon), the freighters OYAMA MARU and NISSHUN MARU left a gap of some 10,000 tons in the enemy's shipping.

In the Admiralty Islands, athwart the western approaches to the Bismarcks, Japanese freighters went to the bottom. Patrolling from Pearl Harbor, TRIGGER (Lieutenant Commander R. S. Benson) sank MOMOHA MARU's 3,000 tons in Admiralty waters on March 15th. TUNA (Lieutenant Commander A. H. Holtz) scored for the Brisbane Force in this area on March 30, sinking KUROHIME MARU, 4,697 tons.

Elsewhere in the Southwest Pacific the attrition war against the Japanese merchant marine went on full blast. Striking in the Java Sea on February 14, TROUT (Lieutenant Commander L. P. Ramage) destroyed the 1,911-ton gunboat HIROTAMA MARU. Torpedoes from THRESHER (Lieutenant Commander W. J. Millican) downed the freighter KUWAYAMA MARU in the same area on February 21, and on March 2 sank the tanker TOEN MARU to subtract a total of 10,900 tons from the Japanese-Java supply line.

One of the loudest blasters in the Southwest Pacific that spring was GUDGEON. Skippered by Lieutenant Commander W. S. Post, Jr., the submarine from Fremantle staged a ravaging raid on the Greater East Asia Co-Prosperity Sphere. GUDGEON's seventh war patrol—her first under command of "Bill" Post—was a short one of three weeks' duration. In this brief excursion, which took her into the Java Sea and Makassar Strait, she sank a freighter and an oil tanker, damaged two luckier merchantmen and engaged in a running gun battle with a sub-chaser.

The freighters were torpedoed soon after the submarine entered enemy water. MEIGEN MARU, 5,434 tons, went down off the Java Coast on March 22nd.

Post reported the liquidation of another AK, but according to Japanese records this *maru* survived the torpedoing.

The sub-chaser fight occurred off Great Masalembo Island. When sighted by GUDGEON's bridge lookout, the enemy patrol vessel was strolling along at some 15 knots. Post put four engines on the line, aiming to close on the enemy's starboard quarter, sweep her deck with 20-mm. fire and then sink the vessel with a shelling from the three-inch gun. Which was all very well until the range shortened to 1,900 yards, the sub-chaser made a sharp veer to the right and the submariners got a good look at their target.

"That Jap patrol boat seemed to open up like an accordion," one of GUDGEON's officers recalled. GUDGEON was chasing a powerful CHIDORI "pinger."

"The CHIDORI seemed undecided what to do," Post related. "So we took the bull by the horns and turned to starboard to keep our battery bearing on his broadside. I hope we scared him as much as he scared us."

Sub and sub-chaser then did a simultaneous ships right, and now the sub-chaser was chasing the sub. As the range closed to a dangerous 1,800 yards, Post fired four torpedoes at GUDGEON's pursuer. Because of the high-speed turn, the helmsman was unable to steady on the firing course, and the torpedoes missed. The salvo forced the CHIDORI to swerve, however, and this gave GUDGEON a moment's initiative. As the enemy hauled over to the submarine's port quarter, the GUDGEON gunners brought their battery to bear. Four times the three-incher flamed and slammed. The CHIDORI retorted with lashing machine-gun fire. But the Japanese were slowed by the shelling. "And just by luck," Post reported, "our fourth shot silenced the Jap's 37-mm. twin mount."

A twin-engine Mitsubishi bomber was something else again. As the echoes of gunfire clattered away, this aircraft made an appearance in the sky. Post ordered a dive and the submariners rigged for a depth charging. But all remained quiet under the Java Sea. Four hours later, Post surfaced and GUDGEON headed north for the Strait of Makassar.

She caught her tanker exactly on the equator, about midway between Borneo and Celebes. Date: March 29th. Latitude: 00-00-00. Tanker: TOHO MARU, 9,997 tons.

Tanker and submarine sighted each other simultaneously, and the oil carrier opened fire without preamble. As the first enemy salvo fell short about 50 yards, three torpedoes from GUDGEON trailed their luminous wakes. Two doomful explosions wrapped the victim in a shroud of smoke, and TOHO MARU began to settle by the stern.

To hasten the settlement, Post ran the submarine

under the equator, and fired a torpedo at the target from the Northern Hemisphere. This shot struck the tanker just forward of the bridge, but the vessel remained stubbornly above water, the Japanese gunners throwing shells in the submarine's direction. Post thereupon sent GUDGEON under the equator once more and from the Southern Hemisphere punched a torpedo into the target. TOHO MARU's demise left a sizable hole in the Japanese-Borneo oil line.

A few hours later, GUDGEON sighted, stalked and torpedoed another Japanese tanker. Evidently this damaged vessel survived. But on her next war patrol —a run from Fremantle to Pearl Harbor—GUDGEON struck a target that did not survive, and the result was the largest hole yet blown in the Japanese transport service.

GUDGEON's homeward journey was by way of the Philippine area where she combed the Sulu Sea between Negros and Palawan. On the eve of April 28 she was driving through dark water tumbled by gusty winds and whisked by intermittent rain squalls. Post had just about decided to write off an uneventful day when—the time: 2345—things began to happen. Lightning splintered in the sky, and there was a ship silhouetted across the water. An ocean liner!

Post and company shocked into action. Headed south, the liner was traveling at racing speed. A radar sweep showed she was unescorted, and it was a good guess she was carrying troops and depending on big engines to get her clear of submarine attack. GUDGEON, already abeam, would have to rely on four Diesels to overhaul this fast transport.

The pursuit lasted a little over an hour, the submarine running like old OREGON coming around the Horn. As GUDGEON closed in directly astern, Post saw the only chance was an up-the-kilt shot, and at 0100 the thumb of the firing officer itched at the key. Four minutes later, Post opened fire—four torpedoes aimed directly at the fleeing liner's rudder. If those fish missed, counter-mined, or prematured—! The ticking seconds seemed to march on to infinity, and then three explosions jolted the night. A distant flash across the sky showed the big liner dragging her stern.

Believing the ship merely damaged, Post sent the submarine to periscope depth and drove forward to deliver the *coup de grâce*. Then, watching through the periscope, he glimpsed the ship's black bow up-angled against the sky—the silhouette slid from view —another burst of eerie light revealed a heaving carpet of water. The radar watch saw it, too. A dwindling pip on the magic screen—then nothing.

"Skipper! That baby's gone!"

This was one of the classic up-the-kilt sinkings

of the war—all over exactly 12 minutes after the first torpedo was fired.

Surfacing to scan the area, GUDGEON found the sea strewn with flotsam, lifeboats thrashing about in the dark, and the water alive with shouting men. The transport, identified as KAMAKURA MARU, was the largest in the Japanese service. She was the former passenger liner CHICHIBU MARU, 17,526 tons.

Later in that patrol, GUDGEON caught a Japanese trawler in the Sulu Sea, sank the craft by gunfire and recovered three Filipinos who had been held captive by the enemy. During this action, Lieutenant (jg) G. H. Pendland, the battery officer, was struck by an ejected cartridge case and knocked overboard. In vain the submarine conducted a two-hour search. This was the one note of personal tragedy in a fighting patrol that GUDGEON concluded in the Sulu Sea May 12 by sinking the 5,862-ton freighter, SUMATRA MARU. In something more than two months' time, Post and his sharpshooting GUDGEON crew demolished 38,819 tons of Japanese shipping.

For the reasons discussed in this chapter, the enemy was unable to maintain the anti-submarine offensive launched in the Rabaul area in the first quarter of 1943. And the Japanese anti-submarine war was as unsuccessful as the related attempt to cope with the logistics problem. The deficiencies in the Japanese A/S system are clearly seen in the demise of the unescorted KAMAKURA MARU. When the Imperial Navy rushed anti-submarine forces to the front, American submarines struck at weakened sectors behind the front. Concentration of escorts in one area left the sea lanes of another exposed. GUDGEON's raid far west of the Solomons could have been another lesson for impetuous Admiral Yamamoto had he lived long enough to study it.

The Admiral did not live that long. Early in April 1943 a flight of Japanese bombers and Zeros struck at Allied shipping off Guadalcanal. The bombers sank a New Zealand corvette, an oil tanker and the destroyer AARON WARD. A few days later a squadron of Army Lightning fighters from Henderson Field raced to Bougainville to repay this attack. The Allies had learned that Yamamoto and members of his staff were flying to Bougainville. Accordingly, the Japanese admiral was struck and killed by American-made "lightning" as his plane came in for a landing.

In any event, he would have arrived too late to turn the South Seas tide. By April the Upper Solomons front had begun to crumble. American aircraft would take over the bulk of the attack on the Bismarcks. Already the U.S. Submarine Force was withdrawing some of its units from the South Pacific and aiming their torpedo tubes toward Japan.

CHAPTER 18

DRIVE ON DAI NIPPON

Portrait of a Submarine Admiral

In a well-known Stateside Bureau during the war, an irreverent naval officer parodied the song, "Don't Fence Me In," with the words, "Don't Ship Me Out!" This pasquil may have pricked a conscience or two on the banks of the Potomac. But at SubLant, SubPac and SoWesPac bases there were few consciences that could be thus troubled. Force commanders had to fight to keep their staff members out of the pressure hulls, and on several warm occasions fleet commanders had to fight to keep their submarine force commanders ashore. A recalcitrant force commander in this respect was Admiral Lockwood who (the story is off the cuff) engaged in a number of vigorous arguments with the Powers that Be, insistently requesting permission to lead a war patrol.

One of the first new fleet submarines to leave Pearl Harbor after Admiral Lockwood became ComSubPac was the USS Scamp. Departing on her maiden patrol for a run in Empire water, Scamp, captained by Commander W. G. Ebert, carried a distinguished passenger. The passenger was Admiral Lockwood.

It has been remarked that submarines are informal naval vessels—for who can strike an attitude in sweatshirt and shorts? Abilities count for more than epaulettes when the plug is pulled. In the democracy of danger submariners learn a mutual respect, and performance is more important than punctilio.

Even so, a submarine crew with an admiral at close quarters could become a little tense during a voyage. True, Admiral Lockwood was a submariner. All in Scamp could see that. Still, he was an admiral, a stranger to most of Scamp's personnel. And his nickname spoken around Pearl, a shade formidable at first hearing, was "The Boss."

For his part, an admiral in a submarine might be a little sticklish were he newly appointed ComSubPac with Cominch and CinCPac watching him and the weight of one of the war's most important Force Commands on his shoulders. But, sitting on Scamp's cigarette deck when she was drumming along on the surface, Admiral Lockwood looked as relaxed as a suburbanite spending the evening on a porch.

The cigarette deck is a pleasant place to relax. That is, until the diving alarm goes off, and then the occupant has to make the longest jump of anyone topside to reach the hatch. While enemy aircraft were not expected between Pearl Harbor and Midway, war admits to no certainties, and a submarine nearing Midway had to keep an eye peeled. Scamp had been making sudden dives as a training aid, submerging at unexpected moments when ordered by the officer of the deck. A dive might be practice, or it might be the real thing. The crew was on its toes. Then—

"One day I was sitting in the wardroom and the diving alarm sounded," Commander Ebert related. *"I eased back to the control room. The boat made the usual dive. Only after we were well down did it suddenly occur to me that there was no admiral around. There was a moment of panic, to say the least. I asked the officer of the deck, and he said he was sure the admiral hadn't been on the bridge when he gave the alarm, although he had been there a few moments before. Well, we finally found the admiral,*

sitting on a bucket in the after torpedo room, shooting the breeze with one of the torpedomen!"

The admiral left the submarine at Midway—which was as far as CinCPac would permit him to go—and SCAMP, after topping off, went on to the Empire. She later acquired a name for herself by sinking the converted seaplane tender KAMIKAWA MARU in the Southwest Pacific in May, downing the Japanese submarine I-24 in the Admiralties in July, and accounting for two passenger-cargomen and a large tanker before the end of her first fighting year.

Admiral Lockwood, too, acquired a name. The name of the force commander who guided SubPac through the scalding tempest of the Pacific War's height—who demanded and obtained a trustworthy torpedo for the torpedo drive on the Empire—who designed the undersea offensive that wrecked the Japanese transport system—who directed his submarines to victory in the greatest naval battles of the war: "The Boss." By that name the U. S. Submarine Force gave him its undeviating respect.

By another, it gave him its man-to-man affection. For Admiral Lockwood fought something more than a war. He fought rule-book thinking and hidebound conformity. He was the implacable foe of "stuffedshirtism." He found time to congratulate a sailor for a job well done, to see that good transportation and quarters were provided for shore-coming submarine personnel, to assure men and equipment everything needed for the maintenance of efficiency. Lockwood saw to the preservation of *élan*, the upkeep of good spirit and good heart.

For the maintenance of morale he obtained the services of old-time vaudeville star Eddie Peabody, former quartermaster who had strummed a banjo in submarines in World War I. He brought into the Force such five-star football and athletic coaches as Dick Harlow, Frank Leahy and Potsy Clark to install a fine program of sports. By the summer of 1943 the patrol-wearied crew putting in at Pearl Harbor or Midway could enjoy a boxing match, a bit of "rug cutting" or a clambake, as taste dictated. This program was continued at such advanced bases as Majuro and Guam. No wearisome setting-up exercises. No compulsory games. Admiral Lockwood sponsored informal recreation and entertainment.

The force responded with *ésprit de corps*—and gratitude. To his friends in the pressure hulls, from mess attendants to captains, Admiral Lockwood was "Uncle Charlie."

New-construction Submarines

At Groton, Connecticut, at Portsmouth, New Hampshire, at Manitowoc, Wisconsin, and several other construction yards, fleet submarines on the GATO model were coming off the line. Here American engineers and artisans, electricians, draughtsmen, mechanics and welders were winning the production war.

This production effort was nation-wide. The submarine whose captains and crews came from every state in the Union was built by labor and capital from every state in the Union, of materials mined, smelted, processed, machined and produced in all corners of the United States. The USS SUBMARINE-FISH, whose skipper may have hailed from Utah or Kentucky, was an amalgam of steel smelted in Pennsylvania or the Midwest, cork which may have come from Florida, rubber from a stockpile perhaps in Illinois. Its copper may have come from Nevada or Colorado, its paint from Delaware, and its camera lenses were probably ground in Rochester, New York. By and large, the U.S. submarine which splashed down the ways was a product as "made in America" as the revolutionary Humphreys frigate or American pine.

What could have been more American than the submarine from the building yard in Wisconsin?—a yard which had established a fine reputation as the builder of Diesel ferries and stalwart Great Lakes craft. Born at this port with the Indian name and launched in Lake Michigan, the Manitowoc submarine acquired its sea legs in the long voyage down the Mississippi, transiting the heart of America to find deep water in the Gulf of Mexico. Submarines going down the Mississippi? Old Man River had not witnessed such a naval spectacle since the Civil War time of Pook's gunboat "turtles," the Federal ironclads of James B. Eads. Submarines off fields of cotton. Submarines going down by the levee. Low bridge—so they had to reach New Orleans before the tall periscopes were installed and they received their complete superstructure. Then away from the Delta and off for Panama the submarine from Wisconsin went to war. American-made of American stuff, these submarines from Manitowoc—and Groton, Portsmouth, Philadelphia, Mare Island—were as industrially homespun as Yankee Bushnell's original.

Shift the submarine production picture to Nippon —an I-boat launched in one of the Emperor's shipyards. Here is a cruiser submarine, and in many respects a good one. Somewhat bigger, perhaps, than the American of the GATO class. With powerful, modern Diesels, heavy armament, excellent sea-keeping qualities.

Toward the building of this boat Japanese engineers, draughtsmen, artisans, welders have contributed great technical skill and fanatical loyalty to

225

Hirohito. In the yard, however, there may be Korean workmen who labor in mechanical obedience to orders but will bear watching if there are war reverses. In this submarine there is steel from the mills of Honshu, copper from the Ashio mines, brass from Buddha's veritable belly. But nickel, bauxite, a dozen other commodities that went into this I-boat had to be imported. And Imperial stockpiles of iron, copper, steel demand constant replenishment from overseas sources—Manchukuo, Korea, China, Indo-China, the Philippines, Malaya, the Netherlands East Indies. Whereas an American submarine may start its voyaging at the headwaters of the Mississippi, the Japanese must fetch their building materials from foreign lands and by many sea routes longer than the Mississippi, before their submarines are constructed. The new-construction I-boat is not indigenous to Japan.

United States submarine and Japanese I-boat furnish a miniature of the entire production war. A miniature, perhaps, of all the wars in modern history in which one opponent had to import in order to produce, while the other, self-sufficient, had but to stop the enemy's imports in order to put him out of the war-business. Those "made in America" submarines were specifically dedicated to stopping Japanese imports.

The first quarter of 1943 reflected the accelerated submarine production in the U.S.A. Peacetime building had averaged about six new submarines a year. Now a spanking new-construction boat arrived at Pearl Harbor almost every other week, the crew ran through final training exercises with the precision of oarsmen preparing for a regatta, and went out to win combat insignia in the contest that is played for keeps.

By March 1943, U.S. submarines were available in sufficient force in the Pacific to exact from enemy shipping a toll that averaged well over 100,000 tons for the remainder of the year. Empire waters bore the brunt of this blasting. Soon after the securing of Guadalcanal, the number of submarines available to the SubPac Force almost doubled as veterans from the South Pacific joined newcomers at Pearl Harbor. For the first time, commitments and strength permitted ComSubPac to concentrate on Empire shipping lanes.

From February until mid-year, CinCPac asked for but one submarine to cover the Marshall Islands area, two or three to cover Truk, and one to cover Palau. This boded ill for Japanese ship traffic off Kyushu, Shikoku, Honshu and Hokkaido. Then in the second quarter of 1943 the number of submarines sent to Empire areas almost trebled that of the first quarter. During the ensuing summer and autumn, nearly half of the SubPac submarines on patrol were covering the sea roads to Yokohama, Kobe, Nagasaki and the other major Japanese ports. About 40% of all shipping sunk in this period went to the bottom close to Japan.

Thus the reinforced Empire blockade tightened its numbing grip. And Tokyo began to feel that pressure early in 1943. Japanese imports were going down, Japanese marine insurance rates were going up, Japanese war production was falling off and some of the local *geisha* girls were beginning to wonder what had become of all those sailors.

Empire Blockaders (*Tarpon's Foray*)

Some of those sailors and the cargoes they carried went down to torpedoes fired by PORPOISE, TRIGGER and HADDOCK operating in Empire waters in January 1943.

PORPOISE (Lieutenant Commander J. R. McKnight) struck at shipping off Hokkaido on New Year's Day to sink RENZAN MARU, freighter, 4,999 tons. TRIGGER (Lieutenant Commander R. S. Benson) tangled with the destroyer OKIKAZE off the coast of Honshu on January 10, and three torpedoes scored two hits which buried the Jap man-of-war in a salty grave. HADDOCK (Lieutenant Commander A. H. Taylor) downed an unidentified freighter in the same area seven days later.

One of the hardest-hitting patrollers off Honshu in the first quarter of 1943 was TARPON. This veteran of the Asiatic Force had weathered many ups and downs since that long-ago retreat from Manila, and her luck had been in need of an overhaul. Now captained by Lieutenant Commander T. L. Wogan, she overhauled two targets on the Tokyo Road, and her torpedoes went straight to the mark. To the bottom on February 1 went FUSHIMI MARU, passenger-cargoman, 10,935 tons. One week later and not far from her first success, she overhauled an ocean liner. Accurate torpedo fire put an end to this queen of the transport service, and down at sea went TATSUTA MARU, 16,975 tons.

The Japanese did not possess many liners of that size. And by this sinking, which preceded the March demise of KAMAKURA MARU in the Sulu Sea, Wogan and his TARPON crew established a precedent and a record. Only three larger merchantmen would be sunk by American submarines in the Pacific War—the aforementioned KAMAKURA MARU, a third liner and a huge oil tanker. And another transport of the same tonnage as TARPON's victim would go under. So TARPON concluded a notable foray. In a single patrol and with two solid punches she had wiped out 27,910 tons of enemy shipping.

In the waters off northeast Honshu and Hokkaido the submarine blockaders met with few *marus*. Because of the game flushed by GUARDFISH and other raiders off Hokkaido the previous year, four of the nine submarines that went on Empire patrol in the first quarter of 1943 were assigned to the traffic lanes between Tokyo Bay and Hokkaido. Targets were scarce, for the enemy, badly bitten, had grown twice shy. Evasive routing and strengthened anti-submarine measures made the blockade of these sea lanes hard to enforce.

Admiral Lockwood's submarines abandoned the northern Honshu-Hokkaido area later in the year to concentrate on the south coast of Honshu and the busy East China Sea. They were not yet numerous enough to put a noose around Nippon. That executionary measure would come later.

Submarine Tactics—Radar plus Periscope

It may seem paradoxical that search radar, increasing the number of night-surface approaches, simultaneously increased the number of night-submerged periscope attacks. The explanation, previously suggested, is fairly simple. A submarine might safely stalk its quarry at a distance, or run up to within two or three thousand yards of the target without too much danger of detection. Visibility conditions called the showdown. Moonlight, varying from bright to dim, could silhouette the submarine as it closed in, and even star-shine could expose the surfaced sub. Hence, in many instances a submerged periscope attack was much safer and surer than an attack launched on the surface. The submarine could approach by surface radar, then go to periscope depth to deliver the punch. In such cases, moon or starlight which would have betrayed the submarine on the surface, now served to expose the target to the eye of the periscope.

Typical radar approach culminating in periscope attack was made by HALIBUT on February 20, 1943. The target was a freighter evidently en route from Kwajalein to Saipan or Guam. This was HALIBUT's fourth war patrol under Lieutenant Commander P. H. Ross.

On the morning of the 20th, HALIBUT was searching along the Empire-Kwajalein track when she sighted the unescorted freighter through the high periscope. The target was 15 miles abeam to starboard. A long run to go before the submarine could gain attack position.

Visibility was excellent, and Ross had to hold HALIBUT beyond range of the enemy lookouts. At the same time it was necessary to keep the target under observation through the high periscope while the

submarine tried to run around the "visibility circle" to reach an ahead position. The freighter appeared to be zigzagging, using large changes of course. Tracking showed her to be making 11 knots. The submarine barely managed to hang on, and after some hours of tag, Ross decided to track all day and close for attack at night. At dusk he ordered HALIBUT to the surface, and put the Diesels on the line to close in on the target. During this phase of the chase, radar fed continuous bearings and ranges to the T.D.C.

A full moon illuminated the night. When HALIBUT had gained a position 11,000 yards ahead of the target, Ross sent the submarine under to avoid detection. At 11,000 yards the target was clearly visible in both periscopes. In the bright moonlight the freighter was zigzagging as though she had the blind staggers, but this antic afforded her no concealment. Holding HALIBUT at shallow depth, Ross was able to obtain radar ranges to use in conjunction with periscope bearings as the submarine bored in.

At 2028, Ross came to attack course for the bow tubes. A few minutes later the target zigged, and he decided to shift to the stern tubes for a 90° track. By now the visibility was so clear there was danger of the submarine's being sighted at shallow depth. Ross took her down to a level below her radar limit, and the last lap of the approach was made by periscope.

At 2059, Ross fired three torpedoes from the stern tubes. Three timed explosions blasted the target. The target went down with a plunge, sinking in a bare two minutes. She proved to be the passenger-cargoman SHINKOKU MARU, a 3,991 tonner. Evidently she failed to get off a radio message as Japanese records list her as missing between Kwajalein and Saipan and sunk on February 18th.

Wahoo on the Warpath

WAHOO's fourth war patrol began on February 23, 1943, when she struck out from Pearl Harbor for the East China Sea and the Yellow Sea. After a week at the Royal Hawaiian, Morton and crew were wound up for action. WAHOO ran on the surface all the way to the Nansei Shoto chain, skirted the north end of this dangerous archipelago and headed up the East China Sea straight for the Yellow.

Morton knew the shallow sea between China and Korea, having cruised it on a tour of duty several years before the war. Submariners called it the "Japanese wading pond." A pond does not give an undersea boat a great deal of depth for diving. But Morton did not intend to spend much of WAHOO's time hugging the bottom. He planned to spend it cutting the sea lanes to Tsingtao and Tientisin, Dairen and Seoul—lanes which linked the conquered China coast, Manchukuo and Korea to Japan.

To match this daring raid an enemy submarine would have had to enter the Gulf of Mexico or the Gulf of Saint Lawrence or some other body of water recessed in the American sea frontier, and run a 1,000-mile round trip through naval defenses. German U-boats managed to approximate this effort, but they never approximated WAHOO's ship-smashing invasion.

WAHOO's northbound run in the Yellow Sea proved disappointing. Morton began to wonder if the enemy's merchant marine had migrated to Nowhere. Not a single target worth the price of a torpedo was sighted until 0800, March 13, and on that date the submarine was off Wung Island, a scant 35 miles from the port of Dairen.

Even then, the target sighted was an inferior article—a small, inter-island steamer which the submariners dubbed "Smoky Maru" because of the black smudge surging from her stacks. Morton pronounced it, "worth one torpedo if you sink it, but not worth two under any conditions." WAHOO bored in, and Morton fired a single. The torpedo missed by a couple of feet, SMOKY MARU being stubbier than estimated. Although the steamer's lookouts failed to see the torpedo wake, Morton decided to abide by his original evaluation. Better wait for bigger game and let this smudge-pot go. Her sinking would have informed the Japs that a submarine was in their pond, and if the news had to come out it might as well be in headlines.

So four more inter-island steamers were allowed to pass. Wanting no part of this trivial traffic, Morton headed WAHOO for Kayo To lighthouse, hoping to come upon the main line from Tsingtao to Shimoneski. Here, too, the pickings were picayune, so he moved WAHOO into the coastal waters of the Shantung Promontory. Off this peninsula the submarine found targets!

The shooting began on March 19th. First victim was a NANKA MARU-type freighter which sank in three minutes, downed by a single torpedo. Morton brought WAHOO to the surface to hunt for survivors. No survivors were found. As the freighter had been unable to radio an alarm, the submarine's presence in the area was still unadvertised.

Two hours later a medium-sized transport hove into view. Morton directed a high-speed chase that culminated in a torpedoing. The disabled ship spied the submarine's periscope and opened fire. A withdrawal seemed sagacious as the vessel was not far offshore and the water was too shallow to risk a

scuffle with any patrol summoned to the scene by the transport's radio. Heading away, Morton took WAHOO across the pond to search the southern approach to the Korean port of Chinnampo.

March 21 brought a SEIWA MARU-type freighter into focus. WAHOO was maneuvered into attack position, and Morton fired three torpedoes at a range of about 1,600 yards. The first hit the target amidships, and there was a blast which knocked a wash basin from the bulkhead of the submarine's forward torpedo room. The Japanese ship was literally disemboweled.

So was another freighter WAHOO torpedoed later in the day. This sinking was less than a dozen miles offshore, and the action was hardly over before two junks came waddling out to investigate the matter. Morton ordered a battle-surface to attack these busybodies, and WAHOO chased them to within two miles of the beach. Returning to look for survivors, the submarine located four swimmers. The quartet refused assistance and there was no time to argue. However, two steamer trunks and a life ring were fished from the water. The life preserver identified the sunken vessel as the SS NITTSU MARU.

"There is never much water in this wading pond. . . . We have to be careful with our angle on dives to keep from plowing into the bottom. Aircraft and patrols have been scarce, because we are in virgin territory. However, she ain't virgin now, and we are expecting trouble soon. We hope to get at least four more ships and then expend our gun ammunition on the way home."

The above was logged by Morton as he shifted WAHOO northward toward the Laotighashan Promontory, ducking sampans and trawlers most of the way. March 23, a freighter was sighted. WAHOO stalked craftily, and Morton fired one torpedo. The ship, a coal carrier, settled slowly while a great, circular film of bituminous dust expanded on the water around her, resembling the inky stain exuded by a wounded squid. Evidently the coaler cried an S.O.S., for as the submarine retired there was a thudding of depth charges in the distance and the angry patrols were out. By that time WAHOO was in open water, hitting a fast clip for Round Island, one of the flagstones on the doorstep of Dairen.

The submariners discovered that the Round Island navigation light had been blacked out. Morton surmised the Dairen shipping had been detoured, and he scouted the port's approaches in search of the evasive route. Its deepest water about 50 fathoms and average depth around 20 fathoms, the Yellow Sea was no place for a submarine to be caught unawares. In water that shallow, depth charges would

MAINTENANCE. *Constant grooming by submarine crews and tender technicians kept submarines in fighting trim. Check-ups and tune-ups were accom-* *plished whenever opportunity presented. Subma-* ***riners take no chances with wear and tear. They*** ***let no grass grow under the keels of their boats.***

WAHOO'S GREAT LEADERS. *Skipper D. W. "Mush" Morton (at right) and exec R. H. O'Kane. With these aces* on her bridge, Wahoo *raised a dust on the warpath, staged a maru-massacre. O'Kane later became captain of Tang.*

TORPEDOED BY GRAYLING, *April 9, 1943,* Shanghai Maru *heads for that bourne from which no traveler returns.*

GRAYLING'S VICTIM *goes under, her back broken by torpedo. The spring of 1943 marked an up-turn in the U. S. sub score. Reason: improved torpedoes, more subs.*

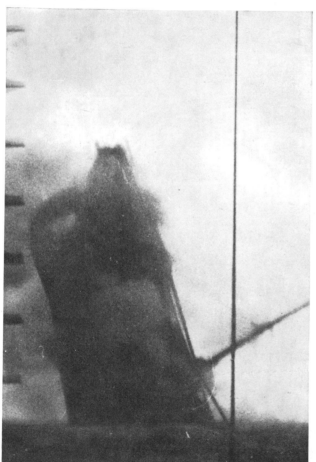

TORPEDOED BY WAHOO, Nittsu Maru *dives to floor of Yellow Sea. Shallow, treacherous, the Yellow was dangerous sea for subs. Wahoo made it dangerous for marus.*

TORPEDOED BY DRUM *near equator in April 1943, freighter goes to nameless grave. Drum watches funeral.*

go off like firecrackers in a bird bath. So WAHOO moved on the hunt with the stealth of a Cherokee. On the afternoon of March 24 the trail was found.

Down the trail came a ship with the lanky silhouette of a tanker. This vessel had to be sunk within an hour, for the port of call was only around the corner. Racing time and tide, Morton sent WAHOO wading in. Three torpedoes sped at the target. Two prematured. The third missed. Driving forward to an ahead position, Morton fired three more. Fragments of the vessel's stern went up like tossed confetti. Five minutes later the ship was under.

The next contact was made early the following morning. A small cargoman. After maneuvering into a good attack position, the submariners were infuriated by another frustrating premature. Morton ordered a battle-surface, determined to riddle the target with gunfire. WAHOO's gunners opened up at 3,800 yards, slamming 4-inch shells into the freighter. Then, as the submarine closed in, the target was raked with 20-mm. fire. When WAHOO pulled away, the little cargo ship was burning like a box of matches.

Thirty minutes later, WAHOO was chasing another freighter. This was a Diesel-powered vessel whose engines made her fairly agile. WAHOO's Diesels were able to overhaul, however, and Morton drove in for another gun action. Running into the teeth of gnashing gunfire, the freighter tried to ram the submarine, but WAHOO skated away with ease and left the cargoman sinking in a bonfire.

During a third gun battle, fought some time later with a 100-ton trawler, the submarine's three 20-mm's. jammed. Shot to sponge, the trawler refused to sink. Aboard WAHOO there was a crate of "Molotov cocktails" which Marines on Midway had given the submarine's crew when she stopped off there. Morton now brought the submarine alongside the riddled trawler and the WAHOO men hurled incendiary bombs at the craft. Although still afloat when the submarine departed, the trawler was reduced to a mass of trash spouting flame and smoke. Most of those aboard it had made their last trawl.

Clearing the area and heading south down the Yellow Sea, WAHOO had but two torpedoes left for her tubes. Morton saved them for the Formosa-Kyushu trunk line. Leaving the Yellow Sea, WAHOO took the opportunity to shoot up two fishing sampans.

The last two torpedoes were fired on March 29 at a freighter on the Formosa-Kyushu line. As this vessel sank with her stern blown off, WAHOO concluded a war patrol which topped the record to that date in number of ships sunk.

Reading the WAHOO-Morton score for this patrol,

no analyst could doubt that the submarine was one of the world's deadliest offensive weapons—one that could massacre the economy of a maritime empire. In 10 days of action this single commerce raider had sunk nine ships. Unfortunately Japan's War Lords and statisticians received no personal instruction from this lesson. At the time, it was brought home only to those Japanese sailors and fishermen who saw the fire too late as they drowned in sea water and blood.

Here is the WAHOO score as officially assessed:

Date	Name	Tonnage	Assessment
March 19	Zogen Maru	1,428	Sunk
March 19	Kowa Maru	3,217	Sunk
March 21	Nittsu Maru	2,183	Sunk
March 21	Hozan Maru	2,260	Sunk
March 23	Unknown Maru	2,427e	Sunk
March 24	Takaosan Maru	2,076	Sunk
March 25	Satsuki Maru	827	Sunk
March 25	Unknown Maru	2,556e	Sunk
March 29	Yamabato Maru	2,556	Sunk

e Estimated tonnage.
  Kowa Maru a transport. All others cargo.

Loss of Pickerel

Captained by Lieutenant Commander A. H. Alston, Jr., PICKEREL left Pearl Harbor on March 18, 1943, to conduct her seventh war patrol. She topped off with fuel at Midway four days later and headed for her assigned area, the east coast of northern Honshu. From those waters she never returned.

She was ordered to remain in her area until sunset May 1, and then head home to Midway. Apparently she never saw this vernal sunset. The Japanese recorded an anti-submarine attack which was launched upon a submersible near Shiramuka Lighthouse, northern Honshu, on April 3rd. The position was outside the area assigned to PICKEREL, but she was the only submarine within reach of Shiramuka Light at that time. Post-war records revealed that Submarine Chaser No. 13 was destroyed by PICKEREL at lat. 40 N., long. 142 E., on that date. And on April 7 she torpedoed and sank FUKUEI MARU, a small freighter, in waters farther north.

The Japanese A/S attack report noted an error in the date, and it is possible this attack occurred later in the month. Meantime, mine plants guarded the coast of Honshu, and small patrol boats roamed PICKEREL's area. After smiting the freighter on April 7, she could have fallen victim to one of these foes.

She was expected at Midway on or about May 6th. When she failed to answer repeated radio calls from her home base, her loss was presumed. It was officially announced on May 12th. PICKEREL was the first U.S.

submarine lost in the Central Pacific. In a cerement of silence, she went down with all hands. Time, place and cause unknown.

More Mines for the Mikado's Merchantmen

During January and February 1943, the Analytical Section on Mine Warfare, established by CinCPac, was engaged in research to determine the most fertile areas for minefields in Empire waters. In March ComSubPac was directed to take advantage of "every opportunity to lay mines by submarine whenever such plants are consistent with patrol areas and tasks assigned." The current torpedo scarcity created ample elbowroom for mines aboard SubPac submarines. Accordingly, RUNNER, SCORPION and STINGRAY were sent westward in April with combination mine-torpedo loads.

STINGRAY (Lieutenant Commander O. J. Earle) headed for the East China Sea to sow her mines off the China coast. Patrolling this area in March, SUNFISH (Lieutenant Commander R. W. Peterson) had sunk a medium-sized freighter. KINGFISH (Lieutenant Commander V. L. Lowrance) had bashed down the 8,154-ton transport TAKACHIKO MARU in the area a few days later. With Japanese ships plowing the coastal waters, the East China Sea was ripe for spring planting. STINGRAY deposited her mines in the approaches to Wenchow. Then she went on to plant a fatal torpedo in the hull of TAMON MARU, an 8,156-ton cargo carrier.

RUNNER, skippered at this time by Commander Fenno, laid 32 Mark 12 mines in the approaches to Hong Kong. Apparently a Japanese hospital ship was damaged by this field some months later, as Tokyo reported the "torpedoing" of such a vessel in the mined area. There were no torpedo attacks made at the time on a vessel of that description.

SCORPION, on her maiden patrol under Lieutenant Commander W. N. Wylie, laid her iron eggs in Japanese waters. Then she ran into fiery action off the coast of Honshu. After the submarine completed her mine plant, Wylie took her on a *maru* hunt. On April 20 she torpedoed and sank MEIJI MARU No. 1, converted gunboat, 1,934 tons. Seven days later her torpedoes stung the passenger-cargoman, YUZAN MARU, 6,380 tons. SCORPION also battle-surfaced and fought a number of running gun battles which resulted in the demolishment of four sampans and a Japanese coast defense craft. During this last action, Lieutenant Commander R. M. Raymond, making the patrol as prospective commanding officer, was killed by an enemy bullet.

"*Each ship of this division,*" wrote the division commander afterwards, "*will dedicate one full tube nest forward to Lieutenant Commander Reginald Marbury Raymond, USN. He was an officer of the highest type, and his irrepressible spirit will continue to inspire all of us. . . .*"

As SCORPION, STINGRAY and RUNNER were concluding their mining missions, two more submarines moved westward to plant iron fields. These were STEELHEAD (Lieutenant Commander D. L. Whelchel) and SNOOK (Lieutenant Commander C. O. Triebel), both conducting maiden patrols.

STEELHEAD planted her mines off Hokkaido. Then Whelchel moved his submarine inshore on another special mission. Standing two miles off the beach, the submariners trained their deck gun on Muroron and proceeded to pump shells into the Nihon Steel Works and the Wanishi Iron Works in a night bombardment that deflated some of the assets of these industrial establishments. This was carrying the production war straight to the heart of Vulcan's furnace —plant managers, metallurgists and steel and iron workers seldom come under the fire of submarines.

SNOOK, too, experienced a lively patrol. She was to plant her minefield in the vicinity of North Saddle Light near Shanghai, and she reached this area on April 30th. Dense fog and the unpredictable currents near the mouth of the Yangtze River gave Triebel and company some onerous navigational hazards to grapple with. While seeking the best water for her mines, the submarine had to run submerged in order to avoid the multitude of junks that wandered in the area. She came within an ace of going aground on Children's Rock, about 30 miles from the mouth of the Yangtze, and at one time she stuck on a mud bar only 65 feet below the surface.

The submarine managed to plane up and over this barrier, but during the next hour and a half of that afternoon she bogged down in the silt time and again. Triebel did some nice jockeying to extricate her from this slough, and finally she crawled into a hole 75 feet deep, and he held her there until nightfall. Then when SNOOK surfaced she almost poked her periscope through the bottom of a junk.

The mines were laid that evening. This two-hour task completed, the submarine felt "very much unburdened." One of the numerous junks was lolling in the offing, and it occurred to Triebel that the Chinese fishermen might be able to give him some information on Japanese shipping.

"*We went alongside looking for an English-speaking Chinaman. . . . They responded in an equally lackadaisical manner to our cheers for Chiang Kaishek or Tojo, but were rapturous at the receipt of a loaf of bread and a can of tomatoes. We got a dozen dry salted fish.*"

SNOOK was carrying some steel fish of American manufacture, so Triebel headed her north up into the Yellow Sea where WAHOO had rampaged. There SNOOK staged a rampage of her own, sinking KINKO MARU and DAIFUKU MARU, a small and medium-sized freighter, on May 5, and a larger one, TOSEI MARU, on the 7th. Running for home base with three ships on the scoreboard, SNOOK and Triebel had begun an outstanding war career.

The mines laid by STEELHEAD and SNOOK were the last to be planted by submarines in the Central Pacific. The torpedo was proving a much more potent weapon, and the torpedo shortage which had made room for mines was almost over. In the Southwest Pacific, mining operations were carried out by submarines until late in the war. But there, as in the Central Pacific, torpedo warfare was the submarines' forte. The *maru* had to come to the mine. The torpedo ran out to meet the *maru*.

Submarine Tactics—Day-periscope Attack

In May 1943, SubPac submarines were dispatched to the northern end of the East China Sea to give the coastal waters of Kyushu their attention. The approaches to Kagoshima and Nagasaki had been previously investigated. Now they were to be continuously patrolled.

Among the submarines dispatched to the area that May was SAURY, under Lieutenant Commander A. H. Dropp. She gave a good account of herself on this, her sixth war patrol. And in so doing, she conducted a daytime periscope attack that critics considered an excellent demonstration of the tactic.

On the afternoon of May 28, SAURY was on the surface, patrolling her area. On the 26th she had sunk the transport KAGI MARU, a 2,300-tonner, and Dropp was on the lookout for something bigger. Weather was calm and the visibility unlimited, although a caravan of low, sooty clouds humped along the northeastern horizon.

SAURY's periscope was up like a mast as she cruised in the placid water. An eye in the crow's nest can see farther than one on a ship's forepeak, and there was no reason for a submarine to forego this obvious advantage when patrolling on the surface. War experience had proved the periscope a valuable surface-lookout instrument whenever the submarine's speed did not cause blurring vibrations. Thus it was that SAURY's periscope watch picked up a target in the northeast before it was sighted by the bridge lookouts. Masts and smoke were spotted by the latter as soon as reported, but the background of horizon-hugging clouds obscured the silhouette. The contact range was about 10 miles, bearing 020° T.

Dropp headed SAURY away, on course 190° T, and stepped up speed in order to check the target's direction of movement. It was soon apparent that the target was overhauling fast. At 1643, a quarter-hour after first contact, it was necessary to dive to escape detection.

The target was identified as a big tanker, steaming along unescorted and zigzagging on courses between 130° T and 208° T. She was empty, and her speed was estimated at 15 knots. Dropp set out to slow her down and fill her to the brim with sea water.

After submerging, SAURY was brought to course 115°. This was approximately the normal approach course. As the approach proceeded satisfactorily, the range closed nicely, and a favorable angle resulted after the tanker made her last zig. Dropp had only to hold SAURY on that course. The approach course thus became the firing course—a nice development.

At 1724, with the range 2,500 yards, Dropp fired a spread of four torpedoes. Depth settings were 18 feet and track was around 110° starboard. Magnetic exploders were set for influence activation. Two minutes and 10 seconds after firing, one torpedo explosion was observed just aft of the tanker's funnel. The cruising speed of the vessel, later identified as the 10,216-ton naval tanker AKATSUKI MARU, was 17 knots. It therefore seemed probable that the estimated speed of 15 knots was too low, and the other three torpedoes missed astern.

The disabled ship was far from sunk. She launched two depth charges, which the submariners at first thought were from a plane. When the explosions were recognized as "embarrassing charges" fired by the tanker, six more torpedoes were fired from SAURY. Four of these scored hits, and the tanker went hustling under the sea.

On May 30, Dropp and company torpedoed and sank the two freighters TAKIMASAU MARU and SHOKO MARU, to conclude a patrol that deprived the Empire of 19,936 tons of shipping. By this it may be noted that the tanker sinking was not the only episode wherein SAURY's tactics were efficient and effective.

Loss of Runner

Heading for the cold seas of the Kuriles, RUNNER, captained by Lieutenant Commander J. H. Bourland, left Midway on May 28 to begin her third war patrol. She was to follow the archipelago down to the Hokkaido coast, and then spend about a month covering the eastern approaches to Ominato and Hakodate. She was to leave this area on the Fourth of July and return to Midway, where she was expected around the 11th. No word was received from her while she was on patrol, and she did not return to

Midway. Efforts to locate her were unavailing, and on July 20 she was reported presumably lost.

There was always a chance that a submarine, which went out into oceanic silence and failed to return, had been stranded on some remote shore, or possibly captured by the enemy. Hence the announcement, "presumed lost," and the lingering hope that war's end would find the crew in a Japanese prison camp. This hope was rewarded in a number of cases, but of RUNNER there remained no trace.

Searched after the war, Japanese records disclosed no anti-submarine actions in her patrol area at the time RUNNER was there. Mines watched the Hokkaido coast, and a minefield may have been responsible for her loss. An unreported attack was another possibility. Japanese records did disclose the fact that RUNNER sank two ships on that patrol—the freighter SEINAN MARU, 1,338 tons, off Ominato on June 11, and the 4,936-ton passenger-cargoman SHINRYU MARU, off the Kuriles on the 26th. With all hands, then, she went down somewhere silently, claimed by the sea.

Pressure below Japan (Trigger vs. Hitaka)

In May, Commander G. R. Donaho brought FLY-INGFISH back from the Hokkaido area with three freighter sinkings to her credit. Donaho ran a smart submarine, and the Japs were now minus SAPPORO MARU NO. 12, AMAHO MARU and KASUGA MARU, sunk in mid-April. But the largest of these steamers was the 2,865-ton SAPPORO MARU, and the accomplishment, measured in tons, was hardly commensurate with the effort.

On maiden patrol off the coast of northern Honshu, POGY (Lieutenant Commander G. H. Wales) found the Maytime pickings equally slim. An ex-gunboat and a small freighter fell to her torpedoes, but big game was not in evidence. SAILFISH (Lieutenant Commander J. R. Moore) took up the northern Honshu blockade in June and sank the freighter SHINJU MARU and the passenger-cargoman IBURI MARU, costing the enemy some 6,900 tons. But as noted earlier in the chapter, the yield in these waters north of Tokyo proved disappointing. The loss of RUNNER late in June decided the issue. ComSubPac withdrew most of his submarines from this northern Empire area. Only HALIBUT and SEARAVEN made full-time patrols in northern Empire waters that summer.

Meantime, the submarine blockade increased the pressure on southern Honshu, Shikoku and Kyushu. Sharp-eyed periscopes kept the approaches to Tokyo Bay under constant surveillance and torpedo explosions set up a continuous, bowling-alley rumble in the East China Sea.

One of the submarines bowling along in the East China Sea that June was GUNNEL. Captained by scrappy Lieutenant Commander J. S. McCain, Jr., this veteran of "Operation Torch" scored a double on her first Pacific patrol. Down went KOYO MARU, freighter, and TOKIWA MARU, freighter—another 13,000 tons of Japanese shipping.

Combing the southern approaches to Tokyo, SAW-FISH (Lieutenant Commander E. T. Sands) torpedoed and sank a medium-sized freighter on May 5th.

Following through in those approaches, TRIGGER (Commander Benson) struck the Imperial Navy a jolting uppercut on June 10 when she torpedoed the aircraft carrier HIYO. This carrier, also called the HITAKA, would undoubtedly have gone down for the count had she been farther from the entrance of Tokyo Bay. As it was, the punch from TRIGGER sent her reeling. Disabled, she could barely hobble into harbor, and the damage dealt her was drastic enough to keep her out of commission for nearly a year.

Another submarine off Tokyo Bay that month was JACK (Lieutenant Commander T. M. Dykers). On June 26, JACK's torpedoes sank the 4,163-ton passenger-cargoman TOYO MARU, and the 5,859-ton freighter SHOZAN MARU. July 4th they accounted for NIKKYU MARU, freighter, 6,529 tons. Having downed some 16,400 tons on this Empire patrol, JACK was embarked on a high-scoring career.

Patrolling the Mandates

While the SubPac Force concentrated on Empire areas during the first nine months of 1943, regular patrols were maintained in the Mandates in accordance with CinCPac's directive. The enemy stiffened his anti-submarine defenses in these areas. And they were notably stiff in the vicinity of Truk. Nevertheless, the submarines covering the sea lanes which tethered the Carolines and the Marshalls to Japan picked off enemy ships with what must have been, to Hirohito's War Council, depressing frequency.

On March 3, HALIBUT (Lieutenant Commander Ross) torpedoed and sank the 6,817-ton passenger-cargoman NICHIYU MARU northwest of Truk.

On April 4, PORPOISE (Lieutenant Commander Mc-Knight) sank KOA MARU, 2,042-ton freighter, off the Marshalls.

May 10 was PLUNGER's day. Plunging into a convoy in the vicinity of the Marianas northwest of Truk, this submarine, under Lieutenant Commander R. H. "Bennie" Bass, hit two good-sized passenger-cargomen with fatal torpedoes. To the bottom went TATSUTAKE MARU, 7,068 tons, and KINAI MARU, 8,360 tons.

TAUTOG (Lieutenant Commander Sieglaff) came up west of the Marianas in June, en route to Pearl Harbor. On June 20 she torpedoed the freighter MEITEN

232

MARU, and 4,474 tons went down in the Mandates.

Throughout July, POGY (Lieutenant Commander G. H. Wales) covered the Empire-Truk main lines. Her luck was indifferent until the 31st when she sighted an aircraft ferry steaming for Truk. Wales engineered two skillful end-arounds, and on the first of August sank MOGAMIGAWA MARU, 7,497 tons.

POGY also sighted a 25-knot Japanese task force composed of two carriers, an auxiliary carrier, several cruisers and escorting destroyers. She tried to overhaul them but failed to gain an attack position.

The Palau blockaders got their share. In January, SEARAVEN, under veteran Commander Cassedy, had made 15 contacts in the Toagel Mlungui vicinity. Cassedy put a torpedo into SHIRAHA MARU, 5,693 tons, on January 14 to sink the freighter.

In April, HADDOCK, under Lieutenant Commander R. M. Davenport, patrolled north of Palau. Under the April sea went ARIMA MARU, 7,389-ton passenger-cargoman, and TOYO MARU, freighter, 1,916 tons. During the late spring and summer months the Pelews were continuously patrolled, but the hunting was poor. TRIGGER made a few contacts off the Malakal entrance, and the other submarines, covering the northern approaches and Toagel Mlungui, made a few. But SUNFISH, east of Palau, found nothing. Shipping in the area was submarine-shy.

SubPac Operational Plan (Target Priority)

On June 24, 1943, ComSubPac published the first Operation Plan drawn up by that command. Sponsored by Admiral Lockwood and devised by his operations officer, Commander R. G. Voge, the plan contained no basic changes in previously issued "Standard Patrol Instructions." But the precepts and missions of the Submarine Force were for the first time stated cogently in one document.

Submarines were to:

(a) Inflict maximum damage to enemy ships and shipping by offensive patrol at focal points.

(b) Plant offensive minefields in suitable enemy waters to destroy enemy ships and to force the enemy to adopt counter-measures.

(c) Undertake other tasks as may be required from time to time by the strategic situation, or based on information which may come to hand. Such special tasks include supporting naval or land forces by attacks on shipping in threatened areas; reconnaissance; transport of troops for raids on enemy bases or installations; landing of agents for intelligence purposes in enemy held territory; evacuation of armed forces or civilians from enemy held territory; delivery of supplies to armed United States or Allied Forces, or to agents in enemy-held territory as may be necessary or desirable.

Target priority in relative order of importance was: Aircraft Carrier (CV); Battleship (BB); Auxiliary Carrier (ACV); Oil Tanker (AO); any man-of-war larger than a destroyer; Transport (AP); Freighter (AK); Destroyer (DD). Standard Patrol Instructions and the Communications Plan were included as annexes.

Invading the Sea of Japan

By July 1943 there was in the entire Pacific Ocean but one area open to enemy shipping which had not been investigated by U.S. submarines. This was Japan's private highway to Asia—the Sea of Japan, lying between the Asiatic mainland and Honshu and Hokkaido.

With but four narrow entrances—one in Russian territory and unavailable, another frozen up for a good part of the year, and the other two guarded by minefields—the Japan Sea was well protected against submarine invasion. Secure behind geographic and military barriers, the traffic arteries which laced Korea and Manchuria to the islands of Nippon were feeding ton after ton of raw material to the voracious Japanese War Machine. In May 1943, ComSubPac produced a plan designed to slash these arteries.

The plan, which was approved by CinCPac, called for the penetration of the Japan Sea early in July. Three submarines were selected to do the penetrating. Those chosen for this perilous venture were PLUNGER (Lieutenant Commander R. H. Bass), PERMIT (Commander W. G. "Moon" Chapple), and LAPON (Lieutenant Commander O. G. Kirk).

Tsushima Strait, separating Japan from Korea, was known to be blocked by mines. Tsugaru Strait, between Honshu and Hokkaido, was similarly blocked. Accordingly, the submarines were to make their entrance through La Perouse Strait, the passage between the northern extremity of Hokkaido and Sakhalin Island. To reach this passage the submarines would have to slip through the tightly linked Kurile chain. They planned to transit Etorofu Strait, cross the southern end of the Sea of Okhotsk and thus enter La Perouse. Little was known of the waters in question, save that they were cold, often fog-shrouded, and in some places dangerously shallow. Shallow water suggested minefields, but as Russian shipping was permitted the use of La Perouse Strait, it was a hopeful guess that its channels were free of mines. The three submarine invaders were instructed to begin shooting at 0000 on July 7, and they were given but 96 hours for hunting. Thereafter they were to keep their fingers crossed and get out through La Perouse before the enemy plugged the exit with mines, bombs and depth charges. To create a diversion on the date of the submarines' exit, NARWHAL (Commander Latta) was dispatched to the Kuriles to make a show of bombarding the airfield on Matsuwa Island.

Salty sweat and exquisite care went into the preparations for this raid. For example, before NARWHAL set out for the Kuriles, her skipper was presented with a painted model of Matsuwa Island—a miniature masterpiece portraying the island's topography and the layout of the enemy air base. Details on weather which might be encountered in the area and the possible location of Japanese mine barriers were briefed for the captains of the invader submarines. But brief was the word for the information available on the Sea of Japan. PLUNGER, PERMIT and LAPON would be the first American submarines to enter that body of water. Somebody nicknamed it "The Emperor's Bathtub." No place for three U.S. subs to be caught bathing!

In the last week of June, Skipper "Bennie" Bass took PLUNGER out of Pearl Harbor and headed, under sealed orders, for Midway. There she met PERMIT and LAPON. Captained by the veteran "Moon" Chapple. PERMIT was ready to start her ninth patrol. LAPON was a newcomer making her first war patrol, but her skipper, O. G. Kirk, was another old hand at torpedo warfare. ComSubPac had seen to it that the raider crews could take confidence in the captains leading this exploit.

As the boats ran westward across the summer seas, some of the lads within the pressure hulls must have been comparing their chances with those of the U-boaters who had invaded the Gulf of Mexico and prowled into the mouth of the St. Lawrence. Or perhaps an invasion of Long Island Sound was more like it, with Block and Fire Island comparable with those which squeezed the waters of Etorofu Strait. The American submariners knew what had happened to U-boats off Block Island. Of course, the Japan Sea was a lot bigger than Long Island Sound. But the entry and exit runs were many hours longer. If the invaders were detected by alert anti-submarine forces, a get-away would be nip and tuck. With emphasis on the Nip!

The three raiders reached the Kuriles on schedule, and transited Etorofu on the surface at night, undetected. Heading southward in Japanese water, they pointed their bows for La Perouse. This unknown strait was the real problem. Entry to the Sea of Japan, it was a likely corridor for ship traffic—Russian, as well as Japanese. The American submariners had been instructed to watch out for the ships of their Soviet ally. But in a race across the foggy Gulf of

Tartary, vessels might be hard to identify—especially if the enemy were in pursuit. This was another hazard to be dealt with.

The weather was chilly, but the submariners approaching La Perouse Strait did some discreet perspiring. Decision was made to dash through the strait at night and on the surface, four-engine speed and all hands at battle stations. Momsen lungs and lifebelts were given to those who felt uneasy about mines.

Running in the deepest part of the channel, the three boats raced through the darkness with all the stealth possible to steaming submarines. A number of small craft were encountered, but they made no move to intercept, and were easily side-stepped. PLUNGER made contact with a small boat only 1,500 yards distant. Bass "pulled the plug." The foreign craft went its way, oblivious of the submarine down below. Evidently the Japanese were not expecting American submarines on the rim of the Emperor's bathtub.

Racing southward from La Perouse Strait, the raider submarines headed for individual patrol areas. LAPON sprinted for the southern end of the Japan Sea. PLUNGER prowled into the middle sea area between Dogo Island and the northern end of Honshu. PERMIT covered the western coastline of Hokkaido.

The weather was propitious, the sea as flat as Lake Michigan, but the raiders found the shooting somewhat disappointing. Opening fire on the tick of the 7th, PERMIT sank the small freighter BANSHU MARU No. 33 off Hokkaido. A few hours later Chapple and company downed the 2,212-ton passenger-cargoman SHOWA MARU. Farther south, PLUNGER waylaid and sank NIITAKA MARU, a 2,478-ton passenger-cargoman. But LAPON, hunting off the coast of Korea, flushed no targets worthy of her steel. However, numerous contacts were made in the northern end of the Japan Sea, which fact was marked for future reference.

The invaders retired as swiftly as they had made their entry. Exit through La Perouse was accomplished at top speed. Like invisible fish the three submarines slipped out through Etorofu while NARWHAL's authoritative 6-inch guns created diversionary uproar at Matsuwa Island. PLUNGER, PERMIT and LAPON drove into the free Pacific with exhilarating news. News that three American submarines could successfully invade the Sea of Japan! News that that body of water was no longer anybody's "private highway" or Imperial Tub. An unpublished headline story that must have disheartened Hirohito.

Saury Has a Scrape

More than one submarine whisked a periscope against the bottom of an enemy ship. But SAURY

(Commander A. H. Dropp) experienced a brush that all but took off her bridge structure as well as her periscope.

On the night of July 30, 1943, while en route to a new patrol area, SAURY was drumming along the road, about halfway between Iwo Jima and Okinawa. No moon, but the night star-spangled and bright with celestial light. Then, at 2225, radar contact! Three ships at long range. At 11,000 yards, they were visible to the submarine lookout—two large vessels and an escort with the silhouette of a destroyer.

On closer inspection the two larger vessels shaped up as a cruiser and a big tanker in column. The destroyer was on the tanker's bow.

SAURY's T.D.C. was out of commission, and Dropp decided to submerge on the target's base course, plot by bearings alone, and then bring SAURY's bow tubes to bear for a zero-angle shot. Dropp sent the submarine down to radar depth on the target's base course. When the Jap ships were about 5,500 yards off, Dropp ordered periscope depth. At a predicted range of 4,000 yards, Sound first picked up the target's screws—poor sound conditions. About the same time the control-room periscope could make out indistinct ship silhouettes. Bearings indicated the ships would pass well to port, so Dropp altered the course to come in for a 90° starboard track. Estimated distance to the track was 1,700 yards.

Depth control was lost twice during the turn, and the periscope was accidentally dunked. By the time SAURY was steadied on the new course, reports from Sound indicated the targets had passed the firing bearing and were much closer than expected. Sound had been as busy as six acrobats, endeavoring to keep track of all bearings, but the operators' stations were in the forward torpedo room, and the approach party was overloaded by bearings from both Sound and periscope. Everything was made more complicated by the large change of relative bearings during the turn. The periscope operator, unable to make out angles on the bow, was badgered by a fogging lens and a leaking periscope gland. Thus the situation when things happened.

Sound reported a bearing of 180° relative. Simultaneously, the periscope revealed the stem of a ship abaft the port beam, and it was getting bigger by the second. Dropp bellowed, "Take her down!" Too late. Before the periscope could be fully lowered, there was a thumping jolt, and SAURY listed about 5° to starboard. She righted for a moment, then listed a second time. Overhead there was a noise that sounded something like an old truck stripping its gears as it rumbled across a wooden bridge. Negative flooded, SAURY hung at 52 feet, but finally coasted

deeper. No depth charges were dropped, but the sound of screws was uncomfortably loud for about half a minute.

When she reached the surface that night, SAURY presented her crew with a sorry silhouette. Her periscope shears looked as though they had been hit by a salvo of dud 16-inch shells and a tornado. The whole structure was listed over like a top hat on the head of a drunk, and the No. 1 periscope above it was bent like the handle of a wrecked umbrella.

Bearded veterans had to agree that SAURY could take it. Stout submarine! She had shaved herself on the keel of a Japanese destroyer!

Submarine Tactics—Down-the-throat Technique

Typical of the down-the-throat shot employed as a defense against escorts was one fired by SAWFISH (Commander E. T. Sands) while she was on her third patrol.

SAWFISH was watching the sea lanes to Nagasaki. Early in the morning of July 27, she made contact with a convoy at the close range of 2,100 yards. Sands put the submarine's stern to the convoy, and opened the range to 3,500 yards. A small patrol boat sighted SAWFISH and opened fire, but the shots were wide of the mark. About 0435 Sands had arrived at the position he wanted, and SAWFISH submerged on the convoy's track.

The formation consisted of four small freighters, one medium-sized freighter and an escort which was identified as a destroyer. Sands intended to pick off the biggest freighter. Then, with the range at 2,500 yards, the convoy suddenly zigged.

The escort had been "pinging," and in order to reduce the submarine's "sound silhouette," Sands kept her bow pointed toward the escort. As the convoy zigged, the escort maintained her course. This brought her plowing head-on toward SAWFISH. Sands decided to stop the DD with a "down-the-throater." He fired four torpedoes with a 1° divergent spread, at a range of 750 yards. As he opened fire, he started deep, expecting a severe depth-charging if the torpedoes missed.

Twenty-five seconds after firing the first torpedo, there was a whacking explosion. The blast was so immediate and violent that the submariners thought it a premature. However, no depth charges were dropped on SAWFISH's heels although one of the freighters dropped a few halfhearted charges some distance away. An hour or so later when SAWFISH came to periscope depth, the convoy had gone over the horizon, and the stern of the escort was just going under. The escort was later identified as a small 700-ton minelayer, one of a type which resembled a destroyer and was easily mistaken for one. And was just as vulnerable to an accurate down-the-throat shot.

"Hit 'em Harder" (Introducing Sam Dealey)

A visitor at the Submarine Base, New London, was dining aboard a newly commissioned submarine. Steak. French fries. Green peas. Salad. A wide wedge of apple pie topped by a cupola of ice cream. And the sort of coffee that father used to make. All this was a far cry from the January sleet outside which was icing the pier and clawing at the bay.

The meal reached the reminiscent stage, the Havanas were lighted and the guest was admiring the officers' mess—not at all the cramped cubicle he had expected aboard a submarine—when a shadow fell across the entry. Pause as a face looked in—the countenance of a young seaman, thin with cold, flakes of snow melting on a worried forehead. In from the night and wet, he was a stranger there—the uninvited. Bowed by the weight of a frozen sea bag, he stood hesitantly, eyeing the bright wardroom and its officers uncertainly. One of the new hands aboard for training, and a little timorous before the command in this unfamiliar submarine, he seemed on the point of an anxious query. Then, wordless, he backed from that cozy threshold and started away.

The submarine's commanding officer, interrupting a story, pushed aside his napkin and stepped into the passage. The guest, who had heard of "Navy braid" and all that, was somewhat surprised to see the commanding officer's extended hand. Captain greeting sailor, the C.O. clasped the boy's damp mitten and smiled down.

"My name's Dealey—what's yours?"

The guest could not remember the sailor's name, but he could remember the lad's look. And he knew he would never forget that captain's. "There," he thought, "is a submarine skipper who's going places, every man in his crew pulling with him." And he was right. They went places—Sam Dealey and his crew in HARDER.

In May 1943, they arrived at the Submarine Base, Pearl Harbor, and after a brief training period they were off on their first war patrol, leaving Pearl on the 7th of June, and fueling at Midway on the 11th. HARDER's maiden patrol area was in Empire waters south of Ise Wan and Nagoya between Shiono Misoki and Oma Saki. She entered the area on the 20th, and on this day made contact with nothing but a small patrol boat. One day without suitable contacts was enough for Dealey, and the next day HARDER was within six miles of the Japanese coast. That evening she was on the trail of a two-ship, single-escort convoy, and her first torpedoes were fired at these merchantmen. Going deep to evade after firing, she bumped the bottom and weathered her first depth-charging, quietly sitting it out on Japanese soil. Dealey and his boys were certain they sank one of the convoy vessels, for the target broke out bright banners of flame. The sinking could not be confirmed, but the vessel was unquestionably damaged.

Concerning the fate of HARDER's next target, there was visible verification. Early in the morning of the 23rd, a northbound, unescorted ship came steaming into view in bright moonlight. Dealey began a careful approach. Just before dawn the vessel sighted HARDER's periscope and opened fire. Dealey retaliated with four torpedoes, one of which struck the enemy ship between bow and bridge. An explosion flared, and the smitten vessel listed about 10° to port, but continued moving at 10-knot speed, trailing oil and zigzagging like a Brahma steer in a rodeo.

A week later HARDER came across the wounded vessel. Deck awash, she had crawled up on a lonely beach to save herself from drowning. And there, apparently, she died. For her name was found in Japanese records examined after the war, and she was listed as sunk—SAGARA MARU, ex-seaplane tender, 7,189 tons.

This tender was not the only vessel damaged by HARDER on her first patrol. On the 24th her torpedoes struck a target, and on the 25th she blasted a three-ship convoy. Anti-submarine vessels drove her under, and results could not be observed, but Dealey and company were confident that a couple of Japanese cargoes got a wetting.

On the day SAGARA MARU's remains were sighted, HARDER picked up two tankers and a freighter heading north. Dealey maneuvered for an overlap, and fired the submarine's last two torpedoes at 700 yards' range. The first shot amputated 50 feet of the freighter's bow, and a timed hit was heard on the tanker. Again results could not be observed, as enemy aircraft in the vicinity made deep submergence advisable. An aerial bomb boomed in the sea as HARDER went down—the closest counter-measure she had yet experienced. The submarine shook it off, and headed eastward. On July 10th, Lieutenant Commander Samuel D. Dealey and crew arrived home at Pearl Harbor and went ashore to receive their combat insignia.

After a refit by "Ma" HOLLAND, HARDER left Pearl Harbor on August 24, fueled at Midway four days later, and was away to take advantage of verbal orders giving her the right to "work over" any vacant submarine areas off the coast of Japan. Of these, there were several, and HARDER filled the vacancies. One night she patrolled so close to the Japanese homeland that Dealey was able to report, "The headlights of many cars moving along the nearby highway remind us of Riverside Drive along the Hudson."

Invading this Nipponese littoral, HARDER sank her first victim (this patrol) not far from Tokyo Bay on September 9th. Exit KOYO MARU, 3,010-ton freighter.

On the 11th, off Mikura Jima Island, she broke the back of YOKO MARU, freighter, 1,050 tons.

For the next eight days, she was "it" in a series of chases and anti-submarine hunts conducted by escorts and patrol planes. Then on the 19th she sank KACHISAN MARU, a little 800-tonner. After which she got a "going over" by a two-day typhoon. On the 22nd she missed shots at two freighters, and in return had her light bulbs granulated by an unpleasantly close aerial bomb.

The following day, six miles from Nagoya Bay, Dealey slammed torpedoes into a freighter and a tanker which had been moving in column. One of these targets blew up with a fury that rocked the submarine as she ducked 80 feet below the surface. Some time later Dealey and company heard another din—"Block Busters" dropped by aircraft which had arrived too late on the scene. The Japanese frequently dropped bombs and depth charges at random, seemingly for their nuisance value. Dealey described such haphazard bombs as the "to-whom-it-may-concern" type. The bombs in this instance did not concern HARDER. Retiring from the scene, she left KOWA MARU, freighter, 4,520 tons, and DAISHIN MARU, tanker, 5,878 tons, deep in the sea behind her.

After firing her last two torpedoes at a convoy on September 28, and battle-surfacing to shoot up two armed trawlers on the 29th, HARDER headed for the barn. She arrived at Pearl Harbor on October 8, a bearded veteran with five ships to her credit for a total of 15,272 tons.

The tonnage total is no measure of the weight behind HARDER's punches—the drive that sent her into the current of Empire coastal traffic, and had her pacing the motorists on Japanese shore roads—the get-it-done leadership and aggressive spirit of Sam Dealey. His submarine, dubbed "Hit 'Em Harder," was going to hit the Imperial Navy one of the sledgehammer smashes it received in reprisal for Pearl Harbor.

Loss of Pompano

Under Lieutenant Commander W. M. Thomas, POMPANO left Midway on August 20, 1943, to start her seventh war patrol. She was to cover the east coast of Honshu from about August 29 to sunset of September 27, and then return to Pearl Harbor for a refit. After leaving Midway, she was never again heard from.

But the Japanese heard from her—or at least saw evidence of her veteran handiwork. Two ships went down to torpedo fire in POMPANO's area that September: AKAMA MARU, cargo, 5,600 tons, on September 3rd; TAIKO MARU, cargo, 2,958 tons, on the 25th.

When POMPANO did not appear at Midway on the expected arrival date, repeated radio calls were sent out in an attempt to locate her. She made no answer, and on October 15, SubPac Headquarters reported her as presumed lost in enemy waters.

As in RUNNER's case, POMPANO's loss was shrouded in the silence and mystery of "cause unknown." The enemy recorded no anti-submarine attack which could have downed her in Empire waters. Japanese minefields guarded the northeast coast of Honshu and the coast of Hokkaido, and POMPANO may have struck a mine. An operational casualty was also possible, or an unrecorded attack. Leaving no trace, the submarine went down with all hands.

Pulling the Trigger

High-scoring war patrols had been conducted in the East China and Yellow Sea by mid-autumn of 1943. One of the outstanding East China Sea patrols was made in September by TRIGGER.

When Lieutenant Commander R. E. "Dusty" Dornin led TRIGGER out of Pearl Harbor on September 1, she was a veteran undersea warrior beginning her sixth patrol. Under Lieutenant Commander R. S. Benson, she had won renown as a raider in Empire waters. Dornin, her new skipper, had pioneered as an officer in GUDGEON. Now, making his first patrol as a submarine commander, he had no intention of letting TRIGGER's reputation collect any barnacles.

Certainly there was no moss growing on her keel as she slipped between Yoran Jima and Okinoyerabu Jima in the Nansei Shoto chain to enter her patrol area on the 16th. And no barnacles were allowed to ornament her outer doors, which opened for action the following evening when the periscope watch picked up a pair of targets—two Japanese vessels steaming on opposite courses.

One ship had the silhouette of a small freighter, and the other resembled a good-sized passenger-cargoman. The distance between them did not permit a simultaneous attack, so Dornin selected the larger for TRIGGER's target. Surfacing the submarine in the dusk, he started her in on the approach. By 2055 TRIGGER was in attack position.

At Dornin's order, four torpedoes spurted from their tubes and, trailing their luminescent tails, rushed at the Jap vessel. The watch on the submarine's bridge tensened expectantly. Two of the "fish" arrowed smack into the target. Then—sweet land of liberty! The Japanese ship lit up like a carnival float, but not from torpedo explosions. These two perfect hits were two perfect duds. TRIGGER had aroused the enemy with blank cartridges!

The excited vessel swung toward the submarine, and Dornin ordered full speed on a fast turn to evade. Guns flamed in the night. The Japanese gunners were not firing blanks. At 700 yards the submarine was visible, and shells began to splash the water around TRIGGER's silhouette. A moon was due, so Dornin ordered the submarine under. Depth charges slammed astern as the crew raced through reloading operations and Dornin maneuvered to gain a new attack position. If anyone smelled sulphur in the conning tower, it was not the first time vigorous English had been inspired by malfunctioning torpedoes.

All tubes reloaded at 2138, TRIGGER was ready for another try. Dornin brought her lunging to the surface, and sent her full speed ahead to run around the now fleeing ship. Two hours later the submarine was once more out in front. Under she went in a bath of bright moonlight to make a submerged periscope attack. At five minutes after midnight the target was in focus. The Japanese vessel was zigging and zagging sharply at one-minute intervals, but these obstreperous capers only slowed her on her base course, and TRIGGER's periscope followed her without difficulty. At 0023, Dornin opened fire.

One of four torpedoes smashed into the vessel's stern. Eight seconds later, Sound reported another hit. All hands in the conning tower snatched quick looks as the ship went down. Going under, the vessel's boilers blew up with a sea-quaking roar. When TRIGGER breasted the surface three minutes after that, she was alone in an expanse of moon-polished water. Not a scrap of wreckage remained to mark the spot where the target had been.

While the "Trigger Men" were still cheering, Dornin set a course to trail the small freighter which had been sighted the previous evening. This vessel escaped in the night, and the sullen dawn promised thick weather. The promise was fulfilled by a ripsnorting typhoon that kept TRIGGER on her toes for the next two days. Nothing could have been torpedoed in those wild and wooly seas, but they flattened out on the 21st, and the afternoon of that day brought a surge of smoke over the horizon.

Directing a submerged approach, Dornin counted six ships in convoy—a big tanker, two smaller tankers, three freighters parading along the horizon with air escort. The convoy outdistanced the submerged submarine and passed out of sight after a three-hour chase. TRIGGER's only chance now was to overhaul on the surface after sundown and cut in for a night attack. At 1923 Dornin surfaced the submarine and started the pursuit on all four engines. A fast run, and TRIGGER was in attack position. Dornin wrote in his patrol report:

Three tankers with the big one leading. It is still fairly light. They should see us, but they don't! At 2056 fired three torpedoes at tanker number one. 2057, fired three torpedoes at tanker number two. Came left with full rudder and full speed. One hit was seen on the after part of tanker number one. Flame shot five hundred feet into the air, lighting up the whole area as bright as day. All six ships could be plainly seen. Eight seconds later, the second torpedo hit her amidships; but nothing could have added to the furious holocaust already taking place. Members of her crew in various stages of dress (mostly in white uniforms) could be seen running forward ahead of the rapidly spreading flames. She was still driving ahead, a brilliant blazing funeral pyre. The men in the bow manned the bow gun and fired three or four times, but she was soon burning throughout her length. The flames were yellow-red, evidently a gasoline fire.

One hit on tanker number two. A small flash amidships, a column of smoke and water were seen and the fire immediately broke out. She was turning away from us when hit.

By this same sharpshooting salvo a freighter in the convoy's far column was hit. TRIGGER's bridge personnel saw the vessel break apart at the middle and sink like a halved brick. The remaining ships in the convoy opened fire at the submarine which was silhouetted in the flame-light. Shells splashed to port and starboard, but none of the geysers was close.

Tanker number three presented a 50 degree starboard angle on the bow, and was closing rapidly, firing his bow gun. We seemed to take a year to pick up speed. Finally steadied with our stern toward him and at 2100 fired three torpedoes aft at this tanker. All missed, probably because we had not steadied enough, and he was swinging toward us, as we realized in a moment.

Dornin then fired a down-the-throat shot at the oncoming tanker. The torpedo struck the tanker's starboard bow, but the Jap gunners continued to shoot at the submarine, and the projectiles began to scythe the air over the bridge. Dornin gave the order to dive, and TRIGGER went under, "with lots of down angle and lots of speed, figuring that the tanker might try to ram or possibly drop some depth charges as he passed over."

The tanker made neither of these gestures. As the submarine tobogganned to a safe level, a rumbling explosion was heard. Fifteen minutes later, TRIGGER was at periscope depth. One burning tanker could be seen. Periscope pictures were taken, and the submariners took turns eyeing the spectacle through the scope. Then Dornin ordered the submarine to the surface, and a sweep disclosed the other ships of the convoy stampeding. Hissing and fuming, the burning tanker went down as TRIGGER started off in pursuit of an escaping freighter.

For the next two hours Dornin drove TRIGGER at first one, then another of the remaining vessels. The enemy gunners fired round after round in a vain attempt to pick off the submarine which was exposed by bright moonlight. Torpedoes were exchanged for shells in this pitched battle, and when TRIGGER finally retired, out of tube ammunition, a canopy of smoke covered a third of the sky and two more *marus* were briskly burning.

Having expended all her torpedoes in nine days of fast action, TRIGGER headed for home, concluding a patrol that came to be called a "nine-day wonder." Behind her she left four verifiable sinkings and possibly one or two more which did not show up in the Japanese record books. Here are the sinkings which were confirmed:

Date	Name	Tonnage	Location
Sep. 18, 1943	Yowa Maru	6,435	2731N, 12657E
Sep. 21, 1943	Shiriya	6,500	2627N, 12240E
Sep. 21, 1943	Shoyo Maru	7,498	2627N, 12240E
Sep. 21, 1943	Argun Maru	6,662	2627N, 12240E

Shiriya and *Shoyo Maru* tankers, others cargo.

The tonnage-sunk total of 27,095 for a single patrol was one of the highest scored by a U.S. submarine to that date. TARPON and SILVERSIDES had bettered it by only a few hundred tons. TRIGGER's niche in the submarine hall of fame was established, and Dornin had proved himself an ace submarine skipper.

Loss of Wahoo

Fresh from a West Coast overhaul, WAHOO headed westward from Pearl Harbor on August 8, 1943, to begin her sixth war patrol. With Commander Morton on the bridge, she was primed for battle, and humming for an area which meant action—the Sea of Japan. Accompanying WAHOO on this foray was PLUNGER, under Lieutenant Commander Bass. Having pioneered the run with PERMIT and LAPON, Bass's submarine was out to show WAHOO the ropes. A *maru*-shooting contest that would knock the bottom out of a lot of enemy shipping was anticipated.

To the bitter disappointment of all concerned, this second invasion of the Japan Sea accomplished little. The fault lay in the torpedo. Targets were plentiful, and both submarines worked long and hard to deliver attacks that were destined to fail before they began.

PLUNGER sank two cargomen—SEITAI MARU, 3,404 tons, on August 20; RYOKAI MARU, 4,655 tons, on the 22nd. This, in spite of deplorable torpedo performance and the fact that she was badgered by motor trouble. On the way up, her No. 2 and No. 4 main motor bearings burned out, putting her port propeller out of commission and forcing her to transit La Perouse Strait on one screw.

WAHOO had the worst possible luck with her torpedoes. Within four days, 12 Japanese vessels were sighted. Nine were hunted down and attacked. To no avail. Morton and his crew were staking their lives in this most hazardous invasion effort. That investment was "honored" by 10 torpedoes that broached, made erratic runs, or thumped against target hulls like derelict motorboats. "Damn the torpedoes!" Morton wrote in wrath. WAHOO's radio crackled out the execrable torpedo's record, and ComSubPac recalled the luckless submarine from the area.

So WAHOO returned to Pearl Harbor to unburden herself of outrageous ammunition and outraged feelings. She did not come back empty-handed, for her deck guns demolished four sampans on the way out of the Japan Sea, and Morton picked up six Japanese fishermen as prisoners of war for questioning by Naval Intelligence. Prisoners, defective torpedoes and feelings were unloaded at Pearl in an atmosphere as pungent as pepper. Rid of the cause, WAHOO took aboard a load of the new Mark 18 electrics, and Morton requested that his submarine be sent back to the Japan Sea for her seventh patrol.

The area's defenders were now on the alert. PLUNGER, coming out through La Perouse Strait, had been forced to dodge two Jap destroyers which were watching the exit. WAHOO left Pearl Harbor on September 9, topped off at Midway on the 13th and headed for La Perouse to run the gantlet. She was trailed by SAWFISH (Lieutenant Commander E. T. Sands) bent on penetrating the Japan Sea in her wake.

Morton's submarine was to make her entry on or about September 20, and patrol the sea below the 43° parallel. SAWFISH was to enter some three days later and cover the area north of WAHOO's. At sunset, October 21, WAHOO was supposed to leave her area, and head for home. She was instructed to report by radio after she made her way out through the Kurile chain. This report was expected about October 23rd.

The transmission from WAHOO was never received. SAWFISH made no contact with her, and she maintained a radio silence that lasted beyond all reasonable hope and became the muteness of interminable tide and infinite sea.

Yet WAHOO was heard from during her seventh and last patrol. Indirectly, and through a foreign agent. That agent was Radio Tokyo, broadcasting to the world a Domei report that a steamer was sunk by an American submarine on October 5 off the west coast of Honshu. The broadcast stated that the vessel was torpedoed near the Straits of Tsushima and sank "after several seconds" with 544 people losing their lives as the ship went down.

This broadcast was reported by *Time* magazine of October 18, under the headline, "KNOCK AT THE DOOR." The magazine's readers were reminded that the torpedoing occurred in waters which were "Japan's historic door" to the mainland of Asia. In these waters, centuries before, Regent Hideyoshi's armada sailed to battle the Koreans. Upon them in 1905 the pugnacious Admiral Tojo had destroyed the Czarist Russian fleet. The magazine "presumed" the submarine knocking at this door was American, and compared the Japan Sea penetration to Gunther Prien's invasion of Scapa Flow and the Jap raid on Pearl Harbor.

The magazine's presumption was correct. What its editors did not know was the fact that other submarines had invaded this sea, and that the submarine in question knocked on the door more than once.

The Japanese recorded an anti-submarine action in La Perouse Strait on October 11, 1943. "Our plane found a floating submarine and attacked it with three depth charges." SAWFISH was depth-charged by a patrol boat while transiting the strait two days before, and the enemy's A/S forces were obviously on the alert in the area. There could be little doubt that the patrol plane's target was WAHOO.

On November 9, WAHOO was officially reported missing. At that time her loss was attributed to enemy mines. The Japan Sea was abandoned as a patrol area, and it was not again invaded until June 1945 when special mine-detecting equipment was available for submarines.

Examined after the war, Japanese records disclosed that WAHOO, in a series of attacks that began on September 29, downed the four ships enumerated below.

So closed the book for one of the greatest submarine teams of World War II—WAHOO and "Mush" Morton. If the philosophy of a combat submariner could be summed up in a single word, one would certainly suffice for Morton's.

"Attack!"

Submarine Tactics—Wolf-packing

WAHOO's thrust into Wewak and invasion of the Japan Sea—GUARDFISH at Rabaul—SEAWOLF at Davao—TROUT at Miri—these were single-handed exploits which characterized the submarine war in the Pacific up to the autumn of 1943. By nature individualistic, the submarine operated for the most part as a lone-wolf raider, its hunting ground a broad patrol area in which it roamed more or less at will, according to the dictates of valor and discretion. The submarine remained one of the few military units capable of acting wholly on its own, far from its base of supplies and unsupported by accompanying forces.

In the last year and a half of the war, American submarine operations were somewhat altered in character. The change was introduced in September 1943 by the formation of the first American "wolf-pack."

The military principle of concentration of force —"getting there fustest with the mostest"—motivated this attack-group experiment. Applied defensively, the principle had developed the convoy system, by way of concentrating friendly forces for mutual protection against submarines. Successful in World War I, this anti-submarine measure was countered early in World War II by German efforts to concentrate their U-boat forces against convoys.

The wolf-pack did not come as a surprise to American submariners. Back in the 1930's the "section attack"—three submarines submerging and maneuvering in concert to trap a target—was assayed by the U.S. Submarine Force. The tactic was soon abandoned. Some critics felt that the restrictions imposed on individual freedom of action, plus the risk of submerged collision, outweighed any theoretical advantage. However, late in 1941 simultaneous night-surface attack by several submarines was given a trial. The outbreak of hostilities interrupted practice maneuvers, and the group-attack method did not reach a final stage of development at that time.

Against the big Atlantic convoys, U-boat concentrations had proved all too effective. In the Pacific,

Date	Name	Type	Tonnage	Location
Sep. 29, 1943	Masaki Maru No. 2	Cargo	1,238	4000N, 13000E
Oct. 5, 1943	Konron Maru	Transport	7,908	3400N, 13000E
Oct. 6, 1943	Unknown Maru	Passenger-Cargo	1,288	3718N, 12933E
Oct. 9, 1943	Kanko Maru	Cargo	2,995	3718N, 12933E

oceanic distances were greater, American submarines were relatively few, Japanese shipping was scattered all over the map. And the character of undersea warfare was influenced by these and other factors which differed from those in the Atlantic.

Nevertheless, the principle of concentrated force could always apply. The matter of employing submarines in concerted effort was intensively studied on the game board and in exercises with American convoys en route to Pearl Harbor. Experiments led to the formulation of a standard coordinated attack doctrine. Given elasticity to meet changing conditions, this doctrine held that an attack group of three submarines would be adequate against the average Japanese convoy.

Tactics were devised for group operation. The three submarines would usually maneuver in line or column, about normal to the expected direction of the convoy's movement. Distance between submarines was prescribed (for the average situation) at somewhat less than twice the range of visibility or radar effectiveness. This arrangement was patterned to broaden the scope of search operations.

When a submarine of the group made contact, she would immediately transmit to her pack-mates the convoy's position and estimated course and speed. Such information was to be amplified whenever possible by the submarine in contact as she closed in and made an attack. If feasible, this first attack was to be delivered on the convoy's flank, away from the other submarines. The attacking submarine then withdrew to play the part of "trailer," while the attack on the convoy was taken up by her two pack-mates who had maneuvered into position on either flank.

Hanging to the convoy's flanks, the "flanker" submarines were to make repeated attacks and end-arounds, and to persist until the convoy was destroyed. Meantime, the submarine in "trailer" position was expected to furnish the "flanker" with information concerning major changes in the tactical situation, and to pick off stragglers or cripples and attack escorts harrying the "flankers." As may be seen, this coordinated attack doctrine was simple and flexible.

By September 1943 there were enough SubPac submarines available to permit a wolf-pack trial. The enemy might have noted that this coordinated attack group came into being at the time he was frantically striving to organize his anti-submarine program and install a convoy system. Force was preparing to meet force, as the occasion demanded.

On September 26 two submarines left home base at Pearl Harbor and headed west for Midway. At Midway they were joined by a third submarine. The three departed together on October 1st—destination, the East China Sea. This was the first American wolf-pack of the war.

The coordinated attack group consisted of CERO (Commander D. C. White), SHAD (Commander E. J. MacGregor), and GRAYBACK (Commander J. A. Moore). It was under group command of Captain C. B. Momsen. Pioneering as a team, the group was not spectacularly successful as to tonnages sunk. GRAYBACK, skippered by "Johnny" Moore, managed to make the list of officially verified sinkings by downing KOZUI MARU, passenger-cargo, 7,072 tons on October 14, and the 7,397-ton ex-light cruiser AWATA MARU on the 22nd. On the 27th SHAD and GRAYBACK teamed up to sink the 9,138-ton transport FUJI MARU. Seven ships were damaged by the three submarines.

No cooperative attacks in accordance with doctrine were made by the group. However, exchange of information between the submarines resulted in the development of numerous contacts. And in that respect the operation was considered significantly successful. Analyzing the group's experience, Captain Momsen recommended that the task group commander should not be embarked on a submarine, but should operate from a shore base where he could collect reports, dispense information and coordinate the activities of his submarines by radio. This recommendation was rejected, mainly because communication facilities were lacking at the time and constant radio transmissions from submarines might be traced by the enemy's radio direction-finders.

A second coordinated attack group left Midway on November 3rd. This wolf-pack—SNOOK, HARDER and PARGO—was led by Commander "Freddie" Warder. Despite communication difficulties, the group made a large number of contacts through cooperative effort. And though attacks did not follow the strictly cooperative pattern, seven ships were downed by the three submarines on patrol in the Marianas area. In his analysis Warder recommended that the pack be directed by the senior commanding officer of the group and expressed the opinion that the presence of the division commander was not imperative.

The American submarine wolf-pack was to hit its stride in the spring of 1944. American wolf-pack tactics did not develop along German lines, for the Pacific struggle bore no exact parallel to the Battle of the Atlantic. The Japanese anti-submarine effort remained sporadic, the Japanese convoy system inefficient. Small attack groups of three or four submarines were adequate, as no large concentration of force was needed to counter the Pacific enemy's A/S measures.

Moreover, the American submarine skipper liked latitude and longitude for individual operation. In union there is strength, but there is also strength in the spirit of independence. American wolf-pack tactics evolved in a manner which blended both virtues—coordinated patrolling to increase contacts, and independent attacks after contact had been made. This blend of cooperation and rugged individualism could not be countered by a robot-minded enemy.

Attrition Review

Inaugurated in September 1943, American submarine wolf-packing marked the end of what might be termed the single-handed submarine offensive against the Japanese homeland. In the 12 months prior to this date, Central Pacific submarines had not only conducted "lone wolf" patrols, but they had constituted the sole American force striking decisively at the heart of the Empire.

The blockade effected during this submarine offensive is clearly indicated on the accompanying chart by the sinkings clustered off the east coast of Japan, spattered through the East China and Yellow Sea and sprinkled across the Sea of Japan. Note that the period represented (from September 1, 1942 to August 31, 1943) does not include such late summer 1943 patrols as TRIGGER's in the East China Sea and WAHOO's in the Sea of Japan.

Note, too, that the Navy and Army air forces scored heavily against enemy shipping in the Solomons and eastern New Guinea areas during this period. But the great bulk of the Southwest Pacific was, in common with the Central Pacific, covered almost exclusively by the submarines.

There was to be no slow-up of the submarine drives against Nippon, the Mandates and the conquered areas of the Southwest Pacific. But the fall of 1943 set the stage for a naval campaign in the upper Solomons, an Army push in New Guinea and an amphibious drive to seize the Gilberts. United States land, sea and air forces were ready to join the submarines in an all-out offensive.

CHAPTER 19

ALEUTIAN CONCLUSION AND ATLANTIC TIDAL TURN

Heating up the North Pacific

While the Japanese were in hot water in the Central and Southwest Pacific, the U.S. and Canadian forces were not permitting the Aleutian waters to freeze over. Throughout the winter of 1942-1943 constant pressure was applied to pinch off the enemy's bases at Kiska and Attu. The Navy kept up steam at Dutch Harbor. The Army Air Force launched heckling raids from its forward Aleutian bases. And only the wildest weather interrupted the relay of submarine patrols.

At the time the fighting was hottest at Guadalcanal, two fleet submarines were dispatched to join the S-boat force at Dutch Harbor.

CACHALOT (Lieutenant Commander H. C. Stevenson) had arrived at that base on October 2, 1942. DOLPHIN (Lieutenant Commander R. L. Rutter) put in there three weeks later.

The veteran fleet submarines found poor pickings in the wintry archipelago. But they added mileage to the areas under patrol and bolstered up the S-boat effort.

Keeping the enemy's bases under surveillance and watching the sea lanes coming north from Japan was a trying task as the winter caterwauled into 1943. The same numbing winds, enormous seas, freak tides, black fogs and maelstromic storms which had assailed the Aleutian pioneers, now thrashed, blinded and flogged the submarining "frontiersmen." A storm might force a submarine to break off contact with an enemy vessel, but the need to surface for a battery charge could not be "called off" because of weather conditions. Not infrequently a submarine had to surface and charge batteries in the teeth of a ferocious gale. During one such instance, S-32 (Lieutenant Commander M. G. Schmidt) was driven into a trough that rolled her 65° to starboard at least three times. Such an experience is hard on the crockery—in a sailor's jaw as well as in the galley.

In mid-January—and no thaw to speak of—S-18, under Lieutenant Commander C. H. Browne, conducted a reconnaissance mission covering the Attu-Semichi Islands area. The mission, which lasted from the 11th to the 26th, could scarcely have been called a harbinger of spring. Yet the Japs, had they been informed, might have taken it as a hint of warmer weather to come.

American Army and Navy forces had occupied Amchitka Island by the end of January—a move that gave them ground for an airfield only 65 miles from Kiska. The landing strip was completed by mid-February, and U.S. fighter pilots were joining American and Canadian planes from Adak in a series of late-winter raids on Kiska and Attu. These air raids soon isolated Kiska. In a move to begin the isolation of Attu, a cruiser-destroyer force under Rear Admiral C. H. McMorris bombarded that island on February 19th.

A heavily screened Jap convoy succeeded in rushing reinforcements from Paramushiru in the northern Kuriles to Attu. As a result of this action, several S-boats were dispatched to cut the Paramushiru-Attu sea lanes. McMorris' surface forces stopped the enemy's traffic, however. Patrolling southeast of the

Russian Komandorskis, the American task group made radar contact on a second Attu-bound convoy on the morning of March 27th. The convoy was strongly escorted and under command of Admiral Hosogaya, IJN. Apparently the Japs, who sighted the oncoming American warships, thought they were meeting a friendly force expected in the area. The resulting Battle of the Komandorskis ended in a decisive Japanese check. Although USS SALT LAKE CITY was damaged by gunfire and the destroyer BAILEY was hit, the Japanese flagship NACHI was all but knocked out of action, and several other Jap warships were damaged. Fearing that American land-based planes would arrive on the scene, Hosogaya ordered a retreat, and the convoy was escorted back to Paramushiru.

It was the last Jap train for the Aleutians. After that fiasco, the Japanese depended on their submarines to supply Attu and Kiska. Thirteen of these had cooperated in the invasion of the Aleutians in June 1942. Now they were to cooperate again—in a reverse operation.

Nautilus and Narwhal to Attu

Japanese I-boats were not the only submarines to land troops on Attu. Early in April 1943, two U.S. submarines were practicing amphibious maneuvers for a scheduled Attu landing.

NAUTILUS was practicing at Pearl Harbor. Lieutenant Commander Brockman needed no indoctrination course in the business of preparing his big submarine for an amphibious operation. At Makin it had been Carlson's Raiders. Now it was 109 Army Scouts to be put ashore in Blind Cove, Holtz Bay, in the northeastern end of Attu.

While NAUTILUS was readying at Pearl Harbor, NARWHAL, under Lieutenant Commander Frank D. Latta, was rehearsing with 105 men and officers of the Seventh Scout Company at San Diego, California, 2,000 miles away.

On April 20, NARWHAL set out for Dutch Harbor. Like her sister submarine on this Aleutian mission, she was jammed to the gills with passengers. Torpedoes and torpedo skids had been removed to make room for wooden and canvas bunks. Sleeping facilities were not exactly Pullman, but there was enough snoring to satisfy the porters. Fresh air, always at a premium on a day-long submerged run, was a problem that had to be solved by the use of oxygen and CO_2 absorbent.

The Army Scouts aboard NARWHAL and NAUTILUS were able to go briskly ashore when the submarines reached Dutch Harbor on April 27th. There, joint disembarkation exercises were conducted, and by May 1, the two submarines were on their way to Attu.

Also en route to Attu was a striking force consisting of battleships IDAHO, PENNSYLVANIA and NEVADA, the escort carrier NASSAU, a number of destroyers, and transports carrying Army troops. Rear Admiral Thomas C. Kinkaid directed the operation.

D-Day had to be postponed for three days due to foul weather. While the ships milled offshore in fog and snowstorms, the two transport submarines maneuvered to keep out of everybody's way. At one time NAUTILUS made a 4,000-yard radar contact on an unidentified vessel, and Brockman jockeyed in for a stern shot. Seen at 1,000 yards, the target proved to be NARWHAL.

May 11 finally brought the order to go in. Around 0300 the submarines rendezvoused off Blind Cove and the Scouts were disembarked in rubber boats. The night was ink-black and the beach was barely visible. NAUTILUS stood by until 0450, showing an infra-red light toward the beach to assist the boats in holding a correct course. NAUTILUS then opened to seaward, following NARWHAL in a planned retirement. Both scouting parties had landed safely.

The battle to take Attu lasted for three weeks. Entrenching themselves in the mountains, the Japanese held out so stubbornly that the Americans had to send for reserves, and 12,000 men were eventually thrown into the fight. At the end, out of ammunition, the Japs made a suicide charge, rushing the American line with knives and bayonets. The *hara-kiri* was all over by May 30th. Japan had lost her major base in the Aleutians.

Grand Finale

On June 2, Attu was declared secure. The battle cost 550 American lives and double that in wounded. The Japanese garrison was practically annihilated.

The next move was to take Kiska. Invasion was scheduled for August 15th. At Adak a force of some 100 vessels was assembled and 29,000 American plus 5,000 Canadian troops were embarked with full battle gear. An ugly contest on the Attu pattern was expected. The upshot came as the war's strangest denouement. When the occupation forces went ashore after a heavy preliminary bombardment, not a single, solitary Jap could be found on Kiska. On August 31, under cover of one of those impenetrable Aleutian fogs, the entire garrison had made a getaway. Japanese fast transports, assisted by 15 submarines, had evacuated it to Paramushiru.

Aleutian Aftermath

While the United States-Canadian forces had been capturing Attu and Kiska, the submarine force from

AWARDS. *In dress uniform, submariners on the left await arrival of Admiral to receive awards, while submarine crew in foreground watches ceremony.*

The Navy's undersea fighters won highest honors. Seven Congressional Medals went to submarine captains. Subs received 36 Presidential Unit Citations.

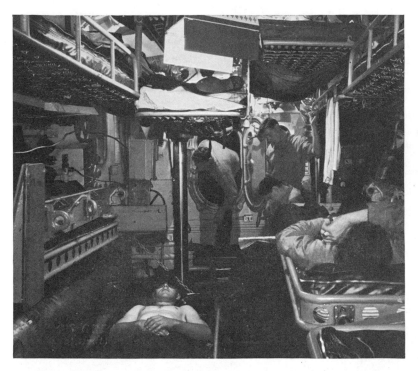

SHUT-EYE. *The off-watch "hits the sack" in the forward torpedo room. Note torpedo alongside man at left; sunlamp overhead for deepsea tan.*

MEDICAL CORPSMAN *at work. Sub Pharmacist's Mates are versatile as doctors.*

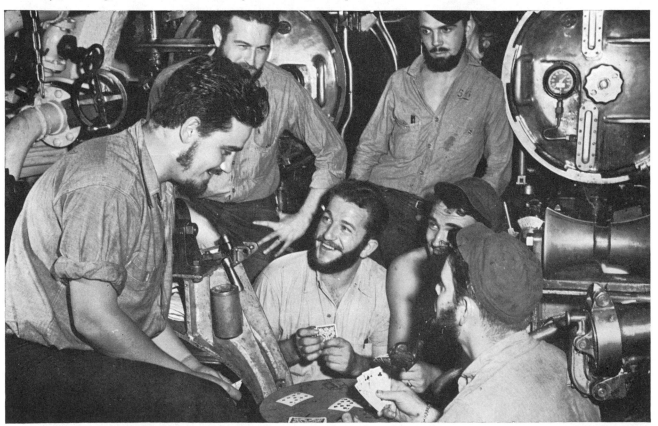

TORPEDOMEN RELAXING. *The whiskers (officially frowned upon) were functional as well as decorative—cut shaving-time to a minimum. Formality does not flourish in submarine navy where performance counts more than protocol. In submarines, where all are in same boat, each man knows his and next man's job; is his brother's keeper.*

Dutch Harbor was on the go out at sea. The S-boats contributed to the Japanese defeat by sinking several AK's and a number of patrol vessels off the archipelago and in the vicinity of the Kuriles.

S-41 (Lieutenant I. S. Hartman) sank SEIKI MARU on May 28th. S-30 (Lieutenant W. A. Stevenson) accounted for the 5,228-ton JINBU MARU on June 11th. On July 2, S-35 (Lieutenant H. S. Monroe) sank BANSHU MARU No. 7, 5,430 tons. The last ship sunk in those waters by an S-boat was the converted gunboat KATSURA MARU No. 2, sunk by S-28 (Lieutenant V. A. Sisler, Jr.) on September 19th.

With the ending of the Aleutian campaign, the "sugar boats" were on the verge of concluding their valorous careers. In October they were slated for retirement or service as training vessels. But they had not yet fired their final shot. One of the last S-boats to go out from the Aleutians on war patrol was S-44 —renowned conqueror of the heavy cruiser KAKO. It was not her lot to end up as a training vessel or in retirement. It was hers to go down in the last S-boat battle of the Pacific War.

Last Shot (Loss of S-44)

On September 26, S-44 stood seaward from Attu, under Lieutenant Commander F. E. Brown, to begin her fifth war patrol—area destination, the northern Kuriles. Submarines had been busy wrecking the Japanese fishing business in those waters, and there was shipping to be found off Paramushiru.

Early in October, S-44 was sighted by an enemy patrol plane which forced her under with several badly aimed depth charges. Then, on the night of October 7, the submarine made radar contact with what appeared to be a small merchantman.

Brown ordered the gunners out on deck and closed in to deliver a surface attack. S-44 was only a few hundred yards from the target when Brown opened fire. A stunning salvo answered the S-boat's deck gun—the ship she had attacked in the dark was a destroyer!

Brown shouted the order, "Clear the deck! Take her down!" The diving alarm sounded as the crew reached the conning tower. But S-44 failed to submerge. A shell had smashed into the control room below the waterline. Now a second projectile exploded in the conning tower, and a third stove in the hull near the forward battery room. In the limbo of flame, smoke and founting spray, the S-boat rolled and lurched under another series of hits as Brown cried the order to abandon and someone flagged a pillow case from the forward battery-room hatch as a signal of surrender. Either the Jap destroyer-men failed to see it in the night, or they were indisposed

to show mercy. The shells continued to smash into S-44 as she went down.

Seven or eight men escaped the sinking submarine, but only two were picked up by the destroyer. These were Chief Torpedoman's Mate E. A. Duva, and Radioman Third Class W. F. Whitemore.

Duva and Whitemore were taken to Paramushiru where they endured the usual grilling, and eventually they were forced to prison labor in the Ashio copper mines. Sole survivors of the S-44, they were released by Allied forces at the end of the war.

Alaska Secured

With the Japanese retirement from Kiska the Aleutian war was ended. American aircraft now had bases within range of Paramushiru, and North Pacific trails had been blazed for a submarine offensive against the Kuriles. The Japanese strike at Alaska had boomeranged into Empire waters.

The Aleutian defeat was more than a military setback for the enemy. The minions of the Emperor were beginning to realize the Rising Sun had passed its zenith. Midway—Guadalcanal—and now the dream of extending the Empire to Alaska was dissipated. Conversely, for the Allies the Aleutian victory, ending the Alaska threat, was a heartening sign that Japan's sun was westering. The United States Submarine Force could take particular pride in its contributions to that victory.

U.S. submarines had pioneered the Aleutian defense. U.S. submariners had helped to slam the door on enemy fingers reaching into "Seward's Ice Box."

Atlantic Tidal Turn

The Squadron Fifty submarines which had participated in "Operation Torch" and patrolled the Bay of Biscay were awaiting new orders in late March of 1943. Roseneath, Scotland, seemed a wallflower base with the war roaring full-tilt along the Mediterranean coast of North Africa and action in Scotland reduced to blackouts and air raids. Hitler's *Festung Europa* was a looming battlement across the English Channel, but it would not be assailed until North Africa and Italy were secured. The Bay of Biscay was a festering spot, but little could be done to squelch Franco Spain's efforts in behalf of Nazi Germany. Restricted to sinking only those vessels positively identified as blockade runners, the submarines had been frustrated at the start, and the six-week patrols off the Spanish coast had been more dangerous than productive.

BARB, HERRING, BLACKFISH, SHAD, GURNARD and GUNNEL assembled at Base Two after nine Biscay patrols had been conducted. The chief topic of talk among the captains was engine trouble. The Diesels installed in this group of submarines were a pre-war type based on German designs. Despite the best efforts of the manufacturers and skilled servicing by the submarine repair forces, this engine refused to function satisfactorily in submarines, and eventually it had to be replaced.

In April 1943 HAKE (Lieutenant Commander J. C. Broach) and HADDO (Commander W. A. Lent) joined Squadron Fifty at Roseneath, relieving GUNNEL and GURNARD. The latter were ordered back to the United States to have their cranky engines removed.

At this time the squadron's patrol areas were shifted to positions off Norway and North Iceland. A few weeks later they were moved to the mid-Atlantic. In these areas the submarines were to hunt U-boats, and they remained available for action in the event of a German breakout from Norway. The Norway breakout did not eventuate, and only one enemy contact was made. On May 25, HADDO sighted a Nazi submarine. She tried to close, but she was unable to gain a firing position and the U-boat slipped away.

After several months it became apparent that the Squadron Fifty submarines were not being used to best advantage. Reason: lack of targets in the Atlantic. Accordingly the squadron was returned to the United States, and the submarines were then dispatched to the Pacific where the undersea war was in full career.

Shortly before the SubRon Fifty boats departed from British waters, the following message was received by Squadron Commander Captain Ives. It was from Rear Admiral C. B. Barry, who had relieved Admiral Sir Max Horton as Admiral of Submarines.

"*. . . The targets that have come your way in European waters have been disappointingly few, but your submarines have invariably seized their opportunity and exploited themselves to the utmost. Their actual contribution has been very great and personal, far beyond numbers of ships sunk or damaged.*"

Captain Ives did not return to the States with Squadron Fifty. He was assigned to naval duty in Europe, where he participated in the Normandy landings in June 1944. After the landings, he was made Port Director of Cherbourg. On August 2, 1944, he lost his life when a car in which he was traveling was ambushed by a party of Germans.

The U-boat War

The Battle of the Atlantic was by no means decided at the time of the North African invasion. Through 1942 the U-boat war had rampaged, torpedo against depth charge, and during the first 10 months of that year it looked as though Hitler's submarines might win. In the summer of 1942 Allied vessels off the American coast were being sunk at a rate of about one a day, and the eastern seaboard was littered with the residue of torpedoed tankers and drowned cargomen. In mid-ocean the U-boat attacks were almost as numerous. Between January 1 and November 1, 1942, the U-boats sank some 878 Allied ships—approximately 4,587,000 tons.

During the last two months of 1942 the sinkings dwindled. Allied A/S measures were beginning to tell. The North Africa invasion provided the Allies with bases in Morocco and Dakar for air patrols in the South Atlantic. British and American forces based in the United Kingdom, Greenland, and Iceland were scoring with increasing frequency in the North Atlantic. From Newfoundland to Brazil the American sea frontier was patrolled by anti-submarine vessels and aircraft. In the first six months of 1943 the Atlantic tide turned decisively against the U-boat. In that period 150 Nazi submarines were sunk.

Attempting to halt these reverses, German Admiral Doenitz made what came to be recognized as a serious mistake. He ordered his submarines fitted with anti-aircraft guns. But the surface gun was never the submersible's strong weapon. The U-boat that tried to shoot it out with an attacking aircraft missed its calling, while the aircraft itself seldom missed.

In one respect the Nazi Navy suffered a handicap in common with the Japanese. Vaunted scientists that they were, the Germans were unable to match the Allies in the field of technology and in the laboratory. From the Battle of the Atlantic, future historians may well conclude that the totalitarian state or government which demands "regimented thinking" shackles itself in the world of science. Certainly the government which forces its scientists to think in goose-step is on a back road, and during the early part of the war many German physicists, chemists and educators were literally set to marching in uniform. In December 1943 Admiral Doenitz issued a top secret order containing the appeal,

IT IS ESSENTIAL TO VICTORY THAT WE MAKE GOOD OUR SCIENTIFIC DISPARITY AND THEREBY RESTORE TO THE U-BOAT ITS FIGHTING QUALITIES

As a result of this entreaty, German scientists who had been drafted were recalled from the front to assist in the creation of the Naval Scientific Directional Staff. This body was similar to the Scientific Council which, organized by Admiral King and composed of civilian scientists, operated with the Tenth Fleet (the coordinating agency for anti-submarine warfare). Late in the field, the German Naval Scientific Directional Staff was unable to overcome the Allied lead, and the "scientific disparity" bemoaned by Admiral Doenitz contributed much to the Nazi defeat in the Battle of the Atlantic.

The struggle between U-boat and Allied A/S forces presents an interesting drama in competitive inventing. When German naval strategists devised the U-boat wolf-pack to operate in seas beyond the range of land-based aircraft, Allied naval strategists countered with small escort carriers to take the aircraft to sea. Similarly, when Nazi scientists invented an acoustical torpedo designed to steer itself toward the noise of a ship's screws, Allied inventors produced a "noisemaker" to be towed from a vessel's stern and divert the torpedo.

Hitler's scientists tried to frustrate supersonic detection by coating the U-boat hulls with rubber. When this shield proved unavailing, they tried to defeat sonar by means of *pillenwerfer*—large chemical pellets which, discharged from a submarine, created in the water a bubbling disturbance calculated to confuse echo-ranging. These gimcracks were effective to some extent, but Allied sonar operators soon learned of the ruse and were able to probe through it.

Allied laboratories produced another submarine detector which harassed the U-boats. This was the sonobuoy—a buoy equipped with sound gear and an automatic radio sender which could transmit a warning when a submerged submarine entered its field. But it was radar that grayed the hair of the U-boat commanders. The German scientists countered with tinfoil streamers to create false radar "pips," and "search receivers" to pick up radar beams and give warning of radar-equipped craft in the offing. The Allied answer was skilled radarmen who could recognize the deceptive "pip," and S-band radar which could not be detected.

Late in the war, the German scientists employed the *schnorkel* extension stack. This was an air tube—in effect, a windpipe extending from the submerged submarine to the surface. Serving as an air intake and exhaust for the engines, it permitted the U-boat to operate on Diesel propulsion at periscope depth, thus giving the submarine a higher submerged speed, and eliminating the necessity for a surface-run battery charge. *Schnorkel* was a most important innovation in submarining. But it came too late to rescue the foundering Nazi Cause.

Between July 1943 and June 1944 some 199 U-boats were sunk by Allied A/S forces. By superhuman effort the Germans might have been able to replace the submarines. But no mortal effort could replace the many experienced U-boat captains and skilled crews lost with these vanquished undersea boats. Before the Nazis capitulated on V-E Day, a total of some 781 German submarines had been sunk and approximately 30,000 German submariners had been drowned in action.

Seen in historical perspective, these figures will not detract from the U-boat's reputation as an engine of destruction. In the Atlantic the U-boat force destroyed almost 3,000 Allied vessels—approximately 14,000,000 tons of Allied shipping. It did not do so well against Allied naval vessels, although it smote the Royal Navy an excruciating blow at the war's outset. American naval losses to the U-boat were the destroyers JACOB JONES and LEARY, the destroyer escorts FISKE and FREDERICK C. DAVIS, five Coast Guard cutters, and the escort carrier BLOCK ISLAND.

Admiral Doenitz made some plaintive excuses at war's end. Hitler, he said, had not prepared to fight a naval war against the Anglo-Saxon powers. To do so, Der Fuehrer should have had 1,000 U-boats available at the war's beginning. The Nazi submarine admiral described radar as the U-boat's Nemesis. It was, he asserted, *"next to the atomic bomb, the most decisive weapon of the war."*

Of course, before radar or any detection device could be brought into play against the enemy, men had to be trained to operate the new instruments. Keeping pace with the demand for expert radarmen and sonarmen was the Navy's need for skilled personnel to man the A/S vessels and aircraft that tracked down and blasted the U-boat after it was detected. United States A/S forces received much of their training in the Atlantic. And U.S. submarines played an increasingly important role in that training. The efficient program launched by Admiral Edwards before the war was successfully continued throughout 1942 and expanded in 1943.

Operational Training Command

In April 1943, the Operational Training Command, Atlantic Fleet, was established with Rear Admiral D. B. Berry in charge. Bermuda was selected for the Destroyer-Destroyer Escort Shakedown Training Center. Captain J. L. Holloway, Jr., the first officer-in-charge of the Shakedown Group, recommended the location. He had been there with his destroyer squadron and the submarines stationed at Ordnance Island had cooperated in anti-submarine training. Holloway was favorably impressed by the local facilities. With submarines available and operating from an established base, the activity was ready to go.

So operational control of Submarine Squadron

Seven stationed at Bermuda was shifted from the Commandant Naval Operating Base, Bermuda, to Commander Operational Training Command. The Squadron Seven submarines were old hands as "trainers." Veteran patrollers originally engaged in hunting the U-boat, they had from the first linked their services with those of the other A/S forces in the Bermuda area.

The DD's and DE's which were built in East Coast and Gulf of Mexico shipyards were now sent to Bermuda for shakedown training. Anti-submarine vessels of all types reported to the Center for refresher exercises. Eventually some 10 to 12 new trainees were arriving every week. The number of submarines engaged in this activity (originally two) increased as the program expanded. Foreign submarines frequently participated.

With the curtailment of the destroyer escort building program early in 1945, the Shakedown Center at Bermuda was no longer needed, and the activity was transferred to Guantanamo, Cuba.

A/S Development Detachment

The Anti-Submarine Development Detachment was organized in July 1943. Its mission was to aid in the development of anti-submarine measures and devices. The activity employed submarines to test new anti-submarine equipment and newly devised A/S tactics.

The Development Detachment was set up at the Naval Air Station, Quonset, Rhode Island, and its operations were conducted in Long Island Sound. In 1944 a branch was established at Fort Lauderdale, Florida, where weather conditions were prevailingly favorable. ComSubLant furnished the submarines for this activity which promoted the anti-submarine effort until the end of the war.

Loss of R-12

Only two United States submarines were lost in the Atlantic during World War II. Both were lost in 1943.

R-12 (Lieutenant Commander E. E. Shelby) was proceeding off Key West, Florida, on June 12th. She was underway to take up her position for a torpedo practice approach—a maneuver she was demonstrating for Lieutenants A. G. D. Almeida and J. L. De Moura of the Brazilian Navy.

The submarine was rigged for diving and riding the vents. On the bridge were Lieutenant Commander Shelby, two officers and three men. About 1220, as Shelby was in the act of turning the O.O.D. watch over to another officer, the collision alarm sounded below and word was passed to the bridge that the forward battery compartment was flooding.

Shelby immediately gave the order to blow main ballast and close the hatches. Water plunged up over the superstructure as he spoke. And then, with a hollow roar, the seas closed in and R-12 was gone.

The disaster occurred in a calamitous 15 seconds. With the exception of Lieutenant Commander Shelby and the two officers and three men who were with him on the bridge, all hands were lost, including the two Brazilian officers—a total of 42 lives. Fortunately, some 18 of the submarine's normal complement were ashore on liberty at the time.

The R-boat went down in 600 feet of water. A Court of Inquiry pronounced the cause of the sinking as unknown, but probably due to rapid flooding of the forward part of the submarine through a torpedo tube.

Loss of Dorado

DORADO, the second submarine to go down in the Atlantic, was lost some time in October. Newly commissioned, under Lieutenant Commander E. C. Schneider, she departed New London, Connecticut, on October 6, and headed for Panama. She was never heard from thereafter.

Commander-in-Chief, United States Fleet, commenting on the Court of Inquiry report, listed three possible causes for DORADO's loss. These were: operational casualties; enemy action; attack by friendly forces.

The standard practice of imposing bombing restrictions within a 15-mile area on either side of an unescorted submarine's course in friendly water was observed. All forces concerned were notified of DORADO's route. However, a patrol plane which was assigned by Commandant, NOB, Guantanamo, to furnish air coverage for a convoy scheduled to be in DORADO's vicinity on October 12, received faulty instructions concerning the bombing restriction area. On the evening of October 12, this plane sighted an unidentified submarine. German submarines were known to be in the area, and the plane attacked, dropping three depth charges. Around midnight the plane sighted another submarine. The submarine failed to answer recognition signals, and opened fire on the plane. It seems probable that this was a U-boat armed with one of Doenitz' anti-aircraft guns.

The submarine sighted and depth-charged by the plane two hours earlier may have been DORADO, for she was due in the area at that date. There was also the possibility that DORADO encountered a German submarine in the Caribbean. Chance meeting with a lurking enemy—a shot in the dark—a torpedo—such undersea battles had been waged in the area.

Lack of evidence forced the Court of Inquiry to adjudge the cause of DORADO's loss as unknown.

Somewhere in the Atlantic—perhaps in action off Cuba—she went down with all hands.

French and Italian Submarines (for Training Purposes Only)

Late in 1943 two French submarines were made available for the A/S training activity under United States supervision. Five more were added to the A/S training program in 1944.

After the invasion of Sicily, the Allied entry into Naples and the landing at Anzio (in January 1944), Italian submarines were obtained for the A/S training activity. Five of these came across the Atlantic in February 1944. When the Italian boot proved to be a foot of clay and Mussolini's Navy collapsed lock, stock and barrel, three more Italian submersibles were brought to the United States.

These foreign submarines were assigned by ComSubLant to Submarine Squadron Seven. They reported for duty with the DD-DE Shakedown Group in Bermuda and later at Guantanamo, and a few were assigned at various times to Key West, Fort Lauderdale, Casco Bay and other A/S training centers. The French and Italian subs were excellent for training purposes. Of heavy hull construction, they could out-dive the older American R- and S-boats. And they made good substitutes for the newly commissioned fleet submarines which had formerly participated in the training program and could now be sent non-stop to the Pacific for combat duty.

The French and Italian submarines were not the equals of the American fleet-type, however. The Vichy French submarine navy had become disorganized and its boats were sorely in need of refit and repair. The Italian submarines reflected the mediocre industrial plant which had spawned them—equipment fairly good, but not up to American standards.

The French and Italian submarines which were entered into the A/S program in 1943-1944 were the following:

FRENCH

ARGO	*(Lieutenant de V. Blachere)*
AMAZONE	*(Lieutenant de V. Bordeaux)*
CENTAURE	*(Lieutenant de V. Tual)*
F. S. ARCHIMEDE	*(Capitaine de Caruette F. Bailleux)*
ANTIOPE	*(Lieutenant de V. Auge)*
CASABLANCA	*(Lieutenant de V. Bellet)*
LA GLORIEUX	*(Lieutenant de V. Piot)*

ITALIAN

VORTICE	*(Lieutenant G. Manunta)*
MAREA	*(Lieutenant A. Russo)*
ENRICO DANDOLO	*(Lieutenant A. Turcio)*
TITO SPERI	*(Lieutenant C. Celli)*
GOFFREDO MAMELI	*(Lieutenant C. Buldrini)*
ONICE	*(Lieutenant F. Boggetti)*
GIOVANNI DA PROCIDA	*(Lieutenant R. Castracane)*
ATROPO	*(Lieutenant A. Galzigna)*

Good for training duty, the Italian submarines also provided the Allies with interesting information on the European end of the Axis. In the newer models, material shortages were well advertised. Parts normally made of copper, brass or bronze were fashioned of iron or steel. It could be presumed that Germany's U-boats were being fed similar *ersatz*.

But as early as the summer of 1943, it was evident that Hitler's Fortress Europa could not last a thousand years. The Germans were losing the war at sea. The Axis was cracking.

United States submarines, no longer needed in the Atlantic, were going through the Panama Canal in steady procession—a parade of periscopes heading toward the setting sun.

CHAPTER 20

TORPEDO!

Fire under Water

"Submarine" and "Torpedo" are subjects which go hand in hand, and a history of one must of necessity include a study of the other. The undersea boat and the undersea explosive charge experienced their development in the same cradle of the deep. Fathered in New England by David Bushnell, they were fostered simultaneously by the American nautical genius, Robert Fulton. The submarine was invented for the express purpose of carrying an underwater demolition charge into battle, and the modern mobile torpedo evolved as an engine designed to deliver the charge to the target.

Obviously, torpedo performance has a direct influence on all submarine operations. It is up to the submarine to locate the target, to adjust the torpedo appropriately, and to unleash it at the proper time. Once sent into action, the torpedo must "carry the ball." Let it fumble, falter or otherwise fail, the whole play goes askew. Such failure may cost the submarine its life.

It goes without saying that battles as well as submarines might be lost through torpedo failure. And an entire campaign could be threatened, were submarines forced to fight it with faulty weapons. As was stated in an early chapter of this text, the U.S. Submarine Force entered the war with such a weapon. It was not until late in 1943 that this serious situation was adequately remedied. The trials and tribulations which the submariners suffered under this handicap compose a story that merits the telling—in behalf of the Navy's torpedo, the men who made good with it, and the men who made it good.

Temperamental Tin Fish

Mr. Whitehead's mobile torpedo, carrying 18 pounds of guncotton and able to maintain a submerged speed of 6 knots, was a wonderfully intricate device. But, in comparison with a modern submarine torpedo, it was a contrivance as simple as a Naphtha launch.

Weighing approximately 1½ tons, with a maximum effective range of over 9,000 yards, the modern, self-guiding submarine torpedo is, in effect, a small robot submarine. Those employed by the U.S. Navy at the beginning of World War II were ejected from the torpedo tube by compressed air. Once ejected, they could level off at a preselected depth, follow a curve to seek out a predetermined course, and then go streaking down this straight course on a bullet-line for the target. Imagine a projectile which, when fired from a gun, could swerve to right or left to head for a target around a corner! A projectile also possessed of the ability to dive and then rise to the level of a suitable trajectory! The torpedo, of course, was not a projectile, but such were its wizardish capabilities.

Steam, generated by forcing a spray of water through a torch of burning alcohol, supplied motive power. Steering was controlled by means of a gyroscopic mechanism. A delicate hydrostatic device, reacting to water pressures, governed depth control. The explosive carried in the torpedo's warhead contained about a quarter of a ton of T.N.T. The blast was detonated by an exploder mechanism which worked by contact (direct hit on the target) or by magnetic influence when the torpedo passed through a steel ship's magnetic field. Certainly the torpedo with which U.S. submarines entered the war was a remarkable weapon—one of the most complex engines of destruction ever produced. It had one drawback, however. All too often it "didn't work."

In action it proved to be a curiously temperamental performer—not unlike the prima donna who stars brilliantly on one occasion and indulges a tantrum on the next. Monday the torpedo might run beautifully—"straight, hot and normal," as the submariners express it. Thursday it might jump along the surface or explode en route to the target. Friday it might hit the target but fail to explode. Sunday it might sink a destroyer four miles away. The only reliable feature of the torpedo was its unreliability.

Defective torpedoes are not easily brought to book —especially those which display a multiplicity of defects. The brand in question made circular runs, porpoised, ran "cold," sometimes refused to run at all. These malfunctionings were infrequent and could generally be attributed to personnel errors—poor preparation or faulty adjustment. More baffling were the defects inherent in the design of the torpedo and the exploder mechanism. As has been described, the torpedoes ran deeper than set depths. They exploded prematurely, sometimes close to the submarine immediately after arming, sometimes near the target, the blast simulating a hit, but not near enough to inflict crippling damage. Again, they might be duds, striking and failing to explode. Such caprices had their origin in the torpedo's make-up and the exploder mechanism's character, and they frustrated correction in a most diabolical manner.

For each flaw concealed the next, making it impossible to detect and correct all of them simultaneously. The deep-running torpedo hid the premature skeleton in its closet, and it was not until deep running was corrected that prematures rattled out into the open. Prematures were the product of that Pandora's Box, the magnetic exploder. Then when this device was inactivated and torpedoes were fired for contact hits, the dud came to the fore as a major problem.

Perhaps most baffling of all was the fact that these torpedoes, when they did work according to Hoyle, ran through their paces with a perfection that left nothing to be desired. They sank enemy shipping—thousands of tons of it—and therein lay much of the difficulty in locating their flaws. The always hard-to-analyze human element contributed to the problem. Torpedoes, after all, are adjusted, aimed and fired by human endeavor. Faulty judgment, errors in calculation, mishandling, poor maintenance, all these could account for torpedo misbehavior. Thus the torpedo troubles were not easily traced to their source, readily diagnosed and speedily remedied. Submarine warfare was too complex and the torpedo too complex a weapon for easy "trouble shooting."

Nevertheless, there were many officers in the Submarine Service who believed that the torpedo could and should have been corrected long before it was. They pointed to the speedy action taken in the matter when someone of Admiral Lockwood's caliber stepped in. These officers—and they were the ones who staked their lives on torpedo performance—were up in arms against the doctrinaire and bureaucratic inertia that refused to recognize or properly

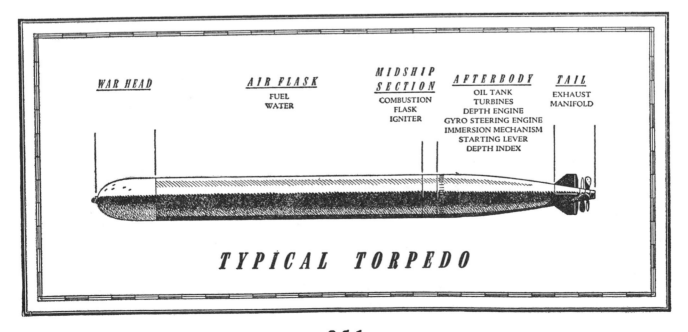

WAR HEAD

AIR FLASK
FUEL
WATER

MIDSHIP SECTION
COMBUSTION
FLASK
IGNITER

AFTERBODY
OIL TANK
TURBINES
DEPTH ENGINE
GYRO STEERING ENGINE
IMMERSION MECHANISM
STARTING LEVER
DEPTH INDEX

TAIL
EXHAUST
MANIFOLD

TYPICAL TORPEDO

diagnose the difficulty and thereby impeded the cure. Massive military organizations, with their interdepartmental ramifications and internal complications, resist change. They may move at a glacial pace where the speed of an avalanche is imperative. And there were several top-level officers of the ordnance organization who ascribed all torpedo faults to errors of the operating personnel, and chose to define "dud" as a "skipper's alibi to explain his miss." So for almost two years the U.S. submarine effort was seriously retarded by defective torpedoes. And it was not until the autumn of 1943, and then only after the forces afloat had stepped in to solve the problem, that the submariners were supplied with a weapon worthy of their skill.

Mark 10 and Mark 14

Until the Mark 18 electric torpedo first went to sea in September 1943, the torpedoes most widely used by the U.S. Submarine Force were the Mark 10 (for S-class submarines) and the Mark 14 (for fleet type). A few other Marks were pressed into service in the early months of the war to relieve the torpedo shortage. Their number was small and their characteristics had no far-reaching effect on submarine operations.

The Mark 10 torpedo was a veteran with well over a decade of service experience. Twenty-one inches in diameter, it weighed 2,215 pounds when ready for a war shot. Its steam turbines gave it a range of 3,500 yards at a speed of 36 knots. The warhead carried 497 pounds of T.N.T.—later, 485 pounds of torpex. The Mark 3 exploder with which it was fitted was a simple contact device, designed to detonate the head upon impact with the target.

The Mark 14 torpedo, 21 inches in diameter, was longer, heavier, faster, and had a range greater than the Mark 10's. When the war broke out, it was the most recent model in quantity production. It had two speed adjustments so that it could be fired either with a speed of 46 knots to a range of 4,500 yards, or, in low power, with a speed of 31.5 knots to a distance of 9,000 yards. The low-power setting was rarely used, and to expedite production during the latter part of the war, the Mark 23 torpedo, which was essentially a Mark 14 with low power eliminated, was introduced. (In this discussion the Mark 14 and Mark 23 are considered synonymous.)

The original Mark 14 warhead contained 507 pounds of T.N.T. Improvements made during the war boosted the explosive charge, in several stages, up to 668 pounds of torpex. The warhead was fitted with the Mark 6 exploder. This exploder was an extremely complicated mechanism. It was designed to explode from impact when the torpedo made a direct hit on the target. And it was also designed to explode by magnetic induction when passing through the magnetic field under and around any vessel built of iron or steel.

The Mark 6 exploder had been a long time in development, and its production had been a top secret. In fact, it had emerged behind such dense veils of secrecy that at the time of Pearl Harbor it was little more than a rumor to many submariners. It was not issued to submarines until the summer of 1941, and even then only commanding officers and torpedo officers were allowed to know about it. It was soon apparent that torpedomen would have to be informed, if they were to acquire some experience in handling the device. But at the outbreak of war, the secret had been so cherished that there was practically no service experience with this exploder. And as events later proved, it was this Mark 6 exploder, rather than the Mark 14 torpedo itself, which played the arch villain in the melodrama of malfunction.

Ironically enough, before the United States entered the war, the Germans had discovered that their magnetic influence exploder was too erratic for submarine employment. In operation similar to the American, the German influence device had proved full of "bugs," and after many trials in action, the U-boaters had discarded it. Only equally rigorous testing could have exposed the Mark 6 before it went into war service. Yet, because of the manner in which torpedo target practices were conducted, submarine operating personnel could not have subjected the exploder to peacetime testing.

The torpedo is an expensive engine, the Mark 14's costing in excess of $10,000 apiece. As a consequence, economy dictated they could not be expended for training purposes. When they were fired in target practice, neither the warhead nor the exploder was used. Instead, an exercise head was employed. This exercise head was filled with water, and it was so designed that at the end of the torpedo's run the water was expelled. This reduced the weight of the torpedo, and brought it to the surface where it could be recovered. In order to prevent damage to the target or to the torpedo, regulations called for a depth setting which insured that the torpedo would pass under, rather than hit the target.

Such target-practice procedure provided a check on the submarine commander's ability to make an approach and an accurate attack. It also tested the abilities of the torpedomen, and to some extent the abilities of the torpedo. But it provided no check on the exploder mechanism. Nor did it provide a check on deep-running torpedoes. (Shallow runners would have exposed themselves by striking the target.)

The checking of a torpedo's running depth was a function of the proving range at Naval Torpedo Station, Newport, Rhode Island. The testing of the exploder and warhead was also Newport's responsibility. The submariners had to accept these matters on faith. The U.S. Navy entered the war with an entire generation of submarine personnel who had never seen nor heard the detonation of a submarine torpedo.

Deep Running

Torpedo defects began to crop out as soon as the submarines went into action. Difficulties with the depth performance of the Mark 14, and the tests and corrective measures taken, have been discussed in a previous chapter. By August 1942, misses caused by erratic depth performance of the Mark 14 had been eliminated.

The Mark 14 was not the sole offender in this regard. When Lieutenant W. G. "Moon" Chapple took S-38 into Lingayen Gulf in that first dark December of the war, his Mark 10 torpedoes misbehaved. At that time the main landing on Luzon was taking place, and Japanese invasion craft were coming over the horizon in herds. The reader may recall that in one foray, Chapple fired a full salvo of four torpedoes—a shot at each of four heavily burdened transports which had already anchored or hove to. The four torpedoes missed.

Chapple had set the torpedoes to run at a depth of 12 feet. Attempting to rationalize four misses at four "set-up" targets, he concluded that the enemy was using shallow-draft vessels for the landing. So he set his remaining torpedoes for nine feet. This depth setting was on the two torpedoes that sank HAYO MARU.

On the 5th of January, 1942, the Bureau of Ordnance informed Commander Submarines, Asiatic Fleet, that the Mark 10 torpedoes ran four feet deeper than set. This belated announcement of a serious defect in a torpedo which had long been in service might have been demoralizing. But at that date, no more than 15 or 16 war shots had been fired by the S-boats. Those shots had been for contact hits, and the submarine captains usually gave such shots a five-foot safety factor.

During World War I the British Navy had discovered that its submarine torpedoes were running four feet deeper than set, and the matter had been well documented. As deep-running was a pit into which another had fallen, it seemed to many U.S. submarine captains that American technicians of a later era could have circumvented that particular difficulty. As it was, the four-foot error in depth performance of the Mark 10 was not nearly so pronounced as the deeper errors of the Mark 14, which ran 10 or 11 feet below the setting.

However, the depth-performance requirements of the Mark 10 were most exacting. For this torpedo had to hit the target in order to inflict damage. Thus a miss with the Mark 10 was literally as good as a mile, whereas the Mark 14, detonated by magnetic influence, would explode if it passed under the target. Fortunately the Mark 10 trouble was detected and corrected early in the war. Not so with the Mark 14's peculiar difficulties. No sooner were its depth defects ironed out than it revealed its tendency to premature or go dud. As these wrinkles had their source in the magnetic exploder, an explanation of the action of this mechanism is in order.

Magnetic Exploders

T.N.T. is an explosive not easily detonated. Under normal circumstances neither fire nor shock will cause it to explode. The cast T.N.T., resembling a block of solid resin, must be acted upon by a detonation wave. In the torpedo warhead this wave is produced by the firing pin striking the primer cap, which in turn sets off the detonator positioned within a cavity in the base of a booster charge. The explosion of the detonator sets off the booster. The booster produces the detonation wave which causes the T.N.T. to explode. So not one explosion, but a series of three which occur with the rapidity of chain lightning, creates the final blast.

The function of the exploder is to inaugurate this series at the proper moment. The Mark 6 exploder, weighing 92 pounds and carried in a cavity in the bottom of a warhead, was designed to release its firing pin either upon contact with the target or upon passing through the target's magnetic field. This dual capacity—to work from impact or from magnetic influence—was a much-prized feature of the mechanism. Equipped with an exploder which could be activated by magnetic influence, the torpedo did not have to make a direct hit. Theoretically, a close shave was as fatal as a strike, and under certain circumstances it could be more damaging.

The exploder mechanism contained another important feature—a device which "disarmed" the torpedo for safe handling. In the unarmed condition, the detonator was withdrawn from the booster cavity. This safety feature prevented any accidental shock, concussion or jolt from setting off the booster and the main charge. When the torpedo was fired, its rush through the water activated a spinner which operated a chain of gears that moved the detonator into the booster cavity. This was accomplished after a run of about 450 yards, and the torpedo was then "armed." During the arming run several delayed-action switches automatically closed, vacuum tubes were warmed up and the exploder was ready for business.

The 450-yard arming run was a feature which served to protect a submarine from the explosion of its own torpedo close aboard. But the full 450 yards were not required for this protection. The extended arming run served another purpose. During the first lap of a run, a torpedo is subject to drastic changes of speed and direction. It hunts its depth setting and seeks its pre-set course. The shock of these spurts and swerves might be sufficient to detonate the exploder, either magnetically or by inertia. The arming mechanism was therefore designed to complete its task after the torpedo perturbations had smoothed out. The 450-yard run gave the torpedo time to calm down, steady on course and hit its stride.

Having accomplished the 450-yard dash, the armed torpedo was all set to explode. But now another contrivance stepped in as a control. This was an "anti-counter-mining" device, designed to prevent the torpedo from being blown up by a near-by explosion such as might occur when several torpedoes were fired in rapid salvo. It would not do to have one torpedo blast detonate other torpedoes which were trailing in for a hit. Hence the delicate anti-counter-mining control—sea pressure acting on a diaphragm to keep the firing pin locked when the pressure head was over 50 feet. A pressure wave from an explosion acted on the diaphragm to prevent the firing of the exploder for the duration of the wave. Delayed release prevented firing of the exploder until after the second wave of detonation had passed.

So the armed torpedo would explode only when it passed through the magnetic field of an iron or steel vessel, or struck the hull of a vessel—that is, if the exploder mechanism were working properly. The contact feature of the Mark 6 exploder was a relatively simple affair. If the torpedo struck an object with sufficient force, the impact caused an inertia element to be dislodged. This contrivance released the firing pin which set off the works. The magnetic influence feature employed a more complicated device. Subtle electronics were involved. When the torpedo passed through a ship's magnetic field, the electromotive force (E.M.F.) generated in the exploder's induction coils underwent a change. Amplified by vacuum tubes, this change of E.M.F. caused release of the firing pin.

What was the extent of a ship's magnetic field? How close did the torpedo have to come to bring the exploder under the "influence"? At the war's beginning, submariners were instructed to set torpedoes to run 10 feet under a battleship's keel or five feet under the keel of a lighter vessel. This presumably allowed a good margin—considerably below the stated depths there would be sufficient magnetic field density to activate the influence mechanism. Operating with both contact and magnetic features, the torpedo was capable of exploding anywhere from the target's waterline down to 15 or 20 feet below the keel.

Sponsors of the magnetic exploder asserted that the device not only expanded the target—gave the submariners a wider mark to shoot at—but induced an explosion which was much more destructive than the direct-hit blast. Literature, correspondence and instructions on the subject repeatedly stated that an explosion a few feet under the bottom of a vessel was *"three times as effective as one against the side."* This was undoubtedly true in the case of the capital ship whose side armor, compartmentation, blisters or protective bulkheads served to shock-absorb the blast of a side hit. However, in 1943 the Bureau of Ships issued a report on investigations made to determine the manner in which a number of ships went down after they were hit by German torpedoes. The report noted that more ships sank from loss of stability than from loss of buoyancy. In other words, the torpedoed vessels capsized first and then flooded, rather than sank from direct flooding caused by torpedo explosion. The report went on to state that side hits were more liable to cause loss of stability than hits under the keel. These findings certainly contradicted the earlier correspondence and literature.

But there could be no gainsaying that a workable magnetic exploder widened the target for torpedo marksmanship. The hitch came in the qualifying adjective "workable." The principle of the magnetic exploder was new to naval warfare. The contact exploder, dating back to the spar torpedoes of the Civil War, was an old and tried device of proven merit. Nevertheless, the Mark 14 torpedo with the Mark 6 magnetic exploder was the primary submarine weapon when the war began.

With the Jap invaders coming down like the Assyrians on Sennacherib, it was no hour to experiment with untried innovations.

Malfunctions vs. Morale

In 1939 and 1940 the German Submarine Force was plagued by torpedo failures. Gunther Prien and other ace U-boat skippers reported prematures and duds—troubles which were seated in the German influence exploder. And because accurate depth control was not imperative if influence exploders operated properly, the German torpedo was wanting in depth performance. Both of these defective features had to be corrected before the U-boats could hope to win in the Atlantic.

Admiral Doenitz reported that torpedo failures seriously undermined the morale of the U-boat crews, and drastic steps were taken to restore their confidence in their chief weapon. The tricky influence exploder was withdrawn from service, and a dependable contact exploder was issued in its place. The torpedo's running faults were corrected. The German torpedo was scoring with appalling efficiency by the time the United States entered the war, and the morale of the U-boat force was correspondingly high.

The U-boaters were spared that concatenation of defects that made American experience with the cranky Mark 14 a two-year nightmare. Moreover, the German's torpedo troubles were alleviated by a general background of victory, whereas the American submariners had to sweat through their difficulties at a time when the enemy was winning one battle after another. If it is true that only in defeat can a military force show the caliber of its morale, the U.S. Submarine Service was put to the ultimate test.

The Philippines invasion alone was sufficiently punishing. The frustration and disillusionment of individual submarine crews could only have been heightened by the knowledge that the entire Manila force, driven from pillar to post, was unable to stem the enemy's advance. To the 28 submarines of the Asiatic Fleet had fallen the bulk of the northern Philippines defense. Twenty-eight submarines—a squadron against an armada. Yet, given a good weapon they might have seriously impeded the foe. But armed with a defective torpedo—

Lingayen Gulf—five submarines on hand—only one Japanese transport sunk out of an invasion fleet of more than 80 ships! January, and the seas around the Philippines aswarm with enemy shipping. Only three Japanese vessels downed by American submarines in the area! February, only three! Four in March! Almost four months of warfare in the Southwest Pacific, and a scant 13 vessels sunk by the hard-fighting American submarines!

It remains for some future statistician to analyze the dozens of torpedo shots fired in those four desperate months. To sift through the maze of controversial reports—separate the wheat of verifiable torpedo hits from the chaff of prematures which looked like bull's-eye explosions—trace the deep-runners which missed the mark—estimate the number of duds which thumped in futility against stout targets. Due to the confusion of those early war reports and the fantastic difficulties involved in tracking down torpedo failures, such an analysis probably defies the making. But the historian may refer to the experience of SARGO's captain, Lieutenant Commander Jacobs (13 shots for zero hits), for a clue to the agonizing situation. Certain it is that the entire Philippines defense, from the day of the enemy strike to Wainwright's surrender, was hampered by the wretched performance of American submarine torpedoes.

As for submarine force morale—

There were casualties. Not many. Not as many as might have justifiably been expected. But a few commanding officers, introspective after repeated failures to score, asked to be relieved of command so that others might try where they had failed. And those skippers who were determined to hit it out and grit it out were burdened by the knowledge that they fought with a blunt weapon. Or was the fault really theirs? Had they missed those shots, fired too early or too late, miscalculated? Honest self-confidence forced to fence with a haunting ghost of doubt.

Hard on the submarine captain, the situation was equally hard on the crew. The crew of a submarine is a team—perhaps more interdependent than most. One fumble on a football field may not lose the game, but a fumble aboard a submarine can cost the life of all hands. The captain directs the approach, is responsible for the attack and gives the order to fire the torpedo. Often he alone sees the target. Those in the conning tower, in the engine room, in the torpedo room must rely on his ability and his judgment. He in turn relies on the crew to perform ably each duty which is demanded during approach and attack maneuvers. The torpedo fails to hit? The captain at the periscope, the sound man who checked the range, the officer at the T.D.C., the chief torpedoman's mate —any one of a dozen men may have been responsible.

Repeated and unexplained failures invite mutual mistrust, engender suspicions that can break down the solidarity of a team. The commanding officer who sees a torpedo miss under circumstances that favored a hit is compelled to investigate the performance of his torpedo crew. The torpedo crew that knows its work has been ably performed is led to suspect the control room. Queries may cause resentment or breed uneasiness. If nothing succeeds like success, nothing is more depressing than continued and inexplicable failure.

Throughout the long retreat to Australia, the period of pioneer Empire patrols, the Solomons struggle, the Aleutian battle, the efforts of the submarine forces were consistently sabotaged by torpedo troubles. But morale stood on its feet and shook its fist. That some of the pioneer submarine teams did not disintegrate, that the force held together as solidly in the trough of adversity as on the crest of the wave is testimony to the courage, resolution and resourcefulness of the men who commanded and served in the Navy's submarines.

Prematures

Worst morale saboteur was the unexplained miss caused by erratic depth performance or failure of the torpedo to explode. These malfunctions often defied detection. Fired in battle, the guilty torpedo could not be hauled in for examination, and the miss could be blamed on innocent parties.

Less sinister, although equally baffling, was the premature—the torpedo that exploded too soon. When a premature blasted the water there was no mystery about what had happened. "Why" might remain an unanswered question, but it could generally be assumed that the fault was the torpedo's. The submarine captain, the fire control party, the torpedo crew were exonerated. Range finding, attack maneuvers and judgment were not involved. The blankety-blank fish went off ahead of time.

But the premature was dangerous. On occasion it could be far more dangerous than a miss. Of course, if the blast were so ill-timed as to occur a moment after firing, the submersible could be wrecked. There is no record of a submarine destroyed by a premature, but American submarines were frequently jolted by these precipitate explosions, and the risk gave the submariners another mental hazard to contend with.

Prematures imperiled submarines in another and most dangerous manner. They warned the enemy of the submarine's attack. Opportunity, knocking but once, might blow sky-high in a geyser of water well off the target ship's beam. Not only could the vessel then maneuver to evade, but the submarine's approximate position was revealed to the escorts. Having fired an engraved announcement of its whereabouts and intentions, the submarine would be subject to immediate counter-attack and perhaps receive a severe "going over." Proof is unobtainable, but it is entirely possible that prematuring torpedoes contributed to the loss of one or two American submarines.

The submarines were made disagreeably aware of prematures in the opening months of the war. However, the percentage seemed small, and it was not until after the depth-control difficulty had been corrected that the extent of the premature problem became apparent. When running deep, torpedoes were unaffected by the action of surface waves. Also, some of the early torpedoes ran so deep that the anti-counter-mining device kept the firing pin locked during the run and while the torpedo passed under the target. But when these malfunctions were corrected and the torpedoes began to run at shallower depths, the perturbations caused by the motion of the sea or by surges in the torpedo power-plant sometimes activated the delicate exploder and caused the torpedo to premature. Thus the percentage of prematures was abruptly increased by the correction of the depth-control difficulty.

In the magnetic exploder lay another cause for prematures. When set to run at a depth which was less than the draft of the target vessel, a torpedo entered the horizontal component of the ship's magnetic field some distance from the vessel's hull. Under certain circumstances, the exploder would go into action at that instant when the torpedo entered this magnetic field, and the torpedo would blow up about 50 feet from the side of the ship. These prematures, seen through a submarine's periscope, looked like perfect hits. The explosions were correctly timed, and an eruption of water, directly in line with the target, obscured the vessel from view. More than one Japanese ship was found to be undamaged after its sinking was reported by a submarine skipper who had been deceived by a premature.

Emerging in the wake of the depth-setting trouble, the premature problem raised its ugly head in the autumn of 1942, and the submarine forces found themselves confronted by another bugbear. By year's end the bugbear was full grown, and it pursued the submariners well into 1943. One of the submarines badgered by this difficulty was SCAMP. In March 1943, while on her first patrol and making her first attack, SCAMP fired a three-torpedo salvo in which all three torpedoes prematured shortly after arming. Of SCAMP's first nine torpedoes fired on that patrol, five prematured. The depth settings had been between six and ten feet. SCAMP had then inactivated her remaining torpedoes with ComSubPac's permission.

The premature problem was a heartbreaker for the force which had battled it out with deep-running. To Admiral Lockwood and all those who had pitched in to correct the torpedoes' depth performance, this new wrench in the machinery was beyond endurance. And what couldn't be endured had to be cured with the greatest possible dispatch. What prematures could mean to a superlatively able captain and topnotch submarine crew is revealed between the lines in TUNNY's report of an attack on a Japanese aircraft carrier formation southwest of Truk on April 9, 1943.

Tunny vs. Carrier Formation

In April 1943, the Japanese were busily engaged in running airplanes into Truk, whence they were usually flown to New Britain for duty on the Bismarck-Solomons front. For this brisk enterprise, the Imperial Navy was employing aircraft carriers, both combat and escort.

At this date, TUNNY was patrolling in the Caroline area. During her first war patrol, concluded in February 1943, she had experienced torpedo troubles which included a dud and a premature. Now she was hoping for better luck. And it seemed to be coming her way when, at 2100 on the night of April 8, she received information that a convoy had been sighted trucking southwest of Truk. TUNNY's skipper, Lieutenant Commander J. A. Scott, lost no time in putting the submarine between the reported convoy and its destination.

At 2228 the following night, TUNNY made radar contact with the convoy at a range of about 1,500 yards. Using radar ranges and bearings, Scott plotted the enemy's course as 060° and his speed as 18 knots. This high speed served to identify the contact as the carrier group which had been reported.

Scott ordered the submarine trimmed down to awash conditions to reduce her silhouette, and put her on four-engine speed to pull ahead of the convoy. At 2237 the convoy changed course to 085° T, which placed the submarine dead ahead. Scott slowed TUNNY to two-thirds speed and headed in to attack with decks awash.

On TUNNY's starboard bow was a large carrier or auxiliary carrier. On her port bow two escort carriers were in column. There was a destroyer on each bow of the formation. TUNNY, still on the surface, headed for the center of the enemy disposition. Scott intended, upon reaching attack position, to swing left, fire the six bow tubes at the two-carrier column, and the four stern tubes at the single carrier. This plan was thwarted when the submarine suddenly picked up a group of three small boats, apparently motor torpedo boats, about one point on the port bow. The range to these craft was only 300-500 yards. TUNNY had to turn away and dive to avoid detection.

Making a swift change of plans and equally rapid changes in his firing set-up, Scott came right to a course that gave him a 90° track, and ordered TUNNY to 40 feet. The T.D.C. set-up was for a stern tube shot at the leading ship of the two-ship column. At 2248, Scott fired four torpedoes from the stern tubes, range 880 yards. Four hits were heard shortly thereafter.

In the meantime, the executive officer, Lieutenant Commander R. M. Keithly, was on the periscope, trying to pick up the single carrier for the bow tubes. He was encountering some difficulty because the recent course-change had left the convoy formation a little ragged and the ships were not in their correct relative positions. The periscope was almost blind in the night's blackout, and practically nothing could be seen unless the target were first approximately located. However, this game of blind man's buff did not last long. Some obliging Jap on the carrier came to Keithly's assistance by opening up with a signal lamp. Keithly was thereby enabled to get a periscope bearing, and it gave the radar a nice check just before the bow tubes were fired. Six torpedoes were shot at the target, range 650 yards, zero gyro angle, longitudinal spread. The first three sounded like smashing hits.

As an example of expert technique in approach and attack, TUNNY's performance had everything. This was probably the first time in history that a submarine had been presented with the opportunity of making a simultaneous bow and stern tube attack, with aircraft carrier targets for both tube nests. Many submarine officers had dreamed of such a situation, but here was the first time it materialized. It was also the last.

Scott proved himself more than worthy of the situation. His radar tracking was good. He used his surface speed daringly to obtain a favorable attack position. He retained the initiative by remaining on the surface until the last possible moment. He planned to deliver this attack from the best possible position.

When the torpedo boats unexpectedly appeared and Scott was suddenly forced to change his plans, TUNNY's fire control party proved sufficiently flexible to follow the abrupt transition without confusion. Ten torpedoes were properly fired at minimum ranges, and the crew operated as smoothly as a synchronized set of precision machines.

"In the history of the war," wrote a critic, *"probably in the whole history of submarines, this attack stands out as tops. It was art for art's sake."* But unfortunately it went for naught. The Japanese escort carrier TAIYO (OTAKA) received some damage which did little to interfere with her schedule. Apparently no other Japanese ships were damaged. The blasts TUNNY heard and reported as hits were undoubtedly prematures caused by defective exploders.

The Exasperating Mark 6

So confidence in the reliability of the Mark 6 exploder waned rapidly during the first six months of 1943. Imperfections in its exploder mechanism repeatedly came to light, necessitating an exchange of considerable correspondence between the submarine forces and the Bureau of Ordnance. As the intricacies and behavior characteristics of the previously secret mechanism became known to many, many were the theories and suggestions for its improvement. Brush riggings were found to be imperfect, and leaky base plate castings, which had slipped by factory inspection, were discovered. Minor design changes were made by the Newport Torpedo Station and the torpedo shops afloat submitted each exploder mechanism to exhaustive and rigid tests before issue to individual submarines. Everything possible, short of designing a completely new influence-exploder, was done. And still torpedoes blew up shortly after arming or exploded at harmless distances from targets.

On April 27, 1943, the Bureau of Ordnance stated that the Mark 6 was susceptible to prematuring when set for 12-foot depth or less. The Bureau recommended inactivation for contact shots. On May 3, BuOrd informed Admiral King, Commander-in-Chief U.S. Fleet, that the effectiveness of the Mark 6 would be increased 10 to 30 per cent by increasing the arming distance from 450 to 700 yards. On May 7, the Bureau recommended that the device be rendered operative north of 30° north magnetic latitude, and torpedoes set to run at keel depth. South of 30° south magnetic, the Mark 6 should be rendered inoperative. Between these latitudes (advised the Bureau) torpedoes should be set to run at keel depth or less, and the influence exploder should be kept operative.

On May 27, Admiral King told BuOrd that the recommended change in torpedo-arming distance was not acceptable. The Commander-in-Chief U.S. Fleet stated that he concurred in a recommendation by Admiral Lockwood that the Mark 6-Mod. 1 exploder be replaced at the earliest possible moment by a simple, fool-proof magnetic exploder.

On July 24, Admiral Nimitz, Commander-in-Chief Pacific Fleet, ordered ComSubPac and ComDesPac (destroyers, too, had suffered torpedo trouble) to inactivate magnetic exploders on all torpedoes. The next day BuOrd asked CinCPac what reasons had led to this decision. CinCPac replied that it had been made *because of probable enemy counter-measures, because of the ineffectiveness of the exploder under certain conditions, and because of the impracticability of selecting the proper conditions under which to fire.* That settled the magnetic exploder for Admiral Lockwood's submarines. The influence device was put out of business, and the SubPac Force was rid of the contraption. But on July 11 Admiral Ralph Christie, then Commander Submarines, Southwest Pacific, directed that the magnetic feature be retained in his force and specified the depth settings to be used against various types of ships. His Headquarters in Fremantle, ComSubSoWesPac was not under CinCPac's command and hence was not bound by the latter's order of June 24th.

A Bureau of Ordnance letter on the Mark 6 exploder dated August 31, 1943, outlined the advantages to be obtained by the magnetic feature's use. According to BuOrd the chief advantages were:

(a) Saving the misses which would occur when torpedoes, otherwise satisfactory, run deep, or incident to error in depth setting or in estimate of target draft.

(b) Sometimes greater damage from under bottom explosions to capital ships, the sides of which are compartmented to localize torpedo damage.

The letter went on to discuss the conditions under which the exploder might be expected to work and those under which it would not. Magnetic latitude, target's magnetic course, conditions of degaussing, beam of target, draft of target and depth of torpedo were factors to be taken into account.

Reasoning as follows, ComSubSoWesPac (Commander Submarines, Seventh Fleet) continued to send his submarines to sea with activated Mark 6 magnetic exploders:

(1) Because it saved some hits.

(2) Because it is our only defensive weapon against the anti-submarine craft.

(3) If we discard it, it is gone forever.

Southwest Pacific (Seventh Fleet) submarines continued to have trouble with prematures. On July 13, one of GROUPER's torpedoes exploded close aboard and showered the submarine with fragments. During an attack made by SILVERSIDES on her sixth patrol in August 1943, the first two torpedoes of a four-torpedo salvo prematured, permitting the target to evade and escape. On the same patrol the SILVERSIDERS had two more prematures. Returning from another patrol on October 11, GROUPER's captain recommended the inactivation of the Mark 6 exploder with this comment: *"It would appear far better to sink the enemy vessels encountered—when targets in certain areas are so hard to find and attack—than to continue spoiling good chances just to prove that a really useless mechanism can be made to function a fair proportion of the time."*

But it was not until March 1944, after all attempted remedial action had failed and prematures had become the bane of the Southwest Pacific Force, that SoWesPac submarines were ordered to inactivate the magnetic feature of their exploders.

Duds

When Admiral Lockwood, in June 1943, ordered the inactivation of the magnetic exploder device, his force believed that its torpedo worries were all but over. Submarine commanders were more than willing to forego the advantages claimed for the magnetic exploder, in order to obtain torpedo hits against the sides of enemy ships. There was at that time no reason to doubt that the contact mechanism of the exploder was anything less than reliable.

A small percentage of duds had been previously observed, but these deadhead torpedoes which hit and failed to explode were comparatively rare. A few failures of even the simple contact exploder had to be expected. Although less complex than the magnetic device, the contact device was still an intricate mechanism. Any mistake in its final check and installation might result in a flooded exploder or one that otherwise failed to function.

TAUTOG on October 28, 1942, had identified one of the first duds. One of two torpedoes fired by the submarine was clearly heard by Sound to strike the target without exploding. On January 2, 1943, Commander Task Force Fifty-one recalled THRESHER from patrol to check her torpedoes because of exploder failures on both magnetic and contact shots. On her next patrol (in March) THRESHER presented evidence of four dud hits.

So the dud made its sly appearance, showing up here and there at unexpected and always unwelcome occasions. A last straw to break the camel's back of confidence in the Mark 6 exploder! That it did not break the spine of submarine force morale indicates the sort of backbone which supported that fighting organization.

The dud was a hard offender to track down. Its extensive delinquency became apparent only when the other torpedo "bugs" had been exterminated and enemy ships continued to survive what should have been fatal submarine encounters. But the dud was to be smoked out, and the smoking began in earnest on July 24, 1943, when the submarine TINOSA had a chance to play Annie Oakley with a "sitting duck."

Tinosa vs. Tonan Maru

The "sitting duck" was TONAN MARU No. 3—a prize longe coveted by American submarine captains. She and her sister ship, TONAN MARU No. 2, had been built as whale factories for processing whales and rendering the blubber at sea. They had later been converted into oil tankers for government use. With a gross tonnage rating of 19,262 tons, each was a whale of a tanker. About twice the size of the average merchant oil carrier, they were the largest tankers that Japan possessed.

Imaginative submarine skippers liked to study this mammoth in the silhouette book and dream of her coming within attack range. TINOSA, captained by Lieutenant Commander L. R. "Dan" Daspit, was patrolling westward of Truk when the dream became a reality. A reality of such dreamlike sublimity that Daspit wanted to rub his eyes. For there was the giant tanker, unescorted! Steaming across the seascape with all the complacency of an ocean monster that believed itself a king among minnows. At any rate, the huge tanker was worth a king's ransom in the coin of wartime shipping, and Daspit set out to collect the prize forthwith.

When contact was made with this tremendous target, TINOSA had 16 torpedoes on hand—all that remained to her after several previous encounters with enemy shipping. Daspit lost no time in bringing his submarine to attack position. He opened fire on the tanker with a spread of four torpedoes, using a large track angle. The range was high—about 4,000 yards—but TINOSA had been unable to close the target's track, and Daspit was forced to accept the unfavorable track angle and lengthy range.

Two torpedoes of the salvo hit near the tanker's stern. The vessel stopped dead in the water and veered in a manner which placed the submarine about two points on her port quarter. Daspit quickly fired two more torpedoes. Both exploded resoundingly. TONAN MARU No. 3 belched smoke and settled slightly by the stern.

Here was a situation almost too good for verity—the big ex-whale factory dead in the water like a mired hippopotamus—not an A/S vessel in the vicinity—submariners with plenty of time at their disposal to finish off the target at will. The tanker's sizable deck guns prohibited a surface assault, but TINOSA could and did close in for a torpedo attack calculated to blow the helpless vessel to blazes.

Carefully Daspit selected a position 875 yards off the tanker's beam and fired one torpedo. The torpedo was heard by Sound to make a normal run. At the moment when the sound of the torpedo's screws stopped abruptly, Daspit at the periscope saw a fishy splash at the point of aim. There was no explosion. A dud.

Deliberately Daspit lined up for another attack, fired another torpedo. Again the torpedo's run trailed off into silence. Two more torpedoes were fired with great care and precision. If silence was golden (under the circumstances it was not!) TINOSA had hit the jackpot. Certainly she was hitting the target—at that range a blind man could not have missed. But TONAN MARU No. 3 remained as fixed in the scene as a taxidermist's exhibit in a showcase. For all their content of torpex or T.N.T., the warheads of TINOSA's torpedoes might as well have been stuffed with sawdust.

So the submarine skipper's dream distorted into a nightmare of impotence. One of those blue, bad dreams in which the prize dances forward only to decay before the eye, and the gold of success, deteriorating at touch, becomes the glue of futile failure. Another skipper thus foiled by duds and robbed of one of the war's great trophies might, himself, have blown up from spontaneous combustion. But Daspit held down the safety valve on his temper. He was a young man with an inquiring and experimental turn of mind, deliberate and unhurried by nature. After the first dud he had resolved to get to the bottom of the matter. And as it turned out, his investigative procedure produced results of greater import than the demolishment of this one fat Japanese target.

What Daspit demolished was any lingering question as to the culpability of the Mark 6 exploder. Altogether he fired eight torpedoes, launching them one after the other from a theoretically perfect position—on the target's beam, using a 90° track angle. The shooting extended over a period of several hours. Before each torpedo was fired it was withdrawn from the tube and all adjustments were checked. Fire control was methodical, as cool as leisure could make it. Working the T.D.C., Lieutenant C. E. "Ebbie" Bell, another calm and capable young officer, did his job with surgical precision. The Torpedomen operated as a well-disciplined unit, and TINOSA played her part as an excellent submarine. Eight hits were scored (including that made by the first dud). And eight times the shots ended in deafening silence where there should have been thundering explosions.

Daspit's careful and finely calculated selection of the best possible track angle was later proved as a reason for the exploder failures. Had the torpedoes struck the target glancing blows, as was the case in the first two salvos, the exploders might have worked. Fired at a 90° angle, whereby they struck the target squarely with normal impact, they failed to work. One torpedo was seen to hit the tanker, jump clear of the water like a playful bass, and sink. The tanker sat there like the broadside of a barn as TINOSA pelted her with eight duds.

Daspit ceased shooting when a last torpedo remained on board. He wanted to take that torpedo back to Pearl as a sample for magnifying-glass analysis. Fifteen torpedoes expended on a single target—twelve hits—and TONAN MARU No. 3 remained obdurately afloat.

Japanese rescuers raced out and towed the great tanker safely into Truk while TINOSA, a disillusioned submarine, headed home to Pearl Harbor. But the big oil carrier had suffered a little damage, and in

playing the part of a monster guinea pig for the torpedo experiment of Daspit and company, she had served the U.S. Submarine Force well. TINOSA mourned the fact that the ex-whale factory was not sunk. But the story that Daspit brought back with him from the Carolines contributed more to the ultimate defeat of Japan.

Shooting the Trouble

When TINOSA reached Pearl Harbor, and a thorough examination of her remaining torpedo failed to disclose any errors in adjustment, the fat was in the fire. Admiral Lockwood decided to dispense with unheeded dispatches and tackle the Medusa-headed torpedo problem himself. Decisions on the part of Admiral Lockwood meant action. His first act was to order the firing of two torpedoes against the submerged cliffs at Kahoolawe.

The test shots were fired, and one of the two torpedoes proved to be a dud. This Mark 14 blank was recovered and examined. The examiners found that the exploder mechanism had released the firing pin, but the pin had not hit the primer cap with sufficient force to set it off.

What next occurred was an exemplary demonstration of what could happen when a complex technical problem, hitherto bottled up in a jar labeled "Secret," was uncorked for the analysis of many able minds. All the available talent at Pearl Harbor joined in cooperative effort to solve the problem, bringing to its solution a variety of skills and techniques. Commander Service Force loaned an ordnance technician, Lieutenant Commander E. A. Johnson. Johnson, working with Commander A. H. Taylor and Lieutenant Commander H. A. Pieczentkowski, devised a unique test procedure. Warheads loaded with cinder concrete in place of torpex, but equipped with exploders, were dropped on a steel plate from a height of 90 feet. This duplicated the forces generated by a torpedo when it struck the side of a steel ship. And seven of the first 10 warheads dropped duplicated the performance of duds by failing to explode. Seven contact duds out of 10—and the war already in its twentieth month!

The impact test corroborated the findings at Kahoolawe. The exploder's firing pin would release, but it would strike with insufficient force to set off the primer cap. However, if the steel plate were set so that the warheads struck it a glancing blow, the exploders invariably functioned properly. This explained why some ships were sunk by torpedoes which struck them glancing blows at the turn of the keel or against the side, whereas solid and normal hits might fail.

"TIN FISH." Loading torpedoes from a tender at an advanced base. Such specimens as the one shown weighed well over a ton. Improved warhead carried 668 pounds of torpex—enough to blow the average maru *Galley West.* U.S. subs in the Pacific fired 14,748 torpedoes at Japs, sank over 1100 ships.

TORPEDOES MAKE STRANGE BEDFELLOWS. *Torpedomen lose no sleep over unarmed "fish." Rollers "under bed" are part of loading gear.*

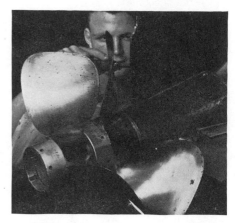

TORPEDO CHECK. *Skilled hand adjusts tail-fin of fish. Checks are frequent.*

TORPEDO TESTING BARGE. *Mark 14 "bugs" eluded detection at Newport.*

DOWN THE HATCH. *Torpedo comes aboard submarine for stowage below. Due to shortage in early part of war, many subs carried mines to enemy waters. In '43, torpedo supply caught up with rapid expenditures.*

LOADING FISH FROM TENDER. *Once U. S. submariners were given dependable torpedoes, Jap Navy suffered.*

With that much information in hand, the inquiry concentrated on the exploder's firing pin. This was a mushroom-shaped device weighing several ounces. When released, spring action forced the pin to move in a direction at right angles to the torpedo axis. Two guide studs controlled the direction of motion which brought the pin into contact with the firing cap. The force of deceleration when the torpedo struck a solid blow was found to be in the neighborhood of 500 times the force of gravity. This force, acting on the firing pin, produced a frictional component of approximately 190 pounds on the guide studs. The firing spring was unable to overcome this friction and drive the pin with adequate force against the cap.

Three corrective measures were tried. Lieutenant Commander Johnson devised an electric inertia switch. The shops of the Pearl Harbor Submarine Base, under Commander D. T. Eddy, and the tender HOLLAND, under the leadership of Captain Perley E. Pendleton, each produced a modified pin. Both of these reduced the weight of the pin to the barest minimum, thus lessening the friction on the guide studs. Each one of the corrections would do the trick, but the electric device was soon shelved in favor of the simpler firing pin modifications.

On September 30, 1943, BARB left Pearl Harbor for patrol, carrying 20 torpedoes equipped with the modified firing pin. And by mid-October enough of the HOLLAND and Submarine Base modifications had been produced to supply all submarines leaving for patrol areas. The Gordian knot had been cut, and the faulty exploder had been corrected. At last—almost two years after the beginning of the war—U.S. submarines went to sea with a reliable torpedo.

Torpedo Shortage

Quality—or, rather, the lack of it—was not the only torpedo problem which bedeviled the submariners in the early months of the war. Quantity was another serious matter. Constituting the greater part of the reserve supply for SubsAsiatic, 233 torpedoes were destroyed during the bombing of the Cavite Navy Yard on December 10, 1942. Quick work and removal under fire saved the remainder. But the loss made the supply problem acute. As has been related, some of the pioneer submarines were sent on patrol only partially loaded with torpedoes. Others, because of the shortage, went out on mining missions. Almost invariably, a submarine returning from patrol with torpedoes on board would transfer them immediately to another submarine about to depart.

At Pearl Harbor the quantity problem was not immediate, for the Japanese raiders had missed the

Submarine Base and the torpedo reserve was left intact. But torpedo expenditures quickly exceeded replacements and the supply situation rapidly deteriorated. In February 1942, ComSubPac reported that the supply on hand, plus expected deliveries during the following six months, would fall more than 200 short of estimated requirements. He requested that drastic measures be taken to overcome the deficiency.

The crisis was relatively brief, considering that this was the first major torpedo war in the U.S. Navy's experience. At the war's outset, the torpedo reserve amounted to a few hundred, while the production of submarine torpedoes was about 60 per month. Before the end of 1942, a total of 2,382 torpedoes had been manufactured to balance an expenditure of 2,010. By January 1943, the production crisis was over. But transportation difficulties slowed delivery, and shortages continued to exist in the Southwest Pacific until mid-1943.

The phenomenal production increase resulted from the foresight and determination with which the Bureau of Ordnance opposed external pressure to retain the long-held torpedo monopoly at Newport, Rhode Island. Efforts to open the Torpedo Station at Alexandria, Virginia, were begun by the Bureau early in the 1930's. Alexandria had been a Torpedo Station in the First World War, but its extensive buildings and facilities had not been used since 1923. When the Nazis exploded the war in Europe and America's eventual involvement became a probability, BuOrd advices were heeded and the Alexandria plant was reopened.

After the United States entered the war, several private concerns were induced to engage in torpedo manufacture. These concentrated on torpedoes for surface ships and aircraft. Most of the submarine steam torpedoes were manufactured at Newport and Alexandria, many of the parts being subcontracted to a diverse list of manufacturers. Westinghouse produced the Mark 18 electric torpedo which, introduced in the late summer of 1943, became the major submarine weapon during the last year of the war. With Newport and Alexandria producing the steam torpedo and Westinghouse the Mark 18 electric, torpedo production kept pace with eventual expenditures which reached as high as 500 per month.

The torpedo shortage, as experienced, had a decided influence on submarine tactics. Commanding officers were encouraged to fire but one or two torpedoes per salvo, even at relatively important targets. In the Southwest Pacific they were instructed to let minor targets go by. Of course, the firing of single shots or two-torpedo salvos greatly reduced the chances of hitting. It also delayed the formulation of a solid doctrine concerning the use of spreads. Where one and two torpedoes were considered sufficient for a target early in the war, a similar target in the war's last year was held to merit a spread of four or even six torpedoes.

When a spread is fired, a hitting percentage of 50 is the optimum. A higher percentage indicates incorrect spread procedure, for the torpedoes are normally diverged to cover at least twice the target's length along its track. On the other hand, while they limit the hitting percentage, spreads greatly increase the chance of getting one or two hits, and thus increase the percentage of successful attacks. It is a maxim of naval warfare that it is the number of hits, rather than the percentage which counts.

Early endorsements on patrol reports frequently applauded extreme economy, even parsimony in the use of torpedoes. This encouraged commanding officers to wait for set-ups. And to some extent it discouraged aggressive action whenever the tactical situation seemed difficult or doubtful. Fortunately, the need for parsimony did not long prevail. Thanks to those at BuOrd who pushed the Alexandria plant —thanks, too, to the manufacturing resources of American industry—the torpedo supply problem was rapidly solved. The submarine forces were thus spared a prolonged torpedo famine and the stringencies of bitter frugality.

The Electric Torpedo

Early in 1942 a German electric torpedo was captured. This torpedo was turned over to the Westinghouse Electrical Manufacturing Company which was asked to produce a Chinese copy for American use.

Many difficulties were encountered. The production of a Chinese copy was not feasible. Several parts of the German torpedo were not adaptable to American manufacturing procedure. The functions of other parts were not fully understandable. And the German torpedo could not be adapted for launching from the tubes of American submarines.

The program for the development of the electric torpedo presently stalled. But in April 1943, the Naval Inspector General was called upon by the Commander-in-Chief U.S. Fleet to investigate electric torpedo development and determine the reason for the delay in getting that weapon into production. The Inspector General reported:

"The delays encountered were largely the result of the manner in which the project was prosecuted and followed up. These difficulties indicate that the liaison officers of the Bureau of Ordnance failed to follow up and to properly advise the Westinghouse Company and the Exide Company during the development of the Mark 18 torpedo. . . . The Torpedo Station had its own electric torpedo, the Mark 2, and the personnel assigned to it appear to have competed and not cooperated with the development of the Mark 18. . . . Failure to provide experienced and capable submarine officers to the Bureau for submarine torpedo development has been a very serious matter and has contributed largely to the above deficiencies."

The electric torpedo had been sponsored by the German High Command primarily because it was "wakeless"—a feature that made its detection difficult and gave the target little chance to evade. Moreover, when the first American torpedo of this type reached the proving range, the technicians discovered that the depth control of the electric torpedo was superior to that of the steam torpedo. Also the electric torpedo did not go deep on its initial dive after being launched, and the impact exploder was free of the "bugs" which infested the steam torpedo's exploder. In the bargain, the electric torpedo could be manufactured at a fraction of the cost of the steam torpedo, and with a great saving in man-hours. Its chief disadvantage was slow speed—28 to 30 knots as compared with 46 for the steam torpedo in high power. Nevertheless, submarine officers who assisted in proving the first electrics were enthusiastic, and they urged the Navy to procure electric torpedoes as soon as possible.

The electric torpedo was subject to its share of infant diseases. The first ones taken to sea lacked hydrogen burning circuits and therefore had to be frequently withdrawn from the tubes for ventilation. Several instances of hydrogen fires and explosions occurred. One fire on the FLYINGFISH heated the warhead until the torpex melted and ran. There were some erratic runners, sinkers, and slow runners. The torpedo's tail vanes were found weak and had to be strengthened. Cold water and consequent low-battery temperature caused the torpedo to run slow, and several misses were due to this unforeseen obstacle. Hot runs in the tubes, following depth-charging, were caused by failure of the guide studs. Warping of the thin shell of the battery compartment resulted in "binding" in the tubes. But these difficulties, encountered through experience, were relentlessly tracked down and swiftly eliminated. Much of the corrective work on the electric torpedo was accomplished at the Submarine Base, Pearl Harbor, where the torpedo shop under Commander M. P. Hottel conducted tests and experiments to improve the ventilation of the torpedo and burn out the hydrogen generated by the storage battery.

The electric torpedo did not meet with the instant favor of the submariners. Many commanding officers were skeptical—not only because of the tactical limitations imposed by its low speed, but because of the difficulties always encountered with a new weapon. For a long time electrics were taken on patrol on a voluntary basis. But the electric torpedo steadily acquired popularity. The wakeless feature, dependable depth performance, shallower depth settings permitted and the simple contact exploder which it carried were much appreciated. Admiral Lockwood enthusiastically pushed the torpedo's employment, and vigorously attacked the difficulties encountered in its use. Thirty per cent of the submarine torpedoes fired in 1944 were electric. In the last six months of the war the percentage rose to 65.

So the history of the American submarine torpedo came full-circle. The name "torpedo" was bestowed upon the invention by Robert Fulton, who borrowed the term from the *torpedo electricus*—the cramp fish which kills its prey by electrocution. The hand-placed underwater bomb—the spar torpedo—the mobile steam torpedo—and now one powered by electricity—at long last, with the launching of the Mark 18, the "tin fish" had come into its own.

Coincidentally with the advent of the Mark 18, the American torpedo problem of World War II was pretty well liquidated. The liquidation of Japan had yet to be accomplished.

Situation Summary

The war would have been foreshortened and many American lives saved had a reliable torpedo been available from the beginning.

That was the consensus of the veteran U.S. Submarine Force—an opinion universally shared by the submarine officers who fought the Battle of the Pacific. The conclusion defies contradiction, but a brief summary suffices to prove the point.

U.S. submarines sank many major Japanese men-of-war—ships in the carrier and cruiser categories, and one specimen in the battleship class. Yet, of the total sunk, less than 15%—just three major warships, to be specific—were sent to the bottom before the exploder faults were corrected. Even so, the three warships destroyed dealt the barest minimum of credit to the faulty Mark 6 exploder. For S-44 sank the heavy cruiser KAKO with Mark 10 torpedoes which were fitted with the simple contact exploder. NAUTILUS sank SORYU after the Japanese carrier had been lamed by American aircraft, her hull plates bomb-weakened. And the third of these vessels, TENRYU, sunk by ALBACORE, although classified as a light cruiser, was an old-timer, little larger than a modern destroyer.

Compare these first three sinkings with the successes scored later. In the last half of the war U.S. submarines using the corrected exploder sank over six times the number of major warships downed by torpedo attack in the first half. Japanese merchantmen also went to the bottom with greater speed and consistency. There was no TONAN MARU NO. 3 exhibition during the last 18 months of the Pacific conflict.

The torpedo trouble was well cured by the end of 1943. It had been a tragically expensive muddle. The cost to the United States war effort in lives, dollars and time remains incalculable.

CHAPTER 21

SOUTHWEST PACIFIC PUSH

Navy's Move

Admiral Halsey's Third Fleet began its drive for the Upper Solomons on June 30, 1943, with the capture of Rendova Island. Opposition was weak, and the island was secured by amphibious forces in a matter of hours.

New Georgia, farther north, was the next stop. Army and Marine detachments were started for the beachheads by July 4, and surface forces entered Kula Gulf the following day to cover a landing and blast enemy installations on Kolombangara Island. During this operation the destroyer STRONG, damaged by shellfire from land artillery, was torpedoed—apparently by an enemy submarine. While rushing to STRONG's rescue, a destroyer crashed into her, and she sank forthwith.

In an effort to save New Georgia, the Japanese rushed a relief force of seven destroyers from Bougainville. The American striking force (three cruisers and four DD's) under Rear Admiral W. L. Ainsworth, reentered Kula Gulf to intercept the Japs. In the resulting Battle of Kula Gulf, the Japanese flagship was demolished, and the remainder of the relief force fled. The cruiser HELENA was sunk in the action.

The Japanese dispatched from Bougainville another relief force—the light cruiser JINTSU and five destroyers. Ainsworth, with three cruisers (HONOLULU, ST. LOUIS, and the New Zealand light cruiser LEANDER) and ten destroyers, intercepted the enemy force off Kolombangara on July 12th. During the Battle of Kolombangara, JINTSU was sunk by shellfire and the American destroyer GWINN was lost. The defeat discouraged the Japanese from further attempts to relieve New Georgia with major fleet units. On August 5 the American ground forces captured Munda airfield, and a few days later New Georgia was secured.

Vella Lavella Island was the next American step. To block this move, the Imperial Navy sent four destroyers with troop reinforcements steaming for the threatened base at Vila. The Japs were spotted by an American plane, and intercepted in Vella Gulf by a task group of six U.S. destroyers under Commander Frederick Moosbrugger. Three Jap destroyers were obliterated in the action that followed. American losses: none. Thereupon the Japanese decided to evacuate their garrison on Vella Lavella.

On the night of October 6 an American destroyer group under Captain F. A. Walker contacted the Jap evacuation force of six destroyers. Result: the Battle of Vella Lavella. In this engagement the enemy lost one DD. USS CHEVALIER was sunk and the destroyers O'BANNON and SELFRIDGE were severely damaged. Destroyer reinforcements arrived in time to turn the tide for the hard-hit Americans, but Japanese transport craft got through to Vella Lavella and took off the garrison.

This left Bougainville the last Japanese stronghold in the Solomons—a tough nut for the cracking. To crack it Admiral Halsey assembled the biggest surface and air fleet he had yet been able to muster in the Solomons. This included SARATOGA, back on duty after repair, and the light aircraft carrier PRINCETON. Halsey began to apply the pressure in mid-October. American and New Zealand troops were landed in the Treasury Islands, a jump away from Bougainville, on October 27th. While this amphibious move was being made, cruisers and destroyers under Rear Admiral A. S. Merrill created a diversion by bombarding enemy posts on Buka and in the Shortland Islands. The SARATOGA-PRINCETON carrier force, under Rear Admiral Frederick C. Sherman, feinted an attack on Bougainville's east coast at the end of October. This drew the enemy's eye from the western beaches of Empress Augusta Bay where Admiral T. S. Wilkinson moved in on the morning of November 1 with an occupation force of 7,500 Marines.

Bougainville's garrison called for help, and Japanese Headquarters rushed four cruisers and six destroyers from Rabaul. This force was spotted by American planes, and Halsey countered by ordering Merrill's cruiser-destroyer force to Empress Augusta Bay. The American force consisted of the light cruisers MONTPELIER, CLEVELAND, COLUMBIA and DENVER and eight destroyers. The enemy's cruisers were MYOKO and HAGURO (CA's) and SENDAI and AGANO (CL's). In the ensuing Battle of Empress Augusta Bay, the Jap cruiser SENDAI was sunk, two Jap destroyers collided and were disabled, HAGURO was damaged and MYOKO rammed and sank a companion destroyer. U.S. destroyers SPENCE and THATCHER collided in the action, and the destroyer FOOTE received serious battle damage—the only severe casualty suffered by Merrill's force. The thrashed Japanese raced back to Rabaul.

Alarmed by the smash at Bougainville, the Japanese High Command dispatched part of Admiral Kurita's Second Fleet to the Solomons-Bismarck front from Truk. Kurita's cruisers reached Rabaul on November 5th, just in time to receive a lambasting from the planes of SARATOGA and PRINCETON which had been ordered by Halsey to strike at air reinforcements flown into Rabaul from Truk. Halsey followed this naval air strike with another on November 11th. Kurita's Second Fleet cruisers had pulled their chestnuts out of the fire by leaving Rabaul after the first air onslaught, but the second clearly knocked the Japanese off balance.

This follow-through punch at Rabaul canceled all Jap hopes of reinforcing Bougainville. Some 27,000 Japanese troops remained on Bougainville, but they might as well have been in Alcatraz. American aircraft controlled the sky over them, and the U.S. Navy controlled the surrounding seas. Isolated and trapped, the Japanese on Bougainville were as helpless as POW's. Military action against them was not worth the effort, so they were by-passed. The Upper Solomons campaign was over.

While Admiral Halsey's Third Fleet was expelling the Imperial Navy from the Solomons, MacArthur's forces were not neglecting the enemy in New Guinea. September 1943 found Vice Admiral Kinkaid's Seventh Fleet operating in New Guinea waters (under area command of General MacArthur) to the detriment of Japanese communication lines around such outposts as Lae, Salamaua and the Trobriand Islands.

Lae and Salamaua were occupied by American-Australian troops in mid-September. Late in the month the Australians captured Finschafen. Seventh Fleet surface forces suffered their first major loss during this campaign when a Japanese I-boat torpedoed and sank the destroyer HENLEY. By November the Japanese positions on the northeast coast of New Guinea were completely neutralized.

The Seventh Fleet now participated in an amphibious move on New Britain—a thrust calculated to paralyze the enemy's naval base at Rabaul. Seventh Fleet forces spearheaded the invasion, blasting at Arawe on the south coast of New Britain in mid-December. There was surprisingly little resistance, and MacArthur's troops captured the local airfield in less than a week. The day after Christmas, Marines were put ashore on the north coast at Cape Gloucester. Enemy aircraft struck at the beachheads, and the destroyer BROWNSON was sunk. But the Jap planes were shot down like geese in open season, and reserves could not be mustered to continue the attack. Navy shells and air bombs had already shattered the enemy's shore defenses, and the Marines were soon driving inland.

Thus the Japanese power-house in the Bismarcks was blanked out. The Japs continued to hold their Rabaul citadel and the neighboring base at Kavieng, New Ireland. But these strongholds were like stymied castles on a chessboard—major pieces which had been outflanked and reduced to impotence and were no longer worth the taking. Like Bougainville, they could be by-passed. The game was over for the Japanese in the South Seas.

So the long arm of Japan, which had encircled the Bismarcks and reached through the Solomons, was amputated in the last quarter of 1943. And Rabaul was left as the residual stump. But before the amputation—long before—the arm had withered almost to the point of atrophy. Compare its resisting power, July through December 1943, with its offensive might in the spring and summer of 1942. Where were the battleships, the aircraft carriers, the cruiser divisions, the caravans of freighters, tankers, troop transports and munition ships which had carried the tidal-wave offensive from the Philippines to Guadalcanal? Where were the guns and men of yesteryear?

But five Japanese cruisers fought in the defense of

the Upper Solomons against the forces of Halsey's Third Fleet. Major units of Kurita's Imperial Second Fleet raced from Truk to Rabaul and back to Truk again, without fighting a surface battle. Admiral Ozawa's Carrier Fleet at Truk launched 250 planes which flew to Rabaul, but Ozawa's carriers never steamed south into the South Seas conflict. Backbone of the enemy's Upper Solomons defense was the destroyer force, supported by a few squadrons of land-based aircraft.

Where was the Imperial Army? It had taken American ground forces almost seven months to win Guadalcanal—Rendova was little more than a skirmish. New Georgia was mopped up in six weeks, and Bougainville was neutralized in a month. Savage jungle fighting followed some of the landings in the New Guinea-Bismarck area, but the Japanese were weak in the air and the coastal defenses of New Britain were flabby. Where were the troops, the anti-aircraft weapons, the planes?

Answer: Japan had been unable to solve the transport problem. The Japanese lost the Battle of Logistics long before they lost the battles of Kolombangara, Vella Lavella, Empress Augusta Bay and Arawe. Long before they were plucked by the Allies, Japan's South Seas bases were pumpkins dying on a vine of withered supply lines.

That vine was blighted by the U.S. Submarine Force.

Transportation Torpedoed

With the withdrawal of the "loaned" Pacific Fleet submarines in the first quarter of 1943, the SoWes-Pac Force based in Australia was reduced to its former quota of 20 submarines. Of these, 12 operated under Commodore Fife's Brisbane Command (Task Force Seventy-two) as a component of Admiral Halsey's Third Fleet. Eight were under the operational control of Rear Admiral Christie at Fremantle and were a component of Vice Admiral Kinkaid's Seventh Fleet. In October 1943 four more submarines were added to the Fremantle command, and the SoWesPac Force totaled 24—12 operating from Brisbane, 12 from Fremantle. As the enemy was swept out of the Upper Solomons in November, several of the Task Force Seventy-two submarines were shifted to the Fremantle command, but the SoWesPac Force ended the year with the 24 quota. These SoWesPac submarines not only covered the Solomons-Bismarck-New Guinea area, but submarines of the Fremantle force patrolled as far west as Malaya, covered the Celebes and Philippines areas, and worked in the South China Sea.

Here was certainly a demonstration of a little bit going a long way to do a lot—an accomplishment that would have been impossible but for several contributing factors. One factor was the arrival of SJ radar which increased the submarine's search range and permitted more surface (faster and farther) running. Another was the gradual improvement in the Mark 14 torpedo (not yet perfect, by any means, but better).

Advanced fueling bases also added many miles to submarine cruising range and area coverage. On the west coast of Australia, Exmouth Gulf was opened as a fueling station in August 1943. It remained in operation until the closing months of the war. Submarines "topping off" at Exmouth instead of at Fremantle were saved about 700 miles of travel, time and Diesel oil. A few weeks after the Exmouth Gulf station was opened, Port Darwin was put in operation as a mid-patrol fueling point. No longer under threat of air attack, this northwest Australian port was also used as a torpedo supply base. As such it was particularly handy, for the growing popularity of night-surface attacks had greatly increased torpedo expenditure. Frequently a submarine fired a load of torpedoes within a few days' time, and wanting to make a quick reload and return to its area, it found Darwin a convenient way-station.

The task force on the east coast of Australia had also been quick to set up advanced fueling and operating bases. Tulagi, the first of these, was a going concern early in 1943. The submarine rescue vessel COUCAL served the TF72 submarines as a roving fueling station. From Jomard Pass in the Louisiades, where she first supplied submarines in September 1943, she moved northward as the Allies advanced in the Upper Solomons. Late in the fall, the tender FULTON steamed into Milne Bay, and submarine refits were conducted there as well as at Brisbane. When the Australians occupied Finschafen, Langemak Bay became a forward fuel stop for submarines.

But fueling stations, SJ radar and better torpedoes did not decrease the SoWesPac workload—only increased the submarine's capacity to tackle the job. As the submarine became more capable, more work was loaded on its shoulders. During the Upper Solomons campaign, the Task Force Seventy-two submarines were variously employed (at Admiral Halsey's direction) in support of fleet operations. Fremantle submarines participated in Seventh Fleet operations in the New Guinea-Bismarck area. These duties, in addition to the undersea war of attrition—the campaign that torpedoed the enemy's transportation system in the South Seas.

That campaign went on without a slow-down. It went on while submarines performed all manner of special missions and duties. A submarine might lay mines, transport coast watchers and intelligence agents, evacuate refugees, rescue marooned aviators, go out scouting or prowl on reconnaissance. But en route, on station or on the way back, its torpedoes were ready for enemy shipping—nearly every mission was tantamount to a war patrol. Jack-of-all-trades, the submarine's chief job was to sink enemy ships. In the South Seas battle the SoWesPac submarines remained on the job.

They did not fight the South Seas undersea war of attrition without assistance. The traffic lanes coming southeast from Palau, south from Truk, southwest from the Marshalls and Gilberts were covered for many miles by submarines from Pearl Harbor under operational control of Admiral Lockwood. Blockading the enemy's bases in the Mandates, the SubPac submarines stopped many a convoy on its way to New Guinea, the Bismarcks, and Bougainville in the spring, summer and autumn of 1943. And many a ship with cargo intended for the South Seas front was stopped north of the Mandates and in the waters off Japan—at the very roots of the transport-system vine.

Of course, every *maru* sunk in the Central Pacific was not bound for the Solomons or Bismarcks. But much of the Japanese shipping in the Mandates was directly or indirectly supplying the Solomons-Bismarck-New Guinea front. Draw a hypothetical east-west line 9° north of the equator. A box score listing the Japanese shipping sunk in Pacific waters below this latitude, May through December 1943, serves to suggest the part played by submarines in cutting the enemy's supply lines during the closing months of the Solomons battle. In a broad belt of ocean extending from the Gilbert Islands to the waters off the east coast of Mindanao and bounded by the 9° parallels north and south of the equator, *maru*-hunting submarines scored as shown in the table on the following page.

When the war ended, the Japanese troops on Bougainville meekly surrendered. Patiently they had been waiting since early in 1943 for reinforcements and relief that never came. Toward the last, facing starvation, they had gone in for gardening. Their little vegetable patches (they could hardly have been called victory gardens) were all that kept them alive. In western New Guinea some of the Japanese garrisons were in similar straits. And in other corners of the Southwest Pacific there were little outposts where the enemy, by-passed, was left marooned. Long after the Armistice which ended World War I, German troops were found in deep pockets of the African interior, waiting for the Kaiser's forces to rescue them. It seems possible that on some remote South Seas island or hiding in New Guinea's jungly interior, there may today be a little company of Japanese Crusoes awaiting a victorious Co-Prosperity Sphere and triumphal relief.

If so, they are in for a long wait.

Submarine Support of Fleet Operations (Solomons-Bismarck-New Guinea Drive)

During the Upper Solomons drive the primary mission of the Brisbane (TF72) submarines was, as has been pointed out, the interruption of the enemy's surface operations and the cutting of his Solomons, Bismarcks and Eastern New Guinea supply lines. Submarine support of Halsey's Third Fleet consisted mainly of this war of attrition. And the same applied to the Fremantle submarine activities in the Seventh Fleet's area.

Moreover, Task Force Seventy-two worked in meshed-gear cooperation with the Third Fleet throughout the Upper Solomons campaign. Every special assignment that could possibly be carried out was undertaken by the Brisbane Force. These assignments included minelaying, scouting, conducting sounding surveys, landing of coast watchers and reconnaissance. The submarines based at Fremantle undertook similar missions. During the May-December period of the South Seas push, SoWesPac submarines accomplished the following special missions:

May 25, 1943: TAUTOG (Lieutenant Commander Sieglaff) landed two Mohammedan agents on Kabaena Island.

May 25: GATO (Commander R. J. Foley) made sounding reconnaissance of Numa Numa Bay, near Choiseul in the Solomons. The previous month-end she had landed 16 coast watchers and Australian intelligence troops on Teop and evacuated a party of missionaries.

June 4: SILVERSIDES (Lieutenant Commander Burlingame) planted a minefield in Steffan Strait between New Hanover and New Ireland.

July 31: GUARDFISH (Lieutenant Commander N. G. Ward) landed a survey party on the west coast of Bougainville.

September 1: GREENLING (Lieutenant Commander J. D. Grant) landed survey parties in the Shortland Islands and in the Treasury group.

September 20-28: GUARDFISH (Lieutenant Commander N. G. Ward) landed a reconnaissance party on the west coast of Bougainville.

September 29: GATO (Commander R. J. Foley) landed a reconnaissance party on the east coast of Bougainville.

September 29: PETO (Commander W. T. Nelson)

Date	Submarine	Commanding Officer	Ship Sunk	Type	Tonnage
May 4	Seal	H. B. Dodge	San Clemente Maru	Tanker	7,354
May 11	Grayback	F. C. Stephan	Yodogawa Maru	Cargo	6,441
May 17	Grayback	F. C. Stephan	England Maru	Cargo	5,830
May 18	Pollack	B. E. Lewellen	Terushima Maru	Ex-gunboat	3,110
May 20	Pollack	B. E. Lewellen	Bangkok Maru	Ex-light cruiser	5,350
May 27	Finback	J. A. Tyree	Kochi Maru	Cargo	2,910
May 28	Scamp	W. G. Ebert	Kamikawa Maru	Converted seaplane-tender	6,853
June 8	Finback	J. A. Tyree	Kahoku Maru	Ex-gunboat	3,350
June 11	Finback	J. A. Tyree	Genoa Maru	Cargo	6,785
June 11	Silversides	C. C. Burlingame	Hide Maru	Cargo	5,256
June 13	Sargo	F. S. Carnick	Konan Maru	Passenger-cargo	5,226
June 17	Drum	B. F. McMahon	Myoko Maru	Passenger-cargo	5,087
June 19	Growler	A. F. Schade	Miyadono Maru	Passenger-cargo	5,196
July 25	Pompon	E. C. Hawk	Thames Maru	Cargo	5,871
Aug. 22	Swordfish	F. M. Parker	Nishiyama Maru	Cargo	3,016
Sept. 2	Snapper	M. K. Clementson	Mutsure	Frigate	860
Sept. 4	Albacore	Oscar Hagberg	Heijo Maru	Ex-gunboat	2,627
Sept. 5	Swordfish	F. M. Parker	Tenkai Maru	Cargo	3,203
Sept. 8	Drum	B. F. McMahon	Hakutetsu Maru No. 13	Cargo	1,334
Sept. 11	Narwhal	F. D. Latta	Hokusho Maru	Cargo	4,211
Sept. 18	Scamp	W. G. Ebert	Kansai Maru	Passenger-cargo	8,614
Sept. 30	Pogy	G. H. Wales	Maebashi Maru	Passenger-cargo	7,005
Oct. 1	Peto	W. T. Nelson	Tonei Maru	Passenger-cargo	4,930
Oct. 1	Peto	W. T. Nelson	Kinkasan Maru	Cargo	4,980
Oct. 8	Guardfish	N. G. Ward	Kashu Maru	Cargo	5,460
Oct. 18	Silversides	J. S. Coye	Tairin Maru	Cargo	1,915
Oct. 24	Silversides	J. S. Coye	Tennan Maru	Cargo	5,407
Oct. 24	Silversides	J. S. Coye	Kazan Maru	Cargo	1,893
Oct. 24	Silversides	J. S. Coye	Johore Maru	Passenger-cargo	6,182
Nov. 4	Tautog	W. B. Sieglaff	Submarine Chaser No. 30	Subchaser	100
Nov. 10	Scamp	W. G. Ebert	Tokyo Maru	Passenger-cargo	6,486
Nov. 13	Thresher	H. Hull	Muko Maru	Transport	4,862
Nov. 17	Drum	D. F. Williamson	Hie Maru	Ex-supply ship	11,621
Nov. 22	Tinosa	L. R. Daspit	Kiso Maru	Cargo	4,071
Nov. 22	Tinosa	L. R. Daspit	Yamato Maru	Cargo	4,379
Nov. 25	Albacore	Oscar Hagberg	Kenzan Maru	Cargo	4,705
Nov. 25	Searaven	M. H. Dry	Toa Maru	Tanker	10,052
Nov. 26	Tinosa	L. R. Daspit	Shini Maru	Cargo	3,811
Nov. 26	Ray	B. J. Harrel	Nikkai Maru	Converted gunboat	2,562
Nov. 26	Raton	J. W. Davis	Onoe Maru	Cargo	6,667
Nov. 28	Raton	J. W. Davis	Hokko Maru	Cargo	5,347
Nov. 28	Raton	J. W. Davis	Yuri Maru	Cargo	6,787
Nov. 30	Gato	R. J. Foley	Columbia Maru	Passenger-cargo	5,618
Dec. 3	Tinosa	L. R. Daspit	Azuma Maru	Passenger-cargo	6,646
Dec. 4	Apogon	P. Schoeni	Daido Maru	Ex-gunboat	2,962
Dec. 13	Pogy	R. M. Metcalf	Fukkai Maru	Passenger-cargo	3,829
Dec. 20	Gato	R. J. Foley	Tsuneshima Maru	Cargo	2,926
Dec. 21	Skate	E. B. McKinney	Terukawa Maru	Cargo	6,429
Dec. 29	Silversides	J. S. Coye	Tenposan Maru	Cargo	1,970
Dec. 29	Silversides	J. S. Coye	Schichisei Maru	Cargo	1,911
Dec. 29	Silversides	J. S. Coye	Ryuto Maru	Cargo	3,311
Dec. 31	Greenling	J. D. Grant	Shoho Maru	Cargo	1,936

The above list is not definitive. It merely indicates the intensity of the submarine attrition-war in an area fronting on and including the Solomons-Bismarck-New Guinea theater at the time of the Allied advance in the South Pacific. In this period and area U.S. submarines sank the enumerated 28 cargo vessels, 12 transports (passenger-cargo), 2 oil tankers and 10 miscellaneous vessels; altogether 52 Japanese vessels loaded with troops, guns, food stores, munitions, gasoline and men.

concluded an unsuccessful two-day search for a Fifth Air Force crew lost somewhere off Wewak, New Guinea.

September 29: GROUPER (Commander M. P. Hottle) landed 46 men and 3,000 pounds of freight on the south coast of New Britain, and took off Captain A. L. Post, USAAF.

During September: SCULPIN (Commander L. H. Chappell) reconnoitered Thilenius and Montague Harbor on the south coast of New Britain.

October 25-28: GUARDFISH (Lieutenant Commander N. G. Ward) landed a reconnaissance party on the west coast of Bougainville.

October 30: SCAMP (Commander W. G. Ebert) reconnoitered in the Solomons.

October 30: TAUTOG (Lieutenant Commander W. B. Sieglaff) bombarded Fais Island.

December 25-January 2, 1944: PETO (Commander W. T. Nelson) reconnoitered and landed personnel on Boang Island in the Solomons.

Practically all amphibious landings were preceded by submarine reconnaissance or by advance scouting parties landed by submarine, or both. The number of enemy fleet units in the Solomons-Bismarck-New Guinea area fluctuated as the Japs ran occasional task groups down from Truk to reinforce the Eighth Fleet based at Rabaul. Coast watchers stationed by submarines in the Upper Solomons and Bismarcks furnished much valuable information on these enemy ship movements.

But the open seas below Truk were also watched—by periscope and radar's long-range "eye." Submarines were employed on offensive reconnaissance north of the prevailing weather front and south of Truk. In these waters they were to intercept southbound enemy fleet detachments and report on enemy fleet movements—information which was most vital to the American surface forces during the Upper Solomons campaign.

However, the employment of submarines on a far-flung scouting line in search of enemy fleet detachments proved to be largely ineffective. Before the Bougainville landings were made, five or six submarines were assigned to patrol south of Truk to watch for and report any Japanese warships which might be standing southward to contest the Bougainville operation. One submarine was stationed directly off Truk, and the remainder were deployed in a scouting line. Despite the fact that the entire cruiser strength of Admiral Kurita's Second Fleet sortied from Truk and steamed south to Rabaul, passing through or around the submarine scouting line, not one of the enemy warships was sighted by the scouting submarines. Unfortunately, GROWLER, who was stationed closest to Truk, had been forced to leave station because of electrical difficulties, just before Kurita's cruisers sortied. Even had GROWLER been there, however, the enemy could have steamed out by a different pass and probably proceeded to Rabaul undetected.

This strategic employment of submarines in scouting line below Truk had come as a result of conference with Admiral Halsey and his staff, who apparently considered it the most direct way submarines could support the fleet. The zero accomplishment emphasized the submarine's limitations in the field of open-sea scouting. Undoubtedly the same number of submarines deployed on the enemy's known traffic lanes would have inflicted great damage on his shipping, and so have been of more value to the fleet.

The only enemy naval vessel sunk by a SoWesPac submarine in the South Pacific during the Upper Solomons campaign was the Japanese submarine I-24. She was sunk off New Hanover on July 27 by SCAMP (Lieutenant Commander W. G. Ebert). On her next patrol SCAMP disabled a destroyer escort, and on November 12, off New Hanover, she damaged an AGANO-type cruiser. Only poor visibility and a rush of A/S vessels to the rescue saved the heavy cruiser from being blown to the bottom. But it was undoubtedly *hors de combat* for the remainder of the campaign.

To the South China Sea in 1943 (Bowfin's Patrol)

While Task Force Seventy-two cooperated with the Third Fleet in the Upper Solomons campaign and Pearl Harbor submarines patrolled the Mandates, the submarines from Fremantle were striking far west of the Solomons-Bismarck-New Guinea front to disrupt Japanese traffic in the South China Sea.

Four major shipping routes connected Singapore with the main ports of the Greater East Asia Co-Prosperity Sphere. One of these routes followed shallow water along the Malay coastline, crossed the Gulf of Siam, and trailed up the coast of Indo-China to Hong Kong, Shanghai and points north. Another main-line route went from Singapore over to northwest Borneo and veered on a coastwise course up into the Philippines. A branch line of this route trekked over to Indo-China, crossing the so-called "Dangerous Ground"—a sketchily surveyed stretch of water between Cochin China and Palawan. The third major route went directly southeast to the Netherlands East Indies, and a fourth—the traffic lane from Singapore to Palau, Truk or Rabaul—trailed eastward through the Balabac Straits between Palawan and Borneo. As the southeast anchor of the Greater East Asia Co-Prosperity Sphere, Singapore was as important to Japan's expanded Empire as Manila Cut the lines which held this anchor, and the Sphere might not drift away, but certainly the anchor would be lost. And the anchor was worth holding on to for its own intrinsic value—Singapore was the chief port of Indonesia with its priceless rubber and rich mines.

The northern end of the Singapore-China trunk line was covered by SubPac submarines on Empire and East China Sea patrols. But the southern segment of the route which crossed the Gulf of Siam and trailed in the South China Sea was covered, as previously noted, by the SoWesPac submarines of the Fremantle Force. To the Fremantlers also fell the Malay Barrier and Philippine patrols. A large order for Admiral Christie's eight submarines.

After the retreat to Australia in 1942, the South China Sea had been too remote, submarines too few and torpedoes too scarce for anything like adequate area coverage. SEADRAGON had been there, as related. The first submarine minelaying operation had been conducted in those waters late in 1942. The few other abbreviated patrols did little more than serve notice on the Japanese that the South China Sea was not immune to submarine warfare.

In the summer of 1943, however, the South China Sea came in for more attention. The enemy was sending an increasing number of convoys down the Asian coast and into the Philippines. An increasing number of oil tankers traveled the sea lanes from Singapore and Borneo. These tankers were upped on the submarine priority list and the growing merchant marine activity was marked for diminution.

In September 1943, BOWFIN was sent out to the South China Sea under Lieutenant Commander Willingham to look over the situation. Covering the northern part of the area, this submarine—it was her maiden patrol—demolished a large barge, destroyed a two-masted schooner and sank (September 25) KIRISHIMA MARU, passenger-cargoman, 8,120 tons. As will be seen, she was merely becoming acquainted with the area.

Two days after the sinking of KIRISHIMA MARU, the Japanese lost a large transport in the same area. She was KASHIMA MARU, 9,908 tons, torpedoed and sunk by BONEFISH, under Lieutenant Commander T. W. Hogan.

Having destroyed this troopship, BONEFISH went on to sink a bigger one. On October 10, Hogan tracked down and sent down the 10,086-ton transport TEIBI MARU. The South China Sea was becoming unsafe for troop carriers.

BONEFISH concluded this patrol by sinking ISUZU-GAWA MARU, freighter, 4,212 tons. When she headed back to Australia she left behind her 24,206 tons of liquidated Japanese shipping.

KINGFISH (Lieutenant Commander V. L. Lowrance) took up the South China Sea patrol in October. She began by planting a minefield off the southwest corner of Celebes Island, squarely across a Japanese shipping lane from Makassar City. She continued on to land six British agents with 4,000 pounds of radio equipment on a hostile Borneo beach. On October 20, in South China Sea water, she sank SANA MARU, freighter, 3,365 tons.

With KINGFISH ending her patrol, BOWFIN was sent out again, this time under Lieutenant Commander W. T. Griffith. Bound for the South China Sea, she left Exmouth Gulf on November 4, her prospective course charted along the usual route through Lombok and Makassar Strait, Sibutu Passage and Balabac Strait. Five days out, not far from Makassar, she battle-surfaced to shoot up a convoy of five schooners. She sank four of these sailing vessels before a patrol plane drove her under. Hit by BOWFIN's 4-inch shells, the wooden ships went down like rocks—a phenomenon that convinced Griffith they were loaded with machinery or other heavy cargo.

Griffith and his boys were only warming up. Entering Sibutu Passage on the night of November 11, BOWFIN battle-surfaced again to set fire to a pair of small oil tankers. This gun action was fought in bright moonlight within a range of Japanese shore batteries on Sibutu Island, but the shooting was over and BOWFIN was under before the coast artillerymen knew what it was all about.

BOWFIN cruised for a short time in the waters off Mindanao, found no targets, and proceeded west across "Dangerous Ground" toward Cape Varella. Rain, wind, heavy seas and a fleeting submarine contact. Nothing to radio home about. Midnight, November 25-26, she was approaching Fisherman's Islands in the sort of weather that makes a poor sailor wish he'd never heard of a foc'sle head and "graveyard watch." Sheeting black rainstorm and seas of India ink. Blindfold for a ship's lookout—worse for a wave-smothered periscope—but nothing to stop radar.

At 0200, BOWFIN's SD picked up several large "pips"—distance two miles and one mile. Three minutes later the inquiring SJ contacted something off in the night, 1,000 yards distant.

"I first thought I had blundered into the beach or some small islands, although I had 75 fathoms of water," Griffith noted in the log. *"Came hard left to clear out to seaward, and backed emergency to keep from ramming an enormous tanker!"*

A few minutes later the submarine backed full to keep from ramming another big tanker. Griffith realized he was in the midst of a Japanese convoy, northward bound. Five ships showed up on the radar screen with visibility practically zero and a blind spot ahead on the SJ due to improper tuning. However, after an hour and a half of tracking, Griffith knew the disposition of these targets. The ships were moving by two's in parallel columns 4,000 yards apart, the fifth ship trailing between the columns with an escort.

Griffith directed an approach on the leading vessel in the nearest (the starboard) column. At 0351 he fired three torpedoes. One struck the tanker's bow, and in the glaring blast the ship's bow section and foremast disintegrated. A second torpedo exploded amidships. As the tanker settled by the head a tide of liquid flame spread across the water. The men on BOWFIN's bridge could see the tanker's broken silhouette and smell the burning gasoline. The vessel's deep-toned whistle wailed a disaster call in the night.

Meantime, Griffith had shifted the submarine for a torpedo shot at the second ship. As the volcanic blast of a hit lit up this second target, BOWFIN had to back emergency to keep from ramming the torpedoed tanker which had veered around broadside within 300 yards of the submarine.

Griffith did some fast maneuvering. Explosions that sounded like depth charges were going off to starboard. The torpedoed tanker, its foredeck awash, was almost on top of BOWFIN. The second vessel, damaged, wallowed in the sea about 1,500 yards beyond. Deciding to finish off the tanker before the escort could arrive on the scene—the other ship could wait—Griffith swung BOWFIN for a stern-tube salvo, and fired three torpedoes at 1,200 yards. One hit under the tanker's stack, and the whistle choked off as if its throat had been plugged.

BOWFIN was steered off into darkness for a quick reload, then Griffith skirted the scene of action for a last look. Rain was smothering the gasoline fires, and in the dim and smoky light the big tanker was slowly sinking in a sea of fumes. The second vessel was gone—like Charon's ferry in the night-draped Styx.

Griffith headed BOWFIN toward Cape Varella to search for the rest of the convoy. At 1050 a periscope sweep brought a 5,000-ton freighter into view. Attempting a submerged approach, Griffith encountered trouble with depth control, and surfaced to accomplish a fast end-around. Four torpedoes scored four hits, blowing the AK completely to pieces.

As Griffith maneuvered the submarine over to the flotsam-strewn water where the freighter had exploded, a small OTORI escort vessel came climbing over the waves about 1,500 yards away. The seas were too rough for the six-foot depth-setting required

for a torpedo shot at this A/S craft, and Griffith headed BOWFIN away.

The following day, BOWFIN found another target— a small coastal steamer—which was disposed of with three torpedo shots. Then, early on the morning of the 28th, BOWFIN received a contact report from the submarine BILLFISH operating in the area—a convoy was in the vicinity. Shortly after the reception of this news, BOWFIN was on the track of five large ships which were steaming under escort.

Griffith directed a surface approach, and at 0313 making a surface attack, he fired four torpedoes at the leading (and largest) target. Four hits sank the ship in as many minutes.

At 0317 Griffith fired two more bow torpedoes. These smashed into the second vessel, leaving her awash to the bridge. At this juncture the third vessel of the convoy, which had been moving in column off BOWFIN's beam, turned and headed straight for the submarine. Gunfire blazed as the ship opened up with a 5-incher at 500 yards. The second shot hit the submarine. The shell ricocheted from the deck into the superstructure and exploded between the pressure hull and the starboard induction pipe. The blast carried away the low-pressure air lines aft, ripped open part of the main induction pipe, and destroyed the ventilation lines.

Griffith fired two stern-tube shots at the attacking ship. That ended the Japanese gunnery. Both torpedoes hit, and the vessel went down, sagging in the middle like a weighted hammock. With this target out of the way, Griffith sent BOWFIN in pursuit of the remainder of the convoy.

While the last two torpedoes aboard were being loaded, the submarine overhauled the quarry. Griffith drove in for an attack on the largest vessel, calculating the set-up carefully. At 0353 he fired the torpedoes. The first prematured at 500 feet, and its explosion deflected the second, sending it on a course wide of the mark.

"This premature cost us two sure hits and a 7,000-ton vessel," Griffith commented afterwards. (The submarines of SoWesPac were still using the Mark 6 exploder.)

So BOWFIN headed home from the South China Sea. But her war patrol was to have a P.S. On December 1 she made contact with a four-ship convoy north of Celebes. Griffith tracked, and then radioed the convoy information to BONEFISH on the chance that Hogan's submarine, then in the area, could intercept. The following day BOWFIN sighted a 75-ton oil-carrying yacht in Makassar Strait. Griffith ordered a gun attack, and BOWFIN's sharpshooters destroyed this unwary craft.

Her main induction patched and her patrol report crammed with action, BOWFIN arrived at Fremantle on December 9th.

"They fought the war from the beginning to the end of the patrol," Admiral Christie lauded BOWFIN's submariners. And for this outstandingly aggressive and successful patrol, BOWFIN was awarded the Presidential Unit Citation. For the Japanese merchant marine she had contrived the following obituary:

Down at sea Nov. 9: four cargo schooners, 425 tons
Down at sea Nov. 11: two small oil tankers, 800 tons.
Down at sea Nov. 26: Ogurasan Maru, tanker, 5,069 tons.
Down at sea Nov. 26: Tainan Maru, freighter, 5,407 tons.
Down at sea Nov. 27: Van Vollenhoven, freighter, 691 tons.
Down at sea Nov. 28: Sydney Maru, passenger-cargo, 5,425 tons.
Down at sea Nov. 28: Tonan Maru, tanker, 9,866 tons.
Down at sea Dec. 2: one oil-carrying yacht, 75 tons.

The tonnage of the schooners and small tankers sunk by gunfire is an estimate and probably on the light side. But the tonnages of the larger vessels were determined by post-war inquest, and a conservative adding machine, excluding the tonnages of the small craft, gives the total as 26,458 tons. BOWFIN's was therefore one of the season's high-scoring patrols. This patrol, with that of BONEFISH, marked the beginning of the end for Japanese merchant shipping in the South China Sea.

Submarines to the Philippines

The campaign to reoccupy the Philippine Islands began long before American landing craft nosed up against the Leyte beaches. United States submarines had never surrendered the usage of Philippine waters, and early in 1943 they began to visit the islands on special missions that were as intriguing as the "sealed orders" under which the captains sailed. The guns were still slamming on Guadalcanal when the first of these missions was undertaken by GUDGEON. January 14, 1943, this submarine, under Lieutenant Commander Stovall, landed a party of six Filipinos captained by Major I. A. Villamor, and one ton of equipment near Catmon Point on the island of Negros.

TAMBOR (Lieutenant Commander S. H. Armbruster) landed a Lieutenant Commander C. Parsons, USNR, and party, with 50,000 rounds of .30-cal. ammunition and 20,000 rounds of .45-cal. ammunition, plus $10,000 cash, near Pagodian Bay, Mindanao, on March 5th.

In April, GUDGEON was back again, this time under Lieutenant Commander W. S. Post, on a mission to land an officer, three men and three tons of equipment near Pucio Point, Panay. Post was never the man to let a mission interfere with the war of attrition. Putting first things first, on April 28 he drove GUDGEON in to attack a target no submarine would wish to overlook. So the Japanese lost KAMAKURA MARU, 17,526-ton transport—the biggest to go down to date in the Philippines. This sinking had a sequel on May 12, when GUDGEON, her mission completed, torpedoed and sank SUMATRA MARU, 5,862-ton freighter. The dead as well as the quick were making quiet landings on the beaches of the Philippines.

May 26, TROUT (Lieutenant Commander A. H. Clark) landed a party of agents with $10,000 and two tons of equipment on Basilan Island, P.I. On June 12 she was in Pagodian Bay on the south coast of Mindanao, unloading 6,000 rounds of .30-cal. ammunition, 2,000 rounds of .45-cal. ammunition, and a party of five under Captain J. A. Hammer, USA. From this hidden cove TROUT evacuated five officers. One of these, Lieutenant Commander C. Parsons, USNR, seems to have had a peculiar penchant for submarine rides in the Philippines. Revisiting Mindanao on July 9, TROUT picked up Parsons and carried him on another inter-island excursion.

THRESHER (Lieutenant Commander H. Hull) was at Catmon Point, Negros, July 9th. There she landed four commandos, 5,000 pounds of stores, 20,000 rounds of .30-cal. ammunition and 20,000 rounds of .45-cal. ammunition.

On July 31, GRAYLING (Lieutenant Commander J. E. Lee) delivered a ton of supplies and equipment to certain parties at Pucio Point, Pandan Bay, Panay. Under Lieutenant Commander E. Olsen the same submarine arrived in Pandan Bay on August 31 with two more tons of cargo.

BOWFIN (Lieutenant Commander Willingham) delivered similar supplies to waiting hands at Binuni Point, Mindanao, on September 2nd. Nine evacuees were taken off. Three weeks later she was delivering supplies, mail and money to interested receivers in the neighborhood of Sequijor Island where she picked up nine more passengers.

And on October 20, CABRILLA (Commander D. T. Hammond) was at Negros to take aboard four men and the aforementioned Major Villamor.

These activities, had they been noticed, would have led the Japanese to suspect that things which did not meet their eyes were happening in the southern Philippines. Who, they might have asked, was this Major Villamor? And the busy and mysterious Lieutenant Commander Parsons who rode submarines around the Philippines as though they were taxis around Times Square! Presently, reports did begin to filter into General Homma's Headquarters —a Japanese scouting party shot down—an outpost raided—a motor convoy ambushed in the jungle. Homma was aware that all the Americans in the Philippines had not been captured, and native guerrilla fighters were beginning an organized resistance. It took him longer to learn that undersea boats were supplying the "underground" war.

One of the submarines which torpedoed shipping in the Philippines area in the autumn of 1943 was the veteran TROUT (Lieutenant Commander Clark). Surigao Strait looked as familiar as Main Street when she entered that waterway on September 9, making a roundabout passage from Fremantle to Pearl with instructions to patrol the Davao area en route.

But a submarine she encountered in the strait did not look familiar. It looked like a Japanese I-boat. So Clark opened fire and sank I-182, the third Japanese submarine destroyed by a United States submarine that year.

On September 23, TROUT sank two more Japanese vessels—the freighter RYOTOKU MARU, 3,483 tons—and the passenger-cargoman, YAMASHIRO MARU, 3,429 tons. But TROUT was just "passing through," and lending support to the Philippine guerrilla movement by attacking enemy shipping and sinking Japanese Army supplies.

Loss of Grayling

The Imperial Navy lost I-182 on September 9, and on that same day a U.S. submarine was seen in Lingayen Gulf, and the Japanese passenger-cargoman HOKUAN MARU reported fighting a submarine action in the "Philippine area." The submarine seen in Lingayen Gulf may have been GRAYLING, ordered to patrol the approaches to Manila on that date, or the submarine driven off by HOKUAN MARU may have been GRAYLING. On August 23 she had completed her special mission to Pandan Bay, Panay, by delivering a cargo of supplies to the local guerrillas. Then she left to reconnoiter Tablas Strait and hunt traffic off Manila. Pandan Bay was the last anchorage she ever made.

Early in the year GRAYLING had conducted two patrols in the Philippines, under Lieutenant Commander J. E. Lee. Her eighth war patrol took her out of Fremantle on July 30, Lieutenant Commander R. M. Brinker serving as her captain. August 19 she reported the damaging of a 6,000-ton freighter near Balikpapan. The following day in Sibutu Passage she sank a small tanker of the TAKI MARU type, and took one survivor prisoner after destroying the oiler by gunfire. Her Pandan Bay arrival and departure was reported by the Panay guerrillas.

At war's end, Japanese records revealed the sinking of MEIZAN MARU, 5,480-ton passenger-cargo ship, in the Tablas Strait area on August 27th. GRAYLING was due in the area at that time, and it seems likely the *maru* in question fell prey to her torpedoes.

Apparently GRAYLING herself went down some time between the 9th and 12th of September. Commander Task Force Seventy-one requested a transmission from GRAYLING on the 12th. Her radio spoke no answer. On September 30, 1943, she was officially reported "lost with all hands."

Narwhal Enters the Guerrilla Movement

Of all the submarines that left Australia to go to the Philippines on special mission, the veteran NARWHAL engaged in the greatest number of these "cloak and dagger" exploits. Late in October she headed out on her first secret mission—a run to the island of Mindoro with peripatetic Lieutenant Commander Parsons, 46 tons of stores and two parties of specialists. Captain of NARWHAL was Lieutenant Commander F. D. Latta, who had been on her bridge when she transported a company of Army scouts to Attu.

NARWHAL was in good hands. Any naval captain who could name a submarine's four engines "Matthew," "Mark," "Luke" and "John" was an officer of unusual capacities. The Biblical Diesels responded by outrunning two Japanese A/S vessels in the Mindanao Sea. And presently NARWHAL was moored alongside a Japanese registry schooner, the DONA JUANA MARU, unloading part of her stores.

This extraordinary business was followed by a junket even more remarkable. Leaving Mindoro, NARWHAL proceeded coolly to Nasipit Harbor, Mindanao (where she went aground in 20 feet of water, and got off not quite so coolly), then tied up at Nasipit dock where a Filipino band played "Anchor's Aweigh" as the supplies brought in by the submarine were unloaded. If the strains of "Anchor's Aweigh" marching off in the Philippine sunshine sounded a little fantastic to the invading submariners (where was the war?) the 32 evacuees, including baby, who came aboard for the return voyage to Australia, could assure NARWHAL's crew that Jap soldiery cracked the whip in Manila. Someone brought aboard a copy of the Manila *Tribune,* dated November 11, 1942, featuring a story that the old SEALION had been raised and was in Dewey Drydock, her interior dismantled and her hull undergoing study. SEALION—that must have been a century ago. And Wainwright's men—or what was left of them—were still in the prisons and stockades in the interior. But help was on the way, coming aboard such submarines as NARWHAL.

In Australia NARWHAL received another set of

sealed orders. Again she headed for the Philippines, this time loaded with 90 tons of ammunition and stores, and carrying a party of eleven Army operatives. "Matthew," "Mark," "Luke," and "John" made the run in good time, and on December 3 the submarine was unloaded near Cabadaran, Mindanao. There, a party of eight (including Lieutenant Commander Parsons) was picked up for the return trip. NARWHAL then proceeded to Alubijid, Majacalar Bay, to take aboard three women, four children and two men. Latta stepped up the four engines to 17 knots as the submarine left this bay—the place had an unhealthy look. At dawn (the date was December 5) the lookout sighted a Japanese steamer, but it proved small enough to be a target for the deck guns.

"The sinking of this ship," Latta noted, "was especially good for morale aboard. These special missions are trying."

NARWHAL was only beating a path. Under Latta she would accomplish two more special missions to the Philippines. And before October 1944 was on the calendar she would have completed nine—going in to the beaches with supplies, ammunition, equipment for the hard-fighting guerrillas, and coming out with evacuees and information.

Fought by Filipinos and Americans of the "underground," the guerrilla war spread through the Philippines in the winter of 1943-44 like a brush fire eating through a forest. Enemy positions were reconnoitered, fortifications uncovered, installations marked for destruction, and large segments of the Japanese defense were undermined before the invasion blow was struck. Landing arms, equipment and secret agents on isolated beaches, U.S. submarines supplied the guerrilla forces with the wherewithal for war. Information brought out by these secret mission submarines implemented MacArthur's assault plans and influenced fleet operations when the drive to retake the Philippines was finally launched.

Loss of Cisco

The Japanese High Command did not remain impervious to the increasing submarine activity in Philippine waters and the adjacent South China Sea. Guerrilla endeavors and shipping losses in these areas were countered by tightened coastal patrols and antisubmarine reinforcements.

On September 28, patrolling Japanese aircraft spotted a shimmering oil slick in the Sulu Sea, due west of Mindanao. Submarine with leaking fuel tanks! The planes flashed the word to A/S surface craft and roared down on the attack.

"*Found a submarine tailing oil,*" the airmen stated in a terse report. "*Bombing. Ships cooperated with*

us. . . . The oil continued to gush up even on tenth of October."

By this it would seem that the Japanese A/S attack was persistent and deadly. Surface vessels joined the planes in the bombing, and the spot where the submarine lay was watched for twelve days. So was lost the USS Cisco and all hands, under Lieutenant Commander J. W. Coe.

There is little doubt about the submarine's identity. Venturing out on her first war patrol, Cisco had headed west from Port Darwin, Australia, on September 18, 1943. A few hours later she returned to Darwin, reporting trouble with the main hydraulic system. Repairs were made that night and she left Darwin the following morning. Ominously enough, as Cisco made her second departure, a Japanese plane was reported over Darwin at 20,000 feet. The aircraft may have been more than an omen. Undoubtedly it spotted the submarine and advised Japanese Headquarters of Cisco's westerly course.

Nothing was heard of Cisco after she left Port Darwin. But her patrol area was charted as a large rectangle in the South China Sea between Luzon and French Indo-China. To reach this area, she was scheduled to cross the Celebes Sea, transit Sibutu Passage, cross the Sulu Sea and go on through Mindoro Strait. On September 28, the day of the Japanese onslaught on the oil-leaking submarine in the Sulu Sea, Cisco was due to be covering that lap of her westward journey. No other United States or Allied submarine was scheduled in those waters at that time.

In the submarine forces, "Red" Coe had made a name for himself as one of the ablest and keenest submarine commanders. As the pioneer captain of S-39, the hard-hitting skipper of SKIPJACK, the author of a classic in Navy correspondence (Subject: paper work) and an all-round American submariner, Coe personified the type of leader who held the line when the going was worst in the undersea war.

The submarine war was moving west. GRAYLING and CISCO had been in the vanguard of a drive that was to break the Japanese grip on Singapore and free the Philippines.

Depth-charging of Puffer

PUFFER came back from the East Indies-Philippines front in late October with a depth-charging story long to be remembered in the Submarine Service. Even in the formal language of a naval report the narrative packs a dramatic punch, and the episode remains a notable example of Japanese attack and submarine reaction in the A/S war. Between the lines one sees a vivid picture of a submersible under fire—the doings within the pressure hull—the reflexes of assailed machines and men. Perhaps the most extraordinary feature of the detailed experience is the psychological footnote at its conclusion. Here is the story:

On October 9, 1943, PUFFER, under Lieutenant Commander M. J. Jensen, was patrolling the northern waters of Makassar Straits. Mid-morning she was on the track of a large Japanese merchant ship. At 1110 she hit the merchantman with two torpedoes. The target stopped dead in the water and assumed a list, but refused to sink. Thereupon, at 1119 Jensen fired two well-intended torpedoes from the stern tubes. One of these prematured. The other torpedo missed or was a dud. So Jensen maneuvered for another attack.

The merchantman's escort, a CHIDORI-class torpedo boat, had been seen earlier in the morning, but was at this time nowhere in the offing. Left to defend herself, the damaged merchant ship opened fire on the submarine, blazing away with small-caliber guns.

Then, at 1125 three distant depth charges were heard by PUFFER's sound operator, and a few minutes later there was "pinging" and Sound reported fast screws approaching. Jensen decided to clear the vicinity. He still hoped to finish off the merchantman, however, so he did not order deep submergence. Then the attack came, unexpected as a rain of lightning bolts.

At 1145 six depth charges exploded near the submarine. During this barrage, the conning-tower hatch and the conning-tower door lifted off their seats and reseated, admitting a shower of water as they did so. A number of sea valves backed off their seats. A plug in a sea-valve casting in the after torpedo room was loosened, and water spurted from this leak, jetting from under the plug in a flat stream the size of a knife blade. The submariners were afraid to tighten the plug, for if it were broken instead of only loose, any attempted repairs would worsen the fracture.

PUFFER's rudder and the stern planes had apparently suffered damage, for their operation was noisy and the motors appeared to be overloaded. Gaskets were found blown out of the main engine air-induction valve and the ventilation supply valves. Considerable miscellaneous and minor damage was reported, and flakes of cork and splinters of glass were everywhere. PUFFER went deep.

Ten minutes later another depth charge slammed near-by. Fifteen minutes after that, four depth charges went off overhead, staggered in depth. It was evident the enemy was able to follow the submarine. The slow venting of the main induction and air supply trunk, as they flooded past the ruptured gaskets, may have been leaving a trail of air bubbles. Or there might have been oil leaks. The current

interfered with evasive maneuvers (when PUFFER's ordeal was finally over, she surfaced in the same place where she submerged—all her underwater running had been just enough to overcome the racing current).

Practically all of the damage done to PUFFER was inflicted during the first attack. Thereafter she remained at a deep submergence, held down by the obdurate tenacity of the CHIDORI "pinger." Most of the enemy's depth charges went off close by and directly overhead, but they were not set deep enough to crush the submarine with their explosions. But the torpedo boat was not to be easily eluded. After dropping a string of charges, she would sidle off, only to return an hour or two later to make another try. The enemy's perseverance and the ease with which he located the submarine were most unnerving.

PUFFER's crew had difficulty with her depth control. There was a lot of water in the bilges, and the main induction and supply lines were flooded. The leak in the after torpedo room continually added to the weight aft, and the trim pump was unable to pick up a suction on the after torpedo-room bilges. Gradually the submarine worked her way deeper until the control room was at an alarming depth level. There was a 12° angle on the boat when the motors moved her at slow speed. Few submarines had ever gone so deep—and the fact provided a mental hazard hard to overcome.

Meantime, the air conditioning was stopped to conserve power and prevent noise. A bucket brigade was formed to control the bilge water and forestall the grounding out of the electrical motors. After PUFFER had been submerged about 12 hours, CO_2 absorbent and oxygen were used. The specific gravity of the battery electrolyte went so low it could no longer be read on the hydrometer.

PUFFER had not been severely damaged. She had no insoluble problem of ship handling. Jensen's evasion maneuvers were conventional and correct. The anti-submarine attack made upon her was unique only in the stubborn perseverance with which it was conducted and the consistency with which the enemy tracked PUFFER and depth-charged her position. The submarine had been submerged since 0525, and it was late in the day when a second anti-submarine vessel joined the first at 1820. These enemies hammered at PUFFER until well after midnight. The last depth charges were dropped at 0115 on the morning of October 10, but the Japs remained over PUFFER making "dry runs" until 1225 that day. Thirty-one hours after PUFFER first submerged, and more than 25 hours after her attack on the merchantman, the enemy finally left, and the counter-attack was over.

After Sound reported "pinging" had stopped, Jensen decided to remain at deep submergence until after nightfall. PUFFER was in difficult trim, and an immediate attempt to rise to periscope depth might have ended in loss of control. Safety tanks, negative, auxiliary tank, and after trim had been blown dry and had pressure in them. There was a 12-inch pressure in the boat already, which practically prevented the venting of these tanks into the boat. The submariners endured until 1910 when PUFFER surfaced direct from deep submergence into bright moonlight, almost 31 hours after diving. She surfaced with a sharp port list, caused by the free water and the flooded induction lines, and it was nearly an hour before the crew could bring her to an even keel. Listing as she was, the submarine made a helpless target, for the crew was unable to use the 3-inch deck gun. Contact with an enemy patrol was made about 15 minutes after surfacing. Jensen maneuvered to evade, and PUFFER was not attacked. At 0450 on the morning of October 11, she was able to make a trim dive, and no serious leaks were found. Jensen held her down all that day to rest the crew and then headed PUFFER for home.

The mechanical features of PUFFER's experience—what happened to her machinery, and the measures taken to keep her going—these were not the chief items of interest in her report. Submarines had endured worse "goings over," suffered more damage, gone perhaps as deep. What was of paramount concern to the Force Command was the reaction of PUFFER's personnel—how the submariners stood up under it, how they behaved, what they were thinking about during the long ordeal. New machines and new techniques would enter submarining in the next decade. But the mechanics of the human mind vary little with the passing of generations—men reacted to stresses and strains yesterday much as they will tomorrow. So the conduct of PUFFER's crew was carefully studied for clues in behaviorism. Her patrol report was psychoanalyzed, so to speak, and from this analysis a number of interesting conclusions were drawn.

The mental can never be divorced from the physical, and the reactions of PUFFER's crew can be seen as intimately related to the submarine's condition—particularly its air conditioning. When that was shut off, the heat became insufferable. Temperature of 125° F. was reported in the maneuvering room. The forward torpedo room was suffocatingly hot. The after torpedo room and the engine room were the coolest compartments in the submarine, but the almost glutinous humidity was higher in the cooler rooms than in the hot spots, and the steam-room atmosphere

was like a drug. Decks and bulkheads became clammy with condensed moisture. Rivulets of sweat would form and follow behind a towel rubbed over a man's body. The men gasped for breath and slipped on the greasy decks.

Although the temperature in the after torpedo room was probably well over 100° F., men going from the maneuvering room reported that they shivered and shook as with a chill. The human body possesses no mechanism for reducing its temperature below ambient wet-bulb temperature. It was therefore probable that in such places as PUFFER's maneuvering room the men developed a high fever. While there were no reports of delirium, the sudden chill indicated that such fever did exist.

Sweating like boxers, the submariners thirsted for cool drinks. But fruit juices, coffee, and water soon reached room temperature. Frequently the swallowing of these warm liquids induced immediate vomiting. Yet thirst was so great the men were constantly drinking, vomiting, drinking again. Profuse sweating and inability to keep down liquids produced many cases of severe dehydration. No one in the submarine cared to eat anything.

The bucket brigade, fighting the mounting water in the motor room bilges, struggled against extreme fatigue. Hourly the air in the submarine worsened. Despite the use of CO_2 absorbent and oxygen, the atmosphere was utterly foul toward the end of the dive. Breathing was sluggish and resultant headache was severe. An officer making the rounds from control room to after torpedo room had to stop and rest several times on the journey. He found a number of the men in a state of physical collapse. From the stupor in which they sank, it became impossible to rouse them to go on watch. As the hours wore on, stations were manned by volunteers. Some of the crew were past the stage of caring what happened.

Both officers and men stated that their first mental reaction to the enemy attack was anger. They were infuriated at everything and anything. They were particularly angry at themselves for having allowed themselves to be caught in such a predicament. They cursed themselves for having offered to serve in submarines. They cursed the enemy A/S vessel for its persistence. They spent much time daydreaming about what they could do to the torpedo boat above them, and discussing such fantastic ideas as discharging acid around the enemy craft to eat holes in its hull. Anyone compelled to take a beating without being able to fight back finds it one of the world's hardest punishments to endure, and the submariners who stood it for 31 hours would not soon forget the experience.

WILL THE NEXT ONE STRIKE? Men in USS Puffer *listen to thunder of depth charges as a persistent enemy tags their submarine. Heat, fouling air and prolonged suspense could try the nerve of all hands in a submerged sub under fire. Puffer's ordeal lasted 31 hours. Other subs survived worse ordeals.*

MOTORMAC ADJUSTING VALVE in submarine's engine room. Maze of operating gear makes sub world's most complex vessel.

HANDS UP! Trout captures Jap lugger off Indo-China. Craft may have radio, Jap officer below decks.

TORPEDOED BY SILVERSIDES in SoWesPac area, Johore Maru settles bottomward. Few U. S. subs sank more ships or tonnage than Silversides, skippered at this date (October 1943) by Comdr. J. S. Coye—a great sub-captain.

TORPEDOED BY PADDLE, Ataka Maru sinks off the coast of Honshu (August 23, 1943). Another twist to the blockade tourniquet that was stemming Imperial commerce and numbing Japan.

TORPEDOED BY TAMBOR, Eisho Maru pauses for photo before taking the fatal plunge. U. S. subs (spring of 1943) were blockading Truk and Palau.

The suspense proved the hardest thing to bear. PUFFER's officers stated that because of this fact, the ordeal was harder on the men than on the officers. When on watch, the officers were in the conning tower or control room. At such times they knew the proximity of the enemy, the state of the battery, what was being done to evade. For the most part, they were busy in some manner or other. Many of the men, however, not engaged in some useful task, could only sit and think, and imaginations were fed by lack of information. To remedy this, the officers occasionally went through the boat and described what was happening overhead. Use of the public-address system proved annoying, as the feeling existed that its noise might disclose the location of the submarine. The conning-tower telephone talker passed information to the other talkers on the fire control telephone circuits. This was found to be best for spreading the word, and later became standard practice.

PUFFER's crew recorded a word of solid advice for those who might have to go through a similar experience: "Find something to do, and keep busy." Men who were idle suffered more from the imprisonment—the realization that an hour or so had gone by since the last attack, and another attack would come soon. Then to hear the approaching vessel, the "pinging" of her echo-ranging as she deliberately and methodically probed for the submarine, followed by the rush of racing screws and the thunderous detonation of a depth-charge salvo—this repetitious build-up and climax, worsened by anticipation, resulted in the hardest sort of nerve strain.

None of the officers reported any difficulty in reaching decisions, but they pointed out that no involved or rapid-fire calculations were called for. The major issue was whether or not to surface and fight it out with the gun—a desperate resort when the opponent was a heavily armed CHIDORI. Another question concerned the choice between speeding up the motors for evasive action, or conserving the remaining battery and waiting where they were until dark. In this connection, one of the enlisted men reported that he was asked to vote for or against an immediate rise to the surface. He expressed himself as willing to go along either way, but he refused to accept the responsibility of a commitment one way or the other. Apparently few of PUFFER's company advocated a gun action in daylight. The submarine carried a 3-inch. Several of the men thought the armament inadequate—with a pair of 5-inch guns they could have given a good account of themselves on the surface. But in any event, a submarine in PUFFER's situation could not well have risked a gun duel with a CHIDORI.

As time went by, dragging leaden minutes into endless hours, as the air fouled into a sewerish gas, as men's sweating bodies weakened in the enervating heat, morale wilted, and in some cases expired. One man suggested flooding everything and getting it over quickly with mass suicide. Another, who had received a minor but most painful injury, appeared incapable of understanding what went on about him. Toward the end of the long submergence, officers as well as men apparently reached the conclusion that they would never come out of it alive. The ease with which the enemy repeatedly located the submarine forced them to this depressing conclusion. Pessimism was climaxed when, after remaining at deep submergence for many hours, all hands were ordered to put on life jackets.

In the engine room a man broke out of his locker three cans of pineapple juice and passed them around. It seemed no longer necessary to save anything "for when things got worse." Everyone questioned had a vivid recollection of the tremendous psychological blow that was dealt by the order to don life jackets. The order was given to provide against a sudden contingency which might force PUFFER to the surface. Experience had demonstrated that, in event of accident and emergency, life jackets saved lives. But the adverse reaction in PUFFER's case suggested that a crew should be prepared for such a seemingly drastic eventuality before the order is given. All critics of PUFFER's report pointed out that the mental state of a submarine's crew is the determining factor in a life-or-death issue under the sea. Deterioration of crew morale can be as disastrous as damage to the submarine's machinery. For this reason, critics considered it a mistake to shut down PUFFER's air conditioning. A submarine crew in a tight situation is exceedingly allergic to noise—a squeaky pair of sandals was recalled by one of PUFFER's crew. Nevertheless, the crew would have accepted the noise of the air-conditioning machine and ventilation blowers in preference to the stupifying heat and humidity. In restrospect, the submariners agreed that the operation of the air-conditioning machine would have been less dangerous than the cataleptic mental reaction induced by heat exhaustion and fatigue.

Despite the fact that there were few duties to perform, PUFFER's company got little sleep. An officer stated that in four hours off watch he napped for about 15 minutes. He recalled this with bitterness because the nap was broken by the order to don life jackets. The steaming, hothouse atmosphere was at once a soporific and a narcotic. Huddled around anything that seemed cool—an uninsulated portion of the hull, or an exposed circulation water pipe—the submariners panted, muttered and stirred as though in the grip of somnambulistic nightmare.

After the submarine surfaced and was out of danger, its crew recovered physically with great rapidity. Within 24 hours, all were physically normal. But for days thereafter, there was evidence of mental strain. If the diving officer wanted to work the vents, he had to pass the word quietly through the boat beforehand. Coming without warning, the noise of opening the vents had been enough to bring every man out of his bunk, standing.

PUFFER's officers arrived at a number of conclusions, and these were noted by the Force Command. When a submarine had gone through such an experience, its crew should be broken up. The sharing of PUFFER's ordeal welded her men together in a fraternal, almost mystic bond, and no newcomer was able to penetrate the inner circle. Men who subsequently made several successful patrols on PUFFER were still "outsiders"—not members of the gang. They hadn't been through THE depth-charging.

Another observation was recorded for submariners of the future: "Be slow to form an estimate of a man's value before you have seen him under stress." Most of the men who were on their feet, working to save themselves and the ship when PUFFER's long dive was over, were not the previous "leaders" of the crew. Those who lasted out were of a more phlegmatic disposition—the ones who didn't bother too much when things were running smoothly.

PUFFER's experienced critics left for the submarine force this curtain line: *The worriers and the hurriers all crapped out, leaving the plodders to bring home the ship.*

Loss of Capelin

Even before the landings on Bougainville and MacArthur's drive on New Britain, the Japanese High Command saw handwriting on the wall—or was it a graph of merchant ship losses?—and set to work on those "previously prepared positions" to which high commanders who have overextended their lines like to make "strategic withdrawals." With Halsey's Third Fleet in the Upper Solomons and MacArthur's troops holding the northeast coast of New Guinea from Milne Bay to the end of the Huon Peninsula, Tokyo was evidently beginning to suspect that the Bismarcks might one day become untenable. Accordingly, Japanese engineers were working on plans to build a powerful fortress on the island of Halmahera, to defend the Celebes area in the event that the Allies might drive on toward the Malay Barrier.

It was in this area that CAPELIN may have been lost—the last submarine to be lost to the Southwest Pacific Force in 1943.

One of the newcomers to the Pacific, CAPELIN had set out on October 31 to conduct her first war patrol. She was captained by Commander E. E. Marshall, who had previously commanded CUTTLEFISH. On November 11 she sank the 3,127-ton Japanese freighter KUNITAMA MARU. Five days later she returned to Port Darwin with a defective conning-tower hatch mechanism, troublesome bow planes and a bad radar tube.

Repairs at Darwin were quickly made—Commander Marshall was satisfied that the submarine was in fighting trim—and CAPELIN once more stood seaward. She was to patrol in the Molucca and Celebes Seas, investigate Kaoe Bay, Halmahera, and hunt shipping in Moratai Strait, Davao Gulf and the vicinity of the Sarangani Islands.

Nothing was heard from CAPELIN after her belated leave-taking of Darwin. The Japanese recorded an attack on an American submarine off Kaoe Bay on November 23rd. CAPELIN was due in the Halmahera area about that time. However, the Japanese attack was of short duration as the contact was uncertain and soon lost. Evidence that CAPELIN was the target remained less than circumstantial.

BONEFISH reported sighting a U. S. submarine on December 2, just north of the equator in waters assigned to CAPELIN on that date. An attempt to reach CAPELIN by radio on December 9 proved unavailing, and subsequent radio transmissions remained unanswered. Official conjecture included the possibility of an operational casualty or a minefield explosion.

In the Celebes Sea? Molucca Passage? The Molucca Sea? The waters closed over CAPELIN and she went down with all hands.

CHAPTER 22

CENTRAL PACIFIC OFFENSIVE

Operation Galvanic

The young men with fur on their chins and chests could feel a bristling in the air. Coming back from patrol, they could scent it in the atmosphere—as noticeable as the autumn snap back home where the frost would be bracing the landscape and down the road would come a smell of burning leaves. No frost here in the islands of pineapple and three-fingered *poi*. But an atmosphere reminiscent of hunting—a gathering of guns—a massing of big smoke. Things were looking up at Pearl Harbor.

"I tell you, Joe, these fast carrier task forces are going places. What with a new YORKTOWN and this ESSEX and LEXINGTON—"

"And the smaller carriers—INDEPENDENCE, PRINCETON, BELLEAU WOOD and LISCOME BAY."

"Telling me? Listen, sailor, I got the word. Just this morning from a buddy at the U.S.O. He—"

"Scuttlebutt! But Nimitz has got something cooking. This big stuff isn't here for nothing. It's good to see the surface navy around again."

The big warships were gathering, and the submariners were glad to see it. And if the above dialogue is fictional, the fact that Nimitz had something on the fire in the autumn of 1943 is history.

The Solomons push was a first round, a preliminary in what was to develop as a steamroller Pacific drive. In winning control of the Upper Solomons, the Allied forces threw the enemy back in the South Pacific and started him worrying about his Malay Barrier defenses. Round two—a smash at the Gilbert Islands—was calculated to crush the easternmost stronghold of Japan's expanded Empire and hurl the foe back on his heels in the Central Pacific. While Halsey's Third Fleet was starting the Upper Solomons campaign, Admiral Nimitz was completing plans for "Operation Galvanic"—the drive to take the Gilberts.

Ten submarines cooperated with the carrier task forces and amphibious landing forces in "Operation Galvanic." Long before D-Day submarines reconnoitered the target islands, investigated the fortifications, studied the approaches and hit at the Japanese traffic. NAUTILUS and ARGONAUT had been there the previous year with Carlson's Raiders. And two months in advance of D-Day, NAUTILUS was in the Gilberts at Apamama on a mission intimately connected with the projected offensive. Details of this drama-packed Apamama mission will presently be recounted.

As seen on the chart on page 285, the Gilbert Islands (Makin, the Tarawa Group and Apamama) lie like a cluster of fruit on the end of a laden branch. Other clusters are the near-by Marshalls and Carolines, and the branch—conceive it as composed of sea lanes—comes down from the Marianas in the northwest.

Key islands of the enemy's Central Pacific transport system, the Marianas (Guam and Saipan) were the distributing point for war supplies freighted down from Japan and destined for the Mandate outposts. From Saipan and Guam the cargoes followed the southeast sea lanes to the Carolines, Marshalls and Gilberts.

Here, then, in the Central Pacific, as in the South and Southwest Pacific, the submarines on patrol, fighting the war of attrition, supported fleet operations by intercepting Japanese convoys, damaging or sinking Japanese troop and cargo transports and otherwise disrupting and destroying Japanese shipping. While it is impossible to estimate the tonnage which left the Marianas for the Gilberts in the spring, summer and autumn of 1943, it is certain that a considerable share of the shipping sent southeast from Saipan and Guam was tagged for delivery to Makin or Tarawa. After the Makin raid, the Japs made a determined effort to reinforce the Gilberts (an effort that showed in the Tarawa defense) and the guns and men came by way of the routes described. It can therefore be assumed that many of the ships sunk by U.S. submarines patrolling off the Marianas, Carolines and Marshalls in the first nine months of 1943 carried cargoes and troops for Tarawa and Makin. In this respect the attrition war fought by SubPac contributed to the ultimate success of "Operation Galvanic." Over the sunken skeletons of dead supply ships the American invasion forces drove in to the Gilbert beachheads.

Pre-Galvanic Attrition War

Unlike the South and Southwest Pacific, thickly strewn with islands and stepping-stone archipelagoes, the Central Pacific has far horizons and endless reaches of latitude and longitude uninterrupted by any landfall. Island groups are as few and far between as oases in the Sahara. Shipping lanes, like caravan lanes, follow established navigational routes —in peacetime. In wartime, with oceans of latitude for evasive routing, a convoy may travel in as many roundabout directions as there are points on the compass. This open-sea shipping presents the hunting submarine with a problem not unlike the Touareg Saharan raider's. The raider may roam the great open spaces for days, and then miss his quarry over the next dune. The Touareg, therefore, lies in wait near a terminal oasis. So it is with the hunting submarine.

The vast expanses of the Central Pacific were not patrolled in haphazard, hit-or-miss fashion. There was the Empire blockade and the Truk blockade— submarine concentrations on shipping focal points. Around the Pelews, the Marianas, the Marshalls and Gilberts the SubPac patrols were blocked out as part of a carefully designed pattern. Seven patrol areas boxed in the Marshalls and Gilberts. The waters off Saipan and Guam were similarly covered. Pacific Fleet submarines traveled in these designated areas with much the same regularity as planets in their orbits.

"Operation Galvanic" struck at the Gilberts on November 21st. From the previous spring to that date, SubPac submarines operating in the Central Pacific between the 10° and 24° parallels, in an oceanic belt which embraced the Marianas and northern Marshalls, waylaid, sank or damaged dozens of Japanese merchant ships. POMPANO, THRESHER, NAUTILUS, SEADRAGON and POLLACK torpedoed and damaged enemy vessels in that area during this period.

In March, the submarine WHALE, under Lieutenant Commander A. C. Burrows, sank the 6,486-ton freighter KENYO MARU off the Carolines. In May she was back to sink SHOEI MARU, a smaller freighter, in the same area. August 8, she sank NARUTO MARU, aircraft ferry, 7,149 tons, in waters nearer the Marianas.

On March 28, TUNNY torpedoed the 10,672-ton transport SUWA MARU off Wake. The ship was beached and later finished off by FINBACK and SEADRAGON.

SEAWOLF (Lieutenant Commander R. L. Gross) got two off the Carolines in April—the cargoman KAIHEI MARU, 4,575 tons, and an old destroyer, Patrol Boat No. 39.

PLUNGER (Lieutenant Commander R. H. Bass) in May sank two large passenger-cargomen off the Carolines, as reported in a previous reference to the Mandates patrols.

PORPOISE (Lieutenant Commander C. L. Bennet) sank MIKAGE MARU No. 20, 2,718-ton passenger-cargoman, off the Marshalls in July. PIKE (Lieutenant Commander L. D. McGregor) sank SHOJU MARU, a similar-sized AP in the same general area on August 5th. As already related, POGY (Lieutenant Commander G. H. Wales) destroyed the aircraft ferry NOGAMIGAWA MARU, in those waters on August 1st.

ON OCTOBER 6, off the Carolines, TINOSA and STEELHEAD cornered the large tanker KAZAHAYA and sent her down in a gush of blazing oil.

And in November, with "Galvanic's" D-Day coming up on the calendar, the attrition war in the Mandates gained momentum. SARGO (Lieutenant Commander P. W. Garnett) sank TAGA MARU, freighter, and KOSEI MARU, passenger-cargoman, to down some 6,000 Japanese tons west of the Carolines on the 9th and 11th.

HARDER (Lieutenant Commander Dealey) broke loose on the 19th and 20th, sinking UDO MARU, HOKKO MARU, and NIKKO MARU, three freighters in a row, to deposit some 15,000 tons of cargo beneath waves to the eastward of the Marianas. HARDER was wolf-packing at the time with SNOOK (Lieutenant Commander C. O. Triebel) and PARGO (Lieutenant Commander I. C. Eddy)—the pack operating under Commander "Freddie" Warder. SNOOK accounted for

YAMAFUKU MARU, passenger-cargoman, 4,928 tons, and the freighter SHIGANOURA MARU, 3,512 tons. PARGO destroyed the two freighters, MANJU MARU and SHOKO MARU for a total of some 7,500 tons. Warder's attack group, striking while the Gilberts campaign was at its height, cost enemy shipping in the Marianas area over 31,000 tons.

These spring-to-December attrition sinkings (taken at random—there were others) deprived the enemy in the Gilberts of thousands of rounds of ammunition, thousands of pounds of food, thousands of items of war gear. At the easternmost end of the Central Pacific transportation vine, the Gilbert Islands were "out on a branch." Tarawa proved thorny and poisonous. But the vine in this area, even as in the Solomons, had been blighted by the fire of submarine torpedoes. Tarawa's fall was assured.

Preliminary Operations (Submarine Lifeguarding)

In August, 1943, the new Pacific Fleet aircraft carriers and light carriers with their supporting cruisers and destroyers were organized into Task Force Fifteen, under Rear Admiral Charles A. Pownall. This fast carrier task force (nucleus of what later became Task Force Fifty-eight) was to pull the trigger of "Operation Galvanic." But by way of preparatory overtures, it was to conduct a series of hit-and-run raids.

In planning these raids, Admiral Pownall considered the problem of rescuing airmen who might be downed at sea. Could ComSubPac furnish a submarine to be stationed near each target island for the purpose of rescuing downed airmen? Admiral Lockwood not only could, but did.

Pacific Fleet submarines had engaged in similar activities before. PIKE, TRITON and FINBACK had cooperated with aircraft during a strike at Midway in December 1942. In April 1943, TARPON had patrolled off Naru and Tarawa to loan navigational aid to planes making air strikes. On May 16, WHALE had played the same role off Wake. While navigational assistance was the primary duty in these missions, the submarines were given the additional duty of rescuing any aviators forced down at sea. Rescues had not been necessary during the patrols enumerated, but an idea had germinated. Now, in the autumn of 1943, it was to reach the budding stage.

As a result of Admiral Pownall's requests, SNOOK (Lieutenant Commander C. O. Triebel) was on station off Marcus Island when the planes of Task Force Fifteen roared out of the blue on September 1st. The strike punished the island like a tornado. There was no opportunity for submarine rescue work, as American losses were unusually light.

STEELHEAD (Lieutenant Commander D. L. Whelchel) was on duty off Tarawa on the 20th when planes from LEXINGTON, PRINCETON and BELLEAU WOOD dropped 80 tons of bombs on this Gilbert Island base. Again there was no occasion for submarine rescue work.

The first successful submarine lifeguard mission was performed during the strike on Wake, made October 6-7 by Task Force Fourteen, under Rear Admiral A. E. Montgomery. This strike, a combined aircraft-cruiser bombardment, hit the island with hurricane fury. The enemy had been forewarned, however, and a number of American planes were shot down. While the battle was at its height, the submarine assigned to lifeguard duty in the area accomplished several daring rescues. She was SKATE, under the captaincy of veteran Commander E. B. McKinney.

SKATE's lifeguard patrol did not begin happily. At dawn on October 6, the day of the first strike, she was savagely strafed by an enemy plane. In this action, Lieutenant (jg) W. E. Maxon was seriously wounded. His wounds did not appear fatal, however, and SKATE continued her patrol.

At 0545 on the morning of October 7, SKATE sighted several squadrons of American planes which were searching for the target island. Signals were exchanged, and the dive bombers were informed as to Wake's direction.

At 0915 SKATE's bridge personnel were watching the furious bombardment. On the search for downed aviators, McKinney moved the submarine on a line about six miles offshore. At 1043 several heavy shells landed in the sea close by, and McKinney ordered SKATE under. When the submarine again surfaced at 1128, she received the word that three airmen were down.

McKinney trimmed down and headed SKATE shoreward in the direction given. The rescue party—Ensign Francis Kay; William A. Shelton, Gunner's Mate 3; and Arthur G. Smith, Torpedoman's Mate 3—crouched on SKATE's bow as the submarine moved in. Japs on the beach opened fire, and shells began to drop around SKATE, but the aviators were there in the water and the submarine lifeguard swam resolutely to the rescue.

Lieutenant H. J. Kicker was plucked from a rubber boat. A few minutes later, SKATE was alongside an aviator who was struggling in the water. As the swimmer appeared exhausted, Torpedoman's Mate Smith swam to him with a life ring. The rescued airman was Ensign M. H. Tyler.

Search for a third airman off Peacock Point was interrupted by an attacking Jap dive bomber. A bomb shook the submarine as she dived, smashing her searchlight and damaging the bow-buoyancy vent-operating mechanism. Repairs were quickly made, and SKATE surfaced after eluding the planes.

Meantime Lieutenant Maxon's condition had worsened. This casualty presented ComSubPac with a difficult question for decision. When Maxon's condition was first reported, ComSubPac requested that Com Task Force Fourteen arrange for a destroyer to rendezvous with SKATE and take off the wounded officer. SKATE was directed to attempt this rendezvous. If it did not eventuate, she was to proceed to Midway at best speed upon completion of her special mission.

On the afternoon of October 7 the air strike was over. Having been unable to effect the rendezvous with the destroyer, McKinney headed SKATE for Midway at top speed as directed. Maxon was now in a most critical condition, and all hands were pulling to save his life.

But the ruthless urgency of war intervened. As SKATE was stepping out for Midway, a message came in from Admiral Montgomery—nine aviators were adrift on life-rafts in the vicinity of Wake. The decision was up to ComSubPac who had to weigh the prospects of Maxon's chances for life against the equally slim prospect of locating nine airmen adrift in the open sea. The decision was made, and SKATE was ordered to return to Wake and hunt for the nine until all chances of rescue were exhausted.

On the morning of October 8, Lieutenant Maxon succumbed to his wounds—two days before SKATE could have reached Midway, had she continued the homeward race at top speed. In any event, Lieutenant Maxon did not lose his life in vain. On October 9, off Wake, SKATE picked up another aviator and three more were recovered the next day, to bring the total to six aviators rescued.

After this successful rescue effort, the commanding officer of LEXINGTON radioed to SKATE: "*Anything on LEXINGTON is yours for the asking. If it is too big to carry away, we will cut it up in small parts.*"

From that time until V-J Day no important carrier strike was made without one or more submarines on the scene of action as lifeguards.

Submarine Photographic Reconnaissance (Nautilus with a Candid Camera)

In planning for the Gilbert Islands campaign, Rear Admiral R. K. Turner, who was in command of Amphibious Forces, requested photographic reconnaissance of Makin, Tarawa and Apamama by submarine. Admiral Nimitz approved the request, and Admiral Lockwood picked NAUTILUS as the submarine to do the job.

Periscope photography had been under consideration before the war, and steps had since been taken to obtain suitable cameras and adapt them for periscope use. But little experimental work in reconnaissance photography had been done. Lieutenant Commander Parks, pioneering one of the first reconnaissance missions, had taken photographs of enemy shorelines. Other captains had photographed sinkings with notable success. Periscope cameras had been designed primarily for the photographing of enemy ships and action scenes.

However, reconnaissance photographs must contain exact and minute detail if they are to prove of any value for intelligence purposes. The camera-eye must be clear. And the picture, taken from a range of several thousand yards, must be sharp enough to reveal the presence or absence of machine-gun positions, artillery, or other defense installations on enemy beachheads, camouflaged or otherwise. Intelligence experts can recognize camouflage—the clearer the picture, the easier such recognition. But no pre-war study had been exclusively devoted to such periscope photography. The techniques of periscope photographic reconnaissance were wartime developments. A major portion of the credit for their successful development goes to NAUTILUS—the first submarine to conduct a full-fledged photo reconnaissance mission.

In selecting her for the task, Admiral Lockwood made a fortunate choice. Her captain at this time, Commander W. D. Irvin, was unusually thorough and painstaking in everything he undertook. Moreover, unknown to ComSubPac when the choice was made, her executive officer, Lieutenant Commander R. B. Lynch, was a camera enthusiast, experienced in the art of photography.

At Pearl Harbor Submarine Base, brackets for the mounting of the camera on the periscope were built. The necessary photographic supplies were taken aboard NAUTILUS, and an enlisted rated photographer was assigned to the submarine for temporary duty. (The photographer could have used six hands, and on all subsequent photo reconnaissance missions two enlisted photographers were aboard.) The lower sound room was fitted up to be used as a darkroom and photographic laboratory for processing the exposed film. Processing on board was necessary in order to permit the retaking of any pictures which did not turn out satisfactorily. Thus equipped, on September 16, 1943, NAUTILUS departed on her mission.

Brady, setting out with his little black wagon to photograph the battlefields of the Civil War, was no more of a novice than Irvin, setting out with

NAUTILUS to photograph the beachheads of Makin, Tarawa and Apamama. In either case the venture was dangerous, the camera work untried and the ultimate outcome uncertain. Brady had one advantage—his black wagon did not have to penetrate the enemy's lines.

NAUTILUS was equipped with several cameras. The Eastman Medalist was standard issue, and NAUTILUS also carried a National Graflex, Series II, and an "Eastman 35" which was specially designed for periscope photography. The Medalist camera was considered the finest in the field, but it lacked a reflex viewfinder. The "Eastman 35" and the Graflex had this feature, but it was soon apparent that all of these cameras were inadequate for the job at hand.

The submarine periscope embodied a number of peculiarities which made periscope photography difficult. When the periscope was raised, vibrations within the submarine or the movement of the periscope through the water caused the periscope's head to vibrate. These vibrations, magnified as the light strikes the lenses and passes down the tube, created a blurred photograph unless high-speed camera shutters were used. However, the efficiency of light transmission through the periscope was something like 35% in high power, and this "dim view" necessitated low shutter-speeds.

Lacking a viewer, the Medalist camera proved impractical. The "Eastman 35" produced too small a picture. The Graflex, which caught the first and one of the finest submarine combat pictures of the war, was not suitable for the present operation. Fortunately for the NAUTILUS mission, Lieutenant Commander Lynch happened to have his own camera aboard.

This camera, a Primarflex, had a single-lens reflex viewfinder and a focal-plane shutter which was ideal for the work in prospect (a focal-plane shutter stops action better than a between-lens shutter). Lynch's Primarflex was pressed into service, and NAUTILUS' camera problem was over. In fact, the Primarflex solved the periscope photography problem for the U.S. Submarine Force. All subsequent submarine photo reconnaissance missions were performed with this type of camera. Ironically enough, it was of German manufacture. It could not be imported for love or money, but the Bureau of Aeronautics (in charge of all matters appertaining to photography in the Navy) could and did advertise for the camera in various photographic trade journals. These unusual "want ads" netted ten Primarflex cameras. Stored at PRISIC (Photographic Reconnaissance and Interpretation Section, Intelligence Center) the second-hand cameras were eventually issued to the submarines sent out on photo reconnaissance missions. Thus a camera made in Germany contributed to the downfall of Japan.

The tactical problems which had to be solved by NAUTILUS were as difficult as the photographic one. Reefs around the atolls prevented camera work at short ranges, and the danger of detection by enemy lookouts or sentries limited the raising of the periscope head to a height of about six feet. A mental hazard was introduced by the possibility of minefields along the coastline. But these were perils incident to any submarine reconnaissance mission off an enemy base.

Procedure on this first photographic reconnaissance mission set the pattern for those that followed. A whole roll of 12 pictures was taken at each periscope exposure. The field being eight degrees in high power, the periscope was rotated about four degrees after each camera shot to give a picture overlap of three or four degrees. Before the exposure of each roll of film, the position of the submarine was accurately fixed by landmarks. This position was marked on the chart, and a notation of the number of the film roll exposed in that position was made. Also vectors were drawn to show the included angle covered by the film roll. Following the exposure of each roll, the submarine moved down the coast a short distance to repeat the process. An overlap of about fifty per cent on each successive roll insured against leaving "holidays."

After the film was developed, each photo was mounted so as to match with the next. In this manner, a continuous panorama of the coastline was obtained.

The work of NAUTILUS on this Gilbert Islands mission did more than solve the problems of technique and procedure. It also established the value of this type of reconnaissance. As a consequence of the standards set by Irvin and crew, every amphibious operation in the Pacific thereafter was preceded by submarine photographic reconnaissance.

The arranging of these reconnaissance missions evolved into a fixed pattern. Commander Amphibious Forces would request CinCPac to have the submarine reconnaissance conducted. CinCPac would evaluate the request and, if he considered that the information to be gained would compensate for the loss of the submarines' patrol effort, he would direct ComSubPac to carry out the mission. ComSubPac would then select a submarine for the job, and would request JICPOA (Joint Intelligence Center, Pacific Ocean Area) to prepare detailed instructions for the conduct of the reconnaissance, and to detail photographers from PRISIC for temporary duty. Then

JICPOA would compile all the available information concerning the islands involved—would list navigational aids, tidal data, prominent landmarks and so on—and would specify the exact photographic coverage desired. In some cases JICPOA prepared special area charts to assist the submarine. The tie-in with JICPOA spared the submarine useless effort in compiling either nonessential information or information which had previously been obtained.

An officer from PRISIC was then assigned to work with the engineer and repair department of the base. His job was to install the camera brackets on the periscope, see that the cameras were properly adjusted to give best results, and train the submariners in their use. Finally, the photographers and photographic equipment would go aboard, and the submarine would sail.

The success of submarine photographic reconnaissance was dependent to a great extent upon the geographic contours of the enemy coast. Islands surrounded by outlying reefs, or hemmed by long stretches of shoaling water, defeated periscope photography—the submarines could not get in near enough to obtain pictures with worthwhile detail. Where the island waters were deep right up to the shore (as at Iwo Jima) pictures of great value to Intelligence were obtained. Good periscope pictures had to be taken at ranges of less than one mile, and the best were taken at something like 500 yards. With a submarine drawing a minimum of 60 feet at periscope depth—add a desired safety factor of at least 20 feet under the keel—there were many enemy islands where shallow water held the submarines offshore three or four miles. In such cases, pictures taken were of little value, although they did show the general silhouette of the shoreline.

Each photo reconnaissance mission normally involved the taking of between one and two thousand individual pictures. Upon the submarine's return to port, the prints, negatives and accompanying charts were turned over to JICPOA for processing and interpretation by PRISIC. Enlarged reproductions of the vital panoramas were then included in the intelligence section of the amphibious operation plan.

The intelligence value of a submarine photographic reconnaissance mission could be judged only by the commander of the amphibious forces that used the information obtained. That the information was of value is evidenced by the consistency with which submarine periscope reconnaissance was requested for every amphibious operation.

Before the war was ended, 14 photographic reconnaissance missions were undertaken by U.S. submarines. With the exception of one, all were carried out. Swordfish, the last submarine assigned such a mission—in conjunction with the last amphibious operation in the Pacific—was lost, apparently en route, with all hands.

The submarines which went out on these missions were the following:

Submarine	Commanding Officer	Month Conducted	Area Reconnoitered
Nautilus	W. D. Irvin	September 1943	Tarawa, Makin, Apamama
Seal	H. B. Dodge	November 1943	Kwajalein
Spearfish	J. W. Williams	November 1943	Jaluit, Kwajalein, Wotje
Tarpon	T. B. Oakley, Jr.	December 1943	Wotje, Maloelap, Mili, Kwajalein
Searaven	H. M. Dry	January 1944	Eniwetok
Seal	H. B. Dodge	January 1944	Ponape
Thresher	D. C. MacMillan	March 1944	Oroluk, Nomi
Greenling	J. D. Grant	March 1944	Saipan, Tinian, Guam
Salmon	H. K. Nauman	April 1944	Ulithi, Woleai, Yap
Seawolf	R. B. Lynch	June 1944	Palau
Burrfish	W. B. Perkins	July 1944	Palau, Yap
Spearfish	C. C. Cole	November 1944	Iwo Jima
Swordfish	K. E. Montross	December 1944	Okinawa

"THERE IS A PORT OF NO RETURN—" Captain John Cromwell goes down with stricken Sculpin to prevent seizure and possible enemy extortion of *special information confided to his care. The sea will keep his secret well, and his name will become a naval synonym for valor. "Sailor, rest your oar—"*

TARGET! HIT! SINKING! *Blasted by* Tunny, *a maru drowns in Carolines.* Tunny's *Comdr. Scott was great attack artist.*

CAPTAIN JOHN P. CROMWELL, *posthumously awarded the Congressional Medal of Honor.*

WHEN SUBMARINERS MEET. *In port after patrol, deep-sea sailors engage in exchange of ideas. How many did you get? Where's Charley? What's new? These and* similar *questions were traded by rival crews. Lads above seem engrossed in some sort of friendly game. Obviously* not the *crews of* Lapon *and* Raton. *(Story in next chapter.)*

Submarine Support of Fleet Operations (Galvanic Campaign)

For "Operation Galvanic" the United States assembled the largest armada yet seen in the Pacific. The naval force totaled 118 warships (including 13 battleships and 19 carriers of various types) plus a fleet of transports, supply ships and auxiliaries. The armada was divided into three groups—the assault force, under Rear Admiral R. K. Turner—the carrier force, under Rear Admiral C. A. Pownall—the shore-based air force, under Rear Admiral J. H. Hoover. Vice Admiral R. A. Spruance, recently appointed Commander of the Fifth Fleet, was in over-all command.

Capture of Tarawa was the major objective, with Makin and Apamama as secondary objectives. Apamama was correctly judged to be the weakest of the three islands. Unfortunately the strength of Tarawa, the central stronghold, was underestimated, as was that of Makin in the north. The Japanese held out on these islands much longer than was expected. The campaign was as a flash fire compared to the long-smoldering conflagration in the Solomons. But flash fires are hot and murderous—as was the fighting at Makin and Tarawa.

Ten submarines cooperated with the carrier task force and the amphibious landing force in "Operation Galvanic." These submarines were THRESHER, APOGON, CORVINA, SCULPIN and SEARAVEN (stationed in the Carolines); SEAL, SPEARFISH and PLUNGER (in

the Marshalls); PADDLE (stationed off Nauru); and NAUTILUS (operating in the Gilberts).

Controlling factors during this operation were weather conditions for the carrier strikes and surf conditions on the beach at Tarawa on D-Day. Weather in the Pacific moves from west to east. With the enemy controlling the oceanic areas west of the Gilberts, there were no Allied weather stations which could supply the information required. The submarine forces took over this task.

PADDLE (Commander R. H. Rice) was assigned an enlisted aerologist and furnished with weather observing instruments and pibal balloons for taking upper air soundings. She took station to the north of Nauru Island (about 300 miles west of Tarawa) where, each sunset from D−5 day until D+4 day, she sent a weather report which included wind direction and velocities of the upper air.

NAUTILUS (Commander W. D. Irvin) carrying eight officers and 70 men of the Amphibious Reconnaissance Company performed lifeguard services at Tarawa on D-2 and D-1. On sunset of D-1 day she closed in on the beach at Tarawa to observe surf conditions, which she reported by radio. She then proceeded to Apamama to land her Reconnaissance Company.

The tactical disposition of submarines supporting "Galvanic" was based on two general assumptions. The first: Any enemy naval interference with the landing would probably emanate from Truk. The

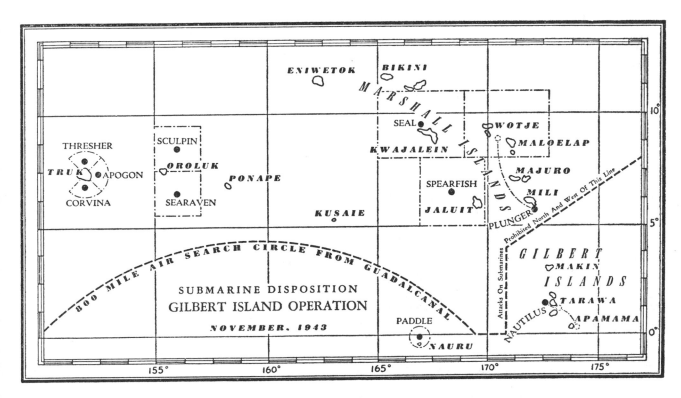

SUBMARINE DISPOSITION
GILBERT ISLAND OPERATION
NOVEMBER, 1943

second: Enemy forces would choose a northerly route to avoid detection by land-based search planes from Guadalcanal, and would probably fuel en route, either at Eniwetok or Kwajalein in the Marshalls.

Accordingly, submarines were not disposed between Truk and Tarawa, but were stationed close to the entrances of Truk to detect any enemy sortie, and along the routes between Truk and the Marshalls (see map). Captain J. P. Cromwell was embarked in SCULPIN, with orders to form, if so directed by dispatch, a coordinated patrol group—a wolf-pack—consisting of SCULPIN, SEARAVEN, and either SPEARFISH or APOGON. The enemy fleet commanders decided to avoid the Gilberts altogether, and submarine offensive operations were therefore confined to the sinking of enemy merchantmen bringing supplies to Truk. PLUNGER (Lieutenant Commander R. H. Bass) on lifeguard duty at Mili, rescued one American aviator. But two submarines were lost during this operation, and NAUTILUS had a narrow escape.

Nautilus at Apamama

Commander Irvin's NAUTILUS was handed a complicated set of instructions in connection with the amphibious detail of "Operation Galvanic." NAUTILUS' primary mission was to transport to Apamama and put ashore a Marine detachment—eight officers and 70 men of the Amphibious Reconnaissance Company, Fifth Amphibious Corps. This was to be accomplished while Tarawa and Makin were under attack.

In conjunction with this transport operation, NAUTILUS had several secondary missions. En route to Apamama she was to conduct a lifeguard patrol off Tarawa during the carrier strikes on that island, which were scheduled for D-2 and D-1 day. At sunset of D-1 day (the eve of the Tarawa landings) NAUTILUS was to observe surf conditions on the Tarawa beaches and report same by radio. These duties performed, she was to proceed to Apamama and land the Reconnaissance Company of Marines.

A sea-bag full of orders—but submariners were becoming inured to multiple operations. NAUTILUS had carried Marines to the Gilberts before. She had already reconnoitered Apamama with a candid camera. She had operated with an amphibious armada in the Aleutians. Lifeguard duty and surf observation were relatively easy assignments compared with the business of transporting and landing troops. However, to engage in all these tasks, she would have to look lively and shake a leg. Any hitch could endanger many lives and, of course, the enemy would be only too happy to sink a submarine.

NAUTILUS left Pearl Harbor on the morning of November 8 with the Marines. Eight days later she was in the vicinity of the Gilberts, and she received a message that she might expect to find Japanese troops on Apamama. Two days later (November 18) she was on lifeguard patrol off Tarawa. The sky roared. Planes from Admiral Pownall's carriers raced in from the horizon to blast Tarawa with load after load of bombs. All that day and the next the aerial bombardment continued. NAUTILUS maintained a sharp lookout, but no downed aviators were sighted.

At sundown of the 19th (the eve of the amphibious landings) Irvin moved his big submarine shoreward to observe surf conditions, as directed. Night closed in, and with it a horde of surface ships converging on Tarawa from all directions.

The commander of the assault force had been previously asked to prescribe the exact route for NAUTILUS to follow at this time. The detail was imperative in capital letters, for a submarine moving at random in the path of onrushing assault forces would be in more jeopardy than a jaywalker on the Indianapolis Speedway. The night was as black as an old-time kitchen range—Tarawa glowing like a red-hot stove lid in the dark—and flitting silhouettes were everywhere. Heading for her next objective, Apamama, NAUTILUS followed the specified route with pencil-line exactitude.

At 2154 Irvin was maneuvering NAUTILUS to clear a reef. Radar contact was made with the warship approaching at a businesslike 25 knots. The battery was low, the air supply was low, the reef was too near for comfort and submergence seemed the worse of two evils. Unlikely the oncoming vessel was a Jap, although its approach was decidedly belligerent. Irvin readied the recognition signals. Then—2159. A blaze of gunfire from the warship. From the submarine the green flare of the recognition comet. Too late—the salvo landed. Smash! NAUTILUS was hit by a 5-inch shell from the destroyer USS RINGOLD.

The projectile struck the conning tower, ripping into the superstructure. Perfect fire control and perfect marksmanship! The projectile failed to explode. Not so perfect ordnance!

But this imperfection—one fluke in a thousand—saved NAUTILUS. Sparks spurted from the conning-tower bilges, but there was no blast and resulting fire. The concussion caused damage, however. And another salvo was heard as the submarine went deep. One close explosion ruptured a water line to the port main motor cooling system and started leaks in the bilges. Water streamed in torrents down the conning-tower hatch, the gyro went out of commission, the main induction flooded and only fast and efficient damage control prevented serious trouble.

As it was, it was serious enough. After NAUTILUS ducked under, there appeared to be three surface vessels tracking her (Irvin was now of the opinion they were Japs) and depth charges were expected at any moment. To make matters worse, there was no density layer for the submarine to hide under. The reef was another hazard to be circumvented. Irvin decided to work the submarine slowly southward, making the most of a favorable current. The un-exploded projectile was too lucky for any further favors from the gods, and everyone aboard, including the Marines under Captain J. L. Jones, USMCR, was doing some industrious sweating. To quote Commander Irvin's log:

"We felt time was running out fast. We had an important date at Apamama and we were going to keep it if we had to surface and fight our way through the horde that was molesting us. The 78 Marines we had aboard were stoic but they were unanimous in the attitude that they would much prefer a rubber boat on a very hostile beach to their present predicament. We managed to assure them they would get their boat ride and it was certain none of them would be hesitant about leaving the ship when landing time came."

By early morning of November 20, NAUTILUS was on the surface and running for Apamama. She reached her destination that afternoon. Convinced that torpedo rooms on assailed submarines were not as comfortable as foxholes, the Marines went ashore with a will.

NAUTILUS remained at Apamama that night and for the next several days, during which time she took off two wounded men and supported the landed company with a shore bombardment of enemy positions. With the occupation of Apamama accomplished, the submarine headed back for Pearl Harbor—mission successfully completed.

In the Officers' Club of the Submarine Base, Pearl Harbor, there is on display an unexploded 5-inch shell. Those best acquainted with this eccentric projectile tip their hats each time they pass it. The hat-tippers are those submariners who were aboard NAUTILUS on the night of November 20, 1943. They doff as one would to an acquaintance—but not exactly a friend.

Loss of Corvina

To participate in the Gilbert Islands campaign, CORVINA (Commander R. S. Rooney) left Pearl Harbor on November 4 and proceeded to Johnston Island. After "topping off" with fuel at Johnston, she headed westward to take her station directly south of Truk. Her mission was the same as that of the four other submarines in the Carolines and the two in the Marshalls. She was to intercept and attack any enemy naval force which might sortie and attempt to rush to the defense of the Gilberts.

CORVINA was ordered to patrol as close in to Truk as enemy anti-submarine forces permitted. It was a dangerous patrol off the southern gateway of Japan's Central Pacific Gibraltar. And this was CORVINA's maiden patrol.

On November 30, after the surface force operations in the Gilberts had been completed, CORVINA was transferred to the Task Force Seventy-two (Brisbane) Command. Dispatches to this effect were radioed to the submarine on two successive nights, and she was directed to acknowledge the messages. There was no acknowledgment by CORVINA.

It was possible for a submarine to miss radio transmissions, due to enemy interference, and a few days later CORVINA was directed to proceed to Tulagi. She made no reply to this transmission. On December 23, CORVINA was officially announced as lost with all hands.

According to Japanese records, one of their I-boats encountered an American submarine directly south of Truk on November 16. Three torpedoes were fired at the American, and two hit, "causing a great explosion sound." There was a swirl of water, and the submarine was gone.

CORVINA's first and only war patrol was ended. So far as is determinable, she was the only United States submarine sunk by a Japanese submarine during the war.

Loss of Sculpin—Captain John P. Cromwell

CORVINA's loss was shrouded in mystery until war's end. The destruction of SCULPIN, the second submarine lost during "Operation Galvanic," was soon suspected by the Force Command, although details were not known until her survivors were recovered from the Japanese prison camps. Then it was discovered that SCULPIN's loss had a tragic aftermath—an epilogue which only Fate could write as the conclusion for a chain of events.

The day following CORVINA's departure, SCULPIN (Commander Fred Connaway) headed out of Pearl Harbor for Johnston Island and a patrol station in the Carolines. After "topping off" with fuel, she left Johnston on November 7. She replied to no radio transmissions thereafter.

SCULPIN's patrol station was directly north of Truk —her mission to intercept and attack any Japanese force which sortied from Truk's northern gateway during the Gilbert Islands campaign.

On the possibility of tactical advantage, a plan had

287

been devised whereby three of the submarines stationed in the Carolines and Marshalls could combine forces as a wolf-pack and deliver a coordinated attack on the enemy. Aboard SCULPIN was Captain John P. Cromwell who was to take charge of the coordinated attack group if the wolf-pack were formed.

The group was to consist of SCULPIN, SEARAVEN and either APOGON or SPEARFISH. Its formation was to be directed by dispatch, and in the event that the group was formed, Cromwell was to direct its operations by low-frequency radio from SCULPIN.

On the night of November 29, ComSubPac ordered the formation of the group. APOGON was named as the third submarine of the trio. No rendezvous orders were issued by Captain Cromwell, however.

Forty hours later (and no word from SCULPIN) ComSubPac sent new orders, directing SCULPIN to proceed to Eniwetok and observe enemy shipping in the Marshalls. These and other orders for SCULPIN were transmitted during the next several days. From the submarine—silence. On December 30, SCULPIN was announced as presumably lost.

After the war her survivors told the story. On the night of November 18, she made radar contact with a fast enemy convoy, and her commander directed an end-around at full power. Closing in at dawn on the attack, the submarine was detected and the convoy zigged toward her, forcing her deep. About an hour later, surfacing to start another end-around, she was sighted by a rear-guard destroyer. She made a quick dive and was depth-charged.

SCULPIN suffered only minor damage during this barrage. But the depth gage was put out of commission, and when the diving officer attempted to bring the submarine to periscope depth, the gage stuck at 125 feet. As a result, SCULPIN broached. She went under immediately, but the enemy had sighted her, and the attack was at once resumed.

About noon, November 19th, a string of 18 depth charges exploded around her. SCULPIN was badly hurt. The blasts dented her pressure hull, started serious leaks, damaged her steering gear and diving planes. Commander Connaway decided to surface and fight it out with the deck guns. The order was passed, and SCULPIN battle-surfaced, rising from the deep like a wounded leviathan.

Attacking the Japanese destroyer, the submarine put up a furious battle. But she was no match for the heavily armed DD. A shell from the destroyer smashed into SCULPIN's conning tower, and another crashed through the main induction. On the bridge Commander Connaway and Gunnery Officer Lieutenant Joseph R. Defrees, Jr., were killed. Lieutenant N. J. Allen was killed by the explosion in the conning tower. Standing at their posts, men died on the bridge and in the control room as SCULPIN rolled in torment under the enemy's punishing fire.

Lieutenant G. E. Brown, the diving officer, succeeded to command. With shells bursting around the submarine and the conning tower torn open, he decided to scuttle and gave the order, "All hands abandon ship!" The crew struggled into life jackets and clambered out of the hatches. Vents open, the submarine plunged from sight, making her final dive.

About 12 men "rode the ship down." Among them were Captain Cromwell and Ensign C. G. Smith, Jr., who refused to leave the stricken submarine. Forty-two of SCULPIN's crew, including three of her officers, got overside and were taken prisoner by the Japanese destroyer. One of the men was immediately thrown by his captors back into the sea because he was badly wounded. Another man escaped this diabolical treatment by wrenching free of the sailors dragging him to the rail, and joining his companions.

Captain Cromwell, who went down with the submarine, did so because he possessed vital information concerning "Operation Galvanic" and other war plans—information which might be extracted by torture. SCULPIN would keep these secrets well, and her captain chose to confide them into her keeping rather than risk the extraction of the information he possessed. For this action, Captain John P. Cromwell, wolf-pack commander, was posthumously awarded the Congressional Medal of Honor.

SCULPIN's survivors were taken to Truk where they were questioned for ten days. After this grilling, they were embarked on two carriers (21 on one, and 20 on the other) and started for Japan. Only one of these parties reached Japan for eventual imprisonment and hard labor in the Ashio copper mines. Of the other group (the party of 21) only one man reached Japan. The events of this tragic aftermath will presently be recounted. It was the fate of these SCULPIN survivors to start for Japan aboard the carrier CHUYO.

Torpedoing of Liscome Bay

Although the Imperial Navy's surface forces at Truk were not sent out to contest the Gilbert Islands occupation, the American assault forces met savage resistance.

About 400 Japanese soldiers and a similar number of Korean construction workers were garrisoned on Makin. But, despite a terrific bombardment from heavy surface craft, the forces on Makin defended the atoll fiercely. Some 6,500 U.S. Army troops went ashore, and it was only after a three-day battle that the island's capture was announced in the message, "Makin taken." American casualties were light, while the Japanese soldiery was wiped out (or committed suicide) almost to a man.

On Tarawa, defended by narrow Betio Atoll, the enemy had concentrated about 4,800 Japanese troops and Korean laborers. A honeycomb of concealed defenses, pillboxes and machine-gun nests, Betio proved an unexpected stumbling block to the American amphibious force attempting to storm the island. The Japanese garrison was finally annihilated after four days of bloody fighting in which almost a thousand Marines were killed.

The Navy's surface forces at Tarawa were to suffer their share of the casualties. Japanese opposition in the air was negligible, but one Jap torpedo bomber raced through the anti-aircraft screen and damaged the light carrier INDEPENDENCE. Japanese submarines wreaked greater havoc. The destroyer FRAZIER sighted, rammed and sank an attacking I-boat. But another enemy submarine succeeded in torpedoing the escort carrier LISCOME BAY. LISCOME BAY exploded like a powder-box. Flames burst through her flight deck and hurled burning planes 200 feet in the air. Floods of blazing oil spread around her as she settled, killing many of her men. The vessel sank in half an hour. Over 700 died in this sinking, those lost including the commander of the escort carrier support group, Rear Admiral H. M. Mullinnix.

In the sinking of CORVINA and LISCOME BAY, the Japanese Submarine Force was nearing the conclusion of its prowess. It would down but one more major United States warship in the Pacific. But United States submarines had barely begun their war against the warships of Japan.

Attrition Continued (A David Meets a Goliath)

While the Fifth Fleet was concentrating on the Gilbert Islands area and ten Pacific Fleet submarines were operating in "Galvanic," the remainder of the SubPac Force was hitting the enemy's shipping closer to home. Torpedoes crashed in the waters off Japan while the guns were thundering at Tarawa, and as the echoes from the Gilberts died away in December, explosions were booming along the Marshall and Caroline sea lanes to the north, and there were oceanic blasts below Dai Nippon.

HALIBUT (Lieutenant Commander I. J. Galantin) got the 4,653-ton freighter EHIME MARU west of Truk on November 2.

On the 9th and 11th, SARGO (Lieutenant Commander P. W. Garnett) sent down 6,000 tons more, same area, by sinking TAGA MARU and KOSEI MARU.

SNAPPER (Lieutenant Commander M. K. Clemenson) sank KEURYU MARU, 4,575-ton cargoman, off Honshu on the 29th.

On the 23rd, GUDGEON (Lieutenant Commander W. S. Post) sank the transport NEKKA MARU, 6,784 tons, and the frigate WAKAMIYA, in waters off Kyushu.

GUNNEL (Lieutenant Commander J. S. McCain) destroyed the passenger-cargoman HIYOSHI MARU, 4,046 tons, below Kyushu on December 4. Four days later, SAWFISH (Lieutenant Commander E. T. Sands) deposited SANSEI MARU, passenger-cargoman, 3,267 tons, on the bottom in the same area.

HERRING (Lieutenant Commander R. W. Johnson) downed HAKOZAKI MARU, 3,948-ton passenger-cargoman, off Honshu on the 14th. A little farther to the north, GURNARD (Lieutenant Commander C. H. Andrews) struck two freighters on the day before Christmas—TOFUKU MARU and SEIZAN MARU No. 2—for a combined sinking of some 7,800 odd tons.

Meantime, SKATE (Commander McKinney) was hunting just north of Truk. December 21 she sank TERUKAWA MARU, a 6,429-ton freighter. Christmas Day she sighted bigger game, and forthwith slammed a torpedo into the superbattleship YAMATO.

Flagship of the late Admiral Yamamoto, this 63,000-ton monster was game of overwhelming size. Packing 18.1-inch guns, vitals shielded by a "torpedo-proof" underwater protection system, she and her twin sister, MUSASHI, were the world's biggest battle-wagons. There were to have been triplet giants, but the third behemoth, SHINANO, was converted during construction into a 59,000-ton aircraft carrier. YAMATO, the first-born (commissioned in 1941), had been at Midway, where she had circumspectly retired without firing a shot. Now, off Truk, the pride of the Imperial Navy was damaged by an undersea torpedo.

SKATE—a submarine David, indeed—was unable to down this mighty Goliath. But the big BB's "torpedo-proof" underbelly was not quite so invulnerable as her sponsors had hoped. Staggering away, she lived to fight another day, but her time would come. A time was coming for all three of these colossal sisters.

Dramatic though it was, the SKATE-YAMATO meeting was not the biggest submarine story of the late autumn-December 1943 attrition war. One of the most dangerous places on the globe for Japanese shipping during that period was the East China-Yellow Sea area where TRIGGER, SEAHORSE and GRAYBACK were on the rampage. While that was going on, TINOSA, off Palau, staged a devastating foray. And while these raiders were making life unbearable (and unlivable) for Japanese seamen, SAILFISH, heading for the Bungo Suido, encountered and sank the third major warship to go down from submarine torpedo fire in the Pacific.

Each of the forenamed submarines was captained

by a topnotch skipper. And the patrol report of each contained tactical data which the Force Command underlined as worth the attention of students of undersea warfare.

Submarine Tactics—Maintaining Position on Escorts

In a previous chapter it was remarked that radar's wartime growth was so rapid that ideas concerning its tactical usage never crystallized into dogmatic doctrine. And veteran submarine captains, discussing such tactics as the night-radar approach, were quick to assert that "it all depended."

One of the factors upon which "it all depended" was the number and position of a vessel's or convoy's escorts. To some degree, escort activity, or the possibility of it, influenced most approaches. And a method of attack which always had to be considered was that devised as a submarine kept positional check of the escorts.

According to the vagaries of Japanese A/S measures, a ship or convoy coming down the track might be accompanied by one or a cordon of escort vessels. These escorts might materialize as converted gunboats, old destroyers, CHIDORI torpedo boats, motorized frigates or heavy-gunned DD's, depending on the convoy's importance and the number of A/S units available. Obviously it was necessary for the approaching submarine to keep close tabs on these combative vessels, and when the escorts were numerous and active, the methods of approach and attack depended to a great extent on their maneuvers. The approach officer had to be continuously informed on the relative position of convoy, escorts and submarine, and this maintaining of position on escorts may be seen as a vital function, controlling to a large degree the tactical *modus operandi*.

Here radar entered the picture with the Plan Position Indicator (PPI scope)—one of the newer scientific developments of 1943. "Continuous information" had been previously obtainable only in a broad sense of the term. But with the advent of this instrument, the maneuvers of a convoy's escorts became as easy to follow and check as the moves of a checker game on a television screen.

Of course, there were surprises. In warfare as in life the only certainty is change—no submarine attack ever followed an exact pattern. However, an attack made by TRIGGER, night of November 1-2, 1943, on a big convoy about 150 miles southeast of Kyushu, aptly demonstrated tactical maneuvers involving the maintenance of position on escorts.

TRIGGER was conducting her seventh patrol. She was under Lieutenant Commander R. E. (Dusty) Dornin, and the "TRIGGER men" were out to uphold their reputation as some of the master marksmen of the submarine forces. At 2025 on the evening of November 1, TRIGGER made radar contact on her first target—a convoy at 10,000 yards. From that moment on she had a busy night's shooting.

As soon as contact was established, Dornin started tracking. The radar screen revealed some dozen ships zigzagging on course between 140° and 180° at a speed of 8 knots. Formation shaped up as two ragged columns. Shortly after contact Dornin was able to determine that there was one escort ahead and one astern, vigilantly patrolling the port side of the convoy. "Dusty" therefore stepped up the speed, and sent TRIGGER around the head of the convoy to try the starboard side. There, Dornin continued his tracking, carefully examining the convoy to determine a course of action.

About an hour after the initial contact, he moved in for a surface attack. The night was hat-black, and neither the escort (at 1,800 yards) nor the ships (at 3,000) could be seen. The night could not conceal them, however, from the penetrating "eye" of radar. TRIGGER was equipped with a Plan Position Indicator. On the PPI's circular screen, a series of concentric circles indicated approximate range, and radial lines gave a rough indication of relative bearings. The device proved invaluable to TRIGGER, engaged in a fast game of tag-in-the-dark with a large convoy. On the PPI screen the "pips" grew, faded, moved about and blended like microbes under the lens of a high-powered microscope. This constant play of movement, as the ships and escorts changed disposition, would have been most difficult to follow without the aid of the PPI.

As Dornin drove in to attack, the whole convoy zigged, and two more escorts showed up on the starboard side. That made four A/S vessels to contend with. Dornin broke off the attack and opened the range in deference to a more opportune time and better position.

During the next half-hour, he started to close in on several occasions. Each time TRIGGER approached the convoy, an escort blocked the way, and Dornin withdrew to try again. While this maneuvering was going on, convoy and escorts were serenely unaware of the submarine's presence, although the A/S vessels were unusually active in their patrolling.

At 2200, the distance to the nearest escort opened out to 3,000 yards. Given this chance to strike, Dornin maneuvered in once more. He planned to fire ten torpedoes at the three nearest ships and the opportunity seemed at hand. About ten minutes after he started the drive in, however, the two leading ships zigged, presenting zero angle on the bow, and the PPI showed the leading escort closing up. At this juncture, a likely target was presented by two overlapping freighters—one in the near and one in the far column. At 2217, Dornin fired three torpedoes at the near freighter, hoping to catch the far freighter with any misses. Sixty seconds after firing, there resounded a smashing hit in the bow of the No. 1 freighter. A half-minute later, there was a slam-bang hit amidships in the far freighter. The near ship settled by the bow, fatally stricken. Blown skyward from the second ship, tons of debris fell helter-skelter in the night, splashing in the sea around the near-by vessels of the convoy. Eruptions of dark smoke rolled up from this torpedoed target, and Dornin swung TRIGGER to reverse course then, and went to full ahead on four engines.

PPI now showed a pip on the starboard bow, and another astern at 1,800 yards' range. Bridge lookouts saw two escorts coming out of the smoke, zero angle on the bow and bones in teeth. Dornin took TRIGGER down to 300 feet. Two "pinging" escorts made alternate runs, dropping twenty depth charges during the next hour or so. The submarine got out from under, and came back for more.

At 0025 the following morning (about two hours after the first attack) Dornin brought her up to radar depth and found all clear. Reload operations were begun. At 0050 TRIGGER surfaced and went full speed ahead in pursuit of the running convoy.

About an hour later radar contact was again established. The ships had evidently scattered like panicked cattle, leaving one of their number behind—a three-island freighter, no escort, making 8 knots, and not zigzagging. At 0203 Dornin fired three torpedoes at this vessel, range 1,200 yards. One was seen to hit. After the blast, the ship did not appear to be sinking, so Dornin resumed the attack. As TRIGGER closed in, the freighter opened fire with bow and stern guns, but the shooting was wild. At 0216 Dornin fired three more torpedoes at 1,700 yards. This salvo scored two hits in the forward part of the vessel. The freighter sank, bow first, in a vertical dive. Dornin ran TRIGGER over to the spot, hoping to pick up survivors. Apparently all hands had gone down.

Twenty minutes later another radar pip was darting across the screen. At 0310 the target was in sight—a large vessel making about 8 knots. There appeared to be no escorts in the vicinity. At 0321 Dornin fired three torpedoes at this target. All three struck the luckless ship. When the smoke cleared away, she was awash aft, and her bow was broken off and sticking straight up in the air. The bow sank without ado, but the after portion remained afloat for several minutes.

As TRIGGER was advancing through a sea of oil, lifeboats were sighted and men were heard crying out. Dornin immediately reversed course to look for survivors, but found only one shattered lifeboat, nobody at the oars. At dawn it was necessary to dive, and the submarine had to stay under throughout the day. But that evening the search for survivors was continued. One life-raft with three souls aboard was found. Dornin steered TRIGGER over to the raft. The relics in the life-raft would make no move to assist in their rescue. As the submariners tried to maneuver alongside, the raft drifted away in the darkness, and could not afterwards be found.

In remarking on this convoy battle, Dornin later pointed out that the maximum range of SJ was 20,000 yards on land masses, but only 10,000 yards on ships. New instruments of higher power and longer range were being issued to submarines at the time, but TRIGGER still had the low-powered transmitter. Had TRIGGER been equipped with one of the new radars, Dornin believed he could have shot a full load of torpedoes into that single convoy. As it was, twelve torpedoes were fired, and the sinking of three ships appeared as a certainty. Japanese records, however, identified only two—YAWATA MARU, cargo, 1,852 tons, and DELAGOA MARU, passenger cargo, 7,148 tons.

Two days later TRIGGER had her sights trained on another convoy—three freighters escorted by two planes and a destroyer. Maintaining a position on the aircraft escorts was a proposition the PPI was not equipped to handle. Dornin started an early-morning periscope approach, choosing the largest freighter for his target. But before TRIGGER could reach attack position the convoy zigged, spoiling the shot at the big cargoman. Then the formation made a zag, and the second ship lined up for a long-range shot while ship No. 3 was a give-away at 1,200 yards. Unhandily, the submarine had but four torpedoes left forward. Dornin opened fire at 0814, shooting three of these at the farther freighter, range 2,400 yards, and one at the nearer. Then he sent TRIGGER deep to evade a "going over."

Sound heard two blasts, but the time lapse was too long for them to have been torpedo explosions. Then the depth charges thundered down. The destroyer-men apparently had TRIGGER located, but the DD's runs were futile. An hour later, thinking the enemy out of the way, Dornin ordered the submarine to periscope depth. Surprise! The periscope had barely broken water when five depth bombs smashed the sea around the submarine.

"They scared hell out of us," Dornin narrated. "Concluded they were aircraft bombs, and went deep again. The destroyer regained contact, guided by the planes, no doubt, and dropped a few more depth charges." TRIGGER remained submerged until dark.

On November 13, TRIGGER's tubes were trained on another target, and down at sea went NACHISAN MARU, passenger-cargo carrier, 4,433 tons. Eight days later, Dornin fired the last four torpedoes at a small freighter off the south coast of Honshu, thereby sinking EIZAN MARU's 1,681 tons. Her patrol completed, all torpedoes expended, TRIGGER headed for home base. Behind them, the "TRIGGER men" left some 15,000 tons of merchant shipping at sea bottom, and Dornin had given a notable demonstration of the night radar approach with maintenance of position on convoy escorts.

Submarine Tactics—The Submerged Radar Approach

In the foregoing account of the TRIGGER vs. convoy engagement on the night of November 1-2, it was stated that Dornin at one juncture brought the submarine up to "radar depth." This meant that the submarine's superstructure was barely awash and the upper part of her conning tower was exposed. Advantage: a diminished silhouette while surface radar could operate. Disadvantage: the lookouts were limited to radar and periscope, submarine mobility was as sluggish as though she were wholly submerged, and not only had she lost the surface speed so advantageous for attack, but she was extremely vulnerable to a depth-charge or ramming counter-attack.

Accordingly, submerged radar approaches were never popular. During 1943 and 1944 only 71 submerged radar attacks were made. With the introduction of the ST radar late in the war, the tactic was more widely employed. The ST, housed in the periscope, could be raised and lowered with that instrument—a device which permitted radar operation at periscope depth. The SJ, mounted on top of the periscope shears, necessitated operation at the radar depth previously described. Preferring to work either on the surface or far enough under it to avoid a ramming, submarine commanders resorted to "radar depth" only when desiring to make a cautious survey of the situation—as in the TRIGGER instance—after the submarine had been submerged and was rising to commence or resume an attack. In the early days of the SJ, after radar contact was thus made and the periscope spotted the target, the submarine frequently went to periscope depth and the attack was guided by periscope observation at the finish.

Such an attack was conducted by Lieutenant Commander J. A. (Johnny) Moore, captain of GRAYBACK during that submarine's eighth war patrol. This was the patrol (East China Sea area) in which GRAYBACK was a member of the first American submarine wolf-pack to sally forth against the enemy in the Central Pacific. As related in an earlier chapter, GRAYBACK, SHAD and CERO, under group command of Captain C. B. Momsen, embarked in CERO, had loped out of Midway on October 1st. GRAYBACK made her first killing of the season on October 14, sinking the 7,072-ton passenger-cargoman KOZUI MARU on that date. Eight days later she made her second killing. It was in this attack that Moore employed the submerged radar approach.

At 1627 on October 21, GRAYBACK, patrolling submerged in the central waters of the East China Sea, sighted masts. Closing to 9,000 yards, she discovered two large ships escorted by three destroyers, all on southerly course. The two big ships bore a striking resemblance to naval auxiliaries. Moore determined to strike them. However, GRAYBACK was unable to get any closer submerged. She sent out contact information on her sound gear for the benefit of her pack-mates, and at 1815, Moore surfaced the submarine and went ahead full speed, trailing the convoy. At 1937 GRAYBACK was in radar contact with the enemy, obtaining radar bearings and ranges every two minutes. The enemy's speed plotted at 15 knots. Moore stepped up GRAYBACK's speed, pulling for an end-around.

The enemy's high speed made the run-around a lengthy process, but the distance covered improved GRAYBACK's position by taking her into deeper water and the Japan current where protective sound layers would aid her when the time came to evade. Also, delay of the attack until after moonrise permitted use of the periscope during the approach.

At 11,000 yards, with the target on the starboard bow, Moore took GRAYBACK down to periscope depth. After obtaining a trim, he planed her back up and continued radar tracking submerged. With the range at 6,600 yards according to radar, Moore went back down to periscope depth. Bearings were then obtainable both by sound and periscope.

The chase had lasted until well past midnight, and it was the morning of the 22nd when GRAYBACK closed in. At 0347 the convoy appeared to zig 15° to the left, and two minutes later Moore began firing the bow tubes. Target bearings were checked by periscope during the firing.

Forty-eight seconds after the first torpedo was fired, a hit was observed. At ten-second intervals, three succeeding hits were heard. These hits were not observed because Moore was busy trying to pick up the second target and swinging GRAYBACK's stern tubes to bear. Poor visibility in the direction of this vessel saved her from destruction. While Moore was still trying to discern the No. 2 target, GRAYBACK was forced deep by one of the three destroyers. Racing up at high speed, the DD dropped a booming pattern of close depth charges, and GRAYBACK got out from under just in time.

The "large ship" sunk by GRAYBACK on this occasion was the ex-light cruiser AWATA MARU, 7,397 tons. A fitting culmination for an expert demonstration of the submerged radar approach made with the SJ.

But the SJ was on its way to obsolescence before another year was out. Perhaps more typical of late 1943 submarining were the routine approaches and attacks made by GRAYBACK during her December patrol. During this patrol, her ninth, she sank two freighters, a sampan and a small net tender in the East China Sea, and damaged another freighter. Her sunken victims were GYOKUREI MARU, 5,588 tons; KONAN MARU, 2,627 tons; KASHIWA MARU, 515 tons. In addition, on December 19 she sank the Imperial Navy destroyer NUMAKAZE in the waters off Okinawa.

Few submarines fought the war harder and more efficiently than GRAYBACK, and few submarine captains were more adept at their exacting profession than Johnny A. Moore.

Submarine Tactics—"Typical" Daylight Approach

While it was suggested that Moore's December tactics were typical, the adjective "typical" is subject to modification. The highly successful approach was by no means the average, and every submarine approach was tailored to fit an individual situation. Unlike the game of chess—wherein the opening gambits, although legion, are limited by a fixed number of pieces, restricted moves and a two-dimensional field of operation—submarine warfare contains as many variations as three-dimensional space, four-dimensional imagination, and the cranky whimseys of the Jay Factor may contrive. Its situations, then, are as diverse as the fingerprints of humankind. The submarine approaches made in World War II varied accordingly. A typical approach? One might be described, yet its details would remain as individualistic as the whorls of a selected fingerprint.

However, an attack made by TINOSA on a two-ship convoy off Palau, November 22, 1943, illustrates a successful daylight approach that might well serve as a prototype were a similar situation to develop. At that time on her fourth war patrol, TINOSA was captained by Commander L. R. Daspit—the young officer whose inquisitive turn of mind had gone far to expose the defects of the Mark 14 torpedo. Daspit was the sort of commander who did not leave all the

calculating up to the T.D.C. His executive officer, Lieutenant Commander "Ebbie" Bell, also had a head on his shoulders. Again it will be noted that submarine warfare with its infinite tactical possibilities and manifold operational problems demanded young men with brains as well as brawn. The officer who was mentally in a groove would not do. Affairs at Palau did not run in a groove, as will be seen, and had TINOSA's commander had a one-track mind the submarine might have ended up, scoreless, on a siding.

TINOSA had left Midway on October 27 to patrol along the Truk-Empire route and then in the vicinity of Palau, after which she was to proceed to Fremantle for duty with the SoWesPac Force. North of Truk she made one contact on a MOGAMI-class cruiser. Daspit maneuvered into a favorable position ahead, but the target escaped by making a couple of fortunate zigzags.

November 15, TINOSA was patrolling off Toagel Mlungui, the western entrance to the Palau lagoon. The pass was found to be well guarded by surface patrols with air cover whenever any activity was pending. Traffic bustled in and out of the pass. In three days TINOSA made contact with three convoys and several independent ships, including a small tanker and a destroyer. Night chase of a merchant vessel spotted at sunset had ended when the target materialized as a properly lighted hospital ship. On none of the "legal" contacts had it been possible to obtain attack position. When the submarine's speed was above 6 knots, a noise developed in the superstructure and this was evidently sufficient to attract the alert patrols. TINOSA was depth-charged on one occasion after trying a fast approach, and the surface patrol was evidently addicted to the use of depth charges every now and then, with or without submarine contact.

As the enemy was now aware that a submarine was off Toagel Mlungui, Daspit withdrew on the 18th to patrol along the Palau-Molucca Passage track. On the 22nd, he returned to the vicinity of Palau, this time electing to cover Malakal Passage, the eastern entrance to the lagoon. Before sunrise on the 22nd TINOSA was patrolling at periscope depth off Malakal.

Early dawn established the presence of the usual channel-guarding surface patrol. No aircraft were sighted. But if the activity around Toagel Mlungui were an indication, they could be expected in the vicinity of any worthwhile torpedo targets. Daspit continued the patrol at periscope depth. In deference to possible aircraft, periscope exposures were limited to a quick sweep every three minutes. It had been pretty well established that peacetime apprehension

293

of aircraft detection was exaggerated—a submarine at periscope depth was not apt to be spotted by a plane, and brief periscope exposures were relatively safe, even when made in the vicinity of such a base as Palau. In Tinosa's case the exposures were worth the risk.

At 0741 smoke was sighted to the southeast, and Daspit ordered battle stations. As the target was probably headed toward the passage through the reef, and as Tinosa was between the ship and its destination, there was no need of preliminary maneuvers to establish direction of movement, nor was there any necessity to come to a normal approach course. Holding the submarine at periscope depth, Daspit headed directly for the target.

Seven minutes later the smoke was made out to be a convoy—two freighters in column with two escorts, one escort leading and one trailing. Approaching on nearly the reverse of the convoy's base course, Tinosa passed almost within hailing distance of the leading escort. It was tentatively identified as a light mine-layer—the stern differing considerably from a destroyer's. The examination was not too lengthy as Daspit was concentrating on the target and his chief concern with the escort was to get past it without detection. Seen from afar, the trailing escort was readily recognized as a submarine-chaser.

The convoy was zigzagging radically every four minutes. Daspit's approach tactics were comparatively simple. He kept Tinosa headed down the range at slow speed, pointed in the general direction of the convoy. There was a chance that the submarine might be left too much "back on the bow" by a haphazard zigzag, but the problem was much simplified by the knowledge that the convoy must be headed towards the opening in the reef. The approximate base course was thus a certainty, and the danger of Tinosa's being misled from the track by a radical zig was greatly reduced. The convoy's speed plotted as 10 knots. This checked on T.D.C. Sound's count of the propeller turns was consistent with the 10-knot estimate. Everything was in order. The approach, which had taken a little over an hour, had reached the attack stage.

Having selected a fat ship for Target No. 1, Daspit sent the submarine boring in. The freighter made her last zig. There was time to adjust Tinosa's course without undue hurry. She came around to the course for 110° starboard track and a salvo from the stern tubes.

"Shooting will be by check bearing."

"Final bearing and shoot—up scope."

At 0838 Daspit fired three Mark 14 torpedoes, gyro angle 182, depth setting 8 feet, range 700 yards.

Thirty seconds later there was a whacking hit. All three torpedoes hit. The freighter rolled over on her side and settled rapidly. The escorts wheeled around like puzzled watchdogs. Daspit was swinging Tinosa hard right to bring the bow tubes to bear on the second freighter. It would have been touch and go to get around in time had not the target made the wrong maneuver and swung hard right rudder. At first glance, it looked as if she were going to ram, but she swung on by. By 0842 she steadied down, and was directly in line for a straight bow shot.

Daspit fired three torpedoes from the bow tubes, track 95° port, range 1100 yards, gyro angle 004. Two torpedoes smote this freighter and left her going down by the stern.

Tinosa was now between two sinking targets, with torpedo tracks extending in both directions, making an "X" to mark the submarine's position. It was time to go deep, and for the first time since contact, Daspit ordered Tinosa below periscope depth, speeding up and changing course 90° as he did so.

Although "X" marked the spot of Tinosa's dive, the two stunned escort vessels failed to trap her. So she made her getaway after demonstrating a "typical" (note the quotation marks) daylight approach. The Japanese ships which participated in this demonstration were the cargo carriers Kiso Maru, 4,071 tons, and Yamato (unlucky name) Maru, 4,379 tons.

Daspit and company did not stop there. On November 26, revisiting the Toagel Mlungui neighborhood, they sank Shini Maru's 3,811 tons. And on December 3 they slammed another warhead into the 6,464-ton passenger-cargoman Azuma Maru. When Tinosa completed this patrol, Japanese statisticians subtracted some 18,000 tons of shipping from the Palau merchant service. Probably they did the subtracting with the aid of an abacus. Daspit and crew did it with torpedoes and brains—plus the proper approach tactics.

Seahorse vs. The Japanese Merchant Marine

Lieutenant Commander Slade D. Cutter received orders to take his submarine Seahorse out of Midway on October 20, 1943, and patrol south of the Empire in the East China Sea. When Cutter put aside his chewed cigar and stalked out of the Gooney Bird Hotel to saddle up, misfortune was in the making for the Japanese merchant marine.

No submarine captain of World War II liked a fight better than Slade D. Cutter. His penchant for this sort of activity, backed by six-feet-two of physique, had won him the heavyweight boxing championship of the Naval Academy. His easygoing disposition and mild manner camouflaged a combative instinct that verged on the titanic.

SEAHORSE galloped out of Midway on October 20 and returned in mid-December. During this time she destroyed three trawlers, damaged a number of unidentified merchantmen and sank three freighters, a passenger-cargo carrier and a large tanker. Cutter's tactics? They reflected his ring personality. He got in and punched. He struck when the enemy's guard was down, and when the guard wasn't down, he knocked it down. SEAHORSE's approaches and attacks were therefore somewhat on the order of cavalry charges, executed with overwhelming dash and vigor. Which is not to imply that Cutter wasn't an expert in the saddle.

Nine days out on the road, Cutter reared SEAHORSE up in a battle-surface to sink the first trawler by gunfire at 2,400 yards. The next day the second trawler was holed with the gun. While this craft was settling, a boarding party from SEAHORSE recovered charts, publications and log. The following day at sunset SEAHORSE battle-surfaced for an attack on Trawler No. 3. The Japs aboard this vessel tried to ram the submarine, but SEAHORSE's sharpshooting gun crew smashed the craft to pieces before it was close.

A few hours after this slam-bang gun action, SEAHORSE contacted a convoy as big as a desert caravan —17 ships, including escorts.

By 0315 on November 1, Cutter had the submarine in position for a submerged attack. The sudden intervention of an escort close aboard, with zero angle on the bow, forced SEAHORSE to go deep.

Twenty minutes later, Cutter had the submarine again on the surface—the escorts had drifted off—and he commenced an end-around. At dawn two "echo-ranging" CHIDORI's prevented an attack, and sometime later explosions and fire announced that another U.S. submarine was attacking the convoy.

Not to be cheated of his quarry, Cutter hung on. At 0048 on November 2, he fired three torpedoes at a freighter in the seagoing caravan, and saw this target sink. Four hours later he emptied three tubes at a large tanker and three more at a medium freighter. Two hits in each target boomed and flared. The two CHIDORI "pingers" now started after the submarine with a vengeance. Cutter put spurs to SEAHORSE and galloped away from the CHIDORI's with four engines on the line. At dawn SEAHORSE dived to spend a quiet day under the surface, reloading. Her victims of November 2 were CHIHAYA MARU, 7,089 tons, and UME MARU, passenger-cargo, 5,859 tons.

Two more contacts later in the week had Cutter and SEAHORSE going again, but the ships evaporated. Then on November 5, Cutter began an approach on

a ship stranded on a reef around Gyo To. Thick fog blinded the periscope, and only quick thinking and skillful submerged maneuvering kept SEAHORSE from being grounded by the treacherous current. But the fog suddenly lifted and the reef was revealed.

On November 17, early in the morning, two freighters and two escorts were contacted. Cutter directed a submerged approach. At the firing point, a final periscope sweep disclosed a destroyer close aboard with zero angle on the bow and obvious intentions. Cutter sent SEAHORSE deep and for the next hour the submarine was on the receiving end of a well-executed depth-charge attack. Intermittent depth-charging and sound-searching continued for ten hours after the destroyer had lost contact. SEAHORSE lay low until the DD was gone.

Then on the 22nd two freighters escorted by three destroyers were contacted. After skillfully maneuvering to get under the enemy's guard, Cutter fired four torpedoes from periscope depth at one target. Two hits sank this vessel. The destroyers depth-charged without making contact. In an hour and a half, at 0418, SEAHORSE was able to surface some distance from the sinking scene and beat a hasty retreat. Behind her (under water) was DAISHU MARU, a 3,322-ton freighter.

Radar contact at dusk, November 26, put the finger on two large tankers and a corpulent freighter with three escorts riding herd. Cutter charged in with SEAHORSE and there ensued another running battle. After repeated attempts to attack after dark on the surface, the submarine's situation was endangered by her proximity to the mined Straits of Tsushima. Cutter's determination to get these targets before they escaped into the Straits led him to fire four torpedoes, 3,750 yards range, at one tanker. Two hits resulted—a tribute to the SEAHORSE fire control party—and the tanker blew up like a can of overheated gasoline. Dodging one escort, Cutter drove SEAHORSE in once more and let the second tanker have four stern shots at 3,100 yards. Again two hits, but the results seemed disappointing. Then small flames sprouted all over the target and suddenly she was wiped from the seascape by a dazzling blast which lit up the sky like daylight. One escort tracked at zero speed as SEAHORSE retired—apparently the A/S vessel was injured by the explosion. Japanese records would confirm only one of these sinkings—the 7,309-ton tanker SAN RAMON MARU. If the other tanker did not go down, it certainly went up, hence the authorities credited SEAHORSE with a 4,000-ton "unknown."

On November 30, SEAHORSE contacted three medium AK's with a small AK and PC acting as escorts.

At nightfall Cutter began a difficult approach, no bow tubes available. Time and again he maneuvered into attack position, only to have this zigzagging convoy turn away. Then, at 2240 three of the ships opened fire on SEAHORSE. Cutter reined SEAHORSE in, then dogged the group, and at 0038 on December 1 she was in position and fired four stern tubes. One torpedo prematured 50 seconds after leaving the tube. The whole convoy promptly opened fire. In the din of explosions, no one could determine whether the blasts were from shells or torpedoes.

Working the angles in all dimensions—third, fourth and Jay Factor—Cutter jockeyed SEAHORSE out from under the barrage. Having demolished 27,579 tons of the enemy's East China Sea shipping, SEAHORSE headed for the barn.

She would not be in the stable for long. January would see her charging down the road to the Mandates, and before another year was out her record would be Apocalyptic. Cutter was to end the war as the third highest scorer on the tons-sunk list.

Sailfish vs. Japanese Escort Carrier

1745: Surfaced in typhoon weather. Tremendous seas, 40-50 knot wind, driving rain, and visibility, after twilight, varying from zero to 500 yards.

2348: Radar contact bearing 114°T (154° relative), range 9,500 yards. Commenced tracking (ship contact #1).

2351: Estimated target course 320°T, speed 18 knots.

2352: Radar contact on another and smaller target just to right of and 900 yards closer than first contact (ship contact #2).

2353: Radar contact on a third target about same size as first contact and located 1,000 yards beyond the first contact (ship contact #3).

2355: Radar contact on a fourth target smaller than the other contacts and 900 yards closer than No. 2 contact (ship contact #4).

2356: Have still only managed to build up speed to twelve knots since initial contact. With these fast targets at close range, have abandoned any idea of a methodical approach, the seas are mountainous with a driving rain. Can't see a thing but blackness and water with the water mostly in my face.

2358: Came left to 300°T to get off the track of the near target (believed to be a destroyer).

So reads Lieutenant Commander R. E. M. Ward's report, SAILFISH's tenth war patrol; date: December 3, 1943; time: early evening until midnight.

On the stroke of midnight the log continues:

0000: Near target close aboard on starboard quarter turned on what appeared to be a good size searchlight with a greenish tinge to it, directed at us and apparently signalling. He could not have seen us so assume he was signalling to someone else near us or he had a doubtful radar contact.

0001: Dove to 40 feet and came right to course 340°T for bow shot at biggest pip. We are 400 yards off track of near destroyer. All targets seem to be in line of bearing, roughly 280-100 degrees true with 900-1,000 yards between targets. Although initial radar contact was not made until a range of 9,500 yards, the picture looks as though we are on the left flank of a fast group of men of war, consisting of a destroyer, then possibly a cruiser, then a carrier or battleship, then another carrier or battleship with possibly something beyond that. Selected nearest of the two largest pips as our target.

0009: Near destroyer passing close aboard to starboard and ahead.

0012: Fired tubes 1, 2, 3, and 4, by radar setup, range 2,100 yards, gyro 53° to 37° right, track 108 to 120 port, torpedoes set at 12 feet, using spread of 1¾° right, 1¾° left, 5° left, and 5° right. Times of hits indicate torpedoes one and four were the hitting torpedoes. Commenced swinging left to bring stern tubes to bear. Heard two torpedoes hit.

0016: Two depth charges fairly close. Went deep and started crossing astern of target.

0017 to
0152: Nineteen depth charges, none very close. Completed reload.

0158: Surfaced and commenced running up target track to intercept possible cripple. Unable to make much speed without shipping black water.

0230: Radar contact bearing 310°T, range 8,400 yards. Commenced tracking (ship contact #5).

0240: Tracking shows target to be circling. The pip is small, yet can't believe radar would pick up a destroyer at 8,400 yards tonight. Commenced easing in slowly. At times the pip has an edge on it giving a momentary indication of another target very close to the one we are tracking.

0430: Target settled down on a northwesterly course, speed 2 to 5 knots. Radar pip now looks like we may have two targets very close together.

0550: Morning twilight and visibility improving fast, rain has stopped, but bridge is still shipping water, targets tracking with speed varying from 1 to 3 knots, range 3,500 yards. With visibility improving so rapidly must fire soon, hence have decided to fire three bow tubes on the surface and then attack again in daylight by periscope, making reload during approach.

0552: Fired tubes 1, 2, and 3, range 3,200 yards, gyros 002°, 00-½°, and 004-½°, estimated track 148° starboard, TDC speed 1 knot, torpedoes set at 10 feet, spread of 0°, ½° right, and ½° left.

0557: Observed and heard two torpedo hits. First hit looked like a momentary puff of fire, second hit looked like and sounded (on the bridge) like a battleship firing a broadside—even with the locomotive rumble so characteristic of sixteen inch shells. Commenced swinging ship to bring stern tubes to bear in case if target started going somewhere.

0558: The Nips started celebrating by firing star shells and heavy AA tracers from at least a dozen guns located at the point of the torpedo explosions, but didn't seem to know where we were because the shooting was directed everyplace but towards us. It's a good show, but despite the illumination I can't see the target.

0600: Tracers coming our way now—plenty of them.

0601: Submerged. Commenced checking torpedoes and reloading.

0603 to

0605: Four depth charges not near us.

0748: Finally see something—*Aircraft Carrier, range about 10,000 yards*, dead in water (ship contact #6). Nothing else in sight.

Impatiently continuing check of torpedoes. All tubes were flooded during each preceding attack. Gyro pots of one torpedo aft and one forward are flooded necessitating reload.

The carrier, stopped dead in the water, had been hit by two torpedoes.

That spoke volumes for the improvements which had been made on the Mark 14 exploder. It also spoke for a brand of fire control and the sort of submarine marksmanship that hell and the highest water could not frustrate.

Ward himself was not sure he had scored a hit in that wild typhoon. But the captain of the Japanese carrier was sure. At once he had flashed the message, "We are torpedoed."

But Japanese communications had broken down—only the cruiser MAYA received the carrier's first S.O.S.

The destroyer URAKAZE noticed from maneuvers that one of the vessels in the convoy was apparently in trouble, but she received no instructions and continued on her course.

At 0030 the carrier radioed a dispatch to Tokyo. *"Hit by one torpedo at 0010. Fire in crew's quarters forward. Able to proceed. Position 3230N., 14350 E."* In reply, Japanese Headquarters ordered URAKAZE to escort the damaged carrier and the other carrier in the convoy.

This message did not get through. A tow was then ordered for the crippled vessel, but the storm apparently canceled this assistance.

Then, at 0600, the damaged carrier was struck by another SAILFISH torpedo.

"Hit by torpedo," she radioed frantically. *"Can make no headway. Position 3155N., 143E."* Far distant, the carrier ZUIHO received this message and ordered the warships in the damaged carrier's vicinity to go to her assistance.

One of these, apparently URAKAZE, was sighted by SAILFISH.

0748: Momentarily sighted tops of a destroyer apparently standing by the carrier (ship contact #7). The picture now indicates that we have a badly damaged carrier plus one destroyer. If there were a cruiser here with 85 foot tower and 125 foot mast he'd show up like a sore thumb compared to the carrier's 60 foot flight deck. Depth control is extremely difficult due to mountainous seas. When we are at 60 feet there is nothing but green waves with the scope looking into or under a wave most of the time. At 55 feet we damn near broach and still can only see about twenty percent of the time. I am convinced that the carrier is a dead duck but there should be someone else around besides a single destroyer, yet there is nothing else in sight from 55 feet and no screws on sound. Am passing carrier down port side from aft forward, range about 1,500 yards. He has many planes on deck forward and enough people on deck aft to populate a fair size village. The only visible evidence of previous hits is a small list to port and a small drag down by the stern. The number of people on deck indicates they are prepared to abandon ship—a reassuring picture.

Ward maneuvered SAILFISH abeam of the stalled carrier.

As there were still no other Japanese ships in sight, he steered the submarine around into position to aim the stern tubes at the target for a straight stern shot.

0940: Fired tubes 5, 6, and 7, TDC range 1,700 yards, gyros 182° 185¾°, track 88 port, torpedoes set at 12 feet, using a spread of 0°, 8° right, and 2° left. All torpedoes heard running normal.

0942: Two hits (time indicates 2,700 yard torpedo run) heard on sound and throughout the boat, followed by a very heavy swish on sound then by exceptionally loud breaking up noises heard not only on sound but also very clearly throughout the boat. Although I had the periscope up anticipating the pleasure of watching the hits, depth control was so lousy that we were at 60 feet when the torpedoes hit and all I could see when the scope was out of the waves was a skyful of tracers being shot up into the air from the carrier's bearing. Ordered right full rudder and came to 70 feet to come around for bow shots. Can't figure how I made the range. Have been using a carrier flight deck height of 60 feet on the stadimeter.

0944 to

0945: Two depth charges not too far away.

0950: Completed turning. Still hear the breaking up noises.

0951: At 55 feet for a look. Nothing in sight on, or either side of, generating bearing. Made sweep to look for the destroyer and sighted a heavy cruiser of the TAKAO or NACHI Class. Commenced swinging hard left to bring bow tubes to bear (ship contact #8).

297

0952: Angle on the bow 10 starboard and he is still swinging towards, range 3,300 yards. Between my surprise at having underestimated the range to the carrier (2,700 yard torpedo run instead of 1,700), the fairly close depth charges from a destroyer I still hadn't been able to see, the surprise sighting of the cruiser racing our way with her forefoot showing over the waves, and the boat starting to broach with her left full rudder, I ordered 90 feet, and thus threw away the chance of a lifetime. Picked him up on sound and attempted to get a ping range on the QC head. Took turn count on JK head of 220, indicating 18 knots. By the time data was obtained from sound to allow even a chance of a hit he was astern and fading out fast. The Monday morning quarterbacks can have a field day on this attack! To top it all off, I have personally criticized the sinking of the SORYU, where the towing cruiser could have been gotten first, then the carrier at leisure—yet, I didn't go up ahead of the carrier and make *absolutely* certain that this wasn't a similar set up. This cruiser was undoubtedly on the off bow of the carrier.

0954 to
1004: Seven depth charges not too close. Destroyer screws fading in and out. Keeping them abaft the beam.

1330: Periscope depth. A careful fifteen minutes look at depths between 52 and 60 feet reveals nothing. I am convinced the carrier has been sunk and the cruiser has gotten clear.

1400: Set course to proceed to area.

2400: One full day's work completed.

The carrier, hit a third time at 0942, had gone down at 0948. Conducted from start to finish in a dragon-toothed typhoon, the battle had lasted ten hours. Ward had no need to worry about the comments of the "Monday morning quarterbacks." Vice Admiral Miwa, Commander Japanese Submarines, cited the SAILFISH performance as a striking example of what submarines could accomplish by relentless and persistent attacks.

Malign fate. A favor on one hand, and cruel deprivation on the other. Veteran of the Pacific War, the escort carrier sunk by SAILFISH had been one of Japan's busiest—made frequent runs as an aircraft ferry to Truk. She was CHUYO. And aboard her on this fatal return trip to Japan were the 21 SCULPIN survivors who had been placed in her hold at Truk.

Only one of these SCULPIN men survived the sinking of CHUYO. A final irony—that SCULPIN should have been the submarine which stood by during the SQUALUS rescue in 1939 when SQUALUS sank off the Isle of Shoals. SQUALUS—raised and renamed SAILFISH.

1943 Summary

As 1943 draws to a close, the Pacific submarine war is roaring into high gear. Last sinking of the year is scored in waters off the Solomons by GREENLING (Lieutenant Commander J. D. Grant)—victim, the freighter SHOHO MARU, 1,936 tons.

The submariners may now look back on 1943 with satisfaction—a year that begins in disappointments engendered by torpedo trouble, and ends in a mood of triumph, with Allied forces driving ahead on all fronts and United States submarines leading the drive.

Limited offensives are ended, and the big push is begun. Surface fleets, air fleets, land forces are ready for the advance to the Philippines, the shove to Tokyo. The submarine forces are in good fettle. There are, at the end of 1943, some 75 fleet submarines in the Central Pacific, representing a net increase of 22 during the year. Three new tenders—BUSHNELL, ORION and EURAYLE—reported for duty in 1943, and two of these have been serving in the Central Pacific, thus making a total of six tenders operating with SubPac. Material shortages and consequent deprivations are over.

Torpex in February—contact exploders in June—the electric torpedo in October—these improvements have contributed heavily to the 1943 score. Tactics developed and established—the radar attack, the end-around, wolf-packing—have implemented the expanding submarine offensive. The lifeguard submarine and periscope photographic reconnaissance are innovations soon to become integral features of submarine support of fleet operations. The sinking of CHUYO appears as handwriting on the wall for the Imperial Navy. With dependable weapons, new tactics, new capabilities, the submariners are far ahead of New Year's Day, 1943. As one man, the submarine forces in the Pacific speak up for the forthright and inspiring leadership of Admiral Lockwood.

The year has exacted casualties. Seventeen submarines. Eight of the SubPac Force—seven in the Southwest Pacific—two in the Atlantic. The loss is heavy. But the Germans have lost over five times this number in 1943. The enemy in the Pacific has lost 22.

And Japanese merchant shipping losses have mounted to a peak approaching crisis—some 300 Japanese ships of 500 tons or over have been sunk by U.S. submarines alone. Japanese oil is becoming watery. The 20 large tankers lost by Japan—some 17 or 18 to submarine torpedoes—do not entirely account for the shortage which is becoming acute. Hundreds of tons of aviation gasoline and crude oil shipped in barrels went down aboard cargo vessels—leaving thirsty throats among the Emperor's tanks and planes.

The success of the submarine attrition war against the Japanese merchant marine may be seen in the

298

table below (statistics from the U.S. Strategic Bombing Survey). Note the mounting tonnages beginning in March 1943, and that summer's increase in "days on offensive patrol." Note, too, the bulky tonnage-total subtracted from the enemy's merchant shipping in November.

Japan is now unable to balance sinkings with replacements. Merchant ship construction, originally under control of the Ministry of Transport, is at this time under control of the Imperial Navy—a measure introduced in the summer of 1942. Military supervision has "put the heat" on the building industry, but the merchant shipyards of Nippon are far in arrears. As of March 1943, Japan's merchant losses totaled a million and a quarter tons. And on that date, her merchant fleet, despite frantic shipbuilding efforts, has shrunk 7½% below its December 1941 size.

This shrinkage is largely due to the war of attrition waged by submarines. The enemy's shipbuilding index rises in 1943 (272 vessels in May; 392 in November). But his ships go down faster than his index goes up. Total ship construction in 1943: 796,000 tons. Total losses (mainly to submarines): 1,803,000 tons. Replacement of less than 45%. Even Tokyo's statisticians can see there is no percentage in that!

The conclusion to be drawn is equally inescapable: Japan must have merchant shipping to prosecute the war—Japanese merchant ships are being sunk faster than the shipyards can replace them—therefore, Japan is now losing the war.

"Submarines," admitted Admiral Nomura, under post-war interrogation, "*initially did great damage to our shipping. And later the submarines, combined with air attack, made our shipping very scarce. Our supply lines were cut and we could not support these supply lines. . . . Our experts knew that it was necessary to have 3,000,000 tons of shipping just for civilian living in Japan.*"

The admiral added that another 3,000,000 tons of merchant shipping were required in order to maintain the Imperial Japanese Army and Navy in the field.

With a scant 5,000,000 tons afloat in December 1943, civilian living in Japan is not so good. Everything is declining in quantity and quality, including morale. Drugged though they are with nationalistic propaganda, the Japanese people are not entirely blind. Their leaders cannot fabricate textiles out of talk, nor rice out of wordage. Perfumed smoke from all the shrines of Shinto cannot hide the signs in the sky.

Night over the Aleutians—sunset in the Solomons and Bismarcks—sundown in the Gilberts—long shadows reach across the Pacific from the north and east and cross the face of Japan. Thunder rumbles in the Mandates. The wind is rising in the Philippines. In Tokyo the glass is falling. The Japanese brace themselves for the coming storm. The warnings are coming from all corners of the Asian Pacific—warnings that contain the Japanese code-word for "submarines."

Month	*Merchant ships sunk by submarines*	*Merchant tonnage afloat*	*Submarine offensive*	
			Number days on offensive patrol	*Number of torpedoes expended*
December 1941 through February 1943 ..	717,708	6,076,553	425	132
1943				
March	109,447	5,771,398	442	299
April	105,345	5,732,762	448	263
May	122,319	5,630,243	437	237
June	101,581	5,536,304	659	389
July	82,764	5,487,600	532	297
August	80,799	5,465,238	858	387
September	157,002	5,430,804	697	461
October	118,847	5,320,196	648	423
November	231,684	5,262,937	572	454
December	131,531	5,034,778	407	251
10-month total	1,241,319			

NEW SUBMARINES COMMISSIONED IN 1943

NAME	FIRST COMMANDING OFFICER	NAME	FIRST COMMANDING OFFICER

BUILT AT ELECTRIC BOAT COMPANY

NAME	FIRST COMMANDING OFFICER
BLUEFISH	Lt. Comdr. G. E. Porter, Jr.
BONEFISH	Lt. Comdr. T. W. Hogan, Jr.
COD	Lt. Comdr. J. C. Dempsey
CERO	Lt. Comdr. D. C. White
CORVINA	Lt. Comdr. R. S. Rooney
DARTER	Lt. Comdr. W. S. Stovall, Jr.
ANGLER	Lt. Comdr. R. I. Olsen
BASHAW	Lt. Comdr. R. E. Nichols
BLUEGILL	Lt. Comdr. E. L. Barr, Jr.
DACE	Lt. Comdr. J. F. Enright
DORADO	Lt. Comdr. E. C. Schneider
FLASHER	Lt. Comdr. R. T. Whitaker
FLOUNDER	Comdr. C. A. Johnson
GABILAN	Lt. Comdr. K. R. Wheland
JACK	Lt. Comdr. T. M. Dykers
LAPON	Lt. Comdr. O. G. Kirk
MINGO	Lt. Comdr. R. C. Lynch, Jr.
MUSKALLUNGE	Lt. Comdr. W. A. Saunders
PADDLE	Lt. Comdr. R. H. Rice
PARGO	Lt. Comdr. I. C. Eddy

BUILT AT MANITOWOC SHIPBUILDING CO.

NAME	FIRST COMMANDING OFFICER
POGY	Lt. Comdr. G. H. Wales
POMPON	Lt. Comdr. E. C. Hawk
PUFFER	Lt. Comdr. M. J. Jensen
RASHER	Comdr. E. S. Hutchinson
RATON	Lt. Comdr. J. W. Davis
RAY	Lt. Comdr. B. J. Harral
REDFIN	Lt. Comdr. R. D. King
ROBALO	Lt. Comdr. S. H. Ambruster
ROCK	Lt. Comdr. J. J. Flachsenhar

BUILT AT MARE ISLAND NAVY YARD

NAME	FIRST COMMANDING OFFICER
TINOSA	Lt. Comdr. L. R. Daspit
TULLIBEE	Lt. Comdr. C. F. Brindupke

BUILT AT PORTSMOUTH NAVY YARD

NAME	FIRST COMMANDING OFFICER
STEELHEAD	Lt. Comdr. D. L. Welchel
BALAO	Lt. Comdr. R. H. Crane
BILLFISH	Lt. Comdr. F. C. Lucas, Jr.
BOWFIN	Comdr. J. H. Willingham, Jr.
CABRILLA	Lt. Comdr. D. T. Hammond

NAME	FIRST COMMANDING OFFICER
CAPELIN	Lt. Comdr. E. E. Marshall
CISCO	Lt. Comdr. J. W. Coe
CREVALLE	Lt. Comdr. H. G. Munson

BUILT AT CRAMP SHIPBUILDING CO.

NAME	FIRST COMMANDING OFFICER
DEVILFISH	Lt. Comdr. E. C. Stephan
DRAGONET	Lt. Comdr. J. H. Lewis
ESCOLAR	Comdr. W. J. Millican

BUILT AT MARE ISLAND NAVY YARD

NAME	FIRST COMMANDING OFFICER
SEAHORSE	Comdr. Donald McGregor
SKATE	Lt. Comdr. E. B. McKinney
TANG	Lt. Comdr. R. H. O'Kane
TILEFISH	Lt. Comdr. R. M. Keithly

BUILT AT PORTSMOUTH NAVY YARD

NAME	FIRST COMMANDING OFFICER
APOGON	Lt. Comdr. W. P. Schoeni
ASPRO	Lt. Comdr. H. C. Stevenson
BATFISH	Lt. Comdr. W. R. Merrill
ARCHERFISH	Lt. Comdr. G. W. Kehl
BURRFISH	Lt. Comdr. W. B. Perkins, Jr.

BUILT AT ELECTRIC BOAT COMPANY

NAME	FIRST COMMANDING OFFICER
PERCH	Lt. Comdr. B. C. Hills

BUILT AT MANITOWOC SHIPBUILDING CO.

NAME	FIRST COMMANDING OFFICER
GOLET	Lt. Comdr. J. S. Clark
GUAVINA	Lt. Comdr. Carl Tiedeman

BUILT AT PORTSMOUTH NAVY YARD

NAME	FIRST COMMANDING OFFICER
SANDLANCE	Lt. Comdr. M. E. Garrison
PICUDA	Lt. Comdr. Albert Raborn
PAMPANITO	Lt. Comdr. C. B. Jackson, Jr.
PARCHE	Lt. Comdr. L. P. Ramage
BANG	Lt. Comdr. A. R. Gallaher
PILOTFISH	Lt. Comdr. R. H. Close
PINTADO	Lt. Comdr. B. A. Clarey
PIPEFISH	Lt. Comdr. W. N. Deragon
PIRANHA	Lt. Comdr. H. E. Ruble
PLAICE	Lt. Comdr. C. B. Stevens, Jr.
POMFRET	Comdr. F. C. Acker

BUILT AT MARE ISLAND NAVY YARD

NAME	FIRST COMMANDING OFFICER
SPADEFISH	Comdr. G. W. Underwood

PART IV

PACIFIC SWEEP
(1944)

Then rose from sea to sky the wild farewell—
    Then shriek'd the timid and stood still the brave—
Then some leap'd overboard with dreadful yell,
    As eager to anticipate their grave. . . .
And first one universal shriek there rush'd,
    Louder than the loud ocean, like a crash
Of echoing thunder; and then all was hush'd,
    Save the wild wind and the remorseless dash
Of billows. . . .

                                           BYRON

CHAPTER 23

OCEANIC HOUSECLEANING

(JANUARY-JUNE 1944)

The Broom

Back in the middle of the Seventeenth Century a stout Dutch fleet under sturdy Admiral von Tromp shot the ambition out of decadent Spain's sea power, and went on to hand the English a historic drubbing. As a symbol of Dutch intentions to sweep the enemy from the ocean, a broom was lashed to the masthead of each of von Tromp's warships. Cromwell's captains replied by tying whips aloft. Although the Dutch failed to win control of the seas, they shattered a British blockade, and von Tromp's brooms, symbolizing naval victory, were soon adopted by naval custom.

America's Revolutionary captains flew brooms as signals of triumph. Not too often, but Paul Jones and one or two others swept several of the King's warships into Davy Jones' dust-bin. And Preble's Boys in 1812 came back from battle with brooms aloft. The custom presently was laid aside with shoe-buckles, ear-rings and the nine-tailed cat. But in World War II it reappeared, appropriately revived by U.S. submarines which had operated in the Netherlands East Indies with the Dutch cruiser TROMP.

The SoWesPac submariners took it up with enthusiasm. And as the undersea war spread across the Pacific, the old broom-at-masthead symbol spread with it. No, it was not surprising to see a battle-bitten S-boat or a war-scarred fleet submarine come sliding into harbor with triumphant broom on high. "Sweep" became the word for it in 1943. There were many new submarines that year, making good the adage about new brooms. In 1944 the sweeping was accelerated so that before year's end a fitting symbol for U.S. submarines would have been a vacuum cleaner.

This oceanic housecleaning was going full blast in January when "Operation Flintlock" was scheduled to strike the Marshall Islands. Having secured the Gilberts, the United States was ready to unleash in the Central Pacific an offensive designed to obliterate or neutralize Japan's Mandate bases and carry through to the Philippines. The drive on the Marshalls was the first move on the calendar.

The Japanese anticipated a Central Pacific push and strove to build a sea wall to withstand the threatened onslaught. After defeat in the Upper Solomons and loss of the Gilberts, the Imperial High Command pulled back the defense perimeter to a secondary line which extended from the Bonin Islands to the Marianas, and on down through the eastern Carolines to central New Guinea. As bastions in the wall, Saipan, Truk and Palau were bases to be held at all cost. Although the Allies were not so advised by Tojo, the great Bismarck base at Rabaul and the Marshall strongholds of Kwajalein and Eniwetok were already conceded untenable. Truk was shaky, but could be bolstered to withstand siege. Admiral Kurita's Second Fleet was to hold out there as long as possible without adequate air support. Ozawa's carrier force had steamed north to Japan to replace the planes massacred in November at Rabaul. Once this force recovered its wings, it could rejoin Kurita, and the two fleets could serve as roving bulwarks in the line.

The above is oversimplified, but it furnishes a generalized picture of the enemy's strategic intentions as the calendar opened at 1944. However, the conception of a defensive sea wall embodies a fallacy. Figurative or literal, no wall could go deep enough to prevent the passage of submarines. At least, no wall the Japanese were able to construct could block the number of U.S. submarines by that time operating in the Pacific. While the Japanese worked to set up "secondary lines" and consolidate "previously prepared positions" on an "outer defense perimeter," the raiders and blockaders of SubPac and SubSoWesPac roamed the Empire's "Inner Zone" and the deepest recesses of the Co-Prosperity Sphere.

Submarines supported the fleet in the assault on the Marshalls. After the Marshalls were swamped, they cooperated with Task Force Fifty-eight when the Navy launched a series of carrier air strikes at Truk, Saipan and Palau. These sea-air operations ("Hailstone" and "Desecrate") of February and March 1944 were followed by the Marianas Campaign ("Operation Forager") in June. Submarines participated in each of these large-scale operations. And when the Palau Campaign ("Operation Stalemate") and the Leyte Campaign ("King Two") developed in the autumn, submarines were in the forefront of these onslaughts that brought down crashing the last major bastions of Japan's Outer Empire.

The parts played by submarines as direct participants in these carrier-air strikes and smashing "triphibious" offensives are detailed in ensuing chapters titled *Submarine Support of Fleet Operations* and *Submarines vs. The Japanese Navy*. The present chapter is concerned with the war of attrition which undermined the enemy's defenses and prepared the way for the great Pacific drives.

Every base-capturing amphibious push was preceded by a concentrated submarine campaign to cut the enemy's service of supply and weaken the target garrison by depriving it of military stores and troop reinforcements. With their brooms the submariners sweep the open-sea lanes before each oncoming drive as sweepers clear the ice before the oncoming "stone" in the game of curling. But long before the crushing air strikes and massive offensives were launched, submarines had blown holes in the enemy's sea wall and blasted the very moats of his Imperial citadel, the home Empire.

It is obvious, therefore, that the torpedo attack on the enemy's outer supply lines, and the attrition campaigns which softened the fortification of the Inner Zone and made quicksand of the foundations under the enemy's home citadel, were in no way divorced from the "island-hopping" offensives waged by United States forces in the Pacific in 1944. If the point seems labored, it is reiterated because the more spectacular submarine exploits of World War II—the dramatic special missions and great submarine battles—have been detailed in this volume at the expense of scores of anti-shipping patrols numerically beyond the limits of book-covers and conducted with a precision and regularity which would seem mundane. These hard-plugging, day-in, day-out patrols, with their sweepings here and sweepings there, all but swept away Japan's merchant marine and thereby reduced the Empire's war effort to virtual impotence. Japan—the home islands—remained to be reckoned with to the last. But as early as January 1944, when the United States all-out Pacific offensive was just getting under way, the Japanese Empire was dissolving to dust under the attrition sweep of submarine brooms.

Attrition vs. Japanese Empire

The attrition war waged by U.S. submarines against Japanese shipping can be seen as a triple-purpose operation. Its moves were aimed at three elementary objectives. First: the cutting of supply lines between Japan and the Empire's outlying military bases—a move obviously related to military strategy. Second: the cutting of transportation lines between conquered territories and the home Empire—a move to prevent the exploitation of those territories and thus deprive the Japanese homeland of foodstuffs and vital raw materials. Third: the cutting of transportation lines between the home Empire and colonial and other foreign markets—a move to liquidate the enemy's overseas commercial enterprises. To some extent, all three objectives were related. But the last two, calculated to disrupt Japan's foreign trade and stifle her domestic industries, blended to achieve an ultimate and most important objective—the ruination of the Empire's economy. This, it might be said, was the chief objective of the submarine attrition war. An examination of the target—Imperial Japan's economy—is in order.

Needless to say, the economy in question is not the type which has a limited reference to frugality. Reference here is to the economy of Economics—of supply and demand, production and consumption, the distribution of goods and the accumulation of wealth. "Economy" is one of those fuzzy words so all-embracing as to defy thumbnail definition. It is, according to one dictionary, *"the practical adjustment, organization, or administration of affairs or resources, especially the industrial resources of a state."* This same authority defines the adjective "economic" as *"pertaining to money matters or wealth, or to the means and methods of living well and wisely."* Thus an Empire's economy appertains to such diverse matters as Imperial organization and financial well-being, with the emphasis on industrial resources. The commercial implications are obvious.

For an Empire is—when divested of its flags and furbelows—nothing more than a union or federation of states, or a ruler nation with subject colonies, organized for commercial advantage. If the Empire is a union or federation, the advantages may be mutual and equally shared by the member states. The colonial Empire is patently organized for the principal benefit of the suzerain—the ruling nation. In any case, an Empire is a business organization comparable to a corporation or a holding company. It buys, manufactures, sells, competes for markets exactly as does any business firm. Which is to say, it is operated for economic gain.

Historians have long remarked the relationship between wars and economy. Invariably the wars of aggression in modern history have been power plays on the part of nations determined to expand the national income by seizure of foreign markets, or enslavement of weaker peoples for cheap labor, or capture of valuable territory. Just as invariably, the aggressors have screened their mercenary motives behind the high-sounding verbiage of a "righteous cause"—the need for "Living Space"—protection for racial groups related to the Fatherland—"Manifest Destiny"—cultural crusade—divine will—the rescue of "national honor." Stripped of these masquerades, the basic motive is exposed as an ambitious tradesman. Wars of aggression are deliberate grabs for wealth or the sources of wealth. Literally, they are waged to make money. Witness the naïve propaganda of the Japanese, promising a "Co-Prosperity Sphere."

As the aggressor nation's objective is economic gain, the target for counter-attack is clearly discernible. Destroy the aggressor nation's hope for profit—put its national or imperial economy on the red side of the ledger—and that nation's war effort collapses like a bankrupt brokerage house. Of course, military reverses in the field may bring about such a collapse by demolishing the enemy's expensive War Machine. Or the prolongment of resistance to the point where the aggressor can no longer afford the military cost may result in the desired collapse. Another means to that end—and a most direct means—is an attack on the enemy's commercial system. Since an Empire—in particular, a colonial or maritime Empire—is chiefly engaged in foreign (overseas) trade, any disruption of that trade is bound to undermine the Empire's economy.

Hence the naval blockade, which, reduced to its least common denominator, is a strategic measure designed to dead-stall a maritime nation's commerce. A blockade may also serve important military objectives. It may bottle up an enemy fleet, or deprive that fleet of basing facilities. But the blockade which interferes with merchant shipping is largely devoted to wrecking the enemy's foreign trade, ruining his export business, preventing the delivery of imports. Deprivation of imports may strangle the enemy's war-making ability by choking off his food supply, or throttling the flow of raw materials demanded by his shipyards, aircraft plants and gun factories. While this hampers his military endeavors in the field, it also hinders his industrial endeavors on the home front. Industrial dislocations do more than slow up war production. They threaten the wartime profits of manufacturers, the wartime wages of workmen. They may reduce the value of a corporation's stocks and bonds to so much wallpaper. Shut down a single industrial firm—say, a manufacturer of aircraft propellers—and national economy suffers. It experiences similar pangs when a tea shop closes down for lack of tea, a shoemaker shuts his doors for lack of leather, or a merchant who exports goldfish ends up in a breadline because he is cut off from the foreign buyer. Prior to the advent of atomic destruction, perhaps nothing short of counter-invasion could put a maritime nation "out of business" as decisively as a successful blockade.

The submarine blockade of Japan's home islands was contrived to put the Japanese Empire out of business. So were the attrition campaigns waged in the Philippines-Malaya-Netherlands East Indies theater. It was remarked at the beginning of this volume that few nations were more dependent on shipping than Japan. The Empire's foreign trade was dependent on shipping. And most of Japan's domestic trade was waterborne. For the home islands were almost as aquatic as Venice. Japan's principal cities were seaports. The mountainous character of the islands limited railroading to a few short lines. Interior highways were negligible and neglected. Coastwise shipping carried most of the local freight, and inter-island steamers served to link the chief ports of the archipelago.

Moreover, the mountainous Japanese islands produced few of the commodities necessary for the maintenance of a large population, much less an industrial plant striving to manufacture a surplus of goods for overseas sale. In the matter of food alone, Japan had to import about 20% of the total supply needed for home consumption. Nearly all of the sugar came from overseas, along with large percentages of rice and wheat, and over 50% of the salt, soy beans and corn. About a third of the raw materials necessary for industry were imported. All of the cotton, wool, rubber, phosphorite, nickel, asbestos and bauxite came from overseas sources. More than 50% of the iron ore, coking coal, scrap iron, petroleum, lead, tin, hides and hemp—to name a smattering of vital items —was shipped in. Only in raw silk, sulphur and one or two other minor products was Japan wholly self-sufficient. It was on this score that the nation's expansionists justified Japanese imperialism. And in passing it might be observed that it was the unbounded ambition of that imperialism and the brass-knuckle methods of its advancement that brought Japan into conflict with the democratic nations. But the point concerns the merchant marine. If the Empire had to engage in foreign trade to prosper, Japan had to import to survive. Thus the submarine attack on Japanese shipping struck at the enemy's most vulnerable spot.

The Japanese freighter sunk off Kagoshimo, the Japanese ore barge sunk off Bandjermasin—any Japanese merchant vessel sunk anywhere rang up a loss in the Imperial cash register. In fact, the sinking would ring up several losses. First, the ship itself—an item of considerable value. Then the cargo—of variable value, depending on the merchandise or commodities and the need. Then the loss in manpower and time—items not to be overlooked in a commercial budget. And perhaps the loss of a foreign customer (if the ship were carrying exports) or an industrial consumer (if the vessel were hauling raw materials to a domestic manufacturer—say, a textile factory—depending on this shipment).

To estimate the damage dealt the Empire's economy by the submarine attrition war, one must have at least a superficial knowledge of Japan's history as a foreign trader. A brief review will furnish the background picture.

After Nippon was opened to world commerce in 1854, the Japanese nation became highly industrialized. Adept at manufacturing, the Heavenly Kingdom was soon competing with other great powers for markets in every quarter of the globe. Japan's methods were aggressive and frequently unethical, but hardly more so than those of the other imperialistic powers in the race for markets during the ambitious Nineteenth Century. Suffice it to say that the Japanese were more than willing to back their ambitions with fire and sword, and by the turn of the century, the Empire was a going concern.

The progress of Japan's foreign trade is reflected by a few statistics. In 1900 Japan did an export business of approximately 204 million yen, and an import business of 287 million yen. The foreign trade

total (exports plus imports) of over 491 million yen was gratifying. But as imports exceeded exports, this created what economists call an "unfavorable trade balance." Japan was buying more than she was selling. Think of a nation as a bicycle factory or a grocery store, and it is evident that it will profit little if it continually buys more than it sells. Japan's up-and-coming Empire builders were determined to rectify this unprofitable situation.

If a bicycle manufacturer wishes to increase his profits, he may do several things. He may produce more bicycles for sale (by expanding his plant and obtaining more production materials). He may reap more profit per bicycle by cutting production costs (sometimes done by manufacturing with cheaper labor and—or—cheaper production materials). He may increase sales by developing new markets (with astute business methods, high-pressure salesmanship, or—as would a racketeer—guns, bombs and brass knuckles).

Japan's Empire builders entered Twentieth Century competition with all these methods at their disposal. A brief war (1904-1905), forced upon Japan by Czarist Russia, gave the Japanese expansionists their opportunity. In winning the Russo-Japanese War, the Japanese knocked out Czarist Russian rivalry in the Far East. Japan emerged as a first-class power with foreign markets and industrial resources in Manchuria and Korea. Or, to apply the "bicycle maker's formula," Japan could step up production with more and cheaper materials, could cut production costs with cheaper labor, and could go to town in Manchuria and Korea with sales. Formerly a sort of novelty shop, Nippon was now in Big Business.

The expansion of Japanese foreign trade during and immediately after the war with Czarist Russia is revealed in the following table. (Totals in yen.)

Year	Japanese Exports	Japanese Imports	Total Foreign Trade
1904	319,260,000	371,360,000	690,620,000
1905	321,533,000	488,538,000	810,071,000
1906	423,754,000	418,784,000	842,538,000
1907	432,412,000	494,467,000	926,879,000

Note that the trade balance is chronically unfavorable, but foreign trade is steadily increasing. One reason for the unfavorable trade balance: shortage of raw materials for the Japanese industrial plant. But Manchuria and Korea were now to be exploited.

In 1912 Japan's foreign trade figures totaled over a billion yen—more than double the figure for 1900. But as imports exceeded exports by about 90 million yen in 1912, the trade balance was still unfavorable.

During World War I, the Empire's foreign trade

continued to expand, and the Japanese cashed in by doing business while the manpower of Europe was prostrate in the trenches. The favorable trade balance is shown below (in *yen*).

Year	Japanese Exports	Japanese Imports	Total Foreign Trade
1915	703,306,000	532,449,000	1,235,765,000
1916	1,127,468,000	756,427,000	1,883,895,000
1917	1,603,005,000	1,035,811,000	2,638,816,000
1918	1,962,100,000	1,668,143,000	3,630,243,000

In 1920 Japan's foreign trade total went well over 4 billion *yen*, with an export business of 1,948,391,000 *yen*, and an import business of 2,336,174,000 *yen*. Business was still expanding, but the trade balance was once more unfavorable.

This condition persisted until 1935. In that year the Japanese Empire did an export business of approximately 2½ billion *yen*, and an import business of approximately the same. The trade balance almost broke even. Then in 1938 it was better than even. And in 1940 the Japanese export business rang the bell at 3,655,850,000 *yen*, while imports amounted to 3,452,725,000 *yen*. Exports were better than 200 million *yen* above imports. Japan, so to speak, was once more in the money. What had happened?

One of the things that had happened was the China War. Having conquered all the way from Peking to Foochow, Japan, the aggressor nation, had acquired vast, new markets, an immense body of cheap labor and miles of valuable territory. She had also acquired Axis partners who had launched another European war. The Empire was now prepared to boom as never before. While the nations of Europe were locked in a death struggle, Japan's industrialists could flood the newly captured markets and the markets of the world with seas of goods—goods manufactured by what amounted to slave labor, from raw materials plundered from the conquered Asiatic territories. That these territories were deliberately stolen and thousands of helpless humans had been butchered in such massacres as the rape of Nanking and the bombing of Shanghai, did not disturb the Shintoist conscience of Japan. Neither did the prospect of holding the captive populations in virtual slavery. Were not the Sons of Heaven born to conquer and rule? Meantime, clothing, pottery, toys, glassware, machinery, cotton goods and raw silks would pour into Manchuria, Korea, Kwantung Province, India, Africa, South America and the United States. Japan would hit the jackpot!

But several adverse developments interrupted this happy project. To begin with, the Imperial Army and Navy, high in the saddle after the conquests in China, wanted to continue conquering. Why stop at China, the militarists argued, when Indo-China, Siam, the Malay States and the Netherlands East Indies lay practically defenseless at Nippon's feet? Imagine the trade possibilities in those areas! Borneo oil alone would make the Empire rich! Japan was already the world's third maritime power. Here was her chance to become the greatest maritime power in the world!

Then, even as the fingers of Japanese tycoons itched for this new source of *yen*, the democratic nations of the world said, "No!" For Democracy had fostered a moral concept previously disregarded in international relations. Democracy was putting the emphasis on human relations. America had suffered through a great civil war to abolish slave labor. Now, in the Twentieth Century, the United States was prepared to recognize the independence of the Philippines. Great Britain was negotiating to establish the freedom of India and Burma. The democratic nations of Europe were joined in a struggle to stop the predatory Nazi and Fascist totalitarian empires. To stop the equally predatory "Prussia of the East," the United States threatened to clamp an embargo on American exports to Japan and discontinue the purchase of raw silk from Japan. These moves were intended to frustrate the drivers of the Japanese War Machine, heavily dependent on scrap iron for munitions, and to sober the *yen*-hungry industrialists. Raw silk was the No. 2 item on the Japanese export list, and the United States had been buying 85% of the output.

But the itch for *yen*, so often more compelling than common sense, drove the Japanese leaders to try the war gamble. Gearing for the conflict, the nation maintained a fairly even trade balance in 1941, although the foreign trade total fell about 1½ billion *yen* below the 1940 figure.

In 1942, with the Pacific conquest going well, the export-import balance was more favorable. But foreign trade fell off another 2 billion *yen*.

In 1943 the foreign trade total slightly bettered the figure for 1942, but the trade balance tipped unfavorably, with imports exceeding exports by about 300 million *yen*.

Here are Japan's foreign trade figures (in *yen*) for 1940-1943:

Year	Japanese Exports	Japanese Imports	Total Foreign Trade
1940	3,655,850,000	3,452,725,000	7,108,575,000
1941	2,650,865,000	2,898,565,000	5,549,430,000
1942	1,792,547,000	1,751,637,000	3,544,184,000
1943	1,627,350,000	1,924,350,000	3,551,700,000

This table tells the story of a Japanese foreign trade decline. In 1940—the year before Pearl Harbor—Japan's foreign trade totals something over 7 billion *yen*. In 1943 it is down to around 3½ billion *yen*—about a billion American dollars below the 1940 mark.

Compare this table with those registering Japan's foreign trade during the Russo-Japanese War period and the period of World War I, and the story assumes sharper significance. During the Russo-Japanese War, the Empire's business expanded. During World War I the Empire's business boomed. During World War II the Empire lost business. In short, the Pacific War, as of 1943, was not a paying proposition.

While the quoted figures apply only to foreign trade, it should be noted that every business enterprise in Japan was affected by foreign trade. A Tokyo laundry, for example, could run out of soap because soap manufacturers could not obtain fats. Shortage of fats could be due to scarcity of cattle. Scarcity of cattle could be due to a shortage of fodder caused by a lack of fertilizer for arid fields. This lack could well be due to submarines sinking ships which carried fertilizer, or ships which carried exports intended as payment for cargoes of fertilizer. Of course, the primary cereal loss would be more damaging to national economy than the tail-end shortage of laundry soap. But the point is that an Empire's foreign trade and domestic business go up or down together like the House that Jack Built. And, as the figures indicate, by the end of 1943 Japan's business was falling off.

The comment concerning submarines sinking ships which carried fertilizer suggests the part played by U.S. submarines in Japan's commercial decline. Other factors had a bearing in the matter. Before the outbreak of World War II much Japanese freight had been carried by foreign vessels. For example, in 1937 some 54% had been carried by Japanese merchantmen and 46% had been carried by vessels under foreign flags, principally British, American, German and Norwegian. The war, of course, prevented Japan from chartering these foreign ships for her Imperial trade. The war also automatically deprived the Empire of foreign markets and raw material sources in North and South America, Africa, India and Europe. However, Japan had expected to maintain the volume of her foreign trade by conquest and exploitation of the Asiatic coast from Hong Kong to Burma, seizure of the Philippines and Netherlands East Indies, and extension of the Empire to New Guinea. It was assumed that business within the Co-Prosperity Sphere would more than make up for the loss of American, European and African

trade. As this business was entirely dependent on shipping, which, in turn, was entirely dependent on the Japanese merchant marine—and as U.S. submarines were practically the only agents attacking Japanese shipping in the Co-Prosperity Sphere during the first two and a half years of the war—the submarine achievement becomes apparent.

Were a corps of expert accountants given exact tonnage figures and an inventory of every cargo sunk in the Pacific, they might be able to assess the precise amount of damage done to Japanese economy by the submarine war of attrition. Delays to shipping caused by bottlenecks at ports under blockade—time lost due to convoy travel and evasive routing—damage to cargoes water-soaked but not sunk—these would also enter the calculation. The figures are unobtainable. But it is clear that the submarine blockade and the attack on overseas shipping knocked much of the bottom out of Japan's foreign trade.

So this chapter featuring the attrition war might be aptly titled *Submarines vs. Japan's Economy*. Suitable sub-titles could read: *Submarines vs. Farm Machinery—Submarines vs. Coal and Iron—Submarines vs. Soy Beans—Submarines vs. Teapots—Submarines vs. Phosphates—Submarines vs. Kimonas—Submarines vs. Bamboo—Submarines vs. Silk Stockings.* Or, *Submarines vs. the Tokyo Stock Exchange.*

The submarines fighting the attrition war were vs. any shipload of anything that contributed to Japan's economic wealth. Textiles, bric-a-brac, any sort of manufactured article outward bound from Japan. Incoming tons of rice, bauxite, pig iron, oil, fish. But the submariners with their brooms were sweeping away something a lot more important than exports and imports. They were sweeping away the profits of the Toa Shipping Combine, of Mitsubishi Heavy Industries, Ltd., of the Aichi Aircraft Company, of the Nissan Automobile Company, of the Shoda Engineering Corporation, of the Nippon Gakki Seizo (Musical Instrument) Manufacturing Company. They were sweeping away the assets of the Zabitsu brokers and the Mitsui bankers, of Mr. Moto the contractor and Papa San the rickshaw salesman. They were sweeping the *yen* out of Japan's economy, and turning the war into an unprofitable business.

January Sweeps

Three sinkings inaugurated the attrition offensive on January 1, promising the Nipponese an unhappy New Year. HERRING (Lieutenant Commander R. W. Johnson) sank NAGOYA MARU, 6,072-ton cargo-aircraft ferry in the East China Sea. RYUYO MARU, 6,707-ton freighter was sunk by PUFFER (Lieutenant Commander F. G. Selby) off the coast of Mindanao. And

RAY (Commander B. J. Harrel) sank the converted gunboat OKUYO MARU, 2,904 tons, off Halmahera. On the first day of January 1944, submarines cost Japanese shipping 15,683 tons.

One of the busiest sweepers of the month was SEAWOLF, under Lieutenant Commander R. L. Gross. The submarine's insigne, a Disney wolf with a dripping torpedo in its teeth, might have appropriately been sketched as wearing a dust-cap on this patrol. Four Japanese ships fell afoul of the WOLF on the path near the Nansei Shotos. The WOLF played four kinds of havoc with this convoy.

Down at sea on January 10 went ASUKA MARU, cargo, 7,523 tons, and GETSUYO MARU, cargo, 6,440 tons. Down at sea on January 11 went YAHIKO MARU, cargo, 5,747 tons, and down at sea on the 14th went the 3,651-ton cargo carrier YAMATSURU MARU. When SEAWOLF headed home from this Nansei Shoto patrol she had swept from Empire waters a total of 23,361 gross tons of Japanese shipping.

Farther up the Honshu coast, there was TAUTOG (Lieutenant Commander Sieglaff). Down went the freighter SAISHU MARU, 2,082 tons, on January 3, followed by the freighter USA MARU, 3,943 tons, on January 4th. Off Shikoku two more cargo carriers were swept away—ERIE MARU, 5,493 tons, and CHOSEN MARU, 3,110 tons—sunk on the 11th and 24th respectively, by STURGEON (Lieutenant Commander C. L. Murphy, Jr.). In adjacent Japanese waters, SWORDFISH (Captain K. G. Hensel) accounted for YAMAKUNI MARU, passenger-cargo carrier, 6,921 tons; DELHI MARU, converted gunboat, 2,182 tons; and KASAGI MARU, converted salvage vessel, 3,140 tons; on the 14th, 16th and 27th respectively. Between them these three submarines (TAUTOG, STURGEON and SWORDFISH) on Empire patrol that January swept away some 27,000 tons of Japanese merchant shipping. Nothing spectacular. Nothing in headlines. Merely attrition-war routine.

In the Mandate areas where the enemy was attempting to stiffen his outer defense lines, the January attrition war hit a somewhat swifter stride. Here the brooms went faster as there was more to sweep. And some of the routine brooming done at this time in Mandate waters (while the preliminary strikes at the Marshalls were under way) swept warships as well as merchantmen into the dust bin.

For example, there was ALBACORE, under Commander J. W. Blanchard. Patrolling south of the Carolines, she sank the 2,629-ton ex-gunboat CHOKO MARU, on January 12th. And on the 14th she destroyed the Imperial Navy destroyer SAZANAMI—the first Japanese DD to go down that year. SKIPJACK would sink another on the 26th, and GUARDFISH would down still another on February 1, but these submarines were units in "Operation Flintlock." ALBACORE was on routine patrol when she sank SAZANAMI. And as an incident in the war of attrition it was a broom-straw in the wind.

Now SEAHORSE came charging down from Pearl Harbor to sweep the seas around Palau. Another galloping patrol with Slade Cutter in the saddle and disaster for enemy shipping in the Pelews.

On the morning of January 16, while en route, SEAHORSE made periscope contact on a vessel with four escorts. Cutter had jockeyed his submarine into excellent position for a submerged stern-tube shot with Mark 18 electric torpedoes, but the target zigged away. With all four escorts fairly close and on the HORSE's side of the target, Cutter held fire and circled off to get clear and start an end-around. Suddenly and without warning, a depth charge exploded nearby. In the next hour an A/S vessel dropped five more depth charges, all close. Cutter wanted no part of that, and concentrated on submerged evasion.

At 1607, however, SEAHORSE was on the surface with four engines on the line, chasing. At 2009 Cutter made a surface attack and three hits demolished NIKKO MARU, freighter, 784 tons.

During the following two days no contacts were made, and the Horsemen worked on temporary repairs to the main induction, which had been damaged by depth charges. On the 19th, Cutter closed Fais Island for reconnaissance.

After entering her area, SEAHORSE contacted two enemy cargo ships with three escorts on January 21st. Cutter tracked all afternoon, then, making a late-evening surface attack, fired three torpedoes at one ship, and surprised himself by getting two hits in this target and one in the second ship, which he had intended to attack later. Both vessels stopped and opened fire, shooting wildly in every direction, while the escorts dropped random depth charges. SEAHORSE loitered at safe distance, while Cutter walked the periscope around. He saw one target sink, and then he fired four torpedoes, in pairs, at the other. A defect in the forward target bearing transmitter (T.B.T.) caused these to miss. Skirting the target, Cutter loosed two stern torpedoes for two hits. Down went the ship. These vessels were later identified as YASUKUNI MARU, 3,025-ton freighter, and IKOMA MARU, 3,156-ton passenger-cargoman.

On the evening of January 28, SEAHORSE contacted three freighters and five escorts coming out of the Malakal Passage entrance to Palau. Noting that the escorts were keeping on a line of bearing between submarine and the targets, Cutter spurred the submarine ahead for a submerged approach. At dawn, the convoy changed course, and SEAHORSE remained some distance submerged astern. At dusk Cutter ordered the submarine surfaced. By 2150 he had the HORSE in position for an attack. But the escorts, displaying an uncanny ability to intervene, frustrated the attack until after midnight.

At 0132, January 30, a radical target-zig to the right threw the two escorts far back on the quarter and gave SEAHORSE her opportunity. Ensued a race between SEAHORSE and the escorts for position, but the former's speed advantage put her out in front, and at 0149 Cutter fired three torpedoes for three hits. The target ship "sank with 90° rise bubble." She was TOKO MARU, a 2,747-ton freighter.

At dawn SEAHORSE lost radar contact with the rest of the convoy. However, she soon regained it and maintained contact by keeping station on a steadily pinging escort as the convoy milled around. In mid-afternoon the convoy split, and under cover of darkness that evening SEAHORSE resumed surface search. It was some time before the submarine could locate the quarry, but Cutter was as patient as he was persistent when the game called for these dogged qualities. Late that night SEAHORSE was running the convoy down. At dawn she had the quarry in sight.

Throughout the day of January 31 she trailed the convoy's smoke as it trudged along the horizon. Radar tracking began at nightfall, and at 0019 on February 1, Cutter opened fire. Four torpedoes from the after tubes—no hits. At 0200 two stern-tube shots netted a double zero. All torpedoes exploded at end of run —misses probably due to the fleeing convoy's lucky zigs. At 0300, with only two after-torpedoes remaining, and all hands exhausted after a chase of 81 hours, Cutter ordered a dive at 10,000 yards' range to begin a submerged radar approach. At 0352 the final torpedoes were fired at 1,050 yards, the convoy's three escorts all within 1,500 yards. The depth-charge counter-attack lasted half an hour. At 0443 SEAHORSE reared to the surface to view the scene of her latest sinking. A mass of gasoline flames, with drums still exploding, the target, TOEI MARU, 4,004-ton AK, was going under. That evening Cutter headed SEAHORSE for the barn with four new victims on her battle flag.

Another SubPac submarine on duty off Palau was GAR (Lieutenant Commander G. W. Lautrop, Jr.). Two freighters fell prey to GAR. On January 20 she sank KOYU MARU, 5,325 tons. Three days later she swept away TAIAN MARU, 3,670 tons.

While SEAHORSE and GAR were sweeping around the Pelews, THRESHER (Lieutenant Commander D. W. MacMillan) was going after Japanese cargoes off the northern coast of Luzon. A veteran with pioneer experience, THRESHER was an expert sweeper, and as industrious as she was adept. On January 15 she sank two freighters, TATSUNO MARU and TOHO MARU. On the 27th, KIKUZUKI MARU and KOSEI MARU were brushed to the bottom by this hard-driving submarine. By this quartet of sinkings, THRESHER deprived Japanese shipping in the Philippines area of some 14,000 tons.

In the meantime, TINOSA (Lieutenant Commander D. F. Weiss) was sweeping in the South China Sea. Her broom caught a convoy on January 22nd; whereupon the Japanese lost KOSHIN MARU, passenger cargo, 5,485 tons, and SEINAN MARU, freighter, 5,401 tons.

So the submariners swept cargo after cargo from the sea lanes of the Western Pacific while "Operation Flintlock" stormed over the Marshall Islands. On January 31 the tireless TRIGGER (Lieutenant Commander Dornin), patrolling in the Carolines, concluded a record month by obliterating YASAKUNI MARU, converted submarine tender, 11,933 tons.

The random sinkings mentioned in the foregoing account provide apt examples of attrition warfare aimed at the three objectives previously discussed. In action off Palau, SEAHORSE and GAR were engaged in cutting a supply line to an outlying military base. TINOSA in the South China Sea and the submarines patrolling Philippine waters were cutting transportation lines from conquered territories to the home Empire. And the submarines in Empire waters were blockading Japan at close quarters, stopping export shipping at the source and import shipping at the terminal.

The sinkings reported are only a representative sample of that month's sweepings. In January 1944, U.S. submarines swept some 50 Japanese merchant vessels into oblivion. Into oblivion with the 50-odd merchant vessels went cargoes which included everything but the proverbial kitchen sink—and it may be that even that homely item was on one of the manifests.

Total merchant tonnage lost to U.S. submarines that month approximated 240,840 tons. This topped the tonnage sunk by U.S. submarines in any previous month of the war. And reference to the table on page 524 in the Addenda will show that in January 1944 the submarines sank a greater tonnage than they downed in the first seven months of the Pacific conflict.

Worse, from the Japanese standpoint, was yet to come. Improved torpedoes, better radar, new submarine tactics—these were factors calculated to make the war entirely uneconomical for an Empire dependent on shipping. Another and most important factor was the increasing number of submarines in the Pacific—submarines with well-trained crews and experience-trained skippers. Such a submarine with such a crew and skipper surfaced into prominence in February 1944. Her name was soon to echo across the Pacific like a bell—a ship's bell struck by a steel mallet. TANG!

Tang in Action

If there were something in the pseudo-science of Onomancy—the belief that names exert a fateful influence over their owners—certainly the Japanese who went to sea in World War II could have made something of it. BARB! WAHOO! TRIGGER! DRUM! These are names alive with sound and imagery, and the submarines so christened lived up to them. Not to mention FLASHER and RASHER! And those submarines with names which included HORSE, LION, SWORD, SILVER, GUARD, WOLF, ARCHER and SPADE.

Here a TAUTOG, POGY or SNOOK will step in to argue the matter, with every right. But the fact is that the submarines mentioned in the foregoing paragraph—submarines with vivid names—composed the majority of leaders in the ships-sunk and tonnage-sunk lists. TANG—with her sharp, resonant name—was no exception.

Built at Mare Island, she was commissioned in October 1943, and Lieutenant Commander Richard H. O'Kane was given her command. Veteran submariner, O'Kane had previously served as "Mush" Morton's exec in famous WAHOO—experience of a high order. Now he was to give TANG (and Japanese shipping) the benefit of that experience.

On January 22, 1944, the submarine departed from Pearl Harbor to conduct her first war patrol. So she began the career that was to send her name ringing through submarine history.

During the first two weeks of her maiden patrol, TANG served as one of the submarines cooperating in "Operation Hailstone," the carrier-air strike aimed at Truk in early February. This strike had originally been planned for April, but the rapid subjugation of the enemy's Marshall Islands strongholds put the Pacific offensive two months ahead of schedule. Assigned a station west of Truk, TANG was to cover the escape routes in that direction and destroy any Japanese ships attempting to flee the bombed Caroline base.

Early in the morning of February 17, while Truk was smoking like a volcano, TANG made radar contact on a two-ship convoy under powerful escort of a destroyer and five smaller A/S vessels. O'Kane tracked, determined the convoy's course and speed, then bored in for an attack.

TANG was nearly in position ahead when the starboard flanking escort suddenly swerved toward the submarine. With the A/S vessel 7,000 yards off, O'Kane gave the order to go deep.

Five depth charges were dropped in a haphazard pattern, and the escort shuffled away. Fifteen minutes later, O'Kane resumed the approach at radar depth, ignoring a few more charges which were dropped at random by the meandering escorts. When the range closed to 1,500 yards, O'Kane cut loose with a four-torpedo salvo aimed at the nearest merchantman. Three hits blasted the target. TANG's commander watched at the periscope as the vessel sank by the stern while the escorts ran hither and yon in futile frenzy. First blood for Tang was GYOTEN MARU, a 6,854-ton freighter.

Five nights later, TANG was in the vicinity of the Marianas where Saipan was under carrier-air attack. Again O'Kane and company played the backfield with orders to down any fugitive shipping.

Along came a Japanese convoy—three freighters protected by a destroyer and three A/S vessels. O'Kane directed a speedy surface attack. After tracking the convoy for half an hour, he maneuvered TANG into firing position on the port bow of one of the freighters and about 4,000 yards from the nearest escort. An unpredicted zig deranged the set-up for a moment, but O'Kane regained position, and the freighter came on nicely. When the range was 1,500 yards (TANG dead in the water and holding her breath), O'Kane let the freighter have it with four torpedoes spread over the target's length. The vessel blew to pieces and sank before TANG could complete an evasive turn. An infuriated escort rushed the submarine, but TANG seemed to find a couple of extra knots in her engines, and she outdistanced this counter-attacker in short order. In fragments strewn across the sea behind her, she left FUKUYAMA MARU, 3,581-ton passenger-cargoman.

TANG circled back on the convoy for a second attack. This time the leading escort conveniently wandered too far ahead of the target vessel. O'Kane succeeded in maneuvering TANG into the position formerly occupied by the escort. Then, stopping the submarine to wait for the precise moment, he fired four torpedoes. The first two struck the freighter in the stern, just aft of the stack. The third torpedo hit forward of the bridge. A dazzling explosion lifted the vessel almost out of the water, and dropped her back on a broken spine. The blast shook TANG like a depth-charge barrage, but quick checkup showed no serious damage done the submarine. The freighter that went under was eventually identified as YAMASHIMO MARU, 6,776 tons.

Tang spent the following day in comparative peace and quiet. Then, in the forenoon of February 24, a tanker, a freighter and a destroyer came into focus of her hunting periscope. Efforts to gain satisfactory position for a day-periscope attack were frustrated by rain squalls and the convoy's zigzagging. Contact was maintained, however, and O'Kane managed a night-surface attack. Four torpedoes terminated in three hits which destroyed the freighter.

While the freighter was expiring, the tanker opened fire fore and aft, and the Jap destroyer, then nearly 3,000 yards away, hurled shells in every direction. Tang did some evading. While doing so, she did not lose contact with the enemy "upstairs." When dawn arrived, O'Kane had the submarine in position for a submerged attack. Lookouts were all over the tanker's deck when O'Kane fired four torpedoes at the vessel. The resulting explosion hurled men and debris sky-high in a thunderhead of smoke. The ship sank by the stern, and was under water in four minutes. And Tang went to deep submergence as the depth charges started booming down. Japanese records would name this "tanker" a cargo ship—Echizen Maru, 2,424 tons.

The next day brought another merchantman over the horizon, and Tang sank Choko Maru, cargo, 1,794 tons. Her final maiden-patrol attack was made after moonset on February 26th. Late that afternoon, a contact was established, and Tang picked up another convoy. A transport, a freighter and four escorts composed this target group. O'Kane maneuvered Tang into attack position on the frantically zigzagging transport, and fired four torpedoes. All missed astern as the transport speeded up. But Tang, O'Kane and company could not hit everything.

And 16 hits out of 24 torpedo shots was masterful marksmanship for a submarine on her first war patrol. The five vessels sunk, depriving the enemy of some 21,000 odd tons, won Tang and O'Kane immediate notice.

Those names, linked together, were to go on submarining through the spring, summer and autumn until they melded into one word for the Japanese merchant marine. Nemesis!

Submarine Tactics—The "Minimum Silhouette Method"

One procedure employed in the conduct of night radar approaches was the "minimum silhouette method." Both experience and logic pointed out that the probability of being sighted was at a minimum when the submarine presented its bow to the target. The maneuver was taught at the Prospective Commanding Officer's School at New London. For each

submarine speed, a family of curves for various target-speeds was devised. For any given target speed, angle on the bow, and range (as determined by the curve), a submarine could keep its bow pointed toward the target, and end up in a favorable attack position on the target's beam. That, at least, was the theory. In practice, modification was necessary as the target ship maneuvered and its escorts changed position.

On February 1, 1944, Hake (Lieutenant Commander J. C. Broach) put this theory into practice with a nicety. She was conducting her first Pacific war patrol after two patrols in the Atlantic. Her first shot at Japanese shipping was fired in the Formosa-Nansei Shoto area on January 12, when she torpedoed and sank the 9,547-ton transport Nigitsu Maru. The last day of January found her far to the south, off the island of Halmahera. At 0030 on the following morning, she made a radar contact at 20,000 yards—almost 12 miles! A few minutes later the contact was discovered as a convoy of three cargo vessels with two small minesweepers as escorts. Radar tracking determined the convoy's speed at 8 knots. The ships were not zigzagging, probably because they were near land.

Broach succeeded in gaining a position ahead of the convoy and about 2,500 yards from the track on the starboard side. The night was dark, but the visibility was good. At 8,000 yards the target was sighted from the bridge. One escort was on the starboard bow and the other was patrolling astern. The starboard-bow escort was the only one occupying an interfering position.

The convoy moved against a land background, whereas the submarine was silhouetted against the light sea horizon. So as soon as the convoy was sighted, Broach presented Hake's bow to the target, and kept it that way. Presently the leading escort passed ahead. With the largest ship of the convoy on a 78° starboard track, range 2,000 yards, Broach fired three torpedoes from Hake's forward tubes at the two smaller freighters which presented an overlapping target at this juncture.

Two hits splashed the darkness with fire, and the largest of the three ships was seen to sink with her back broken. One of the smaller freighters appeared to be settling. Broach turned Hake to the right, put the escort astern, and built up to full speed. Pandemonium broke loose in the submarine's wake—a carnival of blowing whistles, flashing lights and general hullabaloo in the convoy. The radar pip on the torpedoed freighter grew weaker, and when the range was 10,000 yards, abruptly disappeared. Searchlights were raying out like a Japanese fan as Hake also abruptly disappeared. However, she reappeared later, which was not the case with TACOMA MARU, 5,772 tons, and NANKA MARU, 4,065 tons. Their silhouettes were minimized to the vanishing point. HAKE's minimum silhouette was a slim one which Broach used to advantage when a light horizon threatened to expose the submarine to the inshore target.

February Sweeping (Introducing Some Champions)

SNOOK, PLUNGER, POGY, FLASHER, RASHER and PUFFER all accomplished some vigorous sweeping during the second month of 1944. There were others—the Pacific's Oriental carpet was broad enough for all the brooms available. But the forenamed were among the busiest, and their work can stand as exemplary.

SNOOK (Lieutenant Commander C. O. Triebel) needed no introduction to attrition warfare. Captained by one of the aces of the Submarine Service, this veteran of the SubPac Force had already downed nine Japanese merchantmen when she headed for Empire waters on January 6, 1944. En route she encountered a converted gunboat steaming along west of the Bonins. Triebel fired a torpedo which disemboweled this vessel, and down went MAGANE MARU, 3,120 tons.

SNOOK went on to join the blockaders who were littering the beaches of Japan with burned-out hulks and soggy merchandise. Triebel's submarine proceeded to sweep a sizable mass of litter into the coastal waters of western Kyushu. Patrolling the approaches to Nagasaki, she torpedoed a corpulent cargoman on February 8th. On the 14th she sank another freighter; on the 15th, still another. Then, homeward bound and off the Bonins on February 23, she struck a passenger-cargo carrier not far from the spot where she downed the converted gunboat on the way out. When she concluded this patrol, SNOOK had swept five vessels under the Japanese fringe of the Pacific carpet. The sweepings—MAGANE MARU, LIMA MARU, NITTOKU MARU, HOSHI MARU NO. 2 and KOYO MARU—amounted to 20,046 tons.

While SNOOK was enforcing the blockade below Nagasaki, PLUNGER (Lieutenant Commander R. H. Bass) was performing similar duties off the Kii Suido. A lot of war had run under her bridge since the day she had pioneered in those same waters carrying the first radar set into battle. Now, in February 1944, that exploratory patrol seemed as long ago as the visit of Matthew Calbraith Perry. Her original SD aircraft warning installation had been a wonderful innovation. On her present run, PLUNGER carried the modern SJ. The T.B.T., new camouflage, accurate torpedoes and a score of innovations were on hand for this, her tenth, war patrol. The previous nine had been successful, so she made it ten straight.

On February 2 this veteran from pioneer days caught up with TOYO MARU NO. 5 and TOYO MARU NO. 8—sister freighters who were no match for PLUNGER. After disposing of this pair she experienced poor hunting in waters where the enemy had grown torpedo-shy. PLUNGER herself was responsible for some of this shyness. On previous Empire patrols she had sunk six merchantmen in Japan's coastal waters, and TOYO MARU NO. 8 was her eighth in the home islands area. Then, on the open road between Tokyo and the Bonins, she caught another freighter on February 23rd. Down went KIMISHIMA MARU and home went PLUNGER, concluding a run that cost the enemy 9,577 tons. Not a large tonnage, but the average for a hard-working submarine in an area where targets were not too plentiful.

Meantime, POGY (Lieutenant Commander R. M. Metcalf) found all the sweeping she could handle off Formosa. Japan's second largest colony (Korea being the largest), this big island lying at the toe of the Nansei Shoto chain was an important source of food for the home Empire. About 80% of the sugar consumed in Japan was imported from Formosa, as was some 38% of Japan's rice imports. Only the United States, Korea and India had sent larger shipments of commodities to Nippon, and Japanese exports to Formosa were correspondingly large.

Well aware of the colony's economic status in the Empire, SubPac Headquarters had marked the Formosa area for special attention in the summer of 1942. Thereafter it had been continuously patrolled. And now, with the war moving westward, Formosa's importance was increasing in the strategic as well as the economic field. For the island stood as the main way-station on the Malaya-Netherlands Indies-Philippines trunk line to Japan. Linking the East China and the China Sea, Formosa Strait served as a "protected" waterway for Japanese ship traffic north or south bound. The word "protected" is in quotes because the protection was not entirely literal. Roaming the southern end of Formosa Strait were U.S. submarines. In February 1944, for example, there was POGY.

On February 10 this submarine made contact with a convoy in Bashi Channel off the southern tip of Formosa. Riding herd was a Japanese destroyer. To Metcalf and his crew this was so much "pogy bait," and they lost no time in maneuvering to attack. For its part, the Imperial Navy lost the destroyer MINEKAZE, and the Japanese merchant marine lost the 5,500-ton passenger-cargoman MALTA MARU.

Metcalf headed the submarine northward up the east coast of Formosa, and on the 20th of February she caught a convoy on the Tropic of Cancer. Skillful approach and sharpshooting attack sent torpedoes slamming into Taijin Maru, freighter, 5,154 tons, and Nanyo Maru, freighter, 3,610 tons. Sugar? Rice? Sewing machines? Military gear? Whatever the cargoes, they never reached their destination.

Three days later, in Nansei Shoto waters, Pogy blew the bottom out of another freighter—Horei Maru, 5,888 tons. With a DD and four marus to their credit, Metcalf and company hoisted the broom and headed homeward. This submarine's February patrol cost the Japanese some 21,000 tons of Formosa shipping.

The thud of torpedo fire off Formosa had been echoed by torpex blasts in the China Sea. On February 5 one of these blasts had sunk Taishin Maru, a small freighter, in the tropical waters between Mindoro and the Caiamian Islands. On Valentine's Day more blasting in the same area swept Minryo Maru and Hokuan Maru, larger freighters, out of a convoy.

The submarine responsible for this din in the western Philippines was a newcomer operating with the Fremantle Force. On this, her maiden patrol, she had downed an ex-gunboat en route to her area. And the three cargomen off Mindoro gave her a first-patrol score of some 10,000 tons. But that was only a beginning—a cornerstone for a pyramid.

For before the year was out this submarine from Fremantle would amass a tonnage total monumental in U.S. submarine history. Three others—Tautog, Tang and Silversides—sank more ships. Spadefish, another newcomer, sank as many. But Flasher (captained first by Lieutenant Commander R. T. Whitaker and later by Lieutenant Commander G. W. Grider) was the greatest tonnage sweeper of them all. In 1944 this single submarine sank more shipping than was sunk by the entire U.S. Submarine Force in the first four months of the Pacific War!

Neck and neck with Flasher in this tonnage race (and only a few tons behind her on V-J Day) was Rasher. Out of Manitowoc in 1943, Rasher had reported to the Fremantle Force in the autumn of that year. Her torpedoes had already downed five Japanese ships when she headed west from Australia on February 19, 1944, to conduct a patrol in Netherlands East Indies waters.

Her skipper at this time was Lieutenant Commander W. R. Laughon, a crack marksman with torpedoes. Working with Laughon was one of those expert crews that functioned as a smooth-running team. Their performance on this patrol helped to lay the foundation for Rasher's immense tonnage score.

On February 25 she caught an enemy convoy off Bali. Dodging the escorts, Rasher bored in on the attack, and Laughon's deadly torpedo shots scored a double. First, Tango Maru, a 6,200-ton freighter, went dancing to the bottom. Then Ryusei Maru, 4,797-ton passenger-cargoman, joined the freighter on the sea floor. Rasher went on northward through the Strait of Makassar into the Celebes Sea. There she demolished a good-sized merchantman. For the next three weeks she found little to shoot at, but on the way home she sighted and sank another freighter off Bali. So this Rasher patrol, which extended through the month of March, subtracted from the enemy's merchant marine another 20,000 tons.

Rasher was only limbering up. Like Flasher, she would get in her biggest licks later in the year. Flasher did not hit her stride until July. Rasher's mightiest sweep came in August when she was captained by Commander H. G. Munson. Had some clairvoyant in Tokyo been able to foresee the tonnages torpedoed by Flasher and Rasher, the Board of Directors of Japanese Empire, Inc., might have abdicated sooner than it did. Between them, the two SoWesPac submarines sank more shipping, merchant and naval, than the Japanese lost from all causes in the first quarter of 1942.

However, the handkerchief of ignorance remained over Tokyo's eyes. Serious losses showed up on the graph, that was true. Twenty thousand tons here. Twenty thousand tons there. But in February 1944 the battle front was still a long way from Honshu, and the Empire's militarists were disinclined to worry over the problems of bespectacled economists.

On the American side, January's sinkings had caused exuberance in Submarine Headquarters. And February's returns were not all in before ComSubPac and ComSubSoWesPac knew their submarines were setting a new record. From the North Pacific to the Java Sea, Japanese shipping lanes were under torpedo fire and Japanese cargoes were going down in wholesale lots. And commodities were not the only items swept away. For instance, there was the transport sunk by Puffer.

This submarine will be recalled as the one which sweated out a classic depth-charging on her maiden patrol and provided the force with an interesting dossier on submarine psychology. Puffer's crew was determined to contrive something more than a case history. Having been on the receiving end, all hands were eager to repay the compliment, and the submarine's present skipper, Lieutenant Commander F. G. Selby, was out to give them every opportunity. No man was resting on the oars as Puffer prowled the South China Sea this February on her third war patrol.

The opportunity arrived on February 22 in the

form of a Japanese ocean liner off the Natoena Islands on the road between Singapore and Brunei, Borneo. When PUFFER made this contact, the crew knew its ship had come in. The ship grew bigger and bigger as the submarine bored in on the approach. Selby maneuvered for attack position; barked the order, "Fire—!" The spread torpedoes opened a fan of phosphorescent wakes. Explosions boomed, and the target listed and went under. PUFFER's depth-charging debt was paid.

The liner was TEIKO MARU, troop transport, 15,105 tons. With a single swipe PUFFER had wiped out one of Japan's biggest merchant ships—the third largest sunk thus far by U.S. submarines in the war.

The sinking sent PUFFER's broom flying higher than the pigstick on a battleship's mainmast. Hereafter no one would worry about the morale situation in this submarine. Some months later, during a scrimmage with a Japanese submarine tender, PUFFER was treated to a barrage of 30 depth charges that sent the cork and light bulbs flying. Selby reported the comment made by one old-timer afterwards.

"Boy, those were close! I was so scared I smoked half a package of my own cigarettes before I knew what I was doing!"

When a torpedoman under fire pauses to check his own supply of smokes, he is displaying the aplomb of the iron-skinned veteran. The submariners fighting the attrition war in 1944 were in need of iron skins. By January 1944 the Japanese Grand Escort Fleet was in full operation. The First Escort Squadron and the Second Escort Squadron were providing surface escortage for convoys, and the 901st Air Squadron was contributing some air cover. While many of the enemy's A/S measures were eleventh hour, they were nonetheless dangerous when encountered. Almost every Japanese convoy was now accompanied by several heavily armed gunboats, a CHIDORI or two, a destroyer or some other type of anti-submarine vessel, and the attacking submarine usually had to deal with a counter-attack.

No U.S. submarines were lost in January 1944, but as the attrition sweep gained momentum in February, casualties were inevitable. One near casualty occurred in the middle of the month. The enemy in this instance bore no allegiance to the Japanese Empire, but was a foe the submariners could never afford to ignore, as the following episode indicates.

Submarines vs. Old Devil Sea

While the attrition offensive swept forward in a mounting tide of submarine successes, "it was to be remembered" (to borrow a Navy phrase) that this tidal wave was not the only one in the Pacific. Man's war-tides may be mighty, but in that vast ocean west of America there are tides which can overpower the work of man.

"That Ole Devil Sea." Placid on Monday, and a rip-roaring bedlam of sky, wind and water by Tuesday afternoon. Currents that follow all the man-made rules of navigation in the winter only to go off on their own hook in the spring. Water-spouts and doldrums and other peculiar phenomena. Such as waves that loom up out of nowhere to engulf an island. Or capricious, over-sized swells that come suddenly whaling up astern from out of nowhere and swamp a submarine.

When a submarine, hatches open, is swamped by such a wave, she is "pooped." So it is reported in the submariner's vernacular. It could happen. It did happen. And it can happen again. The ocean's way, perhaps, of letting submariners know that Neptune continues to rule the Seven Seas in spite of guns, Diesel engines, radar and other man-made gadgets. Consider the experience of SAURY, veteran fleet submarine. On the night of February 12, 1944, she was about a day's run west of Midway, returning from patrol. Drumming along on the surface, she was making normal time, and the crew was engaged in such routine activities as standing lookout, polishing brightwork and plucking at the hairs on a forearm. Probably the officers were thinking of refreshments at the Gooney Bird Hotel, and some of the men were wondering if a good USO show would be around.

Then at 2225, without warning or previous omen, a large wave overtook the submarine from the quarter, shouldering her over in a 40° portside list, and causing her to yaw 140°. Adding injury to insult, the wave swooped up and over SAURY's bridge, sending green seas through the conning-tower hatch and main induction.

SAURY's crew rushed into action. The main control cubicle had grounded out, causing a small electrical fire. This was promptly extinguished, but there were other bedevilments. The auxiliary-power panel, both high-pressure air compressors, master gyro, air-conditioning units, fathometer and Kleinschmidt feed-pump grounded. A full voltage ground on the forward battery had the electricians jumping for a while.

Although SAURY was composite drive and had two direct-drive engines for propulsion, her captain, Lieutenant Commander A. H. Dropp, thought it best to lie to and repair the damage before proceeding. In half an hour auxiliary power was restored. But repairs to the main control cubicle took almost a full day, and it was 26 hours before the gyro was running.

Fortunately the "pooping" had happened outside of enemy waters. Dire consequences could have resulted, otherwise, for SAURY was unable to dive on her motors for 21 hours.

The arrangement of maneuvering room in the after engine room, common to submarines of the SAURY class, made her type particularly vulnerable to flooding through the main induction. The after engine-room induction came into the compartment above, and was directed at the forward end of the control cubicle. Presumably this design was intended to cool the control cubicle. But the design possessed, in addition, the gratuitous feature of thoroughly sousing the cubicle whenever water was taken through the induction.

Dropp and company got the submarine home without further misadventure, but all hands agreed they could have dispensed with the "pooping" experience. Since SAURY had, some months before, bent her periscope on the keel of a Japanese destroyer, it seemed as though this last scrape was spite on the part of Lady Luck.

SAURY was not the only submarine "pooped" by the puissant Pacific. PERMIT swallowed a large mouthful of the Sea of Japan in July 1943 just after she attacked a convoy southwest of La Perouse Strait. The submarine was surfacing to chase the fleeing convoy remnants when, whoosh! an avalanche of water slopped over her stern, inundating the bridge and flooding the conning tower. Two feet of brine buried the pump room deck-plates, and the submariners had to haul clear and submerge to make repairs. It was four days before PERMIT's radar was resuscitated. The wave that doused this submersible undoubtedly saved many tons of Japanese shipping.

BAYA (Lieutenant Commander A. H. Holtz) got the treatment late in September 1944. Holtz had made it a habit to surface with all hands at battle stations. On the night of the 25th, while on patrol in Luzon Strait, BAYA reaped benefits from this procedure.

At 2005 BAYA submerged in a rough sea after making a plane contact. About 30 minutes later she surfaced, and the executive officer, engineering officer and quartermaster went up to the bridge. The sea was rambunctious, but no more so than earlier in the evening—nothing to worry a salty submarine crew. With the boat "well blown up" and the bridge personnel topside, the main induction was opened, preparatory to starting the engines. Next moment a hill of ocean hovered over BAYA's stern. Then it rushed forward with a roar and whirled the three submariners off the bridge as a millrace might whirl three corks downstream.

BAYA shuddered, staggered and gulped. Her patrol report concludes the story.

> Boat started to settle. Blew all ballast tanks. Started to take water in the conning tower. Main induction was closed, both conning tower hatches were closed, all bulkhead flappers were closed.

> Surfacing in the area with all hands at battle stations paid dividends this time. Main induction was partially flooded and about 12 inches of water were taken in the conning tower. Boat settled to 45 feet. Drained conning tower, blew up, and surfaced. Maneuvered for about twenty minutes to pick up two officers and one quartermaster, all hands including the C.O., grateful that our plane friend did not bother us during this period. There was no damage that a few hours of hard work could not remedy.

Enemy area or harbors of home—wherever he cruises, the submariner remains vigilant. There is never any truce with "that Ole Devil Sea."

Loss of Grayback

No truce with sea or enemy, the submarine war of attrition went careening into the last week of February 1944. Breaking a record, the SubPac and SubSoWesPac sweepers worked overtime to sink ships on the 29th of that Leap Year month. Before the month was out, the Japanese had lost more merchant shipping to submarines than in any previous month of the war.

Success demands its price, however, and the submariners paid it. Radar, electric torpedoes, night camouflage and other boons did not eliminate operational hazards or end the danger of counter-attack. They gave the submariners a chance to fight harder, to strike the enemy more often—and to risk their lives more frequently in mortal combat.

One of February's high-scoring sweeps was staged by GRAYBACK, under the leadership of Commander J. A. (Johnny) Moore. Pioneer veteran of the first war year, GRAYBACK was on her tenth patrol. Dispatched to the East China Sea, she left Pearl Harbor on January 28, topped off with fuel at Midway, and headed west. On February 12, she received orders to conduct an eight-day patrol in the broad strait between Luzon and Formosa before proceeding to her East China Sea area.

On February 19, in Bashi Channel, she sank two freighters—TAIKEI MARU, 4,739 tons, and TOSHIN MARU, 1,917 tons. Five days later, heading northward off the east coast of Formosa, she encountered a convoy. Moore directed a series of attacks, and a torpedo salvo sank the 10,033-ton tanker NAMPO MARU. With but six torpedoes remaining, she attacked another

BATTLE SURFACE! A victim of Tambor's *deck-guns, this Japanese subchaser is en route to the bottom. U.S. submarine gunners swept scores of small craft from the surface of the Pacific. Gun duels were risky. But Jap patrol boats and A/S craft, not worth a torpedo, had to be liquidated. Subs did the job.*

TORPEDOED BY PUFFER (Comdr. F. G. Selby). Liner Teiko Maru *rolls over and goes deep off Borneo. Ex* French D'Artagnan, *this big troop transport was 3rd largest maru sunk by U. S. subs to that date (February 1944).*

TYPICAL JAP SAMPAN *being investigated by U. S. sub. These ragtag craft made picket-line off Jap coast.*

HULL DAMAGE TO SCAMP. *From enemy bomb, April 7, 1944. Struck off Davao Gulf while diving, Scamp suffered severe injuries. (Picture shows portside at frame 78.) Heroic damage control by skipper and crew saved life of sub.*

convoy the following day. When the report of this action was received on February 25, GRAYBACK was ordered to return to Midway. Apparently she never received this radio message, for she continued on and penetrated the Nansei Shoto chain, entering the East China Sea. There, on February 27, with her last two torpedoes, she sank her last ship—CEYLON MARU, freighter, 4,905 tons. That sort of showdown was typical of her skipper, "Johnny" Moore.

GRAYBACK was expected at Midway on March 7th. She did not come home. On February 27 (the Japanese dated it the 26th) a Japanese carrier plane had discovered a submarine on the surface, lat. 25-47 N., long., 128-45 E. According to Japanese report, the attacking aircraft "made a direct hit on submarine, which exploded and sank immediately." Summoned to the spot, several A/S vessels continued the onslaught, dropping depth charges where bubbles rose. The water heaved and quieted. A dark lake of oil welled up to the surface marking the place where the submarine went down.

GRAYBACK was gone. But when the final count was in, her name was still "up there" among those of the high-scoring leaders. Fourteen enemy ships had been downed by her torpedoes, and the vanquished included a submarine, an ex-light cruiser and a destroyer. On her last war patrol she sank 21,594 tons of Japanese shipping.

Loss of Scorpion

Early in 1944, perhaps on a day in February, the Submarine Force lost SCORPION. Captained by Commander M. G. Schmidt, she had departed Pearl Harbor on December 29, 1943, and headed for a patrol area in the northern East China Sea and Yellow Sea. This was SCORPION's fourth war patrol. During her first three patrols, under the captaincy of Lieutenant Commander W. N. Wylie, she had sunk four ships and damaged a freighter and a large tanker. She was acquainted with the Yellow Sea, and a fighting patrol was in prospect.

After topping off at Midway, the submarine resumed her westward run on January 3rd. Then, on the morning of January 5, Schmidt reported that one of the crew had fractured an arm, and requested a rendezvous with HERRING, at that time in SCORPION's vicinity. The rendezvous was made that afternoon, but heavy seas prevented transfer of the injured man. The following day Schmidt reported the case "under control." SCORPION went on.

She was never seen or heard from again. Somewhere in the Pacific?—the East China Sea?—the Yellow Sea?—SCORPION went down with all hands. Japanese records give no clue to the submarine's fate, although

a Japanese I-boat was known to have been in SCORPION's area on February 16th. Also there were mine lines across the entrance to the Yellow Sea. A thin barrier, but it is possible that SCORPION struck one of these. The sea closed in around her—where and when remain unknown.

Loss of Trout

On February 29 a Japanese convoy was waylaid by a submarine at lat. 22-40 N., long. 131-45 E. During the ensuing battle, a ship was badly damaged and the 7,126-ton passenger-cargoman SAKITO MARU was sunk.

TROUT was the only U.S. submarine operating in that vicinity at that date. Under Lieutenant Commander A. H. Clark she had left Pearl Harbor on the 8th to conduct her eleventh war patrol. She topped off at Midway and resumed her journey on the 16th, heading for a patrol area which extended from the 130 E. meridian westward through Luzon Strait to the China coast.

She did not report the convoy attack, and the SAKITO MARU sinking was not known to SubPac Headquarters until after the war. TROUT was due to return to Midway about April 7th. She never made port. Her loss remained a mystery until war's end, and then a search of Japanese records disclosed the convoy attack and the counter-attack which must have been TROUT's final battle.

So closed the book of a veteran famous for her gold-carrying exploit, her fighting patrols, her adventurous special missions to the Philippines. Off Midway on December 7, 1941, she had seen the first flashings of the enemy's naval guns. She had run the iron gantlet to Corregidor. Twelve Japanese ships had fallen prey to her torpedoes, the list including the I-boat sunk in Surigao Strait in September 1943. For her second, third and fifth patrols TROUT had been awarded the Presidential Unit Citation. If she were, indeed, struck down in battle by an A/S hunter-killer group on February 29, TROUT ended her war career as she began it—fighting.

February Finale

TANG, SNOOK, POGY, RASHER, PUFFER, GRAYBACK—setting the pace for Pearl Harbor and Fremantle, these six submarines swept more than 100,000 tons of Japanese shipping out of existence in February 1944. In the last week of February, submarines from another base were heard from. These were BALAO and GATO, carrying their brooms for the Brisbane Force.

The war was by-passing the Solomons-Bismarck area which had been the battle front for the submarines from eastern Australia. The boats from Brisbane were already blockading the Admiralties and cutting the supply routes from Palau and Halmahera to Japanese bases at Hollandia and Wewak, New Guinea. With the advance of United States and Allied forces in the New Guinea theater the submarines from eastern Australia would soon be possessed of an advanced base in the Admiralty Islands. In the meantime, under the skillful direction of two-fisted Commodore Fife, the Brisbane task force hammered at the enemy as he struggled to barricade the approaches to the southern Philippines.

Indestructible GATO (Lieutenant Commander R. J. Foley) veteran "goal-keeper" of the Brisbane Force, was patrolling north of Hollandia on February 26th. Steaming into the equatorial seascape, DAIGEN MARU No. 3 advanced to meet destruction. Foley supplied the accurate torpedo fire, and the 5,256-ton passenger-cargoman was blasted out of the enemy's New Guinea supply system.

BALAO (Lieutenant Commander C. C. Cole) found good hunting along a route that took her through the Arafura Sea, around the northwestern tip of New Guinea up to the Sonsorol Islands below Palau. Cole fired some fast shots to down the passenger-cargoman NIKKI MARU in the Arafura Sea on February 23rd. Five days later, off the Sonsorols, the submarine downed the freighter SHOHO MARU and the passenger-cargoman AKIURA MARU. The accumulated 15,383 tons made BALAO's a generous contribution to the month's total.

The final February figures—some 54 Japanese merchant ships sunk by U.S. submarines for a total 256,797 tons—produced an overwhelming minus for the jugglers of Japanese economy.

Comparing these figures with the four or five merchantmen, the approximate 16,000 tons downed by U.S. submarines in February 1942, the Japanese economists must have experienced a desolating sense of loss. Where were the profits of past wars—where the gains of this war's first drive when the Imperial forces were sweeping ahead all the way from Paramushiru to Christmas Island? American submarines were doing the sweeping, now. All the way from Christmas Island to Paramushiru.

Sandlance to Paramushiru (Exit the CL Tatsuta)

By New Year's Day, 1944, the heightening war-tide in the Central and Southwest Pacific had put an end to submarine patrols from the Aleutians. The few S-boats which had remained after the Jap withdrawal were failing rapidly. And their arduous patrols between Attu and Paramushiru found too few targets to make them worth the effort.

As these war and storm-battered veterans could not cover the whole Kurile Islands area and the Sea of Okhotsk, it was decided to discontinue the Dutch Harbor Submarine Command. The icy sea embraced by Kamchatka, and the 1,000-mile Kurile Chain were assigned to the patrol of submarines from Pearl Harbor.

The first Kurile patrol conducted by SANDLANCE marked the end of S-boat patrols in the North Pacific. Captained by Commander M. A. Garrison, SANDLANCE arrived off Paramushiru on February 24, and proceeded to give enemy shipping off this northernmost Japanese base her undivided attention.

It was SANDLANCE's maiden patrol. And she made it good by lancing three freighters and a passenger-cargoman with her torpedoes. Of these, only one, the 3,548-ton freighter, KAIKO MARU, torpedoed on February 28, was sunk in the Paramushiru area. After this sinking, the LANCE headed south down the Kurile Chain, fighting blows and blizzards. At the lower end, March 3, she sank AKASHISAN MARU, freighter, 4,541 tons.

On March 13, SANDLANCE had her big day. Midnight of the 12th found her off Hachijo Island, surface-running on the southbound road for Honshu. Shortly after 13 came up on the calendar, a plane-contact forced the submarine to dive. The sea was moonlit, and Garrison held her under for about two hours. Then, at 0240, he ran up the periscope to find SANDLANCE in the middle of a convoy.

This was a big outfit—at least five merchantmen under guard of three formidable escorts. One escort silhouette shaped up as that of a light cruiser, TENRYU class. SANDLANCE had only six torpedoes left in the munitions larder, and Garrison determined to make them count.

He fired two after tubes at a freighter, two more at the light cruiser, and two bow tubes at a second freighter. All three targets were hit.

Down went KOKUYO MARU, cargo, 4,667 tons. Disabled, the second cargoman wobbled away. And with a great, thundering roar, the correctly identified light cruiser went to the bottom, destroyed by one torpedo hit.

SANDLANCE also went down. She stayed down—deep under a 16-hour counter-attack in which 102 depth charges were dropped. Many of these seemed accurate in range and deflection, but apparently they were set for shallow depths. SANDLANCE was hugging a depth far below this barrage.

With the thunderstorm crashing overhead, the submarine crept, halted, listened, edged away. When it was over, Garrison and company set out for home. For this one patrol, SANDLANCE was awarded the Presidential Unit Citation. Pretty adept performance for a maiden. With her lance she had swept away, among other things, the Imperial Navy's light cruiser TATSUTA.

Spring Cleaning (March and April)

In March and April the sinking tonnages declined precipitately. One reason: fewer targets. Another: the Japanese were reorganizing the convoy system and holding ships in port to wait for escorts. The net result—a smaller number of vessels at sea—meant a slow-up in torpedo warfare.

During January 1944, the Japanese merchant tonnage afloat approximated 4,947,000 tons. By a tremendous shipbuilding effort, the Japanese had constructed some 126,000 tons of steel vessels the previous December, supplemented by about 108,000 tons in January. This Herculean endeavor, which launched 103 new merchantmen, produced a building index nearly six times greater than the peak in 1941. Nevertheless, the Japanese merchant tonnage afloat dropped to approximately 4,723,000 tons in February. And in March it was down to about 4,320,000 tons—a three-month decrease of some 600,000 tons. United States submarines were largely responsible.

One of those responsible for the March decline was BOWFIN (Lieutenant Commander W. T. Griffith). On a run which would take her from Fremantle to Pearl Harbor, she went by way of Robin Hood's barn to patrol the Halmahera-Celebes traffic lanes. Above Halmahera on March 10, she sank the freighter TSUKIKAWA MARU. Two weeks later, off the southern tip of Mindanao, she bored into a convoy, and Griffith's sharpshooting accounted for two more cargo haulers—SHINKYO MARU and BENGAL MARU. Having dumped some 15,000 enemy tons into the deep, BOWFIN headed for Hawaii with broom on high. That famous broom would presently make one of the strangest sweeps of the Pacific War—a story related in a subsequent chapter.

While BOWFIN was off Halmahera, PICUDA (Lieutenant Commander A. L. Raborn) was hunting in the Carolines. On maiden patrol from Pearl Harbor, she picked off three targets as a starter. Her opening shots on March 2 sank the ex-gunboat SHINKYO MARU, 2,672 tons, not far from Truk. On the 20th she downed HOKO MARU, a small freighter, in the vicinity of Yap. On March 30, south of Guam, she sent the 5,873-ton cargoman ATLANTIC MARU to the bottom of the Pacific. Raborn and company were off.

On March 6 a Japanese transport with a distinguished name was torpedoed and sunk northwest of the Marianas by a submarine with an equally distinguished name. The transport was AMERICA MARU, 6,070 tons. The submarine was NAUTILUS (Commander W. D. Irvin).

In the China Sea area between Hainan and the northern tip of Luzon, the submarine LAPON (Lieutenant Commander L. T. Stone) patrolled the Singapore-to-Japan trunk line. On March 8 she slashed into this line to cut TOYOKUNI MARU out of a convoy. After sinking this 5,792-ton freighter, she chased and overhauled NICHIREI MARU, freighter, 5,396 tons, for another kill on the 9th. Nine days later in the same area, she waylaid and sank HOKUROKU MARU, 8,359-ton passenger-cargoman. The total of 19,747 tons was one of the month's top scores, and Stone and company concluded a memorable patrol. LAPON's next patrol—presently recounted—proved equally memorable.

In Empire waters off Kyushu, POLLACK (Lieutenant Commander B. E. Lewellen) torpedoed the small freighter, HAKUYO MARU, on March 20, and the 2,814-ton passenger-cargoman TOSEI MARU on April 3rd. Sweepings taken at random.

And then on March 13 there was TAUTOG (Lieutenant Commander Sieglaff) in the Kuriles, sending RYUA MARU and SHOJIN MARU and their 3,800 combined tons to the bottom. It is not at all surprising to discover this submarine in the Kuriles in March 1944. Since the day she opened fire on the enemy attacking Pearl Harbor, where hadn't she been? One might readily assume that had Jap shipping been routed *via* Orion, sooner or later TAUTOG's periscope would have been off Betelgeuse. Such was the persistence with which she ran up her prodigious score. And off Betelgeuse, TAUTOG might have made a night-surface attack, driving in to shoot by starlight with her officers and lookouts on the bridge.

Radar, of course, was the big night-attack instrument. By the end of 1943 all submarines had the SJ and favored the PPI. But radar did not entirely replace the human eye, which, on occasion, was sharper than radar. Radar for making contact, tracking, closing the range, solving the target's course and speed. Eyesight for accurate visual bearings just before firing. Frequently the two means supplemented each other nicely, and the approach made by radar would be followed by a "visual" night-surface attack.

TAUTOG and "Barney" Sieglaff demonstrated this technique as they headed home from the Kuriles that March. Their course did not take them by Orion, but it did take them south of Erimo Saki, Hokkaido, where, on the night of March 16, the demonstration was made.

Submarine Tactics—Radar-"visual" Night Attack

It was 1825 when TAUTOG surfaced after an all-day submerged run and went about the business of charging low batteries. At 1843 she made a radar contact to the northeast, and the crew lost interest in the battery charge.

The contacted target was moving at slow speed (initial range 19,000 yards), so Sieglaff decided to track and plot on the surface while TAUTOG jammed a few amperes into the battery at the same time.

Topside, the bridge personnel scanned the night with sharp-eyed binoculars. Surface haze smoked up off the water—one of those icy sea mists cold enough to put a bead on the end of a Norseman's nose. While this lowered the visibility, it also served to screen the submarine's approach. With her camouflaged silhouette slimmed by the "minimum silhouette method" there would be little chance of lookout detection, and apparently the enemy was not using radar.

TAUTOG's radar soon described the "pips" as a seven-ship convoy with at least one escort. The convoy was zigzagging and spread out in a loose formation that made it difficult to discern all the vessels on hand. Sieglaff selected for target No. 1 a ship on the starboard flank. The convoy's speed was 9 knots, a slow pace which enabled Sieglaff to pick his own good time for a drive in on the flank.

Using radar as a guide, TAUTOG closed in. At 3,000 yards the lookouts were able to pick up the target as a black blotch in the night. T.B.T. and radar were checked against each other as the range was closed to 1,500 yards. Both the T.B.T. operator and the radar operator spotted a second ship almost in line with and behind the target. At 2021 Sieglaff fired four torpedoes from the bow tubes, set for 12-foot depth. One minute and three seconds after firing, one torpedo hit the mark, and the black blotch blew asunder in a great splatter of flame.

In the meantime, the O.O.D. had been observing the escort on the starboard bow. This vessel now turned toward TAUTOG and charged like a wrathful bull. Radar verified the range at 2,500 and Sieglaff gave the order to go down. As the submarine was going down, two torpedo explosions were heard. Sieglaff and company felt sure they had hit the ship which had been observed beyond the target.

No depth-charge attack developed, Therefore, at 2100 TAUTOG was up to periscope depth. The night was too dark to see anything through the periscope. Sound heard distant screws, however. So Sieglaff ordered radar depth. Radar made a sweep but picked up nothing. Sieglaff then shoved TAUTOG to the surface.

Once on the surface, radar picked up the convoy at 10,000 yards. Where the previous attack had been made there was nothing but night. The fleeing convoy was zigzagging radically between 90° and 180°, making 9½ knots.

TAUTOG now had three torpedoes forward and seven aft. Again Sieglaff drove in on the starboard flank, and in this attack he fired the three bow torpedoes at a range of 2,700 yards. As TAUTOG was swung right full rudder to bring the stern tubes to bear, one torpedo smashed into the target, and the night thundered. Sieglaff then fired the four stern-tube torpedoes at a range of 2,850 yards. Three explosions blazed and roared, two of them bull's-eye hits. The smitten ship was seen to be sinking.

At this climax, an escort was detected, attempting to close in on TAUTOG. Sieglaff put the A/S vessel astern, and at 17 knots TAUTOG headed out for Midway. The escort depth-charged the ocean astern with 14 heavy blasts. One fish the explosions did not kill was TAUTOG.

Students of submarining will note that the execution of a night-surface attack at decisive torpedo range required a dark or misty night. Bright moonlight would have prevented such an attack as the one described, for the submarine's approach would certainly have been detected. However, had the night been moonlit, Sieglaff would have probably attacked at periscope depth, supplementing radar information with periscope check on the targets. As it was, conditions made possible the surface attack which gave TAUTOG the advantage of fast maneuvering speeds and bridge-lookout vision. Visual bearings, generally more accurate than radar bearings, could (as in TAUTOG's case) put the final finger on the enemy at firing time.

In the Sieglaff-TAUTOG demonstration off Erimo Saki, the finger was put on the 5,460-ton passenger-cargo carrier, NICHIREN MARU. And the escort washed to the bottom in the foray was the Imperial Navy's destroyer SHIRAKUMO.

Loss of Tullibee

Late in March TULLIBEE was lost in a manner at once singular and tragic. Under Commander C. F. Brindupke, she had left Pearl Harbor on March 5 to conduct her fourth war patrol. She put into Midway to top off with fuel, and then, leaving Midway on the 14th, proceeded to her area.

TULLIBEE's area was in the open sea north of Palau where she was to cooperate as a unit in "Operation Desecrate," the carrier-air strike scheduled to hit Palau on March 30th. But after her departure from Midway TULLIBEE was not heard from again.

When no word was transmitted by the submarine in April, she was presumed lost, and her loss was officially announced on May 15th. The circumstances of the TULLIBEE disaster were not known until the end of the war, when C. W. Kuykendall, Gunner's

Mate 2, was released from the Ashio copper mines in Japan. He was the lone survivor of TULLIBEE.

He told a heartbreaking story. TULLIBEE had reached her station off the Pelews on March 25 (five days before the carrier strike at Palau) and on the night of the 26th she had made radar contact with a convoy. Brindupke put the submarine on the track. Rain squalls obscured visibility as TULLIBEE stalked her quarry, which proved to be a transport, three freighters, two A/S vessels and a destroyer.

Radar information gave the convoy's speed and course, and Brindupke twice started to close for the attack, but withheld fire because of the blinding rain. Meantime the escorts, detecting a submarine in the vicinity, were dropping random depth charges. As the sea boomed and spouted, Brindupke drove TULLIBEE in a third time, and fired two bow torpedoes at the invisible target—the big Jap transport.

Kuykendall was among the lookouts on the bridge at this time, peering blindly into the gusting rain. Perhaps a minute and a half after the torpedoes were fired, a stunning explosion rocked the submarine. Kuykendall was hurled into the sea.

Struggling in the water, he could hear men shouting and crying out in the night around him. Half-conscious, he swam automatically. Nightmare in a rainstorm—and then the outcry around him died away. He was fully conscious now—there was a last shout or two in the darkness—then the crushing silence of rain and sea. Kuykendall swam alone throughout the remainder of the night. He never again saw anything of TULLIBEE and his companions.

At 1000 on the morning of March 27, an escort vessel spied the swimming gunner's mate. The Japs fired on him with spiteful machine guns, and then, tiring of the sport, sidled over to pick him up. Kuykendall learned from his captors that the transport TULLIBEE had fired upon had been hit by a torpedo. After the usual grilling and brutal Oriental Third Degree, he was sent to Japan to sweat it out as a prisoner of war.

TULLIBEE had not been sunk by the Japanese. Of that, Kuykendall was certain. Range and bearing of the enemy escorts put them out of position for an immediate counter-attack, and they could not have spotted the submarine on that squally night. There could be but one explanation for the explosion which downed the submarine, and the timing of the blast substantiated it. TULLIBEE had been hit by one of her own torpedoes which had made a circular run.

Scamp Gets Home

On the morning of April 7, 1944, SCAMP (Lieutenant Commander J. C. Hollingsworth) was patrolling south of Davao Gulf. In those hot waters she sighted some big game—an enemy task force of six cruisers, screened by destroyers and aircraft. The sea was blue glass, and while attempting to reach attack position SCAMP was detected. Down she went, and down came the depth charges—a barrage of 22 blasts. She remained at deep submergence for several hours and then returned to periscope depth. Finding the horizon clear of enemy ships, Hollingsworth surfaced the submarine at 1423 in order to send out a contact report.

Communications could not be established. And at 1543, with SCAMP still attempting to transmit, a float plane was sighted coming directly out of the sun at an altitude of about 1,500 feet. Hollingsworth immediately gave the order, "Take her down!" followed by "Rig ship for depth charge!" and "Left full rudder!"

A moment later there was hell to pay. The payment was recorded as follows in Hollingsworth's patrol report:

Boat had seven degree down angle and was passing forty feet with rudder full left when bomb or depth charge landed port side of frame seven seven. Terrific explosion jarred boat. All hands not holding on to something were knocked off their feet. All power was lost. Emergency lights turned on. Boat began to take a large up angle and settle fast. All main vents were open at the time of the explosion, and failed to close by hydraulic power. The diving officer noted the hydraulic controller was on the "off" position having jarred to "off" by the explosion. The hydraulic plant was started and main vents closed. Diving officer began blowing everything.

Boat had slowed only slightly when passing 280 feet. With all tanks dry—a large up angle and still going down at 320 feet. Boat settled finally, hung for a time and started up rapidly. During this time the following reports were being received. "Fire in maneuvering room!" —"All power lost!"—"Thick toxic smoke in maneuvering room and after torpedo room!"—"All hands aft sick!"— "Forward engine room pressure hull dished inboard!"— "Pressure hull crews wash room dished inboard!" "Rudder jammed hard port!"—"Motor room taking water fast!" "Main induction drains showing a full stream!"

Decided: the section watch would have to fight it out— we would not go to battle stations or fire quarters—that if we passed fifty feet going up we would surface and fight it out with deck guns. The diving officer, Lieutenant P. A. Besheny, had charge of the control room. He was doing everything humanly possible to balance the boat, issuing orders clearly, calmly and fast. The control-room watch was having trouble keeping up with the orders, and doing a marvelous job. The diving officer ordered men not required elsewhere to the forward torpedo room to help take the angle off the boat. The men came through the control room like fullbacks and arriving in the forward torpedo room were packed between the tubes like sardines. By venting and flooding everything the boat was caught at fifty-two feet and started down again.

We went down and up three times and had started down a fourth time before power was regained. Lieutenant T. S. Sutherland had charge in the maneuvering room. The situation there was bad. All hands were violently sick but sticking it out trying to get main power. The angles the boat was taking did not help them. (Later figured we were 20 tons heavy aft during this time.)

Too much cannot be said for J. R. McNeill, CEM(A), who, violently sick, kept going throughout the entire time until power had been regained. Without his courageous and efficient action this boat would have been lost. W. R. Fleurney, EM2c, made three trips to the motor room to rig it for depth charge and passed out from the effects of the phenolic smoke on the third trip. Lieutenant Sutherland entered the motor room and brought him out. Artificial respiration was given immediately in the after torpedo room bringing him around.

The entire electrical gang acted in the highest traditions of the service throughout the entire period. As the boat started down for the fourth time and with air banks getting low the maneuvering room reported they were making two thirds on the starboard shaft, and five minutes later two thirds on the port shaft. Never received a happier report. Shortly afterwards the diving officer leveled off at one fifty feet. The rudder was finally placed amidships by hand. A broken bottle of chlorex in the crews wash room was thought to be chlorine gas from the after battery. Both battery wells were dry. Operation of the main vents shook the entire boat and sounded like depth charges. Safety vent leaked and caused the diving officer much trouble.

This thrilling battle report concludes:

We had made one complete circle before the rudder was placed amidships. Seven thousand gallons of Diesel oil which had been released from No. 5B, plus the blowing and venting of main ballast tanks, must have convinced our aviator friend that we were sunk—or else he did not have another bomb. There were no bombs during above period, approximately fifteen minutes. The commanding officer takes pleasure in making the following two statements. *There was no confusion! All hands did their job well and silently!*

Depth charges were still thudding to eastward at 1830, as SCAMP moved off, traveling deep. Once in the clear, Hollingsworth headed for the Admiralty Islands. The radio transmitter had been put out of commission, but by early morning, April 10, Sparks managed to get off a message describing SCAMP's condition. The force commander ordered DACE (Lieutenant Commander B. D. Claggett) to rendezvous with SCAMP and escort her to Seeadler Harbor in the Admiralties. Accompanied by DACE, the injured submarine limped into Seeadler on the morning of April 16th.

After emergency repairs by the USS TANGIER at Seeadler, SCAMP proceeded to Milne Bay, New Guinea, for drydocking. From there she went to the Navy Yard for permanent repairs.

Loss of Gudgeon

Leaving Pearl Harbor on April 4, 1944, GUDGEON (Lieutenant Commander R. A. Bonin) was beginning her twelfth war patrol. Ton after ton of enemy shipping had been sunk by GUDGEON since that long-ago day when she pioneered the road to Tokyo, Captain Grenfell in command, and on the way home sank I-173, the first enemy naval vessel to be destroyed by a U.S. submarine. In the South China Sea, the Battle of Midway, the Philippines, the Bismarck Archipelago, the Mandate areas—GUDGEON had fought all over the Pacific. For her first eight patrols, she had received the Presidential Unit Citation. Departing now for a patrol area just north of the Marianas, she sailed with the confidence of an old sea-fighter who knew the trail and what lay beyond.

She entered the Valley of the Shadow. In the seas north of the Marianas the Japanese were rushing troopships, munition convoys, all available reinforcements to Saipan and on down to Truk and Palau. Jap aircraft winged the sky between the Bonin Islands and Guam. Admiral Toyoda, new Commander-in-Chief of the Combined Fleet (Admiral Koga had been killed late in March in a plane crash), was determined to hold the Marianas line. Defenses were being buttressed with every possible support, and the A/S forces around the Marianas were strengthened. Into these perilous waters went GUDGEON.

On April 18, Japanese planes sighted a submarine some 166 miles off the island of "Yuoh." The aircraft attacked and dropped bombs. "The first bomb hit bow. Second bomb direct on bridge. Center of the submarine burst open and oil pillars rose." So reported the Japanese.

However, there is no island of "Yuoh" in the Pacific. Neither in English nor in Japanese is there an approximation of this name for an island, and the Japanese may have erred in decoding, or there may have been error in subsequent translation. At the time of the attack GUDGEON was due off the island of Maug in the northern Marianas. There was no similar attack reported by any U.S. submarine on that date, and GUDGEON could have been the target.

On May 11, a message was transmitted to GUDGEON, ordering her to leave her area for a special assignment. This message was not acknowledged. The following day, SANDLANCE, SILVERSIDES and TUNNY, patrolling in the Marianas, heard distant depth-charging. SANDLANCE was off Saipan, and the barrage seemed to be about 10 miles away. The Japanese recorded an anti-submarine attack made by aircraft and A/S vessels on that day, but SANDLANCE herself was target for a bomb and depth-charge attack not long after she heard the distant barrage. Was GUDGEON the victim of this ambiguously reported assault?

On May 14 GUDGEON was ordered to return to Midway. She never returned.

The "Horsemen" Ride Again

That April, SEAHORSE was out of the barn again. Cutter took her charging into the Marianas, plunging into the thick of it where GUDGEON, SANDLANCE and the others encountered depth charges and aircraft bombs. SEAHORSE encountered them, too. She was there early in the month. Her rampaging attacks on the 8th and 9th of April may have caused the Japs to rush in the A/S reinforcements later met by GUDGEON, SILVERSIDES and SANDLANCE.

Off Guam on the 8th, SEAHORSE overhauled a Japanese convoy. These waters had once been American —still were, in United States opinion and in the opinion of sea-cavalryman Cutter. The shreds of a Rising Sun flag might be flying over Guam's airfield, but Cutter wanted the convoy to know it was trespassing. He told it so with torpedoes.

Crash! Down went ARATAMA MARU, 6,784-ton converted submarine tender. Slam! KIZUGAWA MARU, cargo, 1,915 tons went down. The chase went into another day and a third trespasser, BISAKU MARU, 4,467-ton freighter, went booming under the sea.

Commander Cutter then galloped SEAHORSE up the road to Saipan to see what enemy shipping could be found off that Marianas base. Off that base on April 20 was the submarine RO-45. Cutter rode down this enemy as Sheridan would have ridden down a mule on the pike to Winchester. A blast of torpedo fire! Down went RO-45.

Seven days later AKIGAWA MARU, cargo, 5,244 tons, was blown to the bottom by a salvo from SEAHORSE. There went the last torpedoes. Having deprived the Marianas defense of four Japanese ships and a submarine for a total of 19,375 tons, Cutter led his "Horsemen" home.

Late April Sweeps

In March 1944, by an almost superhuman effort, the Japanese construction yards turned out some 256,000 tons of new merchant vessels. Approximately one-third of Japan's steel production had been allocated to merchant-ship building, and the yards were working in a hammer-and-tongs frenzy to make up for shortsighted leadership and previous optimism. The 89 merchantmen launched (22 were oil tankers) marked the summit of the Japanese ship-building effort. Throughout the remainder of that year the yards worked at forced draught, but they were unable to repeat their March performance. Nor did they ever manage to recover lost ground. Replacement tonnages in almost every month lagged far behind tonnages sunk by U.S. submarines—and other agents took a toll of merchant shipping in this climax of the war.

In March the submarines accounted for some 106,000 tons of Japanese shipping. In April they downed approximately 95,000 tons. TRIGGER, FLASHER, HALIBUT, PADDLE and POGY were among the busier sweepers in the attrition war during the latter part of April.

Under Lieutenant Commander Fritz Harlfinger, the "Trigger Men" were on blockade duty north of Palau. While thus engaged on April 27, they sank the passenger-cargo carrier MIIKE MARU—an 11,739-ton liner. The sinking of this vessel left a large vacancy in the Japanese transport service.

In the Halmahera area on April 16, PADDLE (Lieutenant Commander B. H. Nowell) destroyed the passenger-cargoman MITO MARU and the freighter HINO MARU No. 1, thereby leaving a 9,000-ton vacuum for the enemy's overworked shipyards to fill.

In the Nansei Shoto area, HALIBUT (Lieutenant Commander I. J. Galantin) sank TAICHU MARU, passenger-cargoman, on April 12th. On the 27th she downed GENBU MARU, passenger-cargoman, and KAMOME, a small minelayer. The two merchant ships totaled 5,000 tons, and the minelayer some 450. Nothing big, and yet the small transports may have carried electronic gear, important mail, an important passenger—who knew?

On April 29, FLASHER (Lieutenant Commander Whitaker) smashed up the 644-ton gunboat TAHURE and the 1,000-ton steamer SONG GIANG MARU, in the coastal waters of French Indo-China. Mice, it would seem, yet all part of the enemy's war effort. The gunboat, for instance, might have otherwise been available for the defense of TEISEN MARU, the 5,050-ton freighter sunk by FLASHER out in the China Sea on May 3rd.

On patrol in the Bungo Suido area, POGY (Lieutenant Commander R. M. Metcalf) was carrying on the Home Empire blockade. Opportunities were not knocking overloudly. But on the night of April 28, a Japanese submarine showed its silhouette, and POGY opened fire. The fire destroyed the Imperial Navy's I-183. Metcalf and company carried the blockade into May and sank two medium-sized freighters, SHIRANE MARU and ANBO MARU, 7,000 more tons which the Emperor's overworked transport experts would never replace.

Meantime, the Emperor's transport experts were faced with something new in U.S. submarine strategy. Born at SubPac Headquarters in April was an operational plan designed to intensify and accelerate the attrition war.

Some submarines had been patrolling key areas where enemy activity was in a constant ferment. Others, visiting these same areas a month later, had found shipping slack with few targets to shoot at. Long runs to Paramushiru, the Yellow Sea or the Sea of Okhotsk were more arduous than cruises from Midway to the Carolines, or from the newly opened advance submarine base at Majuro (where the first refit was accomplished in April, 1944) to Palau.

Submarine Operational Plan, 1944

The new submarine operational plan was devised to spread the attrition-war effort among the boats going out on patrol by equalizing the attack opportunities and dividing the burdensome runs, share and share alike.

The plan contained other important operational features and strategic elements. As these remain under official Navy "security," they cannot be divulged in the present text. Therefore, in the interests of naval security, permit the borrowing of a leaf from tight-lipped President John Adams (bulkhead of the Navy, he was, too) who referred to certain parties he did not care to mention, as "X," "Y," and "Z." By this diplomatic codification, the submarine plan in question may be called the "XYZ Plan." Veteran submarine captains will recognize the reference, future submarine captains will become acquainted with the plan if it is employed in their time, and the present editors can go on with the story.

To complement the "XYZ Plan," new names were given to patrol areas formerly designated by number. And submarines went out to hunt in the "Hit Parade," "Convoy College," "Dunker's Derby" and "Speedway." One area was most appropriately titled "Maru Morgue."

The submarine warfare conducted in these areas was much along the same line as before—there were no changes in the techniques of contact, approach and attack. By April 1944 submarine tactics had become patterned, and only one or two new tactical moves would be introduced before the end of the

war. Plan "XYZ" was merely an operational device calculated to step up the pace of the attrition war and give each submarine an opportunity to strike a "productive" field.

Sponsored by Admiral Lockwood and his operations officer, Captain R. G. Voge, the plan met with the instantaneous approval of the force. That the plan worked is evident in the havoc dealt the enemy by U.S. submarines in the remainder of 1944.

May Marathon

January had been a banner month. February had been better. May 1944 was better yet. By the middle of the month the statisticians at submarine headquarters were adding up another record tonnage. And at month's end the score was over the top. The May total—approximately 265,000 tons of merchant shipping sent to the bottom—marked a new high for the submarine attrition war, and a new low for the graphs in Tokyo.

A list of submarines which sank a *maru* or two that month practically runs the roster's alphabet. ANGLER, ASPRO, BANG, BARB, BURRFISH, CABRILLA, CERO, COD, CREVALLE, FLASHER, FLYINGFISH, GUITARRO, HERRING, LAPON, PARCHE, POGY, POMPON, PUFFER, RASHER, RAY, SPEARFISH, STURGEON, TAMBOR, TINOSA and TUNNY—these and others came home with triumphant brooms.

Four submarines led the field with high individual scores.

SANDLANCE (Commander M. A. Garrison) destroyed five *marus* off the Marianas to deprive the Saipan supply system of 18,328 tons:

Date	Name	Type	Tonnage
May 3, 1944	Kenan Maru	Cargo	3,129
May 11, 1944	Mitakesan Maru	Passenger-Cargo	4,441
May 14, 1944	Koho Maru	Cargo	4,291
May 17, 1944	Taikoku Maru	Cargo	2,633
May 17, 1944	Fukko Maru	Passenger-Cargo	3,834

TAUTOG (Lieutenant Commander T. S. Baskett) sank four Japanese merchantmen in the Kuriles area for a total of 16,038 tons:

Date	Name	Type	Tonnage
May 2, 1944	Ryoyo Maru	Passenger-Cargo	5,973
May 3, 1944	Fushimi Maru	Passenger-Cargo	4,935
May 8, 1944	Miyazaki Maru	Passenger-Cargo	3,944
May 12, 1944	Banei Maru No. 2	Cargo	1,186

GURNARD (Lieutenant Commander C. H. Andrews) swept the vessels enumerated below from the Celebes Sea. The three ships sunk on May 6 were torpedoed off the Celebes port of Menado. The large tanker sunk off the southern tip of Mindanao climaxed an outstanding patrol. In downing 29,795 tons, GURNARD chalked up one of the highest single-patrol tonnage-scores of the Pacific War:

Date	Name	Type	Tonnage
May 6, 1944	Tenshinzan Maru	Cargo	6,886
May 6, 1944	Taijima Maru	Passenger-Cargo	6,995
May 6, 1944	Aden Maru	Passenger-Cargo	5,824
May 24, 1944	Tatekawa Maru	Tanker	10,090

And here is SILVERSIDES (Lieutenant Commander J. S. Coye) sweeping the seas between the Marianas and the Carolines with her famous broom. Six ships for a total of 14,150 tons:

Date	Name	Type	Tonnage
May 10, 1944	Okinawa Maru	Cargo	2,254
May 10, 1944	Mikage Maru No. 18	Passenger-Cargo	4,319
May 10, 1944	Choan Maru No. 2	Converted Gunboat	2,631
May 20, 1944	Shosei Maru	Converted Gunboat	998
May 29, 1944	Shoken Maru	Cargo	1,949
May 29, 1944	Horaizan Maru	Cargo	1,999

From the northern entrance to the Strait of Makassar—where CABRILLA on May 26 sank the 8,360-ton ex-seaplane tender SANYO MARU—to the northern Kuriles where HERRING and BARB carried the fight, the SubSoWesPac and SubPac patrollers were in action. For the most part, the sinkings followed the well-established pattern.

For a variation, on May 14 ASPRO teamed up with BOWFIN in an attack on BISAN MARU, a 4,500-ton freighter, which failed to survive the dual assault. And on May 22 PICUDA joined forces with Army aircraft to down the 3,172-ton freighter TSUKUBA MARU off Hong Kong. The American submariners (and, of course, the Japanese) were remarking an increasing number of United States and Allied aircraft off the Indo-China and South China coasts. Planes of the Fourteenth AF were now roaming over the Gulf of Tonkin and Formosa Strait where, a few months before, Allied planes had been a rarity. Needless to say, the patrolling submarines welcomed the sight of American eagles in those recessed areas. Glimpse of a friendly plane could break the monotony.

And other unexpected meetings with old friends could break the monotony of a routine patrol. One such meeting, which occurred in May 1944, provided the Submarine Service with another of those salty anecdotes. The episode is recounted below.

Lapon vs. Raton

By the spring of 1944, U.S. submarines were cruising in good hunting areas like schools of fish. One consistently good hunting ground was the South China Sea. Early in the war, the western reaches of this great sea had been relatively secure for Japanese ship traffic. That security no longer existed. Patrolling the approaches to Singapore, Bangkok, Saigon, Haiphong, Kiungshan and Hong Kong, submarines from Fremantle chased the marus from one harbor to the next. The northbound convoy that escaped attack below Bangkok was liable to get it off Saigon. If its luck held out at Saigon, it might be blown to pieces off Hue. The same was true of a southbound convoy. Individual submarine patrol areas covered most of the South China Sea, and the submarines ranged these areas like sheriffs on watch for bands of smugglers who were running from county to county.

The locale of this story, then, is along a figurative "county line"—the boundary between two submarine patrol areas. Actually, a third submarine area was on the chart, but its extent remains unknown because the submarine was of Japanese extraction. Thus three submarines became involved in a rapid-fire incident. The moral to be drawn (if any) could have to do with the old apothegm about two being company and three a crowd.

LAPON (Lieutenant Commander L. T. Stone) left Fremantle on April 25 to conduct her fourth war patrol in a South China Sea area below Saigon. Her previous patrol in March, reported earlier in this chapter, was a high-scoring 19,000-tonner. A new-construction boat out of Groton, Connecticut, in 1943, LAPON was keeping up her end of the undersea war. When she reached her patrol area early in May she was on her mettle.

Three weeks of combing the southern approaches to Saigon provided little action. Then on May 24, with about a week of time-in-area remaining, she picked up a Japanese convoy. Stone and company were off in hot pursuit. A slam-bang torpedo attack spelled finish for WALES MARU, a 6,586-ton passenger-cargoman, and BIZEN MARU, freighter, 4,667 tons. Having sent some 11,000 enemy tons to sea bottom, LAPON reloaded and looked around for other marus to conquer.

While she was looking, she received the news that game of another caliber had been sighted in her area —a Jap submarine was in the vicinity! These were fighting words to Stone and company. The watch was alerted and all hands strained at a leash of anticipation.

Enter RATON (Lieutenant Commander J. W. Davis) also hunting the South China Sea for bear. Like LAPON she was conducting her fourth war patrol. She, too, had set herself a mark to shoot at by downing some 18,000 tons during a three-day fracas the previous December. Commissioned at Manitowoc in

1943, with Davis on her bridge, she, too, was a new-comer out to give the enemy battle.

She had left Australia on the 10th of May, and had reached her patrol area a few days later. That area was located almost due south of LAPON's. Even as LAPON went into action on May 24, RATON opened fire—far to the south in the vicinity of the Tambelan Islands. After sinking the frigate IKI at this lower latitude, RATON ran northward up the South China Sea. She thereby approached the area assigned to LAPON.

Surface and undersea areas may be marked on charts. But the water, weather and other physical characteristics of the sea have a way of blending at the boundary lines. The waves that washed LAPON's area rolled on into RATON's. The vista was all one. Even the time of day may seem common for adjacent sea areas although man-made clocks declare it otherwise. RATON, it should be noted, was keeping time an hour later than LAPON. Thus the morning of May 27 bathed both submarines with dawn's early light, but at 0500 for LAPON, it was 0400 for RATON.

What time was it, then, for the Japanese submarine reported in this vicinity? The answer must remain insoluble, for it depends on the whereabouts of the submarine in question, and at 0500 on the morning of the 27th, LAPON was still looking. At that hour she was about 200 miles southeast of Saigon, cruising submerged and making wary periscope sweeps. The Jap was presumably anywhere.

And while time was of the essence in one respect, in another it was of little consequence. No matter how one's chronometers are set, a torpedo is a torpedo. Whether it strikes at 0515 (Hypo) or 0615 (Item) is a matter of small moment. LAPON's chronometers indicated the time at 0503 (Item) when, according to Stone's patrol report:

> Sighted submarine identified as enemy on base course about 035°. Determined to be of the I-68 Class as found in ONI-14.
>
> 0504: Turned away for stern tube attack.
> 0513: Fired first of two torpedoes at range of 1,400 yards, track 53° port. Before firing the last two torpedoes, the previous certainty that this was an enemy submarine was lessened in the mind of the Commanding Officer, and fire was checked. Between the time of sighting and firing the submarine changed course to the west about 60°, either on a zig or on a broad sweep.
> 0517: Went to 200 feet.
> 0518: Heard two explosions as of torpedoes exploding at end of run.

Meanwhile RATON's skipper (Lieutenant Commander Davis) was jotting down some observations of his own. These were timed according to chronometers set for "Hypo"—an hour behind LAPON's "Item." But the date was May 27, and the morning was young.

0430: Interference on SJ radar screen. Appears to be another SJ and on bearing 290°–300 T. Lat. 7°-32'N Long. 108°-51'E.
0535: Lost interference on SJ radar screen.
0615: Ship shaken up considerably by either two underwater explosions or by striking submerged object. People in forward torpedo room thought we had struck something or had been struck by something. Commanding Officer was in control room at time, en route to the bridge, and it appeared to him to be two heavy muffled explosions nearby on port side. Went hard right and steadied on course 035°T (at time of explosion we were on course 350°T going ahead full on three main engines, 17 knots). After making turn the J.O.O.D. reported thin oil streak about 1,000 yards on port beam. No other disturbance sighted in water. . . .

LAPON arrived home at Fremantle on June 6th. RATON came indignantly into harbor on the 23rd. No one who compared reports could doubt that she had been fired upon by LAPON. The positions checked within two miles, and the timing was all too simultaneous.

Undoubtedly RATON's crew had some comments to make, and submariners acquainted with Davis were careful not to jostle his elbow for a long time afterward. RATON an I-boat! But LAPON could be forgiven under the circumstances—with an enemy known to be in the vicinity, and torpedo warfare what it was.

So far as is known, the LAPON-RATON case was the only shooting of its kind in World War II. In numerous instances, U.S. submarines were tracked by U.S. submarines—and finally identified as friendly. This single brush in the South China Sea was the only time an American submarine fired at one of its own family.

The wonder is that undersea warfare did not generate a whole series of Hatfield-McCoy embroglios. When one considers the element these undersea fighters operated in—the difficulty of submarine identification—the submarine concentration in areas that contracted as the war progressed—the record seems remarkable. Mix Japanese submarines into the picture, and it is apparent that American submarine skippers were masters of the fine art of "recognition."

Spring 1944 Summary

The masters of the Japanese merchant marine were now grappling with some alarming statistics. Submarine attacks had averaged 77 per month for the first half of 1943. With June 1944 coming up on the calendar, submarine attacks for the first half of 1944 were averaging 115 per month. Although Japanese shipyards were staging a back-breaking building drive which would launch some 877,000 tons in the first half of 1944—a tonnage greater than the yards produced in all of 1943—the rate of sinkings due to submarine action more than doubled that which prevailed in the first half of 1943. Thus replacements were outstripped by losses even as new ships raced from the yards.

At the end of May 1943, the Japanese merchant tonnage afloat approximated 5,630,000 tons. At the end of May 1944, the tonnage afloat was down to 4,308,000 tons. This shrinkage of over 1¼ million tons bore evidence to the intensified submarine effort which was largely responsible for the reduction.

The accompanying chart graphically indicates the scope and score of the submarine sweep which abolished over 1½ million tons of Japanese merchant shipping during the nine-month period represented (September 1943-May 1944). Note the carrier air strikes which smothered shipping in the Marshalls, at Truk and Palau, and the sinkings scored by Army Aircraft in the Bismarck-New Guinea theater and along the China coast during this period. Note, too, that some of the sinkings overlap, even as the targets overlapped in various areas.

A comparison of this chart with the one which displays Japan's merchant shipping losses for the first nine months of the war shows the elimination of great open spaces once enjoyed by Japanese ship traffic. It also suggests the elimination of thousands of tons of Japanese merchandise, machinery, food, raw material.

The Empire's economy could not long hold together under this strain. By the late spring of 1944 it was coming apart at the seams. Mr. Smith on Main Street, Middletown, U.S.A., might be saving threadbare tires for Sunday motoring. But Mr. Moto on the Ginza, Tokyo, had given up motoring entirely and was worrying about his next meal. American manufacturers and industrialists worried about production and were troubled by bottlenecks. Japanese industrialists and manufacturers were experiencing anxiety about their own necks.

Crux of the Empire's economic situation was, of course, the transportation problem—a problem rendered insoluble by submarines. When the Japanese tried to solve it by shortening their shipping lines and concentrating their forces, they merely reduced the mileage for patrolling submarines and invited counter-concentrations of force. Thus in June 1944 the tightening of the Japanese convoy system was countered by the coordinated attack group. The convoy was now assailed by the submarine wolf-pack.

Wolf-pack operations are detailed in the next chapter, as are several of the great "lone wolf" battles which drove Japanese convoys to the bottom that June. The Empire's merchant marine losses were not as heavy in tonnage as those suffered in May, but the merchant service, literally, did not have so much to lose.

Some 48 Japanese merchantmen fell to submarine torpedoes in June. Routine sinkings. Ships of average size. But Japanese merchant shipping losses for the month approximated 195,000 tons.

Again, success demanded its price, and in June two U.S. submarines were lost. Both went down in action in northern Empire waters where the enemy was consistently dangerous.

Loss of Herring

HERRING (Lieutenant Commander D. Zabriski, Jr.) left Pearl Harbor on May 16 and set out for the Kuriles to conduct her eighth patrol. Five days later she topped off with fuel at Midway. On May 31 she made rendezvous with BARB (Lieutenant Commander E. B. Fluckey) in anticipation of a cooperative patrol. The submarines exchanged information and parted company.

A few hours after leaving HERRING, Fluckey's submarine made contact with a Japanese convoy. As BARB was starting an approach, she heard distant depth-charging and assumed HERRING had attacked and was under counter-attack. Some time later BARB picked up a prisoner who revealed that HERRING had sunk an escort vessel of the convoy BARB was tracking. The downed escort was the frigate ISHIGAKI.

HERRING's attack had scattered the convoy, and BARB trapped, torpedoed and sank two of the fleeing vessels—KOTO MARU, a small freighter, and MADRAS MARU, a 3,802-ton passenger-cargoman. On May 31, HERRING destroyed the third merchantman of the convoy—HOKUYO MARU, freighter, 1,590 tons.

HERRING then attacked a freighter and a passenger-cargoman lying at anchor off Point Tagan, Matsuwa Island, in the Kuriles. According to Japanese records, this attack was made on June 1st. It resulted in the sinking of HIBURI MARU and IWAKI MARU—3,214 and 4,365 tons, respectively. During the action, a shore battery spotted the invading submarine and opened fire. The Japanese gunners reported two direct hits on the conning tower. "Bubbles covered an area about 5 meters wide and heavy oil covered an area of approximately 15 miles."

HERRING's loss was not suspected by ComSubPac until late in June, and Headquarters did not know the details until after the cessation of hostilities. If the Japanese report were accurate, she was the only U.S. submarine sunk by a land battery during the war.

Loss of Golet

GOLET (Lieutenant Commander J. S. Clark) left Midway on May 28 and headed for an area off the northeast coast of Honshu where she was to conduct her second patrol. A door of silence closed quietly behind her, and SubPac Headquarters never heard from her again.

GOLET was scheduled to start back from her area on July 5, and on the 9th a message which required acknowledgment was dispatched to her. When she made no answer, ComSubPac directed that a sharp lookout be maintained along the approach routes to Midway—an emergency procedure based on the assumption that the mute submarine might be unable to transmit. Another long wait—fading hope—and by July 26 the submarine was presumed lost.

The time and place of GOLET's final battle remained a mystery until war's end. Then Japanese records disclosed an A/S attack, dated June 14, 1944, made on a submarine at lat. 41-04 N., long. 14-130 E. "On the spot of fighting we later discovered corks, raft, and so on, and a thick pool of oil. . . ."

GOLET was the only U.S. submarine at that time in the immediate area. Thus it was apparent that she went down with all hands in battle off northern Honshu on June 14th.

Japanese Economic Crisis

The end of June found the Japanese merchant marine with 4,189,319 tons of shipping afloat—some 758,000 tons below the January figure, and almost two million tons below the figure for December 7, 1941. Summarizing the first half of 1944, the Tokyo experts must have known that Japan's merchant marine could no longer sustain such heavy losses and keep its head above water.

Nor could the Empire's economy afford the lost exports and imports which went with the sinkings. The tons of foodstuffs, munitions, clothing, textiles, coal, fertilizer, ores, machinery going to sea bottom day after day spelled ruin for the Empire's foreign trade and starvation for Japan's domestic industries.

By the end of June 1944 raw material shortages in Japan were hampering production in almost every industrial field. The coal shortage was causing grave concern. Rubber stockpiles were rapidly dwindling. Aircraft producers were using up their reserves. A bauxite shortage threatened aluminum production.

Japanese industry was falling back on substitutes. Iron and steel were substituted, when possible, for copper. The aluminum industry attempted to substitute alunite for bauxite. Aircraft builders substituted wood or glass for plastic. Dozens of other substitutions were attempted, but in most cases it was a matter of borrowing from Peter to pay Paul. And *ersatz* is seldom "just as good" as the genuine article.

There was one item which defied substitution. And it was an item as vital to the Japanese war effort as human blood. Japan's home industries might limp along for a time on makeshifts and imitations. The Japanese people could conceivably dispense with meat or soy beans and live on a near-starvation diet of fish and rice. But the Imperial Army, the Imperial Navy and the Imperial Air Force could not budge without this particular item, and no reasonable facsimile was available. Like salt, it was a "must" on Japan's import list. Unlike salt, it was demanded in enormous quantities.

Undoubtedly the submarine attack on the supply lines carrying this vital item contributed much to Japan's ultimate downfall. Even as it slowed the Imperial War Machine, it disorganized the Japanese shipbuilding industry and shook the props under the Empire's tottering economic structure. This submarine effort—a campaign of the war on merchant shipping—had been under way since the summer of 1943. Gaining momentum, it struck with full force in the first quarter of 1944, and by June of that year the damage had been done. One of the great submarine drives of the attrition war, the campaign deserves a detailed recounting. The remainder of this chapter is devoted to the story.

Cutting the Japanese Oil Line

During the first quarter of 1944, U.S. submarines concentrated on an attrition operation that was to drain the vitality of the Japanese war effort as a blood-letting would debilitate a haemophiliac.

Life blood of the Imperial War Machine was oil. High-octane gasoline for planes. Diesel oil for warships and transports. Fuel for the Army's tanks, trucks, tractors. Lube oil, crude oil, petrol—oil by the thousands of barrels—oil by the thousands of tons—oil was demanded in such quantities that the importation of petroleum was Japan's No. 1 wartime imperative.

Without oil the Imperial Navy would rust at anchor, the Army and Air Force would jolt to a halt, the merchant marine would be stranded. Without oil the whole, great, glittering War Machine would stall with all the futility of a flivver out of gas. Any motor mac could see it. Obvious to a schoolboy. Yet Japan's military leaders were as strangely remiss regarding oil requisites as they were in other similarly obvious matters—for example, the need for a convoy system.

With few oil resources in the homeland, the Japanese War Lords wagered everything on the exploitation of the petroleum fields of the Netherlands East Indies. From Sumatra, Java and Borneo would come the oil for the War Machine. The conquered Dutch wells and refineries could furnish an inexhaustible supply, and Japanese tankers would haul the oil to Nippon. Fly in this ointment was the fact that the supply of oil tankers was not so inexhaustible as the supply of oil. Fascinated by the ointment, Japan's War Lords overlooked the fly.

At the time her militarists started the war, Japan possessed a comparatively modest tanker fleet of some 575,000 tons (excluding Navy oilers). Some 90,000 additional tons were constructed by Japanese shipyards in 1942 and the first six months of 1943. Tankers captured or salvaged during this period added about 70,000 tons to the figure. And "conversions" provided an additional 136,000 tons. From the total, 871,000 tons, an approximate 85,700 tons were deleted by war action. The subtraction, wrought in the main by submarines, left Japan about 785,000 tons of oil tankers afloat as of July 1, 1943.

On the surface this looked most impressive. A year and a half of warfare, and only 12 tankers had gone down—three in 1942, and nine in the first six months of 1943. Of this insignificant dozen, U.S. submarines had accounted for a scanty nine, Army aircraft had accounted for one, operational casualty had claimed another, and the largest had been sunk by an unknown agent, perhaps a drifting mine. The list below summarizes the losses in discussion.

Japan, then, had forfeited to submarines something less than 62,000 tons of tanker shipping in the war's first year and a half. This loss (and loss from all causes) was more than balanced by the 90,000 tanker-tons constructed in Japanese shipyards during that time. With the additional "conversion" tonnage, plus the tonnages acquired by capture or salvage, the Japanese tanker fleet was well out in front by the summer of 1943. That is, it was bigger than it had been at the war's beginning, and it had served to carry the necessary oil throughout the period in question. All of which, as has been stated, looked impressive on the surface.

But under the surface there were factors which robbed the peach of some of its bloom. For one thing, the period in question bracketed the months when Japan was on the offensive and consolidating her gains. Now she could reap no more captured tonnages, and hereafter when she converted dry-cargo vessels into oil carriers she would be borrowing from Peter to pay Paul. Future replacements, therefore, depended largely upon building, and by the summer of 1943 Japanese shipyards were already behind schedule.

Meantime, the War Machine had been consuming oil in quantities beyond pre-war calculation. Reserve supplies in Japan were ebbing, and even the enlarged tanker fleet was hard-pressed to maintain an adequate flow between the Netherlands East Indies and the homeland. The Empire's Mandate and South Seas bases were also on the delivery list, and Japanese tankers were running themselves ragged in a race to meet the demand.

And under the surface was another factor which might have troubled those in charge of the Japanese tanker effort—the U.S. submarines.

During the first year of the war, the Japanese tanker fleet had been remarkably immune from submarine attack. There were reasons for this immunity. The average tanker is faster on its feet than the lumbering cargo vessel, and its comparatively high speed makes it an elusive target. Undoubtedly many tankers were spared in 1942 by defective torpedoes. And in that year there were not enough submarines available to cover the remote zones of tanker operation.

Date	Tanker	Tonnage	Sunk By	Northern Honshu
Mar. 1, 1942	Kaijo Maru No. 2	8,636	Grampus	Makassar Strait
Mar. 4, 1942	Erimo	6,500	S-39	Off Formosa
May 25, 1942	Tokyo Maru	902	Pompano	Off Truk
Jan. 18, 1943	Toei Maru	10,023	Silversides	East China Sea
Mar. 2, 1943	Toen Maru	5,235	Thresher	Sulu Sea
Mar. 10, 1943	Kaijo Maru	3,270	Army Aircraft	Locale
Mar. 28, 1943	Funakawa Maru	868	Marine Casualty	Off Truk
Mar. 29, 1943	Toho Maru	9,997	Gudgeon	Java Sea
Apr. 17, 1943	Nisshin Maru No. 2	17,579	Cause Unknown	East China Sea
May 4, 1943	San Clemente Maru	7,354	Seal	Off Truk
May 28, 1943	Akatsuki Maru	10,216	Saury	Makassar Strait
June 15, 1943	Sanraku Maru	3,000	Trout	Below Celebes

With their sources in Sumatra, Java and Borneo, the main oil arteries pulsed northward into the South China Sea where they joined the big Singapore trunk line for the run to Japan. Northward up the South China Sea, northward past Formosa, northward up the East China Sea ran the line. Far behind the Solomons and Mandates front this oil route was deep within the Co-Prosperity Sphere—a great jugular vein protected by the outposts of the Malay Barrier, the battlements of the Philippines and the shielding Nansei Shoto chain. Probing submarines had been too few in number to put a drain on this vein in 1942. Nevertheless, they had pricked it. And in 1943 they went on probing. The four tankers which were bled from this arterial line in the first half of 1943 only hinted at the increasing submarine effort.

Preoccupied with casualties in other categories, the Japanese were not particularly worried by this anti-tanker hint. With an extraordinary lack of foresight, they seem to have assumed that the immunity enjoyed by their tanker fleet would continue for the war's duration. U.S. submarines were blockading the home Empire, roaming the East China and Yellow seas, raiding in the Kuriles. The Aleutian goose was cooked. The Solomons front was caving. The war was beginning to move westward, and the merchant marine was calling for help. But the oil fleet—*Banzai!*—was magically safe. With its security presumably assured, there was no need for a high-pressure building program, although some additional tonnages were scheduled. However, warships and dry-cargo vessels came first. The lucky tankers could get along.

Had the Japanese glimpsed the Operation Plan published by ComSubPac on June 24, 1943, they might have furrowed their brows over the tanker situation with some concern. The reader may remember that this Plan, promulgated to the Submarine

Service, listed target priority in the following order: aircraft carrier (CV); battleship (BB); auxiliary carrier (ACV); oil tanker (AO); any man-of-war larger than a DD; troop transport (AP); cargo carrier (AK); destroyer (DD). Thus the oil tanker (AO) stood a high No. 4 on the priority parade, outclassed as a target only by aircraft carriers, battleships and auxiliary carriers, and outclassing heavy cruisers, light cruisers and everything else afloat. The Japanese were, of course, in the dark concerning this arrangement. They were soon to see the light.

An oil tanker is, perhaps, one of the most inflammable vessels in creation. A loaded munitions ship may be more so, but once its cargo is unloaded the danger is over, whereas an empty tanker may retain explosive fumes, and a loaded tanker is, figuratively, a torch awaiting a match. Petrol is red-flag cargo under any circumstance. Woe to the careless sailor caught snatching a smoke on this vessel's foredeck, war or peace. The tanker is endangered by a spark. Figure, then, its vulnerability to a torpedo loaded with torpex, as in 1943.

Long and rakish with lean flanks and funnel aft, the AO has other vulnerable characteristics. Her low freeboard may serve to reduce her silhouette, but there is no mistaking her for what she is, once sighted. Moreover, low freeboard puts the great bulk of her under water where the torpedo is in its element. High speed gives the tanker a margin of safety, but her volatile cargo means a holocaust when she is hit, and the odds make six of one or half a dozen of the other. They began to show up in the autumn of 1943.

In July and August of that year no Japanese tankers were sunk. Then something happened to the magic. Three tankers went to the bottom in September. Two went down in October. Seven were sunk

Date	Tanker	Tonnage	Sunk By	Locale
Sept. 21, 1943	Shiriya	6,500	Trigger	East China Sea
Sept. 21, 1943	Shoyo Maru	7,498	Trigger	East China Sea
Sept. 23, 1943	Daishin Maru	5,878	Harder	Off Honshu
Oct. 6, 1943	Kazahaya	8,000e	Tinosa and Steelhead	Off Truk
Oct. 31, 1943	Koryo Maru	587	Rasher	Makassar Strait
Nov. 8, 1943	Kyokuei Maru	10,570	Bluefish	South China Sea
Nov. 8, 1943	Tango Maru	2,046	Rasher	Makassar Strait
Nov. 13, 1943	Kyokuyo Maru	17,548	Cause Unknown	East China Sea
Nov. 25, 1943	Toa Maru	10,052	Searaven	Off Truk
Nov. 26, 1943	Ogurasan Maru	5,069	Bowfin	South China Sea
Nov. 27, 1943	San Ramon Maru	7,309	Seahorse	East China Sea
Nov. 28, 1943	Tonan Maru	9,866	Bowfin	South China Sea
Dec. 27, 1943	Kyeui Maru	10,171	Flyingfish	Below Formosa Strait
Dec. 27, 1943	Kyoko Maru	5,792	Ray	Below Celebes
Dec. 30, 1943	Ichiyu Maru	5,061	Bluefish	Off S.W. Borneo

in November. And three were downed in December. Thus in the last four months of 1943 a goodly 15 tankers were obliterated—more than Japan had lost in the previous 20 months of warfare.

As is apparent in the foregoing list, U.S. submarines accounted for 14 of the number, while one (again the largest) went down from a cause unknown.

Anyone interested in addition will note that the above tonnage figures add up to an approximate 111,000 tons, of which submarines were responsible for about 95,000 tons. Taken in a four-month period, this was a sizable bite out of the Japanese tanker fleet, and it must have been apparent to the authorities in Tokyo that the bloom was off the peach.

Tokyo might have noted, too, that three of the lost tankers were torpedoed in the East China Sea behind the Nansei Shoto chain. And eight were sunk in the waters barricaded by the Malay Barrier and the seas in the shelter of the Philippines. In other words, the shipping lanes which lay deep within the Co-Prosperity Sphere were no longer beyond the range and coverage of continuous submarine patrol. This was particularly noticeable in the Java Sea-Celebes-South China Sea area where torpedo warfare was growing hotter and hotter. Certainly the main line from Singapore to Japan, the great jugular vein which pumped East Indies oil to the home Empire, was now menaced. The day of tanker immunity was over.

Still, the Japanese oil authorities seem to have misread the signs, although the autumnal losses of 1943 did invite anxiety. Fifteen tanker sinkings were not to be disregarded. But a moderate building and conversion program had served to provide replacements. At the end of December 1943, Japan's tanker fleet boasted a total weight of 873,000 tons.

So, in spite of the losses, it was some 300,000 tons bigger than it was at the war's beginning. But the war, too, had grown bigger. Bigger by leaps and bounds. Grown to a size beyond the tanker fleet's service capacity. It had been necessary to dragoon many dry cargomen into service, and thousands of barrels of oil and aviation gasoline were being carried by freighters and coastal steamers. But this was a "hauling" rather than a "sinking" emergency.

In short, as the Japanese saw it, the problem was one of oil transport rather than tanker defense. Core of the problem was shipbuilding. Even so, the need for freighters was more immediate than the need for tankers. And the Imperial Navy's needs retained top priority in the yards. So tanker construction could go into second gear, but a shift to high was not imperative. Although the War Machine's oil reserves were going perilously low, enough oil could be hauled

to keep the engines running. As for tanker defense, the new convoy system on the Singapore main line could handle that. The jugular vein had been snipped here and there, but the incisions were insignificant.

If the Japanese reasoned as above, they were due for a rude awakening. It was the morning of 1944. U.S. submarines bristling with brooms were prepared for a big spring housecleaning. Or—to rig a more appropriate metaphor—U.S. submarines had their razors sharpened for that jugular vein which carried the lifeblood of the Japanese war effort.

AO Attrition

Ever since the publication of ComSubPac's Operational Plan, the Japanese tanker had traveled in deadly peril. The No. 4 target for submarines, with torpedo preference over cruisers, troop transports, destroyers! Even so small a vessel as the 587-ton KORYO MARU, downed by RASHER in October 1943, had been endowed with this target priority. Thus ISSHIN MARU, a 10,000-tonner, proceeding off the Honshu coast on New Year's Day, 1944, was asking for it. FINBACK (Commander Tyree) gave it to her on the 2nd, and the season's anti-tanker campaign was well begun.

On January 3 the Japanese petroleum line lost two oil tankers in the South China Sea above Borneo. These were RYUEI MARU, 5,144 tons, and BOKUEI MARU, 5,135 tons. Both were torpedoed and sunk by KINGFISH under the captaincy of Lieutenant Commander H. L. Jukes, veteran S-boat skipper, who had come back from the Aleutians with a taste for oil fires. KINGFISH ignited still another on January 7, and down in flames went FUSHIMI MARU No. 3, tanker, 4,292 tons.

Meantime, RASHER (Lieutenant Commander W. R. Laughon) in an adjacent area off Borneo torpedoed a tanker, and the 7,251-ton KIYO MARU went under in an oily smudge. That same day and not many miles distant, torpedoes from BLUEFISH (Lieutenant Commander G. E. Porter) hit HAKKO MARU, 6,046 tons, to deposit one more AO under the South China Sea.

The attack now shifted to the Carolines where submarines were on the watch off Truk. January 14 was a bad day for tankers in that area. Especially bad for NIPPON MARU, whose 9,975-ton bulk fell afoul of SCAMP (Lieutenant Commander W. G. Ebert) and went to the bottom shortly thereafter. It was equally disastrous for KENYO MARU, a 10,022-tonner torpedoed by GUARDFISH (Lieutenant Commander N. G. Ward).

So the Japanese lost eight oil tankers to submarines in the first month of 1944. Interesting note: with the exception of FINBACK on Empire patrol, the scoring submarines were operating with the Southwest Pacific Force—KINGFISH, RASHER and BLUEFISH from Fremantle—SCAMP and GUARDFISH out of Brisbane. The torpedoed tanker tonnage amounted to 57,865 tons. But the month was not yet over, for on the 24th a Navy carrier plane stepped in and sank another tanker off Truk.

With nine oilers erased in one month for a total loss of 64,000 and some odd tons, the Japanese must have realized that the war had caught up with their tanker fleet. If any optimism inspired a hope to the contrary, it was extinguished in the ensuing month of February.

Tanker sinkings for the month began on the 3rd when TAMBOR (Lieutenant Commander R. Kefauver) torpedoed GOYO MARU, 8,496 tons, on the main line in the East China Sea.

There was a lull until the 16th when Army aircraft sniped a medium-sized oiler off the western tip of New Ireland.

Then the sky fell on the tanker fleet at Truk on February 17th. The specimen sunk late in January by a carrier plane had been a straw in the wind—a wind that developed into "Operation Hailstone." This was the first U.S. carrier-air strike at the enemy's big Caroline base. Detailed in a later chapter, the operation enters the tanker story at this point because of its specific bearing on the topic.

Truk itself was the "Hailstone" target. All the shipping in the harbor was included, and the Navy's carrier planes sank a great, thundering mass of it. Tankers were more or less incidental. The waves of raiding aircraft hit everything in sight, and everything in sight included some Japanese oil tankers.

Among those present was an enormous ex-whale factory—TINOSA's former guinea pig!— the notorious TONAN MARU No. 3. Saved from death in 1943 by dud torpedoes, this monster was now unable to escape the fire from the sky. Down she went in the Truk holocaust with all her 19,209 tons. Four other AO's went down with her. When the great raid was over, Japan had lost five tankers in that single day, for a total deprivation of some 52,000 tons.

This tanker smash was decidedly painful. Yet the pain was that of a pinch to a man struck over the head with a sledge. The lost tanker tonnage was buried under an avalanche of shipping destruction. Truk was knocked flat. And it was not until the Jap naval base picked itself up, so to speak, shook its fractured head and fumbled at its ribs, that the tanker injury was felt.

Then before the Japanese oil officials could recover from the shock, disaster struck the tanker fleet in another quarter. At Truk the damage had been dealt by waves of rampaging aircraft. Now it was dealt by a single rampaging submarine!

Jack the Tanker Killer

Out of Groton, Connecticut, in the spring of 1943 had come the submarine USS JACK. Typical of the new-construction boats, she went out to the Pacific armed with the latest in modern battle equipment— new radar devices—new supersonic gear—new everything including a splendid machine for the manufacturing of ice cream. Surely her captain, Lieutenant Commander T. M. "Tommy" Dykers, had reason to be proud of this spanking undersea warship as he brought her into Pearl Harbor for her battle orders.

JACK. The name was not too distinguished. Nothing as fine as SILVERSIDES, as scrappy as TRIGGER, or as sharp as BARB. Yet its flavor was certainly nautical. There had been Jacks in the Elizabethan Navy. There was the one who had sailed for years in song, "over the bounding main." For generations the name had been coupled with "tar." And now the submarine so christened sailed out to take destiny by the horns and win for the name of "Jack" a distinction which would make it remembered in naval history.

On her maiden patrol conducted in Empire waters, she waded in two-fisted and sank some 16,000 tons of Japanese merchant shipping. Her next patrol, made in the autumn of 1943, was luckless, and she returned home empty-handed. She was then dispatched to Fremantle to join the Southwest Pacific Force. And from Fremantle, on January 16, 1944, she was dispatched to a patrol area in the South China Sea.

So her big moment arrived—at four o'clock in the morning of February 19, 1944, as she cruised along the Japanese traffic lane which connected Singapore with the distant Empire. The sea was a heaving carpet of warm velvet, softened by the dim light of a quarter moon. Faint starshine added to the luminescence, but it took strong binoculars to pick up anything on the horizon's curve. The lookouts on the submarine's bridge and up in the periscope shears were straining their eyes at the glasses. Wait—what was that off there? At 0358 one of the watch had spotted something.

Black as a cat the silhouette crept into view—a long, rakish craft with funnel aft—a tanker unmistakably. Then as JACK's bridge personnel went tense, another tanker was outlined on the horizon. Then another! And still another! And then one more! And there was JACK with her sights trained on five black tankers all in one picture—an oil convoy! Dykers and company went into action as one man.

During the approach, the convoy's formation shaped up. The ships were moving in two columns—four tankers in the main column, and one tanker leading three escort vessels on the flank. One of the escort vessels was a destroyer.

The submarine concentrated on the high-priority targets. By 0442 JACK had reached attack position, Dykers opened fire with a spread of three bow torpedoes aimed to catch the third tanker in the near, main column as it overlapped a target in the far. He fired a fourth torpedo at the last tanker in the main column. This target was struck by two torpedoes. The hits flared at the waterline, there was a dazzling spurt of flame, and then the tanker exploded like a colossal bomb, hurling up a tower of blazing gasoline that seemed to spatter against the ceiling of the night.

Two of the three torpedoes fired in the first salvo were heard to strike something in the far column, but the blinding blast of the tanker prevented identification of these hits. A lake of burning oil spread across the scene of the tanker's demise, and skirting this fiery lake at top speed came the destroyer, shooting wildly. Dykers pulled the submarine away from the milling convoy and started an end-around to make another attack.

Daylight found the tanker convoy once more under way, and through the heat of morning JACK raced at four-engine speed, traveling in an arc that would bring her out in front of the quarry. At 1445, some 42,000 yards out in front, she submerged. Three hours later, the four tankers hove into view, traveling in box formation with no escorts anywhere in evidence.

Down the track they came, like pins irresistibly drawn toward a magnet. Four Japanese ships whose masters, disregarding all warning, seem to have determinedly set a course for Avernus. By what reasoning had they dismissed an escorting destroyer? Why, having suffered one submarine attack, did they suppose they could escape another? The answer to this enigma is sealed somewhere in the Japanese mentality. Or perhaps it is in a code book at the bottom of the South China Sea. Like so many similar moves on the part of the Japanese, the reckless disposition of this oil convoy remains in the realm of mystery.

In no mood to look gift oilers in the teeth, JACK accepted the situation and bored in with a ready will. At 1849 Dykers fired four torpedoes from the stern tubes at two of the tankers which were overlapping. Two shots hit the leading target, and one

torpedo smashed into the tanker in the background. Fifteen million gallons of gasoline went up with a fiery roar. Two tankers went down, incinerated under a mountain of greasy smoke.

An hour later, Dykers surfaced the submarine. The two remaining tankers had separated. One, standing off to the north, had picked up an escort. The other, running westward into dusk, was alone. Dykers sent JACK on a race to catch the lone tanker. The fugitive was zigzagging desperately—which slowed its escape—and the submarine soon overhauled. At 8,000 yards, Dykers fired three bow torpedoes at the galloping target.

Things went askew. The first torpedo failed to run. The second missed the mark. The third ran erratically and passed astern of the tanker. As JACK turned away after this futile salvo, the Japanese tankermen opened fire with a 5-incher. Some of the shells fell close aboard as Dykers once more closed the range and the bow tubes were being reloaded.

The tanker was zigzagging wildly, but by carefully tracking the target on each of its radical twists and turns, Dykers presently had its number. At 2233 he fired a salvo of four torpedoes which scored three hits. Flame exploded from the tanker's vitals and rolled across the seascape like incandescent surf. JACK headed away from the red glare in the night.

"During this attack," Dykers reported, "we picked up what appeared to be one of the mysteriously missing escorts coming up from the south. He was making about 17 knots and managed to close the range to 8,000 yards before it was too late for him to do any good. He'll have a hard time explaining to Tojo why he left his sheep."

Dykers also noted: "Making the second attack on this tanker caused us to lose the last of the five and his escort. Stood off in the direction in which he disappeared at full power, but was unable to regain contact. Would sure like to have made it a clean sweep."

Although four tankers in a row were superlative sweeping, JACK might have scored again a few days later when she encountered another South China Sea convoy. This four-ship group with escorts included a single AO. Dykers promptly selected the tanker as Target No. 1, but during the attack the submarine ran out of torpedoes. The tanker limped away with the fleeing convoy.

"An excellent cruise," Dykers logged in conclusion. "After getting well south of Lombok we had a crossing-line ceremony with all the costumes and torture apparatus of a peacetime crossing. Even the Polliwogs enjoyed it. There was lots of damage to the enemy, spectacular fireworks, only two submerged

333

days, no depth charging, good food including ice cream almost every day, very little ship trouble, and good weather. Needless to say, morale is soaring."

High jinx in the Court of Neptune—ice cream—fireworks—the submarine, it would seem, had nearly everything. Sailing home over the bounding main, she could be confident that she had distinguished the name of JACK. At war's end that name was going to stand among the top 10 on the scoreboard recording tonnages sunk by individual U.S. submarines. But perhaps JACK would be best remembered as the submarine which downed four Japanese tankers in one day—a feat of AO attrition unequalled by any other U.S. submarine in the war. Here is the record:

Date	Tanker	Tonnage	Location
Feb. 19, 1944	*Kokuie Maru*	*5,154*	*1434N., 11411E.*
Feb. 19, 1944	*Nanei Maru*	*5,019*	*1434N., 11411E.*
Feb. 19, 1944	*Nichirin Maru*	*5,162*	*1545N., 11535E.*
Feb. 19, 1944	*Ichiyo Maru*	*5,106*	*1545N., 11548E.*

Reviewing the AO war, one may note that only one other submarine extracted a heavier tonnage from the Japanese tanker fleet in a single patrol. That submarine was FLASHER, in December 1944. But JACK's blow was perhaps more excruciating, landing as it did in the wake of the Truk debacle.

The Tanker Sweep Continues (Destruction vs. Construction)

JACK's foray of February 19 did not conclude the tanker attrition for that month. Ten days of February 1944 remained. And on the 23rd, 24th and 25th, three more Japanese oilers were subtracted from the tanker fleet.

The first of these, OGURA MARU No. 3, was downed off Morotai by COD (Lieutenant Commander J. C. Dempsey). Cost to the enemy's oil line: 7,350 tons.

The second was sunk by GRAYBACK (Lieutenant Commander J. A. Moore) in the East China Sea. This was NAMPO MARU, 10,033 tons.

Largest of this month-end trio was the tanker downed on the 25th—NISSHO MARU, 10,526 tons, torpedoed and sunk south of Mindanao by HOE (Lieutenant Commander V. B. McCrea).

It must have come over the Japanese, then, that in the first eight weeks of 1944 they had lost a total of 21 oil tankers—almost as many as they had lost in all of 1943. Moreover, one of the 24 lost in 1943 had been an operational casualty, while all of the 21 lost thus far in 1944 were victims of enemy action. Obviously enemy action—in particular, U.S. submarine action—was threatening the existence of the tanker fleet. As this jeopardized the fuel supply for the entire War Machine, it was a serious threat, indeed.

While the Japanese oil authorities were digesting this seriousness, the 4th of March arrived on the calendar. On that date the tanker OMINESAN MARU, 10,536 tons, was sent to the bottom of the South China Sea by BLUEFISH (Lieutenant Commander C. M. Henderson).

There ensued a doldrum in the AO attrition war which was not the fault of the submarine effort. So many tankers had been either damaged or sunk in the January-February onslaught that there were gaps in the oil transport system. Also an abnormal number of tankers were tied up for repairs. Working on non-stop schedules, they had all but burned out their bearings, and some had completely broken down. Finally, the convoy system created a slow-up, as the tankers, now thoroughly alarmed, waited in port for escorts. All of which meant fewer AO targets for the hunting submarines.

However, on March 27, HAKE (Lieutenant Commander J. C. Broach) found a tanker off southwest Borneo in the Java Sea. Down in flames went YAMAMIZU MARU, 5,174 tons.

This concluded the submarine score of tanker-sinkings for the year's first quarter. The score: 130,421 tons.

But the quarter was not yet over for the Japanese tanker fleet. On the 30th of March the sky fell upon it again. The occasion was "Operation Desecrate," the Navy's first carrier-air strike at Palau. As at Truk the planes caught a lot of merchant shipping and plastered it unmercifully. Seven tankers were buried beneath the Palau plaster. When the bombing was over, 47,501 tons were deleted from the already shrunken oil fleet.

Addition of the 130,421 tons sunk by submarines, the 99,501 destroyed at Truk and Palau by Navy's aircraft, and Army Air's contribution of 5,461 tons, sums up the tanker fleet's total loss for the year's first quarter as some 235,000 tons. This was more than the Japanese shipyards had been able to build in the preceding 10 months. Tokyo's tanker experts were suddenly aware that destruction had outstripped production.

The sinking figures, incidentally, apply only to vessels of over 500 tons. They do not include small oil carriers. Nor do they include the numerous other craft which went down in the oil-carrying service. Were these minor tonnages added in, the total loss to the Japanese oil-transport system would mount considerably. As it was, the loss in orthodox tanker tons was sufficient to frighten the oil officials in Tokyo.

Already they had launched a program to step up tanker construction. This belated rush to build had begun the previous autumn when the strain on the oil line was growing oppressive. At the turn of the year the building pressure was heightened. And by the end of March 1944 the shipyards were giving tankers everything they could give.

The construction rush is reflected in the following statistics: During the year 1942 the Japanese built seven tankers (20,316 tons). In the first half of 1943 they built 16 tankers (68,670 tons). In the last six months of 1943 they built 38 tankers (186,257 tons). And in the first three months of 1944 they built 46 tankers (154,754 tons).

On the surface, then, it would look as if the builders were doing all right. But under the surface there were the losses which outstripped the building. Despite the race to construct, the Japanese were falling behind in the game, and they had cause to regret their dilatory tanker program. (For a complete set of statistics on Japanese ship construction, see Addenda, page 523.

For the tanker rush was not only tardy, but it deranged the entire shipbuilding effort. Heretofore, heat had been on the yards to produce freighters and passenger vessels. When the emphasis shifted to tankers, the other categories suffered. During 1942 and 1943, tankers had constituted about 25% of the shipyard output. In the first quarter of 1944 they appropriated 32⅕% of the output. And for the remainder of 1944 they embraced 37½%. Thus as tanker production climbed, it reduced the building percentage in other categories. Yet the demand in those other categories remained at an emergency level. Previous quota arrangements were accordingly upset, and in other respects the building program went akilter.

Japan was like the bride with three eggs, who wanted to make an omelette and bake a cake. If she used one egg for the cake, the omelette would be skimpy. If she put all the eggs in the omelette, the cake would be tough. In an attempt to compromise—2⅓ eggs for the omelette; ⅔ egg for the cake—she ended up with scrambled eggs and a half-baked cake.

So the vessels rushed from Japanese shipyards were scrambled and half-baked. Although not up to American standards, the quality had been fairly good for the first two war years. Now compromise and haste caused deterioration. Makeshifts and *ersatz* went into the recipe. Inferior ingredients produced an inferior article. Second-rate marine engines created an epidemic of breakdowns at sea which plagued Japanese shipping for the remainder of the war. To speed construction, such security features as reinforced bulkheads and double bottoms were in many cases eliminated. This made the ships more vulnerable to submarine, air or any sort of attack. The upshot was that while "quantity" made a jump in the spring of 1944 and maintained a high level until the end of that year, "quality" suffered a serious decline. In this respect, tankers and merchant vessels in other categories suffered equally.

One may note that the rush to build tankers was responsible for much of the scramble and half-baking, and U.S. submarines were largely responsible for the rush to build tankers. But the building jam is only a part of the tanker story. And that story is only a part of the main drama, which concerns the Japanese effort to supply the War Machine with oil, and the American effort to cut off the oil supply. In this battle over oil, submarines and tankers were the chief antagonists. But—as noted below—the results must be measured in barrels.

Submarines vs. Oil Imports

Statistics can be brief. At the start of the war, Japanese oil imports averaged 300,000 barrels a month. By the end of 1942 oil imports were well over a million barrels a month. This supplied the War Machine with a sufficiency during that favorable year.

Then, in the first quarter of 1943 Japanese oil imports slacked off. But in the second quarter they rose to a monthly high of 1,500,000 barrels. This would have looked gratifying on the graph had not the War Machine been gulping oil at a rate which accelerated as the conflict heightened. Like the inebriate whose thirst increases after a couple of beers, Japan's military effort was demanding more and more fuel. When oil imports dropped to 1,200,000 barrels a month in the last half of 1943, consumption was threatening to drink up importation and drain the reserves.

The shortage caused sobriety in Tokyo on New Year's Eve. And by the end of January 1944, sobriety had become anxiety. In that month oil importation had fallen under a million barrels. In February the figure dropped to 900,000 barrels. In March it was still only 900,000. And in April—despite tanker construction—despite convoys—despite everything the oil authorities could do—oil importation dropped to 700,000 barrels!

Now this drop in oil imports in the winter of 1943 and the first quarter of 1944 hit the Japanese military effort at the heart. Of course, any stricture in the oil system affected the enemy's military effort. A pinch in the Admiralties or a smash at Truk and Palau caused wrenches and recoils. But the heart of the military effort was the home Empire. Reduction of the supply of lifeblood oil to that heart could cause a convulsion. Such a reduction—and submarines were largely responsible for it—convulsed Japan's whole military effort in the spring of 1944. And in one specific instance it forced the Imperial Navy to make a move which was to change the whole face of the war.

The reader may recall that after the smashing American air raid on Rabaul in November 1943, Admiral Ozawa's carrier fleet, bereft of planes, retired to Japan. There Ozawa's carriers intended to pick up and train new aircraft squadrons. But when Ozawa arrived in Japan he found a serious oil situation. Tanker losses caused by U.S. submarines had so reduced the flow from the Netherlands East Indies that the home islands were running out of gas. With a fuel famine threatening, the Imperial Navy's High Command thought it best to dispatch Ozawa's carriers to Singapore, where they would be nearer the wells of Borneo, Sumatra and Java.

Thus the spring of 1944 found Ozawa's carrier fleet training at Singapore—far from the Second Fleet of Admiral Kurita which had been driven from Truk to Palau. The oil emergency then compelled these fleets to base at Tawi Tawi in the Sulu Archipelago. Their effort to reach the Marianas from that recessed base resulted, as will be seen, in the Battle of the Philippine Sea and catastrophic defeat for Japan. It may be noted that the submarine forces which played a stellar role in that engagement also forged a key link in the chain of events which brought it about. Had Ozawa been able to fuel his carriers in Japan instead of Singapore—had Kurita been able to fuel in the Pelews—but the alternatives fray out in futile speculation. As it was, the Japanese admirals had no alternative. Torpedoes and air bombs had wrecked the oil line to Palau. The petroleum shortage in Japan was established fact.

Submarines sank no tankers in April, but they reduced the main-line oil flow, nevertheless. For they forced the Japanese tanker fleet to employ the sluggish convoy system—a resort that slowed oil transportation to snail's pace. Although Japanese tanker replacements reached a new high in March, oil deliveries to Japan, as has been remarked, fell to 700,000 barrels in April.

Only 700,000 barrels! Less than half the amount imported in June 1943. In Tokyo oil headquarters there were signs of panic. The synthetic oil industry, which had been neglected, was squeezed for more production. Scouts searched the home Empire for new oil resources. Every possible lead was tapped. And the oil fleet was reshuffled in an effort to find more tankers for the main-line Empire run.

Here is another interesting angle to the tanker story. In May 1942 about 42% of the tanker fleet had been engaged in hauling oil from the Netherlands East Indies to Japan. During 1943 the percentage of tankers so engaged steadily climbed. By the end of February 1944 a good 80% of the tanker fleet was hauling oil on the main line. The percentage increased in March and April. Yet 1944 oil imports slumped on a down grade from 1,000,000 barrels in January to 700,000 barrels in April.

Now fully aware of the War Machine's dependence on oil—or call it the dependence of battles on barrels —the Japanese strove with every available device to overcome the import deficit. Shipbuilding—conversion—convoys—allocation of more tankers to the NEI-Japan run—everything possible was done to quicken the flow of lifeblood to the Empire's heart.

In May, oil importation slumped to 600,000 barrels.

Again submarines were the agents chiefly responsible. As recounted below—

The Jugular Vein Is Bled

In the spring of 1944, the submarine drive on Japan's main oil line was (to use the military term for it) intensified. This intensification was in part due to strategic planning, and in part due to the increases in submarines available to the Southwest Pacific Force.

In December 1943 the SubSoWesPac Force contained 24 submarines. These were divided about evenly between the Brisbane and Fremantle Commands. Then in January 1944 the SubSoWesPac quota was raised to 30 submarines. And in May 1944 it was raised to 36. The increase in submarine strength was accompanied by a progressive shift of SoWesPac submarines from Brisbane on the east coast of Australia to Fremantle on the west. By May 1944 the Brisbane task force had been reduced to six submarines. The balance (30) were operating out of Fremantle.

This shift within the SoWesPac Force matched the set of the war-tide to the westward as the Japanese retired from the Solomons and retreated in New Guinea. In January 1944 the Bismarck Archipelago was practically neutralized, and the Allied forces in the Southwest Pacific were pushing for the Admiralties. Manus, the key island in the Admiralties, fell on March 14th. This island, redolent of pearls and copra, became a main staging area for Admiral Kinkaid's Seventh Fleet. Its Seeadler Harbor was one of the finest in the Southwest Pacific. To Seeadler in May went the submarine tender EURYALE. Manus thereby became an advanced base for the SubSoWesPac Force. And submarines operating from

Seeadler Harbor had an open-sea run which put them within easy reach of the Celebes.

Meantime MacArthur's forces, leap-frogging up the New Guinea coast, drove into Hollandia and Aitape on April 22nd. By mid-May they were closing in on Geelvink Bay, the big dent in the western end of New Guinea. These moves pushed the Southwest Pacific front still farther westward. As the front moved westward, the Allied forces drew closer to the Java Sea-Celebes-South China Sea area. With the Solomons left far behind and Rabaul by-passed, SoWesPac submarines were able, in the spring of 1944, to concentrate on Netherlands East Indies waters and the Singapore-Empire main line. As the largest of the tributary oil arteries originated in Borneo, and the major portion of the oil trunk line traversed the South China Sea, the SoWesPac submarines were in a position to deal the Japanese tanker fleet the season's hardest blows.

The first blow was struck early in May. And it was a stunner. It was delivered by the submarine CREVALLE—a newcomer from the Portsmouth Navy Yard in 1943. Under Lieutenant Commander H. G. Munson, CREVALLE had reported to Fremantle late in that year and conducted two successful patrols. On April 4, 1944, with Lieutenant Commander F. D. Walker, Jr., on her bridge, she stood out from Fremantle and headed for the waters off Northwest Borneo.

She was patrolling in the vicinity of Brunei on April 25 when she downed a small ex-net tender. Aside from that the hunting was slow. And Walker and company were wondering if all the big ones had migrated elsewhere, when the biggest one they had ever seen came steaming down the pike.

CREVALLE's crew went into action with the speed of firemen aroused by a five-alarm call. But in this case the fighters were to set the fire. Maneuvering into attack position, CREVALLE was aiming her tubes at an enormous oil tanker—a vessel almost as large as the elephantine TONAN MARUS.

The tanker was as full of explosive vitality as a bottle of nitroglycerin. The torpedoes did not miss. The jolt may have been felt in Brunei, some 150 miles to the southward. Certainly it registered on the graph in oil headquarters in Tokyo. For, on May 6, 1944, crashing to the bottom of the South China Sea went NISSHIN MARU, 16,801 tons. CREVALLE had downed the largest oil tanker (and, incidentally, the third largest merchant vessel) sunk by submarines thus far in the Pacific War.

While the Japanese oil authorities were bemoaning this loss, the 7th of May brought them more bad news. This was a sinking closer to home—the tanker

ROSSBACK, 5,894 tons, torpedoed off the Suido between Shikoku and Kyushu. Responsible for the sinking was the submarine BURRFISH (Lieutenant Commander W. B. Perkins), one of the blockaders from Pearl Harbor.

The next tanker subtraction was the work of GURNARD (Lieutenant Commander C. H. Andrews). Veteran submarine from the Atlantic with a veteran skipper, GURNARD had seen a lot of action since her transfer from Europe to the Pacific front. Patrolling as a SubPac unit, she had sunk five merchantmen in northern Philippine and Empire areas before she went south to Fremantle. Her first SoWesPac patrol took her to the Celebes Sea late in April 1944.

As previously related, she struck a convoy off the Celebes port of Manado on May 6, and abolished three good-sized Japanese merchantmen. Eighteen days later, off the southern tip of Mindanao, she caught up with a large tanker. Andrews sent the submarine boring in. The torpedoes ran true, and GURNARD concluded a lively patrol by depriving the Japanese tanker fleet of TATEKAWA MARU, 10,090 tons.

On June 5 the AO attack was shifted to the Sulu Sea, where PUFFER (Lieutenant Commander F. G. Selby) was patrolling between North Borneo and the Philippines. Along came the tankers ASHIZURI and TAKASAKI. Torpedoes from PUFFER smashed into this pair and sank both of them for an estimated tonnage total of 4,666 tons.

Three days later the tanker SHIOYA was steaming off Manado in the Celebes Sea. She could not have been in more dangerous water. For it was occupied on that date by the submarine RASHER, whose torpedoes had already destroyed three oil tankers and an assortment of eight other Japanese vessels. Operating out of Fremantle, under Lieutenant Commander W. R. Laughon, she was not the submarine to miss an important target like an AO. And she did not miss SHIOYA. Loss to the Japanese oil fleet was estimated as 4,000 tons.

On June 11 the tanker ASANAGI MARU, 5,142 tons, fell to REDFIN (Lieutenant Commander M. H. Austin) in the Sulu Sea. REDFIN at that time and place was looking for bigger game off the enemy's naval base at Tawi Tawi. But there was nothing to prevent her from taking the bird in hand, and the Japanese oil line lost another unit.

On June 25 SAN PEDRO MARU, 7,268 tons, proceeding off the west coast of Luzon ran into torpedoes from JACK (Lieutenant Commander A. E. Krapf). The submarine which had conquered a tanker convoy in February was glad to paint another oiler's flag on the conning tower.

337

SEAHORSE (Lieutenant Commander Slade D. Cutter) scored the last tanker-sinking for the month on June 27th. The victim, MEDAN MARU, 5,135 tons, was downed by Cutter and crew in Bashi Channel between Formosa and Luzon. This was the ninth tanker sunk by submarines in the second quarter of 1944.

The tanker sinkings by SEAHORSE, REDFIN and RASHER were incidents fringing on the Battle of the Philippine Sea. That fleet-smashing engagement drowned out the torpedo fire of the attrition war as a howitzer barrage would blot out a scattered volley of rifle shots. U.S. submarine participation in the battle is reported in a later chapter. Japanese tanker participation is pertinent to the immediate discussion. Two 10,000-tonners were sunk by Navy aircraft during the battle. This raised the Japanese tanker loss for the month of June to eleven.

While the Imperial Navy assessed depressing losses incurred in the Battle of the Philippine Sea, the Japanese oil authorities were anguished by their own peculiar problem. Terms of that problem involved the statistics shown at the right.

Between January 1, 1944, and June 30, 1944, Japan had lost 43 oil tankers. Of these, U.S. submarines sank 27. The submarine score is listed below.

Thus, in the first six months of 1944, submarines downed approximately 189,000 tons of oil tankers. Additional tonnages sunk by naval aircraft and other agents raised the tanker loss to an approximate 335,000 tons. By a tremendous shipbuilding effort, Japan had constructed about 280,000 tons of tankers during this same period. The constructed tonnage, plus about 15,000 tons of conversions, left the tanker fleet short some 40,000 tons—not a bad figure, considering. The fleet had lost some weight since December 1943, but it still contained an impressive 837,000 tons.

However, tanker tonnage was not the critical figure. The critical figure concerned the quantity of oil reaching Japan. And the table below was the one which chilled the heart of oil headquarters in Tokyo.

Japanese Oil Imports: First six months of 1944

January	1,000,000 barrels
February	900,000 barrels
March	900,000 barrels
April	700,000 barrels
May	600,000 barrels
June	600,000 barrels

In these declining importation figures the evidence was plain. The oil was not getting home to Japan

Date	Submarine	Tanker	Tonnage	Locale
Jan. 2, 1944	Finback	Isshin Maru	10,000	Off Honshu
Jan. 3, 1944	Kingfish	Ryuei Maru	5,144	South China Sea
Jan. 3, 1944	Kingfish	Bokuei Maru	5,135	South China Sea
Jan. 4, 1944	Rasher	Kiyo Maru	7,251	South China Sea
Jan. 4, 1944	Bluefish	Hakko Maru	6,046	South China Sea
Jan. 7, 1944	Kingfish	Fushimi Maru No. 3	4,292	South China Sea
Jan. 14, 1944	Scamp	Nippon Maru	9,975	Off Truk
Jan. 14, 1944	Guardfish	Kenyo Maru	10,022	Off Truk
Feb. 3, 1944	Tambor	Goyo Maru	8,496	East China Sea
Feb. 19, 1944	Jack	Kokei Maru	5,154	South China Sea
Feb. 19, 1944	Jack	Nanei Maru	5,019	South China Sea
Feb. 19, 1944	Jack	Nichirin Maru	5,162	South China Sea
Feb. 19, 1944	Jack	Ichiyo Maru	5,106	South China Sea
Feb. 23, 1944	Cod	Ogura Maru No. 3	7,350	North of Morotai
Feb. 24, 1944	Grayback	Nampo Maru	10,033	East China Sea
Feb. 25, 1944	Hoe	Nissho Maru	10,526	South of Mindanao
Mar. 4, 1944	Bluefish	Ominesan Maru	10,536	South China Sea
Mar. 27, 1944	Hake	Yamamuzi Maru	5,174	Java Sea
May 6, 1944	Crevalle	Nisshin Maru	16,801	South China Sea
May 7, 1944	Burrfish	Rossback	5,894	Off Honshu
May 24, 1944	Gurnard	Tatekawa Maru	10,090	Celebes Sea
June 5, 1944	Puffer	Ashizuri	2,166e	Sulu Sea
June 5, 1944	Puffer	Takasaki	2,500e	Sulu Sea
June 8, 1944	Rasher	Shioya	4,000e	Celebes Sea
June 11, 1944	Redfin	Asanagi Maru	5,142	Sulu Sea
June 25, 1944	Jack	San Pedro Maru	7,268	South China Sea
June 27, 1944	Seahorse	Medan Maru	5,135	South of Formosa

from the Netherlands East Indies. Japan had sent the pitcher to the well too often. In this case, the well had not dried, but the pitcher had cracked.

And it had cracked beyond repair. In July, although Japan's tanker losses were only 48,000 tons, oil imports sank to 360,000 barrels. By autumn they were down to a monthly 300,000 barrels. This at a time when the Imperial Navy's battle fleets were being driven in upon the home Empire and almost every warship which reached Japan was panting for fuel oil.

Not obvious, then, in the sinking list or quoted tonnage and barrel figures is the influence which the AO attrition war exerted upon the enemy. The diminution of the oil supply in the first six months of 1944 had a most profound effect on the Japanese war effort. As has been noted, it threw the entire shipbuilding program out of adjustment. It put an added burden on the overloaded convoy system. It forced the Imperial Navy's strategists to make disadvantageous moves. It created production bottlenecks, transportation slow-downs and military setbacks. The exact costs to the enemy may never be assessed. But they are certainly attributable to the submarine attack on Japan's main oil line.

To quote *The War Against Japanese Transportation,* published by the United States Strategic Bombing Survey (1947): *"Had submarines concentrated more effectively in the areas where tankers were in predominant use after mid-1942, oil imports probably could have been reduced sooner and the collapse of the fleet, the air arm, merchant shipping and all other activities dependent upon fuel oil hastened. With the lag required to shift the emphasis of shipbuilding to tankers, Japan could never have caught up even temporarily with the rate of sinkings that might have been produced by such preference. And the fuel shortage might have been acute at the end of 1943 rather than a year later."*

The criticism implied in the above does not take into account the torpedo difficulties and other harassments which badgered the submarine forces in 1942

and 1943. But it does underline the importance of the AO attrition drive which went into high gear in the first half of 1944.

As will be recounted, that drive was continued throughout the ensuing summer and autumn, with such drastic results that at year's end the Japanese Total Mobilization Bureau reported to the Emperor's War Cabinet: *"The preservation of liaison between the southern occupied territories and Japan is an absolute necessity for . . . the maintenance of national material strength. It is recognized that if the resources of the south, especially petroleum, are abandoned, with the passage of time we will lose our ability to resist attack."*

The Total Mobilization Bureau was a little late in its observation. Perhaps it knew all along and had not wished to disturb the Cabinet's peace of mind. Or perhaps, with characteristic Japanese optimism, it had refused in the spring of 1944 to recognize the fact that the Empire oil line was done for.

One can summon to mind a picture (in the style of Low or Herblock). A barrel-shaped Japanese figure in Gilbert and Sullivan garb, facing a submarine in human form. The pair posed as duelers—the stout Japanese (his sash is labeled "Oil Transportation") brandishing an Oriental sword, the submarine brandishing a Navy cutlass. It can be seen that the cutlass has just made a flashing swipe, and the Shogun warrior's throat shows a thin line which curves from ear to ear. However, the Shogun warrior is smiling, albeit a rather worried smile.

"Ai!" he exclaims. "You missed me!"

"Yeah?" says the submarine. "Just wait 'til you move your head!"

There in a chestnut shell is the Japanese oil drama. But the picture is not quite complete. In the background, sketch a horrified little Jap—a servant with a basin and gauze bandage. Label the basin, "Salvage," and the bandage, "Replacements." The little figure—call him "Statistics"—stares at a loss. He knows. It is too late for first aid when the jugular vein has been cut.

CHAPTER 24

CONVOY AND WOLF-PACK

(SPRING AND SUMMER)

Wolf-packs into Action

During the Revolutionary War and the War of 1812, the Atlantic was combed by flocks of American sea raiders who all but chased the British merchant service off the ocean. The attrition war conducted by these Yankee privateers was self-assertive and individualistic as the captains engaged. Competition was cutlass-keen, and for the privilege of attacking a target, some of these skippers were not above sharpening their cutlasses on ardent competitors. Even that burly hero, John Barry, got to bickering over prize money. Privateering eventually threatened to wreck the British Empire's foreign trade but, had the raiders operated as coordinated attack groups, Lloyd's of London might well have gone bankrupt in a season.

In World War II, American deep-sea raiders were again sweeping an Empire's merchant marine from an ocean's surface. The attrition war conducted by U.S. submarines was individualistic enough for any independent captain's liking. And it retained this free-swinging character throughout the conflict. However, in the late spring of 1944 the "lone wolf" patrol was merging with the wolf-pack as more and more submarines were assigned to attack groups patterned along the CERO-SHAD-GRAYBACK and the SNOOK-HARDER-PARGO lines.

Several submarine groups had gone patrolling since the 1943 try-outs. Methods had been modified and wrinkles ironed smooth. But American wolf-packs had not immediately emerged in force because there were not enough submarines available for packs, and Japanese convoys were too small to warrant mass attack.

In the spring of 1944 the situation was sufficiently altered to put a new complexion on the matter. The war's arenas were swiftly shrinking. American submarines were becoming relatively numerous. Japanese convoys were being enlarged and provided with fairly formidable guards. The elimination of some

shipping routes and the shortening of others had bunched the muscles of the enemy's convoy system. And while this contraction strengthened the foe somewhat, it also invited submarine concentration in compact areas.

The accompanying chart shows the network of Japanese convoy routes belatedly established in 1943 and early 1944, and subject to disestablishment as the Allied offensive drove westward. Even as some of these routes were set up, they were summarily abandoned.

The route from Truk to the Marshalls was abandoned in December 1943 as American carrier raids began to thrash the Marshalls area. Menaced by the Allied drive in the South Pacific, the Truk-Rabaul line was simultaneously inactivated.

In January 1944 the Palau-to-Hollandia route, under threat of land-based air attack, was lopped off. At the same time, escort service was stopped on the run from Moji to Shanghai, and the escort vessels were transferred to the Japan-Formosa runs.

In February, after the carrier-air smash at Truk, the convoy route from Palau to Truk was eliminated. In March the line from Kyushu to Palau was canceled, as the merchant service wished to end this long

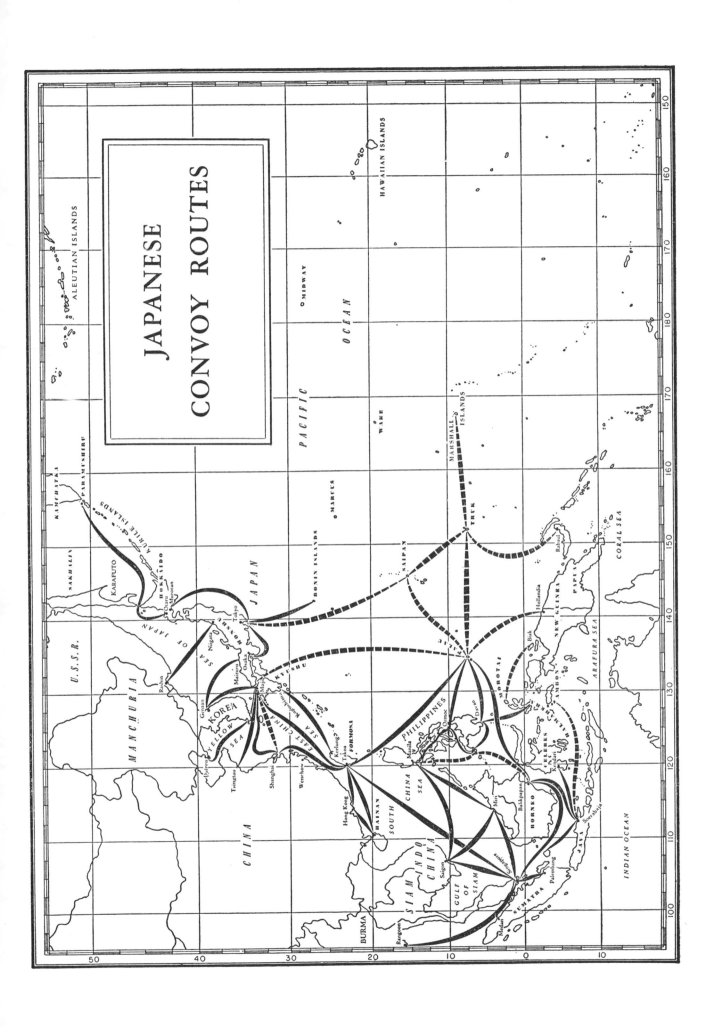

JAPANESE
CONVOY ROUTES

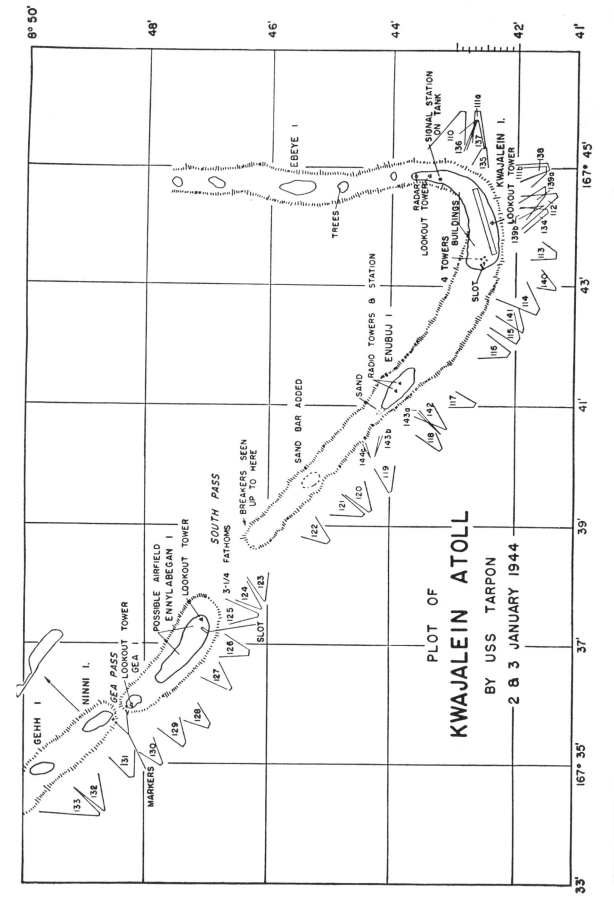

PLOT OF
KWAJALEIN ATOLL
BY USS TARPON
2 & 3 JANUARY 1944

SUBMARINE CARTOGRAPHY. Above chart of Kwajalein, made by Tarpon, is excellent example of work done by U.S. subs on recon-naissance. Early in war few good charts of NEI waters were available; Jap Mandate waters were question-marked. Subs charted them.

open-sea run through submarine water. In May the convoy runs from Morotai to Biak and Soerabaja to Ambon went out of business. The Balikpapan-Manila line was closed down in June—a closure enforced by submarine activity in the Sulu and Celebes seas. And in June all convoy routes to Saipan were eliminated as United States forces invaded the Marianas.

Thus, by the summer of 1944, the land, air, sea and undersea offensives in the Central and Southwest Pacific had forced the enemy to abandon the convoy routes portrayed as dotted lines on the chart. Driblets of shipping might reach such isolated outposts as Rabaul and Truk—Japanese submarines carried cargoes to starving garrisons on occasion—but organized convoying on these routes was ended. On the routes remaining, all Japanese shipping hugged the coastline wherever possible, taking advantage of shallow water and short lifeboat hauls to *terra firma*. On some runs, daylight travel was adopted as an anti-submarine measure, and on the main lines the heaviest escorts available were pressed into convoy duty.

So the Japanese added size and weight to their convoys and to some extent improved their defenses. And United States submarines countered with wolf-packing. The packs from Pearl Harbor and Fremantle operated in the manner described in Chapter 18 —that is, they employed American tactics which emphasized cooperative search rather than coordinated attack. Methods were still in the processing stage late in the spring of 1944 when a SubPac group headed west from Midway to patrol the waters lying between the Marianas and Luzon Strait. The operations of this group—calculated to support the triphibious drive on Saipan—established the American version of wolf-packing along some of the lines it would follow for the remainder of the war. As an eminently successful enterprise, conducted in a fashion which set the pace for the 1944 coordinated attack group, the patrol of "Blair's Blasters" is herewith recounted in some detail.

Blair's Blasters

In mid-May—at the time this wolf-pack patrol was shaping up—the Marianas were securely held by the Japanese, and the convoy routes to Saipan, the key stronghold, were a-bustle with merchant shipping. Traffic was particularly heavy on the Honshu-to-Saipan run. Heavy with troop transports, munitions cargoes and vessels loaded with war gear rushed to reinforce this important bastion of Japan's oceanic defense line. The "Blasters" were to patrol throughout the month of June and range as far west as Luzon strait. But as action eventuated, the wolf-pack did

most of its shooting during one rip-snorting week in the vicinity of the Honshu-to-Saipan road.

Under group command of Captain L. N. Blair, the "Blasters" left Midway on May 21st. The group consisted of SHARK II (Lieutenant Commander E. N. Blakely), PILOTFISH (Lieutenant Commander R. H. Close) and PINTADO (Lieutenant Comander B. A. Clarey). Presently the group was roaming in the Marianas vicinity, and action began on May 31 on the Honshu-Saipan road when SILVERSIDES, in an adjacent area, broadcast a report concerning a convoy which could be intercepted by the "Blasters."

The SILVERSIDES broadcast was on the air about 0500. Four hours later SHARK II made contact with the convoy and reported its movements to PINTADO and PILOTFISH. Blair then attempted to engineer a coordinated attack exactly in accordance with doctrine. He directed PINTADO to the convoy's starboard flank, SHARK II to port, and PILOTFISH was positioned as trailer.

But while the submarines were jockeying for position, the convoy made a radical change in course. This swerve placed SHARK II, the "port flanker," on the convoy's starboard side. Although doctrine provided for such a contingency, it did not provide for a series of radical changes, and when the convoy suddenly veered again, the submarine navigators were left in a sea of confusion.

As a result, the convoy escaped attack on May 31st. But shortly after midnight, on June 1, PINTADO submerged to make a periscope attack. Again the convoy zigged away, leaving PINTADO off-side. In the meantime, PILOTFISH had lost contact, but had picked up another broadcast from SILVERSIDES reporting a second convoy in the vicinity. PILOTFISH proceeded to go after this convoy.

SHARK II was now in position to attack the first convoy, but Blakely broke off his submarine's approach when SILVERSIDES was observed driving in for an attack. The convoy escaped SILVERSIDES. But there its luck evaporated, for it zigged in a direction which gave PINTADO another chance. Clarey directed a fast surface attack, sending PINTADO across the sea at a gallop to strike the convoy in the dark before dawn. At 0457, he fired six torpedoes for five smashing hits in a freighter and a single in another ship. Down went TOHO MARU, 4,716 tons.

Meanwhile, SHARK II found herself in the path of a third convoy. Blakely tried for a periscope attack, but the convoy managed to evade after the SHARK submerged. This same convoy was contacted by PINTADO an hour and a half after sunrise. PILOTFISH joined the pursuit, and SILVERSIDES entered the game of tag. The upshot was a three-ring circus—Japanese ships running, U.S. submarines chasing, and Jap aircraft arriving on the scene to chase the U.S. submarines.

The hurly-burly lasted throughout that day. No sooner would a submarine raise an inquisitive periscope than a Jap plane, flying interference, would force it under. Bobbing up and ducking like prairie dogs, the wolf-packers were unable to maintain contact with the first two convoys, but PILOTFISH persistently trailed convoy No. 3. All night the convoy ran northwestward with the submarine at heel. Morning of June 2, the chase was still going on. And by evening of the 2nd, all three "Blasters" were in contact with the convoy.

A quirk of fate, aided by smart submarining, gave SHARK II the opportunity to attack. The submarine was experiencing her maiden patrol, but she waded in like a battle-trained veteran. Blakely opened fire at 2300, and deadly torpedoes blew the bottom out of CHIYO MARU, a 4,700-ton freighter.

The chase continued throughout the third day of June as the punished convoy legged it for Japan and the "Blasters" doggedly pursued. PINTADO attempted several approaches, but failed to gain attack position. Then, late that afternoon, her periscope picked up a large convoy coming southward. The ships running for Japan were empty; the newcomers, heading for Saipan, were loaded to capacity. With these vessels in view, the "Blasters" were presented with a fine new flock of targets.

At 1000 on the morning of June 4, Captain Blair ordered PILOTFISH to position herself ahead of the Saipan-bound convoy. PINTADO was directed to position 30° on the convoy's starboard bow, and SHARK II was positioned 30° on the convoy's port bow. Boxed in, the convoy would get it on the nose from PILOTFISH, and if the ships veered to right or left they would run into either PINTADO or the SHARK.

PILOTFISH was ordered to attack the convoy at 1600, and plans called for follow-up strikes by SHARK II and PINTADO at half-hour intervals. As the submarines reached their respective positions earlier than anticipated, zero hour for the opening attack was moved up to 1400.

Again the wolf-pack plan for a coordinated attack was frustrated by an unexpected move on the convoy's part. At 1430, SHARK II and PINTADO submerged to make scheduled periscope attacks on the convoy's flanks. Just as the submarines started to bore in, the convoy altered its base course. The shift left PILOTFISH 30° on the port bow, PINTADO 60° on the port bow, and SHARK II dead ahead. But this time, business went on while alterations were being made.

The only submarine in position to deliver an attack, SHARK II struck while the iron was hot.

Blakely opened fire on the oncoming caravan of merchant ships, and one well-aimed salvo sank the 6,886-ton freighter KATSUKAWA MARU.

Off rushed the convoy with the wolf-pack in headlong pursuit. Sundown—midnight—another morning —the convoy streaking for Saipan and the "Blasters" determined it should never get there. Daytime, June 5, PILOTFISH and PINTADO gained positions on either bow of the convoy. But when the submarines submerged to bore in, the convoy veered on a new tack. The course change put both submarines on the same bow with PINTADO in a hopeless position. PILOTFISH was able to continue her approach, but in diving under the sound screen, she lost contact with the convoy.

However, SHARK II managed an independent attack that evening. Blakely and company were by now old hands at torpedo warfare, and the SHARK struck the convoy like a scourge. Two ships fell prey to her steel teeth—TAMAHIME MARU, freighter, 3,080 tons, and the 7,006-ton passenger-cargoman TAKAOKA MARU.

Then, just before midnight, PINTADO regained position for a strike, and Clarey ordered her under to begin a night-periscope attack. A few minutes later PILOTFISH was also boring in for a strike at the convoy. Only PINTADO managed to reach attack position. Clarey fired four shots, and the uproar sounded like a sinking. Japanese records failed to confirm the loss of a vessel at this point, but there was no doubt whatever concerning the outcome of a second PINTADO attack, delivered by Clarey and crew the following noon. Driving full tilt into the scrambled convoy, Clarey fired killing torpedoes into two cargo-laden freighters—KASHIMASAN MARU, 2,825 tons, and HAVRE MARU, 5,652 tons.

Not long after this sustained anti-convoy campaign, "Blair's Blasters" were forced to quit the Marianas area because of the impending invasion by United States surface forces. After leaving the Honshu-to-Saipan highway, the "Blasters" encountered slim picking. SHARK II, low on fuel, returned to Midway, her place being taken by TUNNY. On July 1 the group put into Majuro for refit, and the wolf-pack patrol was over.

In spite of "doctrinaire" difficulties and tactical troubles, the "Blasters" had knocked the stuffing out of some 35,000 tons of enemy shipping. In intercepting the convoy bound for Saipan and sinking five heavy-laden vessels, they had deprived the Marianas stronghold of hundreds of tons of urgently needed equipment. Nearly half of a Japanese division was drowned in this marine debacle, and the surviving soldiery reached shore without guns and battle gear.

Analysis of the "Blaster" patrol substantiated previous doubts concerning the practicability of the coordinated attack doctrine. Again it was obvious that action spoke louder than words on paper. It was also obvious that wolf-pack submarines, searching cooperatively and attacking individually, could give the enemy a terrible blasting.

I Went to Convoy College

Two packs loped out of Pearl Harbor in mid-June to take up the attrition war where the "Blasters" left off. These were "Parks' Pirates" under group leadership of Commander L. S. Parks, and the "Mickey Finns" under Captain W. V. O'Regan.

The "Pirates"—PARCHE, HAMMERHEAD and STEELHEAD—left Midway on June 17 to patrol the waters south and southwest of Formosa. In the seas somewhere ahead of them were the "Finns"—GUARDFISH, PIRANHA, THRESHER and APOGON—their bows also pointed toward Formosa. A patrol area set up in accordance with the newly devised "XYZ Plan" had been established in the waters lying between Formosa, Luzon and the Asiatic mainland. This area was known as "Convoy College." Both wolf-packs were now to enter "Convoy College" where they would major in torpedo warfare.

Glance at the chart, page 340 and note the strategic importance of this area. At the Formosan port of Takao six main-line convoy routes converge. There are the lines from Moji and Shanghai curving down through Formosa Strait. There are the direct runs from Hong Kong and Hainan; the main Singapore-to-Japan trunk coming up through the South China Sea; the line from Formosa to Palau, cutting directly across Luzon Strait. Japanese shipping was not entirely confined to these runs, for some of it raced along the eastern coast of Formosa, and Bashi Channel (directly below Formosa) was alive with traffic. The campus of "Convoy College," then, was one of the busiest shipping areas in the Co-Prosperity Sphere. The "College" was officially opened when GUARDFISH entered the area on July 30th.

PIRANHA (Lieutenant Commander H. E. Ruble) began the shooting for the "Mickey Finns" on July 12th. The target, caught off northern Luzon, was the 6,504-ton passenger-cargoman NICHIRAN MARU. Four days later, at the western side of the strait, PIRANHA's torpedoes smashed into another passenger-cargoman, and down went the 5,733-ton SEATTLE MARU.

On that same day, GUARDFISH (Lieutenant Commander N. G. Ward), ranging in waters southwest of PIRANHA, struck a convoy above Lingayen Gulf. In the ensuing battle, the passenger-cargoman JINZAN MARU, 5,215 tons, sank, followed by the 5,836-ton

freighter MANTAI MARU. The convoy fled southward. GUARDFISH chased. Another attack, delivered the following day, sent HIYAMA MARU, freighter 2,838 tons, plunging to the bottom. GUARDFISH circled to the northward and caught a second convoy two days later about midway between Hainan and the northern tip of Luzon. Ward cut loose with some more sharpshooting, and TEIRYU MARU, a 6,550-ton freighter, sprawled under the sea. Having subtracted 20,461 tons of shipping from the Japanese merchant marine, GUARDFISH, the first entrant, graduated from "Convoy College" with flying colors.

Meantime, THRESHER (Lieutenant Commander D. C. MacMillan) had struck still another convoy on July 17th. Two freighters—SAINEI MARU and SHOZAN MARU—were downed by the torpedoes of this veteran, for a total of some 7,700 tons.

So the "Mickey Finns" concluded a wolf-pack foray which cost the enemy about 41,000 tons of merchant shipping. Thereafter, "Convoy College" figured prominently in the "XYZ Plan," and it was to become the Alma Mater of many an all-American wolf-pack. As the Allied offensive closed in on the Philippines, enemy shipping congested the "College" area, and throughout the summer and autumn of 1944 there were usually two or three wolf-packs rampaging across the campus.

As was the case with the "Blasters," the "Finns" profited from cooperative search, but found the coordinated attack doctrine too cumbersome for employment. This feature of wolf-packing was presently shelved in favor of independent action on the part of attacking submarines. Rugged individualism remained the sparkplug of the American submarine effort. A most dramatic demonstration of that individualism was staged by one of "Parks' Pirates" during an action fought in "Convoy College" on the first day of August. The "Pirate" was PARCHE. And the action was one that wrote the name Lawson P. Ramage in indelible ink across a page of submarine history.

Parche vs. All Hell (Commander Lawson P. Ramage)

PARCHE, HAMMERHEAD and STEELHEAD ("Parks' Pirates") were off Formosa on the morning of July 30, going about their business like any well-organized submarine wolf-pack. So far, business had been slow and pretty much routine—that is, slow and routine so far as submarine warfare is concerned.

Then, at 1030 in the morning of the 30th, STEELHEAD (Commander D. L. Whelchel) sighted a convoy's smoke. STEELHEAD trailed. The convoy was under an umbrella of air protection, and Whelchel's submarine was unable to attack during the day. But at 2015 Steelhead got off a message to pack-mate Parche, giving the course and speed of the Japanese ships. Ramage put Parche on the estimated track and sent her plunging along the surface, top speed.

Midnight, and the two submarines were overhauling the quarry. By 0300, morning of the 31st, Steelhead was boring in on the attack. At 0332 Whelchel opened fire, aiming six torpedoes at a tanker and a large freighter. One torpedo was seen to hit the freighter, and a few moments later a mushroom of black smoke surged up from the tanker. Whelchel maneuvered to fire four stern shots at another freighter. Two Japanese rockets soared in the night, signaling the convoy's alarm.

These flares were seen by Parche. Ramage's submarine had made contact with one of the convoy's escorts about 30 minutes earlier, and was driving forward with crew at battle stations to strike the convoy's flank. Glare of the rockets now revealed several large ships in silhouette and three escorts rushing about. One of the escorts was ahead of Parche and to the starboard. Two were on the submarine's port, between Parche and the convoy. As one of these was bearing down on Ramage and company, Ramage decided the pattern needed some fast alteration.

Running the submarine at full speed, he started a circular swing to draw away from the oncoming escort. The A/S vessel continued on its course while Parche continued her circle which brought her in behind the stern of the second port-side escort.

"This reverse spinner play apparently confused the opposition," Ramage recalled afterward. "Parche was now between the escorts and their convoy, but while this maneuver was going on, the entire Jap convoy had reversed its field and was now headed directly for Parche."

Ramage picked out the closest target for the first shot—a medium-sized freighter. But the range had been overestimated. Before the set-up could be made, the ship was only 450 yards away. Sharp full right rudder slid the submarine out of the freighter's path, and Parche's bridge personnel could almost feel the breeze as the freighter went by at a scant 200 yards.

Ramage swung the submarine and opened fire with two bow shots. The alerted freighter managed a lucky zig, and the torpedoes missed. But the freighter's swing blocked the rush of an escort, and a moment later Parche's lookouts spotted two tankers off to starboard. Starting a run for these targets, Ramage got in a stern shot at the freighter, and a thumping explosion registered a hit. A five-minute dash brought Parche within torpedo shot of the tankers.

Ramage fired four torpedoes at the leading tanker, then swung Parche hard right to fire three at the second tanker. The leading tanker collected the first salvo from cutwater to wake. The first torpedo blew the ship's bow to pieces. The next three ploughed into the tanker's mid-section, quarter and stern. The ship went under immediately, leaving only a small patch of burning oil to mark the spot. The second tanker, struck near the bow by two torpedoes, staggered and slowed down, but kept on going. So did Parche, and she didn't slow down.

Every escort in the convoy and all of the remaining ships were now wheeling and milling. As though his submarine were a PT-boat, Ramage (whose *nom de guerre* was "Captain Red") drove into the center of the traffic jam, shooting everything. The convoy shot back everything. Ensued the maddest surface action yet fought by a submarine in the Pacific. Weaving and dodging through the convoy like a rodeo broncho attacking a herd of wild bulls, Parche struck at one *maru* after another. Ramage fired torpedo after torpedo as the enemy returned fusillades of glowing tracer and screaming shells. The scene blazed and roared with the din of an exploding fireworks factory. Hard right, hard left, the submarine swerved and veered. In her forward and after torpedo rooms the sweating men grunted, swore and labored like Vulcan's blacksmiths to load the tubes. Above, the T.D.C. operator "played the organ" at pinwheel pace, somehow keeping up with the spate of target data which came down from the bridge. On the bridge, at 0423, Ramage and companions were watching two A/S vessels close in—and Ramage was planning the next dodge—when a small, fast *maru* loomed up on the starboard bow, rushing to ram.

"We felt like a mouse at a bridge party," Ramage described the sensation. "I called the engine house to pour in all the oil they had."

Halfway across the rammer's bow, Ramage threw Parche's rudder full right. Ship and submarine passed in the night with elbow room at less than 50 feet. This, as any navigator knows, is the width of a safety-razor blade. The shave left Parche boxed in by small craft on both sides and an oncoming passenger-cargo vessel looming up like the Flatiron Building dead ahead. Left with no alternative but a down-the-throat salvo, Ramage fired three bow shots at the advancing menace. The first torpedo missed. The next two were on the nose. The ship came to a rumbling stop as if she had run her bow into a mud bank. Ramage drove the submarine forward, then swung hard left to bring the stern tubes to bear. Firing a single, he saw the torpedo strike the vessel amidships. At 0442, as Ramage was maneuvering in for a final shot, the ship put its heavy head under the sea. Then, with a rush, it was gone.

344

Ramage glanced about for something else to shoot at, while the residue of the convoy, firing indiscriminately, looked for the submarine.

"There were still several small craft and escorts around, but no worthwhile targets that we could see. I decided to put some distance between us and this hornet's nest."

As PARCHE hauled clear, distant explosions could be heard. STEELHEAD was attacking a remnant of the convoy which had run in that direction. At 0449 Whelchel fired four torpedoes at a large passenger-cargoman, and another salvo of four at a big freighter. The freighter was seen to sprout lifeboats and then go under. Whelchel was maneuvering to finish off the passenger-cargo carrier when an enemy plane attacked in the morning dusk and drove STEELHEAD deep.

PARCHE, in the meantime, was putting the "hornet's nest" astern. As she hauled away, one of the A/S vessels challenged her by searchlight, sending "AA-AA." This somewhat surprising flash was noted by a PARCHE signalman, Courtland Stanton, with the comment: "Those Japs probably have a lot of forms to fill out, too."

Doubtless one of the forms filled out by the Japanese convoy's survivors reported the loss of some 39,000 tons of merchant shipping. As determined by post-war inquest of the Joint Army-Navy Assessment Committee, STEELHEAD was responsible for the sinking of the 7,169-ton freighter DAKAR MARU and the 8,195-ton transport FUSO MARU. Both submarines were credited with the destruction of the 8,990-ton transport YOSHINO MARU. And PARCHE was credited with the sinking of KOEI MARU, a 10,238-ton tanker, and MANKO MARU, passenger-cargoman, 4,471 tons.

The Submarine Service credited Commander Lawson P. Ramage with something more. That credit is expressed in the following paragraphs—excerpts from the monograph with which the Submarine Force Board of Awards recommended Commander Ramage for the Congressional Medal of Honor:

THE PERSONAL DARING AND OUTSTANDING SKILL DISPLAYED BY THE COMMANDING OFFICER IN HIS SERIES OF ATTACKS AGAINST A LARGE HEAVILY ESCORTED ENEMY CONVOY, CONSISTING OF TANKERS, TRANSPORTS, AND FREIGHTERS, CONTACTED ON 31 JULY, IS ONE OF THE OUTSTANDING ATTACKS IN THE SUBMARINE WARFARE TO DATE, WITH ACTION PACKED INTO EVERY MINUTE OF THIS FORTY-SIX MINUTE BATTLE AGAINST THE ENEMY. ATTAINING THE ULTIMATE IN AGGRESSIVENESS, EXCEPTIONAL COURAGE, PERSONAL HEROISM, AND BEARING, THE COMMANDING OFFICER SAGACIOUSLY AND WITH CONSUMMATE SKILL, FIRED NINETEEN TORPEDOES IN FORTY-SIX MINUTES TO OBTAIN FOURTEEN OR FIFTEEN HITS IN THIS BRILLIANT NIGHT SURFACE ATTACK.

BY A BRILLIANT ACT OF STRATAGEM THE COMMANDING OFFICER PENETRATED THE STRONG ESCORT SCREEN; AND, ALTHOUGH HEMMED IN ON ALL SIDES BY SHIPS AND ESCORTS TRYING TO MANEUVER AND DELIVER COUNTER-ATTACKS, HE DARINGLY CLOSED TO A FAVORABLE FIRING POSITION FROM WHICH TO LAUNCH HIS TORPEDOES. WITH A WELL EXECUTED STERN SHOT, HE SUCCEEDED IN DAMAGING A FREIGHTER. FOLLOWING UP WITH A SERIES OF BOW AND STERN SHOTS, HE SANK THE LEADING TANKER AND DAMAGED A SECOND TANKER. DESPITE THE GRAVE PROBLEM OF MACHINE-GUN FIRE AND FLARES FROM ESCORTS, NEAR PROXIMITY OF VESSELS, SOME AS CLOSE AS 200 YARDS, HE SUCCESSFULLY DELIVERED TWO FORWARD RELOADS TO SINK A TRANSPORT. AT THE SAME TIME, HE COMMENCED MANEUVERING TO AVOID NEAREST ESCORT'S GUNFIRE AND OBTAIN A STERN SHOT AT DAMAGED TANKER THAT HAD NOW MANNED HER GUNS. AS HE REACHED A FIRING POSITION, THE FIRST FUSILLADE OF TANKER'S 4" OR 5" SHELLS PASSED CLOSE OVERHEAD AND SLIGHTLY FORWARD. BECAUSE OF THE ACCURACY AND INTENSE FIREPOWER OF ADDITIONAL ENEMY 20 MM. AND 40 MM. INCREASING THE POSSIBILITIES OF CASUALTIES, ALL LOOKOUTS AND SPARE HANDS WERE SENT BELOW, WITH THE EXCEPTION OF THE BRIDGE QUARTERMASTER WHO VOLUNTEERED TO REMAIN ON THE TBT. THE COMMANDING OFFICER, WITH UTTER DISREGARD FOR PERSONAL SAFETY, COURAGEOUSLY REMAINED AT HIS STATION, ON THE BRIDGE, DESPITE THE HAIL OF BULLETS AND SHELLS, IN ORDER TO MANEUVER HIS SHIP MORE EFFECTIVELY AND SCORE HITS WITH HIS STERN TUBES. SIMULTANEOUSLY WITH HIS SINKING THE DAMAGED TANKER AND WHILE TRYING TO CLOSE A LARGE TRANSPORT, HE WAS FORCED TO COMMENCE EVASIVE MANEUVERS TO AVOID A FAST TRANSPORT OR FREIGHTER BEARING DOWN, APPARENTLY INTENT ON RAMMING HIM, AND ALSO IN ORDER TO AVOID CONCENTRATED MACHINE-GUN FIRE OF THE TWO NEARBY ESCORTS. WITH BULLETS AND SHELLS FLYING ALL AROUND, HE ORDERED EMERGENCY FULL SPEED AHEAD AND SWUNG THE STERN OF PARCHE AS SHE CROSSED THE BOW OF THE ONRUSHING TRANSPORT OR FREIGHTER, CLEARING THIS ENEMY SHIP BY LESS THAN FIFTY FEET! ALTHOUGH NOW BOXED IN BY ESCORTS AND THE LARGE TRANSPORT DEAD AHEAD, THE COMMANDING OFFICER DELIVERED THREE

SMASHING DOWN-THE-THROAT BOW SHOTS AND STOPPED THE TARGET. WITH HIGH SPEED AND EXPERT SEAMANSHIP, HE TENACIOUSLY ATTACKED AGAIN, SCORING A KILLING HIT WITH A RELOADED STERN TORPEDO.

AT BREAK OF DAWN, WITH ENEMY ESCORTS' COUNTER-ATTACKS BECOMING TOO ACCURATE TO JUSTIFY FURTHER ATTACK AND RISK, PARCHE CLEARED THE AREA, THUS HAVING DAMAGED ONE ENEMY SHIP AND SUNK FOUR OTHERS IN FORTY-SIX MINUTES. IN ANOTHER ENCOUNTER, A 300 TON PATROL VESSEL WAS SUNK BY GUNFIRE.

THE COUNTER-ATTACKS OF THE ENEMY AGAINST PARCHE DURING HER SERIES OF AGGRESSIVE SURFACE TORPEDO ATTACKS UPON THE CONVOY ON 31 JULY 1944 WERE PROBABLY THE MOST INTENSIVE AND THOROUGH COUNTER-ATTACKS EVER ENCOUNTERED BY A SUBMARINE ENGAGED IN SURFACE APPROACHES AND ATTACKS AGAINST THE ENEMY. ONLY EXCEPTIONAL SEAMANSHIP, OUTSTANDING PERSONAL HEROISM AND EXTREME BRAVERY OF PARCHE'S COMMANDING OFFICER SAVED THIS SUBMARINE FROM SERIOUS DAMAGE IF NOT TOTAL DESTRUCTION BY ENEMY GUNFIRE AND RAMMING.

THE COMMANDING OFFICER'S COURAGE AND FEARLESS ACTIONS IN REMAINING ON THE BRIDGE OF HIS SUBMARINE DURING INTENSE AND ACCURATE ENEMY GUNFIRE IN ORDER TO MAINTAIN THE OFFENSIVE AT ALL TIMES, ENABLED HIM TO CONTROL HIS SHIP SKILLFULLY AND EFFICIENTLY, LAUNCH HIS TORPEDOES EFFECTIVELY AND EVADE THE ENEMY'S VIGOROUS EFFORTS TO DESTROY PARCHE.

Between the lines of official rhetoric, one sees a young man with carrot-colored hair and clamped jaw, clinging to the bridge-frame of an embattled submarine and determined to fight it out against all opposition. Queried about the action later, Ramage made brief reply to an interviewing journalist:

"I got mad."

Commander Lawson P. Ramage received the Congressional Medal of Honor.

Tang Rings the Bell

In the old days, Lloyd's of London made it a practice to ring a solemn bell whenever word of a ship's loss reached that insurance office. During the War of 1812, Yankee privateers all but wore out the clapper, so consistently did they arouse the bell's doleful bonging. Had the custom persisted and been adopted in Tokyo for World War II, the Japanese capital in the summer of 1944 would have resounded with a ceaseless tolling. In the last week of June and

first of July, one submarine alone sank ships enough to sound the tocsin of a great marine disaster.

The submarine was TANG. And the disaster began on June 8 when, under captaincy of Commander Richard H. O'Kane, TANG slid away from Pearl Harbor to begin her third war patrol. East China and Yellow Sea areas were her destination. And her patrol was destined to be one of the great convoy-smashers of the war—another individualistic exploit of the type that characterized American submarining.

First contact was made in the East China Sea southwest of Kagoshimo on the night of June 24th. Convoy! Six large ships herded along by "at least sixteen escorts." After counting the escorts, another skipper might have preferred a submerged approach. O'Kane drove in on the surface, selected two targets, and fired three-torpedo salvos at each. Explosions set fire to the night as the submarine went down to listen to depth charges, rushing propellers and breaking-up noises. O'Kane's conservative report claimed a freighter and a large tanker. Japanese reports failed to agree, recording the loss of three freighters and a medium tanker. Final check-up, made after the war, identified TANG's victims as two freighters and two passenger-cargomen.

Five days after these sinkings, O'Kane and company were making periscope sweeps southwest of Korea along the Dairen-to-Kyushu convoy route. Just before noonday, an unescorted freighter steamed into view. As the *maru* was on a course which prevented submerged overhaul, O'Kane turned TANG away, ordered the submarine to the surface and started a fast end-around. Four hours later the submarine, submerged, was boring in. O'Kane fired two torpedoes at the target. Both missed. TANG went deep to evade a depth-charging, then O'Kane ordered her to the surface to chase. This time he concluded the end-around with a surface attack, closing in to a range of 750 yards. A single torpedo, fired point-blank, broke the hapless freighter in two. TANG's bridge personnel watched grimly as the halved vessel sank.

TANG's next quarry was sighted the following morning (July 1) while the submarine was still cruising on the surface. O'Kane directed a periscope attack on two targets which were eventually identified as a small freighter traveling in company with an 878-ton tanker. First to go down was the freighter. When this vessel was hit, the tanker reversed course and fled. TANG trailed submerged until dusk. Then O'Kane brought her up for an end-around which terminated in a periscope attack. Two shots and one hit blew the tanker into shards of fire.

On the Fourth of July TANG scored another double. The fireworks began at dawn—ship-masts on the

COME AND GET IT! "Red" Ramage and Parche *serving it up hot to the Japanese. In this night-surface attack on a heavily guarded convoy off Formosa,* the lone sub played havoc with the enemy. "Commanding Officer courageously remained at his station on the bridge to maneuver his ship more effectively."

THREE IN ONE OILER! *Torpedoed by* Hake *off Karimata Strait,*
Jap tanker Yamamizu *breaks in three! One way to increase fleet!*

COMDR. L. P. RAMAGE. *Awarded Congres-*
sional Medal of Honor for daring action.

BIG SMOKE! *Tripled tanker (see*
above) creates oleaginous smudge.

SAVED! *British and Australian survivors of Jap prison ship* Rakuyo Maru, *tor-*
pedoed by Sealion II. *Rescue was by* Sealion, Growler, Queenfish *and* Barb.

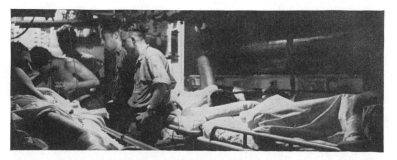

RESCUED P.O.W. *One of Britishers from*
Rakuyo Maru *is landed by submariners at*
Saipan. Brutalized P.O.W.s cheered sinking.

RAKUYO SURVIVORS *treated for shock and exhaustion aboard one*
of submarines. Men were emaciated from overwork on starvation diet
while in captivity. Four subs picked up 159—seven died en route home.

horizon—an end-around—a submerged approach on what O'Kane took to be a "16,000-ton seaplane tender." The water shoaled rapidly and the submarine's keel was about to scrape bottom when O'Kane backed off and fired three torpedoes. Two hits smashed the ship. And when the submarine surfaced to clear the area, about 50 survivors were thrashing around in the water and some 34 fishing boats were milling in the scene. The "seaplane tender" proved to be a good-sized freighter.

Late that afternoon, smoke was sighted and TANG was off again. The submarine overhauled the ship. O'Kane tracked to determine the vessel's zigzag plan, then submerged for a radar-periscope approach. Two torpedoes sped on their way, and another good-sized freighter plunged, booming, to the bottom. O'Kane ordered TANG to the surface, and then maneuvered to pick up a survivor clinging to an overturned lifeboat. The submariners had to catch the lifeboat with grapnels and threaten with a Tommy-gun before they could induce the shivering survivor to come on board.

The following night TANG was searching the waters off Dairen. A round moon painted the sea with lunar light, and presently a Japanese freighter came over the horizon. O'Kane directed a submerged approach, and fired the submarine's last two torpedoes. Both found the mark. Another freighter was wiped from the Dairen-Kyushu line.

So TANG concluded the most destructive anti-merchantman patrol of the Pacific War. Officially credited with 10 sinkings, O'Kane and company set a record. No other U.S. submarine sank as many ships during a single war patrol. No other, in one patrol, sank a greater merchant tonnage. And only three other submarines—RASHER, FLASHER and ARCHERFISH—downed heavier tonnages of Japanese shipping (merchant tonnage plus naval) in one war patrol.

Here is TANG's devastating score:

Ten ships for a total 39,160 tons! For this, her third consecutive outstanding patrol, TANG was awarded the Presidential Unit Citation—the first of the two she was to receive.

In July 1944 the building yards of Japan constructed 106,612 tons of merchant ships. Compare this replacement tonnage with the tonnage sunk in a period of two weeks by a single submarine, and TANG's achievement is as significant as the doom of the Japanese merchant marine was apparent. Had there been a Lloyd's bell in Tokyo at the time of TANG's third patrol, it would have sounded the Empire's death-knell.

Loss of S-28

On July 3, S-28 left the Submarine Base, Pearl Harbor, to conduct training exercises with the Coast Guard cutter RELIANCE. Captained by Lieutenant Commander J. G. Campbell, the S-boat was employed in the training of enlisted personnel and in sonar exercises with ships under ComDesPac.

S-28 made two practice torpedo approaches on RELIANCE, and the following day (July 4) these exercises were continued. At 1730 the submarine dived to begin a submerged approach. At 1820, with the submarine 4,700 yards distant, RELIANCE lost sound contact and was unable to pick it up thereafter. No distress signals had been heard, and there was no echo of an explosion. S-28 had suddenly gone deep.

The alarmed Coast Guard vessel summoned other vessels from Pearl Harbor, and a search for S-28 was begun. The submarine could not be located. On the afternoon of July 6 an ominous stain of Diesel oil was found on the surface—the only sign of possible disaster.

As S-28 went down in 1400 fathoms of water, salvage would have been impossible. The Court of Inquiry which investigated the sinking recorded the opinion that S-28 lost depth control "from either a material casualty, or an operating error of personnel or both." It was noted that the submarine was in good

Date	Name	Type	Tonnage	Locale
June 24, 1944	Tamahoko Maru	Passenger-Cargo	6,780	East China Sea
June 24, 1944	Tainan Maru	Cargo	3,175	East China Sea
June 24, 1944	Nasusan Maru	Passenger-Cargo	4,399	East China Sea
June 24, 1944	Kennichi Maru	Cargo	1,938	East China Sea
June 30, 1944	Nikkin Maru	Cargo	5,705	Yellow Sea
July 1, 1944	Taiun Maru No. 2	Cargo	998	Yellow Sea
July 1, 1944	Takatori Maru No. 1	Tanker	878	Yellow Sea
July 4, 1944	Asukazan Maru	Cargo	6,886	Yellow Sea
July 4, 1944	Yamaoka Maru	Cargo	6,932	Yellow Sea
July 6, 1944	Dori Maru	Cargo	1,469	Yellow Sea

material condition and that "the officers and crew aboard S-28 were competent." Negligence or inefficiency on the part of any "person or persons" therefore seemed unlikely.

The sea closed over the S-boat quietly, and she went down with all hands.

Loss of Robalo

On July 2, ComSubSoWesPac received a contact report from ROBALO stating that she had seen a FUSO-class battleship with air cover and two escorting DD's just east of Borneo. It was the last message received from this submarine which had left Fremantle on June 22 to patrol in the South China Sea. It was ROBALO's third war patrol. Her captain was Commander M. M. Kimmel.

When she did not reply to inquiring transmissions, she was presumed lost. It remained for Philippine guerrillas and a U.S. Navy man, who had been held prisoner at Puerto Princessa Prison Camp on the island of Palawan, to report ROBALO's story. On August 2, an American soldier on a work detail in the prison yard picked up a note dropped from the window of a cell. The soldier passed it to a fellow prisoner of war, a Navy yeoman, who succeeded in conveying the information to Mrs. Trinidad Mendosa, wife of the guerrilla leader, Dr. Mendosa. The note had been dropped by a survivor of ROBALO. It disclosed the fact that the submarine had gone down on July 26, two miles off the west coast of Palawan. The survivors believed ROBALO had been sunk by the explosion of her after battery.

An officer and three men managed to swim ashore from the stricken submarine. They were Ensign S. L. Tucker; Floyd G. Laughlin, Quartermaster 1; Wallace K. Martin, Seaman 3; and Mason C. Poston, Electrician's Mate 2. Upon reaching a small barrio in the jungle northwest of the Puerto Princessa camp, the four were captured by Japanese M.P.'s. The Japs had imprisoned them as guerrillas. Their note stated that they were the only survivors of ROBALO.

Headquarters doubted that a battery explosion could have sunk the submarine, and it seemed probable that ROBALO had struck a mine. The four who survived this disaster were never recovered. After the war it was discovered that a Japanese destroyer had removed them from Palawan on August 15th. The destroyer's destination was unrecorded. Apparently it never reached its intended destination.

Bowfin Doesn't Miss the Bus

Here is another submarine story of the caliber that will keep the cigars glowing and the anecdotes going so long as the smoking lamp is lit.

On August 10, 1944, BOWFIN (Lieutenant Commander John H. Corbus) went in for a close-up look at Minami Daito, an island centrally located in the Nansei Shoto chain. There was a narrow channel and a bay beyond, and the periscope found several ships of a convoy heading in to moor alongside a new concrete wharf. Corbus decided to go in and get them the following morning. So BOWFIN did.

The approach was a ticklish one, but the submarine tiptoed in, and the Jap AK's were lined up there like so many tramp steamers at Hoboken. BOWFIN was ready, and Corbus, squinting at the periscope, drew a careful bead on a target alongside the quay. Then he paused. A bus had rumbled out on the wharf, and a group of Japs was piling down the steamer's gangplank—obviously a shore party. There was a lot of bustle and chatter as these passengers boarded the bus. Corbu felt he could enliven the proceedings.

He fired three torpedoes at a freighter which was anchored off the quay, and three more at the ship alongside. A hit smashed the anchored freighter, throwing up a great cloud of smoke and debris. Another torpedo struck the vessel at the quay. And apparently a torpedo struck the quay itself for there was a mighty blast that filled the air with powdered cement. When the smoke cleared away, that section of the quay where the bus had been loading was obliterated. So was the bus.

Corbus turned BOWFIN on her tail and sent her seaward. Some A/S vessels chased, and the submarine was treated to more than the usual "going over." But afterwards the submariners were sure it was worth it. To date, at least, BOWFIN remains the only submarine able to claim, "Two ships, one quay, one bus."

Unfortunately the vessels torpedoed could not be identified, and BOWFIN was credited only with the 6,754-ton passenger-cargoman TSUSHIMA MARU, sunk at a later date on that patrol. But the post-war assessment committee listed only vessels of over 500 tons. The steamers at Minami Daito may have been smaller. And nowhere on the submarine inventory list was there a column labeled "Buses."

The Paluan Bay Convoy

On August 21, 1944 there occurred an epic battle between a SubSoWesPac wolf-pack and a Japanese convoy. Submarines at this period were patrolling the South China Sea from one end to the other, and contacts made by one submarine were frequently broadcast to and exploited by another down the line. So it happened that a convoy attacked by RAY on August 18 in Southern Palawan Passage subsequently fell afoul of Haddo, Harder, Guitarro, and Raton.

Japanese convoys were proceeding warily in the Palawan area, usually traveling with strong escort by day, and scuttling into some safe anchorage at nightfall.

Ray (Lieutenant Commander W. T. Kinsella) was patrolling off Balabac Strait when she encountered the convoy in question—five tankers, several transports and an assortment of cargo vessels adding up to some 12 or 13 ships. There were at least five escorts with this *maru* herd. Kinsella put Ray on the track and was able to fire six torpedoes at a tanker in a daylight submerged attack. Down went Nansei Maru, 5,878 tons. The A/S vessels staged the usual depth-charge party, which Ray evaded by means of a convenient density layer. When it was over Ray had lost contact, and Kinsella headed her up Palawan channel, hunting the fugitive convoy.

That night three escorts were contacted, but Ray was unable to locate the convoy. Kinsella was certain it had anchored some place during the night. So he headed his submarine on up Palawan passage, hoping to regain contact as the convoy crossed Mindoro Strait.

Kinsella's reasoning proved correct. At 0520 on August 20, the watch sighted the convoy's smoke 13 miles away. Ray was submerged at 0525 with the convoy still out in front; then, two hours later, Kinsella ordered her to the surface and attempted an end-around. The attempt was thwarted by the convoy's air cover.

For the rest of the day Kinsella dodged the air cover, ordering high-speed surface runs between air contacts, and quick dives as the planes closed in. By afternoon, he had decided the convoy was headed for Paluan Bay, on the westernmost tip of Mindoro, to anchor there for the night. Running the gantlet of air cover, Ray headed for the spot, Kinsella hoping to get in an attack as the convoy entered the bay. At 1700 Ray sighted the Japs entering the bay. A mile off the coast and too far out for an attack, the submarine was unable to close.

Like a cat at a mouse hole, Ray loitered off the entrance of the bay. The convoy was safe in the shallow harbor with an alerted escort force patrolling the entrance. But it would have to sortie some time to get on with the journey.

Ray was not long alone in her vigil. At 2036, about an hour after surfacing, she was in touch with another SoWesPac submarine. The newcomer was Harder (Commander S. D. Dealey). Kinsella was soon talking to Dealey in person—conversation by megaphone. Dealey was in tactical command of a wolf-pack en route to an area off the west coast of Luzon. Following Harder along the route was Haddo (Lieutenant Commander C. W. Nimitz, Jr.). Hake, the third submarine of the group, was too far astern to get into the excitement that eventuated, but Dealey got off a message to Haddo to rendezvous off Cape Calavite. Haddo received the word at 2125, and came on at full speed for the rendezvous.

At 0130 on August 21, Haddo slid up alongside Harder, and Dealey and young Nimitz discussed attack plans with Kinsella.

It was agreed that Haddo would attack from the west, Harder from the southwest, and Ray from the northwest. These plans were based on the assumption that the convoy would sortie at dawn and head north The assumption proved correct.

Ray Attacks

At 0457 Ray was submerged at a point one mile off the coast and three miles south of Cape Calavite Light. At 0551 her watch sighted the convoy coming out of Paluan Bay. Four minutes later there were three thumping explosions that sounded like torpedo hits from Harder. This touched off a series of depth-charge attacks that went on intermittently throughout the morning.

Ray was unable to observe the results of Harder's attack. The water was undulating glass, and periscope observation had to be brief. Harder drew most of the enemy's A/S attention. There was only one destroyer escort to seaward of the convoy, well aft of the leading ship.

The first ship in column was a 7,000-ton transport and Kinsella picked this vessel for his target. Only four torpedoes remained aboard the submarine at this climax of an energetic patrol, and Kinsella fired all four at the oncoming passenger-cargoman. Just as the tubes were fired, the target changed course 20° to the left to follow the coastline. The first three torpedoes missed ahead, but the fourth slammed in right under the stack. The escort charged, and Ray went deep, hunting a protective density layer. There was no protective layer. The first 40 depth charges were close, forcing Ray to an abysmal depth. To the north another submarine was being worked over, and the sea was full of thunder. When the storm abated, Ray climbed to periscope depth. One escort was circling the point of attack. The convoy was rounding Cape Calavite. Ray's target was not in sight, for the simple reason that it was under the sea. The ship was Taketoyo Maru, passenger-cargoman, 6,965 tons.

Haddo Attacks

In the meantime Haddo, in accordance with plans, had closed in on Paluan Bay, halting only when she made contact with the destroyer that was patrolling off the entrance. At 0419, with the DD 6,000 yards on her starboard bow, HADDO submerged. Nimitz held her under for a time, then planed her up to radar depth. At 0515, he saw the convoy start to sortie—an elongated column of ships.

The sea was placid and warm with low, oily swells. Air cover for the convoy could be expected. Nimitz planned to run north, squeezing the convoy between HADDO and the coast, until he got a set-up on a good target. Periscope exposures were kept to a minimum, and HADDO went to 80 feet and proceeded at 4.5 knots between looks. The leading ship crossed ahead, and the range was 6,000 yards. The column extended back into the bay, and unless something untoward happened, an attack was in the cards.

At 0554 depth-charging started on all sides of HADDO and continued without interruption until 0616. Taking a quick look, Nimitz saw two escorts on his port beam and three on his starboard side, all of them about 3,000 yards away, dropping depth charges as fast as they could get them overside. The seascape resembled a vista of Old Faithfuls, and in HADDO's conning tower the din was so loud that Nimitz had to shout to make himself heard.

At 0619 HADDO saw a ship ahead struck by a torpedo. This was RAY's target. RAY's attack touched off another depth-charge barrage. HADDO was closing in range, as Nimitz hunted a suitable target. At 0625 he saw three ships astern of the one torpedoed by RAY veer out of column and head in HADDO's direction. This was the awaited opportunity. The vessels made an overlapping target nearly three ships long. At 0627 Nimitz fired the first shot of a six-torpedo salvo from the bow tubes—two torpedoes at each of the three targets.

Immediately after firing, HADDO went deep, anticipating air bombs. Five timed torpedo explosions were heard. The sixth torpedo exploded much later than the others—either an end-of-run explosion or a hit on the island of Mindoro. A depth-charge attack followed in which over 100 charges were dropped by the Jap A/S vessels. At 0720, when HADDO had her next look, one ship was burning like a wooden shed, and to the right a dense pall of smoke was smudging the day.

Harder's Action

HARDER's part in the action is largely a matter of conjecture. At 0555 both RAY and HADDO heard and saw a depth-charge attack apparently directed at neither of them. RAY heard what sounded like torpedo explosions at the beginning of this A/S attack.

They were probably HARDER's torpedoes. The following morning HARDER was in megaphone contact with HADDO, and Dealey and Nimitz plotted another foray against "the Nips." But HARDER was subsequently lost on this patrol and her attack report went down with her.

The Jap convoy was not to escape after HADDO concluded her attack. During the preceding night, GUITARRO, under Lieutenant Commander E. D. Haskins, had moved up to take a position just south of Cape Calavite Light. Also under Haskins' tactical direction was RATON (Lieutenant Commander M. W. Shea). Haskins assigned RATON a station just north of Cape Calavite Light and close inshore. GUITARRO and RATON took up the game where HADDO left off.

Guitarro Attacks

At 0457 on the morning of August 21, GUITARRO was submerged on station. At 0555 she heard a distant depth-charge attack. A few minutes later, her watch sighted smoke to the southeast. When masts materialized under the smoke, Haskins estimated the range at 18,000 yards. Haskins readied GUITARRO and began the approach. The master gyro-compass follow-up system was out of commission. So GUITARRO was steered by auxiliary gyro, matching T.D.C. and conning tower compasses with auxiliary gyro by hand.

At 0620 Sound heard torpedoes fired and a minute or two later listened to hits followed by a prolonged depth-charge attack. At 0640 the convoy was headed north, and Haskins had obtained a position dead ahead. Ten minutes later the whole convoy zigged radically to the right, and headed close inshore to Calavite. This put GUITARRO considerably off the track.

Haskins immediately came to normal approach course and ordered high speed. Off Cape Calavite there was an unfavorable current of 1.3 knots, which handicapped all efforts to close the range. The target group consisted of two large tankers in column, followed by a large cargo ship. Farther aft there were other ships, but the visibility against the shore background was poor and identification was impossible. To the south a burning ship appeared, and three Japanese escorts were intent on depth-charging a submarine in the vicinity. The explosions were thunderous even at a distance. This activity left the near-by convoy unguarded.

Fortunate situation for GUITARRO. She had been caught far off the track by the zig, and she had to use full speed to get in. An alert escort would certainly have picked her up. As it was, the preoccupation of the escorts and the pandemonium of the depth charges enabled GUITARRO to close in.

350

Even so, GUITARRO's speed was barely sufficient. The first tanker went by out of range. The second tanker did likewise. The third vessel, a cargo ship, would also have been beyond range of GUITARRO's Mark 18 torpedoes if something hadn't disturbed her equanimity. At 0717 Haskins saw this freighter fire a gun in the submarine's direction and alter course radically toward GUITARRO. Either GUITARRO had been sighted or the freighter had made some kind of a false contact. But after a moment the Jap ship resumed her original course. The gunfire had evidently been a signal for the escorts. Three CHIDORI "pingers" came racing up.

For GUITARRO the freighter's maneuver proved most fortuitous. It decreased the range about 600 yards, which put the cargo ship just inside the range of the Mark 18's. At 0721 Haskins got off a salvo of four electrics at a range of 3,700 yards. The escorts were coming up fast and Haskins ordered GUITARRO deep. During the next dozen minutes, 50 depth charges were dropped, all of them heavy and all close. GUITARRO received a roughing-up and moderate damage.

Nearly four minutes after the torpedoes were fired, Sound heard the first hit. The hit was not observed but the ship's screws stopped, and a bedlam of breaking-up noises followed.

Final assessment credited GUITARRO with a passenger-cargoman—apparently the last victim in the assailed convoy. RATON had submerged that morning off Cape Calavite, and at 0557 she heard depth-chargings. A few minutes later, smoke was sighted at a distance of 25 miles. Shea maneuvered the submarine into the normal approach course, but the distance was too great and she was unable to make contact. Nevertheless, she was on the field as short-stop. And in submarine warfare, as in baseball, they also serve who only stand and wait.

Post-war investigation disclosed that the Paluan Bay convoy suffered the fatalities listed below.

The tonnage total—28,242 tons—is another good example of teamwork running up a score. But perhaps more impressive are the precision and dispatch with which six submarines were able to concentrate on one embattled Japanese convoy and blow it to pieces in spite of daylight-running coast-hug-

ging, alerted air cover and strong surface escorts,

However, these Japanese anti-submarine measures were not entirely ineffectual—a fact evidenced by the loss of HARDER shortly after the Paluan Bay foray. HARDER's valiant story—a destroyer battle—is told in the following chapter. For inside information on Japanese A/S measures during this period, one may turn to the experience of another famous submarine, the personal observations of another ace submarine skipper.

The submarine: BARB. The skipper: Lieutenant Commander E. B. Fluckey.

Barb vs. A/S Measures (Introducing Lieutenant Commander Fluckey)

On April 28, 1944, Eugene B. Fluckey became commanding officer of BARB. There was no such demonstration of the elements as presumably took place when Buddha was born—no rivers flowing backwards, no portentous comets in the Asian sky. But Japanese star-gazers, if any remained on the flanks of Fujiyama, may have seen some bursts of light that spring in the direction of the Kuriles. Bursts of light caused by torpedo explosions—explosions which sank the following ships:

Date	Name	Type	Tonnage
May 31	Koto Maru	Cargo	1,053
May 31	Madras Maru	Passenger-Cargo	3,802
June 11	Toten Maru	Cargo	3,823
June 11	Chihaya Maru	Cargo	1,161
June 13	Takashima Maru	Cargo	5,633

In the Pacific a new constellation was on the war's horizon—a stellar phenomenon of the first magnitude, composed of a star submarine named BARB, an ace crew of submariners, and a skipper named Fluckey. There were certainly disturbances at sea to mark the advent of Fluckey and BARB.

The skipper they came to call "Lucky." And the submarine, a "lucky sub." Lucky in opportunity, perhaps—in hitting so-called productive areas. But the marksmanship that hits when the targets are on hand, and the submarining that gets a boat out from under an A/S barrage depend on something more

Submarine	Ship Sunk	Type	Tonnage
Ray	Nansei Maru	Tanker	5,878
Ray	Taketoyo Maru	Passenger-Cargo	6,965
Haddo	Kinryo Maru	Passenger-Cargo	4,390
Haddo	Norfolk Maru	Passenger-Cargo	6,576
Guitarro	Uga Maru	Passenger-Cargo	4,433

Nansei Maru sunk August 18. All others sunk August 21.

than chance. That something is apparent in the cold-steel nerve with which Fluckey and company went submarining through such A/S opposition as they encountered late in the summer of 1944.

When BARB made her ninth war patrol (August 4 to October 3) in "Convoy College," Japanese anti-submarine methods were at the summit of their development. BARB's ninth was a highly successful patrol during which she operated as a member of "Ed's Eradicators"—one of the outstanding wolf-packs of the war. TUNNY and QUEENFISH were pack-mates. Captain E. R. Swinburne was group commander.

Fluckey wrote the following description of the anti-submarine measures BARB ran into during the patrol. The tactical indications of Japanese homing on radar make surprising reading in view of post-war information which tends to confirm the fact that Japanese aircraft were not equipped to home on U.S. submarine-radar. And Fluckey's writing makes seat-edge reading in any case. Here was a naval officer whose pen was as dynamic as his sword.

Anti-submarine measures were a bit terrific. Briefly these consisted of 73 enemy plane contacts, 5 bombings, 141 depth charges labeled BARB, assorted depth charges and bombs aimed at submarines in general, gunfire from a CHIDORI which illuminated us, and torpedoes from the CHIDORI or possibly the REDFISH. Some of SEALION's torpedoes passed close aboard, but only required lowering the periscope as a safety measure until torpedoes had passed by.

Air cover for convoys is heavy, never less than two planes and as high as eight or even more. The three convoys we encountered were at night. On two of these, the night flier evidently was called for after the QUEENFISH attack, for he came sweeping in and made his radar contact while we were inside the screens about a minute before we fired. We expected him to bomb, but evidently he didn't make sight contact.

Day air patrol was heavy—along the Manila-Hongkong route, the Takao-Singapore route, and on Formosa-Philippine routes. These could generally be avoided by the customary up-and-down tactics of a submarine. We were caught with our pants down once in the daytime by a high-flying, all silver colored (beautiful camouflage) Nell which dove on us out of the sun and bombed. The other two daytime bombings occurred because we were a bit over-ambitious in chasing a convoy which had thumbed its nose at us. Several planes had forced us down, then we tried to outrun one on the surface and came in second best. Later after a couple of hours surface running we were caught in the bombsights of a plane emerging from a plane locker and were bashed again. This plane cover for the convoy extended at least 100 miles, but the QUEENFISH had excited them. Night air patrol was particularly heavy. . . . Bright

moonlight nights were their specialty. At one time we were driven down by plane and watched TUNNY being bombed. Her position was boxed by float lights which burned for one hour. Float lights were also laid, evidently marking the course on which she submerged. Later, a brilliant green magnesium parachute flare was dropped. We were bombed shortly after midnight the same night, and later at periscope depth observed our submergence position marked by float lights. . . . One of these bombs left bomb fragments and tail vanes on deck, and minor damage was sustained.

At dawn one morning while southwest of Takao we observed 8 Nells returning to their Baku Naval Base in groups of 1, 2, 3's. All were camouflaged with light gray paint.

After our second attack (small AE sunk) about 5 anti-submarine vessels encircled us, sometimes pinging, sometimes listening. Evasion was accomplished by passing under them on a steady course at 100 rpm with a few zigs thrown in. Gradient, 6 degrees.

The CHIDORI killer group encountered were extremely capable of taking care of themselves once alerted. Their sound men must have been experts. On our second surface approach we were challenged at 3,600 yards. We turned tail. At 3,950 yards the CHIDORI illuminated us with search light and commenced firing simultaneously. We evaded by submergence. On the follow-up approach at radar depth while he was after someone else, three torpedoes came from his direction and passed fairly close down our starboard side. These may possibly have been from the REDFISH, for the QUEENFISH had fired across our bow a short time before. If the REDFISH did not fire, the CHIDORI did. CHIDORI then dropped a string of charges on someone. Shortly after the charges, we fired with him on a steady course at 1,500 yards. As our third torpedo was leaving the tube, he practically spun on his heel and came after us. A nice pattern of depth charges bracketed us. His sidekick then joined the BARB party. One stayed on our beam pinging with hand keying while the other came up from astern listening. Since the dropper was passing parallel to us and a bit to port, we kept our course and speed, knowing he would drop to port. He did. Charges were close and set at 250-300 feet. In the turbulence following we took off and lost them.

After our last attack on the surface, we could not clear a CHIDORI escort 750 yards away, closing rapidly, without being sighted and rammed in the force 4 sea; so submerged, turned in a circle to the right to avoid the sinking ships and then cut across the stern of the formation. Many depth charges were dropped, all well astern.

Three lifeboats from the brand new freighter we sank on 31 August were equipped with black and yellow vertically striped sails.

The freighter with the pretty lifeboats was OKUNI MARU, 5,633 tons. QUEENFISH downed the tanker

CHIYODA MARU, 4,700 tons, in the action mentioned. SEALION II, in an adjacent area, sank the minelayer SHIRATAKA. With QUEENFISH, REDFISH and CHIDORI's firing in the vicinity, and BARB's periscope ducking torpedoes from SEALION, the campus of "Convoy College" was lively on the night of August 31st.

As a matter of fact, the A/S opposition encountered by BARB was the Japanese answer to a wolf-pack campaign which had turned the Formosa-Luzon Strait area into a *maru* death-trap. On the southern border of "Convoy College" in mid-August RASHER had rampaged, staging a shipping massacre that downed the second largest tonnage credited a U.S. submarine for one patrol, and simultaneously accounted for the second largest merchantman sunk by submarines in the Pacific War. Because this RASHER rampage also featured the sinking of one of the Imperial Japanese Navy's escort carriers, the patrol is reported in Chapter 26, *Submarines vs. The Japanese Navy*.

Wolf-packing with "Ed's Eradicators," BARB herself sank a Japanese escort carrier in the scalding waters of "Convoy College." This feat is also reported as a naval action.

Altogether Swinburne's "Eradicators" accounted for 51,661 tons of Japanese merchant and naval shipping. And they concluded their wolf-pack patrol as participants in one of the most dramatic submarine exploits of the war—a rescue unparalleled in submarine history. Other participants were GROWLER, SEALION II and PAMPANITO—"Ben's Busters"—a wolf-pack operating in "Convoy College" at the time. The rescue episode is recounted later on.

Another wolf-pack ripping up shipping in the Formosa-Luzon Strait area late in the summer was "Donk's Devils," a group composed of SPADEFISH, REDFISH and PICUDA. The operations of "Busters" and "Devils" merged with those of "Ed's Eradicators" to make "Convoy College" the hottest submarine battle-ground in the Pacific at that season.

Donk's Devils and Ben's Busters (Introducing Spadefish)

Under group leadership of Commander G. R. Donaho, "Donk's Devils" left Pearl Harbor on July 23, and headed for "Convoy College." The practice of employing a wolf-pack captain who was not a submarine commander had been revised in favor of appointing one of the submarine commanders as group leader. In this case, Donaho in PICUDA directed pack operations. REDFISH sailed under Commander L. D. McGregor, Jr. And the group included a newcomer—SPADEFISH—a Mare Island Navy Yard product under Commander G. W. Underwood. Fate was to decree that this submarine on maiden patrol was to deal the pack's hardest blow at the enemy.

SPADEFISH scored first on August 19, slamming torpedoes into a passenger-cargoman off northwest Luzon. Victim was TAMATSU MARU, 9,589 tons. One of the war's hardest-hitting submarine patrols was under way.

Three days later, Underwood and company caught a tanker. Down went HAKKO MARU NO. 2, 10,023 tons. Then PICUDA stepped in on August 25 to score a double—the Japanese destroyer YUNAGI and the 1,943-ton freighter KOTOKU MARU. A few miles to the southward REDFISH punched a killing torpedo into the freighter BATOPAHA MARU, 5,953 tons.

As has been related, "Ed's Eradicators" and "Ben's Busters" were in adjacent patrol areas, and torpedoes were traveling in all directions on the night of August 31st. Evidently the Japanese wished to break up this concentration, and early in September they routed a convoy along the east coast of Formosa. If evasive routing were intended, the effort failed as an anti-submarine measure. On September 8, SPADEFISH and Underwood were off the east coast of Formosa. Underwood put the submarine on the track. And NICHIMAN MARU, NICHIAN MARU, SHINTEN MARU and SHOKEI MARU were shoveled under by SPADEFISH.

Deeper in the interior of "Convoy College," PICUDA and REDFISH struck a convoy on September 16th. PICUDA nailed the passenger-cargoman TOKUSHIMA MARU, and REDFISH picked off OGURA MARU NO. 2, a 7,311-ton tanker. The submarines then swung to the southern border of the area. And on September 21, PICUDA sank the freighter AWAJI MARU and REDFISH downed the 8,506-ton transport MIZUHO MARU.

This concluded the sweep by "Donk's Devils"— a sweep which set a new American wolf-pack record, as may be seen by the tabulated score on page 354.

The SPADEFISH patrol, downing six ships for a total 31,542 tons, won for that submarine and Underwood a secure position in the galaxy of U.S. submarine stars. And in sinking a tonnage total of 64,448 tons, "Donk's Devils" returned to Pearl Harbor with the highest wolf-pack score to date. Had the Japanese added this figure to the tonnage sunk by "Ed's Eradicators," they would have noted that these two wolf-packs in "Convoy College" sank more merchant shipping than Japan's yards, working full blast, were able to construct that August. This, exclusive of the tonnage simultaneously downed by "Ben's Busters."

The "Busters" loped out of Pearl Harbor in mid-August. Group Commander Oakley captained the submarine GROWLER. She was followed westward by

Date	Submarine	Ship Sunk	Type	Tonnage
Aug. 25, 1944	Picuda	Yunagi	Destroyer	1,270
Aug. 25, 1944	Picuda	Kotoku Maru	Cargo	1,943
Sept. 16, 1944	Picuda	Tokushima Maru	Passenger-Cargo	5,975
Sept. 21, 1944	Picuda	Awaji Maru	Cargo	1,948
Aug. 25, 1944	Redfish	Batopaha Maru	Cargo	5,953
Sept. 16, 1944	Redfish	Ogura Maru No. 2	Tanker	7,311
Sept. 21, 1944	Redfish	Mizuho Maru	Transport	8,506
Aug. 19, 1944	Spadefish	Tamatsu Maru	Passenger-Cargo	9,589
Aug. 22, 1944	Spadefish	Hakko Maru No. 2	Tanker	10,023
Sept. 8, 1944	Spadefish	Nichiman Maru	Cargo	1,922
Sept. 8, 1944	Spadefish	Nichian Maru	Cargo	6,197
Sept. 8, 1944	Spadefish	Shinten Maru	Cargo	1,254
Sept. 8, 1944	Spadefish	Shokei Maru	Cargo	2,557

PAMPANITO (Commander P. E. Summers) and SEA-LION II (Commander E. T. Reich).

As has been noted, SEALION II was in action on the night of August 31 when BARB's Commander Fluckey took particular note of the enemy's anti-submarine effort in "Convoy College." Hitting the first target for the "Busters," Reich's submarine bashed to the bottom the 1,345-ton minelayer SHIRATAKA.

Then the "Busters" withdrew to another quarter of the playing field, and began a patrol along the Singapore-to-Japan main line. About one o'clock in the morning of September 12 the wolf-pack made contact with a Japan-bound convoy. The three submarines maneuvered to intercept. Then it was that GROWLER fired the first shot in a drama that began as a submarine-convoy battle and ended with an epic rescue.

Meriting a detailed account, the rescue drama is related as an episode apart from the wolf-pack campaign which decimated Japanese shipping in "Convoy College." When "Ben's Busters" concluded their patrol, they had sunk 37,634 tons of that shipping.

Thus three Pearl Harbor wolf-packs—"Ed's Eradicators," "Donk's Devils," "Ben's Busters"—in approximately one month's time downed a grand total of some 150,000 tons of Japanese merchantmen. As these vessels strewed their cargoes across the sea bottom and their crews and passengers across the tumbling surface, Japan's leaders must have known that the Rising Sun had also been torpedoed.

But the submarine attack was not confined to the waters of "Convoy College."

Pintado Gets the Whale

While wolf-packs were ganging up on "Convoy College" and roaming the waters of "Hit Parade"— an "XYZ area" established off the eastern coastline of Japan—lone submarines were on the prowl in many areas. These "lone wolves" continued to operate throughout the war, and in numerous instances they did so much damage to convoys that the enemy took them for wolf-packs. Outstanding example was TANG. Another "lone wolf" that blew a big hole in Japanese merchant shipping in the summer of 1944 was PINTADO.

Captained by Commander B. A. Clarey, this submarine headed westward from Pearl Harbor on July 24 to conduct her second war patrol. Area assigned: the northern waters of the East China Sea.

On August 6 PINTADO caught a freighter below Kagoshimo on the Kyushu-Formosa run, and that was the end of the 5,401-ton SHONAN MARU. As the submarine proceeded with her hunt, the going looked average. Then, late in the afternoon of August 22, her periscope picked up a target that looked a whole lot bigger than average. A bulge of smoke coming up from the southwest sent PINTADO tracking forward. By 1800 Clarey had the periscope trained on a large Japanese convoy which was traveling in three-column formation. Four modern-looking freighters paraded in the starboard column. Three large oil tankers and two new passenger-cargomen paraded in the port column. Two anti-submarine vessels paced along on either flank of the convoy, and a CHIDORI torpedo-boat "fish-tailed" in the lead, "pinging" this way and that like a cocky drum major performing at the head of a band. But Clarey was not interested in the escorts. What fascinated Clarey was the convoy's center column—a transport led by an oil tanker. An abnormally large oil tanker with two big smoke stacks abreast of each other aft—a silhouette as unmistakable as Noah's Ark!

Indeed, had PINTADO come across Noah's famous cattle-boat at this point almost midway between Kagoshimo and Wenchow, Clarey and company could not have been more surprised. For here was one of the largest oil haulers in creation—perhaps the biggest Japanese merchantman on the sea! Here was that great ex-whale factory twin of the monster which once escaped TINOSA. Here, marching in this convoy's center column, was TONAN MARU NO. 2.

Commander B. A. Clarey had seen this "dream boat" before. That was on October 10, 1942, when AMBERJACK (Lieutenant Commander J. A. Bole, Jr.) made a periscope inspection of the Imperial Navy's harbor at Kavieng. Executive officer of AMBERJACK at that time was Lieutenant Commander B. A. Clarey. And there in Kavieng Harbor was this same ex-whale factory in service as a plane-carrier hauling aircraft to the Bismarck Archipelago.

AMBERJACK skirted the group of small islands at the harbor entrance, and Bole fired four torpedoes, range 3,100 yards, down Nissel Pass. Hits thundered under the whale factory's stern, and TONAN MARU NO. 2 sat in Kavieng Harbor with her rump in the mud, her after compartments flooded and sea water swamping her engines.

Eventually the vessel's engineering spaces were pumped out; the Imperial Navy raised her and she was laboriously towed to Japan where she was refitted and put into service as an oil tanker. And now she was in front of PINTADO's periscope and Clarey's eyes—the revivified TONAN MARU NO. 2, as big as life and twice as handsome.

"It was difficult for me to believe that this could possibly be the same ship," Clarey wrote afterwards. Was he staring, perhaps, at the NISSIN MARU? No, the vessel was undoubtedly the ex-whale factory whose twin had been sunk by Navy bombers at Truk. And it was time the whole family was exterminated. Commander Clarey described the action as follows:

We maneuvered into position ahead of the center of the convoy because we wanted to attack and sink, if possible, the largest ship. Evidently the Nips believed this position to be the safest place for the most valuable ship in the convoy. By six o'clock we had attained position directly ahead of the convoy, right on the track of the whale factory which was zig-zagging alternately to the right and left. At 6:15 we ordered "battle stations submerged," at which time we took a sounding obtaining a depth of 210 feet, rigged ship for depth charges, and proceeded to a firing position. During these maneuvers a CHIDORI torpedo boat anti-submarine vessel, the leading escort, was coming in our general direction and at one time passed about 75 yards ahead of our periscope. At this time he was so close it was impossible to see the whole ship through the periscope. He finally passed clear, not having detected us and, about 11 minutes later, we fired four torpedoes from the stern tubes at the whale factory from a range of about 1200 yards. About a minute and a half after firing, two torpedoes were heard and observed to hit the target.

One hit forward and one amidships. Immediately after firing we turned in order to bring the bow tubes to bear and at one minute after seven fired six more torpedoes at the whale factory and the overlapping tankers in the port columns. All torpedoes were set at six feet. Two of the torpedoes from this last salvo ran erratic. One circled and crossed twice over the PINTADO; it could be distinctly heard as it passed over the engine room. The other torpedoes ran straight. About 2½ minutes later two more hits were heard and the leading tanker in the far column burst into flame over its entire length like an ignited, gasoline-soaked log. The second of these hits was obtained in the tanker next astern.

On again looking at the whale factory it was, by this time, burning briskly from bow to stern. The sun had set about ten minutes past six and it now, being a little after seven, became quite dark. We decided to seek deeper depths and pull away from this area in order to surface as soon as possible, reload our torpedoes and try to attack this convoy again that night.

We avoided escorts and depth charging during the next hour and a half, during which time we heard in the distance a series of tremendous, rumbling-type explosions. A little before 9 o'clock we came back to periscope depth and saw the most incredible sight. Two burning ships were sighted billowing smoke and flame hundreds of feet into the air and the fire from a third ship could be seen near by. Two escorts could be seen milling about in the vicinity of the burning ships. We left the periscope up this time and called all hands to the conning tower to give them a look at the evening's work.

Shortly before 10 o'clock we surfaced and started our search for the remainder of the convoy. As we skirted the area of the damaged ships we could see three enormous and very distinct fires at a range of about five to six miles. A pall of dense, black smoke covered the entire sky, darkening the area around the scene. We continued to search for the remainder of the night and all of the next day but were unable to again locate the convoy.

Evidently the two medium-sized tankers which were struck escaped destruction. But the elephantine two-stacker, identified after the war as none other than TONAN MARU NO. 2, was from that date forward an ex-ex-whale factory.

In the previous chapter it was remarked that Japan's oil imports dropped from approximately 1,000,000 barrels in January 1944 to 600,000 barrels in June. In July, Japan's oil importations fell to approximately 400,000 barrels. Reports conflict for August, but one authority gives the oil importation figure as 300,000 barrels. Certainly the Japanese oil situation was critical in the summer of 1944. And the barrel statistics emphasize the importance of such an oiler as TONAN MARU NO. 2.

The Navy's airmen often spoke of "shooting fish in a barrel." Putting reverse English on the expression, Clarey and his companion submariners had proceeded to shoot barrels in a whale. No Jonah torpedo saved the leviathan on this occasion. The warheads did their work, and the great ex-whale factory plunged to sea bottom. With that blow, PINTADO deprived the Japanese tanker fleet of 19,262 tons. And in so doing, she sank the largest merchantman to be downed by a U.S. submarine in the war.

Loss of Flier

To conduct her second war patrol, FLIER (Commander J. D. Crowley) left Fremantle on August 2 and headed for area waters off Saigon, French Indo-China. On the evening of August 13 she was transiting Balabac Strait, traveling on the surface. At 2200 a thunderous explosion rocked the submarine. Oil, water and debris showered the bridge. Crowley was thrown from his feet and several others on the bridge were injured. Air rushed from the conning tower hatch and there was a roar of flooding water followed by frantic outcry from those below. Lieutenant J. W. Liddell, the executive officer, was blown through the hatch. Men struggled up the ladder behind him. FLIER, still making 15 knots, sank a minute after the explosion.

Thirteen survivors, including Commander Crowley, started a desperate swim in the direction of land. At first they tried to keep together. Then the tide swept some of the weaker swimmers away from the others. Lieutenant W. L. Reynolds and Ensign P. S. Mayer, both badly injured, were unable to swim on. Lieutenant P. Knapp became separated from the group and disappeared in the night. Crowley decided the best chance was to strike out for coral reefs northwestward. The sky was overcast, but an occasional play of lightning helped to keep the swimmers oriented. The moon rose at 0300, August 14, and the going seemed somewhat easier in the silvered water.

But a little while later, Lieutenant J. E. Casey, who had been blinded by oil, quietly slipped away. Realizing it had to be every man for himself, Crowley told all hands to swim on as best they could toward the land which was now in sight.

The sun came up in a crimson welter and the sky blazed. All morning the swimmers labored on. At 1330 five of the group—Commander Crowley, Lieutenant Liddell, Ensign A. E. Jacobson, G. A. Howell, Chief Radio Technician, and E. R. Baumgart, Motor Machinist's Mate 3—caught a floating palm tree. Clinging to this flotsam, they succeeded in reaching the beach of Mantangule Island. There they found Quartermaster J. D. Russo, who had swum the

entire distance. And later they were delighted to encounter D. P. Tremaine, Fire Controlman 3, and W. B. Miller, Motor Machinist's Mate 3.

On this jungly island, FLIER's survivors lived like Crusoes for five days. On August 19 they found friendly natives who guided them to a U.S. Army Coast Watcher Unit on Palawan. The coast watchers provided communication facilities, and arrangements were made for evacuation by submarine.

In small boats the FLIER survivors were embarked on the night of August 30 to make the rendezvous offshore with the submarine REDFIN. After a hair-raising excursion, during which they had to skirt a Japanese ship anchored near the rendezvous point, they reached the objective and were safe aboard REDFIN on the morning of August 31st.

So concluded one of the most harrowing submarine adventures of the Pacific War. The survivors who made the long swim were grateful for the luck and stamina that kept them going. But they would never forget those who were unable to "make it" after FLIER struck the mine.

The Saving of USS Crevalle

"If I omit my practicing for one day, I know the difference. If I miss it for two days, the critics know it. And if for three days, the audience knows it."

The above declaration by Paderewski, world-famed concert pianist, will have meaning for submariners who know the value of the split second and the virtue of reflex action—the appropriate reflex action. A great pianist is, of course, a master technician who (art and all that to one side) makes his living by manual dexterity. A submarine sailor (artist in his line) also makes his living by manual dexterity. And there are occasions when the hand, trained to be quicker than the eye, is called upon to save his very life.

Motor reflexes—actions that are automatic—come from practice and more practice, and are "perfected" only by hours, days and weeks of unforgiving drill. Like a pianist at Carnegie Hall, a submarine technician cannot pause to think something over in the middle of a performance. Once the show is on, he must carry through at top speed. No "stage fright," no "sour notes," no ineptitude at his instrument are permissible.

Concerning reflex action and the automatic ability to do the right thing at the drastic moment, a perfect demonstration was given aboard the USS CREVALLE in September 1944. The performer was an enlisted man, Robert L. Yeager, Motor Machinist's Mate 1.

Yeager, take a bow!

Here is the story.

On the morning of September 11, CREVALLE (Lieutenant Commander F. D. Walker, Jr.) was moving north of the Postiljon Islands to enter Makassar Strait. At 0611 she made a routine trim dive, and at 0624 she surfaced. Fifteen seconds later the ship took a sharp down angle and resubmerged with upper and lower conning tower hatches open.

Officer of the Deck Lieutenant Howard J. Blind and W. L. Fritchen, GM2, were swept from the bridge as CREVALLE went down. The submarine had been making standard speed, and as she went under she continued to make this speed, which drove her down in a precipitous nose-dive. The sea roared into the conning tower, flooding the control room and pump room. The diluvial torrent was deafening and drowned out shouted orders and yells of alarm.

Apparently Lieutenant Blind managed to unlatch the opened hatch cover as CREVALLE burrowed under, for the upper hatch seated at 150 feet. This stopped the inrushing deluge. But the flooded submarine was heading for the bottom when MotorMac Yeager who was in the crew's space sprang to the telephone.

Unable to get in contact with any officer, Yeager took matters into his own hands. Ascertaining that standard speed was still rung up, he ordered, "All back full!" This checked CREVALLE's downward plunge and removed the appalling angle on the boat. In thinking at top speed and acting even faster to give that one command, Yeager undoubtedly saved the submarine.

For CREVALLE had reached 190 feet before she started to back up. With the maximum down-angle, water in the control room was above the forward-battery door and the pump room was completely flooded. In the conning tower the water was arm-pit deep. Had CREVALLE continued her nose-dive, she might never have regained depth control.

Two minutes after she plunged under, CREVALLE broached on the surface, backing full. Machine guns were manned immediately, and search was begun for Fritchen and Blind. Fritchen was soon recovered. But although Blind's head was glimpsed, he disappeared a moment later and was never sighted again.

CREVALLE was in a bad way. Everything in the conning tower, the control room and the pump room was grounded out, including the radio transmitters. Fortunately nothing was sighted and the submariners were able to make temporary repairs on the surface. That night the water-logged submarine was headed for Darwin.

Inquiry was unable to determine the cause of CREVALLE's accidental submergence. Evidently, after making her trim dive, she surfaced with vents open, and after the escape of the initial blow of air, she settled. The in-plunging flood prevented those in the conning tower from pulling the hatch lanyard—presumably it was only after Lieutenant Blind unlatched the hatch from topside that the deluge finally closed it.

More than one submarine surfaced with open vents, and it became customary for the diving officer to report, "Ready for surfacing. Vents shut!"—the second announcement inserted as a reminder. It also became the custom to surface with the lower conning tower hatch shut to minimize possible flooding.

Motor Machinist's Mate Yeager was awarded a citation and congratulated for the "initiative" and "presence of mind" with which he manned the phone and gave the appropriate order. An officer noted, *"His experience as battle-station stern planesman since commissioning had probably qualified him better than any man aboard to make such a decision."*

Actually, Yeager had little time to do any deliberate "deciding" in those flying few seconds of uproar and emergency between the moment CREVALLE plunged and the moment he reached the phone. He was there in a flash, hand on button. In another flash he had given the order. These were motor responses, and the right ones. Hand and mind in the groove after months of training, days of practice and routine exercises, hours of drill, drill, drill. The motor machinist's mate was a trained technician who saw the thing to do and did it instantaneously.

Thus was CREVALLE saved.

Prisoner-of-war Rescue by Submarines

In March 1944 the Japanese at Singapore were cheering the completion of a railroad which had been built by the slave labor of British, Australian and native POW's. This iron trail had cost the lives of 22,000 prisoners, abject victims of the Tojo treatment which included a starvation diet, brutal floggings and finger-snap medical care. The survivors of this barbarous railroading were worked from March to September on the docks at Singapore, while the Japs waited for ships, delayed by the submarine menace, to transport them to Japan. There they were to slave in the Emperor's factories and mines.

On September 6, a convoy of six ships with five escorts left Singapore for Japan. Crammed aboard RAKUYO MARU were 1,350 English and Australian captives. Some 750 of their fellows were stuffed like cattle into the holds of another ship. Of the four other ships of the convoy, one was a heavily laden transport, another was a large freighter carrying rubber and rice, and the remaining two were loaded oil tankers. Several days after sailing, this group was joined by three passenger-cargomen and two more escorts from the Philippines. On the night of September 11-12, the convoy was proceeding northward in three columns, three ships to a column, the DD SHIKINAMI leading the center column and three small escort vessels riding herd on each flank.

This was the convoy that fell prey to the torpedoes of "Ben's Busters"—GROWLER, PAMPANITO and SEALION. Between 0100 and 0130 on the 12th, all three submarines contacted the convoy by radar some 300 miles off Hainan. The submarines swung into action.

At 0155 GROWLER attacked from the convoy's starboard side, and put a torpedo into HIRADO, the leading escort vessel on the starboard bow. This craft, a frigate, blew up amidships, burst into flames and sank within a few minutes. The sky began to flash, reflecting gunfire from the other escorts, and Oakley's submarine withdrew to make an end-around and a second attack.

At 0524 Commander E. T. Reich drove SEALION into attack on the convoy's starboard side. In two minutes' time, Reich slammed two torpedoes in the passenger-cargoman NANKAI MARU in the center of the formation, another torpedo into a large transport leading the right column, and two more into RAKUYO MARU. The Japanese aboard RAKUYO MARU immediately abandoned. The unfortunate prisoners, left to fend for themselves, somehow got free of the ship and into the water.

At 0653 GROWLER attacked and sank the destroyer SHIKINAMI. Then NANKAI MARU went down about an hour later and RAKUYO MARU sank late in the afternoon.

During the day, most of the Japanese were picked up by escorts, while the prisoners in the water were held at bay by rifles and pistols. By nightfall the miserable men, abandoned, were swimming desperately, or clinging helplessly to mats of wreckage. Nearly all were smeared from head to foot with the crude oil which covered the water's surface. After sundown the prospect of survival seemed slim indeed. But these castaways were to have an unexpected deliverance.

Throughout the day PAMPANITO had tracked the convoy, but had been unable to attack because GROWLER and SEALION were attacking and because the convoy changed course and fled toward Hong Kong. But PAMPANITO hung on doggedly as her captain, Lieutenant Commander P. E. Summers, directed the chase. At 2240, the submarine was in position for a surface attack. Summers fired nine torpedoes at the four remaining merchantmen. Seven torpedoes hit home. One salvo sank the tanker ZUIHO MARU and another sank the 10,509-ton passenger-cargo carrier KACHIDOKI MARU. Now more prisoners of war

struggled desperately in the water as PAMPANITO evaded the escorts, and cleared the vicinity, the submariners unaware, as were those aboard SEALION and GROWLER, that allies were in dire need of help.

On September 14 GROWLER departed the area. But SEALION and PAMPANITO remained. On the afternoon of the 15th, PAMPANITO, passing through the waters where she had made her attack, discovered a crude raft loaded with men. Summers sized up the situation at once and PAMPANITO began picking up survivors as fast as she could locate them.

Her patrol reports tells the dramatic story:

As men were received on board, we stripped them and removed most of the heavy coating of oil and muck. We cleared the after torpedo room and passed them below as quickly as possible. Gave all men a piece of cloth moistened with water to suck on. All of them were exhausted after four days on the raft and three years' imprisonment. Many had lashed themselves to their makeshift rafts which were slick with grease; and had nothing but life belts with them. All showed signs of pellagra, beri-beri, immersion, salt water sores, ringworm, malaria, etc. All were very thin and showed the results of undernourishment. Some were in very bad shape, but with the excitement of rescue they came alongside with cheers for the Yanks and many a curse for the Nips.

It was quite a struggle to keep them on the raft while we took them off one by one. They could not manage to secure a line to the raft, so we sent men over the side who did the job. The survivors came tumbling aboard and then collapsed with strength almost gone. A pitiful sight none of us will ever forget. All hands turned to with a will and the men were cared for as rapidly as possible.

At 1710 of that day (the 15th) PAMPANITO sent a message to SEALION asking help. From that hour forward the submariners raced with darkness. SEALION gave a hand, and the two submarines combed the area, picking up survivors. By 2000 no more men could be safely accommodated aboard the overcrowded submarines. The two headed full-speed toward Saipan. Lieutenant Commander Reich expressed the feelings of the submariners as he wrote, "It was heartbreaking to leave so many dying men behind."

PAMPANITO had rescued 73, and SEALION 54.

As soon as he received the word, ComSubPac ordered BARB and QUEENFISH, then in Luzon Strait, to proceed to the rescue area and hunt for survivors. By the afternoon of September 17, these two submarines were combing the waters where the derelicts had last been seen. As will presently be related, BARB had sunk a Japanese escort carrier the day before.

But Fluckey was always ready for the sort of assignment involving a rescue. He wrote:

0100 (17th). Received orders from ComWolfPack to proceed to survivor area. I heartily agree. As an after thought inserted here, having seen the piteous plight of the 14 survivors we rescued, I can say that I would forego the pleasure of an attack on a Jap Task Force to rescue any one of them. There is little room for sentiment in submarine warfare, but the measure of saving one Allied life against sinking a Jap ship is one which leaves no question, once experienced.

Rescue parties, consisting of crack swimmers, and hauling-out, delivery, and stripping parties, had immediately been organized. BARB and QUEENFISH ran a race against the threat of enemy attack, heavy seas, and wind which was whipping up to typhoon velocity. Incredibly enough, survivors were found and picked up. Swimmers took lines to those who could not be reached from the deck or were too weak to hold fast. The hauling-out parties hoisted the oil-coated, half-conscious men to the deck, where the delivery and stripping parties peeled their wretched clothes and led or carried them below. The search went forward until the afternoon of September 18, when a 60-knot wind forced the two submarines to discontinue and head for Saipan. By that time it was certain that no living survivors remained.

When BARB and QUEENFISH completed their rescue mission, 32 more British and Australian survivors had been rescued. Altogether 159 were picked up by the four submarines but seven died before the submarines reached port. Concerning their condition and the care given them, Lieutenant Commander Summers of PAMPANITO wrote:

The problem of habitability was an acute problem with the seventy-three survivors aboard plus our complement of eighty officers and men, but by careful planning and supervision the situation was kept under control and all hands fared very well. The survivors were long used to being in cramped space and even the small space allotted them brought no complaints. The crew was crowded too but cheerfully stood their regular watches and "nurse-maid watch." All survivors, except six of the more critical cases, were berthed in the after-torpedo room. This required ingenuity in devising bunks from torpedo racks and deck space, but with two in each bunk and three or four in each torpedo rack most of them made out better than you might imagine. All men were infected to various extents with beri-beri, scurvy, malaria, and other skin irritations. Strict segregation from the crew was necessary. Two officers were assigned to manage the problems and a two man "nurse-maid watch" was kept in the after torpedo room in addition to the Pharmacist's Mate and two volunteer assistants (one Ship's Cook and one Seaman) who were working continuously. The first problem was getting the men on board. In their weakened condition and due to the fact that they were covered with heavy crude oil, the actual recovery was quite a task. Many of the men could help themselves but the majority had to be lifted bodily on board.

The next problem was to make an attempt to clean some of the oil off before sending them below to treat their immediate medical needs. Several required hypo shots but for the most part a little oil wiped from their eyes and mouth, a wet rag to cool their parched salt-sore lips and throats, and a strong "Yankee" hand to help them get below were sufficient. While still topside their clothes were cut away and they were given a diesel oil sponge bath to remove most of the heavy crude oil. Getting the weakened ones down the hatch was quite a job until in the middle of one recovery operation, three planes were sighted (turned out to be false contact). You should have seen them run for the hatch when the words "Jap planes" were passed. Once below, the main problem was further examination to determine their injuries and sicknesses. Water was their most acute need and they were given plenty (in small amounts at first). Hot soup, tea, and broth followed, and they were soon sleeping the sound sleep of thoroughly exhausted men.

BARB's Commander Fluckey, inimitable stylist, wrote:

A word on the survivors. All were covered with a heavy coating of oil received when they drifted through an oil slick their second night on the rafts. This undoubtedly saved their lives. They were in the water or on their small wooden life rafts for a period of 5 days before being picked up. This in addition to 3 years of prison life under the Japs which included bashings, beating, starvation (all survivors were 25-50 lbs. underweight) malaria, dysentery, pellagra, sores, ulcers, etc., had left them in terrible physical condition. The at first dubious, then amazed, and finally hysterically thankful look on their faces, from the time they first sighted us approaching them, is one we shall never forget. Several of them were too weak to take the lines thrown them. These were rescued by the valiant efforts of Lieutenant Commander R. W. McNitt, Lieutenant J. G. Lanier, and Houston, C. S., MoMM2c who dove in after them. Too much credit cannot be given to the crew for their superb performance and willing efforts in the production line we had formed from the deck party who picked them up, stripped them, and passed them on to the transportation gang to get them below, where they were received by the cleaners who removed the oil and grease, then on to the doctors and nurses for treatment, thence to the feeders, and finally to the sleepers who carried them off and tucked them in their bunks.

The appreciation of the survivors was unbounded. Even those who couldn't talk expressed themselves tearfully through their glazed, oil-soaked eyes. We regret there were no more, for we had found it possible, by taking over every square foot of space aboard ship, sleeping three to a torpedo rack, etc., to accommodate a hundred.

Last of the Convoy Routes

In July the Japanese convoy run from Formosa to Palau was abandoned and Palau-bound convoys were routed through Manila. In August, when the United States offensive struck the Pelews, all runs to Palau were abruptly terminated.

In August the convoy run from Hong Kong to Hainan was ended. The ships were transferred to the hard-pressed Singapore run.

In September the convoy run from Formosa to Hainan went out of operation. The route lay athwart the "Convoy College" area. The closure imposed a severe deprivation on Japan's iron-mongers, for a sizable percentage of Japan's iron ore imports had come from Hainan. However, bottoms were needed to haul bauxite—lack of which had created a crisis in Japan's aluminum industry.

By the end of summer, 1944, Japanese shipping was almost entirely confined to the South China Sea, the East China and Yellow Seas and Empire waters. Japan would never replace the tremendous merchant and naval tonnages lost as the Allied drive thundered westward and U.S. submarines tore the network of convoy routes to ribbons.

The torpedo warfare which raged in "Convoy College" inspired in Japanese mariners a pessimism which spread throughout the merchant service. Heretofore, crew morale had been relatively staunch. Merchant sailors had volunteered willingly enough, and there had been few desertions. But mounting fatalities in this field of endeavor dampened Sailor San's readiness to ship before the mast. Overwork, nerve strain, poor rations and Spartan discipline discouraged volunteering. Casualties and slow recruiting resulted in a shortage of able-bodied seamen and competent engineers and deck officers. Concerning the submarine's responsibility for the deterioration of morale in the Japanese merchant marine, *The War Against Japanese Transportation*, published by the United States Strategic Bombing Survey (1947), has this to say:

Inquiry into the greatest fear of merchant seamen produced various answers. The consensus of opinion appeared to be that crews in general feared air attack the most, but ship captains with a more realistic outlook on their chances of survival feared submarine attack the most. Mine explosions were apparently not an important factor. . . .

Ship captains in general with long experience at sea and a better "knowledge of the world" than the average Japanese, knew that Japan was defeated by the summer of 1944 after the fall of Saipan when the percentage of losses on the Manila and Singapore runs skyrocketed in spite of all the Japanese convoy efforts. The captain of one of the last ships to reach Singapore from Japan (in January 1945) stated as follows: "When I was in Manila for repairs in the summer of 1944 and learned of the heavy submarine losses of ships crossing the Bashi Straits from Formosa to Luzon, I and my associates began to fear that the war was beginning to be lost."

If a captain in Manila had this hint, the masters in Tokyo must have certainly been possessed of the word. The accompanying chart portraying Japanese merchant ship sinkings in June, July and August, 1944, must have had its equivalent in the office of the Japanese Ministry of Transport.

Yet the war was to drag on for another murderous year. And in attempting to "save face," the military leaders of Japan would lose all. Even before the year 1944 was out, the Japanese convoy system had shrunk to a few rag-tag routes.

In September the lines from Davao to Halmahera and Manila to Saigon, Indo-China, were abandoned. The Singapore-to-Madan line closed down in October—a tanker run cut off by submarines in Malacca Strait. To save escort vessels, the line from Miri, Borneo, to Saigon was abandoned in November, and direct communications between the North Borneo oil fields and Indo-China were cut. That same month the Miri-to-Manila line went out of business; the run from Singapore to Balikpapan was terminated; the Soerabaja-Balikpapan run was ended; the runs from Manila to Ormoc and Davao were canceled.

In January 1945 submarines forced the closure of the Singapore-Rangoon route, and the tanker line from Singapore to North Borneo, slashed by submarines, was shut down for lack of tankers.

Thus, at the beginning of 1945, only the Singapore-to-Japan trunk line with a few branches in the South China Sea, and the routes in the East China Sea, the Yellow Sea and Japan's home waters remained available to Japanese convoys. Japan, in the autumn of 1944, had lost shipping contact with all but a fragment of her conquered Southwest Pacific empire. U.S. submarines from Pearl Harbor and Fremantle were the agents chiefly responsible. Storming across "Convoy College" and ranging over the South China Sea, "lone wolves" and wolf-packs* torpedoed the convoy system out of the heart of the Co-Prosperity Sphere.

---

* A complete list of SubPac and SubSoWesPac wolf-packs may be found in the Addenda.

CHAPTER 25

SUBMARINE SUPPORT OF FLEET OPERATIONS

The Pattern

As was stated in an earlier chapter, the pattern for submarine support of offensive fleet operations had been cut by the time the Gilbert Islands were secured. The scouting line in the Battle of Midway—reconnaissance before landings in the Solomons—weather reporting and beacon duty in the Solomons and off Morocco—troop transport at Makin and in the Aleutians—photo reconnaissance, lifeguarding and scouting patrols during the Gilbert strike—these established the design.

The test of fire and water had processed this aspect of submarine warfare. Several elements had been eliminated. Beacon submarines were no longer required. NAUTILUS performed the last troop-carrying mission when she transported Marines to Apamama. There was no future need for such submarine transport service. And NAUTILUS' harrowing experience had underlined the dangers inherent in this type of operation with amphibious forces in the vicinity.

But (with the exception of the submarine scouting line) the other tested features had come to stay. From January 1, 1944, to V-J Day, submarine cooperation with the fleet in the major air strikes and amphibious campaigns would include the following activities:

1. Submarine concentrations to cut the enemy's supply lines to the target areas. (Discussed as a campaign of the attrition war.)

2. Submarine photographic reconnaissance of beachheads marked for amphibious landings and enemy military or naval installations marked for future reference.

3. Submarine lifeguarding during air strikes.

4. Submarine scouting duty in the target area and off enemy bases to report enemy movements and intercept and attack enemy forces which sortied to oppose the attacking United States forces.

5. Submarines stationed to intercept and attack fugitive shipping attempting to flee the target area.

As the United States air-sea offensive drove toward Asia, submarine lifeguarding became a mission of major importance. Its dramatic development will be summarized in a subsequent chapter. This chapter briefly reviews the moves made by U.S. submarines supporting the fleet as reconnaissance, scouting and fighting units during the 1944 Pacific push.

"Operation Flintlock"

The campaign to seize control of the Marshall Islands was a logical follow-through after the Gilberts capture. Lessons had been learned at Tarawa, and Admiral Nimitz prepared to knock out the enemy's last defense installation before a soldier set foot on a beachhead. D-Day was dated January 31, 1944. As a preliminary operation, the Fifth Fleet, under Vice Admiral Spruance, was to bomb and blast the target islands into target ash-heaps.

Weeks before D-Day was set for "Operation Flintlock," SubPac submarines were taking shots in the Marshall group. Camera shots. The submarines engaged in this photo reconnaissance work were SEAL (Lieutenant Commander H. B. Dodge), SPEARFISH (Lieutenant Commander J. W. Williams), TARPON (Lieutenant Commander T. B. Oakley, Jr.) and SEARAVEN (Lieutenant Commander M. H. Dry). The missions were begun in November and continued through the fore part of January. The submarines reconnoitered Kwajalein, Jaluit, Wotje, Maloelap, Mili, Eniwetok and Ponape, taking pictures with the enthusiasm of tourists and the daring of adventure-story newsreel men.

Original "Operation Flintlock" plans projected an invasion of Wotje, Maloelap, Mili and Jaluit—the eastern fringe of the Marshalls. CinCPac decided, however, to go straight to the point and attack Kwajalein, the key stronghold in the west. This unorthodox move—by-passing the bastions and striking at the central citadel—took the enemy completely by surprise. Although the Japanese High Command had concluded that the Marshall Islands were "expendable," the island garrisons had been ordered to hold out to the last ditch. This was tantamount to an order for mass *hara-kiri*, but the sacrifice was intended as a delaying action.

The sacrifice proved eminently futile. Spruance's Fifth Fleet weighed in at something like 2,000,000 tons. Task Force Fifty-eight alone contained six large carriers, five light carriers, eight battleships, six cruisers and 36 destroyers, and was under the aggressive leadership of fisty Admiral Marc A. Mitscher. Landing and assault forces under Rear Admiral Turner were composed of 297 ships, and 53,000 Marine and Army assault troops. Before the troops were moved into the area, striking planes and battleships pounded Kwajalein to a pulp. Not a single palm tree was left upright on this, the largest atoll in the Pacific. Dazed by this "Spruance haircut," the defenders put up nothing like the resistance expected. About 5,000 of the 8,600 Japs on Kwajalein were massacred in the "softening up" bombardment. The remainder did some shooting, but it was all over by February 5th.

Majuro Atoll, a fine fleet anchorage and a primary objective, offered no resistance whatever. The enemy had abandoned before the attack. By April, as has been noted, Majuro was open for business as an American naval base with an advanced submarine base located on Myrna Island.

Spruance staged an unexpected encore by making a northwest leap at Eniwetok. Given another haircut, this secondary Marshall base fell in two days. "Operation Flintlock" was over eight weeks ahead of schedule. The United States controlled the Marshalls. Except for occasional visits by American planes which used them as practice targets, Jaluit, Wotje, Maloelap, Mili and Wake were out of the war.

As Admiral Kurita made no attempt to oppose "Flintlock," the submarines assigned to the operation had relatively little to do. These submarines were PERMIT (Lieutenant Commander C. L. Bennett),

SKIPJACK (Commander G. G. Molumphy), GUARDFISH (Lieutenant Commander N. G. Ward), SEAL (Lieutenant Commander H. B. Dodge), SUNFISH (Lieutenant Commander E. E. Shelby) and SEARAVEN (Lieutenant Commander M. H. Dry). PERMIT, SKIPJACK and GUARDFISH were stationed off the northern, eastern and southern entrances to Truk. Their tactical disposition followed the "Galvanic" design. The Japanese Second Fleet did not emerge in force. However, several units emerged. One, the destroyer SUZUKAZE, not only emerged, but it presently submerged. It did so at the instigation of several torpedoes fired by SKIPJACK on the night of January 25-26. Six days later, GUARDFISH, south of Truk, destroyed the destroyer UMIKAZE. These DD destructions were in conformance with ComSubPac's instructions, which contained the following paragraph:

THE PRIMARY MISSION OF ALL SUBMARINES IS ATTACK EXCEPT IN CASE WITH A CONTACT WITH A LARGE ENEMY TASK FORCE MOVING TOWARD THE VICINITY OF FLINTLOCK OPERATION CONCERNING WHICH THERE HAS BEEN NO PREVIOUS CONTACT REPORT. IN SUCH CASE THE PRIMARY MISSION OF THE FIRST SUBMARINE MAKING CONTACT IS TO SEND OUT A CONTACT REPORT AND THEN TO ATTACK. CONTACT REPORTS SHOULD BE SENT IF FORMATIONS OF ENEMY PLANES ARE SIGHTED BUT NOT ON SINGLE PLANES.

Similar instructions were included in all ComSubPac orders issued to submarines supporting fleet operations. Some of the captains felt that the "report before attack" requirement compromised their chances at enemy targets. To report, of course, the submarine, if submerged, had to surface and transmit a radio message. In any case, there would be delay and the possibility of the submarine's being detected. However, the value of a timely contact report which warned the fleet against a possible surprise attack during amphibious operations considerably outweighed whatever advantage might be gained by a single submarine's intervention.

SEAL, SUNFISH and SEARAVEN, stationed off Ponape, Kusaie and Eniwetok as scouts with additional duty as lifeguards if air strikes on those islands were made, had less to do than the submarines off Truk. "Operation Flintlock" was over almost before it began. On photographic reconnaissance missions, the three submarines had already performed valiantly. Between November 17 and December 15, 1943, SEAL had reconnoitered 88 islands of the 96 in the Kwajalein group, and had photographed 56 of them. During the week of January 23-31, SUNFISH made photographic reconnaissance of Taongi Atoll and Kusaie

Island. SEARAVEN, during this period, took panoramic views of Eniwetok. The Fifth Fleet struck when it saw the picture.

"Operation Hailstone"

While "Flintlock" was still on the planning table at Pearl Harbor, Admiral Spruance developed tentative plans for the first carrier strike on Truk—"Operation Hailstone." This strike was originally set for April 15th.

The carrier attack on Truk was daring in its conception. Truk was the strongest of the enemy's Pacific outposts. Its air defenses were known to be formidable, and with Japanese aircraft on Ponape and possibly on Kusaie to cover the eastward approaches, it seemed impossible for a striking force the size and weight of Task Force Fifty-eight to approach Truk undetected.

"Hailstone" plans were therefore hinged on the assumption that the TF58 carriers would be detected, and the flat-tops and planes would have to fight their way in through land-based air opposition. It was assumed that the Japanese warships and merchantmen inside Truk Atoll would probably flee westward to Palau, northwest toward the Marianas, or southward toward Rabaul and Kavieng.

Accordingly, the submarines that were detailed to "Operation Hailstone" were to be deployed to cut off these escape routes. ComSubPac drew up his tentative plan for submarine support of "Hailstone," and it was approved by both CinCPac and Commander Fifth Fleet—this before the campaign to seize the Marshalls was begun.

"Flintlock" exploded, and Kwajalein fell. Eniwetok fell. Spruance jumped the date of "Hailstone" to February 17, and a dispatch was sent to ComSubPac to put the submarine "Hailstone" into gear. The submarine disposition previously agreed upon was not altered by the change in schedule. Two lifeguards —DARTER and SEARAVEN—were stationed at Truk, and one lifeguard—SEAL—at Ponape. The other "Hailstone" submarines—SKATE, ASPRO, BURRFISH, DACE, GATO, SUNFISH and TANG—were disposed along the escape routes as shown in the chart below.

During the forenoon of February 17, Admiral Spruance ordered his task force in a counter-clockwise sweep around Truk. The long guns slammed their salvos and enemy ships went down. But gun targets were not too plentiful. Unbelievably enough, Mitscher's carriers made the approach on Truk undetected. The enemy was first aware of the strike when the American planes roared over the early-morning horizon. The Jap Zeros buzzed up like bees from a jostled hive, and the American Hellcats shot

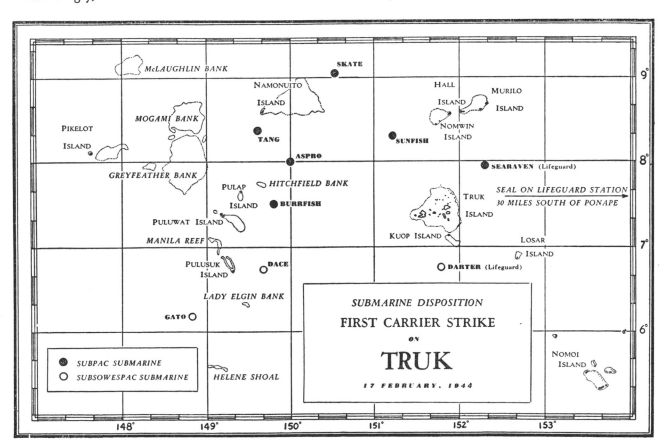

363

them down by the dozen. Dozens more were demolished before they could take off. Vice Admiral Kobayashi, after holding Truk on the alert for two weeks, had ordered the planes grounded and disarmed the very day before the "Hailstone" attack. This misguided action left Truk practically defenseless, for Kurita had rushed the Second Fleet to Palau after the fall of Kwajalein. With over 100 Zeros demolished by the first wave of Hellcats, Truk was practically prostrate when Mitscher's bombers and torpedo planes roared in. The bombs fell on the shipping in the atoll like rocks dropped in a basket of eggs. And after torpedo planes caught and sank a light cruiser, there was little left for Spruance's BB's. That little—a mine craft, a destroyer and a training cruiser—was soon gunned out of existence. Again the bombers roared over Truk to smash up the basket as well as the eggshells.

As fugitive ships did not get very far from the assaulted base, most of the "Hailstone" submarines off Truk sat on their hands. TANG, as has been related, sank a large freighter about 100 miles to the northwest of Truk, but this was a routine action not connected with the carrier strike. The same might be said for the sinking scored by SKATE. This occurred on the evening before the "Hailstone" strike, with SKATE about the same distance from Truk as TANG. However, SKATE's victim was a warship, and the sinking had an aftermath which linked it to "Operation Hailstone." Accordingly it is herewith recounted as a part of that operation.

Skate vs. Agano

The Japanese light cruiser AGANO had been one of the busiest of the Imperial Navy's CL's. She was new, she was fast, and running around the South Pacific in 1943 she had been identified at various times as everything from a pocket battleship to a heavy cruiser of the KAKO class.

This last was what she looked like to SKATE's captain when she jammed her nose over the horizon late in the afternoon of February 16th. Lieutenant Commander W. P. Gruner, Jr., was on his first patrol as captain of a submarine. AGANO was the sort of target no new submarine skipper would want to miss. Gruner did not miss.

In a superbly executed submerged attack made at sundown, he fired four torpedoes at the target and scored three or four hits. AGANO had survived numerous bombings, and a previous submarine attack in which she had been damaged by SCAMP. This time she did not survive. Groaning in mortal hurt, the cruiser lolled in the evening sea, waiting for a destroyer to come to her rescue. The destroyer was late.

Several hours after the torpedoing, AGANO gurgled her last and went down.

Her survivors were picked up by the destroyer MAIKAZE. This DD was sunk the following day by the guns of Task Force Fifty-eight. AGANO was the second light cruiser downed by a U.S. submarine. The SANDLANCE-TATSUTA shooting came a month later. SKATE's February kill established her fame as one of the big-game hunters of the war.

"Hailstone" Sequel

The smashing success of the carrier strike at Truk called for a repeat performance. And one was staged just six days later on the enemy's strongest base in the Marianas—Saipan. The submarines were deployed as at Truk with instructions to destroy escaping ships.

To serve in this "Hailstone" sequel, the submarines APOGON, SEARAVEN, SUNFISH and SKIPJACK were placed on the arc of a circle with a 30-mile radius from Mount Tapotchau, Saipan, on bearings from that peak of 312°, 291°, 270° and 250° respectively. TANG was stationed as safety man in a position 60 miles to the westward, to act upon contact reports received from the inner circle. SUNFISH was given additional duty as lifeguard during the strike, which was scheduled to hit Saipan on February 23rd.

This time a Jap patrol plane sighted Mitscher's carriers, and the American task force had to fight its way in against air opposition. Given the alarm, shipping in Tanapag Harbor fled to the westward. In spite of detection, only six U.S. planes were lost during the strike, and not a single one of Mitscher's ships was damaged. Saipan installations were subjected to a thorough pounding. And the bleeding *marus* received their share.

The rush of shipping from Tanapag Harbor gave the submarines their chance. Early in the morning of February 23, SUNFISH (Lieutenant Commander Shelby) sank a freighter escaping from Saipan. After daybreak, she caught and sank a second freighter. TANG, in her safety position to the westward, staged a three-day shooting match. Between midnight on the 22nd and the morning of the 25th, O'Kane's submarine sank four fugitive ships. This action was described in a previous chapter as "attrition." What better definition?

"Operation Desecrate"

"Flintlock" had flattened the Marshalls as a steamroller flattens gravel. "Hailstone" had similarly flattened Truk, Saipan and Tinian. American losses were amazingly small—less than 400 troops at Kwajalein—the carrier INTREPID damaged by a torpedo plane, and 25 planes lost in the Truk strike—six planes lost in the strike at Saipan and Tinian. On the other hand, the enemy lost some 17 merchant ships at Truk, three cruisers (including AGANO), three destroyers, a mine vessel and almost 300 planes. Losses in the Marianas totaled a half-dozen cargo vessels and several dozen planes.

Extent of the damage dealt the enemy at Truk and in the Marianas was not known to American headquarters at the time, and hindsight suggests that a knockout might have resulted from an immediate follow-up punch in the Marianas. However, General MacArthur urgently requested naval support for a projected drive in New Guinea, and the Fifth Fleet was dispatched to the New Guinea area. The enemy seized the opportunity to rush reinforcements to Truk, the Marianas and Palau.

Late in March, Ozawa's carrier force and Kurita's Second Fleet were positioned off Tawi Tawi, in the Sulu Archipelago. It was at this time that Admiral Koga was killed, flying on an inspection tour of the Tawi Tawi area. Command of the Imperial Fleet passed to Admiral Toyoda. Coincidentally, the first carrier-air strike on Palau—"Operation Desecrate"— was slated for March 30th.

To reach this objective, Task Force Fifty-eight, now in the New Guinea area, had to run a gantlet of enemy airfields located on the north coast of New Guinea and in the western Carolines. Here, again, it was assumed the carriers would be detected and enemy ships would flee the target atoll. As at Truk and Saipan, submarines were stationed in position to intercept the fugitives.

TULLIBEE (Commander C. F. Brindupke), BLACK-FISH (Lieutenant Commander R. F. Sellars), BASHAW (Lieutenant Commander R. E. Nichols), TANG (Lieutenant Commander R. H. O'Kane) and ARCHER-FISH (Lieutenant Commander G. W. Kehl) were stationed counter-clockwise in the order named, on the arc of a circle with a 60-mile radius from Toagel Mlungui Passage.

Thus situated they could cover all escape routes. TUNNY (Commander J. A. Scott), close in to the westward of Toagel Mlungui, and GAR (Lieutenant Commander G. W. Lautrup, Jr.), stationed east of Peleliu Island, were assigned lifeguard duties. The "Desecrate" strike was to include Woleai and Yap. PAMPANITO (Lieutenant Commander P. E. Summers) was stationed as a lifeguard at Yap, and HARDER (Lieutenant Commander S. D. Dealey) was assigned to similar duty off Woleai. Of the submarines enumerated BLACKFISH and BASHAW were from Brisbane, under force command of Commodore Fife. The others were SubPac submarines.

Task Force Fifty-eight was detected on the day preceding the strike. This gave most of the enemy ships in the Pelews a chance to escape, and they fled northwest. Apparently they raced through the sector which had been guarded by TULLIBEE. If such was the case, the disaster which overtook this submarine four days before the strike was a dual calamity. With but one exception the enemy vessels escaped without damage.

That exception was a big one. At sunset on the eve of the strike, TUNNY (Commander J. A. Scott) made contact with Japan's newest battleship and flagship of the Japanese fleet. This was the monster MUSASHI, 63,000-ton twin sister of the giantess YAMATO. Scott drove TUNNY in on the attack, and here was another David-Goliath performance. The able Scott fired six expertly aimed torpedoes, but an alert escort warned the battleship just in the nick. As she swung to comb the tracks, MUSASHI was hit twice near the bow. Had the hits been aft or in the engine spaces, the huge BB would probably have been slowed, and Mitscher's carrier planes might have caught and sunk her the next day. As it was, she was not disabled. Like YAMATO (damaged by SKATE), she made a getaway, and her come-uppance was deferred.

The Marianas Campaign ("Operation Forager")

Two thousand miles southwest of Pearl Harbor, Majuro Atoll provided the SubPac Force with a fine forward base and rest camp. The camp was built in 15 days by men of the tender SPERRY. The tender also put her wing over the incoming submarines that slid from time to time into the lagoon.

Majuro was also busy in April and May as a fleet anchorage. Then early in June 1944, the blue lagoon was bustling with unusual activity. The Fifth Fleet was steaming out on "Operation Forager"—the invasion drive on the Marianas.

From the point of view of the submarine forces, the Marianas Campaign and the Battle of the Philippine Sea which followed were—so far as submarine support of fleet operations was concerned— the high points of the war. Some naval strategists consider the action history's outstanding example of the successful employment of submarines in a major fleet engagement. Effective scouting, efficient communications, intelligent handling and several smashing torpedo attacks combined to give the Submarine Force a leading role in a victory which meant the beginning of the end for the Imperial Navy.

Not since the Solomons campaign had the Japanese fleet offered battle, and the last engagement between surface forces in the Central Pacific had been at Midway. The fast carrier task force of the Fifth Fleet was spoiling for a fight. Mitscher, promoted to vice admiral, had no fear of anything Toyoda could send against him, and the carrier airmen were keyed up for a fleet engagement.

The Marianas invasion promised action. Moving on Saipan, the U.S. amphibious forces would be entering the Japanese inner defense ring. The Japanese would oppose this amphibious move with every defensive weapon they could muster—of that Nimitz was certain. The Fifth Fleet's primary task was to support the Saipan landings and to protect the amphibious forces carrying out the operation. Enemy interference with the operation would come from enemy-held water considerably to the west, and scouting by planes would require support from units of the Fifth Fleet. These would have to leave the Saipan and proceed to the Philippines area—a move that was practically out of the question. So submarines were once more called upon to serve as vedettes on guard against the possible sortie of an enemy force.

The first landings at Saipan were scheduled for June 15th. Submarine lifeguards were supplied for the air strikes which preceded the landings, and at least one submarine was to be on duty at Truk, Woleai and Palau for observation purposes and lifeguard service at those strategic points. ComSubPac's operation plan for "Forager," which contained the above directive, made no definite commitments for the tactical disposition of submarines. It was expected that the campaign might be a prolonged struggle, and that the number of available submarines would vary. Consequently, the submarine disposition to be used was expressed in general terms as follows:

SUBMARINE PATROLS DURING THE PAST SEVERAL MONTHS HAVE BEEN CONCENTRATED IN THE VICINITY OF MARIANA ISLANDS AND ALONG THE TRAFFIC ROUTES FROM THE JAPANESE EMPIRE, TRUK, PALAU, AND THE PHILIPPINES IN ORDER TO WEAKEN BY ATTRITION REINFORCEMENTS OF ENEMY TROOPS AND SUPPLIES BEING SENT TO THAT AREA. THOSE PATROLS WILL BE CONTINUED DURING THE PERIOD OF FORAGER OPERATION EXCEPTING THAT THOSE IN THE IMMEDIATE VICINITY OF THE MARIANAS WILL BE RETIRED IN ORDER TO CLEAR THE AREA FOR THE ADVANCE OF OUR SURFACE FORCES. DURING FORAGER OPERATION SUBMARINES, AS AVAILABLE, WILL BE PLACED IN INTERCEPTION POSITIONS TO THE SOUTHWEST OF THE MARIANAS AND ON THE APPROACHES TO THE MARIANAS FROM THE JAPANESE EMPIRE TO ATTACK AND DESTROY ENEMY FORCES APPROACHING THE MARIANAS AND ESCAPING THEREFROM, AND TO FURNISH ADVANCE WARNING OF THE APPROACH OF ENEMY TASK FORCES.

Before "Forager" was concluded, 28 SubPac and SoWesPac submarines were ordered from regular patrol stations or given special assignments to participate in the operation. But submarines had reconnoitered the target area weeks before the campaign was planned.

In March, GREENLING (Lieutenant Commander J. D. Grant) had photographed Saipan, Tinian and Guam. In April, SALMON (Lieutenant Commander H. K. Nauman) conducted a photo reconnaissance mission covering Ulithi, Woleai and Yap.

As has been related, the Japanese fleet had concentrated at Tawi Tawi in the Sulu Archipelago. The enemy was expecting a thrust at the Marianas, and advices from Rabaul indicated a simultaneous Allied strike at Wewak, New Guinea. In an effort to base the fleet as close as possible to these scenes of impending action Admiral Toyoda had ordered Kurita and Ozawa to the Tawi Tawi anchorage. The fuel situation also motivated this move. The oil shortage was critical (for reasons previously discussed) and Japanese fleet oilers were scarce. A base near the wells of Borneo was therefore desirable.

Allied reconnaissance located the Japanese naval concentration, and ComSubSoWesPac sent HARDER, REDFIN and BLUEFISH to maintain a watch in the vicinity. HAKE, BASHAW and PADDLE were stationed southeast of Mindanao to cover that route to the Marianas. ComSubPac stationed PINTADO, PILOTFISH and TUNNY in Luzon Strait. FLYINGFISH was placed at San Bernardino Strait and GROWLER at Surigao Strait. Thus all avenues from Tawi Tawi to the Marianas were covered by submarines. The Kurita-Ozawa forces would be sighted if they went north of the Philippines, through Luzon Strait; through the Philippines via San Bernardino or Surigao Strait; or south of the Philippines by skirting Mindanao. If they charted a course south of these strategic points, they would be seen by Hollandia-based search planes.

In addition, five SubPac submarines were placed north and west of the Marianas to watch the approaches from the Empire. And ALBACORE, SEAWOLF, BANG, FINBACK, STINGRAY, MUSKALLUNGE, PIPEFISH, SEAHORSE and CAVALLA were disposed to the westward of the Marianas, in waters lying between Palau and the 20° parallel. Neither the number nor position of the submarines in this open-sea area was fixed. Some of those named were on the move to relieve other submarines guarding the Philippines straits. All were shifted from day to day as information on the Japanese fleet was received and ComSubPac moved his units into intercepting positions. This submarine disposal could not have been better conceived and it remains as an example of masterful

366

submarine strategy. That strategy was followed by masterful battle tactics on the part of the submariners who went into action. The brilliant submarine successes which supported the fleet in the Battle of the Philippine Sea are detailed in the ensuing chapter, *Submarines vs. the Japanese Navy*.

In the Marianas storm center, the Japanese also fared badly at the hands of the submarines participating in "Forager." Case in point: the convoy destruction by "Blair's Blasters." When American invasion forces hit the beachheads of Saipan, Tinian and Guam, they were opposed by some 50,000 Japanese troops. About half of this number was concentrated on Saipan. But several regiments had arrived without arms. The Japanese commander, General Saito, was forced to ration munitions. Air crews were faced with a gasoline famine. U.S. submarines had cut the convoy lines, and hundreds of Japanese troopers, intended as reinforcements, had perished far at sea.

The Palau Campaign ("Operation Stalemate")

Projectiles and bombs were still crashing on the Marianas beachheads when SEAWOLF (Lieutenant Commander R. B. Lynch) was camera-shooting off Palau. SEAWOLF's June photographic mission was followed up by BURRFISH's (Lieutenant Commander W. B. Perkins) in July. These photo reconnaissance missions boded ill for Japanese installations in the Pelews.

Perkins and his submariners did more than take pictures. One type of information vitally important to amphibious forces was the depth of water, nature of the shoals and the type of bottom along the coast where a landing was planned. Pot holes, sand bars and jagged coral could easily impede a landing. Depth information was necessary for obvious reasons, and upon it hinged the use of Higgins boats, LST's, alligator tanks, DUKW's and plain shoe leather. In many localities the only way this information could be obtained was by sending landing parties into the beaches in small boats under cover of darkness to take surreptitious soundings. And submarines were the only vessels which could transport these exploring parties without detection.

Such ventures were invariably hazardous, and the BURRFISH mission was tragically so. Along with her photographic work, the submarine was directed to carry out landing party reconnaissance on the beaches of Palau and Yap. The landing party was organized by the Commander Amphibious Forces. It was headed by Lieutenant Charles E. Kirkpatrick, USN, and consisted of one other officer and nine picked men, who were past masters in small-boat handling and scouting.

BURRFISH was off Peleliu on July 30th. Bright moonlight prevailed for a number of successive nights, and the first landing was not attempted until the night of August 11th. On this excursion, the shore party picked up much valuable information. Other Peleliu beaches were not explored, however, as enemy radar was operating in the vicinity.

On August 14, BURRFISH proceeded to Yap. There, on the night of the 16th, a landing was made on the southern tip of Yap Island. A third landing was attempted on the island of Gagil Tomil (in the Yap group) on the night of August 18th. Something went amiss. Three men—Howard L. Roeder, Chief Gunner's Mate; Robert A. Black, Quartermaster 1; John C. MacMahon, Specialist 1—failed to return to the submarine. The remaining two members of the party —John E. Ball, Chief Boatswain's Mate, in charge of the group, and Emment L. Carpenter, Carpenter's Mate 3—told the story quoted in Lieutenant Kirkpatrick's report:

> The boat containing this party was launched at 2006 and given a course to land on the beach about 3,000 yards away. The instructions to the boat crew were to the effect that "if the reef was not passable for landing craft, to not go farther toward the shore, but . . . to search . . . along the reef for possible boat passages." They found the correct point outside the reef, which lay about 1,100 yards from the beach, and the crew, after taking soundings, was debating the feasibility of a landing through the heavy surf when a roller caught them and left them no alternative. They crossed the surf with great difficulty and anchored in 7 feet of water about 1,000 yards from the beach. Roeder, the crew captain, directed Black and Carpenter to swim in toward the beach at the left, while he and MacMahon would go to the right. Each man was armed with 2 knives and a grenade. The rendezvous time at the boat was set at 2245 to allow plenty of time for the boat to leave the beach at 2330. One man, Ball, was left as boat keeper. Carpenter returned to the boat, exhausted, after 20 minutes and he and Ball waited in the boat until 2315, one half hour past the deadline. They then manned the oars and approached the beach to 100 yards, searching. At 0015, 45 minutes past the deadline given to depart for rendezvous with the BURRFISH, they went through the surf once more, abandoned all caution in a last minute effort to pick up the missing men, and flashed their flashlights all around. They had no success, so rowed out to rejoin the submarine.

Landing party reconnaissance of this type was not again attempted during the war. When it was requested by the Commander Amphibious Forces before the Okinawa Campaign, Admiral Spruance, in over-all command of that operation, disapproved the request. Spruance stated that the value of the data obtainable did not justify the risk to personnel. The possibility that detection would give the enemy a "tip-off" concerning the projected operation also militated against such an enterprise.

"Stalemate"—the operation to capture Palau, with Yap and Ulithi as secondary objectives—was under the over-all command of Admiral Halsey. Now that the Admiralty Islands were occupied by Allied forces and Rabaul and Kavieng in the Bismarcks were paralyzed, Palau and Halmahera were the last major barriers east and south of the Philippines. While "Desecrate" had been striking at the Pelews, MacArthur had been mounting a drive against Hollandia. After the capture of Hollandia in late April, this important base served as a springboard which sent the Allied forces bounding to the western tip of New Guinea, only a jump away from Halmahera. That island and Morotai and Talaud beyond were the last obstacle between MacArthur's forces and the Philippines. Although thousands of Japanese troops were camped in western New Guinea, that immense territory was under Allied control. Admiral Kinkaid's Seventh Fleet remained to support MacArthur, and Halsey and his staff were shifted to the Central Pacific to take charge of the Fifth Fleet in the "Stalemate" drive.

Incidentally, the Fifth Fleet was now designated the Third Fleet and Mitscher's TF58 was now designated TF38. The sole difference was one of title and command—the composition of the fleet forces was unchanged. The numerical alteration may have confused the enemy, but its primary purpose was to expedite planning at Headquarters. Halsey and Spruance would now alternate as fleet commanders, and while one conducted an operation at sea, the other would be at Pearl Harbor designing the Navy's next strike.

Halsey's method of submarine deployment differed considerably from Spruance's. Halsey would station submarines at such strategic points as Surigao, San Bernardino, Luzon Straits, and the Bungo Suido, but he also wanted a submarine reconnaissance line to cover a broad front which would extend across miles of open sea. The reconnaissance line devised for "Operation Stalemate" is shown in the chart below.

This line was designated as the "Zoo." It was occupied by three wolf-packs composed of three submarines each. The packs were called "Cats," "Bears," and "Dogs," with Captain C. W. Wilkins in SEAHORSE, Commander A. H. Holtz in BAYA, and Commander R. S. Benson in RAZORBACK as pack commanders. Captain Wilkins was in over-all command of the "Zoo."

The submarine composition of "Cats," "Bears," and "Dogs" is shown on the chart. Note GROUPER stationed as a lifeguard off Palau, and GAR doing lifeguard duty off Yap. GAR retired at sunset on D-4 to relieve HARDHEAD at Surigao Strait, but GROUPER remained on station during this strike.

Halsey's Third Fleet (some 800 ships) drove at Palau on September 15th. After a scorching three-day bombardment, the Marines went ashore. The 12,000 Japanese defenders put up a tooth-and-nail fight, and First Marine casualties were severe. The reduction of Peleliu and Angaur took 10 weeks. But with the fall

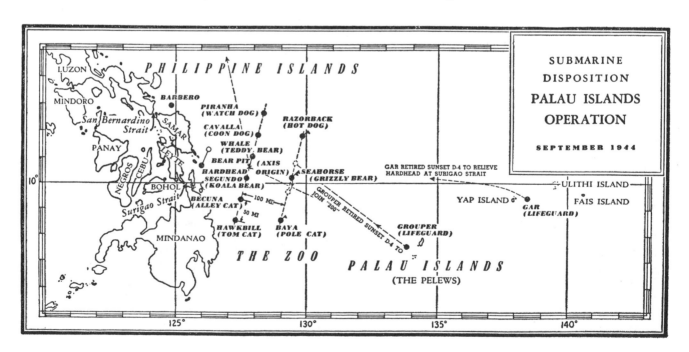

of Palau the last main central Pacific gate to the Philippines was crashed.

While the amphibious landings on Peleliu and Angaur were in full swing, Halsey moved his fast carrier force north and west to strike at Manila. The "Zoo" line was moved to the northward to clear the submarines off the Third Fleet's track. The line was again shifted in the third week of September as Halsey's forces raced on north to attack the northern Philippines, Formosa, and the Nansei Shotos.

"Zoo" was maintained from September 13 until September 25th. But the wolf-packs were unable to make contact with the enemy during this time. Thereafter, the submarine reconnaissance line was not used in the Central Pacific. Admiral Halsey requested such a line for subsequent operations, but Admiral Nimitz did not feel that the results to be expected would justify the effort. He reasoned that submarines patrolling the sortie routes from known enemy bases had more opportunity to inflict damage on the enemy.

The Leyte Campaign ("King Two")

The terms "Stalemate" and "King Two" were borrowed from chess. As a stalemate is a drawn game, the term did not apply to the Palau campaign. The Japs in the Pelews were decisively checkmated.

"King Two"—the opening move of a fast gambit—started a swift game that was to cost the enemy the Philippines. The success of the mid-September raids convinced Halsey that the central Philippines were ripe for a smash. His carrier planes had found the defenses weak, and his conviction was supported by information from a number of sources. One source was photographic reconnaissance. Another was the indomitable undercover agent as personified by the aforementioned Lieutenant Commander Parsons. A third was the patrol report of submarines such as NARWHAL, NAUTILUS, ANGLER and REDFIN.

Even as reconnaissance and the landing of coast watchers supported fleet operations, the landing of secret agents and guerrilla supplies supported the amphibious Philippines offensive. By the autumn of 1944, the guerrilla war was going like a forest fire on Mindanao, Negros and Samar. The submarines which stoked this fire with incendiary war materials blazed the trail for MacArthur's invasion forces.

Performing one of these sub-rosa tasks in the Philippines, ANGLER enjoyed an experience unique in the history of special missions. Navy men who like their Corona-Coronas will appreciate this one.

Philippines Evacuation (Angler Carries the Kiddies)

"There is room aboard a submarine for everything but a mistake."

Students of submarining might paste that proverb in their sea hats and read it every time they doff to someone like CREVALLE's motor machinist's mate—or to those submariners who transported everything from bombs to babes on special missions that rivalled anything in the imagination of Baron Munchausen.

As the war rumbled westward toward the Philippines in the spring and summer of 1944, submarines on special mission were all over the archipelago, running in guns and supplies, landing such agents as "C. Parsons" and picking up evacuees. On February 5, NARWHAL (Lieutenant Commander Latta) was delivering 45 tons of ammunition and stores to guerrillas near Libertad, Panay. Two days later she was at Negros to evacuate 28 men, women and children. She was back early in March with 70 tons of guerrilla supplies and gear, and again she evacuated a party of 28, this time from Nasipit, Mindanao. From there she went to Tawi Tawi for 10 more passengers. Secret cargo and odd assortments of passengers had become mere routine for NARWHAL.

Perhaps some of the oddest passengers ever picked up in the Philippines (or anywhere) were among the group evacuated by ANGLER late in March 1944. Under Lieutenant Commander R. I. Olsen, the submarine was on her second patrol when she received orders directing her to rescue about 20 United States citizens from a rendezvous on the north coast of Panay. A later dispatch mentioned the number to be rescued as 50.

Skipper Olsen, tall enough to take up his own share of deck space, had that feeling a host tries not to show when unexpected guests arrive at a party already running low on beer. Nevertheless, Olsen submerged the submarine about eight miles south of the rendezvous point before daybreak on March 20, and stood in toward the designated position. About 0900 a crowd of people was seen walking behind the tree line on the beach, and an hour later the prescribed signals were hoisted in the palms along the water's edge. The submarine waited offshore, submerged. Then at sunset ANGLER surfaced, crew at battle stations, and with decks awash moved to within about 1,000 yards of the beach.

In the dusk a small banca came alongside, and a Colonel Garcia informed Olsen there were 58 evacuees—did the submarine have room for them all? Olsen replied in the affirmative without hesitation, although he realized only too well the difficulties involved. It was one thing to transport trained troops in a large sub like NAUTILUS which had been readied for the mission. A passenger list which almost equalled the number of operating personnel was another proposition—one that posed problems in food supply, air supply and living space. Moreover, these people were war refugees and many were in urgent need of hospitalization.

However, there is room for everything (but one) aboard a submarine. Within an hour the passengers, including 16 women and children, were aboard. As soon as they were stowed, ANGLER stood seaward for the 12-day run to Darwin, Australia.

The entire ship's company was berthed in the after battery compartment except for torpedo watch-standers, [wrote Olsen, in reference to the cruise]. Concerning the passengers: Men and boys lived in after torpedo room, women and children in forward torpedo room. CPO quarters were inhabited by one woman with a two months old baby, one pregnant woman (8 months), one seriously ill girl (worms—temperature 104°) and two elderly women. Ship was immediately infested with cockroaches, body lice, and hair lice. A large percentage of the passengers had tropical ulcers plus an odor that was unique in its intensity.

All passengers showed signs of prolonged undernourishment. All were suffering from lacerated feet due to the long march to the embarkation point without footgear. One male passenger was temporarily insane, requiring a twenty-four hour watch. Two meals a day with soup at 2400 was put in effect at once, since it was apparent the ship did not have enough food aboard for a full three meals a day. Passengers ate ravenously from their arrival until they left the ship. Food was rationed until the night before our arrival at Darwin.

Habitability forward of the control room resembled the "Black Hole" of Calcutta, a condition which resulted from children urinating and spitting on the deck, body odors and 47 persons sleeping forward of the control room. In spite of a constant watch at the head it proved impossible to teach our passengers the proper use of this vehicle after two years in the hills. . . .

Not all evacuation missions were as uncomfortable as this, but many were as difficult and dangerous. For colorful incident, however, none could surpass the following, recorded in ANGLER's patrol report:

One for the book was the sight of a two-year-old, half Filipino boy smoking (and inhaling) a cigar between gulps of his dinner which he was receiving at his mother's breast.

Aboard ANGLER the submariners would not have made a mistake in any case. But under the circumstances reported, a personnel error was unthinkable. United States Navy men pull a boner? In front of a cigar-smoking baby?

The Undersea Underground

In April the submarines in the Southwest Pacific were busy special-missioning around Borneo. But in

May, CREVALLE, BONEFISH and NARWHAL (under Lieutenant Commander J. S. Titus) were in the Philippines with guerrilla war supplies. During the summer the islands were visited successively by NAUTILUS, SEAWOLF, STINGRAY, REDFIN and NARWHAL. Ton after ton of munitions and stores were landed on secret beaches and distributed to the Filipino jungle fighters. "Joe" was a fierce commando and, as might be suspected of a fellow who was weaned on black cigars, guerrilla warfare was his dish. American submarines worked overtime to keep "Joe's" cartridge belt supplied.

NARWHAL featured as the star in these guerrilla supply missions, running between Australia and the Philippines with something of the nonchalant regularity of a New York-Staten Island ferryboat. Commander Titus made the runs in August and September. Commander Latta was back on the bridge in October. "Matthew," "Mark," "Luke," and "John" kept going like thoroughbred race horses, and more than one company of Japs was cut down in the Philippine interior—thanks to this submarine with the Apostolic engines.

These supply and evacuation missions were always hazardous. NARWHAL experienced a shave in March when, after delivering stores to Colonel Fertig's guerrillas on Mindanao, she contacted an escorted transport offshore. Latta blew the bow off this vessel with a torpedo hit. Then, as the submarine started to go deep, the Jap A/S vessel dropped a depth charge that, according to Latta, "proved to be the closest of the 200-odd NARWHAL had taken in ten war patrols." A few nights later, while unloading supplies at another rendezvous point, NARWHAL was surprised by an enemy destroyer. The DD's guns flashed in the moonlight, and the submarine dug under just in time.

Such surprises by surface craft were not common, but there was always the possibility. Navigational hazards presented another and constant danger to the submarine on this type of special mission.

Often it was necessary to scan a beach closely, preparatory to establishing contact with friends ashore. The submarine would submerge at daylight and approach the coast, usually entering shallow water where a depth-charging could easily prove fatal. At night the boat would surface and move in still closer, running the risk of grounding on shoals and consequent damage or stranding.

NAUTILUS (Lieutenant Commander C. C. Sharp) got into a tight spot during the execution of a guerrilla-supply mission to Cebu, on September 26, 1944. Sharp had closed the beach to 600 yards, and he was maneuvering to keep the submarine in this position while unloading. With radar to tell the range to the beach this was not difficult, but the knotty problem was the fixing of NAUTILUS' position along the beach. Few reference marks could be seen in the dark, but the presence of a shoal near-by made a positional fix imperative.

About 2200 the unloading job was completed, and Sharp, keeping his fingers crossed, ordered the submarine under way to clear the area. Three minutes later, NAUTILUS grounded on Luisan Shoal with 18 feet of water at the bow.

Attempted to back off. Blew all main ballast and variable ballast. Crew topside sallying ship. All efforts futile. About midnight decided to lighten ship and make a final attempt to get off at 0400 when high water was expected.

Lightened ship by sending about 40 tons of cargo ashore; blew 5,900 gallons of reserve fuel overboard; jettisoned 190 rounds of 6-inch ammunition; blew gasoline tanks dry of ballast and burned all secret and confidential matter. The forward and middle ballast tank groups were flooded to hold the ship on the bottom as the tide came in.

By 0330 it was apparent the tide had gone out instead of coming in. NAUTILUS was then up by the bow by 1½° and had a 12° starboard list. Dark as it was, coral heads and sandy bottom were clearly visible on the port side abreast of No. 1 gun. It was now or never for NAUTILUS.

Blew all main ballast tanks. Gradually built up to all back emergency and at 0336 ship began to go astern rapidly, clearing reef.

Safely clear, but sunrise only three hours away. The problem now was how to flood the dry gasoline tanks in less than the normal five hours required. A man-hole plate was removed and the starboard tank flooded relatively quickly. The dive that followed that morning was "breathtaking." It took but 75 seconds to submerge—a fast dive for NAUTILUS.

Four days later after completing another mission, the trim dive took 7 minutes 31 seconds! Obedient in diving, NAUTILUS was intractable in depth control, and the diving officer had to fight to keep the submarine from plummeting to the bottom.

When the gamut of blowing, venting, pumping, full speed and large angles on the boat had finally been run, the submariners realized that, in compensating for jettisoned cargo, some 90,000 pounds of excess variable ballast had been flooded in. In order to secure a fore-and-aft trim it was necessary to shift the remaining 6-inch ammunition from the magazine to the forward torpedo room bilges. A nerve or two had been frayed by the time the emergency was over,

but that was to be expected on a special mission. Veteran of many spine-chilling close calls, NAUTILUS proceeded on her way and successfully performed another special mission on this same patrol.

As has been pointed out, guerrilla supply and refugee evacuation were not the only objectives and accomplishments of these submarine missions. The submarines which penetrated the enemy's lines in the Philippines implemented and promoted an active "underground" which conveyed intelligence information of great value to the Allied forces converging to retake the islands.

Submarine special mission activities in the Philippines from January 1943 to the landings on Leyte in the late autumn of 1944 were summarized by Captain A. H. McCollum, USN, in a memorandum entitled "Résumé of Seventh Fleet Activities Connected with Guerrilla Organization in the Philippines." For some time Officer-in-Charge of the Seventh Fleet Intelligence Center, Captain McCollum was well acquainted with the jigsaw pieces of the mysterious "underground" picture. He wrote:

After the formal surrender of Blue Forces early in 1942, the few Americans who had escaped Prisoner of War or internment camps were hiding in remote areas of the Philippine Archipelago with no rapid and dependable means of passing to our forces such information as they might have. Accordingly it was decided to test the feasibility of landing and supplying small communications and coast watcher units in the Philippines by submarines. The first attempt was made on 14 January 1943 when the GUDGEON successfully landed 6 men and 2,000 pounds of equipment and supplies on the island of Negros. This was followed by the TAMBOR landing a small party with approximately 2 tons of supplies at Labangan, Mindanao, on 5 March 1943. Thereafter, at about 5 week intervals, small parties of personnel with about 2 tons of stores each were landed at various points in the central and southern Philippines by operational submarines as a special mission during their regular war patrol.

The cooperation of the natives in the southern part of the Philippines Area was extremely good, and under the direction of General Headquarters, Southwest Pacific Area, an organization of guerrilla forces was set up along recognized military lines. Efficient functioning of this organization was dependent to a great extent on ability to supply it with a medium of arms, ammunition, medical supplies and funds. The requirements of this supply plus the expansion of the coast watcher and communications net mounted to figures which were impracticable to handle by submarines on war patrol as special missions, hence a special supply unit was organized in October, 1943, with the NARWHAL, NAUTILUS, SEAWOLF and STINGRAY as components, with the primary duty of carrying out supply and evacuation missions in the Philippines Area. That these efforts were highly successful is attested by the rapid growth and efficient functioning of a net of coast watchers, weather observers and aircraft spotters completely covering the central and southern Philippines at the time of our initial landings in Leyte, with additional, but incomplete, coverage of Luzon. This intelligence net employed a total of 120 small radio stations, and the Navy manned and operated two control stations in Mindanao for the purpose of screening the guerrilla traffic and passing directly to Seventh Fleet units such items as were of operational importance. The military supplies brought in by the submarines played no small part in the organization of the natives into effective combat and reconnaissance units; again at the time of the Blue landings on Leyte it is estimated that there were 65,000 organized guerrilla troops in the Philippines south of 12°N. Lat. and they have rendered valuable service in many ways since the campaign started.

Since January 1943, a total of 18 submarines have carried out 39 supply and evacuation missions in the Philippines. During these 39 missions, 1,325 tons of supplies and equipment were landed and delivered into the hands of the guerrillas. Less than 50 tons of supplies were lost or not delivered, and it is believed that none fell into the hands of the enemy. No missions were completely unsuccessful and only 3 were partially unsuccessful. 327 persons were landed during these operations, and 466 were evacuated.

"King Two" Submarines

Word from the underground and the submarines timed the Halsey strikes and the MacArthur drive at Leyte. Mindanao was to be by-passed, and amphibious "King Two" would land like a colossal sledge hammer on the middle of the Philippines—the point where the defenses were weakest. D-Day was set for October 20th.

"King Two" was a Southwest Pacific operation, so the main submarine support was supplied by the SubSoWesPac Force. DARTER, DACE, ROCK, BERGALL, BLACKFIN, GURNARD, COBIA, BATFISH, GUITARRO, ANGLER, BREAM, CERO, NAUTILUS and COD were stationed in strategic positions on a line roughly extending from North Borneo to northern Luzon, where the Southwest Pacific operational area bordered on the waters of "Convoy College." The strategy involved and disposition of submarines are discussed in Chapter 26, Submarines vs. The Japanese Navy.

SubPac submarines supported "King Two" by patrolling the main line from Japan to the Philippines—the waters off the Bungo Suido, the Nansei Shoto area, the rolling seas of "Convoy College." When the Battle for Leyte Gulf developed, ComSubPac had two wolf-packs in Luzon Strait. And two other wolf-packs were en route to Luzon Strait from Saipan—"Roach's Raiders" (HADDOCK, HALIBUT and TUNA) and "Clarey's Crushers" (PINTADO, JALLAO and ATULE), under Commander J. P. Roach in HADDOCK and Commander B. A. Clarey in PINTADO.

The SoWesPac and SubPac submarines enumerated pointed their bows toward high destiny when they headed toward the stations and areas assigned. Entering "King Two" they were soon up to their periscopes in the decisive naval engagement of the Pacific War. The showdown battle and its many actions, fought in the Philippines theater, cannot be detailed in this volume. The great submarine battles fought by DACE, DARTER and the others will be recounted in Chapter 26.

CHAPTER 26

SUBMARINES VS. THE JAPANESE NAVY

Marked Men-of-war

When U.S. submarines set out to "execute unrestricted warfare," every Japanese ship afloat was on the submarine extermination list. But Public Enemy No. 1 was the Japanese man-of-war. The attrition campaign against transports and cargo carriers which kept the submarines on the go around the clock and around the calendar was paced by a relentless hunt for Japanese warships. American submarines were pitted against the Imperial Navy from the first. And they might have hit it harder and sooner had they been armed with a dependable torpedo. As was pointed out in the chapter on torpedoes, the defective magnetic exploder was particularly prone to

err when it entered the expansive magnetic field which surrounded a battleship or an aircraft carrier. Early submarine attacks against vessels of that caliber were invariably frustrated.

The aircraft carrier SORYU, sunk during the Battle of Midway, was already on her last legs when NAUTILUS administered the *coup de grâce*. Sunk by S-44, the heavy cruiser KAKO was blown to the bottom by non-magnetic Mark 10 torpedoes. Sixteen months then elapsed before a U.S. submarine downed another Jap heavyweight. Not that they hadn't tried. But attack after attack had failed to sink the enemy's larger men-of-war. Proof positive that the fault was the torpedo's became apparent when submarines carrying the rectified exploder began to demolish the Imperial Navy's capital ships. SAILFISH started the rally on December 3, 1943, when she downed the escort carrier CHUYO.

In the first quarter of 1944, the submarine drive against the Imperial Navy was getting under way. Straws in the wind, the sinking of the light cruiser AGANO by SKATE, and the SANDLANCE victory over the CL TATSUTA have been reported in previous chapters. Five destroyers were sunk by submarines during that period. Then in April 1944, the drive went into high gear, and by the end of June it attained

the momentum of a steamroller racing downhill.

The onslaught, unleashed by Admiral Lockwood when he corrected the torpedo's faults, developed during the summer of 1944 into a campaign of annihilation. Every U.S. submarine going out on patrol was determined to get her man-of-war. Size was no deterrent—the larger they were, it seemed, the faster they sank. Cruisers succumbed to accurate torpedo fire as speedily as destroyers. Aircraft carriers proved as vulnerable as cruisers. Armor and armament were unavailing. Before the year was over a mighty battleship and a giant aircraft carrier were blown to sea bottom by sharpshooting submarines.

So the "big shots" and lesser gunmen—the capital ships, cruisers and destroyers of that Imperial Navy which dealt death and destruction at Pearl Harbor—were tracked down and obliterated by implacable submarines, much as the Dillingers, "Legs" Diamonds, Capones and "Baby Face" Nelsons of gangdom were tracked down and obliterated by the F.B.I. United States surface and air forces, aided by Allied elements, contributed their share to the extermination campaign. The great naval battles fought by these forces are detailed in other histories. This chapter and its sequel are devoted to the share contributed in 1944 by U.S. submarines.

373

As will be seen, that contribution was sizable—46 Japanese men-of-war and seven Jap submersibles. The total (53 naval vessels) summed up to a loss from which the Imperial Navy never recovered. And the figure does not include four heavy cruisers and a large aircraft carrier which were damaged by torpedo fire and rendered *hors de combat*.

Destroy the Destroyer!

The big submarine headline in April featured the news that it was now open season for DD's. How had the mighty fallen! Had been a time when the lusty destroyer was looked upon by the periscope as the most dangerous of foes—an opponent to be avoided by the submarine unless combat were inescapable. Beware the animal—if asleep, better let it lie. That, at the war's beginning, had been the doctrine.

It was not the doctrine when the calendar reached 1944. By that date 14 Japanese specimens (9 modern and 5 old-timers) had been sunk by U.S. submarines and the depth-charge barrage was a blown-up bugaboo. By pre-war repute a tiger, the Jap DD's reputation had deteriorated to bobcat.

The bobcat had claws. It remained a vicious adversary. However, it was no longer considered big game. As a target, the DD's value had never been particularly high. In the war of attrition the undersea hunters had preferred an AO or a transport, and the destroyer had been taken as something of a pest. Five of these pests were downed by submarines in the first quarter of 1944. (See list below.)

On April 13, 1944, the announcement was made that the hunting season was open. The date was timed by various factors which indicated that the Imperial Navy's destroyer losses (from all causes) had created a serious DD shortage, and the enemy was having great difficulty in mustering these vessels for important convoy and man-of-war escort duty. Acting upon this information, Cominch issued a directive giving destroyers high submarine-target priority immediately under carriers, battleships and cruisers, and over merchantmen of all types. The directive, of course, was not made public, but it was front page news in the quiet code of the "Silent Service."

Patrolling off Zamboanga, REDFIN (Lieutenant Commander M. H. Austin) anticipated the priority season. On April 11, she attacked, torpedoed and sank the destroyer AKIGUMO. After downing this DD, she went on to demolish two passenger-cargo carriers on the 15th and 16th—SHINYU MARU and YAMAGATA MARU, for a total of some 8,000-odd tons.

HARDER and Commander Sam Dealey bagged the next destroyer. This was HARDER's fourth patrol, and she made it in the Marianas area where the waters were still hot from the first Navy air strike. HARDER sighted the target off Guam on April 13—the day of the destroy-the-destroyers directive. Dealey sent the submarine boring in. A well-aimed salvo erased from the surface the Imperial Navy's IKAZUCHI.

HARDER damaged a second destroyer in the same foray, and four days later she sank the 7,061-ton freighter MATSUE MARU. So the big destroyer hunt was on. And on her next patrol, HARDER would strike this enemy the hardest blow dealt the Japanese destroyer force by a single U.S. submarine.

U.S. submarines did not sink any other destroyers in April. But the anti-DD campaign was well begun, and HARDER had set the pace. From the foregoing account of the campaign's inception, it should not be construed that the destroyer was no longer a dangerous antagonist and the depth charge was a squib. HARDER's own final chapter will disclose the contrary. No submarine could afford to trifle with an enemy DD or relax when the dynamite was dropping. But the emphasis had shifted. The CHIDORI "pinger," as an A/S foe, was almost as formidable as a destroyer. A group of *kaibokan* frigates could be as much of a menace to the cornered submersible. Aided by new detection devices and patrol strategems, Japanese aircraft, with which the submarine could not trade blows, were foemen to be avoided. In short, the destroyer was no longer the submarine's arch enemy, but as a man-of-war it was still a "tough guy," as all gunmen are tough.

But its days were numbered. Cominch had given the order, and the "heat was on."

Hunting the Japanese DD

In the spring and summer of 1944, the Japanese destroyer hunt continued with a vengeance. The predatory DD that loomed up over the horizon and came rushing forward with a white moustache under

Date	Submarine	Commanding Officer	Destroyer	Tonnage	Locale
Jan. 14, 1944	Albacore	J. W. Blanchard	Sazanami	1,950	Carolines
Jan. 26, 1944	Skipjack	G. G. Molumphy	Suzukaze	1,580	Ponape
Feb. 1, 1944	Guardfish	N. G. Ward	Umikaze	1,580	Truk
Feb. 10, 1944	Pogy	R. M. Metcalf	Minekaze	1,300	E. of Formosa
Mar. 16, 1944	Tautog	W. B. Sieglaff	Shirakumo	1,950	Hokkaido

its nose was liable to a down-the-throat shot that would stop it as an elephant gun would stop a hyena. Submarine torpedoes—electric and the revised Mark 14—downed a dozen Japanese DD's that spring and summer.

COD (Commander J. C. Dempsey) began the May shooting by sinking the old destroyer KARUKAYA off the coast of Luzon on the 10th.

Off North Borneo, BONEFISH (Commander T. W. Hogan) tracked, torpedoed and sank the Imperial Navy's INAZUMA on the night of the 14th.

Veteran POLLACK, under Commander B. E. Lewellen, downed ASANAGI in the Bonins area on the 22nd.

On June 8, HAKE (Commander J. C. Broach) caught and killed KAZEGUMO off Moro Gulf, Mindanao.

The following night, SWORDFISH (Commander K. E. Montross) sank MATSUKAZE off the Bonins.

On July 25, BATFISH (Lieutenant Commander J. K. Fyfe) put an end to the destroyer SAMIDARE after naval aircraft had driven the DD to beach in the Pelews.

In the meantime, HARDER invaded the Celebes Sea, and there she conducted an anti-DD drive unparalleled in the annals of submarining. As a highlight of the submarine vs. destroyer campaign, the HARDER story is related under an individual heading.

In July the campaign was continued by PADDLE (Lieutenant Commander B. H. Nowell). Day-periscope attack and torpedoing took place in the Celebes Sea on the 6th. Victim was the Imperial Navy's HOKAZE.

Far to the north, USAGUMO went down on the 7th, torpedoed by SKATE (Commander W. P. Gruner) in the Sea of Okhotsk.

On the night of the 7th another DD was bagged in the South China Sea off Luzon. Bagging was by MINGO (Lieutenant Commander J. J. Staley). This was one of the large specimens—a 2,100-tonner—the IJN TAMANAMI.

ASKAZE went down off the west coast of Luzon on August 23, sunk by HADDO (Lieutenant Commander C. W. Nimitz, Jr.).

Off the northwest tip of Luzon, YUNAGI was picked off two days later by PICUDA (Commander G. R. Donaho).

On September 12, GROWLER (Commander T. B. Oakley, Jr.) sank SHIKINAMI in a night-surface action off Hainan.

During the season in which these destroyers were downed, the United States offensive was driving at the Marianas, Palau and the underbelly of the Philippines. Japan was countering with every reserve the War Machine could muster. Some of the above-mentioned destroyers, destroyed by submarines on

attrition patrol, were serving as convoy escorts. Others were on the battle front in the Central and Southwest Pacific. All were vital cogs in the Japanese War Machine. Needless to say that U.S. submarines, by downing them, threw a wrench in the machinery.

Bluegill vs. Yubari

While the destroyer hunt was getting under way, the Imperial Navy lost to submarine torpedoes a man-of-war of another class. This was a vessel rated as a light cruiser (CL)—the third of her ilk to be downed by a submarine that year.

One April day the submarine BLUEGILL was patrolling in the vicinity of the Sonsorol Islands, southwest of Palau. It was BLUEGILL's maiden patrol, and the first command patrol of her captain, Lieutenant Commander E. L. Barr, Jr.

BLUEGILL was after big game. A member of Commodore Fife's Brisbane Force, she was reconnoitering Sonsorol and keeping her periscope peeled for enemy shipping in the neighborhood. Located about midway between Palau and Morotai, the Sonsoral group was suspected of harboring Japanese naval units. BLUEGILL's investigation corroborated the suspicions.

April 27 was the submarine's testing day. On that date she sighted a cruiser and a destroyer prowling off the tiny island like two carnivores against a patch of jungle. The cruiser disappeared behind the island. Barr drove BLUEGILL forward to attack the destroyer.

While the submarine was making the approach, the cruiser suddenly reappeared from behind the island, moving at top speed. Barr managed a quick-change set-up on the T.D.C., swung to the firing course, estimated the time to a fraction, and fired six torpedoes. He observed a smashing hit in the cruiser's fire room —a blast of smoke and flame—heard two more timed explosions as BLUEGILL burrowed under.

So BLUEGILL beat the DD priority by 1,000 tons. Her cruiser victim, the only warship of its class, was the Imperial Navy's YUBARI. Sunk off Sonsorol, the light cruiser YUBARI was no better than a dead goldfish at the bottom of the Emperor's fishpond. Death knows no class.

Harder vs. the DD

On May 26, HARDER slid out of Fremantle, where she had been serviced by the tender ORION, and headed for the Celebes Sea to conduct her fifth patrol. She took with her as observer Captain Murray T. Tichenor, Operations Officer, Submarines Seventh Fleet.

One of HARDER's missions was to pick up a team of British agents from the northeastern coast of Borneo.

To do so, she had to run up through Sibutu Passage, the narrow strait between the southernmost islands of the Sulu Archipelago and the North Borneo coast. As the combined forces of Kurita and Ozawa were in the Sulu Archipelago, based at the old U.S. Asiatic Fleet anchorage at Tawi Tawi, HARDER was impelled to walk softly when she approached this strait. For her principal mission was to scout the Japanese fleet. The task could be accomplished only with circumspection, and silence was golden. Unless, of course, there developed circumstances which made it worthwhile to disturb the peace.

On her way up through the Strait of Makassar, HARDER side-stepped the usual clutter of sailing vessels and fishing fleets which invariably made submarining in those peacock waters an adventure in hazards. Off Tarakan on June 6, she was sighted by a patrol vessel, but she easily evaded this craft. Late that afternoon she was off Sibutu Passage, and shortly after sunset she began the ticklish transit.

She had not gone far when her radar scope displayed a flurry of "pips." Convoy! Coming south through the passage in HARDER's direction! Dealey sent the crew bounding into action, and at 18,000 yards the targets were in view—three large ships which looked like oil tankers. Escorting the tankers were two, possibly three, destroyers. Dealey ordered the submarine to the surface and started an end-around with four engines on the line.

Off HARDER's port beam, the convoy was steaming at 15 knots. And it managed to prolong the chase by changing course and taking a tack away from the submarine. But Dealey and company were not to be outdistanced by these high-priority targets. This was one of those circumstances wherein disturbing the peace was worth it. So the submariners created a considerable disturbance.

As HARDER was completing the end-around, she was suddenly exposed by an unfriendly moon which emerged from a nest of clouds and bathed the bridge with silver light. Twelve thousand yards distant, the nearest Jap DD veered at once and headed for the submarine at top speed. At 8,500 yards, the destroyer tracking dead astern at 24 knots and HARDER's 19 knots laying a white wake as broad as an avenue, Dealy gave the order to submerge. As HARDER burrowed under, the skipper ordered a turn hard left to bring her stern tubes to bear. The destroyer charged headlong, presenting an easy fire control problem. When the range closed to 1,150 yards, Dealey let go with three torpedoes.

Two hits smashed home—one under the warship's bow, the other under her bridge. The destroyer's stern rumped up into the air, and her depth charges started going off. Four minutes later, Dealey brought HARDER to the surface and witnessed the death throes of the 1,500-ton destroyer MINATSUKI.

Dealey then put four engines on propulsion and the convoy chase was resumed. Then another escorting DD veered over to attack the submarine. Dealey fired six torpedoes at this destroyer, but all missed, and it was after midnight before the thunder of the depth charges died away and HARDER could safely surface.

An incident which occurred during the depth-charging illustrates the dependence of a submarine's safety upon the actions of every hand on board. As the crew rigged for depth-charge attack, the regular stern-plane indicator light was de-energized. A new stern planesman, thinking he had lost power, shifted to hand operation. Inadvertently, he put the planes on dive, and before HARDER, already at deep submergence, could be levelled off, she had gone below her test depth. Although this was strictly a "personnel casualty," Commander Dealey gave it a detailed description in his patrol report, "in hope that it may help some other sub to avoid a similar experience."

After this deep-sea plunge, it was too late to catch the convoy, and Dealey ordered a routine submergence before daybreak. Then, early on that morning of June 7, a mast was sighted, and another approach was begun. At 0730 HARDER grazed a submerged reef. Dealey ordered her to the surface, and discovered he had been making an approach on an island—not the first one by a submarine in the war. HARDER rejected this interesting target and went on. Shortly before noon, well along in Sibutu Passage, she was forced deep by a plane. Then, rising to periscope depth, she presently sighted a destroyer at 4,000 yards, small angle on the bow. Crew went to battle stations. Four bow torpedoes were readied. At 3,000 yards, the destroyer headed directly for the submarine's periscope. Angle on the bow varied from port to starboard, as the DD rushed forward, zigzagging. Dealey waited until the enemy was only 650 yards away. Then—

Fired one—two—three in rapid succession. Number four wasn't necessary! Fifteen seconds after the first shot was fired, it struck the destroyer squarely amidships. Number two hit just aft—number three missed ahead. Ordered right full rudder and ahead full to get clear of the destroyer. At range of 300 yards we were rocked by a terrific explosion believed to have been the destroyer's magazine. In less than one minute after the first hit, and nine minutes after it was sighted, the destroyer sank tail first, observed by the Commanding Officer, the Executive Officer and Captain Tichenor.

376

That was the end of the 2,100-ton destroyer HAYANAMI. And it might have been the end of HARDER, if the A/S vessel which rushed up out of nowhere had set the depth charges a bit deeper and dropped them with greater accuracy. Going deep to evade this attack, the submarine spent two hours dodging a furious barrage. Seventeen charges crashed down, and it was some time before HARDER went up to periscope depth.

Then an investigating committee of six sister destroyers was sighted in line of bearing, headed HARDER's way! Dealey decided discretion was the better part of valor, and the submarine went under to sit that one out. A free-for-all with six DD's was out of the question.

Surfacing that night, HARDER headed north at 15 knots to make another try at transiting Sibutu Passage. A hazy and unreliable horizon prevented the obtainment of an accurate position by star sights. And at 2206 a minuscule radar contact at 1,500 yards was picked up dead ahead. Almost immediately a black silhouette—it might have been a submarine's conning tower—was sighted from the bridge. At 1,200 yards it was identified as a "low pinnacle sticking straight up out of the sea, with white foam breaking around it." Grounding was narrowly averted at 400 yards, and Dealey paid tribute to the alert watch-standing of Wilbur Lee Clark, Radio Technician 3, whose timely sighting prevented a scrape which might well have been disastrous. Unexpected rocks and uncharted reefs were commonplace navigational hazards in that area, and only uncommon vigilance and skill on the part of the crews bested these treacherous snares.

HARDER arrived off the rendezvous point, northeast Borneo, on the night of June 8—about 48 hours late, thanks to the Jap destroyers. Three other submarines had unsuccessfully attempted to pick up this party of coast watchers. Now, as a result of careful planning and the able assistance of ace Australian Commando Major W. J. Jinkins, the six intelligence operators were evacuated without ado.

Early morning, June 9, as she was heading away from the rendezvous point, HARDER was forced under by a patrol plane. A bomb exploded just as she went below periscope depth, and the submarine got a shaking up. With the fleet anchorage of Tawi Tawi but 40 miles away Dealey suspected destroyers would be out soon. His suspicions were confirmed. Sound picked up two sets of destroyer screws a little before noon. Dealey elected to lay low at this time. The sea was a blue glass on which a periscope "feather" would have been as ostentatious as the ostrich plume of an opera diva. And in the clear water a submarine,

even at 100-foot depth, might readily be sighted by sharp-eyed aircraft. The destroyers crossed overhead several times without detecting HARDER—Dealey was holding her deep—and early in the afternoon, they departed. HARDER was then headed for the northern entrance of Sibutu Passage.

At 2101 that night a destroyer's silhouette was sighted at 13,000 yards. A minute later another DD silhouette was sighted. The two destroyers were patrolling the narrowest part of Sibutu in line of bearing.

Through the submarine the order rang out, "Battle stations torpedo!" Dealey took her down, and began the approach.

"At 3000 yards both destroyers zigged 30° to their right (with the first presenting at 30° port track) and the picture became 'just what the doctor ordered' for the HARDER." With the targets overlapping, Dealey fired four torpedoes at the first, range 1,000 yards. *"No. 1 appeared to pass just ahead of the first destroyer; No. 2 struck it near the bow; No. 3 hit just under the destroyer's bridge; and No. 4 passed astern of the near target."*

After the first salvo HARDER was swung hard right to avoid hitting this destroyer, and fire was withheld until a new set-up could be made on the second DD.

About thirty seconds after turning, the second destroyer came into view just astern of what was left of the first one, then burning furiously. Just then No. 4 torpedo, which had passed astern of the first target was heard and observed to hit the second target. (No more torpedoes were needed for either.) Meanwhile, a heavy explosion, believed to be caused by an exploding boiler on the first destroyer, went off and the sub (then about 400 yards away) was heeled over by the concussion. At almost the same time a blinding explosion took place on the second destroyer (probably his ammunition going off) and it took a quick nose dive. When last observed by the Commanding Officer and Executive Officer, the tail of the second destroyer was straight up in the air and the first destroyer had disappeared.

Ten minutes after opening fire, Dealey "surfaced to allow others to see the damage, and to make rapid shift to a more quiet neighborhood." Nothing could be seen in the bright moonlight except a large quantity of steam and vapor over the spot of the first sinking and a lighted buoy burning where the second destroyer had been. The destroyer that had been vaporized was the Imperial Navy's TANIKAZE. The second target was never identified. Post-war inquiry led to the conclusion that the vessel may have been an old destroyer, operating as an A/S unit. If the ship went down, her name went down with her, and HARDER was credited with only one DD.

377

While HARDER was on her way out of the vicinity, she was given a brushing by a Jap aircraft that whizzed down from the midnight sky and roared past the submarine's bridge at an altitude of 100 feet, and a scant 300 feet away. Apparently the run was for identification purposes, for the plane did not open fire, and HARDER was able to dive before the first bomb came down. Then the night flyers pelted her until nearly morning. One blast was too close for comfort, but HARDER was becoming accustomed to close shaves.

The following afternoon she sighted a large Jap task force—three battleships, a quartet of cruisers, six or eight destroyers under a canopy of escorting planes. HARDER was about eight miles from the nearest battleship—it looked like one of the MUSASHI supers—when the BB was suddenly screened by black smoke and Sound heard three distant explosions. At this juncture, a destroyer headed straight for HARDER. Evidently a plane of the outer air screen had spotted her in the translucent water. Sound gave a turn count of 35 knots as the destroyer raced for HARDER's periscope, zero angle on the bow.

Angle on the bow still zero and the destroyer was echo ranging right on us steadily! The picture had reached the stage now where we had to hit him—or else! At a range of 1,500 yards three bow torpedoes were fired with gyro angles near zero on a "down the throat" shot. At the same time sound reported fast screws moving in from the starboard beam, but there was insufficient time to take a look. "All ahead, full, right full rudder, take 'er deep!" Fifty-five seconds and sixty seconds, respectively, after the first shot, two torpedoes struck with a detonation that was far worse than depth-charging. By this time we were just passing 80 feet and were soon almost beneath the destroyer when all hell broke loose. It was not from his depth charges—but a deafening series of progressive rumblings that seemed to almost blend with each other. Either his boilers or magazines, or both, had exploded and it's a lucky thing that ship explosions are vented upward and not down.

As it was, the submarine was jolted by the blast. A barometer was kicked out of its fitting, the submariners were thrown from their feet, and a chain sprang from its hook and knocked a man unconscious. When depth charges continued to slam in the wake of this thunderclap, one of the British agents recovering from jungle fever turned to Dealey. "I say, old man, would you mind taking us back to Borneo?"

HARDER spent the next two hours dodging depth charges, aerial bombs, probing "pings" and more of the same. When at last Dealey took her up to periscope depth, she could find no sign of the destroyer target—unless it were a lighted buoy three miles astern of the point of attack. Japanese records fail to name a destroyer sunk at that place and time. Apparently the target was only damaged. But the blasting which had broken the barometer in the distant submarine must have lamed the target ship for life. And Japanese naval leaders were inclined to belittle their losses. Toyoda, for example, reported the sinkings by HARDER as "four destroyers damaged."

Toyoda made another unusual report. He reported that his fleet had been discovered at Tawi Tawi, and the anchorage was surrounded by a great force of submarines. First, a masterpiece of understatement, then a masterpiece of over. His fleet had been discovered, true. But HARDER and REDFIN hardly constituted a great undersea force.

The Admiral, however, was unable to believe that a single submarine could down three fleet destroyers in as many days. He visualized Tawi Tawi as the focal point for a mass submarine concentration, and lacking the DD's to cope with such a situation, he decided it was time for the fleet to get a move on. HARDER, of course, was there to report just such a move.

Watching the Tawi Tawi anchorage on the evening of June 10, she spotted a group of warships steaming southward. As will be seen, HARDER's report of this sortie touched off a train of events that exploded the Battle of the Philippine Sea. After she dispatched this dynamite-laden report, HARDER was ordered to a quieter area. She concluded her fifth patrol on July 10 when she put into Fremantle, her bag bulging with destroyer pelts.

Official post-war assessment credited HARDER with downing three Japanese destroyers in a row and damaging at least two more. Extraordinary shooting for one submarine in a brief period of four days! Perhaps more remarkable than those torpedoings was their after effect—Admiral Toyoda's alarm and the Japanese fleet's precipitate departure from Tawi Tawi. This upset the fleet's previous battle plans, and caused Admiral Ozawa to delay his carrier force in the Philippine Sea, with disastrous results. The strategic consequences of HARDER's anti-DD drive could not be measured in destroyer tons. Nor were they fully known until after the war.

But the destroyer sinkings and the report on the fleet were enough to win for HARDER the plaudits of the entire Submarine Service. For this outstanding patrol Commander Dealey, long recognized as one of the ocean's best submariners, was recommended for the Congressional Medal of Honor.

Loss of Harder (Commander S. D. Dealey)

HARDER left Australia on August 5, 1944, to conduct her sixth war patrol. As has been related, she

© Fred Freeman, 1949

HARDER DOWNS THE DESTROYERS! She is shown surfacing after sinking two Jap DD's with one torpedo spread. This action in Sibutu Passage (night of June 9, 1944) caused Admiral Toyoda to move the Jap fleet precipitately from Tawi Tawi. Harder's skipper was "the submariner's submariner."

SURFACE SEARCH! Lookout topside sweeps the horizon with inquisitive glasses as war-patrolling submarine combs the wave on a hunt for targets.

COMDR. S. D. DEALEY. Posthumously awarded Congressional Medal.

TAUTOG ON TARGET! Going down is a Jap LCI—Transport No. 15, torpedoed off Japan.

RESCUED BY CREVALLE! Evacuees off Negros, P.I., May 11, 1944. Crevalle reported a severe depth-charging. "Conduct of passengers magnificent."

JAP PRISONERS! Taken ashore at Pearl Harbor, sad captives are seen coming across deck of USS Spadefish. Note sinkings marked on Spadefish flag: 4 Jap naval vessels and 17 marus!

was leading a wolf-pack composed of herself, HAKE and HADDO. On the morning of August 21, HARDER joined RAY and GUITARRO in the attack on the Paluan Bay convoy.

After the Paluan Bay battle, HADDO and HARDER made a combined attack on three Jap coast defense vessels off Bataan. These small vessels were speedily demolished, and by that time HAKE, the third submarine of the wolf-pack, arrived on the scene. The wolf-pack continued the hunt.

HADDO destroyed the DD ASAKAZE on the morning of August 23, and then, out of ammunition, headed for Australia. HARDER and HAKE held conference, then departed for their common objective, the waters off Caiman Point.

At 0453, on the morning of August 24, HAKE submerged not far from Caiman Point. HARDER was then in sight 4,500 yards south of her. Presently HAKE heard "pinging" to the southward, and her periscope picked up two ships against the morning sky. HAKE's captain, Commander Broach, sent the submarine boring in. The targets were identified as PHRA RUANG, a three-stack Siamese destroyer, and a Jap minesweeper of less than 1,000 tons. Broach discontinued the attack when the destroyer zigged away, apparently heading for Dasol Bay. The minesweeper loitered off the bay.

At 0647, HAKE, coming to a northerly course, sighted HARDER's periscope dead ahead, perhaps 650 yards distant. Sound reported faint screws on this bearing, so Broach ordered a turn away toward the south. As HAKE turned, Sound heard three strong "pings." A periscope exposure showed the minesweeper veering toward the two submarines.

Broach suspected the enemy had made contact, so he ordered deep submergence. The minesweeper continued to "ping" uncertainly. Then at 0728, HAKE heard 15 rapid depth charges thundering in the distance. Two sets of screws were heard, and the "pinging" went on for some time as Broach maneuvered to evade, heading westward. Two hours and a half later—silence.

That noon there was no sign of HARDER. Her periscope did not appear during the afternoon, and she did not join HAKE that night. Dealey and his good company had fought the final battle.

The account of an A/S attack off Caiman Point was found in Japanese records. The report concluded, "Much oil, wood chips and cork floated in the vicinity."

So perished HARDER and Commander Sam Dealey— one of the greatest fighting teams of the Pacific War. Commander Dealey was posthumously awarded the Congressional Medal of Honor.

Submarines vs. Combined Fleet Strategy (Battle of the Philippine Sea)

Although Admiral Soemu Toyoda, Commander-in-Chief of the Japanese Combined Fleet, could not believe one submersible responsible for such destruction as HARDER wrought in Sibutu Passage, he had, according to his own testimony, already conceived a sincere respect for the prowess of U.S. submarines.

Questioned after the war, he declared, *"Early in the war I think the submarines were the part of the United States Navy which I considered the greatest threat."*

He went on to depone that Japan's downfall resulted, in his opinion, from lack of production, and this lack was due to the home Empire's inability to obtain raw materials from the south. Asked to state the principal reason for this inability to import, he declared, *"The main reason, I think, is that we did not have a sufficient number of ships to begin with, and such as we had, suffered heavy damage owing to your submarines and air action."*

How did he feel about the naval situation when he assumed command of the Combined Fleet after the death of Admiral Koga? *"At that time we had access to oil in Borneo and Sumatra. We were able to obtain supplies directly from the south; so while the stock of oil was almost sufficient for purposes of a fleet, the difficulty was in tankers. I had asked for and obtained about 80,000 tons of tankers for fleet use, but we began to suffer damages through submarine operations; and by the time of the Saipan operation, the greatest hindrance to the drafting of the operation plans was the fact that we did not have sufficient tankers to support it."*

So in June 1944, when "Operation Forager" was preparing to smite the Marianas, the Japanese fleet admiral at Tawi Tawi had submarines on his mind. On his mind also was a plan of action—the "A-Go Plan"—to be set in motion as a counter to an American drive on the Marianas. An offensive thrust at Palau was considered the more imminent, but the Japanese plan was made flexible enough to include the Marianas alternative. This called for a dual attack on the invading United States fleet—first, by Japanese air groups to be rushed to the Marianas from the Bonins; second, by Ozawa's carrier planes, to be rushed to the area from Tawi Tawi. The Imperial Navy flyers were to take off at long range, bomb the American fleet, and then land at evening on the air strips at Saipan, Tinian and Guam. There they would refuel and rearm to resume the attack the following morning. After which they would fly back to Ozawa's presumably waiting carriers.

This operation served a twofold purpose. It

379

permitted the Japanese carrier pilots, who lacked training in night deck landings, to hop from the carriers to the Marianas airfields, and then return to Ozawa's flat-tops by day. And it gave the carrier pilots a chance to "shuttle bomb" the United States Fleet, coming and going. It was assumed that the U. S. Fleet would be so badly punished by land-based planes and carrier aircraft that it would be unable to retaliate when and if the Combined Fleet came within range of the American carrier planes.

The Marianas defense plan was not clumsily contrived. However, since it called for a coordinated attack by land-based planes and carrier planes, perfect timing was imperative. Ozawa's planes and the aircraft from the Bonins would have to reach the area simultaneously, if they were to hit the American fleet full force. Moreover, the carrier planes would have to take off at a point and hour which would permit them to land in the Marianas at evening. Intention, then, was to launch the carrier planes when Ozawa's force, rushing northeastward from the Philippines, reached the 137th or 138th meridian, about two-thirds of the way between the Philippines and the Marianas.

But what if the United States forces were warned about the Combined Fleet's departure from Tawi Tawi? Apparently Toyoda, while worried about submarines, neglected that contingency. On the other hand, Admirals Nimitz, Spruance and Lockwood, planning "Operation Forager," had not overlooked the possibility of interference from Toyoda's fleet. Spruance did not intend to be caught flat by Japanese flat-tops. Therefore, as has been described, U.S. submarines were in the Philippines as well as on Toyoda's mind.

HARDER, REDFIN and BLUEFISH were covering the Tawi Tawi exits. Three submarines were strategically placed on station north of Luzon—three south of Mindanao—one at the eastern entrance to San Bernardino Strait—one at the eastern entrance to Surigao Strait. Then HARDER, on the night of June 6, began her destroyer-shoot in Sibutu Passage. The psychological effect on Toyoda, who was already submarine-conscious, has been reported.

Frightened by the HARDER foray, he pulled the trigger on the "A-Go Plan" as soon as he heard of the preliminary skirmishing in the Marianas. Mitscher's carrier force was spotted by Japanese scouts on June 11 when it was some 200 miles east of Guam. That afternoon American Hellcats raided the key Marianas airfields and destroyed over 100 Japanese planes. General Saito and Admiral Nagumo, in charge of the Marianas, took the raid for a hit-and-run air strike. Japan's military leaders were convinced the American drive was aimed at Palau, and at least 48 hours elapsed before they realized an all-out offensive was bearing down on Saipan. At length, on the morning of June 15, Tokyo Headquarters ordered the "A-Go Plan" into operation. But far to the south at Tawi Tawi, Admiral Toyoda, nervous about submarines, had already set the plan in motion.

Thus it was that HARDER, on the evening of June 10, reported the departure from Tawi Tawi of three battleships, four or more cruisers and some half-dozen destroyers, steaming southward.

The next information came from REDFIN (Commander M. H. Austin) also watching the Sulu Archipelago. Morning of June 13, REDFIN saw six Japanese carriers, four battleships, eight cruisers and a flock of destroyers head northward from Tawi Tawi. Austin's submarine got off this interesting report that evening.

The group sighted by REDFIN was, of course, Ozawa's carrier force. Admiral Spruance now knew the Imperial Navy was on the move. But was it a feint or a fight? Ozawa's force behaved strangely. Sundown, on the evening of June 15, it was spotted by FLYINGFISH (Commander R. D. Risser) emerging from San Bernardino Strait and steaming eastward. Then, instead of striking straight for the Marianas where the offensive was now going full blast, Ozawa's armada proceeded to wander aimlessly around in the Philippine Sea.

Why? Because the fleet's sortie from Tawi Tawi was premature. As a result of Toyoda's jumping the gun on the "A-Go Plan," Ozawa's carriers raced across the Sulu Sea and out through San Bernardino Strait about 24 hours ahead of the operation schedule. Reaching the Philippine Sea ahead of time, Ozawa had to stall until Tokyo gave the word which unleashed the planes from the Bonins. Stalling, he ran his carrier force through circuitous maneuvers which consumed both fuel and time. This shilly-shallying also gave U.S. submarines an opportunity to gain intercepting positions. As will be seen, they made the most of that opportunity.

Meantime, where was the southbound task force which HARDER had sighted? Spruance wanted to know. And the answer to this question came from SEAHORSE (Commander S. D. Cutter).

En route to a patrol station area in Luzon Strait, SEAHORSE was heading northwestward across the open sea between the Philippines and the western Carolines on the evening of June 15th. Normal patrol duties did not prevent her from playing vedette. About the time that FLYINGFISH sent off her headline message concerning Ozawa's emergence from San Bernardino, a hot news flash emanated from Cutter's submarine.

Unfortunately the HORSE developed motor trouble as she trailed, and presently reported that she had lost contact. But the two Japanese forces were now located—the main body east of San Bernardino Strait and the second section coming up from Surigao Strait. Spruance deduced they would rendezvous for fueling before striking for the Marianas. Where? The answer to this all-important question was provided by the submarine CAVALLA.

Cavalla and Albacore vs. Shokaku and Taiho

Captained by Commander H. J. Kossler, CAVALLA, on her maiden patrol, was heading westward to relieve FLYINGFISH at San Bernardino Strait when ComSubPac received the electrifying report from Risser's submarine. CAVALLA was immediately ordered to scout across the estimated track of the Japanese carrier force.

On June 16 at 2300, CAVALLA's radar picked up a convoy of two tankers and three DD's traveling eastward at high speed. Kossler directed an end-around and gained attack position. But his submarine was detected by one of the destroyers and forced deep. About an hour and a half later, Kossler ordered CAVALLA to the surface to transmit the contact report. He then headed her for the Philippines.

Kossler was unaware that this tanker convoy was the key to the puzzle concerning the Japanese fleet's rendezvous point. What was more, if those tankers could be destroyed, Kurita's battleships and Ozawa's carriers would be low on fuel—a shortage that would put a check-rein on their movements. This would give Mitscher's planes a bonanza opportunity to locate and destroy them. ComSubPac lost no time in instructing CAVALLA.

DESTRUCTION THOSE TANKERS OF GREAT IMPORTANCE . . . TRAIL . . . ATTACK . . . REPORT

When these orders were received, Kossler reversed course and started CAVALLA after the convoy at four-engine speed. But by morning of the 17th it was obvious that she could not overhaul the oil argosy. Accordingly, she was ordered to follow along the track at normal cruising speed. The oilers had been moving at 16 knots, but their run was limited, for they were headed toward Spruance's fleet.

CAVALLA lost the tankers, but she found something else. What she found was the task force which HARDER and SEAHORSE had previously contacted. At 2000 on the evening of June 18, the Jap BB's came over the horizon like a herd of elephants. Kossler "pulled the plug." This was in accordance with the

order to report before attacking. Results illustrated the wisdom behind this decree.

As CAVALLA lay low, the battleship force rumbled directly overhead like a munitions train going over a trestle. CAVALLA, far beneath, was undetected. Two hours later she climbed to the surface and transmitted a report which told Spruance that the Japanese Fleet was about 350 miles southwest of Mitscher's Task Force Fifty-eight. There was no doubt now. The enemy was coming out to fight.

CAVALLA was deprived of these big-game targets, but Fate was to present her with another, for the following morning she made contact with Ozawa's carrier force. And in the meantime ComSubPac had informed his submarines in the Philippines area that, the enemy task force having been reported, they now could shoot first and report afterward. This was exactly what the submarine captains wanted. And it was just what Kossler wanted when, peering through the periscope at 1048, he found himself looking at the masts of a large ship under a parasol of Japanese planes. The masts came spiking over the horizon, and were followed by more masts. Now CAVALLA's periscope was focused on a Japanese aircraft carrier which was accompanied by two cruisers and a destroyer. The carrier was identified as one of the SHOKAKU class. Kossler directed a submerged approach on a 90° starboard track, maneuvering for a bow-tube attack.

The carrier resembled a floating beehive. Planes hovered over her in swarms while others skimmed down to her flight deck. The escorting cruisers were moving ahead, but the destroyer on the starboard beam was in a position to give the submarine trouble. Nevertheless, CAVALLA's approach was undetected. At 1118 Kossler fired a salvo of six torpedoes, range 1,200 yards. As the wakes went ribboning toward the target, the DD 1,500 yards away turned toward the submarine. It was time to flood negative and go deep if CAVALLA expected to live to report the attack.

KOSSLER flooded negative. CAVALLA went deep. The depth charges thundered down. But the submarine sidled out from under the barrage. Kossler was presently able to report the action.

HIT SHOKAKU CLASS CARRIER WITH THREE OUT OF SIX TORPEDOES AT ZERO TWO ONE FIVE . . . ACCOMPANIED BY TWO ATAGO-CLASS CRUISERS THREE DESTROYERS POSSIBLY MORE . . . RECEIVED 105 DEPTH CHARGES DURING THREE HOUR PERIOD . . . SUPERSONIC GEAR OUT OF COMMISSION . . . HULL INDUCTION FLOODED . . . NO OTHER SERIOUS TROUBLE . . . SURE WE CAN HANDLE IT . . . HEARD FOUR TERRIFIC EXPLOSIONS IN DIRECTION OF TARGET TWO AND ONE HALF HOURS AFTER ATTACK . . . BELIEVE THAT BABY SANK

Kossler's belief was confirmed by fact. "That baby" went down. And she proved to be SHOKAKU herself —30,000 tons. One of the three largest Japanese aircraft carriers in commission, she was sunk at the very hour when Mitscher's planes were demolishing flight after flight of Jap aircraft as they attempted to reach the Marianas. But this torpedoing was not the only one dealt Ozawa's carrier force on the 19th of June. Some three hours before SHOKAKU was wiped out, ALBACORE struck an even larger carrier. Sixty miles north of the CAVALLA-SHOKAKU battle, this titanic encounter took place.

ALBACORE was at that time under the operational control of ComTaskForce Seventeen—Vice Admiral Lockwood, who served in dual capacity as ComSub-Pac and Commander TF17. The point is underlined because the tactical direction of submarines—a matter handled by the task force commander—played an important part in the development of the Philippine Sea Battle. And Lockwood's expert direction of his submarine task force engineered the opportunity to win a smashing undersea victory.

When CAVALLA contacted and reported the convoy of tankers, Admiral Lockwood deduced that the Japanese fleet intended to refuel somewhere in the vicinity of 13 N., 137 E. He immediately ordered four submarines—FINBACK, BANG, STINGRAY, ALBACORE—to move 100 miles south and SEAWOLF 150 miles south of former station. This placed these five submarines directly across the path of the oncoming fleet. Chess pieces could not have been better deployed by a Capablanca.

To ALBACORE fell the drastic play. A little after 0700 on the morning of the 19th, she submerged to escape the eye of an enemy plane. Her veteran captain, Commander J. W. Blanchard, had an idea the plane meant something. It did. About an hour later, ALBACORE's periscope was watching an aircraft carrier, a cruiser, and the tops of several unidentified ships. Range was 13,000 yards, and angle on the bow 70° to port. Blanchard swung the submarine to a normal approach course. While she was swinging, the periscope picked up a second carrier group.

This group consisted of a flat-top, a cruiser, and several destroyers. Angle on the bow was only 10° starboard—and ALBACORE was in an excellent position for attack. Blanchard promptly seized the better of two opportunities, and came around to the course for a 70° starboard track. At 0801 the submarine had closed the range to 9,000 yards, angle on the bow 15° starboard and distance to the track 2,300. A moment later it was apparent that one of the escorting destroyers was going to run between ALBACORE and the target and block the shot. Blanchard had to swing

to a northerly course to let the destroyer pass beyond the line of fire.

At 0804 the range was 5,300 yards, and ALBACORE 1,950 yards from the target's track. The target's speed plotted at 27 knots. These data were fed into the T.D.C. A periscope exposure made at 0806 checked accuracy. At 0808 Blanchard was ready to shoot. And at that eventful moment, the world's best firing position seemed to fall apart! For as Blanchard ran up the periscope, it was evident that the T.D.C. was not indicating a correct solution.

Blanchard's feelings could be compared to those of a marksman who had drawn a bead on one of the largest rhinos in Tanganyika, only to discover the sights of his rifle were out of kilter. Magnify the rhino into an aircraft carrier and set it moving at 27 knots in front of a submarine at periscope depth, and the captain's situation can be appreciated. Blanchard pulled down the periscope, took a hasty look at the malfunctioning T.D.C.—and already the target had gone by the firing bearing.

Impossible to swing the submarine and keep up with the bearing rate-of-change. It was now or never—accept the solution as correct, and trust to a wide spread to catch the target with a chance hit. Up periscope! Bearings fed the T.D.C. by hand! Time 0809:32. Fire!

Six torpedoes raced at the target, and Blanchard ordered ALBACORE deep. As the submarine went down, a muffled explosion was heard, timed for the run of No. 6 torpedo.

In the submarine forces at this time, "seeing was believing." ALBACORE, deep under the sea, saw nothing. And Blanchard could not believe one muffled explosion meant a sunken carrier. He was disappointed—so much so, he did not bother to transmit a radio report of the attack. When it showed up in his patrol report, submitted to ComSubPac a month later, ALBACORE was credited only with "probable damage." Not until months afterward did the outcome of the encounter come to light. Then a Japanese prisoner of war disclosed that on the morning of June 19 the aircraft carrier TAIHO, torpedoed just as she was gassing planes, had gone down.

Eventually it was learned that the single hit by ALBACORE had ruptured the carrier's gasoline tanks. Aboard the carrier was Admiral Ozawa himself, who managed by means of a destroyer to transfer his person to the carrier ZUIKAKU. He left behind a less fortunate crew. About six hours after the torpedoing, the gasoline fumes from TAIHO's hemorrhaged tanks ignited. And the 31,000-ton aircraft carrier—Japan's newest, and one of the largest in the world—went booming and bellowing to sea bottom. Down with her went dozens of planes and almost her entire crew.

Two first-line carriers sunk by submarines during one eventful morning! The loss of SHOKAKU and TAIHO was a stunner for the Imperial Navy. Toyoda's fleet was still reeling when Mitscher's planes roared overhead on the evening of the 20th and gave it an unmerciful blasting. Down went a fleet oiler, a destroyer and the aircraft carrier HITAKA. Three other carriers, a battleship and three cruisers were damaged by American bombers and torpedo planes.

In the meantime, United States invasion forces were sweeping ashore at Tinian, Guam and Saipan. Of the 400 planes launched into the battle by Ozawa's force, scarcely one got back. By midnight of the 20th, the Japanese Combined Fleet was retreating pell-mell across the Philippine Sea, fleeing for the relative security of Okinawa. Under the fire of submarine torpedoes and air bombs, the Marianas defense plan had disintegrated like a sheet of tissue in a furnace.

SubPac and SubSoWesPac submarines, in intercepting, reporting and attacking the Japanese naval forces, unquestionably proved worth their weight in pressure hulls and permanently established the place of the submersible as a supporting pillar of the fleet. Sinking 61,000 tons of aircraft carriers in one lump, CAVALLA and ALABACORE won front-rank stations in the submarine hall of fame. Front-rank with them stands HARDER, the submarine that deranged the Combined Fleet's operational plan. And not to be forgotten were all those submarines of the past—practitioners of the attrition war which had created for the Combined Fleet a fuel shortage and left a swarm of submersibles in Toyoda's imagination.

Flasher vs. Oi

FLASHER (Commander R. I. Whitaker) left Fremantle, Australia, on June 19, 1944, to conduct her third war patrol in the South China Sea. Action began in the evening of June 28, when Whitaker and company encountered a heavily escorted convoy of thirteen ships. Because of shallow water, Whitaker decided on a surface attack and ended-around to starboard. At midnight FLASHER was on the starboard bow of the leading target group—the two largest ships of the convoy, plus escorts.

Whitaker maneuvered in for the attack. The targets overlapped at ranges of 2,800 and 3,500 yards. And at 0111, morning of June 29, Whitaker opened fire—three bow torpedoes at each target. The first freighter, struck three times, broke in two and sank forthwith. Stopped by two hits, the second vessel, a passenger-cargoman, pumped a volley of shells at the submarine. FLASHER retired on the surface at four-engine

speed. Under the sea behind her she left NIPPO MARU, a 6,079-ton freighter.

July found FLASHER patrolling the coast of Indo-China. Targets were numerous but diminutive, and Whitaker, looking for bigger game, conserved his torpedoes. On the evening of July 7, a medium-sized freighter and escort arrived on the scene. Whitaker took advantage of screening rain to make a fast end-around. At 2,100 yards, he fired four after torpedoes. Explosions spurted in the night, and a burning freighter went under. She was KOTO MARU, 3,557 tons.

With these attrition sinkings, FLASHER was only warming up. On the morning of July 13, she contacted a two-ship convoy, and sent off a contact report to ANGLER and CREVALLE. At 0837 an escort headed for the submarine, and FLASHER had to outrun this busybody on the surface. Thirty minutes later a plane forced her down. The A/S vessel passed overhead at 15 knots without making contact. But FLASHER was unable to regain contact with the convoy.

The next six days proved uneventful—then came the event. Mid-morning of July 19, a ship was sighted as she emerged from the overcast, range 15,000 yards. The O.O.D. ordered submergence, and the approach was begun immediately. Target was identified as a KUMA-class cruiser, escorted by a destroyer. At 1103, the target showed a 30° port angle on the bow, and Whitaker headed the submarine in for a bow shot.

Then, at 1106, the cruiser gave Whitaker a 7° port angle. Whitaker ordered full speed ahead to cross the track for a stern shot. At 1110 four stern tubes were fired. Two hits were heard, and the submarine went deep.

The destroyer dropped a smart pattern of depth charges—15 in four minutes. At 1240 FLASHER was again at periscope depth, and there was the cruiser dead in the water, or with very little way on, obviously disabled. Whitaker closed the range to 3,200 yards, and fired four bow torpedoes spread to cover any speed error. All torpedoes missed. Another barrage of depth charges from the destroyer—another evasion by FLASHER—another rise to periscope depth. Three hours had elapsed since the first shot was fired at the cruiser. Intending to finish the affair, Whitaker rushed a forward reload, holding the submarine at 150-foot depth. FLASHER was almost ready for another go at the target when a thunderstorm of explosions echoed under the sea. At 1651, Whitaker was at the periscope. The Jap destroyer was alone in the seascape. The target, later identified as the 5,700-ton light cruiser OI, had sunk.

On July 25, FLASHER downed a good-sized freighter

to make this an outstanding patrol. The Japs could little afford to lose freighters that summer, and they could less afford the loss of a light cruiser. But worse than the loss of one light cruiser was the loss of two, as occurred during August, with the compliments of U.S. submarines CROAKER and HARDHEAD.

Croaker vs. Nagara

CROAKER was making her first war patrol; her area the East China Sea. Her skipper, Commander J. E. Lee, was a veteran with a record of several previous patrols. Maiden and veteran were equal to the occasion, when, on the morning of August 7, just south of Nagasaki, they encountered a light cruiser of the KUMA class.

The target, zigzagging radically, was escorted by a sub-chaser and a plane. Lee lost no time in firing four torpedoes from the stern tubes. Immediately after the torpedoes were launched, the target made a wide zig away. This doubtless would have caused the whole salvo to miss. But about two minutes later, the cruiser obligingly zagged, and veered back into the line of fire just in time to receive one hit.

The reactions of the sub-chaser and plane were somewhat less than efficient. While they ran around looking for the submarine, Lee was able to give all hands in the control party a periscope look at CROAKER's victim. To widen the audience, Lee and company proceeded to take color movies of the light cruiser's last moments.

This film—The Sinking of CL NAGARA—produced by CROAKER and directed by J. E. Lee—would not have been popular in Tokyo. Pearl Harbor, however, gave it good reviews.

Hardhead vs. Natori

By late August it appeared that the Japanese light cruiser was a standard bag for U.S. submarines on maiden patrol. The trend, started by SANDLANCE and BLUEGILL, and carried on by CROAKER, was stabilized into custom by the submarine HARDHEAD.

HARDHEAD left Pearl Harbor on July 27 to conduct her first patrol. Destination: Philippine waters. A few minutes after midnight on August 18, the submarine, patrolling east of Mindanao, picked up a radar pip suggestive of two targets—one large and one small. HARDHEAD's captain, Lieutenant Commander F. McMasters, was interested in the large. About an hour and a half later he could make out the target through binoculars at 8,000 yards. It looked like a heavy cruiser or a battleship. That was large enough for McMasters.

At 0237 HARDHEAD was in an attack position, and McMasters fired five Mark 23 torpedoes from the bow tubes. He then swung the submarine to the left, and three minutes later fired four Mark 18 electrics from the stern tubes. No hits were seen or heard from the first salvo, although the tracks indicated two hits were in order. From the second salvo, two hits were heard and seen. Flames climbed high up the warship's foremast, and in the glare of light the vessel assumed the proportions of a BB.

The escort headed east at about 10 knots, and McMasters gave chase. Just before dawn the submarine overhauled the quarry, and six torpedoes were fired. Apparently this one escaped. But target No. 1 went down.

On August 31, STURGEON, in the general vicinity of the sinking, fished from the sea a Japanese naval officer and three men. These soggy derelicts identified HARDHEAD's victim as the light cruiser NATORI. This was something of a comedown from the BB visualized by HARDHEAD. Such magnification and subsequent reduction was not uncommon during the war, for perspectives were difficult to judge at night, and silhouettes frequently proved illusory. Even daytime targets had a tendency to expand during the heat of battle and shrink under the cold analysis of inquiry. Yet, there were instances on record wherein large targets were reported as small ones, cruisers resembled destroyers, and destroyers appeared on the radar screen as pipsqueaks. A submarine on maiden patrol could be forgiven if her eyes dilated at her first engagement and her perspective was a little off.

Imperial Navy eyes must have done some dilating, too, when they saw another CL erased from the roster. AGANO—TATSUTA—YUBARI—OI—NAGARA—NATORI—six to U.S. submarines since February! But as NATORI went down in those early hours of August 18, worse news for Japanese Naval Headquarters was coming up.

Rasher vs. Taiyo (Otaka)

Japanese is a curious language. It contains no equivalent of the frank Anglo-Saxon "yes," the French "oui," the Dutch "ja," or the Russian "da." The somewhat indirect Japanese affirmative is "I am listening." Again, the Jap (perhaps to propitiate the gods) refers to fire as "the flowers." This is a pretty idiom—or so it must have seemed to the Japanese until their seamen came home telling about the submarines throwing nosegays around the Pacific and the ships going down all in blossom.

Then one would think a people whose language is so imaginative would have at tongue-tip an endless supply of names—names for freighters, tankers and other seagoing vessels. Curiously enough, in this matter the Japanese frequently resorted to numbers.

Thus there was UNKAI MARU No. 1 and No. 2 and No. 3—up to No. 15. And UNYO MARU from 1 to 8. And SHINSEI MARU from 1 to 18.

On the other hand, some of their naval vessels were given a variety of names. For example, early in the war KASUGA MARU, entering Kwajalein, was attacked by submarines. Doubtless the faulty torpedoes of the period let her live long enough to tell about it—and some time after that, she was steaming under the name of TAIYO. So the Japanese themselves must have been surprised to hear about a string of submarine attacks on an escort carrier dubbed OTAKA. This was an incorrect interpretation of Japanese characters found in captured documents. Result: OTAKA for TAIYO, a confusion that persisted throughout the war. The CVE OTAKA probably experienced more submarine attacks than any other ship in the Japanese Navy. Which is to say a good many torpedoes were fired at the escort carrier TAIYO, one-time KASUGA MARU. However, to a U.S. submarine a Jap escort carrier by any name was just as sweet.

The Japs might have been more surprised had they known the reason behind the longevity of such CVE's as TAIYO. The torpedo trouble, discussed in Chapter 20, needs no elaboration at this point. Except to remind that by the summer of 1944 it was over. As the torpedo defects had now been cured, the immunity of the Japanese escort carrier was ended. TAIYO (OTAKA) had been living on borrowed time. Steaming in Luzon Strait in mid-August, she met the bill collector.

But to begin with, she met REDFISH, patrolling as a member of "Donk's Devils" in "Convoy College." On the evening of the 17th the submarine sighted a convoy and started a surface chase, relaying the convoy's course and speed to her pack-mates PICUDA and SPADEFISH. These submarines were too distant to join the pursuit, and on the morning of the 18th REDFISH attacked on her own hook. Her torpedoes missed the selected target, but while she was shooting, she sighted a Japanese escort carrier. She took one shot at the CVE, and it got away.

The carrier was not to get far. REDFISH noted her course and speed, and then passed this information to another coordinated attack group operating off the northwest coast of Luzon. This SubSoWesPac group—BLUEFISH and RASHER—was under the leadership of Commander H. G. Munson, captain of RASHER. When informed of the REDFISH contact, RASHER was patrolling alone, just below Cape Bojeador. BLUEFISH (Commander C. M. Henderson) had raced off to attack a damaged tanker. The play was all RASHER's.

At 1905 Munson brought her to the surface and headed up the coast, intending to make a sweep as far as Cape Bojeador before BLUEFISH returned. At 2000 RASHER made radar contact with the reported convoy. At 15,000 yards Munson and crew could make out 13 ships with about six escorts.

Munson's description of the approach and attack contained the following observations:

The night was very dark, no moon, completely and thickly overcast with almost continuous rain—absolutely ideal conditions for night attack. Sound gear was of great help in all phases of the action to follow in identifying the escorts by their pinging and was used at this time in "sorting" the convoy. All attacks were made by radar only. Targets were easily detected and tracked at ranges up to 19,000 yards. . . . The speed, number of escorting vessels, great size of this convoy and of the individual ships, plus the intense aerial activity preceding its passage, convinced us that this was an exceptionally important convoy. . . . Took convoy course and tracked from ahead, determined base course 205°, speed 12 knots, zigging 10 degrees either side.

One of the ships turned on a large searchlight, thrusting its ghostly shaft northward down the sky. At 2108, after the light had gone out, RASHER . . .

. . . started in on starboard bow, unable to see any targets when desired firing point reached 1,500 yards ahead of starboard beam escort. Since the mutiplicity of targets . . . confused the radar operator who could not isolate the desired target, swung out at full power 900 yards ahead of the escort. As we steadied on the outbound course, the radar operator solved the bearing problem; we stopped, and at 2122 commenced firing a spread of four torpedoes from the stern tubes, on a 125° starboard track, gyro 5° right, spread 2°, range 2,800. After two torpedoes had been fired, it was doubted that the gyros were matching properly. Ceased fire, drew off and ran up along starboard flank to attack again. As we steadied down, both torpedoes were seen, heard and correctly timed to hit a huge tanker, apparently gasoline laden judging from the appalling explosion with a column of flame 1000 feet high. The entire sky was a bright red. . . . Part of the ship blew off and landed about 500 yards from the remainder of the tanker and both parts burned fiercely for about twenty minutes and then disappeared from sight in one grand final explosion.

The convoy broke up in a pandemonium of flashing lights, gunfire, arching tracers, thundering depth charges. Munson steered RASHER up the starboard side of the water carnival, keeping a distance of 4,000 yards from the hubbub. At 2201, after a reload, the submarine was headed in for another attack. Munson opened fire at 2211.

Fired six bow tubes, on a 71° starboard track, gyro 8° right, spread 2°, range 3,300 yards. Swung left at 2214—fired four stern tubes at a large target immediately to the left and a little farther out, on a 93° starboard track, gyro 13° right, spread 2°, range 3,750 yards.

Three hits were observed, heard and timed for one target off the bow. A second bow target was apparently hit. Two hits were seen, heard and timed on the stern-tube target. And:

Timed a fourth hit that indicated a stern tube torpedo hit on another unidentified target beyond the stern tube target. One half hour later the first stern tube target was plotted at speed zero, four miles from the attack position. Four hours later, while returning through this same vicinity, passed through a thick layer of oil roughly two and a half miles long, in a location only two miles from the last contact with the target.

Escorts rushed about, trying to locate RASHER, but the submarine easily eluded them. At 2245:

Broadcast another contact report as we needed help badly, being nearly fresh out of torpedoes, having but four forward and two aft as we reloaded. . . . 2300: The leading part of the convoy had split into two groups and we picked for our final attack the largest of the two groups remaining, which appeared to consist of at least two large ships in column with one very non-hostile escort on their starboard bow and a third large ship on the port quarter. They had changed base course to 270°. We crossed ahead of the convoy.

At 2230 RASHER was in position for a third attack. Munson fired the remaining four bow torpedoes at the leading target, and the two remaining stern torpedoes were fired at a second target. Three hits were scored on the first target, and two on the second, which exploded with a voluminous bombilation, burned a few minutes and disappeared from the radar screen. Just before midnight, contact was made with BLUEFISH, and Henderson's submarine was put on the trail of the convoy's remnants. RASHER continued to track and send out contact reports. Before the night was over, SPADEFISH (Commander Underwood) intercepted several of the fleeing ships, as did BLUEFISH. By dawn of the 19th, the area was strewn with wreckage and the sea bottom with wrecks. RASHER's score:

Date	Name	Type	Tonnage
August 18	Eishin Maru	Cargo	542
August 18	Teiyo Maru	Tanker	9,849
August 18	Otaka (Taiyo)	Escort Carrier	20,000
August 19	Teia Maru	Transport	17,537
Total: 47,928 tons			

All this on the night of August 18-19 in a battle that lasted less than three hours. But that was the sort of marine massacre which occurred when a submarine skipper fired 18 torpedoes for 16 hits. During the entire action, RASHER remained on the surface. Munson's aggressive conduct of this battle won for himself and his submarine a memorable place in American naval history.

The submarine achieved a notable record. TEIA MARU, the ocean liner which went down in the early hours of August 19, was the second largest merchant ship sunk by U.S. submarines in the war. And the RASHER patrol broke a tonnage record. Two weeks before the convoy battle, she had sunk the 4,739-ton freighter SHIROGANESAN MARU. This sinking, added to the four of the night of August 18-19, gave RASHER a total of 52,667 tons for this patrol. Only one U.S. submarine was to score a larger total during a single patrol.

As for the escort carrier "OTAKA," she was not recognized in the melee, and even that American version of her name was not entered in Munson's patrol report. Unidentified, she sank sometime during the night. A rather ignominious end for the CVE TAIYO.

Coming when it did, the loss of an escort carrier was a severe blow to the Imperial Navy. And American submarines continued to "say it with flowers."

Shad vs. Ihojima

Some hours before dawn on September 19, 1944, SHAD (Commander L. V. Julihn) made contact by radar and sound with a team of two enemy ships. SHAD was then on her seventh war patrol, her area just south of Honshu.

SHAD chased the convoy until dawn, when she submerged to evade a destroyer-type vessel which was busily searching the area. Julihn then directed a submerged approach. At 0553 the target made a sudden swerve that gave the submarine a gratuitously favorable attack position.

With a 90° angle on the bow, Julihn thought he recognized his target as a CHIDORI "pinger." At this silhouette he fired four Mark 23 torpedoes. SHAD was forced deep by a PC-boat before results could be observed. However, three properly timed hits were heard, and Sound reported the familiar breaking-up noises.

Post-war investigators experienced some difficulty in identifying SHAD's September 19 target. At first it seemed the vessel was the cruiser IHOJIMA, 2,500 tons, of Chinese extraction and formerly known as NING-HAI. At a later date, the Army-Navy Assessment Committee listed the vessel as the frigate IOSHIMA, approximately 900 tons. However one spelled it, she

BONE IN TEETH, a Jap DD pursues USS Barb, whose periscope is seen going under on the get-away. The submarine, commanded by Eugene B. Fluckey, has just torpedoed a tanker and the escort carrier Unyo. Date, September 15, 1944, found U.S. subs scoring heavily against IJN. Barb's was a high score.

THERE SHE GOES! *Famous periscope photo by* Seawolf. *Jap Patrol Boat No. 39 in act of diving to bottom after torpedo hit (April '43).*

COMDR. EUGENE B. FLUCKEY. *Awarded Congressional Medal of Honor for daring raid.*

LIGHT CRUISER NAGARA. *Before she met* Croaker. *Result of meeting (at right).*

CROAKER VS. NAGARA. *Jap light cruiser goes down off Nagasaki, August 7, 1944. By this date U.S. subs were hitting IJN with everything.*

AT TOP: *Light cruiser* Oi, *sunk by* Flasher, *July 19, 1944. Center: Seaplane tender hit by* Pargo's *torpedoes. Bottom: Jap Mitsuki-Class destroyers—game for U.S. submarines.*

JAP CL NATORI. *As she looked before sunk by* Hardhead *off Mindanao, August 18, 1944. Sighting her, sub skipper thought her a battleship; sank her posthaste.*

was some sort of naval vessel and SHAD sank her on the day in question.

Barb vs. Unyo

The Imperial Navy was still mourning the loss of TAIYO when another CVE was sunk by torpedo fire on the main line to the southward of Formosa. This escort carrier had the misfortune to fall afoul of "Ed's Eradicators" as they went wolf-packing across the waters of "Convoy College." Some of the eradicating forays of these submarines have been discussed in a previous chapter, as has the part played by BARB and QUEENFISH in rescuing the prisoners of war who survived the RAKYUO MARU disaster. As a pack, the "Eradicators" kept the Japanese in scalding water. In immediate focus is the episode wherein BARB boiled it under the Imperial Navy.

BARB was out on her ninth war patrol—her second under the leadership of Commander Eugene Fluckey. When Fluckey was on the bridge something was bound to happen—there were no exceptions to prove the rule. However, BARB's ninth patrol was "relatively uneventful" until early morning of August 31 when she made contact with an eight-ship convoy. The free-for-all that ensued was one of the liveliest of the season. It was during this battle that BARB torpedoed and sank the 5,633-ton freighter OKUNI MARU.

The submarine sweated out a diabolical depth-charging—58 blasts in all—and then went her way. Planes kept her bobbing up and down for the next few days, and one air bomb exploded close enough to powder a few light bulbs and wrench some fixtures out of place. On September 8, the pack encountered a second convoy. Firing at an escort, BARB experienced a "circular run." Several days after that she tangled with a pair of CHIDORI "pingers" who gave her a going-over. The following day (September 15) the "Eradicators" received word of the prison ship

sinking. Then QUEENFISH and BARB, heading for the rescue area at flank speed that evening, ran into another convoy and more CHIDORI's.

TUNNY had been damaged by an air bomb and forced to leave the pack. So the convoy-eradicating was up to QUEENFISH and BARB. At 2140 QUEENFISH told BARB she was attacking, and Fluckey held off until 2254, when the QUEENFISH onslaught was over. Then, with BARB on the surface, he maneuvered in.

The convoy consisted of five ships which had been moving in two columns of two ships each, with the fifth vessel—a large one—pacing between the pair at the rear. A destroyer led the formation, and escorts trotted along the flanks and quarters. Fluckey selected a large tanker for his target, and drove in. Closing for the attack, he identified the large vessel as a carrier.

Maneuvering on the surface, Fluckey worked for an "overlap" to bring both tanker and carrier in line of fire. While BARB did some fast weaving and darting to attain this position, she was sighted by a CHIDORI that came at her full gun.

When the CHIDORI was a scant 750 yards distant, Fluckey fired the bow nest at the overlapping targets, swung hard right and tried to bring the stern tubes to bear as BARB's six torpedoes sped at the tanker and carrier. No time! The CHIDORI was almost on top of the submarine, and Fluckey "pulled the plug." BARB went under and, by the width of her paint, missed being rammed.

On the way down the submariners heard two hits in the tanker and three in the carrier. One torpedo had broached. But five out of six were enough to settle the issue. A few depth charges were dropped, and as these came down Sound heard a charivari of breaking-up noises.

In the waters boiled by BARB, the 11,177-ton tanker AZUSA was escorting to the bottom the 20,000-ton CVE UNYO.

CHAPTER 27

SUBMARINES VS. THE JAPANESE NAVY (Continued)

Overture to Leyte Gulf

U.S. Marine and Army forces were installed in the southern Marianas by midsummer, and some 25,000 Japanese troops, the residue of the original garrison, prepared to die on the vine. These troops retired to interior positions where they put up a tooth-and-nail resistance. Mopping-up operations did not delay the westbound United States offensive.

Occupation of Saipan, Tinian and Guam gave United States forces control of the Marianas bastion at the edge of Japan's "inner defense zone." From this Central Pacific stage the Navy could launch a smashing drive at the Philippines, the Nansei Shotos or the Japanese home islands. Capture of the Marianas airfields provided Army Air with springboards for the B-29 Superfortresses that were soon to bomb the heart out of Tokyo.

As Japanese convoy runs to the Marianas were terminated, ComSubPac discontinued the "Pentathlon Patrol"—the "XYZ patrol" which had covered the southern Marianas. And "Pentathlon" submarines were now freed to operate in such areas as "Convoy College" below Formosa, "Dunkers Derby" off the Bonins, the "Polar Circuit" off the Kuriles, and "Hit Parade" off eastern Japan.

In the meantime, MacArthur's forces in the Southwest Pacific were girding for the big smash at the Philippines. Influenced by the factors discussed in Chapter 25, MacArthur timed "King Two"—the invasion of Leyte—for the third week in October. After the American occupation of Palau, the Japanese expected a Philippines hurricane, but its date and path troubled the War Lords in Tokyo who could not find the answers in the Japanese almanac.

The Imperial Navy had already devised "Sho-Go" —a plan for the defense of the Philippine Islands. Unfortunately for the inventors, the timing element for "Plan Sho-Go" did not mesh into gear with the high-speed wheels of "King Two." When America's operation roared into action, "Sho-Go" was unready. The Japanese plan had to go off half-cocked, and there is an old and inexorable rule about doing things by halves.

But Japan's military leaders were desperate. The flogging given the Combined Fleet in the Philippine Sea had sent it crawling to Okinawa in the Nansei Shotos—a whipped dragon with its tail between its legs. From there it dragged itself home to its lair in Japan's Inland Sea. It could not, however, curl up and convalesce in this hide-away. At once it had to recuperate for "Operation Sho-Go," and the American offensives in the Central and Southwest Pacific were allowing no time for recuperation.

Moreover, the dragon had arrived home with its fires almost out, and panting with thirst. Only to find drying oil tanks and dusty pumps. So it eventuated that once again the U.S. submarine attack on Japan's main oil line forced the Imperial Navy's strategic hand. From Kure, Japan, Admiral Kurita's Second Fleet was dispatched in July to the southern end of the South China Sea where it was to train near Singapore at the island of Lingga. Questioned later about this move, Admiral Kurita was explicit. *"The shortage of fuel in the home area required training operations at Lingga."*

Thus the main body of the Japanese dragon was compelled to detach itself from the crippled frame and run to a remote haven for sustenance, leaving its wings and lesser members behind in Nippon. The quoted statement by Kurita dissolves any doubt that this cleavage of the Jap Fleet was not a forced move—an expedient to the Imperial Navy's disadvantage. Strategists might question that point, but there can be no gainsaying the crucial oil shortage in Japan and the fact that last-resort expediency is seldom advantageous.

Ozawa's carrier force—the "wings" which remained in Japan—had absorbed the bulk of the punishment given the Combined Fleet in the Philippine Sea. Bereft of three first-line carriers, most of its aircraft and nearly all of its complement of naval pilots, this force had reached home waters in deplorable condition. Fuel shortage or no, it could not put to sea until repairs and replacements were contrived. Repairs could be rushed. New ships and planes might be slapped together in time. But naval aviators were not so readily produced.

Then, while green recruits were being jammed through air schools, the summer burned away. Loss of the 20,000-ton escort carriers TAIYO and UNYO complicated the naval-air problem. The autumnal skies darkened and the glass fell in the Philippines before the Japanese carrier airmen were schooled. No question of separating wheat from chaff—Ozawa's aviators, undrilled in teamwork and untrained in deck landings, were all chaff. The dragon was called upon to fight with its wings clipped.

Halsey and Mitscher brought the issue to a head. After a strike at Okinawa in the second week of October, Halsey led the United States Third Fleet toward Formosa, and Mitscher's carrier planes gave that Japanese bulwark a taste of things to come. Counter-attacking fiercely, Japanese aircraft dealt the new cruisers HOUSTON and CANBERRA a blasting. The cruisers were severely damaged, but the Jap airmen, ignoring their own appalling losses, reported the targets destroyed. They went on to embellish the report with a jubilant announcement of a great victory over Mitscher's carrier force. Thereupon Imperial Headquarters made a rash radio broadcast, declaring that the Japanese Navy was out to abolish the remnant American fleet.

A number of Toyoda's warships did steam south from Japan, hoping to find an abbreviated United States force awaiting slaughter. Air search soon dispelled this phantasy. The Japanese warships took cover while Halsey cheerfully informed Nimitz that the "sunk" cruisers were very much afloat and the Third Fleet was "retiring at full speed toward the enemy."

Halsey's "retirement" sent the Third Fleet steaming in the direction of Leyte Gulf to support the "King Two" offensive. And the Imperial Navy's High Command was left to explain away a lot of hot air. But hot-air explanations were beginning to leave the Japanese people cold. Mr. San and Mr. Moto, weary of phantom victories, were demanding action. The situation in the Philippines theater also demanded action. Having shot off its mouth, the Imperial Navy's High Command was now compelled to shoot off its guns.

According to Admiral Toyoda (post-war reminiscence) the Japanese Navy was hard put to carry out Defense Plan "Sho-Go" at the time the United States offensive struck the Philippines. *"We felt that to take the task force into Leyte was to take a big gamble; and while it would not be accurate to say that we were influenced by public opinion, questions were beginning to be asked at home as to what the Navy was doing after loss of one point after another down south. . . . But since without the participation of our Combined Fleet there was no possibility of the land-based forces in the Philippines having any chance against your forces at all, it was decided to send the whole fleet, taking the gamble. If things went well, we might obtain unexpectedly good results; but if the worst should happen, there was a chance that we would lose the entire fleet. But I felt that that chance had to be taken."*

A lesser Japanese naval officer put it this way: *"We had to do something, so we did our best. It was the last chance we had, although not a very good one."*

These doleful comments bear an acute tonal resemblance to the lament voiced by Captain Concas of the MARIA TERESA when Admiral Cervera ordered the Spanish fleet out of Santiago and a blurting of bugles signaled the foolish attack on the waiting Americans. *"The bugles were the last echo, a signal that four centuries of greatness was ended. 'Poor Spain,' I said to my beloved and noble Admiral, and he answered by an expressive motion."* The Spaniards, of course, were courting suicide. And the Japanese admirals in October 1944 were prepared to make the same gesture. *Hara-kiri* to save face was all part of the tradition.

But Cervera was in it personally, whereas Commander-in-Chief Admiral Toyoda selected Ozawa's carrier force for the suicide. This was a spur-of-the-moment arrangement, not a part of the original "Sho-Go Plan." So impromptu was the decision that, according to Ozawa's Chief of Staff, it was settled

389

by a hasty telephone call. At any rate, Kurita was ordered to bring the main body north from Singapore waters, and Ozawa with his four available carriers was ordered to race south from Japan. A third naval force, under Admiral Shima, was dispatched south from Formosa. The three Japanese forces were to converge on Leyte Gulf, but only Kurita's fleet and Shima's force were supposed to get there.

Ozawa's carriers were to perform a dual mission. The carrier aircraft were to strike at the United States Third Fleet and then (since the pilots were untrained in deck landings) proceed to the airfields of Luzon. The Japanese carriers, their planes gone, would remain in the Philippine Sea to lure the American fleet northward. As decoy ducks, Ozawa's carriers would probably be blown to Kingdom Come. That was realized. But the Imperial Navy—or, at least, Toyoda—was willing to make this sacrifice on the assumption that Kurita's Second Fleet and Shima's force would be able to run eastward through the Philippine straits and attack the American invasion shipping in Leyte Gulf.

Kurita was ordered to demolish McArthur's transports in Leyte Bay, whatever the cost. Here was the Japanese Navy's last chance. For loss of Leyte would certainly mean loss of the Philippines. And loss of the Philippines meant loss of all East Indies oil—a deprivation Japan's sea forces could never survive. In Japanese idiom, this was It. The Imperial Navy was out to do or die. Incidentally, the word "sho" is Japanese for "conquer." Applied to a defensive operation, it seems slightly ambiguous. But the whole "Sho-Go" project was haphazard, mussy-minded and ambiguous. However—

Although destruction seemed in the cards for Ozawa's force, Toyoda's plan of action was not quite as suicidal as Cervera's decision to steam out of Santiago. There was some chance that the carrier decoys might get away. And Kurita's force, built around seven battleships, was a formidable fleet. The battleship group included the monster twins YAMATO and MUSASHI, largest BB's in the world. Thirteen cruisers and 18 destroyers escorted these giants. When Toyoda gave the order to move, one of the world's decisive naval battles was in the making.

U.S. submarines were to have a four-ace hand in the decision.

Submarines Intercept the Enemy

Toyoda's plans were, of course, unknown to the American naval leaders. But information trickled in from various sources. Much could be learned from putting two and two together, and more could be learned from SubPac and SubSoWesPac submarines patrolling off Luzon, off the Nansei Shotos and off Japan. By mid-October it was evident that the Japanese were mustering all available sea forces for a showdown battle in the Philippines.

On October 15, the submarine BESUGO (Commander T. L. Wogan) called the turn when she sighted Ozawa's carrier force coming out of the Bungo Suido. Between 0800 and 0900, three heavy cruisers and one light cruiser were spotted heading southeast into open sea at 18 knots. At 1115, one large, unidentified warship and a destroyer were sighted on the same course, speed 20 knots. The following day BESUGO reported two more heavy cruisers in sortie from the Bungo Suido. Wogan maneuvered to intercept one of these. A torpedo salvo went streaking at the target, and BESUGO reported the cruiser damaged.

Off the Nansei Shoto, SKATE (Commander R. B. Lynch) ambushed one of the cruiser trio which had raced from the Bungo Suido on the 15th. SKATE reported damage to this vessel.

The word from BESUGO and SKATE told Nimitz that the Japanese Navy was coming out for a fight, and Halsey's Third Fleet prepared to meet the threat from the home Empire with appropriate countermeasures. Air search was begun over Surigao and San Bernardino Straits. In the East China Sea and below Formosa the watch was alerted. On October 17, advance units of Kinkaid's Seventh Fleet put Ranger battalions ashore on several islands commanding the entrances to Leyte Gulf. This move was a preliminary to MacArthur's main landings, scheduled for the 20th. The sortie by Ozawa's carrier force did not derange the timetable for "King Two."

D-Day landings were made on schedule. Losses were light, and General MacArthur announced,

OPERATIONS PROCEEDING SPLENDIDLY IN EVERY RESPECT. STRATEGICALLY, ENEMY SEEMS CAUGHT UNAWARES, APPARENTLY IN ANTICIPATION OF ATTACK TO SOUTHWARD. HIS MINDANAO FORCES ARE ALREADY PRACTICALLY ISOLATED AND NO LONGER ARE AN IMMEDIATE FACTOR IN THE CAMPAIGN.

But naval action was impending. On October 21, SEADRAGON (Commander J. H. Ashley, Jr.) reported a Japanese carrier, two cruisers and six destroyers off the southern tip of Formosa. The warships were doing 18 knots on a course that would bring them down the South China Sea along the western coast of Luzon. SEADRAGON attacked the group, and hit the carrier and one of the cruisers. Counter-attack by the escorts forced her deep, and she was unable to ascertain the extent of the damage.

In the same area SHARK II (Commander E. N. Blakely) reported contact with four large vessels and three smaller ones on the same course, rushing at 22 knots. BLACKFISH (Commander R. F. Sellars) reported one carrier, two cruisers and six destroyers steaming toward Luzon.

Far to the north, SEA DOG (Commander V. L. Lowrance), patrolling below Kyushu, sighted a large convoy heading southeast under heavy escort. And ICEFISH (Commander R. W. Peterson) in Luzon Strait reported two heavy cruisers and three destroyers steaming on a run that would take them down the east coast of Luzon.

So SubPac periscopes watched the forces of Ozawa and Shima, and SubPac torpedoes struck at these ships as they raced down on the Philippines. But "King Two," although supported throughout by Admiral Halsey's Third Fleet, was entirely a Southwest Pacific operation. Thus the bulk of the submarine support for "King Two" fell to the SubSoWesPac Force operating with Admiral Kinkaid's Seventh Fleet.

As noted in the chapter, *Submarine Support of Fleet Operations*, ComSubSoWesPac deployed his submarines for "King Two" in positions which covered the South China Sea and Sulu Sea approaches to the Philippines.

Submarines DARTER, DACE, ROCK and BERGALL were stationed in the Palawan Passage area to block the enemy in those waters. BLACKFIN was stationed northwest of Palawan and GURNARD was stationed off Brunei Bay. COBIA was on watch near Sibutu Passage and BATFISH was in the Sulu Sea off northwest Mindanao. Guarding the approaches to Manila were ANGLER and GUITARRO. Farther north, off the west coast of Luzon, were BREAM, CERO, NAUTILUS and COD.

If the Imperial Navy courted a showdown, the United States forces on the sea, over the sea and under the sea were prepared to oblige. The submarines from Fremantle dealt the first hammer blows at the oncoming Japanese.

Bream vs. Aoba

Action off western Luzon was begun early in the morning of October 23 by the submarine BREAM, captained by the veteran Commander W. G. "Moon" Chapple.

BREAM was on the surface 12 miles south of Cape Calavite when she sighted three Japanese warships in column—two heavy cruisers and a light cruiser. The light cruiser was leading the column. Chapple selected the first heavy cruiser for his target, and sent the submarine running in for a surface attack.

Here is an excerpt from Chapple's patrol report:

> Shortly before firing, the cruiser was observed to make a 360° turn to her left, and a very strong odor of gunpowder was smelled by all hands on the bridge and even by some in the conning tower. . . . It is conceivable that when the cruiser turned into the wind he launched a plane and the powder smell was from the catapult charge. . . . Men could be plainly seen running to their battle stations as the big baby drew up on our port quarter only 800 yards away.

At 0324, Chapple opened fire. Six torpedoes fanned out like spectral fingers reaching for the cruiser. At the sixth shot, Chapple gave the order to go down. As BREAM burrowed under, a tremendous flash lit the night and the sea seemed to be thundering as the submarine went deep. The smitten vessel was the heavy cruiser AOBA. She managed to stay afloat, but severe injury eliminated her from the Battle for Leyte Gulf.

Dace and Darter vs. Maya, Atago, Takao

In the early hours of October 23 two other SubSoWesPac submarines were bent on cruiser elimination. These were DACE (Commander B. D. Claggett) and DARTER (Commander D. H. McClintock). The eliminating process began on October 10 when the pair, teamed up as a wolf-pack under the leadership of Commander McClintock, commenced combing the seas between northeast Borneo and that perilous patch of water off Palawan known as "Dangerous Grounds."

On October 11, McClintock was directed by ComSubSoWesPac to conduct a dual patrol that would cover the western approach to Balabac Strait and the southern approach to Palawan Passage. DACE and DARTER were ordered to be on the alert for enemy naval forces which might be northbound from Singapore.

Three days after that, DACE flushed a convoy off North Borneo. Claggett fired fatal torpedoes to score a double and down two good-sized Japanese freighters. But these vessels were small potatoes compared to what was coming.

Coming was the Imperial Second Fleet—Admiral Kurita's battleship force, led by super-battleships YAMATO and MUSASHI. Straight for Palawan this big-gun fleet was heading—an armada of juggernauts that, by comparison, reduced the two submarines in its path to a pair of toothpicks.

Upon reaching Brunei on the northwest coast of Borneo, Kurita's fleet divided into two task forces. Under Vice Admiral Nishimura, two over-age battleships, the rehabilitated cruiser MOGAMI and four destroyers were to pass south of Palawan Island, steam across the Sulu Sea and rendezvous with Shima's Formosa fleet in the Mindanao Sea. This group was then to strike for Leyte Gulf through Surigao Strait. The main body, under Kurita, was to pass north of Palawan, cross the Sibuyan Sea and head eastward through San Bernardino Strait. This force consisted of five battleships, including the two giants, a dozen cruisers and 14 destroyers. Defending Palawan water, DARTER and DACE were certain to contact either one task force or the other. They found themselves pitted against Kurita's main body.

Early in the morning of October 21, DARTER's radio picked up a news broadcast of MacArthur's landing on Leyte. McClintock reasoned that the enemy fleet from Singapore would probably head for the short-cut route to Leyte Gulf—Balabac Strait. Accordingly, he headed DARTER for Balabac, and late that evening the submarine made radar contact with three large warships. DARTER tracked them for seven hours, reporting the contacts.

The ships were traveling at high speed, and the submarine was unable to overhaul. Morning of October 22, McClintock abandoned the pursuit and headed southward for a rendezvous with DACE. Midnight, October 22-23, the two submarines were within hailing distance of each other. One can glimpse in imagination these two little subs drawing together in the tropic dark, two small submarines reduced to the size of minnows by the sea's dark vastness. McClintock's patrol report tells the story:

0000: Speaking to DACE, planning remainder of patrol.
0016: Radar contact.
0017: By megaphone to DACE—"We have contact. Let's go!"
0020: Bearing changing to left. Both subs closing at full power. Came to normal approach course. Targets headed up Palawan passage.

Between now and dawn sent out three contact reports, giving final estimate that ships were a task force of eleven heavy ships. This based on their high speed. Tracking party said that gaining attack position was hopeless due to high target speed (initial estimate, 22 knots). We managed to average about 19 knots. Estimates of enemy speed began to drop until finally it was 15 knots. We had them now! Enemy course 039 degrees true. DARTER was to attack left flank column first, at dawn, with DACE about five miles up the track in position to attack starboard column. Did not attack in darkness, as it was considered vital to see and identify the force which was probably on its way to interfere with the Leyte landing. It was felt that there could be no radical dawn zig due to size of force and narrowness of Palawan passage. Targets did not zig during night.

0425: 20,000 yards dead ahead of port column of heavy ships. Slowed to 15 knots. Biggest ship is last in port column. Picked it as target.
0509: Reversed course, headed towards port column and submerged. (DACE had just passed us to dive to northeast.) DARTER planned to attack from west in half light of dawn at 0540.
0527: First four ships in column identified as heavy cruisers. Fifth one is probably a battleship.
0528: Range is 2,880 yards to first cruiser in column.
0532: Commenced firing bow tubes at leading cruiser. After firing two into him and one spread ahead, target was rearing by so close that we couldn't miss, so spread the remainder inside his length. Then swung hard left (to bring stern tubes to bear) while getting set up on second cruiser.
0533: Torpedoes started hitting first cruiser. Five hits. Commenced firing stern tubes at second cruiser. Whipped periscope back to first target to see the sight of a lifetime. (Cruiser was so close that all of her could not be seen at once with periscope in high power.) She was a mass of billowing black smoke from the number one turret to the stern. No superstructure could be seen. Bright orange flames shot out from the side along the main deck from the bow to the after turret. Cruiser was already down by the bow, which was dipping under. Number one turret was at water level. She was definitely finished. Five hits had her sinking and in flames. It is estimated that there were few, if any, survivors.
0534: Started deep. Evaded. Heard four hits in second cruiser. Felt certain that four hits would sink this one too.
0539: Depth charge attack began. Four destroyers milling about overhead.
0540: Commenced hearing breaking up noises on sound gear, roughly where the targets should be stopped. Noises could be heard through our hull in all compartments. They increased until they seemed to be right overhead and shook the submarine violently. Heavy rumblings and explosions.
0557: Heard four distant torpedo explosions in rapid succession. Probably DACE firing. The Japs must think our submarines are everywhere at once.
From 0600 to 0604 there were tremendous explosions, probably magazines. It is estimated that from 0600 on, our targets' breaking up noises began to combine with those of DACE's targets.
0605: Depth charges began again. Probably meant for DACE this time. A total of about 36 were heard. From this time on more distant breaking up noises and distant rumbling explosions (not depth charges) could be heard until about 0625.
0630: Last of depth charges.

0820: At periscope depth: One ATAGO-class cruiser sighted, range 12,000 yards, at our attack position, listing slightly to starboard and dead in the water. No steam up. Three destroyers were near him and three planes circled the vicinity. No smoke coming from cruiser.

1100: Started in towards cruiser.

1300: Range to cruiser 8,000 yards. Two destroyers patrolling on beam at range of 4,000 yards from target. Four planes circling overhead. Decided we would never get to fire from beam with destroyers where they were, so commenced working around to bow.

1430: Range 7,000 yards to cruiser. Coming in on port bow of target when destroyers both headed towards us. When range about 3,500 yards on closest destroyer, and still coming in, went deep and evaded. Could not attack destroyers since our torpedoes were for the cruiser. Decided to wait until tonight when combined attacks of DARTER and DACE would outwit the destroyers.

1500: Cruiser seen hoisting out a boat. He must have some steam now. Sunset—Too close to cruiser to surface for star sights.

1915: Surfaced. Cruiser in sight on radar. Proceeding to rendezvous with DACE. Sent contact report on the stopped cruiser and estimated composition of the remainder of the Jap force.

2100: Cancelled rendezvous because DACE not yet sighted and reduced visibility rendering immediate attack favorable. DACE ordered to take attack position ten miles from cruiser; bearing 150 degrees true; and DARTER ten miles bearing 050 degrees true from cruiser. (Thought destroyers would attempt to tow cruiser in our direction towards Palawan Barrier Reef.)

2200: Cruiser underway, speed varied from four to six knots; course was erratic as though target was steering with screws. One destroyer patrolling on each beam.

2245: Started in for surface attack in very poor visibility. Planned to attack from starboard quarter, coming in last mile slowly on battery. Told DACE we would attack in 90 minutes and to sink him if we were forced down.

2400: About one hour to run to gain attack position ahead. Making about 17 knots.

0005: (October 25th). Navigator plotting in conning tower. Grounded on Bombay Shoal with tremendous crash.

In the meantime, DACE, having contacted the enemy, was in the thick of it, as noted by DARTER. Interesting to follow Commander Claggett's blow-by-blow account as it synchronizes with McClintock's. At 0532 on the morning of October 23, DACE heard five torpedo explosions and Claggett noted that "DARTER must be getting in."

0534: Four more torpedo hits. DARTER is really having a field day. Can see great pall of smoke completely enveloping spot where ship was at last look. Do not know whether he has sunk, but it looks good. Ship to left is also smoking badly. Looks like a great day for the DARTER. Can see two destroyers making smoke headed for scene. There is much signalling, shooting of Very stars, etc. It is a great show. The big ships seem to be milling around. I hope they don't scatter too far for me to get in. Light is still pretty bad but I have counted eight large ships, battleships or cruisers plus two destroyers. Two of these large ships have been hit so far.

0542: The situation is beginning to clear up. I have now picked a target. It looks like a battleship. Range 7,000 yards.

0545: Have identified target as a heavy cruiser of the ATAGO or NACHI-class. There are two of these, but can now see a larger ship astern. Looks like a battleship! Famous statement: "Will let them go by . . . they are only heavy cruisers!" Shifted targets. He is taking evasive action from the DARTER's position; if he doesn't settle down and present a good set-up, there are two more coming up the line. This is really a submariner's dream . . . sitting right in front of a task force! If I only had some torpedoes aft! After the DARTER's attack the formation has broken up so that I can't estimate too well how the ships were originally formed, but now with better light conditions I have seen the following: two ATAGO or NACHI cruisers leading a battleship or CA (my target); there are two other battleships believed to be the ISE-class in column about 1,500 yards to the westward, and behind my target presenting a zero angle on the bow. There are several destroyers milling around DARTER's position about six miles away. There is one large unidentified ship well to eastward; this looks like either a carrier or perhaps another battleship; however, I can't make him out very well. Total: eight heavy ships, four destroyers.

0552: The two cruisers passed ahead at about 1,500 yards. They were overlapping; appeared to be running screen for my target. Had a beautiful view of them and identified them positively as ATAGO or NACHI-class. My target can be seen better now, and appears to be a KONGO-class battleship. He looks larger than the two cruisers that have just passed ahead. He has two stacks, and superstructure appears much heavier. Sound also reports target screws as heavier and slower than those of cruisers.

0554: Commenced firing a salvo of six bow tubes. Fired One, Two, Three, Four, Five, Six. Took quick look around and saw next battleship still close, so started deep, turning into his wake.

0556: First hit! Second hit! Third hit! Fourth hit!

0601: Heard two tremendous explosions both on sound and through the hull. These explosions were apparently magazines as I have never heard anything like it. The soundmen said that it sounded as if the bottom of the ocean were blowing up. They were obviously shallow as there was neither any shaking of the boat nor water swishing through the superstructure. Nothing could cause this much noise except magazines exploding.

0603: Heard tremendous breaking up noises. This was the most gruesome sound I have ever heard. I was at first convinced that it was being furnished by the DACE, and called for a check of all compartments. Was much relieved to receive reports that everything was all right. Noise was coming from the northeast, the direction of the target, and it sounded as if she was coming down on top of us. I have never heard anything like it. Comment from Diving Officer:

"We better get the hell out of here!"

After about five minutes of these tremendous breaking up noises, continued to have smaller ones and much crackling noises for the next twenty minutes. These noises could be heard on sound and throughout the boat.

0605: First depth charge—not close, but they got progressively closer, and we received a severe working over the next half hour.

1100: At periscope depth. Nothing in sight. Commenced re-load and served breakfast.

1425: Saw tops of masts, headed for same.

1510: Can now make out target as a damaged ATAGO cruiser guarded by two destroyers patrolling well out. He also has air cover. Decided that possibilities of getting in for a daylight attack are pretty slim. Cruiser is definitely stopped at scene of DARTER attack, and there doesn't seem to be much possibility of his getting away. Will clean salt water out of sump this afternoon, get in partial battery charge tonight, and make a submerged night attack.

2256: DARTER says she will try surface attack from quarter. If she is forced down or chased away by destroyers, we are to attack her bow.

2330: Received message that DARTER was making end around to west, was instructed to attack when ready. Commenced end around for better background for submerged attack. Night is dark, but have good horizon to east and will be able to make out target against it.

0007: (October 24th). Received message from DARTER saying she was aground.

Loss of Darter

DARTER was jammed, and in a most precarious position. Making 17 knots, she had ridden up to a draft of nine feet forward, and the reef held her in a relentless clutch. Desperate efforts to get clear were unavailing. The night roared with enemy aircraft. Any moment a Jap warship might come lunging from the dark. The submarine was trapped.

Parenthetically it should be remarked that Commander McClintock had fully realized the dangers involved in the end-around maneuver which had brought DARTER to grief. The incident is considered a classic example of calculated risk. It was regarded by the Submarine Command as one of the unfortunate tactical mishaps always possible in submarine warfare, and McClintock was not held in any way at fault.

DARTER's call to DACE brought Claggett's submarine maneuvering to her aid. Aboard DARTER all confidential papers were burned and secret equipment was smashed. DACE came nosing up through the gloom. Claggett's report of the rescue follows:

0153: Flooded down and approached DARTER. Got line over from bow to DARTER's stern and commenced rescue operations. Salvage impossible. Transferring DARTER personnel via two rubber boats, a slow task. Used up half the battery maneuvering to keep off reef. Current setting me on.

0439: Last boat containing Commanding Officer and Executive Officer of DARTER came aboard. Cast off and backed clear. Received word that demolition charges and warhead were set for 0455, so decided to wait until then before torpedoing.

0500: Heard slight explosion, but can see no damage.

0510: Fired two torpedoes at DARTER. Both exploded on reef.

0530: Fired two more. No apparent damage.

0545: Commenced firing with deck gun. Expended 30 rounds of ammunition. These appeared to do little damage.

0558: Caught by plane in the unenviable position of lying to with 25 men topside. Submerged with ammunition on deck and gun trained out. Heard two explosions which sounded like small bombs. Plane apparently picked DARTER for target.

0805: Surfaced to send message requesting assistance in destroying DARTER.

Redoubtable DARTER was not to be easily destroyed. In mid-morning a Japanese DD prowled up to the reef and lay to. Aircraft hovered over the warship, but this protection was unnecessary as DACE was out of torpedoes. Forced to hold DACE at safe distance, Claggett and McClintock could only stand by helplessly while the enemy inspected the stranded submarine.

That evening Claggett brought DACE to the surface and headed her toward DARTER, intending to use his own demolition outfit for the necessary destruction. But as DACE was closing in on DARTER, enemy "pinging" was heard. It sounded like a Japanese submersible, and the American submariners turned to meet this unseen adversary. Later that night DACE received permission to leave the area.

While DACE was on her way home with DARTER's crew, the submarine ROCK (Lieutenant Commander J. J. Flachsenhar) was dispatched to Bombay Shoal to destroy stranded DARTER. Flachsenhar fired 10 torpedoes at the abandoned submarine. But again destruction was frustrated as the torpedoes exploded in futile fury against the intervening reef.

Finally, on October 31, NAUTILUS (Lieutenant Commander G. A. Sharp) arrived off the shoal with orders to destroy DARTER. Firing point-blank, NAUTILUS' gunners pumped 55 shattering 6-inch shells into the target. As NAUTILUS concluded the bombardment, her commander noted, *"It is doubtful that any equipment in DARTER at 1131 this date would be of any value to Japan—except as scrap."*

So a valiant submarine came to her end. She did not lie alone in those dangerous waters off Palawan. Not many miles from DARTER's shallow grave were the deep-buried bones of Admiral Kurita's flagship, the heavy cruiser ATAGO, sent to the bottom by DARTER's torpedoes. And not far from ATAGO's grave lay the remains of the heavy cruiser MAYA, torpedoed by DARTER's pack-mate DACE.

Hit by torpedoes from DARTER, a third Japanese heavy cruiser, the IJN TAKAO, a floundering cripple, had limped down the Borneo coast to Brunei. From there she went to Singapore where she remained for the duration, paralyzed by a wrecked engine.

Whereas Japanese fatalities on board ATAGO and MAYA had been heavy, no American lives were lost through the DARTER grounding—thanks to expert seamanship on the part of the crew, high-caliber leadership on the part of her skipper, and courageous rescue work by DACE. All hands jubilant over the victory, the conquerors of ATAGO, TAKAO and MAYA made home port.

To preserve the DARTER crew as a crack fighting unit, Headquarters assigned it intact to MENHADEN, then building at Manitowoc, Wisconsin.

Sho-Go Show-Down

It remains for the future historian to analyze with proper perspective the Battle for Leyte Gulf—perhaps the most complex sea fight of the Pacific War—and evaluate the part played therein by submarines. Authorities may disagree concerning American fleet tactics or Japanese strategy. Experts may hold this action or that juncture the turning point. Certain it is, however, that the work of the SoWesPac submarines on the fateful morning which preceded the epic three-day fleet engagement will always be featured in any discussion of the battle which ended the career of the Imperial Navy.

In putting out of action four of Japan's largest and finest heavy cruisers, BREAM, DACE and DARTER decisively influenced the battle's tide. The sinking of ATAGO and MAYA, the damaging of TAKAO and AOBA were setbacks the Imperial Navy could ill afford as it advanced for the final showdown. Two major warships sprawling to sea bottom before the battle fleet had even started its dash through the Philippines! Two more sent hobbling back to port so badly crippled they would never again enter combat! Toyoda must have known, on the morning of October 23, that the gamble was lost.

But the die was cast; there could be no revision of "Plan Sho-Go" at this late date—no backward turning. Dispossessed of his flagship ATAGO, Admiral Kurita transferred himself, his flag and his staff officers to the mighty battleship YAMATO. Had ATAGO sunk more precipitately, this personnel transference might not have been accomplished. But the torpedoed cruiser managed to stay afloat for 30 minutes before taking the plunge.

"It did not interfere with the plan; in fact, it rather improved control. The shift to the YAMATO improved the command possible because she was designated as a flagship and communications were therefore better and the AA defense was also better."

So said Vice Admiral Kurita—afterwards. Leaving one to wonder why, if YAMATO were the better flagship of the two, the admiral did not fly his flag in her in the first place. Certainly a transfer at sea—a hasty packing of code books and a jumpy journey in a launch—must have been inconvenient.

Rear Admiral Tomiji Koyanagi—Kurita's Chief of Staff—seems to have disagreed with Kurita's statement that the shift from ATAGO to YAMATO "improved control." Interrogated after the war, Koyanagi responded as quoted in the following excerpt from a United States Strategic Bombing Survey report.

Q. Do you feel that having your flagship sunk by submarines and having to change flagships had serious consequences on the subsequent conduct of the operation?

A. First we transferred to two destroyers and by the time we passed Palawan Strait we had shifted the flag to YAMATO. It was fortunate that the accident or damage occurred before the battle started. We felt great inconvenience on the destroyer. Communication was only by flashlight.

Q. But once you got aboard the YAMATO did everything go smoothly, was everything all right or was there still trouble?

A. *The most trouble we felt was communication. Half the personnel of the communication staff of the previous flagship was killed in the torpedoing, so lack of personnel caused communications trouble when we got aboard the YAMATO.*

Koyanogi went on to say that it did not "interfere seriously." However, any communications difficulty must have been serious to a fleet on its way to do or die, with an Empire's life in the balance. Kurita himself, when queried about communications, replied:

"I thought that the communications were not entirely adequate partly because, when I switched my flag from ATAGO to YAMATO, communications personnel were divided between two destroyers, one of which had to accompany the TAKAO back to Brunei, and for that reason I consider that the communications were not adequate."

The admiral's reference to TAKAO puts another angle on the torpedoing of this second DARTER victim. A wounded ship frequently proves more burdensome than an abandoned one. TAKAO had to limp away on the arm of an escort, and the escort, as it happened, carried off half of Kurita's surviving communications personnel.

Then, asked if he had received as much information about American forces throughout the Leyte operation as he had expected, Kurita stated, *"From the first I did not think I was getting enough."* Somewhat inconsistently, he attributed this failure to lack of scouting, not communications trouble. Nevertheless, abundant evidence indicates that communications difficulties plagued the Second Fleet. For a time it was out of touch with Nishimura's task force. Messages did not get through to Tokyo Headquarters or Kurita's fleet, as Captain Ohmae, Ozawa's senior staff officer, recalled in post-war testimony.

"Four messages were sent on the 24th from the Japanese Third (Ozawa's) Fleet to Tokyo and to the Second (Kurita's) Fleet. They were not received, and I think the lack of success of the entire operation depended upon that failure of communication."

The U.S. Navy's submariners would be the last deponents to declare that DARTER's torpedoing of ATAGO and TAKAO caused a communications foulup that, in turn, cost the Imperial Navy the Battle for Leyte Gulf. But if the post-war statements of Admirals Kurita and Koyanagi and Captain Ohmae can be trusted, the DARTER foray created much confusion.

Having delayed to change flagships on the morning of October 23, Kurita continued northward with his armada. The Jap battlewagons skirted the Caiamian Islands north of Palawan and swung eastward to clear the southern tip of Mindoro. At the same time,

Nishimura's task force was rushing east across the Sulu Sea to join Shima's task group in the Mindanao Sea. And far to the north, Admiral Ozawa's carrier force was approaching the northeast coast of Luzon. There was nothing wrong with American communications, and Admiral Halsey received a stream of submarine contact reports which gave him a running account of the enemy's moves.

Halsey redeployed his forces to meet the oncoming foe. He stationed one task group (Rear Admiral G. F. Bogan) east of San Bernardino Strait to stop Kurita's emergence from that passage. He sent another task group (Rear Admiral R. E. Davison) to stand by east of Leyte Gulf and reinforce Admiral Kinkaid's Seventh Fleet which was plugging the eastern end of Surigao Strait. A third task group (Rear Admiral F. C. Sherman) was ordered to stand off Luzon and cover the sea lanes coming down from the north. Thus all roads to Leyte Gulf were blocked. As the Imperial Navy discovered on the morning of October 24th.

By mid-morning of the 24th, Davison's search planes had located Nishimura's eastbound force in the Sulu Sea, and American bombs were raining down on this luckless batch of targets. Simultaneously, Kurita's eastbound fleet was spotted from the air as it skirted the southern reaches of Mindoro. Both Bogan and Davison dispatched air squadrons to the scene, and by noon the American naval planes were bombing the daylights out of Kurita's armada.

Battle details must be left to other naval histories, for the concern of this text is submarine operations. A brief sketch will suffice as a background for the undersea actions which followed in the surface-air battle's wake.

Off southeast Mindoro, Kurita's battleship fleet took a terrible blasting. By nightfall every BB in the armada had suffered at least one bomb hit. The heavy cruiser MYOKO, battered and bleeding, was on her way back to Singapore. A destroyer had been bashed to the bottom. And the monster MUSASHI, hit by a tornado of bombs and aircraft torpedoes, had capsized. Kurita, on a reversed course, was heading west.

Thereupon he received a message from Admiral Toyoda—an order which may have caused Kurita to regret that the communication channel between his bridge and the Commander-in-Chief's Headquarters was in any state of repair. The message was this:

ADVANCE COUNTING ON DIVINE ASSISTANCE

It must have been with some misgivings concerning the assistance that Kurita once more headed his punished armada for San Bernardino Strait.

Midnight, October 24-25, Kurita's force reached the

Pacific end of the strait, six hours behind schedule. Steaming out of San Bernardino, the abbreviated battleship fleet raced southward along the coast of Samar, with big guns aimed for Leyte Gulf. And, as darkness grayed into morning of the 25th, it looked as though miraculous aid had, indeed, screened the movements of Kurita.

For Halsey had drawn off the task groups of Bogan and Davison and sent them racing northward to join Sherman's group in an attack on Ozawa's carriers. Thus all available forces of the United States Third Fleet were chasing Ozawa's "decoy ducks" at the hour Kurita's warships charged out through the San Bernardino gateway.

Halsey, of course, had no way of knowing Ozawa's carriers were mere decoys. Attacking Sherman's task group on the morning of the 24th, Ozawa's half-trained airmen joined land-based bombers from Luzon and struck the American group a painful blow. As a result of bomb damage, the light carrier PRINCE-TON blew up, and the cruiser BIRMINGHAM, which had come alongside, was severely blasted. Ozawa's fleet maneuvered erratically off Cape Engano, breaking radio silence, making smoke and doing everything possible to invite attention. Believing the Japanese carriers must at all cost be held away from Leyte Gulf, Halsey assembled his task groups and sent them north to engage Ozawa.

This move was subjected to much post-war criticism, chiefly because Admiral Kinkaid was not immediately notified of the Third Fleet's departure. Left to guard Leyte Gulf with the United States Seventh Fleet, Kinkaid was up against something of a power house. Down came Kurita with four battleships, eight cruisers, 11 destroyers. Although detected and bombed in the Sulu Sea, Nishimura's task force pressed on toward Surigao Strait, the warships having suffered no appreciable damage. At the same time Shima's task group from Formosa was heading for the strait. Had the three Japanese forces succeeded in reaching Leyte Gulf simultaneously, the Seventh Fleet might have been thrown back.

As it was, Rear Admiral J. B. Olendorf, commanding the most powerful task group of the Seventh Fleet, trapped Nishimura and Shima in Surigao Strait. In a brilliant destroyer action, Nishimura's flagship, the old battleship YAMASHIRO, was blown to pieces. Three Jap DD's were demolished by gunfire. Another, damaged, was put to flight. And at 0400 on the morning of October 25, the old battleship FUSO was sunk by shelling from American battleships flanking the entry to Leyte Gulf. Sole American casualty during this engagement: the destroyer ALBERT W. GRANT damaged in collision with the Japanese cruiser MOGAMI. This cruiser, burning and almost out of control, went reeling down the strait.

The fleeing MOGAMI ploughed headlong into the Shima force which had trailed Nishimura's warships into narrow Surigao Strait. Indicative of Japanese confusion, Admiral Toyoda subsequently testified he had no idea Shima was anywhere near Surigao Strait at that time. Moreover, it appeared that Nishimura raced into the strait ahead of schedule, to avoid coming under the command of Shima, his senior officer. There could be but one upshot to this sort of circus. Shima had swallowed enough of it after his cruiser ABUKUMA was torpedoed and disabled by Olendorf's PT-boats and his flagship NACHI was rammed by the floundering MOGAMI. Ordering a retreat, Shima led his battered force back into the Mindanao Sea. There, American aircraft caught up with MOGAMI and ABUKUMA and finished off both cripples. The annihilation of Nishimura's task force was almost total. Only one destroyer escaped the massacre.

Coming down the coast of Samar, Kurita received no word of the Surigao debacle. Nor did he hear from Admiral Ozawa. At 0645, morning of October 25, Kurita's vanguard made contact with an American task unit a few miles northeast of Leyte Gulf. The Jap heavy guns opened fire at long range, and the American ships raced east, laying a smoke screen.

The American task unit—six escort carriers, three destroyers and four DE's—was under command of Rear Admiral C. A. F. Sprague. It had been stationed off southeast Samar to guard against an enemy advance from the north. Southeast of Sprague's unit, a similar task group under Rear Admiral F. B. Stump was stationed. These were the only American forces between San Bernardino Strait and Leyte Gulf. No match for Kurita's battleships, Sprague's carrier group launched its planes and sent out a call for help. But the Third Fleet was far to the north, and Olendorf's battleship force, off Leyte Gulf, in need of fuel and ammunition, could not have reached Sprague's vicinity until afternoon. Stump's carrier group was the only force which could offer immediate aid.

With Japanese cruisers closing in on one flank, destroyers on another and battleships astern, Sprague's destroyers turned to attack the pursuing foe. Snapping and barking at their roaring antagonists, the American DD's slammed a damaging torpedo into the cruiser KUMANO, scored shell hits on several other warships and slowed Kurita's rush. But the destroyers had no chance against the battleships. JOHNSON, SAMUEL B. ROBERTS and HOEL went down under withering fire. Around 0800 the Jap cruisers closed in on the escort carrier GAMBIER BAY and tore her to pieces with shellfire.

By this time Admiral Stump's carrier squadrons were striking the Japanese fleet, and Kurita withdrew northwestward. Japanese aircraft from Luzon continued to pound Sprague's group, and the battle's fury mounted as suicide planes struck the escort carriers KITKUN BAY and SAINT LO. Gutted by explosions, SAINT LO capsized and sank a few moments after her crew abandoned.

Meanwhile, American aircraft were hammering Kurita's warships. Blasted by a bomb, the heavy cruiser SUZUYA caught fire and settled. Heavy cruisers CHOKAI and CHIKUMA were disabled. Ordering the helpless cruisers sunk, Kurita decided to refrain from visiting Leyte Gulf. Completely overstepping previous orders from Toyoda directing him to proceed under any circumstances to Leyte Gulf, Kurita's decision seems to have been based on the ominous silence from Nishimura. Ozawa was equally silent. But no news from the north might be good news, whereas the deathlike hush from Leyte Gulf was depressing. So Kurita headed north intending (according to his post-war testimony) to support Ozawa by locating and attacking the United States Third Fleet.

Or was he, now that the cards were down, reluctant about committing suicide? He had lost the super-battleship MUSASHI and seven heavy cruisers—ATAGO, MAYA, TAKAO, MYOKO, SUZUYA, CHOKAI and CHIKUMA. One more heavy cruiser—KUMANO—was badly damaged. Of his fleet's original dozen, but four heavy cruisers remained available for combat. But he still had mighty YAMATO and three other battleships—a force that might have done damage at Leyte Gulf. Northward he went, however. And in so doing he ran into aircraft from the carriers of Vice Admiral J. S. McCain, whose task group had been ordered east to refuel on October 23 and had come rushing back in answer to Sprague's call for help. Taking off at long range, McCain's airmen roared over the horizon to attack Kurita's remnant fleet. That was enough for Kurita. At sundown he gave up the attempt to run north, and that night he retreated westward through San Bernardino Strait.

Meantime, the Third Fleet forces under Halsey and Mitscher had locked horns with Ozawa's carrier force in the Philippine Sea northeast of Cape Engano. Detected at 0200 on the morning of October 25, Ozawa's carriers ran northward. At dawn Mitscher's aircraft took off for the attack.

Ozawa's force consisted of the large carrier ZUIKAKU, three smaller carriers—CHITOSE, CHIYODA and ZUIHO—battleship carriers HYUGA and ISE, light cruisers OYODA and TAMA, and eight destroyers. Halsey's pursuing forces numbered five large carriers, five light carriers, six battleships, eight cruisers and 41 destroyers. The American carrier planes struck Ozawa's force about 0900. The strikes continued throughout the day. ZUIKAKU went down. CHIYODA went down. ZUIHO went down. CHITOSE went down. By mid-afternoon the remainder of Ozawa's force—with the exception of several destroyers and the light cruiser TAMA—was in headlong flight. The DD's and TAMA were left behind to rescue survivors. As will be seen, these rescuers themselves were soon in need of rescue, for they ran into a nest of SubPac submarines.

During the Battle for Leyte Gulf, 16 SubPac submarines were patrolling the roads between Japan and the northern Philippines. Six were in Empire waters. Three were off northeastern Formosa. The remaining seven were ranging Luzon Strait. And when the Leyte battle exploded, two SubPac wolf-packs of three submarines each were loping toward Luzon Strait from Saipan. These two wolf-packs—"Roach's Raiders" and "Clarey's Crushers"—were rushed to the battle area when word was received that Mitscher's planes were in contact with Ozawa's carriers.

A member of "Roach's Raiders," HALIBUT (Commander I. J. Galantin) was the first submarine to catch up with Ozawa's left-overs. In a submerged attack, made early in the evening of October 25, Galantin fired six electric torpedoes at a target identified as a battleship of the ISE or YAMASHIRO class. The sundown light was deceptive, and the target, at 4,000 yards, looked bigger than she was. Five torpedo explosions were counted. When HALIBUT surfaced three minutes later, nothing was in sight except a capsized hulk. The warship's identity was never positively established. HALIBUT was credited with sinking the destroyer AKITSUKI.

While HALIBUT was scanning the capsized hulk, the submarine's lookouts saw a spatter of blinker lights in the distance. Galantin immediately set course at full speed to investigate this signaling escort. By that time a bright half-moon was in the sky, and a lot of aerial activity.

"Many gunflashes could be seen over the horizon," Galantin noted. *"Thought it better to try to overtake the late ship's escorts than to get mixed up in an all-out naval battle. We were ahead of the main enemy force in the direction of their probable retirement, and if own contact failed to materialize could always drop back on the other enemy units."*

At 2200, while chasing the escort vessel, HALIBUT received a contact report from TUNA and headed to intercept at full speed. About an hour later she made contact with a force of five warships, but this group outdistanced Galantin's submarine.

Meanwhile, "Clarey's Crushers," some 60 miles to the northward, caught the light cruiser TAMA. As detailed later on, the catch was bagged by the submarine JALLAO. Apparently the CL was the last warship lost by Ozawa in the Battle off Cape Engano.

Lockwood's submarines continued to chase Ozawa's running relicts. At 1150 on October 26, SILVERSIDES sighted two battleships racing north. TRIGGER tried to intercept with an end-around, but the BB's changed course and upped their speed.

On October 28, what were probably the same battleships were picked up farther north by SEA DOG (Commander V. L. Lowrance). Lowrance drove his submarine in for an attack, and fired six torpedoes. Just as the salvo was fired, the battleships made a radical zig and the torpedoes missed. Before SEA DOG could get in another attack, the BB team, making 22 knots, was far down the track and highballing for home like the Empire State Express.

Interesting to note that with all this submarining in the Philippine storm center, no U.S. submarines were lost in the Battle for Leyte Gulf. Japanese submarines participating in the Battle for Leyte Gulf were not quite so successful as their American opposites. On October 24, Seventh Fleet surface craft sank I-362 off the Gulf. Three days later, a pair of 2,000-tonners—I-45 and I-54—were detected, depth-charged and demolished in the eastern approaches to Leyte.

The day following the Battle off Cape Engano, planes from Bogan's carriers and McCain's task group located Kurita's fleeing warships in the Sibuyan Sea. Army aircraft joined the chase. Four destroyers and the light cruisers KINU and NOSHIRO were sunk by the pursuing American planes. Kurita's retreat accelerated into a pell-mell rout. Perhaps divine assistance, after all, saved his fleet from complete annihilation. Somehow the remnants reached Brunei, Borneo.

But the Japanese defeat was sufficiently catastrophic. American losses of one light carrier, two escort carriers, two destroyers and a DE, plus loss of the Australian cruiser AUSTRALIA (sunk by *kamikaze* attack during the Leyte landings) were minor compared to Japanese fatalities. These included three battleships, a first-line carrier, three light carriers, eight heavy cruisers (six sunk; two irreparably damaged), four light cruisers, nine destroyers and three submarines. Never in history had a nation lost so much warship tonnage in so short a time.

The Imperial Navy was done for.

The Philippines were lost.

The immediate submarine contribution was something more than the elimination of four heavy cruisers, a retreating light cruiser and a destroyer. And something more than the maladjustment of Kurita's communication machinery, as witness the endorsement of DARTER's fourth war patrol report by Admiral Kinkaid, Commander Seventh Fleet:

The Fourth War Patrol of the USS DARTER embraces one of the most outstanding contributions by submarines to the ultimate defeat of the Japanese Navy. . . . The selection of the time for the attack is considered well advised in view of the difficulty in attacking radar equipped war vessels at night and considering the information desired on the composition of the enemy force. This information, which was promptly transmitted, was the first tangible evidence of the size and magnitude of the forces which the enemy was assembling to dislodge our positions in Leyte. The early receipt of this information enabled our forces to formulate and put into execution the countermeasures which resulted in a major disaster for the Japanese in the second battle of the Philippine Sea.

Jallao vs. Tama

When Admiral Lockwood ordered "Clarey's Crushers" to intercept Ozawa's fleeing carriers, the submarines "poured on the coal." Under the aggressive leadership of Commander B. A. Clarey, the wolfpack consisted of PINTADO (Clarey), JALLAO (Commander J. B. Icenhower) and ATULE (Commander J. H. Maurer).

JALLAO was experiencing her first war patrol. And her captain, Commander Icenhower, was making his first command patrol. Tradition called for the torpedoing of a light cruiser. Icenhower was not the submariner to ignore an established "maiden patrol" custom.

At 2004 in the evening of October 25, JALLAO made long-distance radar contact with a warship off the northeast coast of Luzon. The warship was on a northeasterly course, and clocked in at some 16 knots. JALLAO relayed this information to her pack-mates. Group Commander Clarey in PINTADO promptly maneuvered to team up with Icenhower's submarine.

A brilliant moon illumined the seascape, and JALLAO picked up the target visually at 20,000 yards. Icenhower tentatively identified the Jap warship as a BB, and ordered the torpedoes set for 15 feet. At 2242, range 12,000 yards, he sent JALLAO to radar depth and bored in. When the range closed to 4,000 yards, he ordered JALLAO to periscope depth. The target could now be identified as a CL. Icenhower prepared to carry out the maiden-submarine formalities. To second the affair, Clarey held PINTADO up ahead on the light cruiser's track, thereby giving JALLAO first shot at the target she had flushed.

Icenhower opened fire at 2301, range 1,200 yards. There was some trouble with the submarine's outer doors, and the salvo was limited to three bow shots. One muffled explosion was heard. The torpedoes had

399

evidently missed in depth, for the cruiser, apparently undamaged, turned toward the submarine. Icenhower quickly swung JALLAO for a stern-tube attack, and at the crucial moment the cruiser made another swerve, lining herself up for a fatal salvo. Icenhower fired three stern shots at 700 yards. Three hits sent up geysers of water and flame. PINTADO witnessed the sinking. When JALLAO broke the surface at 2328, Clary informed Icenhower that the light cruiser had gone to the bottom.

The vessel, of course, was TAMA. It seems she had been lamed by naval aircraft during the Battle off Cape Engano, and JALLAO was ultimately credited with a *coup de grâce*. Luckless TAMA was the seventh of her kind to fall to U.S. submarine torpedoes in 1944. She was the eighth CL sunk by American submarines. The British submarine TALLYHO had downed another in January 1944 off Penang to raise the submarine score to nine. Naval aircraft continued to take a heavy toll of this class, and by year's end the breed was almost extinct. A final specimen remained to be downed by submarines in 1945.

"King Two" Aftermath

The successful "King Two" gambit left MacArthur's force in control of Leyte. But a difficult mopping-up operation, a hard drive to Manila lay ahead. The Philippines were lost by Japan—no question of that. But the United States was in the position of the chess player who can announce mate in so many moves; at which time, a sensible opponent resigns. If he refuses to resign, the final moves must be made. The Japanese War Lords—never too sensible—refused to resign. The Imperial Army was dedicated to a *hara-kiri* stand, and reinforcements were rushed to the Philippines by every available means. So the slaughter had to go on.

Monsoon rains delayed the Leyte mop-up in November, but by December the American land forces were scouring the island. Supporting the jungle fighting, detachments of the Seventh Fleet drove through Surigao Strait and blew the enemy out of Ormoc Bay on the western side of Leyte. At year's end the island was declared secure. Japanese losses: 74,261 killed. American losses in dead: 3,135.

Simultaneously Mindoro was invaded, and Japanese forces in the southern Philippines were isolated. Capture of good airfields on Mindoro put the U.S. Army bombers on top of Luzon. With Manila under air assault, the Philippines checkmate was but a move away. Nevertheless, the Imperial Army continued a resistance as furious as it was futile.

Meantime, Kurita's flogged fleet pulled itself together for a dash to the north from Borneo.

Remnants of Ozawa's force had reached Japan, and Kurita had no desire to be caught at the bottom end of the distintegrating Empire. A number of cripples, however, were dispatched to Singapore. Then early in November, after fueling and loading ammunition, YAMATO and her consorts raced from Brunei and headed north for home.

To reverse an expression, the Imperial Navy was out, but it was not yet down. So U.S. submarines continued the all-out hunt for Japanese men-of-war. The minor "gunmen" were nearly exterminated. But as long as some of the "big shots" remained, the "heat" was on. And during November and December 1944, the submarines caught up with some of those "big shots." The torpedoings resulted in sinkings that are epics in submarine history. Sinkings that left the Imperial Navy prostrate on the sea floor.

Guitarro, Raton, Bream and Ray vs. Kumano

Damaged by American destroyers in the battle off Samar, the heavy cruiser KUMANO was detached from Kurita's formation and hurried to Manila for repairs. Her injuries were at once superficial and drastic—she could navigate, but could not fire. Hasty repairs were contrived at Manila. But by the time the cruiser was bandaged up, Kurita's fleet was legging it for Borneo, and "Operation Sho-Go" was on history's junk pile.

With every man-of-war now needed for home defense, KUMANO was ordered out of Manila and sent north early in November with a convoy. She could not have undertaken a more perilous journey. Cruising the waters off western Luzon at this time was the SubSoWesPac wolf-pack led by BREAM (Commander W. G. "Moon" Chapple). Packing with BREAM were GUITARRO (Commander E. D. Haskins) and RATON (Commander M. W. Shea). And independently patrolling an adjacent area was RAY (Commander W. T. Kinsella). Reserved for KUMANO was the fate of running headlong into all four of these submarines.

GUITARRO saw her first. Morning of November 6, Haskins' submarine was patrolling off Cape Bolinao. At 0718—convoy! The target group developed into two heavy cruisers, seven freighters and assorted escorts coming up from the south. Haskins selected the largest plum in the basket, which happened to be KUMANO. The approach lasted about an hour. When GUITARRO gained attack position, Haskins unleashed nine torpedoes—six from the bow tubes and three from the stern tubes. This terrific salvo was fired in 46 seconds! Three timed hits were counted. But the cruiser kept on going.

Six minutes after the GUITARRO attack, BREAM

sighted the northbound convoy. Chapple selected the largest target and sent his submarine boring in. At 0843 he fired the last shot of a four-torpedo salvo at the heavy cruiser. Two timed hits boomed out. KUMANO remained afloat.

At 0846 the oncoming convoy was sighted by RATON. Commander Shea wanted the big heavy cruiser. He opened fire at 0943 and sent six torpedoes streaking at the target. Three sounded like timed hits. KUMANO should have gone to the bottom, but she continued on the surface to play target for RAY.

Kinsella had brought his submarine around to see what the shooting was all about. He was directing an approach on the target when RATON's torpedoes were fired. Some of these torpedoes passed directly over RAY. After wishing them "God speed," Kinsella went on with his own approach maneuvers. At 0946 he fired four Mark 18 torpedoes at the stubborn cruiser. The sea was full of thunder as RAY went deep, but sometimes an empty kettle can make the most noise. When Kinsella ordered his submarine to the surface about an hour later, KUMANO was still there! The cruiser had come to a stop with her bow blown off. A tanker was sidling up to take the warship in tow.

In something less than an hour and three-quarters, 23 torpedoes had been expended on this single target. Kinsella determined to finish off the imperishable vessel. Then, closing in to deliver the death blow, RAY grounded deep under the sea. Damage to the sound cables caused a troublesome leak, and repairs had to be made before the attack could be resumed.

Persistent KUMANO! While Kinsella and crew sweated over the repairs, the pug-nosed cruiser was towed in to the Luzon beach. There she squatted in the shallows, a helpless hulk awaiting her end. It came on November 25 when carrier planes from the United States Third Fleet found her and blew her to pieces.

So aircraft were credited with the execution, while submarines are credited with the capture.

Spadefish vs. Jinyo

They called them "Underwood's Urchins"—SPADEFISH, SUNFISH and PETO. When the pack left Pearl Harbor late in October to conduct a war patrol in the Yellow Sea, Japanese shipping in that body of water was in for trouble. The matter was guaranteed by group leader Underwood, whose submarine SPADEFISH had already dug a large hole in the Japanese merchant marine.

PETO (Commander R. H. Caldwell, Jr.) started the shooting on the 12th. Her shots blew the bottom out of TATSUAKI MARU, freighter, 2,766 tons.

Two days later, Underwood's submarine downed GYOKUYO MARU, freighter, 5,396 tons.

The "Urchins" then encountered nothing until November 17th. On that date they picked up a convoy at the southern end of the Yellow Sea, and when the shooting was over on the 18th, the bottom of the Yellow Sea was the convoy's general location. In the process of burying this mass of merchant shipping, SPADEFISH also dug a hole for a considerable quantity of naval tonnage.

The sea was brassy with midday sun when Underwood's submarine heard the convoy coming. A volley of distant depth charges announced the caravan. At 1434 smoke was in sight. More faraway depth charges at 1543. Then at 1642 five columns of smoke were visible. A Jap plane circled over the convoy like an inquisitive fly, and the masts of four ships came over the horizon at 1651.

The convoy was headed straight for SPADEFISH. As sunset was due in an hour and a half, Underwood decided to let the convoy pass and hit it later with a night-surface attack. He ordered the submarine down to 150 feet, and the convoy rumbled directly overhead, its escort busily "pinging." SPADEFISH heard another depth-charge barrage, and bided her time. At 1754 Underwood ordered periscope depth.

He could make out five bulky merchant vessels and the silhouette of an escort carrier. A number of destroyers and sub-chasers paraded with the formation—a formidable guard. Darkness prevented certain identification, but the carrier resembled a specimen of the OTAKA class, and that was all Underwood needed. SPADEFISH was not alone on the convoy's trail, however. At 1811 an explosion roared in the dusk, and Underwood saw smoke billowing from a freighter ahead of the carrier. Seventeen depth charges boomed in answer to this attack. "Guess some other sub decided not to wait for dark," Underwood noted. "Couldn't see what happened to the target."

At 1834 SPADEFISH was on the surface, and Underwood started an end-around, tracking by radar to determine the exact course and speed of the targets. About 20 minutes later, he received a contact report from SUNFISH—she was trailing an eight-ship convoy three hours behind SPADEFISH's target group. Captained by Commander E. E. Shelby, SUNFISH presently downed two ships of this convoy, accounting for the 6,968-ton freighter EDOGAWA MARU and the 5,463-ton passenger-cargoman SEISHO MARU.

Meantime, Underwood went after the Japanese escort carrier. At 2119 Underwood made one attempt to approach for an attack, but a zig-away by the convoy left him with a long-range shot from abaft the beam. At 2259 SPADEFISH was in position, and at

2303 Underwood fired six torpedoes at the escort carrier, range of 4,100 yards on a 65° starboard track. Executing a rapid turn to the left, Underwood brought his submarine into position for stern shots and fired a four-torpedo salvo at another ship in the formation, range 2,980 yards, 132° starboard track.

Four torpedoes hit the escort carrier. The vessel vomited a mass of flames and started to settle by the stern. Planes rolled off the flight deck as the carrier listed to starboard. A last look showed the vessel *in extremis*, her blazing bow angled skyward, her stern on the bottom in 23 fathoms of water.

One hit was heard from the stern tube salvo, but no damage could be ascertained. SPADEFISH's victim was the CVE JINYO, 21,000 tons—last of the Jap escort carriers to go down to submarine torpedoes.

But Underwood was unsatisfied. Shortly after midnight, he drove SPADEFISH in for another attack. This time the submarine was detected. The counter-attack is best described in Underwood's own words:

. . . Escort opened fire with 40mm. Turned with full left rudder. Ordered the bridge cleared. Helmsman overheard word that we would not dive, mistook it for the word "Dive" and rang up the signal to stop engines and shift to battery power. Before the error could be rectified we had slowed to eight knots, and the escort had closed to 970 yards, shooting with 20mm and 40mm, and with a few heavier caliber shots. He hadn't detected our turn yet so all shots were astern of us. The escort that was on the starboard quarter of the convoy also opened fire, his shots crossing astern and landing on our port quarter. These 40mm tracers do light up the night and also make a hell of a racket. . . . The stern tubes were ready so turned on the after TBT and picked out a target in the direction of the convoy. This was a large escort. . . . fired four torpedoes from stern tubes on a 100° starboard track. Three timed explosions were heard and target's pip disappeared from the radar. The Executive Officer came up to the bridge after firing the torpedoes and saw heavy billowing smoke in the direction of the target. By this time we were getting considerably more than rated horsepower out of our 10 cylinder engines. It was sufficient to pull away from the escort. He had discovered us by this time and his tracers were spraying first one side and then the other of us, only once passing overhead. His gunners were blinded by their own tracers so they would fire a few bursts, then stop and pick up our wake, and then open up in its direction. When they stopped shooting, we would zig about 10 degrees one way or the other, so he wasn't successful in getting on. When the range had opened up to about 2,500 yards he turned away and dropped a string of depth charges. Guess he did that to "save face." His story would be he lost us because we dived. We didn't dive since the water was only 22 fathoms and he certainly had us located. . . .

Outcome of the skirmish: SPADEFISH credited with "probable sinking" of Submarine Chaser No. 156.

Altogether the "Urchins" sank a heavy tonnage on their patrol. PETO added two freighters to the November 18 total—AISAKASAN MARU, 6,923 tons, and CHINKAI MARU, 2,827 tons. And SPADEFISH concluded the score on the 29th with DAIBOSHI MARU No. 6, freighter, 3,925 tons. When Underwood's wolf-pack headed home, it had sunk some 55,000 tons of Japanese shipping in the Yellow Sea.

The destruction of JINYO left the Imperial Navy with but one escort carrier in commission—the CVE KAIYO. When the planes of Task Force Thirty-eight struck the Inland Sea in July 1945, KAIYO was obliterated. She was the last of the five escort carriers built and operated by the Japanese during the war. U.S. submarines had sunk the other four.

Sealion II vs. Kongo

As November waned, U.S. submarines were forced to hunt more and more assiduously for Japanese men-of-war. Big game was conspicuously scarce in the Netherlands East Indies and rapidly vanishing from the surface of the South China Sea. The waters off Luzon promised some shooting while the Imperial forces struggled to retain a toe hold on the northern Philippines. But the best hunting areas at this season were those which hemmed Formosa and lay to the west of the Nansei Shoto chain in the waters of the East China Sea. As has been related, the surviving units of Kurita's Second Fleet, with the exception of some odds and ends at Singapore, had run northward from Brunei in hectic flight. Principal fugitives were the super-battleship YAMATO and battleships NAGATO, KONGO and HARUNA. Their safest route home was by way of Formosa Strait and the East China Sea—the northern end of the trunk line which had once tethered the conquered southern territories to the home Empire.

This oceanic expanse between Formosa and Kyushu was a dangerous sea for American submarines. The northern reaches had long been patrolled by SubPac submarines bent on blockading Kyushu and cutting the shipping lanes to Shanghai. And the Formosa Strait bottleneck was plugged at the southern end by "Convoy College" patrols. Less frequently had U.S. submarines patrolled the southern reaches of the East China Sea—the waters off northern Formosa. Access to this area was difficult. On the west lay the Japanese-held coast of China. On the east lay the great minefield which extended almost all the way from Formosa to Kyushu. To reach the approaches to northern Formosa, a submarine had to skirt the northernmost islands of the

NOT A HOUSING PROJECT, the island of Jap heavy cruiser Atago looms against the sky. It loomed against sea-bottom on October 23, 1944, after USS Darter torpedoed the cruiser off Palawan. Atago's loss made a hole in the Jap fleet racing for Leyte Gulf. Sinking of sister Maya by USS Dace made another.

ESCORT CARRIER JINYO. Before the Spadefish *sank her in November 1944.*

HEAVY CRUISER ATAGO. Before she was sunk by Darter. *For dramatic story of two U.S. subs versus Jap fleet, see text page 391.*

LIGHT CRUISER YUBARI. Before she was sunk by Blue-gill, *April 27, '44. U.S. subs on "maiden" made CL's a habit.*

ESCORT CARRIER TAIYO. Before sunk by Rasher, *August 18, '44. In convoy battle* Rasher *took huge toll.*

LIGHT CRUISER OI, sunk by Flasher. Flasher *sank more Jap tonnage than any other U.S. sub in war.*

LIGHT CRUISER TAMA, sunk off Cape Engano by Jallao *and Navy aircraft.* Jallao *sent her down.*

SCOURGE OF THE JAP NAVY! American submarines like the above struck the Imperial Navy a series of knock-out blows in 1944. Down to the thunder of well-aimed (but good) torpedoes went 28 destroyers; 7 submarines; 8 light cruisers; 2 heavy cruisers; 3 escort carriers; 4 large carriers; and big Battleship Kongo. Latter was sunk by Sealion II.*

Nansei Shoto chain and make the long run southward behind the mine barrier. Once the submarine gained the lower latitudes of the East China Sea, she found herself flanked by a hostile coast on the west and fenced in by mines on the east. This was not the most comfortable hunting ground in the book. But, as has been noted, it was a likely area for home-running Japanese battleships. To intercept such anticipated fugitives, SEALION II (Commander Eli T. Reich) was dispatched to the southern waters of the East China Sea.

The LION left Pearl Harbor on November 1st. This was to be her third war patrol, and the success of her first two under skipper Reich undoubtedly lay behind her assignment to an unusually hazardous patrol area. On her maiden patrol, June-July, she had sunk four freighters with a veteran's precision. On her next patrol, August-September, she accounted for a minelayer and two passenger-cargomen—some 19,000 tons. Crew and skipper were just the submariners to handle a hostile coast on the west, a minefield on the east, and anything else that spelled danger at the southern end of the East China Sea. A Japanese battleship? Why not? To date, U.S. submarines had sunk practically every type of Japanese vessel except a battleship. But they had dented one or two BB's. What was to keep them from downing one? Of course, no hand serving in SEALION actually expected—

But then—

At 0020 on the morning of November 21, SEALION was hunting on the surface some 40 miles north of Formosa in the East China Sea. Lieutenant (jg) Joseph C. Bates had the deck. From the conning tower came the report of a radar contact. Target was unbelievably distant—so distant that Bates at first thought it was land. Probably the coast of Formosa.

Presently, the conning tower reported again. Contact was several thousand yards nearer this time. Maybe phenomenon wasn't land! Bates called the captain, and Commander Reich turned out of his bunk and headed for the bridge in robin's-egg blue pajamas. Topside, the men watched and waited, still uncertain. Then came a report from the conning tower that banished all uncertainty.

"Two targets of battleship proportions and two of large cruiser size! Course 060 True! Speed 16 knots! Not zigging!"

Down the hatch went Reich to jump from pajamas into khaki, and into SEALION's engine room went orders for flank speed ahead on all four main engines. The night was overcast and moonless, but the sea was calm and visibility was good for about 1,500 yards.

The targets had shaped up as a task force on the radar screen. What appeared to be a cruiser was leading the column formation. Then came the two battleships. Then a cruiser in the rear. Port side, flanking the leading cruiser, was an escorting destroyer. To the starboard, flanking each battleship, were two more destroyers. What the radar screen did not show was the massive tonnage of all this war-shipping in comparison with the weight of SEALION II. In a prize ring such a difference in the weight of opponents would have canceled any match then and there. Reich did not bother with finicky prize-ring calculations.

He decided to make a surface approach using radar. This was a daring decision. Submarines were tracking merchant convoys by radar during night-surface approaches, and obtaining excellent results. But such an approach on a naval task force was another matter. The big warships were certainly maintaining an alert radar watch, and premature discovery would put SEALION on the receiving end of a colossal counter-attack. If she were forced to dive, the chances were she would have to go deep and stay deep until the battleships and their escorts cleared the area. However, if she could close in without detection and launch a surprise attack, she might be able to make several strikes before the escorts drove her under. Reich weighed the risks and accepted the odds.

Tracking the course, Reich deduced the Jap warships were bound for Sasebo. This was undoubtedly a unit that had fought in the Battle for Leyte Gulf and was now heading home to salve its scars. Reich and company were determined to interrupt this retirement. SEALION held a course to the westward, starting her end run.

At 0146 SEALION was on the enemy's starboard beam, slowly gaining. As she bent all speed to get ahead, a night wind entered the approach problem and the LION had to claw her way through rising seas. An hour later the submarine was out in front, and Reich picked the second ship in column—the nearest battleship—for his target. As he maneuvered the submarine into attack position the leading cruiser went by. Then an escorting destroyer threatened to intervene. This silhouette, dimly seen from the bridge, was the first visible contact with the enemy task force—until that moment the chase had been conducted entirely by radar. The destroyer, about 1,800 yards distant, was an unwelcome nuisance. Fearing the DD might overlap the battleship in line of fire, Reich set the Mark 18 electrics for a running depth of eight feet.

During the approach, all hands in SEALION had been elated over the prospect of attacking a Jap BB. Now, at close quarters, the mood changed slightly.

This lone submarine, her bow pointing toward the battleship, faced a potential broadside of eight 14-inch guns, eight 6-inch .50-caliber guns, four 5-inch AA guns, and two torpedo tubes. And there was more where that came from, for SEALION faced all the firepower that could be amassed by the other battleship, the two cruisers and the three destroyers. One thinks of a Federal agent with an automatic confronting a gang of felons armed with sawed-off shotguns, rifles and bombs.

At 0256, as the destroyer passed the waiting submarine, Reich fired six bow torpedoes at the battleship, range 3,000 yards. As the last shot left the tube nest, he threw the rudder hard right. This brought the stern tubes to bear on the second battleship in the column. At 0259, range 3,100 yards, Reich fired three stern shots at this target.

Sixty seconds later the SEALIONERS on the bridge saw the mushroom fire of exploding torpedoes and heard three hits on the first battleship. A moment after that they saw at least one hit on the second target—a great sheet of flame that whipped skyward, then burned itself out.

SEALION's bow was pointed away from the enemy, and the submarine ran westward at flank speed while the Jap destroyers charged eastward in pursuit of ghosts. Dull explosions echoed the torpedo blasts. Depth charges rumbled in the sea, and it was evident that the naval task group was as fuddled as the average merchant convoy. By 0310 SEALION was 8,000 yards west of the Jap task force, and Reich slowed the submarine to parallel the enemy's course and rush a torpedo reload.

The enemy warships were doing 18 knots, and Reich now regretted the eight-foot depth setting given the torpedoes. Apparently the hits had only dented the armor belt on the battleships, and another attack was necessary. This would not be easy with the targets moving at 18 knots. To make matters worse for SEALION, the wind was caterwauling, and she was taking solid water over the bridge with plenty of it coming down the conning tower hatch as she put on maximum speed to overhaul the fleeing task force. Traveling at top speed, the submarine held on until sparking commutators on the motors compelled Reich to slow down to full speed. At this pace SEALION could do about 17 knots, bucking heavy seas with safety tank dry and the low pressure blower working hard to keep ballast tanks empty.

A good break was urgent, and at 0450 it came. At that critical moment, the enemy column began to separate into two groups—the cruiser, a battleship and another cruiser in column was pulling ahead. The second group—two destroyers and the battleship which had suffered three torpedo hits—was dropping astern at 12 knots. This was more like it! The LION might get in another attack if she stalked this lagging group. Reich started another end-around, fighting weather that was swiftly developing a hurricane.

By 0512 SEALION was in attack position. Reich slowed her and turned in for the attack. It never eventuated. The battleship with its two escorting destroyers had stopped dead in the water 17,000 yards away. Below decks in SEALION the crew waited on tenterhooks, wondering what the men on the bridge could see. All hands knew that they had resumed a battleship chase. They knew the submarine was ahead of the target, and the attack should come soon. They had gone in once, and now they were going in again, and this time that Jap baby would be on the alert. Stomach nerves tightened to the point of nausea. What was the delay? Why weren't the "fish" sent off? And then it happened.

There was a horrendous explosion. A flash of light came down SEALION's conning tower hatch and illuminated the compartment below. Next came a concussion wave that plucked at breath and clothing like a vacuum cup. The boat shuddered as if shaken by a giant hand. Then there was silence. In the conning tower, tense submariners waited for word from the bridge. Thirty seconds ticked away—in such an eternity the mind can do a lot of thinking. The first thing that entered some minds was a picture of that battleship's turret guns. That explosion and flash suggested a big-gun salvo. The next one might be right on. Then came the word.

"Something's happened up here!"

A few seconds later:

"Our damaged battleship just blew up!"

Reich described the scene later: "We were standing on the bridge on this wild black night, riding the heavy seas. Then without warning there was this brilliant flash. It lighted up the entire sea for miles, like a sunset at midnight. Just as suddenly the ship sank and there was total blackness again."

SEALION did not sit around licking her chops, but immediately took off at flank speed in an attempt to overhaul the warships to the northward. But the riotous weather slowed her, and she was forced to abandon the chase when green seas swept the bridge and a wave cascaded down the conning tower hatch, grounding out some electrical equipment in the control room and in the pump room.

The battleship sunk by SEALION II was the 31,000-ton KONGO. Positive identification came from a Japanese prisoner of war—an officer who had been on one of the ships in the home-bound group, and who was captured two months later. Post-war investigation confirmed the sinking. And it added a postscript to the confirmation. Unknown to the American submariners until war's end was the fact that a torpedo from SEALION's stern-tube salvo, instead of damaging another battleship, had hit and blown to bits the destroyer URAKAZE. A battleship and a destroyer sunk in one slashing attack!

But the battleship alone would have been sufficient. In sinking KONGO, Commander Eli Reich and crew destroyed one of the most powerful warships in the Pacific and won for SEALION II an enduring anchorage in the U.S. Navy's Hall of Fame.

Archerfish vs. Shinano (No. 1 on the "Hit Parade")

ARCHERFISH (Commander J. F. Enright) left Saipan on November 11 to conduct her fifth war patrol. Out of Portsmouth Navy Yard in 1943, the submarine had met with indifferent luck thus far, and there was nothing in the cards to indicate a change. From Saipan she headed north to patrol in the waters of "Hit Parade." Her assigned area lay about 150 miles south of Tokyo—a stretch of water due north of Hachijo Jima in the Nanpo Shoto chain.

Once on the Empire main line from Japan to the Marianas, the Nanpo Shoto islands were now landmarks on the B-29 main line from the Marianas to Japan. ARCHERFISH's primary mission was to act as lifeguard for the first B-29 strikes on Tokyo. She was also to engage in offensive patrolling and shoot at any targets that came her way. But Enright was not anticipating much shooting. American Superforts droned in the sky. ARCHERFISH was not long out before she made contact with three friendly submarines. It could be assumed that Japanese shipping would avoid this lively area. And the first days of the patrol substantiated the assumption. Three small vessels came along, but they were too insignificant to warrant an expenditure of torpedoes. Enright and company watched the air show; otherwise submarining was slow in the Nanpo Shotos.

Early in the morning of November 28, ARCHERFISH received word there would be no air raid that day and she was therefore free from lifeguard duties until further notice. The day was a round of routine monotony. But that evening, when the submarine was about 12 miles off Inamba Shima, something happened. It happened at 2048—radar contact at long range, bearing 028 T. Enright set the machinery in motion and started tracking from ahead.

Within an hour the target was identified as an aircraft carrier, on base course 210, making 20 knots and zigzagging. Only one escort could be located. The sky was overcast but bright moonlight seeped through the clouds, and visibility was good for about 15,000 yards. The horizon was dark to the north, so Enright started his approach on the enemy's starboard flank.

At 2230 an escort was sighted on the target's starboard beam. The position maintained by this escort conspired with visibility conditions to rule out a surface approach on the target from that side. Enright therefore changed course back to the base course. At 2250 the range was decreasing but ARCHERFISH was too far off the track to close in with a submerged approach. Range to the escort was 6,100 yards, and the carrier was 15,000 yards away. So Enright held the submarine on the surface and drove in.

As the range shortened, he sent his lookouts below, and, awaiting gun flashes and splashes, braced himself on the bridge. He could now make out the target group as a large carrier in a cordon of four escorts—one on either beam, one ahead and one astern. A surface attack seemed out of the question, but there was little chance of the submarine's regaining the ahead position required for a submerged approach.

Enright sent out a contact report, hoping to guide some other submarine into an intercepting position. The carrier group was making one full knot better than ARCHERFISH could do at her best. Strive as she would, Enright's submarine was slowly falling behind, and it was evident to her skipper that she would end up far in the rear unless the enemy made an accommodating zig or zag. As it was, the enemy was doing his best to accommodate, but his zags and zigs were not angular enough. However, by careful maneuvering and paralleling the base course, ARCHERFISH managed to hang on.

Many are the pros and cons with regard to zigzagging as a submarine defense. Obviously a target traveling on a straight course at a uniform speed presents the easiest fire control problem to the tracking submarine. On the other hand, zigzagging seldom baffles a well-trained fire control party with modern instruments. The chance that a sudden swerve by the target will adversely affect the submarine's position after she is all set for the attack is about offset by the chance that such a maneuver will improve the submarine's position. There remains the possibility that the target may veer immediately after the torpedoes are fired. But such a course-change would amount to correct evasive action taken before torpedoes had been sighted. So the odds are about Even Stephen. But no navigator—certainly none of Japanese extraction—could deny that zigzagging increases the number of miles steamed in submarine waters, and thereby increases the chances of submarine attack. Moreover, the reduction of target speed, caused by zigzagging, may be just sufficient to enable the submarine to gain an attack position when otherwise it would be left behind. Whatever the theoretical arguments, it remains a fact that ARCHERFISH's target would have escaped had the navigators maintained a straight course.

At 2340 the target group made a radical course-change—a change in the base course to the west. ARCHERFISH was now on the port flank and farther off the track than before. She hung on desperately as the "black gang" coaxed a few more turns from overloaded engines. The chase went on through midnight and into the morning of November 29th. The enemy's zigzag plan allowed the submarine to pull ahead—slowly—slowly. But by 0241 it was obvious that if the carrier held to her base course of 275, the ARCHERFISH situation would be hopeless. Enright sent out a second contact report.

Then came the break. At 0300 the target group made another radical change in course, this time veering to the southwest. The range began to close rapidly, and ARCHERFISH was ahead. The long chase was nearly over. Patience and perseverence were about to move a mountain.

At 0305 Enright came to course 100 and ordered the submarine under. Range to the carrier when ARCHERFISH submerged was 11,700 yards. At 7,000 yards the target could be seen through the periscope. Wait—that baby was going to pass too close! Enright changed course 10° to the left, and now the range shortened to 3,500 yards. At about this point the starboard escort approached the carrier to receive a blinker message. This caused the escort to pass ahead of ARCHERFISH at only 400 yards. The move also served to get the escort out of the way.

At 0316 the carrier zigged away from the submarine. This move put the queen right where Enright wanted her. ARCHERFISH had been a little too close to the target, and the zig gave her a nice position: 1,400 yards range with a 70° starboard track. Because of the late zig, Enright had to accept a larger than normal gyro angle. No matter. At 0317 he fired the first shot of a six-torpedo salvo—Mark 14's set for 10 feet and spread to smash into the target from stern to bow.

Forty-seven seconds later Enright saw and heard the first torpedo hit just inside the carrier's stern, near the propellers and rudder. A great, glowing ball of fire climbed the vessel's side. Then another torpedo smashed home. Enright ordered the submarine deep to evade the inevitable counter-attack. As ARCHERFISH went down, four more timed hits were heard. Breaking-up noises hissed and crackled in the sound gear. Fourteen depth charges boomed in the sea, the nearest some 300 yards away. The last

charge thundered at 0345, but the clash and crackle of a great ship disintegrating deep under the sea continued for another 20 minutes. Finally, silence.

At 0614, Enright put up the periscope for a look. Nothing in sight. Four hours later a thunderous explosion was heard, its source a mystery. Whatever its origin, it came as a salute to the victors of the greatest undersea battle fought in "Hit Parade."

Enright identified the target as a vessel of the HAYATAKA class and accordingly claimed credit for sinking a 29,000-ton aircraft carrier. The facts did not come to light until V-J Day. The Japanese super-battleships YAMATO and MUSASHI, mounting 18-inch guns, were the largest men-of-war ever built by any nation. The Allies were aware that the keel had been laid for a third behemoth of this class—a giant sister to accompany the other two. The name and whereabouts of this third monster remained unknown to the Allies until the cessation of hostilities. Then it was learned that the huge vessel had been converted into a super-aircraft carrier named SHINANO. And her whereabouts was latitude 32-00 N., longitude 137-00 E., where ARCHERFISH had caught and sunk her in the waters of "Hit Parade."

Commissioned on November 18, 1944, she was torpedoed just 10 days later while on her maiden voyage to a safe port for fitting out. SHINANO had a standard displacement of 59,000 tons. Enright and company sank the largest man-of-war ever downed by a submarine. ARCHERFISH leads the hit parade in world history!

Bergall vs. Myoko

Early in December 1943, BERGALL (Commander J. M. Hyde) was patrolling in the South China Sea. For a few December days she encountered relative peace and quiet. Then late in the afternoon of the 13th her high periscope picked up a ship 35,000 yards distant. The sun was westering, and Hyde decided to start an end-around at once to gain an ahead position for a night attack.

This was a bold maneuver. The target was steaming toward Royalist Bank off the southern coast of Indo-China. The coastal waters were shallow—11 to 14 fathoms with several six-fathom spots. In these depths a submerged attack would be difficult, and a submerged retirement would be hazardous. Moreover, the sundown promised a clear evening and the smooth, limpid sea offered little submarine protection. Balancing the risks against the chances of success, Hyde began the chase. Target's speed was plotted at 13 knots, and BERGALL, running on four engines, was soon out in front. She reached attack position about 2000.

One favor—the night was moonless. At 17,500 yards the target could be dimly discerned. The submariners were able to identify it as a large warship. There was an escort on its starboard bow. BERGALL was on the port beam. Hyde determined to remain on the surface, and race the submarine in on the attack as though she were a PT-boat. He reasoned that this audacious charge would take the enemy by surprise and catch him off guard. Again, the risk was calculated. BERGALL was hundreds of miles from assistance, and she lacked a PT-boat's speed. The enemy could out-gun her, and probably run her down, if not stopped by a torpedo hit. Hyde did not intend to miss.

At 2030 the target's silhouette shaped up as that of a heavy cruiser. BERGALL raced forward in the starlight—a leopard leaping in to attack a water buffalo. Afterward, Hyde stated that he was devoting most of his attention to fire control and maneuver, and paying little notice to target identification. At 2037 he opened fire at about 3,300 yards. Target and escort were overlapping at that moment, and the escort now appeared to be a light cruiser.

Six bow torpedoes sped on their way. Two minutes later the night was torn open by a deafening blast. The heavy cruiser was completely enveloped in flames which blanketed her entire length and towered some 750 feet into the air. BERGALL's bridge personnel saw the heavy cruiser break in two as though she were made of cardboard. The fore and aft sections drifted some 1,000 yards apart, creating the illusion of two ships burning in the night.

Because of the dazzling explosion and flame-flare, the submariners could not tell whether the second cruiser had been struck or not. But this warship made no effort to chase BERGALL as she pulled away for a reload. As the escorting cruiser did not open fire, Hyde concluded she had been torpedoed. Then, as he drove BERGALL in to attack this target, the enemy guns suddenly spoke. A two-gun salvo straddled the submarine. One 8-inch shell landed in BERGALL's wake. The second 8-incher pierced the forward torpedo-room loading hatch.

Hyde turned BERGALL away and cleared the battle scene at four-engine speed. But from there on out, the submarine, unable to dive with a large hole in her forward torpedo room, was committed to surface running. A miracle she could run at all!

Hyde was now presented with the problem of making a submarine invisible as it ran an enemy gantlet all the way from French Indo-China, through Karimata Strait and Lombok Strait on down to Australia. The war had by-passed the Netherlands East Indies, but Japanese forces infested the Dutch

islands, and it would be no play on words to say that in those enemy controlled passages BERGALL would be "in dire straits."

But one miracle deserved another. And Hyde and company brought it off. Not by occult means, but by "guts," ingenuity and submarining that were, after all, close to superhuman. After a two-day run, the sweating lookouts sighted ANGLER. When ANGLER came to BERGALL's assistance, temporary repairs were improvised. One officer and 54 men were transferred to ANGLER, while a skeleton crew remained aboard BERGALL to operate the damaged submarine. With ANGLER escorting in case it became necessary to abandon ship, BERGALL started the long voyage home. The submarine reached Fremantle on December 23, after a nerve-wracking journey.

While BERGALL's injuries jeopardized her every mile of travel in enemy water, they were far from mortal, and she was repaired and off to the wars again within a month. Not so her target off the coast of Indo-China. The halved warship was the heavy cruiser MYOKO. The stern half of this vessel ultimately sank. Not to be outdone in miracles, the Jap survivors somehow got the vessel's forward half to Singapore, where it was found at the end of the war. So BERGALL was not credited with a sinking. But that—to Hyde and company—was a mere technicality.

Redfish vs. Unryu

MacArthur's forces invaded Mindoro on December 15th. Eleven days later the Americans on the beachheads were bombarded by a Japanese naval task force. It was not much of a force—two cruisers and some incidental destroyers scraped from the bottom of the barrel. As they approached Mindoro, these left-overs were harassed by American aircraft. They had no air cover. Elderly ISE and HYUGA—battleships with flight decks aft—were too slow to go in with a light bombardment group, and Japanese carriers of more conventional design had become almost as scarce as the brontosaurus.

In fact, but one specimen was available at the time of the American landings on Mindoro. SHINANO, as related, had been sunk by ARCHERFISH on November 28th. JUNYO came to grief on December 9 at the hands of SEA DEVIL (Commander R. E. Styles) and REDFISH (Commander L. D. McGregor). Although JUNYO was not sunk, she was so disabled by this submarine attack that she remained on the binnacle list for the rest of the war. To the Philippines, then, the Imperial Navy was able to dispatch but one last carrier. This was the newly built UNRYU, an 18,500-tonner. She was rushed south by way of the East China Sea.

Hungry REDFISH, having struck at one carrier, was looking around for another. At 1624 on the afternoon of December 19, McGregor's submarine, forced down some moments before by a plane, sighted what appeared to be the masts of a patrol boat coming over the East China Sea horizon. The plane had dropped one fairly close depth charge, and the submariners had an idea something was up. Something was. The masts of another "patrol boat" came into focus, and the periscope was now looking at two destroyers. Almost immediately a Japanese flat-top hove into view. Skipper "Sandy" McGregor clutched the periscope training handles.

"This is a big baby! . . . Battle stations! . . . Torpedo!"

At 1629 the target zigged toward the submarine, presenting a 30° starboard angle on the bow. Exactly eight minutes after sighting the carrier, and without having altered REDFISH's course during the approach, McGregor opened fire with four bow torpedoes at a range of about 6,000 yards. Forty-five seconds later the first torpedo hit. The carrier stopped and listed 20° to starboard. At sight of the torpedo wakes, the vessel had opened up with all guns firing wildly. Now one of the rushing destroyers passed just astern of the submarine, right in line for a salvo from the stern tubes. McGregor fired four shots at the DD, but the torpedoes missed.

While shells and depth charges exploded on all sides, the submariners worked feverishly to load the remaining torpedoes in the after torpedo room. Training the periscope this way and that in an effort to watch all arenas of this wild circus, McGregor shouted for more speed. The destroyers were milling about, the listing carrier was firing her starboard guns at REDFISH, and McGregor himself was ready to explode by the time the first tube could be reloaded.

At 1649½, he fired one Mark 23 steam torpedo. The shot hit the target. UNRYU broke apart like a shattered watermelon, her planes hurled into the air like scattered seeds. The carrier was buried in a cloud of smoke and debris. Then, at 1659, she was buried under the sea. The funeral, all told, had taken 32 minutes.

To escape a similar sea burial, REDFISH went deep. At 150 feet she almost caught it from a pursuing depth charge. The DD's were on top of her, and seven depth-charge blasts exploded close aboard the submarine's starboard bow. The steering gear jammed on hard left, the bow planes jammed on a 20° rise, all hydraulic power was lost, the sound gear went out of commission, and the pressure hull of the forward torpedo room was cracked. There were other casualties. A watertight door, jarring open, struck a man on the head and all but severed his ear.

At 1712 REDFISH was on the sea floor, deep under the surface. She was there more by accident than intent, but the best solution to her difficulties seemed to be to lie low. The enemy overhead tried to locate her foxhole with depth charges, and the barrage went on crashing and rumpusing for about two hours.

At 1904 McGregor finally moved REDFISH from the mud, and half an hour later she was on the surface, running away from the destroyers at flank speed. REDFISH was headed for the barn. But behind her, UNRYU was permanently fastened to the bottom, and the Japanese bombardment force at Mindoro received no carrier support.

THE SCORE
SUBMARINES VS. JAPANESE NAVY (1944)

Date	Submarine	Commanding Officer	Ship Sunk	Tonnage
BATTLESHIP SUNK				
Nov. 21	Sealion II	E. T. Reich	Kongo	31,000
JAPANESE CARRIERS SUNK				
June 19	Cavalla	H. J. Kossler	Shokaku	30,000
June 19	Albacore	J. W. Blanchard	Taiho	31,000
Nov. 29	Archerfish	J. F. Enright	Shinano	59,000
Dec. 19	Redfish	L. D. McGregor	Unryu	18,500
JAPANESE ESCORT CARRIERS SUNK				
Aug. 18	Rasher	H. G. Munson	Taiyo (Otaka)	20,000
Sept. 16	Barb	E. B. Fluckey	Unyo	20,000
Nov. 17	Spadefish	G. W. Underwood	Jinyo	21,000

Date	Submarine	Commanding Officer	Ship Sunk	Tonnage
		HEAVY CRUISERS SUNK		
Oct. 23	Darter	D. H. McClintock	Atago	12,200
Oct. 23	Dace	B. D. Claggett	Maya	12,200
		JAPANESE LIGHT CRUISERS SUNK		
Feb. 16	Skate	W. P. Gruner, Jr.	Agano	7,000
Mar. 13	Sandlance	M. E. Garrison	Tatsuta	3,300
Apr. 27	Bluegill	E. L. Barr	Yubari	3,500
July 19	Flasher	R. T. Whitaker	Oi	5,700
Aug. 7	Croaker	J. E. Lee	Nagara	5,700
Aug. 18	Hardhead	F. McMasters	Natori	5,700
Sept. 19	Shad	L. V. Julihn	Ioshima	900e
Oct. 25	Jallao	J. B. Icenhower	Tama*	5,700
		JAPANESE DESTROYERS SUNK		
Jan. 14	Albacore	J. W. Blanchard	Sazanami	1,950
Jan. 26	Skipjack	G. G. Molumphy	Suzukaze	1,580
Feb. 1	Guardfish	N. G. Ward	Umikaze	1,580
Feb. 10	Pogy	R. M. Metcalf	Minekaze	1,300
Mar. 16	Tautog	W. B. Sieglaff	Shirakumo	1,950
Apr. 11	Redfin	M. H. Austin	Akigumo	1,900
Apr. 13	Harder	S. D. Dealey	Ikazuchi	1,950
May 10	Cod	J. C. Dempsey	Karukaya**	820
May 14	Bonefish	T. W. Hogan	Inazuma	1,950
May 22	Pollack	B. E. Lewellen	Asanagi	1,270
June 6	Harder	S. D. Dealey	Minatsuki	1,500
June 7	Harder	S. D. Dealey	Hayanami	2,100
June 8	Hake	J. C. Broach	Kazegumo	1,900
June 9	Harder	S. D. Dealey	Tanikaze	1,900
June 9	Swordfish	K. E. Montross	Matsukaze	1,270
July 6	Paddle	B. H. Nowell	Hokaze	1,300
July 7	Mingo	J. J. Staley, Jr.	Tamanami	2,100
July 7	Skate	W. P. Gruner	Usugumo	1,950
July 25	Batfish	J. K. Fyfe	Samidare*	1,580
Aug. 23	Haddo	C. W. Nimitz, Jr.	Asakaze	1,270
Aug. 25	Picuda	G. R. Donaho	Yunagi	1,270
Sept. 12	Growler	T. B. Oakley	Shikinami	1,950
Oct. 25	Halibut	I. J. Galantin	Akitsuki	1,900
Nov. 3	Pintado	B. A. Clarey	Akikaze	1,300
Nov. 21	Sealion II	E. T. Reich	Urakaze	1,900
Nov. 25	Cavalla	H. J. Kossler	Shimotsuki	2,300
Dec. 4	Flasher	G. W. Grider	Kishinami	2,100
Dec. 4	Flasher	G. W. Grider	Iwanami	2,100
Dec. 15	Hawkbill	F. W. Scanland	Momo	760
Dec. 30	Razorback	C. D. Brown	Kuretake**	820
		JAPANESE SUBMARINES SUNK		
Feb. 15	Aspro	W. A. Stevenson	I-43	2,212
Mar. 23	Tunny	J. A. Scott	I-42	2,212
Apr. 20	Seahorse	S. D. Cutter	RO-45	965
Apr. 29	Pogy	R. M. Metcalf	I-183	1,630
July 26	Sawfish	A. B. Banister	I-29	2,212
Sept. 15	Sea Devil	R. E. Styles	RO-42	965
Nov. 29	Scabbardfish	F. A. Gunn	I-365	1,470

* Previously damaged by naval aircraft.

Note: In addition to the sinkings listed, five major Japanese warships were knocked out of action. Heavy cruisers Aoba, Takao, Myoko were permanently disabled by Bream, Darter, and Bergall, respectively. The 29,000-ton aircraft carrier Junyo

** Designated as "old destroyers."

(Hayataka), was similarly damaged by torpedoes from Sea Devil or Redfish. Torpedoed by Guitarro, Bream, Raton and Ray, the heavy cruiser Kumano was eventually destroyed by naval aircraft. (And Flounder sank a U-boat in the Java Sea.)

CHAPTER 28

BISECTING THE EMPIRE

Maru Morgue and Maru Cemetery

The last three months of 1944, bracketing the Philippines campaign, sealed the doom of the Japanese merchant marine. Which is to say, the War Lords in Tokyo sealed it as they rushed reinforcements to the Philippines in a frantic effort to contain the American advance. While the Imperial Navy was doing and dying, the Japanese transport service was following suit, and its death throes were as violent as those which racked the IJN.

As is shown by the accompanying chart, Japanese merchant shipping suffered heavy losses in the Philippines area in September. Navy Air was responsible for a large percentage of the toll extracted,

submarines accounting for some 181,000 of the total 424,149 tons sunk that month.

As of October 1, 1944, the Japanese merchant tonnage afloat totaled 3,474,008 tons. By November 1, the total had shrunk to 3,095,820 tons. On December 1, it was down to 2,847,534 tons. And by the end of December it had been further reduced to 2,786,407 tons.

Navy aircraft sank weighty merchant tonnages in the Philippines during October and November, and Army Air came to the fore in December, as shown by the succeeding charts on pages 416, 426 and 432. But submersibles retained the dominant role in the attrition war during the year's final quarter. In spite of intensified carrier and land-based air participation, 55% of the Japanese merchant ships downed in this period were sunk by SubPac and SubSoWesPac submarines.

Majority of the sinkings were in the waters off western Luzon, in Luzon Strait and in Formosa Strait. Here the submarines were concentrated to support "King Two" and to block the enemy's attempt to shore up his crumbling bastions during the Philippines campaign. SubSoWesPac submarines patrolled off North Borneo to watch the Japanese naval anchorage at Brunei and cut off the Borneo oil line.

But it was obvious that the chief logistics support for the Imperial Army in the Philippines would come from Japan and Formosa, hence the SubPac concentration in Formosan waters and Luzon Strait, merging with the SubSoWesPac concentration off western Luzon.

Late in September while the Leyte landings were on the planning board, SubPac Headquarters set up a new "XYZ Patrol" to cover the Nansei Shoto chain. The western and southern boundaries of this patrol area were largely determined by the great East China Sea mine barrier which flanked the archipelago. It would not do to have the "King Two" gambit countered by Japanese pawns moving down through this chain of islands. Submarine patrols could block such moves on the Pacific side and force the Japanese to detour through the East China Sea and move through the Formosa Strait bottleneck. The Nansei Shoto patrol area was given the suggestive name "Maru Morgue."

During an August-September patrol, BARBEL (Commander R. A. Keating) had found some lively small-game shooting off the Nansei Shotos. MIYAKO MARU, YAGI MARU, BOKO MARU and BUSHU MARU had fallen prey to her torpedoes. All small steamers—but the little ones added up, and sometimes carried passengers

410

as important as those on luxury liners. SEA DOG (Commander V. L. Lowrance) downed the converted gunboat TOMITSU MARU and the supply ship MUROTO in this area on October 22nd. But the chief importance of this "XYZ Patrol" area was strategic. As intended, the "Morgue" sent Japanese shipping down the East China Sea and through Formosa Strait to debouch across the waters of "Convoy College." And there the *marus* ended up in a marine cemetery.

As "King Two" hit Leyte and MacArthur's forces pushed from there to Mindoro, the SubPac submarines patrolling Luzon Strait and off southwest Formosa turned "Convoy College" into a potter's field for Japanese ships. The lucky *maru* that escaped this burying ground was slated for sinking in the South China Sea (SubSoWesPac Area) below the 18°-30′ parallel. In these waters, throughout October and November, the Japanese convoys went down like Oriental funeral processions, the burials clamorous with the cymbal-crash of torpedoes, the din of pagan whistles and bells, the ruction of fireworks, the groans and wails of the mourners, the sepulchral rumble of vessels entering the grave. Day and night the Japanese ship burials went on.

CABRILLA, ASPRO, WHALE, SAWFISH, SNOOK, SEADRAGON, ICEFISH, DRUM, ATULE, POMFRET and BANG led the October-November attack in "Convoy College" and adjacent Luzon waters. Some of these submarines operated with coordinated attack groups; others conducted "lone wolf" patrols. But the entire campaign was coordinated as an effort designed to cut Japanese shipping lanes to the northern Philippines.

Carrying torpedoes from Fremantle, CABRILLA (Commander W. C. Thompson) staged a vigorous patrol two weeks in advance of the Leyte landings. On October 1 she was combing the sea southwest of Lingayen Gulf. Along came a tanker convoy, and into action went CABRILLA. When the shooting was over, the Japanese tanker fleet was minus ZUIYO MARU, 7,385 tons, and KYOKUHO MARU, 10,059 tons. This at a time when oil was liquid gold to the impoverished Imperial forces. CABRILLA followed through at the end of the week by sinking two cargomen. Concluding her patrol, she left buried in her wake a good 24,557 tons of enemy shipping.

CABRILLA was patrolling with a wolf-pack composed of herself, ASPRO and HOE, under group leadership of Commander V. B. McCrea in HOE. Working just north of Lingayen Gulf, ASPRO (Commander W. A. Stevenson) downed a large freighter on October 2 and a good-sized passenger-cargoman on the 7th for a total 10,914 tons. Northwest of Lingayen, HOE sank a small passenger-cargoman on the 8th.

Altogether, the pack deprived the Philippines defenders of some 38,000 tons of shipping.

On October 6, WHALE (Commander J. B. Grady) caught a large tanker off northwest Luzon. Down in flames went the 10,241-ton AKANE MARU—another break in the enemy's oil line. Three days later, SAWFISH (Commander A. B. Banister) in a neighboring area overhauled and sank the tanker TACHIBANA MARU, 6,521 tons. On the 23rd, she ripped the bottom out of KIMIKAWA MARU, a 6,863-ton converted seaplane tender.

In the immediate vicinity of the tender sinking, SNOOK (Commander G. H. Browne) struck and sank SHINSEI MARU No. 1, a medium-sized passenger-cargoman. The following day she downed the small tanker KIKUSUI MARU and ARISAN MARU, a bulky freighter. Total cost to the enemy: 16,636 tons.

In Luzon Strait, farther north, SHARK II, BLACKFISH and SEADRAGON were cooperating as a wolf-pack —"Blakely's Behemoths." SHARK II was lost during this patrol, and the enemy swarmed down on SEADRAGON (Commander J. H. Ashley, Jr.).

SEADRAGON was conducting her eleventh war patrol, and the convoy that ran into this veteran had cause to regret it. Freighter EIKO MARU and passenger-cargomen TAITEN MARU and KOKURYU MARU were buried three in a row by the old "Red Pirate." Tonnage total: 15,654 tons.

"Banister's Beagles"—SAWFISH, ICEFISH and DRUM —patrolled an adjacent "Convoy College" area. ICEFISH (Commander R. W. Peterson) sank a freighter on October 24 and another on the 26th. DRUM (Commander R. H. Rindskopf) downed a passenger-cargoman on the 24th and two freighters on the 26th. Combined effort of these two "Beagles" cost the enemy some 25,000 tons.

The "Beagles" and other attack groups roaming "Convoy College" might have found more to shoot at had the submarine blockade of Formosa been less efficient. During October the Formosa Strait bottleneck was tightly plugged at the northern end, and a single submarine served as cork. That submarine was TANG. Lucky was the convoy that escaped TANG's sharpshooting torpedoes. Then she herself—tragic *tour de force*—was downed by her own last shot at the conclusion of this remarkable patrol. The story is featured later in this chapter.

Hardest blow dealt the Japanese transport service in the "College" area at this time was struck by ATULE (Commander J. H. Maurer). She will be remembered as one of "Clarey's Crushers," rushed to Cape Engano waters to intercept Ozawa's carrier group. After JALLAO's bout with TAMA, the "Crushers" went ranging westward through Luzon Strait.

411

Northwest of Luzon on November 1, ATULE ambushed a convoy.

This was no ordinary convoy. Herded along by the escorts was a passenger vessel that outweighed three of the ordinary Japanese variety. When Maurer spotted this ship, he knew ATULE had something. The submarine was on her maiden patrol, and a light cruiser was the traditional target, as JALLAO had demonstrated. However, there was a shortage of Jap light cruisers, and Maurer was more than willing to accept the equally rare Japanese ocean liner. So ATULE dug in. Torpedoes fanned out. Thunder boomed in the sea. And under the sea went the transport ASAMA MARU, 16,975 tons. With her first attack ATULE sank the last Japanese liner of over 15,000 tons to be downed by U.S. submarines in the Pacific War.

Maurer and company did not ship their oars. Twenty days later they sank a minesweeper. And on November 25 ATULE struck another convoy and deposited under the surface an old destroyer and the 7,266-ton freighter SANTOS MARU. For a first patrol ATULE's tonnage score was notable—25,691 tons.

POMFRET (Commander J. B. Hess) covered an area bordering on ATULE's. On November 2 she attacked a convoy and sank a pair of better-than-average passenger-cargomen—ATLAS MARU, 7,347 tons, and HAMBURG MARU, 5,271 tons. On the 25th she downed the small freighter SHOHO MARU.

Clearly marked on the accompanying chart is the success of the submarine campaign to cut the enemy's supply lines prior to and during the October battle for Leyte. Note the sinkings clogging Formosa Strait and Luzon Strait and cluttering the coastal waters of western Luzon and Mindoro. As has been remarked, the South China Sea lanes to Luzon and Mindoro were covered by the SubSoWesPac Force, and the efficient coverage is plainly indicated.

Early in October a wolf-pack composed of HAWKBILL, FLASHER and BECUNA, under Captain E. H. Bryant, opened fire on the Mindoro traffic. FLASHER (Commander R. T. Whitaker) torpedoed a passenger-cargoman on the 4th, and down went TAIBIN MARU, 6,886 tons. On October 7, HAWKBILL (Commander F. W. Scanland, Jr.) teamed up with BAYA to sink KINUGASA MARU, 8,407-ton passenger-cargoman. On the 9th, HAWKBILL and BECUNA (Commander H. D. Sturr) demolished a small freighter off northwest Palawan.

Off southwest Luzon, LAPON (Commander D. G. Baer) dug in on the 10th to nail EJIRI MARU, a 6,968-ton freighter. In the same area BONEFISH (Commander L. L. Edge) demolished a small freighter on the 14th. Northeast of Palawan on that date ANGLER

(Commander F. G. Hess) sank the 2,407-ton transport NANREI MARU. And RATON (Commander M. W. Shea) northwest of Palawan on the 18th caught a convoy and downed SHIRANESAN MARU, freighter, 4,739 tons, and TAIKAI MARU, passenger-cargoman, 3,812 tons.

Off northwest Mindoro, BLUEGILL (Commander E. L. Barr, Jr.) held the undersea line. On October 18 she held it to the extent of one of the best patrol scores in the area. Driven into her bailiwick was the sort of convoy she had been looking for. Barr sent the submarine and the torpedoes boring in. Down went the transport ARABIA MARU, 9,480 tons. Down went CHINZEI MARU, 1,999 tons. Down went HAKUSHIKA MARU, passenger-cargoman, 8,150 tons. Cost to the enemy's Philippine supply line: 19,629 tons.

The biggest merchant ship sunk south of the Philippines storm center in October was the 10,528-ton tanker NIPPO MARU, lowered into a watery grave on the 27th by BERGALL (Commander J. M. Hyde). The tanker lies in the cluster of sinkings charted in the coastal waters of northwest Borneo where submarines were watching the approaches to Brunei. Five of the *marus* downed during October in this strategic little plot were buried by HAMMERHEAD, whose exemplary tactics are discussed elsewhere in this chapter. Suffice it to say at this point that those tactics cost the enemy 25,178 tons of much-needed shipping.

GUITARRO (Commander E. D. Haskins) concluded the October score for the SubSoWesPac Force in the area off southwest Luzon. Her victims were KOMEI MARU, freighter, 2,857 tons, and the 5,872-ton passenger-cargoman PACIFIC MARU.

During November, as shown by the charted sinkings for that month, Japanese merchant shipping off western Luzon came under the concentrated fire of Navy Air. The ATULE and POMFRET shootings in Luzon Strait are marked as the major attrition actions in the "College" area. Most of the SubPac *maru*-attrition occurred as indicated at the northern end of the East China Sea. In the waters off Formosa and northern Luzon, large Japanese merchant convoys had made themselves scarce. However, while SubPac wolf-packs were blocking the southern end of Formosa Strait, "Sandy's Sluggers"—REDFISH, BANG and SHAD—were patrolling off the east coast of Formosa. On November 23 the "Sluggers" trapped a convoy. BANG (Commander A. R. Gallaher) sank a modest freighter and a passenger-cargoman. REDFISH (Commander L. D. "Sandy" McGregor) abolished a 2,345-ton transport.

November sinkings scored by SubSoWesPac submarines are scattered across the South China Sea. BLACKFIN, BARBERO, GUNNEL, BARBEL, JACK,

GUAVINA and MINGO did most of the *maru*-shooting.

On November 4, RATON, BREAM and GUITARRO teamed up to sink KAGU MARU, a 6,806-ton passenger-cargoman, off southwest Luzon. Southwest of the Paracel Islands, BARBEL (Commander R. A. Keating, Jr.) sank a pair of medium-sized freighters on the 14th. JACK (Commander A. S. Furhman) struck a convoy off Saigon, Indo-China, on the 14th, and downed two freighters—NICHIEI MARU, 5,396 tons, and YUZAN MARU No. 2, 6,859 tons.

GUNNEL (Commander G. E. O'Neil, Jr.) staged a busy patrol in the vicinity of the Paracel Islands where she bagged a torpedo boat and the 5,623-ton passenger-cargoman SHUNTEN MARU on November 17th.

Off northeast Palawan on November 14, GUAVINA (Commander C. Tiedeman) added a couple of torpedoes to Navy aircraft bombs and helped spell the finish for a small freighter. On the 21st GUAVINA teamed up with FLOUNDER (Commander J. E. Stevens) to sink GYOSAN MARU, freighter, 5,698 tons. The following day Tiedeman's submarine torpedoed the tonnage out of the 1,916-ton freighter DOWA MARU.

PARGO (Commander D. B. Bell) flushed a tanker southwest of Brunei on November 26th. Down in flames went YUHO MARU, 5,226 tons.

Biggest merchantman downed by SubSoWesPac torpedoes that month was sunk southwest of Brunei on November 25 by MINGO (Commander J. R. Madison). MINGO's victim was the 9,486-ton passenger-cargoman MANILA MARU. The sinking of a *maru* bearing that name was prophetic. For the Japanese had lost their grip on the Philippine capital as surely as they had lost this namesake ship on the run between Singapore and Brunei.

Impavid MacArthur had returned, and returned to stay. The Japanese attempt to reinforce the Leyte front had been frustrated, and the success of the American push was guaranteed. More than 900,000 tons of *maru* shipping had gone to the bottom in October and November—most of it in the Philippines theater—and all hope of logistic support for the Imperial forces on Leyte, Mindoro and Luzon was ended. Over the islands a Japanese twilight would linger for a time, but the Rising Sun had set. Deprived of reserves and replacements, the Imperial garrisons were done for.

Responsible for over 55% of the tonnage subtracted from Japanese merchant shipping during this period, U.S. submarines put a tremendous shoulder to the wheel of the Philippines campaign. No better example of submarine support for an amphibious operation can be found in World War II. And the submarines did more. Cutting the sea lanes to the

Philippines, their October-November attrition drive tore to pieces the Empire's transportation system, severed the Singapore-Japan trunk line, and permanently broke the back of the Japanese merchant marine.

The airmen in the Philippines theater contributed their share, and a goodly share it was. But over the necropolis of "Convoy College" and the cemetery of the South China Sea the submariners reared a monumental score—a colossal *maru* cenotaph on the face of which the table on pages 414-415 is inscribed.

Submarine Tactics—The Attack from Ahead (Night Radar)

Once the time and place of attack were determined and the tracking and approach phases were over, nearly all submarine commanders favored an attack from ahead or on the bow. Such an attack developed rapidly, and thus gave the enemy less opportunity to sight the submarine or make an unexpected maneuver. When the target's speed was relatively high, a position on the bow helped to keep the situation in hand, for no radical course-change could leave the submarine too far out on a limb.

Bow approaches usually produced hits in the head of a convoy column. The Japanese convoy was prone to panic when a vessel in the van was torpedoed. As the stricken *maru* tooted frantically, or wandered off course, disabled, the formation would disintegrate, and vessels and escorts might scatter and race about in the hectic fashion of fowl who scent a fox in the henyard. The confusion usually gave the alert submarine skipper with good radar all the torpedo opportunities he could use.

HAMMERHEAD made an excellent demonstration of the radar approach and bow attack on the night of October 1, 1944, when she struck a convoy off northwest Borneo. Deciding that the best chance of picking up a target lay inside the barrier reef between Furious Shoals and St. Joseph Rock, HAMMERHEAD's skipper, Commander J. C. Martin, took the submarine inside the reef. Uncomfortable water for undersea warfare. Depths average some 110 feet, but there are shallow patches where the bottom is anywhere from 30 to 15 feet below the surface. Martin hoped to get HAMMERHEAD's business over with and have her out in deep water by dawn.

At 2245, radar contact! Ships to the southward, range 16,000 yards. Soon the radar screen showed a convoy of five large vessels and three escorts. HAMMERHEAD was ahead of the convoy, on the starboard bow and only 1,500 yards off the track. Martin maneuvered the submarine out to a position 4,800 yards

413

Japanese Merchant Marine Losses ("Convoy College"—South China Sea)

October-November 1944

Date	Submarine	Commanding Officer	Ship Sunk	Type	Tonnage
Oct. 1	Cabrilla	W. C. Thompson	Zuiyo Maru	Tanker	7,385
Oct. 1	Cabrilla	W. C. Thompson	Kyokuho Maru	Tanker	10,059
Oct. 6	Cabrilla	W. C. Thompson	Yamamizu Maru No. 2	Cargo	5,154
Oct. 7	Cabrilla	W. C. Thompson	Shinyo Maru No. 8	Cargo	1,959
Oct. 2	Aspro	W. A. Stevenson	Azuchisan Maru	Cargo	6,888
Oct. 7	Aspro	W. A. Stevenson	Macassar Maru	Passenger-Cargo	4,026
Oct. 1	Hammerhead	J. C. Martin	Kokusei Maru	Cargo	5,396
Oct. 1	Hammerhead	J. C. Martin	Higane Maru	Cargo	5,320
Oct. 1	Hammerhead	J. C. Martin	Hiyori Maru	Cargo	5,320
Oct. 20	Hammerhead	J. C. Martin	Ugo Maru	Passenger-Cargo	3,684
Oct. 20	Hammerhead	J. C. Martin	Oyo Maru	Passenger-Cargo	5,458
Oct. 2	Pomfret	F. C. Acker	Tsuyama Maru	Passenger-Cargo	6,962
Oct. 4	Flasher	R. T. Whitaker	Taibin Maru	Cargo	6,886
Oct. 5	Cod	J. A. Adkins	Tatshshiro Maru	Cargo	6,886
Oct. 7	Hawkbill / Baya	F. W. Scanland, Jr. / A. H. Holtz	Kinugasa Maru	Passenger-Cargo	8,407
Oct. 6	Whale	J. B. Grady	Akane Maru	Tanker	10,241
Oct. 8	Hoe	V. B. McRea	Kohoku Maru	Passenger-Cargo	2,573
Oct. 9	Hawkbill / Becuna	F. W. Scanland, Jr. / H. D. Sturr	Tokuwa Maru	Cargo	1,943
Oct. 9	Sawfish	A. B. Banister	Tachibana Maru	Tanker	6,521
Oct. 23	Sawfish	A. B. Banister	Kimikawa Maru	Convoy Seaplane Tender	6,863
Oct. 10	Lapon	D. G. Baer	Ejiri Maru	Cargo	6,968
Oct. 12	Ray	W. T. Kinsella	Toko Maru	Passenger-Cargo	4,180
Oct. 13	Bergall	J. M. Hyde	Shinshu Maru	Cargo	4,182
Oct. 27	Bergall	J. M. Hyde	Nippo Maru	Tanker	10,528
Oct. 14	Angler	F. G. Hess	Nanrei Maru	Transport	2,407
Oct. 14	Bonefish	L. L. Edge	Fushimi Maru	Cargo	2,542
Oct. 18	Raton	M. W. Shea	Shiranesan Maru	Cargo	4,739
Oct. 18	Raton	M. W. Shea	Taikai Maru	Passenger-Cargo	3,812
Oct. 18	Bluegill	E. L. Barr, Jr.	Arabia Maru	Transport	9,480
Oct. 18	Bluegill	E. L. Barr, Jr.	Chinzei Maru	Cargo	1,999
Oct. 18	Bluegill	E. L. Barr, Jr.	Hakushika Maru	Passenger-Cargo	8,150
Oct. 23	Snook	G. H. Browne	Shinsei Maru No. 1	Passenger-Cargo	5,863
Oct. 24	Snook	G. H. Browne	Kikusui Maru	Tanker	3,887
Oct. 24	Snook	G. H. Browne	Arisan Maru	Cargo	6,886
Oct. 24	Seadragon	J. H. Ashley, Jr.	Eiko Maru	Cargo	1,843
Oct. 24	Seadragon	J. H. Ashley, Jr.	Taiten Maru	Passenger-Cargo	6,442
Oct. 24	Seadragon	J. H. Ashley, Jr.	Kokuryu Maru	Passenger-Cargo	7,369
Oct. 24	Icefish	R. W. Peterson	Tenshin Maru	Cargo	4,236
Oct. 26	Icefish	R. W. Peterson	Taiyo Maru	Cargo	4,168

Date	Submarine	Commanding Officer	Ship Sunk	Type	Tonnage
Oct. 24	Drum	M. H. Rindskopf	Shikisan Maru	Passenger-Cargo	4,725
Oct. 26	Drum	M. H. Rindskopf	Taisho Maru	Cargo	6,886
Oct. 26	Drum	M. H. Rindskopf	Taihoku Maru	Cargo	6,886
Oct. 26	Rock	J. J. Flachsenhar	Takasago Maru No. 7	Tanker	834e
Oct. 31	Guitarro	E. D. Haskins	Komei Maru	Cargo	2,857
Oct. 31	Guitarro	E. D. Haskins	Pacific Maru	Passenger-Cargo	5,872
Nov. 1	Blackfin	G. H. Laird, Jr.	Unkai Maru No. 12	Cargo	2,745
Nov. 2	Barbero	I. S. Hartman	Kuramasan Maru	Cargo	1,995
Nov. 8	Barbero	I. S. Hartman	Shimotsu Maru	Tanker	2,854
Nov. 3	Gurnard	N. D. Gage	Tamei Maru	Cargo	6,923
Nov. 4	Ray Bream Guitarro	W. T. Kinsella W. G. Chapple E. D. Haskins	Kagu Maru	Passenger-Cargo	6,806
Nov. 1	Atule	J. H. Maurer	Askama Maru	Transport	16,975
Nov. 20	Atule	J. H. Maurer	Minesweeper No. 38	Minesweeper	630e
Nov. 25	Atule	J. H. Maurer	Patrol Boat No. 38	Old Destroyer	820e
Nov. 25	Atule	J. H. Maurer	Santos Maru	Cargo	7,266
Nov. 2	Pomfret	J. B. Hess	Atlas Maru	Passenger-Cargo	7,347
Nov. 2	Pomfret	J. B. Hess	Hamburg Maru	Passenger-Cargo	5,271
Nov. 25	Pomfret	J. B. Hess	Shoho Maru	Cargo	1,356
Nov. 8	Gunnel	G. E. O'Neil, Jr.	Sagi	Torpedo Boat	595
Nov. 17	Gunnel	G. E. O'Neil, Jr.	Shunten Maru	Passenger-Cargo	5,623
Nov. 17	Gunnel	G. E. O'Neil, Jr.	Hiyodori	Torpedo Boat	595
Nov. 8	Redfin	M. H. Austin	Nichinan Maru No. 2	Tanker	5,226
Nov. 8	Hardhead	F. A. Greenup	Manei Maru	Tanker	5,226
Nov. 25	Hardhead	F. A. Greenup	Coast Defense Vessel No. 38	Frigate	800e
Nov. 14	Hardhead	F. A. Greenup	Unkai Maru No. 5	Tanker	2,841
Nov. 14	Hardhead	F. A. Greenup	Kurasaki	Miscellaneous Auxiliary	989
Nov. 14	Barbel	R. A. Keating, Jr.	Sugiyama Maru	Cargo	4,379
Nov. 14	Barbel	R. A. Keating, Jr.	Misaki Maru	Cargo	4,422
Nov. 14	Guavina Navy Carrier-Based Aircraft	C. Tiedeman	Yutaka Maru	Cargo	2,704
Nov. 14	Jack	A. S. Fuhrman	Nichiei Maru	Cargo	5,396
Nov. 15	Jack	A. S. Fuhrman	Yuzan Maru No. 2	Cargo	6,859
Nov. 21	Flounder Guavina	J. E. Stevens C. Tiedeman	Gyosan Maru	Cargo	5,698
Nov. 22	Guavina	C. Tiedeman	Dowa Maru	Cargo	1,916
Nov. 22	Besugo	T. L. Wogan	Transport No. 151	Landing Craft	1,000e
Nov. 23	Bang	A. R. Gallaher	Sakae Maru	Cargo	2,878
Nov. 23	Bang	A. R. Gallaher	Amakusa Maru	Passenger-Cargo	2,340
Nov. 23	Redfish	L. D. McGregor	Hozan Maru	Transport	2,345
Nov. 25	Mingo	J. R. Madison	Manila Maru	Passenger-Cargo	9,486
Nov. 26	Pargo	D. B. Bell	Yuho Maru	Tanker	5,226

from the track, and then turned to come in for a shot on a 90° track angle.

The enemy escorts were "pinging." Sea was calm, but rain curtained the night and the visibility was limited to 7,000 yards. Martin slowed the submarine to 7 knots to reduce the chances of detection. Target was zigzagging about 15° each side of the base course and steaming at 7.5 knots.

When the angle on the bow was about 69° and the range was 5,500 yards, Martin put HAMMERHEAD's bow directly toward the leading ship and drove in. The escorts showed up in the dark rain—one on the port bow, another on the starboard beam, the third bringing up the convoy's rear. The ships were traveling in a ragged column—four freighters and a tanker. Martin decided to fire three bow shots at the leading freighter. Freighter No. 2 was slightly overlapping and a miss on the first ship might hit the second. The remaining three torpedoes from the bow-nest could be fired at freighter No. 3. Then HAMMERHEAD could swing and get in two stern shots at the tanker and two more at the tag-end freighter.

At 2326 the range was 3,800 yards, the track angle for No. 1 freighter 85° with zero gyro. Martin opened fire with the three bow shots. One minute later the bow tubes were clear, and the submarine was swinging to bring the stern tubes to bear. The first torpedoes hit. A bright pillar of flame shot skyward from freighter No. 1 as she blew up. The blast was echoed by a hit on freighter No. 3—a voluminous orange explosion.

Now the after tubes were on with a 10° right gyro and a 3,800-yard range for a 95° track angle. A hit on freighter No. 4 sent up a funnel of flame. Two timed hits on the tanker were counted. White smoke billowed from freighter No. 4, but the tanker did not erupt as did the cargo carriers.

While the submariners worked at top speed to reload HAMMERHEAD's tubes, the rain slackened and visibility improved; whereupon the escorts might have spotted the submarine, but they were dashing hither and yon, chasing shadows. Untroubled by pursuit, HAMMERHEAD slipped away from the dangerous shallows, and reached the quiet embrace of deep water. Behind her she left three torpedoed *marus* on the bottom near Furious Shoals.

HAMMERHEAD's performance was consistently good, for on October 20 she downed two Japanese passenger-cargomen a little farther south off the Borneo coast of Sarawak. Her contribution to the Philippines campaign has been noted as sizable. But her demonstration of the night radar attack from ahead is the case in point. *Maru* mariners seldom fared better when encountering this tactic.

Autumn in Empire Waters ("Loughlin's Loopers")

Although the submarine effort was centered on the Philippines in the autumn of 1944, areas closer to the home Empire were not neglected. CROAKER (Commander J. E. Lee) downed three smallish cargomen off southwest Kyushu in October. On October 25, STERLET (Commander O. C. Robbins) nailed a large tanker off Yaku Island south of Kagoshima, thereby subtracting from the enemy oil line JINEI MARU, 10,500 tons. Hunting in the Kuriles on that day, SEAL (Commander J. H. Turner) sank the 5,742-ton freighter HAKUYO MARU.

In the "Hit Parade" area, GABILAN (Commander K. R. Wheland) demolished a nondescript auxiliary vessel on October 31st. SCABBARDFISH (Commander F. A. Gunn) followed through in November; sank a small freighter on the 16th; and on the 28th, in the waters east of Tokyo, downed the submarine I-365. Patrolling southwest of Kyushu in mid-November, PETO (Commander R. H. Caldwell, Jr.) torpedoed TATSUAKI MARU, AISAKASAN MARU and CHINKAI MARU to strew three more freighters and some 12,000 tons across the sea floor.

Meantime, a new SubPac wolf-pack was ranging over the northern reaches of the East China Sea. Out to shoot its way into submarine headlines, this group was "Loughlin's Loopers"—QUEENFISH, BARB and PICUDA, led by Commander C. E. Loughlin in QUEENFISH. Possessed of a sense of humor as sharp as their other capabilities, the "Loopers" chose to call their boats "Queerfish," "Boob" and "Peculiar." What the Japanese called them is not recorded.

QUEENFISH struck a convoy on November 8 and deleted therefrom two small freighters—KEIJO MARU and HAKKO MARU—and the ex-gunboat CHOJUSAN MARU. On the 15th she caught and sank larger game —AKITSU MARU, aircraft ferry, 9,186 tons. Score for "Queerfish," something over 14,000 tons.

BARB (Commander E. B. Fluckey) went into action on November 10th. Down went the ex-light cruiser GOKOKU MARU, 10,438 tons. Two days later BARB's torpedoes sent down NARUO MARU, freighter, 4,823 tons. Score for "Boob," something over 15,000 tons.

PICUDA (Commander E. T. Shepard) was the "Looper" who knocked the enemy in these waters "for a loop." On November 17 she wiped out the 9,433-ton passenger-cargoman MAYASAN MARU. Wading into a convoy six days later, she sank SHUYO MARU, freighter, 6,933 tons, and FUKUJU MARU, passenger-cargoman, 5,291 tons. Score for "Peculiar," 21,657 tons.

Altogether "Loughlin's Loopers" cost the Japanese merchant marine in Empire waters some 51,000 tons of shipping. And Tokyo was given to understand that a campaign in the Philippines would not relieve the undersea pressure in the north. Now that the major convoy routes below Formosa were either atrophied or amputated, torpedo warfare would louden in the seas embracing the home islands. Japan could look forward to nothing but the winter of her discontent.

But the decimation of Japan's merchant marine had not been accomplished without painful submarine casualties. Seven U.S. submarines were lost in the autumn of 1944—three on one October day. Among those that went down, two were valiant veterans of the war's pioneer period when the Japanese War Machine was thundering down full-tilt on the Philippines instead of frantically retreating.

Loss of Seawolf (A Tragedy of Errors)

No submarine in the Pacific had fought harder in the war than SEAWOLF, pioneer veteran of the Asiatic fleet. Fourteen patrols and 56 torpedo battles had gone into her record since that long-ago day when Lieutenant Commander Warder took her around to Davao Gulf and poked her periscope into the vortex of the Tojo-Yamamoto offensive. Among the first submarines to run from Australia to the Philippines on special mission, she was also one of the last. On her fourteenth patrol, made in August 1944, she transported six agents and 10 tons of supplies to Tongehatan Point, Tawi Tawi, and went on from there to land agents and supplies at Pirata Head, Palawan. While captained by "Freddie" Warder in 1942, she had downed six Japanese ships. In 1943 and the first months of 1944, under captaincy of Commander R. L. Gross, she sank a dozen *marus*. By the autumn of 1944 she had sunk 71,609 tons of enemy shipping. Few submarines had downed as many ships and as much tonnage.

On September 21, 1944, SEAWOLF left Brisbane to begin her fifteenth patrol. She was captained by Lieutenant Commander A. L. Bontier. Eight days later she arrived at Manus in the Admiralties. At this base she received a special mission assignment—she was to carry Army stores and Army personnel to the east coast of Samar in the central Philippines. Stores and passengers were soon on board, and the submarine left Manus a few hours after making port.

While SEAWOLF was en route to Samar, MacArthur's forces were driving at the island of Morotai, the stepping-stone just north of Halmahera. A new submarine safety lane, wherein submarines would presumably be free from attack by friendly forces, had been established in the area directly north of Morotai. SEAWOLF made her passage in this lane.

On October 2, the WOLF notified ComTaskForce 72 that she was bucking heavy seas and running a day behind schedule. This information was promptly relayed to Commander Seventh Fleet.

At 0756 on October 3, NARWHAL sighted SEAWOLF and the submarines exchanged recognition signals. Not long after that a Japanese submarine attacked a Seventh Fleet task group which included the escort carriers FANSHAW BAY and MIDWAY and the destroyer escorts EVERSOLE, EDMONDS, ROWELL and SHELTON. A torpedo struck and mortally injured SHELTON.

ROWELL was directed to stand by the sinking DE and search for the undersea enemy. While ROWELL was circling SHELTON, the damaged vessel reported "sound contact" with a submarine. Although ROWELL did not pick up this contact, depth charges were immediately dropped upon the supposedly detected Jap.

Meantime, the American task group commander dispatched a "hunter-killer" group to search out the Japanese submarine. At 1130 two TBM planes were launched from the large carrier MIDWAY. One of these planes sighted a submarine. The submarine dived and the plane dropped two 325-pound bombs as the submersible went down. The plane had sighted no recognition signals, but this submarine was within the limits of the safety lane. However, the aircraft pilot did not know he was within an attack-restriction area at the time—his information on this detail had been faulty.

Upon receiving a report of this bombing, ROWELL raced to the position given (which had been marked with dye by the plane) and made sound contact on a submarine at 1310. ROWELL delivered six attacks—five with "hedgehogs" (ahead-thrown projectiles) and one with depth charges. After the first "hedgehog" attack, ROWELL heard the submarine send signals by sound gear. The stuttering transmission bore no resemblance to the proper recognition signal, and ROWELL considered it an attempt to "jam" her own sound gear. So she blasted the water with another "hedgehog" pattern. Following this second attack, four or five underwater explosions were heard. Debris was blown to the surface, and ROWELL's crew glimpsed what looked like a section of periscope. A Japanese periscope? Or was it American?

SEAWOLF was never heard from after her exchange with NARWHAL. She did not reach the Philippines, and as Submarine Headquarters assembled the facts, grim evidence of tragedy was revealed.

Four American submarines were in the Morotai area when SHELTON was torpedoed. STINGRAY was in a position estimated as 70 miles distant from the SHELTON torpedoing. NARWHAL was 128 miles away.

DARTER was 260 miles from the scene. And the position which the task group at Morotai had for SEAWOLF was 128 miles distant. However, the position given by SEAWOLF in the message reporting herself a day behind schedule, was within 32 miles of the torpedoing. The U.S. anti-submarine forces at Morotai never received this information. As had been noted, the pilot of the carrier plane which attacked the diving submarine was not even informed that he was in a submarine safety lane and therefore prohibited from attacking any submarine.

After the war it was learned that the Japanese submarine RO-41 was responsible for the SHELTON torpedoing off Morotai. RO-41 was not counter-attacked, and she eventually returned to Japan. The A/S attacks made by ROWELL were 18 miles from the point where SHELTON was hit, and they did not trouble RO-41. As a rule, neither Japanese nor American submarines attempted to "jam" an attacker's sound gear with sound signals. Undoubtedly the signals heard by ROWELL were from SEAWOLF, and the American submarine was desperately trying to establish herself as a friendly unit, in accordance with instructions prescribed.

In view of all the evidence, submarine authorities were practically certain SEAWOLF was sunk by American forces—either by ROWELL's "hedgehog" and depth-charge barrage, or by the bombing from the carrier plane whose pilot was uninformed about the submarine safety lane. Majority opinion of the Board of Investigation: Several individuals were guilty of errors in judgment, but only the commanding officer of destroyer escort ROWELL was subject to censure. Although aware that his DE was operating in a submarine safety lane, he made no exacting effort to identify the undersea target after sound transmissions were heard emanating from the submarine. But the majority of the Board was also of the opinion no disciplinary action should be taken. The officer's errors in judgment were considered "due to over-zealousness to destroy an enemy."

Commander of the task unit and all commanding officers of the ships involved in the "hunter-killer" operation knew they were in a submarine safety lane. They disregarded the provisions governing such a lane because of seemingly compelling circumstances. Three enemy submarine contacts had been reported in the Morotai area during the preceding two weeks. SHELTON had been critically damaged by torpedoes at 0807 on the day in question. Immediately after the attack on SHELTON a submarine sound contact had been made very close to the damaged DE's position. According to the latest Daily Submarine Position Report for the area, the nearest friendly submarine

was no closer than 70 miles from the position of the A/S attack that was made by the carrier plane and ROWELL.

However, had SEAWOLF's position been promptly reported to all concerned, the "hunter-killer" group would have known their contact was within 35 miles of a friendly submarine. In which case, they would have proceeded with more caution. But no correction to the October 3 Submarine Position Report was issued—the correction was incorporated in the Report promulgated the following day. Commander Seventh Fleet had been promptly informed of SEAWOLF's off-schedule run in the Morotai area, but apparently he saw no reason to relay this information further. At that time the Submarine Position Reports were not required by any specific orders of higher authority, but were promulgated on the initiative of ComTaskForce 72. Their promulgation became mandatory two days after the unfortunate action off Morotai.

The SEAWOLF tragedy bears evidence to the jeopardy which threatened every submarine operating in a battle zone, particularly when enemy submarines were in the vicinity. Not only was the submersible imperiled by its undersea foe, but it risked accidental attack by friendly "hunter-killers" who had failed to "get the word" or were otherwise unable to determine the submarine's identity. Yet, such sinkings by friendly forces were remarkably rare on the American side. So far as is known, the possible destruction of DORADO by friendly aircraft in the Caribbean and the probable destruction of SEAWOLF by ROWELL are the only cases of the kind.

Against the magnitude and complexity of World War II, this record stands as a monument to those who planned and coordinated American offensive operations and developed the techniques of recognition.

SEAWOLF's loss was the first in a month that was to cost the Submarine Service grievous casualties. Five U.S. submarines would go down before the end of October, and on one dark day—the 24th—three of these would fight their last battle.

Loss of Escolar

Commander W. J. Millican took ESCOLAR out of Pearl Harbor on September 18 on her maiden patrol. At Midway, where she topped off with fuel, she joined CROAKER and PERCH II to form a wolf-pack. ESCOLAR's captain commanded the group which was named "Millican's Marauders."

The pack put out from Midway on September 23 to conduct a patrol in the Yellow Sea north of the 30° parallel.

ESCAPE FROM USS TANG. Sunk by her own and last torpedo—final shot in an epic convoy battle—the ill-fated submarine lies deep in Formosa Strait. As depth charges rain down, submariners open escape hatch. Strongest goes first with knife to cut away obstacles. (Only 8 Tang escapees gained surface.)

COMDR. R. H. O'KANE. Awarded Congressional Medal of Honor for heroic action.

SUBMARINE CAPTIVE. Blindfolded Jap prisoner is hoisted from hatch by Marines. He will go ashore for searching interrogation.

TORPEDOED BY ASPRO. A freighter assumes the fatal angle. (Probably the Jokuja Maru, sunk on May 15, 1944.)

TANKER GOING DOWN! Torpedoed off Brunei, Borneo, by Pargo. U.S. subs severed Japan's oil lines.

DARTER STRANDED. Two little "Davids"—Dace and Darter—waylaid Kurita's mighty battleship fleet as it raced to contest MacArthur's return to the Philippines. After torpedoing two Jap cruisers, Darter ran aground.

AFTER ABANDONMENT on Bombay Shoal, Darter was wrecked (as shown) by fire of Nautilus to prevent capture.

Seven days later a fragmentary message was received from Millican's submarine.

THIS FROM ESCOLAR . . . ATTACKED WITH DECK GUN, BOAT SIMILAR TO EX ITALIAN PETER GEORGE FIVE OTYI—

ESCOLAR was forced to break off the transmission at this point. But CROAKER and PERCH II made contact with her later, and she reported that she had not been damaged during the gun action.

On October 17, PERCH received a message from ESCOLAR stating that she was in position 33-44 N., 127-33 E., and was heading eastward. This was the last message ever received from ESCOLAR. She should have returned to Midway about November 13th. She did not return.

As was frequently the case with submarines which failed to come back from war patrol, ESCOLAR's fate was to be recorded only in the invisible writing of mystery. Japanese minefields had been planted in the area toward which she was heading. Consensus was that she struck a mine shortly after her October 17 message. No Japanese A/S attack was reported on a submarine in ESCOLAR's area, and a mine seemed the most reasonable supposition. The sea enfolded her, and ESCOLAR went down with all hands.

Loss of Shark II

Accompanied by SEADRAGON and BLACKFISH, SHARK II (Commander E. N. Blakely) left Pearl Harbor on September 23 and headed for Saipan to begin her third war patrol. The three submarines put out from Saipan on October 2, their bows pointed toward "Convoy College" where they were to operate as a wolf-pack—"Blakely's Behemoths." The pack slipped in through Luzon Strait and ranged along the 20° parallel, covering an area about midway between Hainan and the western end of Bashi Channel.

On October 22 SHARK contacted and chased a convoy. The convoy got away. Then on the 24th SEADRAGON received from Blakely's submarine a message stating that she had picked up a lone enemy freighter and was going in on the attack. The Japanese reported this attack as made at 20-14 N., 118-27 E. Apparently SHARK's target was a prison ship carrying 1800 American prisoners of war. After this vessel was torpedoed, the Japanese escorts counter-attacked fiercely. Seventeen depth charges were dropped. "Bubbles, heavy oil, clothing and cork" came to the surface of the exploding sea.

Several U.S. submarines were attacked on October 24 near the position recorded, but none of these torpedoed the Japanese ship in question. Undoubtedly SHARK II was the submarine which sank the prison ship and was counter-attacked in turn.

Because many prisoners of war were being transported to Japan, U.S. submarines had been instructed to search for Allied survivors in the vicinity of Empire-bound vessels which were torpedoed. SHARK II may have been sunk while attempting to rescue such survivors. She was the second U.S. submarine lost on October 24th. The first was DARTER, stranded in the manner described in Chapter 27. The day's third submarine casualty was TANG.

Tang in Formosa Strait (Commander Richard H. O'Kane)

Late in September 1944, Vice Admiral Onishi, Commander-in-Chief of the Imperial Navy's First Air Fleet, proposed a suicidal tactic for his aviators. The Imperial Army in the Philippines was prepared to immolate itself with *banzai* charges. Admiral Toyoda was willing to sacrifice Kurita's Second Fleet and Ozawa's carriers. The Japanese merchant marine was dedicated to a *hara-kiri* performance. It was time for Japan's naval airmen to indulge the Code Bushido with appropriate ceremony. Whereupon Vice Admiral Onishi suggested the *kamikaze*.

The word means "divine wind." Perhaps this was the assistance Toyoda ordered Kurita to count upon when the Second Fleet's commander hesitated about proceeding to Leyte Gulf. And this assistance was not entirely ethereal. When the first *kamikaze* plane smashed into the cruiser AUSTRALIA, American naval commanders were confronted by a new menace.

However, the *Kamikaze* Special Attack Corps was held in check during the Leyte and Mindoro campaigns. Interrogated by an officer of the U.S. Strategic Bombing Survey after the war, Commander Yamaguchi, Staff Operations Officer, 2nd Air Fleet (based at Luzon), gave some interesting reasons.

Q. *After the battle of the 24th and 25th about what was the naval air strength remaining in Luzon? What losses did you suffer?*

A. *We lost about one-third of total strength, and later some reinforcements were made, but very little and very slow.*

Q. *After this battle, what particular missions did the combined First and Second Air Force have?*

A. *The mission . . . was to continue to attack your forces in Leyte. The final objective was to cooperate with Army planes in Leyte Gulf. Additional mission was to protect the Japanese reinforcements of Leyte.*

Q. *When was the reinforcement and defense of Leyte given up?*

A. *This reinforcement and defense was continued until time you occupied Mindoro.*

Q. *When we sent a force and landed at Mindoro, were you able to offer effective air opposition?*

419

A. *Our position was very weak because of the shortage of planes.*

Q. *At that time roughly how many operational planes did you have?*

A. *About 100 planes, both Army and Navy together, and only 50 could be used freely and effectively.*

Q. *Why was that?*

A. *We could not use most of the planes because of the fact we could not receive any parts.*

Q. *Was it because there were no parts in Luzon, because the parts were at other fields and could not be distributed, or what was the trouble?*

A. *They had trouble in production. We were unable to produce in Japan because of lack of raw materials which could not be imported; principally because of submarine attacks. . . .*

Reinforcements "very little and very slow." Planes grounded because of lack of parts. Parts lacking because of production trouble in Japan, created by a lack of raw materials which could not be imported "principally because of submarine attacks." Commander Yamaguchi tells for the Japanese air forces in the Philippines a familiar story. The "divine wind" did not blow its fiery breath across Leyte and Mindoro. During those crucial campaigns it was throttled down to a puff. And the support given MacArthur's Manila-bound troops by *maru*-shooting submarines is reemphasized.

One submarine that contributed Herculean support to the United States offensive was TANG (Commander R. H. O'Kane). By indirect contribution (cargo carriers sunk during previous patrols) she had helped bring about that raw material scarcity which resulted in a shortage of parts for *kamikaze* planes. More direct was the contribution of her October 1944 patrol in Formosa Strait—a patrol which went far to cut down the volume and the speed of Japanese reinforcements.

Commander O'Kane on the bridge, TANG set out from Pearl Harbor on September 24 to conduct her fifth war patrol in the southern reaches of the East China Sea; specifically, the reach between northwest Formosa and the China Coast. Here she would be on the inside of the Formosa Strait bottleneck, in that dangerous area which was hemmed by minefields to eastward and a hostile coast on the west. O'Kane was given the choice of making the long run down through the East China Sea alone, or joining a wolfpack heading for a southern East China Sea area. O'Kane chose to go it alone.

TANG topped off at Midway on September 27, and neither the wolf-pack nor any submarine base heard from her or saw her thereafter. But the Japanese both heard from and saw her. First intimation that she was blockading their Formosa Strait traffic lanes came on the night of October 10-11 when O'Kane and company torpedoed and sank two heavily laden freighters. This was the beginning of a foray that was to be officially described as "the most successful patrol ever made by a U.S. submarine."

Following the action of October 11, the hunting slacked off, and TANG spent the next 12 days in routine search. Then, after a careful analysis of the shipping routes, O'Kane put a finger on the chart. TANG reached that point on October 23rd. And down the road as calculated came a convoy—three cargomen, a troop transport, a tanker or two and pugnacious escorts.

O'Kane decided to stop this convoy with a surface attack. And stop it he did. Driving TANG into the center of the formation, he unleashed a series of ship-puncturing salvos that mangled the *marus* on all sides. Ensued a ferocious free-for-all—freighters blowing up, escorts dashing about in frenzy, the submarine weaving and dodging through a storm of bullets and shells. Looming up out of the battle smoke, the troop transport bore down on TANG to ram her under. Emergency speed and hard left rudder saved the submarine. Then she was boxed in with three burning vessels on one side, and a freighter, a medium transport and several infuriated destroyers charging in on the other. Holding the bridge, O'Kane swung the submarine to attack her attackers. A salvo tore into the freighter and disabled the transport. TANG's tubes were now empty, but O'Kane aimed her bow at the nearest destroyer and sent her charging at the DD. The bluff worked. Unwilling to risk a possible torpedoing, the destroyer veered away. As the night flared and shook with the din of gunfire and shell-bursts, TANG, her tubes unloaded, raced out through the cordon of escorts. Depth charges flailed the sea behind her. Unscathed, she reached quiet water and submerged.

O'Kane reported seven ships torpedoed in this battle. According to Japanese records, only three of these went to the bottom. The remaining four supposedly made port, but if they did so, it must have been the nearest port and not the destination intended. And while the residue of this convoy limped off into some backwater, TANG returned to the surface of Formosa Strait to intercept another.

On October 24, exactly 24 hours after her previous encounter, she picked up this second convoy, another heavily escorted herd of *marus* steaming south to reinforce the Imperial troops on Leyte. O'Kane could make out tankers with aircraft on their lengthy decks and troop transports loaded like camels, their fore and after decks piled high with crated planes. Again O'Kane directed a surface approach. But this time as TANG closed in, she was detected before she reached attack position. Immediately the convoy's escorts swept the sea with random 5-inch and 40-mm. fire. O'Kane held TANG on the surface, driving in. When the range was reduced to about 1,000 yards, O'Kane fired six torpedoes—two at a transport—two at a second transport—two at a near-by tanker. All torpedoes smashed home with a series of shattering blasts that tossed up clouds of fire and debris.

At once the night became livid with the glare of burning ships, spitting guns, larruping tracer and exploding shells. Milling convoy and attacking submarine were exposed in the hell-light as O'Kane maneuvered TANG for a shot at another target. A large transport and a tanker were astern of the submarine, and off the beam a destroyer was charging in at 30 knots. Two DE's rushed at TANG from the other side, and the three burning ships were directly off the bow. For the second time in 24 hours the submarine was boxed in. And again O'Kane's expert handling saved her from destruction by the enemy.

As on the previous night, he rang full speed ahead and sent TANG charging straight at her attackers. But this time the charge was no bluff. Closing the range, O'Kane fired three fast shots to clear the way. The first struck the tanker which promptly spewed a geyser of flame. The second hit the transport and stopped her dead in the water. The third struck the destroyer and stopped this foe with a thunderclap that shook TANG from stem to stern. Sprinting out through the gap, she dashed away from the Jap DE's. The night blazed and boomed in pandemonium astern. O'Kane held the submarine at safe distance while the last two torpedoes were loaded in the tubes.

Loaded into the tubes with these last two torpedoes was Fate, the one factor neither O'Kane, nor TANG's crew, nor TANG herself could dominate. What TANG, crew and O'Kane might have gone on to accomplish, had this factor taken a normal turn, can only be imagined in the light of what they had thus far achieved. Abbreviated as was TANG's fifth patrol, O'Kane and company had already scored the following sinkings:

Date	Name	Type	Tonnage
Oct. 10	*Joshu Go*	Cargo	1,658
Oct. 11	*Oita Maru*	Cargo	711
Oct. 23	*Toun Maru*	Cargo	1,915
Oct. 23	*Wakatake Maru*	Cargo	1,920
Oct. 23	*Tatsuju Maru*	Cargo	1,944
*Oct. 25	*Kogen Maru*	Cargo	6,600
*Oct. 25	*Matsumoto Maru*	Cargo	7,024

* Attacked before midnight, October 24th.

Now Fate was to cut down this fighting submarine at the very hour when she deserved the laurels of victory.

Loss of Tang

O'Kane picked the damaged troopship as the target for a parting salvo. Rushing this way and that, the convoy's rattled escorts gave the submarine an opening, and O'Kane sent her darting through the gap to attack the transport. The crippled vessel was a set-up —as O'Kane gave the order to fire, there was no intimation of impending disaster.

The first torpedo found its groove and ran straight for the mark, trailing its luminescent wake. The second torpedo—TANG's lookouts stared in cold shock! This torpedo swerved sharply to the left, porpoised and made a hairpin turn. A circular run!

O'Kane shouted for emergency speed, and the rudder was immediately thrown over. Too late. Twenty seconds after firing, the terrible boomerang returned from the night and struck TANG in the stern. The blast flung O'Kane and his companions from the bridge. In the submarine's control room men were hurled against the bulkheads, a number suffering fractured arms or broken legs. Mortally stricken, TANG plunged 180 feet to the bottom. Her crew fought its way forward from the flooded after compartments.

Nine submariners had been blown from the bridge into the boiling sea. Three of this group managed to swim throughout the night. One officer, who had escaped from the flooded conning tower, swam with them. O'Kane was among these four swimmers who were picked up by the Japanese the following morning.

The men trapped in the submarine looked Death squarely in the face. After code books and similar publications were burned, these crew members assembled at the escape hatch. Before the escape could be attempted, a Japanese A/S vessel roamed overhead and launched a depth-charge attack. Blast after blast hammered the sunken submarine, bruising her bow and starting a vicious electrical fire in the forward battery. To the men caught at sea bottom, this added torture of blinding smoke and heat seemed the final extremity. But they did not yield to despair and abject resignation. Thirteen of these submariners escaped from the forward compartment. By the time the last man squeezed into the escape hatch, the electrical fire was melting the paint on the bulkhead. Eight of the 13 escapees reached the surface alive. Five were able to swim until morning, when they were picked up.

TANG's nine survivors had to meet another ordeal

421

after their escape from the sea. Aboard the destroyer escort which picked up the nine, there were Japanese survivors from the ships torpedoed by TANG. Blows, kicks and clubbings were dealt the American submariners until the punishment was almost beyond endurance. Yet the torment was suffered with stoicism and stamina.

"When we realized that our clubbings and kickings were being administered by the burned, mutilated survivors of our own handiwork, we found we could take it with less prejudice."

In that statement Commander Richard H. O'Kane displayed a magnanimity and sense of justice that characterized him as a naval officer of extraordinary stature.

When TANG's survivors were recovered from Japanese prison camps at the end of the war, the Board of Awards and Review, Submarine Force, Pacific Fleet, recommended that Commander Richard H. O'Kane be awarded the Congressional Medal of Honor.

FOR CONSPICUOUS GALLANTRY AND INTREPIDITY IN COMBAT, (reads the formal citation) *... AT THE RISK OF HIS LIFE ABOVE AND BEYOND THE CALL OF DUTY....*

THIS IS A SAGA OF ONE OF THE GREATEST SUBMARINE CRUISES OF ALL TIME, THE FIFTH AND LAST WAR PATROL OF A FIGHTING SHIP —THE U.S.S. TANG—ABLY LED BY HER ILLUSTRIOUS, GALLANT AND COURAGEOUS COMMANDING OFFICER, AND HIS CREW OF DARING OFFICERS AND MEN. DURING THIS UNPRECEDENTED PATROL, TANG CONDUCTED A SERIES OF HISTORY-MAKING ATTACKS AGAINST THE ENEMY WHICH PROVED TO BE OF IMMEASURABLE ASSISANCE TOWARD THE ALLIED CONQUEST OF THE PACIFIC....

For contributing that assistance at the critical opening of the Philippines campaign, TANG was awarded her second Presidential Unit Citation. Although the shipping downed by her torpedoes in Formosa Strait did not equal the massive tonnage sunk during her June-July patrol in the Yellow Sea, her single-handed blockade of the Formosa bottleneck was a strategic masterwork.

At the time TANG went down, only one other submarine (TAUTOG) had sunk as many Japanese ships. Only TAUTOG, fighting through to war's end, would sink more than TANG's 24. O'Kane's submarine also had served with outstanding success as a lifeguard, with 22 rescues to her credit. But one other submarine (TIGRONE) would top this rescue score.

Three warships in the United States Navy were twice awarded the Presidential Unit Citation. Two of the honored three were submarines—GUARDFISH (Commanders T. B. Klakring and N. G. Ward) and TANG (Commander R. H. O'Kane).

In Washington, D.C., April 1946, President Truman presented the Congressional Medal of Honor to Commander O'Kane.

The Saving of USS Salmon

In the last week of October 1944, SALMON (Lieutenant Commander H. K. Nauman) was patrolling in the lower latitudes of "Hit Parade." On the night of the 30th, Nauman directed an attack on a Japanese tanker which had been damaged and stopped by TRIGGER. When caught by SALMON off the southern tip of Kyushu, the tanker was guarded by four A/S vessels which were cruising back and forth some 1,000 yards from the crippled oiler, maintaining an alert watch.

Nauman sent his submarine boring in, and fired four torpedoes for two hits. The guards counterattacked furiously, and SALMON went deep. She was leveling off at 300 feet when the enemy located her. Then came the depth charges, and for a few moments the submarine was on the receiving end of a terrific lambasting that forced her down to an appalling depth.

For 17 hectic minutes the assailed submariners fought their battle damage, endeavoring to stop a score of leaks and trying to repair broken machinery. SALMON's hemorrhages could not be stemmed. With the sea gushing into the boat, she would only sink the deeper, and Nauman decided her best chance was to battle-surface and fight it out with the deck gun. The odds on the surface would be one against four, but the odds submerged were hopeless.

When SALMON broke water, she was up moon from the enemy, and the nearest escort was about 7,000 yards away. Either this escort failed to spot the submarine, or purposely delayed the kill until the three A/S vessels farther distant could close in. Whatever the enemy's reason, the attack on wounded SALMON was slow in coming. This unexpected respite gave the submariners time to correct a 15° list and start some of the machinery. Undoubtedly the dilatory onslaught cost the attackers their chance to finish off SALMON.

Nauman ordered the available guns manned and planned his strategy. When the nearest A/S vessel finally headed for SALMON, the submarine gunners held their fire. Every shot had to count, and Nauman was conserving ammunition. Equally wary, the enemy veered away, and then closed on a different tack. A fusillade from the submarine drove the vessel off.

After long minutes of this cat-and-mouse game, the

Japanese decided to ram. At this point, Nauman countered with an old military strategem—a surprise offensive on the attacking enemy. The A/S vessel charged. Nauman snapped the orders. Wheeling on her oncoming foe, SALMON charged with all the velocity she could muster. Firing point-blank, the submarine gunners opened up. Her rush carried SALMON down the side of the A/S vessel, and at a range of 50 yards the submarine fire raked the enemy's deck as CONSTITUTION once raked the deck of HMS GUERRIERE. A spatter of gunnery came back, but it was nothing to bother SALMON. Her marksmen shot the fight out of the A/S vessel. The Japanese gunners were riddled at their posts and the patrol craft was slashed to kindling. When last seen in SALMON's wake, the target appeared to be sinking.

SALMON kept right on going. A second A/S vessel closed in. A few well-directed shots exploded this craft's ambition to duel. And at this climax the Jay Factor supplied a rain squall. It was all the luck needed by the hard-pressed submariners. Nauman sent SALMON racing into the squall, and behind curtains of blowing rain she swam away in the night.

As soon as repairs could be improvised, SALMON's radio called to the submarines in her vicinity. The next night TRIGGER, SILVERSIDES and STERLET were on hand to guard her with a protective screen. This screen was soon augmented by air cover, and the Mariana-based planes escorted SALMON all the way to Saipan. From there she went to Pearl Harbor, where repair engineers reported her damage too extensive to justify costly overhaul. So the submarine was retired from active service. Nauman and all of the SALMON crew were transferred to the submarine STICKLEBACK, then building at Mare Island Navy Yard. As in DARTER's case, Submarine Headquarters wanted to retain this crack crew as a fighting unit.

Loss of Albacore

DARTER, SHARK II, TANG—October 24 was a black-letter day for the U.S. Submarine Service. Somber coincidence that ALBACORE (Lieutenant Commander H. R. Rimmer) should leave Pearl Harbor to begin her eleventh patrol on that ill-starred date. ALBACORE —conqueror of the light cruiser TENYRU, destroyers OSHIO and SAZANAMI, the aircraft carrier TAIHO, two ex-gunboats, a frigate and a sub-chaser. Veteran ALBACORE, whose combative captains and crews had sent more Japanese Navy vessels to lie down below than were sunk by any other single submarine.

She topped off with fuel at Midway four days after leaving Pearl, and then headed west to blockade Japan in "Hit Parade." She was to cover the Pacific approaches to Hakodate and Ominato. Because the coastal waters of this area were mineable, she was ordered to stay outside of water less than 100 fathoms deep. After her departure from Midway, ALBACORE was never heard from again.

Japanese records, examined after the war, suggested that ALBACORE struck a mine off northern Hokkaido. This disaster occurred on November 7, and was witnessed by an enemy patrol craft at lat. 41-49 N., long. 141-11 E. The submarine, evidently detected by the patrol, was running submerged when the enemy heard an explosion under the sea. Thick oil, bubbles, cork, bedding and boxes of provisions swirled to the surface and drifted off on the tide.

ALBACORE went down with all hands, leaving a champion's record behind her.

Loss of Growler

Out of Fremantle on October 20 stood the submarine GROWLER (Commander T. B. Oakley, Jr.), leading a wolf-pack composed of herself, HAKE and HARDHEAD. The pack's destination was an area off southwest Luzon, where they were to join the SubSoWesPac forces blocking the approaches to Manila and Mindoro. Veteran of the Aleutian struggle and the Solomons-Bismarck fighting, GROWLER will be remembered as the submarine which was rammed on the road to Rabaul and saved by the heroic self-sacrifice of Commander Gilmore. Her injuries repaired, she had since made seven war patrols, three of them under her present commander.

Oakley's wolf-pack reached the assigned area on schedule, and then GROWLER's SJ radar developed trouble. Emergency repairs were managed, but spare parts were urgently needed. On November 7 a prospective rendezvous between GROWLER and BREAM was arranged, as BREAM would be able to furnish Oakley's submarine with the necessary spares.

Early in the morning of November 8, GROWLER was en route to the rendezvous point. Freakish luck that at this time her uncertain radar should make contact with an enemy convoy. Oakley relayed this information to HARDHEAD (Commander F. A. Greenup). He directed HARDHEAD to track and deliver an attack on the convoy's port bow. Greenup headed his submarine in the convoy's direction and HARDHEAD soon contacted both the target group and GROWLER.

About an hour later, HAKE (Commander F. E. Hayler) heard two far-off explosions. HAKE was unable to identify these distance-muffled blasts. At the same time, HARDHEAD, approaching the convoy, heard a dull crash that sounded like a torpedo. The convoy zigged away from GROWLER's position, and a few minutes after that HARDHEAD counted three thudding depth-charge explosions.

Followed a silence that lasted for over an hour. During this interlude, HARDHEAD closed in on the convoy's port bow. When the submarine reached the specified attack position, Greenup fired a hitting salvo. Stricken ships listed, slewed off course, belched smoke. Nearing the scene of battle, HAKE witnessed the sinking of the oil tanker later identified as the 5,226-ton MANEI MARU.

The convoy's escorts rushed HARDHEAD, and Greenup's submarine became the target for a whipping counter-attack which was frustrated only by desperately skillful evasion. HAKE, too, was subjected to a wicked depth-charging. It was obvious to both submarines that the enemy's "first team" was on the field. HARDHEAD and HAKE escaped, but the calls were close. And when the storm was over, they were unable to reestablish contact with GROWLER.

When GROWLER failed to keep the appointed rendezvous with BREAM, her loss was suspected. Her continued silence was a confirmation. The punishing counter-attacks on HARDHEAD and HAKE indicated a well-trained Japanese A/S group, and it seemed probable that Oakley's submarine was the victim of these adept "hunter-killers." Yet HAKE and HARDHEAD had noted only three or four explosions at the time when GROWLER closed the convoy, and to those who reviewed the evidence, the brevity of that onslaught left a question mark in GROWLER's wake. Moreover, the Japanese did not record an anti-submarine attack made at that time. And what was the blast which had sounded to HARDHEAD like a torpedo? It could have been an enemy escort's torpedo. But there, again, the Japanese, who reported the convoy's loss of a tanker later that night, made no mention of a torpedo counter-attack. Could one of GROWLER's own torpedoes have prematured or made a circular run? Always a possibility, but one that left no explanation for the succeeding depth-charge explosion.

So the manner of GROWLER's going remains conjectural. She fought her last battle on the night of November 8, and went down in the South China Sea with all hands. Cause unknown.

Depth-charging of Halibut

The SHARK II story and the foregoing account of the attack on Commander Oakley's wolf-pack bear convincing evidence to the fierce opposition encountered by submarines in the Philippines theater. Prepared to accept suicidal losses in the battle for Leyte, the Japanese were nonetheless determined to reinforce the island garrisons, and the transports were given every ounce of protective power that could be mustered. The colossal toll of Japanese shipping was not taken without a hell-and-high-water fight. Every convoy attack invited swift reprisal. The counter-attack might be carelessly delivered by over-confident escorts, or poorly managed. But when well-trained and fully equipped A/S forces were on hand, only expert submarining saved the lives of the undersea fighters.

Crack A/S team and expert submariners battled it out in "Convoy College" on a day in mid-November. In this undersea warfare clash, one observes the Japanese enemy at his best and an American submarine that was better. The submarine was HALIBUT (Commander I. J. Galantin), and the action occurred in Luzon Strait three weeks after the Battle off Cape Engano. HALIBUT, it may be recalled, was operating as a member of "Roach's Raiders," and she had sunk the destroyer AKITSUKI off Cape Engano.

On November 14 the submarine attacked a convoy in Luzon Strait. Counter-attack came as a bolt from the blue. The story is best told in Galantin's report, describing what happened to HALIBUT. Excerpts are quoted below:

The Japs are apparently reverting to their earlier practice using supersonic search around their convoys, for two convoys were contacted by heading in direction of pinging. The pinging, between 16 and 18 Kcs., was ineffective, picking this vessel up only after its presence had been disclosed by other means.

It is believed that our experience of 14 November discloses a new Jap anti-submarine device. Six minutes after we had fired four Mark 18-1 torpedoes and changed course radically, a loud, fast, buzzing sound was heard. Men in the after battery state they heard this pass over four times, approaching from starboard, the direction of the escorts, as well as the direction our torpedoes had been fired. Men in the forward battery do not know which side this device approached from but believe it passed overhead three times. The sound was variously described as high speed screws, a torpedo, and an airplane flying low. The commanding officer has heard Mark 14 torpedoes running erratically and this sound was entirely different. To him, in the conning tower, this sounded as a fast, low-pitched buzzing, increasing in loudness and then decreasing for an estimated total interval of 40 seconds. He had no impression of its circling the ship, but it may have been a succession of similar devices. As the sound faded out, a heavy explosion, similar to a depth charge, occurring fairly close to port caused this vessel to go deep. This explosion was not an aircraft bomb, and no aircraft had been sighted during the approach. Also, at this time, the escorts were still over 2,000 yards away, apparently not having located us yet. With the explosion, they were quickly attracted to us and their pinging became accurate, resulting in a short, very severe depth-charging.

No end-of-run torpedo explosions were heard (depth

of water 1342 fathoms, sea slight swell, few white caps).
It is not believed that this device or devices was one of
our torpedoes running erratic for it is too improbable
to suppose that six minutes after being fired it would
seek us out, pass over us several times, and then
choose to explode close aboard. Neither would its
turning circle permit it to pass overhead more than
once in such a short interval.

It is known from discussion with two experienced
submarine officers who took part in special tests that
at periscope depth it is possible to hear a plane go
overhead if it is *very* low and *very* large. In view of this,
and the heavy air coverage the PINTADO saw, it is possible the planes came over us and dropped markers to
indicate our position and movement, thereby accounting for the unusual speed and accuracy of the depth
charge counter-attack by the surface escorts. However,
conditions for being sighted by aircraft can be described
as only fair, and no torpedo wakes or impulse bubbles
existed.

Evidently HALIBUT was "fingered" by planes
equipped with *jikitanchiki*, the Nipponese version
of the magnetic airborne detector. These planes flew
so low over the water that the submariners could
hear them. After dropping bombs, the aircraft left
markers and called in the convoy's surface escorts.
The A/S vessels ganged up on the submarine. Their
teamwork was good, and they unloaded a depth-
charge barrage that came within a fraction of getting
HALIBUT's number.

One close explosion dished in the port side of the
submarine's conning tower. This blast was followed
by three or four rapid thunderbolts which drove
HALIBUT deep into the black abyss of the sea. Galantin's report details some of the damage.

The forward torpedo room was particularly hard hit.
The skids, with their torpedoes, jumped one foot up,
damaging the torpedoes, all deck plates were dislodged,
and all personnel were thrown into the bilge, one
man being sure he was going through the bottom of the
boat. All sea valves spun open, and the escape trunk
leaked, but they soon brought matters under control.
The pressure hull and tank tops were wrinkled and
numerous bolts sheared. Meanwhile the line from #1
air bank in the forward battery well carried away.
The rush of high pressure air, and the combined odors
of hair tonic, shaving lotion, glypton, and food caused
the personnel in the compartment to believe it was
flooding and that chlorine gas was escaping; hence, they
abandoned and secured the compartment. #1 bank
bled down, creating over 50# pressure in the compartment. This prevented opening the after door or
the flappers.
Since the forward door opens into the torpedo room,
ordered that room to crack the door carefully, checking
for chlorine gas, and letting the pressure equalize if no

gas was present. By opening this door the pressure in
the two compartments was reduced to 28#. Began to
bleed the pressure into the control room through the
trim line hose connections. This was a long, very noisy
process, but finally were able to jack the door open
and help the men in the forward rooms. Both sound
heads could be trained in hand, but with difficulty,
and in the great heat and pressure the men were
working to exhaustion. On surfacing found that a depth
charge had exploded on or very close to the 4" gun
(forward), for the breech cover was smashed and punctured, and the chamber pushed to port.

HALIBUT was badly hurt. Somehow—or, rather,
with know how—her technicians forged temporary
repairs, her engineers maintained life in the machinery, her captain extricated her from Luzon Strait.
Concluding his report, Galantin noted:

For some reason, the Japs shoved off. A little persistence would have paid off handsomely. The beating
the ship took and survived brings our admiration and
respect to the men who designed her, the people who
built the HALIBUT, and those who recently overhauled
her at Bethlehem Steel Company.

A final assessment of HALIBUT's injuries covered
three typewritten pages. After first aid at Saipan and
more repairs at Pearl Harbor, she was sent to the
States where specialists at Portsmouth Navy Yard decided the injuries were too extensive to justify the
necessary overhaul, and HALIBUT was relieved from
active service. A wonder, indeed, that she had survived such battle damage.

It would seem that her captain and crew were also
made of high-grade steel.

Loss of Scamp

SCAMP (Commander J. C. Hollingsworth) left Pearl
Harbor on October 16, topped off at Midway and
set out from there on the 21st to conduct her eighth
war patrol. The area assigned was in the vicinity of
the Bonins. However, on November 9 she was
ordered to stay clear of area waters south of the 28°
parallel during raids on Tokyo by the Superforts
from Saipan. SCAMP acknowledged the dispatch. And
this acknowledgment was the last communication
received from the submarine.

On November 14 SCAMP was ordered to proceed to
the eastern approaches to Tokyo Bay where, at a
designated point, she was to station herself as a lifeguard. November 29, SubPac Headquarters received
word that an enemy minefield had been planted in
the waters off Inubo Saki. This was in the vicinity of
SCAMP's lifeguard station. All submarines in the area
were promptly warned, but for SCAMP the warning

may have been too late. When she failed to return from her lifeguard mission, her loss was presumed. It was officially announced on December 21st.

Post-war inquest uncovered a report by a Japanese patrol plane which had sighted and bombed an "oil slick" in the Tokyo Bay area on November 11th. Guided to the scene by the plane, a coast defense vessel dropped 70 depth charges on the spot where the oil-trail originated. The barrage brought a black tide of oil welling to the ocean's surface.

Two days later GREENLING, on lifeguard station in the area, made radar contact with what might have been a submarine. The contact was indistinct, and GREENLING was unable to track it down. The Japanese reported two A/S attacks in this area on November 16th. In reference to the second, they noted, "Great explosive sounds came as a result." Any or all of these attacks could have been made on SCAMP. Trailing an oil slick, she might have been bombed and damaged on the 11th, and ultimately succumbed to the depth-chargings on the 16th. At some final hour, following her message of November 9, SCAMP's time arrived. There was thunder—or perhaps no more than a murmur—under the sea. Then the silence beyond fathoming. SCAMP and all hands were gone.

"Burt's Brooms" ("Operation Hotfoot")

When Admiral Halsey was planning "Operation Stalemate" for the capture of Palau, plans were also projected for the first full-scale carrier-air attack on the Japanese mainland. The strike was to be made by Task Force Thirty-eight in November, and the operation was titled "Hotfoot." Mitscher's aviators, of course, wished to approach the Tokyo area undetected. The greatest obstacle to a surprise raid was the picket-boat line which the Japanese maintained several hundred miles south and east of the Honshu coast. Although this picket fence could be blown to kindling by assaulting destroyers or fast-shooting planes, the presence of either DD's or carrier aircraft in the vicinity would undoubtedly alert the mainland. Some of the pickets were sure to get off a warning, and Mitscher's punch would be "telegraphed."

Submarines seemed the answer to this "Hotfoot" problem. SubPac blockaders had been attacking and sinking Japanese picket boats off Honshu since early in the war. A few more submarine attacks would not be likely to arouse suspicion. The "Hotfoot" plan included a submarine sweep in advance of TF38—a quick clean-up to clear the route of picket boats.

Preparing for this "Hotfoot" detail, ComSubPac assembled a group of submarines at Saipan early in November. Skippers were readied and submarines were groomed for the impending mission. Supposedly this fleet-support mission was to last no longer than several weeks. But the enemy delayed the operation by throwing everything he could muster into the Philippines campaign. Mitscher's carriers were kept busy as Halsey pursued fleeing Japanese forces hither and yon and the naval airmen rained blows upon the foe in the Luzon area. So "Operation Hotfoot" was postponed from week to week, and the submariners waiting at Saipan sat on their hands. Eventually the "Hotfoot" strike was canceled.

Meantime, to get his submarines into action, ComSubPac proposed an accessory plan. Why not have them sweep the strategic "Hotfoot" area as an overture to the delayed strike? CinCPac approved this plan, and the anti-picket sweep was ordered.

Seven submarines—RONQUIL, BURRFISH, STERLET, SILVERSIDES, TRIGGER, TAMBOR and SAURY—were organized into the wolf-pack. Commander T. B. "Burt" Klakring was placed in charge of the pack. And "Burt's Brooms" left Saipan on November 10, with orders to sweep an avenue approximately 180 miles wide, over which Mitscher's carriers could move toward Japan with relative safety from detection. The submarines were directed to sink every picket boat encountered and to "leave no holidays."

The "Brooms" went out to raise a dust, but the sweeping proved more of a task than expected. Bad weather kicked up the November ocean and sent green seas booming over decks and conning towers. Accurate gunnery was next to impossible. A submarine's low freeboard restricts employment of the deck gun, for the gun crew can keep its footing only in comparatively calm water. Buffeted by foam-capped seas, the "Brooms" ploughed into the Japanese picket line. The targets bobbed and jumped like bubbles in a kettle, and the submarines bounced, rolled and bucked like birch canoes in a rapids. Clutching their leaping mounts, the sub gunners saw black spots before their eyes. Only four picket boats were sunk, and those at considerable risk of life and limb. In the bargain, the operation backfired. Either the pickets were unduly alarmed by the sweep, or the Japanese coast guards grasped the opportunity to test their A/S system. At any rate, all available planes and patrol craft were rushed to the threatened area. Instead of clearing an avenue, the sweep attracted attention and multiplied the swarm of pickets in the target area.

As this result was the antithesis of the one desired, it was apparent that future sweeps would require different tactics. Also apparent was the fact that gun attacks could not be successfully conducted in rough seas by submarine gunners who had to cling to their mounts like broncho busters "pulling leather."

Several "Broom" gunners were almost swept overboard—a type of sweeping that was not in the assignment. The Japanese trawlers in the picket line were heavily armed, and the attacking submarines encountered unexpectedly hot fire. One man aboard TAMBOR and two aboard BURRFISH were wounded. RONQUIL damaged her own stern with a 5-inch shell. Wrenched shoulders, Charley horses, and bruised shins were minor casualties. Liniment and adhesive tape were nothing to pointers, trainers and ammunition passers, but the surface actions were too risky to justify the meager accomplishment.

All in all, "Burt's Brooms" had a knockabout time of it, but the experience was informative and therefore valuable. Headquarters learned that a voice-radio better than the one in current use was needed. So were heavier deck guns. Future picket-boat sweepers would be provided with adequate weapons, more ammunition, and better protection.

December Clean-up

A glance at the statistics concerning Japan's merchant marine losses during World War II will show that merchant sinkings tended to slack off in the last month of each war year. The reason varied with the year, but the cause of the slump in December 1944 is obvious. By that date Japanese merchant tonnage afloat had reached a new low—a level which could be represented as close to "sea bottom." Japan had begun the year with 4,947,815 tons of merchant shipping. As stated at the beginning of this chapter, Japanese merchant tonnage afloat on December 1, 1944, amounted to 2,847,534 tons. Statistics may prove anything in politics, but in war such figures as these prove a shrinkage of some 2,100,000 tons of shipping during a critical 11 months! The Empire's merchant marine was nearing the bottom literally as well as metaphorically. And so much of it was on the bottom geographically that the hunting submarines could find little to shoot at in December 1944.

This target shortage is reflected in the chart portraying Japanese merchant sinkings in December 1944. As shown on the chart, U.S. submarines were patrolling all the way from Christmas Island to the Kuriles. The marus were not readily flushed, and Army Air, bombing the traffic in the Philippines, sank almost as many Japanese merchantmen as did the far-ranging submarines.

Blockading the home Empire, SEA DEVIL (Commander R. E. Styles) ambushed a convoy off southwest Kyushu, and downed two large merchantmen on December 2nd. Sunk by her torpedoes were AKIGAWA MARU, freighter, 6,859 tons, and HAWAII MARU, passenger-cargoman, 9,467 tons. For the remainder of the month, Japanese shipping in home waters was shy to the point of effacement. In a "Hit Parade" area between the Nanpo Shotos and the coast of Honshu, TILEFISH (Commander R. M. Keithly) blew a CHIDORI torpedo boat out of existence. Bagged on the 22nd, this ugly customer was the year's last catch off Japan.

For merchantmen only, the chart does not show the CHIDORI sinking. Neither does it spot the frigate sunk by PIPEFISH (Commander W. N. Deragon) near Hainan Island on December 3, nor the frigate sunk by BLENNY (Commander W. H. Hazzard) off Luzon on the 14th, nor the two large landing craft transports buried by PINTADO (Commander B. A. Clarey) in "Convoy College" on the 13th. But the marus are all there. For instance, the 6,933-ton freighter KENJO MARU, bashed under the coastal waters of western Luzon on December 6 by SEGUNDO (Commander J. D. Fulp, Jr.) and RAZORBACK (Commander C. D. Brown). Same day, same area, SEGUNDO and Navy aircraft demolished the 5,794-ton freighter YASUKUNI MARU.

On December 8 PADDLE (Commander J. P. Fitzpatrick) and HAMMERHEAD (Commander J. C. Martin) teamed up to sink the 2,854-ton tanker SHOEI MARU off southwest Borneo. SEALION (Commander E. T. Reich) in an area southeast of Hainan Island sighted the 7,000-ton supply ship MAMIYA and sank same on the 20th. Patrolling off southwest Luzon, BLENNY struck a freighter on December 23, and down went KENZUI MARU, 4,156 tons. BARBERO (Commander I. S. Hartman) downed a freighter on the road to Borneo Christmas—JUNPO MARU, 4,277 tons.

These December sinkings have been detailed to indicate the scarcity of merchantmen targets in the southern half of the unprofitable Co-Prosperity Sphere. Japanese shipping in home Empire waters had gone into hibernation, but on the sea lanes below Formosa the large maru herds would never reappear.

TREPANG (Commander R. M. Davenport) caught one of the last herds to be trapped by a submarine in Luzon Strait. The marus hove in sight on the evening of December 6th. Davenport directed a night-surface attack, and in a two-hour battle TREPANG torpedoed and sank three cargomen—BANSHU MARU No. 31, JINYO MARU and FUKUYO MARU—for a total of some 13,000 tons. The shooting in "Convoy College" was almost over.

Off the coast of Indo-China two other maru herds were blown from the surface of the December seas. The handiwork was FLASHER's, the targets were high priority, and the tonnage that went to the bottom sent FLASHER's record to the top. But before this tremendous maru-shoot was concluded, another

427

submarine won herself headlines at Headquarters. The story came down from the Kuriles, and the name was DRAGONET.

The Saving of Dragonet

"Surface and bring home your submarine with her forward torpedo room completely flooded!"

Were a force commander to issue the above order to a "bottomed" submarine, he would undoubtedly be reported as a mental case. And were he to issue the order to a submarine operating within range of enemy shore batteries in the Kurile Archipelago his case would be considered serious. Of course, no force commander in his right mind would think of issuing such an order. No submarine skipper could be expected to accomplish such a dangerous and difficult feat.

Yet the order was issued by that most inexorable of force commanders—Fate. And skipper J. H. Lewis of DRAGONET carried it out. Moreover, he brought the submarine to the surface right under the eyes and guns of the Japanese Air Base at Matsuwa Island. Then, defying the wrath of a cyclonic storm, he ran her to Midway!

Drama began on the morning of December 15, when DRAGONET, on her first war patrol, was cruising submerged in the frigid waters off Matsuwa. Commander Lewis' patrol report narrates the highlights of Act One:

0717: In position Lat. 47-57.5N., Long. 153-08.5E., six miles south of Matsuwa To, returning to depth of 100 feet after a periscope observation. At 70 feet, course 090° (T); speed 2 knots, with 2° dive angle, a slight jar was felt and ship broached to 58 feet. This was thought to have been an aircraft bomb. Negative tank was flooded and speed increased to gain depth. Rigged for depth charge attack. Hung at 90 feet with 20° dive angle. Heavy grinding sounds forward and repeated jars. Realized we were aground. Forward torpedo room reported flooding. Collision quarters sounded, and abandoned forward torpedo room. Blew all main ballast tanks and put pressure on compartment salvage air to forward room.

Forward room reported completely flooded. Boat rose to 65 feet with very large dive angle and then began to sink again. Getting noplace, and afraid that stern would clear and be sighted from Matsuwa, ordered all main ballast tanks flooded.

Settled at 92 feet with 16° dive angle and pounding badly.

Could not obtain suction with trim pump on forward trim tank. We were greatly concerned with the heavy pounding and grinding sounds that continued. Essential we get off before ship breaks up.

Act Two of this tense drama follows immediately.

0732: Received report that water was receding in the forward torpedo room.

0735: Blew forward main ballast tank group and safety tank. Angle began to level off and ship rose slowly. Blew after main ballast tank group.

0738: Surfaced under the eyes of shore installations on Matsuwa, exchanged feel of temporary relief for one of shameful nakedness. Cut in all four main generators clearing area at best speed. With all the days of low visibility we have had, today *would* be one of unlimited visibility and ceiling. Shore installations clearly visible on Matsuwa as we ran for it.

0740: Steering normal escape course at emergency ahead speed about 17.3 knots. Large list to port and believe No. 2 main ballast tank has been holed.

The bringing of this water-logged submarine to the surface was a feat to rival the hydraulic wizardry of Houdini. But the escape was not yet accomplished. December 16 staged another climax. Act Three—The Storm:

1800: In cyclonic storm. Barometer dropped 0.13 in one hour. Gale winds and heavy seas. Slowed to 5 knots and changed course frequently to find best sea condition to ride out storm. Bowplanes are still rigged out and pounding continuously. Feels as though ship will come apart. Steadied on course 105° T. Water rising in forward torpedo room. Leak around cable stuffing gland in bulkhead between forward battery and torpedo room causing water to enter pantry. Blew No. 1 normal fuel oil tank in No. 5A and B.F.B.T. in effort to obtain an angle and reduce water level in torpedo room. Developed 20° port list which settled down to a final 10 degrees. Rolling 40° to port. With the large free water surface in flooded compartment it felt that we would roll over. Opened No. 5B flood valve and blew this tank to sea. This leveled the list. Pumped No. 3 auxiliary dry. Taking fuel from the starboard side of No. 6.

Act Four: Morning of the next day. The seas had hauled around to the westward and DRAGONET's bow was riding higher with some six inches of water sloshing over the torpedo-room floor plates. As two torpedoes had been left halfway out of the tubes when the flood rushed in, and the bow planes were pounding heavily in the rough sea, Lewis sent an emergency squad forward to secure the torpedoes and rig in the bow planes by hand. Three officers and two men entered the compartment. The air was foul with the fumes of fuel oil, and oxygen was bled in to the gasping work party. The job was accomplished handily, but at this time the submariners learned that the pressure hull had been ruptured on the port side —a rent above the top level of the forward trim tank. This was dangerous damage, and DRAGONET's difficulties were far from over. On October 18 came the Act Four climax:

> Ship rolled 63° to port and hung there righting herself very sluggishly and settling down with a 20° port list. Mercury spilled out of master gyro and compass went out of commission. Personnel were thrown out of bunks, clear across compartments. Sea filled the port side of bridge, but fortunately did not reach the upper conning tower hatch.

After this barrel-roll in the Pacific, the seas flattened down and DRAGONET proceeded on an even keel to Midway. She arrived on December 20, and all hands went ashore to celebrate a Merry Christmas. The DRAGONET drama was over.

A Navy Yard overhaul was required to put the submarine back into fighting trim. That she reached the yard at all was phenomenal. Or call it a combination of submarine architecture, naval engineering and that amalgam of skill, trained reflexes and grit which made American submariners the sort who could surface a submarine with her forward torpedo room completely flooded and bring her home from the Kuriles in spite of Hirohito and high water.

Early Americans talked of Lewis and Clark. American submariners talk of Lewis and DRAGONET.

Oil Fire off Indo-China (Flasher's Great Patrol)

By December 1944 the Empire's oil importation effort was expiring. It was expiring because U.S. submarines in the first half of 1944 had cut the main oil artery between the Netherlands East Indies and Japan. Paradoxically, the Japanese tanker fleet floated some 868,000 tons. Thus it had been reduced by only 5,000 tons since January 1944, and it was almost 200,000 tons heavier than it had been at the war's beginning. A break-neck building and conversion program had replaced the oil haulers almost as fast as submarines had sunk them. Yet Japan was almost out of gas.

For the Japanese tanker fleet, like the Italian Navy, constituted a fleet in being, rather than a fleet in action. The ships were there, but they could not get anywhere else—that is, with any reasonable degree of safety. And if they did get somewhere else, presumably some place where they could pick up oil, there remained the problem of getting back. Going or coming, this problem was well-nigh insoluble once the convoy system was torpedoed. Hence the problem for the Japanese tanker fleet had been a baffler since the summer of 1944. A few tanker convoys had squeezed through, carrying 300,000 barrels to Japan in September, about 600,000 barrels in October, about 300,000 in November. Not enough to satisfy the Imperial War Machine. Not nearly enough. And every mile of the voyage, a race with death for tanker-men riding in potential iron coffins. So dangerous were these oil hauling runs that the Japanese Government granted tanker crews a 15 per cent bonus which was doubled when the vessel carried gasoline.

Bonus or no bonus, a Japanese tanker convoy steamed straight for the Styx when it cruised the South China Sea in December 1944. Such a convoy was heading for oblivion on the morning of December 4, as it traveled west by south along an open sea lane from Manila to Saigon, Indo-China. Daylight found the tanker group about 300 miles west of Mindoro. Coincidence that these highly volatile ships should run into a submarine named FLASHER!

FLASHER (Commander G. W. Grider) was en route to a patrol area off Camranh Bay. She was operating in a wolf-pack composed of herself, HAWKBILL and BECUNA under group command of Captain E. H. Bryant in HAWKBILL. Her meeting with the oil convoy was not entirely coincidental, for she received a report from HAWKBILL that the oilers were heading in her direction, and Grider promptly set her on the track to intercept. The submarine was then about a third of the way between Palawan and Indo-China. The convoy was not far distant. Evidently the convoy's navigators counted on squally weather to screen its movements. If so, the thinking was overly wishful. Thirty minutes after receiving the word, FLASHER's lookouts, peering through gusts of gray rain, sighted the familiar AO silhouettes. The time was 0749—zero hour for the convoy.

Tracking ahead, Grider sent the submarine under at a point 13 miles distant from the target group and waited for the convoy to come down the line. Along it came, and Grider sent FLASHER burrowing in on the approach. When she had closed the range to about 8,000 yards, a cloudburst blotted the targets from view. The submarine moved steadily forward. And suddenly a Japanese destroyer loomed up in the downpour, range 2,000 yards. Grider let the range shorten to 1,100 yards, at which point he opened fire with a four-torpedo salvo. Two hits boomed out. The destroyer stalled, smoking heavily, and assumed a drunken list.

Grider obtained a quick set-up on a large tanker beyond the destroyer, and fired four stern shots at this target. A hasty periscope sweep showed the damaged DD squatting in the water with her stern under. But as FLASHER's periscope admired this spectacle, a second destroyer rushed out through a wall of rain and bore down on the submarine. With this bone-chewing man-of-war only 700 yards away, Grider ordered the submarine deep. All of which occurred in a matter of seconds. As FLASHER coasted into deep water, two hits on the tanker target were heard. Then the depth charges came slamming down. Sixteen explosions shook the submarine; most of them were close. FLASHER evaded under a good "negative gradient."

At 1053 Grider ordered periscope depth. A brief look showed the tanker afire and settling by the stern. Five hundred yards from the tanker an ASASHIO destroyer was standing by, and a net tender and some assorted escorts were moseying around the burning ship. The submarine scrutinized this scene from a distance of 7,500 yards; then Grider rushed a reload and headed in to attack the DD and finish off the tanker. Rainsqualls blinded the periscope as FLASHER closed the range. But at 1249 a break in the downpour gave Grider a knot-hole look at the targets. Two minutes later he fired four torpedoes at the DD, and two which were set to pass beneath the destroyer and hit the wallowing tanker beyond. Four hits rumbled and roared as the submarine went deep to evade counter-attack. The counter-attack lasted half an hour, and Grider and company were perspiring when it was over. Some of the explosions were king-size and too close for polite language.

At 1410, however, the submarine was again at periscope depth, eyeing the target group. The torpedoed destroyers were nowhere in sight. Three escorts remained in the scene as did the torpedoed tanker which was afire from stern to stem. At sundown Grider moved FLASHER in for a close-up of the flaming AO. By that time the tanker had been abandoned; all escorts had departed. The vessel was burning like a log on a grate.

But the ship was still above water—might be salvageable—so Grider decided to blow her under. He pushed the submarine to within 300 yards of the fiery hulk, lined up for a shot and readied a movie camera. At 1921, with camera trained and everything set, he fired one torpedo.

"When it hit," he reported later, "one of the great shots of the war was lost to posterity."

The shot lost was the sinking of the 10,022-ton oil tanker HAKKO MARU. It was lost because the torpedo explosion blew out the fires in the tanker's hulk, and the camera photographed nothing but darkness and a splatter of ink. But posterity was not the only loser. With the extinguishment of HAKKO MARU, the Empire lost a valuable oil tanker. And in the process the Imperial Navy had lost a pair of large destroyers, namely the DD's KISHINAMI and IWANAMI.

FLASHER's patrol was only beginning. A run of foul weather accompanied her westward to the Indo-China coast, and for two weeks the sea and sky did their best to wash out the hunting. Then, on the evening of December 20, the submarine was off Hon Doi Island, north of Van Fong Bay, not far from Binhdinh. This struck Grider as a good spot for the interception of traffic northbound from Camranh. If a requisite of submarine warfare is the ability to guess the enemy's next move, Grider had it. At 0925 the following morning—contact!

This was a small patrol boat excursioning up the coast. Grider maneuvered his submarine to seaward to let the busybody pass at 3,000 yards. Thirty minutes later the sound of many screws came through the water from the south. Presently FLASHER's periscope was focused on a bustling CHIDORI. Behind this guard, a troop of large oil tankers steamed into view. Grider moved the submarine farther out to sea. The convoy passed within 2,000 yards of FLASHER, but high waves made torpedo performance doubtful and Grider held his fire, watching the convoy as it went by.

At noon the tanker group was well on its way up the Indo-China coastline, and Grider had his submarine 20 miles offshore to begin a long end-around. The seas continued to pile up, and Grider was compelled to order three-engine speed—as fast as he dared drive FLASHER over the hills of water. During the afternoon the submarine lost contact, and the crew was certain the convoy had escaped. By midnight the prospects of an overhaul had apparently gone glimmering. The seas had quieted somewhat, but the convoy seemed to have evaporated. Radar picked up what appeared to be a small island off the Indo-China coast, but could find nothing else in FLASHER's vicinity.

"We had decided to reverse course at 0100," Grider recalled, "when the navigator noticed that Tortue Island was underway!"

This phenomenon soon resolved itself into five large tankers, three escorts and a destroyer traveling through the night at 11 knots. The ships were not zigzagging, but following a circuitous course which traced the shoreline, the tankers inshore and the escorts to seaward. While Grider maneuvered to gain an ahead position, the Jap DD consistently intervened, and as the tanker formation was unusually tight, with the ships traveling in column and some 500 yards apart, an attack from the seaward side was prevented. So FLASHER's skipper decided to try for an attack from the land side.

The tankers were about 12 miles off the beach and about 15 miles south of the pass between Cape

Batangan and Kulao Rai Island. FLASHER was 10,000 yards, 30° on the port bow of the leading ship. As the submarine moved into this position, the DD briefly intervened, then dropped back on the convoy's starboard. One escort now remained on the port bow of the leading ship. The others were on the convoy's starboard flank. Grider drove FLASHER in on the attack. Here is his patrol report description of the battle:

As we started in, a light flashed on the beach abeam, and another one shone from Cape Batangan. These apparently were navigational lights turned on by request. The horizon was hazy in the direction of the convoy. There was a black cloud behind FLASHER, but it was moving away fast.

Started in at 0415. Sighted targets at a range of 6,000 yards. At 0446 began firing three bow tubes at leading tanker. Then shifted to second tanker and fired three at him. Then swung right to bring stern tubes to bear on third tanker. While swinging observed two hits on each of first two tankers.

Just prior to firing the stern tubes, the second tanker blew up and illuminated the area like a night football game.

At 0448 fired four stern shots at the third tanker. He exploded immediately when hit and made the visibility even better. The flames from the second and third targets flowed together like a river on fire.

Swung to course 180 degrees and went ahead flank plus. This put the convoy abeam, but we didn't want to get any nearer the shallow water. Took a fathometer reading: fifty-six fathoms.

As we fired, the destroyer had dropped back to the starboard quarter of the last ship. When we headed south, we sighted him two points forward of our port beam at a range of 4,000 yards. He made one circle to the left and fell into position on FLASHER's port beam, range 3,200 yards. Sent the lookouts below. We could see in full detail with the unaided eye. This weird formation cruised south for about two miles before the destroyer slowed down and dropped aft. Apparently he never saw us. We breathed a prayer of thanks to the camouflage artists and slowed to flank speed.

Shortly after the destroyer dropped back, the first target blew up and added his light to the flames. The entire sea aft was covered with billowing red fire which burned for about forty minutes. All hands came up, two at a time, and had a look. It was something to see. When we passed to leeward of the mess, there was a strong odor of naphtha. The explosions suggested gasoline, but the fire gave off great clouds of heavy black smoke that resembled oil.

All three tankers disintegrated with the explosions; were swallowed in the flames and were not seen again. The destroyer went back to the formation for a moment, then proceeded southward along the coast in the direction from which he had come. No depth charges were dropped. No guns were fired. Apparently they believed they had struck a minefield!

FLASHER opened out to the southeast, sent a message reporting results, then dived for a rest at 0630. Surfaced at 1631, and headed for the barn.

So Grider and company concluded the top-scoring anti-tanker patrol of the Pacific War. There in the coastal waters of Indo-China, at a point about midway between Binhdinh and Hué, they had buried three Japanese oil haulers for a total of 28,646 tons. Then there was the AO sunk on December 4—a 10,022 tonner. By downing these four tankers in a row, FLASHER subtracted from the Empire's tanker fleet a staggering 38,668 tons.

This huge toll was only a little short of the merchant tonnage extracted from the enemy by TANG the previous summer. But with the addition of two DD's, FLASHER topped TANG's June-July total. As shown by the table below, FLASHER's December score added up to 42,868 tons of enemy shipping.

Date	Name	Type	Tonnage
Dec. 4	Kishinami	Destroyer	2,100
Dec. 4	Iwanami	Destroyer	2,100
Dec. 4	Hakko Maru	Tanker	10,022
Dec. 22	Omurosan Maru	Tanker	9,204
Dec. 22	Otowasan Maru	Tanker	9,204
Dec. 22	Arita Maru	Tanker	10,238

Thus FLASHER downed more tanker tonnage than any other U.S. submarine. And shot into second place when it came to merchant tonnage downed in a single patrol. Only RASHER and ARCHERFISH sank greater tonnages (merchant plus naval) during one patrol. Even so, when final tonnage scores (all categories, all patrols) were totaled at war's end, FLASHER surfaced to the top. Her December run with Commander Grider on the bridge put her in the lead of the tonnage-sunk race for the duration.

However, FLASHER's December 1944 patrol added up to something more significant than win, place and show in a box score. What it added up to was a percentage figure that registered the doom of the Empire's transportation system.

For the submarine war of attrition was based on the principle that when shipping losses exceeded the enemy's ability to make replacements, the enemy's seaborne commerce would soon come to an end and his Imperial economic system would perforce collapse. During 1944, and particularly in the year's last quarter, U.S. submarines came within an ace of changing the character of the war at sea.

So long as submarines exacted a toll of only a minor percentage of the Empire's seagoing traffic, the

Japanese war planners were able to devise ways and means of muddling through. If 50% of the cargoes reached the intended destination, it was merely necessary to double the number shipped. Eventually the cost might bankrupt the nation, but there was always the chance of a lucky break in war's roulette, and the Japanese War Lords were wanton gamblers. But when submarines began to sink more than 50% of the cargoes—began to down two-thirds or three-quarters of each convoy—a new principle became involved. This principle had to do with the law of diminishing returns, and when that law went into effect, the enemy was losing "reserve" cargoes along with the "regular." In short, he was "throwing good money after bad"—a gesture the reverse of economical. Finally, when submarines wiped out nine-tenths of a convoy, the loss was close to total, and the percentage for the enemy was utterly ruinous. Of course, the total annihilation of a convoy left the enemy with no percentage whatsoever. At which point the submarine became a weapon for wholesale destruction rather than piecemeal attrition.

American submarines never completely wiped out Japanese shipping in a particular area. But they did reach the two-thirds and three-quarters figures, and some of them—TANG and FLASHER, for example—nearly abolished entire convoys. By means of radar superiority, which permitted submarines like FLASHER to operate on the surface and make a high-speed end-around, U.S. submarines came close in 1944 and 1945 to annihilating the enemy's merchant fleet.

They did annihilate the Japanese effort to import oil. Consumed in the December flash-fires off Indo-China was Japan's last hope of maintaining the Empire's oil line. It would pump for a few weeks longer—a convulsive spurt in January—a brief February flow—but the pulsations were those of an artery fatally severed. Serviceable tankers remained, but the convoy system in the South China Sea was blown galley west. Grider and company could testify to that. They blew a lot of it there.

1944 Summary

New Year's Eve—and American submariners are celebrating the conclusion of a whale of a year. Such a year as old-timers "Freddie" Warder, "Pilly" Lent, Creed Burlingame, "Barney" Sieglaff, "Bull" Wright, "Hal" Bruton, "Jumping Joe" Grenfell and other pioneer veterans of the pressure hulls had never dreamed would exist. At SubPac Headquarters, Operations Officer "Dick" Voge is congratulated by Admiral Lockwood for the winning "XYZ Patrol Plan." In turn, "the Boss" receives congratulations for the triumphant torpedo and the sweeping SubPac

offensive. Down south there are festivities at Fremantle and Brisbane. What a year for SubSoWesPac! For all the submarines in the Pacific, what a sweep! During this historic 1944 the boats with the brooms have swept away approximately 2½ million tons of enemy merchant shipping, and have abolished some 700,000 tons of the Imperial Japanese Navy. Success is the Master of Ceremonies on this New Year's Eve. But—Lest Auld Acquaintance Be Forgot—19 submarines have been lost in this war year.

But the big sweep has carried through, and at year's end 156 fleet-type submarines are operating with SubPac and SubSoWesPac—an over-the-year increase of 33. Five new submarine tenders have reported for duty during 1944—HOWARD W. GILMORE, PROTEUS, AEGIR, ANTHEDON and APOLLO. They bring up the tender total to 14—three of these normally operating with SubSoWesPac.

The year has witnessed changes in the submarine commands. After serving as ComTaskForce in Brisbane since December 23, 1942, Commodore Fife was detached at Milne Bay on March 16, 1944, and ordered to Admiral King's staff in Washington. Now he is back in Australia where, on December 30, he relieves Admiral Christie as ComSubSoWesPac, with H.Q. in Fremantle. Rear Admiral Fife is welcomed back by all hands. And the Submarine Service welcomes another new rear admiral—Admiral C. W. Styer, who became ComSubLant on November 23 of this year.

Gone are the days when force commanders could not muster the necessary submarines for sufficient area coverage; when important shipping lanes had to be neglected; when blockaders had to carry mines instead of torpedoes, and patrollers were forced to go a mile to accomplish an inch. Gone are the days when such maintenance officers as flinty Captain J. M. Will had to comb kangaroo country for spare parts and forge submarine material out of oaths and sweat and baling wire and any other tangible or intangible that came to hand. At the close of 1944 there are enough submarines to rub elbows in vital Pacific areas; enough spares and repair facilities to warm the heart of the most exacting maintenance officer. Tenders are now on hand for all manner of refits and voyage repairs, and bases lie within short-run range of enemy harbors and shipping lanes.

Since the end of July, Saipan has been available as a submarine fueling station. Guam, opened in November, now provides voyage repairs for submarines, and Camp Dealey on Guam is opening up as a rest and recuperation center for submariners. Majuro and Johnston Island have long since been by-passed. Tulagi in the Solomons is far astern. Even Brisbane is passing into history, as its famous task force may find fuel and repairs at Manus. Farther west, the tender ORION has been operating off the New Guinea coast, refitting submarines at Mios Woendi in the Schouten Islands.

These advanced bases and forward-moving tenders keep submarines in combat areas for much longer periods than formerly. For example, in 1942 and 1943, SubPac submarines averaged 23 days on patrol-in-area. In 1944, the average time in area has increased to 27 days. For the patrolling submarine, an extra three or four days in area can mean the addition of hundreds of tons on the score sheet. Multiply these additional tonnages by the number of submarines on patrol, and the increase amounts to thousands of tons per month. These increases are reflected in the table below* which records the colossal tonnages swept from the Japanese merchant marine by U.S. submarines in the 12 months of 1944.

The 1944 table of sinkings records U.S. submarine efficiency at an all-American peak. This has been the submariners' year of victory. Their torpedo war has torn huge gaps in the Imperial Navy's carrier force. They have crushed light cruisers as though they were tin cans; all but exterminated the enemy's destroyers. They have proved the submarine a match for the heavy cruiser; a challenger capable of taking on (and abolishing) a mighty battleship. Convoy destruction has long since reached the status of carnage. From the Malay Barrier to the Mikado's bathing beach, and from there to Matsuwa Island, the ocean bottom is a junk yard strewn with the wreckage of torpedoed Japanese shipping.

The Mitsui Brothers and their kin are no longer in the import-export business; they run ferryboats down the River Styx to extinction. The Imperial Navy is committing suicide. The Japanese oil importation problem has but one solution—unconditional surrender. Mythical to begin with, the Greater East Asia Co-Prosperity Sphere is now little more than a remembered scheme haunting those who sit in General Koiso's Supreme War Direction Council in Tokyo. This council is a gloomy body which was formed on August 5, 1944, three weeks after the fall from grace of Hideki Tojo. That fall—a sequel to the fall of Saipan—has brought a new "board of directors" to govern Japan, Inc. Already the Emperor has asked Koiso to look about for some means of terminating the war, lest its continuance result in the complete collapse of the Empire. But the "directors" temporize, wondering if they can save anything.

Little remains to be saved. Of the conquered real estate which once included the Philippines, Malaya, Borneo and Celebes, the Netherlands East Indies Archipelago, the strategic Mandate islands and the north coast of New Guinea—of this vast Central and Southwest Pacific Empire but a few jigsaw segments remain under Japanese control. Trinkets compared to the enormous gew-gaws and rich valuables which had lain in the Imperial palm at the end of 1942. And now Japan cannot exploit these residual Southwest Pacific holdings. Doubtful if the suzerain can

| Month—1944 | Merchant Tonnages Sunk | Merchant Tonnages Afloat | Submarine Offensive | |
			Number of Days on Offensive Patrol	Number of Torpedoes Expended
January	240,840	4,947,815	824	460
February	256,797	4,723,696	593	383
March	106,529	4,320,802	689	370
April	95,242	4,352,240	775	292
May	264,713	4,308,427	1063	493
June	195,020	4,189,319	824	362
July	212,907	4,041,711	1275	635
August	245,348	3,902,700	1056	581
September	181,363	3,710,446	850	436
October	328,843	3,474,008	1306	799
November	220,476	3,095,820	1317	775
December	103,836	2,847,534	1128	506
Total	2,451,914			

* Compiled from U. S. Strategic Bombing Survey ship sinking list.

433

exploit the holdings closer to home, for the Allies are closing in on Japan. Only two tenuous island chains block the advance—the Bonins and Volcanoes north of the Marianas, and the Nansei Shotos dribbling down from Kyushu to Formosa. The great maritime Empire lies prostrate, divided into two portions—the home Empire in the north and the fragmentary patchwork in the south—neither portion able to support the other.

And Japan's economy is wrecked as decisively as the Imperial fleet which lies on history's trash heap. The algebra of disaster is easily figured in declining import percentages and tonnages of shipping afloat. Two statistical items serve to indicate the economic debacle. In 1942 Japan imported 50,000 metric tons of scrap iron and 2,629,200 metric tons of rice. In 1944, scrap iron imports fall to 21,000 metric tons and rice imports are down to 783,200 metric tons. The merchant tonnages tabulated on page 433 present a mathematical picture of the Empire's shipping situation. At the war's beginning, the Japanese experts had estimated that 3,000,000 tons of merchant shipping were necessary for civilian needs—or, as Admiral Nomura put it, "just for civilian living in Japan." The merchant tonnage afloat at the end of December 1944 totals 2,786,407 tons, and some 700,000 tons of this total must be allocated to the Imperial Army and Navy. So-called "civilian living"

in Japan is becoming precarious existence indeed.

The bankrupt home Empire is doomed and its capital is doomed. Already the Superforts are flying from the Marianas, and bombs are crashing down on the Ginza, burning Tokyo's industrial and residential sections and bringing ruin and despair to Mr. San and Mr. Moto. These air strikes will ignite one of the greatest holocausts in world history.

But the Japanese capital, like the Empire it sponsored, was doomed long before the fire raids of December 1944. Months before the Superforts took off from the Marianas, the Japanese War Machine began to run down. Short of tungsten, lead, bauxite and other "must" raw materials, the manufacturing plants of industrial Nippon have long been unable to furnish the War Machine with many necessary spares and replacements. For some weeks, Japanese shipyards have been out of essential building materials, the Imperial Navy almost out of oil, the Japanese Air Force short of gas.

On December 28, USS DACE torpedoes the last Japanese merchantman to be sunk by a submarine in 1944. This is the collier NOZAKI, estimated at 1,000 tons. Down she goes in the waters off Saigon. Another Japanese furnace is out of coal.

"Happy New Year, boys."

"Happy New Year, skipper. When do you think we'll get home?"

NEW SUBMARINES COMMISSIONED IN 1944

NAME	FIRST COMMANDING OFFICER
BUILT AT ELECTRIC BOAT COMPANY	
BREAM	Comdr. W. G. Chapple
CAVALLA	Lt. Comdr. H. J. Kossler
COBIA	Lt. Comdr. A. L. Becker
CROAKER	Comdr. J. E. Lee
FLIER	Lt. Comdr. J. D. Crowley
SHARK	Lt. Comdr. E. N. Blakely
SEALION II	Lt. Comdr. E. T. Reich
BARBEL	Lt. Comdr. R. A. Keating, Jr.
BARBERO	Lt. Comdr. I. S. Hartman
BAYA	Comdr. A. H. Holtz
BECUNA	Lt. Comdr. H. D. Sturr
BERGALL	Lt. Comdr. J. M. Hyde
BESUGO	Comdr. T. L. Wogan
BLACKFIN	Lt. Comdr. G. H. Laird, Jr.
CAIMAN	Comdr. J. B. Azer
BLENNY	Lt. Comdr. W. H. Hazzard
BLOWER	Lt. Comdr. J. H. Campbell
BLUEBACK	Lt. Comdr. M. K. Clementson
BOARFISH	Comdr. R. L. Gross

NAME	FIRST COMMANDING OFFICER
CHARR	Lt. Comdr. F. D. Boyle
CHUB	Comdr. C. D. Rhymes, Jr.
BRILL	Comdr. H. B. Dodge
BUGARA	Comdr. A. F. Schade
BULLHEAD	Comdr. W. T. Griffith
BUMPER	Comdr. J. W. Williams, Jr.
CABEZON	Comdr. G. W. Lautrup, Jr.
BUILT AT MANITOWOC SHIPBUILDING CO.	
GUITARRO	Lt. Comdr. E. D. Haskins
HAMMERHEAD	Lt. Comdr. G. C. Martin
HARDHEAD	Lt. Comdr. Fitzhugh McMaster
HAWKBILL	Lt. Comdr. F. W. Scanland, Jr.
ICEFISH	Comdr. R. W. Peterson
JALLAO	Lt. Comdr. J. B. Icenhower
KETE	Comdr. R. L. Rutter
KRAKEN	Lt. Comdr. T. H. Henry
LAGARTO	Comdr. F. D. Latta
LAMPREY	Comdr. W. T. Nelson

434

NAME	FIRST COMMANDING OFFICER
BUILT AT PORTSMOUTH NAVY YARD	
STERLET	*Lt. Comdr. O. C. Robbins*
QUEENFISH	*Lt. Comdr. C. E. Loughlin*
RAZORBACK	*Lt. Comdr. A. M. Bontier*
REDFISH	*Comdr. L. D. McGregor, Jr.*
RONQUIL	*Lt. Comdr. H. S. Monroe*
SCABBARDFISH	*Lt. Comdr. F. A. Gunn*
SEGUNDO	*Lt. Comdr. J. D. Fulp, Jr.*
SEA CAT	*Comdr. R. R. McGregor*
SEA DEVIL	*Lt. Comdr. R. E. Styles*
SEA DOG	*Comdr. V. L. Lowrance*
SEA FOX	*Lt. Comdr. R. C. Klinker*
ATULE	*Lt. Comdr. J. H. Maurer*
SPIKEFISH	*Comdr. N. J. Nicholas*
SEA OWL	*Lt. Comdr. C. L. Bennett*
SEA POACHER	*Lt. Comdr. F. M. Gambacorta*
SEA ROBIN	*Lt. Comdr. P. C. Stimson*
SENNET	*Comdr. G. E. Porter, Jr.*
PIPER	*Comdr. B. F. McMahon*
THREADFIN	*Lt. Comdr. J. J. Foote*

NAME	FIRST COMMANDING OFFICER
BUILT AT MARE ISLAND NAVY YARD	
TREPANG	*Lt. Comdr. R. M. Davenport*
SPOT	*Comdr. W. S. Post, Jr.*
SPRINGER	*Comdr. Russell Kefauver*
BUILT AT PORTSMOUTH NAVY YARD	
TENCH	*Comdr. W. B. Sieglaff*
THORNBACK	*Comdr. E. P. Abrahamson*
TIGRONE	*Comdr. Hiram Cassedy*
TIRANTE	*Lt. Comdr. G. L. Street, III*
TRUTTA	*Comdr. A. C. Smith*
TORO	*Comdr. J. D. Grant*
TORSK	*Comdr. B. E. Lewellen*
QUILLBACK	*Lt. Comdr. R. P. Nicholson*
BUILT AT CRAMP SHIPBUILDING CO.	
HACKLEBACK	*Lt. Comdr. F. E. Janney*
BUILT AT CRAMP SHIPBUILDING CO. FINISHED AT PORTSMOUTH NAVY YARD	
LIONFISH	*Lt. Comdr. E. D. Spruance*

PART V

JAPANESE SUNSET
(1945)

Full fathom five thy father lies;
Of his bones are coral made;
Those are pearls that were his eyes:
Nothing of him that doth fade
But doth suffer a sea-change
Into something rich and strange.
                    SHAKESPEARE

CHAPTER 29

TOKYO APPROACH

Sarawak Maru Runs the Gantlet

Perhaps the luckiest merchant ship in the Pacific War, and possibly one of the luckiest in creation, was the 5,135-ton SARAWAK MARU. It might stretch the hawser a bit to call her as lucky as the SANTA MARIA. She probably had a better navigator than did that most fortunate of caravels, and in that respect the odds were in her favor. On the other hand, SANTA MARIA, although steered by the whimsical Admiral of the Ocean Sea, did not have torpedoes and air bombs to contend with as she sought a fast route to the Indies. SANTA MARIA was not a high-priority target. SARAWAK MARU was an oil tanker.

On the last day of 1944, SARAWAK MARU sailed from Japan with a convoy bound for Singapore. The convoy consisted of seven or eight tankers, five dry-cargo carriers and eight escorts. In Formosa Strait on January 8 this *maru* herd was ambushed by a submarine wolf-pack. The tanker HIKOSHIMA MARU was torpedoed and sunk. Tanker SANYO MARU suffered a fatal explosion which was probably caused by a submarine torpedo. Freighter SHINYO MARU and the large passenger-cargoman ANYO MARU were blown under by torpedo fire. Lucky SARAWAK MARU legged it into the Formosan port of Takao with the remainder of the convoy.

At Takao the *marus* came under the wing of the First Japanese Escort Force, a unit of which was added to the convoy's guard. There, too, the convoy came under the wings of attacking United States carrier planes. The bombs thrashed the harbor on January 9, and tankers KAIHO MARU and NANSHIN MARU No. 4 were obliterated, along with two more freighters. SARAWAK MARU escaped injury.

As soon as the crews could pull themselves together, the convoy hauled out of Takao and continued its southward voyage. The formation was hardly under way before one of the escorts broke down and dropped out. Heading southwestward from Formosa,

the convoy ran for Hainan Island. Serving with the escort group which made this run was Lieutenant Commander Noriteru Yatsui, IJN. Yatsui had been navigation officer of the cruiser OI when that man-of-war was torpedoed and sunk by FLASHER the previous July. After this experience, he had been assigned to the staff of the Seventh Escort Unit, First Japanese Escort Force. He spoke a marked respect for submarines when he was interrogated after the war. Asked, *"On what was the emphasis placed in your defense of convoys?"* Yatsui replied, *"Some thought was given to AA, but the major factor was anti-submarine defense."* On behalf of the convoy in question, however, both aircraft and anti-submarine defenses should have been emphasized.

"The convoy was en route south and had reached a position east of Hainan Island," Yatsui recalled. *"At this point a message was received from Headquarters at Takao that another convoy had been attacked near Saigon. This influenced Headquarters to order my convoy to take shelter."*

So the convoy reversed course and ran for shelter into the harbor of Hong Kong. This, it appeared, was a futile defense measure. The day after the convoy reached Hong Kong, American carrier planes reached the same harbor. At Takao the air strike had worked all kinds of havoc. At Hong Kong the havoc was worse. The Navy tanker KAMOI was disabled. Freighters DOSEI MARU and ANRI GO NO. 2 were sunk. And tankers HARIMA MARU, SANKO MARU, MATSUSHIMA MARU and TENEI MARU were pounded to the bottom. The destroyer HATSUHARU and 10 coast defense and escort vessels were mangled in the massacre. And SARAWAK MARU? Somehow she came out of the shambles unharmed.

The reduced convoy now consisted of one freighter, one oil tanker and four escorts. The freighter dropped out of the group and stayed in Hong Kong. That left SARAWAK MARU and the four escorts. She must have felt a trifle conspicuous as she set out to resume the journey down the South China Sea. As conspicuous, say, as the tenth little Indian in the nursery rhyme.

The attenuated convoy crept down the Indo-China coast and scurried across the Gulf of Siam. Off the coast of Malaya it was attacked by a submarine. One of the escorts, damaged, was forced to drop out. On January 27, SARAWAK MARU, the sole surviving merchantman of the original baker's dozen, arrived at Singapore.

Luckier than the SANTA MARIA? Thus far. Columbus' flagship crossed the Atlantic safely, but then the admiral rammed her on the rocks of Haiti. SARAWAK MARU did not ram any rocks. But on March 19, in the Singapore roadstead, this last survivor of a once-formidable convoy rammed an American mine. And so—to quote "Ten Little Injuns"—then there were none.

The accompanying chart, portraying the destruction of the Japanese merchant marine during January 1945, marks the grave of SARAWAK MARU off the southern tip of Malaya (small black triangle).

The chart also marks the graves of the vessels sunk by submarines in Formosa Strait on January 8, and the resting place of the tankers demolished by carrier planes at Hong Kong on the 16th. (Unidentified at the time this chart was produced, the freighters sunk during the Hong Kong air strike are not shown here.)

As for the luck of SARAWAK MARU, one needs only to glance at the gantlet of January submarine patrols extending the entire length of the Japan-to-Singapore run. Of course, nautical miles are considerably longer than they look on a small-scale chart. But if the patrolling submarines had a lot of mileage to cover, so did SARAWAK MARU. Moreover, the submarines patrolling in the East China Sea just north of Formosa Strait were "Loughlin's Loopers." Any vessel which managed to elude this champion wolf-pack was singularly fortunate. Lucky, indeed, was the *maru* that escaped the torpedoes of "Lucky" Fluckey.

Barb's Great Patrol (Commander Eugene B. Fluckey)

To conduct its second patrol as a coordinated attack group, Loughlin's wolf-pack left Guam on December 29, 1944, and headed for the southern end of the East China Sea. This area just inside the Formosa Strait bottleneck promised action. The Japanese front might come back-firing from Manila any day. Formosa was the season's target for China-based Army planes and Navy Air. The drivers of the United States offensive were planning a leap at the Nansei Shotos where Okinawa was on the amphibious agenda. To meet the threat, the Japanese were running reinforcements to the Nansei Shotos and rushing reserves down the East China Sea to Formosa. That island was hotter than Tophet, and the waters around it were a-boil. But if the waters were hot, so were "Loughlin's Loopers," whose previous patrol, as has been related, cost the Japanese merchant marine a tidy 51,000 tons.

New Year's Eve the three submarines were well on their way. As in the autumn, the pack was composed of QUEENFISH (Commander C. E. Loughlin), PICUDA (Commander E. T. Shepard) and BARB (Commander E. B. Fluckey). Once more these "Loopers" were determined to knock the enemy "for a loop." But as Fate spun the wheel of fortune, the play consistently fell to Fluckey's submarine. So this is BARB's story, and no one is better qualified to tell it than her eloquent commanding officer.

On the evening of the third night out, Fluckey noted in his log, "*Celebrated the advent of what we hope is the final year of the war.*" Then, on January 1, 1945, "*The Patrol started by the sinking of a small Japanese craft with gunfire.*"

On January 8 the wolf-pack was roaming the northern reaches of Formosa Strait. About an hour after noon the submarines picked up a large convoy which, trudging southward, was evidently headed for Takao. This was the convoy containing lucky SARAWAK MARU. The wolf-pack containing "Lucky" Fluckey tracked for five hours while PICUDA, the submarine farthest away, was coached to an intercepting position. BARB, as will be noted, held back to give her team-mates time to enter the battle. Fluckey continues the story:

> It would be a snap to get in the center of this outfit. However, it is imperative that we bend them to port, and prevent them from heading towards the shallow China coast. Holding off on the starboard bow. Plan to smack the four goal-poster with the four escorts in the port echelon since she is probably the most

important ship, then use the other three bow tubes on the leading engines-aft job in the starboard echelon, following through with a stern tube attack on the second ship.

Finally at 1724 the skipper sent BARB boring in on a day-periscope attack. His account goes on:

Coming in nicely. Made ready all tubes. Fired six torpedoes.

Left full rudder. All ahead standard. Swinging for stern shot.

Four torpedoes hit close together, the third of which was a tremendous explosion. At the time, being intent on coming stern shot, I idly remarked, "Now that's what I call a good solid hit." I heard someone mutter, "Golly, I'd hate to be around when he hears a loud explosion!"

This, accompanied by the tinkle of glass from a shattered light bulb in the conning tower, and the expressions on the faces of the fire control party, snapped me out of my fixation and the full force of the explosion dawned upon me. BARB had been forced sideways and down, personnel grabbed the nearest support to keep from being thrown off their feet, cases of canned goods had burst open in the forward torpedo room. Later we found a section of deck grating ripped out of the superstructure aft. QUEENFISH later told us that this last ship hit blew up and was obviously an ammunition ship.

Sound reported high speed screws all around. Rigged ship for depth charge. Steadying up and attempting to climb back to periscope depth. A look at our results is paramount. Breaking-up noises.

All screws going away on sound. At periscope depth. A smoke cloud where the torpedoed ship had been. The stern of the transport sticking up at a 30 degree angle with two escorts close aboard. Her bow is evidently resting in the mud. Depth of water, 30 fathoms. One ship is on fire amidships, just above the water line. The whole formation has turned away and appears to be stopped. Amazingly, we appear to have leprosy. All escorts have scampered over to the un-attacked side of the formation. The destroyer has reversed course.

Evidently the ship with her bow resting at 30 fathoms in the mud was the 5,892-ton freighter SHINYO MARU. The ship on fire amidships seems to have been the target in the starboard echelon—the "engines-aft job." Probably the 2,854-ton tanker SANYO MARU. While the convoy floundered in consternation and the escorts dashed in the wrong direction, Fluckey rushed preparations for another attack.

Can feel aggressiveness surging through my veins, since the escorts are more scared than we are. Commenced reload forward. Heading towards convoy, with another ship in our sights. Destroyer suddenly turned towards us! Nice spot for 'down the throat' shot, but no torpedoes forward. Aggressiveness evaporated. Assumed deep submergence of 140 feet. Mud below that.

QUEENFISH and PICUDA attacking convoy.

BARB makes second and third attack.

Three hits observed, followed by a stupendous earth shaking eruption. This far surpassed Hollywood, and was one of the biggest explosions of the war. The rarefaction following the first pressure wave was breathtaking. A high vacuum resulted in the boat. Personnel in the control room said they felt as if they were sucked up the hatch. Personnel in the conning tower who were wearing shortened shirts not tucked in at the belt, had their shirts pulled up over their heads. On the bridge, as the air was wrenched from my lungs, somehow it formed the words, "All ahead flank." The target now resembled a gigantic phosphorous bomb. In the first flash as the torpedoes hit, all we could ascertain was that the target had a long superstructure and a funnel amidships. The volcanic spectacle was awe inspiring. Shrapnel flew all around us, splashing in the water in a splattering pattern as far as 4,000 yards ahead of us. Topside, we alternately ducked and gawked. The horizon was lighted as bright as day. A quick binocular sweep showed only the one ship ahead remaining and a few scattered escorts. No escorts close to the munition ship could be seen. These were probably blown up, and we could claim them as probably sunk, except that I figure that four ships sunk, one probably sunk and one damaged is about all the traffic will bear for a twelve torpedo expenditure.

At this point of the game I was ready to haul ashes. However, the Engineering Officer, who had never seen a shot fired or a ship sunk in five runs, from his diving station, really had his guns out. Frantically, he pleaded that we couldn't let the last ship go; besides he loved to hear the thump, thump, thump of the torpedoes and to see millions of bucks go sky high.

Good sales talk.

Commenced the approach for a stern tube attack on the ship ahead. Then QUEENFISH said she wanted to attack. PICUDA said she would follow QUEENFISH. We had our share, so we gave them the green light. Passed our target (what a temptation) and headed down towards the pass between Formosa and a minefield to make sure nothing escaped.

BARB's victim in this spectacular instance seems to have been the 9,256-ton passenger-cargoman ANYO MARU. Fluckey noted that QUEENFISH concluded the foray by sinking a tanker. The shooting was over. This last victim, cornered by the wolf-pack and downed by QUEENFISH, was the 2,854-ton tanker HIKOSHIMA MARU.

The explosions described by Fluckey's pen highlight the fortunes of such a vessel as SARAWAK MARU. They also serve to highlight the fortunes of Commander Fluckey, nicknamed "Lucky." But "luck is

441

where you find it." And, as someone once remarked, "To find it, you have to look for it." Fluckey was not the officer to loll on Easy Beach waiting for his ship to come in. He looked for the ship. On January 10 he had BARB patrolling northward on the 20-fathom curve along the China coast. Ships were not readily found. For the next week and a half, BARB dodged Japanese patrol planes, ducked around fleets of Chinese junks and sighted nothing bigger than a good-sized canal barge. Fluckey took time out to analyze the enemy's traffic:

> While our forces are hammering Formosa, no shipping is moving around Keelung. All traffic is now running that inshore route along the China coast. No lights have been observed burning along the coast. Consequently, the Japs are running only in the day time, when it is impossible for a submarine to attack along the new, close coast route. Anchorages being used are probably Shanghai, Wenchow, Foochow, and Lam Yit, all of which are well mined and a day's run apart. In conclusion, our prospectus appears poor, unless we can find a suitable opportunity at night to resort to torpedo boat practice.
>
> Basing the remainder of our patrol on the latter assumption, made a complete study of the China coast from Wenchow south to Lam Yit. Recent unknown mining has taken place north of Wenchow. If our assumptions are correct, the present convoy, for which we are searching, is anchored at Foochow tonight (January 21) and will be en route Wenchow tomorrow. To substantiate our conclusions, plan to mingle with the Junk Fleet north of Seven Stars tomorrow afternoon at a point ten miles inside of the 20 fathom curve and 15 miles from the coast where we can observe the passage of our convoy.

The following day two ships were sighted traveling inside the 10-fathom curve in 8-fathom water. The sky was heavily overcast, and Fluckey decided to tackle the targets that night if the overcast blindfolded the moon. BARB tracked the vessels throughout the day, only to lose contact that night. Fluckey deduced that the ships had anchored, and he determined to search the coast—a hazardous venture as the absence of junks offshore hinted at the presence of a minefield. But again luck is where one finds it, and Fluckey was a persistent hunter.

> January 23, at 0030 started an inshore surface search for convoy anchorage. Maneuvering constantly to avoid collision with junks. Present entourage consists of several hundred darkened junks. At 0300 rounded Incog Island and contacted a very large group of anchored ships in the lower reaches of Namkwan Harbor! Slowed to take stock of the situation.

Instead of turning up one ship, BARB's skipper had found an entire convoy! It may now be observed that Dame Fortune makes a final demand of those who court her guerdons. To locate the grab bag is not enough—one must reach in to get the prizes. The manner in which Commander Fluckey reached into the Namkwan grab bag is described below by the practitioner. As a demonstration of astuteness, capability and drive—balancing the odds and then accurately shooting the works—it remains a classic of submarine warfare.

> Fully realize our critical position and the potential dangers involved. Estimate the situation as follows:
>
> a. Recent unknown mining in this vicinity is a known fact. Mines could be laid from Incog Island to Tae Island. However a more effective minefield would be from Incog Island to Pingfong, the eastern entrance to Namkwan Harbor, which would provide a protected anchorage behind it. Since the position of the anchored convoys is too close to this line, assume the latter minefield does not exist. The former, though doubtful, must remain a possibility, particularly in view of the absence of junks.
>
> b. One escort appears to be patrolling several thousand yards northeast and a second escort to the east of the anchored ships covering the most logical position for entry and attack. A third escort is working close to Incog Light, apparently more concerned with keeping himself off the rocks. Visibility is very poor.
>
> c. Assumed the closely anchored columns would be heading about 050 degrees true, heading into the wind and seas with a current of one knot. Plotted the navigational position from which we would attack, making our approach from the southeast.
>
> d. Elected to retire through an area marked "unexplored" on our large scale chart which contained sufficient "rocks awash" and "rocks, position doubtful," to make any over-ambitious escorts think twice before risking a chase. This course would also cross the mass of junks which would be a definite and final barrier to all pursuit.
>
> e. Countermeasures expected will be searchlights, gunfire, and hot pursuit. Against this we will have a stern tube salvo, 40mm's and automatic weapons.
>
> f. Inasmuch as our attack position will be six miles inside the ten fathom curve and 19 miles inside the 20 fathom curve, we will require an hour's run before being forced down. Consequently, our attack must be sufficient to completely throw the enemy off balance. We have four torpedoes forward and eight aft. No time will be available for reload; for a speedy darting knife thrust attack will increase the probability of success.
>
> Figure the odds are ten to one in our favor.
>
> Man battle stations, torpedoes.
>
> Seriously considered placing crew in life jackets, but the atmosphere throughout the boat is electric. The men are more tense than I've ever seen them. Save for

an occasional sounding ". . . six fathoms . . ." the control room is so quiet that the proverbial pin would have sounded like a depth charge. Discarded the idea of life jackets as definitely alarmist, with so many hearts doing flip-flops.

Do not consider it advisable in our present precarious position to send a contact report to the PICUDA. She could not possibly attack before dawn and get out. Will send one after the attack, when our presence is known.

Range 6,000 yards. Made ready all tubes.

Ships are anchored in three columns about 500 yards apart with a few scattered ships farther inshore. This, frankly, must be the most beautiful target of the war. Ships are banked three deep. Even an erratic torpedo can't miss. Estimate at least 30 ships present. Our biggest job will be to prevent too many torpedoes from hitting one ship!

Chose one of the large ships to the left of center of the near column as target.

Fired one. Fired two. Fired three. Fired four.

Right full rudder, all ahead standard. Sounding, five fathoms. Shifted target to right for ships ahead in near column.

Fired seven. Fired eight. Fired nine. Fired ten.

All ahead flank! Commanding Officer manned bridge.

Torpedo number two—hit on target. Timed and observed.

Torpedo number three—hit on target. Timed and observed.

Torpedo number one—hit in second column. Timed and heard.

Torpedo number four—hit in third column. Timed and observed.

Torpedo number six—hit in first column. Timed and observed.

Torpedo number eight—hit in first column. Timed and observed.

Torpedo number five—hit in second column. Timed and observed.

Torpedo number seven—hit in third column. Timed and observed.

Large AK in first column was hit by torpedoes two and three. Target observed to settle and undoubtedly sink.

Unidentified ship in second column was hit by torpedo after turn to right. Damaged.

Large AK, in third column, hit by number four torpedo, shortly thereafter caught on fire. Fire later flared up five or six times then went out in a manner similar to a sinking ship. Ship probably sank.

Torpedo number six hit in the first column. Believed to have hit in ship struck by number two and three torpedoes. Observation not sufficiently accurate to claim additional damage.

Large AK hit by torpedo number eight. Ship belched forth a huge cloud of smoke. Damage.

Unidentified ship in second column hit by torpedo five. The whole side of this ship blew out in our

direction in a manner similar to an ammunition ship or the magazine of a large warship. Ship sank.

Large ammunition ship in third column hit by number seven torpedo. Ship blew up with a tremendous explosion. Ship sank.

Tracers of all descriptions flew out from the two ships which exploded. At the same time several large caliber projectiles estimated 6-12 inch, with tracers, hurtled through the air. A moment after this, searchlights were seen sweeping about for a short while. Smoke from the ships hit, on fire and exploding, completely obscured all ships and prevented any further observation of other damage.

The BARB is now high-balling it for the 20 fathom curve at 21.6 knots, broken field running through the Junk Fleet, wildly maneuvering when some of the junks are inside the sea return. Expect to see a junk piled up on the bow at any second.

Gunfire from well astern. Some poor junks are getting it. Sent contact report to PICUDA.

One hour and nineteen minutes after the first torpedo was fired, the Galloping Ghost of the China Coast crossed the 20 fathom curve with a sigh. Never realized how much water that was before. Life begins at forty fathoms!

Thirty-eight minutes later, it was dawn. Assume the Japs will expect us to submerge, so will stay on the surface!

That evening BARB headed for Midway. She reached that base on February 10th. The Japanese left no record of the ships which were sunk in the Namkwan smash-up, and it has since been impossible to estimate the tonnage downed during that raid. But SubPac Headquarters estimated that BARB's performance would merit a Presidential Unit Citation.

Commander Eugene B. Fluckey, for his

COURAGE, INITIATIVE, RESOURCEFULNESS AND INSPIRING LEADERSHIP, COMBINED WITH BRILLIANT JUDGMENT AND SKILL . . . AN INSPIRATION TO ALL SUBMARINE PERSONNEL,

was awarded the Congressional Medal of Honor.

Submarine Tactics—The Attack from the Quarter

Although the attack from the bow was preferred by most submarine captains, other attack positions had their advocates. Commander Fluckey felt that with radar superiority and a comfortable speed advantage over the average convoy, the inability of Japanese escort commanders to meet unconventional situations should be exploited. To exploit it, he developed the attack from the quarter. Having employed this attack with success during BARB's eleventh war patrol, Fluckey discoursed upon the tactic, writing with his usual (and unusual) facility.

To stimulate discussion of new methods of approach and attack, the following is offered, of possible interest, from our meagre experience, for what it is worth. It is a special situation of a dark night, poor visibility convoy attack.

Fault was found with the standard off bow attack in that an end around was required; usually only two targets presented themselves at the optimum torpedo accuracy range which were readily taken care of by the bow tubes; shifting nests for low parallax stern tube salvo resulted in no suitable target for the stern salvo at a satisfactory range of 1,500-3,000 yards; escorts were passed close aboard; another end around was required for the next attack; and the formation turned, or was so fouled up, another lengthy tracking period was required.

To obviate this second end around on our last patrol, we changed our off bow attack tactics so that our next shift would be a high parallax stern tube set-up, though contrary to doctrine, and we would emerge ahead of the convoy, ready for a reload and another attack. Again no stern tube target was immediately available at hitting ranges, and, while pulling out ahead, we had to cross in front of the convoy to fire the stern tubes at the leader of another column. Per usual the formation became disorganized. It was two hours before targets and escorts were sufficiently settled for another attack, and even then it was poor. Disorganization of the formation, with the targets wandering about, continually changing position, course and speed, was a distinct disadvantage.

Realizing the advantage of maintaining convoy organization, new tactics were developed and tried, which we label the "Barbarian Attack."

Briefly it consists of a quarter attack firing three bow torpedoes at the trailing ship of an outboard column. The sub then turns out at a 60° angle from the convoy course and opens out on the flank to 4,000 yards. Paralleling the formation at this range, fifteen minutes is utilized in tracking and reload while moving up on the next ship. This ship is then attacked from the flank or quarter with a three torpedo bow tube salvo, and the sub again opens out and reloads while tracking the next ship ahead. If this ship is not the leading ship of the column, the procedure is repeated. Assuming it is the leader, a stern tube off bow salvo is fired, and the sub pulls out ahead of formation, ready to reload the stern tubes and proceed with any type of attack desired.

The above method was tested on this patrol with such ease and lack of expected difficulties that attack was only secured to give the rest of the pack a chance. The convoy was contacted at 20,000 yards with the BARB broad on its starboard quarter. Forty-two minutes later the trailing ship was attacked.

The convoy remained organized, used same zig plan and increased speed slightly. Twenty-one minutes after the first attack, the second attack was made on the next ship up the line. Twenty minutes later, the second attack was made, and the BARB passed the next ship ahead at 2,160 yards, foregoing an attack in deference to the rest of the pack. Thus in less than 1½ hours after contact, we found ourselves ahead of the convoy, without making an end around, with all tubes reloaded, and with two concentrated attacks under our belts. Trouble from escorts which were stationed astern, on the flank and off the bow, was nil. As we had anticipated, not seeing us, they turned towards the stricken ship to drop depth charges, maintained course and speed to hold gunnery practice, or, in the case of the exploding AE, were intent upon saving their own necks. If they had turned out to chase us, we had the advantage of a head start on our departure course and at full speed before the torpedoes hit.

Consequently, to us, the tactics of this attack appear ideal in its particular sphere; no end around; the accuracy of concentrated fire; requires only one-third of the time normally used; automatically takes care of reload; minimum escort trouble; maximum convoy organization, and best possible position of sub upon completion of first wave of attacks. Obviously it is flexible and easily adaptable to special circumstances.

January Target Shortage

Once it was torpedoes. Now it was targets. Look as they would, many submarine captains could not find ships in January 1945. In southern backwaters of the Co-Prosperity Sphere, *marus* were becoming as hard to locate as invisible Chloe. Hot though they were, the East China Sea waters off northern Formosa were hardly traffic-jammed. After the convoy battle of the 8th, Commander E. T. Shepard, a skipper as sharp-eyed as any, was unable to flush a target for PICUDA until January 29th. Shepard, who knew what to do with a chance when given it, made the most of the 5,497-ton passenger-cargoman CLYDE MARU. But the pickings were slim. In a neighboring area, pack-leader Loughlin in QUEENFISH found nothing.

Submarines in "Convoy College" enjoyed a holiday. ASPRO teamed up with carrier aircraft on January 3 to sink SHINSHU MARU, an 8,170-ton converted water carrier. This was the month's only major sinking in Luzon Strait.

The big event of January 1945 was the American invasion of Luzon—an amphibious drive by way of Lingayen Gulf to take Manila from the rear. Supporting the landings, Navy Air swept the Indo-China coast with fire, and, as has been related, blasted the harbors of Takao and Hong Kong. This scorching sweep cost the Japanese merchant fleet about 280,000 tons of shipping. With the exception of November 1942, this would be the first month in which the tonnage of Japanese shipping destroyed by aircraft exceeded the tonnage sunk by submarines.

The carrier-air raids in the South China Sea almost brought shipping in that body of water to a standstill. Hugging the coast, a few vessels crawled down to Singapore or up to Hong Kong, but not many were luckier than the aforementioned SARAWAK MARU. One of the submarines patrolling along the coast of Malaya not far from Singapore was BESUGO. She was there for the express purpose of catching any *maru* that tried to sneak down across the Gulf of Siam. On January 6 she caught the large tanker NICHIEI MARU.

On that same day SEA ROBIN nailed a tanker off the east coast of Hainan Island. Thereafter things were mouse-quiet along the submarine-covered lanes in the South China Sea until January 24 when BLACKFIN glimpsed a rat off the coast of Malaya. Commander W. L. Kitch lost no time in torpedoing this rare specimen which was later identified as the Japanese destroyer SHIGURE. Elsewhere in the waters below the 20° parallel the SubSoWesPac submarines skirmished with patrol craft and sank steamers of the tramp variety. But the big ones were far between and few. Closing the month for the SubSoWesPac Force, BOARFISH, on the 31st, sank a fat freighter off Binhdinh, Indo-China, and downed another in teamwork with Army aircraft.

Late in January, SubPac submarines turned up several targets in the waters south of Kyushu and along the convoy routes to the Yellow Sea. Covering the approaches to Kagoshimo, TAUTOG downed a small transport on the 17th and a torpedo-boat tender on the 20th. In the immediate vicinity of these sinkings, SILVERSIDES sank a medium-sized freighter on the 25th. In the Yellow Sea off Tsingtao, ATULE abolished a large freighter on the 24th. Down the line near Shanghai, SPADEFISH struck a convoy on the 28th and buried a bulky frigate and the 7,158-ton converted seaplane tender SANUKI MARU. In "Hit Parade," THREADFIN sank a small transport south of the Bungo Suido.

In the northern reaches of the East China Sea, in the Yellow Sea and in "Hit Parade" the waters would grow warmer as the Allied offensive neared Japan's home ports and the desperate imperialists strove to quicken the flow of war and food supplies. There were freighters and passenger-cargomen in the Sea of Japan. Some big *maru* bottoms were yet to be holed. But from this January forward, the submarine score sheet would display an increasing number of frigates, tenders and converted this-and-thats.

Sinking of USS Extractor

On the evening of January 23, 1945, GUARDFISH (Commander D. T. Hammond) was returning from patrol in a Joint Zone—an area in which both surface ships and submarines are permitted to operate and in which neither can attack the other unless positive of enemy character. GUARDFISH was heading for Guam. At 2038 she made a radar contact at 11,000 yards on a vessel which tracked on course 270 at 11 knots. There were no friendly radar indications, and nothing could be sighted from the bridge. Lacking detail regarding friendly forces in the area, GUARDFISH, while continuing to track, sent in a contact report and requested information. This message was cleared at 2310.

While waiting for a reply, the submarine's commanding officer set a sound watch to listen for possible challenges—the sort which might be issued by a friendly surface ship in a Joint Zone. No challenges were heard. At midnight Hammond sent a dispatch to ComSubPac and ComTaskGroup 17.7 giving position, course and speed of the target, and stating that GUARDFISH would continue tracking and would attack when positive of the target's enemy character. At this time the submarine was on the northern edge of the Joint Zone.

At 0113, morning of the 24th, GUARDFISH received a message from ComSubPac informing her that there were no known friendly submarines in the vicinity of the reported contact, but advising that, as the contact was made in a Joint Zone, the unidentified vessel, if a surface ship, was probably friendly. At 0130 a dispatch was received from ComTaskGroup 17.7— GUARDFISH was to continue tracking. At 0338 another message from ComTaskGroup 17.7 informed GUARDFISH that no known friendly forces were in the vicinity of contact. The message reminded GUARDFISH that she was in a Joint Zone, however.

Hammond held GUARDFISH on the trail as instructed, and at 0542 he ordered the submarine submerged 13,600 yards ahead of the target and 2,000 yards off the track. This put GUARDFISH in a position where she might identify the target at dawn and be within striking distance if the vessel were an enemy submarine. At 0605 the target was identified as a Japanese submarine of the I-165 class, the commanding officer and executive officer viewing it through the scope and using the silhouette book for a studied comparison. Observation was made 10 minutes before sunrise, the sky was overcast with passing light rain squalls, and the target was clearly silhouetted by dawnlight in the east. Fifteen minutes later, Hammond opened fire, estimated range 1,200 yards, track angle 70° starboard. Four Mark 18 torpedoes were fired. Two struck the target. As the vessel sank, the stern tilted against the sky, and it was evident the target was not a submarine.

Hammond sent GUARDFISH to the surface and made for the wreckage. Seventy-three survivors were picked up, all apparently in good condition, a few with minor bruises and lacerations. Six men of the crew were missing and could not be found. GUARDFISH's victim was an American ship—the USS EXTRACTOR!

This tragedy resulted from a concatenation of mistakes. Investigators learned that GUARDFISH had not attempted to identify the target with special identification equipment which was in operating condition and which would probably have disclosed the target's friendly character, since EXTRACTOR's corresponding gear was in use. The submariners had not used this identification equipment because they had no evidence of its employment by the target and because the enemy was known to have used similar gear for deception.

GUARDFISH's commanding officer had relied upon visual identification, and had made six periscope observations, sighting the target at various angles on the bow (between 15° and 50°) at a time when visibility was not the best. Had he waited for an angle on the bow nearer to 90°, the EXTRACTOR would probably not have been taken for a submarine.

Higher authority did not know EXTRACTOR's position in the Joint Zone because orders addressed to her the previous afternoon were received by the ship in a garbled form which made them unintelligible. These orders, dispatched approximately 24 hours before she was contacted by GUARDFISH, directed EXTRACTOR to reverse course and return to port. Her captain did not break radio silence to request a retransmission of the unreadable message. Therefore, officers responsible for knowing EXTRACTOR's whereabouts stated they knew of no friendly surface ship in the position reported by GUARDFISH.

The EXTRACTOR sinking was seen as resulting from the submarine captain's failure to properly identify the target, and the failure of the operations officer at Headquarters, Commander Forward Area, to check EXTRACTOR's whereabouts at the time the submarine reported contact.

To the uninitiated who have never glimpsed a target through a periscope, the mistaking of a ship's silhouette for that of a submarine may seem incomprehensible. But a playing card may serve to illustrate. Draw one—the two of spades. Seen from a distance, an oncoming ship may look no larger than the small two-spot at the bottom right-hand corner of the card. On the next periscope look, it may be as large as the two-spot, bottom center of the card. About that time, the submarine skipper is hurrying preparations for a "down the throat" shot. But the point is that target silhouettes are not as big as barns. Furthermore, they shift, elongate, assume all manner of angles as do shadows moving along a wall. The changing light of daybreak (or clouds at noon, or sundown, or moonshine) and the movements of the sea are other factors which enter the problem. But artists know the illusions created by light and shadow, the tricks of perspective.

GUARDFISH's skipper did not fire in haste, nor was he astigmatic at the periscope. Certainly a communications failure was involved in the EXTRACTOR case. Nevertheless, the burden of positive target identification rests on a submarine attacking in a Joint Zone, and for this reason a Court of Inquiry voted a reprimand for the commanding officer of the submarine.

Loss of Swordfish

SWORDFISH (Commander K. E. Montross) left Pearl Harbor on December 22, 1944, to conduct her thirteenth war patrol in an area off the Nansei Shotos. In addition, she was to carry out a photo reconnaissance mission at Okinawa. Plans for "Operation Iceberg"—the campaign to capture this stronghold—were already incubating, and good photographs of defense installations and beaches would be invaluable. SWORDFISH was provided with special equipment for the vital mission. After the usual topping off at Midway, she headed west for the big bastion in the Nansei Shoto chain.

On January 2, 1945, she was ordered to keep clear of the Nansei Shotos until a series of carrier-air strikes had been conducted. In the meantime, she was to patrol the shipping lanes off Yaku Island below Kyushu. The submarine acknowledged these instructions on January 3rd. Six days later, she was directed to proceed to the Nansei Shoto Archipelago and perform her special mission. Then she was to return to Saipan unless she were unable to transmit by radio, in which case she was to go to Midway.

When SWORDFISH failed to appear at Saipan on the date scheduled for her arrival, it was presumed she had gone on east to Midway, in accordance with instructions. But she never returned to Midway. After unbroken silence was the only answer to repeated attempts to contact her by radio, SubPac Headquarters knew she must be lost.

SWORDFISH may have been lost on the morning of January 12th. On that day the submarine KETE, in the Okinawa area, reported possible contact with a near-by submersible. KETE was unable to positively identify the contact, but SWORDFISH was due in the vicinity at the time. Four hours later, KETE heard prolonged depth-charging. The Japanese failed to record the A/S attack heard by KETE. But it sounded like a heavy barrage, and it could have been aimed at SWORDFISH.

The waters off Okinawa were thickly sown with Japanese mines. Did SWORDFISH strike a mine barrier? Was she sunk by an A/S attack in the vicinity of Yaku? The submarine that sank ATSUTASAN MARU—first Japanese ship downed by a U.S. submarine in the Pacific War—concluded a long, hard-fighting career somewhere in action below Kyushu or off the Nansei Shoto chain. Like so many of her companions in the "Silent Service," she went down silently with all hands, leaving in her wake a valiant record of courageous accomplishment.

Loss of Barbel

Entering the war under Commander R. A. Keating, BARBEL scored her first sinking in the Nansei Shoto area on August 5, 1944. Six ships were sent down by her torpedoes before the end of that year, which found her in Fremantle.

On January 5, 1945, BARBEL, captained by Lieutenant Commander C. L. Raguet, left Fremantle to patrol an area in the South China Sea. She topped off at Exmouth Gulf on the 8th and proceeded to her area via Lombok Strait, the Java Sea and Karimata Strait.

Late in January she was ordered to form a wolf-pack with PERCH and GABILAN and patrol the western approaches to Balabac Strait and the southern entrance to Palawan Passage. On February 3, BARBEL sent a message to TUNA, BLACKFIN and GABILAN—her area was buzzing with Japanese aircraft, and three times enemy planes had attacked her, dropping depth charges. Raguet stated his submarine would transmit further information the following night.

The expected transmission from BARBEL was not received. On February 6, TUNA reported that she had been unable to contact BARBEL for 48 hours and had ordered her to a rendezvous point on February 7th. BARBEL did not appear at the rendezvous. Evidently she never received the message from TUNA.

Japanese aviators reported an attack on a submarine discovered off southwest Palawan on February 4th. Two bombs were dropped, and one landed on the submarine near the bridge. The submarine plunged under a cloud of fire and spray. Unquestionably this was BARBEL, going down in battle, with all hands.

"Mac's Mops," "Latta's Lances" and "Operation Detachment"

Although the "Hotfoot" carrier-air strike on Honshu was canceled because of the Third Fleet's prolonged activities in the Philippines, plans for such a strike were not abandoned. Early in the new year "Operation Detachment" was devised for the capture of Iwo Jima, and a carrier-air strike on Honshu was included in the plan. And, as in the abortive "Hotfoot" operation, a submarine sweep to clear the carrier route of picket boats was projected.

In planning the "Detachment" sweep, ComSubPac could base the project on the experience of "Burt's Brooms." A double sweep was designed—one group of sweepers to clear the path for the aircraft carriers, and a second and smaller group to create a diversion by sweeping an "off the trail" path. The main sweep was to be conducted by a wolf-pack designated as "Mac's Mops." The "Mops" consisted of STERLET, POMFRET, PIPER, TREPANG and BOWFIN, under Commander B. F. McMahon, captain of PIPER. The diversionary sweep was assigned to "Latta's Lances"—HADDOCK, LAGARTO and SENNET under Commander F. D. Latta, captain of LAGARTO.

The sweepers participating in this operation were better equipped than "Burt's Brooms." Mounted fore and aft on each submarine were 5-inch and 40-mm. guns. Improved voice radios were carried. A special high-speed torpedo for attacks on A/S vessels had come into service, and these were distributed to the "Mops." With this lively torpedo, a submarine making an undetected submerged attack could demolish a picket boat before the picket had time to dispatch a warning.

"Latta's Lances"—the diversionary sweepers—were instructed to attack the pickets with gunfire, but not to sink them until they had time to send out a radio alarm. By this stratagem, Latta's wolf-pack would decoy the enemy to the area it was sweeping—divert him from the scene of the main sweep. The "Lances," it may be observed, were to take hold of the thorny end of the stick. And the thornier it was—the more enemy aircraft and A/S vessels they attracted to their area—the better it served the devices of "Operation Detachment."

Latta's wolf-pack began its diversionary sweep on the morning of February 11 at 0800. Striking the picket line in broad daylight, the "Lances" rattled against the pickets and created a fine uproar. In the process they sank two picket boats. The diversion was a complete success.

Armed with the special torpedoes, "Mac's Mops" covered their assigned area on schedule. But they saw no picket boats on which to try their new weapon.

The chart on the following page shows the areas covered by the anti-picket boat sweep and the diversionary sweep. After completing the sweep, the "Mops" and "Lances" continued on to "Hit Parade" patrol areas, as shown.

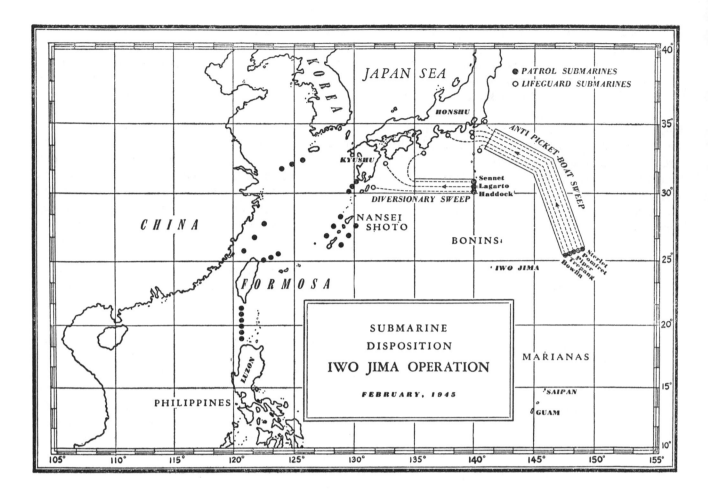

SUBMARINE
DISPOSITION
IWO JIMA OPERATION

FEBRUARY, 1945

As for the carrier-air strike on Honshu—steaming along the path traveled by the sweepers, Mitscher's carriers did not see a single picket. And vice versa. The carrier planes reached Tokyo undetected!

Iwo Jima Campaign

Civilian living in Tokyo was becoming unpleasant in January 1945. Against United States carrier aircraft from the sea and B-29's from the Marianas, the city's AA defenses were about as protective as paper parasols. However, to reach the Japanese capital, the American bombers had to break through the air screens over the Bonins and Volcanoes. The flight from Saipan to Tokyo meant a round trip of 3,000 miles which the Superforts had to make on their own, for the target was beyond the range of fighter escorts. Because Japanese aircraft based in the Bonins and Volcanoes were able to intercept the B-29's, offensive plans called for the capture of a major base within jabbing distance of Tokyo. Okinawa, middle link in the Nansei Shoto chain, was the objective. Only 400 miles from Japan, the island had harbors for the accommodation of the Navy and terrain suitable for good airfields. This stronghold would make a springboard for a final leap at the Japanese homeland.

But before Okinawa could be seized, it was necessary to obtain a fighter-plane base to support the Mariana-based B-29's. Iwo Jima in the Volcano Group was the selection. Capture of this island, the largest of the Volcanoes, would serve to neutralize the enemy's bases in the Volcanoes and Bonins, give fighter support to the Tokyo raiders and clear the way for a drive at Okinawa.

The capture of Iwo Jimo and subsequent invasion of Okinawa were operations assigned to Admiral Spruance's Fifth Fleet. D-Day for the Iwo Jima campaign was set as February 19. The Okinawa campaign, designated "Operation Iceberg," was to hit the beachheads of that island on April 1st. Late in January, Fleet Admiral Nimitz transferred CinCPac Headquarters from Pearl Harbor to Guam in order to direct the dual operation from a front seat in the Marianas.

Submarines played a part in both of these campaigns. From November 28 to December 2, 1944, SPEARFISH (Commander C. C. Cole) was on photo reconnaissance mission in the waters off Iwo Jimo and Minami Jima.

During the Iwo Jima landings, submarines were tactically disposed as indicated on the above chart.

Occupying these stations during the preliminary air strike, they served as lifeguards. Several furnished the Fifth Fleet with weather information.

Iwo Jima is the Marine Corps' story. But the submarines were there. An "XYZ" patrol—"Dunker's Derby"—had been cutting the convoy routes to the Bonins since April 1944. When the Fifth Fleet struck in February 1945, the target islands were already showing signs of a familiar blight.

Hunting the Japanese Submarine (Batfish Breaks a Record)

"The best defense against submarines is other submarines."

So wrote an author whose opinions, in the 1920's, could stir up more controversy than a bear with his paw in a beehive. The writer, of course, was forthright General William "Billy" Mitchell, whose imagination was as far ahead of his time as radar. Taken literally, many of his statements were and are open to argument. But so are many of the statements of arbitrary literalists who strain at gnats while swallowing camels. Mitchell probably wanted to touch off the pros and cons, and his opinions concerning air power and submarine warfare came nearer to hitting the target than scores of conventional shots fired by less independent thinkers.

As for the statement quoted above, submarines may not have been the *best* defense against other submarines during World War II. But U.S. submarines were never employed solely for anti-submarine duty (that is, as normal A/S units were employed) and their licks at enemy submersibles were generally side-swipes taken in passing. Japanese submarines were not high on the target priority list in 1942, 1943 and 1944. Even so, in those 36 months of warfare U.S. submarines downed a significant percentage of their opponents in the undersea field.

It is interesting to note that the first enemy warship sunk by a U.S. submarine was the Jap submersible downed off Midway by GUDGEON (Commander E. W. Grenfell). The brief review of the submarine sinkings scored by U. S. submarines, 1942-1944, shown below may underline the broad meaning of the "Billy" Mitchell observation.

Although the listed sinkings were incidental to the tremendous anti-shipping war and the offensive against the Imperial Navy's surface forces, they were incidents that blasted sizable holes in the enemy's submarine effort. And when U.S. submarines were given the opportunity to concentrate on A/S warfare, that hole was immediately and decisively enlarged. The opportunity developed in the first quarter of 1945, coincident with the shortage of surface targets that followed the gigantic harvest reaped in the autumn of 1944.

After the sinking of LISCOME BAY in the Gilberts, the Imperial Navy's submarines had given a most indifferent account of themselves. Partly responsible was the strategy of the Japanese High Command which shifted the submarines yon and hither, frequently under the operational control of the Imperial

Date	Submarine	Commanding Officer	Ship Sunk	Locale
1942				
Jan. 27	Gudgeon	E. W. Grenfell	I-173	Midway
Apr. 26	Tautog	J. A. Willingham	I-23	Johnston I.
May 17	Tautog	J. A. Willingham	I-28	Truk
May 17	Triton	C. C. Kirkpatrick	I-164	Kyushu
Dec. 20	Seadragon	W. E. Ferrall	I-4	New Ireland
1943				
Jan. 2	Grayback	E. C. Stephan	I-18	Solomons
July 27	Scamp	W. G. Ebert	I-24	New Hanover
Sept. 9	Trout	A. H. Clark	I-182	Surigao St.
1944				
Feb. 15	Aspro	W. A. Stevenson	I-43	Truk
Mar. 23	Tunny	J. A. Scott	I-42	Palau
Apr. 20	Seahorse	S. D. Cutter	RO-45	Saipan
Apr. 28	Pogy	R. M. Metcalf	I-183	Bungo Suido
July 26	Sawfish	A. B. Banister	I-29	Luzon St.
Sept. 15	Sea Devil	R. E. Styles	RO-42	Honshu
Nov. 10	Flounder	J. E. Stevens	U-537	Java Sea
Nov. 28	Scabbardfish	F. A. Gunn	I-365	Honshu

Army. The Japanese Submarine Force seemed to lack a primary mission, a clearly defined program. Imperia Navy leaders sought to retain its services for fleet operations. Generals demanded I-boats for transport and supply. Some strategists thought the submarines should concentrate wholly on naval targets. Others favored emphasis on a campaign to cut Allied transportation lines. The result was a dispersal of effort which sprayed off in all directions when a fire-hose stream was needed to reach the objective.

In the Indian Ocean, Japanese submarines waged unrestricted warfare on Allied convoys, but results were militarily inconsequential as the High Command maintained but a small squadron of some 10 submarines for that campaign. The Nazis contributed a few of their 1,200-ton U-boats to this activity. On November 10, 1944, FLOUNDER (Commander J. E. Stevens) caught one of these Germans poking a nose into the Java Sea. Bang! Down went U-537. The Axis patrollers sank about 70 Allied merchantmen in the Indian Ocean. Over one-third of the available I-boats and RO-boats were engaged, during 1943 and 1944, in transporting supplies to last-ditch garrisons of isolated Pacific bases. The Japanese submariners did a lot of hazardous blockade-running and performed numerous tasks on the order of their evacuation work at Kiska—a remarkable exploit. But that was not fighting an offensive war.

Now, in February 1945, with Okinawa an obvious United States objective, there were indications that the Japanese Submarine Force was out to defend the approaches to the Nansei Shotos. If such was the resolution of its commanders, the resolve came too late. American submarines were on the lookout for their Imperial Navy rivals and those few specimens donated by Doenitz to the Pacific War. On the lookout and eager to devote more time to the hunting of these undersea boats. Primed for battle, they hit the enemy submarine forces a series of stunning blows in the opening months of 1945.

First and hardest blows were landed in February by USS BATFISH. Skippered by Commander J. K. Fyfe, she was working in Luzon Strait on her sixth war patrol when she encountered the undersea enemy. At this date the Japanese were busy evacuating some of their top-rank personnel from Aparri on the north coast of Luzon. I-boats were one way of getting out the evacuees, and as the Japanese had been known to essay these missions, American submarines in the area were alerted. Patrolling in Baboyan Channel, BATFISH had been keeping her radar-eye peeled for submersibles.

The watch picked up results.

At 2250 on the evening of February 9, a radar contact was made at 11,000 yards. BATFISH started tracking. In a few minutes the radar detector began to register strong signals which could only be enemy radar. Commander Fyfe directed a surface approach. At 2331, range 1,850 yards, he fired four torpedoes at the target. All four missed. The moonless night was unusually dark, and the target had not been sighted.

Fyfe started a fast end-around to gain a new attack position. On the next approach he decided to close in to visual range. At one minute after midnight, the lookouts picked up a Japanese submarine at 1,020 yards, and 60 seconds later Fyfe fired three torpedoes. One of these struck the mark. As the explosion roared in the darkness, radar indication on the detector ceased abruptly. As abrupt was the decease of the enemy submarine. The victim was later identified as the Imperial Navy's I-41.

Fyfe circled BATFISH over the spot several times on the off chance of locating a survivor, but none was found. At dawn BATFISH was forced deep by Japanese planes. One of the attackers let fly with a torpedo, but the submarine was faster.

The following evening at 1915, BATFISH again detected enemy radar signals. As it was a signal previously associated with Japanese submarines, there could be little doubt as to the target's identity. Fyfe maneuvered carefully to determine the approximate bearing of this foe. At 2037 the target was sighted by the bridge watch. At 2043, as Fyfe was preparing to open fire, the Japanese submarine submerged.

Apparently the Jap sub had detected BATFISH and ducked. But some 30 minutes after the enemy went under, BATFISH's sound operator reported a swishing noise—the sound made by a submarine blowing her tank! A moment later, radar contact at 8,650 yards. The target submarine had surfaced! Fyfe sent his crew to battle stations and rushed an end-around. When the range was reduced to 6,000 yards, he ordered BATFISH to radar depth and continued the approach. At 2202 he fired four torpedoes. An explosion flashed and roared, and the hit blew the Japanese submarine to pieces. This victim was eventually identified as RO-112.

Two days later BATFISH duplicated the RO-112 shooting almost to a "T." At 0155, morning of February 12, the radar detector picked up this third submarine. BATFISH went to bat. When the range shortened to 7,150 yards the target submarine suddenly submerged. Fyfe headed BATFISH for a position ahead on the track. In about an hour the enemy returned to the surface, and BATFISH regained radar contact at 6,800 yards. Fyfe ordered radar depth. At 0449 the first torpedo hit the mark. Explosion! A

PERISCOPE ON TARGET! Tirante's *skipper squats to spot a maru in shallow channel. Tracking, he feeds information to the fire control party. Range,* target speed, track angle and similar data go into the TDC. Then, "Fire one!" sends a torpedo on its way. A strike! The target slowly sinks from *view.*

COMDR. GEORGE L. STREET. Awarded Congressional Medal of Honor for daring invasion.

TRIGGER-MEN AT GUAM. A hard fighting sub, Trigger was in the Pacific War's thick of it—one of the 3 U.S. subs lost off Okinawa.

UNSUSPECTING MARU poses for Pargo's periscope. SAME MARU, after Pargo removed her bow with a telling torpedo—!

JAP SUB of I-161 class, similar to I-164 sunk by Triton in 1942. Batfish was Jap sub Nemesis.

BATFISH DISPLAYS her war flags: 7 Japanese warships, 8 merchantmen. She downed 3 Jap subs in 3 days.

JAP SUBMARINE I-4. She met her match in Seadragon on December 21, 1942. At war's end Jap subs were about only Imperial Navy units operating. Out of fuel or on the ocean bottom, Jap surface Navy had been swept from the Pacific.

dark geyser. Whirlpool. Another sunken enemy sub.

This submarine vs. submarine performance established BATFISH as one of the champion A/S vessels of the war. Three submarines in three days! When the third enemy submersible—RO-113—went down on February 12, BATFISH turned in a record that was equaled by no other submarine in the Pacific.

Then LAGARTO (Commander F. D. Latta) stepped in to make it a record anti-submarine month for the American undersea arm. The A/S bout came as a sequel to the diversionary anti-picket boat sweep which LAGARTO had led two weeks before. After the "Hotfoot" activity, Latta's submarine headed for a patrol area in "Hit Parade." There, off the Bungo Suido on February 24, LAGARTO sank a small freighter. Not long afterward she spotted a Japanese submersible. Day-periscope attack resulted in a whacking hit. Deep for the last time went RO-49.

As of January 1, 1945, the Japanese had lost a total of 102 submarines. Some 96 or 97 replacements had been rushed from the construction yards. A comparison of these figures with Japanese destroyer figures for the same period—117 lost and 43 replaced—shows that the Imperial Navy exerted a considerable effort to maintain its submarine strength. But battleships, aircraft carriers and cruisers, retaining top priority in the building yards, absorbed most of the available steel. Returning dimpled and bedraggled from long patrols, the I-boats and RO-boats were often unable to obtain repairs and spares. Strive and contrive as it would, the Japanese Submarine Force had in commission or available for duty on March 1, 1945, only 41 submarines. Needless to state, the depleted force had been unable to afford the four submarines obliterated by BATFISH and LAGARTO in February.

Japanese submarines were shy in March. Only two were sunk—both by surface forces in the Nansei Shoto area. But eight were sent to the bottom in April 1945, one of the worst months experienced by the force. Two were sunk in the Bungo Suido area by Army mines. Three were sunk by surface craft. Two were sunk by carrier aircraft. And one was trapped and sunk by the submarine SEA OWL.

In mid-April, SEA OWL (Commander C. L. Bennet) was passing Wake Island when she picked up a submarine contact. The contact led her to Wake, and she picketed the island for several days playing hide-and-seek with the enemy submersible. Finally Bennet's patience wore thin, and on April 17 he decided to go in and get the target. SEA OWL found the Japanese sub playing sitting duck at anchor. That was the end of RO-56.

BESUGO (Commander T. L. Wogan) added to the April A/S score by torpedoing an Axis submarine in the Java Sea on the 23rd. Surfacing after a day-periscope attack, the American submariners ran in to look for survivors and were surprised to fish from the oily sea a German. This dripping catch identified BESUGO's victim as the Nazi submarine U-183. This was the second *unterseeboot* downed in the Java Sea by American submarine torpedoes. The Dutch submarine ZWAARDVISCH had also sunk a U-boat off the north coast of Java (in October 1944). Based at Penang, the German submarines had formerly operated in the Indian Ocean, and their presence in the Java Sea was indicative of the Japanese submarine shortage.

In the last three months of the Pacific War, U.S. submarines sank three of their Japanese rivals. SKATE (Commander R. B. Lynch) sank I-22 on June 10 in the heart of the Japan Sea. On July 15, BLUEFISH (Commander G. W. Forbes) downed I-351 in waters northwest of Borneo. The day before the war ended, SPIKEFISH (Commander R. R. Managhan) sank I-373 in the East China Sea.

Thus a total of 25 enemy submarines (23 Japanese and two German) were sunk by American submarines in the Pacific War. Although at first disposed to belittle the American submarine effort, the Japanese submariners were among the first members of the Imperial Navy to express a revised opinion in this regard.

"American submarine crews were very well-trained, skillful and brave," Vice Admiral Shigeyoshi Miwa, Commander-in-Chief of the Imperial Navy's Sixth (Submarine) Fleet said after the war. *"We did not expect such skillfulness. One instance is our Japanese carrier going home from the south area of the Pacific. That carrier was attacked in the night, wind speed at 20 meters, just a single submarine and the same one attacked twice again the next morning. . . . Another example is the sinking of the KONGO. As Commander of the Sixth Fleet, I discussed this operation by the American submarine with my officers, saying it should be an example to our own forces of a brave, skillful operation."*

Miwa made a curious observation. When asked what type of attack Japanese submariners feared most, he replied that air attack was most feared because, *"Your aircraft with radar attacked at night when the submarine is floating."*

Concerning this testimony, Miwa's interrogators (officers of the Naval Analysis Division of the United States Strategic Bombing Survey) noted: *"This statement is of interest in that only three submarines are known to have been sunk by our night air attack during the entire war, of which two were German and one Japanese, all three of which were sunk in the*

Atlantic Ocean. Of Pacific night air attacks on submarines, four are presently assessed as 'probably sunk.'"

Perhaps equally interesting is the fact that American submarines, employing radar, sank seven Japanese submarines by night attack. All three of the submarines downed by BATFISH were sunk in night actions after detection by radar. And on November 13, 1943, the British submarine TAURUS sank I-34 by night attack in Malacca Strait. Possibly the Japanese were misinformed in regard to the nocturnal agent consistently threatening their undersea boats.

The Japanese lost a total of some 130 submarines during World War II. Of these, five or six were operational casualties; five were downed by causes unknown. In sinking 23 of the 120 which were downed in action, U.S. submarines were responsible for approximately 20% of the losses.

Far-sighted "Billy" Mitchell! Looking into the future—three or four decades into the future—he may have come even closer to the anti-submarine answer than the 20% scored by U.S. submarines in World War II would suggest.

Flounder and Hoe (Traffic Accident)

Circulating in Singapore in 1944 was a saying that one could walk from there to Japan on the tops of U.S. submarine periscopes—or so declared a prisoner of war rescued from the Japanese.

The reporter may have exaggerated the rumor, and the hyperbole itself is subject to punctuation with a grain of salt. However, by 1945 there were areas where American submarines were concentrated with a "density" that left little latitude for figure-skating maneuvers. This is not to imply that the patrollers jostled one another with the enforced intimacy of rush-hour passengers bound for Brooklyn in a New York subway. Nevertheless, the density of the concentration frequently brought several submarines into action against a single target, the attackers maneuvering within a few thousand yards of each other. Example: the GUITARRO-RATON-BREAM-RAY attack on KUMANO.

The accompanying chart furnishes a picture of the American submarine concentration in the seas between Singapore and Japan during March 1945.

Not exactly sardines in a can, these SubPac and SubSoWesPac patrollers. But near enough so that a few hours' run would bring each within hailing distance of the next—and in some instances, nearer than that. Consider the experience of FLOUNDER and HOE, patrolling adjacent areas off the coast of Indo-China. The episode occurred in the last week of February, but the submarine disposition at that time was virtually as shown on the chart for March.

On the afternoon of February 23, FLOUNDER (Commander J. E. Stevens) was cruising along submerged in the vicinity of Pulo Kambir. HOE (Commander M. P. Refo, III) was running submerged in an area just to the north of FLOUNDER's. A 4-knot current had been registered in HOE's area, and believing his submarine on the southern boundary of the area, Refo had set course north in mid-morning. But at 1700, while running at 60 feet, speed 1.8 knots, position 13-30.9 N., 190-29.1 E., HOE came a cropper with a crash.

Refo thought his submarine had struck an undersea rock. The shock seemed to be forward on the starboard side, and the submarine took a 4° up-angle and broached. The commanding officer ordered battle stations and blew all main ballast tanks. Rushing topside, the bridge personnel found all clear—with the exception of an unidentified ship, hull down on the horizon to the northeast. Reports from below were reassuring. No underwater damage; soundheads and pitometer log were operating normally and could be housed easily. So Refo called for four-engine speed to open the range before his submarine was sighted by the vessel over the horizon. A "cut" checked HOE's position; she had under her 65 fathoms of water. At 1711 a Japanese float plane forced her to dive, and Refo took the opportunity to begin an approach on the unidentified vessel. No torpedoes were fired, for the vessel was soon identified as a hospital ship.

Leave HOE as she stalks this disappointing target, and turn back the clock to 1700—at which moment things happened to USS FLOUNDER. Stevens' submarine had been running at 65 feet on course 090 T. on that afternoon of February 23rd. All clear by sound and periscope. Then at 1700 FLOUNDER suddenly was shaken as though seized by a paroxysm—a violent stem-to-stern shudder. FLOUNDER started to go deep. Thirty seconds later, she suffered another spasmodic jolting, and water spurted in through a slashed cable. The shear valve was closed and the leak stopped. Sound excitedly reported a tremendous rush of air and the whish-whish-whish of high-speed screws starting and stopping on the starboard bow.

Stevens needed no little bird to tell him that his submarine had been run over by another submersible. The screw noises faded out. Eleven minutes after the collision, FLOUNDER was again at periscope depth, her scope above water for a look. All was clear at that moment. For HOE was diving to elude aircraft contact just as FLOUNDER's periscope broke water. With nothing in view in FLOUNDER's vicinity, Stevens and crew entertained the hope that they had sideswiped a

452

submerged Japanese submarine and sunk same.

About two hours later FLOUNDER heard a noise of blowing air on the starboard bow, and shortly thereafter she sighted a surfaced submarine some 3,000 yards away. The submarine was retiring eastward at high speed. Stevens tentatively identified the retiring stranger as American, and he learned she was HOE that night when dispatches established the fact that the two submarines had met in a submerged collision.

The damage was fairly extensive. HOE had run over FLOUNDER from starboard to port, just forward of the victim's periscope shears. In passing, HOE's keel sliced a 25-foot gash in FLOUNDER's superstructure directly aft of the 4-inch gun, damaging the vent line to No. 2 normal fuel-oil tank and the 10-pound blow line, and grooving a deep dent in the tank. Stanchions and deck of the forward 20-mm. gun platform were damaged, the SJ mast was bent askew and an antenna was broken. HOE herself got off with a much lighter crash bill—perhaps a couple of dollars for paint.

This was the first and only submerged submarine collision on record. But it leads to the conclusion that if World War II had lasted much longer, U.S. submarine concentrations might have necessitated special instruction in the art of patrolling subjacent as well as adjacent areas.

A facetious thought suggests a future day when undersea lanes may become as congested as Times Square. To prevent underwater collision, periscope heads thrust up in stiff-necked inquiry, and such angry exchanges as "Whaddya want, the whole ocean?" and, "Who the hell are you? Neptune?" deep-sea rules of the road may be necessary. Stop and go signals, 40 fathoms down. Submarine traffic cops. And the old demand, "Let's see your diver's license!"

February 1945 Attrition (and the Vanishing DD)

About 56,000 tons of merchant shipping were sent to the bottom by U.S. submarines in February 1945. Not much more than "Loughlin's Loopers" had downed the previous November. And not a great deal more than FLASHER alone downed in December. The concentration of submarines along the Japan-to-Singapore line, and the carrier air strikes on South China Sea and East China Sea traffic had shattered the main-line convoy system beyond all hope of repair. February shipping waned to a dribble, and the target shortage reduced the submarines' score.

BECUNA, BLENNY, GATO, GUAVINA, FLASHER, HARDHEAD, PAMPANITO, PARCHE, HAWKBILL and SPADEFISH sank merchantmen here and there. BLENNY (Commander W. H. Hazzard) downed the largest of these.

The victim, sunk off Saigon, Indo-China, on February 26 was the 10,238-ton tanker AMATO MARU. Watching the approaches to Singapore, PAMPANITO (Commander P. E. Summers) sank a large freighter on the 6th and a transport on the 8th. GUAVINA (Commander R. H. Lockwood) struck the 6,892-ton freighter TAIGYO MARU off Malaya on the 7th, and two weeks later in waters farther north downed the 8,673-ton tanker EIYO MARU. Total of some 15,500 tons gave GUAVINA the month's best individual score.

BESUGO, BOWFIN, BERGALL, GATO, HAMMERHEAD and HOE sank an assortment of frigates. HAWKBILL sank two sub-chasers. SENNET downed a coastal mine-layer in "Hit Parade." Small game, but the larger specimens were almost extinct. Big-game shooting, as has been related, featured the enemy submarine as the major target.

However, on the evening of February 20, PARGO (Commander D. B. Bell) made contact with a Japanese destroyer off the coast of Indo-China not far from Camranh. Bell directed a night-surface attack on this ancient foe, and torpedo hits terminated the career of the destroyer NOKAZE.

PARGO's victim was the last DD to be downed by U.S. submarines in the Pacific War. Japan had begun hostilities with a destroyer force that totaled 113 DD's. At the end of February 1945 only 37 Japanese destroyers remained in commisssion or available for war duty. (United States destroyers in commission or available at that date numbered 455.) The Imperial Navy's leaders had made no provision for a large-scale destroyer-building program, and the destroyer force was unable to absorb heavy losses. By war's end the Imperial Navy's destroyer losses totaled 126 DD's. U.S. submarines were responsible for the destruction of 39—something over one-third of the number lost.

Naturally, the drastic destroyer shortage heightened the convoy crisis which was threatening to tie up the Japanese merchant marine in February 1945. In that month the Takao-to-Hong Kong convoy run was abandoned to spare merchant vessels the race with death across the southern end of Formosa Strait. The runs from Shanghai to Formosa and Kyushu to Formosa were simultaneously abandoned to spare the *marus* a race with death in the East China Sea. Hence the increasing scarcity of targets for the submarines patrolling along the main line from Japan to Singapore. And even that Imperial "life-line" was soon to be hauled in. A second glance at the chart, page 452 will show why.

Last Run to Singapore (End of the Oil Line)

Somehow a few Japanese tankers won the race with death in February and carried about 300,000 barrels

453

of oil to Japan. In March the last tankers to reach Japan from the south brought in about 150,000 barrels. By the Ides, the oil importation effort was through.

It was through because such tankers as the 5,236-ton PALEMBANG MARU, the 10,016-ton RYOEI MARU and the 5,542-ton HONAN MARU could not run up the South China Sea without adequate protection. Attempting to do so, PALEMBANG MARU was sunk off the Indo-China coast on March 4 by BAYA (Commander B. C. Jarvis). RYOEI MARU went down the next day in the vicinity of Hué, torpedoed by BASHAW (Commander H. S. Simpson). In an adjacent area BLUEGILL (Commander Eric Barr) sank HONAN MARU on March 28th. These were the last big tanker-sinkings scored by submarines in the Pacific War. Smaller oil haulers were blown to blazes here and there in the war's closing months, but BASHAW had torpedoed the last 10,000-tonner in the South China Sea. Pounding the harbors of the home Empire, aircraft would smash up several large AO's and one would foul an Army mine. Such sinkings came as sequels to the submarine attack on the Empire's main oil line. By the end of March 1945 that artery was completely severed—the flow from the south ceased. With it ceased all possibility of sustaining for more than a few months the Japanese war effort.

The severance of the Japanese oil artery had its physical expression in the closure of the Japan-to-Singapore convoy run. The termination of this line in March 1945 was as fatal to the Empire's economy as the simultaneous stoppage of the oil flow from the south was fatal to the Japanese war effort. But in March the convoy service between Japan and Singapore was canceled, and the merchant shipping allocated to this run was pulled off the line in anticipation of an American drive for Formosa or Okinawa.

So the conquered southern Empire was literally if not formally surrendered. The mountains, mines, forests, plantations, oil fields, harbors, markets, rich cities, the populations representing cheap labor—in short, the lands and the peoples thereof geographically located between northern Indo-China and the easternmost isle of the Netherlands Indies could no longer be exploited by Japan. The vast network of transportation lines which had webbed these conquered territories to the home islands had disintegrated like a chart thrown into a bonfire. A few glowing traceries remained, but they would blow away at a puff.

The War Machine almost out of fuel, the Empire facing bankruptcy and inevitable defeat, Emperor Hirohito had held audience with a number of senior statesmen in February. Consensus was that Japan should immediately seek peace. Now in March, Prince Naruhiko Higashikuni advocated peace moves through the mediation of China. But Japan's Army generals bickered, bogging down in windy debate over "national polity," public opinion and morale, discipline and personal safety. While these War Lords tried to screen their failures behind large but indefinable words—one eye hunting for a convenient exit, the while—the war went on.

Loss of Kete

Captained by Lieutenant Commander Edward Ackerman, KETE left Guam on March 1 to conduct her second patrol. Area assigned was in the Nansei Shotos. In addition to normal patrol duty, KETE was to submit weather reports and serve as lifeguard during air strikes on Okinawa.

On the night of March 9-10, KETE ambushed a convoy, and Ackerman did some crack torpedo-shooting. Down went three cargomen in a row—KEIZAN MARU, SANKA MARU and DOKAN MARU for a total of 6,881 tons. KETE reported these torpedoings. And on the night of March 14 she reported the firing of four torpedoes at a cable-laying vessel. As the submarine had only three torpedoes remaining, she was directed to leave her area on March 20 and return to Pearl Harbor. She was to fuel at Midway en route.

KETE acknowledged these orders on March 19th. The next day she transmitted a weather report from lat. 29-38 N., long. 130-02 E. This was the last transmission ever received from Ackerman's submarine.

She should have made Midway by March 31st. After a futile attempt to locate her by radio—two weeks of deepening silence—she was reported as presumed lost. Apparently there were no Japanese A/S attacks on submarines in the waters east of the Nansei Shotos where KETE headed after making her weather report. A mine was unlikely, for the submarine was traveling eastward into open sea. There were more than the usual number of Japanese submarines operating in the waters through which KETE had to pass, and she may have been lost in deep-sea battle with one of these. But the manner of her going remains conjectural. Somewhere en route from the Okinawa area to Midway, she went down with all hands.

Submarine Tactics—Submerged Radar Attack (ST)

The submerged radar attacks of the latter part of the war differed considerably from those made at an earlier date. When SEA ROBIN found a convoy off Bawean Island in the Java Sea late in the evening of March 4, 1945, a night-submerged radar-approach was in the cards. High card was the submarine's ST radar with its antenna in the periscope's head.

454

This was Sea Robin's second patrol. She was captained by Commander P. C. Stimson. SJ radar picked up the convoy about 40 minutes before midnight. Stimson put Sea Robin on the track, and the convoy's base course was found to be 050° T. Speed plotted an estimated 8.5 knots. As the submarine tracked, Stimson worked her toward the head of the convoy to obtain attack position.

The moon was too bright for the usual surface end-around. But occasional clouds dimmed the light, and during these dim-outs a surface approach was feasible. Stimson saw a chance to destroy the whole convoy, which shaped up as one large cargo vessel and two smaller freighters, accompanied by three escorts. *"Decided three times to make a surface attack as the moon clouded over,"* Stimson noted in his log, *"and four times to make a submerged approach as the moon came out bright. Decided we couldn't trust the moon."*

Midnight passed, and the day was March 5th. At 0108 Sea Robin was in a favorable ahead-position. At 11,000 yards' range, Stimson headed her down the true convoy bearing, and dived to radar depth. At 10,000 yards the biggest target showed up nicely on the radar screen. Thanks to the new ST radar gear, the submerged radar approach and the submerged periscope approach could be simultaneous. Because the radar antenna was assembled in the head of the periscope, radar and periscope depths were practically identical. And when visibility was bad and the target was not in periscopic view, radar's eye could take over and radar ranges and bearings could be obtained. When the target could be seen through the periscope, bearings could be taken visually, and simultaneously checked by radar. Meantime, the submarine could operate at periscope depth, which was much safer than the former "radar depth" of the SJ. All of which presented Sea Robin with a favorable situation.

But as Stimson was driving in, the target zigged suddenly, range 2,500 yards, and for a moment it appeared to be headed straight for the submarine. The course then settled down to a 20° starboard angle on the bow, which put Sea Robin close to the track. One of the small freighters, the one on the convoy's port bow, went by at close range. Stimson decided to seize this opportunity—a sharp track and a relatively large gyro angle—and go for the target. The big freighter had an escort on each bow and one on her quarter. Stimson liked the formation.

At 0123 he fired three torpedoes, range 980 yards, 30° starboard track and 54° right gyro. All three torpedoes hit the mark. Flames soared 500 feet in the air. Fragments of freighter soared with the flames and splashed in the surrounding sea. Eager to find a stern-tube target, Stimson at once began a search for one of the smaller vessels. Abruptly the ST radar gave him a range of 350 yards on an escort. Time to go deep and rig for depth charges.

Negative flood jammed closed with 12,000 pounds in negative, and it was necessary to speed up to hold Sea Robin's depth. Slowly the submarine sank. Far below the surface, she ended her descent, settling with 10° rise angle. The stern must have been on the bottom, for the rudder refused to move. Gradually the submariners got her up to a safer depth. Into the sound gear poured a charivari of noises—screws, breaking-up clashings, minor explosions. But no depth charges. Stimson maneuvered to put the sound of screws astern.

At 0240 he ordered Sea Robin to the surface, 6,000 yards from the torpedoed ship. There was an escort vessel 5,800 yards off the submarine's starboard beam, evidently trying to head off Sea Robin and prevent her from going to eastward. Stimson ran around the would-be interference to the northward. And at 0300, radar contact was made with the SJ at 17,000 yards. By 0414 the submarine was well ahead of the remnants of the convoy. It was still too light for a surface approach, so Stimson decided to repeat his submerged radar approach using the ST scope.

At 0430 Sea Robin dived to radar depth. Twenty minutes later she was almost dead ahead, with the range decreasing. Then one of the target ships zigged. Stimson immediately saw his chance and opened fire with the bow tubes at a range of 1,050 yards, 70° port track. When three torpedoes were off, the skipper shifted his attention to the other targets. As he did so, the first torpedo of the salvo hit. The target slewed around, capsized to port and sank stern first, only 300 yards from the submarine.

Now the last freighter was zigzagging for dear life. At a range of 1,780 yards and with a 96° starboard target, Stimson began firing the stern tubes. The target swung hard right. Angle on the bow decreased to zero. After two torpedoes were off, Stimson ceased fire until the target steadied down. The freighter completely reversed course. Through the periscope at night it was hard to determine whether the angle on the bow was port or starboard. Stimson learned it was starboard and fired the remaining two torpedoes.

The first torpedo hit the target squarely in the middle. The freighter broke apart as though it were made of cake. The radar officer at the ST reported, "Split pip." The forward half of the target sank at once. All hands in Sea Robin's conning tower had a chance to watch the stern half sink.

Sea Robin's three victims were Shoyu Maru, 853

tons; NAGARA MARU, 856 tons and MANYO MARU, converted gunboat, 2,904 tons. Added to a 2,500-ton freighter sunk on March 3, they gave the ROBIN a good late-war score. And they furnished the Submarine Service with a deft demonstration of the night-submerged radar attack.

Devilfish vs. Japanese Plane

USS DEVILFISH (Lieutenant Commander S. S. Mann, Jr.), en route to her patrol area, was somewhere west of Iwo Jima on the afternoon of March 20th. Time: 1644. Nothing to disturb the routine. Then, at 1645, the officer of the deck sighted a "Zeke" or "Hap" diving from the clouds astern, range about five miles. Whether the enemy was named "Hap" or "Zeke" was of little moment. Enough to recognize his nationality as Japanese.

DEVILFISH made a quick dive, and while she was passing 50 feet, she heard a bang which sounded like a light bomb some distance away. But a moment later water poured in through the bottom of the SJ mast. This hemorrhage could not be controlled. DEVILFISH's crew worked desperately to stem the cascade which rushed through the hatch into the control room. Electrical circuits were pulled in the conning tower to prevent fire, and eventually the stream of water was funneled into the periscope well. But the damage was considerable. One periscope would not raise and the other had gone blind. The SD was inoperative.

When Mann ordered DEVILFISH to the surface that night, the SD and SJ radar masts were found gashed away. There was an eight-inch hole in the after periscope shears. Two antennae and an underwater loop were destroyed, and the upper bearings of both periscopes were distorted.

Of particular interest to Mann and company were some jagged pieces of aluminum adhering to the damaged periscope shears. Miscellaneous pieces of scrap and a bit of junk which looked like a plane's landing gear were found on DEVILFISH's deck and bridge. Someone picked up a nameplate inscribed with Japanese characters.

It had not occurred to DEVILFISH's captain and crew that their submarine had been the target of a *kamikaze* attack. But the aircraft's calling card settled that. The *kamikaze* had hit DEVILFISH and gone with the wind—the "divine wind." On the basis of the evidence, DEVILFISH was credited with destroying an enemy plane, and the members of her crew were authorized to wear the Submarine Combat Insignia.

Loss of Trigger

TRIGGER, scourge of the Japanese merchant marine, was on the hunt. Captained by Commander D. R. Connole, she had left Guam on March 11 to raid the sea lanes off the Nansei Shoto Archipelago. This was her twelfth war patrol. Sixteen Japanese ships had been sent down by her torpedoes since her first patrol in the Aleutians. For her fifth, sixth, and seventh patrols under the indomitable "Dusty" Dornin, she had been awarded the Presidential Unit Citation. Hers was a proud record, and now she was off to the battle front with the confidence of a decorated veteran.

As was the case with SWORDFISH and KETE, TRIGGER was to perform a special mission in the Okinawa area in addition to her normal patrol duty. She was also to serve as lifeguard during a scheduled carrier-air strike on Okinawa.

On March 18 TRIGGER reported that she had made a seven-hour end-around on a convoy and sunk a freighter. This vessel, later identified as the 1,012-ton TSUKUSHI MARU No. 3, went down at lat. 28-05 N., long. 126-44 E. The remainder of the convoy fled westward.

Because the waters of the East China Sea lying west of the Nansei Shotos were mined, ComSubPac had directed submarines to avoid specific areas which were known to be marked "restricted" on Japanese shipping charts. Captured charts and supplementary information had tipped off the U.S. Submarine Force concerning the general disposition of the minefields. But there were broad avenues through the mine-lines, and the convoy which TRIGGER had attacked was obviously running for one of these open roads. ComSubPac ordered TRIGGER to trail the fleeing convoy and locate, if possible, the enemy's "safety lane" through the mined area.

TRIGGER replied on March 20, stating that she had been held under by A/S vessels for three hours following the convoy attack and had been unable to regain contact after surfacing. Four days later, she was directed by ComSubPac to patrol between 29 N. and 31 N., west of the Nansei Shotos, remaining clear of restricted areas and outside the 100-fathom curve. Then on March 26, she was ordered to form a wolf-pack at a designated rendezvous point with SEA DOG and THREADFIN. The pack, "Earl's Eliminators," was to operate under Commander E. T. Hydeman, captain of SEA DOG.

The wolf-pack message required acknowledgment. On the day it was sent, TRIGGER transmitted a weather report. But she did not acknowledge ComSubPac's dispatch. The weather report was the last message ever received from TRIGGER.

On March 28, SEA DOG reported that she was unable to contact TRIGGER. Thereupon ComSubPac sent TRIGGER another dispatch requiring acknowledgment.

TRIGGER made no reply, and the wolf-pack was disbanded. After numerous attempts to contact TRIGGER by radio, she was finally presumed to be lost. It seems probable that she was sunk by Japanese A/S vessels and aircraft on the afternoon of March 28th.

On that date, SILVERSIDES, HACKLEBACK, SEA DOG and THREADFIN, sharing a common area in Nansei Shoto waters, heard a thunderous depth-charge barrage. THREADFIN tracked down and torpedoed a destroyer escort that day, and was treated to 18 depth charges by way of reprisal. An hour after this onslaught, THREADFIN reported, ". . . . many distant strings of depth charges and several heavy explosions from what was believed to be eastward. It sounded as though someone was getting quite a drubbing."

After the war, investigators learned that the repair ship ODATE had been sunk on March 27 at 30-40 N., 127-50 E. This sinking was in TRIGGER's patrol area. And undoubtedly TRIGGER was the target for the blasting heard by THREADFIN. Participating Japanese aircraft reported the attack as follows: "Detected a submarine and bombed it. Ships also detected it, and depth-charged. Found oil pool, one to five miles in size, the next day."

Only a fatally damaged submarine could have left such an oil pool. And only TRIGGER was in the immediate vicinity of the reported attack. Fighting her last battle, she went down with all hands—the third submarine lost during the preliminary operations which preceded the all-out drive on Okinawa.

Close Call for Spot

After joining some 200 Superforts in a raid which burned out a square mile of Tokyo on February 25, planes of Task Force Fifty-eight loaded up for a strike which blasted Okinawa on March 1st. Battleships of Task Force Fifty-eight, led by Vice Admiral W. A. Lee, steamed to Okinawa on March 24 and proceeded to bombard the island's southeast coast in support of minesweeping activities. These air and sea operations roused a turmoil that made the Okinawa storm center a dangerous area for submarining. The enemy was resisting fiercely, and all hell was on hand to break loose.

Some of it broke loose on SPOT (Commander W. S. Post, Jr.) when that submarine caught a convoy on March 17 in Formosan waters west of the Nansei Shotos. A torpedo salvo downed the 3,005-ton passenger-cargoman NANKING MARU, and another salvo damaged a freighter, which was later finished off by a Navy plane. This end-around brought SPOT into contact with a Japanese minelayer. Exploded a slam-bang gun battle that SPOT's crew had reason to remember. With a force 5-6 sea running, and the gunners struggling to hang on to their slamming 5-incher, SPOT came within a halved hair of being rammed. Swept by flying spray and whistling lead, the submarine dodged away in the darkness and with slight damage considered herself lucky.

Two weeks later she was target in another shooting match, and this time her escape was luckier. Having concluded her run in Formosan waters, she headed eastward on orders to patrol an area on the Pacific side of the Nansei Shotos. Moving east, she sank two enemy trawlers, skirted around the Okinawa maelstrom, and entered her assigned area. There SPOT was put "on the spot."

The experience was unexpected, for she was operating in a Submarine Patrol Zone. This gave her skipper every reason to believe that surface vessels encountered would be enemy, and if they were not enemy, they would, ipso facto, be friends. Thus when radar contact was made at 1845 on the evening of March 31, range 14,400 yards, SPOT was alerted for action. But there was always some possibility that the vessel might be friendly, and when radar interference was detected, SPOT's captain assumed the contact was another U.S. submarine, probably POGY.

An attempt to exchange signals was unsuccessful, however, and at 1849 Post stationed a radar tracking party and headed SPOT for the target. Now strong radar interference similar to that made by an SC radar was detected. Post maneuvered cautiously. At about 9,000 yards the stranger's silhouette could be visually identified as a friendly destroyer or DE. Post thereupon altered course in order to remain close enough to exchange identification signals and yet show enough angle on the bow so that SPOT, in turn, could be identified.

At 1857 the range was less than 7,500 yards. As the destroyer had made no attempt to challenge by light, Post turned his submarine away. According to SPOT the closest range was 4,200 yards. According to the destroyer, the range had closed to 3,000 yards. The destroyer was the USS CASE. Her version of the episode: She made visual challenge for major war vessels five times with Aldis lamp, at ranges between 3,000 and 4,000 yards. SPOT never saw these challenges, and the reason probably lay in the fact that an Aldis lamp must be turned directly on the bearing of a ship to be seen.

The destroyer-men stated that a final challenge was made with a 12-inch searchlight, and then CASE opened fire. Only one small flash of red light was observed by SPOT's bridge personnel a moment before this first salvo, and the red glimmer, as seen from the submarine's position, bore no resemblance whatever to a recognition signal. The next thing the submariners saw was a flash that bore every resemblance to the flame-jet of a destroyer's guns.

As this first salvo passed overhead at 1907, the submariners fired a red "Buck Rogers" pyrotechnic signal. This was seen by those on board CASE, and the destroyer-men ceased fire with the third salvo in the air. The second salvo had smashed into the sea and the third was just hitting the water at 1908 as Post "pulled the plug" and SPOT went under.

No more red stars were fired, but the air in SPOT's conning tower was red, white and blue, and some of the sparkling conversation may have sent a pyrotechnic glow to the ocean's surface. At 1920 sonar recognition signals were exchanged. The destroyer-men stated that CASE had been getting off sonar recognition signals every two minutes during her sweep and that her IFF gear had been on the entire time. Both ships claimed that after exchanging recognition signals neither would exchange visual calls. However, both said they tried to do so.

Fortunately, the night's blind darkness had necessitated full radar gun control, and the salvos fired by the destroyer had missed SPOT. A little more light and they might have been right on her. But then, a little more light and the submarine would probably have been recognized. Theoretical considerations which failed to soothe the ruffled feelings of Post and company.

To begin with, CASE made the attack in a Submarine Patrol Zone where normally she had no right to be. She had been on lifeguard station in position 28 N., 137 E., and upon receiving an aircraft contact report of two unidentified surface targets some 86 miles distant, she set off on an excursion to locate them. Her course took her inside the Submarine Patrol Zone, and although she endeavored to so notify her squadron commander, she had no assurance the message would be delivered. As a matter of fact, the dispatch never got through.

The most precise attack restrictions were imposed on United States surface vessels operating in Submarine Patrol Zones. Unequivocally the orders stated:

Surface vessels will normally keep clear of Submarine Patrol Zones. . . . In an emergency, when surface vessels enter a Submarine Patrol Zone without prior timely notification, they must accept the risk of attack by friendly submarine. . . . Surface vessels shall not attack a submarine unless it has been identified as enemy beyond possibility of doubt.

In commenting on the destroyer's attack on SPOT, ComSubPac made the following statements:

CinCPOA Standard Operating Procedure specifically states that failure to receive reply to a sonar challenge shall not in itself be considered conclusive evidence of a submarine's enemy character. By implication the same should apply to visual challenges. . . .

Commanding Officer of the CASE states: "No report of submarine positions yet received shows one in or near this position." This indicates a condition of dangerous thinking that can not be too strongly discouraged. The Commander in Chief, Pacific Fleet, and the Commander Submarine Force, Pacific Fleet, have scrupulously and consistently avoided informing surface ships and aircraft of the movements of submarines in Submarine Patrol Zones (or in Joint Zones except in proximity to our own bases). Submarines are allowed freedom of movement in those zones, and their positions are not known accurately by this command. The reasoning behind this sound policy is to prevent exactly what occurred in this instance—the inference that a submarine is an enemy because of lack of notification of the presence of a friendly submarine.

SPOT's close shave was paralleled by one given the submarine TORO about four months later. On lifeguard duty at that time, TORO (Commander J. D. Grant) was stationed off Shikoku.

On the evening of July 24 she was drawn off station to search inshore for some aviators reported downed in that area.

At 1800 her air cover departed, and TORO was left to face a friendly task force due in the vicinity that night.

At 2055 the submarine made radar contact on this force, and maneuvered to give it a wide berth. While maneuvering, she was picked up by the USS COLAHAN.

Rushing in at 28 knots, the destroyer endeavored to establish identification by voice radio. Her IFF was used and showed no return. Meantime, TORO was trying to challenge by light signals and other means. Poor visibility conditions frustrated the light and the signaling did not get through. COLAHAN opened fire at a range of 7,400 yards, straddling TORO with the first salvo. The submarine fired a flare and smoke bombs as Grant "pulled the plug," but spray and a rain squall prevented identification. Immediately after diving, TORO challenged by sonar, and again the challenge was futile, for the destroyer's sound gear was inoperative at a speed of 28 knots. COLAHAN did not cease fire with her 5"/38's until 52 rounds had been pumped at the target's position.

Largely responsible for the attack was a communications failure—a garbled message which led the destroyer-men to believe the target was enemy. TORO was considered at fault for not employing her IFF gear and for failing to submerge as soon as she made contact with the oncoming task force—a discretionary measure that would have prevented trouble.

In the SPOT incident, however, there were few if

any extenuating circumstances in the destroyer's favor. When the shooting was over, CASE was on the spot.

The Sinking of Awa Maru

Not 24 hours after the erroneous attack on SPOT, an American submarine operating in an area west of the Nansei Shotos became involved in a torpedoing that induced most tragic results. Ironically enough, the episode occurred on April 1—a day that has implications of its own on the American calendar. This day was also D-Day at Okinawa. And by a singular coincidence, the submarine's patrol area was the one which had been patrolled by SPOT before that submarine was shifted eastward. And the ship which was torpedoed went down within a few thousand yards of the point where SPOT, on March 17, had sunk NANKING MARU.

The victim of this April 1 tragedy was the 11,600-ton passenger-cargoman AWA MARU, one of the last of Japan's large, fast, passenger liners. Normally the sinking of such a prize would constitute a feather in any submarine's cap. Not so in this instance. For on this particular voyage the United States Government had guaranteed AWA MARU safe conduct for the purpose of transporting Red Cross relief supplies to Japanese prisoner-of-war camps in Malaya and the Dutch East Indies.

AWA MARU had departed Moji, Japan, on February 17, to visit Singapore and various Indonesian ports by way of Takao and Hong Kong. On return trip, she was scheduled to arrive in Miture, Japan, on April 4, and safe conduct had been granted for both the outward and homeward passage. Her immunity from attack was dependent upon visual markings—". . . White Cross on each side of funnel . . . Crosses to be illuminated at night . . . Two White Crosses on each side of ship . . . All navigation lights to be lighted . . ." No procedure was prescribed for her identification in the event of fog or low visibility. On such occasions her immunity depended upon a rigid adherence to a specified schedule and track which would be promulgated to all United States and Allied air, surface and submarine forces in the areas concerned.

During the second week in February, a dispatch in plain language giving the schedule, route, description and identifying markings of AWA MARU was broadcast to all SubPac submarines. As was common with important messages to submarines, the broadcast was emphatically repeated—three times on three successive nights—nine times in all. Early in March the Japanese altered the route for AWA MARU's return voyage, and a message conveying this information was sent out in the same manner, same number of transmissions.

The major lap of the hospital ship's voyage was through South China Sea waters patrolled by Sub-SoWesPac. But the first few days of the outward passage and the last few days of the return trip were through areas patrolled by SubPac submarines. Two days before AWA MARU was scheduled to re-enter the SubPac areas, ComSubPac sent a reminder to his commanding officers. In a coded dispatch he stated in effect, ". . . Let pass safely AWA MARU carrying prisoner of war supplies. . . . She will be passing through your areas between March thirtieth and April fourth. . . . She is lighted at night and plastered with White Crosses . . ."

QUEENFISH (Commander Charles E. Loughlin) was the submarine patrolling the area recently vacated by SPOT—the waters just inside the Formosa Strait bottleneck at the southern end of the East China Sea. At 2200 on the night of April 1, Loughlin's submarine made radar contact with a single ship, range 17,000 yards. Loughlin sent the crew to battle stations, and the fire control party started tracking the target. A fog almost as dense as the vapor produced for a smoke screen surged over the water. Visibility was no more than 200 yards. The target was presumed to be a destroyer or destroyer escort because of the smallness of the radar pip, the relatively low range of radar contact, and the ship's high speed. In the blind fog the ship was doing about 17 knots and was not zigzagging.

QUEENFISH paced the target at a distance of 1,000 yards off the track until the range closed to 3,600 yards. Then Loughlin turned her away and slowed to 4 knots. At 2300, the commanding officer and the bridge watch having unsuccessfully strained to get a glimpse of the target, Loughlin fired four torpedoes from the stern tubes. Radar bearings were employed in the fire control, and all four torpedoes hit. The flash of the explosions lit the fog, but the target remained unseen. Rapid disappearance of the radar pip told the submariners they had scored a fast sinking. Loughlin reversed the submarine's course and sent her back to look for survivors. Some 15 or 20 Japanese were sighted clinging to mats of wreckage, but only one could be prevailed upon to come on board. This survivor stated that the ship was the liner AWA MARU.

When word of the sinking reached ComSubPac's Headquarters at Guam, QUEENFISH was immediately ordered to search the scene of the disaster for any remaining survivors and to obtain evidence of the character of the ship's cargo. SEAFOX, operating in the vicinity, was directed to assist in the search. No other

459

survivors could be found, but several thousand bales of crude rubber and numerous tins of an unidentified black granular substance were seen floating on the water. Samples of this residue were picked up by both QUEENFISH and SEAFOX.

The sinking of AWA MARU placed the United States Government in a most embarrassing position, and the reaction from Washington was immediate and peremptory.

. . . ORDER QUEENFISH INTO PORT . . . DETACH LOUGHLIN FROM COMMAND AND HAVE HIM TRIED BY GENERAL COURT MARTIAL

The court, consisting of two vice admirals, two rear admirals and two captains, met at the Headquarters of Vice Admiral John H. Hoover, on Guam. Three serious charges were brought against Loughlin:

"Culpable inefficiency in the performance of duty."

"Disobeying the lawful order of his superior officer."

"Negligence in obeying orders."

Loughlin's defense was based on the theory that AWA MARU, because of the cargo and passengers she carried, had sacrificed her right to safe conduct. Intelligence had learned that on the outward passage the ship had unloaded 500 tons of ammunition, about 2,000 bombs and 20 crated planes at Saigon. On her return voyage, according to the lone survivor, she was carrying a cargo of rubber, lead, tin and sugar, and about 1,700 passengers—a few government officials, but for the most part merchant seamen who had been stranded when their ships had been sunk in Malayan and Indonesian water. The court ruled this testimony immaterial in view of the fact that the safe conduct agreement had placed no restrictions on the cargo to be carried in addition to the relief supplies, and the commanding officer of QUEENFISH, at the time of the attack, had no knowledge of the character of AWA MARU's cargo.

Defense then introduced evidence to show lack of intent. The 3-foot depth-setting used on the torpedoes, and the manner in which they were spread (4½°—approximately 300 feet at target track) proved beyond all reasonable doubt that Loughlin believed he was firing at a short, shallow-draft vessel rather than an 11,000-ton passenger liner. Among the war's most successful submarine skippers, with seven previous sinkings to his credit, Loughlin was not the one to make such elementary mistakes in torpedo fire control.

The true cause underlying the disaster was never brought out in the court martial. Early in the trial, defense counsel admitted that all messages concerning AWA MARU had been received on board QUEENFISH.

But no one at the trial thought to inquire whether or not Loughlin had seen them. And that was the key to the whole disastrous episode. Although Loughlin had seen the coded dispatch of March 28 concerning AWA MARU, none of the messages specifying her route and schedule had been delivered to him. The communicators had paid scant attention to these plain-language broadcasts which were received two weeks in advance of the time AWA MARU was to pass through QUEENFISH's area. Through the dereliction of his communications personnel, Loughlin had "failed to get the word."

Here was a tragedy of carelessness that took a heavy toll of human life, seriously impugned the word of the United States Government and put a smudge on the record of one of the finest officers in the Submarine Service. Acquitted of the first two charges brought against him, Commander Loughlin was found guilty of the third—negligence in obeying orders. He was sentenced to receive a letter of admonition from the Secretary of the Navy.

The Okinawa Campaign—"Operation Iceberg"

The seizure of Okinawa and neighboring islands of the Nansei Shoto chain was the last major "triphibious" operation in the Pacific. The method of submarine participation followed the established formula. SWORDFISH, as related, was dispatched on photo reconnaissance mission to Okinawa. KETE and TRIGGER engaged in weather reporting. Many submarines served as lifeguards during the preliminary strikes and the pre-Okinawa carrier-air raids on Japan. It was during the course of these raids that Mitscher's planes located several remnants of the Imperial Fleet in the Inland Sea and smashed to junk some of the Japanese Navy's last BB's and CV's. The American carrier FRANKLIN went through her ordeal of death and fire at this time. The collapsing Japanese War Machine was still capable of dealing murderous counter-attacks.

In advance of "Operation Iceberg," six or seven submarines were assigned to "Hit Parade" waters off Honshu and Kyushu. Two of these were stationed to watch the Bungo Suido and one to watch the Kii Suido. These posts off the Bungo and Kii were rigidly maintained. If the residual Japanese Fleet attempted to interfere with the Okinawa landings, the sortie would be through one of these two Pacific-side entrances to the Inland Sea.

The assumption proved correct. On the night of April 6-7, a task force consisting of the super-battleship YAMATO, the light cruiser YAHAGI and a number of destroyers sortied through the Bungo Suido for an immolating attack on Spruance's forces. The

Japanese warships were spotted by THREADFIN and HACKLEBACK on watch at the Bungo exit. In accordance with orders, the submarines surrendered their chance to strike, and transmitted a series of contact reports. Acting on the information received from these submarines, Mitscher's airmen descended upon this enemy force on the morning of April 7th.

Giant YAMATO, cruiser YAHAGI and the destroyers HAMAKAZE, ISOKAZE, ASASHINO and KASUMI were bombed to extinction by the carrier planes. The Japanese ships were without air cover, and if hara-kiri was desired, the desire was fulfilled. The super-battleship was first to go in this fiery sacrifice, her steel plates torn open as though they were sheets of tin. Down went the others, hissing, gushing smoke and flame, their decks all acockbill. Only a few American planes were lost in this action which was the dying convulsion of the Imperial Navy.

"We questioned whether there was a fifty-fifty chance," Admiral Toyoda said in post-war reminiscence. "Even in assembling that squadron we had a difficult time getting the necessary 2,500 tons of fuel oil. But . . . it would have been contrary to the tradition of the Japanese Navy not to have sent them."

This bow to tradition, costing hundreds of lives (Toyoda's among the excepted), was as futile as it was spectacular and Oriental. By way of defending Okinawa, it availed nothing—in fact, it relieved Spruance of further worry about interference from the Japanese Navy. The fighting at Okinawa was sufficiently violent for the invading American forces. The Japanese garrison battled fang and claw to hold the island, and the kamikazes scorched Task Force Fifty-eight and the other Fifth Fleet forces with a hot breath far from "divine." BUNKER HILL was severely damaged during the campaign, and INTREPID, ENTERPRISE and HANCOCK were sorely hit. Twelve American destroyers were sunk in the fighting—among them the destroyer MANNERT L. ABELE, named after the captain of GRUNION, lost three years before in the Aleutians.

Over 4,900 Americans in naval uniform were killed during "Operation Iceberg," and about an equal number were wounded. Thirty American ships were sunk and some 50 vessels were severely damaged. Responsible for nearly 80% of these casualties was the Kamikaze Special Attack Corps. The U.S. Navy was staggered by this savage blow from a nation undergoing its death-throes.

Invited by Admiral Toyoda's statement that his squadron was barely able to obtain 2,500 tons of fuel oil, a speculative question arises. What sort of slaughter would have reddened the waters off Okinawa if the Japanese Air Force had not been pressed for high-octane gasoline and Japanese aircraft manufacturers had not run short of aluminum and other building materials in the autumn of 1944? Kamikaze pilots did not need a great deal of training, and in the spring of 1945 there was no dearth of human material ready to die on the sacrificial altar for the god-Emperor. Enough planes, enough gas and the hot "divine wind" might have melted "Operation Iceberg."

But thousands of tons of aviation materials and thousands of drums of aviation gasoline had been sent to sea bottom by the submarine attrition war. These tonnages and tanker cargoes Japan's failing transport system had never been able to replace. Like the remnant Imperial Fleet, the Kamikaze Special Attack Corps was held in check by shortages largely created by the submarine attack on Japanese shipping.

March-April Attrition

While SubPac submarines in March and April were largely devoted to the preliminaries of "Operation Iceberg" and activities which supported the Okinawa offensive, routine patrolling continued in areas far removed from the storm center. The large tanker sinkings in the South China Sea and the convoys swept away by KETE and SEA ROBIN have been discussed. Other bags were small, but they all added up. On March 1 STERLET downed a small freighter off Tokyo Bay. Far to the south SEALION II sank a small tanker off the coast of Malaya on the 17th. Covering the approaches to Saigon, BLENNY flushed a convoy on the 20th and sank two small freighters and a small tanker—one, two, three. On March 25 TIRANTE, operating off southwest Kyushu, sank a small tanker. Three days later she downed a small freighter—the beginning of one of the war's outstanding patrols. In Nansei Shoto waters SPRINGER loaned immediate support to "Operation Iceberg" by sinking a 1,500-ton transport on March 19th. SPADEFISH struck and sank a 2,274-ton freighter at the northern end of the island chain on March 23rd.

The biggest merchant ship sent to the bottom by a submarine in March 1945 was the 10,413-ton transport HAKOZAKI MARU sunk on the 19th by BALAO (Commander R. K. Worthington) in the Yellow Sea. A notable sinking in that it was the last large Japanese merchantman (with the exception of AWA MARU) to go down from the torpedo fire of U.S. submarines.

A Pacific tag-end of the Japanese transportation network was sheared away in March when the convoy run from Tokyo to the Bonins was terminated. The battle for Iwo Jima had cost the U.S. Navy heavy casualties—loss of the escort carrier Bismarck Sea, and Saratoga badly mutilated by the *kamikazes*. Marine casualties (as of March 26) were particularly severe—4,891 killed and about 16,000 wounded. But the Japanese were never able to solve the logistics problem. Only a trickle of supplies and reinforcements had leaked through the submarine blockade, and when the convoy run was abandoned the garrisons in the Bonins and Volcanoes were marooned.

Also discontinued in March was the convoy run from Tokyo to Osaka. This was the first major break in the domestic transportation network. Long under fire by submarines patrolling in "Hit Parade," this coastwise line was already charred when the threat of scorching by American aircraft from Iwo Jima caused the Japanese to haul it in. None too soon. In April the SubPac blockaders tightened the vise on the Pacific coasts of Japan.

Spadefish, Sea Dog, Sennet, Cero and Sunfish downed shipping off Honshu in April 1945. Hardest blows were struck in the coastal waters north of Tokyo, where Cero (Commander R. Berthong) sank a 6,925-ton freighter on the 29th, and Sunfish (Commander J. W. Reed), striking in mid-April, smashed up two convoys in the approaches to Ominato, downing three small freighters and a frigate.

Operating in the northern waters of the East China Sea, the Kyushu blockaders were also closing in. Parche and Springer on April patrols wiped out small craft in this area.

The accompanying chart marking the month's Japanese merchant sinkings shows the shift of undersea warfare to home Empire waters. Submarine patrols are ranged like stepping stones from the Java Sea to the coastal waters of Hokkaido. In the Java and South China Sea hardly a sprinkle of sinkings—a small freighter downed by Gabilan; a 6,886-ton freighter sunk at the mouth of the Gulf of Siam by Hardhead. Most of the shooting is in SubPac territory—"Hit Parade" and the southern reaches of the Yellow Sea.

In April 1945, Japan was still trying to siphon sustenance from China and Manchuria, and Yellow Sea convoys were a last, albeit an expiring, hope. One of these convoys ran into Sea Devil (Commander R. H. Styles) on April 2nd. Down went a good-sized freighter and two smaller cargo-carriers, three in a row. On April 30 another Yellow Sea convoy was ambushed by Trepang (Commander A. F. Faust). Down went a good-sized cargoman. These sinkings fringe the cluster centered in the southern waters of the Yellow Sea. That cluster was the handiwork of Tirante (Commander G. L. Street)—a *maru*-shoot presently to be discussed.

Meantime, as the April chart clearly indicates, targets were growing as scarce as pheasants in the hunting season, but there was no let-up in the attrition effort during the invasion of Okinawa. In March and April 1945, U.S. submarines sank approximately 130,000 tons of Japanese merchant shipping.

They also sank one of the last Japanese warships afloat in the Southwest Pacific.

Gabilan and Charr vs. Isuzu

Isuzu was the last of the light cruisers to fall victim to a submarine torpedo. After the loss of the Philippines, Japanese garrisons were cut off in many fragmentary areas of the East Indies. The "Co-Prosperity Sphere" now resembled Humpty Dumpty after his fall from the wall. All the king's horses and all the king's men would never achieve its reassembly. But surviving units of the Imperial Navy were pressed into service to rescue Army detachments marooned on the scattered fragments and convey them to some concentration point for a general evacuation.

Isuzu was among the relics which were dispatched to the Southwest Pacific to act as transports and expedite the exodus.

In early April 1945, she was steaming on one of the transport runs. Also in early April a wolf-pack consisting of Besugo (Commander H. E. Miller), Gabilan (Commander W. B. Parham) and Charr (Commander F. D. Boyle) was patrolling off the Paternoster and Postiljon Islands in the waters below Celebes. The group was under the leadership of Commander Boyle.

On April 4, the pack made a mid-morning contact with the cruiser and her four escorts. None of the three submarines was able to get in an immediate attack. While hot on the chase, all were forced down by planes, and they were held down for the rest of the day. After dark, however, Besugo regained contact just as Isuzu and her escorts entered Sape Straits. Hotly pursuing, Besugo made the dangerous night passage of the Strait, and sank one of the escorts.

Meantime Gabilan and Charr returned to their patrolling in the vicinity of Bima Bay off the coast of Soembawa Island. At 1500 on April 6, Charr saw the elusive cruiser enter Bima Bay. At 1900 Charr was on the surface, and Group Commander Boyle passed the news to Gabilan, ordering Parham's submarine to guard the eastern half of the entrance to Bima Bay. The following morning at 0255 Charr made radar contact with the quarry and reported the contact to Gabilan. At 0325 Gabilan reported making contact. At 0443 Boyle ordered a message sent to Gabilan advising her that Charr was diving to attack. Before CHARR's radio could transmit this message, word came from GABILAN—she was attacking. Boyle decided to wait out GABILAN's attack on the surface. But at 0520 it was light enough to see the cruiser's silhouette on the horizon, and Boyle took CHARR under.

CHARR was not long under before she discerned that the enemy formation was rambling and confused. The cruiser was moving slowly and wandering in circles. At 0650, the target was identified as a NATORI-class CL, and a periscope glimpse showed her listing slightly and down by the bow. GABILAN had torpedoed her.

Boyle decided it was time to put her out of her misery. Maneuvering CHARR into attack position, he opened fire at 0724. Six torpedoes. Three observed hits.

During CHARR's approach, the British submarine SPARK had entered the play, moving up to recover the ball if CHARR fumbled. The demise of ISUZU was therefore witnessed by the commanding officer of SPARK, who had a fine periscope view of the sinking. Cheers! The Yanks have picked off another one! Counting the one that was sunk by HMS TALLYHO in January 1944, that makes ten light cruisers the Japs have lost to submarines in the last year and a quarter.

Loss of Snook

"Walling's Whalers" left Guam on March 25 to conduct a wolf-pack patrol in "Convoy College" and perform lifeguard missions if so directed by dispatch. The "Whalers" were BURRFISH, BANG and SNOOK, under group leadership of Commander J. F. Walling, captain of SNOOK.

On March 27 SNOOK returned to Guam for emergency repairs. The following day she headed out to rejoin her group. She was ordered to transmit weather reports as she proceeded westward, and these she dispatched daily until April 1 when she was told to discontinue them. On that same day Walling's submarine was ordered to join a coordinated attack group—"Hiram's Hecklers"—under Commander Hiram Cassedy in TIGRONE. The "Whalers" had been disbanded, BANG and BURRFISH having been assigned to lifeguard duty.

TIGRONE was in contact with SNOOK on April 8 and the latter's position at that time was 18-40 N., 111-39 E. On April 9 TIGRONE attempted to communicate with SNOOK, but received no answer. It was assumed Walling's submarine had moved eastward toward Luzon Strait. And on April 12 she was ordered to serve as a lifeguard during a British carrier-air strike. For this duty she was to take station in the vicinity of Sakeshima Gunto, about 200 miles east of northern Formosa. On April 20 the commander of a British carrier task force reported a plane downed in SNOOK's area. The dispatch also stated that the British force commander was unable to contact SNOOK by radio. BANG was then sent to rendezvous with SNOOK. BANG arrived on the scene in time to rescue three British aviators, but she saw no sign of Walling's submarine. By mid-May—the submarine still missing—Headquarters was convinced SNOOK was lost.

The Japanese reported no A/S attacks which could account for the loss of SNOOK. The Sakeshima Gunto area was mined, but SNOOK was fully informed on the location of the minefields. During April and May five Japanese submarines were sunk in Nansei Shoto waters, and a number of Japanese submarines were contacted in the Sakeshima Gunto area at the time SNOOK was to have been there on lifeguard station. Japanese submarine captains had been instructed to watch for U.S. submarines on the surface doing lifeguard duty. This suggests the possibility that SNOOK was sunk by an enemy submarine which was, in turn, destroyed at a later date.

Going down with all hands, SNOOK left behind her a superior record. While captained by Commander C. O. Triebel, she had sunk 14 Japanese ships, and in October 1944 she had accounted for three more. Somewhere in the western Pacific—east of Luzon Strait?—off Sakeshima Gunto?—she fought her last battle of the war.

Tirante vs. Yellow Sea Transportation (Lt. Comdr. George L. Street, III)

Out of Portsmouth Navy Yard in the autumn of 1944 came the USS TIRANTE, on her bridge Lieutenant Commander George L. Street. If she arrived at Pearl Harbor late in the war, she set out to make up for lost time. And she more than made up for it on her first patrol which took her westward to beat the backwaters of the Yellow Sea.

She slid away from Pearl Harbor on March 3, 1945, and she did not return to base until April 25th. During the intervening 52 days, she attacked 12 enemy vessels, downed half of this number, shot up the rest and raised a Yellow Sea storm that snarled up the Japanese transportation lines to Seoul, Dairen, Tientsin and Tsingtao. Altogether a masterful performance for a maiden patroller and a submarine skipper making his first run in enemy water.

TIRANTE downed her first ship on March 25—a small tanker off Kagoshimo. Three days later she sank a freighter southwest of Nagasaki. From there she headed into the Yellow Sea, looking for bear.

The question as always was where to find it. Informed on the Japanese ship shortage, Street did not expect to see prizes swarming all over the seascape. So he set out to look for ships in locales where the Japanese would not expect an inquisitive periscope. After careful analysis he concluded that the *marus* were following evasive routes through shallow coastal waters, heretofore unexplored by submarines. To those shallow waters he took TIRANTE.

As a result, Street's submarine slammed headlong into action on April 9, and on April 14 fought a battle that brought her a Presidential Unit Citation and the highest honors for Lieutenant Commander Street. The saga is told, Navy style, in the following excerpt from the citation with which the Submarine Board of Awards recommended Lieutenant Commander Street for the Congressional Medal of Honor.

WITH EXTREME AGGRESSIVENESS, BRILLIANT PLANNING AND DARING, THE COMMANDING OFFICER TOOK HIS SUBMARINE DEEP INTO THE ENEMY'S INNER DEFENSES IN A METICULOUS SEARCH FOR ENEMY SHIPPING. WITH SAGACITY AND CONSUMMATE SKILL, HE PENETRATED STRONG ESCORT SCREENS IN THE SHALLOW WATER AND LAUNCHED FOUR DEVASTATING TORPEDO ATTACKS WHICH RESULTED IN THE SINKING OF A 1,218-TON FREIGHTER, A 2,220-TON FREIGHTER, A TANKER AND A 5,057-TON TRANSPORT LOADED WITH TROOPS. AFTER THE ATTACK UPON THE TRANSPORT, TIRANTE WAS SUBJECTED TO A SEVERE DEPTH-CHARGING WHICH BOUNCED HER OFF THE BOTTOM. FIGHTING FOR HER LIFE, WITH EXPLOSIONS ROCKING HER FROM SIDE TO SIDE, THIS GALLANT SUBMARINE CAME BACK WITH A VENGEANCE AND LAUNCHED A BRILLIANTLY EXECUTED TORPEDO ATTACK TO SINK A VALUABLE 1,500-TON PATROL VESSEL. IN THE CONFUSION FOLLOWING THE SINKING OF THIS VALUABLE ENEMY COMBATANT UNIT, TIRANTE SKILLFULLY MADE HER ESCAPE.

ALTHOUGH TIRANTE HAD ALREADY SUNK A VERY CREDITABLE AMOUNT OF ENEMY SHIPPING, THE COMMANDING OFFICER REFUSED TO LEAVE THIS DANGEROUS AREA UNTIL THE MAXIMUM AMOUNT OF DAMAGE HAD BEEN INFLICTED UPON THE ENEMY. BY SOUND DEDUCTIONS AND BRILLIANT REASONING, IT WAS DETERMINED THAT THE ENEMY SHIPS WERE USING A CONFINED HARBOR ON THE NORTH SHORE OF QUELPART FOR AN ANCHORAGE. IN ORDER TO REACH THIS ANCHORAGE, HE WOULD HAVE TO TAKE HIS SUBMARINE THROUGH MANY MILES OF SHALLOW WATER IN WHICH HIS SHIP WOULD NOT BE ABLE TO DIVE. THE

HARBOR WAS INEVITABLY MINED, NUMEROUS REEFS AND SHOALS WERE KNOWN TO EXIST, AND THE WHOLE AREA WAS CLOSELY GUARDED BY SHORE-BASED RADAR, NUMEROUS PATROL VESSELS, AND EXTENSIVE AIR COVERAGE. FULLY REALIZING THE MOUNTAINOUS DANGERS INVOLVED, THE COMMANDING OFFICER MADE HIS DECISION—"BATTLE STATIONS. TORPEDO." —A DECISION TO ATTEMPT AN ACT FAR ABOVE AND BEYOND THE CALL OF DUTY.

DISREGARDING THE POSSIBILITY OF MINEFIELDS AND THE FIVE SHORE-BASED RADARS IN THE IMMEDIATE VICINITY, TIRANTE CLOSED THE SHORELINE AND PROGRESSED INTO THE HARBOR THROUGH NUMEROUS ANTI-SUBMARINE VESSELS. THE GUN CREWS WERE AT THEIR STATIONS, AS TIRANTE WOULD HAVE TO FIGHT HER WAY OUT ON THE SURFACE IF ATTACKED. ONCE IN THE INNER HARBOR, THE CURRENT WAS CHECKED AND A RAPID SET-UP WAS MADE ON A NEARBY 10,000-TON TANKER. TWO TORPEDOES WERE SKILLFULLY FIRED AT THIS TARGET AND A GREAT MUSHROOM OF WHITE BLINDING FLAME SHOT 2,000 FEET INTO THE AIR AND A THUNDEROUS ROAR NEARLY FLATTENED THE CREW OF TIRANTE. IN THE LIGHT OF THE BURNING TANKER, TWO NEW MIKURA-CLASS FRIGATES SPOTTED TIRANTE AND STARTED IN FOR THE KILL. QUICKLY BRINGING HIS SUBMARINE TO BEAR ON THE LEADING FRIGATE, THE COMMANDING OFFICER TENACIOUSLY FIRED TWO "DO OR DIE" TORPEDOES AT THIS VESSEL WHICH WAS ENDEAVORING TO BLOCK HIS ESCAPE AND THEN SWUNG HIS SHIP AND FIRED HIS LAST TORPEDO AT THE OTHER FRIGATE.

WITH ALL TORPEDOES EXPENDED, THE COMMANDING OFFICER HEADED HIS SHIP OUT OF THE CONFINED HARBOR AT FULL SPEED JUST AS THE TORPEDOES HIT THE FIRST FRIGATE AND BLEW IT SKY-HIGH. SECONDS LATER, THE SISTER SHIP WAS HIT AND IT, TOO, FOLLOWED A LIKE FATE AND DISINTEGRATED. WITH EMERGENCY FULL SPEED AHEAD, THE COMMANDING OFFICER SLIPPED RIGHT OUT OF THE ENEMY'S HANDS AND PASSED UNDETECTED ALONG THE SHORELINE BEFORE RETIRING TO DEEPER WATER. IN ADDITION TO THIS HISTORY-MAKING OFFENSIVE AGAINST THE ENEMY, A 100-TON LUGGER WAS SUNK BY GUNFIRE, THREE PRISONERS WERE CAPTURED FROM A SCHOONER AND TWO AVIATORS WERE PICKED UP FROM A DOWNED JAP AIRCRAFT.

On October 5, 1945, President Truman presented the Medal of Honor to Commander Street in Washington.

CHAPTER 30

SUBMARINE LIFEGUARDING

Lockwood Says "Wilco"

It all began at the time plans were afoot for the Gilbert Islands campaign. Commanding a carrier task force, Rear Admiral Charles A. Pownall was to conduct a series of preliminary raids on various Gilbert outposts. Marcus Island and Wake were to be included in the foray. These raids would take Pownall's force through waters patrolled by U.S. submarines. While conferring with ComSubPac on the problem of Joint Zone operations, Admiral Pownall suggested the possibility of using submarines in target areas to rescue aviators who were downed at sea.

"Just the knowledge that it was there would boost the morale of the aviators," he said. "Do you think a submarine—?"

But Admiral Lockwood already had the picture. The picture was a Navy carrier plane crash-landing in mid-ocean, desperate pilots adrift in rubber boats or clinging to wreckage, eyes staring hopelessly across a vacant desert of sea—and then a submarine silhouetted in the surface haze—advancing to come alongside—cheers! Admiral Lockwood's response was emphatically immediate and affirmative. Operations Officer Commander R. G. Voge was directed to arrange the necessary details. A program was soon devised. Endorsing the plan for lifeguard submarines, Admiral Lockwood put his stamp of approval on a project that eventually surfaced into second place on the priority list of submarine missions. Lifeguarding was second in importance only to sinking of enemy ships.

The mills of the gods may grind slowly, but at SubPac Headquarters time was of the essence. When the preliminary Gilbert air strikes were planned, the submarine lifeguard program had to be launched in a matter of days. The planning, subject to the admiral's approval, was left up to Commander Voge, who had acquired a reputation for getting things done the best way in the shortest time.

Parenthetically, it might be noted that Admiral Lockwood invariably invited his staff members to "sit in" on important conferences with other flag officers. A three- or four-striper might blink at a roomful of stars, but the staff officer would need little briefing on a project afterward. When Voge pitched into the lifeguard problem, he already knew the picture—he had attended the conference between Pownall and Lockwood. Lockwood's methods were occasionally unconventional, but this was war, and war conforms to conventions only in the imagination of those who keep wishfully hoping for convenient patterns—and always wondering why they never materialize.

So SubPac Headquarters shed its necktie, so to speak, and got on this lifeguarding job. And, as has been related in a previous chapter, SNOOK, STEELHEAD and SKATE performed lifeguard duties at Marcus, Tarawa and Wake, respectively, and SKATE rescued six downed airmen.

Plunger at Mili

The next successful lifeguard mission was performed by PLUNGER (Lieutenant Commander R. H. Bass) during "Operation Galvanic"—the invasion of the Gilberts. Stationed off Mili, PLUNGER rescued one aviator. This fighter pilot had been downed near

Knox Island, a small atoll not far from Mili. PLUNGER raced to the spot at four-engine speed. The aviator was clinging to a yellow rubber lifeboat. As the submarine drew near, a Jap Zero plummeted out of the clouds and skimmed the conning tower with guns blazing.

The rescue party was not yet on deck, but there were about a dozen men on the bridge, including the skipper, the exec, the gunnery officer, the quartermaster, an electrician and four lookouts. Six were wounded when a 20-mm. shell hit the superstructure and exploded, spraying the bridge with shrapnel.

The wounded were rushed below, the bridge was cleared, and Bass ordered a quick dive. PLUNGER went deep, then planed up to periscope depth. The Zero had disappeared; the American aviator was 50 yards away. Sighting the periscope, he waved cheerfully and dug in with the oars, rowing toward the submarine. So PLUNGER rose to the occasion to take aboard Lieutenant (jg) F. G. Schwartz, USNR. Bass then set a course for Makin, where the wounded were transferred to the transport LEONARD WOOD. Fortunately all of the injured recovered. And with seven rescues to its credit, the lifeguard program was a going concern by the time of the Marshall Islands campaign.

The "Reference Point" Method

The lifeguard instructions issued for the Marshall Islands operation introduced the use of the "reference point" method of reporting the positions of downed aviators. This method proved so successful it was adopted as standard procedure.

A pilot in a damaged plane about to ditch had neither time nor opportunity to encode or encrypt a message giving his position. To send this information in plain language was to invite strafing attacks upon himself and upon the lifeguard submarine by enemy aircraft. The solution of this problem was to report position in plain language by giving the bearing and distance from a reference point unknown to the enemy. Such a reference point was specified for the target of each air strike, and the lifeguard submarine assigned that station was given a voice call. The names of comic strip characters were chosen for the voice calls.

The unique voice call served three purposes. It summoned the lifeguards. (The method was instituted for surface ships and rescue planes as well as submarines.) It designated the objective, or geographical reference point. And when preceded by "distance" and followed by "bearing," it described the exact location of the crash. For example USS FIGHTERFISH has been assigned lifeguard station southwest of Oahu and is given the call "Skeezix."

The name "Skeezix" is also given the reference point —say, Barber's Point. The pilot ditching off Barber's Point, or observing a brother aviator's crash in that area, would send, "12 Skeezix 195," which means, "Calling USS FIGHTERFISH . . . Plane crash 12 miles bearing 195 degrees from Barber's Point."

As in the above example, the reference point chosen for an air strike was usually some prominent landmark which could easily be located by both the submarine and the aircraft. To confuse the enemy, a geographical position at sea in the vicinity of the target was sometimes chosen—for instance, the center of North East Pass, Truk, was used for the strikes on that atoll in February 1944.

So the air waves over the Central Pacific were presently jocular with calls for Donald Duck, Moon Mullins, Dick Tracy, Lace and other celebrities from the best-read pages of American newspapers. Unfortunately, the Japanese soon learned of the "reference point" stratagem. Whereupon they threatened to throw a wrench in the machinery by sending out false distress messages, which served to send the lifeguard submarines off on wild-goose chases, or lured them into range of enemy shore batteries. Although there was no definite evidence that the system had been compromised, this unexpected interference created a new problem.

The problem was solved by changing the voice calls daily, prohibiting use of the calls for anything but actual emergency, and choosing call-words which featured the letter "L."—a baffler to the Jap who has more trouble with "L" than a Cockney with an "Aitch." This linguistic device opened new avenues for the exercise of imagination and ingenuity. And the enemy was soon tongue-tied by such unpronounceables as "Lonesome Luke," "Little Lulu," "Soul Mate," "Pollywog," "Lillian Russell," "Languid Love," and "Lollipop." In short, he got "ell."

Following the Marshalls campaign, carrier-air strikes smote the enemy's bases in the Marianas and Carolines. The raids on Truk, Guam, Saipan and the islands in the western Carolines have been briefly discussed in previous chapters. Submarine lifeguards participated in all these strikes, and in every case aviators were rescued. Many of the rescues were accomplished under fire, and in all instances the submarine, operating on the surface, risked attack. The trooper going over the top to crawl through barb wire to his pal would appreciate the jeopardy of the submarine rising from its foxhole to run across open water to a bull's-eye yellow lifeboat. But the submariners were not to be deterred. Danger was their business, and as practitioners of that business they were experts. The one bad mishap which occurred

HARDER AT WOLEAI. She is closing the beach to pick up a downed airman—one of the war's more daring rescues. On lifeguard duty, U.S. submarines saved 504 aviators from capture by the enemy or death in the open sea. (On following page is photograph of Navy flyer awaiting rescue by Dealey's sub.)

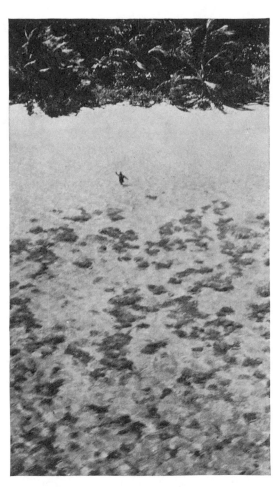

RESCUED BY TANG! Under fire at Truk. Tang picked up 22 airmen. Here are flyers with Tang's ace skipper, O'Kane.

HALOO! Flyer on beach at Woleai hails rescuers. Boiling shoals do not frustrate bold Harder.

SUBMARINE LIFEGUARD. Typical rescue scene, East China Sea. Note crowded raft.

SAFE ON SUB! Three rescued flyers come aboard lifeguard sub. Thanks, boys, that sea is wet! This was a rewarding, welcome sub mission.

USS GAR, LIFEGUARD. Picking up two aviators from the sea. Tigrone (Comdr. Hiram Cassedy) was lifeguard champion: rescued 31 airmen. Such rescues, well prepared for, were common.

during the period in question was the bombing of TUNNY (Lieutenant Commander J. A. Scott) while she was on lifeguard station at Palau. Mistaking her for an enemy destroyer, American carrier planes let fly with a one-ton bomb that missed TUNNY's stern by a scant 10 yards. The explosion caused internal injuries which forced the submarine to abandon her lifeguard duties and do some fast work to save her own skin.

The TUNNY bombing—the only serious misadventure since the fatal wounding of Lieutenant Maxson in SKATE and the casualties suffered by PLUNGER— pointed to the need for maintaining fighter cover over lifeguard submarines. Such cover would not only protect the submarine from attack, but it would increase the efficiency of the lifeguards. The submarine on lifeguard station, unable to distinguish friendly planes from enemy, was forced to dive when any plane approached in a seemingly menacing manner. Then distress calls might be missed by the submerged submarine. Air cover would take care of this situation. Moreover, it would extend the hunt for survivors many miles beyond the range of a searching submarine. However, it was not until TANG (Commander R. H. O'Kane) took station for lifeguard duty during the carrier strikes on Truk on April 30 and May 1, that the importance of fighter cover was conclusively demonstrated.

Meantime, HARDER (Commander S. D. Dealey) at Woleai, and GAR (Commander G. W. Lautrop, Jr.) at Palau accomplished rescues which were the talk of the Submarine Service. GAR recovered eight aviators who had been downed off Palau—a feat unequalled up to that date. At Woleai HARDER recovered one airman. The HARDER exploit—one of the more dramatic rescues on record—merits a detailed accounting. As described by Commander Dealey, the episode vividly portrays the work of a lifeguard submarine in action.

Harder at Woleai

On April 1, 1944, HARDER was off Woleai in the western Carolines—a small island, but important as a "feeder base" for enemy aircraft en route from the home islands to the New Guinea front. At 0840 HARDER was some two miles offshore when Mitscher's planes came roaring in. One of the planes spoke HARDER, reporting a pilot downed off a small island west of Woleai. Dealey sent HARDER racing to the rescue. Excerpts from his patrol report tell the story.

We made full speed on four engines. From here on the picture in the skies looked like a gigantic Cleveland Air Show. With dozens of fighters forming a comfortable umbrella above us, we watched a show that made the Hollywood "Colossals" seem tame. We rounded the southeast coast of Woleai, one to two miles off the beach, and had the perfect "ringside seat." The plastering that the airmen gave this Jap base was terrific! Bombs of all sizes rained on every structure on the island. Several buildings seemed to be lifted and thrown high in the air. Causeways between the various islands were bombed. Oil or gasoline storage tanks blew up covering the island with heavy clouds of black smoke. The runway on the island was hit time and time again with large and small bombs. It was hard to believe that anything could be left on the islands after the first wave of planes had gone over, and yet some bursts of AA fire continued to meet the planes on each attack. The bombers hit Woleai from the south, waited for the smoke to clear, re-formed, and then gave it the works from the east-west course! Fighters seemed to hit the place from all directions, peeling off from high above and diving straight into the AA fire that still persisted. Many looked as if they would go right on thru the blanket of smoke and crash on the islands, but all managed to pull out just above the trees. Fires blazed intermittently on Woleai and most of its adjacent islands, and gradually the AA defense was reduced to a few sporadic bursts.

Fighters now zoomed the HARDER, one mile off the northeast corner of Woleai, and guided us toward the downed pilot.

1145: The pilot was finally sighted on the northwest tip of the second island to the west of Woleai. Battle surface stations were manned, the ship flooded down, and maneuvered into a spot about 1,500 yards off the beach. White water was breaking over the shoals only twenty yards in front of the ship, and the fathometer had ceased to record. Planes now advised us that if rescue looked too difficult from here (and it did!) that a better approach might be made from another direction.

Backed off to make approach from another angle. The aviator had been standing on the beach and was now observed to fall and lie there stretched on the sand. His collapse was undoubtedly due mainly to physical exhaustion, but also to the disappointment in seeing his chances of rescue apparently fade away.

We were then advised by the plane that further air reconnaissance showed the first approach to be the best after all. Reversed course and headed back at full speed. Made ready the rubber boat (no paddles were aboard), and selected Lt. Sam Logan, J. W. Thomason, SC1c, and Francis X. Ryan, MoMM1c, from a large group of volunteers and maneuvered the ship in for a second attempt at rescue. Moved in again until the forward torpedo room reported ". . . bottom scraping forward" (soundings at zero fathom) and worked both screws to keep the bow against the reef while preventing the ship from getting broadside to the waves.

1200: The three volunteers dove over the side and commenced pushing and towing their rubber boat toward the beach, about 1,200 yards away. A line was payed out from the sub to the rubber raft in order to pull it back from the beach. Meanwhile one of the planes had dropped another rubber boat to the stranded aviator who got in and commenced feebly paddling it to sea against the tide.

When the rescue party reached a spot where they could stand up, Thomason was directed to remain with the rubber boat while Lt. Logan and Ryan waded on through the surf toward the aviator. Both were in the breakers now most of the time, and their feet and legs were badly cut by the coral reefs.

After about half an hour, Logan and Ryan, alternately swimming and wading, reached the aviator whose raft had meanwhile drifted farther away. By this time he was thoroughly exhausted. They put him in the raft and by alternately pushing and swimming headed back toward their rubber boat from which a line led to the submarine about 500 yards away.

Meanwhile, a float plane, also attempting the rescue, taxied over the line to the raft, and it parted! The entire rescue party was now stranded.

Thomason was then recalled and managed to swim back to the sub after a hard battle against the tide. Another volunteer swimmer, Freeman Paquet, Jr., GM1c, then dove over the side and finally managed to swim a line to the three men standing just short of the heavy breakers. This line was made fast to the raft, and little by little, the four men were pulled through the breakers and brought back to the ship.

Through the entire rescue, the cooperation of the aviators was superb. They kept up a continuous pounding of the islands by bombs and flew in low to strafe the Japs and divert their attention from the rescue. In spite of this, Jap snipers, concealed in trees along the beach, commenced shooting at the ship and rescue party, and bullets whined over the bridge, uncomfortably close. The rescue could never have been attempted without the protection afforded by the planes. Too much praise cannot be given to the officer and the three men who effected this rescue. Its daring execution, under the noses of the Japs and subject to sniper's fire from the beach, can be classified a truly courageous accomplishment.

The rescued aviator, Ensign John R. Galvin, though physically exhausted, showed a character that refused to admit defeat. It is a privilege to serve with men such as these.

With pilot and rescue party aboard, HARDER was backed clear of the reef and headed seaward. Dealey and his good company would long be remembered for this intrepid rescue.

Tang at Truk

When O'Kane's submarine was assigned lifeguard duty for the late April carrier strike at Truk, Com-SubPac anticipated a successful performance by TANG. But no one expected the record-breaking show which O'Kane and company staged in the turbulent waters off that Caroline stronghold. At 0400 on April 30, 1944, TANG was in her assigned position off Truk Atoll—a station well within the range of the Japanese shore batteries.

Thirty-six minutes later the first planes were sighted. At 0610 the bridge watch saw the first plane go down over Dublon Island. A group of unidentified aircraft forced O'Kane to "pull the plug" a moment later, and the submarine had to stay down for 13 minutes—time lost in evading planes which may have been friendly.

Again on the surface, TANG watched the bombers swarming over Truk. At 1025 the first report of a downed plane came in. O'Kane headed his submarine for the reported position, which was about two miles off Fourup Island. Fighter planes came up to guide TANG to the three survivors who were riding a raft about four miles west of the originally reported position. This trio had bailed out of a Grumman Avenger after the plane had been struck by Japanese shells. Now they were only too happy to have TANG bail them out of the unfriendly sea off Truk.

TANG, with her first three passengers aboard, was hardly under way when another call came in—plane down, two miles east of Ollan Island. To reach this position, TANG had to run within range of the shore batteries on Ollan. O'Kane decided to make the run on the surface and limber up the gun crew in passing. So TANG's gunners pumped 20 rounds in the enemy gun emplacements as the submarine went by. Returning this fire, the Japanese artillerymen opened with a salvo that sent TANG burrowing under. "We didn't spot the second salvo," O'Kane said afterward. "We remained submerged for forty minutes, and then proceeded toward the east side of Truk at emergency speed."

From this position, O'Kane sent TANG in a zigzag search of the area, firing green Very stars at 15-minute intervals, hoping for a return signal from the aviators. One of the men picked up later said he saw the submarine's signal but was afraid to answer it. Hours of futile search ended in a contact with a Japanese submarine. O'Kane sent TANG under to chase; the contact evaporated. When TANG returned to the surface, the crew spread large colors across the deck to assure identification, and the Jap submarine's presence in the area was reported to the task force commander. In return, TANG received the report that a life-raft was drifting two miles southwest of Ollan Island.

"Before we reached this raft a float plane from the NORTH CAROLINA capsized in the cross chop while attempting to rescue," O'Kane recalled. "Another

468

NORTH CAROLINA plane made a precarious landing, and, upon our arrival, was towing both raft and fellow pilot clear of the island. This action was most helpful, for we expected competition from Ollan, and near-by fighters were already strafing the gun emplacements for us."

Later in the day TANG picked up the airmen she had searched for the previous night. This trio gave her a complement of six. Then circling fighter planes directed the submarine to another life-raft. Three more airmen were hauled aboard TANG. And this third rescue was hardly completed before word of three life-rafts adrift off Kuop Island sent O'Kane and company racing for that position.

"As our track took us close by our submarine of the morning, we requested and promptly got good air coverage," O'Kane related. "Off Mesegon Island in the action between Kuop and Truk, we expected to be driven down. But our strafing escorts evidently discouraged any opposition."

Thus O'Kane observed that the enemy gunners consistently refused to fire upon the submarine when American aircraft were in the vicinity. Obviously the Japs did not want to disclose their gun positions to the bombers. O'Kane continued to request fighter cover; the cover was supplied, and the tactic worked with precision and perfection. Thirty-five airmen were shot down during this Truk strike. TANG rescued 22. Most, if not all, of the 13 lost were shot down directly over the target or inside the atoll where they could not be reached.

TANG's record of 22 rescues on a single patrol led the field for over a year. And it settled all question about the value of fighter cover. Thereafter such cover became standard practice for all carrier air strikes. Admiral Mitscher's Operation Plan for the carrier force during the Marianas campaign assigned fighter cover for each lifeguard submarine and specified four tasks to be undertaken by the Submarine Combat Air Patrol. The aircraft were to assist submarine in locating survivors; protect submarine from strafing by enemy planes, or from attacks by small enemy patrol vessels; prevent friendly planes from forcing submarine to dive; act as beacon over submarine so that planes in trouble would know the exact location of submarine and could head in its direction if possible.

TANG's remarkably successful lifeguard mission did more than obtain the desired fighter cover. It created a wide and immediate demand for submarine lifeguard service. Requests now came in from all sides—from bomber commands in the Solomons, the Admiralty Islands, New Guinea, far-off China. As a result of these requests, from early summer 1944

until the autumn of that year one submarine lifeguard was maintained in the vicinity of Truk, and another in the Yap-Woleai area to perform services for shore-based bombers. On July 14, GUAVINA (Commander C. Tiedeman), lifeguarding near Yap, rescued four air-crewmen of a Thirteenth Air Force Liberator which had crashed the previous day. Five days later she picked up eight aviators who had bailed out from another Liberator.

Lifeguard work in the Caroline Islands was at first combined with normal patrolling. Any available submarine was assigned the mission as additional duty. But not long after the Caroline bases were by-passed, Japanese shipping ceased almost entirely in those waters, and the chance to make an occasional torpedo attack became correspondingly rare. When this situation developed, such older submarines as PLUNGER, POLLACK, PERMIT and TARPON, with but six torpedo tubes each, were used exclusively in these "unproductive" areas—a measure which released the newer submarines with 10 tubes for anti-shipping patrols. Eventually the by-passed enemy bases were neutralized to virtual non-existence. When they were no longer good for occasional target practice, the need for lifeguard submarines ceased to exist. During her twelfth war patrol, TARPON was on lifeguard station at Truk from September 2 until October 1, 1944. The squadron commander's endorsement to her patrol report contained the following:

The area around Truk has just about lost all value as an offensive submarine area, and, due to its gradual neutralization by air and surface forces, its value as a submarine lifeguard station is considered questionable.

TARPON was relieved on station by PERMIT, and when PERMIT departed from the area on October 28, lifeguarding in the Carolines was discontinued.

Lifeguarding for Land-based Bombers (Guavina and Mingo)

In July 1944, GUAVINA (Lieutenant Commander Carl Tiedeman) rescued 17 downed aviators in the vicinity of Yap. This heroic enterprise featured submarine lifeguard service for land-based aircraft. Army fly-boys were as delighted as anybody to have a friendly submarine come alongside and pluck them out of the ocean. But the GUAVINA rescues were exceptional. Lifeguarding for land-based bombers in the western Carolines was a slow business. The value of the lifeguards to the bomber commands was mostly psychological. Flight crews were heartened by the knowledge that submarines were out there to give them a hand if their motors conked or the enemy shot them down. However, enemy air opposition had been all but obliterated by the previous carrier strikes. Occupation of the Marianas, Peleliu and Ulithi prevented the foe from sending air reinforcement to those areas. The bombing of these isolated outposts was generally conducted at high altitude, and desultory anti-aircraft fire was the only opposition encountered. Consequently there were few planes shot down and few calls for rescue.

Moreover, the land-based bombers were multi- instead of single-engine aircraft, and seldom was such a plane's power plant entirely destroyed. If one of two engines were shot out of commission, the pilot, instead of heading for the lifeguard submarine, would invariably attempt to reach home base with whatever he had left to go on. In the few instances where the pilots failed to make home, they ditched their planes well beyond the reach of the lifeguard submarines.

When the China-based Twentieth Bomber Command started B-29 strikes on Kyushu in June 1944, from two to four submarines were on duty for each strike, stationed along the outgoing and return routes. Here, too, no rescues were made—for reasons noted above. Also, the strikes were upon a large land mass, and most of the planes that were lost crashed inland.

In Borneo waters, however, a submarine of the SoWesPac Force accomplished a most hazardous and dramatic rescue of Liberator pilots. The submarine was MINGO. Skippered by Lieutenant Commander J. R. Madison, she took up a station off Balikpapan in October 1944 to stand lifeguard for a Thirteenth Air Force Liberator strike.

MINGO reached her station a day ahead of schedule. While marking time, she got into a ferocious shooting match with four oil-hauling trawlers, ran aground, backed off under fire, and had a hot time generally. Cooling off the next day, she ran to the rescue of six airmen adrift in a huddle of life rafts.

On the day after that, the lookouts sighted a small fire on the eastern fringe of Balesang Bay. MINGO scouted in for a closer look. American aviators? Or a trap of some kind. The submariners broke out a rubber boat and, armed with Tommy-guns, paddled in to investigate. Thirty minutes later they returned with four aviators. A fifth paddled out by himself in a native dugout. The five airmen were installed in the submarine. So was the dugout—marked as a present for the Officers' Club in Fremantle.

One of the flyers said he believed five more crewmen were down on the beach a few miles north. Madison headed MINGO for a search in that neck of the woods. The woods of Borneo being about as primitive as was Tarzan's favorite jungle, the submariners proceeded cautiously. Because rescued airmen said they had at first mistaken MINGO for a Jap sub, Madison ordered a large flag secured to the periscope for identification.

As the submarine rounded Cape Biroe, the lookouts saw a flashing light, and noticed a parachute spread out on a clump of rocks. Madison maneuvered in toward the beach. Five more Liberator crewmen were soon aboard. Of the downed aircraft's crew only one man remained unaccounted for.

With the 16 survivors aboard and under the care of the pharmacist's mate, Madison headed his submarine south. MINGO had not gone far in that direction when she was sighted by a high-flying Liberator bomber that made a decidedly menacing scrutiny of the submarine. Madison and company tried frantically to communicate their identity to the aircraft. Twenty minutes of that, and the bomber turned away. All hands exhaled in relief. Six minutes later the bomber was back! All hands inhaled. A 100-pound bomb landed 300 feet broad on MINGO's starboard beam. For some perverse reason, only then was voice communication established between the submarine and the bomber. Perhaps it was because the submariners were all yelling like wild men of Borneo.

MINGO's interesting experience illustrates the fact that lifeguarding for shore-based bomber commands introduced a new problem into the endeavor. Carrier-air operations were usually planned well in advance, and the submarine commander proceeded to his station with detailed instructions in hand. When submarines were suddenly called upon to perform lifeguard services without previous planning, as was the case with land-based strikes, each instance required a long and complicated exchange of instructions between the Submarine and the Air Commands. To rectify this situation, ComSubPac suggested the creation of a standard lifeguard procedure which could be issued in advance to all concerned.

The result was Standard Operating Procedure Number Two ("SOP TWO") dated October 28, 1944. With minor changes, this rescript remained in effect until the end of the war.

"SOP TWO"

"SOP TWO" laid down all the rules for lifeguarding (surface ship as well as submarine) and specified universal radio frequencies for all air-sea rescue communications. Accompanying "SOP TWO" was a secret list of reference points for all Central and Southwest Pacific areas where air strikes might be expected. For each reference point a series of six calls was assigned, the calls changing every 24 hours for six days and then repeating in rotation. As air strikes became more diversified, new reference points were added, and the system was modified when necessary to meet major changes in the strategic situation.

With the issue of "SOP TWO," the dispatch instructions to the submarines were greatly simplified. For example, if Admiral Halsey decided to conduct a carrier strike on Honshu, he would pick out the reference point closest to his target and send a dispatch as follows:

REQUEST SUBMARINE LIFEGUARD NEAR FOX 6 AT 0500 ITEM 10 JULY

Upon receipt of this message, ComSubPac would study the chart to determine how close to that point a submarine could approach. Then he would select a submarine for the job, and send dispatch instructions to her on this order:

AT 0500 ITEM 10 JULY BE ON LIFEGUARD STATION TWENTY MILES BEARING 160 DEGREES FROM FOX 6 . . . CONDUCT LIFEGUARD SERVICES FOR CARRIER BASED PLANES . . . PROCEDURE IN ACCORDANCE WITH SOP TWO

Notice of this dispatch would be sent to Admiral Halsey and the carriers concerned, and the paper work was done. "SOP TWO" explained the entire procedure to be followed, and the listed reference points told the submarine and the carriers the exact position of the reference point in question and the radio call to be employed. "L" words were continuing to baffle the Japs, who mouthed helplessly, attempting to cope with "Bustle Rustle," "Flabby Flanks," "Flashy Lassie" and "Fleshy Flo."

Lifeguarding for the Superforts

By the end of October 1944 submarine lifeguards had rescued a cheering lot of Navy pilots—had won the heart of Army Air—had acquired a standard procedure. All who knew of it were enthusiastic over the project, and the lifeguard submarine basked in the limelight much as her counterpart in civil life basks in the sun on Palm Beach. But the submarine lifeguards were only warming up.

As has been related, the Marianas invasion gave Army Air good air strips for the B-29's, and brought Japan within land-based bombing range. The Superfortresses had been developed for the specific purpose of blasting the home Empire, and the original B-29 raids from China were dress rehearsals for the bigger raids to be staged from Saipan, Guam and Tinian. In November 1944 the Superforts at Saipan were ready, and the strikes were launched, Tokyo serving as No. 1 target. The first of these Tokyo strikes, made by about 100 long-range bombers, was only a sample of the strikes that were to come the following spring when air armadas would assail the Japanese capital.

Some weeks before the opening strike on November 24, 1944, representatives of the Twentieth Bomber Command called on ComSubPac to enlist the services of submarines for air-sea rescue work. Four submarines were placed on the approach and retirement routes for the first strike. And, with the exception of a few occasions when only three were available, four or more submarines were employed during the ensuing strikes.

The original plan had been to control the movements of these submarines from SubPac Headquarters at Pearl Harbor. But this remote control soon proved impractical. Weather conditions over the Japanese homeland governed the timing of the strikes, and these conditions could not be forecast very far in advance. As a consequence, the last-minute postponement of planned strikes became the norm, rather than the unusual. Good lifeguarding required the submarines to remain on the surface during the entire time the planes were in the air, and unless the submarines could be given immediate notice of these snap postponements, they would surface and expose themselves needlessly for strikes that had been canceled. This meant that spot information had to be furnished the submariners to inform them on the exact time of a strike and to feed them data concerning the positions where planes had ditched or where survivors had been sighted in the water. The Submarine Force had already established Commander Task Group 17.7 in a tender at Saipan for the purpose of routing, arranging for escort, and giving voyage repairs and fuel to submarines passing through the Marianas. The duty of controlling the lifeguard submarines and supplying them with information was turned over to this command. Four submarines would be ordered by ComSubPac to the areas concerned, and ComTaskGroup 17.7 was permitted to control their movements within certain limits. For the easy addressing of his submarines in dispatches he quickly dubbed them the "Lifeguard League"—a name that soon took hold with the submariners and aviators. Commander Task Group 17.7 controlled the League until early February 1945, when ComSubPac reassumed its control from advanced headquarters, established in the tender HOLLAND at Guam.

At first the Lifeguard League experienced the difficulties which had previously been encountered while operating with land-based bomber groups. The B-29 aviators had to be educated to the possibilities of rescue by submarine. Submarines were an unknown and uncertain factor to the Superfort boys, and the average, uninitiated B-29 pilot would take his chances on getting a damaged plane home rather than ditch in the vicinity of these little gray subs that might or might not be there when he wanted them.

After the inauguration of the B-29 strikes, more than a month elapsed before the submarine lifeguards rescued their first B-29ers. On December 19, SPEARFISH (Lieutenant Commander C. C. Cole) saved seven air-crewmen from a plane that went down in the vicinity of the Bonins. This was the beginning of a long list, but it was not until March 31, 1945—more than three months later—that the second rescue occurred. Seven more aviators were saved—this time by RONQUIL (Lieutenant Commander R. B. Lander). The next rescue of Superfortress crewmen occurred on April 27, when GATO (Commander R. Holden) picked up 10. From that date onward the rescues were an occurrence as common as the crash of bombs in Tokyo.

Lifeguards for Far Eastern Air

Meantime, requests for submarine lifeguard service continued to come in from other quarters. The invasion of Luzon brought requests in March 1945 for submarine lifeguards to serve Army air forces based at Lingayen. Later, when planes at Clark Field were taking off to strike targets on Formosa and the China coast, lifeguards were requested for those strikes. Here the submariners were presented new problems in communications. The separation of the Far Eastern Air Force and the Submarine Force, Pacific Fleet, red-taped and slowed the exchange of information. This separation was a matter of command echelons rather than mileage. FEAF was a subordinate command of the Commander-in-Chief, Southwest Pacific Area, and the Submarine Force was a subordinate command of Commander-in-Chief, Pacific Fleet. There was no direct channel of communication between these two subordinate commands of two distinct higher echelons, and the following of the normal chain of communication through the command echelons meant delays. The lifeguards were supplied, as requested, off northern and southern Formosa, and near Hong Kong and Hainan. But due to the lag in supplying spot information, these lifeguard endeavors were practically nullified.

To remedy this situation, ComSubPac dispatched Captain Voge to Leyte late in March to confer with representatives of FEAF. As a result of this conference, Commander R. L. Rutter, who had recently relinquished command of the submarine KETE, was established at Fifth Air Force Headquarters at Clark Field, Luzon, for the purpose of coordinating the submarine lifeguard work with FEAF's activities. This arrangement expedited matters, and it continued in effect until May 1945 when ComSubSoWesPac, by arrangement with ComSubPac, took over the additional area south of 23° North and west of 122° East. Thereafter, the Southwest Pacific Force supplied lifeguards for Luzon-based planes.

Texas and National Leagues

Shortly after the landings in Okinawa, Fleet Air Wing One, under the command of Rear Admiral Price, was established at Kerama Retto and started air search across the Yellow Sea and East China Sea. Admiral Lockwood foresaw the lifeguard problems involved, and Commander C. M. Henderson was placed on Admiral Price's staff for temporary duty to coordinate air and submarine work. A part of this involved the exchange of contact information between submarines and aircraft, as well as lifeguard and flying data. After Okinawa was occupied and various bomber commands were established on the island, Henderson moved there to carry out his duties with the Air-Sea Rescue Unit. With two groups of submarines operating as lifeguards—one group for Okinawa-based planes and the other group for Marianas-based planes—the title "Lifeguard League" was dropped. As each submarine group needed an individual title, the lifeguard group for Okinawa planes was designated as the "Texas League" and the group for Marianas planes was called the "National League."

In June 1945, Commander J. D. Adkins was ordered to temporary duty with the Air-Sea Rescue Unit at Iwo Jima. While all the B-29 strikes of Marianas-based planes were controlled from Guam, fighter strikes by P-51 Mustang planes were being run from Iwo Jima, and the Air-Sea Rescue Unit had its headquarters there. So it was from Iwo Jima that information concerning downed pilots was centralized. Adkins' duties were to supply this information to the submarines, along with information concerning fighter cover for the "National League." He also coordinated submarine hunts for survivors with searches by "Dumbo" planes (that famous genre which carried special gear for air-sea rescue work). About the time Adkins was sent to Iwo Jima, Commander Hiram Cassedy became lifeguard liaison officer on ComSubPac's staff at Guam. These three officers—Henderson at Okinawa, Adkins at Iwo Jima and Cassedy at Guam—had all been in recent command of lifeguard submarines (BLUEFISH, COD and TIGRONE, respectively). Thoroughly acquainted with lifeguard missions, they knew the problem from the submarine end and were able to put a lot of power into the project. Cassedy in particular. His submarine TIGRONE had broken the all-Pacific record. And on V-J Day she was on top as the champion lifeguard of World War II. Thirty-one rescues!

Communication and Coordination

In June 1945, at the instigation of Admiral Lockwood, and with the backing of Lieutenant General Barney Giles (at that time in command of Army Air Forces, Pacific Ocean Area, with headquarters at Guam) a series of airman-submariner conferences was arranged. These conferences were attended by representatives from the various air commands and members of the staff of ComSubPac's Advanced Headquarters, plus submarine commanding officers from lifeguard missions. The purpose of the conferences was to iron out communications problems and promote coordination between the submarine and planes—especially the "Dumbo" planes and the fighter cover, who assisted in the search for survivors. Arrangements were made for flight personnel to embark in submarines for training practice in the Marianas, and for submarine commanding officers to make Dumbo flights in B-29 planes. At the invitation of Admiral Lockwood, flight crews were sent to Camp Dealey, Guam's submarine rest camp, for four-day periods. There pilots and submariners became acquainted with mutual problems. In June 1945, a submarine lifeguard lecture team was also organized by ComSubPac to tour the various air bases, giving lectures and showing movies of submarine rescues.

Two hundred and forty-seven air-crewmen were saved by submarines in the months of May, June and July 1945. Among those rescued were Army bomber and fighter crews, Marine Corps fighter pilots, British carrier pilots and Navy search-plane and carrier-plane personnel. A few Japanese pilots (not included in the total) were salvaged for good measure. Most of the rescues were in the Central Pacific, but Sub-SoWesPac lifeguards contributed their share.

Lifeguarding in the Southwest Pacific followed the pattern set in the Central Pacific, but the pace was somewhat slower. In the SubPac areas the long overseas flights were made either by carrier planes or by long-range bombers. Over-water flights were relatively short in the Southwest Pacific, and most of the strikes were made by land-based light and medium bombers or fighters. And since the presence of lifeguard submarines forced the aircraft to identify a sea-going target as "not submarine" before attacking, the Southwest Pacific air commands chose to forego lifeguards for short-range air strikes in order to avoid attack restrictions. Thus the established practice of excluding submarines from areas within the attack-range of shore-based bombers.

Aces High

EVEN IF YOU WERE SHOT DOWN IN TOKYO HARBOR THE NAVY WOULD BE IN TO GET YOU!

So was titled an article by Ernie Pyle, featuring the rescue of Ensign Robert Buchanan by the submarine POMFRET (Lieutenant Commander J. B. Hess) on lifeguard mission off Sagami Nada. Here is the story in POMFRET's log, dated February 17, 1945.

About noon a fighter was reported down in the submarine's area. Trailing the air cover, Hess headed POMFRET into the bay. Groping through an oyster-clammy mist, she navigated entirely by radar, using a "pip" she hoped was the Suro Saki lighthouse. Finally, after approaching uncomfortably close to the shallows in the center of Sagami Nada, she picked up Ensign R. L. Buchanan of the USS CABOT. At this juncture the last of the aircraft cover departed because of low fuel. Hess reported later, "As he faded off the SD screen there was not a friend anywhere." Five or six small Jap vessels were in sight to the northwest as POMFRET followed her retiring air cover. The commanding officer felt sure the Japs had listened to his radio conversation and were aware of POMFRET's naked presence in the area, but the submarine's outward passage was unopposed. This rescue, of course, did not take place in Tokyo Bay, but the "even if" by Ernie Pyle was no exaggeration.

On one occasion an aviator was rescued most unexpectedly. April 2, 1945, SEALION II (Lieutenant Commander C. F. Putnam), patrolling in the South China Sea, sighted a distant object across the water. Running forward, the SEALIONERS picked up Sergeant Bauduy R. Grier of the Fifth Bomber Command. Grier had been adrift in a rubber boat for 23 days!

Probably the all-astounding rescue of the war was one accomplished on a day in June 1944 by STINGRAY (Lieutenant Commander S. C. Loomis, Jr.) within one mile of Agaña airfield, Guam. At the time, the island was still in enemy hands. About 1015 in the morning of this day, fighter planes reported a downed airman adrift near Orote Point. The submarine ran to the designated spot. There she found the desperate aviator playing target for an AA shore battery which was peppering him with a vicious fire. As the submarine approached, a shell exploded 400 yards off her starboard beam. To prevent a salvo from landing squarely on STINGRAY's conning tower, Loomis "pulled the plug." What happened after that is delightfully described in the submarine skipper's patrol report. As follows:

1233: Sighted pilot dead ahead. Had to approach from lee or across wind. Velocity 10 to 12 knots.
1235: Two shell splashes ahead.

473

1238: Two more splashes and burst of AA fire near pilot. Can see him ducking in rubber boat.

1240: Pilot has sighted us and is waving. Holding up left hand which shows a deep cut across the palm.

1303: Approached with about ten feet of number one scope and about three feet of number two scope out of water. Pilot very close and no signs of line ready for scope. Pilot so close I have lost him in number one field. Headed directly for him. Missed.

1319: Three shell splashes on port quarter.

1347: Heard shell land close aboard.

1349: Heard another close one.

1352: Almost on top of pilot. Now, he's paddling *away* from periscope. Missed.

1418: Planes commenced bombing Agana field and shore batteries.

1423: Shell splash, about 500 yards.

1424: Heard shell splash.
Heard another close one.
Heard another close shell.
Heard two more.
Heard one shell.

1440: Heard and saw two splashes close aboard.

1453: Pilot missed the boat again. On this try, he showed the first signs of attempting to reach periscope. Maybe shell fire has made him think that a ride on a periscope might be all right after all. I am getting damned disgusted, plus a stiff neck and a blind eye.

1500: Heard another shell.

1516: Fourth try. Ran into pilot with periscope and he hung on! Towed him for one hour during which time he frantically signalled for us to let him up. His hand was cut badly and it must have been tough going hanging onto the bitter end of the line with one hand while bumping along in the whitecaps.

1611: Lowered towing scope, watching pilot's amazed expression with other periscope.

1613: Surfaced.

1618: Picked up Ensign Donald Carol Brandt, USNR, suffering from deep wound in left hand. Glad to finally get him aboard. He said that during first and third approaches he was afraid periscopes were going to hit him and he tried to get out of the way and come in astern of me. He had been briefed on a rescue like this, but guess the shock of getting hit at 14,000 feet and falling upside down in his parachute from 12,000 feet was too much. And then the shell-fire shouldn't have done him much good either. He's taken quite a running, and taken it well. We're on speaking terms now, but after the third approach, I was ready to make him captain of the head.

The date of this periscope-ride was June 13, 1944.

Anyone who wants to make something out of the date, the 13th, may do so. At any rate, it was a day that the submariners in STINGRAY would not soon forget, and one that the rescued aviator would in all probability remember as long as he lived.

And he, and many more like him, lived because of Submarine Lifeguarding—an enterprise which started as a little extra duty to assist the air forces and developed in the closing months of the war into one of the major tasks assigned U.S. submarines. The success of this remarkable submarine effort can best be measured by the following table.

	Submarine-days on lifeguard station	Number of rescues
1943	64	7
1944	469	117
1945 (to 14 Aug)	2739	380
Total	3272	504

These 504 rescues were accomplished by the 86 submarines listed below:

Archerfish	1	Hammerhead	1	Seafox	11
Argonaut II	1	Harder	1	Sealion II	1
Aspro	6	Hardhead	2	Seaowl	6
Balao	7	Icefish	6	Searaven	3
Bang	1	Jack	1	Searobin	2
Batfish	3	Jallao	5	Seawolf	2
Bergall	4	Kingfish	4	Shark II	2
Blackfish	6	Kraken	1	Silversides	2
Blueback	4	Mingo	16	Skate	6
Bluefish	9	Perch	2	Snook	1
Bonefish	2	Peto	12	Spearfish	7
Bowfin	3	Pintado	12	Spikefish	1
Bream	5	Pipefish	9	Springer	9
Bullhead	3	Plaice	5	Steelhead	1
Cabrilla	6	Plunger	1	Sterlet	8
Cero	3	Pogy	10	Stingray	5
Charr	2	Pomfret	7	Sturgeon	3
Chub	3	Queenfish	13	Tang	22
Cobia	7	Quillback	1	Tench	2
Dragonet	5	Ray	21	Threadfin	4
Finback	5	Razorback	5	Tigrone	31
Gabilan	17	Rock	1	Tilefish	1
Gar	8	Ronquil	10	Tinosa	10
Gato	13	Sailfish	12	Toro	9
Grouper	7	Saury	1	Trepang	10
Guardfish	2	Sawfish	2	Trigger	1
Guavina	17	Scabbardfish	12	Trutta	1
Hackleback	1	Seadevil	15	Tunny	3
Haddock	1	Seadog	1	Whale	15

But the statistics are too laconic. Think of the 504 as American airmen. Good lads, who were saved.

CHAPTER 31

MISSION ACCOMPLISHED

Bankruptcy of an Empire

By May 1945 the submarine attrition war in the Southwest Pacific was almost over. Little remained of the Imperial transportation network which had sprawled across the southern half of the Co-Prosperity Sphere like a parasitical vine. Singapore, one-time terminal of that great trunk line which had extended from Indonesia to Japan, was now nothing more than a useless stump, hardly worth the powder to blow. The submarine and air blockade in the Camranh Bay-Cape Varella area had stopped all Indo-China coastal traffic north of Saigon, and the few nervous convoys which continued to run between Saigon and Singapore were inconsequential.

The Japanese shipping lines between Singapore, Borneo and the Philippines had been chopped away. No Japan-bound convoys plowed the central waters of the South China Sea. The branch line from Singapore to Palembang, Sumatra, and the line from Singapore to Soerabaja, Java, remained in operation, as did the line from Soerabaja to Kendari, Celebes. These lines were still in operation at war's end. Militarily they were worthless to the Japanese—vestigial roots which maintained a sort of life in the Singapore stump.

In Borneo, Celebes, Sumatra, Java, Bali and other islands of the Netherlands East Indies, Imperial Army forces waited glumly for evacuation. No *marus* were on hand to take home these wallflower garrisons. None would come from Tokyo for the bales of cotton, the tons of ore and rubber, the bins of rice, the drums of oil which crammed the Singapore go-downs and crowded the wharves of Netherlands Indies ports. The small convoys that did run to and from Palembang, Soerabaja and Kendari were Toonerville Trolleys compared to the ship trains of yesteryear. Roaming the waters off Java, Sumatra, Borneo and Malaya, SubSoWesPac submarines combed great open spaces in May and lolled in sleepy tropic doldrums in June. Admiral Fife kept some of his boats busy with special

missions and scouting, but the routine patrollers had time for long games of acey-deucey.

The Gulf of Siam was invaded by SubSoWesPac patrollers during this closing period of the war. Believed strewn with mines, the Gulf's interior had long been marked out-of-bounds for patrolling submarines. But in March 1945 the Gulf patrol was resumed by the British submarine TRADEWIND. In April HARDHEAD had covered the approaches to Bangkok. Entering the Gulf in May, BAYA, LAGARTO and HAMMERHEAD found targets. Teaming up with BAYA to attack a convoy, LAGARTO was lost in these waters. (The story is detailed later on in this chapter.) BAYA was frustrated by unexpectedly strong A/S measures. But HAMMERHEAD sank a small tanker off the Malay coast on May 6, and in the same area downed TOTTORI MARU, 5,973-ton passenger-cargoman, on the 15th. Thereafter, traffic between Siam and Singapore was reduced to a trickle.

The passenger-cargoman sunk by the HAMMERHEAD was the largest vessel downed by the SubSoWesPac patrollers that May. Homeward bound from the Gulf of Siam, BAYA sank a 2,500-ton tanker in the Java Sea on the 13th. HAWKBILL caught a minelayer off the Malay coast on the 16th, and, as will be seen, avenged the destruction of LAGARTO. Then nothing fell to SubSoWesPac torpedoes until the 30th when BLENNY ended the month's score for the force by sinking a small freighter in the Java Sea.

And if May's crop of targets was sparse, June's was even more so. On June 8 COBIA struck a convoy on the Saigon-Singapore run and downed a small tanker and the 3,841-ton landing-craft HAKUSA. In a lively battle with a Java Sea convoy on the 23rd, HARDHEAD demolished a shuttle boat and two sub-chasers. Off Bali on June 27, BLUEBACK sank a sub-chaser. This was the sum and substance of the SubSo-WesPac attrition score for June 1945. There could be no doubt that few maru targets remained to be flushed in the Southwest Pacific. The seas below the 18° 30' parallel were practically swept clean. Or, to tailor the phrase to suit torpedo warfare, the waters had been "fished out."

The maru's disappearance from the Southwest Pacific was matched by the Japanese man-of-war's vanishment. During March and April MacArthur's troops had wiped out most of the enemy's last-ditch garrisons in the Philippines, and late in April heavy units of the Seventh Fleet arrived off the coast of North Borneo with Australian invasion forces. Tarakan fell on the first day of May—a capture which gave the Allies an important airfield and rich oil wells. Brunei was next. Early in June efficient mine-sweepers cleared the road into Brunei Bay, and the Australians reached the beaches on June 10th. Allied surface forces and submarines patrolled the approaches to Brunei on the lookout for Japanese warships which might attempt to contest the landings. They patrolled in vain. The Imperial Navy had been dispossessed of the last three cruisers it had held available for duty in this theater. One of these, the light cruiser ISUZU, had been downed in April by GABILAN and CHARR. British aircraft and destroyers had sunk the heavy cruiser HAGURO in May. And on June 8 the British submarine TRENCHANT sank the heavy cruiser ASHIGARA off Sumatra. When the Australians went ashore at Brunei there was not a major Japanese man-of-war afloat in the area.

So submarine warfare in the Southwest Pacific faded out with a sputter of shots, a few scattered torpedo explosions. With the summer of 1945 coming up on the calendar, the SubSoWesPac Force knew the job was done. In the South China Sea, the Java Sea, and the waters off Celebes, the Japanese merchant marine had all but expired and the Imperial Navy was all but extinct. A residue of rusty tramp steamers and minor patrol craft merely emphasized an abolition of merchant and naval shipping which bore evidence to the dissolution of the Japanese Empire. But ever since March, the "conquered" territories of the quondam Co-Prosperity Sphere had been cut adrift from Japan. That was the month when the last convoy from the south reached Kyushu with the last barrel of oil from the Indies. With the arrival of that last convoy the Japanese Empire virtually passed out of existence.

Remained the home Empire—Japan—maritime, insular, and almost totally bereft of industrial resources and commercial outlets. Deprived of foreign markets and the raw materials necessary for the manufacture of exports, Japan could no longer pretend to be in the Empire business. Nor could the island nation, bereft of the raw materials needed for the maintenance of heavy industries, hope to sustain any sort of effective war effort. However, Japan might have been able to survive for a time as a "closed Empire" had the home islands been able to import from Korea, North China and Manchuria such vital necessities for domestic existence as food-stuffs and coal. But Japan's domestic existence was now in the balance. For importation, of course, depended on shipping, and Japanese shipping was dependent on oil. Deprived of all southern oil, the shipping industry in Japan experienced immediate and shocking strokes of paralysis. Reserve stocks had long since dried up, and now that the driblets which had been rationed were not forthcoming, the Japanese merchant service which had thus far survived the war was mortally stricken. In April a considerable tonnage of small vessels was laid up for lack of fuel. In May Japan's harbors were crowded with trawlers, coastal steamers and small freighters waiting for oil. Threatening to dead-stall domestic inter-island traffic, this creeping paralysis began to numb the shipping lines running to China, Korea and Manchuria. For this disease which resulted from the oil famine there could be no cure; inevitably the fuel would be entirely consumed and the Japanese merchant fleet would be totally paralyzed. Had Nippon been menaced by nothing other than this shipping stoppage, her leaders must have known that the nation's ultimate doom was inescapable.

Yet Japan's leaders in the spring of 1945 were disposed to bandy words. Although the Empire was out of business, the stockholders were bankrupt and countless thousands of lives had been squandered in the miserable war enterprise, the Imperial "Board of Directors" continued to harangue and temporize, desperately hunting for personal security and a clever "out." Statesmen with a penchant for diplomatic double-talk hoped they could strike some sort of smart bargain with the Allies. Trying to pull their own chestnuts out of the fire, Army generals talked big generalities about national honor and the need for continuing resistance as a means of maintaining public discipline. What would happen when the Japanese people discovered they had been hoodwinked by mendacious propaganda? Would not the populace revolt if it learned the Emperor was no more of a god than a fisherman? While this windy word-juggling went on, the United States offensive struck Okinawa, and Baron Suzuki became Premier of Japan. Suzuki's cabinet carried on the prolix debate. Calls for help had gone to Nazi Germany, but in March the frantic appeals had been answered by the news that American armies were crossing the Rhine. Soon came the appalling word that one Axis partner was done for—on April 27 a squad of Italian partisans had executed Benito Mussolini and the crowd had strung up the body like a side of beef. In Tokyo the Japanese War Lords could feel their hair rise. The Axis was shattered. The Empire was up in smoke. Still the Army High Command voted to maintain the suicidal resistance and several Imperial Navy admirals, among them Toyoda, were opposed to suing for peace.

Because these Totalitarian militarists had their say, the Pacific War went on. Hundreds of Americans and many thousands of Japanese would lose their lives in the ensuing weeks of a conflict prolonged by a huddle of incompetents who wished only to "save face."

Loss of Lagarto

One of the last U.S. submarines to go down in World War II was LAGARTO. On April 12, Commander F. D. Latta on her bridge, she left Subic Bay in the Philippines to patrol an area in the South China Sea. On her maiden patrol she had led "Latta's Lances" in their successful diversionary anti-picket-boat sweep south of Honshu. Now, on her second patrol, she found nothing to sweep in the South China Sea.

Late in April she was directed to patrol in the Gulf of Siam. There on May 2 she made contact with BAYA (Lieutenant Commander B. C. Jarvis). During the afternoon LAGARTO received word that BAYA was tracking a convoy—a tanker traveling under heavy escort. That night BAYA reported that the enemy escorts, equipped with 10-cm. radar, had detected her approach and driven her off with gunfire. BAYA requested a rendezvous.

The two submarines met early the following morning. Jarvis and Latta discussed attack plans. It was agreed that LAGARTO would dive on the convoy's track when a certain point was reached, and BAYA would strike from a point some 12 miles ahead of LAGARTO. The submarines parted company, and the convoy chase went on.

LAGARTO and BAYA exchanged contact reports during the day, and BAYA overhauled the convoy that evening. Jarvis directed a midnight attack, and again his submarine was driven off by the unusually alert escorts. And what of LAGARTO? Early in the morning of May 4 BAYA tried to contact her teammate. LAGARTO made no reply. BAYA did not hear from her again, and Latta's submarine never returned to port.

The JAPANESE minelayer HATSUTAKA reported an attack on a submarine off the Malay coast near the mouth of the Gulf of Siam at the time LAGARTO was in that vicinity. Apparently HATSUTAKA was one of the radar-equipped escorts operating with the convoy BAYA and LAGARTO had tracked down. The blasting occurred in 30-fathom water—a depth which gave the submersible little chance for evasion—and Headquarters could only assume that LAGARTO was the minelayer's victim.

Yet 30 fathoms would not ordinarily have baffled a submarine captain as experienced as Commander Latta. Skipper of NARWHAL when that big undersea boat had transported troops to Attu, he had followed through with all manner of perilous special missions in the Philippines. Every patrol conducted by this veteran commanding officer had been designated successful. If LAGARTO went down to a minelayer, she must have suffered a freakish direct hit or a phenomenally violent barrage. Perishing in battle, then, she was lost with all hands.

Minelayer HATSUTAKA did not long survive this action. Skulking southeastward down the Malay coastline, she was ambushed on May 16 by another U.S. submarine. As has been noted, this patroller was HAWKBILL. Captained by Commander F. W. Scanland, Jr., HAWKBILL dealt the enemy vessel a killing blow. The torpedoes struck home, and when the smoke and fire unraveled, the minelayer was gone. LAGARTO was avenged.

SubPac Vise on Japan

While the B-29's hammered Tokyo, and American invasion forces battered their way across Okinawa, Admiral Lockwood's submarines concentrated on the blockade of Japan's Pacific ports and the cutting of Japanese shipping lines to China and Manchuria. Patrolling the Yellow Sea in May, RATON sank three small freighters off the Shantung peninsula; SPRINGER destroyed two large frigates on the line from Tsingtao to Moji; SHAD sank a good-sized freighter off southwest Korea. Heading into the Yellow Sea late in May, BILLFISH downed a small freighter off Kyushu, then on June 4 sank a 2,220-tonner southeast of Dairen. SHAD sank another small freighter off the Korean coast on June 7th. SEA OWL demolished a frigate off southwest Korea on the 9th. SEGUNDO sank a small freighter off the Shantung peninsula on the 11th. SEA DEVIL sank still another off this promontory on the 14th. Frigates and small freighters—as these May-June sinkings were tabulated at SubPac Headquarters, it was obvious that *maru* targets were becoming as rare in the Yellow Sea as they were in the seas patrolled by SubSoWesPac.

Game was also rapidly disappearing from the waters of "Hit Parade." Off northeast Honshu early in May, BOWFIN downed a freighter and a small transport. In an adjacent area CERO sank a pair of small freighters. Thereafter nothing fell to the "Hit Parade" blockaders until the forepart of June when TENCH struck a traffic run off Hakodate, where she downed two small freighters, a medium freighter and a small tanker. Later in the month PARCHE sank a small freighter and ex-gunboat in the southern approaches to Ominato.

In the "Polar Circuit" which embraced the Kuriles the SubPac patrollers harried the remnant Japanese fishing fleet, depriving the hungry nation of food supplies which were as vital to the home front as fuel oil. Freight traffic had never been notably heavy in this "XYZ Patrol" area. However, STERLET sank a pair of small cargomen east of Etorufu Island on May 29th. In waters farther north APOGON downed a 2,614-ton transport on June 18, and in the same area CABEZON sank a medium-sized freighter on the 19th.

To the Japanese merchant marine, half-paralyzed by the fuel famine, badgered by air attack, unable to scrape up escorts, repairs or replacements, these losses to submarines in home Empire waters must have come as Ossas of disaster piled on Pelions of ruin. For Japan the reduction of Yellow Sea shipping and the relentless blockade of her Pacific ports meant lengthened breadlines. Even on stringent rations, the home islands were compelled to import large quantities of staple grains. In April 1945 the situation was so critical that nearly all of the available shipping had been ordered to haul only foodstuffs and salt. Now the sinkings in the Yellow Sea, the Kuriles and off northeast Honshu brought the food crisis to a head. But the straws which broke the camel's back in the spring of 1945 came from the brooms of U.S. submarines conducting a June sweep in the Sea of Japan. This sweep, in conjunction with a B-29 mine-laying campaign which blocked the Shimonoseki Straits, ended Japan's last hope of importing from Korea and Manchuria the commodities necessary for the maintenance of bare existence.

While these decisive operations—the last great campaigns of the attrition war—were getting under way,

a SubPac lifeguard reported an incident which gives one a vivid periscope-glimpse of battle action perhaps typical of this period.

Atule Spots Planes

Lifeguard duty not infrequently provided American submariners with a box seat for an air show, and on a number of occasions the up-thrust periscopes watched in fascination as American aircraft shot down enemy planes. But only a few submarines were able to assist the action by vectoring the victors in. ATULE (Comander J. H. Maurer) was one of these.

On May 5, 1945, ATULE was on lifeguard station 12 miles south of Okino Shima. At 0759 Maurer took her down to evade a Jake or Rufe. About an hour later, rising to periscope depth, the submarine sighted her lifeguard plane-cover—a Dumbo B-29. Reassured, Maurer ordered ATULE to the surface.

For a time the morning was peacefully routine. Then the air show began. Commander Maurer's patrol report narrates the action as seen from the submariner's point of view.

1000: Sighted Jake and Rufe coming in on starboard beam. Dumbo was opening out on the port beam at this time. Immediately reported enemy to him by VHF, and received acknowledgment as we dived to periscope depth to watch the show. The Jake passed almost directly overhead, close enough for us to distinguish the type of tail fins on the bomb between his floats. In the meantime, the Rufe began investigating conditions in an adjacent area, leaving his team mate to tackle the monster alone. . . . The fight was short and unequal, and the panorama through the periscope was one of the most unforgettable of the war as the scene unfolded, low over the water and less than two miles away. The C.O. at the periscope was commentator, giving a play-by-play account throughout the ship over all communication systems—mostly by direct voice.

1006: The twisting, weaving Jake received one short and devastatingly deadly barrage from the B-29 (tracers plainly visible), burst into flames aft, and crashed into the sea in a sheet of flame from the exploding bomb and gasoline.

1009: Surfaced. Dumbo thanked us for the assist and departed for home.

1020: Reached scene of crash. One survivor was calling for help, but of the remaining two, one had been completely decapitated, and the other was dead and floating face downward in the gasoline covered water. The survivor, Lt. Masayosi Kojima, a naval observer, was pulled past the grisly body and floating head of his team mate and hauled aboard. He was suffering from shock, second degree burns of the face and hands, flesh wounds in the neck and arm, and gunshot or crash wounds in his right

478

ankle. How he escaped alive from the exploding plane is amazing in itself. . . . The numerous pockets in the clothes, uniform and life-jacket of our English and German speaking P.O.W. provided a wealth of printed matter including identification, seven packs of Jap and one of British cigarettes, calling cards, ration books, club tickets, diary, notebook, flight record, and, of prime importance, two magnetic detector traces and notes concerning them. A thick wad of currency, vial of perfume and other personal items showed he was ready for any eventuality. . . . The time schedule of this action is rather unusual since the total action, from initial sighting, including diving, the attack, surfacing and the rescue, covered only twenty minutes.

Maurer's description of the time schedule as "rather unusual" could be applied, it would seem, to other features of the incident. Everyone seems to have done some fast work, including Lieutenant Kojima with his calling cards, club tickets, currency and perfume.

V-E Day

Somebody at Pearl Harbor stared at a dispatch. At Fremantle a radioman's fingers shook slightly.

It had been expected. Patton was over the Rhine, and on May 2 the Russians had stormed into Berlin and Adolph Hitler had vanished like Mephisto in a cloud of fire and rubble under the Chancellery.

All that had been in the news. But at Pearl Harbor, Guam, Fremantle, Manus and points west, Europe seemed as far away as Mars.

"The Nazis have surrendered! The Allies are in Berlin!"

But the Allies had yet to enter Tokyo. In the Southwest Pacific MacArthur's forces hammered at Borneo. On Okinawa the fighting continued in unabated fury. The Superforts took off for Honshu with their bomb and mine loads. Submariners had only time to clap each other on the back. May 18, 1945, was just another day in the Pacific War.

In SubPac Headquarters at Guam, Admiral Lockwood's staff officers concentrated on charts and discussed the Sea of Japan.

"Operation Barney" (Under-running Enemy Minefields)

Ever since the loss of WAHOO in those waters in the autumn of 1943, the Sea of Japan had been "out of bounds" for SubPac patrollers. Captured documents, old charts, Japanese prisoners and other sources of information had confirmed suspicions that the Japan Sea was guarded by minefields. And until the spring of 1945 such undersea barriers, once located, were scrupulously avoided by submarines.

The Sea of Japan was not to retain its immunity to torpedo warfare. In the autumn and winter of 1944-1945 American scientists and technicians of the University of California Division of War Research worked overtime to develop a mine-detecting device which would permit submarines to penetrate mined areas. This device enabled a submersible to "hear" an enemy mine in the waters ahead. Gear for the clearance of the menace was simultaneously produced. By the spring of 1945 this equipment, thoroughly tested by seven submarines on routine patrol, was ready for the business at hand. For the SubPac Force the business at hand was an invasion of the Japan Sea—the one remaining area on the globe where Japanese shipping steamed more or less on schedule and unmolested. Such an invasion, successfully accomplished, would completely isolate Japan by severing the last of her overseas supply lines. Deprived of even a portion of the imports carried across the Sea of Japan, the already tottering nation would be prostrated. To assure the success of this decisive invasion, the staff at SubPac Headquarters burned many hours of midnight oil in perfecting the plans.

Admiral Lockwood's Operations Officer, Captain R. G. Voge, selected one of his assistants at Guam to take charge of the project. The officer selected was Commander W. B. "Barney" Sieglaff. Conductor of six successful patrols as captain of TAUTOG, Sieglaff brought to the invasion enterprise a veteran's knowledge of undersea warfare and a lively intellect—the right sparkplug for the energizing of such a venture.

Equipped with the new mine-detecting device, nine SubPac submarines assembled at Guam to complete preliminary training. Guiding the final preparations, Commander Sieglaff put skippers and crews through a "third degree" course in Japan Sea navigation and minefield penetration. Shipping routes were studied, area coverage plotted, methods discussed. The Nishi Suido (West Channel) of Tsushima Strait was to be the point of entrance. Exit was to be made through La Perouse. The invaders were furnished with fairly comprehensive information on the minefields which guarded Tsushima Strait, but the exact coordinates of the mine lines were unknown. Everything depended on the mine-detecting gear and the skill of the operators. The apparatus required experts. It had them. The submarines were manned by expert crews and captained by expert skippers. The project had expert direction. Thus success was assured for "Operation Barney."

"Hydeman's Hellcats"

Under group leadership of Commander E. T. Hydeman, the nine submarines that were detailed to "Operation Barney" formed a wolf-pack answering to the name of "Hydeman's Hellcats." The "Hellcats" were subdivided into three task groups—"Hydeman's Hepcats"; "Pierce's Polecats"; "Risser's Bobcats." These "Hellcat" task groups lined up as follows:

"Hydeman's Hepcats"—SEA DOG (Commander E. T. Hydeman); CREVALLE (Commander E. H. Steinmetz); SPADEFISH (Commander W. J. Germerhausen).

"Pierce's Polecats"—TUNNY (Commander G. E. Pierce); SKATE (Commander R. B. Lynch); BONEFISH (Commander L. L. Edge).

"Risser's Bobcats"—FLYINGFISH (Commander R. D. Risser); BOWFIN (Commander A. K. Tyree); TINOSA (Commander R. C. Latham).

Leaving Guam on May 27, the nine submarines headed northwestward, their bows pointing like compass needles for Tsushima Strait. En route, "Risser's Bobcats" performed lifeguard duties, and TINOSA rescued 10 men of the crew of a B-29 which had crashed about 18 miles northeast of Sofu Gan. Sideline issue compared to the venture in prospect—slipping across the northern waters of the East China Sea and stealing through the narrow passage between Korea and Tsushima Island. It was off this island centered in Tsushima Strait midway between Korea and Kyushu that the Czar's Baltic fleet in 1905 was trapped and destroyed by the Japanese. The "Hellcats" would encounter no Japanese fleet, but mines were a certainty. Would the new detection device do the trick? It had its idiosyncrasies. Sensitive as it was, the contrivance detected many submerged objects which were not mines. Fish, for example. Such false contacts registered an alarm, and it took an ace specialist to distinguish the real from the semblance. As is the case with most specialists and technicians, the operators of this mine-detecting gear developed a terminology of their own. Registered by the submarine detecting device, authentic mine-warning signals were termed "Hell's Bells."

With "Hell's Bells" ringing here and there, and not a few false warnings to keep their nerves at attention, the "Hellcats" crept through Tsushima Strait and entered the Sea of Japan on schedule. Shooting was timed to begin at sunset on June 9th. On station before this zero hour, some of the skippers were so tantalized by the sight of Japanese ships traveling unescorted with undimmed lights that they were tempted to jump the gun. Itchy trigger fingers were restrained, however, until all "Hellcats" reached their assigned areas.

Overconfident even at this catastrophic season, the Japanese were caught completely off guard by the invaders at their back door. Astounded by the sudden thunder of torpedo fire off the west coast of Honshu, they could not believe American submarines had entered the Sea of Japan by normal means. Radio Tokyo, always imaginative, announced that the submarines had been "smuggled in."

The smugglers, of course, were eight crack skippers and crews of top-caliber submariners under the high-powered leadership of Commander Earl Hydeman. And if the Japanese were looking for mysterious smuggling equipment they could have found it in the gadget born and bred in the far-off University of California War Research Laboratory at San Diego. Having staked their lives on this apparatus, the "Hellcat" skippers and crews breathed a vote of thanks to science and invention as their boats left the Tsushima minefields astern and proceeded to assigned patrol areas in the Japan Sea.

The "Hepcats" covered the waters off northwest Honshu, cutting the inside shipping lanes to Hakodate and Ominato. Shortly after sunset on June 9, SEA DOG attacked a freighter a few miles north of Sado Shima and downed the vessel with one shot. Before midnight her torpedoes had sunk a second freighter in the same area. Three more cargomen and a passenger-cargo carrier fell to Hydeman's submarine before her foray in the "Emperor's private ocean" was concluded. Pack-mate CREVALLE also opened fire on the 9th, picking off a 2,215-ton cargoman. Commander "Steiny" Steinmetz and company sank another medium-sized freighter on the 10th and a third on the 11th. SPADEFISH, under Commander "Bill" Germerhausen, worked the waters northward from Wakasa Wan to Hokkaido. Three passenger-cargomen were shoveled under on June 10 by this old hand. She downed still another on the 14th and fired her last shots to bury a medium-sized freighter on the 17th.

Ranging the southeastern waters of the Japan Sea, "Pierce's Polecats" had their share of fast action. Commander George Pierce's TUNNY found the action more exciting than the targets. Hunting game, the submarine steamed boldly into the harbors of Etomo Ko and Uppuri Wan, but shipping was not in evidence. Then TUNNY herself played target in a running gun battle with two Jap DD's. As the destroyers dropped their depth charges at a range of 7,000 yards, TUNNY was untroubled by this skirmish. Meantime, SKATE found better shooting around the Noto Peninsula. There, mid-morning of June 10, Commander "Ozzie" Lynch and crew encountered the Japanese submarine I-122. This I-boat's number was up when it zigged across SKATE's bow at a range of 800 yards, thereby collecting two torpedoes of a four-torpedo spread. Two days later SKATE entered Matugashita Cove to attack an anchored convoy. Three "sitting ducks" were downed during this ticklish action. And while SKATE was littering the southwest coast of Honshu with wreckage, BONEFISH, skippered by Commander "Larry" Edge, was strewing the neighboring littoral with similar scrap. To her torpedoes fell the two largest vessels downed by the invading "Hellcats" —a 6,892-ton freighter sunk on the 13th, and a 5,488-ton passenger-cargoman blasted under on the 19th.

Combing the western waters of the Japan Sea, "Risser's Bobcats" slashed at shipping off the east coast of Korea. Captained by Commander "Bob" Risser, FLYINGFISH struck at an assortment of coastal craft which included barges, tugs and scows laden with bricks. On June 10 FLYINGFISH sank a medium-sized freighter, and the following day she downed a small passenger-cargoman. Farther north, "Alec" Tyree's BOWFIN encountered creamy fog, hundreds of friendly Korean fishermen and two marus—a passenger-cargoman and a small freighter. The marus

were dispatched to the bottom on the 11th and 13th respectively. In adjacent Korean waters, TINOSA likewise was enmeshed by fog and fishermen. Fishnets proved more of a nuisance than fog, but neither prevented "Dick" Latham and company from downing the Japanese freighter that steamed into range on June 9th. TINOSA's torpedoes caught a second cargoman on the 12th and nailed two more on the 20th. These were the last marus downed by the June invaders in the Sea of Japan.

The list of sinkings impressively summarizes the handiwork of "Hydeman's Hellcats." (See below.)

Accomplished in 12 days, the sinkings enumerated —27 Japanese merchantmen and an I-boat—cost Japanese shipping a total of some 57,000 tons. For good measure the "Hellcats" shot up a number of small craft. A few marus were damaged by torpedo fire. The tonnage sunk would not have seriously hampered the Japanese in an earlier period of the war, but in June

"HELLCAT" SCORE

Date	Submarine	Ship Sunk	Type	Tonnage
June 9	Sea Dog	Sagawa Maru	Cargo	1,186
June 9	Sea Dog	Shoyo Maru	Cargo	2,211
June 11	Sea Dog	Kofuku Maru	Cargo	753
June 12	Sea Dog	Shinsen Maru	Cargo	880
June 15	Sea Dog	Koan Maru	Passenger-Cargo	884
June 19	Sea Dog	Kokai Maru	Cargo	1,272
June 9	Crevalle	Hokuto Maru	Cargo	2,215
June 10	Crevalle	Kaiki Maru	Cargo	2,217
June 11	Crevalle	Hokuto Maru	Cargo	2,211
June 10	Spadefish	Daigen Maru No. 2	Passenger-Cargo	4,273
June 10	Spadefish	Unkai Maru No. 8	Passenger-Cargo	1,293
June 10	Spadefish	Jintsu Maru	Passenger-Cargo	994
June 14	Spadefish	Seizan Maru	Passenger-Cargo	2,018
June 17	Spadefish	Eijo Maru	Cargo	2,274
June 10	Skate	I-122	Submarine	1,142
June 12	Skate	Yozan Maru	Cargo	1,227
June 12	Skate	Kenjo Maru	Cargo	3,142
June 12	Skate	Zuiko Maru	Cargo	887
June 13	Bonefish	Oshikayama Maru	Cargo	6,892
June 19	Bonefish	Konzan Maru	Passenger-Cargo	5,488
June 10	Flyingfish	Taga Maru	Cargo	2,220
June 11	Flyingfish	Meisei Maru	Passenger-Cargo	1,893
June 11	Bowfin	Shinyo Maru No. 3	Passenger-Cargo	1,898
June 13	Bowfin	Akiura Maru	Cargo	887
June 9	Tinosa	Wakatama Maru	Cargo	2,211
June 12	Tinosa	Keito Maru	Cargo	880
June 20	Tinosa	Kaisei Maru	Cargo	884
June 20	Tinosa	Taito Maru	Cargo	2,726

1945, when their merchant service was falling apart like the One Horse Shay, the blow was comparable to a cyclone after an earthquake. The leaders in Tokyo must have known that Japan could survive few more of these disasters.

The "Hellcats" were elated. They had circumvented the dangerous minefields and given the enemy's shipping arteries in the Japan Sea a memorable clawing. In accordance with plans, Commander Hydeman assembled his pack off La Perouse Strait, and on the night of June 24, running on the surface through cotton-thick fog, the submarines began their dash for the Pacific. Moving in parallel columns, and communicating by voice radio, the "Hellcats" closed up and raced through the Strait at 18 knots. Colors flying, they entered Pearl Harbor on the Fourth of July.

But one tragedy marred this triumphal return. BONEFISH was not among the submarines that made home.

Loss of Bonefish

When BONEFISH entered the Japan Sea with the "Hellcats" she was making her eighth war patrol. As a member of the task group led by Commander Pierce, she was ordered to transit Tsushima Strait on June 5, and to proceed to a patrol area off the west coast of central Honshu. She made the transit on the 5th without misadventure and like the other "Hellcats," she held her fire until the 9th. On the 16th she kept a rendezvous with TUNNY, and her skipper, Commander Edge, reported the sinking of the ship later identified as the 6,892-ton OSHIKAYAMA MARU—the largest vessel sunk by the invading "Hellcats."

At a second rendezvous with TUNNY on the morning of the 18th, Commander Edge asked permission to conduct a submerged daylight patrol in Toyama Wan, a bay farther up the Honshu coast. Permission was granted, and BONEFISH departed for Suzo Misaki.

The "Hellcat" plan called for the transit of La Perouse Strait on the night of June 24th. When BONEFISH did not appear at the assembly point on the evening of the 23rd, the other submarines reluctantly prepared to make the transit. After running through the Strait, TUNNY waited at the Pacific entrance until June 26, hoping to contact her missing pack-mate. TUNNY waited in vain.

Provision had been made for the "Hellcats," in event of emergency, to proceed to Russian waters and claim a 24-hour haven. Too, they had been given liberty to make an exit from the Japan Sea before or after June 24 if circumstances warranted. The submariners hoped that BONEFISH had availed herself of one of these alternatives. But on June 30 the missing submarine was announced presumably lost.

Japanese A/S forces reported an attack on a submarine in Toyama Wan. Savage depth-charging brought to the surface a swirling pool of oil and pieces of splintered wood. The passenger-cargoman KONZAN MARU was torpedoed and sunk in this vicinity on the date in question, and there could be little doubt that BONEFISH was the victim of a severe counter-attack. Going down with all hands, she was the last SubPac submarine lost in World War II.

Tirante off Nagasaki

Although the Yellow Sea and the Sea of Japan were marked for major attrition campaigns, the submarine war did not by-pass Kyushu in June 1945. Early in that warm month TIRANTE (Lieutenant Commander G. L. Street) was patrolling the East China Sea directly off Nagasaki. About 0800 on the morning of the 11th, Street spied a ship alongside the wharf at Ha Shima. This little island is about seven miles southwest of the entrance to Nagasaki—a short run for an excursion steamer, a mere dash for a destroyer, and practically nothing flat for a coast artillery projectile. The waters off Nagasaki were a-bustle with small shipping of all kinds, and since the dark before dawn, TIRANTE had been surrounded by fishing craft, sampans, coasters, and perhaps an excursion boat or two. Japanese destroyers were not likely in this or any area at that date, but coastal batteries could be expected, and it was ticklish territory for submarining. However, 3,000-ton targets were at a premium. The ship at the dock was a novel sight after a long and fruitless hunt, and Street decided to take the bird in hand.

This meant going into the bush after it, and there was a considerable distance to go. TIRANTE would have to move in under a headland and pass within spitting, or at least gunshot, distance of a beach. Street and company remained undismayed. There was the target. Let's go.

The approach was made submerged. There seemed to be no patrol craft in the offing and the absence of minefields could be inferred from the criss-crossing sampan traffic. Dexterous navigation took the submarine past the inside of Mitsue Se Shoals, and she advanced on Ha Shima from the southwest. In these shallows TIRANTE walked as though barefoot on coral. Soundings were taken every five minutes. They were not the only things that were taken. As the submarine crept forward, movies were taken through the periscope. Submarine photography had come a long way since "Lew" Parks went pioneering with a camera in POMPANO. Modern TIRANTE took color movies of this action.

The target vessel measured 310 feet, bow to stern. On her stern was a 4.7 gun, and the crew happened to be standing by. At 1115 TIRANTE was lined up for a shot. Street fired one torpedo, with ½-knot target speed set on T.D.C. to offset the observed current. This was intended as a ranging shot to test the accuracy of the current observation. Rigged to the periscope in time to catch the explosion, the movie camera was buzzing as the torpedo hit home 50 feet forward of the point of aim. Geyser! Smoke-pall! Then the scene cleared and Street could see a hole in the target's bow and an avalanche of coal spilling into the sea. Two sailors who had been leaning over the bow rail were no longer in the scene.

Now the Japanese Navy gunners on the vessel's quarter-deck snapped into action. They were training the gun aft and up, squinting skyward in search of aircraft. Street had planned to run for it on the surface at high speed, but as long as the gunners were aiming at imaginary aircraft there was no need to surface the submarine and disillusion them.

TIRANTE began a swing to the left. Street steadied her down and fired one electric torpedo, aimed to eliminate the ship's gun and its rubbernecking crew. The torpedo ran true, but came to a sudden stop without exploding. Either the torpedo was a dud or it had been stopped by a mud bank or net. And this was not the moment for the freighter's gun crew to sight TIRANTE's SD radar antenna which had been used preparatory to surfacing. Shells began to smack the water around the submarine. The battle was on.

Street set another electric torpedo for shallow depth, aimed it just aft of the freighter's mid-section in order to miss any obstruction that might have stopped the previous shot, and fired. Bull's-eye! When the smoke lifted, the ship was listing 20° to starboard. The stern gun was still there, but its crew had vanished as though whisked away by magic.

With the wreck 1,800 yards astern, Street surfaced TIRANTE and ordered emergency speed. Any minute a shell could be expected, and the submarine's engineers tried to produce a little more than the horsepower rating of her engineering plant. The Diesels were galloping when the SD reported aircraft a mile distant. Those on the bridge could not spot the aircraft, but automatic gunfire from the beach jumped into view, and bullets began to whine around TIRANTE's conning tower. Fortunately this fire was spasmodic and inaccurate. The SD contacts proved to be land, and TIRANTE was safely on her way out when the submariners made an alarming discovery. While the submarine was running at flank speed across the water, her bow planes would not rig in. With these huge fins "catching crabs," TIRANTE had

been bumping along like a sea cow on a gravel beach.

Assembling all hands on the bridge behind the armored section, Street rang up "Stop." Troubleshooters rigged in the recalcitrant bow planes as Japanese shore guns continued to shoot at TIRANTE. All hands were sweating when the planes were finally rigged. And hotter work was in the offing. To clear the shoal spot at Nakano Sone, it was necessary to run directly toward the headland of Nomo Saki. Automatic guns on the bluff-top along the cape opened up on the submarine at a range of 3,000 yards as she skirted the shoals. Racing through a storm of lead, TIRANTE cleared the headland and ran seaward, tagged by angry projectiles. Unharmed, the submarine reached safe water. It had been a Hollywood finish, and it photographed as one of the most spectacular submarine dramas of the war. Produced by TIRANTE and company. Directed by Commander G. L. Street. Filmed in "technicolor"!

Barb Bombards Japan

While "Hydeman's Hellcats" were rampaging in the Sea of Japan and patrollers such as TIRANTE were nuzzling the home Empire's waterfronts, a SubPac raider appeared off the port of Shari on the north coast of Hokkaido and proceeded to blow holes in the center of the city. As might be expected, the submarine that thus employed a town for a target was BARB, captained by Commander E. B. Fluckey. On the assumption that cargo in a warehouse was as valuable as that in the hold of a *maru*, Fluckey opened fire on this snug seaport. BARB was not the first American submarine to bombard a Japanese town, but she was first to give the local citizenry a glimpse of the American rocket's red glare. A rocket-launcher had been installed on the submarine's deck, and the attack was something novel by way of undersea warfare.

The unique bombardment took place early in the morning of June 22, a few hours after BARB's arrival in the area. In the dark of 0234 a dozen 5-inch rockets, screaming in from the sea, exploded in the heart of the Hokkaido town. Wakened from sleep by this display of fireworks, the Shari populace must have thought a shower of meteors had landed on their rooftops. The rockets were launched at a range of 5,250 yards. Apparently the local wardens believed the bombardment an air raid, for they started a radar search of the sky as BARB retired seaward.

Twelve days later Fluckey's submarine was off the island of Kaihyo at the eastern extremity of the Karafuto Peninsula. Here a large seal fishery was operated by the Japanese Government. As BARB moved in on the surface at dawn, Fluckey remarked the stockades of the seal rookery and noted "two beacons, radio antenna and an observation post . . . on the flat top of the island." Commander Fluckey decided to pound the island's top a little flatter. Up from below came the submarine gunners. Barracks, warehouses and buildings were sighted, and the local islanders could be seen running in panic. When the range closed to 1,100 yards, Fluckey gave the order, and BARB's gun crew opened fire. Simultaneously the shore gunners sent machine-gun bullets chattering at the submarine. They failed to hit her. BARB's gunnery was better. Her sharpshooters dropped shell after shell into observation posts, buildings, and a huddle of anchored sampans. A wheel was shorn from a 75-mm. field gun, and an oil dump was set afire. As Fluckey expressed it: *"Really a wonderful sight and the ideal submarine bombardment—sampans destroyed, oil drums tumbled and split, a field piece overturned and a machine gun hanging loose, unattended."*

After this shooting match, BARB lay to for a time to see whether planes would be sent out. Evidently the radio station had been demolished before an alarm could be put on the air. Intending to land a commando party, Fluckey moved BARB in toward the beach. Closer inspection revealed four pill-boxes on the island's plateau, their guns looking directly down at the submarine. BARB's 40-mm. fire was immediately answered, and a discreet withdrawal was in order. However, the front of one pill-box was stove in by a 40-mm. hit which exploded squarely in the slot.

The next morning (July 3) Fluckey again trotted out the rockets. Target this time was the town of Shikuka on the western shore of Patience Bay, Karafuto Peninsula. At 0240 the rockets were away, range 4,000 yards from the beach. Explosions racketed and flared, but no fires were started.

Passing the Fourth of July in quiet cruising, Fluckey and company took time out on the 5th to torpedo and sink SAPPORE MARU NO. 11, a 2,820-ton freighter. Mere routine. The crew was more interested in the skipper's plan for sabotaging a railroad train. A waterproof electrical hook-up had been rigged for a 55-pound demolition charge suitable for planting alongside a railroad track. Coupled with a micro switch, the charge would be set off when a locomotive came larruping along on the rails. Perhaps this enterprise was suggested by the fact that BARB was operating in the Kurile waters of the "Polar Circuit," and that "XYZ Area" was subdivided into patrol areas titled "Day Coach," "Diner," "Club Car," "Locomotive" and "Pullman." BARB was operating in the "Locomotive" subdivision.

A position near Otasamu on the east coast of Karafuto was selected. Train times were noted. The operation was scheduled for a night when clouds darkened the moon. The dark night arrived, and a saboteur party of eight men under Lieutenant W. M. Walker, USNR, went ashore. While the submariners were busy landing their gear, one train whistled by. As its sparks twinkled off in the distance, the saboteurs began their nocturnal work. Then, as the party paddled back to the submarine, another train came highballing up the track.

The party was still paddling furiously when *"Wham!* (quoting Fluckey). *What a thrill! The charge made a much greater explosion than we expected. The engine's boilers blew, wreckage flew two hundred feet in the air in a flash of flame and smoke, cars piled up and rolled off the track in a writhing, twisting mass of wreckage. Cheers!"* A prisoner of war captured later said the newspapers reported a bomb had hit the train and killed 150 passengers.

From train-wrecking BARB turned to ship-sinking, and down went a frigate on July 18th. On the night of July 25, Fluckey directed a rocket-bombardment of Shiritori, a factory town on the Karafuto coast. Thirty-two 5-inch rockets soared into the town, and the retiring submariners saw the flush of a conflagration brighten the sky. Later that night 12 rockets were fired into the town of Kashiho, and another Japanese populace was panicked by blasting and destruction.

Midday, July 26, some large canneries in the town of Chiri were subjected to 43 rounds from BARB's 5-inch gun. The last and probably the most damaging bombardment of this land-strafing submarine patrol was delivered that afternoon at Shibertoro on the west coast of Kunashiri Island. Aircraft were not in evidence, and BARB cruised along the beach in bright daylight looking for targets. A lumber mill, adjacent buildings, fuel tanks and a sampan building-yard were sighted. About 35 sampans were counted—some on the ways and others on the beach. Mill, buildings, and sampan yard were camouflaged to deceive aircraft observation. Obviously the Japanese in the area had not anticipated attack by submarine.

Fluckey sent BARB excursioning past the waterfront to draw fire. As no fire eventuated, the submarine gunners opened up on the shipyard. The yard went up like a tinderbox and the sampans were shattered to kindling. When the submariners returned that evening for a look, the town was a black yawn of charred ruins and smoking embers.

BARB's incendiary raids were match-flares compared to the great fire-raids at that time consuming the industrial and residential sections of Tokyo. But when a lone submarine could roam at will along a nation's coastline, bombard the shore defenses with impunity, wreck a railroad train and reduce a town to ashes, it was apparent that the defenders had reached the exhaustion point.

Japan was prostrate, and the Pacific conflict was nearly over. Fluckey and his raiders suspected they were heading home for good as they set BARB on a course for Midway.

Japan Surrounded

In July 1853 a United States fleet under Commodore Perry opened up the Closed Empire to world commerce. In June 1945, United States fleet submarines reestablished the Empire's status as closed. The blockade is graphically portrayed in the accompanying chart which shows the submarines on patrol in Japanese waters and the pertinent merchant sinkings of that month. (As the chart represents a 30-day period, the "Hellcat" submarines are reduced in number to indicate abbreviated time in area.)

Although the chart does not portray the June sinkings off northern Hokkaido and the patrollers in the Kurile "Polar Circuit," it clearly delineates the submarine vise on the home Empire. Surrounded by SubPac blockaders, Nippon lies as a helpless Gulliver pinned down by a score of Lilliputians. Weakened by malnutrition, Tokyo's heart convulsed by attack after attack, the prone enemy cannot loosen the bonds which the submarines have fastened on his seafaring arm. The Samurai gladiator is through.

Rough statistics present a similar picture of Japan's plight. As of May 1945 Japanese merchant tonnage afloat approximated 2,384,000 tons. Tonnages sunk by submarines in May and June reduced this figure by some 125,000 tons. Mines laid by aircraft subtracted the lion's share of Japanese shipping during this two-month period, accounting for approximately 375,000 tons. This figure includes damage and disablement, but any vessel which suffered a material casualty at this time was to all intents and purposes "sunk." Note the charted sinkings scored by the B-29 mine barrage choking the Shimonoseki Straits between Kyushu and Honshu. Also the merchant tonnage sunk by invading aircraft in the Osaka area. By June's end the Japanese merchant fleet was down to a skimpy 2,058,000 tons.

But the tonnage afloat which remained to the Japanese merchant fleet was not the tonnage in active service. In May and June a large percentage of the merchant fleet was immobilized by lack of fuel. Another sizable percentage was incapacitated by normal wear and tear and abnormal absence of repair facilities. In a desperate effort to feed and supply the home islands, the dazed Government placed all merchant shipping under a War Power Council. Tonnages previously allocated to the Imperial Army and Navy were now thrown into the civilian pool. Even with the addition of military transports, munitions vessels and similar craft, the Council could scrape together only 1,200,000 tons of cargo ships for service in June.

To round out the picture of the Japanese merchant marine's collapse, one must see in the background a panorama of wrecked wharves, mangled loading machinery, roofless warehouses, channels blocked by sunken hulks. Burned-out shipyards, crushed drydocks, vacant machine shops and abandoned offices all contributed to the transportation tie-up and held many marus immobile in Japanese ports. Qualified captains, mates, engineers and able-bodied seamen could be produced by neither bonuses nor bludgeons, and the war's heavy casualties had created a shortage of capable mariners that the War Power Council was unable to alleviate. Neither could it cope with a stevedore problem which had been created by the insatiable Army draft. The transference of cargoes from ships to shore is an intrinsic part of the merchant service, but with characteristic carelessness it had been neglected by the masters of Japanese transportation. As early as the summer of 1944, Chinese and Korean workers had been rushed to Japan to replace drafted stevedores, but efficient stevedoring could not be obtained from enforced coolie labor. In the large seaports of Honshu, patriotic societies, school children, convicts, prisoners of war and Army troops were laboring to move cargoes on battered waterfronts. But everywhere the merchant marine was disintegrating. Even the question of food and clothing for seamen badgered the frantic War Power Council as marus were being delayed while stewards rummaged through impoverished stores in a search for these items. The bombed-out sailor's lodging house and the bomb-smashed residence of the ship-owner added their share of desolation to the vista of ruin.

By the end of June the War Power Council arrived at figures which proved that Japan's water transport was all but aground and the situation was hopeless. There could be no denying the ruthless mathematics. Japan had begun the war with approximately 6,000,000 tons of merchant shipping. At least half of this tonnage was admittedly required for "civilian living" in Japan. Now, after three and a half years of war, the merchant tonnage afloat added up to a scant 2,000,000 tons, and of this tonnage only 1,200,000 tons of ships were serviceable. But not all of this tonnage was in home waters, and not all of

485

the ships at home were available for cargo hauling.

Whereas Japan's war-starting militarists may not have been overly concerned with the demands of "civilian living," the nation's surviving residue of nobles and War Lords must have been seized with alarm for their own living when advised that the civilian merchant service, which had carried 2,991,000 metric tons of cargo in May 1942, hauled only 752,000 metric tons of cargo in June 1945. Not only was Japan's economy on the rocks, but the nation's populace was facing literal starvation.

Still the incompetents around the Emperor continued to pantomime, bluster, berate, and delay surrender. Wooden ships, luggers—anything that could sail and float was pressed into service to haul food, coal and salt to the famine-stricken nation. Realities were evaded by medieval thinking, and figures were juggled to aid self-deception. The War Power Council talked about "total mobilization," a "voluntary" system of ship repair, volunteer stevedoring, expediting this measure and utilizing that. Where fuel, supplies and trained personnel were to come from no "expediter" could say, but it all sounded meaningful in a fog of high-flown, technical words.

So the war dragged on through July.

Maru Mop-up

Had the entire Japanese merchant tonnage afloat been fueled, manned and able to move, the issue was settled by the severance of the shipping lines between Japan and the Asiatic mainland. Without adequate escort, the *marus* could not have lasted many weeks in the Yellow Sea and the Sea of Japan now that those bodies of water were marked for submarine concentrations. The chart for June 1945 may serve as one portraying the SubPac blockade as it persisted for the war's duration. Sinkings dwindled as shipping petered out on the sea lanes, but the submarines maintained the patrols much as shown.

The success of "Operation Barney" called for a repeat invasion performance, and the "Hellcats" were hardly home before other submarines were headed for the Japan Sea. These were STICKLEBACK (Commander H. K. Nauman); PARGO (Commander D. B. Bell); PIPER (Commander E. L. Beach); TORSK (Commander B. E. Lewellen); JALLAO (Commander J. B. Icenhower) and POGY (Commander J. M. Bowers). Each made an independent run under the minefields and all patrolled in the "Emperor's private ocean" until V-J Day.

Another sequel to "Operation Barney" and the successful mine-detection exploit ensued when Admiral Halsey asked Admiral Lockwood for minefield reconnaissance off Kyushu and Honshu. Accordingly,

RUNNER II (Commander R. H. Bass), REDFIN (Lieutenant Commander C. K. Miller) and CATFISH (Lieutenant Commander W. A. Overton) were dispatched to perform these perilous reconnaissance missions. Object was to determine the extent of the coastal field and locate safe channels for the Third Fleet which was preparing to close in on Japan.

On June 1 the Navy's major combatant ships had been released from support duty in cooperation with the forces at Okinawa. The fleet had suffered severe casualties during "Operation Iceberg"—4,907 Navy personnel killed and nearly as many wounded. At this date the fleet command passed to Admiral Halsey, who headed the warships for Kyushu. Submarines advanced to take lifeguard stations in front of Admiral McCain's carriers, but the strike on Kyushu was interrupted by a roaring typhoon that tore the bow from the cruiser PITTSBURGH and seriously damaged some other warships. Halsey led the storm-thrashed fleet back to Leyte Gulf for fuel and repairs, then set out for Honshu in July. Once again SubPac submarines conducted an anti-picket sweep ahead of the carriers.

Commander B. F. McMahon in PIPER was again in charge of the sweep, the submarines in the group going by the name of "Mac's Moppers." These were PIPER, POMFRET, PLAICE and SEA POACHER. Working in conjunction with the sweepers, RUNNER II, REDFIN and CATFISH probed for the minefields with their sensitive detecting gear. The mine detectors found an open path, the "Moppers" on the surface encountered no pickets, and McCain's carrier force moved in. As in "Operation Detachment" the strike was undetected by the enemy.

On July 10 the carrier aircraft hammered Tokyo with a pulverizing weight of bombs. Seven days later Halsey's battleships, joined by 28 British warships, steamed along the Japanese coastline dealing out bombardment after bombardment. In a final raid, the carrier planes flew to the Inland Sea and pounded the Imperial Navy's base at Kure. Blown to pieces was KAIYO, the last Jap escort carrier. Battleships HARUNA and HYUGA were demolished. The old ISE was disabled beyond repair. Cruisers KITAGUMI and OYODO were sunk, AOBA and TONE were disabled and several destroyers were wrecked. When the last carrier plane departed, Japanese sea power was totally defunct. What had been the third largest navy in the world was now shrunk to a couple of small cruisers, some 50 submarines, and not enough destroyers to efficiently escort a half-dozen convoys.

But by this date the despairing War Power Council could scarcely assemble a half-dozen convoys. And the sea lanes of the home Empire were nearly as

486

devoid of *maru*-trains as the waters of the Southwest Pacific where junks, sampans, *dhows, prahus* and luggers were attempting to haul Japanese cargoes. Previously such craft had been allowed considerable freedom by the Allied forces in the Southwest Pacific, as the Allies had not wanted to alienate the natives of the region. However, by July 1945 the native craft assumed military importance as they constituted practically the only means of supplying the enemy garrisons in Malaya and the Netherlands East Indies. Consequently the whole ragtag and bobtail were put on the list of legitimate SubSoWesPac targets, although the submariners were under strict orders to provide for the safety of native crews.

Thus the attrition war in South China and Java Sea waters ended as a pot-shooting contest, the submarines running into shallow bays and harbors to snipe at cockleshell sailing craft and scurrying catamarans and fight gun duels with Japanese patrol boats. In these latitudes at this date the enemy's A/S efforts were little more than weary gestures. A few coast defense vessels and frigates, an occasional plane challenged the submarines. Their depth charges and bombs remained dangerous to the last, but they were too depleted a force to offer anything but token resistance.

For the SubSoWesPac Force, BAYA, BUMPER, HAMMERHEAD, HARDHEAD and LIZARDFISH downed Japanese vessels in July. Largest of these was the 1,189-ton tanker KYOEI MARU NO. 3 sunk on the 20th in the Gulf of Siam by BUMPER. In an adjacent area HAMMERHEAD downed a small cargoman and a little tanker. The other sinkings included a 595-ton torpedo boat and an assortment of sub-chasers. These were the last Japanese targets of torpedo-shooting size to fall to the SubSoWesPac submarines.

But surface gun actions kept Admiral Fife's patrollers on the jump and significant tonnages were downed in these forays. Patrolling in the Gulf of Siam the submarine BUGARA, captained by Commander A. F. Schade, sank 12 junks, 24 schooners, 16 coasters, three sea trucks, one naval auxiliary and a *trengganu*—a total of 57 small craft bulleted to the bottom for an estimated 5,284 tons. All except two of these vessels were boarded; native crews were put safely ashore with their personal belongings. As a touch of spice to this colorful patrol, adventurous BUGARA came across a Japanese ship manned by a Chinese crew under attack by a yelling swarm of Malay pirates. The American submarine rescued the Chinese, sank the Japanese ship and disposed of the piratical Malays. A continuity to rival anything from M-G-M or the pen of Milton Caniff!

Another gun-battler at that time off the Malay coast

was BLENNY, captained by Commander W. H. Hazzard. Stopping native traffic on the road to Singapore, Hazzard treated the targets to 5-inch and 40-mm. fire, machine-gun fire, boarding parties with demolition charges and a 12-gage shotgun to blast holes in wooden bottoms. The sharpshooting submarine ran out of ammunition and was resupplied by other submarines in the vicinity, bullets and shells being sent aboard by means of a breeches buoy. Hazzard saw that the native crews were unharmed, and their personal possessions were handled with care. On this patrol BLENNY sank 63 vessels—a record for the war. The tonnage total, however, added up to some 5,700 tons.

The SubPac patrollers in Empire waters found more to shoot at during July. But not a great deal more. HADDO, striking a convoy in the Yellow Sea on July 1, downed a frigate and two cargomen for a total of 6,126 tons. As has been related, BARB downed a fair-sized freighter off Karafuto on the 5th. TREPANG sank a small transport off Ominato on the 7th. TIRANTE sank a small transport in the Yellow Sea off Tsingtao on the 8th. On the 10th, RUNNER II sank a minesweeper off Honshu and SEA ROBIN downed a small freighter off southwest Kyushu. THREADFIN sank a minesweeper in the Yellow Sea on the 20th.

Operating in the Sea of Japan off northwest Honshu, SENNET (Lieutenant Commander C. R. Clark) concluded the month's scoring for the SubPac Force with a convoy shooting that began on July 28 and ended on the 30th. Down went UNKAI MARU NO. 15, freighter, 1,208 tons. Down went HAGIKAWA MARU, freighter, 2,995 tons. Down went HAKUEI MARU, tanker, 2,863 tons. To the bottom went YUZAN MARU, transport, 6,039 tons. When the torpedoings were over, SENNET had sunk 13,105 tons of Japanese merchant shipping, and Clark and company had fought the last full-fledged convoy battle of the Pacific War.

Last of the I-boats

It speaks something for the submersible's ability to survive that, at a time when Japanese capital ships were in oblivion, the Jap cruiser force was reduced to a CL and a training cruiser, and the Jap DD's could not muster at a good dozen, the Imperial Navy possessed some 50 ocean-going submarines. Not all of these were in operating condition. But in July 1945, when the Imperial Navy's surface forces were virtually non-existent, Japanese submersibles were still in action in the Southwest Pacific and in the waters of the home Empire.

Stationed in Japan during the war, German Vice Admiral Paul H. Weneker, in charge of blockade running by submarines between Japan and Germany, did not think much of the I-boat. After the war he stated:

"The Japanese had poor types of submarines. They were too big for easy handling when under attack, and consequently were too easily destroyed. Then the asdic and sonic and radar equipment was very far behind in development."

Weneker went on to say that a Nazi submarine had been sent to Kure where the Japanese carefully studied the German design. *"But they then came to the conclusion that this type boat was too complicated for construction in Japan."*

Weneker arranged for a Japanese submarine crew to be sent to Germany for training. *"They had, I think, very good training in German boats and German attack methods. But unfortunately they got caught in the North Atlantic in early 1944 while returning to Japan."*

However, this German admiral expressed great respect for the American submarine effort. German submarines, he explained, ran from Germany to Penang or Singapore with such war materials as optical goods, aircraft plans and machine tools for the Japanese. In exchange the U-boats picked up quinine, tin, rubber and other items scarce in Nazi Germany. Personnel were also exchanged in this fashion.

"But this was not so easy an arrangement because of the American submarines on the route between Japan and the South [Singapore]. I knew much of this because of the shipping for which I was responsible. It was terrible. Sometimes the entire convoy including all my material would be lost. It seemed that nothing could get through."

Vice Admiral Miwa, Commander-in-Chief of the Imperial Navy's Sixth (Submarine) Fleet, stated that the average number of Japanese submarines in operation during the war was somewhere between 40 and 45. The force maintained this strength throughout the war. The figure did not include midget submarines. Scores of these two-man subs were built to defend the home islands from invasion; few of them got into action, and at war's end they were found rusting on Japanese waterfronts. When the American offensive was driving on the western Carolines, Admiral Miwa dispatched eight one-man "torpedo-submarines" to Ulithi to attack the United States warships. These midgets were transported by two ocean-going submersibles. Miwa considered them "good weapons." But the American A/S forces treated them as shark-hunters would treat barracuda. Such dwarfs were little more than novelties.

Japanese submarines were not equipped with radar until June 1944. Attempting to defeat Allied radar, the Japanese tried coating submarine hulls with gum, and devised a cork-shaped conning tower which they hoped would deflect radar beams down into the water. Neither of these measures proved effective. Late in the war a greatly reduced superstructure was designed. Miwa stated with pride that he had fostered a plan for submarine "breather tubes" some time before the German *"schnorkel"* stack was introduced. At war's end the Japanese had in commission several 5,000-ton submarines, intended for use as plane-carriers. These unwieldy submersibles did not get into action, but were training when hostilities drew to a close. Miwa testified that he opposed the building of these big submarines as wasteful of construction material and because large superstructures were "a weak point against radar." Toward the end of the war the Imperial Army put its finger in the pie of submarine building, and Miwa felt that the soldiery were getting in over their heads.

"The Navy explained to the Army that building of submarine very difficult, and the Navy wanted to show how to build them; but military did not want to be assisted by Navy, so military themselves built the submarines. . . . I think they were of no use."

Asked who controlled the operations when Navy submarines were supplying Army troops, Miwa declared, *"It was undecided."*

When one considers the Japanese radar situation, the lag in electronics, the material shortages, the sea of confusion in which the Imperial Navy's submariners operated, the hardihood of the submersible becomes even more apparent. Japan's submarine losses were heavy. The I-boats stuck their necks out. But they were hauling supplies in the Southwest Pacific, scouting off the Nansei Shotos and patrolling off the coasts of Japan to the bitter end.

As has been noted in a previous chapter, BLUEFISH (Commander G. W. Forbes) nailed I-351 off northwest Borneo on July 15th. The I-boat was first spotted by BLOWER (Lieutenant Commander N. P. Watkins). Coached into position by BLOWER, Forbes' submarine intercepted the enemy, and a brace of BLUEFISH torpedoes did the rest. Apparently I-351 was caught in the act of hauling gasoline.

On July 29 the submarine I-58 struck the United States Third Fleet an agonizing blow by torpedoing the heavy cruiser INDIANAPOLIS as that warship neared Leyte. This was the last major loss suffered by the U.S. Navy in World War II. The American cruiser sank in 15 minutes. About half of her crew of 1,196 escaped from the sinking vessel, but through a grievous blunder nobody noticed that the cruiser was overdue at her port of destination. When the survivors were picked up four days later—and then quite by accident—only 316 remained.

Just two weeks after this anti-climactic disaster, SPIKEFISH (Commander R. R. Managhan) caught a Japanese submarine in the East China Sea. Late in the evening of August 13, SPIKEFISH made radar contact. Closing in, the American submariners identified the target as a Jap submersible. The wary enemy submerged. Managhan then indulged in a fast guessing game. He guessed that the enemy had reversed course after diving. Acting on that premise, he started SPIKEFISH on the hunt. A few minutes after midnight radar contact was regained.

While the hide-and-seek was going on, Managhan radioed a report to SubPac Headquarters, and a return dispatch advised him that no friendly submarines were in the area. Nevertheless, he decided to wait until daylight to see his quarry. Thereupon, he held SPIKEFISH at periscope depth, and just before dawn she sighted the target. The silhouette betrayed the I-boat's nationality, and Managhan promptly fired six torpedoes.

One survivor was recovered. The prisoner identified the torpedoed submarine as I-373.

Thus the last Japanese submersible destroyed in World War II was sunk by a U.S. submarine.

Loss of Bullhead

Lombok Strait—the narrow passage between Lombok Island and Bali—was patrolled by Japanese A/S vessels throughout the war. In 1943 the Japanese made an attempt to mine the strait, but this move merely sent the SubSoWesPac submarines detouring through neighboring straits and the mining effort was abandoned. Then in 1944 a shore battery of 6-inch guns on the cliffs of Lombok began to throw shells at submarines going through the passage on moonlit nights. In the autumn of that year ComSubSoWesPac ordered his submarines to refrain from offensive action within 120 miles of Lombok—a move designed to conceal the fact that the passage was being used. The Jap shore battery and its attendant radar post were soundly blasted by American planes early in 1945. Yet as late as mid-July at least one gun remained in commission. The battery lobbed shells at LOGGERHEAD as that submarine, running on the surface, assayed the first daylight, above-water transit of the strait.

A few enemy planes also drifted over Lombok during the closing weeks of the war. The area remained as a small cancer spot in the Netherlands East Indies, and U.S. submarines entered the strait with caution.

On the last day of July, BULLHEAD (Lieutenant Commander E. R. Holt, Jr.) left Fremantle to begin her third war patrol. Her orders were to patrol in the Java Sea until September 5, and then head for Subic Bay in the Philippines. Her Java Sea patrol area extended roughly from the island of Bali to the coastal waters of central Java. To reach this area she would transit Lombok Strait.

BULLHEAD reported herself through the Strait on August 6th. Submarines CAPITAINE and PUFFER were to conduct simultaneous patrols in the same area. COD and CHUB also passed through in transit during August, and British submarines TACITURN and THOROUGH were operating in the vicinity. Several anti-submarine attacks were made by the Japanese in the Lombok-Bali area between August 6 and August 15th. On the 6th, a Japanese Army plane depth-charged a submarine off the Bali coast near the northern mouth of Lombok Strait. The pilot claimed two direct hits and reported a gush of oil and air bubbles at the spot where the target went down.

CAPITAINE did not reach the Java Sea until August 13th. On the 12th, en route, she ordered BULLHEAD to take position in a scouting line with herself and PUFFER. She received no reply from BULLHEAD. On August 15 CAPITAINE reported, "Have been unable to contact BULLHEAD by any means since arriving in area." BULLHEAD was gone.

The number of submarines in the area and the multiplicity of A/S attacks delivered leave some doubt as to the day and cause of BULLHEAD's loss. She was probably struck down as she headed west from Lombok Strait on August 6th. With all hands she went down in action—the last United States submarine lost in the war.

The Rising Sun Is Sunk

One of the last periscope attacks of the war was made in the Yellow Sea by BILLFISH (Lieutenant Commander L. C. Farley, Jr.). The day was August 5, 1945. To get a shot at anything like a *maru* at this late date, U.S. submarines were practically crawling into Japanese docks and climbing into the laps of Japanese shipyards. Not too exaggerated a picture when one recalls TIRANTE at Ha Shima and BARB shooting out the street lights of towns on the "Polar Circuit." Now BILLFISH advanced to the very doormat of Dairen harbor at the Manchurian end of the Yellow Sea to find a torpedo target.

There she flushed two small freighters, a sea truck and a PC-boat. Operating in 15- to 20-fathom water, Farley closed in for a shot at one of the freighters, and three torpedoes sank the 1,091-ton KORI MARU. This periscope attack was made in broad daylight, and the submerged submarine streaked away in the shallows before the enemy could get off a single depth charge.

On that same August day Pogy sank the 2,220-ton freighter KOTHIRASAN MARU in the Sea of Japan off the west coast of Honshu. Off the Korean coast, PARGO struck on August 8 to sink the 5,454-ton transport RASHIN MARU in the Sea of Japan. JALLAO downed the 5,795-ton transport TEIHOKU MARU in the middle of the Japan Sea on the 11th.

These August sinkings were drowned out by the explosion that shook the world. For several months Hirohito and Prime Minister Suzuki had been trying to end the hopeless war. Late in June, Prince Konoye was dispatched to Moscow with secret instructions to accept any terms he could negotiate through the Russians, but the Soviet leaders, refusing to deal with Konoye, had promptly informed the United States of these panicky Japanese maneuvers.

On July 26 the Allies issued the Potsdam Declaration, demanding immediate and unconditional surrender. Favoring acceptance of the ultimatum, the Emperor and his Inner Cabinet were once more balked by Japan's reactionary militarists—General Anami, the War Minister, and his two chiefs of staff, General Umezu and Admiral Toyoda—who rejected the terms as "too dishonorable." Struggling in the coils of gold braid and red tape, the Cabinet was unable to break the deadlock. This miserable muddle—the creation of a Government that was an anachronism—could only result in tragedy. Discussions of "national polity," the Tenno System, the Emperor's status as a deity and the need for maintaining that illusion were interrupted on August 6 by the terrible blast at Hiroshima.

Two days later a second atomic bomb wiped out the city of Nagasaki. On that same day the Soviet Union declared war on Japan. Even then the die-hard militarists could not make up what was left of their minds. Capitulate to the atom—an object that could not be seen by the naked eye? Had the hold-outs argued in such fashion, the point would have been no more absurd than the one presented by Admiral Toyoda, the Navy Chief of Staff. On August 13 the Emperor's Cabinet voted 13 to 3 in favor of capitulating to American terms. Admiral Toyoda remained one of the three opposed. His reasons furnish an inside view of that medieval, ritual-bound mentality which had led Japan to disaster.

"The main point . . . had to do with the Emperor's position, since it was the conviction of the Japanese people that the Emperor was a living god above whom there could be no earthly being. It was feared the Japanese people would not readily accept the wording of a reply which placed the Emperor in a subordinate position."

However, 13 of Japan's leaders and the Emperor himself were not inclined to share the viewpoint of the anachronistic admiral. The realities of the situation were that Japan was down and out and any further slaughter of the people would be utterly futile.

On August 14 the Emperor dispensed with evasions, fables and precedent and asked the Government to draft an Imperial rescript to stop the war.

Last Torpedo Shot

The first verifiable sinking of a Japanese ship by a U.S. submarine was scored by SWORDFISH on December 15, 1941, when she downed ATSUTASAN MARU off Hainan. On August 14, 1945, just three years and eight months later, TORSK (Commander B. E. Lewellen) scored the last killing torpedo-shot of the war.

TORSK was patrolling in the Sea of Japan off the southwest coast of Honshu. The previous day she had downed KAIHO MARU, 873-ton freighter—conventional day-periscope attack. Only a few hours before the cessation of hostilities, she encountered and sank Coast Defense Vessel No. 13. Her last torpedo shot was fired at another frigate. Hapless Coast Defense Vessel No. 47 went down in history as the last Japanese vessel sunk by a U.S. submarine in World War II.

Submarines in Tokyo Bay

The "Cease fire" order was in the making as TORSK launched the war's last torpedo shot. When the greatest war in world history ended on August 15 a ring of United States submarines surrounded Japan, the United States Third Fleet stood at the entrance of Tokyo Bay, Army and Navy aircraft clouded the sky, American invasion forces were assembling at Okinawa, Allied armies were coming across the Pacific. Scattered fragments of the Imperial Army were marooned in the Southwest Pacific, the Imperial Navy was at sea bottom, the residual Japanese merchant marine was at the end of its rope.

"I do not believe it would be accurate to look upon the atomic bomb and the entry of Soviet Russia as direct causes of the termination of the war," stated Admiral Toyoda. *"But I think those two factors did enable us to bring the war to an end without creating utter chaos in Japan."*

Oriental casuistry—for Japan was already in a chaotic state, militarily impotent, economically wrecked, financially bankrupt, with famine, death and terror stalking the land. If anything saved the nation from black chaos it was the entry of the United States Pacific Fleet into Tokyo Bay on September 2 and the signing of the surrender instrument aboard the battleship MISSOURI.

MOPPING UP! Submarine gunners blaze away. U.S. subs had to comb the surface for small game in spring of 1945. Marus were scarce. Japan started war with 6 million tons of merchant shipping. By July 1945 only 1 million tons remained. Jap civilian life alone demanded 3 million. Facing famine, Japan was sunk.

ADMIRAL'S FAREWELL. *Taking command as CinCPac in January 1942, Admiral Nimitz raised his flag on sub-* marine Grayling. *He relinquishes command (scene above), boarding submarine* Menhaden *to haul down his flag.*

COMING HOME! *Submariner heaves a line to the wharf; the voyage is over. Good to be on surface again. In port.*

SUBMARINE OVERHAUL. *In floating drydock after war. She may go out soon again—or wind up in mothballs.*

SAIL ON! *Deep, and on the surface, the underwater navy carries out its peacetime missions. World War II took its toll of American submarines—52 were lost in the conflict.* *But seldom, if ever in history, had so small a naval force accomplished so much. Japan's war effort depended on shipping. It was sunk in the main by U. S. submarines.*

In the offing, symbolic, the submarine tender PROTEUS rode at anchor with her brood alongside. With PROTEUS was the rescue vessel GREENLET. Witness to the historic surrender were the submarines ARCHERFISH, CAVALLA, GATO, HADDO, HAKE, MUSKALLUNGE, PILOTFISH, RAZORBACK, RUNNER II, SEGUNDO, SEACAT, and TIGRONE.

Four weeks later a great fleet of submarines was assembling at Pearl Harbor for the long voyage home. As a part of Task Force Thirty under Admiral Halsey, whose flag was in SOUTH DAKOTA, the submarines sortied for the West Coast on the morning of October 9th. The fleet paraded past Diamond Head, and then the task groups proceeded independently, each heading for a home port. Halsey's own task group steamed for San Francisco. Entering San Francisco Bay on the 15th, the warships paraded in column under Golden Gate Bridge. First in column was SOUTH DAKOTA. Then—more symbolism—came the submarines PUFFER, BAYA, KRAKEN, LOGGERHEAD, PILOTFISH and STICKLEBACK. Three destroyers, a light cruiser and three battleships trailed the submarines.

At Pearl Harbor, taking command as CinCPac on December 31, 1941, Fleet Admiral Nimitz raised his flag on the submarine GRAYLING. And on a submarine —the USS MENHADEN—Admiral Nimitz lowered his flag when he relinquished command of the fleet.

That, too, was symbolic.

Empire Liquidated

It has been said that Japan lost the Pacific War when her Imperial forces lost control of the Central and Southwest Pacific. Some consider Midway the turning point. Others point to Saipan. But all agree that Japan's insular conquests could only have been supported and exploited by her merchant fleet. It might be said that Japan lost the Pacific War on the date that her merchant fleet losses exceeded all possibility of replacement.

That date probably arrived in the spring of 1944 when convoy sinkings began to outstrip the 50% margin, and the Japanese, trying to play double or nothing, were too frequently left with nothing. The war was certainly lost on the day the Japan-to-Singapore run closed down. On that day the Empire went out of business, and thereafter Japan was unable to import the fuel and raw materials needed to maintain her War Machine. Then the problem became one of bare sustenance for the home islands.

On the day of surrender, Japan had but 1,800,000 tons of merchant shipping afloat, of which 1,650,000 tons were in home Empire waters. But of this tonnage in the "Inner Zone," only 650,000 tons were serviceable—a mere 12% of the merchant fleet which

had flown the Japanese flag at the war's beginning. Moreover, there was not enough fuel on hand for this residual fleet, maintenance and repair services were at a standstill, and less than half of the available *marus* were operating in August 1945. Having begun the war with some 6,000,000 tons of merchant shipping in action (3,000,000 tons of which were needed for "civilian living" in the home islands), Japan ended up with some 312,000 tons of steel ships manned, fueled and hauling cargo. Former mistress of the East and one of the world's three great maritime powers, Japan now possessed a merchant service about the size of the "Old Fall River Line."

Due to slipshod Japanese records, exact statistics may never be computable. But the part played by United States submarines in Japan's maritime demise is depicted with reasonable accuracy in the figures compiled after the war by the Joint Army-Navy Assessment Committee. According to this authority, United States submarines sank 1,113 Japanese merchant ships (of over 500 gross tons) for a tonnage total of 4,779,902 tons. They "probably" sank an additional 65 vessels, for an extra 225,872 tons. United States submarines also sank 201 Japanese naval vessels—a total of 540,192 naval tons. Thirteen "probables" in this category added 37,434 tons to the naval score. With the few "probables" added to the many certainties, U.S. submarines scored as below:

Number of Merchant Ships Sunk:	*1,178*
Merchant Tonnage Sunk:	*5,053,491 tons*
Number of Japanese Naval Vessels Sunk:	*214*
Japanese Naval Tonnage Sunk:	*577,626 tons*

Again, statistics do not tell a comprehensive story. Figures that run into thousands and millions lose meaning. To understand the submarine score, one must visualize the ships that went down—the great hulls and shining engines that were crushed in the sea's oppressive depths—the cargoes dumped, the lakes of oil spilled, the mountains of machinery destroyed in roaring fires and swirling waters.

One chronometer—delicate ship's timepiece—costs around $200, average market. In chronometers alone (1,178 x $200) U.S. submarine torpedoes cost the Japanese merchant marine $235,600.

The engine-room telegraph of an average ship costs around $400. To the bottom with the merchantmen sunk by U.S. submarines went some $471,200 worth of Japanese engine-room telegraphs.

The average ship's anchor (homely item) costs the merchant owner something over $1,200. Iron is valuable; anchors are heavy. Give but one to a ship, and $1,413,600 in anchors went down aboard the *marus* sunk by submarines in World War II. Almost 1½ million dollars worth of anchors!

But chronometers, engine-room telegraphs, anchors—these were minor gadgets on a seagoing vessel, comparable in scale to the clock; speedometer and hand brake on an automobile. The ship's marine engines, the Diesel plant (coal burners are somewhat less) averages $60,000 to $70,000. Put the figure at $60,000 to include the *maru* coal burners, and at this minimum, submarine torpedoes sank over $70,000,000 worth of marine engines.

Now make the cost of the steel hull and superstructure an arbitrary $100,000 for the purpose of illustration (the actual figure would run much higher). And add $117,800,000 to the red side of the Japanese ledger.

To these figures append the value of cargoes destroyed—the thousands of tons of petroleum, rubber, coal, textiles, raw silk, ore, grain, munitions, war equipment, clothing, chemicals, fertilizer, fish and foodstuffs that went down with ship after ship. Typewriters, telephones, trucks, trinkets, toys, tiles, teapots, tires, tinware, tools, tractors—tons of such manufactured articles (and one can run them through the alphabet) can be added. The monetary values soar into figures that are astronomical.

And what is the value of a man? Engineers have yet to produce a mechanism as intricate and marvelous as the little finger. No scientist has created a camera as wonderful as man's eye. The physicists who grapple with atomic power could not begin to penetrate the mystery of the human brain. Japan might replace the trigger of a gun—the trigger-finger of a sharpshooter who has been drowned aboard a torpedoed transport is not so readily replaced. Japanese shipyards might reconstruct a vessel's bow—the eyes of human lookouts are another matter. Among the passengers who went down in torpedoed passenger-cargomen were scientists, specialists and engineers whose brains were lost to Japan forever. Nearly every *maru* that went under took skilled hands with it. Life is cheap in the Orient, but merchant marine casualties alone—the thousands of drowned seamen and hundreds of marine engineers and ship's officers—added up to a human toll Japan could not afford.

Japan began the war with a well-trained, highly efficient merchant marine personnel. Some 45,000 officers and 77,000 seamen manned the ocean-going fleet. As shown in the table that follows, casualties due to submarine action during the war amounted to more than half of the original merchant marine complement. Although the Japanese were able to meet replacement requirements for a time, the crew

problem became serious late in 1943, and the service was beset by a demoralizing manpower shortage at the end of 1944.

Personnel Losses of Japanese Merchant Marine (Ocean-going Vessels) Dec. 1941-Aug. 1945

Agent	No. of Dead and Missing	Wounded or Otherwise Incapacitated	Total
Submarines	16,200	53,400	69,600
Aircraft	8,100	26,700	34,800
Mines	2,700	8,900	11,600
Total Casualties			116,000

The economic crash of Japan caused by the collapse of the maritime nation's merchant service will keep the analysts and the adding machines busy for a generation. The final figures may never be assessed. Financial losses resulting from the decline in industrial output, the stoppage of overseas commerce, the dislocation of domestic trade, the reduction in agriculture are beyond immediate computation. One cargo of graphite, torpedoed as it left Manchuria, may have shut down for days a plant manufacturing electrodes. Orders unfilled, lost man-hours, idle hands, labor trouble, eventual closure of the plant—the consequences could extend through five files of carbon copies and a volume of bookkeeping. The exact percentage of submarine responsibility for the plant's ultimate closure would be indeterminable.

So it is with the submarine's responsibility for the collapse of Japan's merchant service and the resultant economic crash of that nation. But some light on the economic consequences induced by the U.S. submarine attrition war may be cast by a page of past history. During the American Civil War the indomitable Raphael Semmes, captain of Confederate raiders SUMTER and ALABAMA, destroyed some 70 Northern merchantmen. These depredations cost the Union about $10,000,000 in ship and cargo losses. But these losses were insignificant in comparison to the damage done Northern commerce. Had the Union been dependent on overseas supplies, the work of this one enemy might have caused the North to lose the war, for Semmes all but paralyzed the nation's ocean-carrying trade, and the United States, which had attained second place in world commerce, remained far down the list for the next five decades.

When a single surface raider in the slow-motion era of canvas and cannon-balls could create such havoc, imagine the damage that could be dealt a maritime nation led by Nineteenth Century thinkers in a sea war against a power possessed of a modern fleet of Twentieth Century submarine raiders!

The commentary of a more or less impartial observer adds an interesting footnote to this point. Asked what he considered the causes for Japan's loss of the war, German Vice Admiral Weneker stated that in his opinion Japanese overconfidence, underestimation of the enemy and overextended supply lines which could not be protected were basic causes. *"After that I would say the reasons for their disaster could be classed about as follows in order of importance: First, and by far the worst, were the attacks of the highly efficient American submarines on merchant shipping. Most serious of all, here, was the sinking of tankers and hence the loss of oil from the south. The second factor in importance was the destruction of the Japanese Navy . . . the third was the air bombing attack on this country (Japan)."*

The U.S. submarine war against the Japanese Navy provides more material for speculation. Strategic values must be estimated and included in any assessment of naval losses—the cost to the enemy in offensive moves disrupted, defenses undermined and battle defeats.

Strategists and analysts will argue these computations for the next five decades, for the equations must include many "probable" factors, "X" potentials and other unknowns. But it takes no master strategist to deduce that the carrier torpedoings by ALBACORE and CAVALLA seriously injured the enemy during the Battle of the Philippine Sea, and the heavy cruisers deleted from Kurita's fleet by DACE and DARTER dislocated the Japanese defense of Leyte Gulf. No one need graduate from a war college to perceive the mortal blows dealt Japan's sea power by the submarines which sank KONGO and SHINANO at an hour when the Imperial Navy was reeling. The eight light cruisers blown to the bottom in 1944, the 28 destroyers destroyed, the Japanese submarines abolished —this subtraction wrought by U.S. submarines in that single year's time may be seen as deciding factors which reduced the Japanese Navy to impotence and paved the way for the final drive on Tokyo.

But generalizations, like the figures from the IBM machines, leave much to be taken into account. One (1) battleship—KONGO, for instance—was something more than that. Into KONGO went years of planning, millions of *yen* worth of steel, machine-tooling and equipment, thousands of man-hours, and finally, hundreds of trained navy men. All compressed into "1 BB." Again, into a carrier—UNRYU, for example. Time, money, labor, men were as much a part of this vessel as her hull. So were the planes she carried, the tons of aviation gasoline, and a thousand and three items, including her potential power at that place and time, and her intentions. Figures cannot indicate the value of "1 CVE" when warfare involves such chain-of-events formulae as may cause the loss of a battle for want of a horseshoe nail.

Transmute "nail" into "blueprints," for instance. Blueprints which German aircraft designers and technicians have spirited into Singapore. There these important items are loaded aboard a Japanese submarine for spiriting to Tokyo, while the German experts proceed by plane. Then somebody talks, and the story is overheard by Allied listeners. Presently a dispatch goes to ComSubPac, and Admiral Lockwood's Headquarters leaps into action. Messages are radioed to U.S. submarines along the Jap's prospective route—"Get the I-boat." The submarines converge on the track and lie in wait. The I-boat walks into the ambush. Torpedo wakes streak the surface of Luzon Strait, and an explosion tears a red hole in the dusk. A brief smudge of smoke. A scuffle in the water. Down goes I-29, torpedoed by SAWFISH (Lieutenant Commander A. B. Banister). One (1) Japanese submarine is recorded as sunk. But down with that one (1) submarine went those German blueprints. And those blueprints may have contained material which would have immeasurably strengthened the Japanese Air Force. Obviously SAWFISH sank more than just "1 SS."

Thus the equation becomes one which defies mathematical solution. But even so, the percentage figures have tremendous impact. In 1944, U.S. submarines sank one-third of all the major enemy combat vessels destroyed in the Pacific that year. The 201 Japanese warships and 13 "probables" sunk by U.S. submarines during the war comprised 29% of the enemy war-shipping sunk by all agencies in the Pacific conflict. About 55% of all Japanese shipping (merchant and naval) downed in World War II was sunk by U.S. submarines. Perhaps the graph on the end paper of this book best illustrates this stupendous submarine achievement—an achievement accomplished by a force that consisted of less than 2% of the United States Navy's personnel.

American submarine losses must be taken into account, and the Service suffered heavy casualties. Fifty-two out of 288 American submarines were lost in the war—almost one out of five. But only 48 went down in combat operations, and of these not more than 41 were downed by enemy action. The toll of lives was severe. Personnel strength of the submarine operating forces averaged 14,750 officers and men. The fatalities totaled 3,131 men and 374 officers. The hazards of undersea warfare are indelibly recorded in American casualty lists which show that six submariners lost their lives in the line of duty for every one non-submariner who died in Naval Service (exclusive of aviation). Axis submarine losses, however, were far greater. The Japanese lost 130 submarines, the Italians 85, and the Germans the appalling total of 781.

Again statistics fail the story—for those to whom this book is dedicated, and for those who saw the final victory. The valiant efforts and incomparable achievements of United States Navy submariners cannot be summarized in statistics. Neither graphs nor percentages could measure the leadership of an Admiral Lockwood, the genius of a Captain Voge, the skill of such commanders as Morton and O'Kane, the courage of every submarine's crew. But the American submariners of World War II need no encomiums. From mess attendants to admirals, all were captains courageous. Their war record speaks for them, and the liquidation of the Japanese Empire stands in evidence.

—FINIS-

EPILOGUE

If nothing else, World War II proved the prodigious power of ships (sea and air) capable of operating in the third dimension. It was in that third dimension that Japan lost the Pacific War. He who lived by the Samurai sword died by the air bomb and the submarine torpedo.

The holocaustal incandescence which consumed Hiroshima and Nagasaki could not blind observers to the fact that the maritime Empire was already destroyed. And long before the first mass air-raids smote Tokyo, many Japanese-held harbors in the Southwest Pacific were as deserted as the bays of the moon, and in many of Japan's home seaports there were vacant docks with rusting bollards where only spiders tied their lines. The atomic bomb was the funeral pyre of an enemy who had been drowned.

NEW SUBMARINES COMMISSIONED IN 1945

Name	First Commanding Officer
BUILT BY CRAMP SHIPBUILDING CO. FINISHED AT BOSTON NAVY YARD	
LANCETFISH	Lt. Comdr. R. K. MacLean
LING	Comdr. G. C. Molumphy
BUILT AT CRAMP SHIPBUILDING CO. FINISHED AT PORTSMOUTH NAVY YARD	
MANTA	Lt. Comdr. E. P. Madley
BUILT AT CRAMP SHIPBUILDING CO.	
MORAY	Comdr. F. L. Barrows
RONCADOR	Comdr. E. R. Crawford
SABALO	Lt. Comdr. J. G. Andrews
SABLEFISH	Comdr. R. H. Crane
BUILT AT ELECTRIC BOAT COMPANY	
DENTUDA	Comdr. J. S. McCain, Jr.
CAPITAINE	Lt. Comdr. E. S. Friedrick
CARBONERO	Comdr. C. L. Murphy, Jr.
CARP	Lt. Comdr. J. L. Hunnicutt
CATFISH	Lt. Comdr. W. A. Overton
ENTEMEDOR	Lt. Comdr. W. R. Smith, Jr.
CHIVO	Lt. Comdr. W. R. Crutcher
CHOPPER	Lt. Comdr. Saverio Filippone
CLAMAGORE	Comdr. S. C. Loomis, Jr.
COBBLER	Comdr. J. B. Grady
COCHINO	Comdr. W. A. Stevenson

Name	First Commanding Officer
CORPORAL	Comdr. E. E. Shelby
CUBERA	Lt. Comdr. R. W. Paine, Jr.
BUILT AT MANITOWOC SHIPBUILDING CO.	
LIZARDFISH	Comdr. O. M. Butler
LOGGERHEAD	Comdr. R. M. Metcalf
MACABI	Comdr. A. H. Dropp
MAPIRO	Comdr. V. A. Sisler, Jr.
MENHADEN	Comdr. D. H. McClintock
MERO	Comdr. J. H. Turner
BUILT AT MARE ISLAND NAVY YARD	
STICKLEBACK	Comdr. H. K. Nauman
BUILT AT PORTSMOUTH NAVY YARD	
ARGONAUT	Lt. Comdr. J. S. Schmidt
RUNNER	Comdr. R. H. Bass
CONGER	Lt. Comdr. H. D. Sipple
CUTLASS	Comdr. H. L. Jukes
DIABLO	Lt. Comdr. G. G. Matheson
MEDREGAL	Comdr. W. H. Wright
REQUIN	Comdr. S. D. Cutter
IREX	Comdr. J. D. Crowley
SEA LEOPARD	Comdr. R. E. M. Ward
ODAX	Comdr. F. D. Walker, Jr.
SIRAJO	Comdr. F. L. Harlfinger
POMODON	Comdr. M. H. Dry

ADDENDA

UNITED STATES

SUBMARINES LOST

IN WORLD WAR II

——————————☆——————————

SEALION	GRENADIER	GRAYBACK	TANG
S-36	RUNNER	TROUT	ESCOLAR
S-26	R-12	TULLIBEE	ALBACORE
SHARK I	GRAYLING	GUDGEON	GROWLER
PERCH	POMPANO	HERRING	SCAMP
S-27	CISCO	GOLET	SWORDFISH
S-39	S-44	S-28	BARBEL
GRUNION	DORADO	ROBALO	KETE
ARGONAUT	WAHOO	FLIER	TRIGGER
AMBERJACK	CORVINA	HARDER	SNOOK
GRAMPUS	SCULPIN	SEAWOLF	LAGARTO
TRITON	CAPELIN	DARTER	BONEFISH
PICKEREL	SCORPION	SHARK II	BULLHEAD

——————————☆——————————

There is a port of no return, where ships
May ride at anchor for a little space
And then, some starless night, the cable slips,
Leaving an eddy at the mooring place . . .
Gulls, veer no longer. Sailor, rest your oar.
No tangled wreckage will be washed ashore.

LESLIE NELSON JENNINGS
"LOST HARBOR"

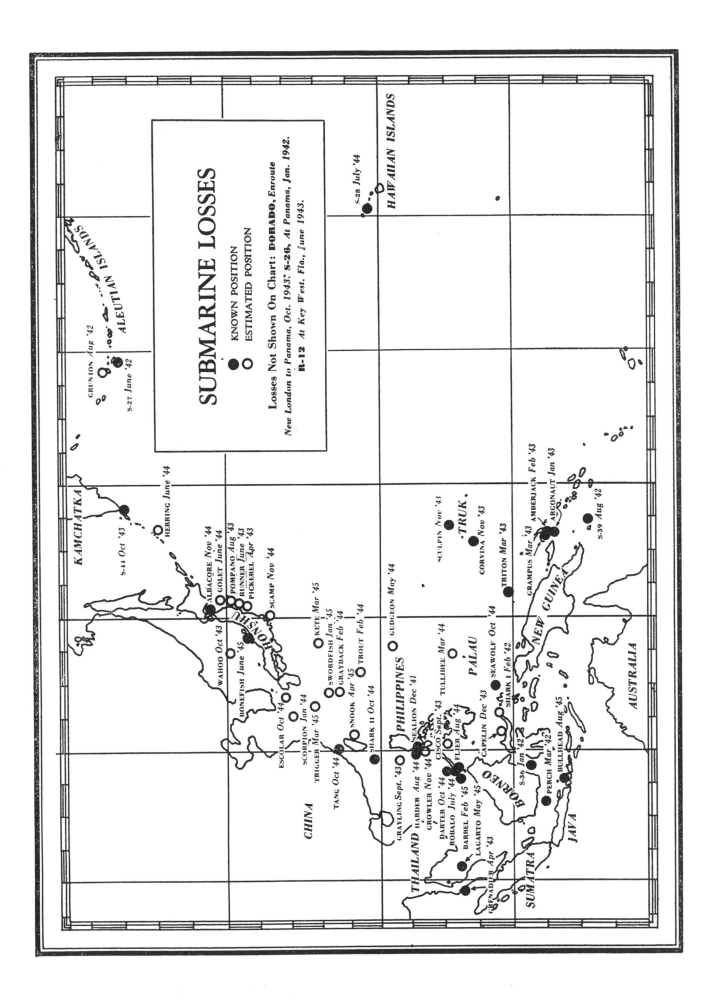

SUBMARINE LOSSES

● KNOWN POSITION
○ ESTIMATED POSITION

Losses Not Shown On Chart: **DORADO**, *Enroute*
New London to Panama, Oct. 1943: **S-26**, *At Panama, Jan. 1942.*
R-12 *At Key West, Fla, June 1943.*

ALEUTIAN ISLANDS

HAWAIIAN ISLANDS

S-28 July '44

GRUNION Aug '42

S-27 June '42

KAMCHATKA

HERRING June '44

S-44 Oct '43

ALBACORE Nov '44
GOLET June '44
POMPANO Aug '43
RUNNER June '43
PICKEREL Apr '43
SCAMP Nov '44

WAHOO Oct '43
BONEFISH June '45

HONSHŪ

KETE Mar '45
SWORDFISH Jan '45
GRAYBACK Feb '44
TROUT Feb '44

GUDGEON May '44

SCULPIN Nov '43

·TRUK·

CORVINA Nov '43

TRITON Mar '43

GRAMPUS Mar '43
AMBERJACK Feb '43
ARGONAUT Jan '43

S-39 Aug '42

NEW GUINEA

ESCOLAR Oct '44
SCORPION Jan '44

SNOOK Apr '45
SHARK 11 Oct '44

PHILIPPINES

SEALION Dec '41

TULLIBEE Mar '44

PALAU

SEAWOLF Oct '44

CHINA

TANG Oct '44

TRIGGER Mar '45

GRAYLING Sept. '43

HARDER Aug '44
GROWLER Nov '44

CISCO Sept. '43
FLIER Aug '44

CAPELIN Dec '43

SHARK 1 Feb '42

S-36 Jan '42

DARTER Oct '44
ROBALO July '44
BARBEL Feb '45
LAGARTO May '45

PERCH Mar '42

BULLHEAD Aug '45

THAILAND

BORNEO

JAVA

AUSTRALIA

GRENADIER Apr '43

SUMATRA

PRESIDENTIAL UNIT CITATIONS

SUBMARINE	FOR PATROLS	COMMANDING OFFICER
Albacore	*2,3*	*R. C. Lake*
Albacore	*7,8*	*J. W. Blanchard*
Archerfish	*5*	*J. E. Enright*
Barb	*8,9,10,11*	*E. B. Fluckey*
Batfish	*6*	*J. K. Fyfe*
Bowfin	*2*	*W. T. Griffith*
Cavalla	*1*	*H. J. Kossler*
Flasher	*3,4*	*R. T. Whitaker*
Flasher	*5*	*G. W. Grider*
Gato	*4,5,6,7,8*	*R. J. Foley*
Greenling	*1,2,3*	*H. C. Bruton*
Guardfish	*1,2*	*T. B. Klakring*
Guardfish (Second Award)	*8*	*N. G. Ward*
Gudgeon	*1,2*	*E. W. Grenfell*
Gudgeon	*3*	*H. B. Lyon*
Gudgeon	*4,5,6,7,8*	*W. S. Post, Jr.*
Haddock	*2*	*A. H. Taylor*
Haddock	*5,6,7*	*R. M. Davenport*
Harder	*1,2,3,4,5*	*S. D. Dealey*
Jack	*1,3*	*T. M. Dykers*
Jack	*5*	*A. E. Krapf*
Nautilus	*1,2,3*	*W. H. Brockman*
Parche	*1,2*	*L. P. Ramage*
Pintado	*1,2,3*	*B. A. Clarey*
Queenfish	*1,2*	*C. E. Laughlin*
Rasher	*1*	*E. S. Hutchinson*
Rasher	*3,4*	*W. R. Laughon*
Rasher	*5*	*H. G. Munson*
Redfish	*1*	*R. D. King*
Redfish	*2*	*M. H. Austin*
Sailfish	*10*	*R. E. M. Ward*
Salmon	*11*	*H. K. Nauman*
Sandlance	*5*	*M. E. Garrison*
Seahorse	*2,3,4*	*S. D. Cutter*

SUBMARINE	FOR PATROLS	COMMANDING OFFICER
Sealion	2,3	E. T. Reich
Silversides	4,5	C. C. Burlingame
Silversides	7,10	J. J. Coye, Jr.
Spadefish	1,2	G. W. Underwood
Tang	1,2,3	R. H. O'Kane
Tang (Second Award)	4,5	R. H. O'Kane
Tinosa	4	L. R. Daspit
Tinosa	5,6	D. F. Weiss
Tirante	1	F. L. Street, III
Trigger	5	R. S. Benson
Trigger	6,7	R. E. Dornin
Trout	2,3	F. W. Fenno, Jr.
Trout	5	L. P. Ramage
Tunny	2,5	J. A. Scott
Wahoo	3	D. W. Morton

NAVY UNIT COMMENDATIONS

SUBMARINE	FOR PATROLS	COMMANDING OFFICER
Aspro	*1*	*H. C. Stevenson*
Aspro	*2*	*W. A. Stevenson*
Atule	*1*	*J. H. Maurer*
Barb	*12*	*E. B. Fluckey*
Bergall	*2*	*J. M. Hyde*
Bluegill	*1,3*	*E. T. Barr, Jr.*
Bonefish	*1,3,4*	*T. W. Hogan, Jr.*
Bonefish	*5,6*	*L. T. Edge*
Bowfin	*6*	*J. Corbus*
Crevalle	*1,2*	*H. G. Munson*
Crevalle	*3,4*	*F. D. Walker, Jr.*
Croaker	*1*	*J. E. Lee*
Dace	*5*	*E. B. Claggett*
Darter	*4*	*D. H. McClintock*
Grayback	*7*	*E. C. Stephan*
Grayback	*8,9,10*	*J. A. Moore*
Growler	*1,2,4*	*H. W. Gilmore*
Growler	*10*	*T. B. Oakley, Jr.*
Guitarro	*1,2,3*	*E. D. Haskins*
Gunard	*2,3,4,5*	*C. H. Andrews*
Haddo	*7*	*C. W. Nimitz, Jr.*
Halibut	*10*	*I. J. Galantin*
Hammerhead	*2*	*J. C. Martin*
Hawkbill	*1,3,4*	*F. W. Scanland, Jr.*
Lapon	*3,4,5*	*L. T. Stone*
Lapon	*6*	*D. G. Baer*
Pargo	*7*	*D. B. Bell*
Permit	*10*	*C. L. Bennett*
Picuda	*1,2*	*A. Raborn*
Picuda	*3*	*G. R. Donaho*
Picuda	*4,5*	*E. T. Shepard*
Plunger	*2,3,4*	*D. C. White*
Plunger	*6,10*	*R. H. Bass*
Pogy	*5,6*	*R. M. Metcalf*

SUBMARINE	FOR PATROLS	COMMANDING OFFICER
Puffer	4	R. G. Selby
Raton	4	J. W. Davis
Raton	6	M. W. Shea
Ray	5,6	W. T. Kinsella
Sea Devil	3	R. E. Styles
Seawolf	4,7	F. B. Warder
Seawolf	10,12	R. L. Gross
Skate	1,2	E. B. McKinney
Skate	3	W. P. Gruner
Skate	7	R. B. Lynch
Sunfish	9	E. E. Shelby
Sunfish	11	J. W. Reed
Swordfish	1,2,4	C. C. Smith
Tautog	2	J. H. Willingham, Jr.
Tautog	5,6,8,9,10	W. B. Sieglaff
Tautog	11	T. S. Baskett
Thresher	13	D. C. MacMillan
Trepang	1	R. M. Davenport
Trigger	9	F. J. Harlfinger

U. S. SUBMARINE
WOLF-PACKS

OCTOBER 1943 ... MAY 1945

SUBPAC FORCE

Pack Commander,
Pack Name
and Submarines

Capt. C. B. Momsen
CERO
SHAD
GRAYBACK

Cdr. F. B. Warder
SNOOK
HARDER
PARGO

Lt. Cdr. C. F. Brindupke
TULLIBEE
HADDOCK
HALIBUT

Capt. G. E. Peterson
PARCHE
BANG
TINOSA

Cdr. F. W. Fenno
"Fenno's Ferrets":
PICUDA
PERCH
PETO

Cdr. D. F. Weiss
TINOSA
SEALION
TANG

Capt. L. N. Blair
"Blair's Blasters":
SHARK
PILOTFISH
TUNNY
PINTADO

Capt. W. V. O'Regan
"Mickey Finns":
APOGAN
THRESHER
GUARDFISH
PIRANHA

Pack Commander,
Pack Name
and Submarines

Lt. Cdr. A. R. Gallaher
BANG
SEAHORSE
GROWLER

Capt. W. D. Wilkin
"Wilkin's Wildcats":
ROCK
SAWFISH
TILEFISH

Cdr. L. S. Parks
PARCHE
HAMMERHEAD
STEELHEAD

Cdr. S. P. Moseley
"Moseley's Maulers":
BILLFISH
SAILFISH
GREENLING

Cdr. G. R. Donaho
"Donk's Devils":
SPADEFISH
REDFISH
PICUDA

Cdr. J. B. Oakley, Jr.
"Ben's Busters":
GROWLER
PAMPANITO
SEALION

Cdr. E. R. Swinburne
"Ed's Eradicators":
TUNNY
QUEENFISH
BART

Capt. C. W. Wilkins
"Wilkins' Bears":
SEAHORSE
WHALE
SEGUNDO

Pack Commander,
Pack Name
and Submarines

Cdr. A. H. Holtz
"Holtz' Cats":
BAYA
BECUNA
HAWKBILL

Cdr. R. S. Benson
"Benson's Dogs":
RAZORBACK
CAVALLA
PIRANHA

Cdr. F. C. Acker
POMFRET
SNOOK
COBIA

Lt. Cdr. G. H. Browne
SNOOK
COBIA

Cdr. A. B. Banister
"Banister's Beagles":
SAWFISH
ICEFISH
DRUM

Cdr. E. N. Blakely
"Blakely's Behemoths":
SHARK
BLACKFISH
SEADRAGON

Cdr. J. S. Coye, Jr.
"Coye's Coyotes":
SILVERSIDES
SALMON
TRIGGER

Cdr. W. J. Millican
"Millican's Marauders":
ESCOLAR
PERCH
CROAKER

Pack Commander,
Pack Name
and Submarines

Lt. Cdr. T. L. Wogan
"Wogan's Wolves":
BESUGO
GABILAN
RONQUIL

Cdr. J. P. Roach
"Roach's Raiders":
HADDOCK
HALIBUT
TUNA

Cdr. B. A. Clarey
"Clarey's Crushers":
PINTADO
JALLAO
ATULE

Cdr. T. B. Klakring
"Burt's Brooms":
SILVERSIDES
SAURY
TAMBOR
TRIGGER
STERLET
BURRFISH
RONQUIL

Cdr. G. W. Underwood
"Underwood's Urchins":
(I)
SPADEFISH
SUNFISH
PETO

Cdr. L. D. McGregor
"Sandy's Sluggers":
REDFISH
SHAD
BANG

Cdr. C. E. Loughlin
"Loughlin's Loopers": (I)
QUEENFISH
BARB
PICUDA

Pack Commander,
Pack Name
and Submarines

Cdr. L. P. Ramage
"Red's Rowdies":
PARCHE
POMFRET
SAILFISH

Cdr. F. W. Fenno
"Fennomints":
PAMPANITO
SEACAT
PIPEFISH
SEARAVEN

Cdr. R. M. Davenport
"Roy's Rangers":
TREPANG
SEGUNDO
RAZORBACK

Cdr. C. L. Bennett
"Bennett's Blazers": (I)
SEAOWL
PIRANHA
SEAPOACHER

Cdr. V. L. Lowrance
"Rebel's Rippers":
SEADOG
SEAROBIN
GUARDFISH

Cdr. W. S. Post
"Post's Panzers": (I)
SPOT
ICEFISH
BALAO

Cdr. W. A. Stevenson
"Steve's Stingers":
ASPRO
CROAKER
SAWFISH

Cdr. M. K. Clementson
"Clementson's Clippers":
BLUEBACK
SEAFOX
PUFFER

Cdr. J. C. Nichols
SILVERSIDES
TAUTOG

Cdr. C. E. Loughlin
"Loughlin's Loopers": (II)
QUEENFISH
BARB
PICUDA

Cdr. W. B. Perkins
BURRFISH
POGY
RONQUIL

Cdr. J. F. Enright
"Joe's Jugheads":
ARCHERFISH
BATFISH
BLACKFISH

Cdr. G. W. Underwood
"Underwood's Urchins":
(II)
SPADEFISH
POMPON
ATULE
BANG

Cdr. A. G. Schnable
"Al's Sharks":
PILOTFISH
FINBACK
RASHER

Cdr. C. B. Stevens
"Clyde's Cannibals":
PLAICE
SCABBARDFISH
SEAPOACHER

Cdr. Frank Latta
"Latta's Lancers":
LAGARTO
HADDOCK
SENNET

Cdr. E. E. Shelby
"Shelby's Shellackers":
GATO
SUNFISH
JALLAO

Cdr. B. F. McMahon
"Mac's Mops":
PIPER
STERLET
TREPANG
POMFRET
BOWFIN

Cdr. J. D. Fulp, Jr.
"Fulp's Fiddlers":
SEGUNDO
SEACAT
RAZORBACK

Cdr. C. L. Bennett
"Bennett's Blazers": (II)
SEAOWL
PIRANHA
PUFFER

Cdr. J. R. Middleton, Jr.
"Middleton's Mobsters":
THRESHER
PETO
SHAD

Cdr. W. B. Sieglaff
"Barney's Boxers":
TENCH
SEADEVIL
BALAO
GROUPER

Cdr. W. S. Post
"Post's Panzers": (II)
SPOT
SEAFOX
QUEENFISH

Cdr. R. W. Peterson
"Pete's Panthers":
ICEFISH
KINGFISH

Cdr. R. G. Latham
"Latham's Locators":
TINOSA
SPADEFISH
TIRANTE

Cdr. Hiram Cassedy
"Hiram's Hecklers":
TIGRONE
BULLHEAD
BLACKFISH

Cdr. J. F. Walling
"Walling's Whalers":
SNOOK
BURRFISH
BANG

Cdr. E. T. Hydeman
"Earl's Eliminators":
SEADOG
THREADFIN
TRIGGER

Cdr. N. J. Nicholas
"Nick's Nippers":
SILVERSIDES
HACKLEBACK
THREADFIN

Cdr. A. C. Smith
TRUTTA
LIONFISH
PARCHE
SUNFISH

Cdr. J. A. Adkins
"Caddy's Caddies":
COD
POMPON

Cdr. R. Kefauver
"Russ's Rustlers":
SPRINGER
TREPANG
RATON

Cdr. B. F. McMahon
"Mac's Moppers":
PIPER
POMFRET
PLAICE
SEAPOACHER

SUBSOWESPAC FORCE

Cdr. R. T. Whitaker
FLASHER
CREVALLE
ANGLER

Cdr. F. D. Walker, Jr.
CREVALLE
ANGLER

Cdr. E. D. Haskins
GUITARRO
RATON
GUNNEL

Cdr. H. C. Munson
RASHER
BLUEFISH

Pack Commander and Submarines	Pack Commander and Submarines	Pack Commander and Submarines	Pack Commander and Submarines
Cdr. S. D. Dealey HARDER HADDO HAKE RAY	*Cdr. J. G. Martin* HAMMERHEAD LAPON PADDLE MINGO	*Cdr. B. C. Hills* PERCH GABILAN SEALION BARBEL	*Cdr. B. A. Clarey* PINTADO HAWKBILL
Cdr. C. W. Nimitz, Jr. HADDO HAKE	*Cdr. J. R. Stevens* FLOUNDER BASHAW GUAVINA	*Cdr. E. L. Barr, Jr.* BLUEGILL BREAM BARBEL	*Cdr. J. H. Campbell* BLOWER BASHAW
Cdr. R. T. Whitaker FLASHER LAPON BONEFISH	*Capt. E. H. Bryant* HAWKBILL FLASHER BECUNA	*Cdr. R. L. Gross* BOARFISH CHARR	*Cdr. P. E. Summers* PAMPANITO MINGO SEALION CAIMAN
Cdr. D. H. McClintock DARTER DACE	*Cdr. Earl Tiedman* GUAVINA BASHAW	*Cdr. T. H. Henry* KRAKEN PARGO	*Cdr. B. A. Clarey* PINTADO CAIMAN
Cdr. V. B. McCrea HOE ASPRO CABRILLA	*Cdr. A. H. Holtz* BAYA HOE CAVALLA	*Cdr. J. R. Stevens* FLOUNDER HAKE PARGO	*Cdr. H. B. Dodge* BRILL CHUB
Cdr. J. A. Adkins COD RAY	*Cdr. H. D. Sturr* BECUNA FLASHER HOE PADDLE DACE	*Cdr. P. E. Summers* PAMPANITO GUAVINA	*Cdr. M. K. Clementson* BLUEBACK BERGALL HAWKBILL BLACKFIN FLASHER BLUEGILL BASHAW
Cdr. E. L. Barr, Jr. BLUEGILL ANGLER	*Capt. E. H. Bryant* HAWKBILL BAYA CAVALLA	*Cdr. E. F. Steffanides* TUNA BARBEL BLACKFIN	
Cdr. W. G. Chapple BREAM GUITARRO RATON		*Cdr. F. D. Boyle* CHARR TUNA BLACKFIN	*Cdr. R. A. Keating, Jr.* ROCK GUAVINA COBIA BLENNY BAYA
Cdr. I. S. Hartman BARBERO REDFIN HADDO	*Cdr. F. C. Lucas, Jr.* CAIMAN BLENNY LAPON	*Cdr. G. W. Grider* FLASHER BASHAW	
Cdr. T. B. Oakley, Jr. GROWLER HAKE HARDHEAD	*Cdr. N. D. Gage* GURNARD GUITARRO	*Cdr. J. M. Hyde* BERGALL BLOWER GUITARRO	*Cdr. J. R. Stevens* FLOUNDER SEAROBIN CHUB
Cdr. Thomas Kinsella RAY RATON BATFISH	*Cdr. T. L. Wogan* BESUGO HARDHEAD COBIA BLACKFIN GURNARD	*Cdr. H. D. Sturr* BECUNA BLENNY GUAVINA BAYA	*Lt. Cdr. W. L. Fey* CAIMAN SEALION MINGO
Cdr. F. A. Greenup HARDHEAD HAKE	*Cdr. A. H. Holtz* BAYA CAVALLA	*Cdr. G. H. Laird, Jr.* HAMMERHEAD BAYA	*Cdr. F. D. Boyle* CHARR BESUGO GABILAN
Cdr. G. E. O'Neil, Jr. GUNNEL MUSKALLUNGE	*Cdr. F. C. Lucas, Jr.* CAIMAN SEALION	*Cdr. H. J. Kossler* CAVALLA HOE HAMMERHEAD	*Cdr. E. L. Barr, Jr.* BLUEGILL BASHAW CROAKER

SUBMARINE
TENDERS
IN THE PACIFIC WAR

PELIAS

HOLLAND   OTUS

CANOPUS *(Lost off Bataan)*

FULTON   ☆   SPERRY

GRIFFIN   BEAVER

BUSHNELL   ORION

PROTEUS

EURYALE

AEGIR

ANTHEDON

APOLLO

CLYTIE

Note: The minesweeper PIGEON (Lieutenant Commander R. E. Hawes) was twice awarded the Presidential Unit Citation. First award for action on December 10, 1941. Second award for action throughout remainder of December 1941. During this period PIGEON performed heroically as a submarine rescue vessel.

U. S. SUBMARINE
SPECIAL MISSIONS
CHRONOLOGY

DATE	SUBMARINE	MISSION
27-28 Jan '42	SEAWOLF (Lt. Cdr. F. B. Warder)	Delivered Corregidor 37 tons of .50-cal ammunition. Evacuated 25 Army-Navy pilots, submarine spare parts and 16 torpedoes.
3 Feb '42	TROUT (Lt. Cdr. F. W. Fenno, Jr.)	Delivered 3500 rounds of 3" AA to Corregidor. Evacuated 20 tons of Philippine gold and silver plus securities and mail.
4 Feb '42	SEADRAGON (Lt. Cdr. W. E. Ferrall)	Evacuated 21 Army-Navy personnel, 23 torpedoes, 4000 lbs. sub spares and 3000 lbs. radio equipment.
14 Feb '42	SARGO (Lt. Cdr. T. D. Jacobs)	Delivered 1 million rounds .30-cal ammunition to Polloc Harbor, Mindanao, evacuated 24 Army enlisted personnel of 14th Bombardment Squadron, late of Clark Field, Luzon.
20 Feb '42	SWORDFISH (Lt. Cdr. C. C. Smith)	Evacuated President Quezon and his party of 9 to San Jose, Panay, and took aboard 13 torpedoes.
24 Feb '42	SWORDFISH (Lt. Cdr. C. C. Smith)	Evacuated American High Commissioner to Philippines Francis B. Sayre and his party of 12, plus 5 Navy enlisted men.
26 Feb '42	S-38 (Lt. H. G. Munson)	Bombarded probable position of radio station at Sangapura, Bawean Is., Java Sea—72 rounds of 4".
27 Feb '42	S-39 (Lt. J. W. Coe)	Landed on Chebia Is., South China Sea, in search of 40 British refugees from Singapore. None on Island.
28 Feb '42	PERMIT (Lt. W. G. Chapple)	Delivered her service allowance of ammunition to Corregidor. Evacuated 51 naval personnel and brought out 3 torpedoes.
1-10 April '42	SWORDFISH (Lt. Cdr. C. C. Smith)	Departed on patrol with 40 tons of food for Corregidor. Undelivered due to surrender of Bataan.
2-10 April '42	SEARAVEN (Lt. H. Cassedy)	Departed on patrol with 1500 rounds of 3" AA ammunition for Corregidor. Bataan surrendered prior to delivery.
5 April '42	SNAPPER (Lt. Cdr. H. L. Stone)	Delivered 20 tons food to Corregidor, evacuated 27 Army-Navy personnel.
8 April '42	SEADRAGON (Lt. Cdr. W. E. Ferrall)	Delivered 7 tons food to Corregidor, evacuated 22 Army-Navy personnel.
11 April '42	SEARAVEN (Lt. H. Cassedy)	Rescued 33 Australian Army personnel from Timor Is., near Koepang, N.E.I.
April '42	THRESHER (Lt. Cdr. W. L. Anderson)	Made weather reports for Doolittle raid on Tokyo.
22 April- 6 May '42	SAILFISH (Lt. Cdr. R. G. Voge)	Departed on patrol with 1856 rounds 3"AA ammunition. Undelivered due to surrender of Corregidor.
3 May '42	SPEARFISH (Lt. J. C. Dempsey)	Evacuated from Corregidor 6 Army officers, 6 Navy officers 11 Army nurses, 1 Navy nurse, 1 civilian woman.

DATE	SUBMARINE	MISSION
10 May '42	PORPOISE (Lt. J. R. McKnight, Jr.)	Rescued 5 Army aviators, crew of plane LB-30, from Island of Ju, between Halmahera and New Guinea.
20 May '42	S-39 (Lt. F. E. Brown)	Reconnoitered Deboyne Is. in Louisiades.
12-19 Jul '42	S-42 (Lt. O. G. Kirk)	Landed and embarked special agent at Adler Bay, near Rabaul, New Britain.
19-20 Jul '42	S-43 (Lt. E. R. Hannon)	Landed and embarked RAAF officer to contact agents on New Ireland.
23-26 Jul '42	S-43 (Lt. E. R. Hannon)	Landed RAAF officer to contact agents on Feni Is. in Bismarcks. Unable to recover.
11 Aug '42	FINBACK (Lt. Cdr. J. L. Hull)	Disembarked and reembarked survey party in Tanaga Bay, Tanaga I., Aleutians. Took soundings.
16-18 Aug '42	ARGONAUT (Lt. Cdr. J. R. Pierce)	Carried 114 men and 7 officers of "Carlson's" Marine Raiders on Makin Island raid.
16-18 Aug '42	NAUTILUS (Lt. Cdr. W. H. Brockman, Jr.)	Carried portion of "Carlson's" Marine Raiders on Makin Island raid. Supported it with gunfire and sank 2 ships in lagoon.
25 Oct '42	WHALE (Lt. Cdr. J. B. Azer)	Laid mines off Hino Misaki, Honshu.
5-6 Oct '42	AMBERJACK (Lt. Cdr. J. A. Bole, Jr.)	Reconnoitered Greenwich I.
15-16 Oct '42	AMBERJACK (Lt. Cdr. J. A. Bole, Jr.)	Reconnoitered Ocean I.
16 Oct '42	THRESHER (Lt. Cdr. W. J. Millican)	Laid mines northernmost part of Gulf of Siam.
19 Oct '42	GAR (Lt. Cdr. D. McGregor)	Laid mines northernmost part of Gulf of Siam.
25 Oct '42	AMBERJACK (Lt. Cdr. J. A. Bole, Jr.)	Delivered 9000 gals. aviation gasoline, 200 hundred-lb. bombs and 15 Army fighter personnel to Tulagi—brought in from Espiritu Santo.
29 Oct '42	GRENADIER (Lt. Cdr. B. L. Carr)	Laid mines middle of Tonkin Gulf.
2 Nov '42	TAMBOR (Lt. Cdr. S. H. Ambruster)	Laid mines in eastern Tonkin Gulf.
2 Nov '42	TAUTOG (Lt. Cdr. J. H. Willingham)	Laid mines just south of Cape Padaran, French Indo-China.
4-8 Nov '42	SHAD (Lt. Cdr. E. J. MacGregor)	Furnished reconnaissance and weather information and acted as special beacon off Mehdia, French Morocco, during U.S. invasion.
4-8 Nov '42	BARB (Lt. Cdr. J. R. Waterman)	Reconnoitered, made weather reports and landed beacon party at Safi, French Morocco.
4-8 Nov '42	GUNNEL (Lt. Cdr. J. S. McCain, Jr.)	Reconnoitered, made weather reports, acted as beacon off Fedala, French Morocco.
4-8 Nov '42	HERRING (Lt. Cdr. R. W. Johnson)	Furnished reconnaissance and weather information and acted as special beacon off Casablanca, French Moroccan coast.

DATE	SUBMARINE	MISSION
4-8 Nov '42	BLACKFISH (Lt. Cdr. J. F. Davidson)	Furnished reconnaissance and weather information and acted as special beacon off Dakar.
14 and 17 Dec '42	SUNFISH (Lt. Cdr. R. W. Peterson)	Laid mines in entrance to Iseno Umi.
17 Dec '42	DRUM (Lt. Cdr. B. F. McMahon)	Laid mines in Bungo Suido.
20 Dec '42	TRIGGER (Lt. Cdr. R. S. Benson)	Laid mines off Inubo Zaki.
30 Dec '42	SEARAVEN (Lt. Cdr. H. Cassedy)	Landed 7 agents on south coast of Ceram Is., Lt. H. P. Nygh, RNNR, in charge.
1 Jan '43	NAUTILUS (Lt. Cdr. W. H. Brockman, Jr.)	Evacuated 29 civilians from Teop Is., Solomon Is., including 17 women and 3 children.
30 Nov '42 15 Jan '43	PORPOISE (Lt. Cdr. J. R. McKnight, Jr.)	Ordered to reconnoiter Tsugaru Strait; uncompleted due to shortage of fuel.
5 Jan '43	GRAYBACK (Lt. Cdr. E. C. Stephan)	Evacuated 6 B-26 survivors from Rendova Is. Acted as beacon ship for TF 67 during bombardment of Munda Bar, Solomon Is.
14 Jan '43	GUDGEON (Lt. Cdr. W. S. Stovall, Jr.)	Landed 6 Filipinos, Major Villamor in charge, and 1 ton of special equipment near Catmon Pt., Negros.
21-22 Jan '43	GREENLING (Lt. Cdr. H. C. Bruton)	Reconnoitered Pak and Tong Is. in Admiralties.
16-26 Jan '43	S-18 (Lt. G. H. Browne)	Conducted reconnaissance in Attu and Semichi Is. area.
21-25 Jan '43	HADDOCK (Lt. Cdr. A. H. Taylor)	Special mission in the Tokyo-O'Shima area.
1-2 Feb '43	GREENLING (Lt. Cdr. H. C. Bruton)	Landed party on east coast of New Britain.
8-10 Feb '43	GROUPER (Lt. Cdr. R. R. McGregor,	Evacuated aviator from Rengi Is.
9 Feb '43	GUDGEON (Lt. Cdr. W. S. Stovall, Jr.)	Evacuated 28 men from south coast of Timor: 21 Australians, 1 Englishman, 1 Portuguese and 5 natives.
17 Feb '43	THRESHER (Lt. Cdr. W. J. Millican)	Reconnoitered Christmas I.
21-23 Feb '43	POMPANO (Lt. Cdr. W. M. Thomas)	Reconnoitered Bikini, Eniwetok, and Rongerik Atolls.
1 Mar '43	STINGRAY (Lt. Cdr. O. J. Earle)	Reconnoitered Eniwetok Atoll and later Taongi.
1-2 Mar '43	GREENLING (Lt. Cdr. J. D. Grant)	Landed party on South Coast of New Britain in Bismarcks.
5 Mar '43	TAMBOR (Lt. Cdr. S. H. Ambruster)	Landed Lt. Cdr. C. Parsons, USNR, and party, 50,000 rounds of .30-cal., 20,000 rounds of .45-cal., and $10,000 currency on south coast of Mindanao, P.I., near Pagadian Bay.
6 Mar '43	TAUTOG (Lt. Cdr. W. B. Sieglaff)	Laid mines southeast coast of Borneo.

DATE	SUBMARINE	MISSION
15 Mar '43	PLUNGER (Lt. Cdr. R. H. Bass)	Reconnaissance of Ujeland and Kalo Is., in Marshalls.
29 Mar '43	GATO (Lt. Cdr. R. J. Foley)	Evacuated 3 nuns, 27 children, 9 mothers and 12 AIF commandos from Teop Is., Solomon Is.
3 Apr '43	DRUM (Lt. Cdr. B. F. McMahon)	Made photographic reconnaissance of Nauru Is.
7 Apr '43	TROUT (Lt. Cdr. L. P. Ramage)	Laid mines near Sarawak, Borneo.
9-12 Apr '43	POLLACK (Lt. Cdr. R. E. Palmer)	Reconnaissance in Gilbert Is.
21 Apr '43	STINGRAY (Lt. Cdr. O. J. Earle)	Laid mines near Wenchow.
22 Apr '43	STINGRAY (Lt. Cdr. O. J. Earle)	Laid mines.
29 Apr '43	GATO (Lt. Cdr. R. J. Foley)	Landed 16 coast watchers and AIF troops and freight at Teopasino Plantation, Teop I., Solomons. Evacuated a number of missionaries, including the Bishop of Bougainville.
30 Apr '43	GUDGEON (Lt. Cdr. W. S. Post, Jr.)	Landed 1 officer, 3 men and 3 tons of equipment near Pucio Pt., Panay, P.I. Evacuated 2 men.
30 Apr '43	SNOOK (Lt. Cdr. C. O. Triebel)	Laid mines off Saddle Is., China.
Apr '43	SKIPJACK (Lt. Cdr. H. F. Stoner)	Reconnoitered Rongerik Atoll and Wake.
19 Apr '43	SCORPION (Lt. Cdr. W. N. Wylie)	Laid mines off Kashima Nada.
20 Apr '43	RUNNER (1) (Lt. Cdr F. W. Fenno, Jr.)	Laid mines near Hong Kong.
1-5 May '43	THRESHER (Lt. Cdr. H. Hull)	Unsuccessful attempt to locate and evacuate personnel in Philippines, who did not appear.
4-11 May '43	NAUTILUS (Lt. Cdr. W. H. Brockman, Jr.)	Transported 109 Army Scouts from Dutch Harbor to Attu, disembarking at Scarlet Beach. Made reconnaissance in Aleutians.
4-11 May '43	NARWHAL (Lt. Cdr. F. D. Latta)	Reconnoitered Attu landing beaches and on 11 May disembarked 105 Army Scouts on Scarlet Beach, Attu.
5-11 May '43	NAUTILUS (Lt. Cdr. W. H. Brockman, Jr.)	Reconnoitered Attu landing beaches and on 11 May disembarked 109 Army Scouts on Scarlet Beach, Attu.
12 May '43	STEELHEAD (Lt. Cdr. D. L. Whelchel)	Laid mines off Erimo Saki.
21 May '43	SKIPJACK (Lt. Cdr. J. W. Coe)	Reconnoitered Rongerik Atoll and Wake Island.
25 May '43	TAUTOG (Lt. Cdr. W. B. Sieglaff)	Landed 2 agents on Kabaena Island.
25 May '43	GATO (Lt. Cdr. R. J. Foley)	Made sounding reconnaissance of Numa Numa Bay, near Choiseul in Solomons to determine suitability for mining.

DATE	SUBMARINE	MISSION
25-27 May '43	SILVERSIDES (Lt. Cdr. C. C. Burlingame)	Reconnoitered Apemama on the 25th and Nauru on the 27th.
26 May '43	TROUT (Lt. Cdr. A. H. Clark)	Landed 6 or 7 agents, $10,000 and 2 tons of equipment on Basilan I., Philippines.
31 May '43	STEELHEAD (Lt. Cdr. D. L. Whelchel)	Laid mines off Erimo Saki.
4 June '43	SILVERSIDES (Lt. Cdr. C. C. Burlingame)	Laid mines in Steffan Strait between New Hanover and New Ireland.
8-11 June '43	SALMON (Lt. Cdr. N. J. Nicholas)	Special missions south of Honshu.
9-12 June '43	SCORPION (Lt. Cdr. W. N. Wylie)	Performed special missions en route area in northern China and Yellow Sea.
12 June '43	TROUT (Lt. Cdr. A. H. Clark)	Landed 5 men, Capt. J. A. Hammer, USA, in command, supplies, 6000 rounds of .30-cal. and 2000 of .45-cal. ammunition. Evacuated 5 officers including Lt. Cdr. C. Parsons from Pagadian Bay, south coast of Mindanao.
12-20 June '43	FLYING FISH (Capt. F. T. Watkins)	Performed special tasks prior to entering area.
20 June '43- 3 July '43	SEARAVEN (Lt. Cdr. H. Cassedy)	Reconnoitered Marcus I., 2 days; performed special tasks, 12 days.
20 June '43- 28 July '43	PORPOISE (Lt. Cdr. C. L. Bennett)	Made reconnaissance of many islands in Marshalls.
1 July '43	GAR (Lt. Cdr. P. D. Quirk)	Landed commando party of 4 on south coast of Timor, Lt. Pives in command.
9 July '43	TROUT (Lt. Cdr. A. H. Clark)	Evacuated Lt. Cdr. C. Parsons, USNR, and four officers from south coast of Mindanao.
9 July '43	THRESHER (Lt. Cdr. H. Hull)	Landed commando party of 4, and 5000 pounds of stores, 20,000 rounds of .30-cal., 20,000 rounds of .45-cal., at Catmon Pt., west coast of Negros.
7-22 July '43	S-38 (Lt. Cdr. C. D. Rhymes, Jr.)	Reconnoitered Uturik, Taka, and Kwajalein Atolls in Marshalls plus Nauru.
12 July '43	TROUT (Lt. Cdr. A. H. Clark)	Landed Capt. J. A. Hammer, USA, on south coast of Mindanao, P.I.
15 July '43	NARWHAL (Lt. Cdr. F. D. Latta)	Bombarded Matsuwa Airfield on Matsuwa To in Kuriles with 31 rounds of six-inch shells. Also reconnoitered several Kurile islands.
25 July '43	SEADRAGON (Lt. Cdr. R. L. Rutter)	Performed special mission in open sea area west of Johnston I.
31 July '43	GUARDFISH (Lt. Cdr. N. G. Ward)	Landed survey party west coast of Bougainville, Solomon Islands.
31 July '43	GRAYLING (Lt. Cdr. J. E. Leo)	Delivered 2 tons of supplies and equipment at Pucio Pt., Pandan Bay, Panay, P.I.
July '43	S-31 (Lt. Cdr. R. F. Sollars)	Reconnoitered Kwajalein.

DATE	SUBMARINE	MISSION
July '43	STURGEON (Lt. Cdr. H. A. Piecentkowski)	Spent 11 days on special missions.
14 July '43- 9 Aug '43	S-33 (Lt. Cdr. C. B. Stevens, Jr.)	Made photographic reconnaissance of west coast of Kiska.
1 Aug '43	MINGO (Lt. Cdr. R. C. Lynch, Jr.)	Reconnoitered and bombarded Sorol I.
9-10 Aug '43	SUNFISH (Lt. Cdr. R. W. Peterson)	Reconnoitered Marcus I.
23 Aug '43	GRAYLING (Lt. Cdr. E. Olsen)	Delivered 2 tons of cargo at Pucio Pt., Pandan Bay, Panay, P.I.
Aug '43	S-35 (Lt. Cdr. J. E. Stevens)	Accomplished special mission in the Kuriles.
30 Aug '43- 2 Sept '43	SNOOK (Lt. Cdr. C. O. Triebel)	Photographic reconnaissance of Marcus I. before and after air strike.
1 Sept '43	GREENLING (Lt. Cdr. J. D. Grant)	Landed shore parties in connection with survey in Shortland I. area and on Treasury Islands.
2 Sept '43	BOWFIN (Cdr. J. H. Willingham, Jr.)	Delivered supplies and picked up 9 persons west of Binuni Pt., Mindanao, P.I.
13-23 Sept '43	GUDGEON (Lt. Cdr. W. S. Post, Jr.)	Reconnaissance of Saipan, Rota, Guam, and Agrihan Is.
16 Sept '43- 16 Oct '43	NAUTILUS (Lt. Cdr. W. H. Brockman, Jr.)	Made photographic reconnaissance of many islands in the Gilberts including Tarawa, Apamama and Makin.
20-28 Sept '43	GUARDFISH (Lt. Cdr. N. G. Ward)	Landed party in connection with reconnoitering west coast of Bougainville, Solomons.
24 Sept '43	SAWFISH (Cdr. E. T. Sands)	Reconnoitered Esutoru, west coast of Sakhalin I.
20-29 Sept '43	GATO (Cdr. R. J. Foley)	Landed party in connection with reconnaissance of east coast of Bougainville, Solomon Is.
27-29 Sept '43	PETO (Cdr. W. T. Nelson)	Searched for Fifth Air Force crew down off Wewak, New Guinea—unsuccessful.
28-29 Sept '43	GROUPER (Cdr. M. P. Hottel)	Landed party of 17 whites and 29 natives, 3000 lbs. freight, and took aboard Capt. A. L. Post, USAAF, from south coast of New Britain.
30 Sept '43	BOWFIN (Cdr. J. H. Willingham, Jr.)	Delivered supplies, mail, and money and evacuated 9 people from Philippines vicinity of Sequijor I.
Sept '43	SCULPIN (Cdr. L. H. Chappell)	Reconnoitered Thilenius and Montagu Harbor, south coast of New Britain, Bismarck Archipelago.
Sept '43	GROUPER (Cdr. M. P. Hottel)	Landed personnel on south coast of New Britain, Bismarck Archipelago.
2 Oct '43	KINGFISH (Cdr. V. L. Lowrance)	Laid mines off southern Celebes.
6 Oct '43	KINGFISH (Cdr. V. L. Lowrance)	Landed 6 agents and 5000 pounds of supplies and equipment on northeast coast of Borneo.
20 Oct '43	CABRILLA (Cdr. D. T. Hammond)	Picked up 4 men including Major I. A. Villamor at Dogo Pt., Negros, P.I.

DATE	SUBMARINE	MISSION
25-28 Oct '43	GUARDFISH (Lt. Cdr. N. G. Ward)	Landed personnel on west coast of Bougainville, Solomons, in connection with reconnaissance.
30 Oct '43	SCAMP (Cdr. W. G. Ebert)	Performed special mission in Solomons.
Oct '43	TAUTOG (Lt. Cdr. W. B. Sieglaff)	Reconnaissance of Palau and Fais and bombardment of Fais Island.
8 Nov '43- 4 Dec '43	NAUTILUS (Cdr. W. D. Irvin)	Reconnoitered islands in Gilberts and on 20 Nov. landed Marine detachment on Apamama. Assisted landing with bombardment.
13 Nov '43	NARWHAL (Lt. Cdr. F. D. Latta)	Delivered 46 tons of stores and landed 2 parties, Lt. Cdr. C. Parsons in command, at Paluan Bay, Mindoro, P.I.
14 Nov '43	TUNA (Cdr. A. H. Holtz)	Landed agent on Sanbergelap Island.
15 Nov '43	NARWHAL (Lt. Cdr. F. D. Latta)	Delivered 46 tons of supplies and evacuated 32 people including 8 women and 2 children at Nasipit, Mindanao, P.I.
17 Nov '43- 15 Dec '43	SEAL (Cdr. H. B. Dodge)	Reconnoitered 88 islands of the 96 comprising Kwajalein Atoll. Photographed 56 of them.
12-24 Nov '43	PADDLE (Cdr. R. H. Rice)	Made weather reports in connection with Gilbert Is. attack.
18 Nov- 13 Dec '43	SPEARFISH (Lt. Cdr. J. W. Williams)	Made photographic reconnaissance of Jaluit Atoll.
2 Dec '43	NARWHAL (Lt. Cdr. F. D. Latta)	Delivered 90 tons of ammunition and stores and evacuated 8 people including Lt. Cdr. C. Parsons and 2 women from Mindanao, P.I.
5 Dec '43	NARWHAL (Lt. Cdr. F. D. Latta)	Evacuated 3 women, 4 children and 2 men including DeVries family from Majacalar Bay, Mindanao, P.I.
13 Dec '43	POMPON (Cdr. E. C. Hawk)	Laid mines southwest of Cochin China.
18 Dec '43	CABRILLA (Cdr. D. T. Hammond)	Laid mines off coast of Cambodia.
13 Dec '43- 4 Jan '44	TARPON (Lt. Cdr. T. B. Oakley, Jr.)	Made photographic reconnaissance of Marshall Is.
25 Dec '43- 2 Jan '44	PETO (Cdr. W. T. Nelson)	Conducted reconnaissance and landed personnel on Boang Is., Solomons, under operational control of CTF 31.
3 Jan '44	BLUEFISH (Cdr. G. E. Porter)	Laid mines off eastern Malayan coast.
4 Jan '44	RASHER (Lt. Cdr. W. R. Laughon)	Laid mines off Cochin China.
5-6 Jan '44	GATO (Cdr. R. J. Foley)	Survey in Green Islands for CTF 31.
15 Jan '44	CREVALLE (Lt. Cdr. H. G. Munson)	Laid mines east of Saigon.
20 Jan '44	TINOSA (Cdr. D. F. Weiss)	Landed agents and 5000 lbs. of equipment off Labian Point, N.E. Borneo.

DATE	SUBMARINE	MISSION
23-31 Jan '44	SUNFISH (Lt. Cdr. E. E. Shelby)	Made photographic reconnaissance of Taongi Atoll and Kusaie I.
29 Jan '44	BOWFIN (Lt. Cdr. W. T. Griffith)	Laid mines off southeastern Borneo coast.
30 Jan '44- 8 Feb '44	BLACKFISH (Cdr. J. F. Davidson)	Conducted reconnaissance survey of Mussau, Tanga Feni Is.
26 Jan '44- 13 Feb '44	SEARAVEN (Lt. Cdr. M. H. Dry)	Made photographic reconnaissance of Eniwetok Atoll.
3-5 Feb '44	GATO (Cdr. R. J. Foley)	Rescued 12 P-38 aviators from open bay, New Britain, shot down over Rabaul.
5 Feb '44	NARWHAL (Lt. Cdr. F. D. Latta)	Delivered 45 tons of ammunition and stores and evacuated 5 servicemen and one British subject near Libertad, Panay, P.I.
17 Jan '44- 6 Mar '44	SEAL (Cdr. H. B. Dodge)	Reconnoitered Ponape I.
7 Feb '44	NARWHAL (Lt. Cdr. F. D. Latta)	Delivered 45 tons of cargo and evacuated 28 men, women, and children in vicinity of Balatong Point, Negros.
22 Feb '44	RAY (Cdr. B. J. Harral)	Laid mines off coast near Saigon.
17 Jan '44- 3 Mar '44	SEARAVEN (Lt. Cdr. M. H. Dry)	Made photographic reconnaissance of Eniwetok Atoll and surrounding islands.
3-5 Feb '44	GATO (Cdr. R. J. Foley)	Special mission accomplished North of Vitiaz Strait in the Bismarck Archipelago.
5 Feb '44- 17 Mar '44	SKATE (Lt. Cdr. W. P. Gruner, Jr.)	Reconnoitered in Caroline Is. mostly around Woleai but also around Ulithi, about 24 Feb.
2 Mar '44	NARWHAL (Cdr. F. D. Latta)	Delivered 70 tons of ammunition and stores and evacuated 28 passengers (women) from Butuan Bay, Nasipit, Mindanao, P.I.
5 Mar '44	NARWHAL (Cdr. F. D. Latta)	Delivered some cargo and received 10 passengers from Tawi-Tawi, P.I. Unloading interrupted by patrol boats.
20 Mar '44	ANGLER (Cdr. R. I. Olsen)	Evacuated 58 persons including women and children from the west coast of Panay, P.I.
22-27 Mar '44	DACE (Lt. Cdr. B. D. Claggett)	Accomplished 2 special missions in the Hollandia-Tanah-Merah area.
14 Mar '44- 7 Apr '44	CABRILLA (Lt. Cdr. W. C. Thompson)	Primarily a reconnaissance patrol of Sunda Strait. Also reconnoitered Flying Fish Cove, Christmas Is.
5-18 Apr '44	THRESHER (Cdr. D. C. MacMillan)	Conducted photographic reconnaissance at Nomei Is.
10-16 Apr '44	HADDO (Lt. Cdr. C. W. Nimitz, Jr.)	Unsuccessful attempt to contact agents on northeastern Borneo for evacuation.
2-29 Apr '44	GREENLING (Cdr. J. D. Grant)	Made photographic reconnaissance of Guam, Saipan, and Tinian Is.
10-16 Apr '44	DACE (Lt. Cdr. B. D. Claggett)	Escorted damaged SCAMP from area to base at Seeadler Harbor.

DATE	SUBMARINE	MISSION
14-20 Apr '44	CABRILLA (Lt. Cdr. W. C. Thompson)	Made reconnaissance patrol in Lombok Strait.
22 Apr '44	REDFIN (Lt. Cdr. M. H. Austin)	Laid mines off Sarawak, Borneo.
15 Apr '44- 7 May '44	SALMON (Cdr. N. J. Nicholas)	Made photographic reconnaissance of Ulithi (5-20 Apr.), Yap (22-27 Apr.), and Woleai Is. (29 Apr.-7 May) in Carolines.
Apr 44	HADDOCK (Lt. Cdr. R. M. Davenport)	Anti-picket patrol south of Jap mainland.
2 May 44	REDFIN (Lt. Cdr. M. H. Austin)	Attempted to locate personnel ashore unsuccessfully. Own men attacked by Japs and narrowly escaped.
11 May 44	CREVALLE (Lt. Cdr. F. D. Walker, Jr.)	Evacuated 48 persons including 28 women and children, and picked up intelligence information from Negros, P.I.
17-19 May '44	BONEFISH (Lt. Cdr. L. L. Edge)	Reconnoitered Tawi-Tawi Bay, P.I.
24 May '44	NARWHAL (Lt. Cdr. J. C. Titus)	Landed 22 men and 25 tons of supplies near Alusan Bay, Samar, P.I.
28-29 May '44	NARWHAL (Lt. Cdr. J. C. Titus)	Unsuccessful attempt to make contact ashore and evacuate personnel in Philippines.
1 Jun '44	NARWHAL (Lt. Cdr. J. C. Titus)	Landed 16 men and 25 tons of supplies and evacuated 2 men near Pagadian Bay, southwest coast of Mindanao.
5 Jun '44	NAUTILUS (Cdr. G. A. Sharp)	Landed 1 man and 98 tons of cargo at Tucuran, Mindanao, P.I.
8 Jun '44	REDFIN (Lt. Cdr. M. H. Austin)	Landed 6 Filipinos on Ramos Is., P.I.
8 Jun '44	HARDER (Cdr. S. D. Dealey)	Evacuated 6 coast watchers from northeast coast of British North Borneo, aided by Major W. L. Jinkins, AIF.
10 Jun '44	HARDER (Cdr. S. D. Dealey)	Reconnoitered Japanese fleet anchorage at Tawi-Tawi, P.I.
12, 14, 19 Jun '44	BREAM (Cdr. W. G. Chapple)	Special mission in 3 parts in vicinity of Morotai, probably weather reports in connection with Palau landings.
13 Jun '44	NARWHAL (Cdr. F. D. Latta)	Bombarded oil tanks at Bula, Ceram I., N.E.I.
20 Jun '44	NAUTILUS (Cdr. G. A. Sharp)	Landed 4 men and supplies and evacuated 17 people including 5 women and 1 German prisoner from Balatong Pt. Negroes, P.I.
20-21 Jun '44	NARWHAL (Cdr. F. D. Latta)	Landed supplies and evacuated personnel in vicinity of Lipata Pt., Panay, P.I.
21-30 Jun '44	S-47 (Lt. Cdr. L. V. Young)	Special mission in New Guinea area.
4 Jun '44- 7 July '44	SEAWOLF (Lt. Cdr. R. B. Lynch)	Made photographic reconnaissance of Palau area.
29 Jun '44- 13 Aug '44	PERMIT (Lt. Cdr. D. A. Scherer)	Made photographic reconnaissance of Woleai, Yap and Elate in Carolines.
9 July '44	NAUTILUS (Cdr. G. A. Sharp)	Landed 22 men and 12 tons of supplies on Pandan I., on west coast of Mindoro, P.I.

DATE	SUBMARINE	MISSION
14 July '44	NAUTILUS (Cdr. G. A. Sharp)	Landed 4 men and cargo near San Roque, Leyte, P.I. for Col. Kangleon's guerrillas.
16 July '44	NAUTILUS (Cdr. G. A. Sharp)	Received special cargo near Balatong Point off Negros, P.I. Delivered to Col. Abacede.
7 Aug '44	SEAWOLF (Lt. Cdr. A. M. Bontier)	Landed 6 men and 10 tons of supplies at Tongehatan Pt., Tawi-Tawi, P.I.
9 Aug '44	SEAWOLF (Lt. Cdr. A. M. Bontier)	Landed 6 men and 10 tons of supplies at Pirata Head, Palawan, P.I.
11-20 Aug '44	BURRFISH (Cdr. W. B. Perkins)	Made photographic and beach reconnaissance of Angaur Palau, 11-13 Aug., and of Yap, 16-20 Aug. Three men were lost in landing on Gagil Tomil I., Yap, 18 Aug.
18 Aug '44	S-42 (Lt. Cdr. P. E. Glenn)	Landed 3 native contact agents on Halmahera I. Lost two of them.
19 Aug '44	REDFIN (Lt. Cdr. M. H. Austin)	Laid mines vicinity of western coast of Sarawak, Borneo.
27 Aug '44	STINGRAY (Cdr. O. J. Earle)	Landed 15 people and 6 tons of supplies at Mayriaira Pt., northwest coast of Luzon, P.I.
30 Aug '44	NARWHAL (Cdr. J. C. Titus)	Landed 20 men and 10 tons of supplies on east coast of Luzon, P.I.
31 Aug '44	REDFIN (Cdr. M. H. Austin)	Supplied guerrillas with ship's small arm ammunition and evacuated 17 people including 8 survivors of USS FLIER on southwest tip of Palawan I., P.I.
1 Sept '44	NARWHAL (Cdr. F. D. Latta)	Landed 20 men and 10 tons of supplies on east coast of Luzon, P.I.
14 Sept '44	PARGO (Lt. Cdr. D. B. Bell)	Laid mines in Natuna Is. vicinity in South China Sea.
15 Sept '44	STINGRAY (Cdr. S. C. Loomis, Jr.)	Landed air-warning party of 1 officer and 8 men plus stores on Majoe I., Molucca Sea.
22 Sept '44	NARWHAL (Cdr. J. C. Titus)	Landed 45 men and 35 tons of cargo on southwest coast of Mindanao, P.I.
25 Sept '44	NAUTILUS (Cdr. G. A. Sharp)	Landed 65 tons of cargo, 20 drums of gasoline and 2 drums of oil on southeast coast of Cebu, P.I. Grounded and narrowly got off after jettisoning much fuel and ammunition.
27 Sept '44	NARWHAL (Cdr. J. C. Titus)	Landed 3 men and 20 tons of cargo on North coast of Mindanao, P.I.
27 Sept '44	STINGRAY (Cdr. S. C. Loomis, Jr.)	Landed 35 tons of cargo on eastern coast of Luzon, P.I.
29 Sept '44	NARWHAL (Cdr. J. C. Titus)	Evacuated 81 POW survivors and 1 doctor from Sindangan Bay, N.W. Mindanao, P.I. Men were survivors of Jap POW ship SHINYO MARU torpedoed 7 Sept. by PADDLE.
30 Sept '44	NAUTILUS (Cdr. G. A. Sharp)	Landed 40 tons of cargo and evacuated 47 men, women and children near Libertad, Panay, P.I. Diving time took 7 minutes-31 seconds.
30 Sept. '44	STINGRAY (Cdr. S. C. Loomis, Jr.)	Landed 3 Army officers and their supplies on east coast of Samar, P.I.

DATE	SUBMARINE	MISSION
17 Oct '44	NARWHAL (Cdr. F. D. Latta)	Landed 11 tons of cargo on northwest coast of Tawi-Tawi, P.I.
19 Oct '44	NARWHAL (Cdr. F. D. Latta)	Landed 37 men and 60 tons of cargo and evacuated 20 women and children plus 6 prospective mess boys and one steward's mate on southwest coast of Negros I., P.I.
23-24 Oct '44	NAUTILUS (Cdr. G. A. Sharp)	Landed 12 men and 20 tons of cargo on east coast of Luzon, P.I.
25 Oct '44	NAUTILUS (Cdr. G. A. Sharp)	Discharged cargo in Dibut Bay, east coast of Luzon, P.I.
27 Oct '44	NAUTILUS (Cdr. G. A. Sharp)	Landed party of 12 men and 20 tons of cargo on east coast of Luzon, P.I.
31 Oct '44	NAUTILUS (Cdr. G. A. Sharp)	Demolition mission on DARTER on Bombay shoal, S. China Sea. Fired 88 rds. of 6 inch for 55 hits.
1 Nov '44	RAY (Cdr. W. T. Kinsella)	Landed 3 men and 2 tons of cargo and evacuated 2 aviators and 3 escaped POW's from west coast of Mindoro, P.I.
3 Nov '44	CERO (Cdr. E. F. Dissette)	Landed 16 men and 17 tons of cargo and picked up 2 naval officers, 1 Army Private and one 12-year-old boy from Masanga River, east coast of Luzon, P.I.
6 Nov '44	GURNARD (Cdr. N. D. Gage)	Laid mines off Sarawak coast, western Borneo.
10-17 Nov '44	SAURY (Cdr. R. A. Waugh)	Anti-picket boat sweep north of Bonin Is.
10-17 Nov '44	TAMBOR (Cdr. W. J. Germershausen)	Anti-picket boat sweep NW to NE of Bonins.
10-17 Nov '44	SILVERSIDES (Cdr. J. S. Coye, Jr.)	Anti-picket boat sweep NW to NE of Bonins.
10-17 Nov '44	RONQUIL (Cdr. H. S. Monroe)	Anti-picket boat sweep NW to NE of Bonins.
10-17 Nov '44	TRIGGER (Cdr. F. J. Harlfinger II)	Anti-picket boat sweep NW to NE of Bonins.
10-17 Nov '44	BURRFISH (Cdr. W. B. Perkins)	Anti-picket boat sweep NW to NE of Bonins.
10-17 Nov '44	STERLET (Cdr. O. C. Robbins)	Anti-picket boat sweep NW to NE of Bonins.
18 Nov '44	BLACKFIN (Cdr. G. H. Laird, Jr.)	Picked up intelligence documents from northern coast of Mindoro, P.I.
20 Nov '44	GAR (Lt. Cdr. M. Ferrara)	Landed 5 tons of supplies on north coast of Mindoro, P.I.
23 Nov '44	GAR (Lt. Cdr. M. Ferrara)	Landed 16 men and 25 tons of supplies on west coast of Luzon, P.I. at Santiago Cove, Luzon, P.I. Picked up documents.
28 Nov '44- 2 Dec '44	SPEARFISH (Cdr. C. C. Cole)	Made photographic reconnaissance of Iwo Jima and Minami Jima. Took pictures of PPI scope showing islands.
2 Dec '44	GUNNEL (Cdr. G. E. O'Neill, Jr.)	Evacuated 11 Allied aviators from Palawan. Supplied guerrillas with arms, ammunition, food and medical supplies.

DATE	SUBMARINE	MISSION
5 Dec '44	HAKE (Lt. Cdr. F. E. Hayler)	Landed available supplies, arms and ammunition and evacuated 19 persons including aviators from Libertad, Panay, P.I.
11 Dec '44	GAR (Cdr. M. Ferrara)	Landed 35 tons of supplies on west coast of Luzon, P.I., near Durigaos Inlet. Picked up 1 naval officer and documents.
16 Dec '44	DACE (Lt. Cdr. O. R. Cole, Jr.)	Laid mines off French Indo-China coast, just west of Pulo Gambir.
12-18 Dec '44	MINGO (Lt. Cdr. J. R. Madison)	Reconnoitered Fiery Cross shoal and Camranh Bay in South China Sea.
15-20 Dec '44	ANGLER (Lt. Cdr. H. Bissell, Jr.)	Escorted damaged BERGALL from South China Sea to Exmouth Gulf, Australia, carrying 55 of her men while so doing.
3-30 Dec '44	BAYA (Cdr. A. H. Holtz)	Reconnoitered for enemy fleet in connection with invasion of the Philippines.
29 Dec '44- 1 Jan '45	HOE (Lt. Cdr. M. P. Refo, III)	Reconnoitered Tizard's Bank in South China Sea and bombarded installations there.
22 Dec '44- 9 Jan '45	TINOSA (Cdr. R. C. Latham)	Special task (probably mine detection) in empire area.
12 Dec '44- 8 Jan '45	COBIA (Cdr. A. L. Becker)	Performed reconnaissance duty off Balabac Strait and in area south of Dangerous Ground.
1 Jan '45	STINGRAY (Cdr. H. F. Stoner)	Landed 27 tons of cargo at Tongehatan Pt., Tawi-Tawi, P.I.
7 Jan '45	BREAM (Cdr. J. L. McCallum)	Reconnoitered Tizard's Bank.
20 Jan '45	NAUTILUS (Lt. Cdr. W. Michael)	Delivered 45 tons of supplies to south coast of Mindanao, P.I. Evacuated 1 Army officer.
23 Jan '45	NAUTILUS (Lt. Cdr. W. Michael)	Delivered 45 tons of supplies to east coast of Mindanao, P.I.
28 Jan '45	TUNA (Cdr. E. F. Steffanides, Jr.)	Reconnoitered NE coast of Borneo. No landing attempted because of enemy activity.
21-26 Jan '45	SENNET (Cdr. G. E. Porter)	Conducted special mission in Bonins area, probably minefield location.
Jan '45	SWORDFISH (Cdr. K. E. Montross)	Lost during reconnaissance of Okinawa.
4-6 Feb '45	PARGO (Lt. Cdr. D. B. Bell)	Reconnoitered, landed and retrieved commando party and bombarded Woody I. in Paracels, South China Sea.
7-8 Feb '45	STINGRAY (Cdr. H. F. Stoner)	Landed 2 coast watchers and equipment on Sekala I., N.E.I.
10-13 Feb '45	STERLET (Cdr. H. H. Lewis)	Anti-picket boat sweep SE of Honshu.
11-14 Feb '45	HADDOCK (Cdr. W. H. Brockman, Jr.)	Anti-picket boat sweep west of Bonins.
11-14 Feb '45	LAGARTO (Cdr. F. D. Latta)	Anti-picket boat sweep west of Bonins.
11-14 Feb '45	SENNET (Cdr. G. E. Porter)	Anti-picket boat sweep south of Honshu.

DATE	SUBMARINE	MISSION
10-13 Feb '45	PIPER (Cdr. B. F. McMahon)	Anti-picket boat sweep southeast of Honshu.
10-13 Feb '45	TREPANG (Cdr. A. R. Faust)	Anti-picket boat sweep southeast of Honshu.
13-21 Feb '45	BURRFISH (Lt. Cdr. M. H. Lytle)	Made weather reports.
11-13 Feb '45	POMFRET (Cdr. J. B. Hess)	Anti-picket boat sweep southeast of Honshu.
3-4 Mar '45	TUNA (Cdr. E. F. Steffanides, Jr.)	Landed 7 AIB personnel and 4400 pounds of stores on northeast coast of Borneo near Labuk Bay.
8 Mar '45	BASHAW (Cdr. H. S. Simpson)	Unsuccessful attempt to locate and pick up men from sailboat off Cape Varella, French Indo-China.
12-13 Mar '45	PIPER (Cdr. B. F. McMahon)	Anti-picket boat sweep south of Honshu.
12-13 Mar '45	BERGALL (Cdr. J. M. Hyde)	Performed special mission in vicinity of Cape Varella, French Indo-China.
12-17 Mar '45	TREPANG (Cdr. A. R. Faust)	Anti-picket boat sweep south of Honshu.
14 Mar '45	BREAM (Cdr. J. L. P. McCallum)	Landed 2 operators on island in Java Sea. Both captured by Japs.
14-16 Mar '45	ROCK (Cdr. R. A. Keating, Jr.)	Landed 4 AIB operators and 3000 lbs. of stores on SW shore of Lombok I., N.E.I.
20-22 Mar '45	PERCH (2) (Cdr. B. C. Hills)	Landed party of 12 men on east coast of Borneo in vicinity of Mahakam River Delta.
25 Mar '45	BRILL (Cdr. H. B. Dodge)	Landed party of two who picked up 5 natives from south shore of Sekala I., Java Sea.
12 Mar '45- 18 Apr '45	BLUEGILL (Cdr. E. L. Barr, Jr.)	Accomplished one special mission to SoWesPac Area. Another one was not completed.
13-15 Mar '45	TUNNY (Cdr. G. E. Pierce)	Special mission, probably mine location in Tsushima Straits.
26 Mar '45	SPADEFISH (Cdr. W. G. Germershausen)	Special mission in Tsushima Straits, probably mine location.
25-28 Mar '45	TINOSA (Cdr. R. C. Latham)	Conducted special mission in vicinity of 28-29N, 127-05E, probably mine detection.
29 Mar '45- 1 Apr '45	SEAHORSE (Cdr. H. H. Greer, Jr.)	Conducted special mission in vicinity of Tsushima Straits, probably mine location.
25 Jan '45- 4 Apr '45	STERLET (Cdr. H. H. Lewis)	Anti-picket boat sweep (12-17 Mar.) and reconnaissance for Jap Fleet.
2 Apr '45	HARDHEAD (Cdr. F. A. Greenup)	Laid mines off Cape Kamao, Cochin China.
9-10 Apr '45	BOARFISH (Cdr. R. L. Gross)	Landed and retrieved 2 AIF men at Tamquan Bay, French Indo-China for reconnaissance.
12-13 Apr '45	BERGALL (Cdr. J. M. Hyde)	Accomplished special mission in N.E.I. Area.

DATE	SUBMARINE	MISSION
15 Apr '45	CHARR (Cdr. F. D. Boyle)	Laid minefield off Malay Peninsula.
15-16 Apr '45	BOARFISH (Cdr. R. L. Gross)	Landed and retrieved 2 AIF commandos near Tourane Bay, French Indo-China for reconnaissance and sabotage. Mined railroad curve and derailed and/or damaged train.
18 Apr '45	ROCK (Cdr. R. A. Keating, Jr.)	Bombarded Batan I. radio station.
18 Apr '45	TIGRONE (Cdr. H. Cassedy)	Bombarded Batan I. radio station.
20 Apr '45	GUITARRO (Cdr. T. B. Dabney)	Laid mines near Berhala I., off northeast coast of Sumatra.
21-22 Apr '45	BONEFISH (Cdr. L. L. Edge)	Conducted special mission in Tsushima or NE of East China Sea, mine detection.
21-25 Apr '45	CREVALLE (Cdr. E. H. Steinmetz)	Conducted probably minefield location search in vicinity of south entrance to Tsushima Straits.
23 Apr '45- 15 May '45	BOWFIN (Cdr. A. K. Tyree)	Special mission in Empire Area.
8 May '45	BREAM (Cdr. J. L. McCallum)	Laid minefield off French Indo-China Coast.
12-22 May '45	PETO (Cdr. R. H. Caldwell, Jr.)	Reconnoitered Marcus.
14 May '45	TINOSA (Cdr. R. C. Latham)	Bombarded Ulul Is.
20 May '45	CHUBB (Cdr. C. D. Rhymes, Jr.)	Accomplished special mission in the vicinity of the north coast of Java.
28 May '45	BLUEBACK (Cdr. M. K. Clementson)	Landed AIB operator near Piring Pt., on north coast of Java.
28-29 May '45	BLUEGILL (Cdr. E. L. Barr, Jr.)	Bombarded, reconnoitered, landed on, and occupied Pratas Is., South China Sea.
23 May '45- 1 June '45	PIRANHA (Cdr. D. G. Irvine)	Reconnoitered and bombarded Marcus I.
16 Jun '45	DEVILFISH (Lt. Cdr. S. S. Mann)	Lifeguarding.
23-29 Jun '45	REDFIN (Lt. Cdr. C. K. Miller)	Special mission off Honshu and Hokkaido, minefield search.
29 Jun '45	BLUEBACK (Cdr. M. K. Clementson)	Landed 2 agents near Tanjong Pelabuhan on north coast of Java.
2 Jul '45	BLUEBACK (Cdr. M. K. Clementson)	Landed 2 agents in Semanka Bay, SW Sumatra.
4-16 Jul '45	RUNNER (2) (Cdr. R. H. Bass)	Minefield location on east coast of Honshu between 36-20 and 37-00N, and 39-11 and 39-20N.
27 Jul '45	COBIA (Cdr. A. L. Becker)	Landed 4 AIB operators at Chewar, Java, N.E.I.

DATE	SUBMARINE	MISSION
2-6 Jul '45	REDFIN (Lt. Cdr. C. K. Miller)	Special mission, south coast of Honshu, minefield location.
3 Aug '45	CAIMAN (Cdr. W. L. Fey, Jr.)	Conducted evacuation of agents near Kendari, Celebes.
9 Aug '45	CAIMAN (Cdr. W. L. Fey, Jr.)	Accomplished mission in vicinity of Sekala I., Java Sea.
9-11 Aug '45	HAWKBILL (Cdr. F. W. Scandland, Jr.)	Destroyed radio station on Tambelan and Jemaja I. by gunfire. Landed commandos at Terampha Town and destroyed stores and installations. Reconnoitered Anambas I. in South China Sea.
11-15 Aug '45	REDFIN (Lt. Cdr. C. K. Miller)	Minefield location search southwest coast of Kyushu.
14-15 Aug '45	CATFISH (Cdr. W. A. Overton)	Minefield location search on east coast of Kyushu.

STATISTICAL SUMMARY

ATTRITION WAR AGAINST JAPANESE MERCHANT MARINE

(From "The War Against Japanese Transportation," published by the United States Strategic Bombing Survey)

Submarine Operations Against Merchant Shipping

	Days of offensive patrol in operating areas	Merchant ships attacked	Torpedoes expended
1941			
December	281	31	66
Subtotal	281	31	66
1942			
January	322	33	78
February	363	36	88
March	363	27	81
April	396	33	82
May	396	63	160
June	446	29	71
July	437	37	93
August	462	59	168
September	454	41	115
October	504	84	242
November	512	42	105
December	512	55	159
Subtotal (13 mos.)	5,167	539	1,442
1943			
January	577	103	283
February	405	55	193
March	442	74	299
April	448	64	263
May	437	62	237
June	659	102	389
July	532	75	297
August	858	105	387
September	697	112	461
October	648	118	423
November	572	106	454
December	407	73	251
Subtotal	6,682	1,049	3,937
1944			
January	824	114	460
February	593	106	383
March	689	96	370
April	775	81	292
May	1,063	137	493
June	824	108	362
July	1,275	168	635
August	1,056	173	581
September	850	127	436
October	1,306	230	799
November	1,317	193	775
December	1,128	115	506
Subtotal	11,700	1,648	6,092
1945			
January	1,066	124	421
February	1,093	93	373
March	1,217	96	367
April	1,045	113	433
May	1,014	89	386
June	1,067	147	522
July	901	124	488
August	338	59	221
Subtotal	7,741	845	3,211
Total	31,571	4,112	14,748

Decline of Japanese Merchant Marine

Month		Merchantmen (minus tankers)	Tankers
		Tonnage afloat first of month	
1941	December	5,421,143	575,464
1942	January	5,464,992	587,245
	February	5,503,083	598,023
	March	5,540,051	606,037
	April	5,544,877	604,985
	May	5,591,077	607,329
	June	5,544,248	606,425
	July	5,569,169	611,883
	August	5,547,609	624,864
	September	5,507,167	631,280
	October	5,524,025	648,368
	November	5,390,402	662,356
	December	5,252,201	662,356
1943	January	5,219,547	686,498
	February	5,087,659	727,935
	March	4,990,454	780,944
	April	4,944,600	788,162
	May	4,862,046	768,197
	June	4,763,634	772,670*
	July	4,702,449	785,151
	August	4,648,216	817,022
	September	4,598,417	832,387
	October	4,475,490	844,706
	November	4,392,732	870,205
	December	4,170,825	863,953
1944	January	4,074,745	873,070
	February	3,884,120	839,576
	March	3,560,295	760,507
	April	3,558,407	793,833
	May	3,509,605	798,822
	June	3,353,961	835,358
	July	3,204,385	837,326
	August	3,049,965	852,735
	September	2,874,564	835,882
	October	2,601,675	872,333
	November	2,256,873	838,947
	December	1,978,572	868,962
1945	January	1,925,436	860,971
	February	1,789,097	679,984
	March	1,908,236	618,748
	April	1,902,734	562,136
	May	1,924,799	460,077
	June	1,857,926	377,840
	July	1,733,627	324,782
	August	1,587,236	275,525
	August 15	1,547,418	266,948

* Oil tankers placed fourth on target priority list at this date.

Japanese Merchant Shipbuilding Effort

Year	Losses (All causes)	Construction	Percent of losses
	Tons	*Tons*	
1942	952,965	260,059	27
1943	1,803,409	769,085	43
1st half 1944	1,776,248	877,372	49
3d quarter 1944	959,900	393,721	41
4th quarter 1944	1,098,229	428,110	39
1st quarter 1945	805,332	380,520	47
2d quarter 1945	802,346	122,642	15

The Decline in Japanese Imports of Bulk Commodities

	1940, metric tons	1941, metric tons	1942, metric tons	1943, metric tons	1944, metric tons	1945, metric tons
Coal	7,011,000	6,459,000	6,388,000	5,181,000	2,635,000	548,000
Iron ore	6,073,000	6,309,000	4,700,000	4,298,000	2,153,000	341,000
Bauxite	275,000	150,000	305,000	909,000	376,000	15,500
Iron and steel	621,000	921,000	993,000	997,000	1,097,000	170,000
Scrap iron	2,104,000	246,000	50,000	43,000	21,000	12,000
Lead	100,100	86,530	10,990	24,500	16,810	4,000
Tin	10,500	5,500	3,800	26,800	23,500	3,600
Zinc	23,500	7,900	8,500	10,100	6,100	2,500
Phosphorite and phosphate	710,400	396,500	342,100	236,700	89,600	23,000
Dolomite and magnesite	409,600	506,300	468,700	437,500	287,100	65,900
Salt	1,728,300	1,438,900	1,499,800	1,425,100	989,700	386,900
Soybean cake	333,900	337,700	449,500	304,500	384,700	163,400
Soybeans	648,500	572,400	698,800	590,600	728,800	606,900
Rice and paddy	1,694,000	2,232,700	2,629,200	1,135,800	783,200	151,200
Other grains and flours	269,300	267,400	823,300	750,100	506,600	231,400
Raw rubber	27,500	67,600	31,400	42,100	31,500	17,900
	22,039,600	20,004,430	19,402,090	16,411,880	10,129,610	2,743,200

Japanese Merchant Marine Ship Losses
(Ships over 500 gross tons)

Year and Month	Army Air[2] No. of ships	Army Air GRT	Navy Land-based Air No. of ships	Navy Land-based Air GRT	Carrier Air[3] No. of ships	Carrier Air GRT	Submarines[4] No. of ships	Submarines GRT	Mines No. of ships	Mines GRT	Surface Gunfire No. of ships	Surface Gunfire GRT	Marine Casualties No. of ships	Marine Casualties GRT	Unknown No. of ships	Unknown GRT	Total No. of ships	Total GRT
1941–1942																		
December	3	16,901					6	31,693			4	22,751	3	7,466			12	56,060
January	1	6,757					7	28,351	1	1,548	3	10,485	4	14,388			17	73,795
February							5	15,975			1	7,170			1	6,788	9	33,248
March	1	4,109			3	21,610	7	26,183	2	14,618			1	4,469			15	78,159
April	2	9,798					5	26,886	2	10,546							7	36,684
May							20	86,110									22	96,656
June	2	12,358					6	20,021			½	4,286	1	3,111			8	32,379
July	2½	20,775	1	9,309			8	39,356					1	5,950			12	67,528
August	½	420					17½	76,652									20	92,331
September	1	7,190					11	39,389			1	3,311	2	11,187			12	46,579
October	5	5,863	3	25,546			25	118,920			1	10,438	2	11,079			32	164,827
November	3	24,510	11	77,607			8	35,358					2	13,377			27	158,992
December		9,859	1	548			14	48,271					3				21	71,787
1943																		
January	9	41,269	2	10,568			18	80,572					2	5,732	1	179	28	122,590
February	3½	19,478					10½	54,276			1	3,121	2	3,187			19	93,175
March	10	37,939					26	109,447							1	1,916	38	150,573
April	7	24,521	1	1,917			19	105,345					2	5,144			27	131,782
May	3	2,060					29	122,319					2	6,581			35	131,440
June	1	953					25	101,581					2	3,298			28	90,507
July	3	4,425					20	82,784					3	7,730			25	98,828
August	1	4,468					19	80,799					4	22,812	1	5,831	23	197,906
September	5	15,429					38	157,002	1	2,663			1	10,718			47	145,594
October	7	15,253					27	119,623					4	4,370			38	314,790
November	20½	70,458	1	5,824	6	26,017	44½	231,683	1	2,455			1		1	544	68	207,129
December	13	36,266	5	14,397			32	121,531					4	8,374			61	
1944																		
January	12	22,823	15	55,184	4	6,738	50	240,840	1	2,428	1	3,535	3	7,214	1	889	87	339,651
February	16	40,983	4	8,207	29	186,725	54	256,797	1	5,307			9	17,584	2	3,956	115	519,559
March	5	13,224	1	2,655	20	86,812	26	106,529			1	2,722	9	16,546			61	225,766
April	8	21,042	1	2,230	2	1,775	23	95,242					1	1,891	1	3,022	37	129,846
May	3½	9,626			1	992	63½	264,713			2	8,742	5		1	557	69	277,222
June	5	7,753	1	966	15	65,146	48	195,020	1	2,284			4	9,110			75	285,204
July	5	7,865			5	9,486	48	212,907	1	1,018			3	4,546			63	241,652
August	6	13,610	1	6,659	5	22,918	49	245,348	7	13,411			3	4,772			65	294,099
September	3	3,258	5	8,095	55	213,250	47	181,363	5	5,964			6	11,519	1	1,428	121	424,149
October	9	23,627	4	12,256	40½	131,308	68½	328,843	2	2,350			6				134	514,945
November	11	37,350	2	8,627	26	120,373	53½	220,476					9	2,232			97	391,408
December	13	54,996	3	4,158	2	8,217	18	103,836					9	20,669			45	191,876
1945																		
January	7½ (1)	20,620 (2,830)	1	549	83½ (3)	283,234 (23,185)	22	93,796	6	17,322	1	584	3 (1)	8,857 (873)	1	543	125 (5)	425,505 (26,888)
February	3	8,593	2	1,677	2	1,384	15	55,746	3 (4)	13,166 (16,293)			4 (2)	6,898 (4,412)			29 (7)	87,464 (31,310)
March	13 (1)	30,931 (10,605)	10½	14,373	15 (3)	27,563 (22,874)	23½	70,727	7	21,402			3 (3)	19,987 (3,711)	1	1,135	73 (12)	186,118 (48,067)
April	14 (6)	18,174 (21,482)	1 (2)	875 (1,725)			18	60,696	16 (9)	20,145 (21,396)			2 (6)	1,812 (5,611)			51 (17)	101,702 (28,732)
May	2 (2)	2,358 (1,760)	29 (5)	57,041 (10,438)			17	32,394	66 (31)	109,991 (106,302)			2 (5)	9,752 (6,426)			116 (43)	211,536 (124,836)
June	2 (2)	11,470 (23,839)	12 (4)	16,163 (4,864)			43	92,267	45 (38)	69,009 (94,176)			4 (4)	3,871 (6,511)	2	3,400	108 (54)	196,180 (129,390)
July	9 (8)	11,802 (23,709)	11 (2)	16,372 (1,743)	43 (23)	113,831 (63,450)	12 (1)	27,408 (803)	34 (44)	63,323 (134,372)			1 (9)	2,220 (10,126)	1	874	111 (89)	235,830 (243,014)
August	10 (14)	22,884 (50,757)	2 (1)	1,715 (880)	2 (5)	1,805 (14,442)	4 (1)	14,559 (880)	8 (21)	18,462 (48,186)	(2)	(8,811)	(4)	(6,664)	(2)	(1,756)	26 (48)	59,425 (123,565)
Total	260 (40)	774,680 (134,892)	130½ (14)	363,518 (19,650)	359½ (34)	1,329,184 (123,951)	1,150½ (2)	4,859,634	210 (147)	397,412 (420,725)	16½ (2)	77,145 (8,811)	116 (34)	308,386 (44,334)	16 (2)	31,632 (1,756)	2,259 (275)	8,141,591 (755,802)
Grand total disabled	300	909,572	144½	383,168	393½	1,453,135	1,152½		356	818,137	18½	85,956	150	352,720	18	33,388	2,534	8,897,393

[1] Figures in parentheses are ships damaged and put out of action for the duration (not included in sinkings).
[2] At least 12 percent of Army air sinkings listed were by Allied planes (Australian, British, Russian, etc.).
[3] At least 23 percent of carrier air sinkings in July 1945 were by British carrier planes.
[4] About 2 percent of submarine sinkings were known to have been the work of British and Dutch subs.
"Half" ships listed above are cases where credit is divided between two attacking agents; tonnage is divided equally.

LEADING INDIVIDUAL
SUBMARINE SCORES
(TOP 25)

NUMBER OF SHIPS SUNK		TONNAGE SUNK	
Submarine	*Ships*	*Submarine*	*Tonnage*
TAUTOG	26	FLASHER	100,231
TANG	24	RASHER	99,901
SILVERSIDES	23	BARB	96,628
FLASHER	21	TANG	93,824
SPADEFISH	21	SILVERSIDES	90,080
SEAHORSE	20	SPADEFISH	88,091
WAHOO	20	TRIGGER	86,552
GUARDFISH	19	DRUM	80,580
RASHER	18	JACK	76,687
SEAWOLF	18	SNOOK	75,473
TRIGGER	18	TAUTOG	72,606
BARB	17	SEAHORSE	72,529
SNOOK	17	GUARDFISH	72,424
THRESHER	17	SEAWOLF	71,609
BOWFIN	16	GUDGEON	71,047
HARDER	16	SEALION II	68,297
POGY	16	BOWFIN	67,882
SUNFISH	16	THRESHER	66,172
TINOSA	16	TINOSA	64,655
DRUM	15	GRAYBACK	63,835
FLYINGFISH	15	POGY	62,633
GREENLING	15	BONEFISH	61,345
JACK	15	WAHOO	60,038
GRAYBACK	14	SUNFISH	59,815
KINGFISH	14	ARCHERFISH	59,800

☆

CLAIM DISCREPANCIES AND
VESSELS DAMAGED

During the war it was frequently impossible to identify a submarine's target. Recognition of the target ship's class was sometimes faulty, and circumstances often prevented on-the-spot verification of a sinking. As has been pointed out in the foregoing chapters, many actions were fought at night or in weather conditions which blurred visibility. Silhouettes sighted at long range by binoculars or periscope could be deceptive. The defective torpedo employed in the first 21 months of the war created many illusory hits, or merely damaged vessels with hits which should have sunk them. Submarine Headquarters demanded "eyesight evidence" and refused to credit claims which were unsupported by proofs (viz., periscope photographs, testimony of survivors, recovered flotsam, intelligence reports or witnessed sinkings). Nevertheless, some sinkings credited to submarines during the war were found to be in error at war's end, and a number of unobserved

sinkings and "probables" were eventually credited to submarines. These post-war revisions were rare—remarkably so, considering the difficulties of identification during action, the hundreds of attacks made by submarines, and the hundreds of targets struck. A check with the Japanese "books" showed that American submariners had been most conservative in their sinking claims and, when it came to "recognition," in the great majority of instances they had hit the nail, as well as the target, on the head.

One type of vessel peculiarly difficult to identify was that known as the AKITSU class. Built to serve as an escort carrier with a full flight deck, the ship had the silhouette of a CVE. But it was used by the Japanese as a landing craft or aircraft transport, and as such was classed by them as a merchantman. In November 1944 CREVALLE torpedoed this specimen one stormy night off Luzon, and reported the sinking of an escort carrier. As no Japanese CVE or vessel of like description was recorded by the Imperial Navy as sunk at that date in that position, it is believed CREVALLE's target, an aircraft transport, escaped with serious damage. Four months later, SUNFISH torpedoed a similar vessel off Saipan. Explosions and flying debris were witnessed by the submariners, but a post-war search of the records failed to disclose a CVE down at that place and time. SUNFISH's victim was finally identified as a large freighter. On November 15, 1944, QUEENFISH downed the original AKITSU MARU in the East China Sea a few miles south of Tsushima Strait, reporting the sinking of an escort carrier. The target was not identified until after the war.

TILEFISH claimed the sinking of a heavy cruiser off the south coast of Honshu on December 22, 1944. The submarine had been troubled by a fogging periscope, and this target was later identified as a CHIDORI tor-pedo boat. The warship IOSHIMA, identified by SHAD as a CL, was classed by the Japanese as a frigate. In November 1943, GUDGEON torpedoed a coast defense vessel which she identified as a light cruiser.

But the Japanese records were found to be incomplete and in numerous cases unreliable. Therefore, mysteries remain. The "cruisers" struck by SEAWOLF off Christmas Island early in the war—a light cruiser struck by SALMON off Indo-China in May 1942—a large warship struck by S-47 in St. George's Channel on the night of September 12, 1942—these torpedoings were not to be found in Imperial Navy records. And several dozen merchantmen claimed as sunk could not be located in Japanese files. In some instances photographed "sinkings" could not be verified, and witnessed explosions which must have blown the target to blazes remained unexplained. The Japanese may have salvaged and repaired some of these torpedoed vessels. The verification of salvage and repair proved so difficult and damages so hard to estimate that, with the exception of a few cases, these features have not been included in this text. It goes without saying that scores of merchantmen were damaged, some to the point of permanent disablement, and thousands of tons of cargo were thereby ruined. Finally, hundreds of small craft (vessels under 500 tons) were swept away by American submarines. These are not included in the following lists (nor are the Axis vessels sunk off Morocco and in the Bay of Biscay by U.S. submarines in the Atlantic). The listed Japanese merchant and naval losses do not score the entire submarine effort. Carefully compiled by the Joint Army-Navy Assessment Committee, the listings stand as the official score for the Pacific War, however, and upon this authoritative assessment the submarine accomplishments recounted in the present volume have been based.

JAPANESE NAVAL AND MERCHANT VESSELS

SUNK DURING WORLD WAR II

BY UNITED STATES SUBMARINES

(Compiled by Joint Army-Navy Assessment Committee)

SUBMARINE AND DATE	NAME OF VESSEL	TYPE OF VESSEL	TONNAGE	LOCATION	SUBMARINE CAPTAIN
USS ALBACORE					
Dec 18 1942	Tenryu	Light Cruiser	3,300	5-11S, 145-57E	
Feb 20 1943	Oshio	Destroyer	1,850	0-50S, 146-06E	R. C. Lake
Feb 20 1943	Unknown	Frigate	750ᵉ	0-50S, 146-06E	
Sep 4 1943	Heijo Maru	Ex-Gunboat	2,627	5-32N, 156-23E	O. E. Hagberg
Nov 25 1943	Kenzan Maru	Cargo	4,705	0-51N, 145-56E	
Jan 12 1944	Choko Maru	Ex-Gunboat	2,629	3-30N, 147-27E	
Jan 14 1944	Sazanami	Destroyer	1,950	5-15N, 141-15E	
Jun 19 1944	Taiho	Aircraft Carrier	31,000	12-22N, 137-04E	J. W. Blanchard
Sep 5 1944	Shingetsu Maru	Cargo	880	32-24N, 134-15E	
Sep 11 1944	Submarine Chaser No 165	Submarine Chaser	170	32-20N, 131-50E	
		10 Vessels	49,861		
USS AMBERJACK					
Sep 19 1942	Shirogane Maru	Passenger-Cargo	3,130	6-33S, 156-05E	J. A. Bole
Oct 7 1942	Senkai Maru	Passenger-Cargo	2,095	1-55N, 153-42E	
		2 Vessels	5,225		
USS ANGLER					
Jan 29 1944	Shuko Maru	Ex-Net Tender	889	23-07N, 142-27E	R. I. Olsen
May 20 1944	Otori Maru	Cargo	2,105	5-40S, 105-27E	
Oct 14 1944	Nanrei Maru	Transport	2,407	11-53N, 121-39E	F. G. Hess
		3 Vessels	5,401		
USS APOGON					
Dec 4 1943	Daido Maru	Ex-Gunboat	2,962	8-15N, 159-06E	W. P. Schoeni
Sept 27 1944	Hachirogata Maru	Cargo	1,999	46-32N, 146-48E	A. C. House
Jun 18 1945	Hakuai Maru	Transport	2,614	50-30N, 155-01E	
		3 Vessels	7,575		
USS ARCHERFISH					
Jun 28 1944	Coast Def Vessel No 24	Frigate	800ᵉ	24-44N, 140-20E	W. H. Wright
Nov 29 1944	Shinano	Aircraft Carrier	59,000	32-00N, 137-00E	J. F. Enright
		2 Vessels	59,800		
USS ASPRO					
Feb 15 1944	I-43	Submarine	2,212	12-42N, 149-17E	H. C. Stevenson
May 15 1944	Jokuja Maru	Cargo	6,440	10-10N, 131-25E	
Jul 28 1944	Peking Maru	Transport	2,288	17-33N, 120-21E	W. A. Stevenson
Oct 2 1944	Azuchisan Maru	Cargo	6,888	18-25N, 120-32E	
Oct 7 1944	Macassar Maru	Passenger-Cargo	4,026	17-54N, 119-57E	
		5 Vessels	21,854		

ᵉ Estimated tonnage.

527

SUBMARINE AND DATE	NAME OF VESSEL	TYPE OF VESSEL	TONNAGE	LOCATION	SUBMARINE CAPTAIN
USS Atule					
Nov 1 1944	Asama Maru	Transport	16,975	20-09N, 117-38E	
Nov 20 1944	Minesweeper No 38	Minesweeper	630e	21-21N, 119-45E	
Nov 25 1944	Patrol Boat No 38	Old Destroyer	820e	20-12N, 121-51E	
Nov 25 1944	Santos Maru	Cargo	7,266	20-12N, 121-51E	J. H. Maurer
Jan 24 1945	Taiman Maru No 1	Cargo	6,888	36-47N, 123-59E	
Aug 13 1945	Coast Def Vessel No 6	Frigate	800e	42-11N, 142-14E	
	6 Vessels		33,379		
USS Balao					
Feb 23 1944	Nikki Maru	Passenger-Cargo	5,857	7S, 135-42E	C. C. Cole
Feb 28 1944	Shoho Maru	Cargo	2,723	6N, 132-53E	
Feb 28 1944	Akiura Maru	Passenger-Cargo	6,803	00-06N, 132-53E	
Jan 8 1945	Daigo Maru	Cargo	5,244	34-28N, 122-39E	M. Ramirezdear-elland
Mar 19 1945	Hakozaki Maru	Transport	10,413	33-09N, 122-08E	R. K. Worthington
Mar 26 1945	Shinto Maru No 1	Cargo	880e	35-14N, 123-44E	
	6 Vessels		31,920		
USS Bang					
Apr 29 1944	Takegawa Maru	Cargo	1,930	19-26N, 118-45E	
Apr 30 1944	Nittatsu Maru	Cargo	2,859	19-11N, 119-10E	
May 4 1944	Kinrei Maru	Cargo	5,947	20-58N, 117-59E	
Sep 9 1944	Tokiwasan Maru	Cargo	1,804	28-53N, 137-42E	A. R. Gallaher
Sep 9 1944	Shoryu Maru	Cargo	1,916	28-53N, 137-42E	
Sep 19 1944	Tosei Maru No 2	Tanker	507	24-56N, 122-14E	
Nov 23 1944	Sakae Maru	Cargo	2,878	24-12N, 122-53E	
Nov 23 1944	Amakusa Maru	Passenger-Cargo	2,340	24-24N, 122-45E	
	8 Vessels		20,181		
USS Barb					
Mar 28 1944	Fukusei Maru	Cargo	2,219	24-25N, 131-11E	J. R. Waterman
May 31 1944	Koto Maru	Cargo	1,053	47-52N, 151-02E	
May 31 1944	Madras Maru	Passenger-Cargo	3,802	48-21N, 151-19E	
Jun 11 1944	Toten Maru	Cargo	3,823	46-58N, 143-50E	
Jun 11 1944	Chihaya Maru	Cargo	1,161	46-58N, 143-50E	
Jun 13 1944	Takashima Maru	Passenger-Cargo	5,633	50-47N, 151-20E	
Aug 31 1944	Okuni Maru	Cargo	5,633	21-14N, 121-22E	
Sep 16 1944	Azusa	Tanker	11,177	19-18N, 116-26E	
Sep 16 1944	Unyo	Escort Aircraft Carrier	20,000	19-18N, 116-26E	E. B. Fluckey
Nov 10 1944	Gokoku Maru	Ex-Light Cruiser	10,438	33-23N, 129-03E	
Nov 12 1944	Naruo Maru	Cargo	4,823	31-29N, 125-19E	
Jan 8 1945	Shinyo Maru	Cargo	5,892	24-31N, 120-28E	
Jan 8 1945	Anyo Maru	Passenger-Cargo	9,256	24-54N, 120-26E	
Jan 8 1945	Sanyo Maru	Tanker	2,854	24-54N, 120-26E	
Jan 23 1945	Taikyo Maru	Cargo	5,244	27-04N, 120-27E	
Jul 5 1945	Sapporo Maru No 11	Cargo	2,820	40-03N, 142-16E	
Jul 18 1945	Coast Def Vessel No 112	Frigate	800e	46-04N, 142-14E	
	17 Vessels		96,628		

SUBMARINE AND DATE	NAME OF VESSEL	TYPE OF VESSEL	TONNAGE	LOCATION	SUBMARINE CAPTAIN
USS Barbel					
Aug 5 1944	Miyako Maru	Passenger-Cargo	970	27-36N, 128-54E	
Aug 9 1944	Yagi Maru	Cargo	1,937	27-52N, 128-49E	
Aug 9 1944	Boko Maru	Cargo	2,333	27-52N, 128-49E	
Sep 25 1944	Bushu Maru	Cargo	1,222	29-50N, 130-06E	R. A. Keating
Nov 14 1944	Sugiyama Maru	Cargo	4,379	15-14N, 112-13E	
Nov 14 1944	Misaki Maru	Cargo	4,422	15-14N, 112-13E	
	6 Vessels		15,263		
USS Barbero					
Nov 2 1944	Kuramasan Maru	Cargo	1,995	4-30S, 118-20E	
Nov 8 1944	Shimotsu Maru	Tanker	2,854	14-01N, 117-17E	I. S. Hartman
Dec 25 1944	Junpo Maru	Cargo	4,277	1-10N, 108-20E	
	3 Vessels		9,126		
USS Bashaw					
Jun 25 1944	Yamamiya Maru	Cargo	6,440	3-36N, 127-14E	R. E. Nichols
Sep 8 1944	Yanagigawa Maru	Cargo	2,813	8-14N, 121-47E	
Mar 5 1945	Ryoei Maru	Tanker	10,016	16-46N, 108-41E	H. S. Simpson
	3 Vessels		19,269		
USS Batfish					
Jan 20 1944	Hidaka Maru	Cargo	5,486	31-28N, 134-52E	W. R. Merrill
Jun 22 1944	Nagaragwa Maru	Passenger-Cargo	990	34-35N, 137-56E	
Aug 23 1944	Minesweeper No 22	Minesweeper	492	8-09N, 134-38E	
Feb 9 1945	I-41	Submarine	2,212	18-50N, 121-40E	J. K. Fyfe
Feb 11 1945	RO-112	Submarine	525	18-53N, 121-50E	
Feb 12 1945	RO-113	Submarine	525	19-10N, 121-23E	
	6 Vessels		10,230		
USS Baya					
Mar 4 1945	Palembang Maru	Tanker	5,236	12-52N, 109-30E	
Mar 21 1945	Kainan Maru	Ex-Submarine Chaser	524	11-55N, 109-18E	B. C. Jarvis
May 13 1945	Yosei Maru	Tanker	2,500e	6-31S, 111-19E	
Jul 16 1945	Kari	Motor Torpedo Boat	595	5-48S, 115-53E	
	4 Vessels		8,855		
USS Becuna					
Feb 22 1945	Nichiyoku Maru	Tanker	1,945	11-28N, 109-06E	H. D. Sturr
USS Bergall					
Oct 13 1944	Shinshu Maru	Cargo	4,182	11-52N, 109-20E	
Oct 27 1944	Nippo Maru	Tanker	10,528	7-09N, 116-40E	
Jan 27 1945	Coastal Minesweeper No 102	Coastal Minesweeper	174	8-37S, 115-39E	J. M. Hyde
Feb 7 1945	Coast Def Vessel No 53	Frigate	800	12-04N, 109-22E	
	4 Vessels		15,684		
USS Besugo					
Nov 22 1944	Transport No 151	Landing Craft (LST)	1,000e	11-22N, 119-07E	
Jan 6 1945	Nichiei Maru	Tanker	10,020	6-57N, 102-57E	T. L. Wogan
Feb 2 1945	Coast Def Vessel No 144	Frigate	800e	4-32N, 104-30E	
Apr 6 1945	Minesweeper No 12	Minesweeper	630	8-13S, 119-14E	H. E. Miller
	4 Vessels		12,450		

SUBMARINE AND DATE	NAME OF VESSEL	TYPE OF VESSEL	TONNAGE	LOCATION	SUBMARINE CAPTAIN
USS BILLFISH					
May 26 1945	Kotobuki Maru No 7	Cargo	991	33-18N, 129-20E	
Jun 4 1945	Taiu Maru	Cargo	2,220	38-32N, 124-45E	L. C. Farley
Aug 5 1945	Kori Maru	Cargo	1,091	38-51N, 121-39E	
		3 Vessels	4,302		
USS BLACKFISH					
Jan 16 1944	Kaika Maru	Cargo	2,087	4-03N, 148-41E	J. F. Davidson
USS BLACKFIN					
Nov 1 1944	Unkai Maru No 12	Cargo	2,745	12-54N, 120-10E	G. E. Laird
Jan 24 1945	Shigure	Destroyer	1,580	6-00N, 103-48E	W. L. Kitch
		2 Vessels	4,325		
USS BLENNY					
Dec 14 1944	Coast Def Vessel No 28	Frigate	800ᵉ	15-46N, 119-45E	
Dec 23 1944	Kenzui Maru	Cargo	4,156	16-50N, 120-18E	
Feb 26 1945	Amato Maru	Tanker	10,238	11-57N, 109-18E	
Mar 20 1945	Yamakuni Maru	Cargo	500	11-17N, 108-55E	W. H. Hazzard
Mar 20 1945	Nanshin Maru No 21	Tanker	834	11-17N, 108-55E	
Mar 20 1945	Hosen Maru	Cargo	1,039	11-17N, 108-55E	
May 30 1945	Hokoku Maru	Cargo	520	4-09S, 114-16E	
		7 Vessels	18,087		
USS BLUEJACK					
Jun 27 1945	Submarine Chaser No 2	Submarine Chaser	300	7-25S, 116-00E	M. K. Clemenson
USS BLUEFISH					
Sep 26 1943	Kasasagi	Motor Torpedo Boat	595	5-50S, 121-57E	
Sep 28 1943	Akashi Maru	Cargo	3,227	6-11S, 126-00E	
Nov 8 1943	Kyokuei Maru	Tanker	10,570	16-44N, 116-22E	
Nov 18 1943	Sanaye	Old Destroyer	820	4-52N, 122-07E	G. E. Porter
Dec 30 1943	Ichiyu Maru	Tanker	5,061	2-45S, 109-10E	
Jan 4 1944	Hakko Maru	Tanker	6,046	7-10N, 108-25E	
Mar 4 1944	Ominesan Maru	Tanker	10,536	5-32N, 109-09E	
Jun 16 1944	Nanshin Maru	Passenger-Cargo	1,422	2-28N, 118-09E	C. M. Henderson
Jun 21 1944	Kanan Maru	Cargo	3,312	4-04S, 116-45E	
Aug 19 1944	Hayasui	Tanker	6,500ᵉ	17-34N, 119-24E	
Jul 9 1945	Submarine Chaser No 50	Submarine Chaser	100ᵉ	2-13N, 105-03E	G. W. Forbes
Jul 14 1945	I-351	Submarine	2,650	4-30N, 110-00E	
		12 Vessels	50,839		
USS BLUEGILL					
Apr 27 1944	Yubari	Light Cruiser	3,500	5-20N, 132-16E	
May 1 1944	Asosan Maru	Cargo	8,812	7-07N, 129-56E	
May 20 1944	Miyaura Maru	Cargo	1,856	2-14N, 128-00E	
Aug 7 1944	Sanju Maru	Cargo	4,642	6-04N, 124-22E	
Aug 13 1944	Submarine Chaser No 12	Submarine Chaser	300	6-17N, 126-09E	Eric Barr
Aug 13 1944	Kojun Maru	Cargo	1,931	6-17N, 126-09E	
Oct 18 1944	Arabia Maru	Transport	9,480	14,06N, 119-40E	
Oct 18 1944	Chinzei Maru	Cargo	1,999	14-06N, 119-40E	
Oct 18 1944	Hakushika Maru	Passenger-Cargo	8,150	14-06N, 119-40E	
Mar 28 1945	Honan Maru	Tanker	5,542	12-39N, 109-27E	
		10 Vessels	46,212		

SUBMARINE AND DATE	NAME OF VESSEL	TYPE OF VESSEL	TONNAGE	LOCATION	SUBMARINE CAPTAIN
USS Boarfish					
Jan 31 1945	Enki Maru	Cargo	6,968	14-55N, 109-01E	R. L. Gross
USS Bonefish					
Sep 27 1943	Kashima Maru	Transport	9,908	10-14N, 109-45E	
Oct 10 1943	Teibi Maru	Transport	10,086	14-44N, 110-19E	
Oct 10 1943	Isuzugawa	Cargo	4,212	14-44N, 110-19E	
Nov 29 1943	Suez Maru	Cargo	4,646	6-22S, 116-35E	T. W. Hogan
Dec 1 1943	Nichiryo Maru	Passenger-Cargo	2,721	1-31N, 120-51E	
Apr 26 1944	Tokiwa Maru	Passenger-Cargo	806	6-12N, 125-47E	
May 14 1944	Inazuma	Destroyer	1,950	5-08N, 119-38E	
Jul 30 1944	Kokuyo Maru	Tanker	10,026	6-03N, 119-54E	
Sep 28 1944	Anjo Maru	Tanker	2,068	13-16N, 120-08E	
Oct 14 1944	Fushimi Maru	Cargo	2,542	16-12N, 119-45E	L. L. Edge
Jun 13 1945	Oshikayama Maru	Cargo	6,892	38-30N, 136-58E	
Jun 19 1945	Konzan Maru	Passenger-Cargo	5,488	37-13N, 137-18E	
	12 Vessels		61,345		
USS Bowfin					
Sep 25 1943	Kirishima Maru	Passenger-Cargo	8,120	9-44N, 111-56E	J. H. Willingham
Nov 26 1943	Ogurasan Maru	Tanker	5,069	12-48N, 109-34E	
Nov 26 1943	Tainan Maru	Cargo	5,407	13-02N, 109-28E	
Nov 27 1943	Van Vollenhoven	Cargo	691	13-01N, 109-30E	
Nov 28 1943	Sydney Maru	Passenger-Cargo	5,425	12-46N, 109-42E	
Nov 28 1943	Tonan Maru	Tanker	9,866	12-46N, 109-42E	W. T. Griffith
Jan 17 1944	Shoyu Maru	Cargo	4,408	18N, 118-37E	
Mar 10 1944	Tsukikawa Maru	Cargo	4,470	1-30S, 128-17E	
Mar 24 1944	Shinkyo Maru	Cargo	5,139	5-27N, 125-38E	
Mar 24 1944	Bengal Maru	Cargo	5,399	5-27N, 125-38E	
Aug 22 1944	Tsushima Maru	Passenger-Cargo	6,754	29-32N, 129-31E	J. H. Corbus
Feb 17 1945	Coast Def Vessel No 56	Frigate	750*	33-53N, 139-43E	
May 1 1945	Chowa Maru	Passenger-Cargo	2,719	41-06N, 144-28E	
May 8 1945	Daito Maru No 3	Cargo	880	39-37N, 142-07E	A. K. Tyree
Jun 11 1945	Shinyo Maru No 3	Passenger-Cargo	1,898	39-23N, 128-59E	
Jun 13 1945	Akiura Maru	Cargo	887	39-13N, 128-07E	
	16 Vessels		67,882		
USS Bream					
Jun 16 1944	Yuki Maru	Cargo	5,704	2-19N, 128-40E	W. G. Chapple
Apr 29 1945	Teishu Maru	Ex-Submarine Tender	1,230	4-11S, 111-17E	J. L. McCallum
	2 Vessels		6,934		
USS Burrfish					
May 7 1944	Rossback	Tanker	5,894	33-14N, 134-40E	W. B. Perkins
USS Bumper					
Jul 20 1945	Kyoei Maru No 3	Tanker	1,189	8-08N, 103-40E	J. W. Williams
USS Cabezon					
Jun 19 1945	Zaosan Maru	Cargo	2,631	50-39N, 154-38E	G. W. Lautrup

SUBMARINE AND DATE	NAME OF VESSEL	TYPE OF VESSEL	TONNAGE	LOCATION	SUBMARINE CAPTAIN
USS CABRILLA	Tamon Maru No 8				
Jan 4, 1944	Sanyo Maru	Cargo	2,705	11-05N, 109-10E	D. T. Hammond
May 26 1944	Maya Maru	Ex-Seaplane Tender	8,360	2-48N, 124-19E	
Jul 17 1944	Zuiyo Maru	Passenger-Cargo	3,145	7-40N, 122-03E	
Oct 1 1944	Kyokuho Maru	Tanker	7,385	16-15N, 119-43E	W. E. Thompson
Oct 1 1944	Yamamizu Maru No 2	Tanker	10,059	16-15N, 119-43E	
Oct 6 1944	Shinyo Maru No 8	Cargo	5,154	17-31N, 120-21E	
Oct 7 1944		Cargo	1,959	17-50N, 119-37E	
		7 Vessels	38,767		
USS CAPELIN					
Nov 11 1943	Kunitama Maru	Cargo	3,127	3-08S, 127-38E	E. E. Marshall
USS CAVALLA					
Jun 19 1944	Shokaku	Aircraft Carrier	30,000	11-50N, 137-57E	
Nov 25 1944	Shimotsuki	Destroyer	2,300	2-21N, 107-20E	
Jan 5 1945	Shunsen Maru	Cargo	971	5-00S, 112-16E	J. H. Kossler
Jan 5 1945	Kanko Maru	Ex-Net Tender	909	5-00S, 112-16E	
		4 Vessels	34,180		
USS CERO					
May 23 1944	Taijun Maru	Cargo	2,825	2-38N, 128-08E	D. C. White
Aug 5 1944	Tsurumi	Tanker	6,500ᵉ	5-50N, 125-42E	E. F. Dissette
Apr 29 1945	Taishu Maru	Cargo	6,925	39-15N, 141-58E	
May 4 1945	Shinpen Maru	Cargo	884	39-28N, 142-04E	R. Berthrong
May 13 1945	Shinnan Maru	Cargo	1,025	39-07N, 141-57E	
		5 Vessels	18,159		
USS CHUB					
May 21 1945	Minesweeper No 34	Minesweeper	492	6-15S, 116-01E	C. D. Rhymes
USS COBIA					
Jul 13 1944	Taishi Maru	Cargo	2,800	27-23N, 140-33E	
Jul 18 1944	Unkai Maru No 10	Ex-Gunboat	855	29-12N, 139-10E	
Jul 18 1944	Nisshu Maru	Cargo	7,785	28-43N, 139-24E	
Jan 14 1945	Yurishima	Coastal Minelayer	720	5-51N, 103-16E	A. L. Becker
Jun 8 1945	Nanshin Maru No 22	Tanker	834ᵉ	8-56N, 105-37E	
Jun 8 1945	Hakusa	Landing Craft	3,841	8-56N, 105-37E	
		6 Vessels	16,835		
USS COD					
Feb 23 1944	Ogura Maru No 3	Tanker	7,350	3-53N, 129-17E	
Feb 27 1944	Taisoku Maru	Cargo	2,473	1-48N, 127-32E	
May 10 1944	Karukaya	Old Destroyer	820	15-38N, 119-25E	J. C. Dempsey
May 10 1944	Shohei Maru	Cargo	7,256	15-38N, 119-25E	
Aug 3 1944	Seiko Maru	Ex-Net Tender	708	1-45S, 126-14E	
Aug 14 1944	Transport No 129	Landing Craft	1,000ᵉ	4-17S, 126-46E	
Oct 5 1944	Tatsushiro Maru	Cargo	6,886	13-01N, 120-15E	J. A. Adkins
Apr 25 1945	Minesweeper No 41	Minesweeper	492	25-53N, 121-08E	
		8 Vessels	26,985		

SUBMARINE AND DATE	NAME OF VESSEL	TYPE OF VESSEL	TONNAGE	LOCATION	SUBMARINE CAPTAIN
USS CREVALLE					
Nov 15 1943	Kyokko Maru	Passenger-Cargo	6,783	14-53N, 119-54E	H. T. Munson
Jan 26 1944	Busho Maru	Ex-Gunboat	2,552	8-27N, 109-12E	
Apr 25 1944	Kashiwa Maru	Ex-Net Tender	976	7-09N, 116-48E	
May 6 1944	Nisshin Maru	Tanker	16,801	7-17N, 116-51E	F. D. Walker
Jul 26 1944	Aki Maru	Passenger-Cargo	11,409	18-28M, 117-59E	
Jul 28 1944	Hakubasan Maru	Passenger-Cargo	6,650	16-18N, 119-44E	
Jun 9 1945	Hokuto Maru	Cargo	2,215	40-54N, 139-48E	
Jun 10 1945	Daiki Maru	Cargo	2,217	40-44N, 139-48E	E. H. Steinmetz
Jun 11 1945	Hakusan Maru	Cargo	2,211	40-43N, 139-51E	
	9 Vessels		51,814		
USS CROAKER					
Aug 7 1944	Nagara	Light Cruiser	5,700	32-09N, 129-53E	
Aug 14 1944	Daigen Maru No 7	Ex-Gunboat	1,289	37-25N, 125-12E	
Aug. 17 1944	Sansho Maru	Cargo	6,862	35-38N, 126-10E	J. A. Lee
Oct 9 1944	Shinki Maru	Cargo	2,211	32-08N, 129-51E	
Oct 23 1944	Byakuran Maru	Cargo	887	35-39N, 126-05E	
Oct 24 1944	Mikage Maru	Cargo	2,761	33-00N, 125-49E	
	6 Vessels		19,710		
USS DACE					
Jul 27 1944	Kyoei Maru No 2	Tanker	1,157	5-25N, 121-43E	
Oct 14 1944	Nittetsu Maru	Cargo	5,993	6-05N, 115-55E	
Oct 14 1944	Eikyo Maru	Cargo	6,948	6-05N, 115-55E	B. D. Claggett
Oct 23 1944	Maya	Heavy Cruiser	12,200	9-29N, 117-20E	
Dec 28, 1944	Nozaki	Ex-Supply Ship	1,000ᵉ	12-39N, 109-30E	D. R. Cole
Jun 10 1945	Hakuyo Maru	Cargo	1,391	47-25N, 149-04E	
	6 Vessels		28,689		
USS DARTER					
Mar 30 1944	Fujikawa Maru	Cargo	2,829	1-56N, 133-00E	W. S. Stovall
Jun 29 1944	Tsugaru	Minelayer	4,400ᵉ	2-19N, 127-57E	
Oct 23 1944	Atago	Heavy Cruiser	12,000	9-24N, 117-11E	D. L. McClintock
	3 Vessels		19,429		
USS DRUM					
May 2 1942	Mizuho	Seaplane Tender	9,000	34-26N, 138-14E	
May 9 1942	Unknown	Cargo	4,000ᵉ	33-48N, 136-08E	
May 13 1942	Shonan Maru	Cargo	5,264	34-39N, 139-10E	
May 25 1942	Kitakata Maru	Cargo	2,380	34-58N, 140-04E	R. H. Rice
Oct 8 1942	Hague Maru	Passenger-Cargo	5,641	34-06N, 136-22E	
Oct 9 1942	Hachimanzan Maru	Cargo	2,461	33-27N, 136-01E	
Oct 20 1942	Ryunan Maru	Cargo	5,106	34-08N, 136-46E	
Apr 9 1943	Oyama Maru	Cargo	3,809	00-32N, 150-05E	
Apr 18 1943	Nisshun Maru	Cargo	6,380	1-55N, 148-24E	
Jun 17 1943	Myoko Maru	Passenger-Cargo	5,087	2-03S, 153-44E	B. F. McMahon
Sep 8 1943	Hakutetsu Maru No 13	Cargo	1,334	2-44S, 141-36E	
Nov 17 1943	Hie Maru	Ex-Supply Ship	11,621	1-48N, 148-24E	
Oct 24 1944	Shikisan Maru	Passenger-Cargo	4,725	20-27N, 118-31E	
Oct 26 1944	Taisho Maru	Cargo	6,886	19-21N, 120-50E	D. F. Williamson
Oct 26 1944	Taihaku Maru	Cargo	6,886	19-21N, 120-50E	
	15 Vessels		80,580		

SUBMARINE AND DATE	NAME OF VESSEL	TYPE OF VESSEL	TONNAGE	LOCATION	SUBMARINE CAPTAIN
USS Finback					
Oct 14 1942	Teison Maru	Transport	7,007	25-22N, 121-15E	
Oct 20 1942	Yamafuji Maru	Cargo	5,359	24-26N, 120-26E	J. L. Hull
Oct 20 1942	Africa Maru	Cargo	9,475	24-26N, 120-26E	
May 27 1943	Kochi Maru	Cargo	2,910	8-41N, 134-02E	
Jun 8 1943	Kahoku Maru	Ex-Gunboat	3,350	9-074, 134-31E	
Jun 11 1943	Genoa Maru	Cargo	6,785	7-36N, 134-17E	
Jun 30 1943	Ryuzan Maru	Cargo	4,720	6-31S, 111-26E	J. A. Tyree
Aug 3 1943	Kaisho Maru	Passenger-Cargo	6,070	5-18S, 111-52E	
Aug 19 1943	Submarine Chaser No 109	Submarine Chaser	200	3-01S, 125-50E	
Jan 2 1944	Isshin Maru	Tanker	10,000°	29-30N, 128-50E	
Sep 11 1944	Hakuun Maru No 2	Cargo	860	27-37N, 140-21E	
Sep 11 1944	Hassho Maru	Cargo	536	27-37N, 140-21E	R. R. Williams
Dec 16 1944	Jusan Maru	Cargo	2,111	27-35N, 141-35E	
		13 Vessels	59,383		
USS Flasher					
Jan 18 1944	Yoshida Maru	Ex-Gunboat	2,900	23-50N, 151-28E	
Feb 5 1944	Taishin Maru	Cargo	1,723	13-09N, 120-24E	
Feb 14 1944	Minryo Maru	Cargo	2,193	13-44N, 120-40E	
Feb 14 1944	Hokuan Maru	Cargo	3,712	13-40N, 120-27E	
Apr 29 1944	Tahure	River Gunboat	644	13-02N, 109-28E	
Apr 29 1944	Song Giang Maru	Cargo	1,065	13-02N, 109-28E	
May 3 1944	Teisen Maru	Cargo	5,050	12-54N, 114-07E	
Jun 29 1944	Nippo Maru	Cargo	6,079	00-43N, 105-31E	
Jul 7 1944	Koto Maru	Cargo	3,557	13-02N, 109-26E	R. I. Whitaker
Jul 19 1944	Oi	Light Cruiser	5,700	12-45N, 114-20E	
Jul 26 1944	Otoriyama Maru	Tanker	5,280	18-10N, 117-56E	
Sep 18 1944	Saigon Maru	Ex-Light Cruiser	5,350	14-11N, 120-02E	
Sep 27 1944	Ural Maru	Transport	6,374	15-40N, 117-18E	
Oct 4 1944	Taibin Maru	Cargo	6,886	15-26N, 119-49E	
Dec 4 1944	Kishinami	Destroyer	2,100	13-12N, 116-37E	
Dec 4 1944	Iwanami	Destroyer	2,100	13-12N, 116-37E	
Dec 4 1944	Hakko Maru	Tanker	10,022	13-12N, 116-37E	
Dec 22 1944	Omurosan Maru	Tanker	9,204	15-04N, 109-06E	G. W. Grider
Dec 22 1944	Otowasan Maru	Tanker	9,204	15-04N, 109-06E	
Dec 22 1944	Arita Maru	Tanker	10,238	15-04N, 109-06E	
Feb 25 1945	Koho Maru	Cargo	850	20-04N, 111-22E	
		21 Vessels	100,231		
USS Flier					
Jun 4 1944	Hakusam Maru	Transport	10,380	22-55N, 136-44E	J. D. Crowley
USS Flounder					
June 17 1944	Nipponkai Maru	Ex-Motor Torpedo Tender	2,681	6-58N, 127-52E	J. E. Stevens

SUBMARINE AND DATE	NAME OF VESSEL	TYPE OF VESSEL	TONNAGE	LOCATION	SUBMARINE CAPTAIN
USS Flying Fish					
Feb 16 1943	Hyuga Maru	Cargo	994	18-30N, 145-47E	
Apr 12 1943	Sappora Maru No 12	Cargo	2,865	41-23N, 141-30E	
Apr 17 1943	Amaho Maru	Cargo	2,769	42-04N, 143-22E	G. R. Donaho
Apr 24 1943	Kasuga Maru	Cargo	1,377	41-43N, 141-21E	
Jul 2 1943	Canton Maru	Cargo	2,820	25-07N, 119-18E	F. T. Watkins
Oct 27 1943	Nanman Maru	Cargo	6,550	12-34N, 134-48E	G. R. Donaho
Dec 16 1943	Ginyo Maru	Cargo	8,613	22-27N, 120-08E	
Dec 27 1943	Kyuei Maru	Tanker	10,171	21-42N, 118-05E	
Mar 12 1944	Taijin Maru	Cargo	1,937	25-53N, 131-19E	
Mar 16 1944	Anzan Maru	Passenger-Cargo	5,493	27-41N, 128-41E	
Apr 1 1944	Ninami Maru	Cargo	2,398	25-56N, 131-18E	R. D. Risser
May 25 1944	Taito Maru	Passenger-Cargo	4,466	11-30N, 134-55E	
May 25 1944	Osaka Maru	Passenger-Cargo	3,740	11-30N, 134-55E	
Jun 10 1945	Taga Maru	Cargo	2,220	41-40N, 129-52E	
Jun 11 1945	Meisei Maru	Passenger-Cargo	1,893	41-47N, 131-44E	
		15 Vessels	58,306		
USS Gabilan					
Jul 17 1944	Minesweeper No 25	Minesweeper	492	33-51N, 138-35E	K. R. Wheland
Oct 31 1944	Kaiyo No 6	Miscellaneous Auxiliary	100ᵉ	32-50N, 134-21E	
Apr 14 1945	Kako Maru	Cargo	762	5-19S, 117-06E	W. B. Parham
		3 Vessels	1,354		
USS Gar					
Mar 13 1942	Chichibu Maru	Cargo	1,520	33-53N, 139-29E	D. McGregor
Dec 8 1942	Heinan Maru	Cargo	661	00-52N, 118-54E	
May 9 1943	Aso Maru	Cargo	703	9-09N, 122-50E	
May 15 1943	Meikai Maru	Passenger-Cargo	3,197	13-07N, 121-49E	P. D. Quirk
May 15 1943	Indus Maru	Passenger-Cargo	4,361	13-07N, 121-49E	
Aug 20 1943	Seizan Maru	Cargo	955	00-58N, 119-01E	
Jan 20 1944	Koyu Maru	Cargo	5,325	6-40N, 134-17E	G. W. Lautrup
Jan 23 1944	Taian Maru	Cargo	3,670	5-45N, 134-45E	
		8 Vessels	20,392		
USS Gato					
Jan 21 1943	Kenkon Maru	Transport	4,575	6-12S, 155-51E	
Jan 29 1943	Nichiun Maru	Cargo	2,723	6-21S, 156-04E	
Feb 15 1943	Suruga Maru	Cargo	991	6-27S, 156-02E	
Nov 30 1943	Columbia Maru	Passenger-Cargo	5,618	1-56N, 147-23E	R. J. Foley
Dec 20 1943	Tsuneshima Maru	Cargo	2,926	1-30N, 148-36E	
Feb 26 1944	Daigen Maru No 3	Passenger-Cargo	5,256	00-55S, 139-02E	
Mar 12 1944	Okinoyama Maru No 3	Cargo	871	00-25S, 132-55E	
Feb 14 1945	Coast Def Vessel No 9	Frigate	800ᵉ	34-48N, 125-58E	R. M. Farrell
Feb 21 1945	Tairiku Maru	Cargo	2,325	35-24N, 125-23E	
		9 Vessels	26,085		
USS Grampus					
Mar 1 1942	Kaijo Maru No 2	Tanker	8,636	4-52N, 151-20E	E. S. Hutchinson

SUBMARINE AND DATE	NAME OF VESSEL	TYPE OF VESSEL	TONNAGE	LOCATION	SUBMARINE CAPTAIN
USS GRAYBACK					
Mar 17 1942	Ishikari Maru	Cargo	3,291	27-05N, 142-05E	W. A. Saunders
Jan 2 1943	I-18	Submarine	2,180	8-49S, 157-09E	E. C. Stephan
May 11 1943	Yodogawa Maru	Cargo	6,441	00-47S, 149-02E	E. C. Stephan
May 17 1943	England Maru	Cargo	5,830	1-00S, 148-40E	
Oct 14 1943	Kozui Maru	Passenger-Cargo	7,072	27-35N, 127-27E	
Oct 22 1943	Awata Maru	Ex-Light Cruiser	7,397	26-48N, 124-56E	
Dec 18 1943	Gyokurei Maru	Cargo	5,588	26-22N, 128-20E	
Dec 19 1943	Numakaze	Destroyer	1,300	26-29N, 128-26E	
Dec 21 1943	Konan Maru	Cargo	2,627	30-24N, 129-53E	J. A. Moore
Dec 21 1943	Kashiwa Maru	Ex-Net Tender	515	30-24N, 129-53E	
Feb 19 1944	Taikei Maru	Cargo	4,739	21-48N, 119-50E	
Feb 19 1944	Toshin Maru	Cargo	1,917	21-46N, 120-06E	
Feb 24 1944	Nampo Maru	Tanker	10,033	24-20N, 122-25E	
Feb 27 1944	Ceylon Maru	Cargo	4,905	31-50N, 127-45E	
		14 Vessels	63,835		
USS GRAYLING					
Apr 13 1942	Ryujin Maru	Cargo	6,243	31-51N, 132-50E	E. Olsen
Nov 10 1942	Unknown Maru	Cargo	4,000e	7-12N, 150-47E	
Jan 26 1943	Ushio Maru	Cargo	749	13-26N, 121-16E	J. E. Lee
Apr 9 1943	Shanghai Maru	Cargo	4,103	13-11N, 121-45E	
Aug 27 1943	Meizan Maru	Passenger-Cargo	5,480	13-13N, 121-23E	R. M. Brinker
		5 Vessels	20,575		
USS GREENLING					
May 4 1942	Kinjosan Maru	Cargo	3,262	8-44N, 150-56E	
Aug 5 1942	Brasil Maru	Transport	12,752	9-50N, 150-38E	
Aug 6 1942	Palao Maru	Passenger-Cargo	4,495	9-04N, 150-54E	
Oct 3 1942	Kinkai Maru	Cargo	5,852	38-46N, 142-02E	
Oct 4 1942	Setsuyo Maru	Cargo	4,147	39-48N, 142-08E	
Oct 14 1942	Takusei Maru	Cargo	3,515	39-33N, 142-15E	H. C. Bruton
Oct 18 1942	Hakonesan Maru	Cargo	6,673	38-46N, 142-03E	
Dec 22 1942	Patrol Boat No 35	Old Destroyer	750e	5-05S, 156-04E	
Dec 30 1942	Unknown Maru	Cargo	4,000e	00-41N, 148-52E	
Dec 30 1942	Hiteru Maru	Cargo	5,857	00-41N, 148-52E	
Jan 16 1943	Kinposan Maru	Cargo	3,261	2-47S, 149-10E	
Dec 31 1943	Shoho Maru	Cargo	1,936	5-18N, 160-16E	J. D. Grant
Nov 7 1944	Kiri Maru No 8	Cargo	939	34-32N, 138-33E	
Nov 7 1944	Kotai Maru	Tanker	975	34-32N, 138-33E	J. D. Gerwick
Nov 10 1944	Patrol Boat No 46	Old Destroyer	820	34-30N, 138-34E	
		15 Vessels	59,234		
USS GRENADIER					
May 8 1942	Taiyo Maru	Transport	14,457	30-40N, 127-54E	W. A. Lent
USS GROUPER					
Sep 21 1942	Tone Maru	Cargo	4,070	31-18N, 123-27E	
Oct 1 1942	Lisbon Maru	Transport	7,053	29,57N, 122-56E	R. R. McGregor
Dec 17 1942	Bandoeng Maru	Passenger-Cargo	4,003	4-54S, 154-17E	
Jun 24 1944	Kumanoyama Maru	Cargo	2,857	34-36N, 139-32E	F. H. Wahlig
		4 Vessels	17,983		

SUBMARINE AND DATE	NAME OF VESSEL	TYPE OF VESSEL	TONNAGE	LOCATION	SUBMARINE CAPTAIN
USS Growler					
Jul 5 1942	Arare	Destroyer	1,850	52-00N, 177-40E	
Aug 25 1942	Senyo Maru	Ex-Gunboat	2,904	22-23N, 120-10E	
Aug 31 1942	Eifuku Maru	Cargo	5,866	25-43N, 122-38E	
Sep 4 1942	Kashino	Supply Ship	4,000e	25-43N, 122-38E	H. W. Gilmore
Sep 7 1942	Taika Maru	Cargo	2,204	25-31N, 121-33E	
Jan 16 1943	Chifuku Maru	Passenger-Cargo	5,857	4-00S, 151-55E	
Jun 19 1943	Miyadono Maru	Passenger-Cargo	5,196	1-38N, 148-14E	A. F. Schade
Jun 29 1944	Katori Maru	Cargo	1,920	19-09N, 120-27E	
Sep 12 1944	Shikinami	Destroyer	1,950	18-16N, 114-40E	T. B. Oakley
Sep 12 1944	Hirado	Frigate	860	17-54N, 114-49E	
		10 Vessels	32,607		
USS Grunion					
Jul 15 1942	Subchaser No 25	Subchaser	300	52-02N, 177-42E	M. L. Abele
Jul 15 1942	Subchaser No 27	Subchaser	300	52-02N, 177-42E	
		2 Vessels	600		
USS Guardfish					
Aug. 24, 1942	Seikai Maru	Passenger-Cargo	3,109	38-12N, 141-30E	
Sep 2 1942	Teikyu Maru	Cargo	2,332	42-08N, 141-15E	
Sep 4 1942	Chita Maru	Cargo	2,276	40-10N, 141-53E	
Sep 4 1942	Tenyu Maru	Cargo	3,738	40-14N, 141-51E	
Sep 4 1942	Kaimei Maru	Cargo	5,254	40-14N, 141-51E	T. B. Klakring
Oct 21 1942	Unknown Maru	Cargo	4,000e	27-03N, 122-42E	
Oct 21 1942	Nichiho Maru	Cargo	6,363	27-03N, 122-42E	
Jan 12 1943	Patrol Boat No 1	Old Destroyer	750e	2-51S, 149-43E	
Jan 22 1943	Unknown Maru	Cargo	4,000e	3-55S, 152-07E	
Jan 23 1943	Hakaze	Destroyer	1,300	2-47S, 150-38E	
Jun 13 1943	Suzuya Maru	Cargo	901	3-08S, 151-24E	
Oct 8 1943	Kashu Maru	Cargo	5,460	00-25S, 146-22E	
Jan 14 1944	Kenyo Maru	Tanker	10,022	5-22N, 141-27E	
Feb 1 1944	Umikaze	Destroyer	1,580	7-10N, 151-43E	
Jul 16 1944	Jinzan Maru	Passenger-Cargo	5,215	18-20N, 119-42E	N. G. Ward
Jul 16 1944	Mantai Maru	Cargo	5,863	18-20N, 119-42E	
Jul 17 1944	Hiyama Maru	Cargo	2,838	18-17N, 119-50E	
Jul 19 1944	Teiryu Maru	Cargo	6,550	20-07N, 118-20E	
Sep 25 1944	Miyakawa Maru No 2	Cargo	873	38-30N, 124-06E	
		19 Vessels	72,424		
USS Guavina					
Apr 26 1944	Noshiro Maru	Cargo	2,333	28-37N, 141-00E	
Jul 4 1944	Tama Maru	Passenger-Cargo	3,052	7-33N, 133,45E	
Sep 15 1944	Transport No 3	Landing Craft	1,500e	5-34N, 125-23E	C. Teideman
Nov 22 1944	Dowa Maru	Cargo	1,916	10-22N, 114-21E	
Feb 7 1945	Taigyo Maru	Cargo	6,892	7-03N, 106-05E	R. H. Lockwood
Feb 20 1945	Eiyo Maru	Tanker	8,673	11-17N, 109-00E	
		6 Vessels	24,366		

SUBMARINE AND DATE	NAME OF VESSEL	TYPE OF VESSEL	TONNAGE	LOCATION	SUBMARINE CAPTAIN
USS GUDGEON					
Jan 27 1942	I-173	Submarine	1,785	28-24N, 178-35E	
Mar 26 1942	Unknown Maru	Cargo	4,000	32-31N, 127-10E	E. W. Grenfell
Mar 27 1942	Unknown Maru	Passenger-Cargo	4,000●	33-53N, 127-33E	
Aug 3 1942	Naniwa Maru	Cargo	4,858	7-37N, 150-18E	W. S. Stovall
Oct 21 1942	Choko Maru	Passenger-Cargo	6,783	3-30S, 150-30E	
Mar 22 1943	Meigen Maru	Cargo	5,434	6-31S, 112-47E	
Mar 29 1943	Toho Maru	Tanker	9,997	00-00N, 118-18E	
Apr 28 1943	Kamakura Maru	Transport	17,526	10-18N, 121-44E	
May 12 1943	Sumatra Maru	Cargo	5,862	12-43N, 124-08E	W. S. Post
Sep 28 1943	Taian Maru	Passenger-Cargo	3,158	15-22N, 145-38E	
Nov 23 1943	Nekka Maru	Transport	6,784	28-49N, 122-11E	
Nov 23 1943	Wakamiya	Frigate	860	28-49N, 122-11E	
		12 Vessels	71,047		
USS GUITARRO					
May 30 1944	Shisen Maru	Cargo	2,201	24-30N, 122-30E	
Jun 2 1944	Awaji	Frigate	900●	22-34N, 121-51E	
Aug 7 1944	Kusakaki	Frigate	900●	14-51N, 119-59E	
Aug 10 1944	Shinei Maru	Cargo	5,135	16-17N, 119-46E	
Aug 21 1944	Uga Maru	Passenger-Cargo	4,433	13-23N, 120-19E	E. D. Haskins
Aug 27 1944	Nanshin Maru No 27	Tanker	834	12-28N, 119-57E	
Oct 31 1944	Komei Maru	Cargo	2,857	15-17N, 119-49E	
Oct 31 1944	Pacific Maru	Passenger-Cargo	5,872	15-17N, 119-49E	
		8 Vessels	23,132		
USS GUNNEL					
Jun 15 1943	Koyo Maru	Cargo	6,435	33-55N, 127-38E	
Jun 19 1943	Tokiwa Maru	Cargo	6,971	32-31N, 126-19E	J. S. McCain
Dec 4 1943	Hiyoshi Maru	Passenger-Cargo	4,046	29-45N, 145-55E	
Nov 8 1944	Sagi	Torpedo Boat	595	16-09N, 118-56E	
Nov 17 1944	Shunten Maru	Passenger-Cargo	5,623	16-56N, 110-30E	G. E. O'Neil
Nov 17 1944	Hiyodori	Torpedo Boat	595	16-56N, 110-30E	
		6 Vessels	24,265		
USS GURNARD					
Jul 11 1943	Taiko Maru	Cargo	1,925	12-53N, 131-49E	
Oct 8 1943	Taian Maru	Cargo	5,655	18-24N, 119-09E	
Oct 8 1943	Dainichi Maru	Passenger-Cargo	5,813	18-24N, 119-09E	
Dec 24 1943	Seizan Maru No 2	Cargo	1,898	34-02N, 136-19E	
Dec 24 1943	Tofuku Maru	Cargo	5,857	33-58N, 136-16E	C. H. Andrews
May 6 1944	Tenshinzan Maru	Cargo	6,886	2-42N, 124-10E	
May 6 1944	Taijima Maru	Passenger-Cargo	6,995	2-42N, 124-10E	
May 6 1944	Aden Maru	Passenger-Cargo	5,824	2-42N, 124-10E	
May 24 1944	Tatekawa Maru	Tanker	10,090	5-45N, 125-45E	
Nov 3 1944	Taimei Maru	Cargo	6,923	5-48N, 111-05E	N. D. Gage
		10 Vessels	57,866		

538

SUBMARINE AND DATE	NAME OF VESSEL	TYPE OF VESSEL	TONNAGE	LOCATION	SUBMARINE CAPTAIN
USS HADDO					
Aug 21 1944	Kinryo Maru	Passenger-Cargo	4,390	13-23N, 120-19E	
Aug 21 1944	Norfolk Maru	Passenger-Cargo	6,576	13-23N, 120-19E	
Aug 22 1944	Sado	Frigate	860	14-15N, 120-05E	C. W. Nimitz, Jr.
Aug 23 1944	Asakaze	Destroyer	1,270	16-06N, 119-44E	
Sep 21 1944	Katsuriki	Surveying Ship	1,540	13-35N, 119-06E	
Nov 9 1944	Hishi Maru No 2	Tanker	856	12-27N, 120-05E	
Jul 1 1945	Coast Def Vessel No 72	Frigate	800	38-08N, 124-38E	F. C. Lynch
Jul 1 1945	Taiun Maru No 1	Cargo	2,220	38-08N, 124-38E	
Jul 1 1945	Konri Maru	Cargo	3,106	38-08N, 124-38E	
	9 Vessels		21,618		
USS HADDOCK					
Aug 22 1942	Unknown Maru	Transport	4,000*	26-07N, 121-29E	
Aug 26 1942	Teishun Maru	Cargo	2,251	27-05N, 121-23E	
Nov 3 1942	Tekkai Maru	Cargo	1,925	32-02N, 126-15E	A. H. Taylor
Nov 11 1942	Venice Maru	Passenger-Cargo	6,571	35-36N, 123-44E	
Jan 17 1943	Unknown Maru	Cargo	4,000*	34-31N, 137-48E	
Apr 3 1943	Arima Maru	Passenger-Cargo	7,389	10-26N, 135-00E	
Apr 8 1943	Toyo Maru	Cargo	1,916	10-26N, 135-00E	R. M. Davenport
Jul 21 1943	Saipan Maru	Transport	5,533	16-18N, 134-09E	
	8 Vessels		33,585		
USS HAKE					
Jan 12 1944	Nigitsu Maru	Transport	9,547	23-15N, 133-49E	
Feb 1 1944	Tacoma Maru	Passenger-Cargo	5,772	1-35N, 128-58E	
Feb 1 1944	Nanka Maru	Cargo	4,065	1-35N, 128-58E	
Mar 27 1944	Yamamizu Maru	Tanker	5,174	3-52S, 109-40E	J. C. Broach
Jun 8 1944	Kazegumo	Destroyer	1,900	6-03N, 125-57E	
Jun 17 1944	Kinshu Maru	Cargo	5,591	6-17N, 126-17E	
Jun 20 1944	Hibi Maru	Passenger-Cargo	5,874	5-35N, 125-15E	
	7 Vessels		37,923		
USS HALIBUT					
Dec 12 1942	Gyokuzan Maru	Cargo	1,970	40-19N, 142-27E	
Dec 16 1942	Shingo Maru	Cargo	4,740	41-10N, 141-32E	
Dec 16 1942	Genzan Maru	Passenger-Cargo	5,708	41-10N, 141-32E	R. H. Gross
Feb 20 1943	Shinkoku Maru	Passenger-Cargo	3,991	15-09N, 159-30E	
Mar 3 1943	Nichiyu Maru	Passenger-Cargo	6,817	10-22N, 145-21E	
Aug 30 1943	Taibun Maru	Passenger-Cargo	6,581	41-53N, 141-10E	
Sep 6 1943	Shogen Maru	Cargo	3,362	42-13N, 142-16E	
Nov 2 1943	Ehime Maru	Cargo	4,653	28-18N, 134-48E	
Apr 12 1944	Taichu Maru	Passenger-Cargo	3,213	28-07N, 129-01E	I. J. Galantin
Apr 27 1944	Genbu Maru	Passenger-Cargo	1,872	27-20N, 128-15E	
Apr 27 1944	Kamome	Coastal Minelayer	450	27-37N, 128-11E	
Oct 25 1944	Akitsuki	Destroyer	1,900	20-29N, 126-36E	
	12 Vessels		45,257		

SUBMARINE AND DATE	NAME OF VESSEL	TYPE OF VESSEL	TONNAGE	LOCATION	SUBMARINE CAPTAIN
USS HAMMERHEAD					
Oct 1 1944	Kokusei Maru	Cargo	5,396	6-30N, 116-11E	
Oct 1 1944	Higane Maru	Cargo	5,320	6-30N, 116-11E	
Oct 1 1944	Hiyori Maru	Cargo	5,320	6-30N, 116-11E	
Oct 20 1944	Ugo Maru	Passenger-Cargo	3,684	4,52N, 113-24E	J. C. Martin
Oct 20 1944	Oyo Maru	Passenger-Cargo	5,458	4-41N, 113-22E	
Feb 23 1945	Yaku	Frigate	900ᵉ	12-39N, 109-29E	
Mar 29 1945	Coast Def Vessel No 84	Frigate	1,000ᵉ	14-30N, 109-16E	
May 6 1945	Kinrei Maru	Tanker	850	8-15N, 102-15E	F. T. Smith
May 15 1945	Tottori Maru	Passenger-Cargo	5,973	9-21N, 102-25E	
Jul 10 1945	Sakura Maru	Cargo	900	9-38N, 101-30E	
Jul 10 1945	Nanmei Maru No 5	Tanker	834ᵉ	9-38N, 101-30E	
	11 Vessels		**35,635**		
USS HARDER					
June 23 1943	Sagara Maru	Ex-Seaplane Tender	7,189	33-45N, 138-10E	
Sep 9 1943	Koyo Maru	Cargo	3,010	35-20N, 140-40E	
Sep 11 1943	Yoko Maru	Cargo	1,050	33-50N, 139-33E	
Sep 19 1943	Kachisan Maru	Cargo	814	33-30N, 135-40E	
Sep 23 1943	Kowa Maru	Cargo	4,520	34-15N, 137-00E	
Sep 23 1943	Daishin Maru	Tanker	5,878	34-15N, 137-00E	
Nov 19 1943	Udo Maru	Cargo	3,936	22-27N, 147-15E	
Nov 19 1943	Hokko Maru	Cargo	5,385	22-27N, 147-15E	
Nov 20 1943	Nikko Maru	Cargo	5,949	22-47N, 147-20E	S. D. Dealey
Apr 13 1944	Ikazuchi	Destroyer	1,950	10-13N, 143-51E	
Apr 17 1944	Matsue Maru	Cargo	7,061	9-22N, 142-18E	
Jun 6 1944	Minatsuki	Destroyer	1,500	4-05N, 119-30E	
Jun 7 1944	Hayanami	Destroyer	2,100	4-43N, 120-03E	
Jun 9 1944	Tanikaze	Destroyer	1,900	5-42N, 120-41E	
Aug 22 1944	Matsuwa	Frigate	860	14-15N, 120-05E	
Aug 22 1944	Hiburi	Frigate	900ᵉ	14-15N, 120-05E	
	16 Vessels		**54,002**		
USS HARDHEAD					
Aug 18 1944	Natori	Light Cruiser	5,700	12-29N, 128-49E	F. McMaster
Nov 8 1944	Manei Maru	Tanker	5,226	13-53N, 119-26E	
Nov 25 1944	Coast Def Vessel No 38	Frigate	800ᵉ	14-22N, 119-57E	
Feb 2 1945	Nanshin Maru No 19	Tanker	834ᵉ	5-40N, 103-17E	
Apr 6 1945	Aracsan Maru	Cargo	6,886	9-37N, 102-48E	F. W. Greenup
Jun 23 1945	Shuttle Boat No 833	Miscellaneous Auxiliary	200ᵉ	5-50S, 114-18E	
Jun 23 1945	Submarine Chaser No 42	Submarine Chaser	100	5-50S, 114-18E	
Jun 23 1945	Submarine Chaser No 113	Submarine Chaser	200ᵉ	5-50S, 114-18E	
Jul 23 1945	Submarine Chaser No 117	Submarine Chaser	200ᵉ	8-10S, 115-29E	J. L. Haines
	9 Vessels		**20,146**		
USS HAWKBILL					
Dec 15 1944	Momo	Destroyer	760	16-00N, 117-39E	
Feb 14 1945	Submarine Chaser No 4	Submarine Chaser	100ᵉ	8-20S, 115-45E	
Feb 14 1945	Submarine Chaser No 114	Submarine Chaser	100ᵉ	8-20S, 115-45E	F. W. Scanland
Feb 20 1945	Daizen Maru	Cargo	5,396	00-42S, 106-18E	
May 16 1945	Hatsutaka	Minelayer	1,500	4-54N, 103-28E	
	5 Vessels		**7,856**		

SUBMARINE AND DATE	NAME OF VESSEL	TYPE OF VESSEL	TONNAGE	LOCATION	SUBMARINE CAPTAIN
USS HERRING					
Dec 14 1943	Hakozaki Maru	Passenger-Cargo	3,948	33-10N, 125-55E	R. W. Johnson
Jan 1 1944	Nagoya Maru	Cargo-Aircraft Ferry	6,072	32-10N, 138-37E	
May 30 1944	Ishigaki	Frigate	860	48-30N, 151-30E	
May 31 1944	Hokuyo Maru	Cargo	1,590	48-00N, 153-00E	D. Zabriskie
Jun 1 1944	Iwaki Maru	Cargo	3,124	48-00N, 153-00E	
Jun 1 1944	Hiburi Maru	Passenger-Cargo	4,365	48-00N, 153-00E	
	6 Vessels		19,959		
USS HOE					
Feb 25 1944	Nissho Maru	Tanker	10,526	5-55N, 126-05E	V. B. McCrea
Oct 8 1944	Kohoku Maru	Passenger-Cargo	2,573	18-32N, 116-13E	
Feb 25 1945	Shonan	Frigate	900ᵉ	17-08N, 110-01E	M. P. Refo
	3 Vessels		13,999		
USS ICEFISH					
Oct 24 1944	Tenshin Maru	Cargo	4,236	19-31N, 118-10E	R. W. Peterson
Oct 26 1944	Taiyo Maru	Cargo	4,168	19-04N, 120-36E	
	2 Vessels		8,404		
USS JACK					
Jun 26 1943	Toyo Maru	Passenger-Cargo	4,163	33-22N, 138-56E	
Jun 26 1943	Shozan Maru	Cargo	5,859	33-22N, 138-56E	
Jul 4 1943	Nikkyu Maru	Cargo	6,529	34-31N, 138-35E	
Feb 19 1944	Kokuei Maru	Tanker	5,154	14-34N, 114-11E	
Feb 19 1944	Nanei Maru	Tanker	5,019	14-34N, 114-11E	T. M. Dykers
Feb 19 1944	Nichirin Maru	Tanker	5,162	15-45N, 115-39E	
Feb 19 1944	Ichiyo Maru	Tanker	5,106	15-40N, 115-48E	
Apr 26 1944	Yoshida Maru No 1	Passenger-Cargo	5,425	18-06N, 119-47E	
Jun 25 1944	San Pedro Maru	Tanker	7,268	16-07N, 119-44E	
Jun 30 1944	Tsurushima Maru	Cargo	4,645	14-25N, 119-47E	
Jun 30 1944	Matsukawa Maru	Cargo	3,825	14-25N, 119-47E	A. E. Krapf
Aug 29 1944	Minesweeper No 28	Minesweeper	492	2-03N, 122-28E	
Aug 29 1944	Mexico Maru	Passenger-Cargo	5,785	2-07N, 122-28E	
Nov 14 1944	Nichiei Maru	Cargo	5,396	11-19N, 109-01E	A. S. Fuhrman
Nov 15 1944	Yuzan Maru No 2	Cargo	6,859	11-20N, 109-03E	
	15 Vessels		76,687		
USS JALLAO					
Aug 11 1945	Teihoku Maru	Passenger-Cargo	5,795	38-03N, 1331-13E	J. B. Icenhower
USS KETE					
Mar 10 1945	Keizan Maru	Cargo	2,116	29-31N, 127-55E	
Mar 10 1945	Sanka Maru	Cargo	2,495	29-31N, 127-55E	E. Ackerman
Mar 10 1945	Dokan Maru	Cargo	2,270	29-31N, 127-55E	
	3 Vessels		6,881		

SUBMARINE AND DATE	NAME OF VESSEL	TYPE OF VESSEL	TONNAGE	LOCATION	SUBMARINE CAPTAIN
USS KINGFISH					
Oct 1 1942	Yomei Maru	Cargo	2,860	33-35N, 135-15E	
Oct 23 1942	Seikyo Maru	Ex-Gunboat	2,608	33-45N, 135-25E	
Dec 7 1942	Hino Maru No 3	Passenger-Cargo	4,391	23-59N, 138-43E	
Dec 28 1942	Choyo Maru	Cargo	5,388	24-46N, 120-40E	V. L. Lowrance
Mar 19 1943	Takachiho Maru	Transport	8,154	26-00N, 122-18E	
Oct 20 1943	Sana Maru	Cargo	3,365	12-36N, 109-30E	
Jan 3 1944	Ryuei Maru	Tanker	5,144	8-06N, 112-30E	
Jan 3 1944	Bokuei Maru	Tanker	5,135	6-58N, 112-02E	H. L. Jukes
Jan 7 1944	Fushimi Maru No 3	Tanker	4,292	9-27N, 117-36E	
Oct 24 1944	Ikutagawa Maru	Cargo	2,220	27-08N, 143-13E	
Oct 27 1944	Tokai Maru No 4	Cargo	537	25-22N, 141-31E	
Oct 27 1944	Transport No 138	Landing Craft	1,000*	25-22N, 141-31E	T. E. Harper
Jan 3 1945	Yaei Maru	Cargo	1,941	30-29N, 142-03E	
Jan 3 1945	Shibazono Maru	Passenger-Cargo	1,831	30-29N, 142-03E	
	14 Vessels		48,866		
USS LAGARTO					
Feb 24 1945	Tatsumomo Maru	Cargo	880*	32-40N, 132-33E	F. D. Latta
Feb 24 1945	RO-49	Submarine	965	32-40N, 132-33E	
	2 Vessels		1,845		
USS LAPON					
Oct 18 1943	Taichu Maru	Cargo	1,906	34-00N, 136-24E	
Mar 8 1944	Toyokuni Maru	Cargo	5,792	19-23N, 116-13E	
Mar 9 1944	Nichirei Maru	Cargo	5,396	19-47N, 116-13E	
Mar 18 1944	Hokuroku Maru	Passenger-Cargo	8,359	19-22N, 116-52E	
May 24 1944	Wales Maru	Passenger-Cargo	6,586	7-16N, 109-04E	L. T. Stone
May 24 1944	Bizen Maru	Cargo	4,667	7-25N, 108-43E	
Jul 18 1944	Kyodo Maru No 36	Passenger-Cargo	1,499	8-22N, 116-40E	
Jul 31 1944	Tenshin Maru	Tanker	5,061	8-22N, 116-40E	
Sep 22 1944	Shun Yuan	Cargo	1,610	15-22N, 119-17E	
Sep 27 1944	Hokki Maru	Tanker	5,599	15-45N, 117-48E	D. G. Baer
Oct 10 1944	Ejiri Maru	Cargo	6,968	16-10N, 119-44E	
	11 Vessels		53,443		
USS LIZARDFISH					
Jul 5 1945	Submarine Chaser No 37	Submarine Chaser	100	8-10S, 114-50E	O. M. Butler
USS MINGO					
Jul 7 1944	Tamanami	Destroyer	2,100	13-55N, 118-30E	J. J. Staley
Nov 25 1944	Manila Maru	Passenger-Cargo	9,486	5-30N, 113-21E	
	2 Vessels		11,586		
USS MUSKALLUNGE					
Aug 21 1944	Durban Maru	Passenger-Cargo	7,163	11-43N, 109-17E	M. P. Russillo
USS NARWHAL					
Mar 4 1942	Taki Maru	Cargo	1,244	28-37N, 129-10E	
Jul 24 1942	Unknown Maru	Cargo	1,500*	45-05N, 147-27E	C. W. Wilkins
Aug 1 1942	Meiwa Maru	Cargo	2,921	41-12N, 141-36E	
Aug 8 1942	Bifuku Maru	Passenger-Cargo	2,559	41-14N, 141-32E	
Sep 11 1943	Hokusho Maru	Cargo	4,211	00-28S, 116-52E	
Dec 5 1943	Himeno Maru	Cargo	834	9-10N, 124-30E	F. D. Latta
Mar 3 1944	Karatsu	River Gunboat	560	8-52N, 123-23N	
	7 Vessels		13,829		

SUBMARINE AND DATE	NAME OF VESSEL	TYPE OF VESSEL	TONNAGE	LOCATION	SUBMARINE CAPTAIN
USS Nautilus					
Jun 25 1942	Yamakaze	Destroyer	1,580	34-34N, 140-26E	
Sep 28 1942	Tamon Maru No. 6	Cargo	4,994	40-35N, 141-50E	
Oct 1 1942	Tosei Maru	Cargo	2,432	41-20N, 141-35E	W. H. Brockman
Oct 24 1942	Kenun Maru	Cargo	4,643	41-24N, 141-50E	
Jan 9 1943	Yoshinogawa Maru	Cargo	1,430	6-13S, 156-00E	
Mar 6 1944	America Maru	Transport	6,070	21-50N, 143-54E	W. D. Irvin
		6 Vessels	21,149		
USS Paddle					
Aug 23 1943	Ataka Maru	Passenger-Cargo	5,248	34-37N, 137-53E	R. H. Rice
Apr 16 1944	Mito Maru	Passenger-Cargo	7,061	2-02S, 127-20E	
Apr 16 1944	Hino Maru No 1	Cargo	2,671	2-02S, 127-20E	B. H. Nowell
Jul 6 1944	Hokaze	Destroyer	1,300	3-24N, 125-28E	
Sep 7 1944	Shinyo Maru	Cargo	2,518	8-11N, 122-40E	
		5 Vessels	18,798		
USS Pampanito					
Sep 12 1944	Kachidoki Maru	Transport	10,509	19-18N, 111-53E	
Sep 12 1944	Zuiho Maru	Tanker	5,135	19-18N, 111-53E	P. E. Summers
Nov 19 1944	Shinko Maru No 1	Cargo	1,200	19-00N, 111-51E	F. W. Fenno
Feb 6 1945	Engen Maru	Cargo	6,968	6-29N, 106-11E	
Feb 8 1945	Eifuku Maru	Passenger-Cargo	3,520	7-04N, 104-46E	P. E. Summers
		5 Vessels	27,332		
USS Parche					
May 4 1944	Taiyoku Maru	Cargo	5,244	20-48N, 118-03E	
May 4 1944	Shoryu Naru	Cargo	6,475	20-48N, 118-03E	
Jul 31 1944	Koei Maru	Tanker	10,238	19-10N, 120-58E	L. P. Ramage
Jul 31 1944	Manko Maru	Passenger-Cargo	4,471	19-10N, 120-58E	
Feb 7 1945	Okinoyama Maru	Cargo	984	29-09N, 129-45E	
Apr 9 1945	Minesweeper No 3	Minesweeper	615	39-06N, 141-57E	
Jun 21 1945	Hizen Maru	Cargo	946	41-19N, 141-28E	W. W. McCrory
Jun 26 1945	Kamitsu Maru	Ex-Gunboat	2,723	39-25N, 142-04E	
		8 Vessels	31,696		
USS Pargo					
Nov 29 1943	Manju Maru	Cargo	5,877	18-23N, 140-18E	
Nov 30 1943	Shoko Maru	Cargo	1,933	14-31N, 140-18E	I. C. Eddy
May 4 1944	Eiryu Maru	Ex-Net Tender	758	7-04N, 129-18E	
Jun 28 1944	Yamagiku Maru	Cargo	5,236	6-50N, 122-41E	
Sep 10 1944	Hinoki Maru	Ex-Net Tender	599	6-27S, 116-48E	
Sep 26 1944	Aotaka	Minelayer	1,600	7-00N, 116-00E	
Nov 26 1944	Yuho Maru	Tanker	5,226	4-55N, 114-06E	D. B. Bell
Feb 20 1945	Nokaze	Destroyer	1,300	12-48N, 109-38E	
Aug 8 1945	Rashin Maru	Passenger-Cargo	5,454	41-23N, 131-25E	
		9 Vessels	27,983		
USS Permit					
Mar 8 1943	Hisashima Maru	Cargo	2,742	41-16N, 142-27E	
Jul 6 1943	Banshu Maru No 33	Cargo	787	43-35N, 140-21E	W. G. Chapple
Jul 7 1943	Showa Maru	Passenger-Cargo	2,212	43-14N, 139-53E	
		3 Vessels	5,741		

SUBMARINE AND DATE	NAME OF VESSEL	TYPE OF VESSEL	TONNAGE	LOCATION	SUBMARINE CAPTAIN
USS Peto					
Oct 1 1943	Tonei Maru	Passenger-Cargo	4,930	4-01N, 143-47E	
Oct 1 1943	Kinkasan Maru	Cargo	4,980	4-01N, 143-47E	W. T. Nelson
Dec 1 1943	Konei Maru	Cargo	2,345	1-02N, 146-42E	
Mar 4 1944	Kayo Maru	Passenger-Cargo	4,368	1-28S, 138-40E	P. Van Leunen
Nov 12 1944	Tatsuaki Maru	Cargo	2,766	31-18N, 125-30E	
Nov 18 1944	Aisakasan Maru	Cargo	6,923	33-50N, 124-44E	R. H. Caldwell
Nov 18 1944	Chinkai Maru	Cargo	2,827	33-39N, 124-26E	
		7 Vessels	29,139		
USS Pickerel					
Jan 10 1942	Kanko Maru	Ex-Gunboat	2,929	6-12N, 125-55E	B. E. Bacon
Feb 15 1943	Tateyama Maru	Cargo	1,990	39-18N, 142-08E	
Apr 3 1943	Submarine Chaser No 13	Submarine Chaser	440	40-00N, 142-00E	A. H. Alston
Apr 7 1943	Fukuei Maru	Cargo	1,113	41-00N, 142-00E	
		4 Vessels	6,472		
USS Picuda					
Mar 2 1944	Shinkyo Maru	Ex-Gunboat	2,672	6-25N, 148-31E	
Mar 20 1944	Hoko Maru	Cargo	1,504	10-06N, 138-10E	
Mar 30 1944	Atlantic Maru	Cargo	5,873	12-15N, 145-42E	A. L. Rayborn
May 22 1944	Hashidate	Gunboat	1,200	21-20N, 117-10E	
Aug 25 1944	Yunagi	Destroyer	1,270	18-46N, 120-46E	
Aug 25 1944	Kotoku Maru	Cargo	1,943	18-46N, 120-46E	
Sep 16 1944	Tokushima Maru	Passenger-Cargo	5,975	21-15N, 121-29E	G. R. Donaho
Sep 21 1944	Awaji Maru	Cargo	1,948	18-43N, 120-52E	
Nov 17 1944	Mayasan Maru	Passenger-Cargo	9,433	33-16N, 124-43E	
Nov 23 1944	Shuyo Maru	Cargo	6,933	34-15N, 128-58E	
Nov 23 1944	Fukuju Maru	Passenger-Cargo	5,291	34-19N, 128-05E	E. T. Shepard
Jan 29 1945	Clyde Maru	Passenger-Cargo	5,497	25-33N, 120-54E	
		12 Vessels	49,539		
USS Pike					
Aug 5 1943	Shoju Maru	Passenger-Cargo	2,022	24-37N, 152-45E	L. D. McGregor
USS Pintado					
Jun 1 1944	Toho Maru	Cargo	4,716	18-13N, 141-19E	
Jun 6 1944	Kashimasan Maru	Cargo	2,825	16-41N, 142-43E	
Jun 6 1944	Havre Maru	Cargo	5,652	16-41N, 142-43E	
Aug 6 1944	Shonan Maru	Cargo	5,401	30-53N, 129-47E	
Aug 22 1944	Sonan Maru No. 2	Tanker	19,262	29-44N, 125-22E	B. A. Clarey
Nov 3 1944	Akikaze	Destroyer	1,300	16-48N, 117-17E	
Dec 13 1944	Transport No 12	Landing Craft	1,900ᵉ	20-34N, 118-45E	
Dec 13 1944	Transport No 104	Landing Craft	1,900ᵉ	20-34N, 118-45E	
		8 Vessels	42,956		
USS Pipefish					
Sep 12 1944	Hakutetsu Maru No 7	Cargo	1,018	33-31N, 135-57E	
Dec 3 1944	Coast Def Vessel No 64	Frigate	800ᵉ	18-36N, 111-54E	W. N. Deragon
		2 Vessels	1,818		

SUBMARINE AND DATE	NAME OF VESSEL	TYPE OF VESSEL	TONNAGE	LOCATION	SUBMARINE CAPTAIN
USS PIRANHA					
Jul 12 1944	Nichiran Maru	Passenger-Cargo	6,504	18-33N, 122-53E	H. E. Ruble
Jul 16 1944	Seattle Maru	Passenger-Cargo	5,773	19-26N, 120-18E	
	2 Vessels		12,277		
USS PLAICE					
Jun 30 1944	Hyakufuku Maru	Ex-Gunboat	986	28-22N, 141-17E	C. B. Stevens
Jul 5 1944	Kogi Maru	Ex-Net Tender	857	27-43N, 141-02E	
Jul 18 1944	Submarine Chaser No 50	Submarine Chaser	300ᵉ	29-22N, 139-14E	
Sep 27 1944	Coast Def Vessel No 10	Frigate	800ᵉ	29-26N, 128-50E	
	4 Vessels		2,943		
USS PLUNGER					
Jan 18 1942	Eizan Maru	Cargo	4,702	33-30N, 135-00E	D. C. White
Jun 30 1942	Unkai Maru No 5	Cargo	3,282	30-04N, 122-54E	
Jul 2 1942	Unyo Maru No 3	Cargo	2,997	30-30N, 120-25E	
Mar 12 1943	Taihosan Maru	Ex-Water Carrier	1,805	7-15N, 159-10E	
May 10 1943	Tatsutake Maru	Passenger-Cargo	7,068	14-29N, 149-00E	
May 10 1943	Kinai Maru	Passenger-Cargo	8,360	14-29N, 149-00E	
Jul 12 1943	Nijtaka Maru	Passenger-Cargo	2,478	43-02N, 140-00E	R. H. Bass
Aug 20 1943	Seitai Maru	Cargo	3,404	42-15N, 139-58E	
Aug 22 1943	Ryokai Maru	Cargo	4,655	42-40N, 139-48E	
Feb 2 1944	Toyo Maru No 5	Cargo	2,193	33-32N, 135-58E	
Feb 2 1944	Toyo Maru No 8	Cargo	2,191	33-32N, 135-58E	
Feb 23 1944	Kimishima Maru	Cargo	5,193	30-30N, 140-20E	
	12 Vessels		48,328		
USS POGY					
May 1 1943	Keishin Maru	Ex-Gunboat	1,434	37-04N, 141-06E	G. H. Wales
May 26 1943	Tainan Maru	Cargo	1,989	37-03N, 141-09E	
Aug 1 1943	Mogamigawa Maru	Aircraft Ferry	7,497	11-16N, 153-34E	
Sep 30 1943	Maebashi Maru	Passenger-Cargo	7,005	6-01N, 139-08E	
Dec 7 1943	Soyo Maru	Submarine Tender	6,081	14-04N, 152-09E	
Dec 13 1943	Fukkai Maru	Passenger-Cargo	3,829	7-07N, 134-31E	
Feb 10 1944	Minekaze	Destroyer	1,300	23-12N, 121-30E	
Feb 10 1944	Malta Maru	Passenger-Cargo	5,500	23-12N, 121-30E	
Feb 20 1944	Taijin Maru	Cargo	5,154	24-12N, 123-20E	R. M. Metcalf
Feb 20 1944	Nanyo Maru	Cargo	3,610	24-28N, 123-31E	
Feb 23 1944	Horei Maru	Cargo	5,588	26-22N, 126-15E	
Apr 28 1944	I-183	Submarine	1,630	32-07N, 133-03E	
May 5 1944	Shirane Maru	Cargo	2,825	33-31N, 135-28E	
May 13 1944	Anbo Maru	Cargo	4,523	34-31N, 138-33E	
Jul 27 1945	Chikuzen Maru	Passenger-Cargo	2,448	37-00N, 134-02E	J. M. Bowers
Aug 5 1945	Kotohirasan Maru	Cargo	2,220	39-52N, 138-52E	
	16 Vessels		62,633		

SUBMARINE AND DATE	NAME OF VESSEL	TYPE OF VESSEL	TONNAGE	LOCATION	SUBMARINE CAPTAIN
USS POLLACK					
Jan 7 1942	Unkai Maru No 1	Cargo	2,225	34-27N, 138-59E	
Jan 9 1942	Teian Maru	Cargo	5,387	35-00N, 140-36E	S. P. Mosley
Mar 11 1942	Fukushu Maru	Cargo	1,454	30-53N, 126-20E	
May 18 1943	Terushima Maru	Ex-Gunboat	3,110	8-45N, 170-30E	
May 20 1943	Bangkok Maru	Ex-Light Cruiser	5,350	5-47N, 169-42E	
Aug 27 1943	Taifuku Maru	Passenger-Cargo	3,520	32-27N, 132-24E	
Sep 3 1943	Tagonoura Maru	Cargo	3,521	34-10N, 140-12E	
Mar 20 1944	Hakuyo Maru	Cargo	1,327	30-53N, 140-42E	B. E. Lewellen
Mar 25 1944	Submarine Chaser No 54	Submarine Chaser	300	28-34N, 142-14E	
Apr 3 1944	Tosei Maru	Passenger-Cargo	2,814	30-00N, 139-44E	
May 22 1944	Asanagi	Destroyer	1,270	28-20N, 138-57E	
	11 Vessels		**30,278**		
USS POMFRET					
Oct 2 1944	Tsuyama Maru	Passenger-Cargo	6,962	21-00N, 121-46E	F. C. Acker
Nov 2 1944	Atlas Maru	Passenger-Cargo	7,347	20-20N, 121-30E	
Nov 2 1944	Hamburg Maru	Passenger-Cargo	5,271	20-20N, 121-30E	J. H. Hess
Nov 25 1944	Shoho Maru	Cargo	1,356	20-18N, 121-34E	
	4 Vessels		**20,936**		
USS POMPANO					
May 25 1942	Tokyo Maru	Tanker	902	27-03N, 127-03E	
May 30 1942	Atsuta Maru	Transport	7,983	26-07N, 129-06E	L. S. Parks
Aug 12 1942	Unknown Maru	Cargo	4,000ᵉ	33-02N, 136-00E	
Sep 3 1943	Akama Maru	Cargo	5,600	41-00N, 141-30E	W. H. Thomas
Sep 25 1943	Taiko Maru	Cargo	2,958	41-30N, 139-00E	
	5 Vessels		**21,443**		
USS POMPON					
Jul 25 1943	Thames Maru	Cargo	5,871	2-40N, 148-26E	E. C. Hawk
May 30 1944	Shiga Maru	Cargo	742	33-15N, 134-11E	
Aug 12 1944	Mayachi Maru	Cargo	2,159	50-28N, 144-09E	S. H. Gimber
	3 Vessels		**8,772**		
USS PORPOISE					
Jan 1 1943	Renzan Maru	Cargo	4,999	39-11N, 141-44E	J. R. McKnight
Apr 4 1943	Koa Maru	Cargo	2,024	13-11N, 161-57E	
Jul 19 1943	Mikage Maru No 20	Passenger-Cargo	2,718	18-34N, 166-20E	C. L. Bennett
	3 Vessels		**9,741**		
USS PUFFER					
Dec 20 1943	Fuyo	Old Destroyer	820	14-44N, 119-55E	
Jan 1 1944	Ryuyo Maru	Cargo	6,707	8-24N, 122-56E	
Feb 22 1944	Teiko Maru	Transport	15,105	3-03N, 109-16E	
May 18 1944	Shinryu Maru	Cargo	3,181	7-36S, 113-12E	F. G. Selby
Jun 5 1944	Ashizuri	Tanker	2,166ᵉ	6-32N, 120-40E	
Jun 5 1944	Takasaki	Tanker	2,500ᵉ	6-32N, 120-40E	
Aug 12 1944	Teikon Maru	Tanker	5,113	13-17N, 120-07E	
Jan 10 1945	Coast Def Vessel No 42	Frigate	800ᵉ	27-01N, 126-34E	C. R. Dwyer
	8 Vessels		**36,392**		

SUBMARINE AND DATE	NAME OF VESSEL	TYPE OF VESSEL	TONNAGE	LOCATION	SUBMARINE CAPTAIN
USS Queenfish					
Aug 31 1944	Chiyoda Maru	Tanker	4,700	21-21N, 121-06E	
Sep 9 1944	Toyooka Maru	Passenger-Cargo	7,097	19-45N, 120-56E	
Sep 9 1944	Manshu Maru	Transport	3,054	19-45N, 120-56E	
Nov 8 1944	Keijo Maru	Cargo	1,051	31-09N, 129-38E	C. E. Loughlin
Nov 8 1944	Hakko Maru	Cargo	1,948	31-09N, 129-38E	
Nov 9 1944	Chojusan Maru	Ex-Gunboat	2,131	31-17N, 129-10E	
Nov 15 1944	Akitsu Maru	Aircraft Ferry	9,186	33-15N, 128-10E	
Apr 1 1945	Awa Maru	Passenger-Cargo	11,600	25-25N, 120-07E	
	8 Vessels		40,767		
USS Rasher					
Oct 9 1943	Kogane Maru	Passenger-Cargo	3,132	3-36S, 127-44E	
Oct 13 1943	Kenkoku Maru	Cargo	3,127	3-47S, 127-41E	E. S. Hutchinson
Oct 31 1943	Koryo Maru	Tanker	589	1-25N, 120-46E	
Nov 8 1943	Tango Maru	Tanker	2,046	00-22N, 119-44E	
Jan 4 1944	Kiyo Maru	Tanker	7,251	5-46N, 108-36E	
Feb 25 1944	Tango Maru	Cargo	6,200	7-46S, 115-09E	
Feb 25 1944	Ryusei Maru	Passenger-Cargo	4,797	7-56S, 115-14E	
Mar 3 1944	Nittai Maru	Cargo	6,484	3-17N, 123-55E	
Mar 27 1944	Nichinan Maru	Cargo	2,750	7-31S, 115-57E	W. R. Laughon
May 11 1944	Choi Maru	Cargo	1,074	3-30S, 126-06E	
May 29 1944	Anshu Maru	Converted Gunboat	2,601	3-40S, 126-58E	
Jun 8 1944	Shioya	Tanker	4,000ᵉ	3-04N, 124-03E	
Jun 14 1944	Koan Maru	Cargo	3,183	4-31N, 122-25E	
Aug 6 1944	Shiroganesan Maru	Cargo	4,739	14-14N, 117-16E	
Aug 18 1944	Eishin Maru	Cargo	542	18-16N, 120-20E	
Aug 18 1944	Teiyo Maru	Tanker	9,849	18-09N, 119-56E	H. G. Munson
Aug 18 1944	Otaka	Escort Aircraft Carrier	20,000	18-16N, 120-20E	
Aug 19 1944	Teia Maru	Transport	17,537	18-09N, 119-56E	
	18 Vessels		99,901		
USS Raton					
Nov 26 1943	Onoe Maru	Cargo	6,667	00-40N, 148-14E	
Nov 28 1943	Hokko Maru	Cargo	5,347	1-40N, 141-45E	
Nov 28 1943	Yuri Maru	Cargo	6,787	1-40N, 141-45E	
Dec 24 1943	Heiwa Maru	Cargo	5,578	2-45N, 127-41E	J. W. Davis
May 24 1944	Iki	Frigate	860	1-17N, 107-50E	
Jun 6 1944	Coast Def Vessel No 15	Frigate	800ᵉ	8-58N, 109-30E	
Oct 18 1944	Shiranesan Maru	Cargo	4,739	12-37N, 118-46E	
Oct 18 1944	Taikai Maru	Passenger-Cargo	3,812	12-37N, 118-46E	
Nov 14 1944	Unkai Maru No 5	Tanker	2,841	17-57N, 117-45E	
Nov 14 1944	Kurasaki	Miscellaneous Auxiliary	989	17-27N, 117-43E	M. W. Shea
May 2 1945	Toryu Maru	Cargo	1,992	37-22N, 123-43E	
May 12 1945	Rekizan Maru	Cargo	1,311	37-23N, 123-42E	
May 16 1945	Eiju Maru	Cargo	2,455	37-39N, 124-11E	
	13 Vessels		44,178		

SUBMARINE AND DATE	NAME OF VESSEL	TYPE OF VESSEL	TONNAGE	LOCATION	SUBMARINE CAPTAIN
USS RAY					
Nov 26 1943	Nikkai Maru	Converted Gunboat	2,562	4-00N, 147-50E	B. J. Harrel
Dec 27 1943	Kyoko Maru	Tanker	5,792	5-00S, 121-22E	
Jan 1 1944	Okuyo Maru	Converted Gunboat	2,904	3-51S, 128-04E	
May 22 1944	Tenpei Maru	Passenger-Cargo	6,094	5-43N, 127-37E	
Jul 18 1944	Janbi Maru	Tanker	5,244	5-21S, 112-30E	
Aug 4 1944	Koshu Maru	Cargo	2,612	3-59S, 117-54E	
Aug 14 1944	Zuisho Maru	Passenger-Cargo	5,289	3-52N, 112-56E	
Aug 18 1944	Nansei Maru	Tanker	5,878	8-48N, 116-58E	W. T. Kinsella
Aug 21 1944	Taketoyo Maru	Passenger-Cargo	6,965	13-23N, 120-19E	
Oct 12 1944	Toko Maru	Passenger-Cargo	4,180	13-31N, 120-19E	
Nov 1 1944	Horai Maru No 7	Cargo	865	13-02N, 120-17E	
Nov 14 1944	Coast Def Vessel No 7	Frigate	800ᵉ	17-46N, 117-57E	
	12 Vessels		49,185		
USS RAZORBACK					
Dec 30 1944	Kuretake	Old Destroyer	820	21-00N, 21-24E	C. D. Brown
USS REDFIN					
Apr 11 1944	Akigumo	Destroyer	1,900	6-43N, 122-23E	
Apr 15 1944	Shinyu Maru	Passenger-Cargo	4,621	6-41N, 123-40E	
Apr 16 1944	Yamagata Maru	Passenger-Cargo	3,807	7-04N, 123-27E	M. H. Austin
Jun 11 1944	Asanagi Maru	Tanker	5,142	6-20N, 120-47E	
Jun 24 1944	Aso Maru	Passenger-Cargo	3,028	9-57N, 125-07E	
Nov 8 1944	Nichinan Maru No 2	Tanker	5,226	13-46N, 116-53E	
	6 Vessels		23,724		
USS REDFISH					
Aug 25 1944	Batopaha Maru	Cargo	5,953	18-33N, 120-34E	
Sep 16 1944	Ogura Maru No 2	Tanker	7,311	21-23N, 121-17E	
Sep 21 1944	Mizuho Maru	Transport	8,506	18-35N, 120-39E	L. D. McGregor
Nov 23 1944	Hozan Maru	Transport	2,345	24-26N, 122-46E	
Dec 19 1944	Unryu	Aircraft Carrier	18,500	28-59N, 124-03E	
	5 Vessels		42,615		
USS ROCK					
Oct 26 1944	Takasago Maru No 7	Tanker	834ᵉ	10-18N, 117-47E	J. J. Flachsenhar
USS RONQUIL					
Aug 24 1944	Yoshida Maru No 3	Cargo	4,646	25-13N, 121-49E	H. S. Monroe
Aug 24 1944	Fukurei Maru	Cargo	5,969	25-13N, 121-49	
	2 Vessels		10,615		
USS RUNNER					
Jun 11 1943	Seinan Maru	Cargo	1,338	41-00N, 141-30E	J. H. Bourland
Jun 26 1943	Shinryu Maru	Passenger-Cargo	4,936	48-06N, 153-15E	
	2 Vessels		6,274		
USS RUNNER II					
Jul 10 1945	Minesweeper No 27	Minesweeper	630ᵉ	39-20N, 142-07E	R. H. Bass
USS S-28					
Sep 19 1943	Katsura Maru No 2	Converted Gunboat	1,368	49-05N, 151-45E	V. A. Sisler

SUBMARINE AND DATE	NAME OF VESSEL	TYPE OF VESSEL	TONNAGE	LOCATION	SUBMARINE CAPTAIN
USS S-30					
Jun 11 1943	Jinbu Maru	Cargo	5,228	50-23N, 155-36E	W. A. Stevenson
USS S-31					
Oct 26 1942	Keizan Maru	Cargo	2,864	50-09N, 155-37E	R. F. Sellars
USS S-35					
Jul 2 1943	Banshu Maru No 7	Cargo	5,430	52-30N, 156-12E	H. S. Monroe
USS S-37					
Feb 8 1942	Natsushio	Destroyer	1,900	5-10S, 119-24E	J. C. Dempsey
Jul 8 1942	Tenzan Maru	Passenger-Cargo	2,776	4-00S, 151-50E	J. R. Reynolds
		2 Vessels	4,676		
USS S-38					
Dec 22 1941	Hayo Maru	Cargo	5,445	16-37N, 120-17E	W. G. Chapple
Aug 8 1942	Meiyo Maru	Transport	5,628	4-52S, 152-43E	H. G. Munson
		2 Vessels	11,073		
USS S-39					
Mar 4 1942	Erimo	Tanker	6,500	4-19S, 108-25E	J. W. Coe
USS S-41					
May 28 1943	Seiki Maru	Cargo	1,036	50-38N, 155-15E	I. S. Hartman
USS S-42					
May 11 1942	Okinoshima	Minelayer	4,400	5-06S, 153-48E	O. G. Kirk
USS S-44					
May 12 1942	Shoei Maru	Converted Salvage Vessel	5,644	4-51S, 152-54E	
Jun 21 1942	Keijo Maru	Converted Gunboat	2,626	9-00S, 160-00E	J. R. Moore
Aug 10 1942	Kako	Heavy Cruiser	8,800	2-1S, 152-15E	
		3 Vessels	17,070		
USS Sailfish					
Mar 2 1942	Kamogawa Maru	Aircraft Ferry	6,440	8-06S, 115-57E	R. G. Voge
Jun 15 1943	Shinju Maru	Cargo	3,617	39-13N, 142-00E	J. R. Moore
Jun 25 1943	Iburi Maru	Passenger-Cargo	3,291	39-34N, 142-06E	
Dec 4 1943	Chuyo	Escort Aircraft Carrier	20,000	32-37N, 143-39E	
Dec 13 1943	Totai Maru	Cargo	3,195	30-55N, 132-33E	R. E. M. Ward
Dec 21 1943	Uyo Maru	Cargo	6,376	32-38N, 132-04E	
Aug 24 1944	Toan Maru	Cargo	2,110	21-29N, 121-18E	
		7 Vessels	45,029		
USS Salmon					
May 25 1942	Asahi	Repair Ship	11,441	10-00N, 110-00E	
May 28 1942	Ganges Maru	Passenger-Cargo	4,382	9-00N, 111-00E	E. B. McKinney
Nov 17 1942	Oregon Maru	Converted Salvage Vessel	5,873	14-46N, 119-44E	
Aug 10 1943	Wakanoura Maru	Passenger-Cargo	2,411	46-58N, 143-30E	N. Nicholas
		4 Vessels	24,107		

SUBMARINE AND DATE	NAME OF VESSEL	TYPE OF VESSEL	TONNAGE	LOCATION	SUBMARINE CAPTAIN
USS SANDLANCE					
Feb 28 1944	Kaiko Maru	Cargo	3,548	50-02N, 155-30E	
Mar 3 1944	Akashisan Maru	Cargo	4,541	45-52N, 149-16E	
Mar 13 1944	Tatsuta	Light Cruiser	3,300	32-58N, 138-52E	
Mar 13 1944	Kokuyo Maru	Cargo	4,667	32-58N, 138-52E	
May 3 1944	Kenan Maru	Cargo	3,129	15-29N, 145-42E	
May 11 1944	Mitakesan Maru	Passenger-Cargo	4,441	14-58N, 145-26E	M. A. Garrison
May 14 1944	Koho Maru	Cargo	4,291	13-42N, 144-43E	
May 17 1944	Taikoku Maru	Cargo	2,633	14-57N, 144-47E	
May 17 1944	Fukko Maru	Passenger-Cargo	3,834	14-55N, 142-30E	
Jul 14 1944	Taiko Maru	Converted Gunboat	2,984	6-00S, 121-30E	
		10 Vessels	37,368		
USS SARGO					
Sep 25 1942	Teibo Maru	Cargo	4,472	10-31N, 109-31E	R. V. Gregory
Jun 13 1943	Konan Maru	Passenger-Cargo	5,226	6-05N, 138-25E	E. S. Carmick
Nov 9 1943	Taga Maru	Cargo	2,868	21-38N, 131-19E	
Nov 11 1943	Kosei Maru	Passenger-Cargo	3,551	27-36N, 130-32E	
Feb 17 1944	Nichiro Maru	Passenger-Cargo	6,534	8-50N, 135-57E	P. W. Garnett
Feb 29 1944	Uchide Maru	Passenger-Cargo	5,275	8-57N, 132-52E	
Apr 26 1944	Wazan Maru	Cargo	4,851	33-30N, 135-27E	
		7 Vessels	32,777		
USS SAURY					
Sep 11 1942	Kanto Maru	Aircraft Ferry	8,606	3-16S, 118-29E	L. S. Mewhinney
May 26 1943	Kagi Maru	Transport	2,343	28-45N, 129-37E	
May 28 1943	Akatsuki Maru	Tanker	10,216	27-32N, 126-08E	
May 30, 1943	Takamisan Maru	Cargo	1,992	30-07N, 124-32E	A. H. Dropp
May 30 1943	Shoko Maru	Cargo	5,385	30-07N, 124-32E	
		5 Vessels	28,542		
USS SAWFISH					
May 5 1943	Hakkai Maru	Cargo	2,921	34-11N, 137-41E	
Jul 27 1943	Hirashima	Coastal Minelayer	720	32-32N, 127-41E	E. T. Sands
Dec 8 1943	Sansei Maru	Passenger-Cargo	3,267	25-20N, 141-46E	
Jul 26 1944	I-29	Submarine	2,212	20-10N, 121-50E	
Oct 9 1944	Tachibana Maru	Tanker	6,521	19-33N, 116-38E	A. B. Banister
Oct 23 1944	Kimikawa Maru	Converted Seaplane Tender	6,863	18-58N, 118-31E	
		6 Vessels	22,504		
USS SCABBARDFISH					
Nov 16 1944	Kisaragi Maru	Cargo	875	28-56N, 141-59E	F. A. Gunn
Nov 28 1944	I-365	Submarine	1,470	34-44N, 141-01E	
		2 Vessels	2,345		

SUBMARINE AND DATE	NAME OF VESSEL	TYPE OF VESSEL	TONNAGE	LOCATION	SUBMARINE CAPTAIN
USS Scamp					
May 28 1943	Kamikawa Maru	Converted Seaplane Tender	6,853	1-36S, 150-24E	
Jul 27 1943	I-24	Submarine	2,180	2-50S, 149-01E	
Sep 18 1943	Kansai Maru	Passenger-Cargo	8,614	00-25N, 146-21E	W. G. Ebert
Nov 10 1943	Tokyo Maru	Passenger-Cargo	6,486	3-36N, 150-34E	
Jan 14 1944	Nippon Maru	Tanker	9,975	5-02N, 140-43E	
		5 Vessels	34,108		
USS Scorpion					
Apr 20 1943	Meiji Maru No 1	Converted Gunboat	1,934	37-10N, 141-25E	
Apr 27 1943	Yuzan Maru	Passenger-Cargo	6,380	38-08N, 143-03E	W. N. Wylie
Jul 3 1943	Anzan Maru	Cargo	3,890	38-08N, 124-20E	
Jul 3 1943	Kokuryu Maru	Passenger-Cargo	6,112	38-08N, 124-20E	
		4 Vessels	18,316		
USS Sculpin					
Oct 7 1942	Naminoue Maru	Transport	4,731	3-51S, 151-21E	
Oct 14 1942	Sumiyoshi Maru	Cargo	1,921	3-20S, 150-03E	L. H. Chappell
Aug 9 1943	Sekko Maru	Passenger-Cargo	3,183	24-51N, 122-12E	
		3 Vessels	9,835		
USS Sea Devil					
Sep 15 1944	RO-42	Submarine	965	34-30N, 145-23E	
Dec 2 1944	Akigawa Maru	Cargo	6,859	30-51N, 128-45E	
Dec 2 1944	Hawaii Maru	Passenger-Cargo	9,467	30-51N, 128-45E	
Apr 2 1945	Taijo Maru	Cargo	6,866	34-18N, 124-04E	R. H. Styles
Apr 2 1945	Edogawa Maru	Cargo	1,972	34-18N, 124-04E	
Apr 2 1945	Nisshin Maru	Cargo	1,179	34-18N, 124-04E	
Jun 14 1945	Wakamiyasan Maru	Cargo	2,211	37-38N, 123-34E	C. F. McGivern
		7 Vessels	29,519		
USS Sea Dog					
Oct 22 1944	Tomitsu Maru	Converted Gunboat	2,933	29-20N, 129-45E	V. L. Lowrance
Oct 22 1944	Muroto	Supply Ship	4,500ᵉ	29-20N, 129-45E	
Apr 16 1945	Toyo Maru	Cargo	6,850	33-24N, 139-31E	
Jun 9 1945	Sagawa Maru	Cargo	1,186	38-13N, 138-43E	
Jun 9 1945	Shoyo Maru	Cargo	2,211	38-11N, 138-45E	
Jun 11 1945	Kofuku Maru	Cargo	753	40-28N, 139-47E	E. T. Hydeman
Jun 12 1945	Shinsen Maru	Cargo	880	40-09N, 139-43E	
Jun 15 1945	Koan Maru	Passenger-Cargo	884	39-53N, 139-40E	
Jun 19 1945	Kokai Maru	Cargo	1,272	43-12N, 140-19E	
		9 Vessels	21, 469		
USS Sea Owl					
Apr 17 1945	RO-56	Submarine	889	19-17N, 166-35E	C. L. Bennet
Jun 9 1945	Coast Def Vessel No 41	Frigate	800ᵉ	34-18N, 127-18E	
		2 Vessels	1,689		

SUBMARINE AND DATE	NAME OF VESSEL	TYPE OF VESSEL	TONNAGE	LOCATION	SUBMARINE CAPTAIN
USS SEA ROBIN					
Jan 6 1945	Tarakan Maru	Tanker	5,135	19-40N, 111-24E	
Mar 3 1945	Suiten Maru	Cargo	2,500	6-29S, 112-48E	
Mar 5 1945	Shoyu Maru	Cargo	853	5-42S, 114-02E	
Mar 5 1945	Nagara Maru	Cargo	856	5-41S, 114-01E	P. C. Stimson
Mar 5 1945	Manyo Maru	Converted Gunboat	2,904	5-56S, 113-45E	
Jul 10 1945	Sakishima Maru	Cargo	1,224	33-39N, 126-40E	
	6 Vessels		13,472		
USS SEADRAGON					
Feb 2 1942	Tamagawa Maru	Passenger-Cargo	6,441	17-16N, 119-48E	
Jul 12 1942	Hiyama Maru	Cargo	6,171	13-48N, 109-33E	
Jul 13 1942	Shinyo Maru	Passenger-Cargo	4,163	13-04N, 109-39E	W. E. Ferrall
Jul 16 1942	Hakodate Maru	Cargo	5,302	12-55N, 109-29E	
Oct 10 1942	Shigure Maru	Cargo	2,445	1-01S, 117-23E	
Dec 20 1942	I-4	Submarine	1,995	5-02S, 152-33E	
Apr 23 1944	Daiju Maru	Cargo	1,279	33-35N, 135-45E	J. H. Ashley
Oct 24 1944	Eiko Maru	Cargo	1,843	20-10N, 118-16E	
Oct 24 1944	Taiten Maru	Passenger-Cargo	6,442	20-31N, 118-32E	
Oct 24 1944	Kokuryu Maru	Passenger-Cargo	7,369	20-33N, 118-34E	
	10 Vessels		43,450		
USS SEAHORSE					
Nov 2 1943	Chihaya Maru	Cargo	7,089	28-37N, 134-47E	
Nov 2 1943	Ume Maru	Passenger-Cargo	5,859	28-37N, 134-45E	
Nov 22 1943	Daishu Maru	Cargo	3,322	33-36N, 128-35E	
Nov 26 1943	Unknown Maru	Cargo	4,000e	33-36N, 128-57E	
Nov 27 1943	San Ramon Maru	Tanker	7,309	33-38N, 129-05E	
Jan 16 1944	Nikko Maru	Cargo	784	12-49N, 150-19E	
Jan 21 1944	Yasukuni Maru	Cargo	3,025	3-19N, 137-02E	
Jan 21 1944	Ikoma Maru	Passenger-Cargo	3,156	3-19N, 137-02E	
Jan 30 1944	Toko Maru	Passenger-Cargo	2,747	6-10N, 138-14E	
Feb 1 1944	Toei Maru	Cargo	4,004	4-21N, 143-16E	S. D. Cutter
Apr 8 1944	Aratama Maru	Converted Submarine Tender	6,784	13-16N, 144-45E	
Apr 8 1944	Kizugawa Maru	Cargo	1,915	13-16N, 144-45E	
Apr 9 1944	Bisaku Maru	Cargo	4,467	15-22N, 145-06E	
Apr 20 1944	RO-45	Submarine	965	15-19N, 145-31E	
Apr 27 1944	Akiguwa Maru	Cargo	3,244	14-50N, 142-23E	
Jun 27 1944	Medan Maru	Tanker	5,135	21-21N, 120-18E	
Jul 3 1944	Nitto Maru	Cargo	2,186	19-28N, 115-41E	
Jul 3 1944	Gyoyu Maru	Passenger-Cargo	2,232	19-28N, 115-41E	
Jul 4 1944	Kyodo Maru No 28	Cargo	1,506	20-20N, 114-54E	
Oct 6 1944	Coast Def Vessel No 21	Frigate	800e	19-27N, 118-08E	C. W. Wilkins
	20 Vessels		72,529		

SUBMARINE AND DATE	NAME OF VESSEL	TYPE OF VESSEL	TONNAGE	LOCATION	SUBMARINE CAPTAIN
USS SEAL					
Dec 23 1941	Hayataka Maru	Cargo	856	17-35N, 120-12E	
May 28 1942	Tatsufuku Maru	Cargo	1,946	7-27N, 116-17E	K. C. Hurd
Nov 16 1942	Boston Maru	Transport	5,477	6-18N, 135-20E	
May 4 1943	San Clemente Maru	Tanker	7,354	6-54N, 134-55E	H. B. Dodge
Aug 24 1944	Tosei Maru	Cargo	531	42-30N, 144-05E	
Sep 9 1944	Shonan Maru	Passenger-Cargo	5,859	47-58N, 148-20E	J. H. Turner
Oct 25 1944	Hakuyo Maru	Cargo	5,742	50-17N, 150-50E	
		7 Vessels	27,765		
USS SEALION II					
Jun 28 1944	Sansei Maru	Cargo	2,386	34-03N, 129-00E	
Jul 6 1944	Setsuzan Maru	Cargo	1,922	29-59N, 122-53E	
Jul 11 1944	Tsukushi Maru No 2	Cargo	2,417	37-24N, 124-31E	
Jul 11 1944	Taian Maru No 2	Cargo	1,034	37-30N, 124-32E	
Aug 31 1944	Shirataka	Minelayer	1,345	21-05N, 121-26E	E. T. Reich
Sep 12 1944	Nankai Maru	Passenger-Cargo	8,416	18-42N, 114-30E	
Sep 12 1944	Rakuyo Maru	Passenger-Cargo	9,419	18-42N, 114-30E	
Nov 21 1944	Kongo	Battleship	31,000	26-09N, 121-23E	
Nov 21 1944	Urakaze	Destroyer	1,900	26-09N, 121-23E	
Dec 20 1944	Mamiya	Supply Ship	7,000e	17-48N, 114-09E	C. F. Putnam
Mar 17 1945	Samui	Tanker	1,458	5-18N, 103-23E	
		11 Vessels	68,297		
USS SEARAVEN					
Jan 14 1943	Shiraha Maru	Cargo	5,693	9-12N, 130-38E	H. Cassedy
Nov 25 1943	Toa Maru	Tanker	10,052	8-20N, 158-00E	M. H. Dry
Sep 21 1944	Rizan Maru	Cargo	4,747	49-16N, 145-29E	
		3 Vessels	20,492		
USS SEAWOLF					
Jun 15 1942	Nampo Maru	Converted Gunboat	1,206	14,20N, 120-20E	
Aug 14 1942	Hachigen Maru	Passenger-Cargo	3,113	5-07N, 119-37E	
Aug 25 1942	Showa Maru	Cargo	1,349	3-55N, 118-59E	
Nov 2 1942	Gifu Maru	Cargo	2,933	6-14N, 126-07E	F. B. Warder
Nov 3 1942	Sagami Maru	Passenger-Cargo	7,189	7-02N, 125-33E	
Nov 8 1942	Keiko Maru	Converted Gunboat	2,929	6-22N, 126-03E	
Apr 15 1943	Kaihei Maru	Cargo	4,575	21-06N, 151-45E	
Apr 23 1943	Patrol Boat No 39	Old Destroyer	820e	23-45N, 122-45E	
Jun 20 1943	Shojin Maru	Cargo	4,739	24-39N, 118-52E	
Aug 31 1943	Shoto Maru	Passenger-Cargo	5,254	28-27N, 123-03E	
Aug 31 1943	Kokko Maru	Cargo	5,486	28-27N, 123-03E	
Sep 1 1943	Fusei Maru	Passenger-Cargo	2,256	31-28N, 127-24E	
Oct 29 1943	Wuhu Maru	Cargo	3,222	22-30N, 115-25E	R. L. Gross
Nov 4 1943	Kaifuku Maru	Passenger-Cargo	3,177	21-22N, 113-20E	
Jan 10 1944	Asuka Maru	Cargo	7,523	27-35N, 127-30E	
Jan 10 1944	Getsuyo Maru	Cargo	6,440	27-22N, 127-31E	
Jan 11 1944	Yahiko Maru	Cargo	5,747	27-10N, 127-28E	
Jan 14 1944	Yamatsuru Maru	Cargo	3,651	28-30N, 133-40E	
		18 Vessels	71,609		

SUBMARINE AND DATE	NAME OF VESSEL	TYPE OF VESSEL	TONNAGE	LOCATION	SUBMARINE CAPTAIN
USS SEGUNDO					
Mar 11 1945	Shori Maru	Cargo	3,087	34-29N, 127-55E	J. D. Fulp
Jun 11 1945	Fukui Maru No 2	Cargo	1,578	37-11N, 123-23E	
		2 Vessels	4,665		
USS SENNET					
Feb 16 1945	Nariu	Coastal Minelayer	720	32-10N, 135-54E	G. E. Porter
Apr 19 1945	Hagane Maru	Cargo	1,901	33-35N, 135-23E	
Apr 28 1945	Hatsushima	Repair Ship	2,000ᵉ	33-58N, 136-17E	
Jul 28 1945	Unkai Maru No 15	Cargo	1,208	39-53N, 139-43E	
Jul 28 1945	Hagikawa Maru	Cargo	2,995	40-17N, 139-50E	C. R. Clark
Jul 28 1945	Hakuei Maru	Tanker	2,863	39-53N, 139-43E	
Jul 30 1945	Yuzan Maru	Passenger-Cargo	6,039	42-36N, 139-48E	
		7 Vessels	17,726		
USS SHAD					
Sep 19 1944	Ioshima	Frigate	900ᵉ	33-40N, 138-18E	L. V. Julihn
May 17 1945	Chosan Maru	Cargo	3,939	35-41, 126-17E	D. L. Mehlhop
Jun 7 1945	Azusa Maru	Cargo	1,370	34-00N, 126-45E	
		3 Vessels	6,209		
USS SHARK					
Jun 2 1944	Chiyo Maru	Cargo	4,700	20-53N, 140-17E	
Jun 4 1944	Katsukawa Maru	Cargo	6,886	19-35N, 138-43E	E. N. Blakely
Jun 5 1944	Tamahime Maru	Cargo	3,080	17-37N, 140-32E	
Jun 5 1944	Takaoka Maru	Passenger-Cargo	7,006	17-37N, 140-32E	
		4 Vessels	21,672		
USS SILVERSIDES					
May 17 1942	Unknown Maru	Cargo	4,000ᵉ	33-28N, 135-33E	
Jul 28 1942	Unknown Maru	Transport	4,000ᵉ	33-21N, 139-24E	
Aug 8 1942	Nikkei Maru	Passenger-Cargo	5,811	33-33N, 135-23E	
Jan 18 1943	Toei Maru	Tanker	10,023	6-21N, 150-23E	
Jan 20 1943	Somedono Maru	Passenger-Cargo	5,154	3-52N, 153-56E	C. R. Burlingame
Jan 20 1943	Surabaya Maru	Cargo	4,391	3-52N, 153-56E	
Jan 20 1943	Meiu Maru	Cargo	8,230	3-52N, 153-56E	
Jun 11 1943	Hide Maru	Cargo	5,256	2-47N, 152-00E	
Oct 18 1943	Tairin Maru	Cargo	1,915	1-00N, 143-16E	
Oct 24 1943	Tennan Maru	Cargo	5,407	2-05N, 144-39E	
Oct 24 1943	Kazan Maru	Cargo	1,893	2-05N, 144-39E	
Oct 24 1943	Johore Maru	Passenger-Cargo	6,182	2-05N, 144-39E	
Dec 29 1943	Tenposan Maru	Cargo	1,970	8-00N, 133-51E	
Dec 29 1943	Shichisei Maru	Cargo	1,911	8-03N, 134-04E	
Dec 29 1943	Ryuto Maru	Cargo	5,311	8-00N, 133-51E	
Mar 16 1944	Kofuku Maru	Cargo	1,920	4-28N, 136-56E	
May 10 1944	Okinawa Maru	Cargo	2,254	11-26N, 143-46E	J. S. Coye
May 10 1944	Mikage Maru No 18	Passenger-Cargo	4,319	11-26N, 143-46E	
May 10 1944	Choan Maru No 2	Converted Gunboat	2,631	11-26N, 143-46E	
May 20 1944	Shosei Maru	Converted Gunboat	998	13-32N, 144-36E	
May 29 1944	Shoken Maru	Cargo	1,949	16-23N, 144-59E	
May 29 1944	Horaizan Maru	Cargo	1,999	16-23N, 144-59E	
Jan 25 1945	Malay Maru	Cargo	4,556	31-18N, 130-08E	J. C. Nichols
		23 Vessels	90,080		

554

SUBMARINE AND DATE	NAME OF VESSEL	TYPE OF VESSEL	TONNAGE	LOCATION	SUBMARINE CAPTAIN
USS SKATE					
Dec 21 1943	Terukawa Maru	Cargo	6,429	9-50N, 151-55E	E. B. McKinney
Feb 16 1944	Agano	Light Cruiser	7,000	10-11N, 151-42E	
Jul 7 1944	Usugumo	Destroyer	1,950	47-43N, 147-55E	W. P. Gruner
Jul 15 1944	Miho Maru	Cargo	515	48-07N, 148-06E	
Jul 16 1944	Nippo Maru	Cargo	1,942	48-12N, 148-03E	
Sep 29 1944	Ekisan Maru	Cargo	3,690	27-12N, 128-18E	
Jun 10 1945	I-122	Submarine	1,142	37-29N, 137-25E	
Jun 12 1945	Yozan Maru	Cargo	1,227	37-07N, 136-42E	R. C. Lynch
Jun 12 1945	Kenjo Maru	Cargo	3,142	37-07N, 136-42E	
Jun 12 1945	Zuiko Maru	Cargo	887	37-07N, 136-42E	
		10 Vessels	27,924		
USS SKIPJACK					
May 6 1942	Kanan Maru	Cargo	2,567	12-05N, 109-35E	
May 8 1942	Bujun Maru	Cargo	4,804	12-00N, 111-10E	J. W. Coe
May 17 1942	Tazan Maru	Passenger-Cargo	5,478	6-22N, 108-36E	
Oct 14 1942	Shunko Maru	Cargo	6,781	5-35N, 144-25E	
Jan 26 1944	Okitsu Maru	Converted Seaplane Tender	6,666	9-22N, 157-26E	G. G. Molumphy
Jan 26 1944	Suzukaze	Destroyer	1,580	8-51N, 157-10E	
		6 Vessels	27,876		
USS SNAPPER					
Sep 2 1943	Mutsure	Frigate	860	8-40N, 151-31E	M. K. Clemenson
Nov 29 1943	Kenryu Maru	Cargo	4,575	33-19N, 139-34E	
Oct 1 1944	Seian Maru	Passenger-Cargo	1,990	28-11N, 139-30E	W. W. Walker
Oct 1 1944	Ajiro	Coastal Minelayer	720ᵉ	28-11N, 139-30E	
		4 Vessels	8,145		
USS SNOOK					
May 5 1943	Kinko Maru	Cargo	1,268	38-39N, 122-36E	
May 5 1943	Daifuku Maru	Cargo	3,194	38-39N, 122-36E	
May 7 1943	Tosei Maru	Cargo	4,363	36-05N, 123-21E	
Jul 4 1943	Koki Maru	Cargo	5,290	28-40N, 124-10E	
Jul 4 1943	Liverpool Maru	Cargo	5,865	28-40N, 124-10E	
Sep 13 1943	Yamato Maru	Transport	9,656	30-06N, 123-33E	
Sep 22 1943	Katsurahama Maru	Cargo	715	39-11N, 123-20E	
Nov 29 1943	Yamafuku Maru	Passenger-Cargo	4,928	18-37N, 139-45E	C. O. Triebel
Nov 29 1943	Shiganoura Maru	Cargo	3,512	18-38N, 139-35E	
Jan 23 1944	Magane Maru	Converted Gunboat	3,120	29-49N, 140-07E	
Feb 8 1944	Lima Maru	Cargo	6,989	32-18N, 129-20E	
Feb 14 1944	Nittoku Maru	Cargo	3,591	33-48N, 128-49E	
Feb 15 1944	Hoshi Maru No 2	Cargo	875	34-23N, 128-12E	
Feb 23 1944	Koyo Maru	Passenger-Cargo	5,471	28-58N, 141-15E	
Oct 23 1944	Shinsei Maru No 1	Passenger-Cargo	5,863	19-44N, 118-25E	
Oct 24 1944	Kikusui Maru	Tanker	3,887	20-54N, 118-19E	G. H. Browne
Oct 24 1944	Arisan Maru	Cargo	6,886	20-31N, 118-32E	
		17 Vessels	75,473		

SUBMARINE AND DATE	NAME OF VESSEL	TYPE OF VESSEL	TONNAGE	LOCATION	SUBMARINE CAPTAIN
USS SPADEFISH					
Aug 19 1944	Tamatsu Maru	Passenger-Cargo	9,589	18-49N, 119-47E	
Aug 22 1944	Hakko Maru No 2	Tanker	10,023	18-48N, 120-48E	
Sep 8 1944	Nichiman Maru	Cargo	1,922	24-46N, 123-15E	
Sep 8 1944	Nichian Maru	Cargo	6,197	24-46N, 123-15E	
Sep 8 1944	Shinten Maru	Cargo	1,254	24-39N, 123-31E	
Sep 8 1944	Shokei Maru	Cargo	2,557	24-39N, 123-31E	
Nov 14 1944	Gyokuyo Maru	Cargo	5,396	31-04N, 123-56E	
Nov 17 1944	Jinyo	Escort Aircraft Carrier	21,000	33-02N, 123-33E	G. W. Underwood
Nov 18 1944	Submarine Chaser No 156	Submarine Chaser	100e	33-07N, 123-09E	
Nov 29 1944	Daiboshi Maru No 6	Cargo	3,925	37-17N, 125-11E	
Jan 28 1945	Kume	Frigate	900e	33-56N, 123-06E	
Jan 28 1945	Sanuki Maru	Converted Seaplane Tender	7,158	33-56N, 123-06E	
Feb 4 1945	Tairai Maru	Passenger-Cargo	4,273	37-18N, 125-22E	
Feb 6 1945	Shohei Maru	Passenger-Cargo	1,092	38-44N, 121-23E	
Mar 23 1945	Doryo Maru	Cargo	2,274	29-31N, 127-41E	
Apr 9 1945	Lee Tung	Cargo	1,853	37-21N, 125-08E	
Jun 10 1945	Daigen Maru No 2	Passenger-Cargo	1,999	43-21N, 140-40E	W. J. Germerhausen
Jun 10 1945	Unkai Maru No 8	Passenger-Cargo	1,293	43-23N, 140-32E	
Jun 10 1945	Jintsu Maru	Passenger-Cargo	994	43-28N, 140-28E	
Jun 14 1945	Seizan Maru	Passenger-Cargo	2,018	47-03N, 142-01E	
Jun 17 1945	Eijo Maru	Cargo	2,274	42-38N, 139-49E	
		21 Vessels	88,091		
USS SPEARFISH					
Apr 17 1942	Unknown Maru	Cargo	4,000e	10-53N, 121-35E	J. C. Dempsey
Apr 25 1942	Toba Maru	Cargo	6,995	17-01N, 120-15E	
Jan 30 1944	Tamashima Maru	Passenger-Cargo	3,560	21-15N, 149-18E	J. W. Williams
May 6 1944	Toyoura Maru	Cargo	2,510	32-16N, 127-08E	
		4 Vessels	17,065		
USS SPIKEFISH					
Aug 13 1945	I 373	Submarine	1,660	29-02N, 123-53E	R. R. Managhan
USS SPOT					
Mar 17 1945	Nanking Maru	Passenger-Cargo	3,005	25-34N, 120-01E	W. S. Post
USS SPRINGER					
Mar 19 1945	Transport No 18	Landing Craft	1,500e	26-33N, 127-11E	
Apr 28 1945	Submarine Chaser No 17	Submarine Chaser	440	32-34N, 128-52E	R. E. Kefauver
May 2 1945	Ojika	Frigate	1,000e	33-58N, 122-58E	
May 3 1945	Coast Def Vessel No 25	Frigate	1,000e	34-38N, 124-15E	
		4 Vessels	3,940		
USS STEELHEAD					
Jan 10 1944	Yamabiko Maru	Converted Salvage Vessel	6,795	31-28N, 137-44E	
Jul 31 1944	Dakar Maru	Cargo	7,169	18-57N, 120-50E	D. L. Welchel
Jul 31 1944	Fuso Maru	Transport	8,195	18-57N, 120-50E	
		3 Vessels	22,159		

SUBMARINE AND DATE	NAME OF VESSEL	TYPE OF VESSEL	TONNAGE	LOCATION	SUBMARINE CAPTAIN
USS Sterlet					
Oct 25 1944	Jinei Maru	Tanker	10,500	30-15N, 129-45E	O. C. Robbins
Mar 1 1945	Tateyama Maru	Cargo	1,148	34-11N, 139-43E	
May 29 1945	Kuretake Maru	Cargo	1,924	46-36N, 144-22E	H. H. Lewis
May 29 1945	Tenryo Maru	Cargo	2,231	46-36N, 144-22E	
	4 Vessels		15,803		
USS Stingray					
Jan 10 1942	Harbin Maru	Transport	5,167	17-40N, 109-20E	
Jun 28 1942	Saikyo Maru	Converted Gunboat	1,292	12-41N, 136-22E	R. J. Moore
May 2 1943	Tamon Maru	Cargo	8,156	27-18N, 121-38E	O. J. Earle
Mar 30 1944	Ikushima Maru	Cargo	3,943	20-42N, 143-00E	S. C. Loomis
	4 Vessels		18,558		
USS Sturgeon					
Mar 30 1942	Choko Maru	Cargo	842	5-39S, 119-00E	
Apr 3 1942	Unknown	Frigate	750e	00-36N, 119-19E	W. L. Wright
Jul 1 1942	Montevideo Maru	Transport	7,267	18-37N, 119-29E	
Oct 1 1942	Katsuragi Maru	Aircraft Ferry	8,033	5-51S, 153-18E	H. A. Pieczent-kowski
Jan 11 1944	Erie Maru	Cargo	5,193	32-56N, 132-02E	
Jan 24 1944	Chosen Maru	Cargo	3,110	32-25N, 133-00E	
May 11 1944	Seiryu Maru	Cargo	1,904	29-30N, 141-40E	C. L. Murphy
Jun 29 1944	Toyama Maru	Passenger-Cargo	7,089	27-41N, 129-09E	
Jul 3 1944	Tairin Maru	Cargo	6,862	38-52N, 129-56E	
	9 Vessels		41,350		
USS Sunfish					
Mar 13 1943	Kosei Maru	Cargo	3,262	29-04N, 129-17E	
Aug 13 1943	Edo Maru	Converted Gunboat	1,299	23-24N, 142-26E	R. W. Peterson
Sep 4 1943	Kozan Maru	Passenger-Cargo	4,180	22-22N, 120-04E	
Feb 23 1944	Shinyubari Maru	Cargo	5,354	15-17N, 145-03E	
Feb 23 1944	Kunishima Maru	Cargo	4,083	15-23N, 145-02E	
Jul 5 1944	Shinmei Maru	Passenger-Cargo	2,577	51-35N, 156-30E	
Jul 9 1944	Taihei Maru	Cargo	6,284	51-17N, 155-34E	
Sep 10 1944	Chihaya Maru	Tanker	4,701	33-52N, 127-41E	E. E. Shelby
Sep 13 1944	Etashima Maru	Cargo	6,435	35-04N, 124-49E	
Nov 17 1944	Edogawa Maru	Cargo	6,968	33-31N, 124-32E	
Nov 18 1944	Seisho Maru	Passenger-Cargo	5,463	33-36N, 124-18E	
Nov 30 1944	Dairen Maru	Transport	3,748	38-06N, 124-39E	
Apr 16 1945	Manryu Maru	Cargo	1,620	39-36N, 142-05E	
Apr 16 1945	Coast Def Vessel No 73	Frigate	800e	39-36N, 142-05E	
Apr 19 1945	Kaiho Maru	Cargo	1,093	42-22N, 142-16E	J. W. Reed
Apr 19 1945	Taisei Maru	Cargo	1,948	42-23N, 142-13E	
	16 Vessels		59,815		

SUBMARINE AND DATE	NAME OF VESSEL	TYPE OF VESSEL	TONNAGE	LOCATION	SUBMARINE CAPTAIN
USS Swordfish					
Dec 16 1941	Atsutasan Maru	Cargo	8,662	18-06N, 109-44E	
Jan 24 1942	Myoken Maru	Cargo	4,124	1-22N, 125-05E	C. C. Smith
May 29 1942	Unknown Maru	Cargo	1,900e	7-33N, 116-18E	
Jun 12 1942	Burma Maru	Cargo	4,584	10-08N, 102-34E	
Jan 19 1943	Myoho Maru	Cargo	4,122	5-30S, 156-00E	J. H. Lewis
Aug 22 1943	Nishiyama Maru	Cargo	3,016	2-40N, 137-10E	F. M. Parker
Sep 5 1943	Tenkai Maru	Cargo	3,203	1-10N, 142-10E	
Jan 14 1944	Yamakuni Maru	Passenger-Cargo	6,921	33-16N, 139-30E	
Jan 16 1944	Delhi Maru	Converted Gunboat	2,182	34-04N, 139-56E	K. G. Hensel
Jan 27 1944	Kasagi Maru	Converted Salvage Vessel	3,140	33-31N, 139-36E	
Jun 9 1944	Matsukaze	Destroyer	1,270	26-59N, 143-13E	K. E. Montross
Jun 15 1944	Kanseishi Maru	Cargo	4,804	29-30N, 141-11E	
	12 Vessels		47,928		
USS Tambor					
Aug 7 1942	Shofuku	Converted Net Tender	891	9-22N, 170-12E	
Aug 21 1942	Shinsei Maru No 6	Passenger-Cargo	4,928	6-45N, 158-10E	S. H. Ambruster
Nov 3 1942	Chikugo Maru	Cargo	2,461	20-18N, 108-39E	
May 29 1943	Eisho Maru	Cargo	2,486	17-35N, 110-45E	
Jan 29 1944	Shuntai Maru	Cargo	2,253	27-22N, 128-29E	
Feb 3 1944	Ariake Maru	Cargo	5,000	29-11N, 124-45E	
Feb 3 1944	Goyo Maru	Tanker	8,496	29-11N, 124-45E	R. Kefauver
Feb 12 1944	Ronsan Maru	Passenger-Cargo	2,735	27-43N, 128-35E	
May 26 1944	Chiyo Maru	Cargo	657	20-30N, 141-45E	
Aug 13 1944	Toei Maru	Cargo	2,324	48-56N, 149-03E	W. T. Germerhausen
Jun 2 1945	Eika Maru	Passenger-Cargo	1,248	20-30N, 107-57E	
	11 Vessels		33,479		
USS Tang					
Feb 17 1944	Gyoten Maru	Cargo	6,854	8-04N, 149-28E	
Feb 22 1944	Fukuyama Maru	Passenger-Cargo	3,581	14-47N, 144-50E	
Feb 23 1944	Yamashimo Maru	Cargo	6,776	14-45N, 144-32E	
Feb 24 1944	Echizen Maru	Cargo	2,424	15-16N, 143-12E	
Feb 25 1944	Choko Maru	Cargo	1,794	15-50N, 144-21E	
Jun 24 1944	Tamahoko Maru	Passenger-Cargo	6,780	32-30N, 129-35E	
Jun 24 1944	Tainan Maru	Cargo	3,175	32-30N, 129-35E	
Jun 24 1944	Nasusan Maru	Passenger-Cargo	4,399	32-30N, 129-35E	
Jun 24 1944	Kennichi Maru	Cargo	1,938	32-30N, 129-35E	
Jun 30 1944	Nikkin Maru	Cargo	5,705	35-03N, 125-08E	
Jul 1 1944	Taiun Maru No 2	Cargo	998	34-33N, 125-12E	
Jul 1 1944	Takatori Maru No 1	Tanker	878e	34-27N, 123-46E	R. H. O'Kane
Jul 4 1944	Asukazan Maru	Cargo	6,886	35-22N, 125-56E	
Jul 4 1944	Yamaoka Maru	Cargo	6,932	36-05N, 125-48E	
Jul 6 1944	Dori Maru	Cargo	1,469	38-40N, 123-40E	
Aug 11 1944	Roko Maru	Cargo	3,328	34-12N, 136-19E	
Aug 23 1944	Tsukushi Maru	Transport	8,135	34-37N, 137-50E	
Oct 10 1944	Joshu Go	Cargo	1,658	25-20N, 121-32E	
Oct 11 1944	Oita Maru	Cargo	711	25-40N, 121-30E	
Oct 23 1944	Toun Maru	Cargo	1,915	24-57N, 120-25E	
Oct 23 1944	Wakatake Maru	Cargo	1,920	24-57N, 120-25E	
Oct 23 1944	Tatsuju Maru	Cargo	1,944	24-57N, 120-25E	
Oct 25 1944	Kogen Maru	Cargo	6,600	25-06N, 119-31E	
Oct 25 1944	Matsumoto Maru	Cargo	7,024	25-06N, 119-31E	
	24 Vessels		93,824		

SUBMARINE AND DATE	NAME OF VESSEL	TYPE OF VESSEL	TONNAGE	LOCATION	SUBMARINE CAPTAIN
USS Tarpon					
Feb 1 1943	Fushimi Maru	Passenger-Cargo	10,935	34-16N, 138-17E	
Feb 8 1943	Tatsuta Maru	Transport ·	16,975	33-45N, 140-25E	T. L. Wogan
		2 Vessels	27,910		
USS Tautog					
Apr 26 1942	RO-30	Submarine	965	18-11N, 166-54W	
May 17 1942	I-28	Submarine	2,212	6-30N, 152-00E	
May 25 1942	Shoka Maru	Cargo	4,467	4-07N, 143-32E	J. H. Willingham
Aug 6 1942	Ohio Maru	Passenger-Cargo	5,872	13-51N, 113-15E	
Oct 27 1942	Unknown Maru	Passenger-Cargo	4,000e	10-20N, 108-43E	
Dec 25 1942	Banshu Maru No 2	Cargo	1,000e	9-00S, 124-00E	
Jan 22 1943	Hasshu Maru	Passenger-Cargo	1,873	5-40S, 120-35E	
Apr 9 1943	Isonami	Destroyer	1,950	5-26S, 123-04E	
Apr 9 1943	Penang Maru	Cargo	5,214	5-29S, 123-02E	
Jun 6 1943	Shinei Maru	Cargo	973	7-00N, 123-37E	
Jun 20 1943	Meiten Maru	Cargo	4,174	15-57N, 140-55E	
Nov 4 1943	Submarine Chaser No 30	Submarine Chaser	100	7-34N, 134-00E	W. B. Sieglaff
Jan 3 1944	Saishu Maru	Cargo	2,082	33-44N, 136-02E	
Jan 4 1944	USA Maru	Cargo	3,943	34-09N, 136-50E	
Mar 13 1944	Ryua Maru	Cargo	1,925	47-41N, 152-41E	
Mar 13 1944	Shojin Maru	Cargo	1,942	47-41N, 152-41E	
Mar 16 1944	Shirakumo	Destroyer	1,950	42-25N, 144-55E	
Mar 16 1944	Nichiren Maru	Passenger-Cargo	5,460	42-25N, 144-55E	
May 2 1944	Ryoyo Maru	Passenger-Cargo	5,973	48-04N, 153-16E	
May 3 1944	Fushimi Maru	Passenger-Cargo	4,935	45-28N, 149-56E	
May 8 1944	Miyazaki Maru	Passenger-Cargo	3,944	41-49N, 141-12E	
May 12 1944	Banei Maru No 2	Cargo	1,186	40-01N, 141-58E	
Jul 8 1944	Matsu Maru	Cargo	887	40-56N, 141-27E	T. S. Baskett
Aug 2 1944	Konei Maru	Cargo	1,922	33-57N, 136-20E	
Jan 17 1945	Transport No 15	Landing Craft	1,500e	31-09N, 130-29E	
Jan 20 1945	Shuri Maru	Motor Torpedo Boat Tender	1,857	33-37N, 128-40E	
		26 Vessels	72,606		
USS Tench					
Jun 2 1945	Mikamisan Maru	Cargo	861	41-22N, 141-28E	
Jun 4 1945	Ryujin Maru	Cargo	517	40-54N, 141-29E	T. S. Baskett
Jun 9 1945	Kamishika Maru	Cargo	2,857	41-52N, 141-08E	
Jun 10 1945	Shoei Maru No 6	Tanker	834	41-20N, 141-29E	
		4 Vessels	5,069		
USS Threadfin					
Jan 30 1945	Issei Maru	Passenger-Cargo	1,864	33-30N, 135-31E	
Mar 28 1945	Mikura	Frigate	900e	31-49N, 131-44E	J. J. Foote
Jul 20 1945	Minesweeper No 39	Minesweeper	630e	35-01N, 125-42E	
		3 Vessels	3,394		

SUBMARINE AND DATE	NAME OF VESSEL	TYPE OF VESSEL	TONNAGE	LOCATION	SUBMARINE CAPTAIN
USS Thresher					
Apr 10 1942	Sado Maru	Cargo	3,039	34-52N, 139-15E	W. L. Anderson
Jul 9 1942	Shinsho Maru	Motor Torpedo Boat Tender	4,836	8-43N, 167-33E	
Oct 31 1942	Unknown Maru	Cargo	3,000e	4-40S, 118-54E	W. J. Millican
Dec 29 1942	Hachian Maru	Cargo	2,733	4-45S, 113-54E	
Feb 21 1943	Kuwayama Maru	Cargo	5,724	7-53S, 119-13E	
Mar 2 1943	Toen Maru	Tanker	5,232	3-29S, 117-17E	
Jul 1 1943	Yoneyama Maru	Passenger-Cargo	5,274	00-20N, 119-32E	H. Hull
Nov 13 1943	Muko Maru	Transport	4,862	8-57N, 152-36E	
Jan 15 1944	Tatsuno Maru	Cargo	6,960	19-45N, 120-40E	
Jan 15 1944	Toho Maru	Cargo	4,092	19-45N, 120-40E	
Jan 27 1944	Kikuzuki Maru	Cargo	1,266	22-11N, 119-12E	
Jan 27 1944	Kosei Maru	Cargo	2,205	22-11N, 119-12E	D. C. McMillan
Jul 17 1944	Sainei Maru	Cargo	4,916	19-04N, 119-26E	
Jul 17 1944	Shozan Maru	Cargo	2,838	19-04N, 119-26E	
Sep 18 1944	Gyoku Maru	Cargo	6,854	35-05N, 124-24E	
Sep 25 1944	Nissei Maru	Cargo	1,468	37-32N, 124-33E	J. R. Middleton
Sep 26 1944	Koetsu Maru	Cargo	873	37-13N, 123-48E	
		17 Vessels	66,172		
USS Tilefish					
Dec 22 1944	Chidori	Torpedo Boat	527	34-33N, 138-02E	R. M. Keithley
Mar 5 1945	Minesweeper No 15	Minesweeper	492	29-30N, 129-33E	W. F. Schlech
		2 Vessels	1,019		
USS Tinosa					
Nov 22 1943	Kiso Maru	Cargo	4,071	7-09N, 134-34E	
Nov 22 1943	Yamato Maru	Cargo	4,379	7-09N, 134-34E	L. R. Daspit
Nov 26 1943	Shini Maru	Cargo	3,811	6-56N, 134-38E	
Dec 3 1943	Azuma Maru	Passenger-Cargo	6,646	6-29N, 131-28E	
Jan 22 1944	Koshin Maru	Passenger-Cargo	5,485	7-22N, 115-05E	
Jan 22 1944	Seinan Maru	Cargo	5,401	7-22N, 115-05E	
Feb 15 1944	Odatsuki Maru	Cargo	1,988	10-03N, 126-54E	
Feb 16 1944	Chojo Maru	Transport	2,610	9-15N, 127-05E	
May 4 1944	Taibu Maru	Cargo	6,440	20-54N, 118-14E	D. F. Weiss
May 4 1944	Toyohi Maru	Cargo	6,436	20-51N, 118-02E	
Jul 3 1944	Konsan Maru	Passenger-Cargo	2,733	32-24N, 128-46E	
Jul 3 1944	Kamo Maru	Passenger-Cargo	7,954	32-24N, 128-46E	
Jun 9 1945	Wakatama Maru	Cargo	2,211	37-32N, 129-10E	
Jun 12 1945	Keito Maru	Cargo	880	37-47N, 129-10E	R. C. Latham
Jun 20 1945	Kaisei Maru	Cargo	884	35-39N, 130-29E	
Jun 20 1945	Taito Maru	Cargo	2,726	36-04N, 130-26E	
		16 Vessels	64,655		
USS Tirante					
Mar 25 1945	Fuji Maru	Tanker	703	31-08N, 130-30E	
Mar 28 1945	Nase Maru	Cargo	1,218	32-15N, 129-55E	
Apr 9 1945	Nikko Maru	Transport	5,507	36-50N, 123-55E	
Apr 14 1945	Juzan Maru	Passenger-Cargo	3,943	33-25N, 126-15E	
Apr 14 1945	Coast Def Vessel No 31	Frigate	800e	33-25N, 126-15E	G. L. Street
Apr 14 1945	Nomi	Frigate	900e	33-25N, 126-15E	
Jun 11 1945	Hakuju Maru	Cargo	2,220	32-37N, 129-45E	
Jul 8 1945	Saitsu Maru	Passenger-Cargo	1,045	38-48N, 121-28E	
		8 Vessels	15,886		

SUBMARINE AND DATE	NAME OF VESSEL	TYPE OF VESSEL	TONNAGE	LOCATION	SUBMARINE CAPTAIN
USS TORSK					
Aug 13 1945	Kaiho Maru	Cargo	873	36-16N, 136-08E	
Aug 14 1945	Coast Def Vessel No 13	Frigate	800ᵉ	35-42N, 134-35E	B. E. Lewellen
Aug 14 1945	Coast Def Vessel No 47	Frigate	800ᵉ	35-42N, 134-36E	
		3 Vessels	2,473		
USS TREPANG					
Oct 1 1944	Takunan Maru	Cargo	751	30-32N, 138-17E	
Oct 11 1944	Transport No 105	Landing Craft	1,000ᵉ	33-18N, 137-42E	
Dec 6 1944	Banshu Maru No 31	Cargo	748	18-54N, 120-49E	R. M. Davenport
Dec 6 1944	Jinyo Maru	Cargo	6,862	18-54N, 120-49E	
Dec 6 1944	Fukuyo Maru	Cargo	5,463	18-59N, 121-05E	
Feb 24 1945	Usuki Maru	Cargo	875ᵉ	33-58N, 136-18E	
Mar 3 1945	Nissho Maru No 2	Converted Gunboat	1,386	34-05N, 139-54E	
Apr 28 1945	Transport No 146	Landing Craft	1,000ᵉ	32-24N, 128-40E	
Apr 30 1945	Miho Maru	Cargo	4,667	34-20N, 123-58E	F. A. Faust
May 4 1945	Minesweeper No 20	Minesweeper	492	34-16N, 123-37E	
Jul 7 1945	Koun Maru No 2	Passenger-Cargo	606	41-21N, 141-28E	
		11 Vessels	23,850		
USS TRIGGER					
Oct 17 1942	Holland Maru	Cargo	5,869	32-21N, 132-04E	
Dec 22 1942	Teifuku Maru	Cargo	5,198	34-52N, 139-49E	
Jan 10 1943	Okikaze	Destroyer	1,300	35-02N, 140-12E	R. S. Benson
Mar 15 1943	Momoha Maru	Cargo	3-103	00-00N, 145-00E	
Jun 1 1943	Noborikawa Maru	Cargo	2,182	35-02N, 140-14E	
Sep 18 1943	Yowa Maru	Cargo	6,435	27-31N, 126-57E	
Sep 21 1943	Shiriya	Tanker	6,500	26-27N, 122-40E	
Sep 21 1943	Shoyo Maru	Tanker	7,498	26-27N, 122-40E	
Sep 21 1943	Argun Maru	Cargo	6,662	26-27N, 122-40E	
Nov 2 1943	Yawata Maru	Cargo	1,852	28-49N, 134-50E	
Nov 2 1943	Delagoa Maru	Passenger-Cargo	7,148	28-55N, 134-43E	
Nov 13 1943	Nachisan Maru	Passenger-Cargo	4,443	32-57N, 125-06E	R. E. Dornin
Nov 21 1943	Eizan Maru	Cargo	1,681	36-40N, 125-31E	
Jan 31 1944	Nasami	Coastal Minelayer	443	9-50N, 147-06E	
Jan 31 1944	Yasukuni Maru	Converted Submarine Tender	11,933	9-21N, 147-02E	
Apr 27 1944	Miike Maru	Passenger-Cargo	11,739	8-20N, 134-53E	F. Harlfinger
Mar 18 1945	Tsukushi Maru No 3	Cargo	1,012	28-05N, 126-44E	
Mar 27 1945	Odate	Repair Ship	1,564	30-40N, 127-50E	D. R. Connole
		18 Vessels	86,552		
USS TRITON					
Feb 17 1942	Shinyo Maru No 5	Cargo	1,498	32-14N, 127-14E	
Feb 21 1942	Shokyu Maru	Cargo	4,184	32-10N, 126-28E	W. A. Lent
Apr 23 1942	Unknown Maru	Trawler	1,000ᵉ	28-22N, 153-18E	
May 1 1942	Calcutta Maru	Passenger-Cargo	5,339	28-07N, 123-45E	
May 6 1942	Taiei Maru	Cargo	2,209	28-42N, 123-50E	
May 6 1942	Taigen Maru	Passenger-Cargo	5,660	28-19N, 123-38E	
May 17 1942	I-164	Submarine	1,635	29-25N, 134-09E	C. C. Kirkpatrick
Jul 4 1942	Nenohi	Destroyer	1,600	52-15N, 173-51E	
Dec 24 1942	Amakasu Maru No 1	Water Carrier	1,913	19-16N, 166-37E	
Dec 28 1942	Omi Maru	Passenger-Cargo	3,393	6-23N, 160-17E	
Mar 6 1943	Kiriha Maru	Cargo	3,057	00-00N, 145-0 E	G. W. McKenzie
		11 Vessels	31,788		

SUBMARINE AND DATE	NAME OF VESSEL	TYPE OF VESSEL	TONNAGE	LOCATION	SUBMARINE CAPTAIN
USS TROUT					
Feb 10 1942	Chuwa Maru	Cargo	2,719	25-30N, 122-38E	
May 2 1942	Uzan Maru	Cargo	5,014	33-26N, 135-52E	F. W. Fenno
May 4 1942	Kongosan Maru	Converted Gunboat	2,119	33-32N, 136-05E	
Sep 21 1942	Koei Maru	Converted Net Tender	863	6-54N, 151-51E	
Jan 21 1943	Unknown Maru	Cargo	2,984ᵉ	11-25N, 109-22E	L. P. Ramage
Feb 14 1943	Hirotama Maru	Converted Gunboat	1,911	4-11S, 117-45E	
Jun 15 1943	Sanraku Maru	Tanker	3,000	5-09N, 119-38E	
Jul 2 1943	Isuzu Maru	Cargo	2,866	13-36N, 121-49E	
Sep 9 1943	I-182	Submarine	1,630	10-33N, 125-31E	A. H. Clark
Sep 23 1943	Ryotoku Maru	Cargo	3,483	21-17N, 142-00E	
Sep 23 1943	Yamashiro Maru	Passenger-Cargo	3,429	21-17N, 142-00E	
Feb 29 1944	Sakito Maru	Passenger-Cargo	7,126	22-40N, 131-50E	
		12 Vessels	37,144		
USS TULLIBEE					
Aug 22 1943	Kaisho Maru	Passenger-Cargo	4,164	10-09N, 147-25E	
Oct 15 1943	Chicago Maru	Passenger-Cargo	5,866	24-35N, 120-31E	C. F. Brindupke
Jan 31 1944	Hiro Maru	Converted Net Tender	549	15-23N, 145-35E	
		3 Vessels	10,579		
USS TUNA					
Mar 4 1942	Unknown Maru	Cargo	4,000ᵉ	32-33N, 133-26E	
May 15 1942	Toyohara Maru	Cargo	805	33-34N, 125-09E	J. L. De Tar
Mar 30 1943	Kurohime Maru	Cargo	4,697	00-22S, 147-46E	A. H. Holtz
Dec 12 1943	Tosei Maru	Cargo	5,484	2-44N, 126-14E	J. T. Hardin
		4 Vessels	14,986		
USS TUNNY					
Feb 8 1943	Kusuyama Maru	Cargo	5,306	22-40N, 119-12E	
Apr 2 1943	Toyo Maru No 2	Cargo	4,163	7-23N, 149-13E	
Apr 7 1943	Kosei Maru	Passenger-Cargo	8,237	8-50N, 147-06E	J. A. Scott
Jun 28 1943	Shotoku Maru	Converted Gunboat	1,964	14-10N, 145-03E	
Mar 23 1944	I-42	Submarine	2,212	6-40N, 134-03E	
May 17 1944	Nichiwa Maru	Cargo	4,955	14-45N, 142-40E	
		6 Vessels	26,837		

SUBMARINE AND DATE	NAME OF VESSEL	TYPE OF VESSEL	TONNAGE	LOCATION	SUBMARINE CAPTAIN
USS Wahoo					
Dec 10 1942	Kamoi Maru	Cargo	5,355	4-56S, 154-58E	M. G. Kennedy
Jan 26 1943	Unknown Maru	Cargo	4,000e	2-37N, 139-42E	
Jan 26 1943	Buyo Maru	Transport	5,447	1-55N, 139-14E	
Jan 26 1943	Fukuei Maru No 2	Cargo	1,901	1-55N, 139-14E	
Mar 19 1943	Zogen Maru	Cargo	1,428	38-29N, 122-19E	
Mar 19 1943	Kowa Maru	Transport	3,217	38-27N, 122-18E	
Mar 21 1943	Nittsu Maru	Cargo	2,183	38-05N, 124-33E	
Mar 21 1943	Hozan Maru	Cargo	2,260	38-11N, 124-33E	
Mar 23 1943	Unknown Maru	Cargo	2,427e	38-37N, 121-01E	
Mar 24 1943	Takaosan Maru	Cargo	2,076	39-01N, 122-25E	
Mar 25 1943	Satsuki Maru	Cargo	827	38-10N, 123-26E	D. W. Morton
Mar 25 1943	Unknown Maru	Cargo	2,556e	38-13N, 123-24E	
Mar 29 1943	Yamabato Maru	Cargo	2,556	30-26N, 129-41E	
May 7 1943	Tamon Maru No 5	Passenger-Cargo	5,260	40-05N, 141-53E	
May 9 1943	Takao Maru	Passenger-Cargo	3,204	38-57N, 141-49E	
May 9 1943	Jinmu Maru	Cargo	1,912	38-57N, 141-49E	
Sep 29 1943	Masaki Maru No 2	Cargo	1,238	40-00N, 130-00E	
Oct 5 1943	Konron Maru	Transport	7,908	34-00N, 130-00E	
Oct 6 1943	Unknown Maru	Passenger-Cargo	1,288	37-18N, 129-33E	
Oct 9 1943	Kanko Maru	Cargo	2,995	37-18N, 129-33E	
		20 Vessels	60,038		
USS Whale					
Jan 13 1943	Iwashiro Maru	Cargo	3,550	9-54N, 167-07E	J. B. Azer
Jan 17 1943	Heiyo Maru	Passenger-Cargo	9,815	10-13N, 151-25E	
Jan 27 1943	Shoan Maru	Passenger-Cargo	5,624	14-15N, 153-43E	
Mar 23 1943	Kenyo Maru	Cargo	6,486	17-16N, 144-56E	
May 26 1943	Shoei Maru	Cargo	3,580	14-17N, 144-53E	A. C. Burrows
Aug 8 1943	Naruto Maru	Aircraft Ferry	7,149	24-12N, 142-51E	
Jan 16 1944	Denmark Maru	Cargo	5,870	23-09N, 135-14E	
Apr 9 1944	Honan Maru	Cargo	5,401	33-50N, 128-01E	J. B. Grady
Oct 6 1944	Akane Maru	Tanker	10,241	19-40N, 118-05E	
		9 Vessels	57,716		

DATE	NAME OF VESSEL	TYPE OF VESSEL	TONNAGE	LOCATION	AGENTS
Jan 26 1943	Tokai Maru	Passenger-Cargo	8,358	13-27N, 144-37E	SNAPPER / FLYING FISH
Mar 28 1943	Suwa Maru	Transport	10,672	19-13N, 166-34E	TUNNY / FINBACK
Oct 6 1943	Kazahaya	Tanker	8,000ᵉ	10-01N, 148-31E	SEADRAGON / TINOSA / STEELHEAD
Oct 27 1943	Fuji Maru	Transport	9,138	28-25N, 128-04E	SHAD / GRAYBACK
Jan 17 1944	Tarushima Maru	Cargo	4,865	22-45N, 135-00E	WHALE / SEAWOLF
May 14 1944	Bisan Maru	Cargo	4,500	9-00N, 133-34E	BOWFIN / ASPRO
Jul 26 1944	Tosan Maru	Passenger-Cargo	8,666	18-13N, 117-50E	CREVALLE / FLASHER
Jul 31 1944	Yoshino Maru	Transport	8,990	19-10N, 120-58E	STEELHEAD / PARCHE
Aug 12 1944	Shimpo Maru	Tanker	5,135	13-17N, 120-07E	PUFFER / BLUEFISH
Oct 7 1944	Kinugasa Maru	Passenger-Cargo	8,407	14-30N, 115-48E	HAWKBILL / BAYA
Oct 9 1944	Tokuwa Maru	Cargo	1,943	12-46N, 118-02E	HAWKBILL / BECUNA
Oct 30 1944	Takane Maru	Tanker	10,021	30-14N, 132-50E	TRIGGER / SALMON / STERLET
Nov 4 1944	Kagu Maru	Passenger-Cargo	6,806	15-54N, 119-45E	RAY / BREAM / GUITARRO
Nov 21 1944	Gyosan Maru	Cargo	5,698	10-39N, 115-05E	FLOUNDER / GUAVINA
Dec 6 1944	Kenjo Maru	Cargo	6,933	18-57N, 120-58E	SEGUNDO / RAZORBACK
Dec 8 1944	Shoei Maru	Tanker	2,854	4-03N, 111-31E	PADDLE / HAMMERHEAD
Jan 8 1945	Hikoshima Maru	Tanker	2,854	24-37N, 120-30E	BARB / PICUDA / QUEENFISH
Apr 7 1945	Isuzu	Light Cruiser	5,700	7-38S, 118-09E	CHARR / GABILAN

SUNK BY UNITED STATES SUBMARINES
AND NAVY CARRIER-BASED AIRCRAFT

DATE	NAME OF VESSEL	TYPE OF VESSEL	TONNAGE	LOCATION	AGENTS
Jun 4 1942	Soryu	Light Aircraft Carrier	17,500	30-13N, 179-17W	NAUTILUS / Navy Carrier-Based Aircraft
Jul 25 1944	Samidare	Destroyer	1,580	8-10N, 134-38E	BATFISH / Navy Carrier-Based Aircraft

DATE	NAME OF VESSEL	TYPE OF VESSEL	TONNAGE	LOCATION	AGENTS
Sep 9 1944	Eiyo Maru No 2	Tanker	5,061	8-11N, 122-40E	PADDLE *Navy Carrier-Based Aircraft*
Oct 25 1944	Tama	Light Cruiser	5,700	21-23N, 127-19E	JALAO *Navy Carrier-Based Aircraft*
Nov 14 1944	Yutaka Maru	Cargo	2,704	12-40N, 120-40E	GUAVINA *Navy Carrier-Based Aircraft*
Dec 6 1944	Yasukuni Maru	Cargo	5,794	18-51N, 121-07E	SEGUNDO *Navy Carrier-Based Aircraft*
Jan 3 1945	Shinshu Maru	Converted Water Carrier	8,170	21-57N, 119-44E	ASPRO *Navy Carrier-Based Aircraft*

SUNK BY UNITED STATES SUBMARINES AND LAND-BASED AIRCRAFT

DATE	NAME OF VESSEL	TYPE OF VESSEL	TONNAGE	LOCATION	AGENTS
Feb 19 1943	Hibari Maru	Cargo	6,550	6-45S, 155-50E	GATO *Navy Land-Based Aircraft*
May 22 1944	Tsukuba Maru	Cargo	3,172	21-20N, 117-10E	PICUDA *Army Aircraft*
Jan 31 1945	Taietsu Maru	Cargo	6,890	14-55N, 109-01E	BOARFISH *Army Aircraft*
Mar 17 1945	Ikomasan Maru	Passenger-Cargo	3,173	26-08N, 119-56E	SPOT *Navy Land-Based Aircraft*

Mothballs
☆

INDEX

570